Street by Street

ESSEX

PLUS BISHOP'S STORTFORD, CHESHUNT, FELIXSTOWE, HAVERHILL, HODDESDON, IPSWICH, ROMFORD, SUDBURY, WALTHAM ABBEY

Enlarged Areas Basildon, Chelmsford, Clacton-on-Sea, Colchester, Harlow, Harwich, Southend-on-Sea

Ist edition May 2001

© Automobile Association Developments Limited 2001

This product includes map data licensed from Ordnance Survey® with the permission of the Controller of Her Majesty's Stationery Office. © Crown copyright 2000. All rights reserved. Licence No: 399221.

Published by AA Publishing (a trading name of Automobile Association Developments Limited, whose registered office is Norfolk House, Priestley Road, Basingstoke, Hampshire, RG24 9NY. Registered number 1878835).

Mapping produced by the Cartographic Department of The Automobile Association.

A CIP Catalogue record for this book is available from the British Library.

Printed in Italy by Printer Trento srl

The contents of this atlas are believed to be correct at the time of the latest revision. However, the publishers cannot be held responsible for loss occasioned to any person acting or refraining from action as a result of any material in this atlas, nor for any errors, omissions or changes in such material. The publishers would welcome information to correct any errors or omissions and to keep this atlas up to date. Please write to Publishing, The Automobile Association, Fanum House, Basing View, Basingstoke, Hampshire, RG21 4EA.

Ref: MX028

Key to map pages	ii-iii
Key to map symbols	iv-1
Enlarged scale pages	2-21
Street by Street	22-419
Index – towns & villages	420-421
Index – streets	422-462
Index – featured places	462-469

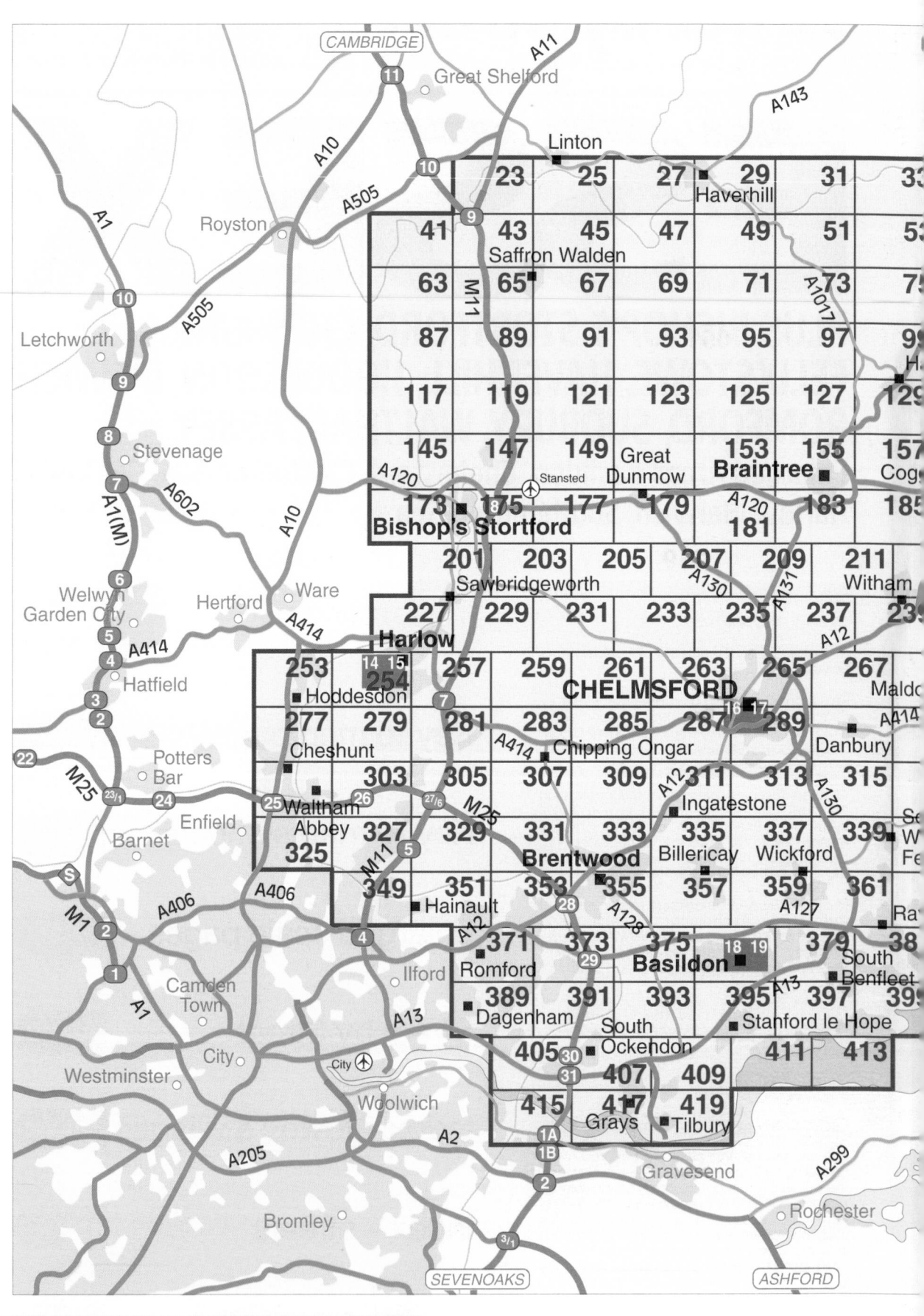

ii

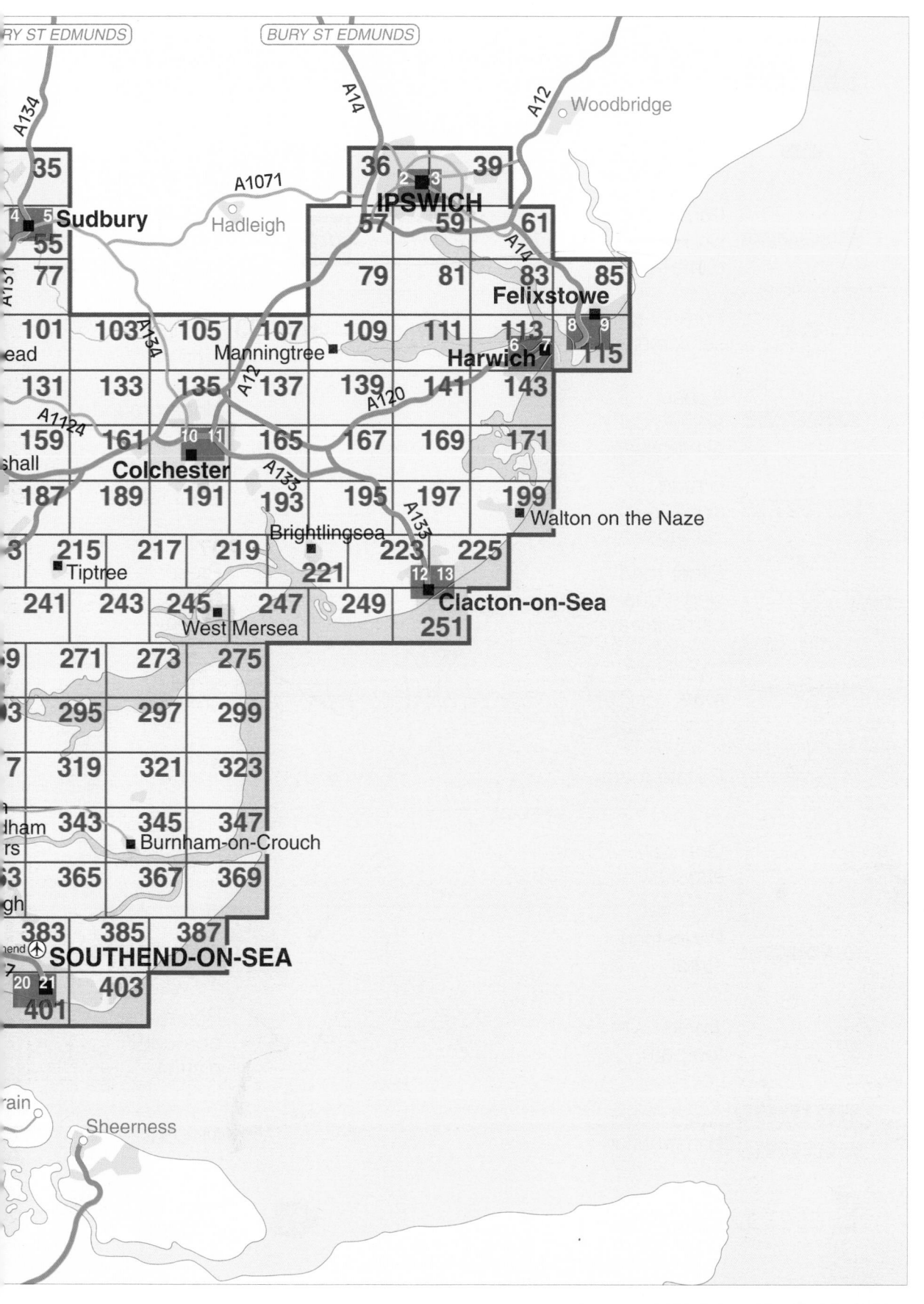

A134

A14

A12

Woodbridge

35

A1071

36 2 3 39

IPSWICH

4 5 Sudbury

Hadleigh

57 59 61

55

A14

77

79 81 83 85

Felixstowe

A151

101 103 105 107 109 111 113 8 9

Manningtree 115

ead 6 7

131 133 135 137 139 141 143 4

A134

A12

A120 Harwich

A1124

159 161 10 11 165 167 169 171

Colchester

A133

187 189 191 193 195 197 199

Walton on the Naze

3 215 217 219 223 225

Brightlingsea

Tiptree 221

A133

241 243 245 247 249 12 13

West Mersea 251 Clacton-on-Sea

9 271 273 275

3 295 297 299

7 319 321 323

ham 343 345 347

rs Burnham-on-Crouch

3 365 367 369

gh

383 385 387

end SOUTHEND-ON-SEA

7

20 21 403

401

rain

Sheerness

3.6 inches to 1 mile **Scale of main map pages 1:17,500**

0 1/2 miles 1

0 1/2 1 kilometres 1 1/2 2

Junction 9	Motorway & junction		P+	Park & Ride
Services	Motorway service area			Bus/coach station
	Primary road single/dual carriageway			Railway & main railway station
Services	Primary road service area			Railway & minor railway station
	A road single/dual carriageway			Underground station
	B road single/dual carriageway			Light railway & station
	Other road single/dual carriageway		++++++++++++	Preserved private railway
	Restricted road		LC	Level crossing
	Private road		•—•—•—•—•	Tramway
← ←	One way street		-------------	Ferry route
	Pedestrian street		....	Airport runway
	Track/ footpath		—·—·—·—·—	Boundaries-borough/ district
	Road under construction		▼▼▼▼▼▼▼▼▼	Mounds
	Road tunnel		93	Page continuation 1:17,500
P	Parking		7	Page continuation to enlarged scale 1:10,000

River/canal
lake, pier

Aqueduct
lock, weir

465
▲
Winter Hill

Peak (with
height in
metres)

Beach

Coniferous
woodland

Broadleaved
woodland

Mixed
woodland

Park

Cemetery

Built-up
area

Featured building

City wall

A&E

Accident &
Emergency
hospital

Toilet

Toilet with
disabled facilities

Petrol station

PH Public house

PO Post Office

Public library

i Tourist Information
Centre

Castle

Historic house/
building

Wakehurst
Place NT

National Trust
property

M Museum/
art gallery

† Church/chapel

Country park

Theatre/
performing arts

Cinema

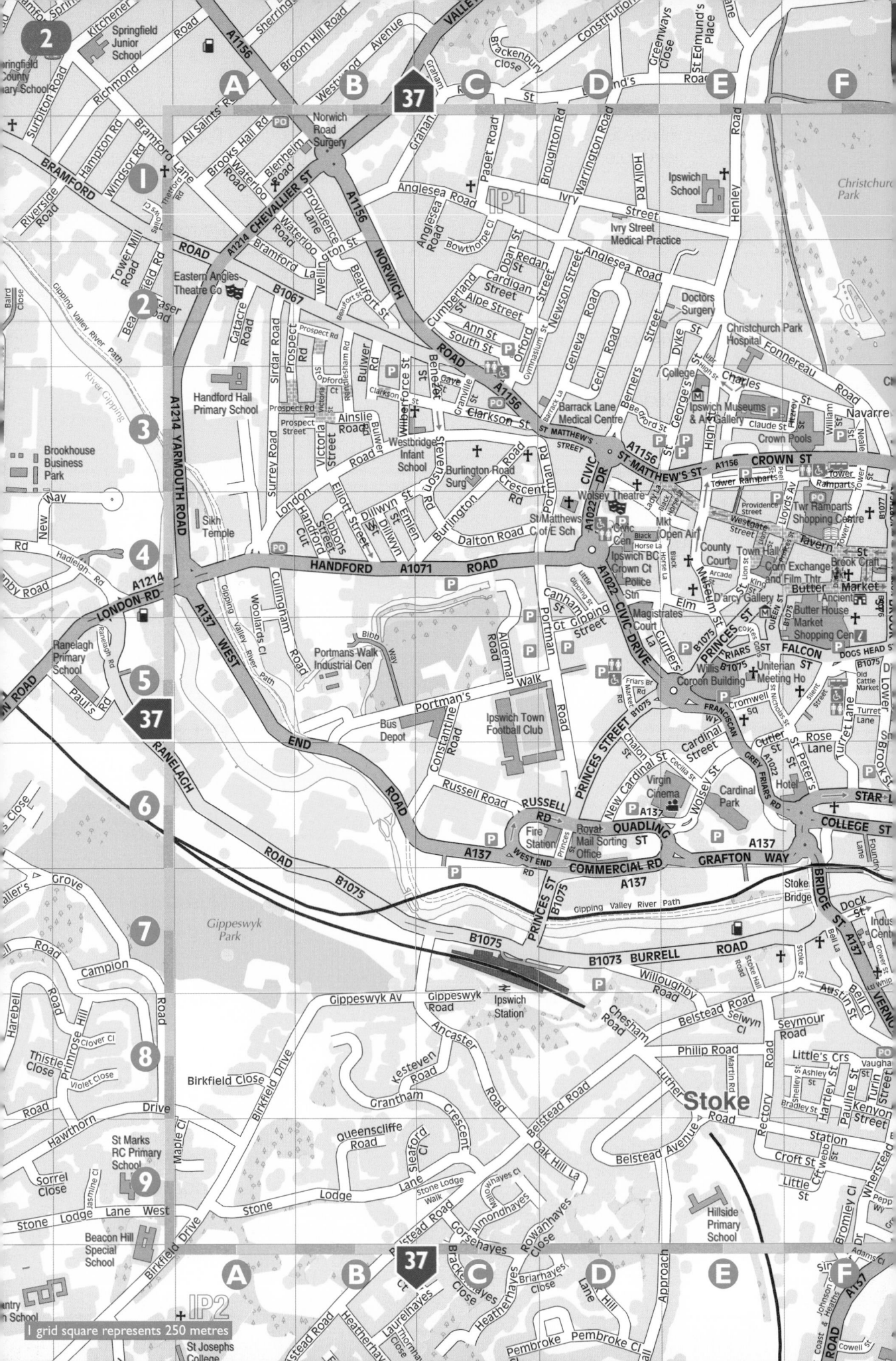

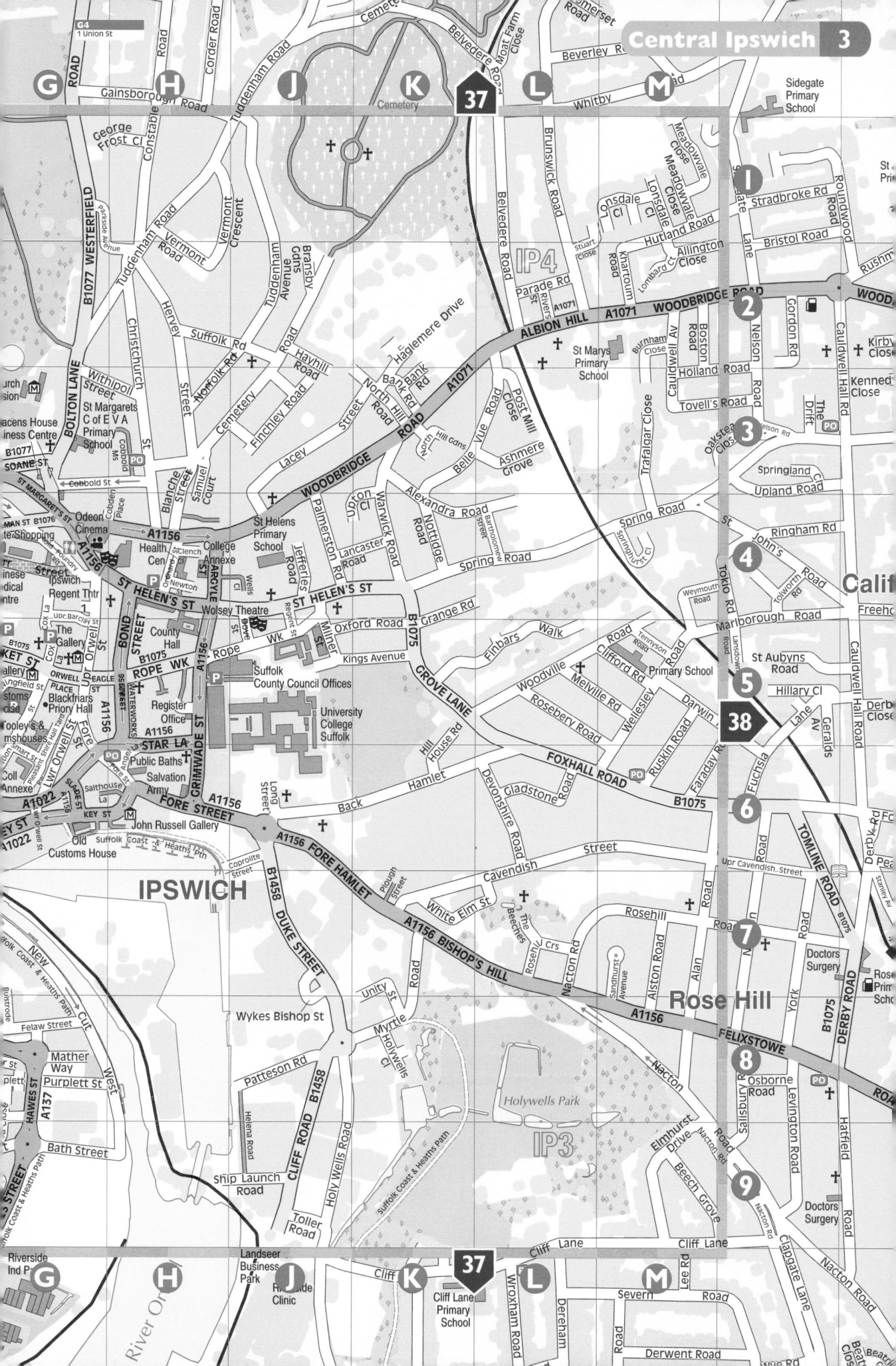

J7
1 Hordle Pl
2 Hordle St

L2
1 St Austin's La

L3
1 Angelgate Esp
2 Church La
3 Golden Lion La
4 Outpart Eastward

113

G H J K L M

ESBJERG; HAMBURG
HOEK VAN HOLLAND

1

Harwich Harbour

2

Castlegate
Street

THE QUAY
Hotel
Eastgate St
King's Quay
Street

King's Head St

Market St

Wellington Rd

Harwich Town
Sailing Club

3

WEST STREET
Church
Street
A120(T)
PO
Street
Guildhall
B1352

St Helen's
Green

GEORGE
STREET

Bath
Side

Road
Pepys
Street

Coke
St

Albemarle St

Harwich
Town Station

Station
Rd

Harbour
Crescent

4

Maria St

A120(T)

Stour

Vansittart
Street

George
Street

Ferndale
Road

Road
Harbour
Crescent

Harbour Crs

5

Canning
St

Alexandra
St

Talbot
St

Ingestre
Street

Albert
Street

Harwich County
Primary School

LC

Alexandra
Rd

Ferndale
Road

Main
Road

Mayflower Av

The Redoubt

Harbour Crs

Mayflower
Avenue

Essex Way

114

HARWICH

Grafton Road

Park Rd

B1352

Barrack
Lane

Beacon Hill
Av

6

Dovercourt
Station

A120(T)

Park
Road

Cwynne
Road

Waddesdon Rd

East
Street

Victoria
Street

Station
Road

HIGH STREET

7

Station
Lane

Nelson Rd

Paddock
Close

Pattrick's Lane

Hill Road

PO

Kingsway Hall Art and Theatre

Orwell
Road

Milton Rd

Bay Rd

Essex Way

King George's
Avenue

B1352

7 2

KINGSWAY

Mill Lane

Bagshaw Rd

Empire Rd

Marine Pde

B1414

Hillcrest
Court

Cliff Road

Brooklyn
Road

Hillcrest
Court

8

Harwich &
Parkeston
Football Club

Portland Crs

Oakland
Road

Portland Avenue

Dovercourt

Hotel

MARINE PARADE

Essex Way

Langley Cl

Road

Lee
Avenue

Second
Avenue

First Av

Hotel

B1414

Elmhurst
Road

Third Av

9

ONK'S ROAD

B1414

Beach
Road

St George's AV

Lower Marine Parade

G H J K L M

143

The Port of Felixstowe

1 grid square represents 250 metres

Felixstowe Station

G · H · J · K · L · M

Cornwall Road

Kemsley Rd · Chester Rd · Devon Rd · Road · West

Beacon Fld · Broom Fld · James Boden Cl

Grange Close

Hawn Wy · Valley · Walk

A154

Andrew's Road

Fleetwo · St Andrew's Road · Croutel

Norchwood Arts Gallery · Gainsborough Road

Cemetery · Langley Avenue

Nursery Wk · Deben High School

Eagles Cl · Cobbold Road · Cowley Road · Penfold Road · York Rd · Ranelagh Road · Felix R · Constable Rd · Quilter Rd · Barton Road

Felixstowe General Hospital · Cobbold Road · Roa

Oak Cl · Oak Close · Wadgate Rd

Thorn Way · Mill Lane

Goyfield Av · Newry Avenue · Surrey Road · Princes Gdns · Princes Lane · Mill Lane · Crescent Rd · Tomline Road · Leopold Road · A1021 · Highfield Road · A1021 · Hamilton Road · Victoria Street · Cobbold Rd · Montague Rd · Chevaler Rd · Cambridge Rd

Deben Way Avenue · Chaucer Road · Queen's Road · A1021 · Brownlow · Hamilton Gardens

Suffolk Coast &

Stour Avenue · Butley Road · Kings Fleet Rd · Waveney Road

Garrison Lane · Garfield Road · Tower Road · Orwell Road · A1021 · Crescent Road · Leopold Rd · Orwell Rd · B1082 · Orwell Rd · Stanley Rd · PO · Hamilton · Spa Pavilion Theatre

ORWELL · Queen's Rd · Leopold Gdns · Htl · Bent Hl · Undercliff Rd W · B1082

Coronation Drive · Anne St · Charles Rd · Way · Avenue

Garrison La · A154 · Riby Road · Bacton Rd · Victoria Road · Garfield Rd · Garfield Cl · Princes Rd · Wolsey · South Hill · Convalescent Hl · UNDERCLIFF RD W

Lincoln Terrace · FELIXSTOWE

Holland Rd · UNDERCLIFF RD WEST · B1082

Cavendish Rd · Granville Rd · Felixstowe Pier

Langer Park Industrial Estate · Holland Road · Sea Road · Suffolk Coast & Heaths Path

Manning Rd · Russell Road · Beach Road W

Marina Gdns · Eaton Gdns · LANGER ROAD · A154 · Buregate Rd · Arwela Road · Sea Road

County Primary School · Manwick Road · St Edmund's Road

Platters Road · Sea Road · Suffolk Coast & Heaths Pth

AV · A154 · BEACH STATION RD · LC · Micklegate Rd

Levington Rd · Nacton Road · A154 · Beach Station Rd · PO · Sea Road · Pretyman Rd

Orford Rd · Tacon Rd · Orford Road

LANGER ROAD

A154

Manor Terrace · A154 · Landguard Rd · Manor Rd

85

115

G · H · J · K · 115 · L · M

I · 2 · 3 · 4 · 5 · 115 · 6 · 7 · 8 · 9

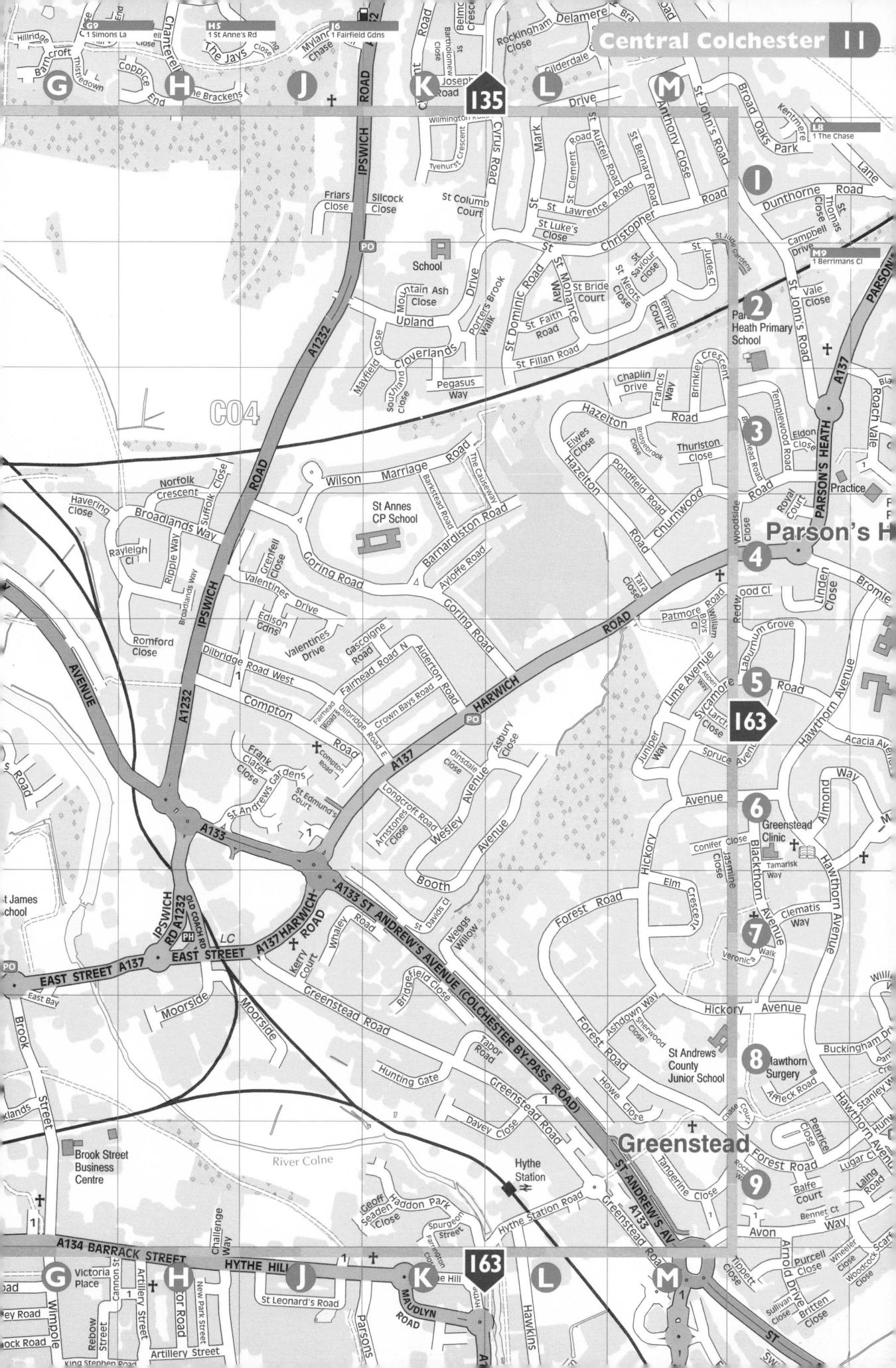

135

163

Parson's H

Parson's Heath

Greenstead

Park Heath Primary School

Greenstead Clinic

St Andrews County Junior School

Hawthorn Surgery

St Annes CP School

School

Brook Street Business Centre

Hythe Station

River Colne

St James School

Practice

Roads and labels:

IPSWICH ROAD
A1232
CO4
HARWICH ROAD
A137
AVENUE
A133
A133 ST ANDREW'S AVENUE (COLCHESTER BY-PASS ROAD)
EAST STREET A137
IPSWICH RD A1232
OLD COACH RD
EAST STREET
A137 HARWICH ROAD
A134 BARRACK STREET
HYTHE HILL
ST ANDREW'S AV A133
Greenstead Road
Moorside
Forest Road
Hawthorn Avenue
Blackthorn Avenue

Grid references: G H J K L M (top and bottom), 1 2 3 4 5 6 7 8 9 I (right side)

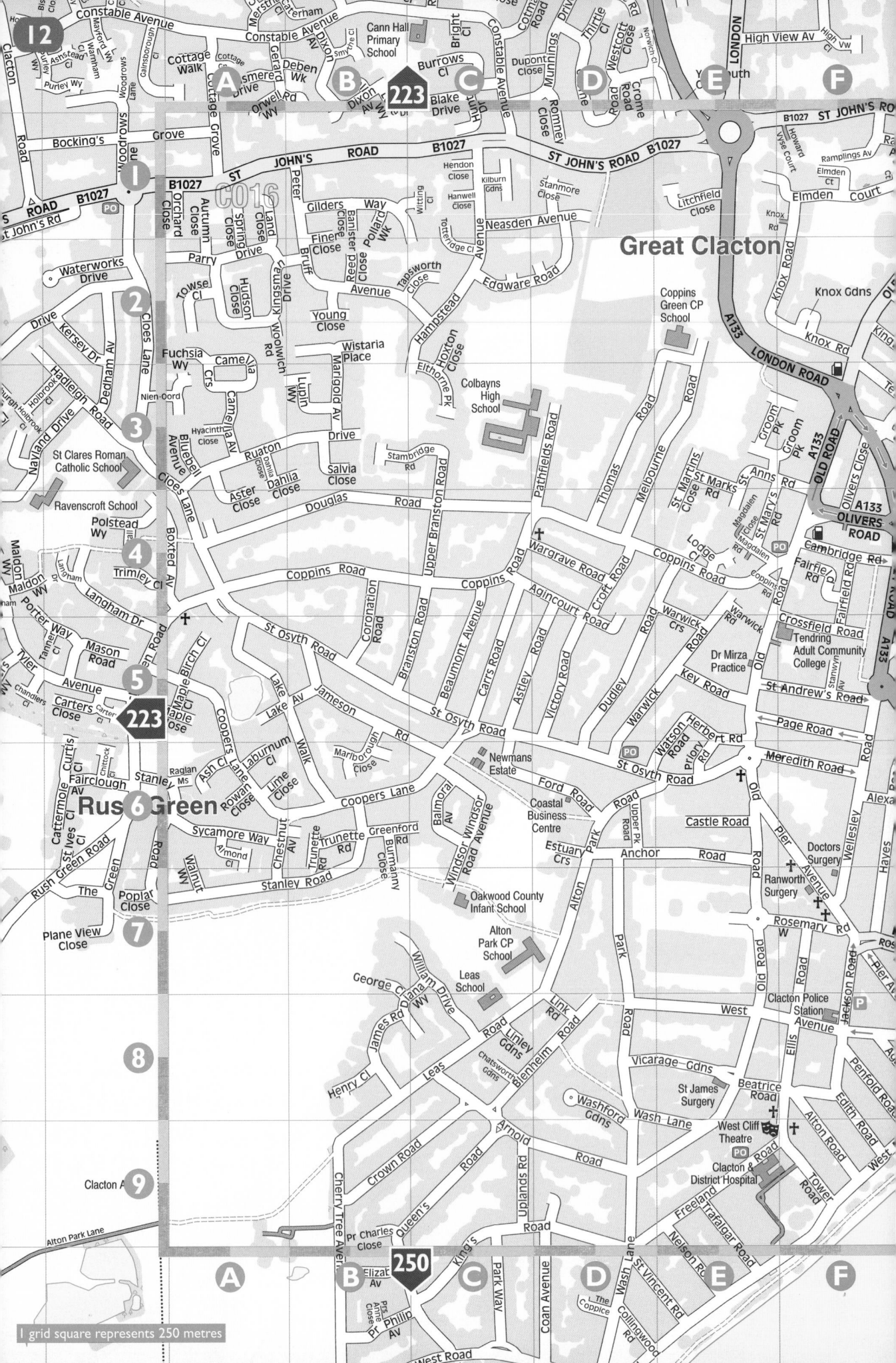

CLACTON-ON-SEA

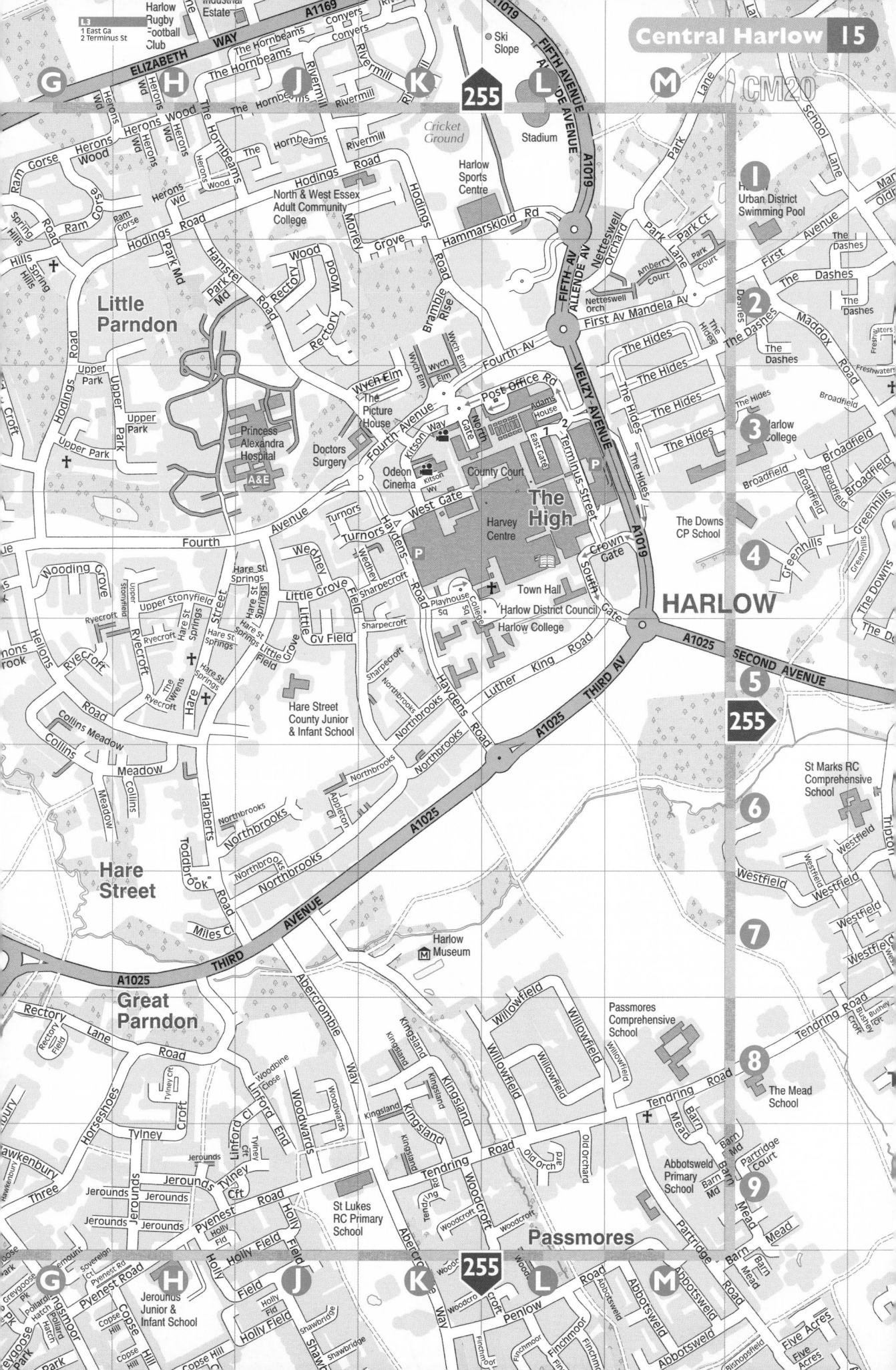

CM20

L3
1 East Ga
2 Terminus St

Little Parndon

Hare Street

Great Parndon

Passmores

HARLOW

The High

Princess
Alexandra
Hospital

North & West Essex
Adult Community
College

Harlow
Rugby
Football
Club

Harlow Sports
Centre

Cricket
Ground

Stadium

Ski Slope

Urban District
Swimming Pool

Harlow
College

Harvey
Centre

County Court

Town Hall

Harlow District Council

Harlow College

Odeon
Cinema

The
Picture
House

Doctors
Surgery

Adam's
House

Post office Rd

The Downs
CP School

St Marks RC
Comprehensive
School

The Mead
School

Abbotsweld
Primary
School

Passmores
Comprehensive
School

St Lukes
RC Primary
School

Hare Street
County Junior
& Infant School

Harlow
Museum

Jerounds
Junior & Infant
School

A&E

Playhouse
Sq

255

255

255

G H J K L M

I
2
3
4
5
6
7
8
9

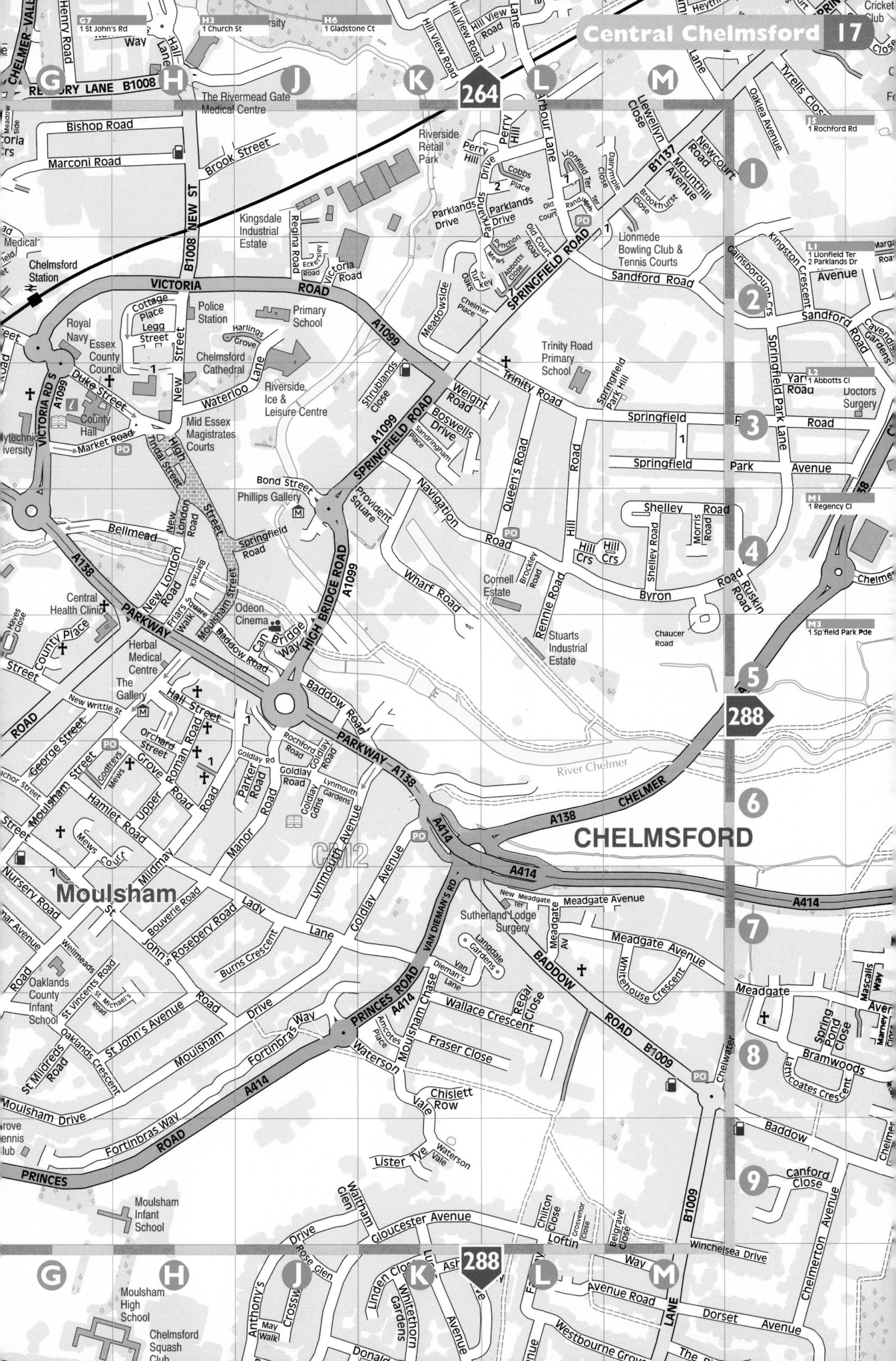

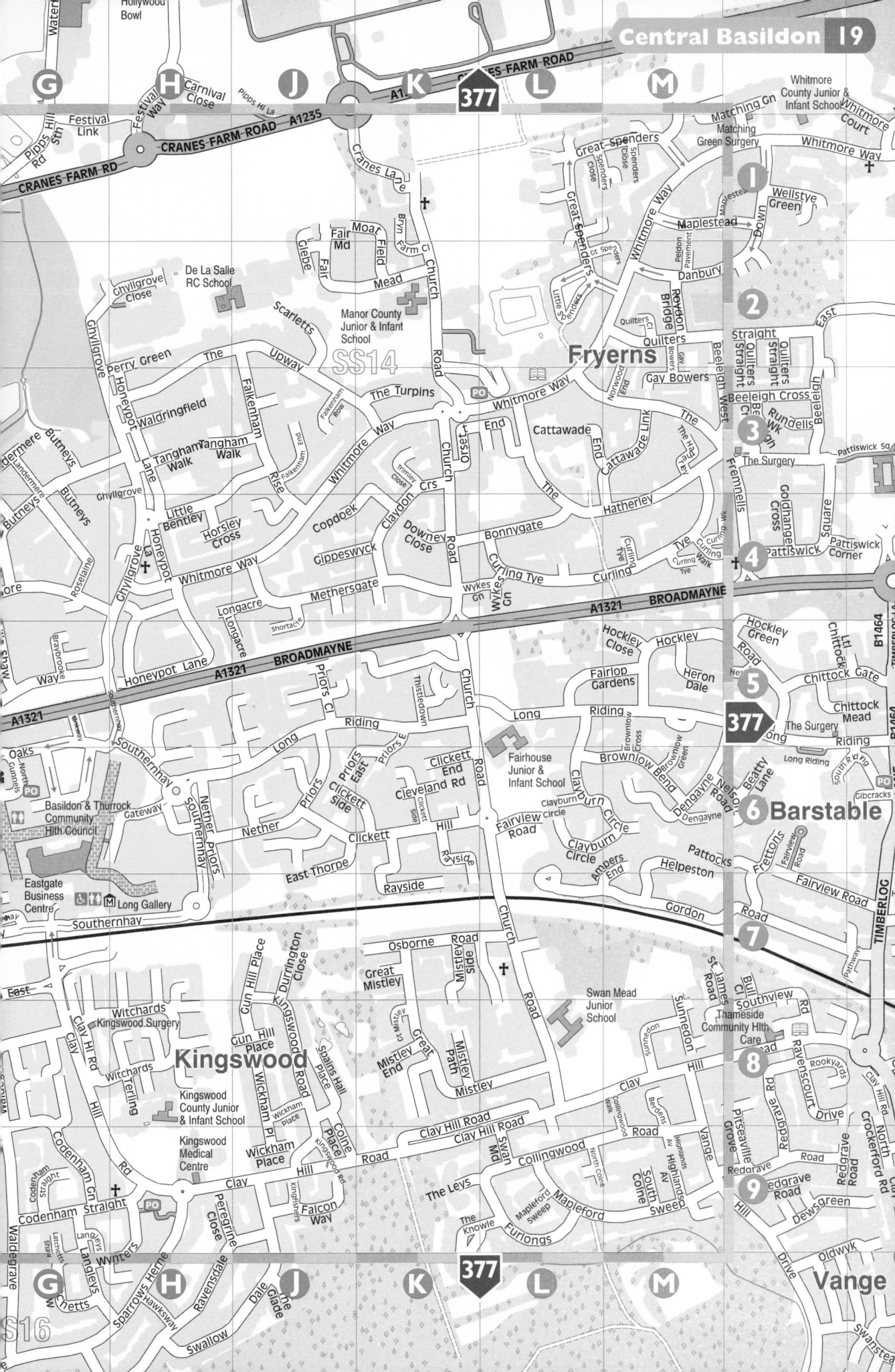

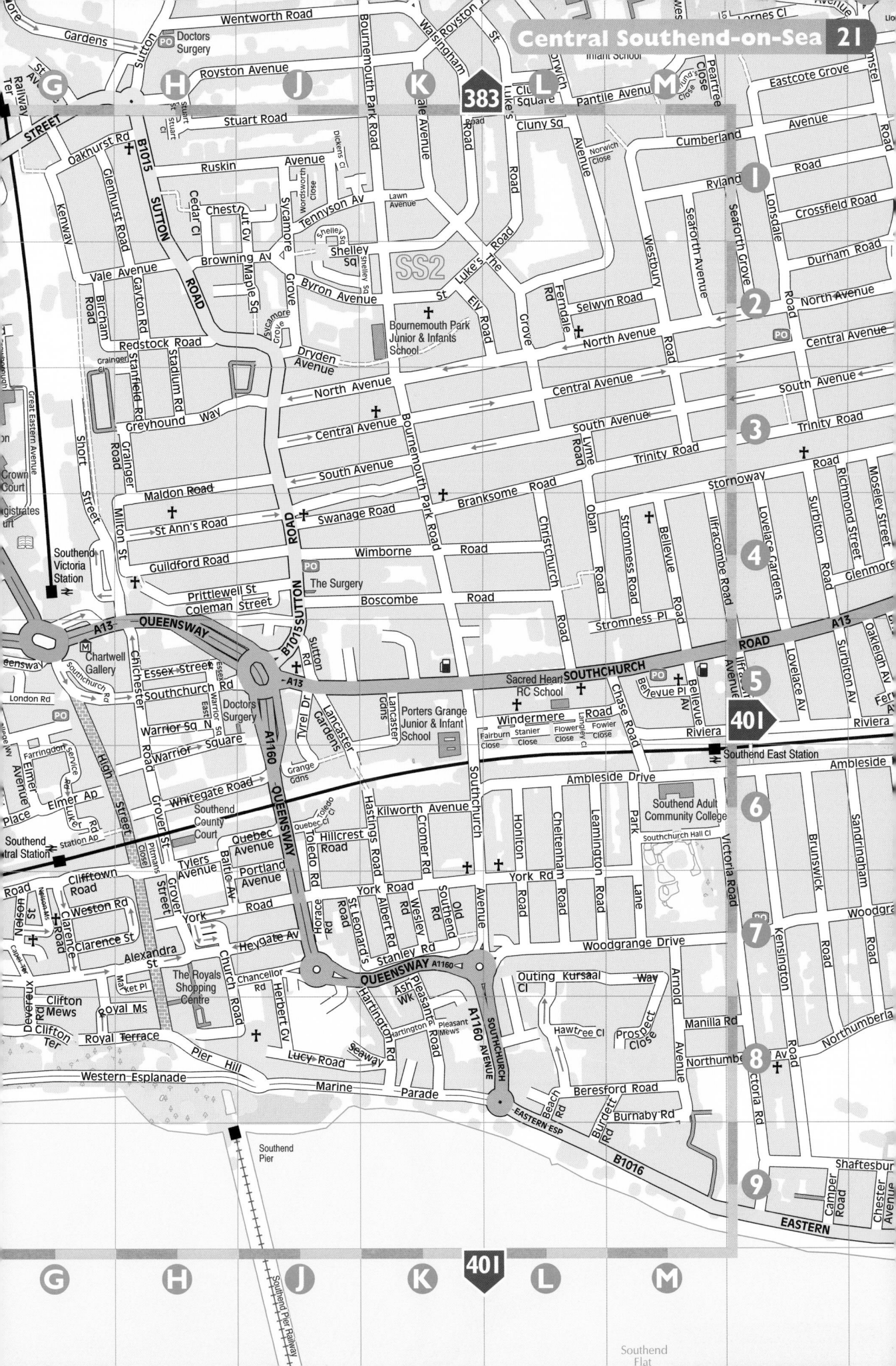

383

G H J K L M

Gardens
Wentworth Road
Sutton
PO Doctors Surgery
Royston Avenue
Stuart Road
Royston Road
St Luke's Square
Pantile Avenue
Infant School
Peartree Close
Eastcote Grove
Cumberland
Avenue
Railway Ter
STREET
Oakhurst Rd
B1015
Ruskin
Cliff Square
Cluny Sq
Norwich Close
Lonsdale
Ryland
I
Road
Crossfield Road
Kenway
Glenhurst Road
SUTTON ROAD
Cedar Cl
Chestnut Gv
Avenue
Dickens Cl
Wordsworth Close
Tennyson Av
Lawn Avenue
Seaforth Grove
Seaforth Avenue
Durham Road
2
Vale Avenue
Bircham Road
Gayton Rd
Maple Sq
Sycamore Grove
Browning Av
Shelley Sq
Byron Avenue
SS2
St Luke's Road
Ely Road
The Grove
Ferndale Rd
Westbury
Selwyn Road
North Avenue
PO
Central Avenue
North Avenue
Redstock Road
Stanfield Rd
Stadium Rd
Grainger Cl
Dryden Avenue
Bournemouth Park Junior & Infants School
South Avenue
3
Trinity Road
Greyhound Way
Grainger Road
North Avenue
Central Avenue
Central Avenue
South Avenue
Bournemouth Park Road
Branksome Road
Lyme Road
Trinity Road
Stornoway
Road
Lovelace Gardens
Surbiton Road
Richmond Street
Moseley Street
Maldon Road
St Ann's Road
Milton St
Swange Road
Wimborne Road
Christchurch
Oban Road
Stromness Road
Bellevue Road
Ilfracombe Road
Glenmore
4
Southend Victoria Station
Guildford Road
The Surgery
PO
Boscombe
Road
Stromness Pl
Crown Court
Short Street
Prittlewell St
Coleman Street
A13 QUEENSWAY
B1015 SUTTON ROAD
A13
SOUTHCHURCH
ROAD
A13
5
401
Chartwell Gallery
M
Essex Street
Southchurch
Chichester Rd
Essex Rd
Warrior East
Doctors Surgery
Sutton Rd
Lancaster Gdns
Sacred Heart RC School
Chase Road
Bellevue Pl Av
Bellevue Av
Riviera
Southend East Station
London Rd
PO
Warrior Sq N
Warrior Square
A1160 QUEENSWAY
Tyrel Dr
Porters Grange Junior & Infant School
Windermere
Road
Langley Cl
Fowler Close
Ambleside
Riviera
Farringdon service
High Street
Whitegate Road
Grange Gdns
Fairburn Close
Stanier Close
Flowery Cl
Southchurch Park
Ambleside Drive
Oakleigh Av
Surbiton Av
6
Southend Central Station
Elmer Avenue
Elmer Ap
Grover St
Quebec Avenue
Toledo Cl
Quebec Cl
Kilworth Avenue
Cromer Rd
Hillcrest Road
Hastings Road
Honiton Road
Cheltenham Road
Leamington Road
Southend Adult Community College
Southchurch Hall Cl
Victoria Road
Brunswick Road
Sandringham
Woodgra
Station Ap
Clifftown Road
Weston Rd
Tylers Avenue
Baltic Av
Portland Avenue
York Road
St Leonard's Road
Albert Rd
Wesley Rd
Old Southend
York Rd
Woodgrange Drive
Kensington
7
Nelson Mews
Clarence Road
Clarence St
York Road
Heygate Av
Stanley Rd
Avenue
Road
Devereux Rd
Alexandra St
The Royals Shopping Centre
Chancellor Rd
Church Road
Herbert Gv
Hartington Rd
Ash Wk
Pleasant Pl
QUEENSWAY A1160
Outing Cl
Kursaal
Way
Arnold Avenue
Manilla Rd
Northumberla
Clifton Mews
Royal Ms
Clifton Ter
Royal Terrace
Pier Hill
Lucy Road
Seaway
Hartington Pl
Pleasant Mews
A1160 SOUTHCHURCH AVENUE
Hawtree Cl
Prospect Close
Northumberland Av
Beresford Road
8
Western Esplanade
Marine Parade
Southend Pier
Beach Rd
Burdett Rd
Burnaby Rd
Shaftesbur
Camper Road
Chester Avenue
9
Southend Pier Railway
EASTERN ESP
B1016
EASTERN

G H J K L M

401

Southend Flat

A B C D E F

I

2

3

River Cam or Granta

LC

Hinxton

North End Road

Duxford Road

Mill Lane

Hunts Lane

High Street

A1301

4

Church Green

PH

New Road

A11(T)

Field Farm

5

Ickleton Road

LC

A1301

6

Cemetery

Brooklampton Street

Duxford Road

Stump Cross

Dell's Farm

M11

7

Butcher's Hill

Mill Lane

Church Street

Abbey Farm

Abbey Street

Frogge Street

River Cam or Granta

PO

B1383

NEWMARKET ROAD

B184

WALDEN ROAD

Birds Close

Back Lane

Priory Close

Southfield

Ickleton

The Stackyard

Coploe Road

Hyll Close

Jackson's

Meadow Lane

Spencer Rd

Stanley Road

The Elms

The Willows

Our Acres

Jackson's

Rookery Close

Pilgrims

8

M11

Carmen St

Eastgate

PO

Church Street

Primary School

Schools

Rookery

The Surg

Rose Lane

High Street

Manor Lane

School Street

Surgery

South Street

Great Chesterford

A B C D E F

Frogge St

Ickleton Road

LC

1 grid square represents 500 metres

E8 1 Wakefield

B8 1 Icknield Cl

Hinxton Grange

G H J K L M

Chalky Road

I

2

3

4

24

5

6

7

8

Abington Park Farm

Cambridgeshire County
Essex County

Park Farm

Cow Lane

Crave Hall Farm

Icknield Way Path

Burtonwood Farm

Icknield Way Path

Icknield Way Path

w Lane

Icknield Way Path

G H J K L M

A1307

A1307

Harcamlow Way

1

2

3

Dean Road

4

26

Bartlow

Camps Road

PO †

Harcamlow Way

5

Westoe Farm

Hills Farm

Harcamlow Way

6

River Bourn

7

Harcamlow Way

8

Whitensmere Farm

G H J K L M

45

Waltons

Newnham Hall Farm

Steventon End

Harcamlow Way

Over Hall Lane

Horseheath

A   B   C   D   E   F

Linton Road

Haverhill Road

Audley Way

Cornish Close

Harcamlow Way

Howard's Lane

Cardinal's Green

Horseheath Green

A1307   PARK HILL

Horseheath Park

Shardelow's Farm

Mill Green

Road

Main Street

New Road

Shudy Camps Park

Main Street

Shudy Camps

Carsey Hill

Parkway

Blacksmiths Lane

Church Road

Haverhill

Bartlow Road

Claydon Close

High Street

Camps Hall

Whitens Farm

Church   Lane

Castle Camps Primary School

Ca   Ca

A   B   C   D   E   F

I
2
3
4
25
5
6
7
8

46

1 grid square represents 500 metres

K2
1 Horsham Cl
2 Shardlow Cl

L2
1 Bramble Cl
2 Reynold's Cl
3 Ruskin Cl
4 Stubbs Cl

M2
1 Cambridge Wy
2 Hawthorn Rd
3 Meadowsweet Cl

G   H   J   K   L   M

A1307

Hanchet End

Hanchet Hall

Barsey Farm

Hazel Stub

Nosterfield End

HAVERHILL

Parkway Middle School

Castle Manor Upper School

Castle Middle School

St Felix RC Primary School

Burton End CPSchool

Clements CP School

Doctors Surgery

Haverhill Hall

Horseham Hall

Suffolk County
Essex County

Moat Farm

47

G   H   J   K   L   M

M5
1 Buckingham Rd
2 Norton Rd

M4
1 The Causeway
2 Greenwood Cl
3 Horseshoe La
4 Yerril Gdn

M3
1 Castle Wk

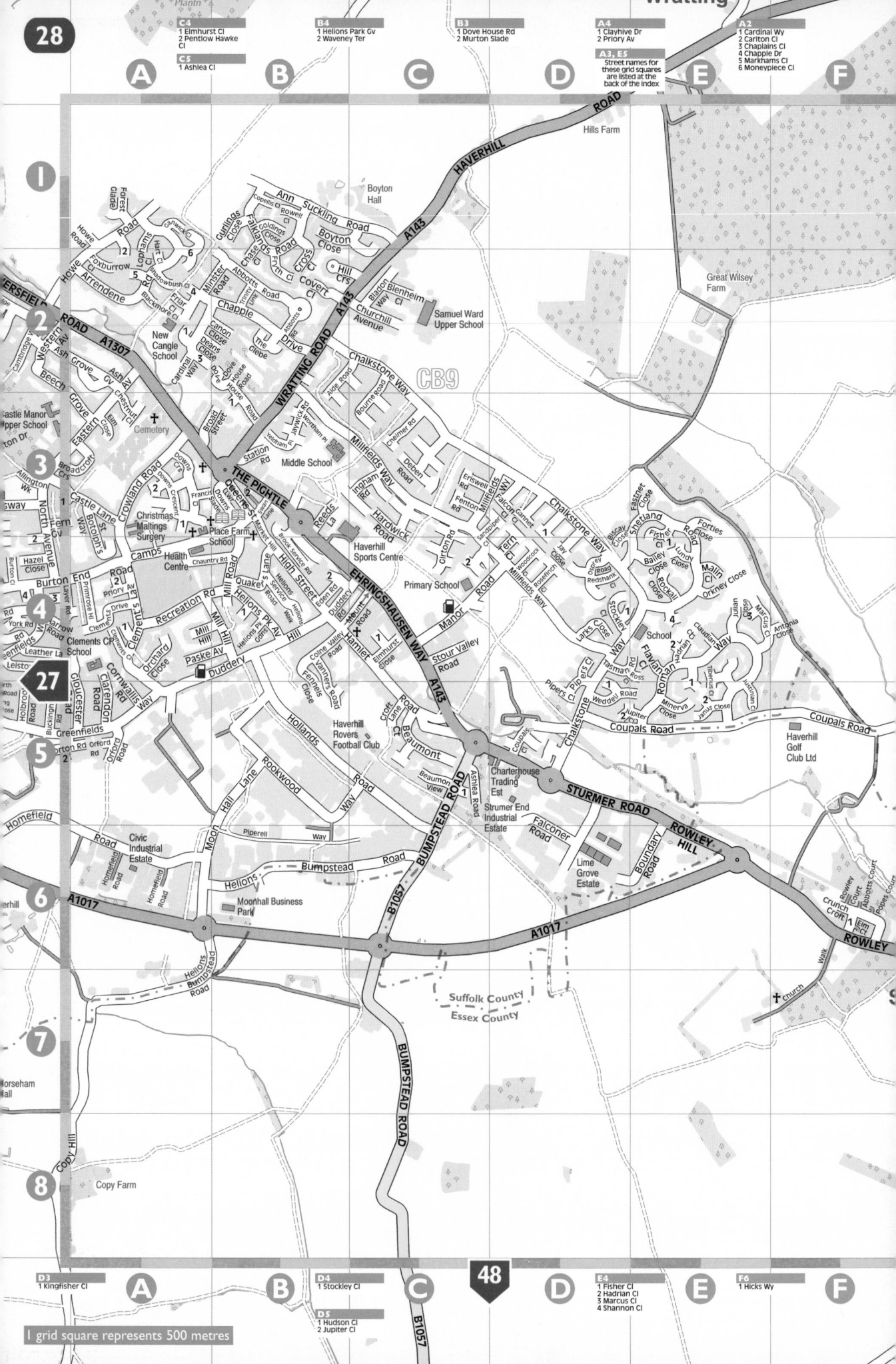

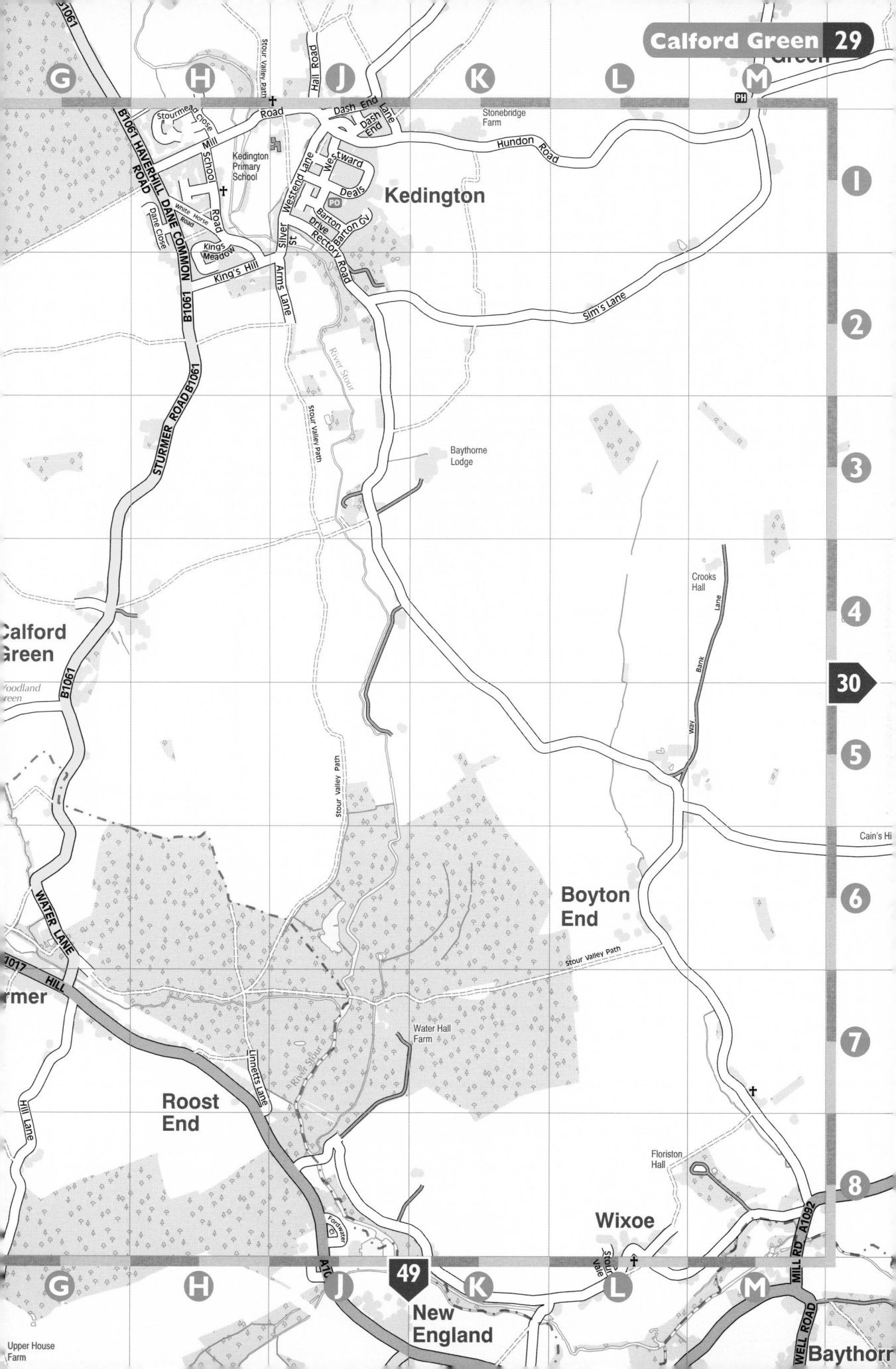

G H J K L M

Green
PH

1

Stourmead Close
Road
Dash End
Dash End
Westward
Deals
Stonebridge Farm
Hundon Road

B1061 HAVERHILL DANE COMMON
Mill School Road
Kedington Primary School
White Horse Road
PO
Barton Barton Gv
Drive
Rectory Road
Kedington

King's Meadow
King's Hill
Silver St
Arms Lane
Westend Lane

2
Sim's Lane

River Stour
Stour Valley Path

STURMER ROAD B1061

Baythorne Lodge
3

Crooks Hall
4

Calford
Green
Woodland Green
B1061

Way
Bank Lane
30

5
Cain's Hi

WATER LANE
Boyton
End
6

B1017 HILL
rmer
Linnetts Lane
Stour Valley Path
7

Roost
End
River Stour
Water Hall Farm
†
Floriston Hall
8

Hill Lane
Fordwater
A10
Stour Vale
Wixoe
†
Mill Rd A1092

G H J K L M
Well Road
New
England
Upper House Farm
Baythorn

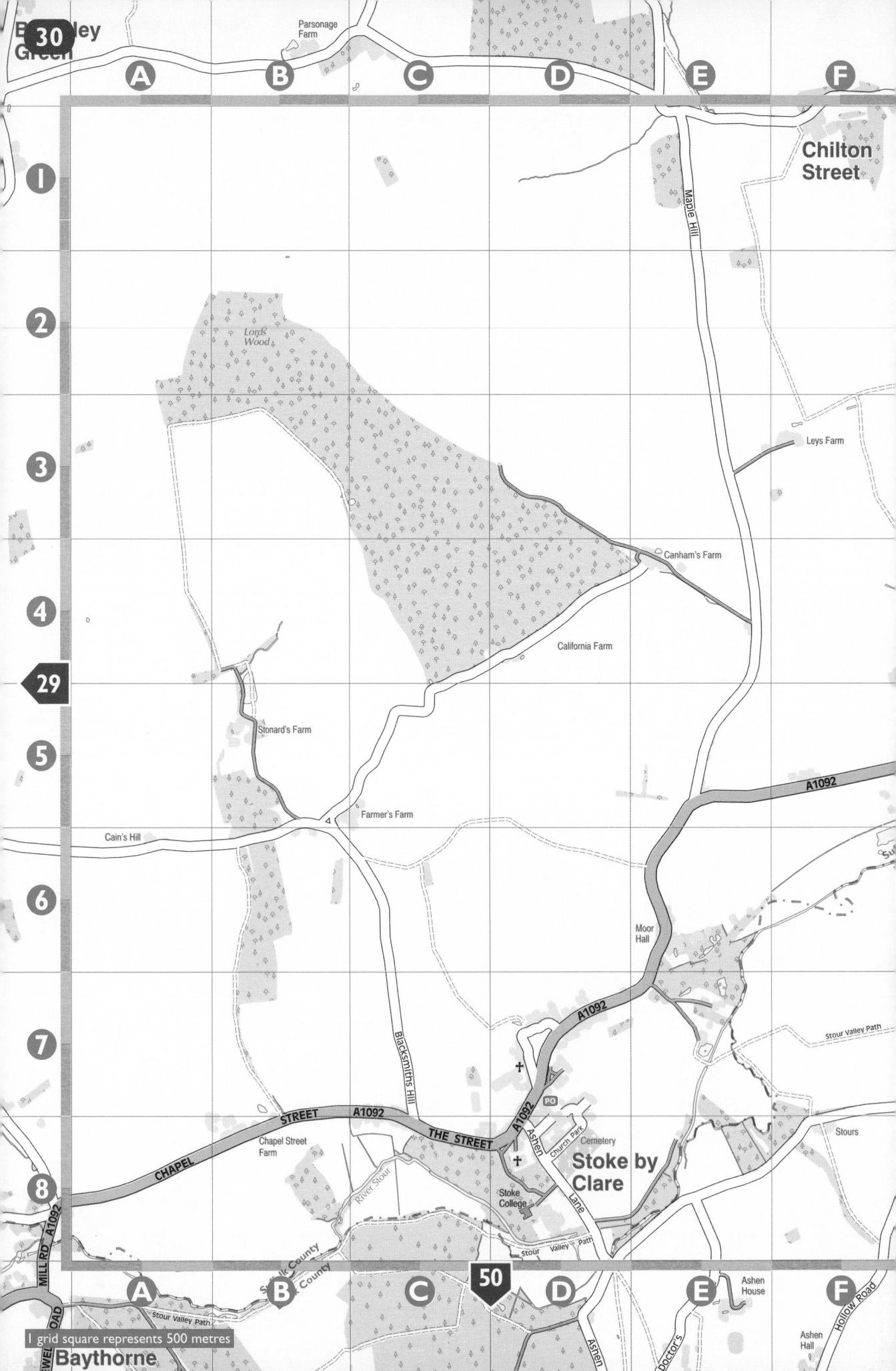

K4
1 Riverbank Cl

G H J K L M

I

Stour Valley Path

Hou
Hall

Wentford
Farm

Wentford

B1063

Clare Road

2

B1063

Hermitage
Farm

Wentford
View

March
Place

Mortimer
Place
De
Burgh
Place

Hertford Road

Hertford Rd

Hertford Road

Hermitage Meadows

SNOW HILL

BRIDEWELL STREET B1063

Gilbert
Road

Clarence Road

Hermitage Farm

A1092

ROAD

3

Upper
Common

Common St

Police
Station

Clare
Primary School

Erbury Place

Cosford
Close

Gosford
Close

Guildhall Surgery

Cemetery

B1063

CALLIS STREET

CHURCH STREET

Clare

Stour Valley Path

Clare
Middle School

CAVENDISH

Bench Barn
Farm

The Gallery

Stonehall Surg

High Street

NETHERGATE ST

WELL LANE

CD

Station
Road

Matting Lane

1

PH

Mill Road

Bailey

Clare Castle
Country Park

Highfield

River Stour

4

32

County
County

River Stour

Mill Farm

STOKE

A1092

ROAD

Westfield

Granary Close

Lutus Cl

Ashen Road

Stour Valley Path

Hickford Hill

Claredown
Farm

5

6

Hollow Road

Ashen Road

Claret
Hall

Bradley hill
Farm

Stour Valley Path

7

8

G H J K L M

Butler's
Farm

Ovington

A   B   C   D   E   F

E1
1 Church Cl

D1
1 Manor Cl
2 Peacocks Cl

Blacklands
Hall

1

Houghton
Hall

r Valley Path

Stour Valley Path

Peacocks Cl

Peacocks

2

Nether
Hall

1

Nether Rd

Nether Rd

1

Water Lane

Cavendish

The Commons

Stour Valley Walk

Cavendish
Primary
School

PH PO

A1092 HIGH ST LOWER

MEI

2

Greys Close

Sue Ryder
Foundation

ST

Pentlow Dr

ciuanie
orch

Cavendish
Hall

POOLE STREET A1092

River Stour

Pentlow

B1

STOUR STREET

3

A1092

A1092

Mill Lane

Bower Hall

River St

4

Larks in the Wood

31

Sch

5

Pentlo

Paine's
Manor

Shearing
Place

6

Pannell's
Ash

7

Paul's
Hall

Church Street

8

**Church
Street**

Brown's

Church street

A   B   C   D   E   F

I grid square represents 500 metres

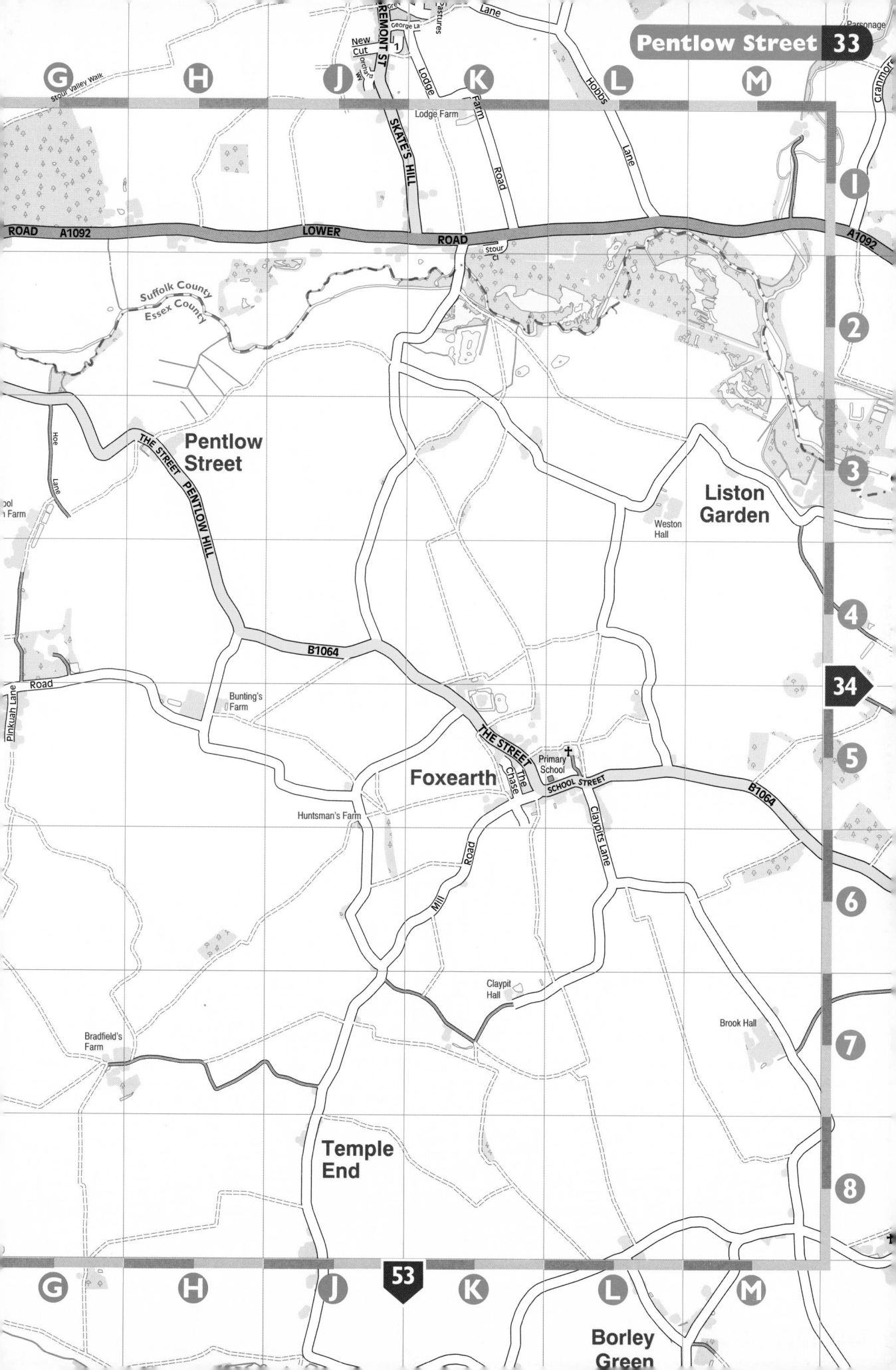

G H J K L M

I

2

3

4

34

5

6

7

8

G H J K L M

53

Parsonage

George La

New Cut

REMONT ST

SKATE'S HILL

Lodge

Farm

Road

Lodge Farm

Hobbs

Lane

Cranmor

ROAD A1092 LOWER ROAD A1092

Stour
Cl

Suffolk County
Essex County

Pentlow
Street

THE STREET PENTLOW HILL

Hoe

Lane

Liston
Garden

Weston
Hall

ool
n Farm

B1064

Pinkuah Lane

Road

Bunting's
Farm

Foxearth

THE STREET

The Chase

Primary
School

SCHOOL STREET

B1064

Claypits Lane

Huntsman's Farm

Mill

Road

Claypit
Hall

Brook Hall

Bradfield's
Farm

Temple
End

Borley
Green

Stour Valley Walk

A   B   C   D   E   F

Parsonage Farm

Lane

Crannoregreen

St Edmund Way

Steeds Meadow

D3

1

Farm

High St

Harefield

A1092

Burton's Farm

WINDMILL HILL

WESTGATE STREET

B1092

Church Wk

Stour Va Wk

B1064

2

Cranbrook Lane

School Lane

Melford Hall (NT)

Bull Lane

3

River Stour

Chad Brook

PH

PO

Hotel

Smalley Ga

Spicers La

Cock And Bell La

Chantry

M Gallery

Woollards Gdns

The Long Melford Practice

Shaw Road

Cordell Place

Cordell Road

Chadburn Road

Middle Way

Raile Walk

Hill Cl

Sampson Dr

Palmerswent

Cl

Lakforth

King's

4

Stour Valley Walk

Meeting Fld

New Rd

St Catherine's Rd

HALL ST

The Limes

Laurel Dr

1

Olivers Cl

Olivers Cl

Olivers Cl

LONG MELFORD

33

Liston Lane

Long Melford Primary Sch

Swan Lane

Swanfield

Swanfield

5

Liston

Stour Valley Walk

LITTLE ST MARY'S

SOUTHGATE ST

Rivish La

Rivish Way

Roman Dr

Roman Wy

Cox's Old Dr

Lepton Dr

Southgate Gdns

6

B1064

Station Rd

STATION RD

Martyns Rise

Westrodes

The Drays

St Stephen Close

Ropers Lane

RODBRIDGE HL

Rodbridge House

Mills Lane

7

B1064

BORLEY ROAD

B1064

Rodbridge Corner

SUDBURY ROAD

A134

8

C010

Stour Valley Walk

Lower Road

Hall Road

Borley

54

Bor Hall

River

A134

Pembroke Rd

Canterbury Road

Chaucer Road 7

Lancaster Rd

Gloucester Rd

Clermont Av

Hoxter

Highview Close

Lane

A   B   C   D   E   F

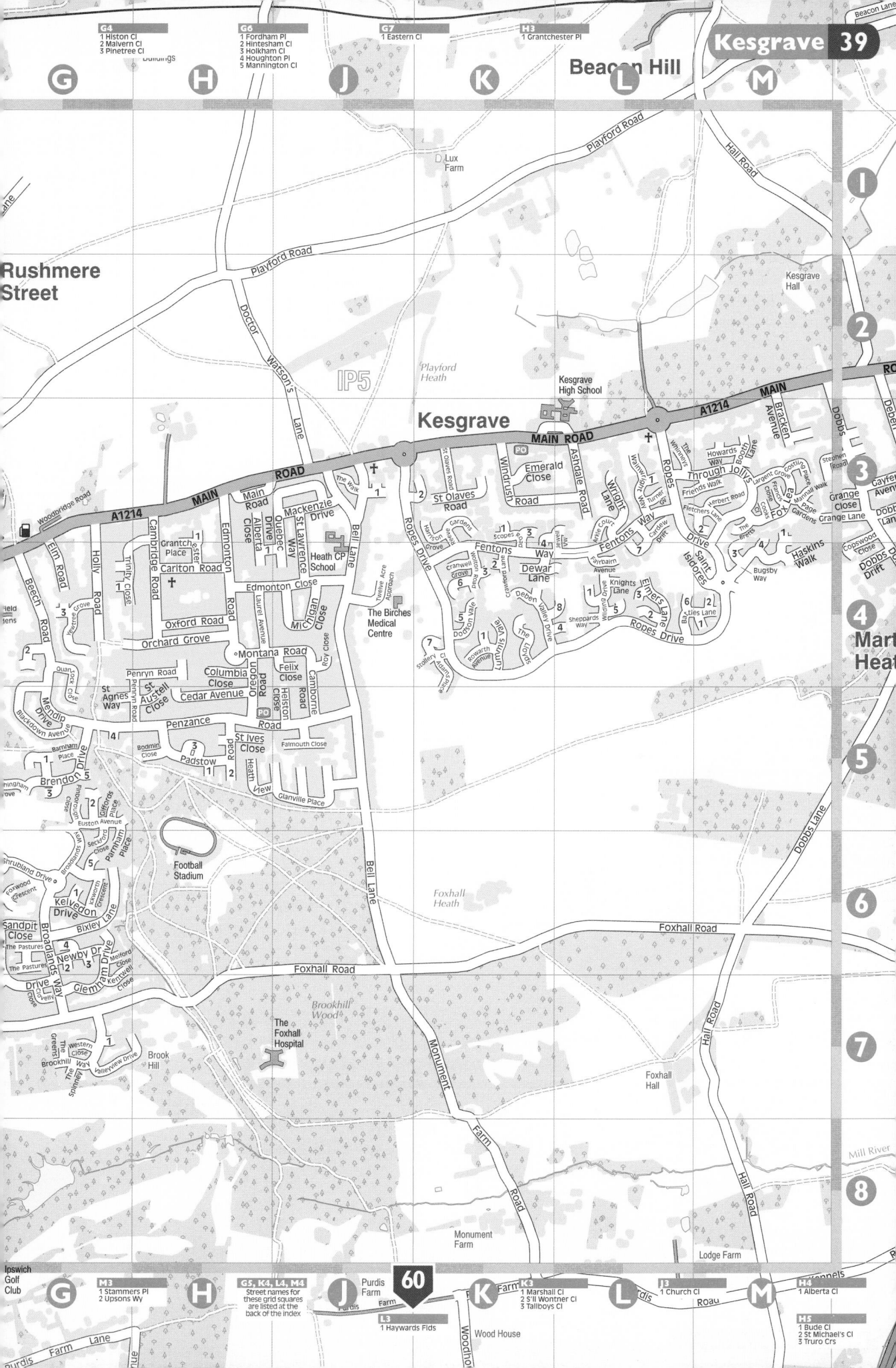

G   H   J   K   L   M

Beacon Hill

Rushmere
Street

Beacon Lane

Playford Road

D Lux
Farm

Kesgrave
Hall

Playford Road

Playford
Heath

IP5

Kesgrave
High School

A1214   MAIN   RO

Woodbridge Road

A1214   MAIN   ROAD

Kesgrave

MAIN   ROAD

PO

Bracken Avenue

Dobbs Lane

Debe

Howards
Way

Through Jollys

Gayfer Aven

Grange
Close

Dobb
Lan

Grange Lane

Copswood
Close

Main
Road
Drive

The Walk

St Olaves Road

Emerald
Close

Windrush

Wright
Lane

Ropes

Friends Walk

Fletchers Lane

Herbert Road

Francis
Close

Page
Gardens

Marshall Walk

Haskins
Walk

Du
Dri

Elm Road

Holly Road

Cambridge Road

Trinity Close

Grantchester
Place

Edmonton
Road

Alberta
Drive

Quebec
Way

Mackenzie
Drive

St Lawrence
Way

Bell Lane

Ropes Drive

St Olaves
Road

Harton
Grove

Gardens

Scopes Road

Fentons
Way

Ante Court

Turnel
Gr

Cardew
Drift

Fentons
Way

Wainwright Way

Saint Isidores

The Brens

Bugsby
Way

Beech Road

Grove

Edmonton Close

Cariton Road

Michigan
Close

Laurel Avenue

Cranwell
Grove

Crawford
Grove

Deben
Close

Dewar
Lane

Fairbairn
Avenue

Knights
Lane

Elmers Lane

Battles Lane

St Agnes
Way

Oxford Road

Montana Road

Columbia
Close

Oregon
Road

Roy Close

Felix
Close

Doddon Vale

Rowarth
Avenue

Stollery

Adams

Sheppards
Way

Ropes Drive

Orchard Grove

Penryn Road

Penryn Road

St Austell
Close

Cedar Avenue

Camborne
Road

Helston
Close

PO

The Lloyds

Windle

Deben Valley Drive

Mendip
Drive

Blackdown Aven

Quant

Barnham
Place

Penzance

St Ives
Close

Padstow

Bodmin
Close

Falmouth Close

Heath
View

Glanville Place

Brendon
Drive

Findon

Gibbons

Euston Avenue

Seckford
Close

Parham
Place

Football
Stadium

Foxhall
Heath

Bell Lane

Dobbs Lane

Shrubland Drive

Foxwood
Crescent

Broadlands

Kelvedon
Drive

Bixley Lane

Ixworth
Crescent

Sandpit
Close

Broadlands
Way

The Pastures

Newby Dr

Melford
Close

Kentwell
Close

Foxhall Road

Foxhall Road

Drive

Glemham
Way

The Greens

Western
Close

Valleyview Drive

Brook
Hill

Brookhill

Brookhill
Wood

The
Foxhall
Hospital

Monument

Farm

Foxhall
Road

Foxhall
Hall

Mill River

Hall Road

Ipswich
Golf
Club

Monument
Farm

Lodge Farm

I   2   3   4   5   6   7   8

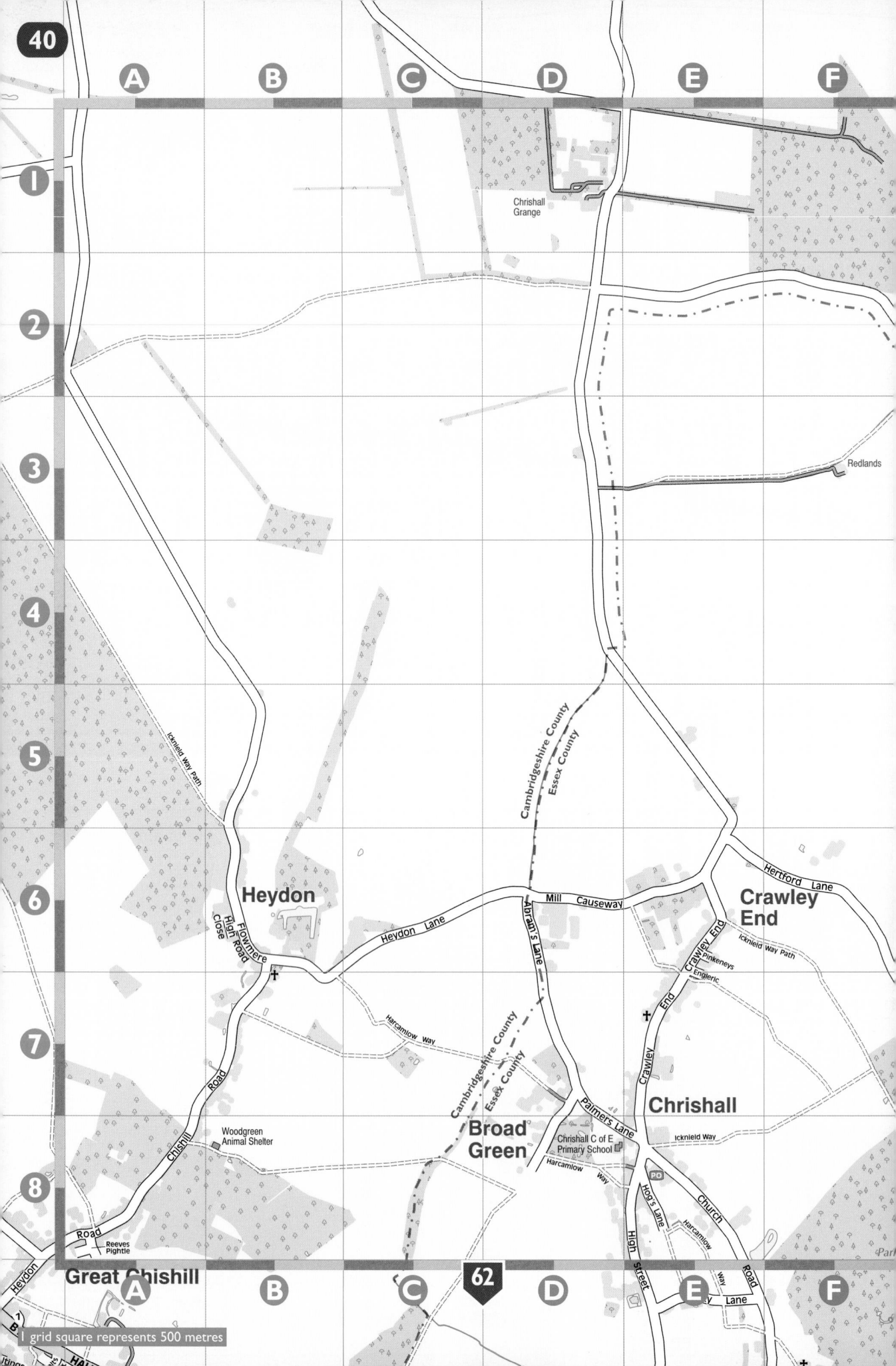

G H J K L M

1

2

3

4

42

5

6

7

8

Rectory Farm

Ickleton Granges

Grange Road

Royston Lane

Cambridgeshire County
Essex County

Lodge Farm

Valance Farm

The Poplars

Quickset Road

New Jersey Farm

Elmondbury

Elmdon

Strethall

Hartford Lane

Heydon Lane

Ickleton Road

Elm Court

Horseshoe Close

Hollow Road

Icknield Way

Icknield Way

Essex Hill

Freewood Lane

Freewood Farm

G H J K L M

63

Lofts Hall

ood

Ickleton
The Stackyard

A B C 22 D E F

I

Great
Chesterford

2

Junction 9

River Cam or Granta

Valance
Farm

3

Bordeaux
Farms

Strethall
Field

4

5
The
Poplars

Strethall Road

6

ethall

7

Catmere
End

Howe
Wood

Strethall Road

Littlebury

8

Littlebury Green Road

A B C D E F

Howe
Hall

1 grid square represents 500 metres

G7
1 Kents Yd
2 Meadow Clays
3 Rectory Cl

L7
1 Limefields
2 Little Walden Rd

M8
1 Aspin Ms
2 Buckenhoe Rd
3 Byrd's Farm La
4 Chalklands
5 Cornwallis Pl
6 Doddenhill Cl
7 Fair Leas

G   H   J   `23`   K   L   M

1
2
3
4
44
5
6
7
8

Ickhield Way Path

Rectory Farm

Chesterford Park

Pelts Lane

High Street

Little Chesterford

Emanuel Wood

WALDEN ROAD

B184

THE SLADE

Springwell

B184

B1383

Rowley Hill Farm

SPRINGWELL ROAD

LITTLE WALDEN ROAD

B1052

Westley Farm

Westley Lane

B1052

CAMBRIDGE ROAD

Roman Way

Walden Road

Northend

Church Walk

HIGH ST

Mill Lane

River Cam or Granta

B1383

LONDON ROAD

WINDMILL HILL

The Vineyard

Spring Wood

Golf Course

Saffron Walden Golf Club

BRIDGE ST

Saffron Walden Town Football Club

St Marys Primary School

Castle Street

Castle Street Surgery

The Museum

Little Walden Road

Rookes

St Marys View

Crocus Fields

mbert Cross

Shrublands

Goddard Way

Corner Park

Morris Harp Way

Goddard Cross

Usterdale Road

Castle Cross

Brook Avenue

de Bohun Court

Neville Road

How Howard Road

Ashdon Road

MILL LANE

Thorncroft

The Wayback

School

G   H   J   `65`   K   L   M

White
Farm

Camps
Hall

Ca
Ca

church

Cast
Prim
School

1

Langley
Wood

Castle Farm

2

**Camps
End**

Cooper's
Farm

3

Browning's
Farm

Winsey Farm

Cambridgeshire County

Essex County

Little Biggin
Common

4

Olms
Gree

45

5

Bourne
Farm

Great
Bendysh
Wood

Olmstead
Hall

6

7

Swan's
Farm

Park Farm

**Radwinter
End**

Little Bendysh Wood

8

Godfrey's
Farm

Bendysh
Hall

Winc
Hall

Ashdown Road

Golden Lane

I grid square represents 500 metres

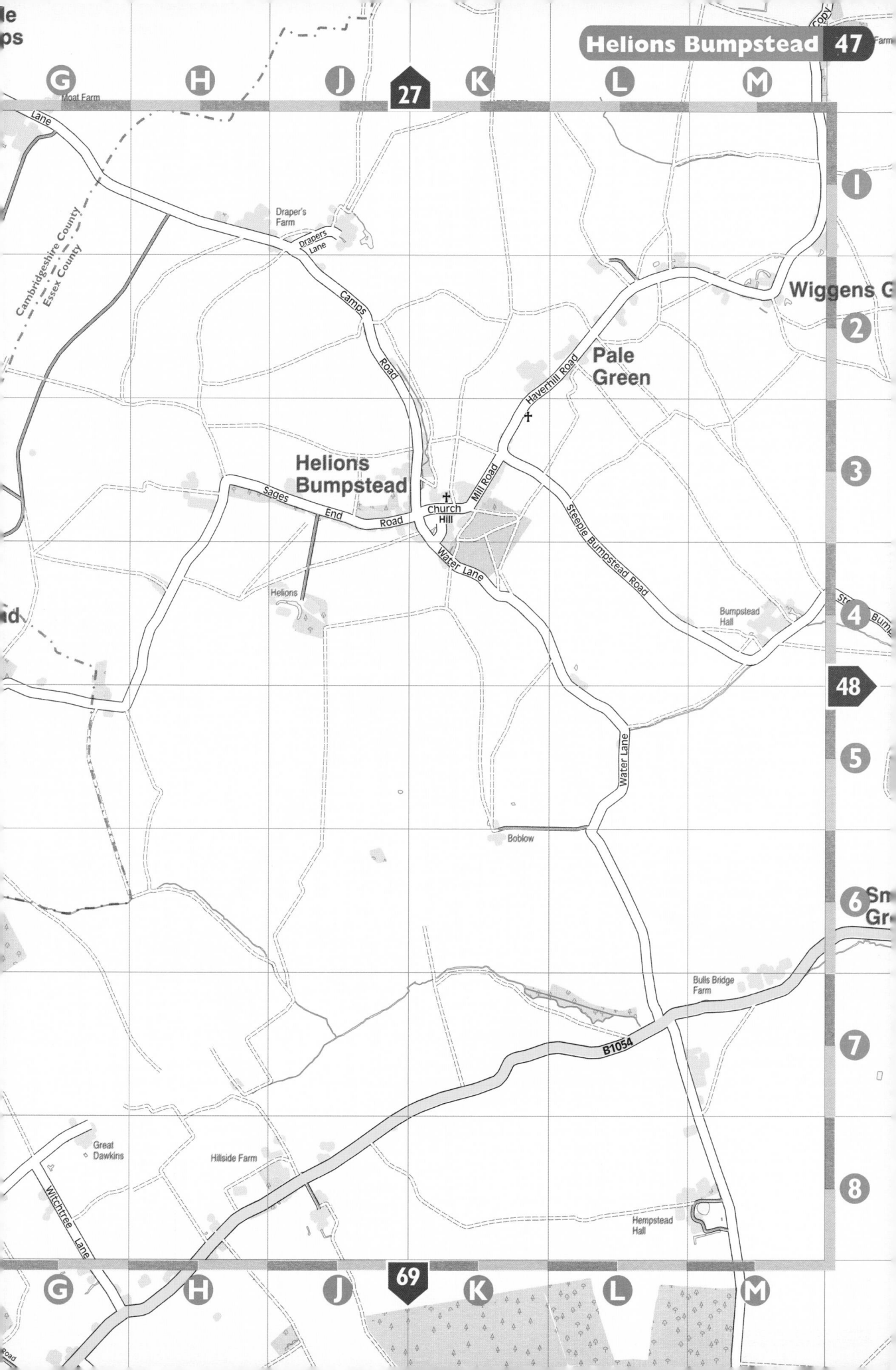

G H J **27** K L M

I

Moat Farm
Lane

Draper's
Farm

Drapers
Lane

Cambridgeshire County
Essex County

Camps Road

Wiggens G

2

**Pale
Green**

Haverhill Road

3

**Helions
Bumpstead**

Sages End Road

Church
Hill

Mill Road

Steeple Bumpstead Road

St
Bum

4

Helions

Water Lane

Bumpstead
Hall

48

5

Water Lane

Boblow

6 Sm
Gr

Bulls Bridge
Farm

Great
Dawkins

Hillside Farm

Witchtree Lane

7

B1054

8

Hempstead
Hall

G H J **69** K L M

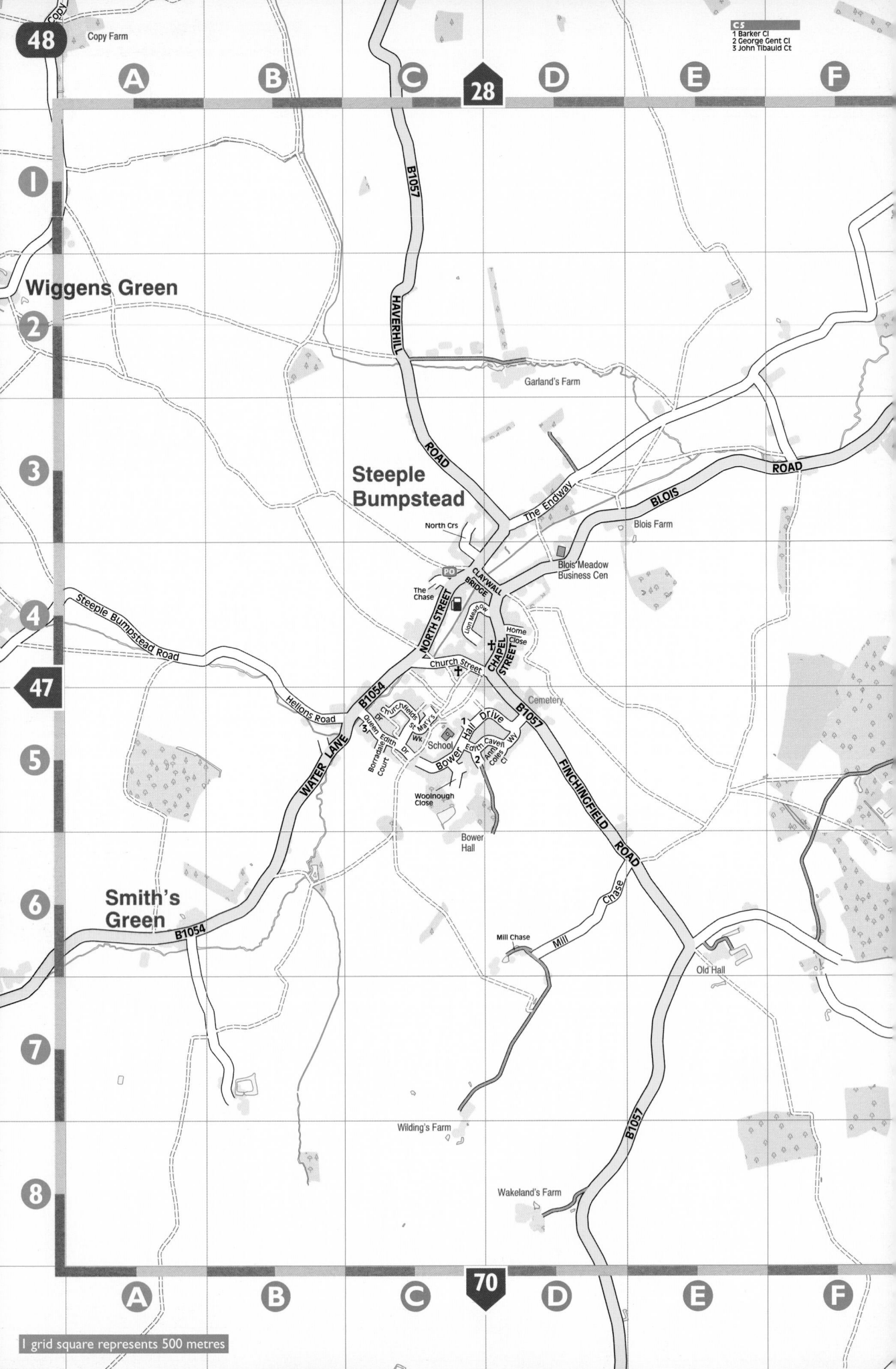

Copy Farm

A B C 28 D E F

1

Wiggens Green

2

B1057

HAVERHILL ROAD

Garland's Farm

3

Steeple
Bumpstead

The Endway

BLOIS ROAD

Blois Farm

North Crs

Blois Meadow
Business Cen

PO

The Chase

CLAYWALL
BRIDGE

NORTH STREET

Lion Meadow

Home
Close

CHAPEL STREET

4

Steeple Bumpstead Road

47

Hellons Road

Church Street

Cemetery

B1054

Church Fields

St Mary's

WK

Queen Edith Dr

Borradaile Court

School

Bower Hall Drive

1

Cavell

Edith
Amb
Cole
Ct
Cl

2

B1057

WATER LANE

Woolnough
Close

FINCHINGFIELD ROAD

5

Bower
Hall

6

Smith's
Green

B1054

Chase

Mill Chase

Mill

Old Hall

7

B1057

Wilding's Farm

8

Wakeland's Farm

A B C 70 D E F

I grid square represents 500 metres

G

H

J 29

K

W L oe

M

New England

Floriston Hall

Upper House Farm

1 Baythorn End

B1054

2

B1054

Rylands Farm

A1017

FOUR ASH HILL

MILL RD A1092

A1017 RIDGEWELL ROAD

Fell Road

Station Road

3

THE

Fell Road

Whitleys

4

Birdbrook

Moat House

The Street

Moat Road

50

Daw Street

5

Stud Farm

Frinkle Green

Three Chimneys Farm

6

Stambourne Road

Essex Hall

Whitehouse Farm

Park Wood

Wesley End Road

7

Wesley End Road

8

Hill Farm

Birdbrook Road

Chapel Road

Way

En 71

Mill Road

Stambourne

Church Road

G

H

J

K

L

M

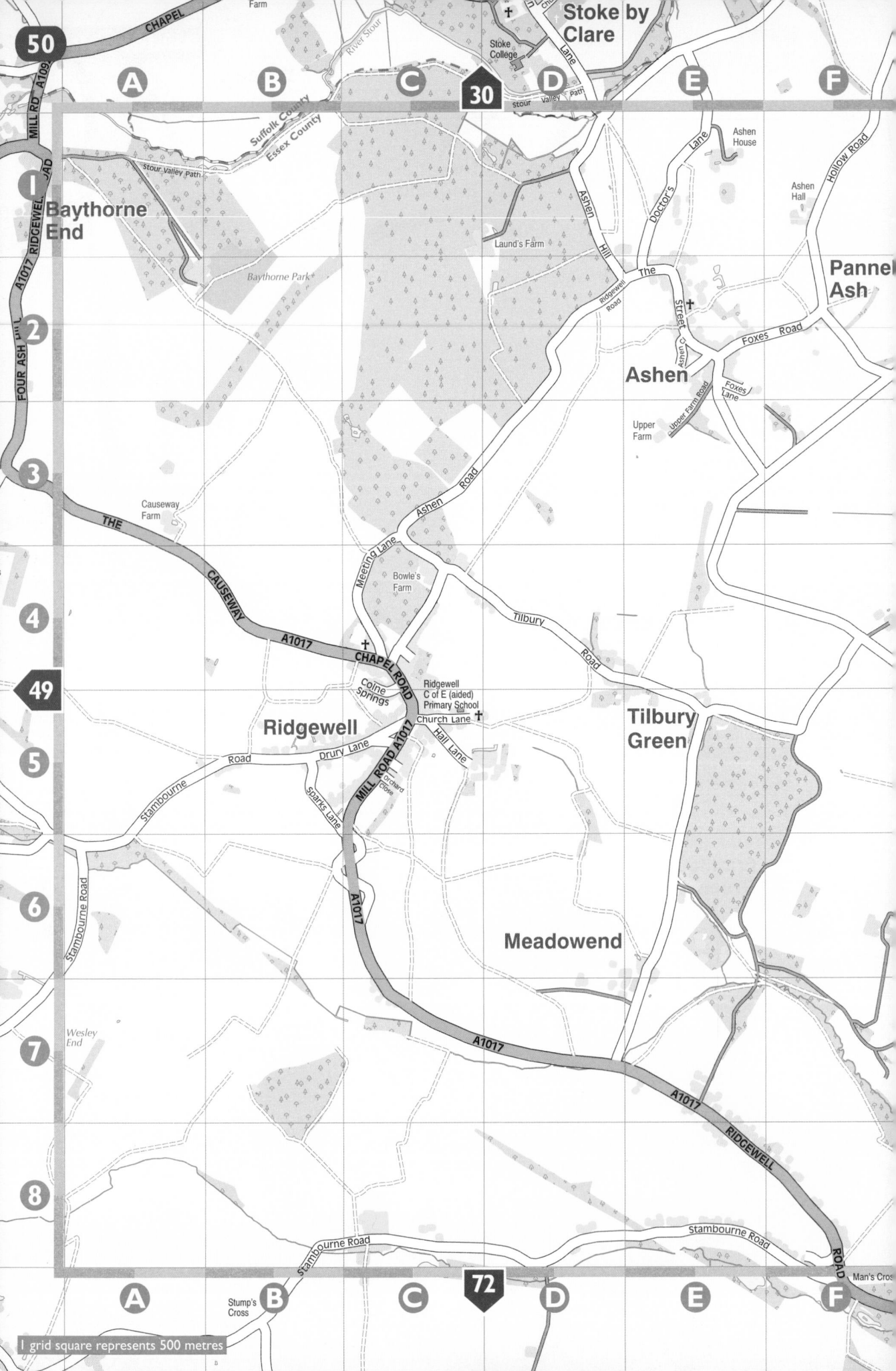

G H J 31 K L M

I

Butler's Farm

2 Bel
t F

Ovington Hall

Ovington

Ashen Road

3

Silver End

Gage's

Know Gree

Gage's Road

Wakeshall Lane

Wakeshall Farm

Marshy Lane

4

52

Park Farm

5

Twelve Acre Wood

Belchamp Road

Mashay Road

6

Tilbury Hall

Tilbury Juxta Claire

Tilbury Court

Red House

Mashay Road

7

Spencers

Little Yeldham

Hydewood Road

School Road

North End Road

Tilbury Road

Mill Lane

8

The Hyde Farm

Road

Hall Green

Nor

Gr Yeldham

Primary School

A1017

Upper Yeldham Hall

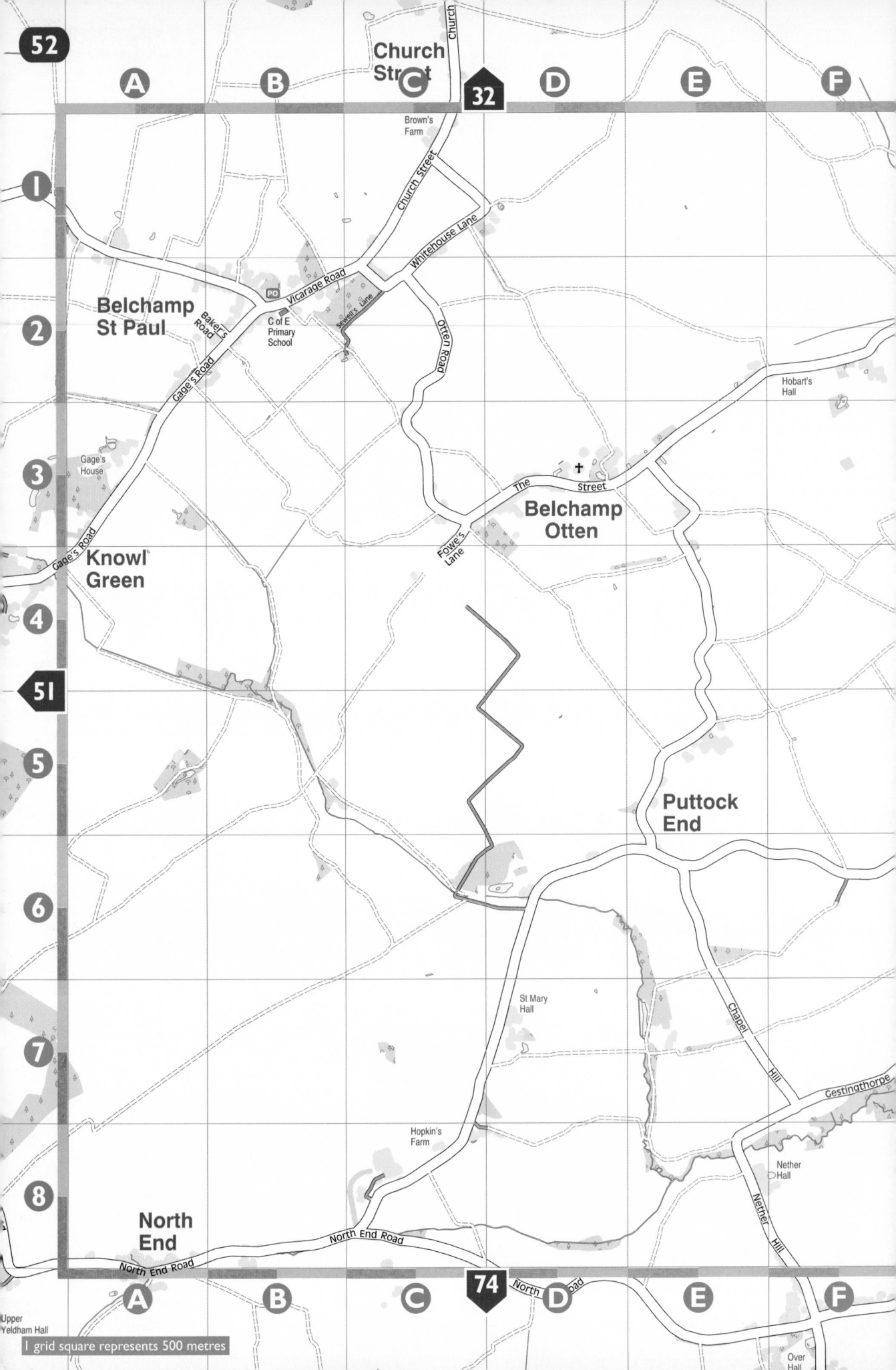

52

A   B   Church
Street   C   32   D   E   F

Brown's
Farm

1

Church Street

Whitehouse Lane

Belchamp
St Paul
PO   Vicarage Road

2

Baker's Road
Gage's Road
C of E
Primary
School

Sewell's Lane

Otten Road

3

Gage's
House

The Street

Belchamp
Otten

Gage's Road

Knowl
Green

Fowe's Lane

4

51

5

Puttock
End

6

St Mary
Hall

Chapel Hill

7

Gestingthorpe

Hopkin's
Farm

Nether
Hall

8

North
End

North End Road

Nether Hill

North End Road

A   B   C   74   North   D   Road   E   F

Upper
Yeldham Hall

1 grid square represents 500 metres

Over
Hall

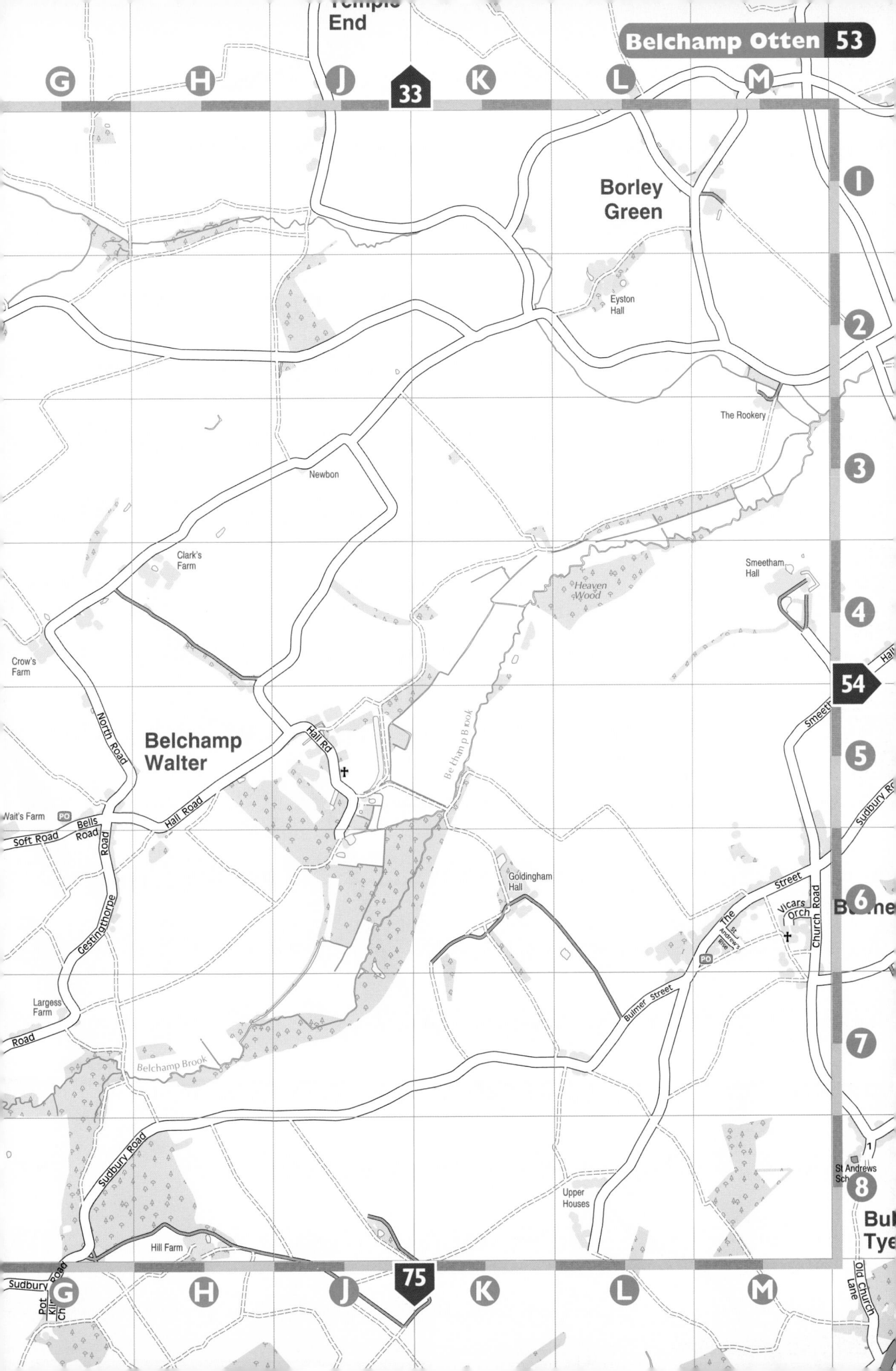

Temple End

G H J **33** K L M

I

Borley Green

Eyston Hall

2

The Rookery

3

Newbon

Clark's Farm

Heaven Wood

Smeetham Hall

4

Crow's Farm

54

5

North Road

Belchamp Walter

Hall Rd

Betham p B rook

Sudbury Rd

Wait's Farm PO

Bells Road

Hall Road

Soft Road

Smeeth

Gestingthorpe Road

Goldingham Hall

Street

Vicars orch

Bu

6

The St. Andrew's Rise

Church Road

Largess Farm

Road

PO

Bulmer Street

7

Belchamp Brook

Sudbury Road

Upper Houses

St Andrews Sch

1

8

Hill Farm

Bu Tye

Sudbury

Pot Kiln Ch

G H J **75** K L M

Old Church Lane

A   B   C   D   E   F

Valley Farm

Pigeon's Lane

The Grange

Washbrook Street

Was

Wood's Hill

Fen Farm

Lower Barn Road

Chattisham

The Street

Spring Road

Church Lane

Fen Vw Back

Dales Vw

Fen Vw

Chattisham Road

Coles Green

Hollow Road

Saxon Lane

Wenham Road

Elm Lane

Birch House Farm

Mace Green

Hotel

Rookery Farm

Wenham Road

The Grange Farm

Wenham Thicks

Redhouse Farm

Brockle Wood

Parkhouse

Folly Lane

Lane Farm

A12(T)

Grove Farm

Clay Hall

London Road

Bentley Long Wood

Jermyns Farm

tle enham

Pond Hall

A   B   C   D   E   F

Broom Way

Glebe End

Hawbridge

1 grid square represents 500 metres

A B C **39** D E F

I

Ipswich Golf Club

Purdis Farm

Purdis Farm Lane

Purdis Farm Lane

Mon Farm

A2
1 Porter Rd
2 Routh Av
3 Whitethorn Rd

Lodge Farm

Purdis Road

Wood House

Woodhouse Lane

Bucklesh

Purdis Farm Lane

Foxglove Crs

Essex
Access
Close

Hazel Drive

Warren Heath

Murrills

Berry Close

Mount
Drive

Road

1 3

Bucklesham Road

Mill Lane

Penny Lane

2

Suffolk Showground

Civil Service Sports Club

2

FE OWE ROAD

FELIXSTOWE ROAD

A1156

Felixstowe

Road

Elmham Drive

Straight Road

3

Yale Business Park

uestern Road

Nacton Heath

Havens

Ho

FELIXSTOWE ROAD

LC

Felixstowe

Road

A14(T)

A1156

4

A14(T)

A14(T)

Seven Hills

Felixstowe

59

actor
d

Square
Covert

5

Ipswich Road

Amberfield School

Amberfield

Mill Piece

Sawmill
Lane

Workshop Lane

PO

Finney's Drift

6

Park Farm

The Street

Nacton

Nacton Primary School

Ipswich

Road

7

Levington Road

Red House Walk

Church Road

Bridge Road

Church

Orwell Park School

Shore Lane

Suffolk Coast & Heaths Path

8

Orwell Park House

Broke Hall

A B C **82** D E F

Brightwell

G H J K L M

H2
1 Church Cl
2 Forge Cl

Valley
Farm

Kennels Road

A12(T)

Steel's
Farm

Main
Road

Church Lane

7

2

St Mary's Pk

Bucklesham

Green Crescent

Levington Lane

Field
View

PO

Bucklesham
Primary
School

Bucklesham
Hall

IP10

Kembroke
Hall

Chapel Road

Heath
Cottages

Tenth Road

Tenth Road

Kirton Road

Redhouse
Farm

Levington Lane

A14(T)

Levington
Heath

Law's Drift

Law's

A14(T)

Bridge Road

Walk Farm

LC

Croft House

Lane

ington

Strattonhall D

Stratton
Hall

G H J **83** K L M

Lower House

Jackson Rd

New

swic

I

2

3

4

5

6

7

8

Road

A   B   C   **40**   D   E   F

Reeves
Pightle
Road

Great Chishill

Heydon

Hall Lane

Waller's Close

The Hall

1

2

3

B1039

Building End Road

Hollow Road

Bury Lane

Chalky Lane

Church Road

High Street

Hog's Lane

PO

Harcamlow Way

B1039

Harcamlow Way

**Building
End**

Common Lane

Building End Road

Chiswick
Hall

4

5

*Chrishall
Common*

Cambridgeshire County

Essex County

Harcamlow Way

*High
Wood*

6

7

Park Lane

River Stort

Duddenhoe
Grange

8

Harcamlow Way

The Hall

The
Causeway

A   B   C   **86**   D   E **Upper
Green**   F

Park Lane

Bull Lane

Langley

1 grid square represents 500 metres

G H J **41** K L M

Freewood Lane

Freewood Farm

Essex Hill

Lofts Hall

I

2

B1039

B1039

3

Hope Farm

Pond Street

Cogmore

4

New Farm

B1039

64

Cemetery

School Lane

Knole Lane

5

Bridge Green

Brooksies

Duddenhoe End

Rockells Farm

6

Ostler's Gn

Cooper's End

Beard's Lane

Long Lane

7

Newland End

Hobs Aerie

Beard's Lane

8

Cosh Farm

Harcamlow Way

Clavering Farm

Hamplt

A B C **42** D E F

I

Howe
Hall

† **Littlebury
Green**
Thomas
Walk

2

*Green
Wood*

Chestnut Avenue

M11

3

4

1039

63

5

Long Lane

ROYSTON ROAD

B1039

B1039

M11

Nats
B1039 STATIC
†
church street
†
Bea
Bus
Park

PH

**Wenden
Ambo**

Chinnel Lane

DUCK Street

Rookery

6

Clanverend
Farm

7

Hobs
Aerie

8

A B **88** C D E F

Harcamlow Way

Harcamlow Way

itch

B1
1 Ferguson Cl

A4
1 Peal Rd

A3
1 Burnsall Cl
2 Stanleys Farm Rd

A1
1 Bradley Ms
2 Dawson Cl
3 Hamilton Ms
4 Nightingale Ms
5 Whiteshot Wy

A B C **44** D E F

1

Corner
Goddard Way
West
Wynard
Lane
Neville
Howard
Road

The Wayback

Mill Lane

Thorncroft
Harvey
Way
De Vigier
Avenue

School

Elizabeth
Close

Carnation
Everitt
Road
Way
Elizabeth
Way

Ashdon Road
Saffron
Business
Centre

Saffron
Walden
Hospital

Hollyhock
Road

Shepherds
Way

RADWINTER   **ROAD**

B1053

Pounce
Hall

Sewards
End

B1053

**SAFFRON
WALDEN**

Cemetery

Prospect
Place

Shire
Hill

2

Carmarthen
Butler Close
Victoria Avenue

B184

St Thomas
Moore RC
Primary School

Monks
Hill

Rylstone
Way

Shire
Hill
Farm

Shire Hill La

Shire Hill La

WALDEN ROAD

The
Dreys

Tylers

The
Towers

3

Peaslands
Road

Old
Mill Road

Railey
Road

Antigua
Road

Winstanley Road

Tukes
Way

THAXTED

Lord Butler
Leisure Centre

Thaxted Road

Bears
Hall

Cole End Lane

Tiptoft
Farm

4

The
Glebe

65

Katherine
Semar
Junior School

Herberts

THAXTED   ROAD

B184

Gunters

Cole End Lane

**Cole
End**

5

Road

pits

Roos Hill

6

The
Roos

Cole End Lane

7

Debden
Road

Peverel's
Wood

THAXTED   ROAD

B184

Thaxted Road

Abbots

New House
Farm

8

Pamphillions

A B C **90** D E F

Debden
Common

E2
1 Dragon's Gn

Airfield

Wimbish

THAXTED ROAD

Walden Av

Carver
Barracks

Rowney
Av

Howe

Newhouse

1 grid square represents 500 metres

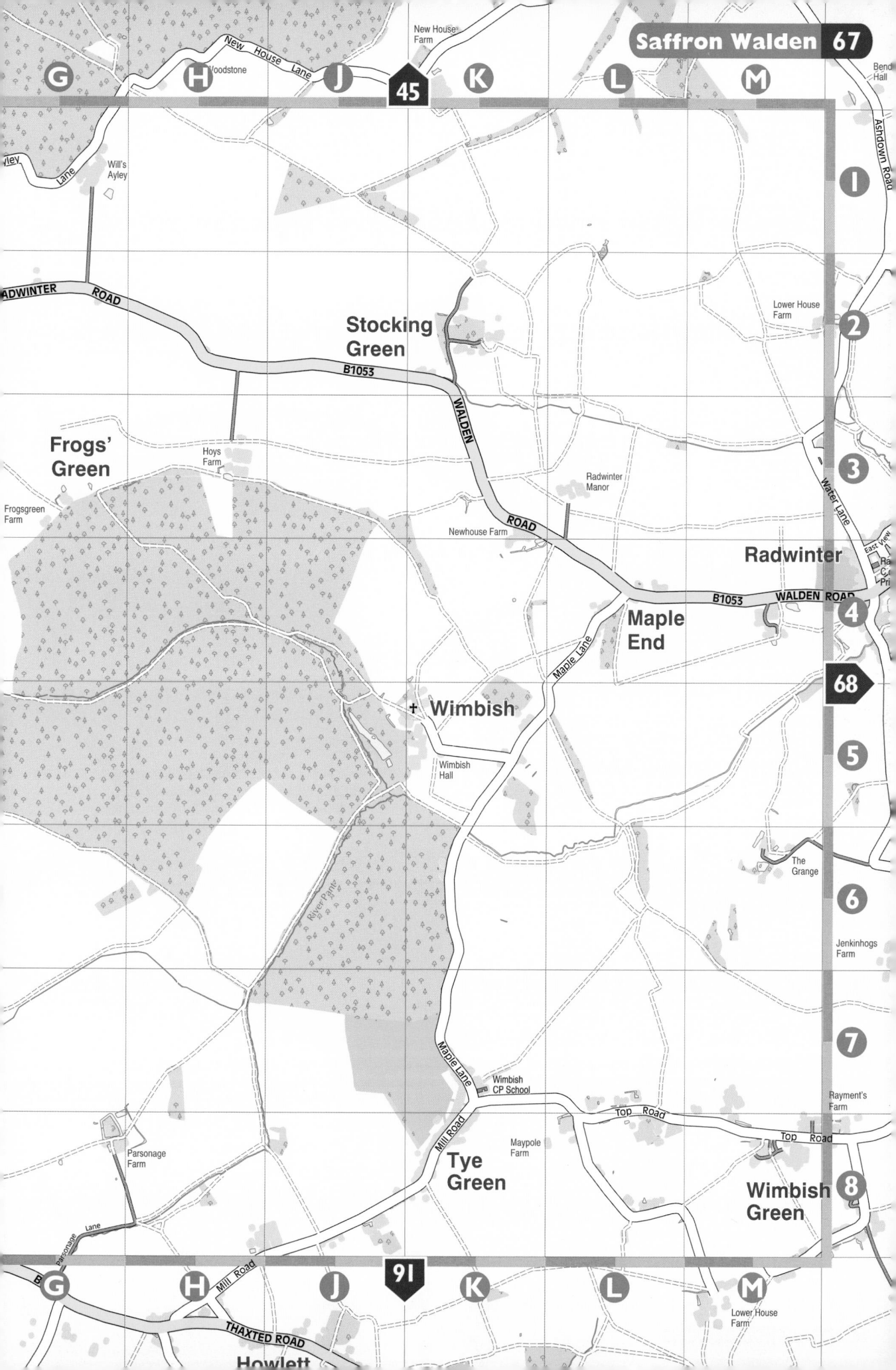

G H J **45** K L M

New House Lane

Woodstone

New House Farm

Bend Hall

I

Will's Ayley

Ayley Lane

RADWINTER ROAD

Lower House Farm

2

Stocking Green

B1053

WALDEN

Water Lane

3

Frogs' Green

Hoys Farm

Frogsgreen Farm

Radwinter Manor

East View

Radwinter

Ra C Pri

Newhouse Farm

ROAD

B1053 WALDEN ROAD

4

Maple End

68

Maple Lane

+ **Wimbish**

5

Wimbish Hall

The Grange

6

River Pant

Jenkinhogs Farm

7

Maple Lane

Wimbish CP School

Rayment's Farm

Mill Road

Top Road

Top Road

8

Parsonage Farm

Tye Green

Maypole Farm

Wimbish Green

Parsonage Lane

Mill Road

B

THAXTED ROAD

Lower House Farm

Howlett

A   B   C   46   D   E   F

I

Ashdown Road

Golden Lane

Bent Hall

Cowlass Hall

Lower House Farm

2

Godfrey's Farm

Wincelow Hall Road

Wincelow Hall

coac

HILL ROAD

3

Water Lane

Selland's Farm

B1054

Longcroft

Moss's Farm

adwinter

East View Close

PH

Radwinter C of E Aided Primary School

WALDEN ROAD

4

67

5

B1053

B1055

Anser Gallows Farm

The Grange

6

Jenkinhogs Farm

River Pant

Top Road

Sparrow's Hall

7

Rayment's Farm

Top   Road

Brockholds

Win ush Green

8

Byeballs Farm

Bush Road

Tindon End Road

House

A   B   C   92   D   E   The Dovehouse   F

1 grid square represents 500 metres

Dawkins

Hillside Farm

STREET

Witch Lane

Harvey Way

Boyton's Lane

Road

Hophouse Farm

Hempstead Wood

Hempstead Hall

Lakehouse Farm

Hempstead

Pollards Cross

Church Road

Field's Farm

Calthorpes Farm

Spain's End Farm

Howses

Free Roberts

Parsonage Farm

Old House Farm

Lower

Howe Lane

Sparepenny Lane North

Great Sampford

Sparepenny Lane South

Parsonage Farm Lane

Hawkes Farm

Great Sampford County Primary School

Homebridge

Willetts Field

B1053

Maynards

B1051

G   H   J   K   L   M

I   2   3   4   70   5   6   7   8

47   **93**

T G

G H J 49 K L M

Birdbr Road

Mill Road

Chapel End Way

† PO

Stambourne

Church Road

†

Cornish Hall End Road

Stambourne Green

Dyers Road

I

Revels Farm

Finchingfield Road

Tagley

Elm's Farm

2

Nortons

3

Craig's End

Mor Farr

4

Levitt's Farm

Finchingfield Road

72

Gooseley's Farm

5

Harrow Hill

Bradfie

Hole Farm

Thurston Farm

Robinhood End

Le Hurst

6

7

Gainsford End

†

Mill Lane

Mill Farm

8

Gainsford Hall

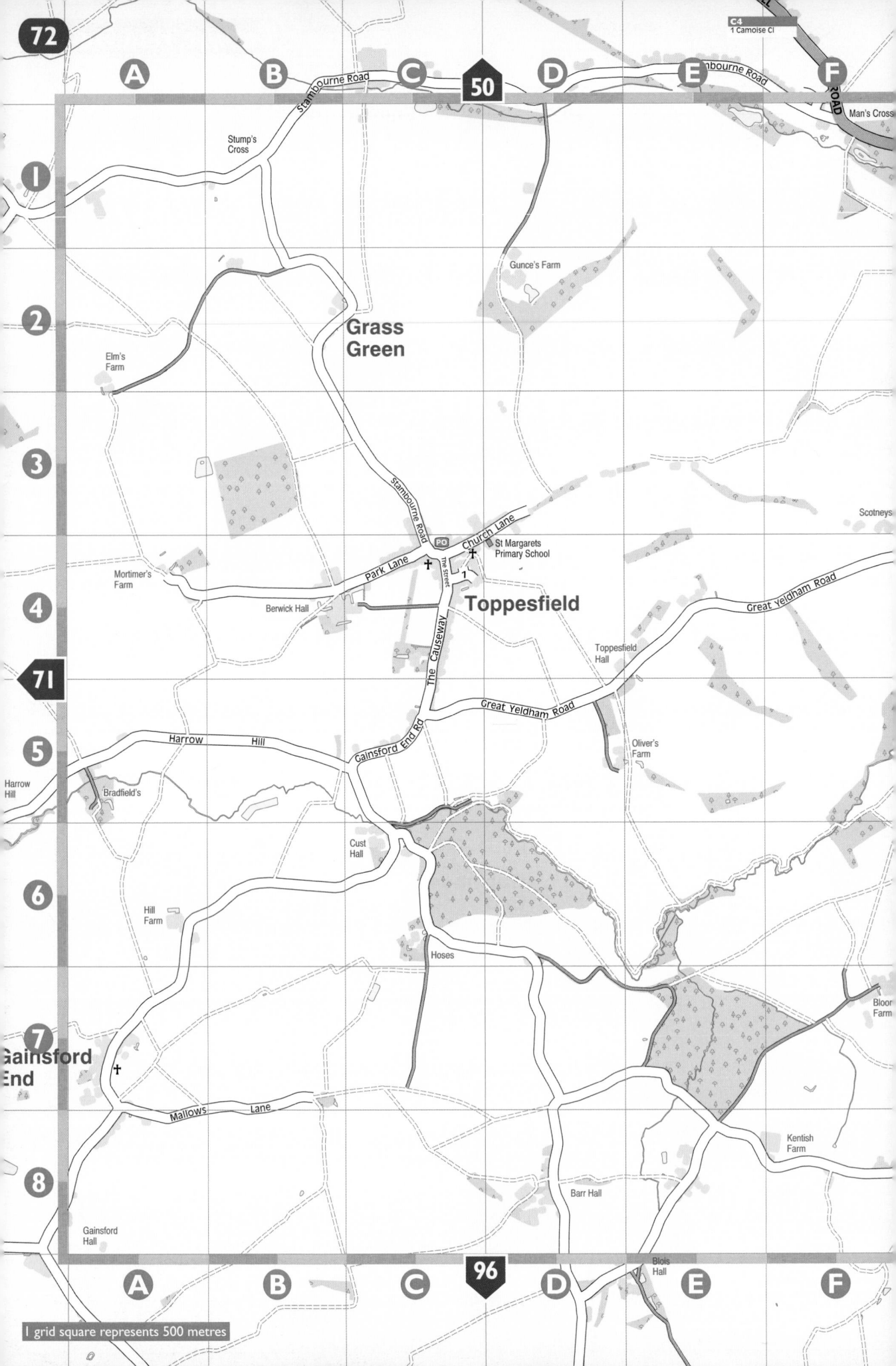

56

C1
1 Farthings Went
2 Jermyns Cl
3 The Queech
4 Roundridge Rd

B2
1 Dodmans
2 School Cl

A2
1 Aisthorpe

A B C D E F

tle
enham

Jermyns
Farm

Grove Farm

Pond
Hall

1

Windmill
Hill

Days
Road

Dawes
Close

Broom Way
Hawbridge
Glebe
End
Longfield
Rylands
Peter's Grove
Penn
Close
The Pightle
London Rd

Mill Cl

Catespray
Ash
Thorney
Crotchets
Close
Penny
Meadow
Bowylands
Road

Winding
Piece

Little
Tufts
Great Tufts

Capel St Mary

Days Green

The Street
Cedars
Lane
Plough
Road
Coombers

Capel St Mary
School

Chapel
Link Rd
Gate
Road
Letton
Stockmers End
Rembrow
Sawyers
Chalkners Cl

Tawney
Lane
Smithers
Close
Busney
Close
Playfield
Road
White
Road
Mowlands
Horse
Homefield
Long
Perry

Barnfield
Caroggs
Butcher's
Lane
The Street
The Old
St
London Rd

Snowcroft

PO

2

Friars
London

A12(T)

Red
Lane

Capelgrove

3

Potash
Grove
Farm

Pound
Lane

Potas

Bluegate
Lane

Road

Tawneys
Farm

Old
London
Pound Lane

Manor
House

Case
Lane
Bentley
Highfields

The Link
West Mill
Garden
East Mill
Gn
Silver
Leys
Church
Road
Station Road
Grove Road
South
PO
Link Lane

4

5

Chaplain's
Farm

Dodnash
Wood

6

Martins
Glen

7

Rookery
Farm

Dodnash
Priory
Farm

The Grange

8

Mission
Lane
Fisher's Lane
East
End
Gravelpit Lane
Gravel Pit Lane

MILL
East End Road
Park
Road

Broom
Knoll

East End

Park
House

slough

Road

Highlands

A B C D E F

G   H   J   **57**   K   L   M

Bentley Manor

Hubbard's Hall Farm

House

I Ho Par

Coxhall Road

Tattingstone White Horse

White Horse Hill

School Road

Hill

Lemons Hill

2

3

Bentley Park

Church Road

Falslaff Manor

Bentley Primary School

Tattingstone

The Box Gallery M

The Close

4

Church Road

Glebe Cl

Green La

Tattingstone C of E V CP School

80

Church Road

Station Road

Back Lane

Pond Hall Farm

Tattingstone Place

5

The Heath

Tattingstone Wonder

6

Stutton Lane

Argent Manor Farm

Coppey Farm

Folly Farm

Vale Lane

White House Farm

7

Bentley Lane

Holly Lane

Bentley Lane

Vale Farm

8

Jimmy's Lane

Woodfield Lane

G   H   J   **109**   K   L   M

Lewis Lane

Creps

MANNINGTREE

Stu

G **H** **J** **59** **K** **L** **M**

I

Home Farm

Suffolk Coast & Heaths Path

Cat House

Hall Point

MAIN ROAD

Manning's Lane

Pratt's La

Ipswich High School for Girls

Woolverstone Park

Suffolk Coast & Heaths Path

2

Pin Mill

PH

Woolverstone

Harkstead Lane

Glebe Lane

PO

B1456

MAIN ROAD

Orwell Rise

Mill Road

3

Whitehouse Farm

Walnut Tree Farm

Richardsons Lane

Collimer Cl

Rectory Field

Woodlands

School

Andrew's Dr

Church St

Hollow La

Wendy Close

St

4

MAIN ROAD

Chelmondiston

PO

Bylam Lane

82

Harkstead Lane

Bylam Farm

Ling's Lane

5

Holbrook Gardens

New Road

Brick Kiln Road

Red House Farm

Ling's Lane

Grove Lane

6

Harkstead Road

Ipswich Road

Lovers Lane

7

Holbrook Lodge

The Vale Farm

Harkstead Hall Farm

8

Lower Holbrook

Slushy Lane

Church Lane

Old Church School

Fish Pond Hill

Lower Houses Road

Rectory Road

G **H** **III** Harkstead **K** **L** **M**

Holbrook Rd

The Street

Walnut La

PO

er VW oad

Shing

Coast & He

A   B   C   60   D   E   F   L

I

2

Pin
Mill
PH

Suffolk Coast & Heaths Path

Clamp
House

3

Orwell
Rise

Pinmill Road

River

Orwell

Rectory
Field

Chelmondiston

Hollow La

Collimer Cl

Andrew's Dr

Wendy
Close

Hill Farm La

4

MAIN   ROAD   B1456
PO

81

5

B1456

Red House
Farm

Wade's Lane

Charity
Farm

6

Pear
Tree
Farm

The Drift

Shotley Hall

Shotley Walk

7

Warren Lane

Erwarton Walk

B1456

Rence Park
Farm

8

Shotley

THE   STREET
PO

The
Surgery

A   B   C   112   D   E   F

The Street

Orwell Park
House

Broke
Hall

Church

I grid square represents 500 metres

G8
1 Rose Ct

ngton

G   H   J   **61**   K   L   M

I

Strattonhall Drift

Stratton
Hall

2

Morston
Hall

Morston Hall Rd

Morston
LC

LC

Suffolk Coast & Heaths Path

Suffolk Coast &

3

**Thorpe
Common**

Thorpe Lane

Suffolk Coast & Heaths Path

River

4

Grimston

84

Hill House

**Trimley
Lower
Street**

5

**Church
End**

Orwell

Crane's
Hill

6

Frogs Alley

Frogs
Alley

*Trimley
Marshes*

7

Oldhall Road

8

well View Road

Suffolk Coast

71

B1456

Shotley
Primary
School

G   H   J   **113**   K   L   M

Over Hall

*Shotley
Marshes*

B1456

E6
1 The Kempsters
2 Welbeck Cl

D5
1 Carriage Cl
2 Heathgate Piece
3 The Wheelwr'hts

C5
1 St Mary's Cl

C3
1 Crowswell Ct
2 Heath Ct

B3
1 High Hall Cl

B4
1 Brick Kiln Cl

Falkenham

A   B   C   D   E   F

1

Lower
Falke

Kirton Road

Trimley St Martins
County Primary School

Back Lane

Suffolk Coast & Heaths Path

2

A14(T)

Trimley
St Martin

Heathfields

Mill Close

Red House Cl

Capel Close

Sandy Close

Capel   Hall   Lane

Capel Hall Lane

Brook Lane

Suffolk Coast & Heaths Path

3

Thorpe Lane

LC

Grimston Lane

Cavendish Road

Old Kirton Road

Kirton Road

Blue Barn Close

St Martins Green

Meadow Cl

Jasmine Cl

A14(T)

Capel
Hall

4

High Road

PO

High Road

Church Lane

Thurmans   Lane

Fell Meadow

Thomas Rd

Great Rd

Way

A14(T)

Candlet

83

5

Grimston Hall

Caymers Lane

Laud's Lane

The Josselyns

Drover's Ct

Brotherton Av

Faulkeners

Dawson Dr

3

Punchard Way

2

Langstons

6

Keeper's Lane

Trimley
St Mary

LC

Stennets

St Mary's Cl

Manor Road

The Nest
Branch Surg

The Avenue

Second Av

Station

New

Road

Trimley Station

Addington Road

Primary School

Black Barns

Hunters End

Dains Pl

Burnham

Farriers Went

Spritelee End

Eastlands Ct

Spriteshall Lane

CANDLET RO

IP11

Ascot Drive

Walton
Surgery Rd

Longcroft

7

Cordy's Lane

Searson's
Farm

Chatsworth Crs

Clickett Hill

PORT OF FELIXSTOWE ROAD

Hawkes Lane

High Street

Maidstone Road

Causton
County
Junior School

Orwell
High
School

Infant
School

King Street

Crown St

Margaret St

8

Suffolk Coast & Heaths Path

Long
Fld

Runnacles
Way

Winton Cl

Avenue

Hall Fld

Garden Fld

Aldringham Ms

Hintlesham Dr

Mellis Farm

Haven Close

Cricket Fld

Grange Road
Primary School

Cemetery

Treetop

Falcon

Alexandra

Grange
Close

Lane

Maidstone Rd

Vicarage Road

Avenue

E7
1 Barnfield

E8
Street names for
this grid square are
listed at the back of
the index

F7
1 Cross St

F8
1 Beacon Fld
2 Broom Fld
3 Crossgate Fld
4 Hamilton St
5 James Boden Cl
6 Maidstone Rd

A   B   C   **114**   D   E   F

Blofield Rd

A14(T)

A15A

1 grid square represents 500 metres

Oyster

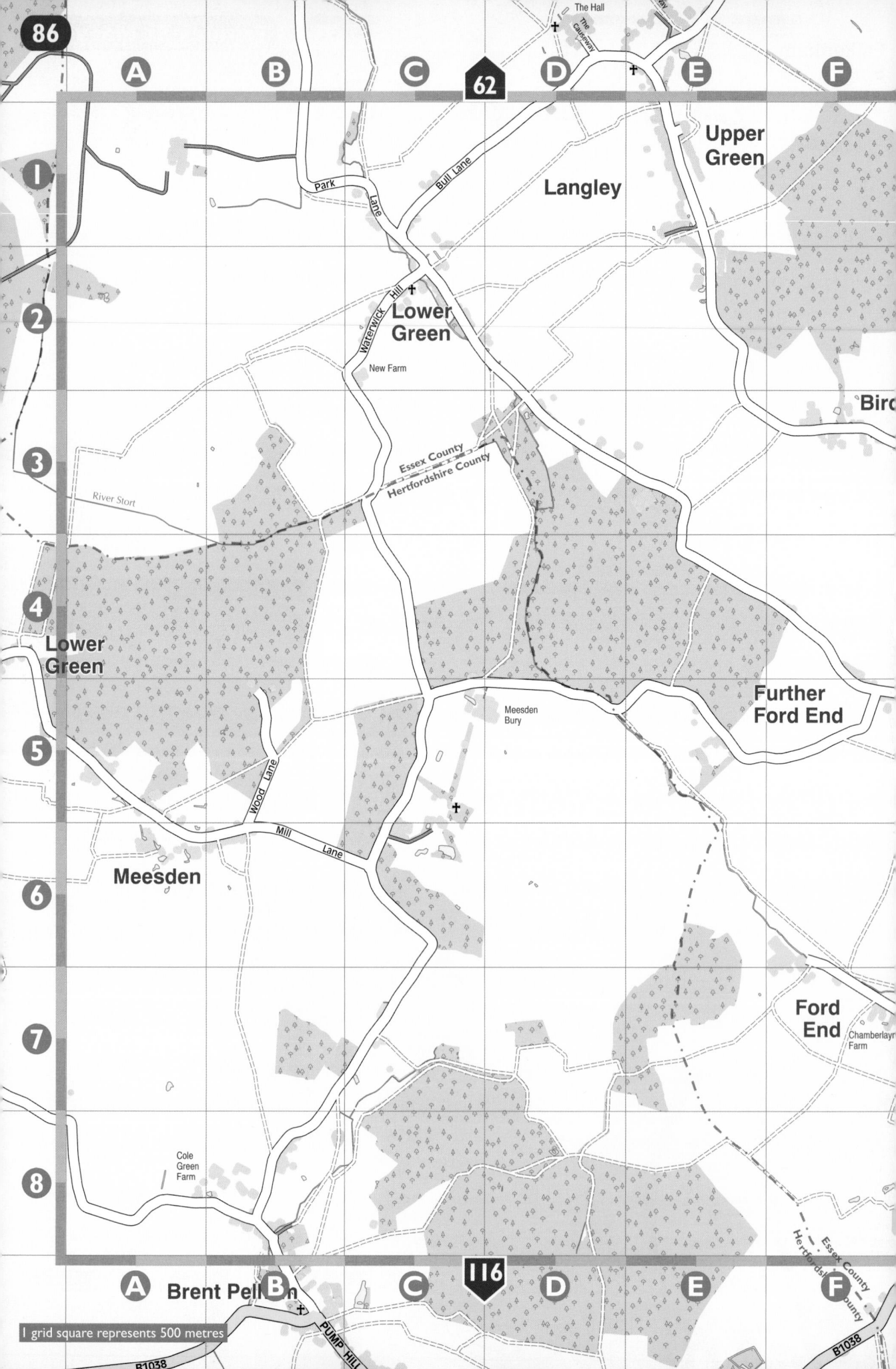

(A) (B) (C) **62** (D) (E) (F)

1

Park Lane

Bull Lane

Langley

Upper Green

2

Waterwick Hill

Lower Green

New Farm

Bir

3

River Stort

Essex County

Hertfordshire County

4

Lower Green

Further Ford End

Meesden Bury

5

Wood Lane

6

Mill Lane

Meesden

Ford End

Chamberlayr Farm

7

8

Cole Green Farm

1 grid square represents 500 metres

(A) **Brent Pell** (B) (C) **116** (D) (E) (F)

Pump Hill

B1038

Essex County

Hertfordshire County

B1038

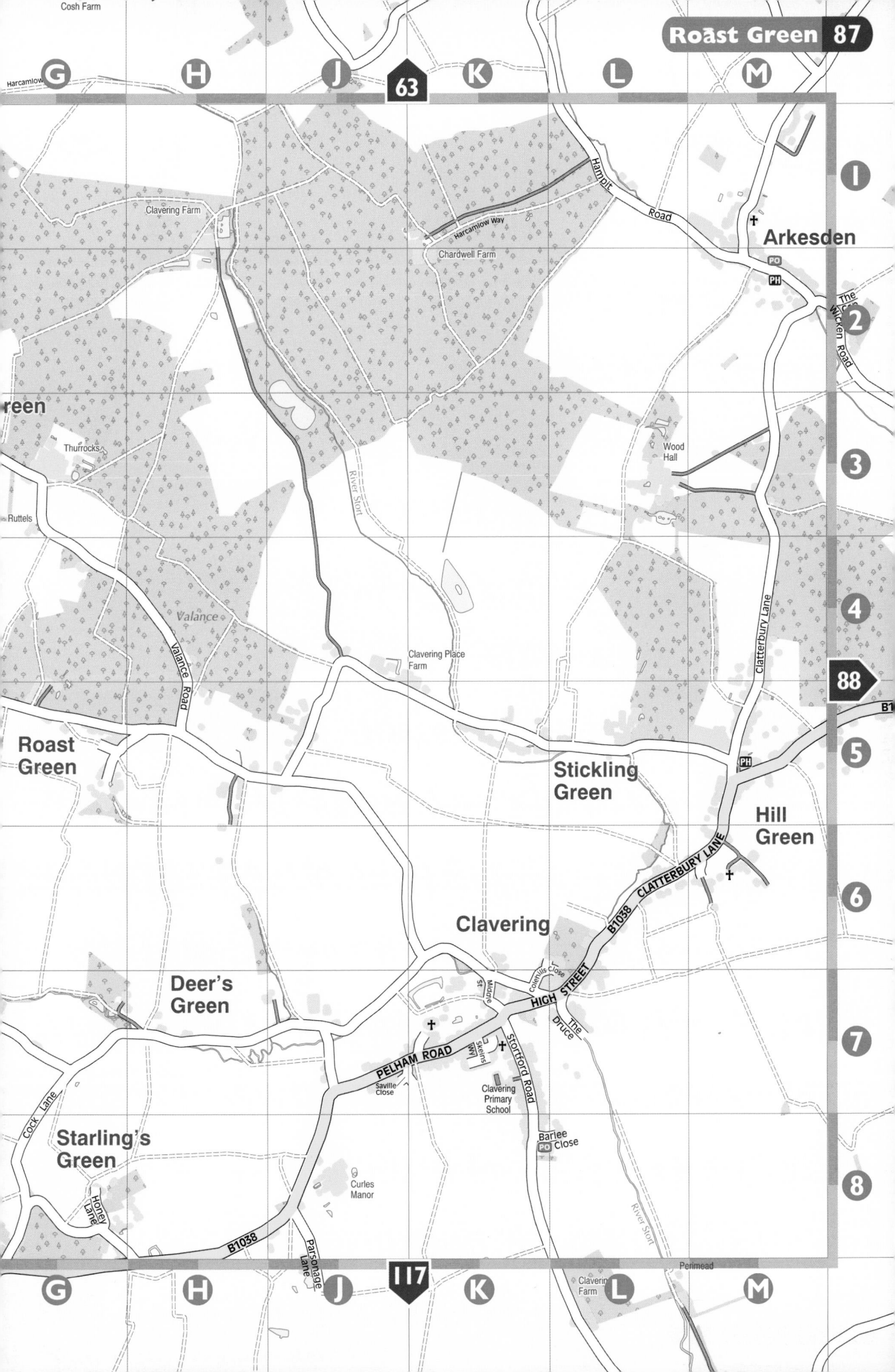

G H J **63** K L M

I

Cosh Farm

Harcamlow

Clavering Farm

Harcamlow Way

Chardwell Farm

Arkesden

PO
PH

The Wicken Road

2

reen

Thurrocks

Wood Hall

3

Ruttels

River Stort

Clatterbury Lane

4

Valance

Valance Road

Clavering Place Farm

88

B1

Roast Green

Stickling Green

PH

5

Hill Green

6

Deer's Green

Clavering

Colehills Close

CLATTERBURY LANE

B1038

HIGH STREET

Middle St

The Druce

7

Starling's Green

Cock Lane

PELHAM ROAD

Saville Close

Steins Wy

Storrtford Road

Clavering Primary School

Bariee Close

PO

8

Honey Lane

Curles Manor

B1038

Parsonage Lane

River Stort

Perimead

Clavering Farm

G H J K L M

65

I

2

3

4

90

5

6

7

8

Shortgrove Hall

Debden Common

Brick House Farm

B1383

CAMBRIDGE ROAD

Whiteditch Lane

Grammar School

Water Lane

BELMONT HILL

Bury Water Lane

School Lane

Gaces Acre

Tenterfield

Gilbey Green

Meadowford

Newport Gallery

Church St

PO

B1038

WICKEN ROAD

The Surgery

Chapel Close

Cherry Garden Lane

Frambury Lane

Bullfields

B1383 HIGH STREET

Pond Cross Farm

Frambury Lane

Newport CP School

Station Road

Newport Station

Newport

Debden Road

Harcamlow Way

Harcamlow Way

Debden Water

Bromley Lane

Harcamlow Way

Ringers

Debden Road

Harcamlow Way

Harcamlow Way

River Cam or Granta

The Spinney

LONDON ROAD

M11

B1383

Waldegraves

High Street

Widdington

Church Street

The Hall

Hamel Way

Cornells Lane

Mole Hall

Wood End

Hollow Road

Newport Drive

B1383

M11

North Hall Road

River Cam or Granta

Quendon

Prior's Wood

G H J K L M

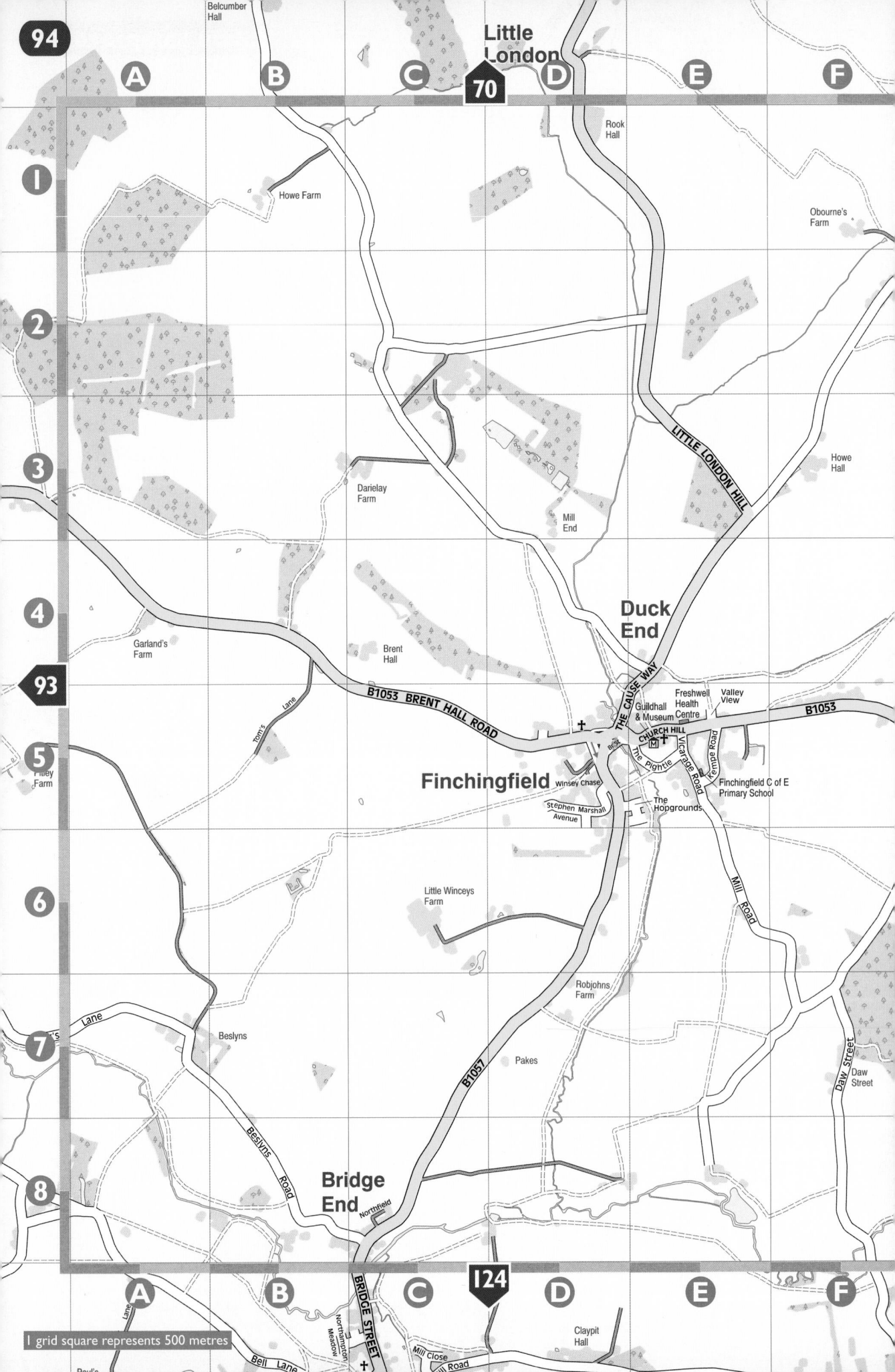

A   B   C   72   D   E   F

Gainsford
Hall

Barr Hall

Blois
Hall

1

Birdgreen
Farm

2

Redhouse
Farm

Flower's
Hall

Tattersall's
Farm

3

Morris
Green

Wethersfield
Airfield

Lane

Sugar

Deek's
Farm

4

95

Whitehall
Farm

5

Fairy
Farm

Wright's
Farm

6

New
Barns

7

Brickkiln
Green

Lower
Green

Pouches
Hall

Patten's
Farm

8

School
Green

Widleybrook   Lane

PH

Widleybrook

Lane

A   B   C   126   D   E   F

Baker's
Farm

Blackmore
End

G **H** **J** **73** **K** **L** **M** **I**

L1
1 Abbey Meadow
2 Elm Cl
3 Grays Mead
4 Hawthorns
5 Oak Wk
6 Willowdene

L2
1 Brook Meadow
2 Parkfields
Grave's 3 St Peters Vw
Hall

L3
1 Warburton Av
2 Webster Cl

Rookwoods

Christmas Field

dingham County ondary School

Highstreet Green

Sible Hedingham

Carter's Farm

Oxford Lane

Oxford Mdw

Station Road

Friars Close

Castle Mdw

Beech Grove

Wethersfield Rd

Rectory Road

Church St

Cyanet Court

Brook Ter

Burnt House Farm

Cuckoo Hill

Hostage Farm

Cuckoos Farm

Parkfields

Alexandra Road

Recreation Road

Gibson Road

Spurgeon Close

Summerfields

Spring Wy

Hilton House Surgery

Alderford St

School Road

Hills Rd

St Peters C of E Primary School

Hawkwood Road

Sparrow Close

Hilton Mdw

Swan Chase

A1017 POTTER STREET

2

3

School Road

Cobbs Fenn

Lamb Lane

Lamb Lane

4

Forry's Green

Bayker's Farm

98

5

Inmham Hill

Horn Hill

Pevor's Farm

Southey Green

HEDINGHAM ROAD A1017

6

Listonhall Chase

7

Cutmaple

Hawkwoods

Liston Hall Farm

Bound Farm

Wh re

8

M3
1 Colne Rd
2 Hawkwood Rd
3 Jubilee Ct
4 Willow Mdw

M2
1 Brook Meadow
2 Spurgeon Cl

M1
1 Bewick Ct
2 Everitt Wy

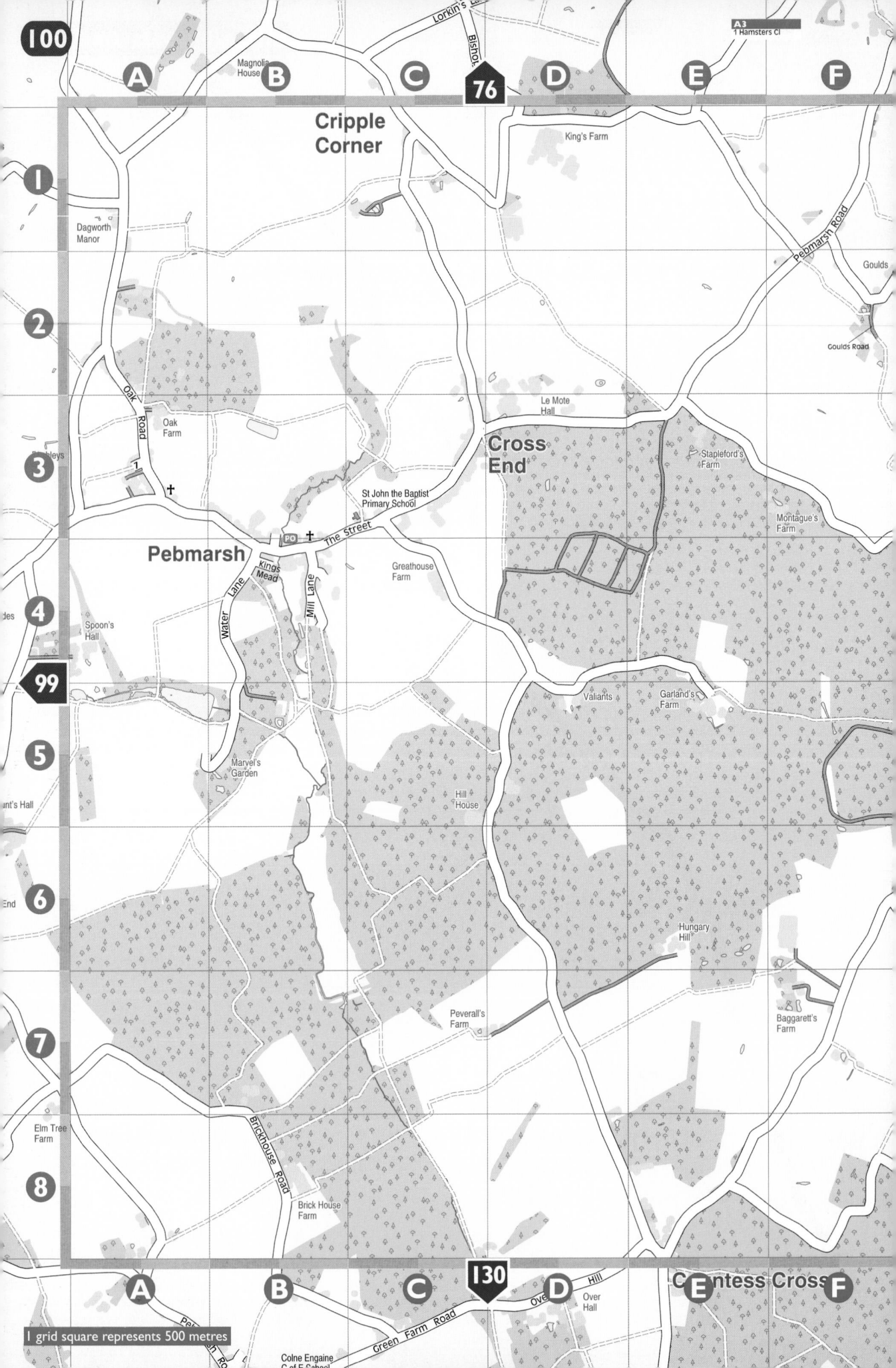

A Magnolia House B C 76 D E F

Cripple Corner

1

Dagworth Manor

2

Oak Road

Oak Farm

3 Buckleys

Le Mote Hall

Cross End

Stapleford's Farm

St John the Baptist Primary School

The Street

Pebmarsh

PO

Kings Mead

Montague's Farm

Greathouse Farm

4 Spoon's Hall

Water Lane

Mill Lane

99

Marvel's Garden

5

Valiants

Garland's Farm

Hill House

unt's Hall

6 End

Hungary Hill

7

Peverall's Farm

Baggarett's Farm

Elm Tree Farm

Brickhouse Road

8

Brick House Farm

A B C 130 D Over Hill E Centess Cross F

Green Farm Road

Colne Engaine C of E School

Pebmarsh Road

Goulds

Goulds Road

1 Hamsters Cl A3

King's Farm

Lorkin's Bishop

Alpha...e

M3
1 Hamlet Ct
2 Parsonage Gv

G H J 77 K L M

I
2
3
102
4
5
6
7
8

Clees Hall

Shrub Farm
Hewitts

Langley Hill

Springett's Hill

Hill Farm

Speck's Farm

The Ferriers

C08

Bures Station

Lamarsh Hl

Maltings

Station HIV

Water La
The Paddocks
New Cut
1
2

BRIDGE ST
Wharf La
The Wharf

Normandie W. Cambridge

B1508

Peyton Hall

Horne's Green

Fishpits

Baker's Hall

Colne Road

Ravensfield Farm

Butler's Farm

Pricketts Hall

Craig's Lane

LC

Daw's Cross

Mount Bures

Lower Jennies

Valley Green Farm

White's Farm

Cambridge Bro

Hall Road

Catley's Farms

Moreland's

Little Loveny Hall

Great Loveney Hall

Chappel Road

Robert's Hill

Fordham Road

Weirstock Farm

Jupe's Hill

Inworth Lane

Bal

G H J 131 K L M

G H J K L M

I
2
3
4
104
5
6
7
8

G H J K L M

133

Brunning's

Radley's Farm

Harper's Hill

Farthing Hall

Guinea Wiggs Farm

Rickland Farm

Wissington Grange

Hill Farm

The Westerings

HARPER'S HILL A134

Constable

Campions Hill

Wissington Grove

Campion Lane

Wiston Road

Bures Road

Creem's

River Stour

Bures Road

Wissington

Stour Valley Path

Naylands Road

Ware Road

Bowdens

Stour Valley Path

Lower Dairy House

Lane

Bowdens Lane

Stour Valley Path

School Lane

C of E ool

The Grange

Garnons Chase

Bottengoms

School Road

Fishponds Hill

Collets Chase

Stour Valley Pth

Little Horkesley

Malting Farm

Cockrell's Farm

Cockrell's Rd

MAIN

Little Horkesley Road

Wood Hall

Long's Farm

ROAD

Holts Road

Holts

Vinesse Road

Workhouse Road

Crabtree

Knowles's Farm

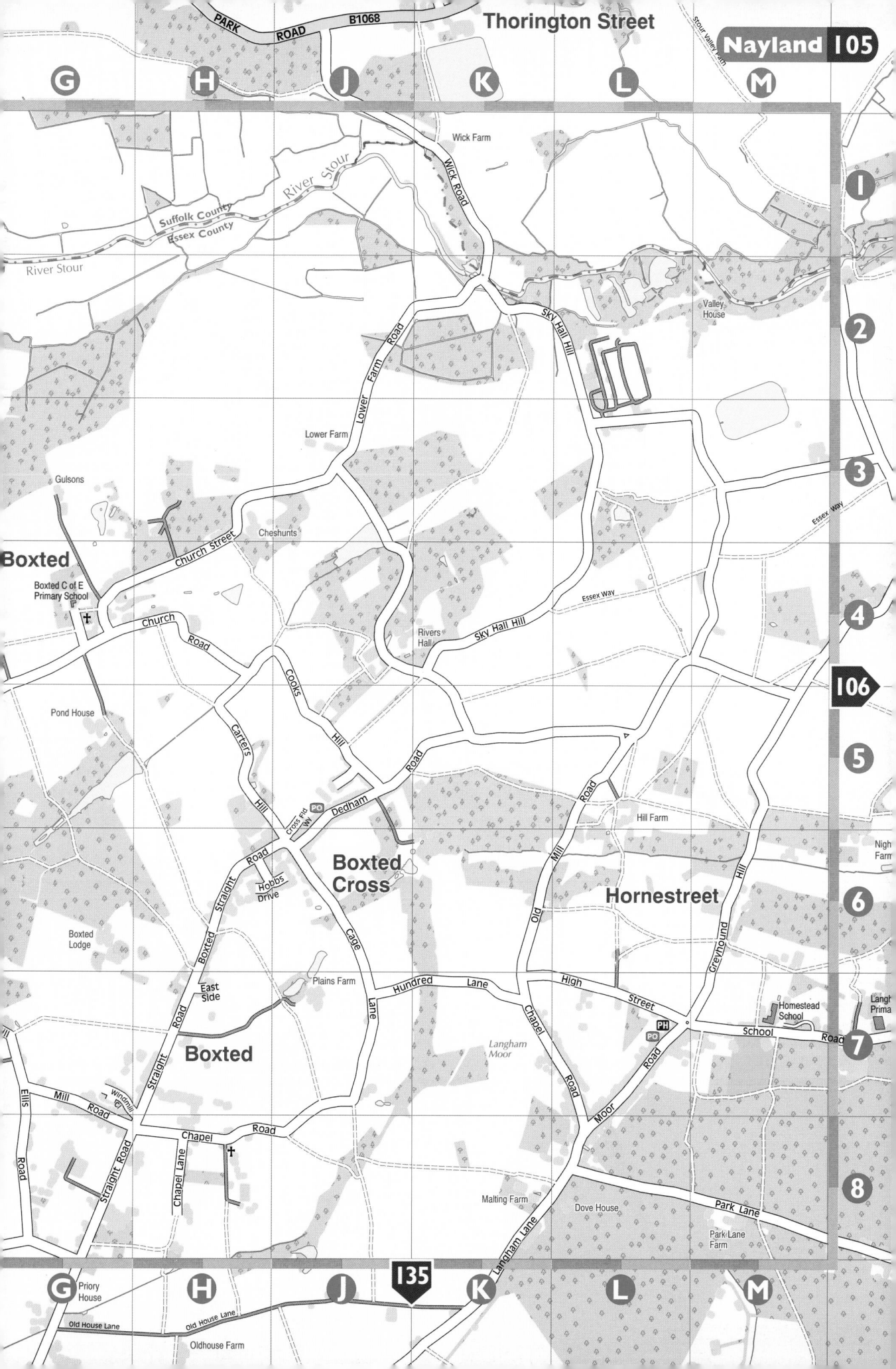

79

H7
1 Chapel Cut
2 Kerridge's Cut

H8
1 Brunswick House
Cut
2 Swan Ct

J8
1 Cambria Cl

G   H   J   K   L   M

Woodfield Lane

MANNINGTRE

Lewis Lane

Crepping Hall

Hyam

I
Stu

STUTTON ROAD

B1080

THE STREET

Brantham
Court

Newmill   Lane

The   Chase

Brantham
Hall

Upper
Street

Manor Lane

2

Queech
Farm

Queech Lane

3

Seafield
Bay

Stutton
Mill

Newmill
Creek

4

110

5

Suffolk County
Essex County

6

Mistly
Towers

The Cr

Mistley

HIGH STREET

PO

PH

Mistley Station

Essex Way

School Lane

Beckford
Rd

California Rd

HARWICH

Anchor
End

Stourview

Mistley Norman
C of E
Prim Sch

Remercie Rd

Portliol

Seafield
Av

Stourview
Cl

Nether
Hall

LC

7

Shrubland Road

Furze
Hill

ROAD

AVENUE

Middlefield
Rd

Rigby

Av

Westmorland
Close

B1352

BRICKMAN'S HILL

STATION ROAD

Ship Lane

Stour
Lodge

Shore Lane

8

New
Mistley

Essex Way

Essex

Road

Heath

G   H   J   K   L   M

139

Mistley
Heath

Bradf

G H J **81** K L M

Lower
Holbrook

Harkstead

Slushy
Lane

River Vw
Road

PO

Holbrook Rd

The Street

Walnut
Tree La

Shore
Lane

Coast & Heaths Path

Suffolk Coast & Heaths Pth

Fish Pond Hill

Old
Church
School

Lower
Houses

Rectory

Road

Road

I

Rat Hill

2

Knights Farm

Beaumont
Hall

3

Nether
Hall

4

112

Suffolk County
Essex County

5

6

Shore
Farm

Essex Way

Stone Lane

Copperas
Bay

7

Strandlands

Essex Way

Wrabness
Station

Black Boy Lane

Station Road

Wrabness

PO

Rectory

Road

Dimbols
Hall

Primrose
Hill

Stour
Wood

Stourwood
Fm

WRABNESS

WRABNESS ROAD

B1

Home F

8

Essex Way

G H J **141** K L M

HARWICH ROAD B1352

A B C **82** D E F

Shotley

The Surgery

Garde

Kingsland Av

Queensland

Kingsland

1

The Street

Church Lane

PH

Erwarton

Rat Hill

Hill House Farm

Shop Corner

Ness Road

2

Suffolk Coast & Heaths Path

Ness Farm

Beaumont Hall

3

Erwarton Bay

Suffolk Coast & Heaths Path

4

◄ III

Suffolk County
Essex County

Stour

5

River

Car F Term

West Dock R

6

Refinery Road

Foster

Occu Heal

Ray Lane

Edward

7

Ray Farm

Ray Lane

East Newhall

8

WRABNESS ROAD B1352

Home Farm

LUNNISH HILL

WRABNESS RD

Essex Way

Pond Hall Farm

A120(T)

A120(T)

Upper Dover

A B C **142** D E F

Michaelstowe

Chevy Ct

Michaelstowe Close

Clayton Rd

Payhaven

Valleyd

MAIN

Rowlands

CHAS

PO

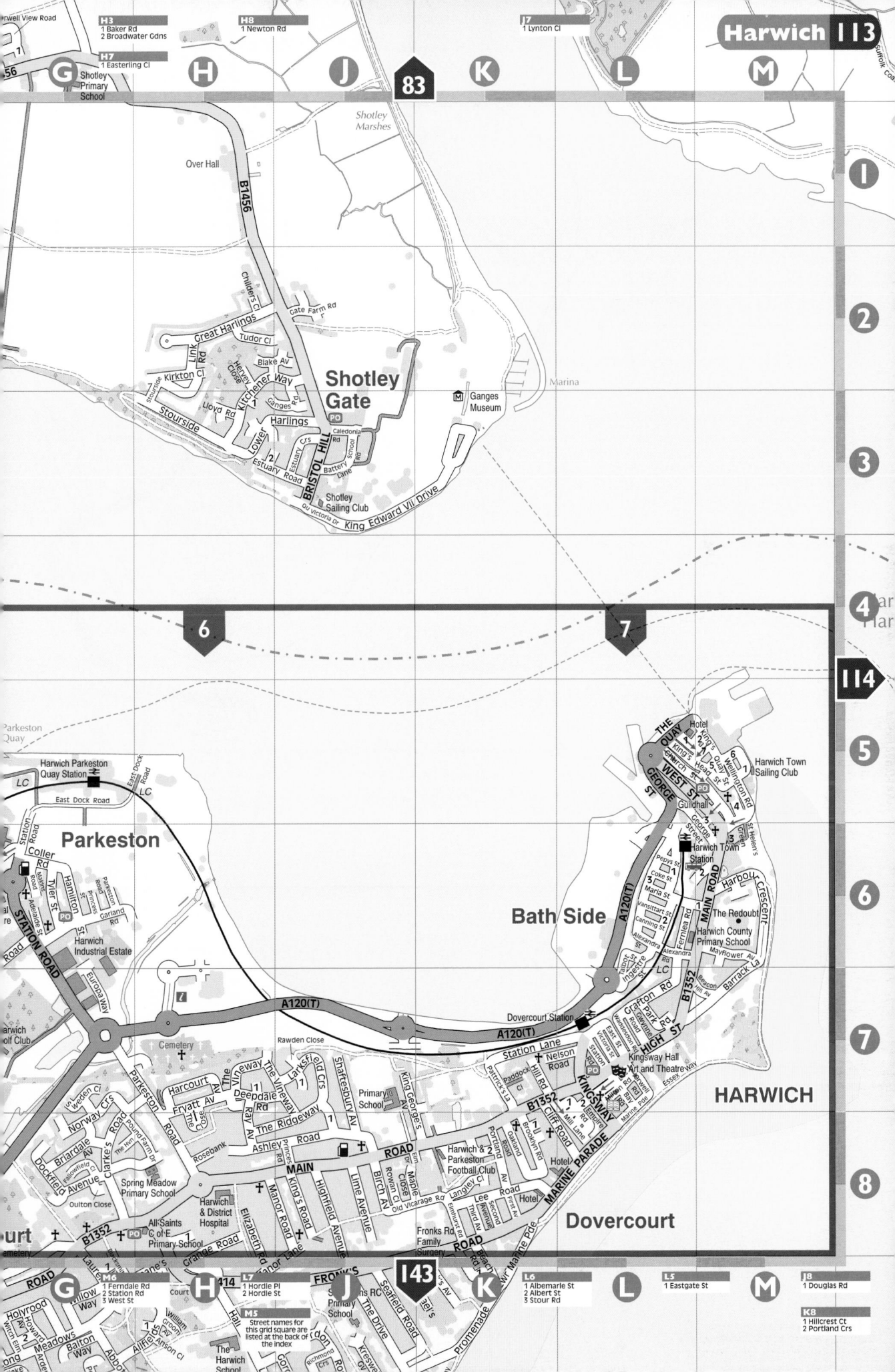

G   H   J   **83**   K   L   M

I
2
3

6   7

4
114
5
6
7
8

Shotley Marshes

Over Hall

Shotley
Gate

Shotley
Sailing Club

Ganges Museum

Marina

Childers Cl
Gate Farm Rd
Great Harlings
Tudor Cl
Blake Av
Link Rd
Kirkton Cl
Hervey Close
Kitchener Way
Ganges
Lloyd Rd
Harlings
Lower
Stourside
Estuary Road
Crs
Caledonia Rd
Battery Lane
BRISTOL HILL
PO
Qu Victoria Dr   King Edward VII Drive

B1456

Parkeston
Quay

Harwich Parkeston
Quay Station
East Dock Road
East Dock Road
LC

Parkeston

Coller Rd
Tyler St
Hamilton
Parkeston Road
Princess Road
Garland Rd
Adelaide St
PO
Harwich Industrial Estate
STATION ROAD
Europa Way
Harwich Golf Club

A120(T)

Cemetery

Rawden Close

A120(T)

THE QUAY
Hotel
King's Head St
Quay St
Wellington Rd
WEST ST
Church St
GEORGE ST
Guildhall
George Street
Harwich Town Station
Pepys St
King's
Harwich Town
Sailing Club
St Helen's
Main Road
Harbour Crescent
Bath Side
Coke St
Maria St
Vansittart St
Canning St
Alexandra
Fernlea Rd
The Redoubt
Harwich County
Primary School
Mayflower Av
Talbot Rd
Ingestre St
Grafton Park
LC
B1352
Beacon
Barrack La

Dovercourt Station
Station Lane
Nelson Road
St Patrick's La
Paddock
Kingsway Hall
Art and Theatre
PO
HIGH ST
Fryatt Av
Harcourt
The Vineway
The Vineway
Deepdale Av
Ray Av
Larksfield Crs
Shaftesbury Av
The Ridgeway
Primary School
King George's Av
CLIFF ROAD
KINGSWAY
B1352
Mill Lane
Norway Crs
Briardale Av
The Hvn
Roseberry
Ashley Road
Princes Rd
MAIN
ROAD
Birch Av
Harwich & Parkeston
Football Club
Hotel
MARINE PARADE
HARWICH
Dockfield Avenue
Clarke's Road
Norway Crs
Spring Meadow
Primary School
Oulton Close
Manor Road
King's Road
Highfield Avenue
Lime Avenue
Elm Rd
Maple Rd
Rowan Av
Old Vicarage Rd
Langley Cl
Lee Road
Third Av
Second Av
First Av
Hotel
Dovercourt
All Saints
C of E
Primary School
Harwich & District Hospital
Grange Road
Elizabeth Avenue
Manor Lane
Fronks Rd
Family Surgery
FRONKS
ROAD
Lwr Marine Pde
Beach Rd
Promenade
B1352

G   **114**   **H**   **143**   **J**   **K**   **L**   **M**

M6
1 Ferndale Rd
2 Station Rd
3 West St

L7
1 Hordle Pl
2 Hordle St

L6
1 Albemarle St
2 Albert St
3 Stour Rd

L5
1 Eastgate St

J8
1 Douglas Rd

K8
1 Hillcrest Ct
2 Portland Crs

M5
Street names for
this grid square are
listed at the back of
the index

FELIXSTOWE

Felixstowe Pier

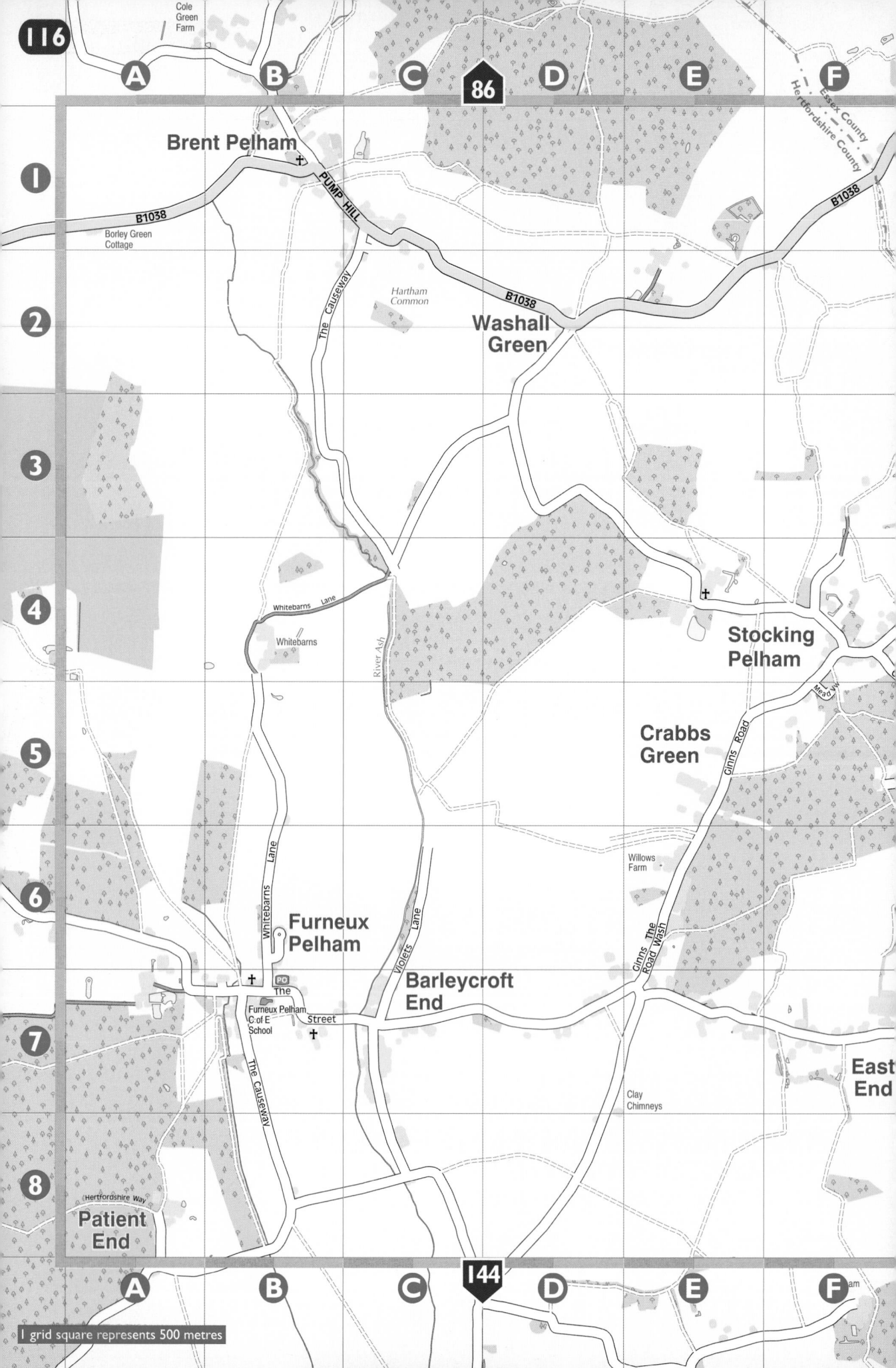

Cole Green Farm

A   B   C   D   E   F

Brent Pelham

1

PUMP HILL

B1038

Borley Green Cottage

Hertfordshire County
Essex County

B1038

B1038

2

The Causeway

Hartham Common

Washall Green

3

4

Whitebarns   Lane

Whitebarns

River Ash

Stocking Pelham

Meadow

5

Crabbs Green

Ginns Road

6

Whitebarns Lane

Furneux Pelham

Willows Farm

The Road Wash

Ginns

7

PO

The

Violets Lane

Barleycroft End

Furneux Pelham C of E School

Street

East End

8

Hertfordshire Way

Clay Chimneys

Patient End

A   B   C   D   E   F

am

1 grid square represents 500 metres

Green

G H J 87 K L M

Curles Manor

Honey Lane

Parsonage Lane

B1038

Clavering Hall Farm

Perimead

River Stort

I

Dewes Green

Berden Priory Farm

Dewes Green Road

Highlands

2

Dewes Green Road

Benhams Lane

Bonnetting Lane

Vicarage Lane

St Nicholas St Fld

Berden

Little London

3

The Street

Church Drive

Sawpit Lane

Potash

4

118

The Crump

Peyton Hall

5

Park Green

Lane

Brick House End

Battle's Wood

6

7

Maggots End

Sheepcote Lane

8

Mount Pleasant

Butt

Lane

145 Mallows Gr

Stewarts Way

G H J K L M

Man

A   B   C   88   D   E   F

F2
1 Thistley Crs

Harca

1
B1383

Brick
Kiln
Lane

2
Greys
Hollow

1 PO

Brick Kiln
La

Rickling
C of E
Primary School
PH

**Rickling
Green**

3
Potash Farm

Harcamlow Way

Belcham's
Lane

Brixton Lane

Lane

4
River Stort

Broom
Wood

117

B1383

5
Harcamlow   Way

Patmore
Fields

Brixton Lane

6
Wade's
Hall

7
Pinchpools

Bollington
Hall

Harcamlow   Way

Pinchpools Road

8
Harcamlow   Way

Harcamlow   Way

Stewarts Way
The
Anderson
Close

The
Hall

A   B   C   146   D   E   F

e
Lane

Street

†

Manuden

1 grid square represents 500 metres

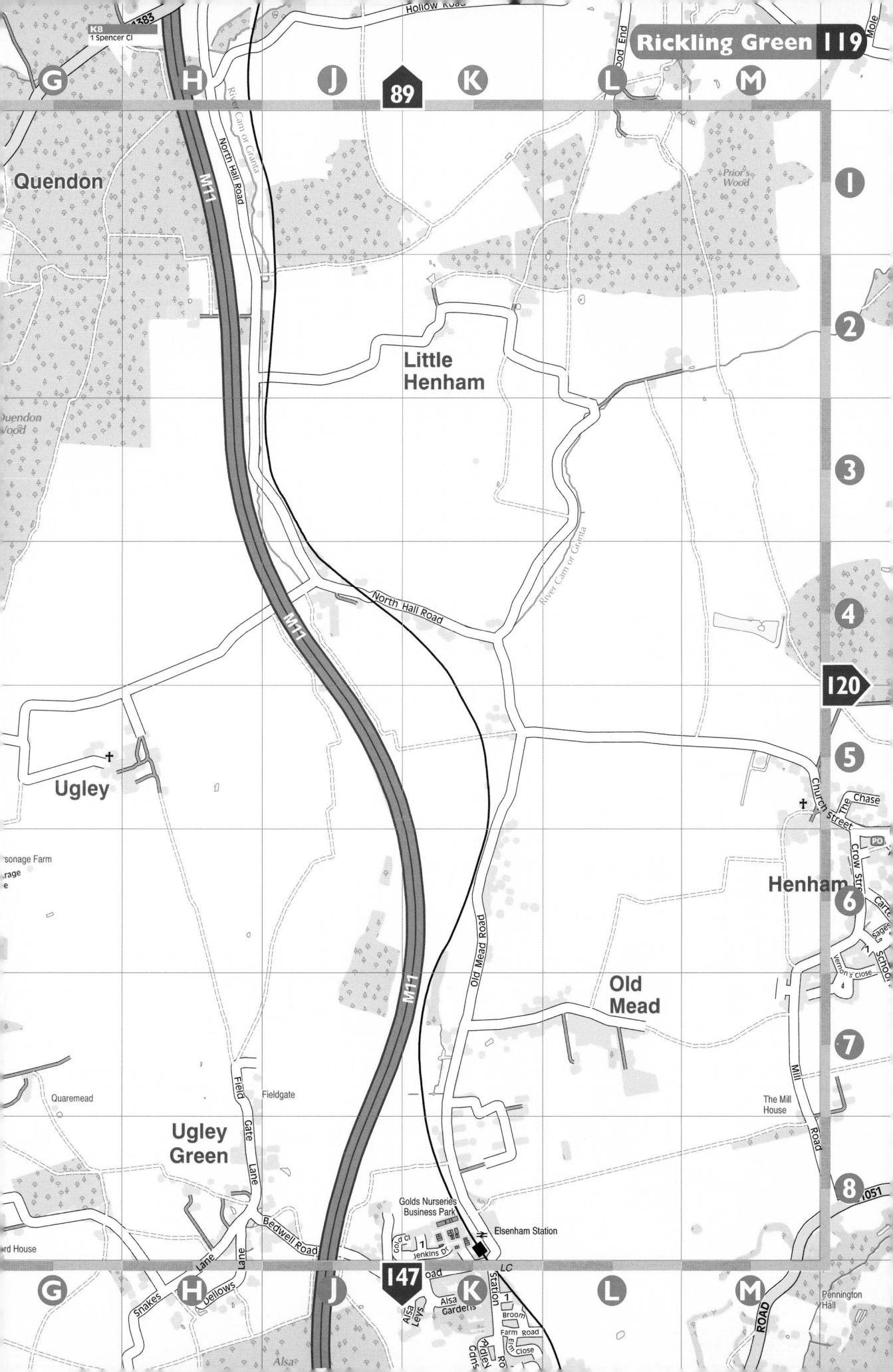

K8
1 Spencer Cl

G H J 89 K L M

Quendon

1

Quendon
Wood

2

Little
Henham

3

North Hall Road

River Cam or Granta

North Hall Road

4

120

Ugley

5

The Chase

Church Street

Crow Street

Henham

6

PO

Cart
sages

School

Vernon's Close

parsonage Farm
rage

Old
Mead

7

Mill Road

The Mill
House

Quaremead

Field Gate Lane

Fieldgate

Ugley
Green

8

1051

Bedwell Road

Snakes Lane

Jellows

Golds Nurseries
Business Park

Elsenham Station

Gold Cl
Jenkins Dr

1

LC

G H J 147 K L M

Alsa Leys

Alsa
Gardens

Broom
Farm Road

Adley Gard

Close

Station Road

ROAD

Pennington
Hall

ord House

The Driv

perden
End

Water Hall
Farm

Richmond's
in the Wood

eggatts
Farm

Loves
Farm

Cutlers
Green

Bolf

Stanbrook

Buckingham's
Farm

Ham
Hill F

B1051

Armigers

122

Fol Mill Lan

River Chelmer

Fitch W

Sharpes Farm

B1051

**Sucksted
Green**

Broadfans
Farm

Chaureth
Hall
Farm

B1051

Fitch Way

Chickney

Tingates

Wolsey's

B1051

Coldarbour
Farm

Tilty Hill
Farm

Hotel

**Church
End**

Cranham
Road

Broxted

Fitch Way

Abbe

View

**Duton
Hill**

A **B** **C** **D** **E** **F**

92

Thaxted

B1
1 Orange St
2 Stony La
3 The Tanyard
4 Town St

Blunt's Farm

I

NEWBIGGEN
The Drive
The Maypole
Back Lane   Clare COL
Weaverhead Close
Mead
Vicarage
Margaret Street
The Surgery
WATLING STREET
Orchard Lane
Wedow Road
Brook View
Copthall Lane
Magdalen Green
Barnards Field

MILL END
Fishmarket Street
St Clements
Thaxted Primary School

Bolford Street

Bardfield
End Green

2

B1051 PARK STREET

DUNMOW ROAD

B184

Fitch Way

Prior's Hall

3

Stanbrook

The Maltings
Star Mead

4

Buckingham's Farm

Hammer Hill Farm

Dovehouse Farm

Richmond's
Green

121

Monk
Street

Holder'
Green

5

Folly Mill Lane

Mayes Pl

B184

Fitch Way

River Chelmer

Sibley's Green

6

Cowels Farm Lane
Cowels Farm

7

Fitch Way

Moathouse Farm

8

Wolsey's Farm

Little Cambridge

Dove House

Gallows
Green

Hyde Farm

Greenarbour

Gallows Green Road

A **B** **C** **D** **E** **F**

B184

Blamster's Hall

150

Lane

Breach

1 grid square represents 500 metres

Hill

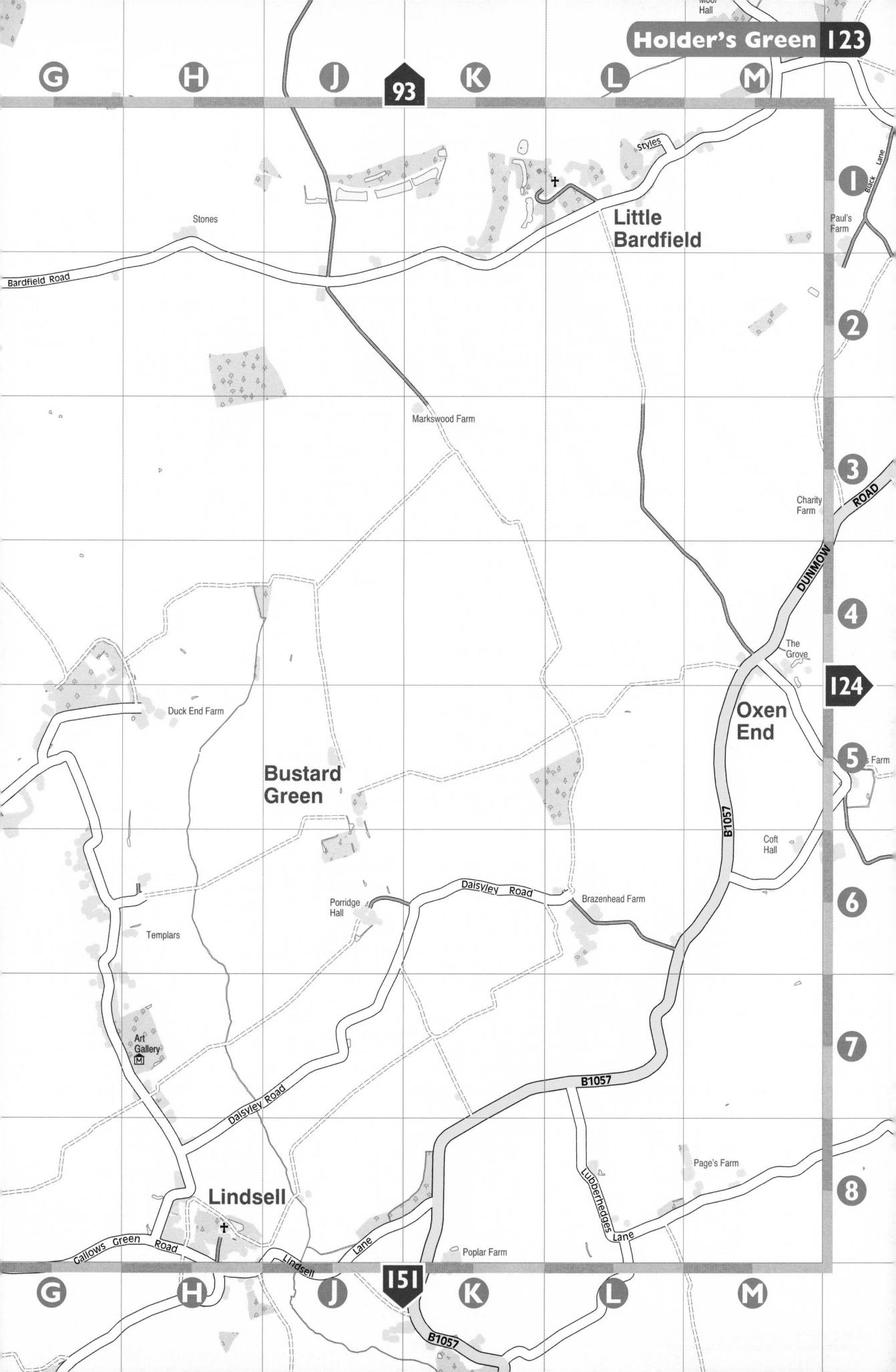

G H J 93 K L M

I

Paul's Farm

Black Lane

2

Stones

Little Bardfield

Bardfield Road

3

Charity Farm

DUNMOW ROAD

Markswood Farm

4

The Grove

124

Duck End Farm

Oxen End

5

s Farm

Bustard Green

B1057

Coft Hall

6

Templars

Porridge Hall

Daisyley Road

Brazenhead Farm

Art Gallery

7

Daisyley Road

B1057

Page's Farm

Lubberhedges Lane

8

Lindsell

Gallows Green Road

Lindsell Lane

151

Poplar Farm

B1057

G H J 151 K L M

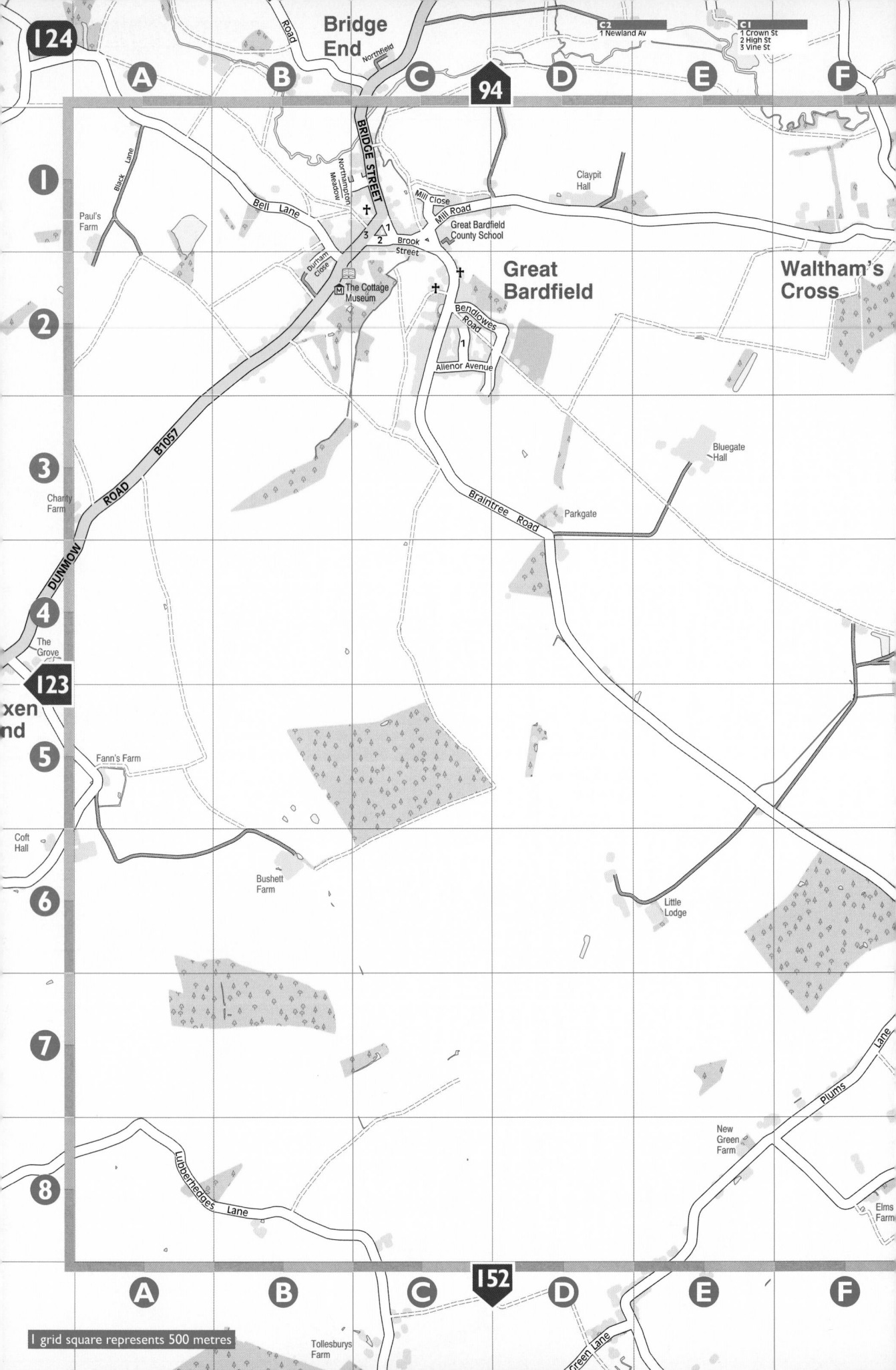

Bridge
End

A   B   C   D   E   F

Northfield

C2
1 Newland Av

C1
1 Crown St
2 High St
3 Vine St

1

Paul's
Farm

Black Lane

Bell Lane

Mill Close

Mill Road

Claypit
Hall

BRIDGE STREET

Northampton
Meadow

3   7
2
1

Brook
Street

Great Bardfield
County School

Great
Bardfield

Waltham's
Cross

2

Dunam
Close

The Cottage
Museum

M

Bendlowes Road

1

Alienor Avenue

3

Charity
Farm

DUNMOW   ROAD   B1057

Braintree   Road

Parkgate

Bluegate
Hall

4

The
Grove

xen
nd

5

Fann's Farm

Coft
Hall

6

Bushett
Farm

Little
Lodge

7

Plums   Lane

New
Green
Farm

8

Lubberhedges   Lane

Elms
Farm

A   B   C   D   E   F

Tollesburys
Farm

Green Lane

1 grid square represents 500 metres

M3
1 Edmund Gn
2 Woodland Wy

M4
1 Greenways

G H J **97** K L M

Whit
ree

I

Bounce's
Farm

Farm

Shardlowe's
Farm

2

Halstead

A1017

Highlands

Home
Farm

Meadway

Ches'nut
AV

Halstead
Rd

Gosfield
Primary School

THE STREET

A1017

3

Gosfield

Gosfield Lake
Golf Club

St Margarets
Preparatory
School

Hall

Drive

Church

Road

Nun's Meadow

PO
PH

1
1

Greenfield

Parkhall
Farm

Parkhall Road

Gosfield
Lake

†

The
Limes

4

A1017

128

Parkhall
Wood

Parkhall Road

5

Ayleward's
Farm

BRAINTREE

ROAD

New Road

Peterfield's

6

Harmas
Farm

Peterfield's
Farm

Bovingdon
Wood

Gosfield
Wood

A1017

Iron Pear
Tree Farm

7

Fennes

Road

GOSFIELD ROAD

HALSTEAD

ROAD

Fennes

Foley
House

A131

Boon's Farm

8

Boul

G H J **155** K L M

**High
Garrett**

GARRETT

Sunnyfields
Road

Trotters'

Whiteash
Green

H1
1 Broton Dr
2 Elizabeth Wy
3 Upper Chapel St

E3
1 The Tythings

E2
1 Clovers
2 De Veres Rd
3 Monklands Ct
4 Mount Ri
5 Oxford Rd
6 Warren Rd

E1
1 The Pippins

A B C 98 D E F

HALSTEAD

Halstead Town
Football Club

Box Mill Lane

Sloe Hill

Sloe House

Beridge Road

Slough Farm Road

Butler Road

Broton Drive

Chapel St

High Street

The Centre

3 2

Stanley Road

Colne Valley

Chapel Hill

Primary School

Orchard Av

Dooley Road

Trinity Street

The Surgery

Halstead
Business Cen

Fac

Factory La

I

Gosfield
School

2

Halstead Road

Russell's Road

The Grange

The Grange

Russell's Farm

Blamster's
Farm

New Street

Windmill Road

Acorn Av

A131

Trinity Road

PO

Kings Road

Park

Knowles Close

Godwin Cl

Warren Road

Mount Pleasant

Neale Road

Oxford Road

Mitchell Ave

West Rd

Rayner Way

School Cha

Highlands

Halstead
Rd

Gosfield
Primary School

3

Gosfield

PO
PH
Greenfield
The
mes

1

Park Lane

A1017

127

Mount HL

Prior Cl

Blamster's Cfs

Conway
Close

White Link Rd

Abels Road

Bourne Cl

Holmes Road

Ramsey Rd

West
Yard

Ronald Road

Horse

Tweed Close

Clare Close

Conies Road

Parker Way

Roundacre

Tolnds

South

Grange
Close

Firwood's
Rd)

4

5

BOURNEBRIDGE HILL

A131

Russell's Road

Upper Beakley
Farm

Oak Road

Letche's
Farm

Bourne Brook

Froyz Hall
Farm

Aylett's Farm

Plaistow Green Road

Gladfen Hall

6

New Road

Peterfield's Lane

A131

Penny
Pot

Plaistow
Green

eterfield
arm

7

Rayne Hatch
Wood

Highbarn Hall

Ward's Farm

ROAD

8

Rayne
Hatch
Farm

Boultwood's Farm

A B 156 C D E F

I grid square represents 500 metres

G1
1 Bois Hall Gdns
2 Morley Rd
3 Saxon Cl

G2
1 Kingfisher Mdw
2 Swallow Wk

G3
1 Bentall Cl

G **H** **J** 99 **K** **L** **M**

SUDBURY

Greenwood
School

Ramsey
School

Colne
Road

Maple
Close

Abbot's
Shrub

Westwood
Farm

Brook Street

I

2 Brook
Farm

HEAD ST

Chipping
Hill

Cemetery

Upper Fenn
Road

Fenn Road

COLCHESTER A1124 ROAD

Fifth Avenue

Fourth Avenue

Bluebridge Industrial
Estate

Second Avenue

First Avenue

Harvey St
Weavers Row
Gardeners Road
Courtauld
Close

Kestrel
Rise

Netter
Court

Third Avenue

Brook Farm
Close

River Colne

Elms Hall

Elms Hall Road

3

Elm Drive
Ravens
Av
R Johnston
Close
Cooks
Close
Well
Field
Stanstead
Hills
River
Close
Meadow Close

Bluebridge House

A1124

Colne
Valley

Banmeo Brook

4

Greenstead
Hall

A1124 STONEBRIDGE HILL

HALS

I30

Parley Beans
Farm

Stanstead
Hall

5

Don
Johns

Nightingale
Hall

6

Church Road

Greenstead
Green

Burton's Green Road

PO

Whitings

Lodge
Farm

7

Perces

8

G **H** 157 **K** **L** **M**

J urton's
Green

Mann's Farm

Markshall Wood

Clavering's Farm

Lancaster Way

H1
1 Coggeshall Wy
2 Haubourdin Ct
3 Hawthorn Cl

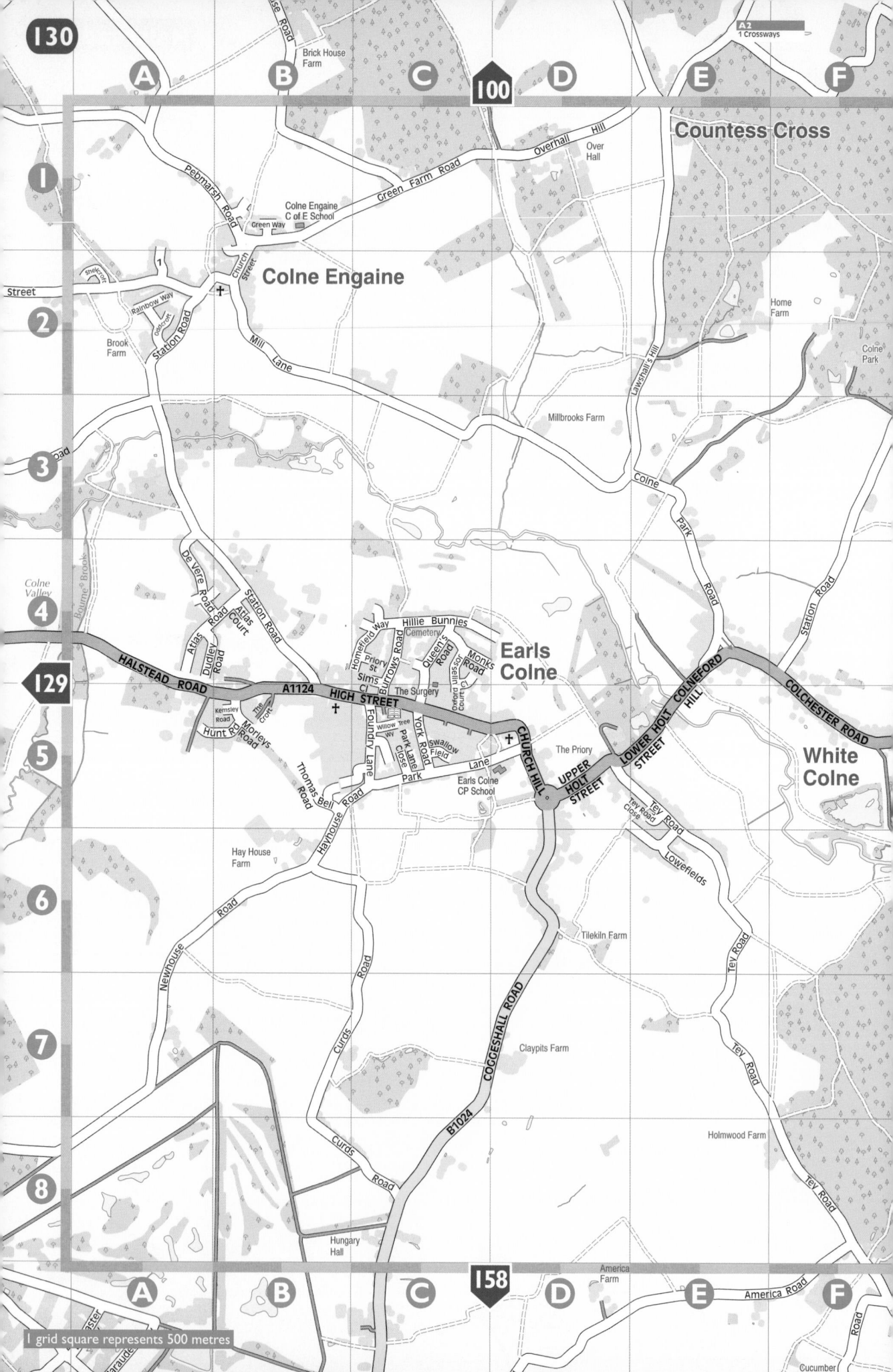

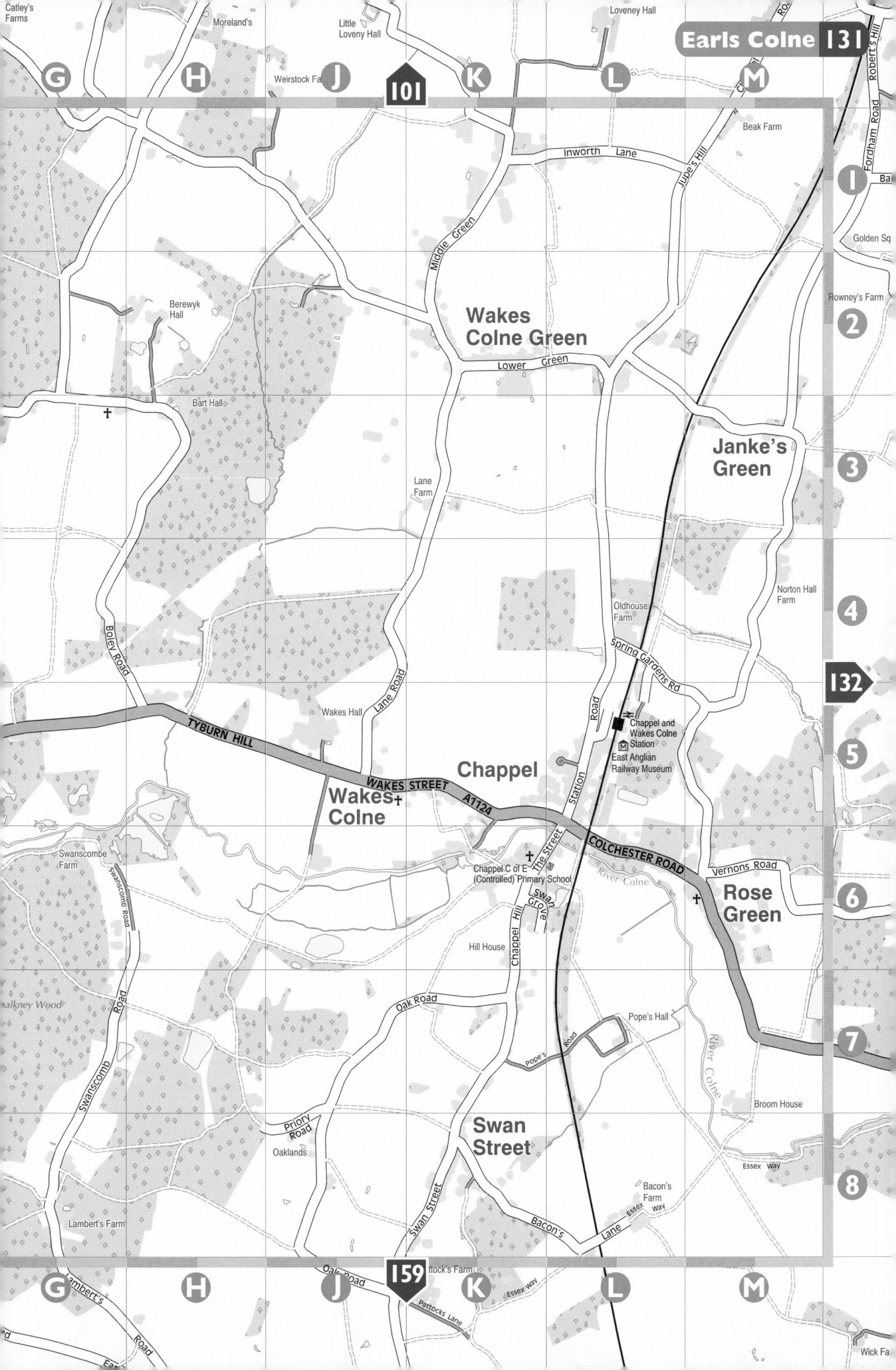

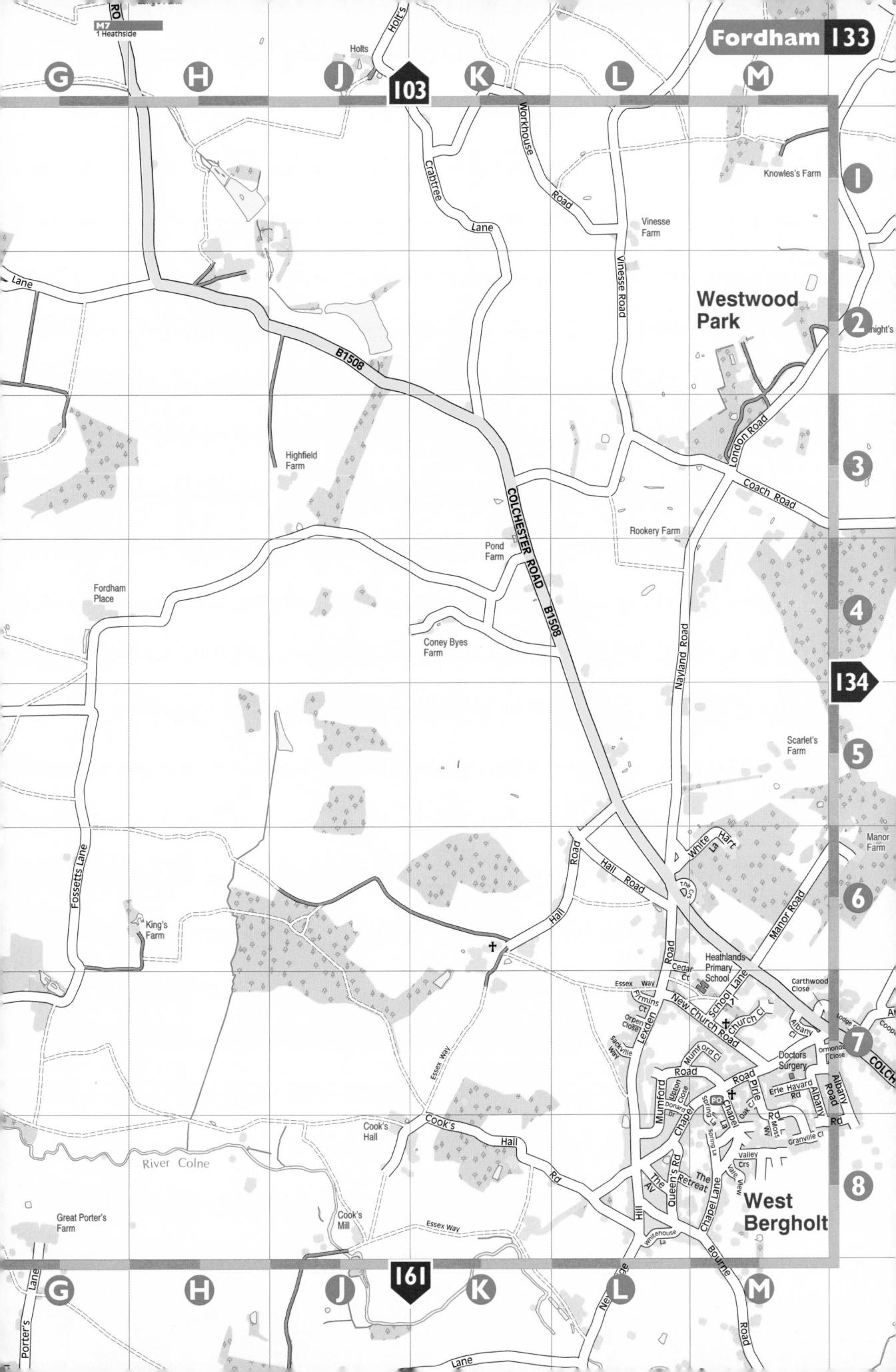

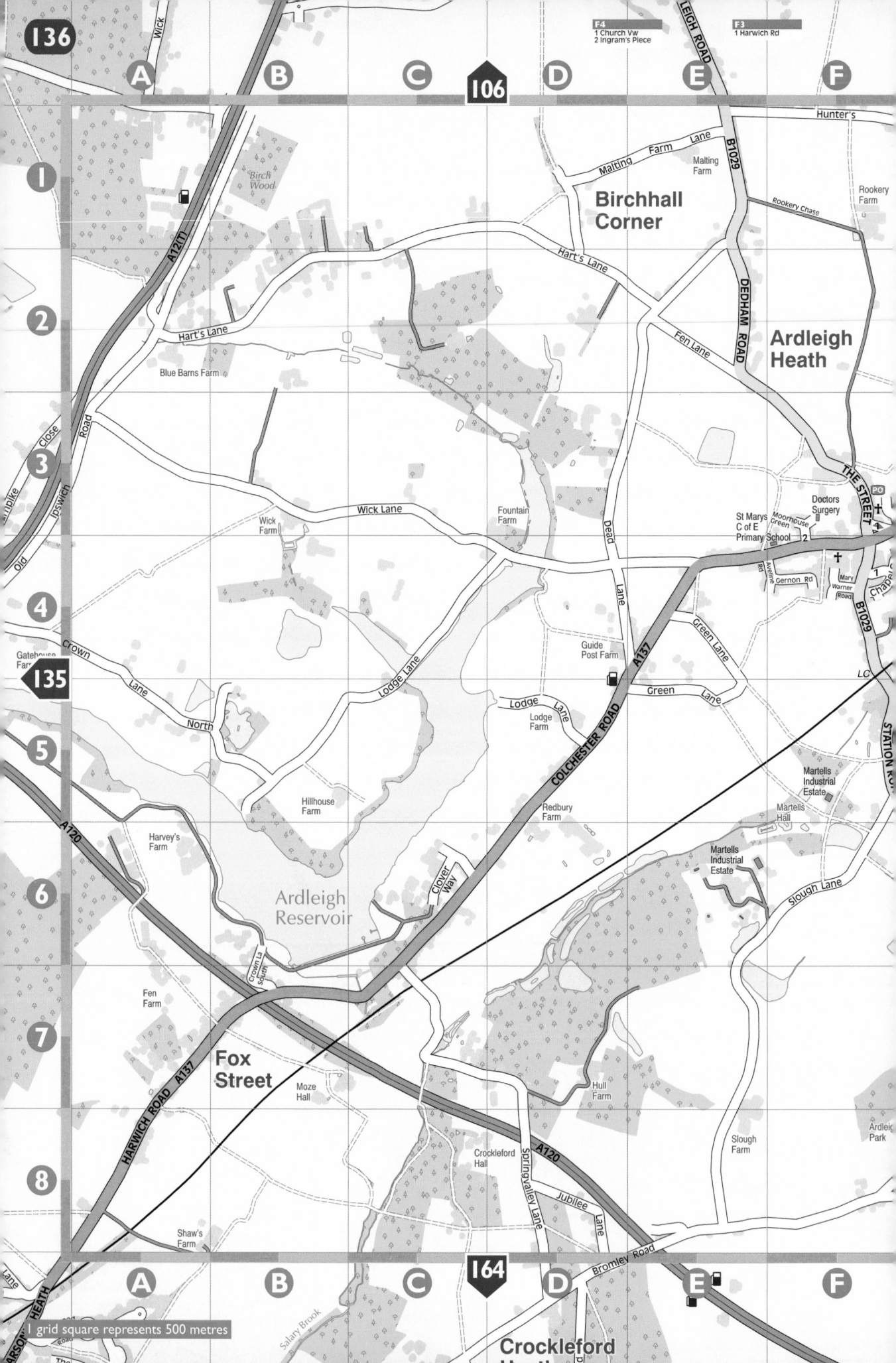

A B C **106** D E F

LEIGH ROAD

Hunter's

Malting Farm Lane

Malting Farm

B1029

Rookery Chase

Rookery Farm

Birchhall Corner

Birch Wood

Hart's Lane

DEDHAM ROAD

Fen Lane

Ardleigh Heath

Hart's Lane

Blue Barns Farm

THE STREET

PO

Doctors Surgery

Wick Lane

Fountain Farm

Moorhouse Green

St Marys C of E Primary School

Gernon Rd

Mary Warner Road

Chapel

B1029

Wick Farm

Dead Lane

Ipswich Road

Close

Old Turnpike

Gatehouse Farm

Guide Post Farm

Green Lane

LC

135

Crown Lane

Lodge Lane

Lodge Lane

Lodge Farm

COLCHESTER ROAD

A137

Green Lane

STATION ROAD

North

Martells Industrial Estate

Martells Hall

Hillhouse Farm

Redbury Farm

Martells Industrial Estate

Harvey's Farm

A120

Clover Way

Slough Lane

Ardleigh Reservoir

Crown La South

Fen Farm

Hull Farm

Slough Farm

Ardleigh Park

Fox Street

HARWICH ROAD A137

Moze Hall

A120

Crockleford Hall

Springvalley Lane

Jubilee Lane

Bromley Road

Shaw's Farm

A B C **164** D E F

ARSONS HEATH

Salary Brook

Crockleford

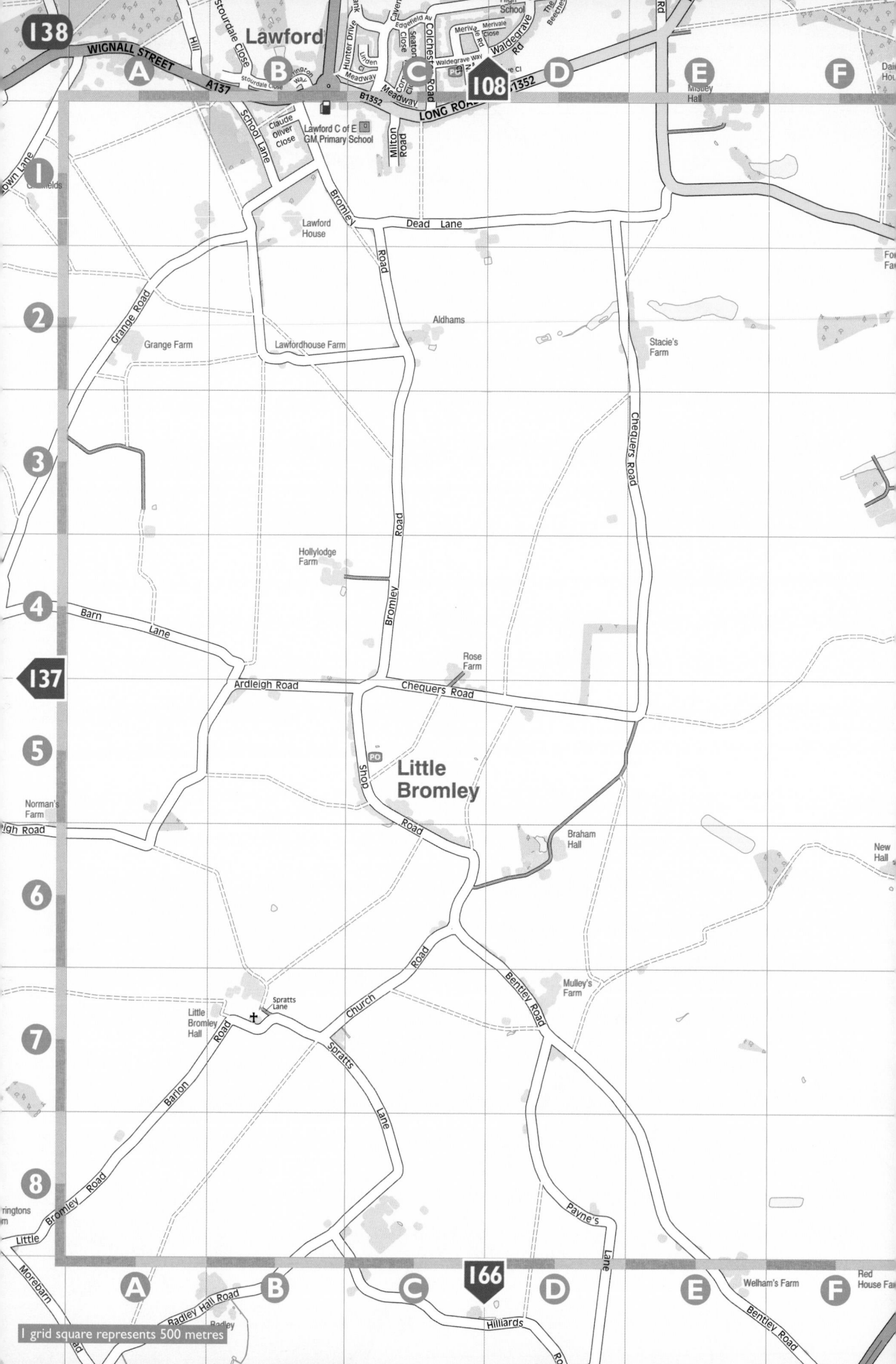

New Mistley

Middlefield Rd
Westmorland Close
Rigby Av
Furze Hill

Essex Way

G H J 109 K L M I

Essex Way

Mistley Heath

Bradfield

Heath Road

C011

Windmill Road

Mill Lane

Home Farm

Bradfield Primary School

Lodge

Station Road

The Street

Wix

2

Straight Road

King St

Dunning Close

PO

Crownail Lane

Heath Road

3

Steam Mill Road

Heath

Bradfield Heath

y Hall

Barrack St

Cansey Lane

Dairyhouse Lane

Ellis Rd

4

Bradfield Hall

Cansey Lane

140

CLACTON ROAD

B1035

Cansey Lane

Goldenferry

5

Horsleycross Street

Cansey Lane

6

Bradfield Lodge

Crossman's Farm

A120

Abbott's Hall

CLACTON ROAD

Cansey Lane

Colchester Rd

7

Goose Green

Horsley Cross

A120(T)

8

A120(T)

Harwich Road

B1035

Hempstall's Farm

Tendring

Brocketts Hall

A · B · 110 · C · D · E · F

1

Bradfield

HARWICH ROAD B1352

Essex Way

School
Jacques Hall

Lonbarn

Priory
Farm

Wheatsheaf Lane

Street

Shore

LONBARN HILL

SPINNEL'S HILL

HARWICH ROAD

Spinnel's
Farm

2

Barn
Farm

Bluehouse
Farm

Wix
Road

3

Pond
Hall

Willow
Hall
Lane

Willow
Hall

Dairyhouse Lane

Carbonells

4

Dairy
House

Bradfield Road

Dairyhouse Lane

Bradfield Road

Wix Abbey

Spinnel's

Lane

5

Wix
Lodge

WIX BY-PASS

Wix CP
School

PO
Abbots Close

Bradfield Road

Harwich Road

Wix

6

A120(T)

Colchester Road

Daleview Avenue

Glebe Close

Clacton Road

Clayhall

7

Calsey Lane

Spring
Farm

Honeypot Lane

Wix Road

Dengewell
Hall

8

Tendring Road

Colchester Road

Frith's Farm

Stonehall Lane

Col r Road

Stones Green Road

A · B · C · D · E · F

1 grid square represents 500 metres

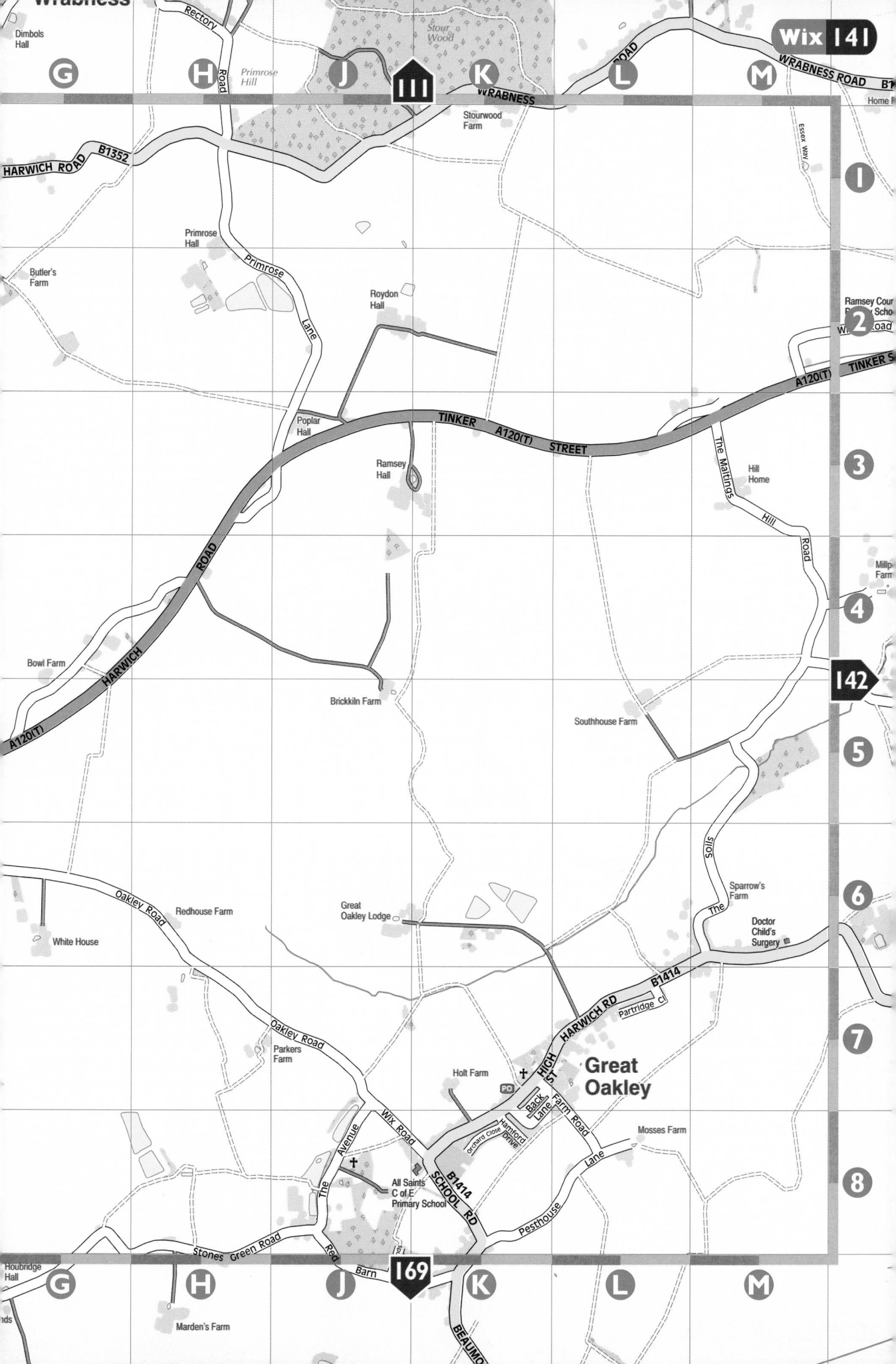

Dove**L**ourt   **M**

G   **H**   **J**   **113**   **K**

G2
1 Musgrave Cl
2 Nightingale Cl
3 Oxenford Cl
4 Shackleton Cl

1 Blackthorn Rd
2 De Vere Wy

1 Washington Rd

Oulton Close

All Saints
C of E
Primary School

Harwich
District
Hospital

B1352   PO

ROAD

Holyrood

Willow
Way

B1414

Deane's Cl

Deanes Court

St Josephs RC
Primary School

St Michael's
Road

Howard
Meadows

William
Groom

The
Harwich
School

Queen's
Rd

Coral
Cl

The Drive

Seafield Road

Promenade

Old Vicarage Rd

Balton
Way

Abbott
Road

Alfred
Anson Cl

Gordon
Way

Richmond
Crs

Kreswell
Gv

Harwich
Sports Centre

Hudson Close

Wick

West End Lane

Dovercourt
Swimming Pool

Whinfield
Av

Low Road

St Denis

Louvain Rd

Vienna Cl

Brussels

Bruges Cl

W End La

Promenade

Essex Way

Essex Way

I   1

2

3

4

5

6

7

8

G   **H**   **J**   **171**   **K**   **L**   **M**

K1
1 St George's Av

H2
1 Acorn Cl
2 Newport Cl
3 St Edmunds Cl

Pennyhole
Bay

Patient End

Hertfordshire Way

A   **B**   **C**   **D**   **E**   **F**

Hixham Hall

1

Hole Farm

2

Hertfordshire Way

Hertfordshire Way

Kitchers

Gravesend

Patmore Heath

Patmore Hall

3

Albury Hall

Barncroft

4

Harcamlow Way

Harcamlow Way

Mill Lane

Hertfordshire Way

Clapgate

Albury School

Parsonage Lane

Albury

5

Upwic Green

Albury Lodge

6

Upwick Hall

Piggott's Farm

7

Albury End

River Ash

8

STANDON

A   **B**   A120   **C**   **D**   **E**   **F**

Albury Road

Little Hadham

Church End

STORTFORD RO

Lloyd-Taylor Close

Little Hadham

1 grid square represents 500 metres

G   H   J   **117**   K   L   **M**

Mallows Green

Mount Pleasant

Butt   Lane

Stewarts Way

1
Mar

Mallows Green Road

Uppend

Dogden la

Mallows Gree

Watery Lane

Parsonage Farm

2

Harcamlow Way

3

Essex County

Hertfordshire County

Harcamlow   Way

Farnham Green

Chatter End

Harcamlow Way

4

Waterside (School)

146

Bourne Brook

Farnham School

Rectory Lane

Globe Crescent

Farnham

5

Level's Green

The Common

6

Mill Hill

Walnuttree Green

7

A120

8

Wickham Hall

G   H   **173**   J   K   L   M   Fox

Green

G4
1 Lower St

K1
1 Cranmore Cl

K2
1 Saunders Cl

G

H

Bedwell Road

J

119

K

Golds Nurseries
Business Park

Elsenham Station

kins Dr

L

M

1051

I

Pennington
Hall

rford House

Snakes Lane

Bellows Lane

New Road

Station Road

Alsa Levs

Alsa
Gardens

LC

Broom

Farm Road

1
Close

Pidley
Gdns

De Mandevill

Otzlers
Rd

Park Road

Hallies
Wd

Elsenham

Alsa
Wood

The Surgery

The
Croft

Cem

HENHAM

B1051

2

Alsa
Lodge

Alsa
Street

Norman
House

Fourways

HIGH ST

PH

ROAD

Alsa
Business Park

Leigh
Drive

Glebe

PO

Hall Road

Church Lane

3

May Walk

STANSTED ROAD

Stansted
Rd

Robin Hood Rd

Mill Cl

B1051

Call End Lane

Stansted House

M11

Rush
Lane

LC

**Fuller's
End**

Tye Green Road

4

148

ROVE HILL

Castle
Walk Clinic

Tye
Green

5

ted
et Station

Churchfields

The Arthur Findlay
College

M11

Burton
Bower

Claypit Hill

6

CM24

St Mary's

The Mountfitchet
School

Church Road

Old Buryloge
Lane

Burton End

Belmer Road

7

Foresthall Rd

Parsonage Lane

Parsonage Farm

Bury Lodge Lane

Sixth Avenue

8

Parsonage Farm
Indusrial Estate

M11

Monks
Farm

G

H

J

175

Ninth Avenue

Seventh Avenue

Third Av

Second Av

enth Av

K

L

M

End

G H J **121** K L M

Broxted

Broxted Hall

Hotel

Cranham Road

Moor End Farm

Brown's End Road

Muscombs

Water Lane

Harcamlow Way

Flemings Hill Farm

Harcamlow Way

Brookend

Bamber's Green

Sheering Hall

Lane

The Grange

Tilty

Harcamlow Way

Goodfellows

Perryfields

Easton Lodge

River Roding

Du n Hill **1**

Abbey View

Flitch

2

3

Rebecca Meade

The Endway

Blocks Md

4

150

Easton Farm

5

Little Easton

Glebe Lane

6

Mar Rc

7

Park Road

8

G H J **177** K L M

(A) (B) (C) **122** (D) (E) Gallows Green (F)

Gallows
Green

Hyde
Farm

Gallows Green Road

Abbey V

1 Duton
Hill

Blamster's
Hall

B184

Breach
Lane

Breach

2

3

Rebecca
Meade

Millend
Green

Little Rakefairs

Andrews Farm Lane

Andrews
Farm

The Endway

The Endway

Bigod's
Wood

Brocks Md

4

149

Great
Easton

B184

Easton
Farm

5

Bigods Hall
Farm

Maysland

6
Little
Easton

Glebe
Lane

Butchers
Pasture

Manor
Road

DUCK

Street

Bigods Lane

Lower
Hall

Marks
Farm

7

Park Road

Elmbridge
Farm

rk Road †

8

B184

Bigods Lane

Ravens
Farm

Dunmow
Sports
Centre

The
Parsonage

Chur

(A) (B) (C) **178** (D) (E) (F)

BEAUMONT HL

CHURCH
END

CHURCH STREET

St Edmunds
Flds

Frey

B184

Page's Farm

Lindsell

G   H   ✝   J   Lane   **123**   K   Poplar Farm   L   e   M

Gallows Green Road

Lindsell

Lubbernedd

I

B1057

Simpkins

Duck
End

Holt's Farm

2

Stebbing Brook

Lashley
Hall

B1057

3

Bran
End

B1057

Rosemary La

Bran End
Fields

4

Brick   Kiln   Lane

Clay
Lane

152

Brook Fields

Marshall's Piece

Pound Gate

Park Side
Fields

5

Garden

William's
Farm

Spike House

Stebbing
Park

High   Street

PO

Stebbing 6

BROADWAY

Dunmow
Farm

Mott's
Yard

Watch House Road

Wh

Old House

Mill Lane

✝

✝   Ruffels
Field

THE

7

CM6

Haydens

8

Tooley's
Farm

uches
end

Merks
Hall

G   H   J   **179**   K   Brook   L   M

Homelye Farm

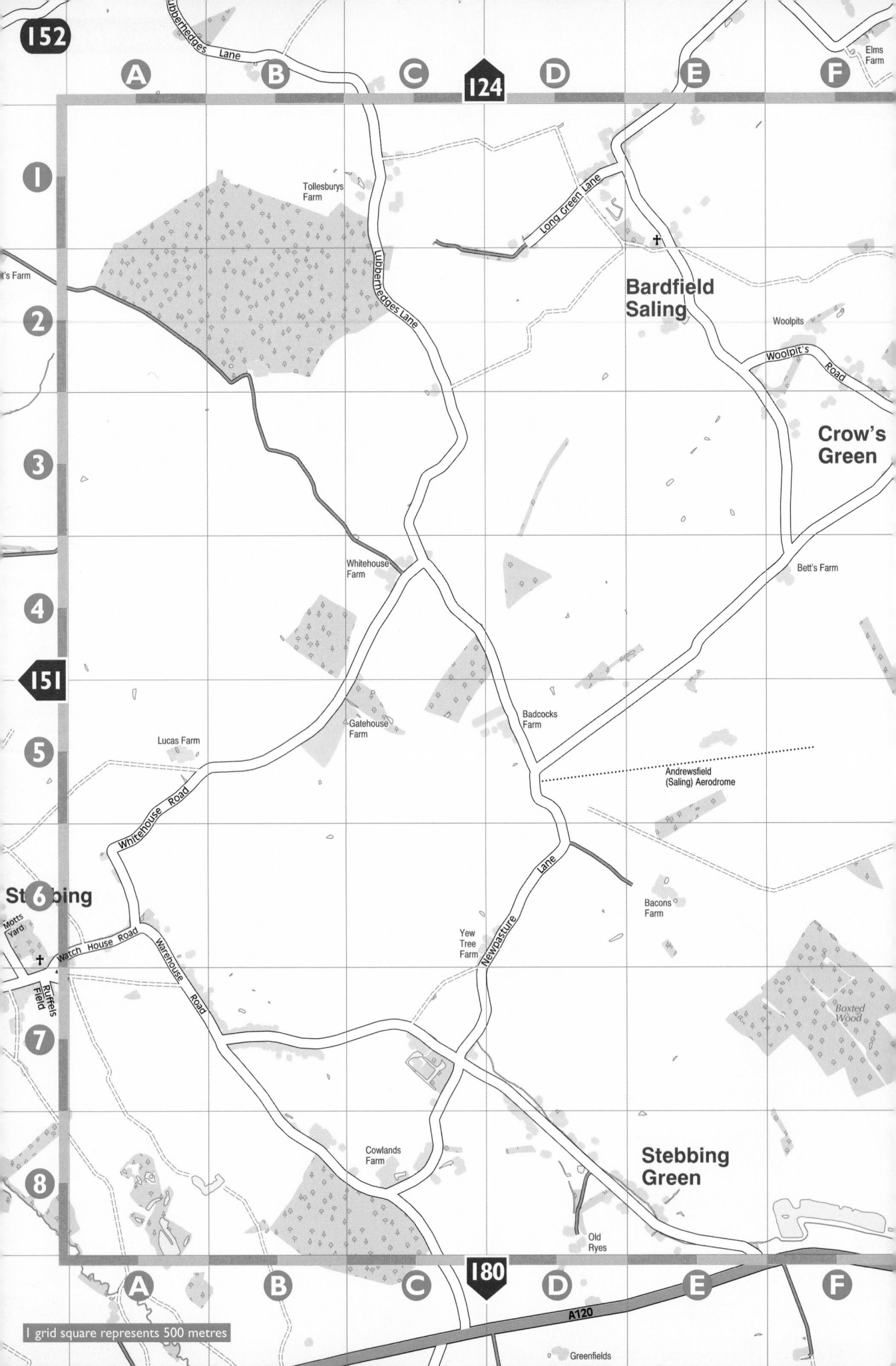

A   B   C   124   D   E   F

1

Ubberhedges Lane

Lubberhedges Lane

Tollesburys Farm

t's Farm

2

Long Green Lane

†

Bardfield Saling

Woolpits

Woolpit's Road

3

Crow's Green

Whitehouse Farm

Bett's Farm

4

151

Badcocks Farm

Gatehouse Farm

5

Lucas Farm

Andrewsfield (Saling) Aerodrome

Whitehouse Road

St**6**bing

Motts Yard

Watch House Road

Bacons Farm

†

Warehouse Road

Ruffels Field

Yew Tree Farm

Newpasture Lane

7

Boxted Wood

Cowlands Farm

Stebbing Green

8

Old Ryes

A   B   C   180   D   E   F

A120

Greenfields

G   H   J   **125**   K   L   M

Shalford Green

Bartlett's F

Jasper's Green

Water

1

Lowlands Farm

2

Bardfield Road

Cold Hall Farm

3

Pudneys Farm

Piccotts Lane

Great Saling

Piccotts Farm

PO

Vicarage Close

Piccotts Lane

Saling Grove

Mount's Farm

Hall Rd

4

154

5

Onchor's Farm

Old Hall

6

Pods Brook

Shalford Road

7

Rumley Wood

Moor's Farm

Pound Farmhouse

Duckend Green

8

Blake House Farm

Blake End Gallery

Moors Lane

Rayne CP School

Cape C

G   H **Blake End**   J   **181**   K   L   M

B141

A120

DUNMOW

Pods

eyside

Capel Road

Brunwi

Rayne

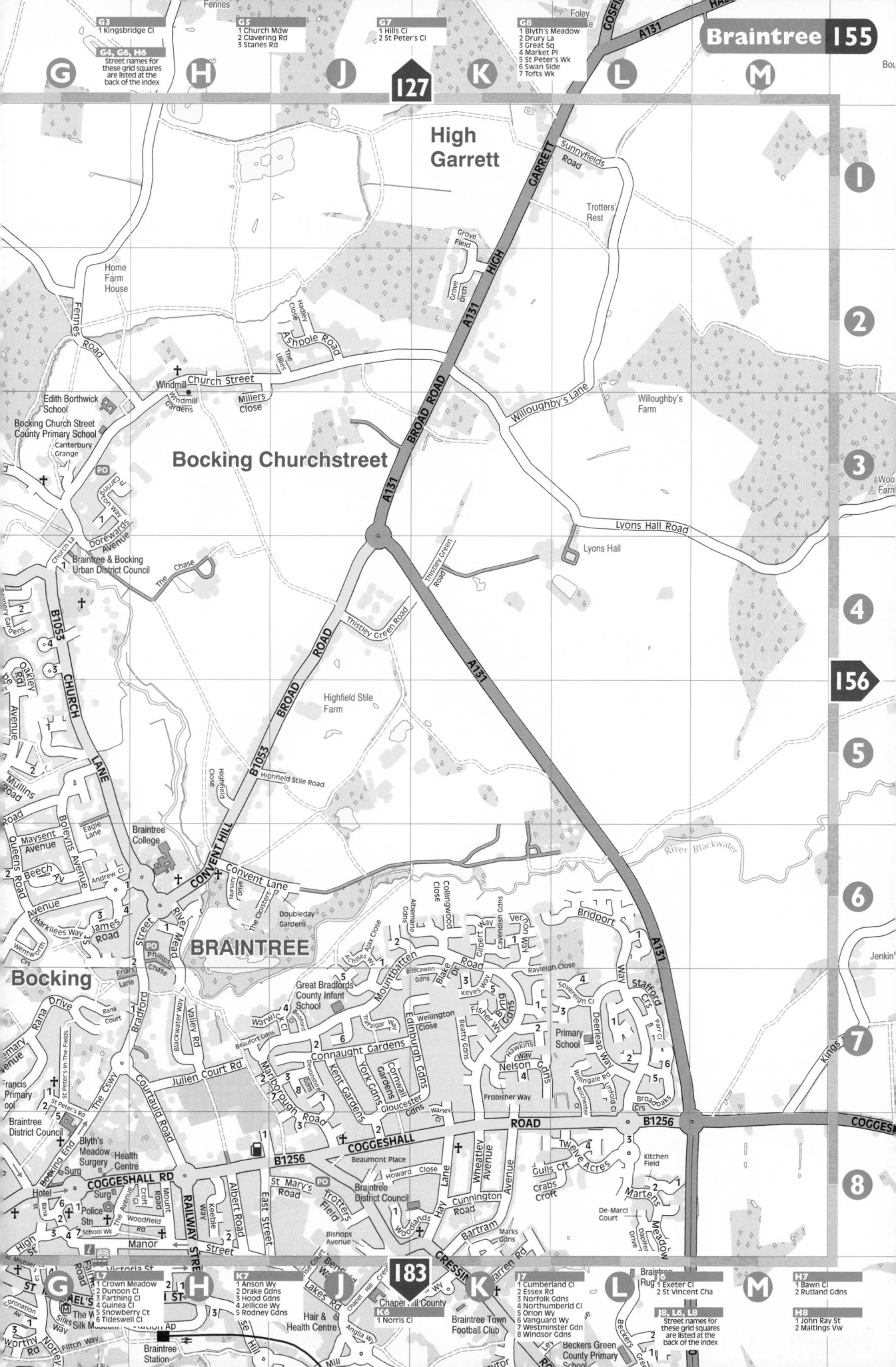

High Garrett

Bocking Churchstreet

Lyons Hall

Highfield Stile Farm

River Blackwater

BRAINTREE

Bocking

Braintree College

Great Bradfords County Infant School

Braintree Town Football Club

Braintree Station

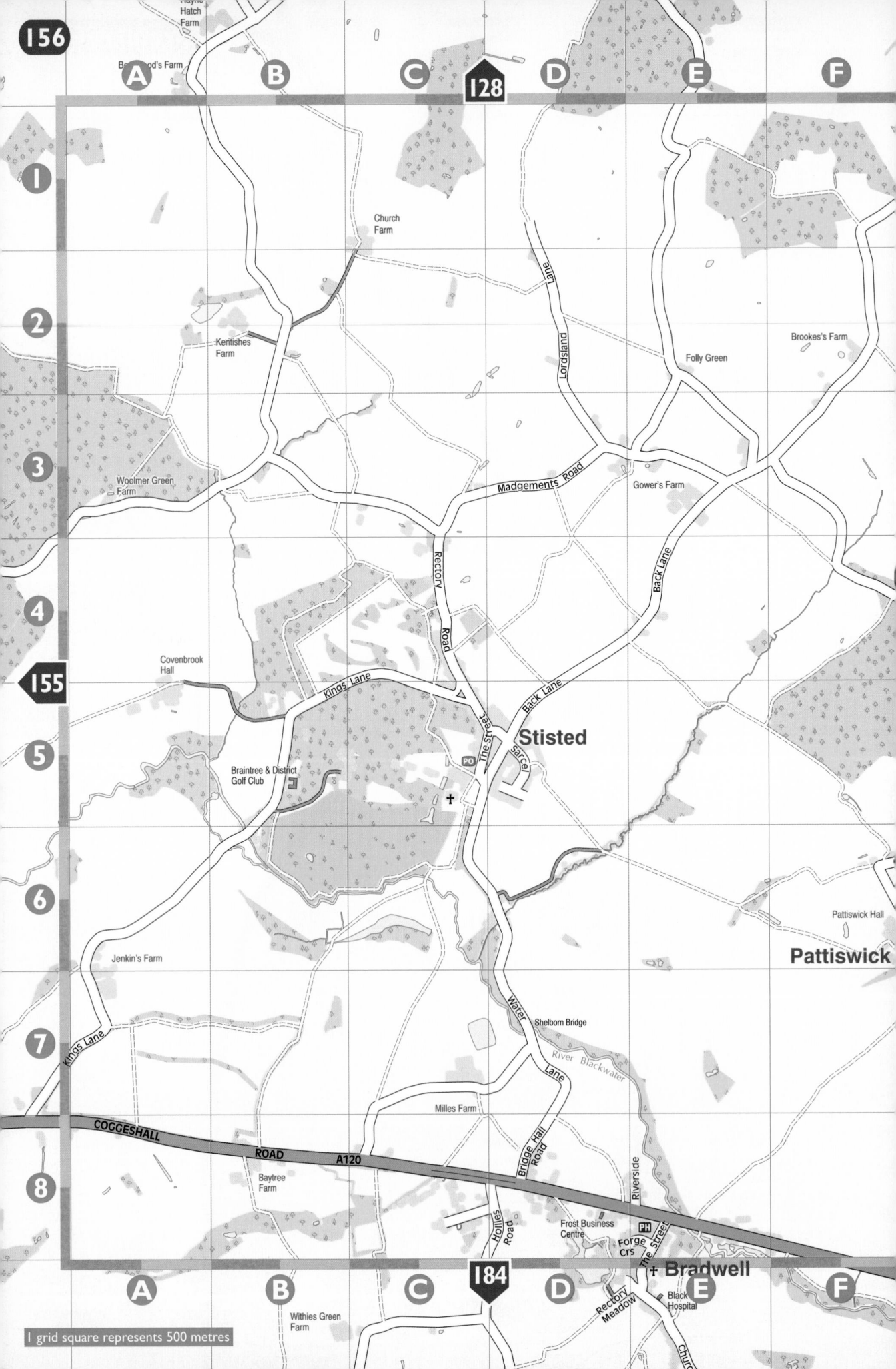

G H J **129** K L M

I
2
3
4
158
5
6
7
8

Perces

Lodge Farm

Clavering's Farm

Burton Green

Mann's Farm

Markshall Wood

Nunty's Lane

Great Nunty's Farm

Nunty's Lane

Great Monks Wood

Markshall

Woodhouse Farm

Marks Hall Arboretum

Potash Farm

Bungate Wood

Marygolds

Marks Hall Road

Robin's Brook

Compasses Road

PH

Church Road

Road

Hovells Farm

Cradle House

Holfield Grange

Tilkey

Ambridge Road

G H J **185** K L M

Coggeshall

Whiteshill Farm

Coggeshall Road

Coggeshall Road

COGGESHALL RD

Highfields

Robin Rd

Coggeshall

Great Tey

Little
Tey

East Gores

K3
1 Holliland Cft
2 Tambour Cl

M8
1 Honywood Cl

Lambert's Farm

G H J K L M

I
2
3
4
160 LC
5
6
7
8

Wick Farm

Lambert's Road

Earls Colne Road

Teycross Farm

Oak Road

Pattock's Farm

Pattocks Lane

Bacon's

Bacon's
Farm

Essex Way

Essex Way

Essex Way

Belt's
Farm

Tey Road

Chappel Road

Newbarn Road

Lower Langley

Chrismund Way

Greenfield Drive

Whitmund Way

Great Tey
Primary School

Farmfield
Road
Harvesters'
Way

Garden
Fields

Essex Way

Moor Road

Moor Farm

Florie's Road

Brookhouse Road

Abraham's Farm

The Street

The Chase

Brook Road

Coggeshall Road

Coggeshall Road

Roman River

Walcott's
Hall

Essex Way

Essex Way

Teybrook Farm

Little Hey
House

Trumpingtons
Farm

Roman Brook

Roman River

East Gores Road

Upper Hall
Farm

Great Tey Road

Salmon's Lane

Bracks Lane

Church Lane

Godbolt's Farm

A120

COGGESHALL ROAD

Elm Farm

Elm Lane

Mott's Lane

Godmans
Lane

Primary
School

Mandeville
Rd

Wilson's

Domsey
Bank

Stane Fld

Patten
Cl

Keable Lane

Hawkmark End

LC

A   B   C   132   D   E   F

Fordstreet

C7
1 The Rookeries

A8
1 Cornwalls Dr
2 Kingsbury Cl
3 Maybury Cl
4 Steele Cl

Wash Farm

1

Wick Farm

New Road

Fiddlers Hill

2

Bourchier's Hall

New Road

Gallows Green

Green Lane

A1124

HALSTEAD

Bullbanks Farm

Fiddler's Farm

Foxes Lane

3

Hoe Farm

Rectory Road

Tey Road

Hardings Cl

Church Gv

The Chase

Hines Cl

Aldham

Thurgoods Farm

Chippetts

Daisy Green Road

Daisy Green

4

Church House Farm

Rectory Road

Brook Road

Chippetts Farm

159

LC

Roman River

Aldham Hall

5

Kemp's Farm

Turkey Cock Lane

Mo Fa

6

Brook Road

North Lane

A12(T)

Copford Place

Foundry La Hedgelands

Queensbury Avenue

Copford End

Queensbury Av

Dorothy

Curtice Cl

PK

Willow

Grantier

Marks Tey Station

Hotel

London Road

B1408

Windmill Ct

7

Church Lane

Station Rd

A12(T)

LONDON RD

A12(T)

Mill Road

Doctors Surgery

Copford

Allendale Drive

Ashwin Avenue

School Road

8

Hawkmark End

Well Side

Patten Cl

Bury Cl

Northern

London Road

The Crescent

Hall Chase

Hall Road

Domsey Bank

Ba

Jays Lane

Keable

LC

Dobbies La

Potts Green

Marks Tey

A   B   C   188   D   Copford C of E Primary School   E   F

Copford Green

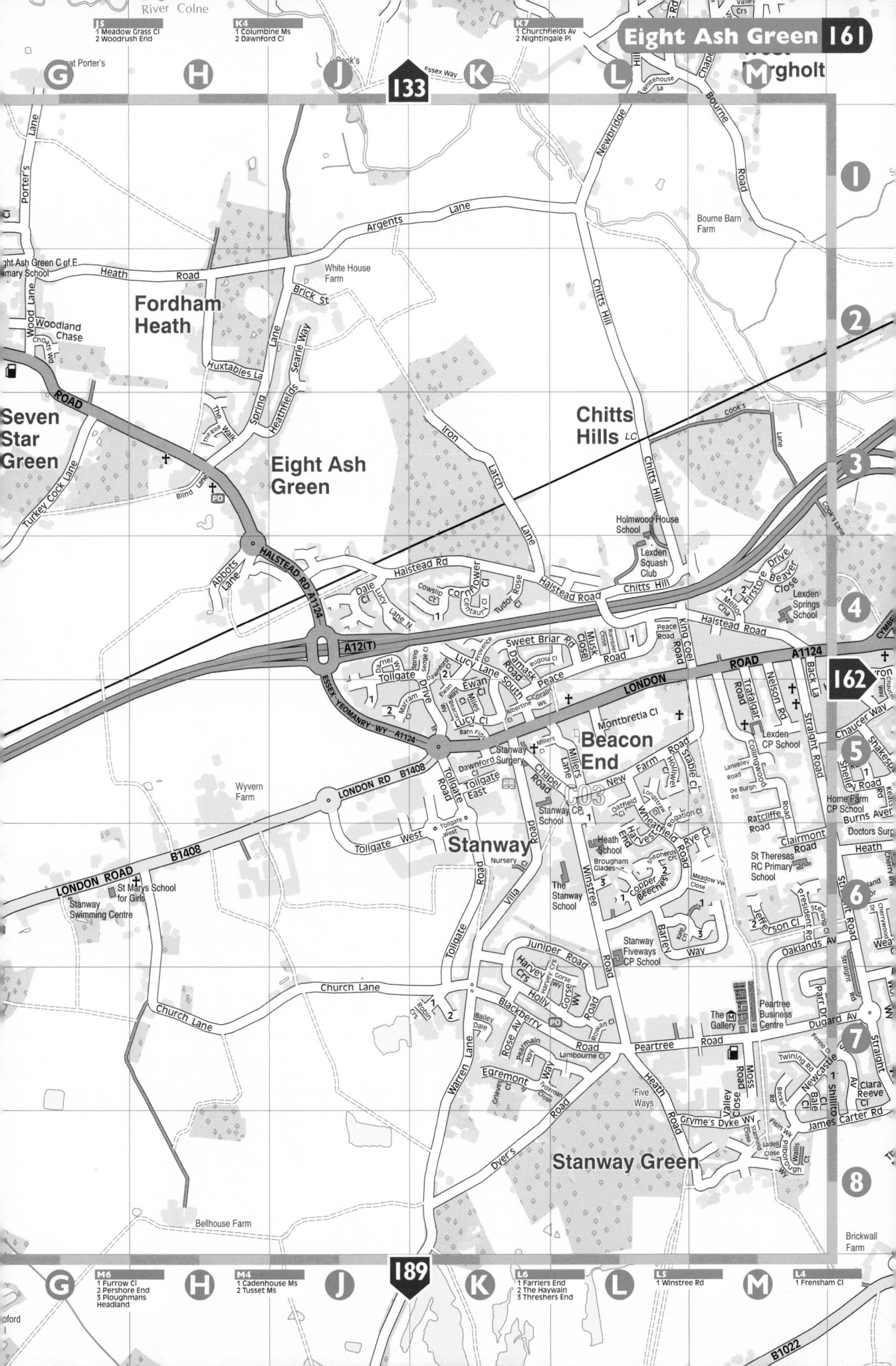

River Colne

J5
1 Meadow Grass Cl
2 Woodrush End

K4
1 Columbine Ms
2 Dawnford Cl

K7
1 Churchfields Av
2 Nightingale Pl

West
rgholt

G   H   J   **133**   K   L   M

I

Great Porter's

Cook's

Essex Way

Argents   Lane

Bourne Barn Farm

Chitts Hill

Newbridge Road

Porter's Lane

Eight Ash Green C of E mary School

Heath   Road

Brick St

White House Farm

2

Fordham Heath

Wood Lane

Woodland Chase

Chats Wd

Huxtables La

Searle Way

Heathfields

Spring Lane

The Walk

The Rise

Seven Star Green

ROAD

Chitts Hill

Cook's Lane

Chitts Hills
LC

3

Eight Ash Green

Iron Latch Lane

Holmwood House School

Lexden Squash Club

Firstore Drive

Beaver Close

Cook's Lane

Turkey Cock Lane

Blind Lane

PO

HALSTEAD RD · A1124

Abbots Lane

Halstead Rd

Corntower Cl

Dale Cl

Lucy Lane N

Cowslip Ct

Tudor Rose Cl

Centaur

Halstead Road

Chitts Hill

Mellor Cl

Lexden Springs School

Lexden Squash Club

4

162

A12(T)

ESSEX YEOMANRY WY · A1124

Tollgate

Brspring

Daylesford

Ewin

Provence

Lucy Lane South

Damask Cl

Sweet Briar Rd

Peace

Musk Close

Rambler

Peace Road

King Coel Road

Halstead Road

ROAD   A1124

Back La

Nelson Rd

Straight Road

Iron

CYMBE

Chaucer Way

Shakes

Ewan Wy

Miles

Lucy Cl

Albertine

Coralli Wk

LONDON

Montbretia Cl

Lexden CP School

Trafalgar Road

Sheln Road

Burns Aver

5

Wyvern Farm

LONDON RD · B1408

Barn Flds

Dawnford Cl

Stanway Surgery

Miles

Millers

New Farm Road

Hollwell

Stable Cl

Lanvalley Road

Collingwood Rd

De Burgh Rd

Ratcliffe Road

Clairmont Road

Home Farm CP School

Doctors Surg

Heath

Chern Wy

6

Tollgate Road

Tollgate East

Chapel Road

Miles Lane

Beacon End

C03

Stanway CP School

Wheatfield Road

Vestheath

Oatfield Cl

Longthorn

Bogation Cl

Longfield

Rye Cl

St Theresas RC Primary School

Jefferson Cl

President Rd

Cherrywood

Weat

St Marys School for Girls

Stanway Swimming Centre

Tollgate West

Stanway

Nursery

Heath School

Shepherds Cft

Brougham Glades

Copper Beeches

Meadow Vw Close

Barley Way

Oaklands Av

Straight Rd

LONDON ROAD   B1408

The Stanway School

Winstree Road

Villa

3

Stanway Fiveways CP School

The Gallery

Peartree Business Centre

Dugard Av

7

Church Lane

Church Lane

Tollgate Road

Juniper Road

Harvey Crs

Holly

Gorse Wy

Blackberry

Robin

Balley Dale

Rose Av

Pearmain Way

Peartree Road

Lambourne Cl

Heath Road

Moss Road

Newcastle Av

Shillito Cl

Clara Reeve Cl

Warren Lane

Egremont Way

Grieves

Trjentan Close

Five Ways

Gryme's Dyke Wy

Valley

James Carter Rd

Twining

Becker

8

Bellhouse Farm

Dyer's

Stanway Green

Pilborough

Ladell Close

Brickwall Farm

G   H   J   **189**   K   L   M

M6
1 Furrow Cl
2 Pershore End
3 Ploughmans Headland

M4
1 Cadenhouse Ms
2 Tusset Ms

L6
1 Farriers End
2 The Haywain
3 Threshers End

L5
1 Winstree Rd

L4
1 Frensham Cl

B1022

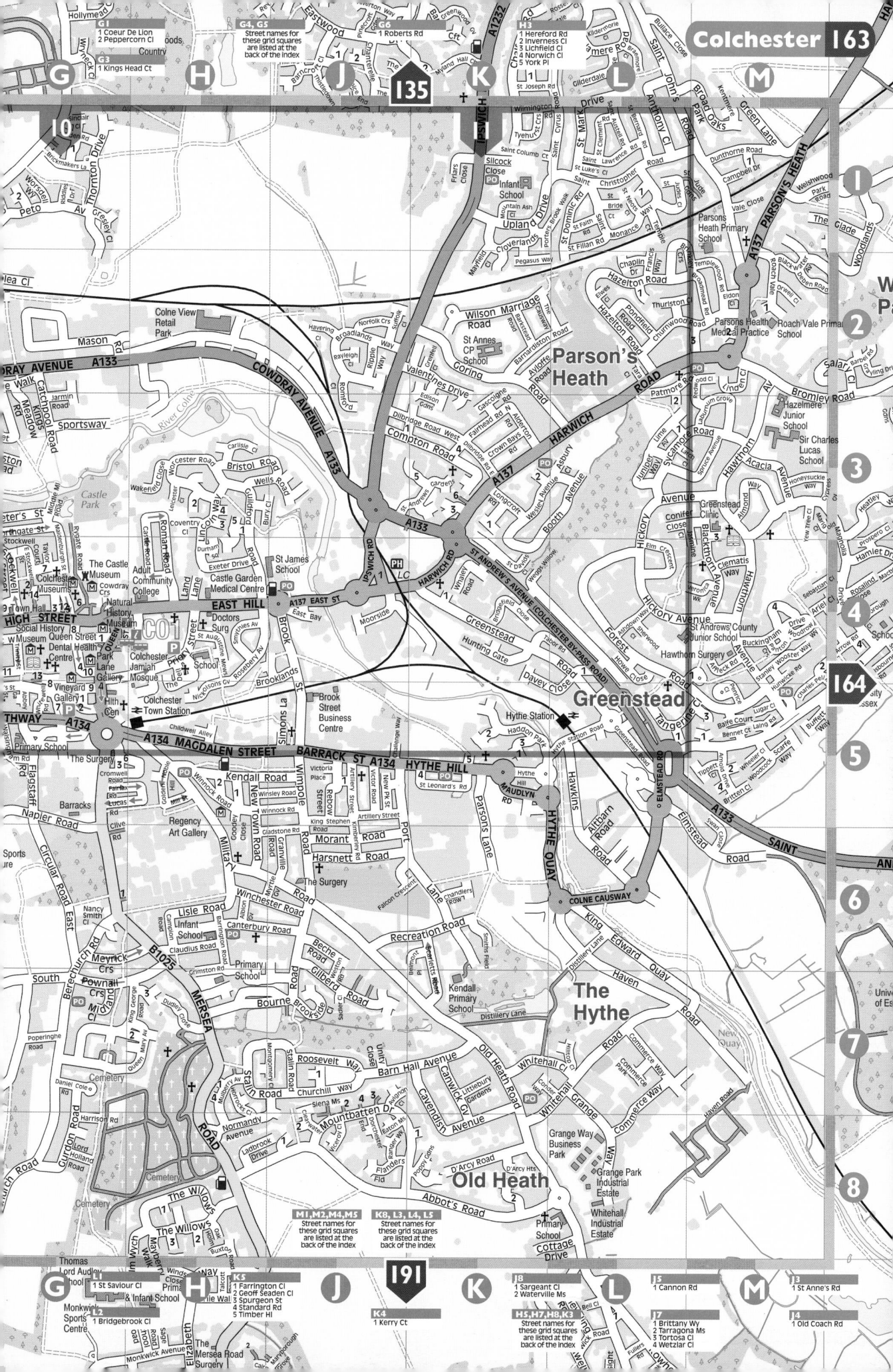

G H J K L M

All Saints
C of E
Primary School

141

B1414

Stones Green Road

The

Red Barn Lane

Woodup

SCHOOL R

Pesthouse Lane

Houbridge
Hall

Marden's Farm

BEAUMONT ROAD CROSS HILL

Moze Cross

I

2

Old Moze
Hall

B1414

Goff's Lane

HARWICH ROAD

Oldhouse Farm

Potland

New Moze
Hall

3

Beaumont

B1414

Church Lane

HARWICH ROAD

Beaumont Hall

170

4

5

Beaumont
Quay

Quay Lane

White
Home

6

**Thorpe
Green**

Golden Lane

7

Golden Lane

Landermere
Hall

Walton Road

8

Thorpe
Lodge

New
Hall

Kentshill Farm

G H J K L M

St. Michael's
Lane

Vicarage
Lane

B1

The

Town Road

New Av

Palmerston
Road

Lonsdale
Road

Spencer
Road

Kendle
Grove

B1414

ROAD

197

Walton

Road

142

A B C D E F

I

2

169

3

4

5

6

7

8

A B C D E F

198

Oakley Creek

Pewit
Island

Hamford   Water

Skipper's
Island

Kirby Creek

Horsey
Island

The
Wade

Marsh
Home

Birch
Hall

1 grid square represents 500 metres

Road

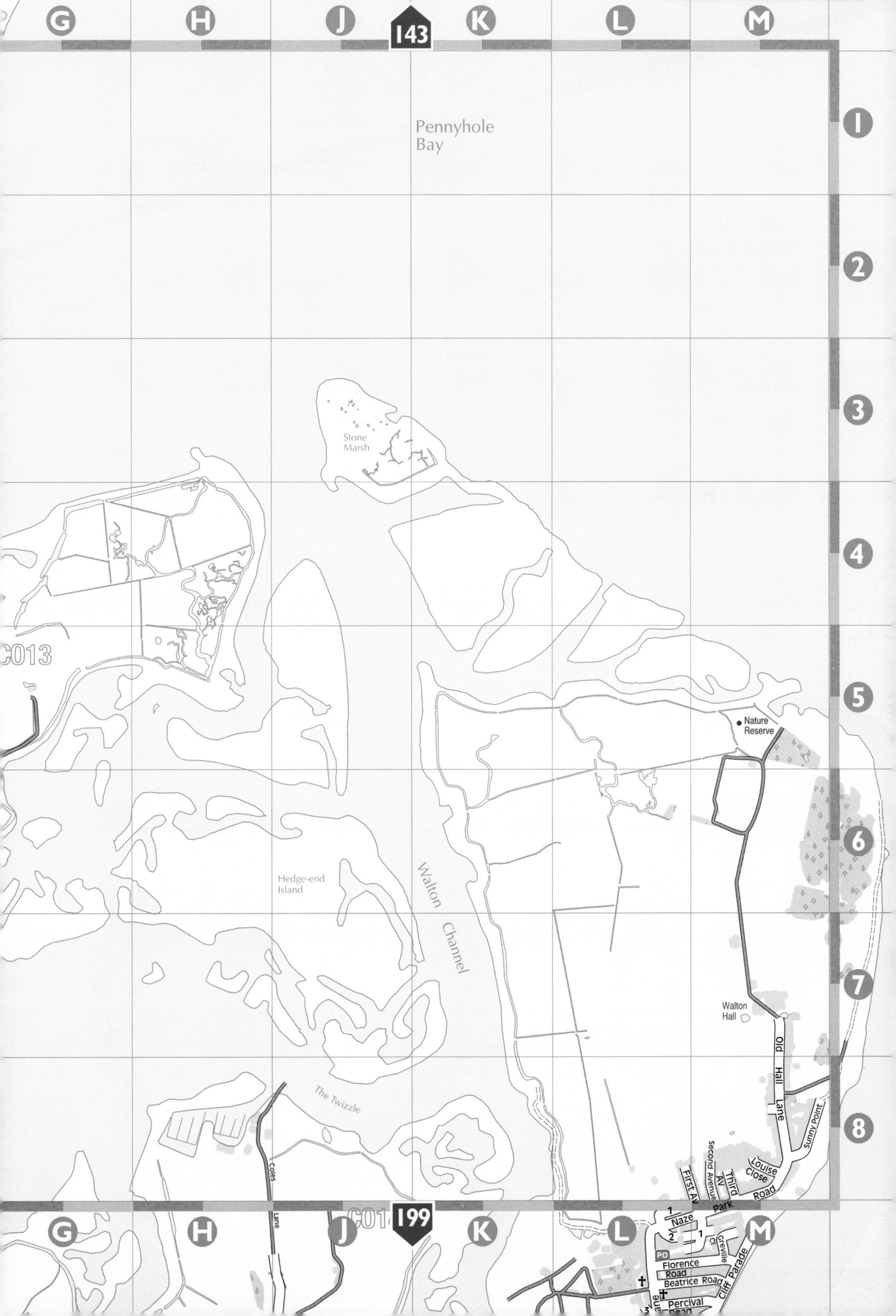

G   H   J   **143**   K   L   M

Pennyhole
Bay

Stone
Marsh

C013

Hedge-end
Island

Walton Channel

Nature
Reserve

The Twizzle

Walton
Hall

Old Hall Lane

Sunny Point

Coles Lane

First Avenue
Second Avenue
Third Av
Naze Park
Louise Close
Greville Road
Cliff Parade
PO
Florence
Road
Beatrice Road
Percival
Road

1
2
3
1
1

I
2
3
4
5
6
7
8

STANDON ROAD

A120

A **B** **C** **144** **D** **E** **F**

Watts Cl

Albury Road

Little Hadham

STORTFORD ROAD

A120

Church End

1

Little Hadham Place

Lloyd·Taylor Close

The Smithy

2

Lodge Farm

Ridgeway

Home Farm

PO

Green Street

Chapel Lane

Hadham Ford

PH

Ford Field

3

Millfield Lane

New Road

Ford Hill

The Grove

4

Westfield Bury

Bridgefoot

Acremore Street

Clintons

Bury Green

5

River Ash

Lordship Farm

6

Barns Lane

WINDING HILL

7

B1004

Exnalls

Much Hadham

HIGH STREET

Church Lane

B1004

Dane Bridge

Homestalls

8

Oudle Lane

Hertfordshire Way

Danebridge Road

Dane Br Lane

Warr Farm

A **B** **C** **D** **E** **F**

Hadham Cross

The Barn School

Moor Place

Health

Parsonage Farm
Indusrial Estate

M11

Bury Lodge Lane

Bury
Lodge

Eleventh Avenue

Ninth Avenue

Tenth Av

Second Av

First

Seventh

Third Av

P

Round Coppice Road

PRIORY WOOD
ROUNDABOUT

Monks
Farm

147

Long Border Rd

Taylor's End Rd

Long Border Road

I

2

3

CM22

Junction 8

Threnhall Avenue

A120

**Start
Hill**

Bury Lodge Lane

Thremhall
Priory Farm

A120 DUNMOW ROAD

Flitch Way

4 A120

Takele
et

176

**Tilekiln
Green**

Harps Farm

Forest Way

*Hatfield
Forest*

5

Hatfield
Forest NT

6

**Bedlar's
Green**

The Street

Beggar's Hall

Three Forest Wy

Harcamlow Way

Way

Three Forests Way

Harcamlow Way

Three Forests Way

Church Road

The Grove

Three Forests Way

Harcamlow
Way

7

**Hallingbury
Street**

Forest
Lodge

*Collin's
Coppice*

Forest Way

Little Barrington
Hall Farm

8

llingbury

Ladywell

202

Lodge
Farm

Bridgefoot
Farm

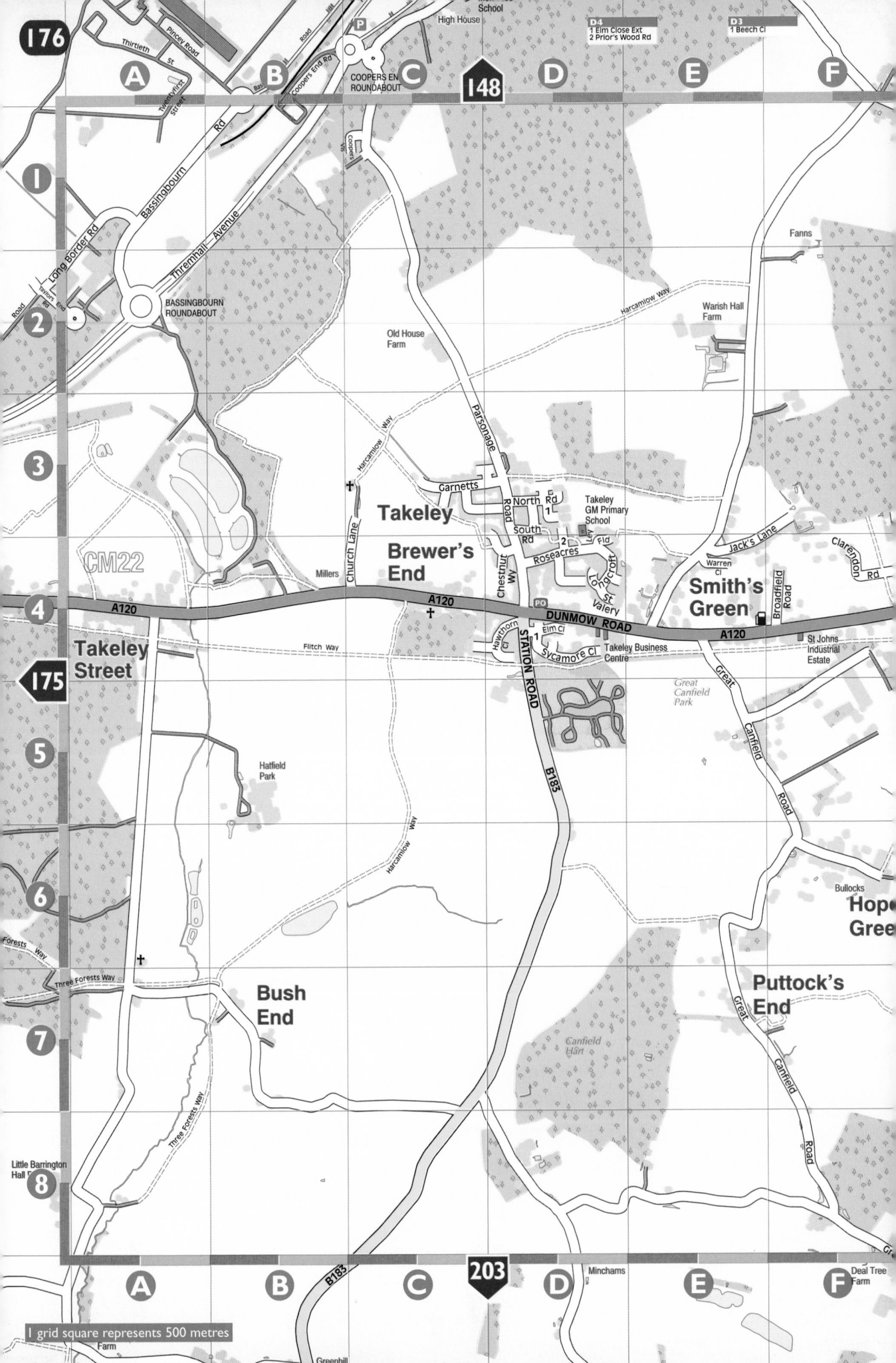

A B C 148 D E F

School
High House

Fanns

I

Long Border Rd
Bassingbourn Avenue
Thremhall Avenue
Pincey Road
Bell Road
Coopers End Rd

P
COOPERS EN
ROUNDABOUT

A120

Warish Hall
Farm

Harcamlow Way

Road
Taylor's End
Thirtieth St
Twentyfirst Street

2 BASSINGBOURN
ROUNDABOUT

Old House
Farm

3

CM22

Takeley

Brewer's
End

Garnetts
North Rd
South
Rd
Roseacres
Takeley
GM Primary
School
Jack's Lane
Clarendon
Rd
Warren
Cl

Smith's
Green

Broadfield
Road

4 A120 A120 Flitch Way DUNMOW ROAD PO A120
St Johns
Industrial
Estate

Takeley
Street

175

Church Lane
Millers
Chestnut Wy
Hawthorn Cl
Station Road
Elm Cl
Sycamore Cl
Longcroft
St Valery
Fld
Takeley Business
Centre

Great Canfield
Park

Great Canfield Road

5

Hatfield
Park

Harcamlow Way

B183

6

Forests Way

Hope
Green

Bullocks

Three Forests Way

Bush
End

Puttock's
End

Three Forests Way

7

Canfield
Hart

Great Canfield Road

8 Little Barrington
Hall

A B 203 C D E F
B183 B183 Minchams Deal Tree
Farm

Farm Greenhill

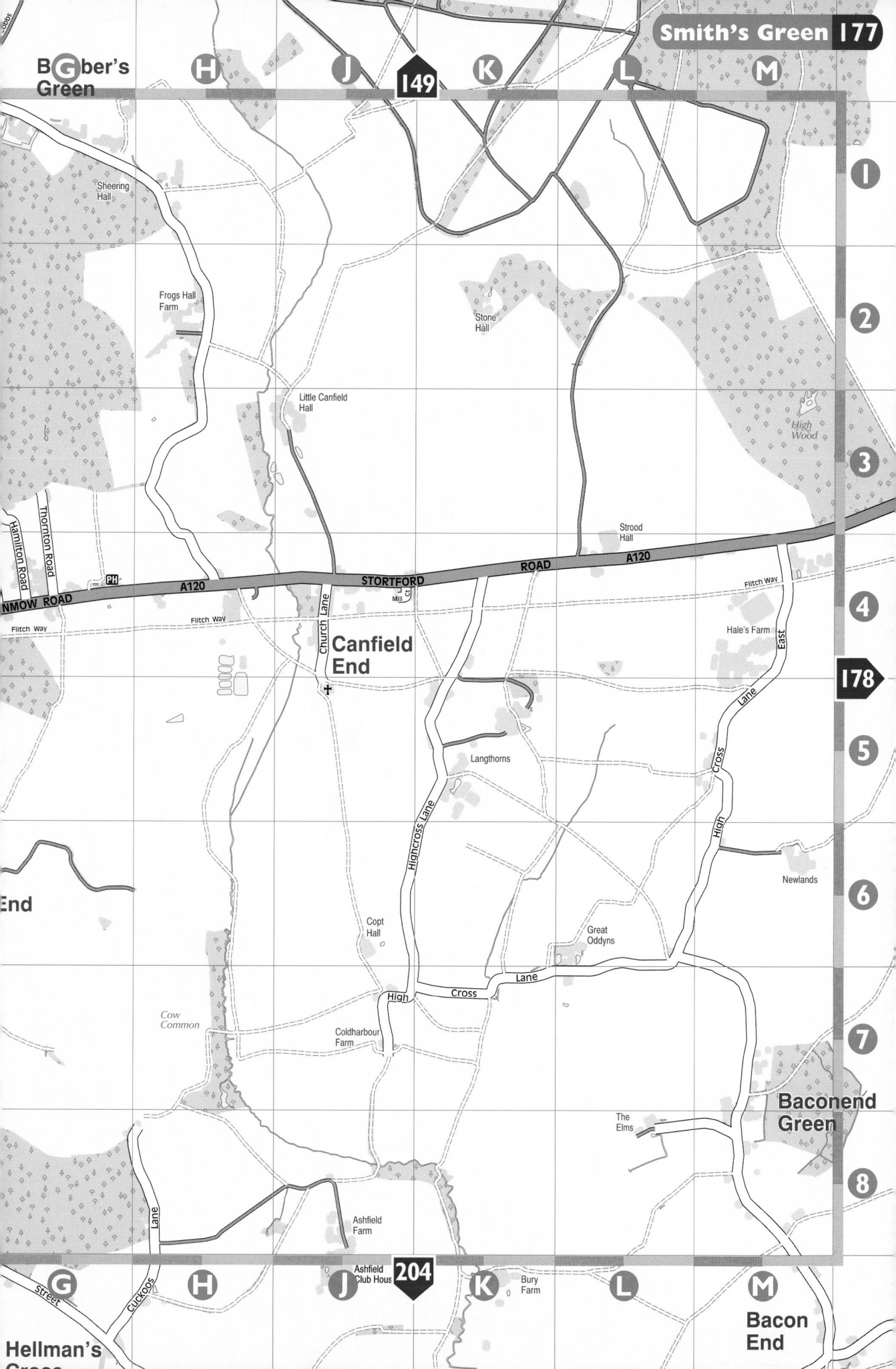

E2
1 Gibbons Ct
2 Market Pl
3 Maynard Cl

D2
1 Rosemary Cl
2 Rosemary Crs
3 Rosemary Crs
4 Wells Ct

D1
1 Bradley Cl
2 The Poplars

C2
1 Juniper Ct
2 Laurel Dr

B184

150

A **B** **C** **D** **E** **F** Chur

Church End

1

Dunmow Sports Lane

The Parsonage

Ravens Farm

Newton Hall

Helena Romanes School

The Charters

Church Gdns

BEAUMONT HL

CHURCH Street

CHURCH END

St. Edmunds Flds

St. Edmunds Flds

Millers Cft

Windmill Close

Riverside

2

Woodside Way

Larch Way

Pine Av

Cypress

Woodlands Park Drive

Newton Green

The Wad

Emblems

Godfrey Way

Godfrey Way

Godfrey Way

Berbice Lane

Coones Lane

Godfrey Way

Downs Crs

Infants School

The Downs

NORTH STREET

Counting House Lane

The Mattings

Knights Way

The Dell

3

High Wood

STORTFORD ROAD

A120

Folly Farm

Stortford Lane

Stortford Road

Jubilee Ct

Green Lane

Rosemary Lane

The Downs

Mill Lane

Crayfields

Tenterfield

Chelmer Dr

Wenmore

The Dell

Braintree

Great Dunmow Town Council

Hotel

Chequers La

Angel Lane

B184 HIGH STREET

The Book Gallery

Dunmow C of E Junior School

High Stile

South Vw

High Meadow

The Surgery

Uttlesford District Council

High Flds

The Avenue

Oakcroyd Avenue

Sunbank

Flitch Way

Flitch Way

Springfields

Woodview Road

Medical Surgery

New Street

Hasler's Lane

Station Road

Station Yard

CHELMSFORD

Flitch

Normansfield

4

East

Butters Lane

Flitch Industrial Est

Ash Grove

Lukin's Dr

Ongar Road Trading Est

Lower Ml

Nursery

Upper Ml Flds

Heywood Lane

B184

ONGAR ROAD

RD

177

Olives or Shingle Hall

B184

ONGAR ROAD

Lukin's Dr

Hoblong Industrial Est

5

Minchins

Clapton Hall

Clapton Lane

Hill Lane

6

Newlands

Tanners

Bedfords

Pharisee Green

B184

Trutons

Puttocks

7

Baconend Green

Pharisee House

Philpot End Lane

Mountain's Farm Road

Coopers

Marte

8

Brands Farm

Halfway House

Mountains Farm

Sallets Green

A **B** **C** **D** **E** **F**

205

con d

Dove's Lan

Lane

Roffey

I grid square represents 500 metres

Philpot

GREAT DUNMOW

G5
1 Chelmsford Rd

H7
1 Hylands Cl
2 Miller's Cl

L4
1 Moors La

G

H

J

151

Tooley's
Farm

K

L

M

Brookend

I

Merks
Hall

Homelye Farm

Homelye Chase

Throws

A120

Bramble Lane

2

Ford Farm

BRAINTREE   ROAD   A120

Braintree
Road

3

PH

The Street

Little
Dunmow

4

Chelmsford Road
dustrial Est

Grange   Lane

The Grange

St Mary's
Pl

Brook Street

Bayleys

180

side
Road

ak Ind Park

Langleys

Flitch Way

Flitch Way

Brook   Street

5

A130

Brick
House

River Chelmer

6

Broadgroves

Mill Field

Berners End

Watts Close

A130

The Chase

Barnston
Lodge

Barnston

Rayfield Close

Barnston Green

CHELMSFORD   ROAD

Absol
Park

7

Parsonage Lane

8

High Easter Road

G

H

**Wellstye
Green**

J

206

K

**Onslow
Green**

L

M

nnett's Lane

North

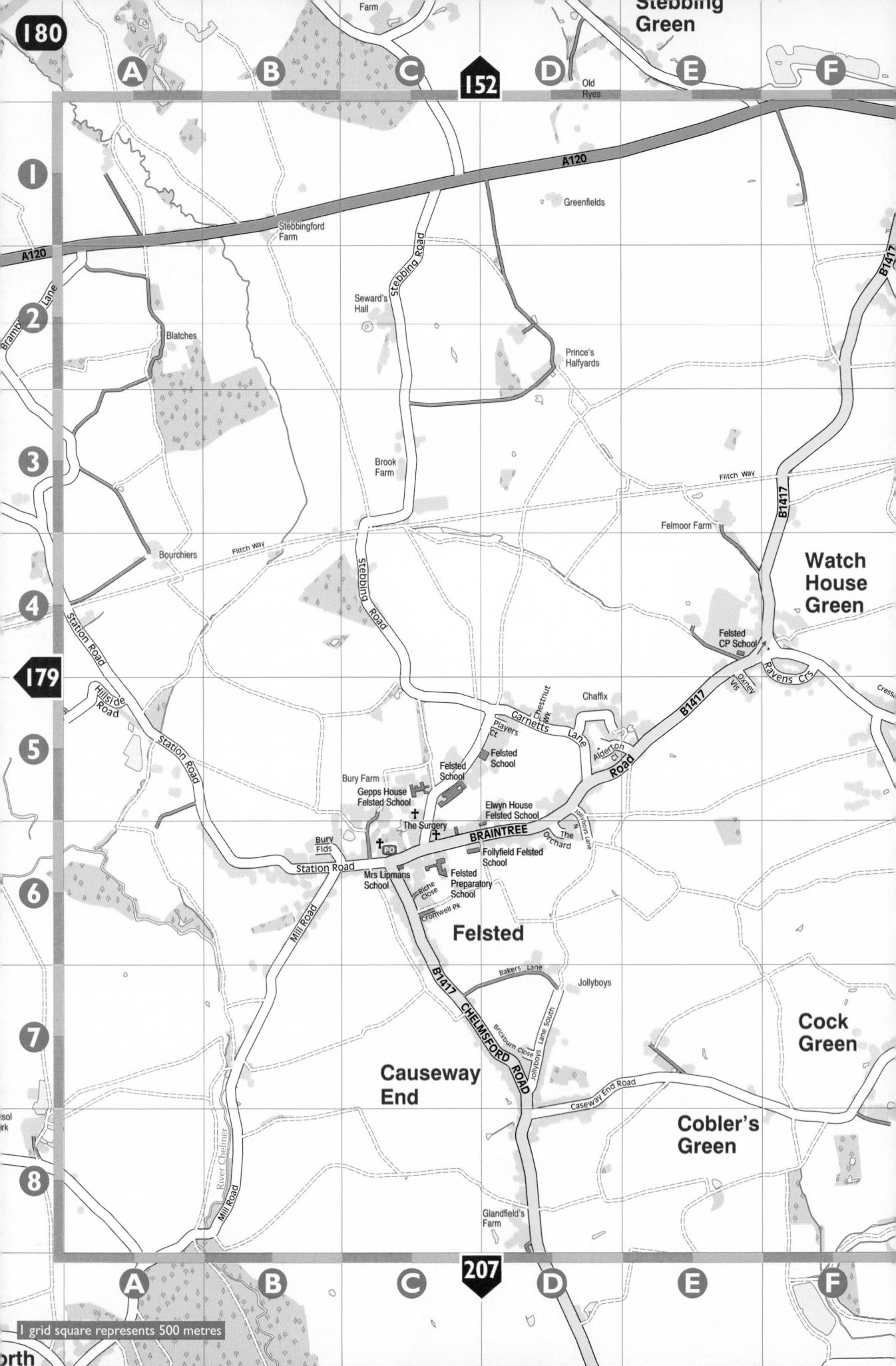

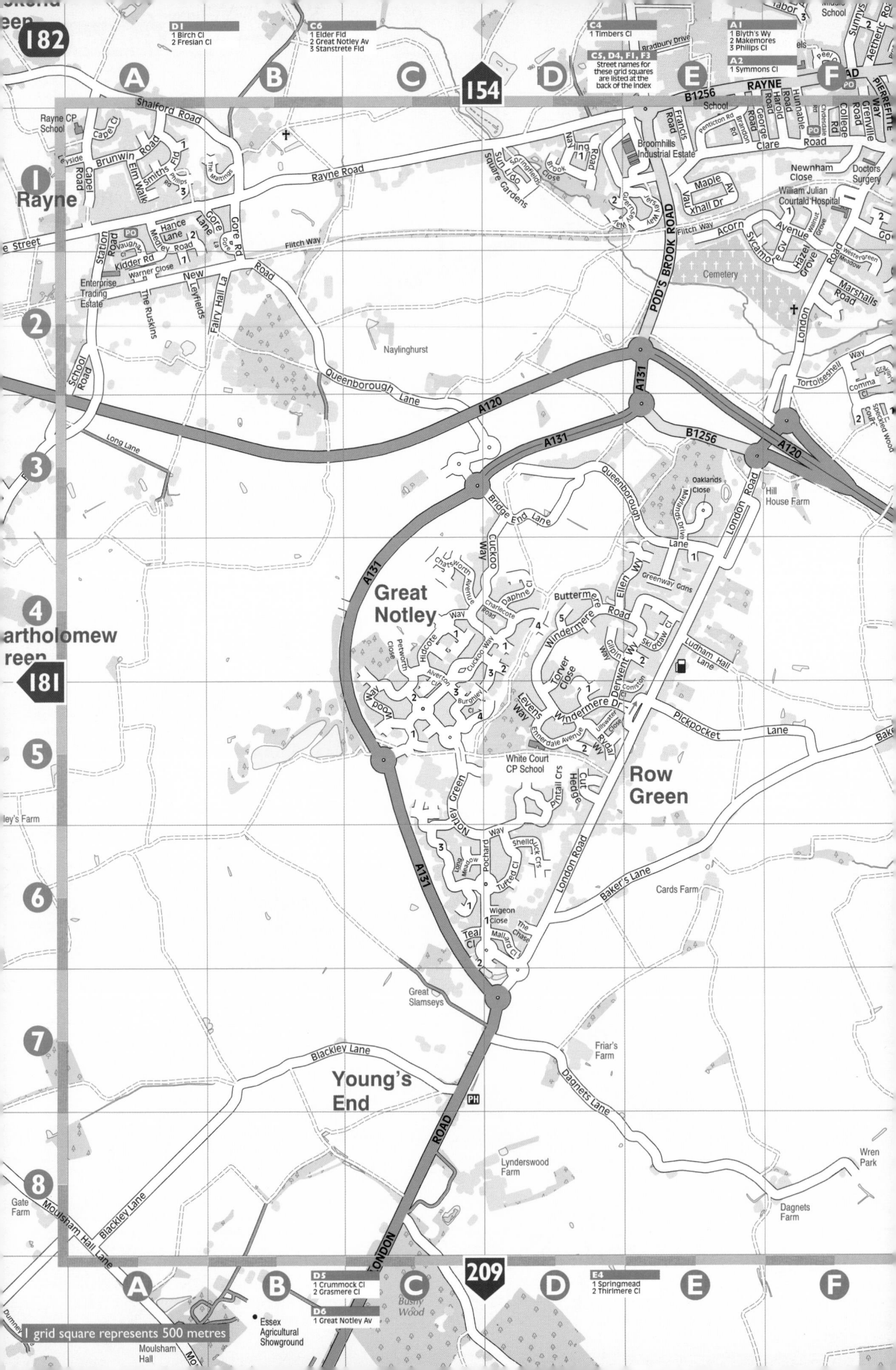

G H J 157 K L M

Holfield Grange

Coggeshall Road

Whiteshill Farm

Coggeshall Road

COGGESHALL ROAD A120

Highfields

Coggeshall

Paycoc House

Watery Lane

Road

Bradwell Hall

West Street

Grigg's Farm

Coggeshall Town Football Club

2

River Blackwater

Essex Way

Essex Way

Essex Way

Essex Way

Curd Hall Farm

3

Herons Farm

Cuthedge Lane

Haywards

Cuthe

4

186

5

Woodhouse Farm

Sheepcotes Farm

Allshot's Farm

6

Storey's Wood

7

Felix Hall

Western Road

Park Gate Road

Parkgate Farm

Park Road

Porter's Farm

Shrivener's

Leapingwells

8

G H J 212 K L M

Hollo

Ford Farm

Broad

A   B   C   158   D   E   F

A120

Surrex

Skye
Green

COLCHESTER ROAD

ggeshall

Coggeshall Surgery

Paycocke's
House (NT)

Grange
Barn (NT)

Grange Farm

**Coggeshall
Hamlet**

Pointwell
Lane

Scrip's Farm

White Barn

Monk's Farm

Pantlings
Lane

Felix
Hall

Park
Farm

Feeringbury

River Blackwater

Frame Farm

Coggeshall
Hall.

Old Mill
Lane

B1024

COGGESHALL ROAD (FEERING)

B1024

The Street

PO

Gore P

Cemetery
Cemetery

Feering
Primary
School

Millers Mead

Waterhill Rd

Mill
Lane

River
Blackwater

Sherwood Way

Hunt
Close

Driffield
Close

Feering
Hill
Court
John Raven

FEERING HILL

Greenways

Observer
Way

Feering

Kelvedon Station

Station
Road

Doucecroft
School

INWORTH ROAD

LONDON

Kelvedon St Marys
C of E
Primary School

Swan Street

Thresh
Farm

A   B   C   D   E   F

1 grid square represents 500 metres

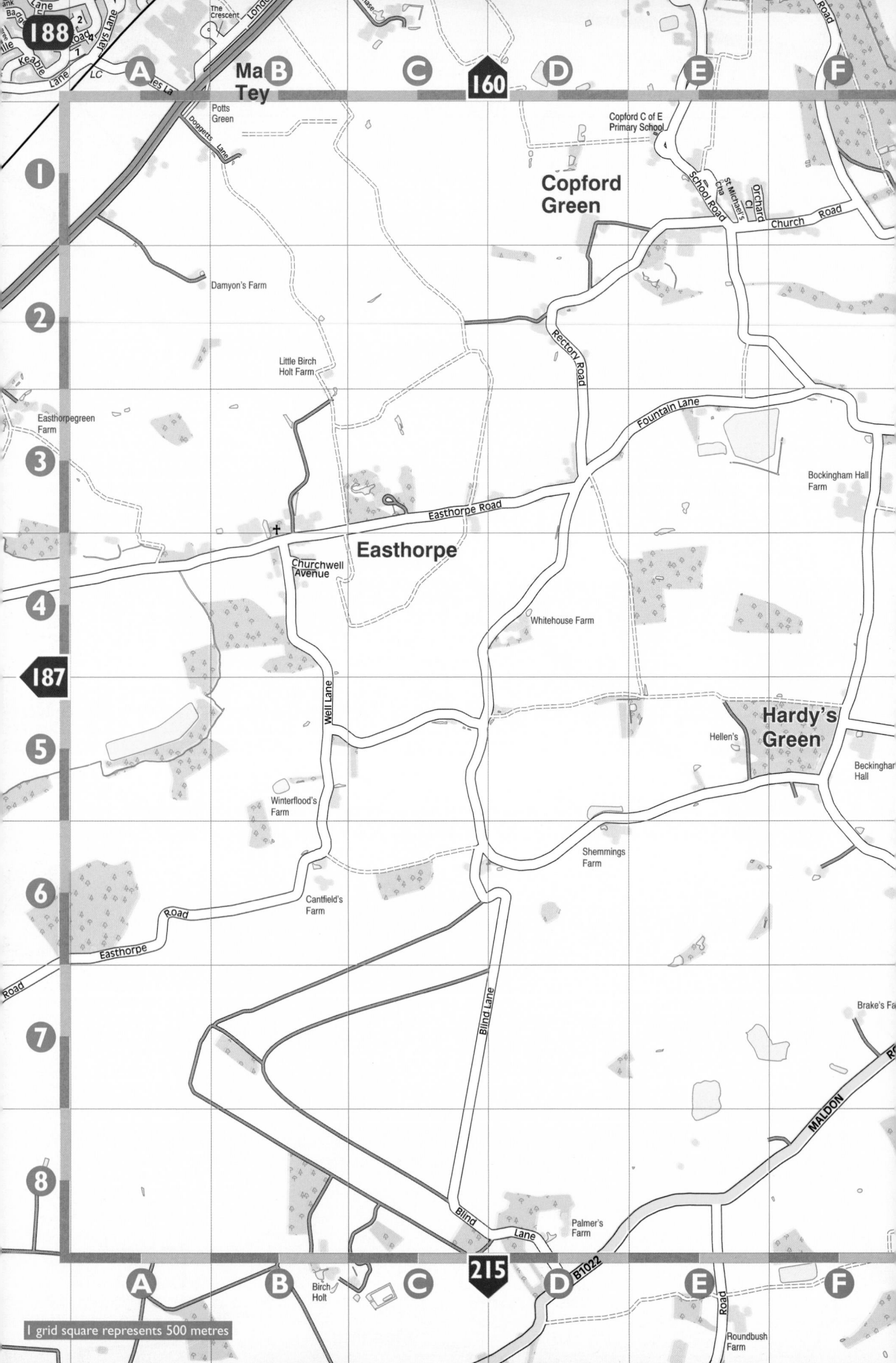

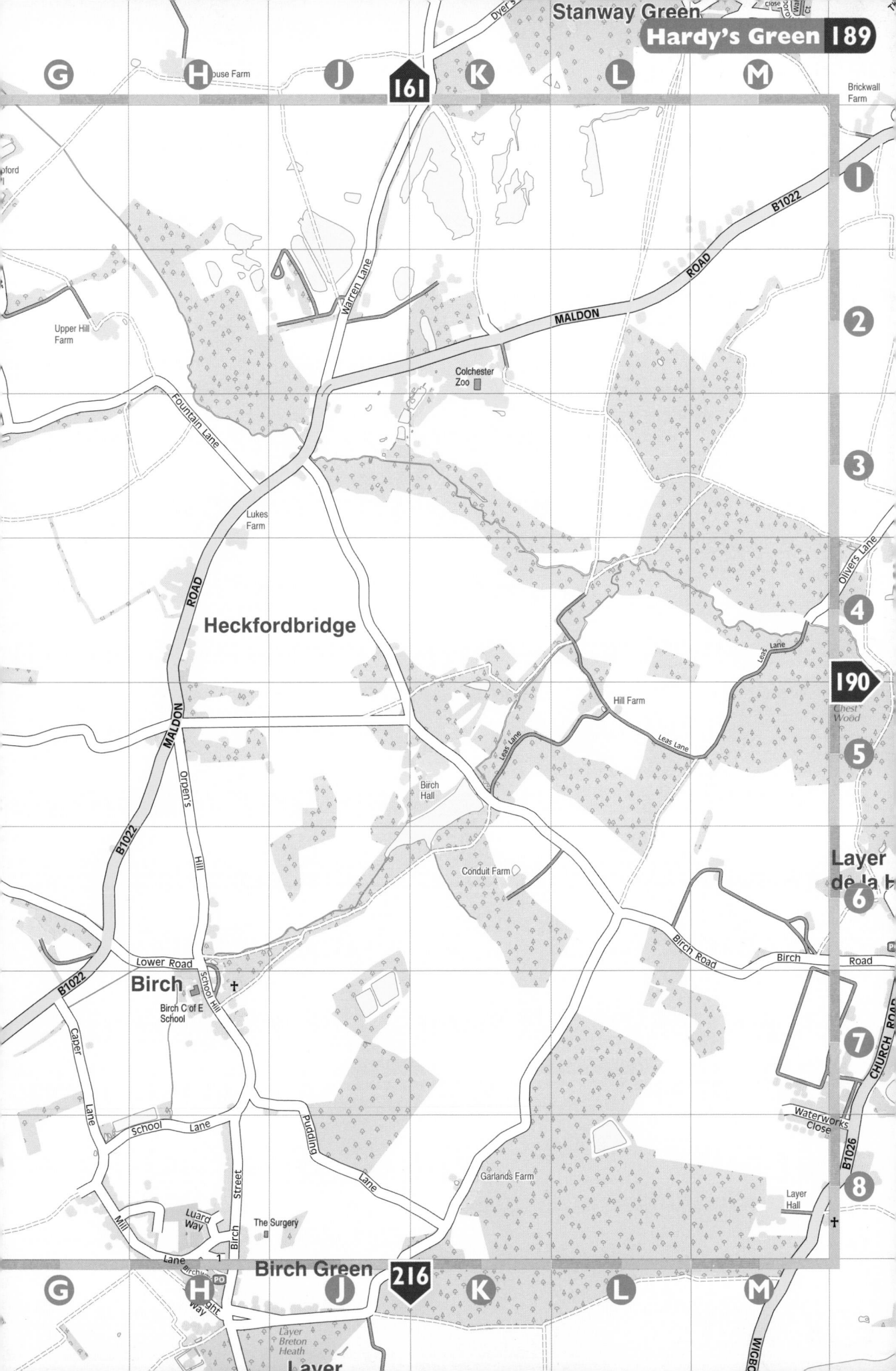

G H House Farm J **161** K L M Brickwall Farm

1

Upper Hill Farm

MALDON ROAD B1022

2

Warren Lane

Colchester Zoo

3

Fountain Lane

Oliver's Lane

Lukes Farm

4

Hill Farm

190

Chest Wood

Heckfordbridge

Leas Lane

Leas Lane

5

MALDON

Birch Hall

Orpen's

Hill

Layer de la H

6

B1022

Conduit Farm

Birch Road

Birch Road

Lower Road

B1022

Birch

School Hill

Birch C of E School

7

CHURCH ROAD

Waterworks Close

Caper

B1026

Lane

School Lane

Pudding

Layer Hall

8

Mill

Lane

Birchill

Street

The Surgery

Luard Way

Lane

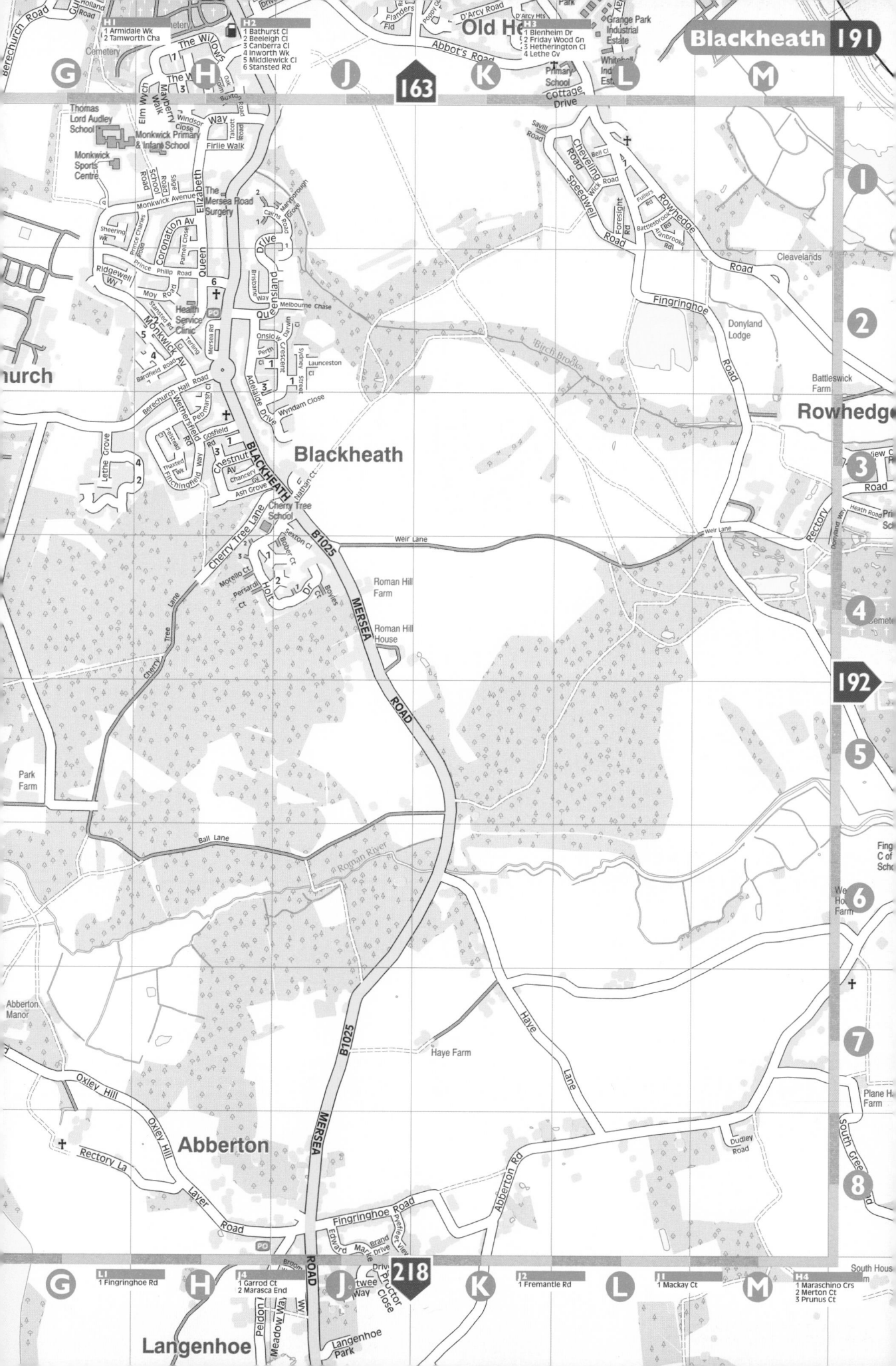

G   H   J   **165**   K   L   M

H4
1 The Chequers

J3
1 Ash Rd
2 Bramley Cl
3 Chestnut Rd

J4
1 De Staunton Cl

FRATING HILL A133

I

ng
Lodge

Frating

2

Rectory   Ro

Church Road

Cockaynes Lane

Blue
Gates

Hockley
Farm

Hockley
Place

3

B1027

Cockaynes

Alresford
Business
Centre

Tenpenny
Farm

Heath Road

Coppice Road

Orchard Road

Station Road

Oak Tree
Crs

Worcester
Crs

Cox Road

Alresford
Alresford Station

Laxton Road

Hawkins Road

Coach Road

LC

Elm
Crs

Poplars Cl

Crestlands

Tenpenny Brook

4

B1027

Furze   Crs 1

Conifer   ane

Wivenhoe Road

1

SAINT OSYTH ROAD

Brook
Farm

194

Church Road

St Andrews

Alresford
Primary
School

Alresford
Grange

5

Ford Lane

Alresford
Hall

TENPENNY HILL

B1027

6

Sixpenny Brook

Brick Kiln Lane

Tenpenny
Heath

Alresford Lodge

The Ford

7

Tho
Farm

Plumpton's
Farm

B1

Alresford Creek

8

BRIGHTLINGSEA ROAD

Gatehouse
Farm

Aldbo
Poin

G   H   **220**   J   K   L   M

Ford Lane

Moverons Lane

Wapping ane

Moverons

A · B · C · **166** · D · E · F

Frating Green

1 — Frating — The Grange

MAIN ROAD — PO — Binnings — The Cedars Farm — Ivy Lodge — Heckford's Road

2 — Frating — Rectory Road — Slough House Farm — Brook Farm — Sturrick Farm — Moors Close

GREAT BENTLEY ROAD — B1029

3 — Hockley Place — SCHOOL LANE — STATION RD — Great Bentley Road — Bentley Brook — Thorrington Road — Finch Dri — Parkfield Rd 1 — Robin Close — Linnet Way — Cherrywoods — The Path — Doctors Surgery — **Great Bentley** — Crabtree Farm

B1029 FRATING ROAD — Lufkins Farm — Great Bentley Road — PO — Morella Close — Great Bentley CP School — Hallw Road — Keeble Court — Birch — Station Road — Avenue — Cedar — Great Bentley Station — LC — Plough Road

4 — LC — LC

5 — STATION ROAD — B1029 — Whitehouse Farm — Frating Abbey — Frating Abbey Farm Road

PENNY HILL — Church Road — Clover Drive — Hazel Close — **Thorrington** — Rosemary La — Aingers Gre

6 — Tenp Heat — B1027 — Heathlands 1 — CLACTON ROAD — PO — Chapel La

7 — Thors Farm — B1029 — B1027 CLACTON ROAD — The Lodge

ROAD — B1027 HOLLYBUSH HILL — Dia

8 — Gatehouse Farm

A · B · C · **221** · D · E — Marsh Farm Lane · F — Greatmarsh Farm

G3
1 Rowan Cl

G6
1 The Paddocks
2 St Mary's Rd

G   H   J   167   K   L   M

I

A133
COLCHESTER ROAD

Fisher's Farm

Admiral's Farm

Shair Lane

Brett's Hall

Hawk Farm

B1033
COLCHESTER ROAD

2   Hilltop   Hilltop Crs

WEELEY BY-PASS ROAD

Swallow's Row

Weeley Road

Risby's Farm

2

3

Wee
Sta

St Andrews C of E
Primary School

A133

Lane

St Mary's Farm

Lover's   Lane

The Tye Road

Gutteridge   Hall

Gutteridge Hall

4

196

Tye
Homestead

The Tye Road

Coppice Farm

5

Wenlock

Weeley Rd

Colles Brook Road

Aingers

Green   Road

Wick

Moynes Farm

Road

Bentley Road

Norwood
Lodge

A133

Plough Road

1   2

Highbirch Road

College Farm

6

Colles   Brook   Road

South Heath Road

Straight Road

St Osyth
Wick Farm

Wick Lane

High
Birch

Maldon
Wood

7

Ampers Wick

**South
Heath**

Milton
Wood

Rectory R

8

G   H   J   222   K   L   M

Highbirch Road

y's La

G4
1 Edward Rd

H2
1 Beldams Cl

Walton Road

G   H   J   169   K   L   M

Thorpe Lodge

New Hall

Kentshill Farm

olden Lane

St Michael's Road

arage Lane

The Crs

New Town Road

New Thorpe

Palmerston Road

Lonsdale Road

Spencer Road

Kenilworth Grove

Argyle Road

B1414

LANDERMERE ROAD

The Spennells

Rolph Lane

1

I

Walton Road

B1033

HIGH STREET

Argyle Road

College

Rolph C of E Primary School

PO

Abbey

CJ

Byng Crs

Thorpe-le-Soken

2

Snea Hall

The Surgery

Mill Lane

ABBEY STREET

Hall Lane

FRINTON ROAD

White Ldg Crs

Damant's Farm

Lane

SNEATING HALL LANE

King's Farm

B1034

B1033

3

ange Farm

B1414

Thorpe Hall

Thorpe Cross

Malthouse

STATION ROAD

Thorpe-le-Soken Station

1

Thorpe Park Lane

Rice Bridge Industrial Est

B1033

4

THORPE

198

AD

B1414

Lodge Road

Thorpe Park

Pork Lane

LC

Birch Hoe Farm

5

Holland Brook

P

6

Little Clacton Lodge

Holland Brook

7

Tan Lane

Lodge Road

Parkgate Farm

Dairy House

Mill Lane

8

Clacton

G   H   J   224   K   L   M

Holland Road

Redland Farm

ope Road

Cook's Green

Little

reat Holland Common Road

G4, G5, K3
Street names for
these grid squares
are listed at the
back of the index

H3
1 Ockendon Wy
2 Pulpitfield Cl

H4
1 Little Bakers
2 Rochford Wy

J3
1 Brian Bishop Cl
2 Cartbridge Cl
3 The Ridge
4 Wardle Cha

L3
1 Brian Bishop Cl
2 Cartbridge Cl
3 The Ridge
4 Wardle Cha

G H J 171 K L M

C014

I
2
3
4
5
6
7
8

The Frinton &
Walton Heritage Museum

Walton &
Frinton Yacht Club

Walton GM
Primary School

Frinton & Walton
Swimming Pool

Standley
Rd

PRINCE'S ESP

WALTON-ON-THE-NAZE

KIRBY

B1034
ROAD

The Surgury

Churchfield
Rd

HIGH STREET

Cemetery

Walton-on-Naze
Station

ROAD

The
Promenade

Walton
WALTON

Central Avenue

Hamford
CP School

Tendring
Sixth Form
College

Seaview
Heights

Southview
Drive

Southcliff

Way

Pole Barn Lane

Greenway

Glebe Way

School

Winchester
Road

Eton Road

Oxford
Road

Cambridge
Road

Raglan Road

Esplanade

Esplanade

Frinton
Summer Thtr

The
Crescent

Queen's Road

Cherry
Tree
Surg

CONNAUGHT AVENUE

B1033

Esplanade

The Greensward

Avenue

Esplanade

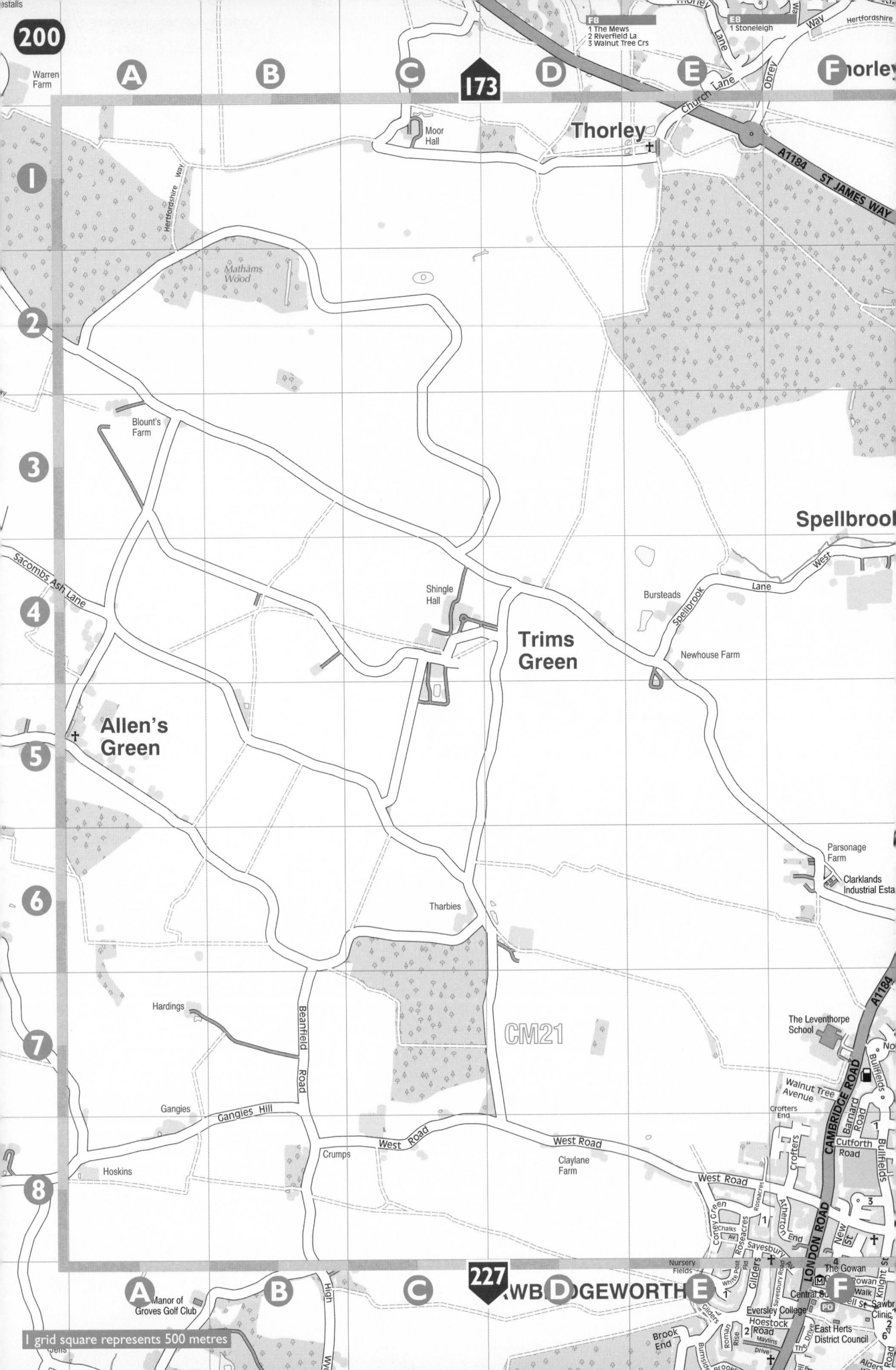

StreeG

174

Latchmore Bank

Port Lane

Church Road

Anvil Cross

Howe Green House School

Howe Green

Morleys

1 The Beadles

Highland Road

Hawthorn Rise

Thorley Way

Pig Lane

Lane

LATCHMORE BANK

Hallingbury Close

New Barn Lane

Normandale Farm

New Barn Lane

M11

Wood Green

2

Thorley Wash

Hertfordshire County

Essex County

Brookside Business Centre

Staddles

Dell Lane

Little Hallingbury C of E Primary School

Hatch Gn 1

Little Hallingbury

3

B1383

A1060

Spellbrook Lane East

Dell Lane

LC

Spellbrook JMI School

Sawbridgeworth Road

PO

Wright's Green

Goose Lane

Lane

Sutton Acres

Goose

Goos

4

A1184

Gaston House

Gaston Green

Back La

LOWER ROAD A1060

Pinchpole Paddocks

Wright's Green

202

Tednambury Farm

Old Mill Lane

Grinstead

Lane

Mott's Green

Little Hallingbur Park

5

Little Bursteads

Sawbridgeworth Road

Road

Three Forests Way

Little Hallingbury Hall

Cemetery

South House

M11

Stone Hall

6

Queen's Cl

Kecksky's

Reedings Way

River Stort (Navigation)

Hallingbury Road

Three Forests Way

7

H

Redd Rd

Great Hyde Hall

STORTFORD

Mill La

Sawbridgeworth Station

Little Hyde Hall

Sawbridgeworth Road

Sawbridgeworth Road

8

The Maltings Industrial Estate

LC

Cowick

228

Three Forests Way

Moorings

Forestw

Church Walk

Foreburg

Hedger

Sappers Close

Ash

Groves

The Mdw

Harcamlow Way

Stort Valley Way

Sheeri

Quickbury

G **H** **J** **K** **L** **M**

202

A B C 175 D E F

1 Morleys Ladywell

Hallingbury Park

Lodge Farm

2 Woodside Green

Wall Wood

The Woods

Three Forests Way

3 Monk's Wood

Forest Hall

Forest Farm

Goose Lane

Three Forests Way

4 Forest Way

Ryes Lane

201

5 Little Hallingbury Park

Three Forests Way

FEATHERS HILL

The Marsh

6 Corringales

OLD STREET HILL

Town Farm

7 Camp Farm

STORTFORD

Mill Lane

Broomfields

B183

Ongars

Lea Hall

8 Sawbridgeworth Road

ROAD A1060

Home Pastures

The Heath

Cox Ley

Wagon

Broomfields

West Hayes

Clipped Hedge

Shaw

The Surgery

Beehive Ct

Hatfield Heath C.P. School

Pond Lane

Hatfield Heath

CHE 229 D ROAD E F Lancasters

Friars Lane

A B C Drive D E F

1 grid square represents 500 metres

G   H   J   **176**   K   L   M

Helln Cros

1

2

3

4

204

5

6

7

8

Minchams

Deal Tree Farm

Green Stree

Bridgefoot Farm

Greenhill

B183

Hatfield Regis Grange

Whiteheads

Cannons

Boxley Lane

Taverners Green

Barrington Hall

B183

Braintris

Woolard's Ash

Pincey Brook

Crabbs Green Farm

Broomshawbury

DUNMOW ROAD

HIGH STREET

PO

St Marys C of E Primary School

Broad St

Hammonds Road

Cage End

Medlars Rd

Cannons

The Surgery

Cage End Cl

Duke Orch

Lane

Bar hfield

Hatfield Broad Oak

Stanways

Needham Green

Three Forests Way

Anthonys

Philpotts

Popla Farm

Pierce Williams

Row Wood

Walkers

Three Forests Way

G   H   J   **230**   K   L   M

Prows

G   H   J   **178**   K   L   M

1

Mountains Farm

Sallets
Green

Roffey

**Philpot
End**

2

Garnetts Wo

Gowers
Farm

DUNMOW ROAD

Watery Lane

Doves Lane

3

G

Rands   Road

Bishops
Green

Mudwall

Broadgates

4

Attridge's Farm

Roding

County
Farm

206

Porters

Barnfiel

5

Poplar

High
Trees
Farm

Peakins

Maidens

6

Chimballs   Bushbarns

Loves

Greens
Farm

7

Hopkins

8

School Lane

Hill
Farm

Gepps
Close

Haydens

G   H   J   **232**   K   L   M

St
Cr

High Easter

Sallets
Green

1

**Wellstye
Green**

**Onslow
Green**

**North
End**

Parsonage Lane

Bennett's Lane

Great
Broadfields Farm

2

Garnetts Wood

Black Chapel Lane

Pyes
Farm

3

Hall Chase

Garnetts

Coppice Lane

Parkgate

Lawn Hall

4

Quoins

205

Barnfield

5

Cromps

Little
Leys

Oldpar
Farm

Maidens

6

Yewtree

Blunts

7

Upper
Harveys

8

Essex Way

Grange Road

A

**Stagden
Cross**

The Street

Acreland
Green

B

C

233

D

Pleshey
Grange

E

Vicarage Road

F

1 grid square represents 500 metres

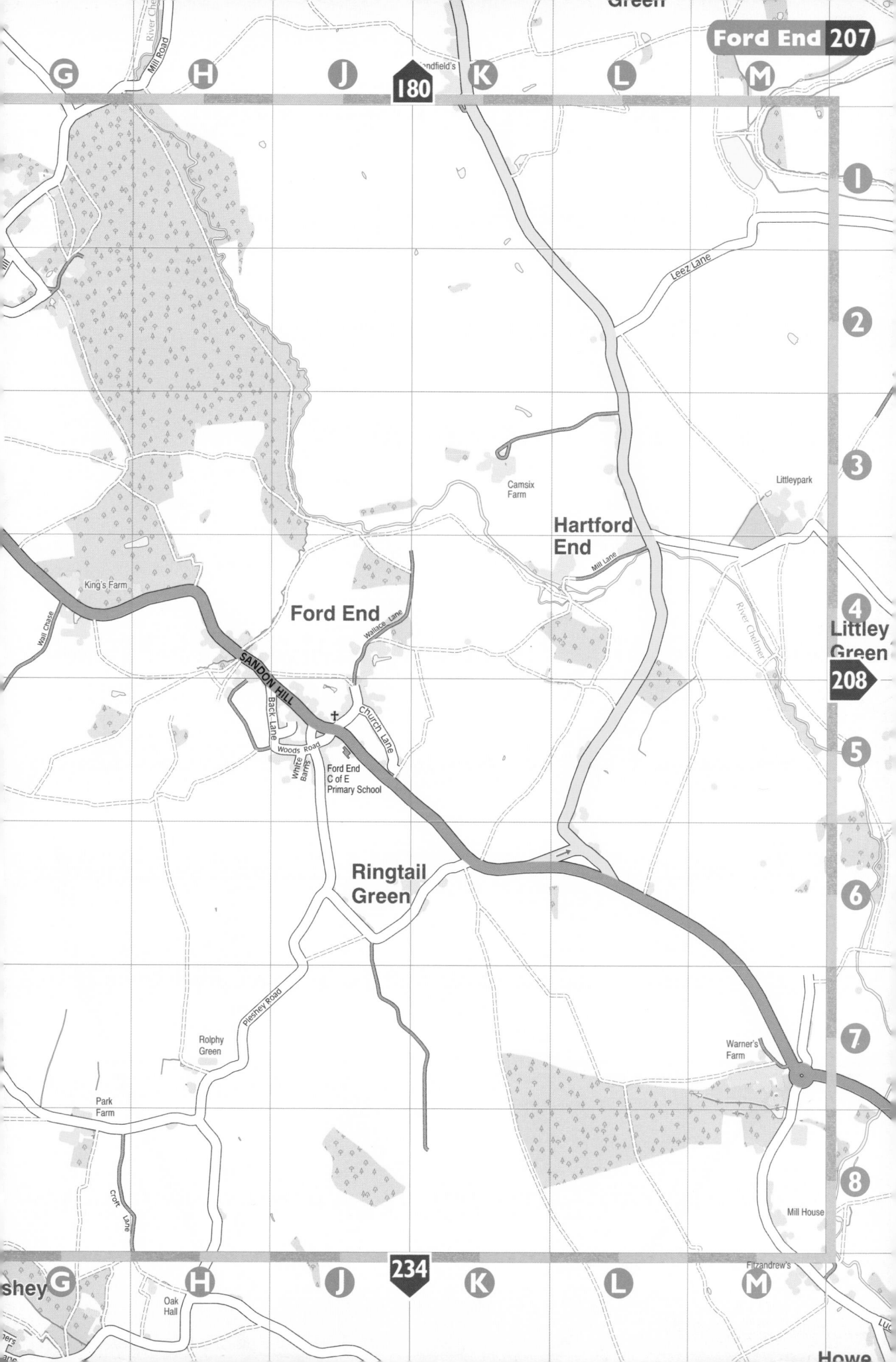

G H J **180** K L M

I
2
3
4
Littley Green
208
5
6
7
8

Leez Lane

Littleypark

Camsix Farm

Hartford End

Mill Lane

River Chelmer

King's Farm

Wall Chase

Ford End

Wallace Lane

SANDON HILL

Back Lane

Church Lane

Woods Road

White Barns

Ford End C of E Primary School

Ringtail Green

Pleshey Road

Rolphy Green

Park Farm

Croft Lane

Warner's Farm

Mill House

Fitzandrew's

Oak Hall

Howe

A B 181 C D E F Gate Farm MOU

1

Howletts

Dumney Lane

Leighs Lodge

Dumney Lane

Lodge Lake

Lavender Lake

River Ter

2

Warren Park Farm

Breams Farm

Dumney Lane

3

Littleypark

Mattock's Farm

Church Lane

Rectory Lane

S

4

Littley Green

†

Ro Fa

Whites Lane

5

Mabb's Farm

Old Shaw's Farm

† Church Lane

Little Leighs

Essex Way

THE CRESCENT

6

Lowle Farm

A131 STRAWBROOK HILL

7

Essex Way

Whitbreads Farm Lane

Liberty Hall

8

Mill House

Chatham Green

Essex Way

A130

Andrew's

A B 235 C D E F

ESSEX

A131

Waltham House

Howe

1 grid square represents 500 metres

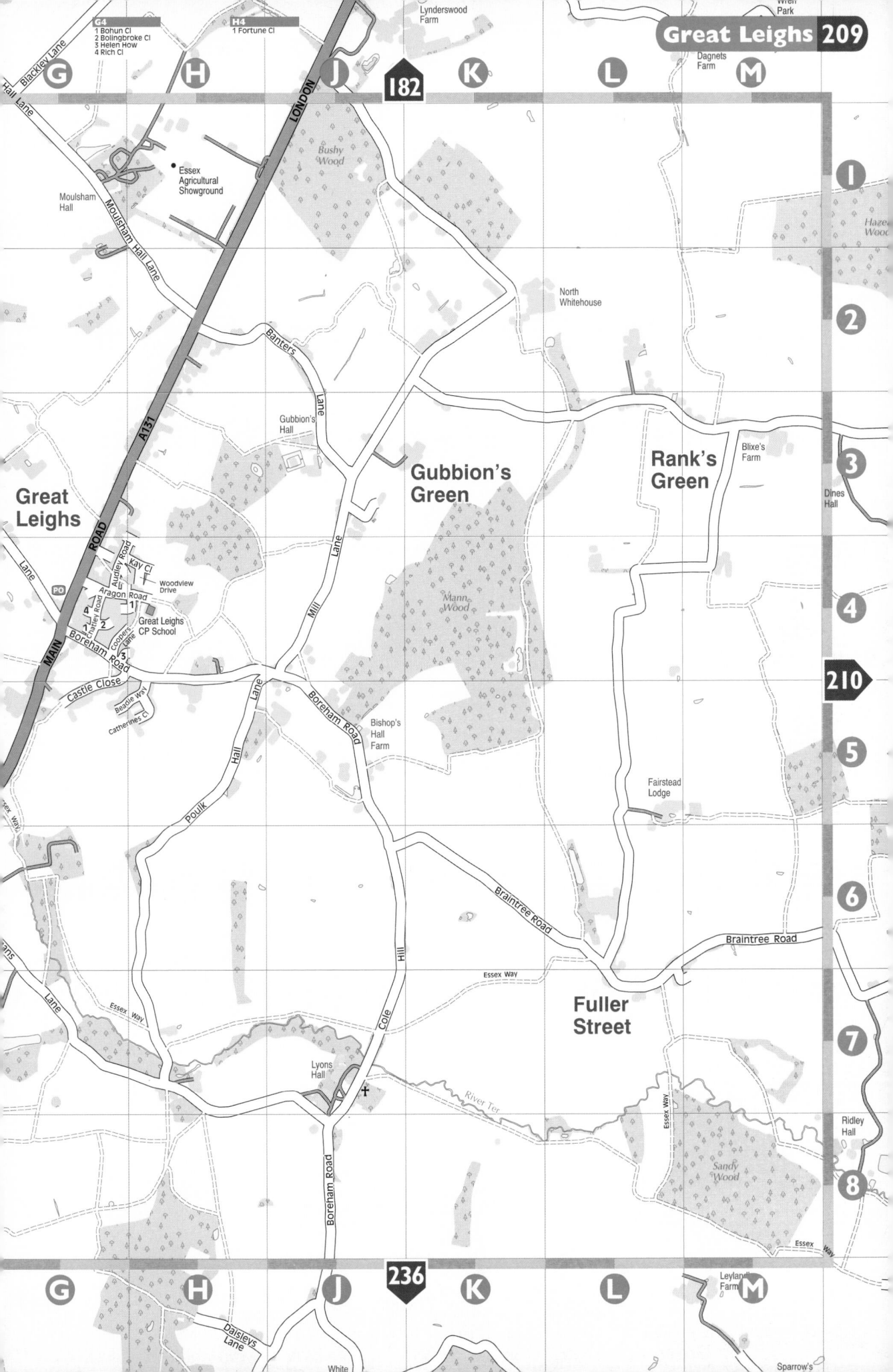

G4
1 Bohun Cl
2 Bolingbroke Cl
3 Helen How
4 Rich Cl

H4
1 Fortune Cl

G **H** **J** 182 **K** **L** **M**

Blackley Lane

Hall Lane

Moulsham Hall Lane

Moulsham Hall

Essex Agricultural Showground

Bushy Wood

Lynderswood Farm

Wren Park

Dagnets Farm

I

Hazel Wood

2

North Whitehouse

Banters Lane

A131

LONDON ROAD

Gubbion's Hall

Mill Lane

Gubbion's Green

Rank's Green

Blixe's Farm

3

Dines Hall

Great Leighs

Lane

PO

MAIN ROAD

Audley Road
Kav Cl
Aragon Road
Woodview Drive
Cranley Road
Coopers Lane
Beadle Way
Catherines Cl
Castle Close

Great Leighs CP School

Boreham Road

Mann Wood

4

210

Poulk Hall Lane

Boreham Road

Bishop's Hall Farm

Fairstead Lodge

5

Essex Way

Cole Hill

Braintree Road

Braintree Road

6

Essex Way

Fuller Street

7

Lane

Essex Way

Lyons Hall

River Ter

Essex Way

Ridley Hall

Sandy Wood

8

Boreham Road

Leyland Farm

G **H** **J** 236 **K** **L** **M**

Daisleys Lane

White

Sparrow's

Essex Way

A　B　C 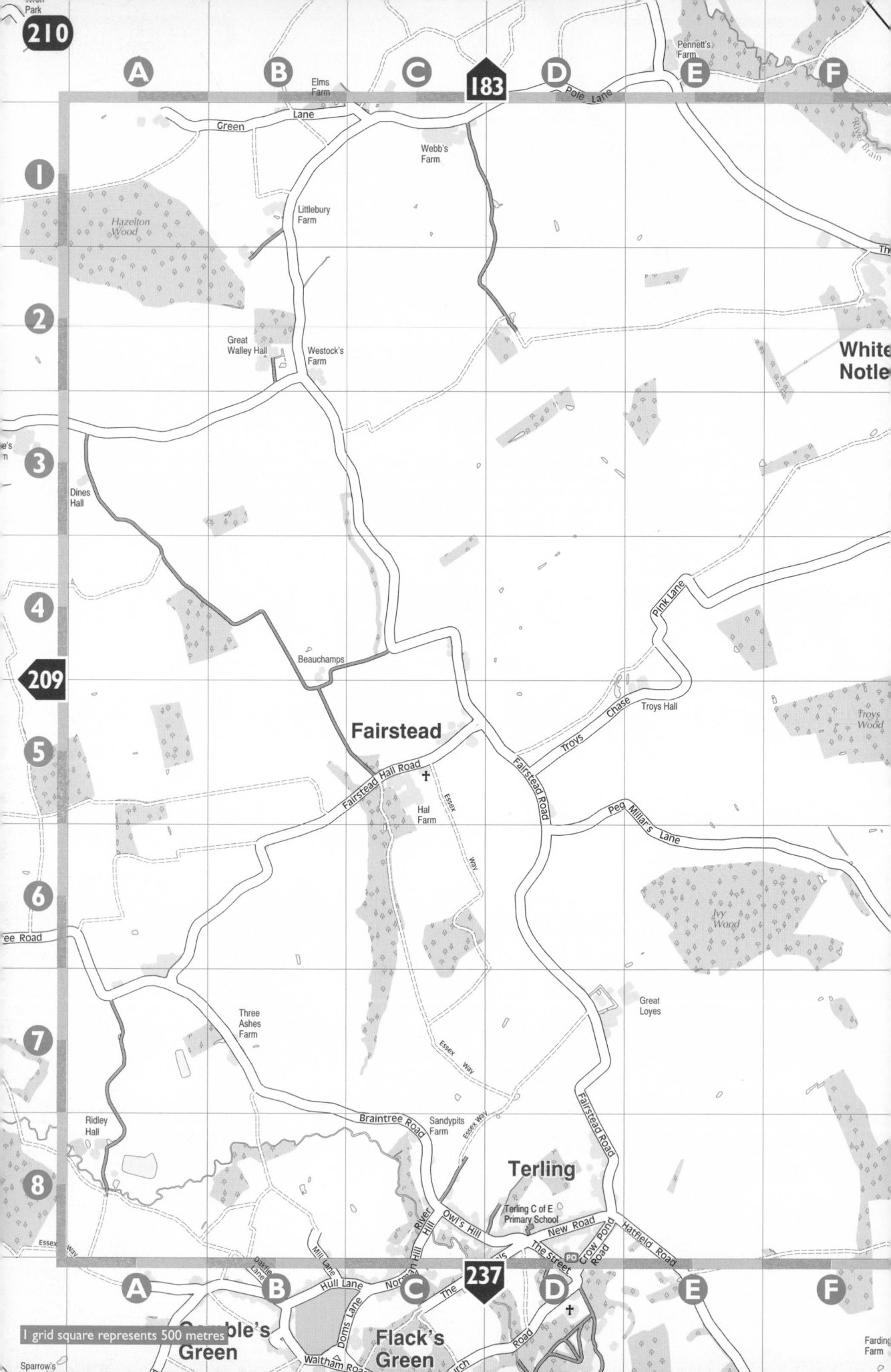 183 　D　E　F

Owen Park

I

Hazelton Wood

Green　Lane

Elms Farm

Webb's Farm

Littlebury Farm

Pole　Lane

Pennett's Farm

River Brain

Th

2

Great Walley Hall

Westock's Farm

White Notle

3

Dines Hall

e's n

4

Beauchamps

Pink Lane

209

Troys Chase

Troys Hall

Troys Wood

5

Fairstead

Fairstead Hall Road

†

Hal Farm

Essex　Way

Fairstead Road

Troys

Fairstead Road

Peg　Millar's　Lane

6

ee Road

Ivy Wood

7

Three Ashes Farm

Essex　Way

Great Loyes

Fairstead Road

Ridley Hall

8

Braintree Road

Sandypits Farm

Essex Way

Terling

Essex

Way

Terling C of E Primary School

New Road

Crow Pond Road

Hatfield Road

River

Owl's Hill

Norman Hill

The

PO

The Street

Farding Farm

Sparrow's

A　B　C 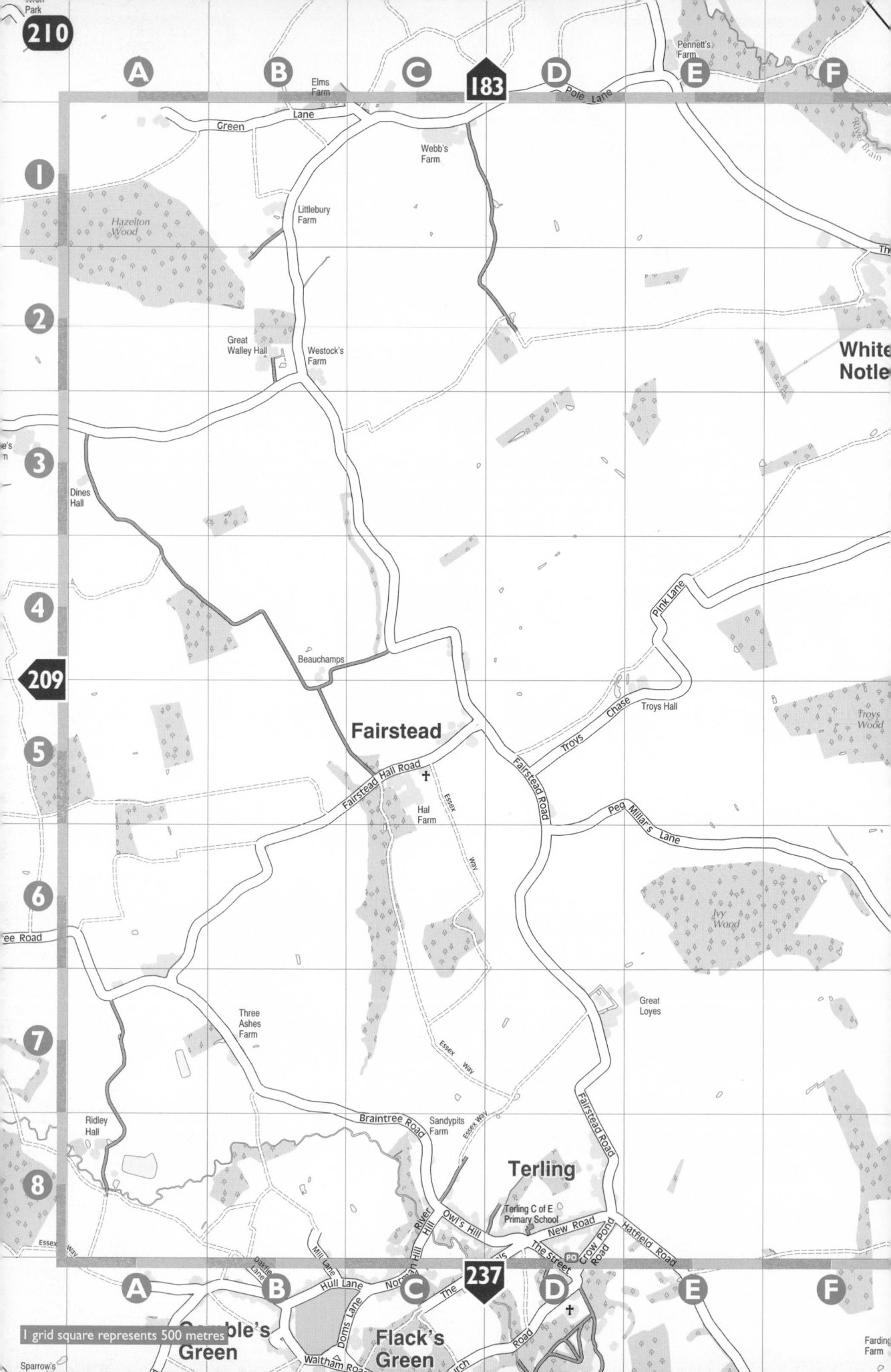 237 　D　†　E　F

Dokile Lane

Mill Lane

Hull Lane

Doms Lane

Waltham Road

ole's

Green

Flack's Green

rch　Road

G   H   J   188   K   L   M

Birch
Holt

Smythe's Green

Palmer's
Farm

B1022

Roundbush
Farm

1

Winter's Road

Duke's Farm

2

Roundbush Road

Haynes
Green

Haynes   Green   Road

*Layer
Wood*

3

Layer
Marney
Tower

Layer Marney

Wick Farm

Stockhouse Road

Newbridge Road

4

216

Viners
Farm

5

Road

Rockingham's
Farm

6

wbridge Road

*Long
Wood*

7

Layer Brook

Park
Farm

8

**Paternoster
Heath**

Park Lane

rook
ose

erry La

PO

The
Folly

Knight

Brook   Road

Hawthorn
Road

orn Way

stockhouse cl

D'ARCY

242

G   H   J   K   L   Barn Hall
Farm   M

**Tolleshunt
Knights**

A B C D E F

189

Birch Green

Mill

Birch Street

The Surgery

1
Birchway
PO

Lane

Straight Way

Layer Breton Heath

Layer Breton

1

Winter's Road

Shatters Road

Lower Road

Layer Breton Hill

Bumblebee Farm

2

Garlands Farm

B1
1 Hollingtons Gv

Layer Hall

WIGBOROUGH ROAD

3

Layer Breton Hall

Rows Farm

B1026

Farm

4

◀ **215**

C05

5

Layer Brook

B

6

ROAD

Staffor

School

7

Garr House Farm

B1026

LAYER

8

Abbot's Wick Farm

Abbots Wick Lane

Sherwin's Farm

Lower Moulsham's Farm

Great Wig

A B C D E F

243

ROAD

CESTER

Maldon Road

1 grid square represents 500 metres

G   H   J   190   K   L   M

I

2

Abberton Reservoir

3

Peldon
Lodge

Peldon

4

Malting Road   Peldon Road   Lodge Lane

218

5

Peldon †

St Ives Road

Church Road

PO

6

Corner

Harvey's Farm

Lower   Road   Newpots Close   Mers

Road

Newpots Lane

7

Wigborough   Road

Moulsham's
Farm

Copthall
Grove

Sampson's
Farm

Sampson's   Lane

lyde Farm

Church Lane   †

8

chool Lane

Peldon Road

Little
Wigborough

Copt Hall Lane

New
Hall

ough

Chestnuts
Farm

Peldon Road

owse's Farm

G   H   J   244   K   L   M

A B C 191 D E F

1

Langenhoe

Glebe House

Langenhoe
CP
School

Langenhoe
Park

Crouch House
Farm

Lodge   Lane

Pete Tye
Common

Pantile
Farm

Peldon   Road

Peldon   Road

2

3

Peldon   Road

Haxells
Farm

Langenhoe Hall Lane

Langenhoe
Hall

4

Pete
Hall

COLCHESTER   ROAD

5

B1025

Langenhoehall
Marsh

Moor
Farm

Mersea

6

Kemps
Farm

Road

Mersea   Road

7

Lane

Sampson's   Lane   Newpots

THE

8

STROOD

Bonner's
Saltings

A B C 245 D E F

Ray Island
Nature Reserve

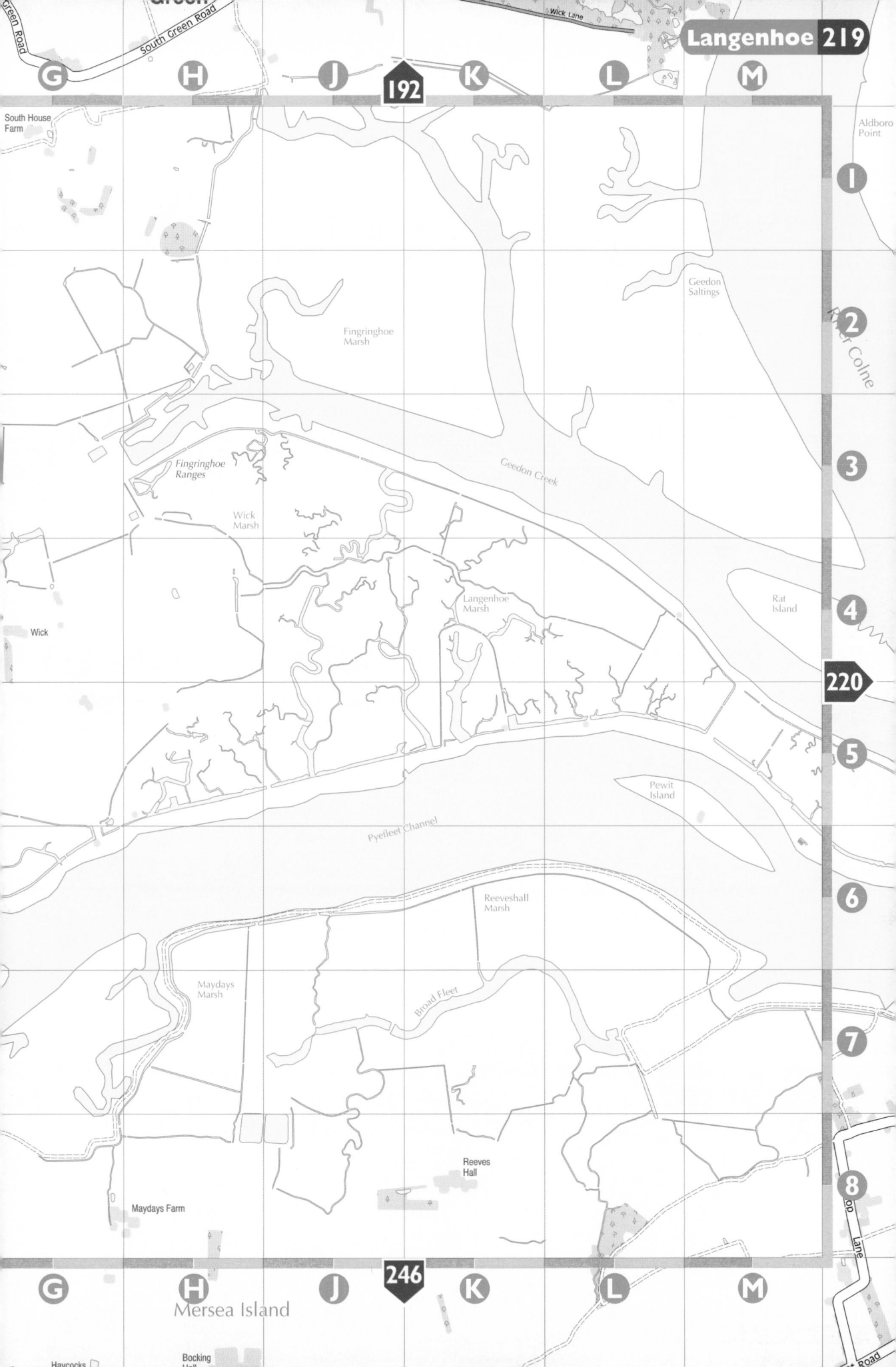

South Green Road

Wick Lane

G H J **192** K L M

South House
Farm

Aldboro
Point

1

Geedon
Saltings

River Colne

2

Fingringhoe
Marsh

Geedon Creek

3

Fingringhoe
Ranges

Wick
Marsh

Langenhoe
Marsh

Rat
Island

4

Wick

220

5

Pewit
Island

Pyefleet Channel

6

Reeveshall
Marsh

Maydays
Marsh

Broad Fleet

7

8

Reeves
Hall

Maydays Farm

op Lane

G H J **246** K L M

Mersea Island

Havcocks

Bocking

A B C D E F

193

Aldboro
Point

Ford Lane

Moverons

Wapping Lane

Moverons Lane

Moverons Lane

BRIGHTLINGSEA ROAD

Gatehouse
Farm

†

River Colne

CHURCH

Samson's

Fordwich
Place

St Andrews Rd

Deal Way

Maltings Road

R Romney Close

ROAD

Sarre Way

The Colne
Community
School

BRIGHTLINGSEA

Farm Walk

Manor House Way

Pertwee Close

B1029

Lodge Lane

Marennes
Crescent

Pyefleet

Chestnut Way

Upper Park Rd

Dean Street

Well Street

Spring Chase

Elm Dr

Ash Cl

Park

Drive

Walnut Way

Cedar Av
Planton
Way

Willow Close

Birch

Beacon Cl

Lower Park Way

Junior
Sch

Western Rd

York Rd

STATION RD

Colne Rd

219

Colne
Medical Cen

Way

Oyster Tank

Sailing
Club

Promenade

Western Prom

Westmarsh
Point

St Osyth
Stone Point

East Essex
Aviation Society
& Museum

M

Ivy House

Nature
Reserve

Ivy Lane

Mersea
Stone

East Road

North
Barn

Shop Lane

247

A B C D E F

Broman's
Farm

Broman's Lane

Cudmore Grove
Country Park

1 2 3 4 219 5 6 7 8

G3
1 Hastings Pl
2 Wincheisea Pl

G4
1 Recreation Wy

G5
1 George Cut
2 Hall Cut
3 Thomas St
4 Wellington St
5 Windsor Ct

G H J 194 K L M

1

B1027

2

FLAG H

Greatmarsh Farm

Morses

Lowermarsh Farm

3

Eastmarsh Point

Churchill Cl
Red Barn Road
Folkards Lane
Morses Lane
Stoney Lane

Dover Road
Regent Cl
Sandwich Road
Belfield Av
Cinque Port Road
Kent Close
Campernell Close

Brightlingsea United Football Club
Stanley Av
Chapel Road
Granville Way
Robinson Road

4

Lower Farm

Bayard Av
Beaumont Avenue
George Av
Edward Avenue
Albert Rd
Richard Charles Close
Anne Cl
Margaret Close
Elizabeth Wy
John St
Whitegate Rd
Greenhurst Road
Creekhurst Close
Hurst Close
Fair Close

Freelands

222

5

PO
High Street
Chapel Rd
Link Rd
Tower Cut
Mill Street

Hurst Green

Flag Creek

New Street
Sydney St
Tower Street
Lime Street
Back Waterside Lane
Ophir Rd

University Yacht Club
Colne Yacht Club

Brightlingsea Creek

6

Cindery Island

Brightlingsea Creek

7

St Osyth Creek

Colne Way
New Way
Norman Way
W Wall
Cruce Way
Mersea View
Seaview Ter
Roman Way
Allen Way
Lydia Drive
Oakmead
Alpha Rd
Road
Colne View
Beacon Way

Cow Lane

Point Clear Road

8

Mill Dam Lake

G H J 248 K L M

PO
Hts
Dumont Avenue

H5
1 Kirkhurst Cl

H4
1 Hill House Ct

Point Clear Road

G6
1 Copperas Rd
2 Francis St

Wigboro Wick Lane
Point Clear Road

South Heath

St Osyth Heath

St Osyth

195

221

249

1 grid square represents 500 metres

GS
1 Bournemouth Rd
2 Hall Cl
3 Quilters Cl
4 Southview Dr
5 Sundale Cl

Clacton

Road

Manor Road

Church Lane

Long

Lane

MAIN ROAD

PO

Frinton on Sea
Lawn Tennis Club

Hotel

The Greensward

G

H

J

198

K

L

M

Frinton
Golf
Club

CLACTON ROAD

B1032

Golf
Course

Holland Gap

Sandy Point

Chevaux de
frise Point

FRINTON ROAD

B1032

Manor Way

Way

Holland
Haven

3

arwood Av

Aylesbury Drive

octors
urg

Saxon Wy

Viking Wy

Crende

Way

5

Haven Av

The Esplanade

Brighton Road

2

1

4

oad

Cha
Parade

G

H

J

K

L

M

I

2

3

4

5

6

7

8

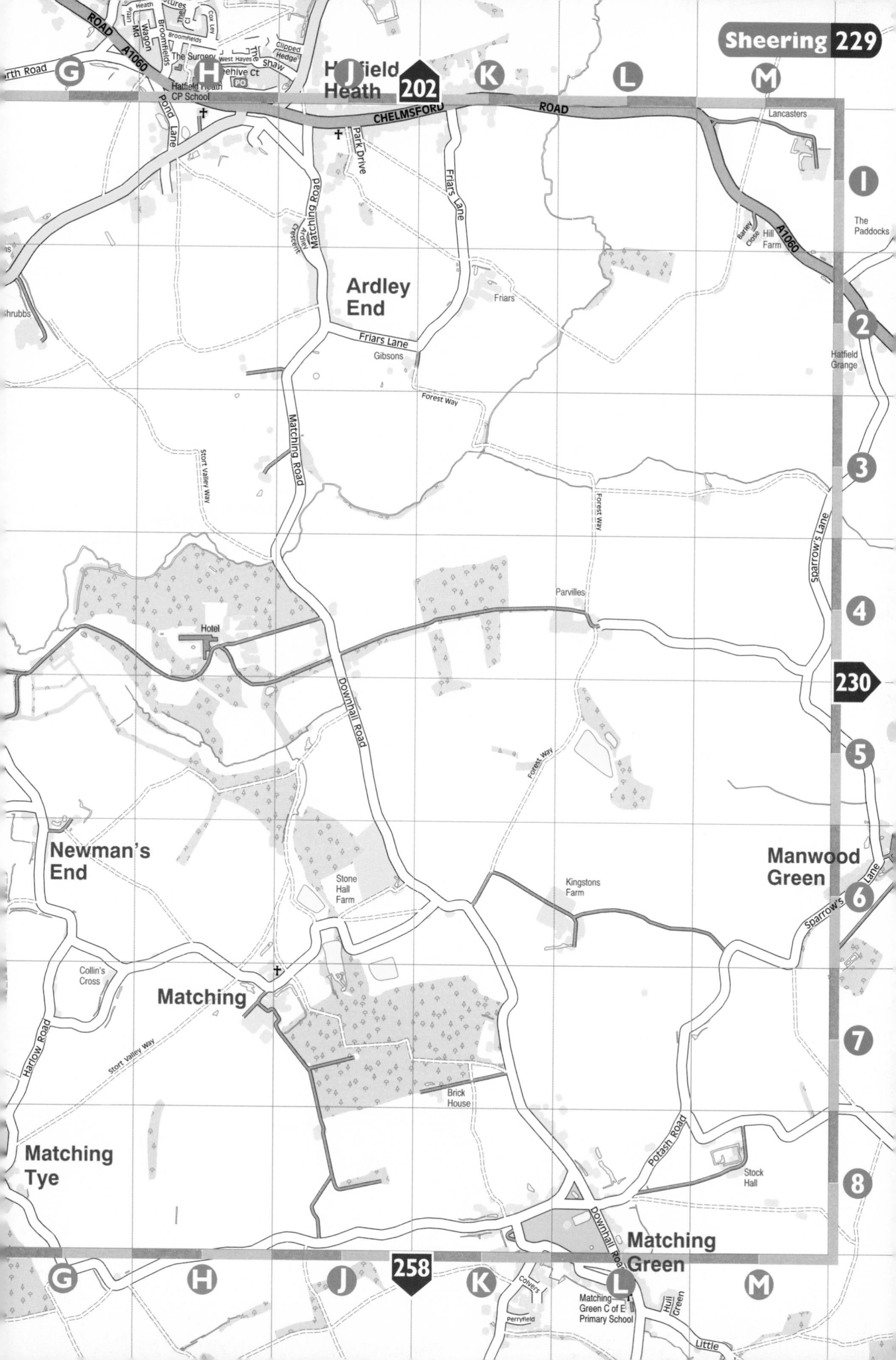

G
H
J
Hatfield Heath 202
K
L
M

CHELMSFORD ROAD

Lancasters

I

The Paddocks

2

Hatfield Grange

Barley Close
Hill Farm
A1060

3

Sparrow's Lane

Ardley End

Friars

Friars Lane

Gibsons

Forest Way

Matching Road

Stort Valley Way

Matching Road

Archer Crescent

North Road

Pond Lane

ROAD
A1060

Park Drive

Friars Lane

Broomfields
The Surgery
Beehive Ct
Hatfield Heath CP School
PO
West Hayes
The Shaw
Clipped Hedge
Cox Ley
Heath

Parvilles

Forest Way

4

230

Hotel

Downhall Road

Forest Way

5

Newman's End

Stone Hall Farm

Kingstons Farm

Manwood Green

6

Sparrow's Lane

Collin's Cross

Matching

Stort Valley Way

7

Harlow Road

Brick House

Matching Tye

8

Potash Road

Stock Hall

Downhall Road

Matching Green

G
H
J
258
K
L
M

Colvers
Perryfield
Matching Green C of E Primary School
Hill Green
Little

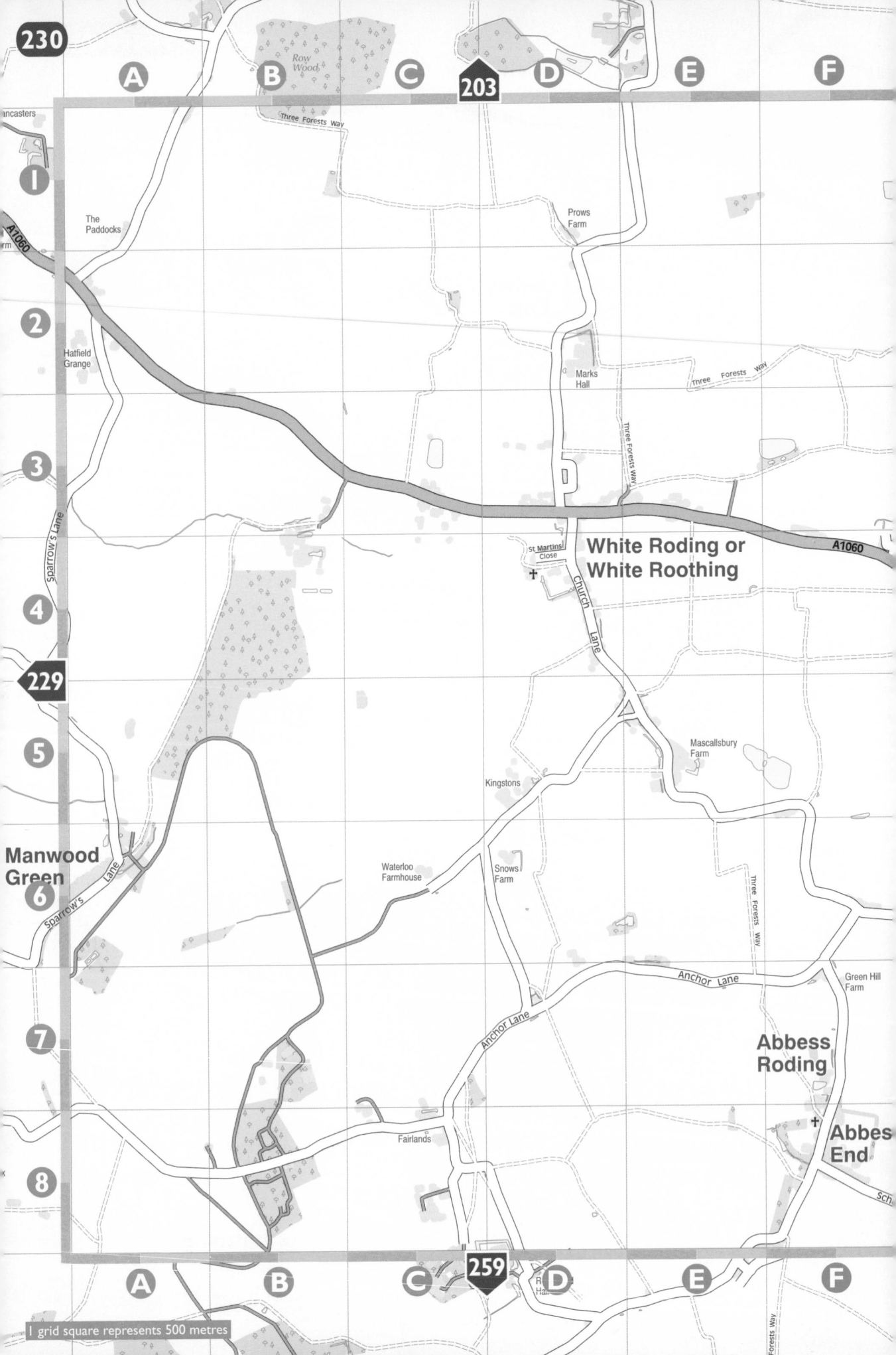

A **B** Row Wood **C** 203 **D** **E** **F**

Lancasters

Three Forests Way

1

The Paddocks

Prows Farm

A1060

2

Hatfield Grange

Marks Hall

Three Forests Way

3

A1060

St Martins Close

White Roding or White Roothing

Church Lane

4

Three Forests Way

229

Mascallsbury Farm

5

Kingstons

Manwood Green

Sparrow's Lane

6

Waterloo Farmhouse

Snows Farm

Anchor Lane

Green Hill Farm

Sparrow's

Three Forests Way

Anchor Lane

7

Abbess Roding

Fairlands

Abbess End

8

Sch

A **B** **C** 259 **D** **E** **F**

R Hall

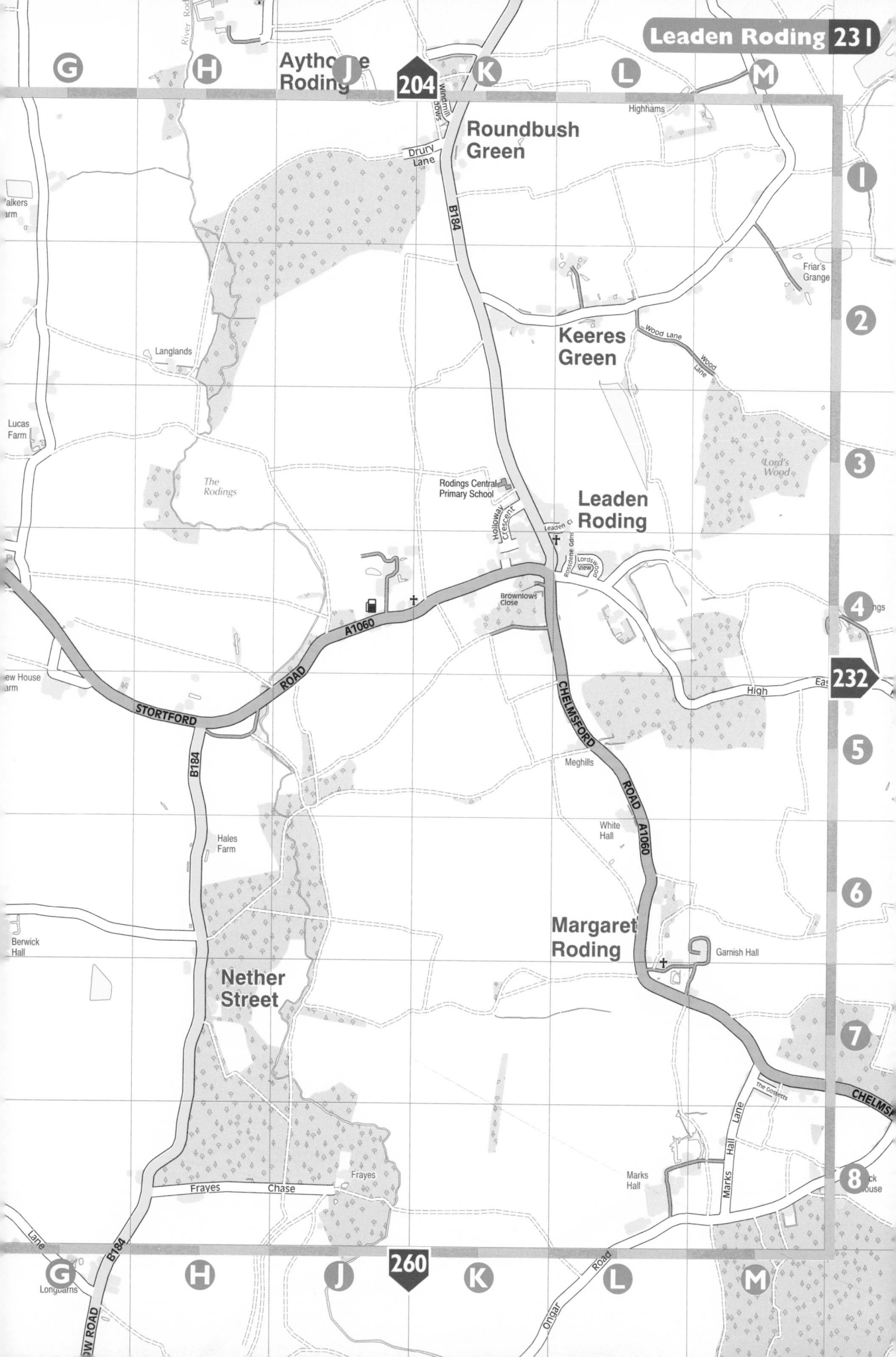

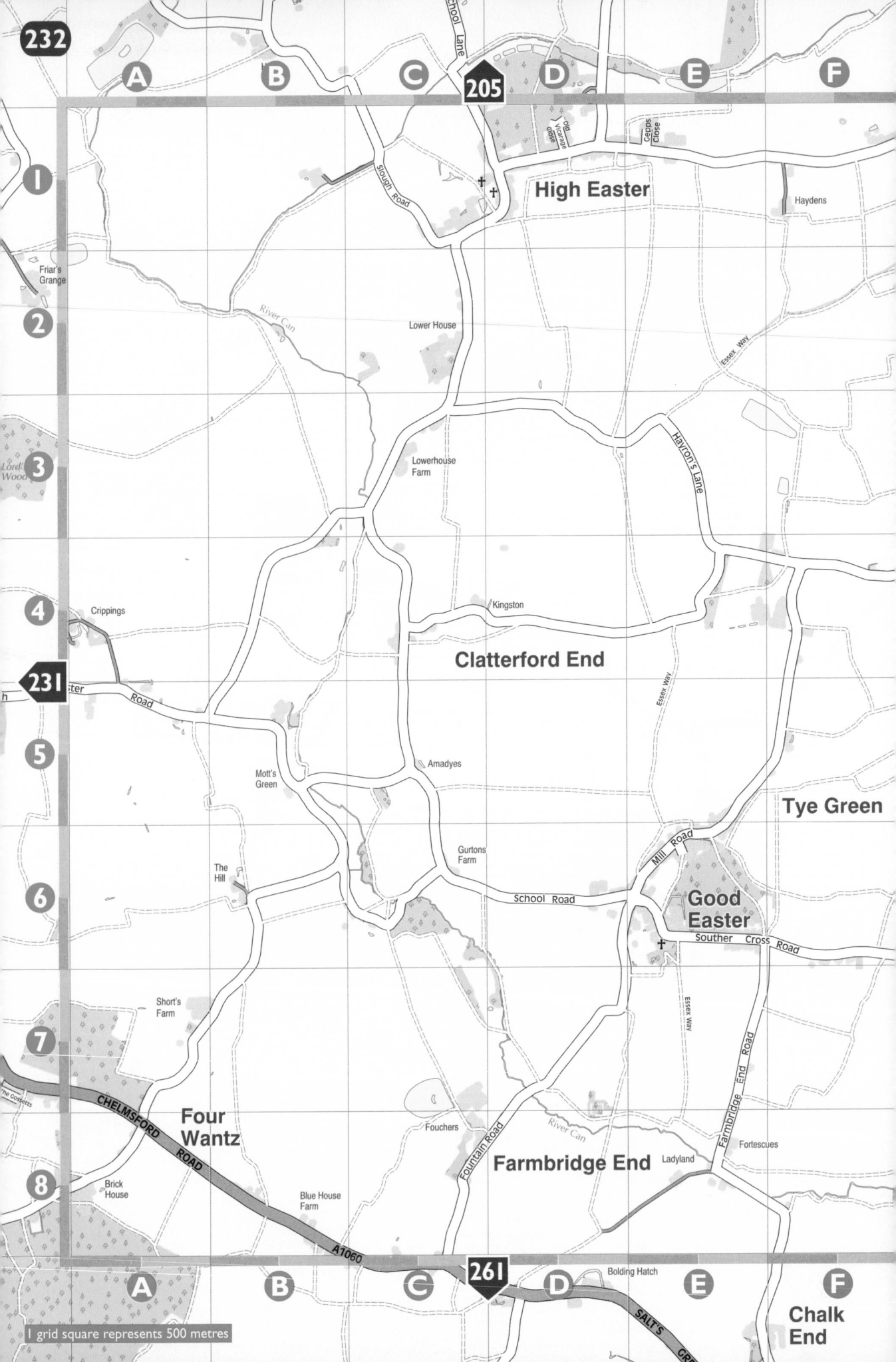

232

A   B   C   **205**   D   E   F

1

Friar's Grange

Lord's Wood

2

River Can

Lower House

3

Lowerhouse Farm

High Easter

Haydens

Essex Way

Hayron's Lane

4

Crippings

Kingston

231

ster Road

Clatterford End

Essex Way

5

Mott's Green

Amadyes

Tye Green

6

The Hill

Gurtons Farm

School Road

Mill Road

Good Easter

Souther Cross Road

Essex Way

7

Short's Farm

Farmbridge End Road

The Gorselts

Four Wantz

CHELMSFORD ROAD

Fouchers

Fountain Road

River Can

Fortescues

Farmbridge End

Ladyland

8

Brick House

Blue House Farm

A1060

A   B   C   **261**   D   Bolding Hatch   E   F

SALT'S CRE

Chalk End

1 grid square represents 500 metres

Pleshey

Stagden Cross

Acreland Green

The Street

Raylands

Pleshey Grange

Grange Road

Woolmers Mead

Vicarage Road

Back Lane

Essex Way

Pump Lane

Plesheybury

Linsteads

Duckers Lane

Baileys

Elbows

Armours

Bedfords

Fridays

Bards Hall

Mashb

234

Barrack Road

Smallshoes

Gatehouse

Wares Road

Wares

Little Newarks

Mashbury

Langley's Farm

Great Newarks

Howletts Hall

262

Essex Way

G H J K L M

1
2
3
4
5
6
7
8

A B **207** C D E F

Pleshey

Oak Hall

1
Woolmers Mead
Back Lane

Pump Lane

†
2

Waltham Bury

Essex Way

Bury Lane

3
Fitzjohn's Farm

Barrack Lane

Brook Mead

High Houses

Great Waltham

Cherry Garden Road
Glebe Meadow
School
Duffue's Clo
South Str

Mashbury Road

4

233
Israel's Farm

Humphrey's Farm Lane

Humphrey's Farm

Breeds

Hoe Lane

5

Fanner's Green

6
Broa Gree

Partridgegreen

Beadle's Hall

Walnut Tree Farm

7
Dyers Hall

†

Chignall Smealy

8
Woodhall

263
Woodhall Farm

A B C **263** D E F

Gray's Farm

Mill Hous

Fitzandrew's Farm

G4
1 Bakers Mead

H1
1 Parsonage La

H8
1 The Millars

Chatham Green

G H J 208 K L M

A130

ESSEX

REGIMENT

WAY

A131

Luck's Lane

owe Street

PO

Waltham House

Chatham Hall Lane

Park Farm

Essex Way

Essex Way

Scurvy Hall Lane

Great Stonage Farm

I

Long's

2

3

Chatham Hall

Chatham Hall Lane

B1008

Wolmers Hey

Hatchfields Ray Mead

Upper Moors

Dicky Moors

Little Waltham C of E Primary School

Sheepcotes Lane

Sheepcotes Farm

4

236

Chelmsford Road

Minnow End

PO

The Street

Chapel Drive

Winckford Close

Sorrill Close

Brook Hill

The Surgery

Church Hill

Rectory Close

Little Waltham

Wheeler's Hill

Wheeler's Hill

Leighs Rd

Power's Farm

5

Lark's Lane

's

Roman Road

Manor Crescent

Chelmer Avenue

Back Lane

River Chelmer

A130

6

B1008

Rolphs Farm

ESSEX REGIMENT WAY

Pratts Farm Lane

Pratt's Farm

7

King Edward Grammar Sports Ground

Woodhouse Lane

Wood House

Back Lane

Pratts Farm Lane

Domsey Lane

Belsteads

Broomfield Hospital

Hospital Approach

Court 1

The Windmills

Anglia Polytechnic University

Nash Drive

Road 1

Mandeville Way

Ayletts

3

Blasford Hill

Butlers Farm

Channels Golf Club

8

Chelmer Valley High School

G H

Church

Avenue

Road 1

Broomhall Road

Whyte Mead

J 264 K

Belsteads Farm Lane

L

K5
1 Hazeldon Cl

M

J8
1 Constance Cl
2 Gernon Cl
3 Warren Cl

Jubilee Avenue

Terling

G H J K L M

210

Owl's

Terling C of E
Primary School

The Street

PO

Crow Pond Road

Hatfield Road

Oakfield Lane

Hull Lane

Mill Lane

Norman Hill

Doms Lane

The Dismals

Gamble's
Green

Flack's
Green

Waltham Road

Church Road

Terling Place

Waltham Road

Terling Hall Road

Roll's
Farm

River Ter

Farding's
Farm

Taylor's
Farm

Whitelands

Witham Road

Hatfield Road

I

2

3

4

238

5

6

7

8

Ringer's
Farm

Terling Hall Road

Terling
Hall

Porridge
Pot

Lost
Wood

Toppinghoehall
Wood

Terling Hall Road

Termitts
Chase

Hatfield
Wick

Berwick
Place

Wallace's
Lane

Waltham Road

Toppinghoe
Hall

Chantry
Farm

Chantry Lane

Hogwells

266

A12(T) MAIN ROAD

B1137

A12(T)

THE

Hatfield
Place

Hall Lane

G H J K L M

G

H

J

212

K

L

M

I

Moss Road

White Lane
Chipping Hill
Moat Farm Chase
Station Rd
Easton Road
Braxted Lane
Coleman's Farm

Witham Station
G

Collingwood Road
B1018
Guithavon Valley
The Surgery
The Avenue
Newland Street
Fanmead
Chess Lane
Stepfield
Little Braxted
Braintree District Council
The Witham Health Centre
Barwell Way
Alvercorn Way
Wheaton Road
River Blackwater

Guithavon Street
Town Hall
Kings Chase
Greenfield
Freebournes Road
Pryor Close
Perry Road
Perry Way

Bramston Sports Centre
B1389
Fern House Surgery
Maldon Road
River View
Blackwater Lane

The John Bramston School
Bridge St
Howbridge Road
Laurence Avenue
Sauls Bridge Close
Claysmiths Drive
Carraways
River Brain

Wickham Rd
Dengie Cl
Infants School
Maltings
Holy Family RC Primary School
Pelly Av
Elizabeth Avenue
Pitt Avenue
Sauls Avenue
B1018
Constance Cl
Benton Close
Benton Hall
Chase
Glen Acres
Sewells Farm
Hale's Farm

Ashby Road
Scarletts Close
Ishams
Blue Mills
Halfacres
Blue Mills Hill

Oliver's Farm
B1018
ROAD
Sparkey Wood
Glebe Farm
Chantry Wood
240

Howbridge Hall Rd
MALDON ROAD
Heathgate
Witham Road
Birch Rise

Wickham Place
B1018
Wickham Bishops
Welands Close
Welands
Holt Dr
The Warrens
Beech Green
Poney Cha
6

Hatfield Road
Mope Lane
Leigh Drive
Byron Dr
Church Close
Church Road
Blacksmiths Lane
Longmead
The Street
School Road
Grea

Roots Lane
Grange Road
Back
Cra
7

Station Road
Hill Place
Wickham Hall Lane
Whitehouse Farm
8

Smallands Hall Farm
268
Blackwater

G

H1
1 Armiger Wy
2 Bevington Ms
3 Charlotte Wy
4 Kynaston Pl
5 Oliver Pl
6 Wakelin Wy

H

H4
1 Gay Bowers Wy
2 Hodges Holt
3 Lifchild Cl
4 Sparkey Ci

J

268

K

H3
1 Edinburgh Ci

L

H2
1 Barley Flds
2 Blackman Wy

M

H1
1 Boone Pl
2 Du Cane Pl
3 Horner Pl
4 Lockram La
5 Mayland Rd

A B C D E F

1

Church

The Avenue

Great Braxted
Hall

Noak's
Cross

Sextons Lane

Braxted R

Braxted Road

2

Broomfield's
Farm

PH

Tiptree

Bung Row

PO

Braxted Lane

M

Great Braxted

3

Threadgold's
Farm

's Farm

4

Lea Lane

Green Man Lane

Carters Lane

Braxted Hill

Maclarens

Mountains Road

Mountains

Rookery Lane

Kings Rd

Brickspring Lane

Spring La

Mill Road

Eaton Way

Chapel Road

Mount Pleasant Est

**Great
Totham**

5

Rise

Beacon Road

The Surgery

Finch's

Goat Lodge Road

Beacon Hill

Mountains

COLCHESTER ROAD

B1022

Mount Lodge
Chase

Totham Hill Green

**Totham
Hill**

6

The Warrens

Beech
Green

Poney Chase

PO

The Street

The Arbour Lane

ksmiths Lane

School Road

Kelvedon Road

Great Totham Road

PH

Walden

Great Totham
County Primary
School

Walden House

Walden Close

Staplers Pk

Staplers Hearth

2

Beckingham Road

Forrester
Park Golf &
Tennis Club

7

Roots Lane

Longmead

Back Lane

Maypole Road

Crabb's Farm

Prince

Of

Wales

Road

Catchpole Lane

1

Morton Road

Foster Road

Harvey

Brook Cl

Woodside

Pixie Chase

Heron Way

School Road

**Great
Totham**

Seagers

Millways

MALDON ROAD

Hall Road

8

Captains Wood Road

ain's
Wood

Jepcrack's Farm

Church Road

A B C D E F

Spickets Brook

Sheenna

I grid square represents 500 metres

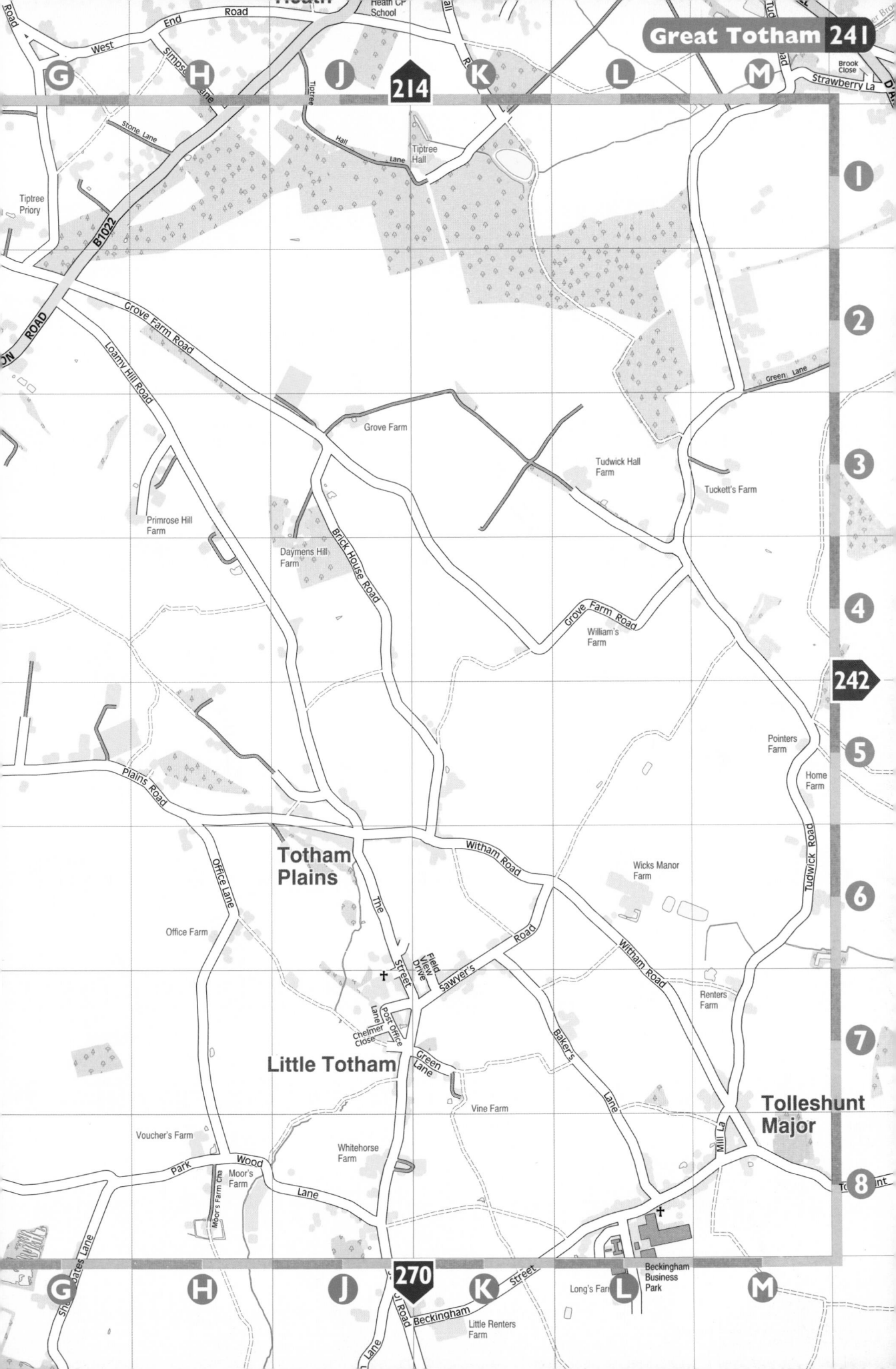

G H J **216** K L M

1

2

3

4

244

5

6

7

8

Rowse's Farm

Abbotts Hall

Maldon Road

Maldon

COLCHESTER ROAD

B1026

Barnhall Road

The Street

Mill Lane

Rose Lane

Salcott Street

Salcott Creek

Salcott-cum -Virley

WHITEHOUSE HILL

B1026

Hotel

Spital Farm

Bridge Farm

Colchester Road

ROAD B1026

Old Hall Farm

Old Hall Lane

Back Road

Bourchier's Hall

Guisnes Court

Gorwell Hall

ESBURY

ROAD

Back Road

272

Carrington Farm

Station Road

Thurstable Road

Mallard Close

Genesta Close

Shamrock Close

Endeavour Close

Valkyrie Close

Thurstable Close

Thurstable Way

Thurstable

North Road

Abbots Wick La.

Abbot's Wick Farm

Sherwin's Farm

G H J **272** K L M

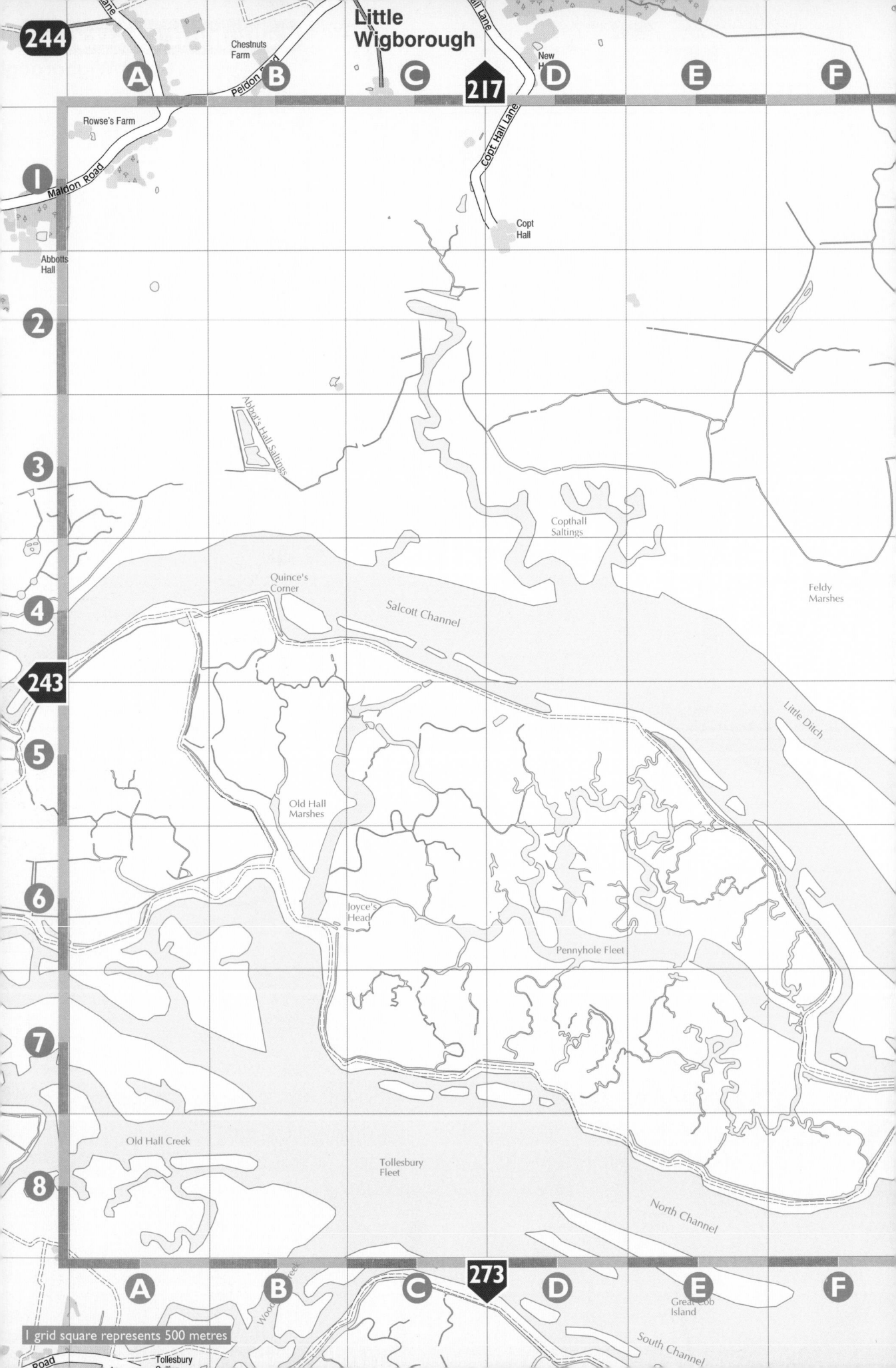

A   B   C   D   E   F

**Little
Wigborough**

217

New

Rowse's Farm

Chestnuts
Farm

Peldon Road

Copt Hall Lane

I   Maldon Road

Copt
Hall

Abbotts
Hall

2

3

Abbots Hall Saltings

Copthall
Saltings

Feldy
Marshes

Quince's
Corner

4

Salcott Channel

243

Little Ditch

5

Old Hall
Marshes

6

Joyce's
Head

Pennyhole Fleet

7

Old Hall Creek

8

Tollesbury
Fleet

North Channel

A   B   C   273   D   E   F

Great Cob
Island

South Channel

Road

Tollesbury

Wood Creek

G   H   J   218   K   L   M

218

J4
1 Cypress Ms

K4
1 Langwood
2 Trinity Ms

K6
1 Kingsland Cl

I
2
3
4
246
5
6
7
8

Bower
Hall

Blu
Row

Ray Island
Nature Reserve

Strood Channel

Sampson's
Creek

Thorn
Fleet

Mersea
Fleet

Besom Fleet

Cobmarsh
Island

Mersea
Quarters

Quarters
Spit

East Mersea Road

STROOD

B1025

COLCHESTER ROAD

Wellhouse
Farm

Weathercock

Dawes Lane

Brierley
Avenue

East Road

The Cross

Cross
Way

Constable
Close

Gdn
Farm

Garden
Farm

Windsor

Oakwood

Oakwood Road

Suffolk Av

Norfolk
Avenue

East Avenue

Stable
Mews

Sable
Cl

Beveney
Avenue

Fairhaven

Empress

Seaview

Estuary Park

MILL ROAD

B1025

KINGSLAND

Colchester Road

Trinity Close

Lawns
Close

Chadsworth
Road

Upland
Crescent

Woodstock
Cl

Upland Road

The
Surgery

Elmwood

Avocet
Close

Qu Anne
Drive

Rainbow
Road

Oakwood
Dr

Kingsmere Close

Gainsborough

Hogarth Close

Lea Side

Empress
Dr

King
Charles
Rd

Alexandra Av

Osborne
Drive

Westwood
Drive

Esplanade

Whittaker Wy

Woodfield
Drive

Bricknouse

Curlfleet

Buxey
Close

Spruce
Cl

Pine
Grove

High Street North

Reymead
Close

Vince
Close

Grays
Close

BARFIELD RD

Rushmere
Close

Qu Anne Rd

Prince Albert Road

Willoughby Av

Broomhills

The
Coverts

Victoria

Shear
Crs

Dabchicks
Sailing
Club

Carriers Cl

The Lane

City Road

Stonehill
Way

Firs Chase

Firs Hamlet

Blackwater
Drive

Rosebank
Road

Cemetery

Strood
Close

Firs
Road

St Peter's Road

Mersea Avenue

New
Captains
Road

Churchfields

Captains
Rd

B1025 HIGH ST

Vince
Close

Victory   Road

WEST
MERSEA

Coast   Road

West Mersea
Museum

PO

Church Rd

Melrose Road

Mersea Community
& Sports Centre

Yorick
Road

The
Pharos
Lane

Meadow
Lane

Mersea
Island
GM Sch

Grove Avenue

Beach   Road

Kingsland Road

Kingsland
Beach

G   H   J   274   K   L   M

M5
1 Queenbury Cl

L5
1 Birch Wood Cl
2 Goings La
3 Qu Anne Gdns
4 Richmond Rd
5 Thornwood Cl

L4
1 Carrington Ct
2 Oakwood Gdns

246

A B C 219 D E F

Mersea Island

Reeves
Hall

Bower
Hall

Haycocks

Maydays Farm

Bocking
Hall

Meeting Lane

PO

East Road

CO5

Blue Row

East Mersea Road

East
Mersea

Church Lane

Chapmans Lane

Weathercock

Lane

East Road

Cross Way

Rewsalls
Farm

Mersea Flats

The Cross

245

Cross Lane

Waldegraves Lane

Waldegraves
Farm

Avenue

Park Rd

Westwood Drive

Cross Lane

sborne
Rd

245

275

A B C 275 D E F

1 grid square represents 500 metres

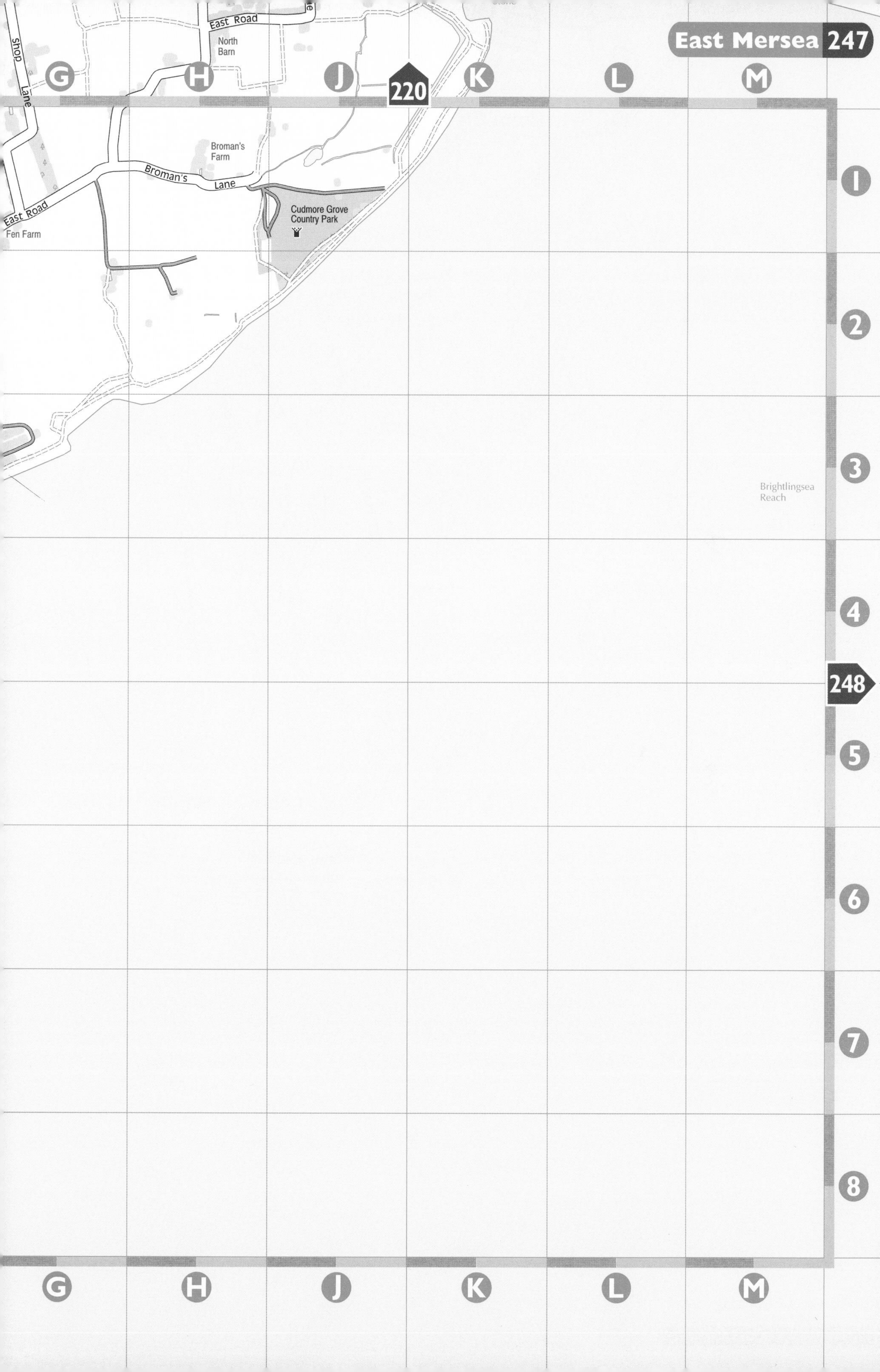
East Road
North Barn
Shop Lane
G
H
J
220
K
L
M
Broman's Farm
Broman's Lane
East Road
Fen Farm
Cudmore Grove Country Park
1
2
3
Brightlingsea Reach
4
248
5
6
7
8
G
H
J
K
L
M

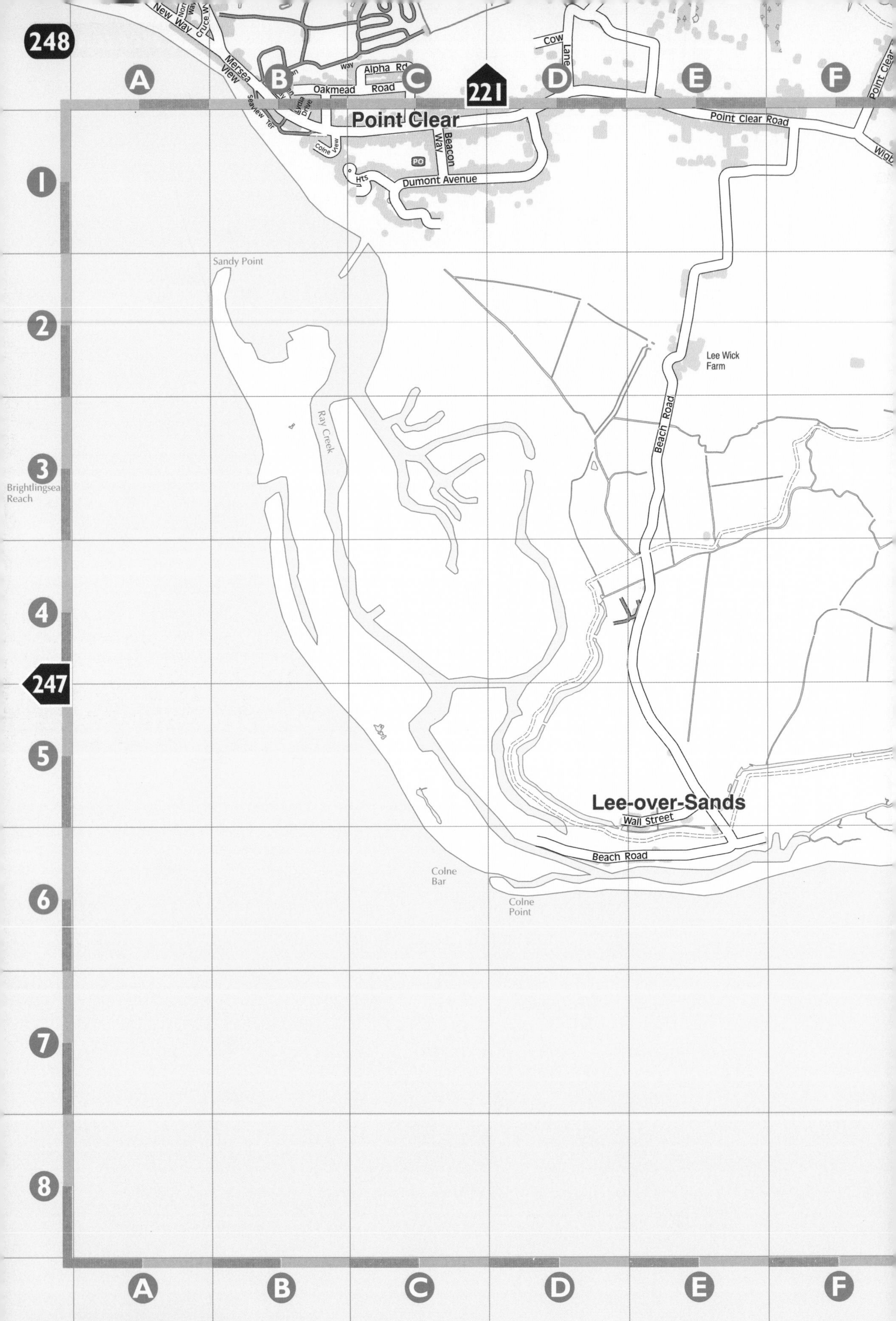

A B C D E F

New Way
Mersea View
Seaview Ter
Colne Way
Lydia Drive
Alpha Rd
Oakmead Road
Cow Lane

Point Clear

Point Clear Road

Beacon Way
PO
Hts
Dumont Avenue

Wigt

I

Sandy Point

2

Lee Wick Farm

Beach Road

3

Brightlingsea Reach

Ray Creek

4

5

Lee-over-Sands

Wall Street

Beach Road

6

Colne Bar

Colne Point

7

8

A B C D E F

I grid square represents 500 metres

CLACTON-ON-SEA

Clacton Pier

13

224

G   H   J   K   L   M

1
2
3
4
5
6
7
8

G   H   J   K   L   M

A B C D E F

PO

1 Hickman Cl
2 Overlord Cl
F8

Swallow Grove
Farm

Prior's
Close

odland Road

ly Road Cl

Postwo

Prior's Wd

Woodside

Heath

The Harlings

LONDON ROAD

College Road

Haileybury
College

College Road

The
Meadow

Hailey Lane

Hailey Lane

1

Balls
Wood

The
Roundings

The
Roundings

Brides
Farm

2

B1197

Woollensbrook

Elbow Lane

3

B1197 HERTFORD ROAD

Box
Wood

Goose
Green

Mangrove Lane

4

Elbow Lane

Dalmonds

Box Lane

Lord Street

High
Leigh

5

Monks
Green

Highfield
Wood

Hoddesdonpark
Wood

6

HOD

owheath
Wood

Cock Lane

A10(T)

7

Stratfield

Woodstock Road

Sutton Lane

Norris Grov

Alamein
Close

Gold
Close

Chingf
Close

Pulham
Avenue

Sheriden
Walk

Carnaby Road

Baas Lane

8

Pembridge Lane

Wood House Lane

A B C D E F

276

Cold
Hall

Baas Hill

Allard Way

Highfield
Drive

Baas Hill
Close

Bell
Lane

Tudor

Beam

Badgers

Stubbs Lane

Paradise
Wildlife

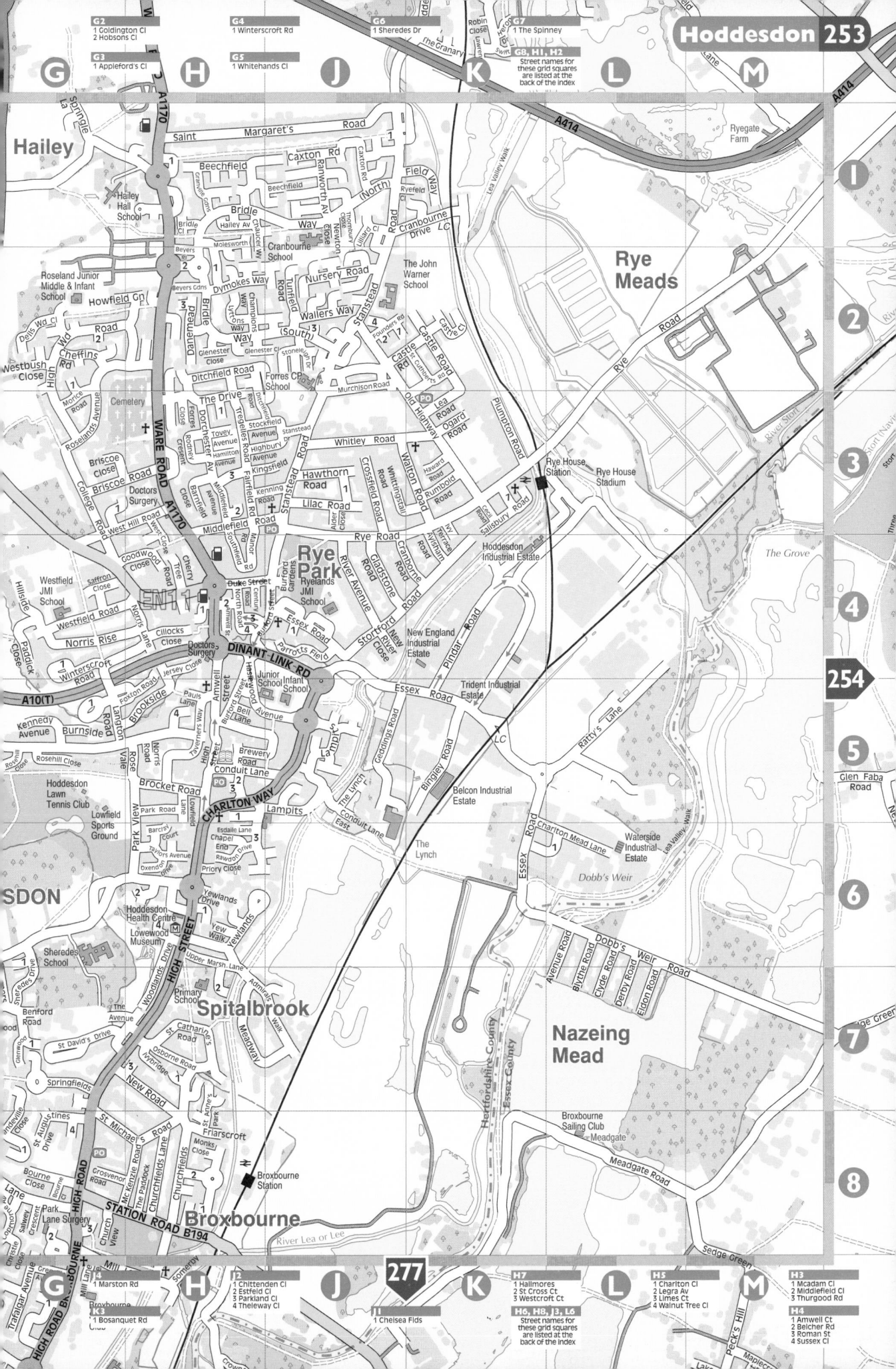

Hailey

Rye Meads

Saint Margaret's Road
Caxton Rd
Beechfield
Beechfield
Cranville Gdns
Bridle Way
Cranbourne School
Ranworth Av
Ryfeld
Cranbourne Drive

Roseland Junior Middle & Infant School
Howfield Gn
Ware Road A1170
Dymokes Way
Nursery Road
The John Warner School

Westbush Close
High
Roselands Avenue
Briscoe Close
Briscoe Road
Doctors Surgery
Wallers Way (South)
Stanstead Road
Founders Rd

Cheffins Rd
Morice Road
Cemetery
The Drive
Whitley Road

Rye Meads

College Road
Doctors Surgery
West Hill Road
Middlefield Road
Forres CP School
Murchison Road
PO
Lea Road
Ogard Road
Plumpton Road
Rye House Station
Rye House Stadium

Hawthorn Road
Lilac Road
Whittingstall Road
Rumbold Road
Salisbury Road

Rye Road

Westfield JMI School
Goodwood Close
Cherry Tree
Duke Street
Rye Park
Gladstone Road
Cranbourne Road
Aysham
Hoddesdon Industrial Estate

Westfield Road
Norris Rise
EN11
North Road
Century
Ryelands JMI School
Essex Road
New England Industrial Estate
Pindar Road
254

A10(T)
Winterscroft Road
DINANT LINK RD
Amwell Street
Junior School
Infant School
Essex Road
Trident Industrial Estate

Kennedy Avenue
Burnside
Brookside
High
Pauls Lane
Bell Lane
Geddings Road
Bingley Road
Belcon Industrial Estate
Ratty's Lane
Glen Faba Road

Rosehill Close
Brewery Road
Conduit Lane
Brocket Road
Park Mead
Charlton Way
Lampits
The Lynch
Conduit Lane East
Chariton Mead Lane
Waterside Industrial Estate

SDON
Hoddesdon Lawn Tennis Club
Lowfield Sports Ground
Esdaile Lane
Chapel End
Priory Close
Essex Road
Dobb's Weir

Sheredes School
Hoddesdon Health Centre
Lowewood Museum
High Street
Yewlands Drive
Yew Walk
Upper Marsh Lane
Dobb's Road
Blythe Road
Clyde Road
Derby Road
Eldon Road
Avenue Road
Weir Road

Benford Road
The Avenue
Spitalbrook
St. Catharine's Road
Osborne Road
Meadway
Admirals Walk
Nazeing Mead

Springfields
New Road
St Michael's Road
Friarscroft
Monks Close
Broxbourne Sailing Club
Meadgate
Meadgate Road

St Augustines Drive
Grosvenor Road
Churchfields Lane
Broxbourne Station
Hertfordshire County
Essex County

Bourne Close
STATION ROAD B194
Broxbourne
River Lea or Lee
Sedge Green

277

G H J **228** K L M

Churchgate C of E Primary School

Feltimores

Nicholas chool

Hobbs Cross Road

Franklins Farm

M11

Chalk Lane

Hobbs Cross

Forest Way

Forest Way

Housham Tye

Carter's Green

Matching Park

Stort valley Way

oyt Gree

New Way Lane

Faggotters Lane

CM17

Roffey Hall

New Way

Threshers Bush

New Way La

Green Lane

Foster Street

Foster Street

Tilegate Green

258

School Lane

Tilegate Road

Hall Farm

Magdalen Laver

Stort Valley Way

Great Wilmor

Stort Valley Way

Wynter's Farm

Willow Pl

Hastingwood Road

Rolls Farm

Tilegate Road

Spencers Farm

Wynter's Grange

Street

Hastingwood

Humphreys

Shanks Brook

Paris Hall

Stort valley Way

Sewalds Hall Farm

Greens Farm

Stort valley Way

Stort

Weald Lodg

G H J **281** K L M

Kents Lane

I

2

3

4

5

6

7

8

Mat ye

Rainbow

Road

ow Tye

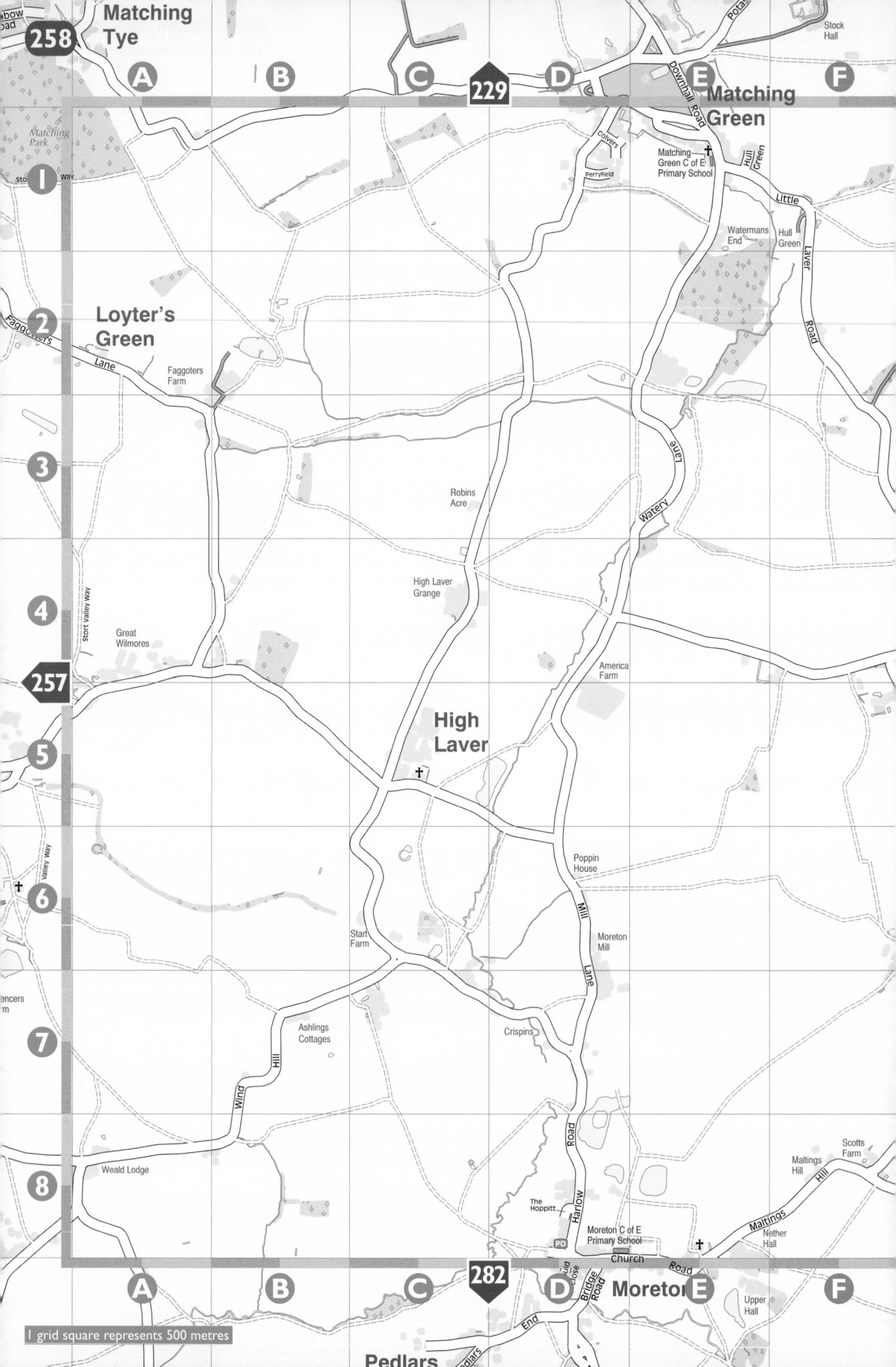

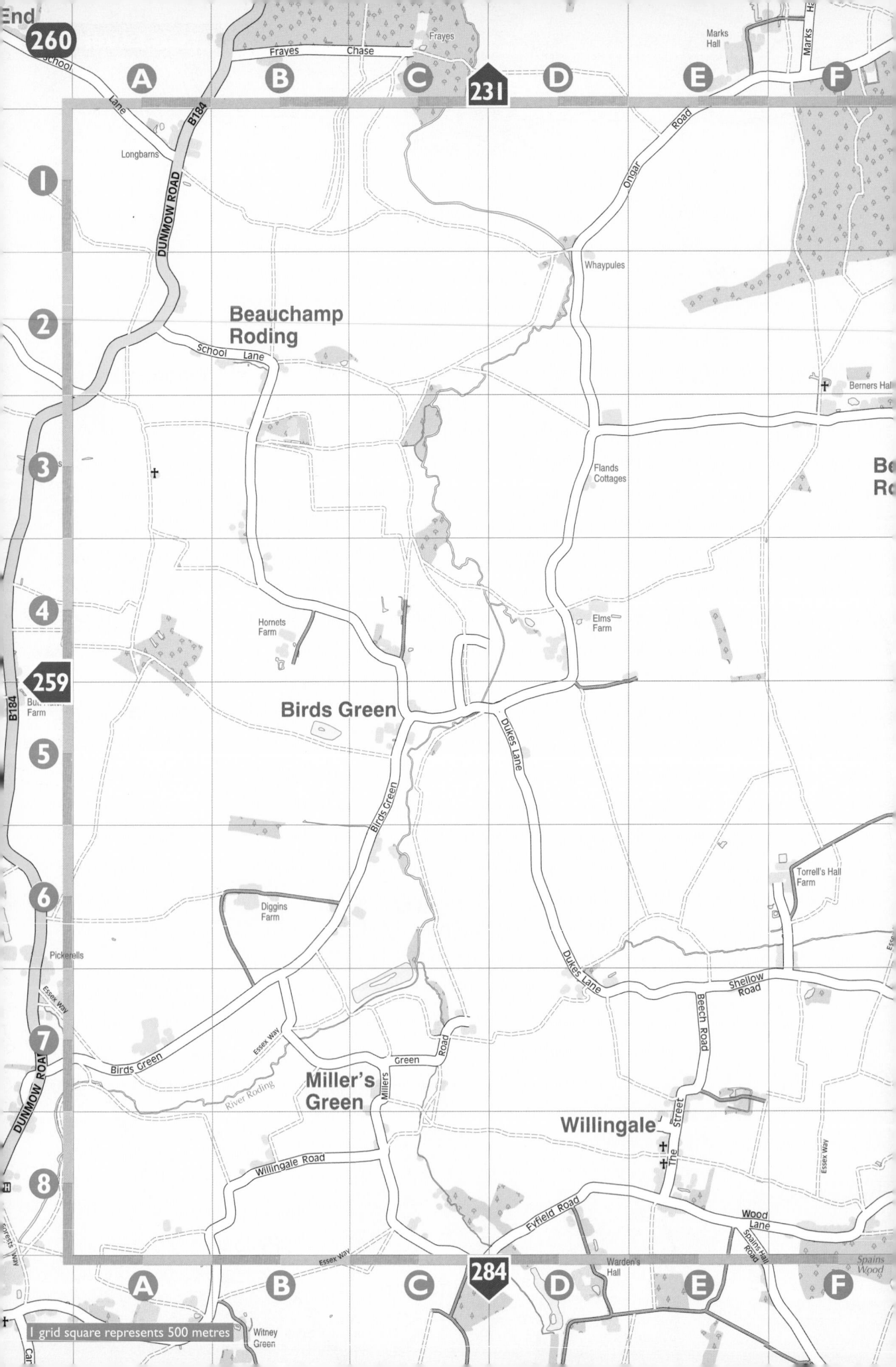

ROAD

Brick House

Blue House Farm

Ladyland

G

H

J

232

A1060

K

L

M

Bolding Hatch

SALT'S GREEN

Chalk End

I

2

Fountain

Pepper's Green

Essex Way

ners ing

acre ottages

Ne Ha

3

Mountneys

Newla

4

Essex Way

262

Rowe's Farm

Elms Farm

5

Elms Road

Skreens Park Farm

6

Windmill Farm

Shellow Cross Farm

Tye Hall

hellow all

Shellow Bowells

Skreens Park

7

Sawyer's Farm

Patience Bri

8

Wood Lane

Stays Lane

G

H

River Lane

Quires Green

285

J

K

Butt Hatch Farm

L

M

Pooty Pools

Wall's Green

A   B   C   D   E   F

233

Langley's
Farm

Howletts
Hall

Chignall
Hall

1

2

A1060

Hill Farm

Little Boyton
Hall

Boyton
Hall

3

Newland
Hall

Newland Brook

4

Boyton
Cross

261

Dukes

5

Elms Road

Lightfoots

Roxwell

PO

Roxwell C of E
Primary School

The Street

Mill
Close

St. Michael's Drive

Church Green

Thatcher's
Farm

6

Tye
Hall

Roxwell Brook

Galleons Hill

Green Lane

Vicarage

Road

Blackwall
Bridge

A1060

ROXWELL

Street

Hoestreet

7

Stonehill
Farm

Stonehill Road

Hoe

Lane

8

Patience
Bridge

Green Lane
Farm

Hillcroft

Gravelly

Lane

A   B   C   D   E   F

286

Benedict
Otes

Ne C ey G en

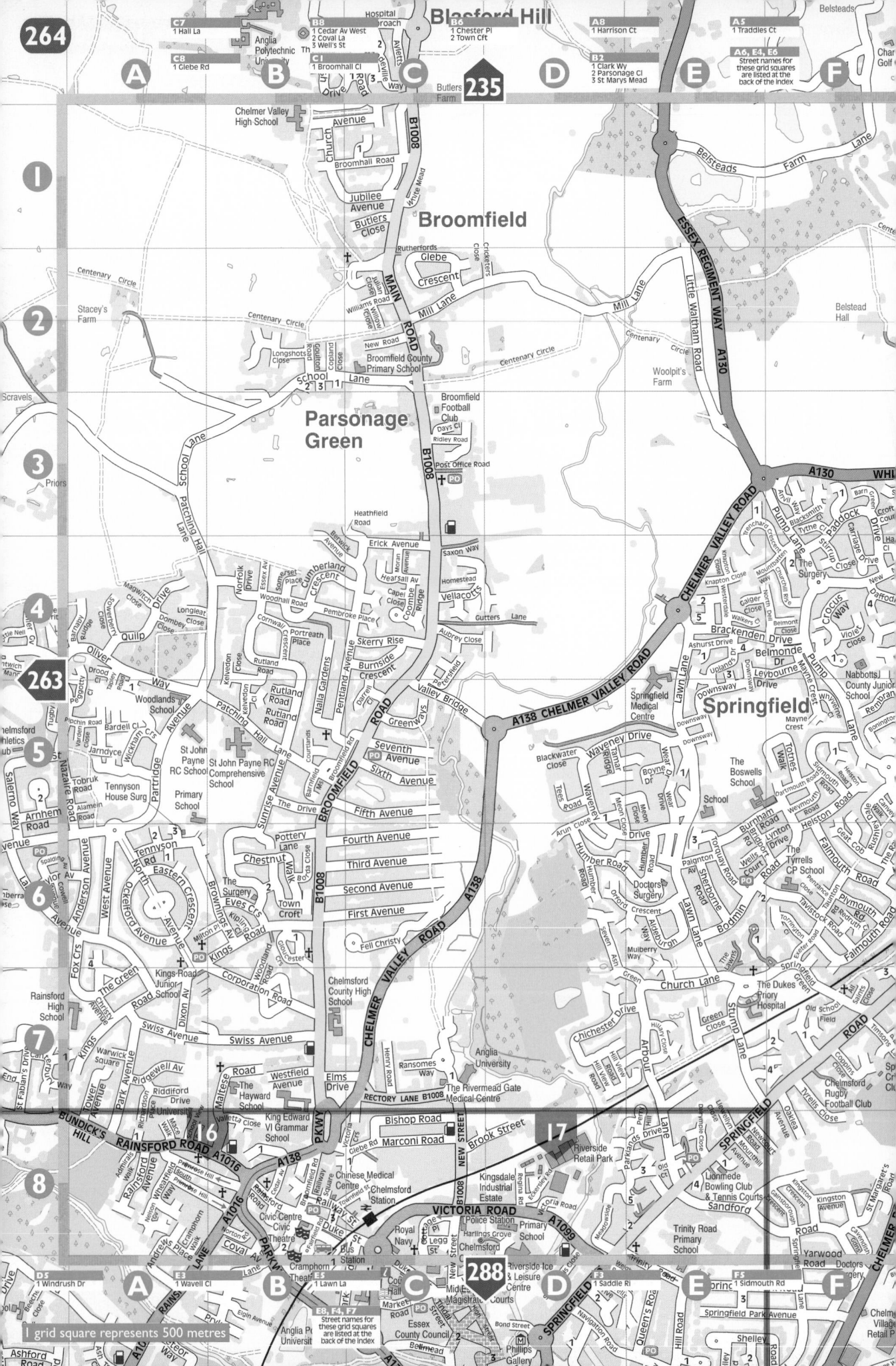

G H J 236 K L M

I
2
3
4
266
5
6
7
8

236
289
266

G3
1 Goldenacres

G4
1 Hunters Wy
2 Vermeer Ride

G5,G8,H6,M2
Street names for these grid squares are listed at the back of the index

G6
1 Dahlia Cl
2 Lavender Ct
3 Wallasea Gdns

H3
1 Clachar Cl
2 Dunmore Rd
3 Hopkins Cl
4 Leapingwell Cl

H7
1 Brook End Rd
2 Clarence Cl
3 Milison Bank
4 Pocklington Cl
5 Sutton Mead
6 Wilkinsons Mead

L3
1 Howards Cl
2 The Larches

G8
1 Golding Thoroughfare
2 Kirk Pl
3 Samuel Manor
4 Stanley Rl

G7
1 Emberson Ct
2 N'umberland Ct

Mount Maskall
Generals Lane
Centenary Circle
Bulls Lodge
Generals Lane
A12(T)
Main Road
B1137
A130
A130
Boreham
Church Road
Old Forge Road
The Laurels Surgery
Butterfield Road
St Andrews Road
Old Lodge Farm
Hart Lane
White Hart Lane
Hunters Way
Martingale Drive
The Bishops C of E & RC Primary School
Colchester Road
A138
A130
B1137
Hedgerows Business Park
Springfield Lyons
Sheepcotes
Winsford Way
Fordson Road
A12(T)
Chelmer Road
Springfield Rd
A138
Cuton Hall Lane
Chelmer Village Way
Cuton Hall
Centenary Circle
Phillow's Farm
Dukes Park Industrial Estate
Montrose
Richmond Road
Beaufort Road
Chelmer Village Way
Chancellor Avenue
Cornelius Vale
Ward Path
A12(T)
Hammond's Farm
Kingsford Drive
Junior School
Chelmer Village
Brook End Road
Clements Close

G H J **238** K L M

1

Sportsmans
Lane

The
Priory

Nounsley

Priory
Farm
Road

Jenkin's
Farm

Gray's
Farm

Lea Grove

2

Fairfields

Crabb's Hill

wden Hall Lane

Nounsley Road

Priory
Close

Manor Road

Deverel
Avenue

Ulting Road

Butlers

River Ter

Mowden Hall Lane

3

Cardfield's
Farm

Fairwinds
Farm

Ashfield   Farm   Road

Ulting Grove

4

Chelmer & Blackwater Navigation

Burnfords

Lane

Ulting Hall Road

268

Ulting Wick

Church
Road

Cemetery

Crouchman's   Road

Ulting Farm

Ulting

5

Bassett's
Farm

Ulting Lane

Chelmer & B

River Chelmer

The   Causeway

6

Retreat Farm

Tofts Chase

Manor   Road

Hoe Mill
Barns

7

Bassetts

Lane

West   Bowers

Little London Lane

Raven's
Farm

Road

Hoe   Mill   Road

Blue   Mill   Lane

Gibbs

Spring Elms Lane

Spring Elms

Common Lane

Stivvy's Road

Gun Hill
Farm

Rectory   Road

Mead
Pastures

Woodham Walter
C of E
Primary School

PO

8

Little   Baddow   Road

The St

Church Hill

G H J **291** K L **Woodham Walter** M

Woodham
Walter
Common

The
Wilderness

240

270

293

G6
1 Long Common
2 Rainbow Ms

G7
1 Roman Cl

G8
1 Coach La
2 Silver St

H7
1 Creasen Butt Cl

G H J K L M

Spickets Brook

Sheepcoates Farm

Jepcrack's

Langford Grove

Captain's Wood

Totham Lodge

South Wood

Sains Hall

Scraley Road

Sligborough Road

Broad Street Green

Howell's Farm

Poplar Grove Farm

Poplar Grove Chase

Slough House Farm

Lofts

Chigboro Farm

Scyila Close

Ash Grove

Chestnut Av

e Road

Sycamore

Scraley Road

Heybridge Swifts Football Club

Heybridge

Grapnells Farm

Heywood Way

Wood Road

Oak Road

Maple Avenue

Rowan Walk

Larch Walk

Heybridge CP School

The Surgery

Drapers Sports Club

Salcote Hall

Langford Road

Holloway Road

Kingston Chase

Gill Close

Doubleday Drive

Beeches Road

Crescent Road

Elizabeth Way

Regency Ct

Ten Acre Approach

Abbotsmead

Wood Lane

Everest Way

Hunt Avenue

Hillary Cl

Stock Chase

Towers Road

Cedar Chase

Globe Road

Elm Avenue

Redshank Drive

Lapwing Dr

Heron Way

Kingfisher Close

Lawling Avenue

Wagtail Drive

Coopers Avenue

Limbourne Drive

Steeple Close

Ramsey Close

Drapers Chase

Everest Way

Bentalls Industrial Estate

The Street Industrial Estate

Bentalls Shopping Cen

Benbridge Industrial Estate

Anchor Lane

Longfield Medical Cen

HEYBRIDGE STREET

Heybridge House Industrial Estate

Cemetery

Thirslet Drive

Mayland Close

Virley Close

Goldhanger Road

B1026

Road

Hadrians Way

Temple Way

Harvest Way

Galliford Road

Bates Road

Spring Lane

Hall Bridge Rise

Freshwater Crs

Hall Road

Colchester Road

B1018

Heybridge Ap

A414

The Causeway B1018

Blackwater Trading Estate

Station Road

MALDON

Riverside Industrial Estate

Fullbridge

Cromwell Lane

Primary School

Beeleigh Road

West Chase

Maldon Court School

Market

Gate Street Mews

Bull Lane

High Street

Maldon Town Council

River Chelmer

Chelmer & Blackwater Navigation

Heybridge Basin

Blackwater Sailing Club

The Stiles

Harfred Avenue

Chapel Lane

Burrswood Place

Collier's h

Wellington Road

Fambridge Road

Mount Pleasant

The Plume School

Maldon District Council

Downs Road

Victoria Road

Butt Lane

The Hythe

St Mary's Lane

Maldon Primary School

Maldon Museum

M8
1 Maritime Av
2 Spinnaker Dr

K7
1 Southey Cl

M7
1 Saltcote Maltings

K6
1 Avocet Wy
2 Curlew Cl
3 Dunlin Cl
4 Fir Tree Wk
5 Kittiwake Dr
6 Sanderling Gdns

J5
1 Hazelwood Ct
2 Heywood Ct

H8
1 Chequers La

J7
1 Coates Cl
2 Swan Ct

G H J K L M

Collier's h

1 I
2
3
4
5
6
7
8

G

H

J

242

K

L

M

Beckingham
Hall

hunts

MALDON ROAD

Brook House
Farm

I

White
House
Farm

2

Hyde Farm

Pa.. Lane

3

Church Road

B1026

CM9

Joyce's Chase

Highams Chase

Wycke
Farm

4

Goldhanger

Higham
Farm

Joyce's Chase

Joyce's
Farm

Lauriston
Farm

272

5

Tolleshunt

Gore
Saltings

6

Goldhanger Creek

7

8

The Stumble

Tolleshunt

G

H

J

295

K

L

M

The Chase

272

272

A B Gorwell Hall C 243 D E E1 1 Estuary Ms F

I

White House Farm

Pages Lane

2

3

Wycke Farm

271

4

5

6

7

8

Prentice Hall Farm

Prentice Hall Lane

Carrington Farm

North Road

B1023 WEST STREET

St John's Street

Doctors Surgery
St John's Court

Cemetery

Elysian Gdns

Tollesbury

Church Street

Station Road

Mallard Close
Genesta Close
Shamrock Close
Endeavour Close
Valkyrie Close
Thurstable Close

New Road

Thurstable Road
Thurstable Way

Hasler Road
Sceptre Cl

Kents
Grass

The Chase

HIGH ST EAST STREET

PO

School

The Mount

Woodrolfe Road

Orchard Close
Kings Wk
Crescent Rd

Darnet Rd

Mell

Woodrolfe Far Lane

Monk Walk

Mell Road

Woodrolfe Road

Wy

Bohuns Hall

Mell Farm

Decoy Farm

Rolls Farm

Thirstlet Creek

A B C 296 D E River Blackwater F

1 grid square represents 500 metres

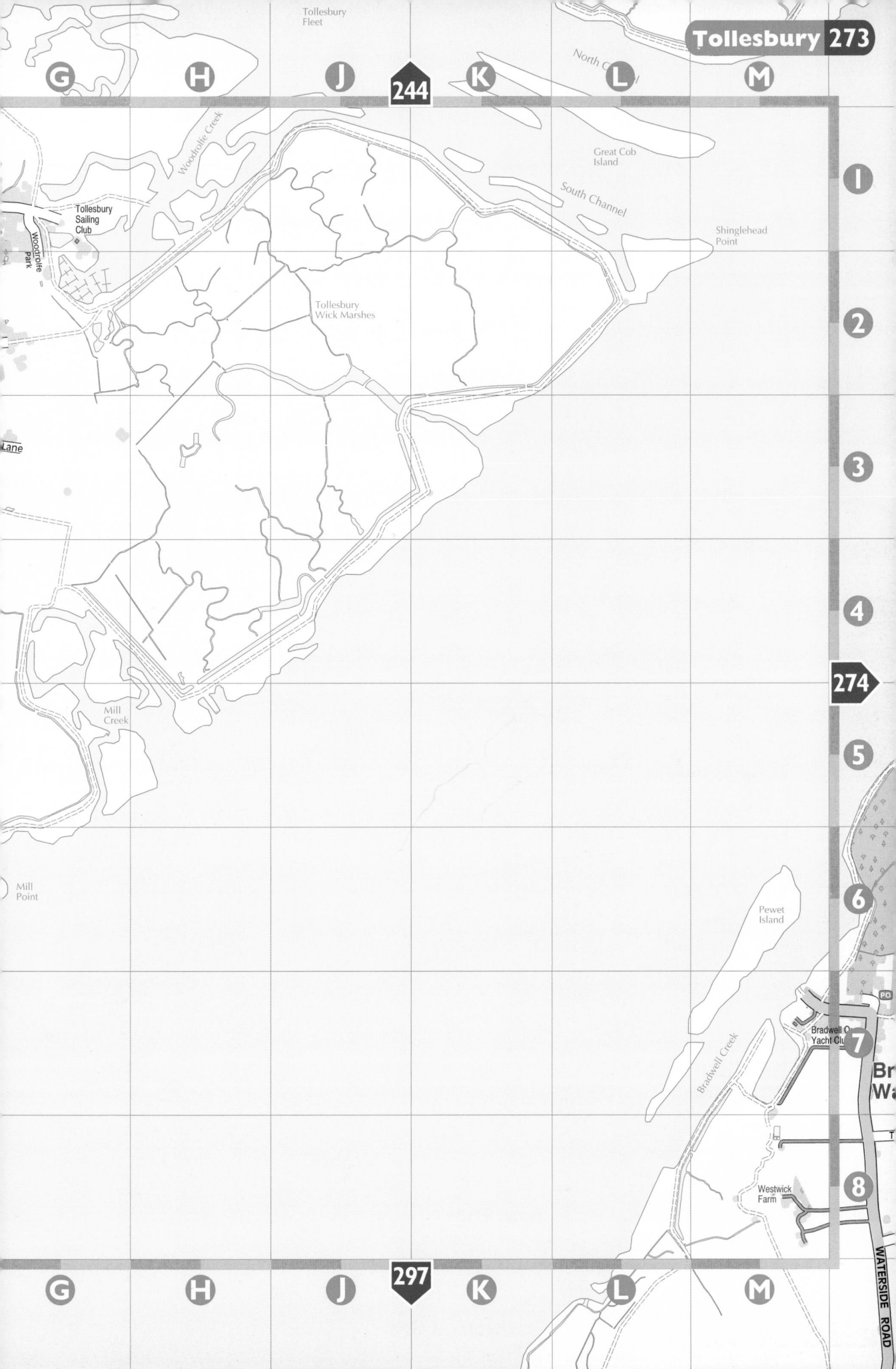

G　H　J　K　L　M

244

I

Tollesbury
Fleet

North C

Great Cob
Island

South Channel

Shinglehead
Point

2

Woodrolfe Creek

Tollesbury
Sailing
Club

Woodrolfe
Park

Tollesbury
Wick Marshes

3

Lane

4

274

Mill
Creek

5

Mill
Point

Pewet
Island

6

PO

Bradwell O
Yacht Clu

7

Bradwell Creek

Br
Wa

Westwick
Farm

8

G　H　J　K　L　M

297

WATERSIDE ROAD

C8
1 Buckeridge Wy

A   B   C   245   D   E   F

1

2

3

4

273

5

Bradwell
Nuclear Power
Station

6

ewet
land

PO

Bradwell Quay
Yacht Club

7

**Bradwell
Waterside**

Trusses Road

Down
Hall

East Hall
Farm

Eastlar

Eastend Road

East Hall

8

estwie
arm

Woodyards

East End

Eastend Road

Eastend Road

Munkins
Farm

A   B   C   298   D   E   F

High Street

South St

Kingswood Court

Bate Dudley Dr

PD
St Cedds
Primary School

Bradwell on Sea

Bradwell
Lodge

Hockley Close

Hockley

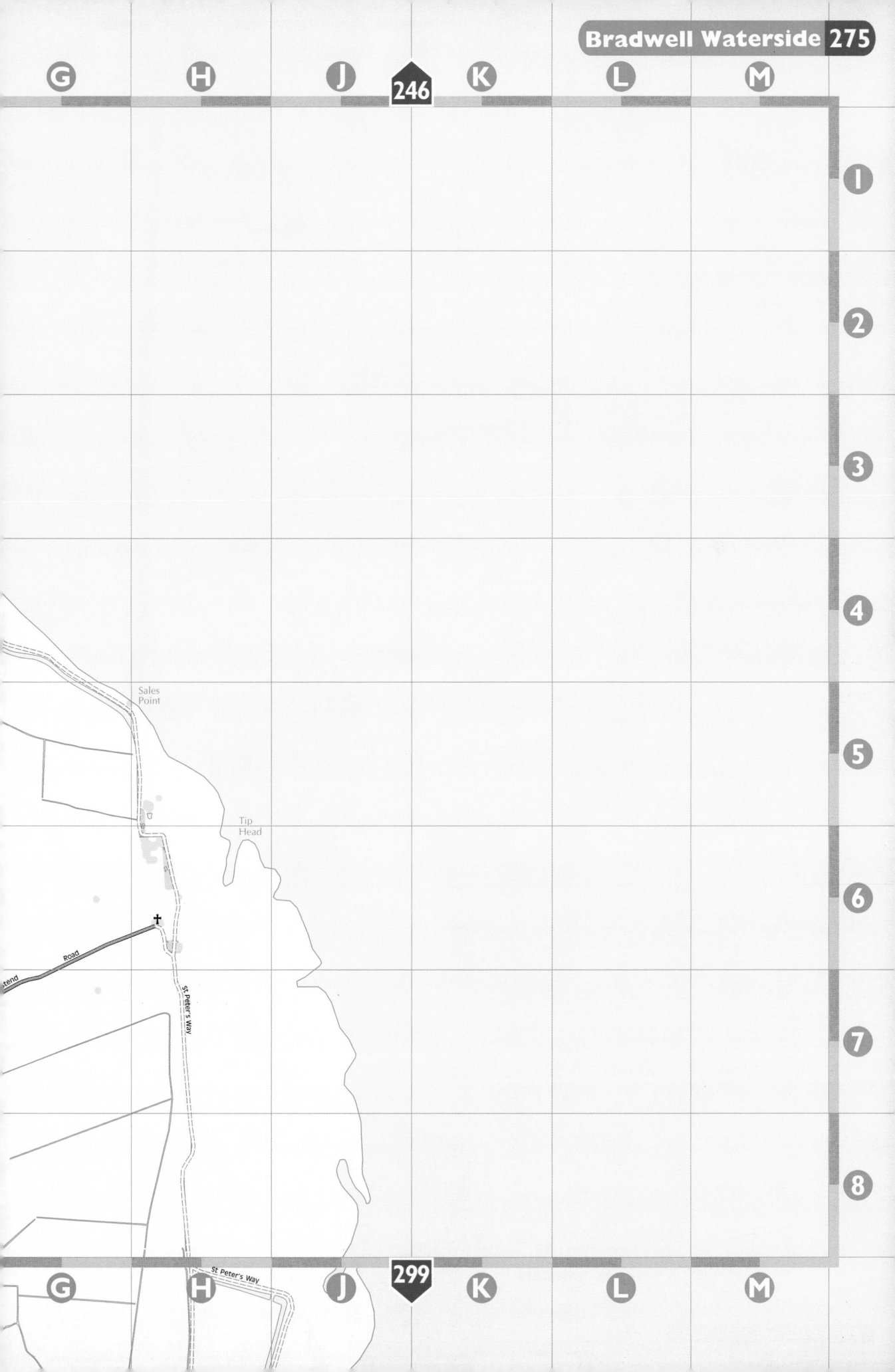

Sales
Point

Tip
Head

Road

St Peter's Way

St Peter's Way

A   B   C   **254**   D   E   F

**Broadley
Common**

I

Stoneshot Common

A2
1 Hoecroft

Three Forests Way

Hoe Lane

Betts Lane

Back Lane

Nazeing

Nazeing Common

2

Palmers Grove

Wheelers Close
Hoe Lane
Sunnyside Lane

Road
1
Barnfield Close

Mayflower Close
Crooked W'y
Nazeing P School
Mead
Barnard Acres
Tovey Close

Middle Street

Nazeing Park School

Back Lane

3

Curtis Farm

Middle

Stort Valley Way

Nazeingwood

Perry Hill

Perry Hill

Middle Street

Nazeing Golf Club

Belchers

Belchers Lane

4

**Bumble's
Green**

277

Nazeing Common

Stort Valley Way

5

Laundry Lane

Waltham Road

Allmains Cl
Bumbles Gn Lane
The Hts

Nazeing Parish Council

**Nazeing
Gate**

The Avenue

**Nazeing
Long Green**

Felsteads

6

Waltham Road

Harold's Park Farm

B194

7

Galleyhill Green

8

Galleyhill Wood

Claverhambury

Claverhambury Road

**Aimes
Green**

May Farm

Clave...bury Road

A   B   **302**   C   D   E   F

Deerpark Wood

EN9

Pa.. Farm

Three...

1 grid square represents 500 metres

1 Holmes Meadow
2 Savoy Wd

1 Chestnut Wk

255

Kingsm

G **H** **J** **K** **L** **M**

EPPING ROAD
B181

Richmonds Farm

Parsloe Road

Phelips Road

Maxwell Wd

Jack's Hatch

Parndon Wood

Dorrington Farm

Fernhill Cottage

1

Lodge Farm

Three Forests Way

Little Canons Farm

Gibbon's Bush Farm

Stort Valley Way

Little Marles Farm

Rye Hill

Rye Hill Road

2

Marles Farm

3

Common

Epping Long Green

Stort valley way

Magpies

Elm Cl

Green Cl

EPPING ROAD

Pump Lane

Epping Green

Carters La
1

Epping Upland C of E Primary School

280

4

B181

Pinch Timber Farm

Upland Road

5

Hunter's Hall Farm

Chambers Manor Farm

Epping Upland

Takeley Manor

6

Gills Farm

Three Forests Way

B181

Cobbin's Bridge

7

Cobbin's Brook

Bury Farm

B181

LINDSEY

8

B181

G **H** **J** **303** **K** **L** **M**

B182

G H J **257** K L M

Paris Hall

1

Stort Valley Way

Kents Lane

Weald Lo

Weald Bridge Road

Weald Bridge

2

Ash

ANE

Stort Valley Way

Little Weald Hall

North Weald Golf Club

A414

Stort Valley Way

Wyldingtree

3

Ravley Lane

Merlin Way

Weald Hall

Lane

Vicarage Lane

Church Lane

Vicarage Lane

A414

New House Farm

Tower Close

St Andrews Close

Bluemans Lane

Bluemans End

Hows Mead

Tyler's Green

4

HIGH ROAD

A414

282

St Andrews C of E (gm) Primary School

The Pavilions

Oak Piece

School Green Lane

Beamish Close

Thorpe Lane

B181

5

North Weald Airfield

Queens Road

The Elms

Princes Close

HIGH

ROAD

Emberson View

NORTH WEALD BASSETT

The Limes Medical Centre

Higham View

Thornhill

PO

6

Lancaster Road

George Avey Cft

Bassett Gdns

The Birches

Higham View

Ongar Park Hall

Merlin Way

Hampden Cl

Wellington Rd

HIGH ROAD

7

B181

Blenheim Way

York Road

Dukes Cl

PH

Station Road

Epping Forest Railway

Roughtallys

Hurricane Wy

Park Cl

Watermans Wy

Kiln Road

Pike Way

Hawks Hl

Roughtalley's Wood

8

Cold Hall Farm

Mill Lane

Essex Way

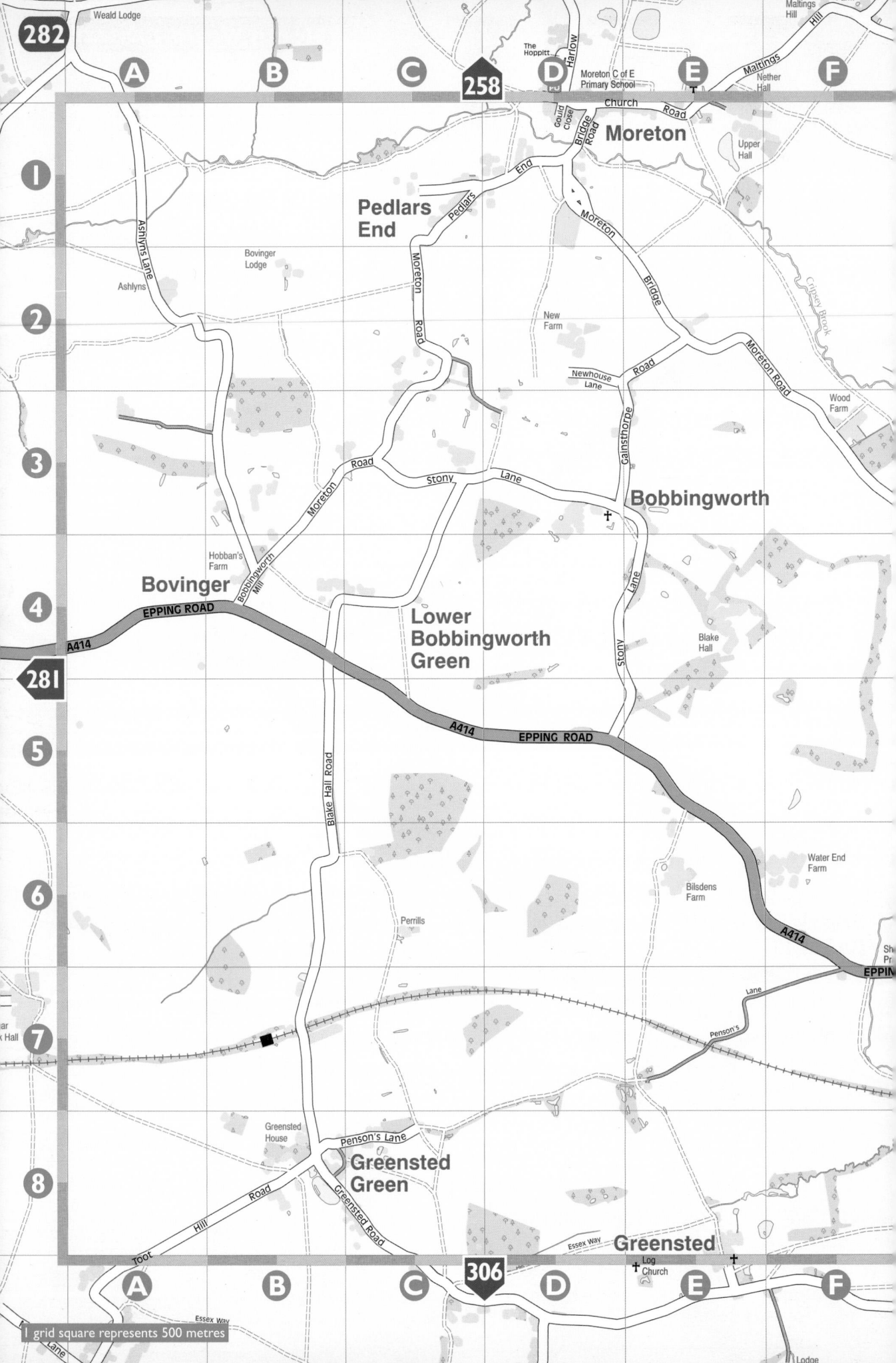

A   B   C   258   D   E   F

I

Weald Lodge

The Hoppitt

Moreton C of E
Primary School

Church   Road   Nether
Hall

Maltings
Hill

Harlow

Moreton

Upper
Hall

Maltings
Hill

Cripsey Brook

Ashlyns Lane

Ashlyns

Bovinger
Lodge

**Pedlars
End**

Pedlars   End

Moreton   Road

Gould
Close

Bridge
Road

Moreton

2

New
Farm

Newhouse
Lane

Road

Moreton   Bridge   Road

Moreton Road

Wood
Farm

3

Moreton   Road

Stony   Lane

Gainsthorpe

✝

Bobbingworth

Hobban's
Farm

Bobbingworth   Mill

Bovinger

4

EPPING ROAD

**Lower
Bobbingworth
Green**

Stony   Lane

Blake
Hall

A414

281

5

A414   EPPING ROAD

Blake Hall Road

Water End
Farm

6

Perrills

Bilsdens
Farm

A414

Sh
Pr

EPPIN

7

ar
k Hall

Lane

Penson's

8

Greensted
House

Penson's Lane

Toot   Hill   Road

Greensted Road

**Greensted
Green**

Essex Way

Greensted

Log
Church
✝

✝

A   B   C   306   D   E   F

Essex Way

Lane

Lodge

G6
1 Betjeman Wy
2 Kimpton's Cl

G7
1 Aukingford Gdns
2 Aukingford Gn

L1
1 Roding Cl

G **H** **J** 259 **K** **L** Fyfield **M**

Fyfield Road

Moreton Road

Pennyfeathers Farm

Clatterford End

Lampetts

Essex Way

B184 7

Walker Avenue

Houchin Drive

Fyfield Dr Walkers
C of E
Primary School

Queen Street

PO

Cannons Lane

Essex Way

I

Harriets Farm

2 nd
Green

Essex Way

Cross Lees Farm

Herons   Lane

Herons Farm

CM5

3

Bundish Hall

Three Forests Way

4

Folyats

ONGAR ROAD

Little Forest Hall

Essex Way

284

Shelley

Church Lane

Boarded Barns Farm

Norton Lane

Three Forests Way

5

Nortor
Mande

B184

FYFIELD ROAD

Brookfields

Moreton Road

Shortlands Avenue

Ongar War Memorial Hospital

Coles Close

Shelley Close

Clare Mews

Ongar Leisure Centre

Essex Way

6

Cripsey Avenue

Acres Avenue

St Peter's Avenue

Queensway

Springfield Close

County School

Essex County Council

High Road Ongar (Chelmsford Road)

CHELMSFORD ROAD   A414

7

1 2

Mark's Avenue

Great Lawn

Great Stony School

The Johns

Mayflower Way

Roding View

High Ongar CP School

PO

The Street

High Ongar

Barron's Close

Bowes Drive

pping Forest Railway

Churchill Close

Onslow Gardens

Three Forests Way

St Peter's Way

Nash Hall

Cemetery

Love Lane

Ongar & District Sports Club

Ongar Parish Council

Bansons Way

St Peter's Way

Essex Way

Millfield

8

Ongar Health Centre

Banson's Lane

Shakletons

St Peter's Way

sex Way

A128

OAD

G Millbank Avenue **H** Castle Street **J** CHIPPING
ONGA 307 **K** **L** **M**

Fair Close

Fairfield Road

Glebe Road

Rodney Road

HIGH STR

Stanley Place

Greensted Road

PO

Mill Lane

St Peter's Way

Willingale Road

Fyfield Road

Wood Lane

Spains Hall Road

Spains Wood

Warden's Hall

1 Cannons Lane

Essex Way

Witney Green

Essex Way

Spains Hall Road

Spains Hall

2 Cannon's Green

Essex Way

Rockhills

Norton Heath Road

Norton

3

Willingale Road

4

Offin's Cottages

Hulke's Farm

283

5 Norton Lane

Norton Lane

Spriggs

Dodd's Farm

Norton Manor

Norton Mandeville

Norton H

Norton Heath Road

6

A414

The Orchard

Chevers Hall

Spurriers

Fingrith

7 CHELMSFORD ROAD A414

Cozen's Farm

Paslow Hall

King Street

Rookery Road

Rookery Farm

8

King Street

St Peter's Way

Way

Nine

1 grid square represents 500 metres

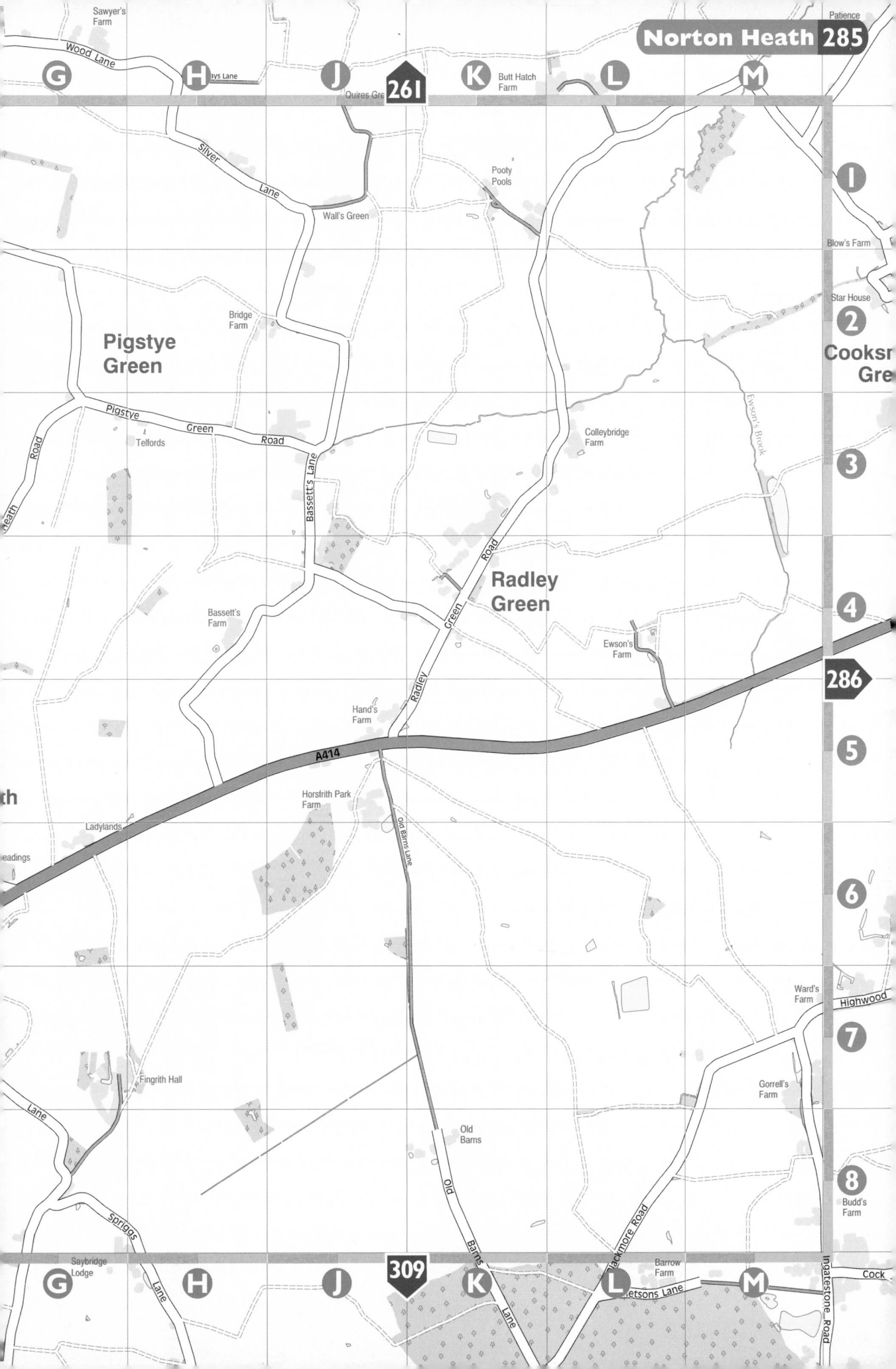

A B C D E F

262

I

Newney Green

Patience
Bridge

Green Lane
Farm

Benedict
Otes

Victoria

Blow's Farm

Star House

2 Chapel Lane

Cooksmill
Green

A414 Ongar Road

3 Little Oxney Green

Brainwood
Farm

Highwood Road

4 A414 ONGAR ROAD

285

The Causeway

Wyse's
Cottage

Lee Farm

Wyse's Road

5 Highwood Road

Highwood

Edney
Common

6 Sparrows Close

Jordan's
Farm

Fithlers Hall
Farm

Nathan's Lane

Loves
Green

Ward's
Farm

Highwood Road

County
Primary
School

7

Pool's Lane

Gorrell's
Farm

Writtle Park

8

Budd's
Farm

Coptfold
Hall

Ingatestone Lane

Cock Lane

A B C D E F

310

Furness
Farm

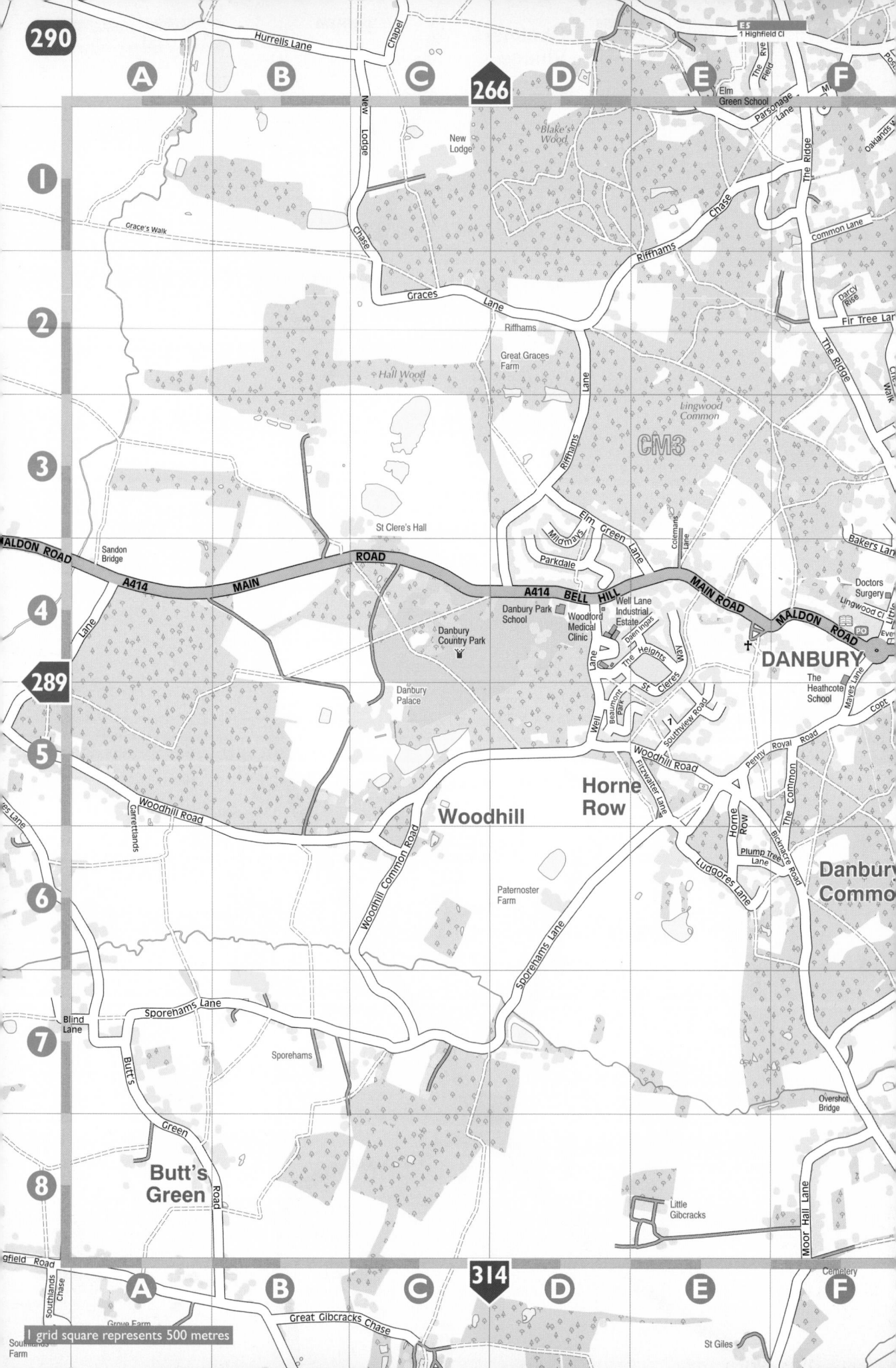

266

289

314

A **B** **C** **D** **E** **F**

1

Grace's Walk

Hurrells Lane

New Lodge

Chapel

New Lodge

Blake's Wood

1 Highfield Cl

Elm Green School

The Rye Field

Parsonage Lane

Oaklands

2

Riffhams

Chase

Common Lane

Graces Lane

Riffhams

Darcy Rise

Fir Tree Lane

The Ridge

3

Great Graces Farm

Hall Wood

Riffhams Lane

Lingwood Common

CM3

Bakers Lane

St Clere's Hall

Elm Green Lane

Colemans Lane

Cliff Walk

The Ridge

4

MALDON ROAD

Sandon Bridge

A414 MAIN ROAD

A414 BELL HILL

MAIN ROAD

MALDON ROAD

Danbury Park School

Danbury Country Park

Woodford Medical Clinic

Well Lane Industrial Estate

Mildmays

Parkdale

Well Lane

Daen Ingas

The Heights

Doctors Surgery

Lingwood Cl

DANBURY

PO

5

Danbury Palace

Woodhill Road

Garrettlands

Lane

Beaumont Park

St Cleres

Southview Road

Penny Royal Road

The Heathcote School

Mayes Lane

Copt

6

Woodhill Road

Woodhill Common Road

Woodhill

Paternoster Farm

Horne Row

Fitzwalter Lane

Sporehams Lane

Horne Row

Ludgores Lane

Plump Treece Lane

Bicknacre Road

The Common

Danbury Common

7

Blind Lane

Sporehams Lane

Butt's

Sporehams

Overshot Bridge

8

Butt's Green

Green Road

Little Gibcracks

Moor Hall Lane

Cemetery

gfield Road

Southlands Chase

Southlands Farm

Great Gibcracks Chase

St Giles

A **B** **C** **D** **E** **F**

1 grid square represents 500 metres

Woodham Walter

Runsell Green

Woodham Mortimer

Gay Bowers

Hyde Chase

MALDON

G3
1 Clarks Farm Rd
2 Fairleads

G4
1 Belvedere Rd

H4
1 Baxters
2 Belvedere Rd
3 The Hawthorns

267

315

292

Woodham Walter
C of E
Primary School

The Wilderness

Oak Farm

Lodge Farm

Warren Golf Club

Twitty Fee

Woodham Walter Common

Litchborough Park

Golf Course

Brock's Farm

Thrift Wood

Old London Road

A414

A414 CHELMSFORD ROAD

Little Meadows

Conduit

Nursery Farm

Tyndales

Hyde Woods

B1418 SOUTHEND ROAD

Little Grange

Hyde Chase

Little Meadows

MALDON ROAD

HYDE LANE

B1418

Tyndales Lane

Mill Lane

Slough Road

White Elm Farm

Klett's Farm

Bicknacre

Peartree Lane

WHITE ELM ROAD

Cock

Burnham

Gun Hill

Little Baddow

Common La

Herbage Park Road

Church Hill

Oak Farm Road

The St

Woodham Mortimer Road

Bryant's Lane

Tit Lane

Tom

Rectory

Post Office Lane

Marplits Road

Goat

Chimney Pot

House

Hackmans Lane

Birchwo

1 Brook Cl

Runsell Lane

Runsell Close

Runsell View

Jacks Lane

Dockwra La

Rumsey

Hopkirk Close

Nursery Lane

Simmonds

Armstrong Close

Hay Gn

The Leeway

Primary School

West Belvedere

Danbury Clinic

Belvedere Close

Belvedere Road

Little Fields

Hopping

Wyncroft Surgery

The Avenue

Hoynors

Mill Lane

Gay

Bowers Lane

Jubilee Rise

Pedlar's Path

Potters Close

Capons Lane

Hawks Close

Mill Fields

Meadows Green

Barley Mead

Diston

Danbury Vale

Hyde Green

Cherry Garden Lane

Landsdale

Hyde Lane

Southdown Chase

Augustine Way

Western Rd

Blenheim Close

Bicknacre Road

Elm Acres

G H J K L M

I 1 2 3 4 5 6 7 8

269   294   317

G1
1 Friars La
2 Greenways
3 New St

G3
1 Courtland Ms
2 Falcon Ms
3 Randolph Cl

H1
1 America St
2 Wantz Hvn

G3
1 Chichester Wy
2 Francis Ms
3 Mermaid Wy
4 Nelson Crs
5 Tideway

H1
1 Chelmer Ter

H4
1 Memory Cl

L2
1 Dryden Cl
2 Johnston Wy
3 Ridgeway
4 Shelley Cl
5 Spencer Cl

M2
1 Brooke Sq
2 Burns Cl
3 Drayton Cl
4 Sassoon Wy
5 Warwick Cl

Mundon

A B C D E F

I
2
293
5
6
7
8

Club

The Colliers

Collier's
Reach

Hilly
Pool Point

Osea

270

Decoy
Point

River Blackwater

West Point

Northey
Island

CM9

Southey
Creek

Cooper's
Creek

Iltney
Farm

Bramble
Hall Farm

New Hall Lane

Garlands

Blackwater
Farm

White
House
Farm

Brookmead
Farm

Wash

Brick House
Farm

Lane

Mundon
Hall

Mundon Creek

s Way

1 grid square represents 500 metres

I

The   Chase

2

CM9

Osea
Farm

Osea
Island

East Point

Stansgate Abbey
Farm

3

4

296

Mundon
Stone Point

Steeple
Creek

5

6

Lawling Creek

Mayland Creek

St Peter's   Way

Canney   Road

Canney Road

7

8

Steeple

Sea Parade

Harlow
Sailing Club

St Peter's Way

Hall

Grange
Farm

A   B   C   **272**   D   E   F

River   Blackwater

1

2

The
Stone

St Lawrence Bay

Sea View Promenade
Riverton Drive   Tinnocks Lane
St   Lawrence   Drive
Sea View

Wick Farm

**Ramsey
Island**

Mountview Crescent

Bay Vw

Main Road

Seaway
Sunny Way

gate Abbey

3

High View
PO
Beachy
Cl
Moonten Aveune

sgate Abbey

Ramsey
Marsh

Main Road

4

The Plovers

295

Beacon Hill
Farm

5

Steeple
Wick

Mott's
Farm

Brad

6

St Lawrence Hill

Stansgate Road

7

Kings
Farm

Steeple Road

Black House
Court Farm

8

St Peter's Way

Bradwell   Road

Poplars
Farm

West
Newlands

East
Newlands

Garden Flds

The   Street

Grange
Farm

A   B   C   **320**   D   E   F

1 grid square represents 500 metres

G H J **273** K L M

I

B1021

2 Orplands

3

MALDON ROAD

Maldon Road

Highfield

Bradwell Wick

Bradwell Hall

4

Bradwell Brook

298

Byhams

Mark

ROAD

5 Sampsons

al Road

BRADWELL

Blackbirds

B1021

6

East Hyde

St Lawrence Road

Brook Road

St Peter's Wa

St Lawrence

St Nicholas Road

NORTH STREET

Tilling

West Hyde

St Peter's Way

The Sq

Chance

7

Tillingham St Nicholas C of E Primary School

Casey Lane

Mill Rd

Vicarage Lane

PH

Lane

PO

Birch Rd

Stowe's Lane

Stows Farm

Chapel La

Brick House Farm

Marlborough Av Bakery Close

B1021 SOUTH ST

Tillingham Medical Centre

Reddings

Englefields

8

Grange

Southminster Road

B1021

G H J **321** K TILLINGHAM ROAD L M

Reddings

High House Farm

298

A Bodyards B East End C 274 D E F

Kingswood Court Eastend Road Bare Dud

I

WATERSIDE ROAD

High Street

Kingswood Court

St Cedds Primary School

Bradwell on Sea

Bradwell Lodge

Bacons

Hockley Close

Hockley Lane

Hockley

B1021

South St

2 Maldon Road

Maldon Road

Delameres

Bacons Chase

Maldon Road

3 Curry

Hockley Lane

Sandbeach

4 St Peter's Way

Weatherwick

297 Packards

5 Mark Road

St Peter's Way

Mark Farm

Dots & Melons

6 St Peter's Way

Marsh Road

Marshhouse Decoy Pond

St Peter's Way

Tillingham Marsh Road

Leggatts

Marsh Road

7 Chance... Mill Rd

Marsh Road

Marsh House

Casey Lane Mill Rd

Birch Rd

B1021 SOUTH ST

Tillingham Medical Centre

8 Tillingham Marshes

Grange Road

Bridgemans Farm

A B C **322** D E F

Midlands Howe

I grid square represents 500 metres

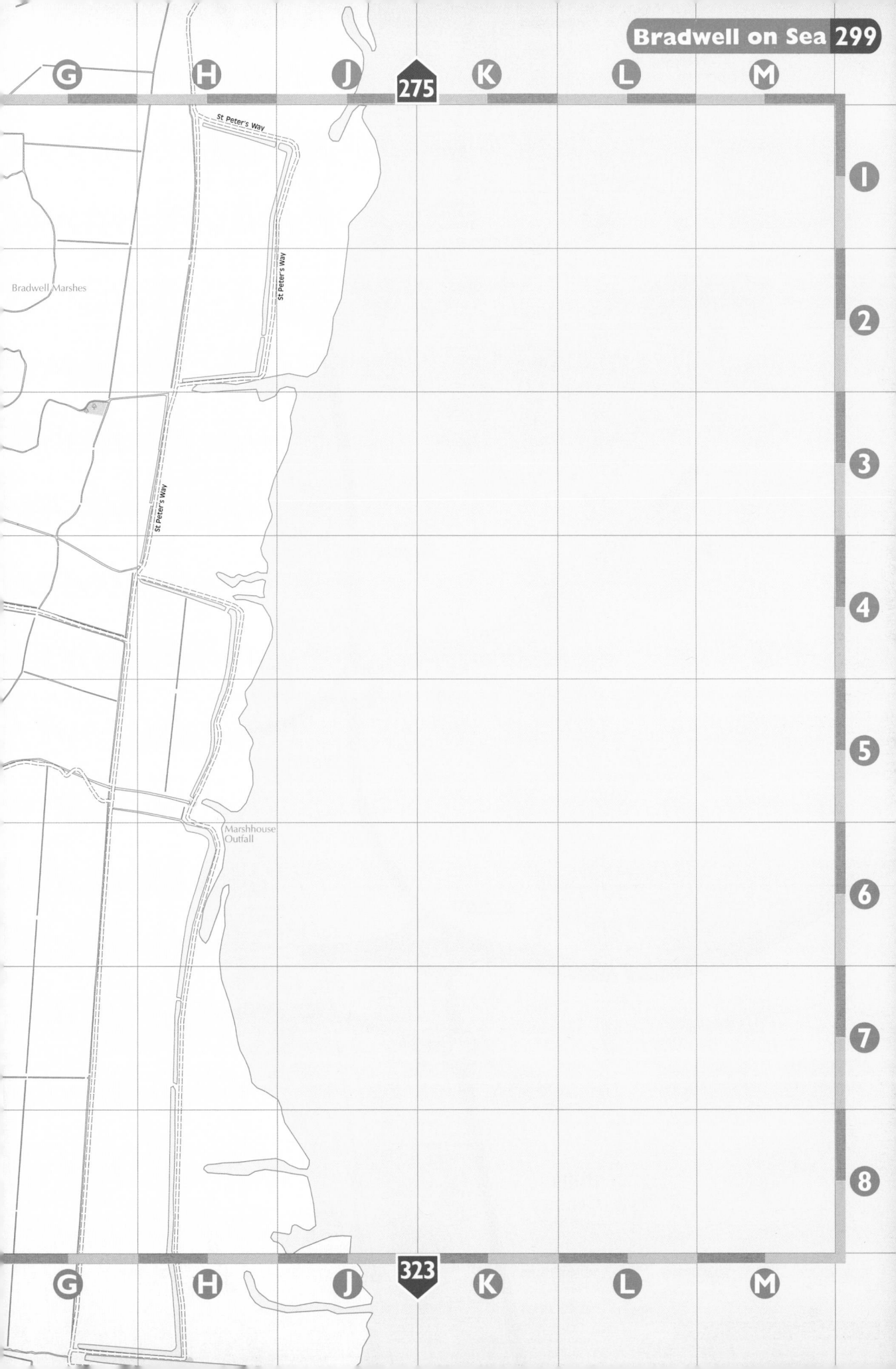

St Peter's Way

St Peter's Way

St Peter's Way

Bradwell Marshes

Marshhouse
Outfall

275

323

G H J K L M

1 2 3 4 5 6 7 8

G   H   J   **277**   K **Holyfield**   L   M

I

HOLYFIELD ROAD B194

2

Monkhams Hall

Fishers Green

Dallance House

Breaches Farm

Galleyhill Road

CROOKED MILE B194

3

Cornmill Stream

Old River Lea or Loop Road

WALTHAM ABBEY

4

Marie Gardens
Valley Close

Parklands
Drayson Close

302

Essex County

Hertfordshire County

Cheshunt Marsh

The Straits

Middle Road

Powdermill Way

Powdermill Lane

ABBEYVIEW A121

CROOKED MILE

Waltham Holy Cross Junior School

King Harold Comprehensive School

5

Amwell Court

Flagstaff Close

Beaulieu Drive

Llewelyn Surgery

The Surgery

Tudor Way

Monkswood Avenue

The Gladeway

Broomstick Hall Road

Eastbrook Road

Rounton Road

HONEY LANE

Cheshunt Station

Lea Valley Walk

Horsemill Stream

Town Hall

Waltham Holy Cross Council

Health Centre

Sun Street

Essex Co Council

FARM HILL ROAD A121

Halfhides

A121

Stonyshotts

Meadowcross

6

MANOR CROSS ROAD A121

STATION ROAD

HIGHBRIDGE STREET

Grove Court

Quaker Lane

SEWARDSTONE ROAD

Howard Business Park

Roundhills

Ruskin Avenue

Doctors Surgery

Fishers Close

Barbel Close

River Close

Queen's Drive

Gordon Road

Lea Road

Abbey Court

Mead Court

Orchard Gardens

Audrey Gardens

Howard Close

Denny Avenue

Caldbeck

Gilsland

Bryanstone Rd

Britannia Business Centre

Brook Road

Alexandra Way

Middle & Infant School

Long Croft Drive

Industrial Park

Abbey Mead Ind Park

Brooker Rd

Cartersfield Road

Cemetery

Cemetery

Pinnacles

Roundhills

Beatty Rd

New Ford Road

Cemetery

Waltham Abbey Swimming Pool

M25

7

SON AVENUE

Lower Island Way

Centre Way

Quinton Way

Lodge Lane

Beechfield Wk

East Way

8

Bridle Close

Tysoe Avenue

Black Ditch Way

Black Ditch Road

Sewardstone Way

South Way

SEWARDSTONE ROAD

Avey L

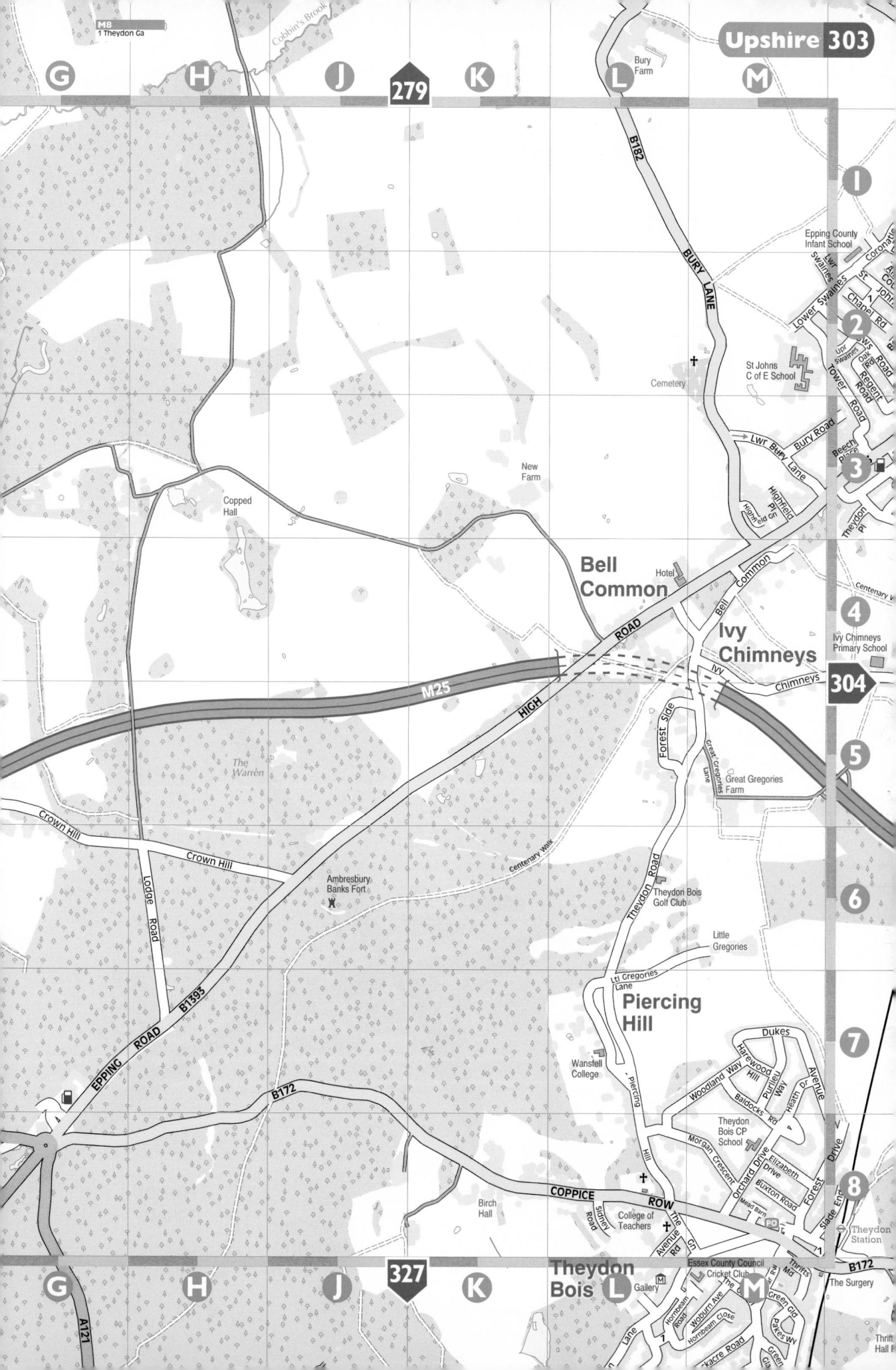

Roughtalley's
Wood

G   H   J   K   L   M

Cold Hall
Farm

281

Essex Way   Essex Way

Essex Way

Mill   Lane

I

**Colliers
Hatch**

Does
Farm

Hill Crest
Road

Cumley
Road

Epping Road

School Road

To
Hi

2

Epping Road

Freemans
Farm

Toot Hill
Golf Club

Blakes

3

Mount
Farm

Knightsland
Wood

Banks Lane

Tawney Common

Tawney Lane

Nickerlands

4

Tawney
Common

Woodhatch

306

**Mount
End**

5

Beachet
Wood

Tawney Common

Berwick   Lane

6

Berwick

Tawney Lane

Little
Tawney Hall

7

Howfields

25

Coleman's
Farm

Three Forests Way

8

✝

**Theydon
Mount**

✝

**Stapleford
Tawney**

G   H   J   329   K   L   M

Three Forests Way

✝   ney Hall

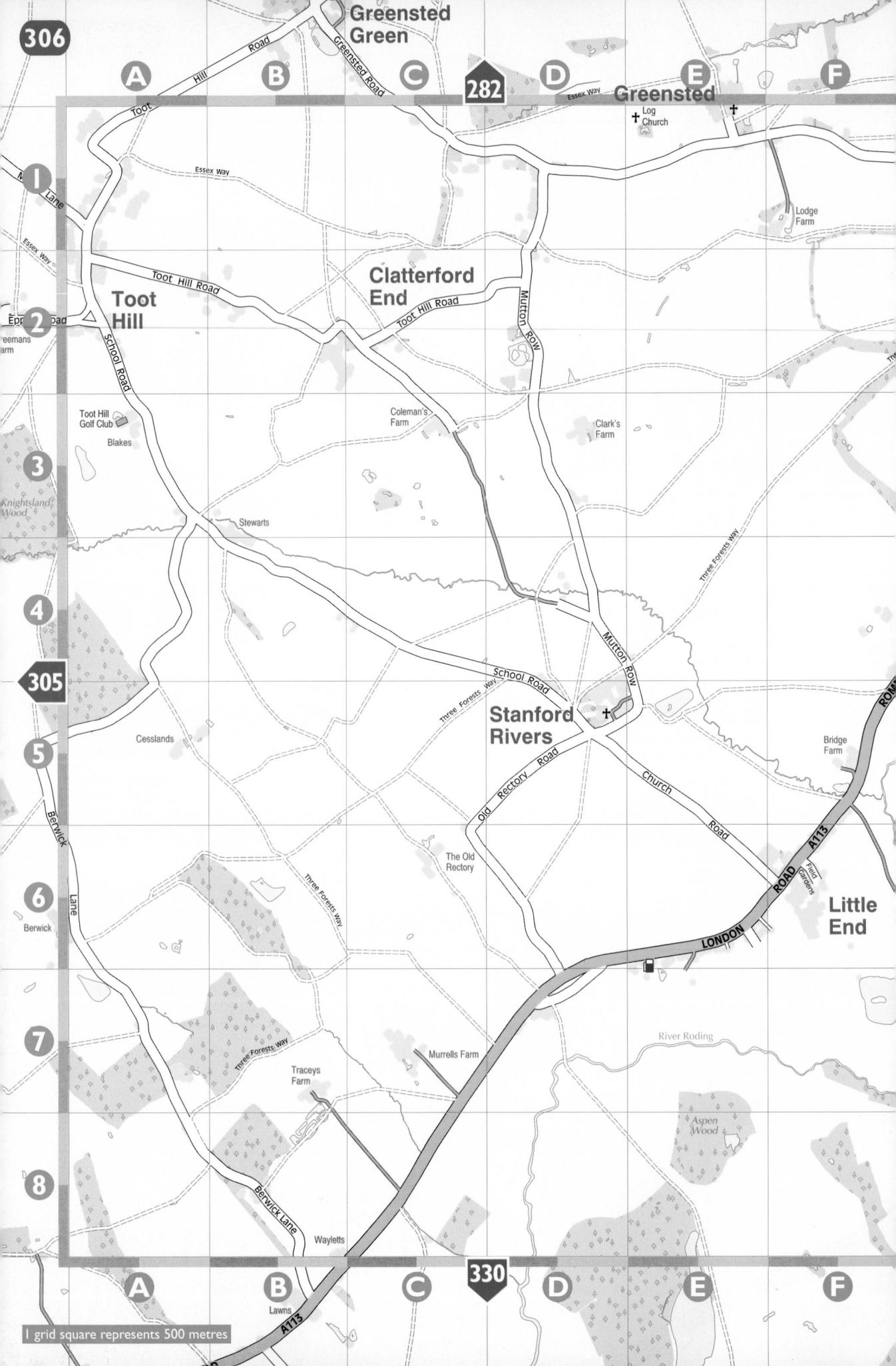

CHIPPING ONGAR

Marden Ash

Hallsford Bridge

Kelvedon

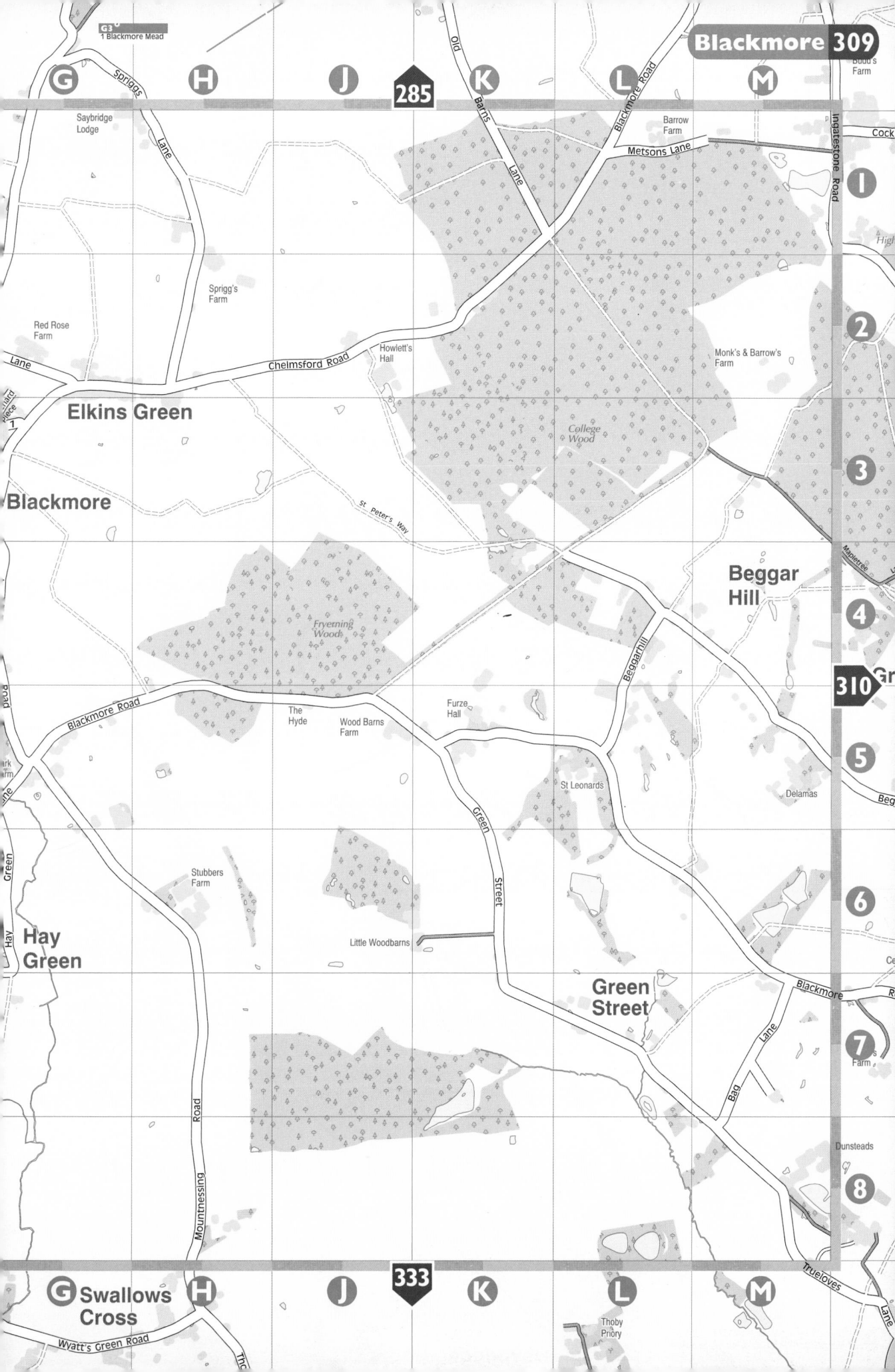

G H J **285** K L M

1 Blackmore Mead

Spriggs Lane

Saybridge Lodge

I

High

Sprigg's Farm

Red Rose Farm

Lane

Howlett's Hall

Chelmsford Road

Elkins Green

2

Monk's & Barrow's Farm

Barrow Farm

Metsons Lane

Cock

Ingatestone Road

Blackmore

St Peter's Way

College Wood

3

Mapletree Lane

Beggar Hill

Fryerning Wood

310 Gr

4

Blackmore Road

The Hyde

Wood Barns Farm

Furze Hall

Beggarhill

St Leonards

Delamas

5

Beg

Stubbers Farm

Green Street

6

Hay Green

Little Woodbarns

Green Street

Blackmore R

Ce

Bag Lane

7

Farm

Mountnessing Road

Dunsteads

8

Wyatt's Green Road

Thoby Priory

Trueloves Lane

A **B** **C** **D** **E** **F**

286

D8
1 Summerfields

D7
1 Star La

C8
1 The Furlongs

C7
1 Bakers Ms
2 Chapel Cft
3 Exley Cl
4 Market Pl
5 Mellor Cl
6 Rectory Cl

Budd's Farm

Cock Lane

Ingatestone Road

High Woods

1

2

Ivy Barns Lane

Wells & Sheds

Dawes Farm

Ivy Barns Lane

3

St Peter's Way

Handley Barns

Handley Green

Mill Green Road

Maplertree Lane

Dog Kennel Lane

Marg Prima

4

Harding's Farm

Harding's Lane

CM4

309

Mill Green

Little Hyde Lane

Little Hyde Farm

Roman Road

Church Lane

Margaretti Hall

5

Delamas

Beggarhill

Mill Lane

The Grange

Lane

Back Lane

Little

6

Fryerning

Cemetery

Little Hyde Lane

A12(T)

B1002

INGATESTONE BY-PASS

HIGH STREET

7

Blackmore Road

Dodd's Farm

Ingatestone County Infant School

Trimble Close

Wadham Close

Pemberton Avenue

Steen Fryerning Disney Close

Willow Green

School

Woodlands Close

New Road

Roman Rd

B1002

Docklands Avenue

Park Drive

Pine Drive

Stock Lane

Ingatestone & Fryerning C of E Primary School

Meads Cl

The Meads

Norton Road

Bakers La

Four Hands Gallery

A12(T)

Cameron Close

HIGH STREET B1002

Deaconene

Fairfield

Stock Lane

8

Dunsteads

Pemberton Avenue

The Furlongs

The Belvoir

Avenue Road

Barrington

Maningham Chase

Pledge Close

Wall Close

Country Drive

Station Lane

Post Office Road

The Paddocks

PO

Bell Mead

The Lynes

Ingatestone Station

INGATESTONE

Stock Lane

Trueloves Lane

The Heythrop

Whadden Chase

The Quorn

Gatehouse Mews

LC

Petre Bryant

Roman Road

The Leas

Rye Wall

Tudor Close

B10

334

A **B** **C** **D** **E** **F**

Heybridge

G

H

J

287

K

L

M

I

Margaretti

A12(T)

Lodge Farm

2

River Wid

3

Whitesbridge Lane

Swan Lane

Crondon
Hall

312

Bearman's
Farm

A1016

A12(T)

White's Place

Durrant's
Farm

Maldon Road

Molehill
Common

Margaretting

Wantz Road

Penny's Lane

B1002

Orton Close

Parsonage Lane

Peacocks

School

Canterburys

LC

Margaretting
Tye

St. Peter's Way

4

5

Crondon
Park

6

St. Peter's
Way

Fristling
Hall

St. Peter's Way

Swan Lane

Crondon Park Lane

7

St. Peter's Way

Ramsey
Tyrells

Tye
Green

Stock Road

8

Greenwoods
Stock

Falkner
Close

Birch Lane

Myin Meadow

Swan Lane

Dakyn Drive

Stock C of E
Primary Sch

High Street

Common Road

Garden
End

Valentin

G

H

J

335

K

L

M

Back

Vernon Corner

Brookman
Road

Hightrees

School Lane

B1007

Bakers
Field

Mill Road

Thornton
Place

PO

The
Square

Common Lane

The
Paddock

The

A   B   C   **288**   D   E   F

1

Lodge Farm

Running Mare Lane

Thriftwood School

Skinner's Lane

1 Twitten La

Coat Hall Lane

B1007 STOCK ROAD

PO

Walters Close

Roughtons

Lane

Centenary Circle

Bekeswell Lane

Pyms Road

Watchouse Road

Grey Ladys

Cannon

Pavitt Meadow

Rignals

Margaretting Road

Chelmsford District Council

Birches Walk

Pyms Road

The Street

Chaplin Close

The Limes

James Croft

Galleywood County Infant School
St Michaels C of E Junior School

Barnard Road

Home Mead

Galleywood

Baddow Park

Mill Hill

London Hill

Galleywood Common

Wood Farm

B1007

Ponds Road

Rous Chase

Badgers

Well

Moretons

Barnard Road

Lower Green

Lower Green

Centenary Circle

2

A12(T)

Margaretting Road

Avila Chase

Pyne Gate

Colvin Chase

Milligans Chase

Centenary Circle

A12(T)

3

A12(T)

Bakers Lane

Gay Bowers Farm

4

Oldbarn

B1007 ROAD

Little Peverels

311

Temple Farm

5

Forest Lodge

STOCK ROAD

Ship Road

West Hanningfield Hall

Hall Lane

West Hanningfield Road

6

Forest Wood

Foxborough Chase

Wantz Corner

Ship Road

7

Downham Road

Foxborough Farm

Kents Farm La

Lower Stock Road

B1007 STOCK ROAD

Keelings

Lower Stock Road

Slough House Farm

St. Peter's Way

8

Greenwoods Stock

Falkner Close

Birch Lane

St. Peter's

Steel's Farm

336

Seamans Lane

Seamans Lane

The Paddock

Common Road

Myrrh Meadow

Meadowgate

Mill Lane

Leatherbottle Hill

Garden End

Valentines

A   B   C   **336**   D   E   F

Howe
Green

G7
1 Middlemead
2 Middle Mead Cl

G · H · J · 289 · K · L · M

Brook Farm

Centenary Circle

Great
Mascalls

Brook Lane

A12(T)

Little and Great Sir Hughes Lane

Little
Sir Hughes

**Little
Mascalls**

Great
Sir Hughes

Peveril
Hall

W Hanningfield Road

Tanfield
Tye

Chalklands

Alexander
Mews

East Hanningfield Road

Southlands
Chase

Grove

Southlands
Farm

SOUTHEND ROAD

Old Southend Road

A130

Downhouse

Little Claydons
Farm

Bushy
Wood

314

St Peter's Way

Hill Farm

Patten's Farm

Tinsley Farm

Link
House Farm

Blind Lane

St Peter's Way

A130

St Peters C of E
School

Helmons Lane

Church Road

Church La

West Hanningfield

Middlemead

Barnard's Farm

Canon
Barns

2

1

G · H · J · 337 · K · L · M

Middlemead

A13

I

2

3

4

5

6

7

8

Rudley Green

292

A B C D E F

Cock Clarks

Birchwood Road

Hackmans Lane

Scotts Farm

Lodge Lane

ROAD B1010

New Hall

Hazeleigh Hall

St Peter's Way

Purleigh CP School

Hawthornes

Westerings 7

Callowood Croft

PO

The Glebe

Church Hill

Purleigh

1 Corporation Farm

St Peter's Way

Birchwood Road

Pump Lane

Mill Lane

Mill Hill

Walton Hall

Chapel Lane

Howegreen

Flambird's Chase

315

Hackmans Lane

Great Whitmans

Farther Howeg

Flambirds Farm

Howe Green Road

Hackmans Lane

Great Canney

Three Rivers Golf Club

Cold Norton

Charity Farm

Hagg Hill

Golf Course

Stow Maries

Hawe's Wood

Stow Road

The Street

Woodham Road

PH

Church Lane

Honey Pot Lane

Crows Lane

Wellinditch

340

A B C D E F

1 grid square represents 500 metres

Hackmans Lane

G5
1 Henney Cl

G   H   J   **293**   K   L   M

I

Blind Lane

Purleigh
Wash Farm

Blind Lane

Mundon

LANE   B1010

Simmonds   Lane

St Peter's Way

Sparrow
Wycke

St Peter's Way

West
Chase

2

Purleigh   Street

Eastcroft

B1010

Clock
House

Wood Lane

Limbourne
Park Farm

St Peter's Way

Roundbush   Road

Parsonage Chase

FAMBRIDGE   ROAD

Burnham   Road

Parsonage
Farm

3

Roundbush

Maldon   Road

Hale's
Farm

4

St Andrew's
Farm

318

Old
Redgate Farm

Mayfa...
Indus...
Estate

Thatcher's
Croft

5

Cherry Blossom Lane

Crown Road

Victoria Road

Junction   Road

Green Trees   Avenue

Station   Road

1

Clarke Rise

...tchingdon   Road

Ferris Avenue

Station
Crescent

County
Primary
School

Burnham Avenue

Purleigh
Grove

PO

Crofton

B1018   COLD   NORTON   ROAD

B1010

6

en

The Fairways

FAMBRIDGE ROAD

Newport
Avenue

Norton
Hall

St Stephens Road

7

Purleigh
Barns

FAMBRIDGE   ROAD

London
Hayes

8

G   H   J   **341**   K   L   M

Little
Cooks

B1010

...ER BURNHAM ROAD   B1012

Marsh House
Farm

LOWER BURNHAM ROAD   B1010

A   B   C   294   D   E   F

1

Mundon Hall

St Peter's Way

2

May

Limbourne Park Farm

Lawling Hall

3

Butterfields

4

317

Mayfair Industrial Estate

Brook Hall

5

Ramsey Chase
Latchingdon C of E Primary School
Ludgrove
Meadow Way
Bridgemans Green
Steeple Road

THE STREET   B1018   Buchanan Way
Canary Close
St Michaels Close
Snorenam Gardens
Heritage Way
Lawlinge Road

Good Hares

6   B1018   BURNHAM ROAD   B1018

Latchingdon

B1018

Red Lyons Farm

7

Snoreham Hall

Rectory Lane

London Hayes

8

Scatterbrook Farm

Rosedale Farm

A   B   C   342   D   E   F

Tyle Hall

B1010

River View

H8
1 Summerdale

G   H   J   295   K   L   M

Steeple

St Peter's Way

Hall Farm

Grange Farm

The Street

Garden Fids

I

Sea View Parade
Harlow Sailing Club
Nipsells Chase
North Drive
Promenade
Sea Green Av

Nipsells Farm

St Peter's Way

2

Dock Road

Worcester
Orchard Drive
Derby Cl
Bramley Way
Mayland Branch Surgery
Katonia Av
Barrett
Bramble Gdns
Hillcrest
Nipsells Chase

Mill Road

Mayland

3

Maylandsea CP School
The Drive
Wembley Avenue
Princes Avenue
Smiths Av
Curlew Av
Teal Av
Tern Cl
Drake Av
Heron Way
Green Cl
Mayland Cl
Mallards
Industrial Estate
Mayland Gn

Maldon Road

Lower Farm

Steeple Road
Woodland Park Chase

Grange Avenue

Highlands

320

4

Highlands Hill

5

Green Lane

Mayland Hill

Mayland Hall

6

Warden's Farm

Bovill Uplands

Mayland Court

BURNHAM ROAD
Garden Close
PO
(SUMMERHILL)
Lower Chase

7

SOUTHMINSTER ROAD   BUTTON'S HILL   B1018

Joyce's Farm

Dairy Farm

Dairy Farm Road

Highfield Rise
7
Woodlands
Austral Way
Oakwood Court
Upper Chase

8

The Endway

High House

G   A. horne   J   343   K   L   M

FAMBRIDGE ROAD   BURNHAM   ROAD   The Endway

Althorne Lodge

A B C 296 D E F

E8
1 The Brambles
2 The Wellingtons

E7
1 Elsden Cha
2 Regents Cl

C7
1 Queen St

West
Newlands

East
Newland

Garden
The Street

Bradwell
Road

Poplars
Farm

Grange
Farm

†

1

Batt's
Farm

Batt's Road

Asheldham   Brook

2

Badnocks
Farm

3

Park
Farm

4
Foxhall
Farm

Foxhall Road

319

Lunendales

Steeple Road

Sheepcotes

5

Squeaks
House

Sheepcotes Lane

CRIPPLEGATE

6
Mayland
Court

Northend

Homefield

NORTH END

New Moor
Close

Queenborough Rd

Pump Md Cl

Spells Cl

Coombe Road Ely

Combe Road

NORTH STREET

Chard Rd

New Moor Crs

Prior's Way

Cherry
Orchard

Hallmark
Industrial Est

7
B1018 SOUTHMINSTER ROAD SCOTTS HILL

Steeple
Road

Steeple Mdw

Crown Way

Dow Ct

Crown

Hillside Road

Rupert Rd

Munsons Av

Queenborough Rd

B1021 NORTH STREET

Station Road

The Maltings

The Malti
Industrial

Scott's Farm

QUEEN STREET

PANTILE
HILL

HIGH STREET

PO

Falcon Road

Wonston Road

House St

SOUTHMINSTER

Southfield

Southminster
Medical Cen

The Chase

St Leonards C of E
Va Junior School

Southminster
Infant School

Southminster
Station

Tattersalls

Hall Road

Hall Road
Industrial Est

Caidge Farm

Kings Croft

Kings Road

Lavender

Primrose Walk

Dukes Avenue

Princes Av

Meadow
Vicarage

Smyatts

Rose Drive

Buttercup Way

8

Endway

High House

High House

A B 344 D E F

Filey Road

Old Heath Road

Gleaner Road

Scarborough Road

Scalby Road

Whitby Road

BURNHAM ROAD

sborough Chase

Goldsands Road

G H J K L M

297

I

Grange

Reddings

Reddings

TILLINGHAM ROAD B1021

Hill Farm

High House Farm

Bacons

Glebe Lane

2

Moynes Farm

Asheldham Grange

Rushes Lane

TILLINGHAM ROAD

B1021

Manor Road

Glebe Farm

Keelings Lane

3

Manor

Dengie

Keelings

Keelings Road

Cemetery

Landwick Farm

Landwick Lane

SOUTHMINSTER ROAD

Hall Road

New Hall Farm

4

Asheldham

CMO

322

Oldmoor

5

TILLINGHAM ROAD

Asheldham Brook

6

Newmoor

North Wycke

7

8

Wraywick Farm

G H J K L M

345

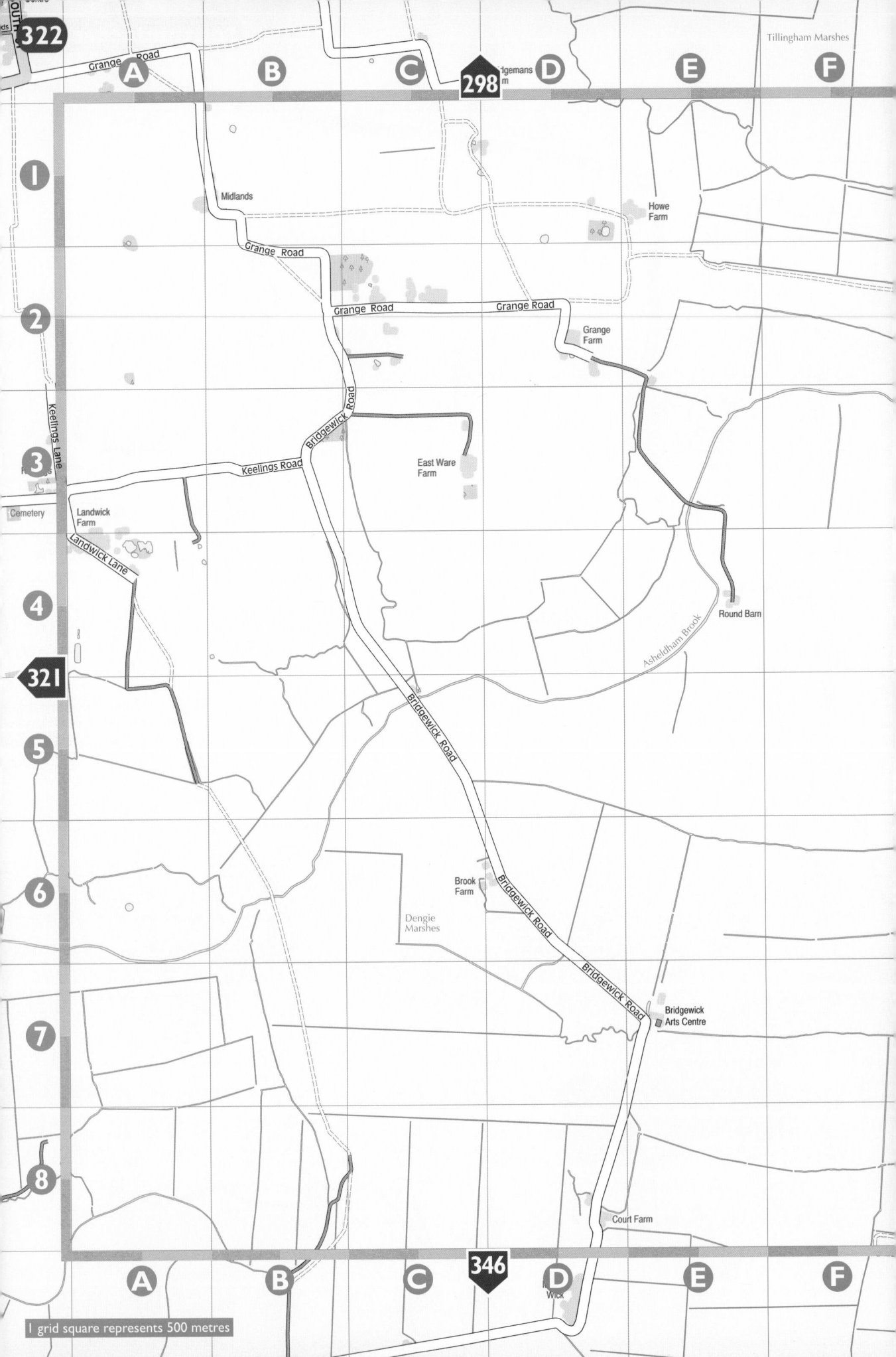

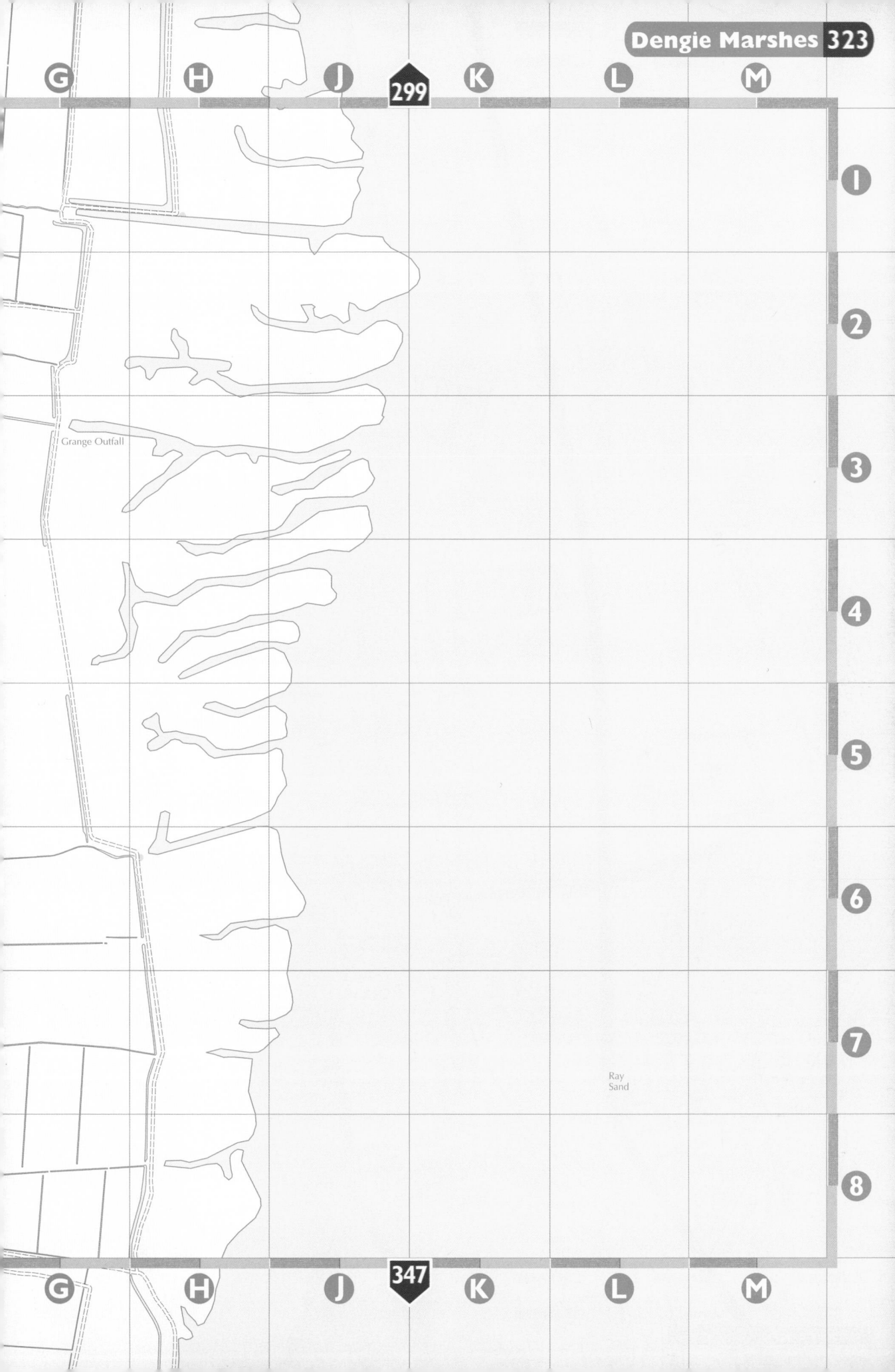

Grange Outfall

Ray
Sand

G8 1 Cranleigh Gdns

H2 1 Garden Wy

H3 1 Firs Dr
2 Monkchester Cl

H4 1 Maple Ga
2 Roundmead Cl

H5 1 Thistle Mead

G **H** **J** **303** **K** **L** **M**

Theydon Bois

Theydon Gallery

College of Teachers

Essex County Council Cricket Club

The Surgery

Thrift Hall

I

Ripley Grange

Debden Green

2

Debden Road

Debden Lane

Ripley View

Davenant Foundation School

Theydon Park Road

3

Broadstrood

Camplions

The Beacons

Stanmore Way

Clay's Lane

Goldings Rise

Bracken Close

Cleland Path

Wren Ter

Grosvenor Drive

Chester Road

Castell Road

Hereward Green

Willingale Road

The Hereward County School

The Summit

Whitakers Way

Hill Way

Wroths Pth

Stony Pth

Goldings

Lower Rd

Goldings Road

Coles Green

England's Lane

Cotford Rd

Grosvenor Close

Chandler's Rd

Oak Tree

Mowbrey Gdns

Collard Ave

Audley Gdns

4

Harwater

Millsmead Way

Sedley Rise

Dr Goldings Hill Clnc

PO

Hillcroft

Hillyfields

Brady Avenue

Goldingham Avenue

Thatchers Cl

Manson Drive

Jessel Drive

St John Fisher RC Junior School

328

Ashfields

Grasmere Close

Essex County Council

Marjorams Avenue

The Greens Close

Pyrles Lane

Fairmeads

Mead Of Cecil

Colebrook Lane

Burney

Manock Drive

Etheridge Road

Willingale Road

Rookwood Ave

Rockwood Gdns

5

St John's Road

The Heights

Purlip Hill

CHURCH HILL

RECTORY

Doctors Surgery

Lawton Road

Convers Way

Harvey Gdns

Appleton

Paley Gardens

Westall Road

Rochford Green

Kingsley Road

Rockwood

A121

Church Lane

Cemetery

Hill Top Close

Roundmead Avenue

Wellfields

Newplace

Hatfields

Nursery Cl

Sandford Ave

Doubleday Rd

Path

The Thomas Willingale GM School

The Broadway

Langston Rd

6

Doctors Surg

The Uplands

Loughton Cricket Club

Clerks Piece

Eleven Acre Rise

West View

Whitehills

Burney Way

Newmans Lane

Elmores

LANE

A1168

Loughton Hall Clinic

Essex County Council

Barrington Gn

Vere Road

Fort Road

Burton Rd

Epping Forest District Council

PO

Torrington Drive

Lethall Road

Prospect Business Park

Sparleleaze

Trap's Hill

Rowans

Wy

Hill

Border's

Special School

Colson Path

Honeycroft Gdns

Barrington

Rochford Gn

Rochford Green

Business Centre

Loughton

Shelley Grove

Doctors Surgery

Alderton Hall Lane

Greenfields

Deepdene

Roding Valley High School

Honeycroft

Deepdene

Colson Rd

Debden Station

7

Alderton Hill

The Lindens

Doctors Surgery

Alderton County Junior & Infant School

Parkmead

Bushfields

Poundfield Road

Chequers

Road

Lushes Ct

Oakwood Hill Industrial Estate

Oakwood Hill

Debden Sports Club

Epping Forest District Council

River Roding

A113

ABRIDGE ROAD

Hogarth Reach

Barncroft Rd

Monksgrove

Marie Cl

Oakwood Hill Industrial Est

Three Forests Way

M11

Junction 5

8

Stonards Hill

Alderton Hill

Oakwood Way

River Road

Highwood Lane

CHIGWELL LANE

Pudding Lane

Valley Close

Makern Gardens

Kenilworth Gardens

Southern Drive

PO

South Vw Road

Three Forests Way

Avondale Drive

Broomfield

Drayton Av

Home Farm

G **L1** 1 Hornbeam Rd

L5 1 Austen Cl

H **K3** 1 Hereward Gn
2 Mowbrey Gdns

J **349** **K** **J5** 1 Beech Cl

J7 1 Longcroft Rl
2 Lushes Rd

L **L4** 1 Colebrook Gdns
2 Swanshope

M **H7** 1 Barncroft Cl

J3 1 Pyrles Gn

Theydon
Mount

Stapleford
Tawney

G **H** **J** 305 **K** **L** **M**

I

Great
Tawney Hall

Three Forests Way

Shales
More

Suttons
Manor
Clinic

2

Skinners Farm

Epping Lane

Tawney Lane

London Rd

Suttons

Suttons Manor
Clinic

3

Lee Forests Way

Arnolds Farm

ONGAR ROAD A113

London Rd

M25

**Passingford
Bridge**

Albyns Lane

River Roding

4

Hammonds
Farm

Bons Farm

Albyns

330

Havering
Cricket
Club

5

B175

**Curtis
Green**

Church Lane

RM4

6

Curtis Mill Lane

Stapleford
Abbotts County
Primary School

7

STAPLEFORD ROAD

Stapleford
Hall Farm

Hook Lane

Grove
House

Gutteridge Lane

8

Hook Lane

High
House Farm

**Stapleford
Abbotts**

Road

Knolls Hill
Farm

G **H** **J** 351 **K** **L** Brook
Indust.
Estate **M**

Bournebridge Lane

**Nuper's
Hatch**

330

A B C **306** D E F

I

LONDON ROAD A113 Wayletts Lawns

Berwic

Suttons Manor Cl

2 Mitchells Farm Shonks Mill Road Rose Hall Farm Navestock Hall Farm Shonks Mill Road

† Navestock Hall Farm

3 Howletts Hall Church Road

4 Mill Lane **Navestock Heath** Murthering Lane

329 Havering Cricket Club Old Road **Sabine's Green**

5 Loft Hall

Curtismill Green M25

6 Brook Farm **Horseman Side**

Curtis Mill Lane Jenkins Farm

7 Murthering Lane

Tyseahill Farm Curtis Mill Lane Horseman Side **Waterhales**

8 The Paddocks M25

Watton's Green

A Tysea Hill B C **352** Navesto Comm D E F

Goatswood

Asheton Farm

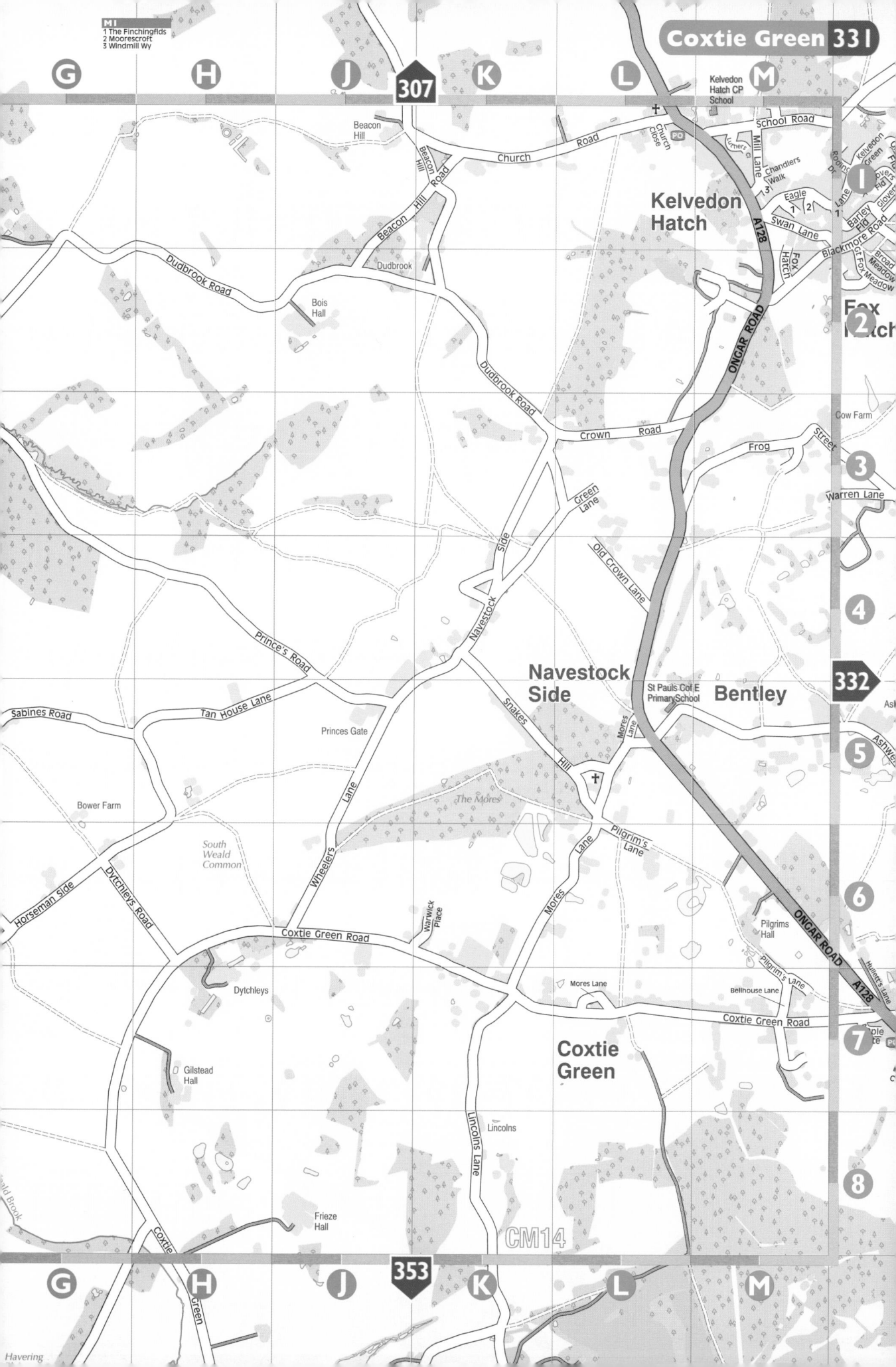

M1
1 The Finchingfids
2 Moorescroft
3 Windmill Wy

G   H   J   **307**   K   L   M

Kelvedon
Hatch CP
School

Beacon
Hill

Church   Road

Church
Close

PO

School Road

Chandlers
Walk

**Kelvedon
Hatch**

Beacon Hill

Beacon Hill Road

Swan Lane

Eagle

Barley Fld

Blackmore Road

Broad
Meadow

Ct Fox
Meadow

Meadow

Dudbrook Road

Dudbrook

**Fox
Hatch**

Bois
Hall

Dudbrook Road

Cow Farm

Crown   Road

Frog

Street

Green
Lane

Warren Lane

Old Crown Lane

Navestock Side

Navestock Side

Prince's Road

**Navestock
Side**

St Pauls Cof E
Priman School

Bentley

332

Sabines Road

Tan House Lane

Princes Gate

Snakes Hill

Mores Lane

Ashwe

Ash

Lane

Bower Farm

The Mores

Wheelers Lane

South
Weald
Common

Pilgrim's
Lane

Mores Lane

Pilgrim's Lane

Pilgrims
Hall

ONGAR ROAD

Horseman Side

Dytchleys Road

Coxtie Green Road

Warwick
Place

Mores Lane

Bellhouse Lane

Pilgrim's Lane

A128

Dytchleys

Mores Lane

Coxtie Green Road

Huletts Lane

Gilstead
Hall

**Coxtie
Green**

Lincolns Lane

Lincolns

CM14

Coxtie Green

Frieze
Hall

d Brook

Havering

332

A B C **308** D E F

C1
1 Steeple Wy

B8
1 Darlington Ct
2 Hazelwood Gdns

A7
1 Willowdene

A1
1 Littlebury Ct
2 Lyndale
3 Matching Fld
4 Short Cft

1

Chandlers Walk
Eagle

Kelvedon Green
Roding Dr

Glovers Fld
Glovers Fld

Blackmore Road
Place Farm

Hallam

Church Lane

Rectory Chase

Brook Lane

Peartree Green

Brook La

Pettits Lane

Swan Lane
Fox Hatch

Barley Fld
Stocks
Elmtree Av
Stocksfield
Short Cft
Briarwood
Blackmore Road
Broad Meadow

Stocks Lane

Place Farm

Doddinghurst
C of E
Junior School

Doddinghurst
County
Infant School

Middle Green
PO

Harpers

Parsonage
Field

2

**Fox
Hatch**

Broad Meadow Lane

Dagwood

Lane

Peartree Lane
Lime Grove

Apple Tree
Crescent
Willow
Close

Peartree Close

Park
Meadow

Mountnessing Lane

Doddinghurst Road

Dagwood
Farm

Days Lane

Park
Farm

Park
Wood

CM15

3

Street

Cow Farm

Warren
Warren Lane

Cowes Farm

Solid Lane

America
Farm

Doddinghurst Road

4

Wishfields
Farm

Sumner's
Farm

331

Ashwells

**Crow
Green**

Hall Lar

5

Ashwells Road

Well
Lane

Days Lane

Brickhouse
Farm

6

Pilgrims
Hall

ONGAR ROAD
A128

Pilgrims Lane

Hillcrest
Lane

Green Road

Green Road

Crow Gn Lane

Lascelles
Close

Alderton Close

Hall Lane

Beads

**Pilgrims
Hatch**

Canterbury
Tye Hall

7

Apple
Gate
PO

Georges Drive

Crow

Ash Close
Vale Close
Pilgrims Close
Orchard Lane

Catherine Close

Priory Close

Danes Wy
Danes Way

Lancaster
Gloucester Rd
Cornwall Rd
Daffodil Av
Tulip Cl
Iris Cl

Honeysuckle Cl
Lilac Close

Magnolia Way

Doddinghurst Road

A12(T)

A1

Danbury
Close

The Firs

Larchwood
Gardens

King George's

Balmoral Road
PO

Harewood
Rd
Sandringham
Rd
Albany
Rd

Wisteria
Lorraine Rd
Crown
Lavender Av

8

Langtons

Broomwood Gdns
Ongar Rd

County Junior
& Infant
School

Marlborough
Road

Kensington
Road

Osborne
Road
Windsor Rd

Clarence Road
Carisbrooke
Rd
Elizabeth
Rd

Bishop's
Rd
Philip Cl

Viking Way

A12(T)

Hurst

St Kilda's Rd

Sawyer's
Hall

Robin Hood

Hedley

St Helens
Junior
School

Shenfield Rd

Shenfield

A B C **354** D E F

C7
1 Heather Cl
2 Mimosa Cl

Warescot Rd
Kimpton Av
Sawyer's

1 grid square represents 500 metres

Swallows Cross

Mountnessing

Hutton

J8
1 Willow Cl

K7
1 Barnston Wy
2 Oakland Gdns

K8
1 Beaumont Gdns
2 Bradwell Gn
3 Felstead Cl
4 Fielding Wy
5 Horksley Gdns
6 Normanhurst
7 Paglesfield
8 Waltham Cl

G H J 309 K L M

I
2
3
4
334
5
6
7
8

G H J 355 K L M

M8
1 Ardleigh Gdns
2 Magdalen Gdns
3 Willingale Cl

M3
1 Hope Cl

L8
1 Carswell Cl

L7
1 Carpenter Pth
2 Wild Cl
3 Woodside Cl

334

INGATESTONE

Heybridge

Padham's Green

1 grid square represents 500 metres

G   H   J   313   K   L   M   I

2

Lacey's Farm

Bromley Lodge

Hanningfield Reservoir

Middlemead

Hall Farm

Church Lane

South Hanningfield Road

South Hanningfield

Coalhill

Marks La

Chalk Street

3

4

338

Hawkswood Road

Warren Road

Warren Road

Warren Rd

Runningwell

5

Brock Hill

Flemings Farm

6

Brock Hill Road

Sudbury Road

Sudbury's Farm

School Road

7

The Grange

Brock Hill

Castledon Road

De Beauvoir Farm

Downham Hall

The Greenway

Waverley Crs

Lindon Road

Downham Road

Brock Hill

Brock Hill Dr

South Hanningfield Way

Meadow Lane

8

G   H   J   359   K   L   M

Delmar Gdns

Grange Road

Cariton Road

Station Rd

Swallow Rd

Lapwing Rd

Church End

Viking Wy

Tidworth Av

Runwell Parish

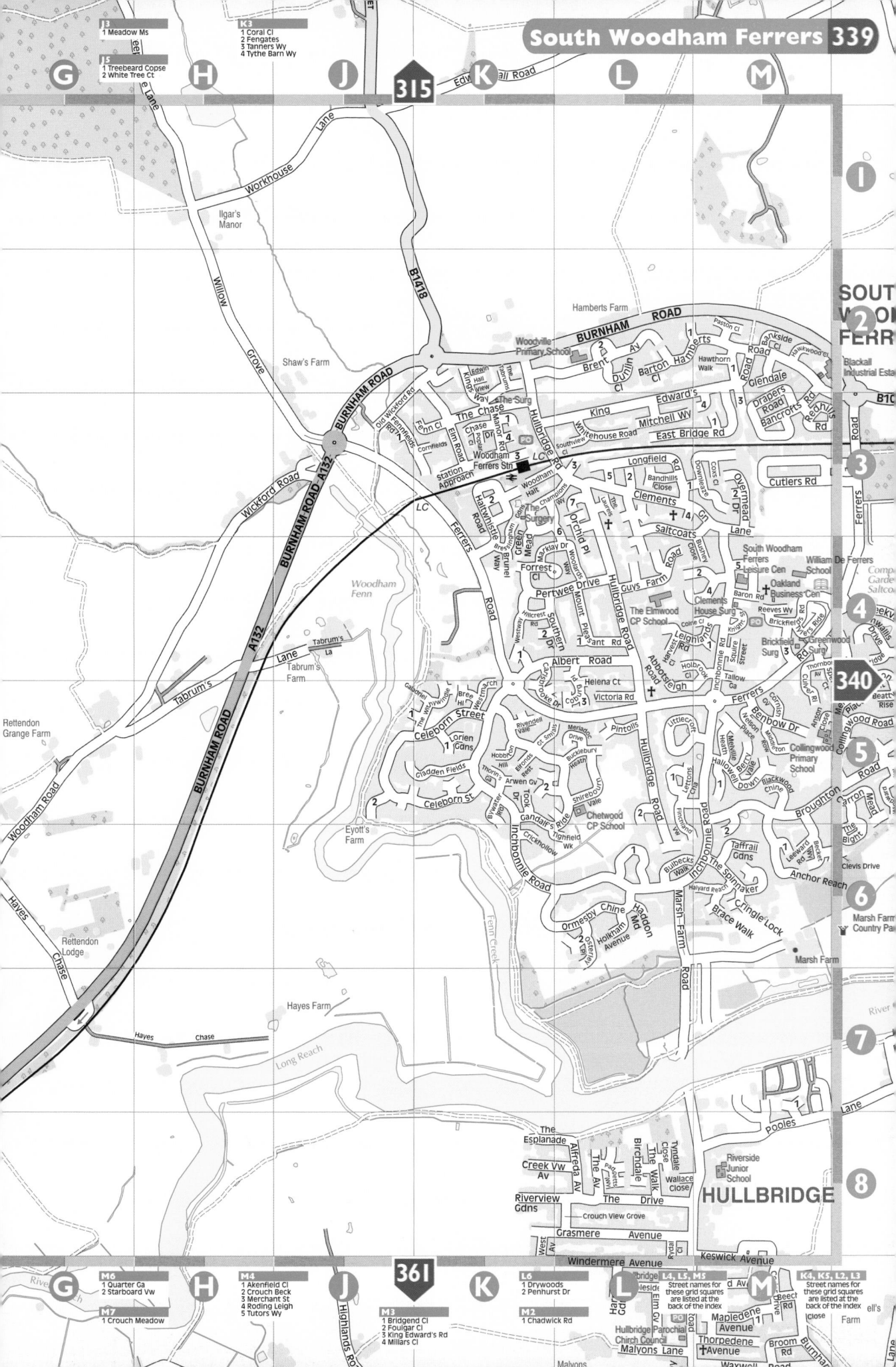

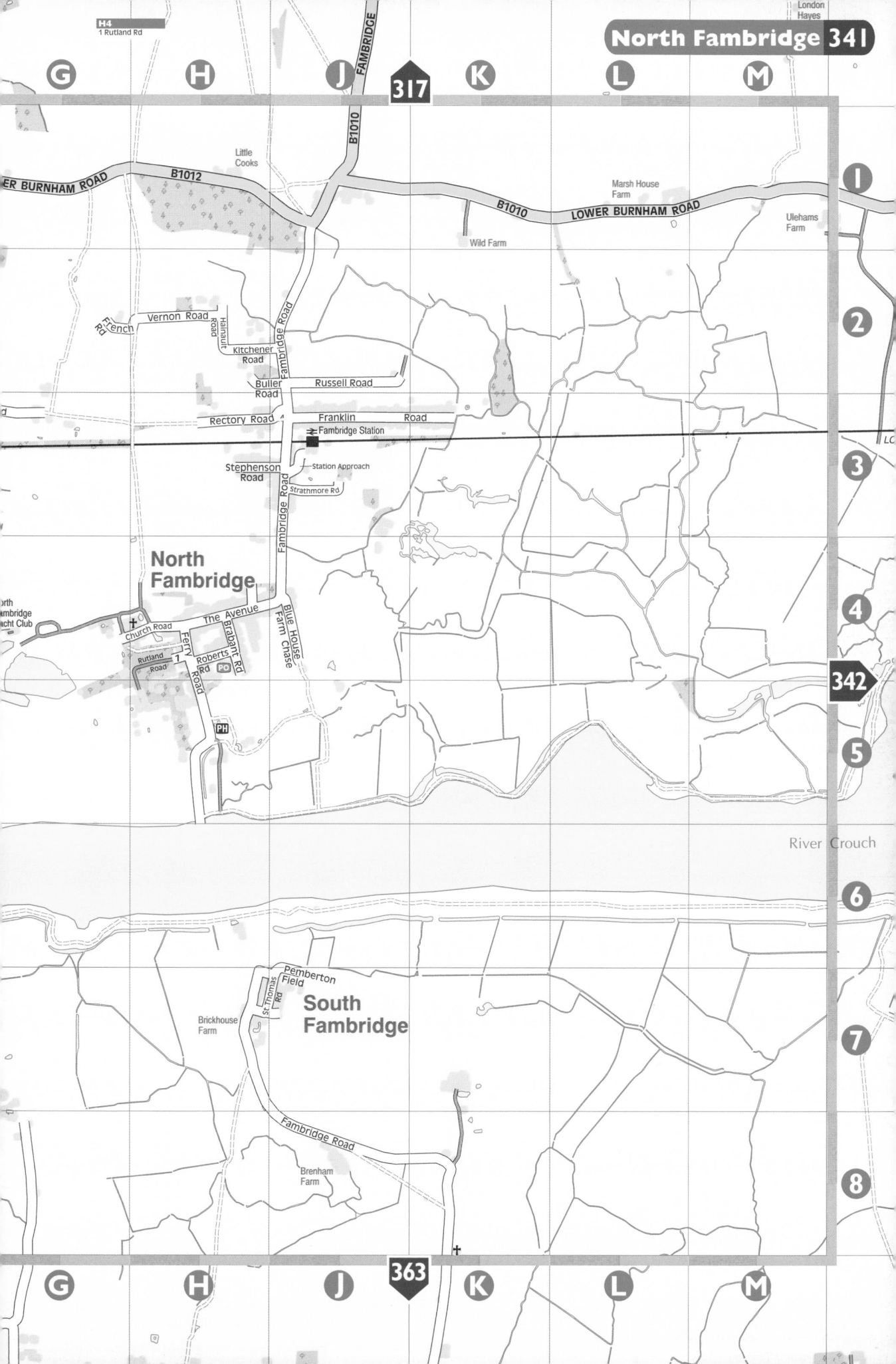

G   H   J   K   L   M

317

FAMBRIDGE

B1010

H4
1 Rutland Rd

Little Cooks

ER BURNHAM ROAD   B1012

Marsh House Farm

B1010   LOWER BURNHAM ROAD

Ulehams Farm

I

Wild Farm

2

French Rd   Vernon Road

Hainault Road

Fambridge Road

Kitchener Road

Buller Road   Russell Road

Rectory Road   Franklin   Road

Fambridge Station

3

LC

Stephenson Road   Station Approach

Strathmore Rd

Fambridge Road

North Fambridge

4

North Fambridge Yacht Club

Church Road

The Avenue   Brabant Rd

Blue House Farm Chase

342

Ferry Road

Rutland Road   1

Roberts Rd   PO

PH

5

River Crouch

6

Pemberton Field

St Thomas Rd

Brickhouse Farm

South Fambridge

7

Fambridge Road

Brenham Farm

8

G   H   J   **363**   K   L   M

London Hayes

A　B　C　**318**　D　E　F

Scatterbrook
Farm

Rosedale
Farm

Tyle
Hall

Chestnut Farm

Summerdale
Road

Chestnut Farm Drive

B1010

River View
Terrace

Ulehams
Farm

1

Stamfords Farm

2

Althorne
Station

LC

3

Bridgemarsh Creek

4

341

Bridgemarsh
Island

5

Landsend
Point

Easter
Reach

River Crouch

6

Roach Valley Way

7

Upper
Raypitts
Farm

Roach Valley Way

8

Pudsey
Hall

A　Pudsey　B　C　**364**　D　E　Cays Lane　F

Canewdon

Roach Valley Way

Butts Paddock

G H J **319** K L M

I

2

3

4

5

344

6

7

8

G H J **365** K L M

Highfield Rise

Highlands

Austral Way

Oakwood Court

Upper Chase

Barnes Farm

Althorne

FAMBRIDGE ROAD

BURNHAM ROAD

The Endway

The Endway

High House

Althorne Lodge

Station Road

LC

LC

Bridgemarsh Lane

Andrews Farm

Stoke's Hall

B1010

MALDON ROAD

Elm Farm

Pinners

Creeksea Lane

Ostend

Creeksea Hall

Burnham On Crouch Golf Club Ltd

LC

Black Point

Ferry Road

River Crouch

Cliff Reach

Ferry Road

Creeksea

Ferry Road

White House

Old Fleet

River Crouch

Lion Wharf

Creeksea Ferry Road

Ferry Road

Creeksea

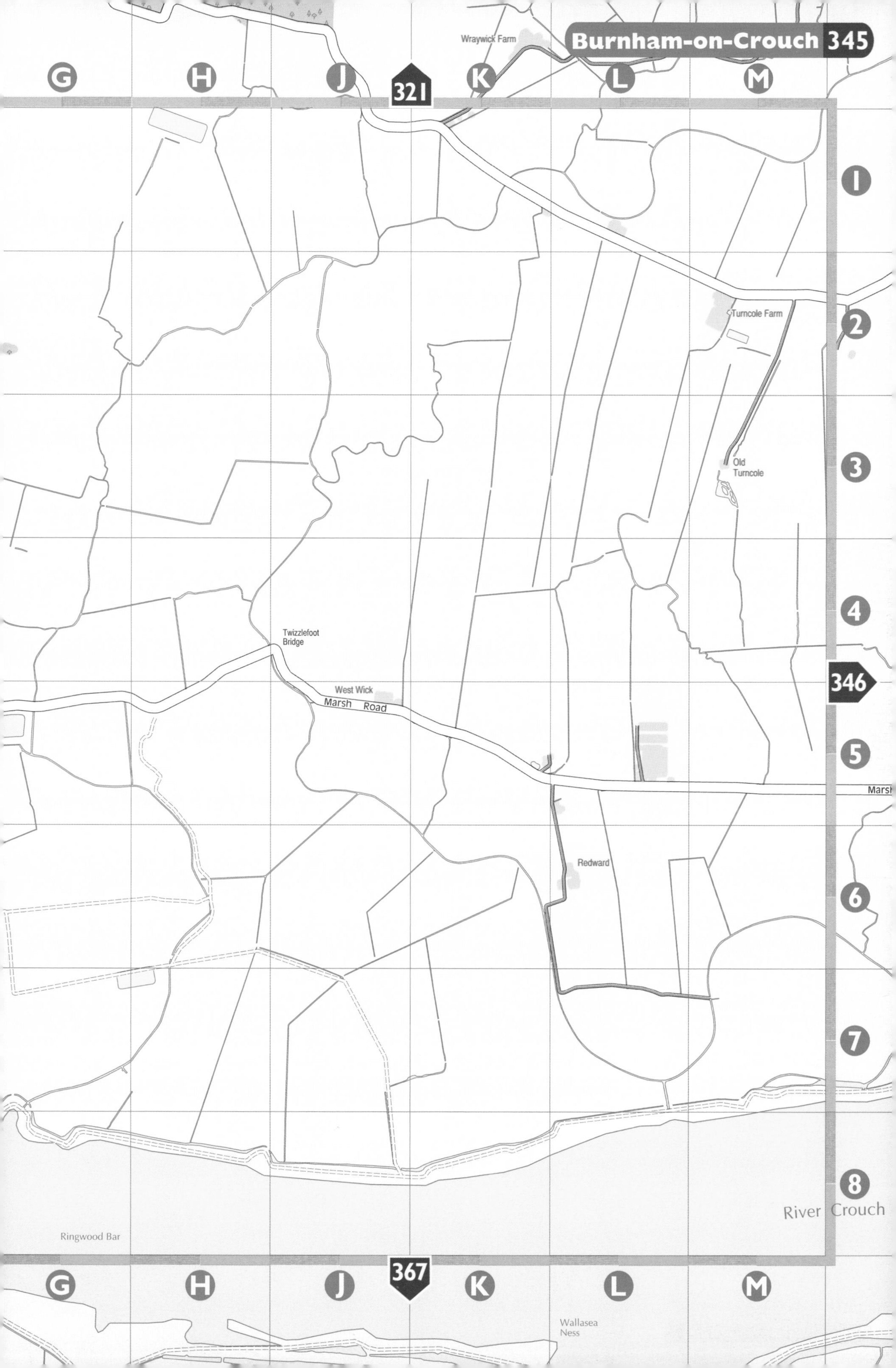
Wraywick Farm
G
H
J
321
K
L
M
1
2
Turncole Farm
Old Turncole
3
4
Twizzlefoot Bridge
West Wick
Marsh Road
346
5
Marsh
Redward
6
7
8
River Crouch
Ringwood Bar
367
G
H
J
K
L
M
Wallasea Ness

Ⓐ   Ⓑ   Ⓒ   322   Ⓓ   Court Farm   Ⓔ   Ⓕ

Middle
Wick

1

2

3   **Montsale**

4   Deal
Hall

345

5   Coney
Hall

East
Wick

Marsh Road

6   Holliwell Farm

7

8
River Crouch   River Crouch

Ⓐ   Ⓑ   Ⓒ   368   Ⓓ   Ⓔ   Ⓕ

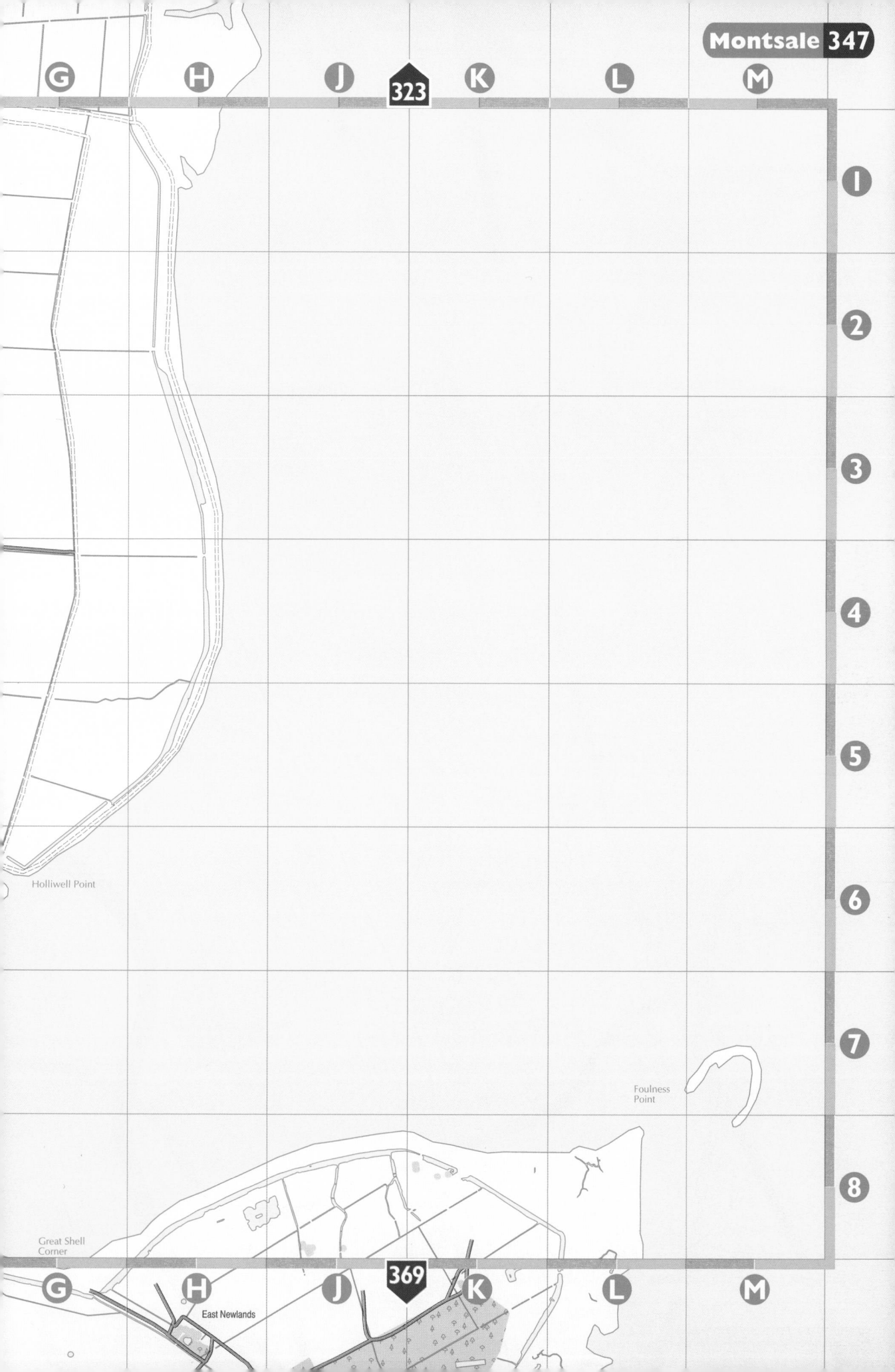

323

G H J K L M

I

2

3

4

5

6

7

8

Holliwell Point

Foulness
Point

Great Shell
Corner

G H J K L M

369

East Newlands

G6
1 Swindon Gdns

G7
1 Amersham Wk

G8
1 Barnsley Rd
2 Camborne Wy
3 Gleneagles Cl
4 Melksham Cl
5 Wednesbury Gn

331

CM14

G

H

J

K

L

M

1

2

3

4

5

6

7

8

Havering Plain

Hou Hatch

Weald Park (Country Park)

Wrightsbridge Road

Weald Road

Wealdside

St Vincent's Hamlet

Rochetts

Essex County Council

Brookweald Cricket Club

M25

Weald Road

St Peters C of E Primary School

South Weald

Wigley

Bush Lane

354

Weald Park Wa

Talbrook

Leonard Rd

The Gv

Havering College of Further & Higher Education

Mascalls Gdns

A12(T)

Hotel

BROOK STREET

Brook Street

Dagnam Park

Dycorts School

Settle Road

Kings Wood School

Sedgefield Crescent

Swindon Lane

Wickford Dr

Oakley Dr

Sheffield Drive

Dagnam Park Drive

Tiverton Gv

Bedale Road

Stratton Road

Tamworth Road

Dagnam Pk

Maylands Golf Club

M25

Junction 28

A1023

Nags Head Lane

Doctors Surgery

Redruth Road

Redcar Road

Leamington Road

Kirby Close

Petersfield Cl

Petersfield Avenue

Penrith Road

Penzance Road

Retford Road

Kenilworth Av

Fair Cross Av

Woodstock Av

COLCHESTER ROAD

Maylands Wy

Homeway

Craven Gardens

Mount Avenue

Essex County Havering

Boyles Court

Mead Infant School

Colne Drive

Brook Way

Paines

Neot's

Amersham

Harold Court School

Church Road

Geoffrey Av

David Drive

Court Avenue

Haldon Rise

Elgin Av

Thurso Cl

A12(T)

Harold Park

Ingreway

Harold Court

CHESTER ROAD

Sunnydene Cl

Sussex Avenue

Bates Rd

Waterside Close

Royston

Bates Industrial Est

G

H

J

K

L

M

M3
1 Wingrave Crs

J7
1 Dagnam Park Sq
2 Fairford Cl

372

H8
1 Birkdale Av
2 Firham Park Av
3 Hoylake Gdns

H7
1 Dagnam Pk Gdns
2 Penzance Gdns

H6
1 Stratton Wk

M5

Ridgeway

Arundel Rd

Harold Wood Station

356

A   B   C   **334**   D   E   **F** Foose Green

1 Kenilworth Cl

I

2

CM12

3

4

355

5

6

7

8

Herongate

A   B   C   **375**   D   E   **F**

Oak...aven...
woodwoo...
sh...
7 Close

A129
Hutton Lane
Church Lane
Bushwood
Hunters Chase
North Drive
Foxes Grove
Tally-Ho Drive
A129 LONDON
Courtland...
Springfield...
Gar...ens
2 Lodge Close
3
...edon
Drive
Hutton...

Great Cowbridge Grange

Blunts Wall
Blunts Wall Road
Blunts...
Billericay Town Football Club

Creaseys Farm

Elmshaws Farm
Wiggin's Lane

Tye Common Road
Salmon's Farm
Sudburys Farm Road
Babshole Farm
Blind Lane
Wiggins Lane

Tye Common Road
Hatches Farm
Hatches Farm Road
Botney Hill Road

Heron Hall
Blind Lane
Botney Hill Farm
Botney Hill Road
Green Lane
Chase Farm

Mount Thrift
Billericay Road
Dunton Lodge
Billericay Road
Dunton Road

1 grid square represents 500 metres

Down
Hall

337

G | **H** | **J** | **K** | **L** | **M**

I

2

3

4

360

5

6

7

8

Runwell

Nevendon

SS12

Castledon Farm

River Crouch

Doeshill Farm

Great
Bromfords

Cricketers Retail
Park

378
Burnt
Mills

G | **H** | **J** | **K** | **L** | **M**

127

Herons
Gate
Trading Est

Martin Road

Southend Arterial Road

A127

I grid square represents 500 metres

A132
RUNWELL ROAD
338
A130

Battlesbridge
Battlesbridge Station
Battlesbridge Motorcycle Museum
Hawk Hill
Hawk La

Runwell
River Crouch
Southlands Farm

SS11

River Crouch

Rawreth Shot

Burrells Farm

Church Road
St Nicholas C of E Primary School
Chelmsford Road

Rawreth

Infant School
Beauchamps Drive
Royal Oak Dr
Beauchamps High School

Shot Farm

Enfield Rd
Oak Av

A129 SOUTHEND ROAD

Shotgate

Old London Road

Bruce Grove
First Avenue
Fanton Chase
Wakescoline

Hotel

WICKFORD
The Robert Frew Medical Centre
Capitol Industrial Cen
Hurricane Way
Sopwith Crescent
Hurricane Cl

Dollymans Farm

Doublegate Lane

LONDON ROAD

Sappers Farm
Fanton Hall Farm

Fairway
Park
Fanton Av
Road

Pantile Farm

Harrow Road

343

G **H** **J** **K** **L** **M**

New Hall

Lambourne
Lane

Hall

Road

Lambourne
Hall

Saltings

I

Creeksea Ferry Road

Creeksea Ferry Road

Paglesham Creek

2

Roach Valley Way

Loftmans
Farm

3

West
Hall

PH

**Paglesham
Churchend**

4

Roach Valley Way

366

Ballards Gore

Paglesham Road

Ingulfs

East
Hall

5

Biggins Farm

South
Hall

6

Roach

Valley

Way

Roach Valley
Way

Stannetts

7

Hampton Barns

Roach valley way

Barton Hall

8

384

G **H** **J** **K** **L** **M**

Waldens

Roach

River Crouch

G   H   J   345   K   L   M

Ringwood Bar

1

Wallasea
Ness

2

Brankfleet

Wallasea
Island

Crow
Corner

3

The
Quay

Monkton
Barn

4

368

5

River Roach

Quay Reach

6

Potton
Point

Horseshoe
Corner

7

The Middleway

8

G   H   J   386   K   L   M

Ringwood Bar

River Crouch

A   B   C   346   D   E   F

River Crouch

1

Clark's
Hard

2

Nase
Wick

3

Monkton
Barn

4

367

†

PO

Churchend

Lodge Farm

5

Foulness Island

6

Priestwood

East Wick

Rugwood Farm

7

Eastwick
Head

8

Great
Burwood Farm

A   B   C   387   D   E   F

Rugwood Head

I grid square represents 500 metres

G H J 347 K L M

East Newlands

Great Shell Corner

Courtsend

The Chase

New Mouse Farm

Fishermans Head

1
2
3
4
5
6
7
8

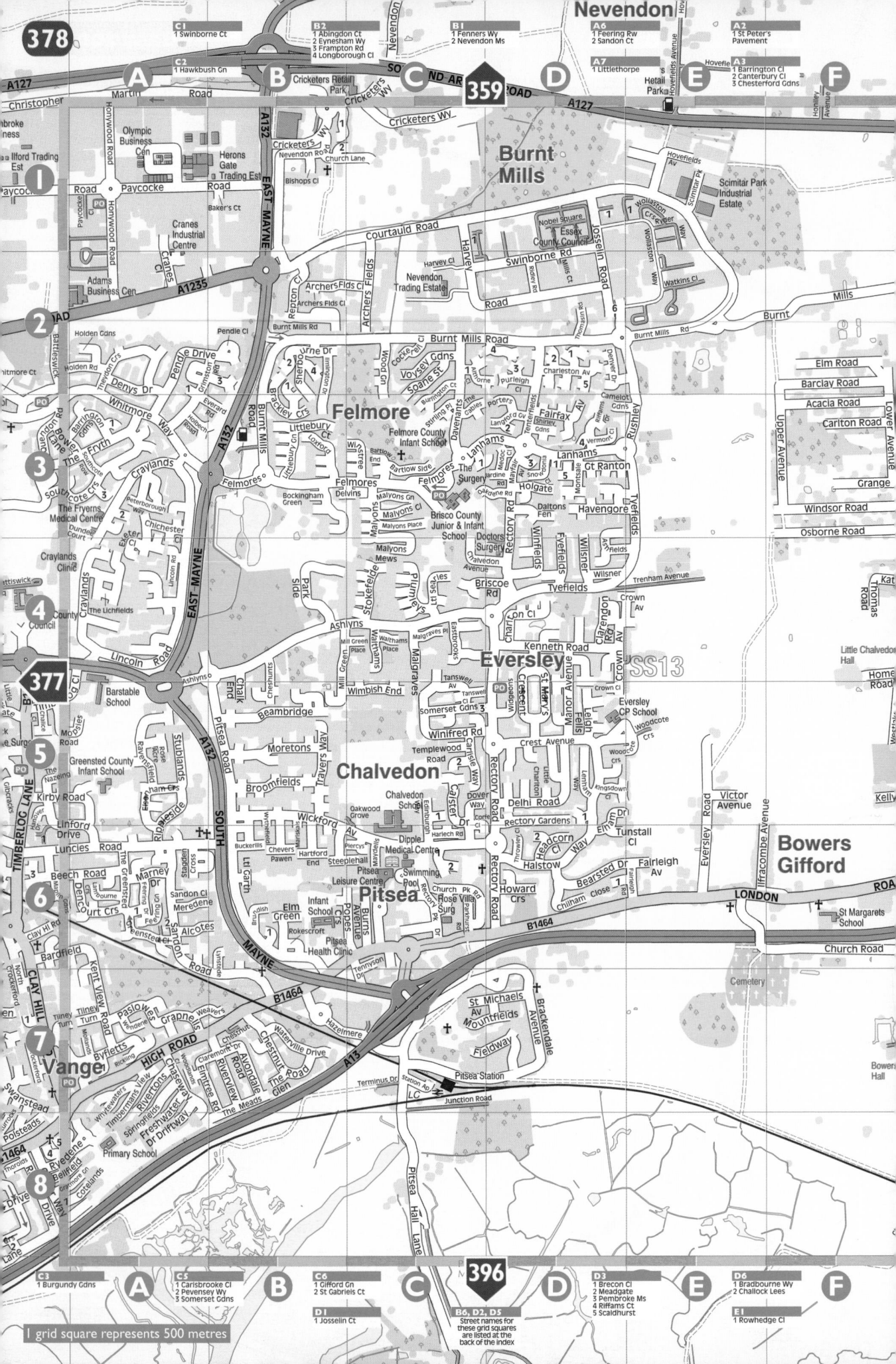

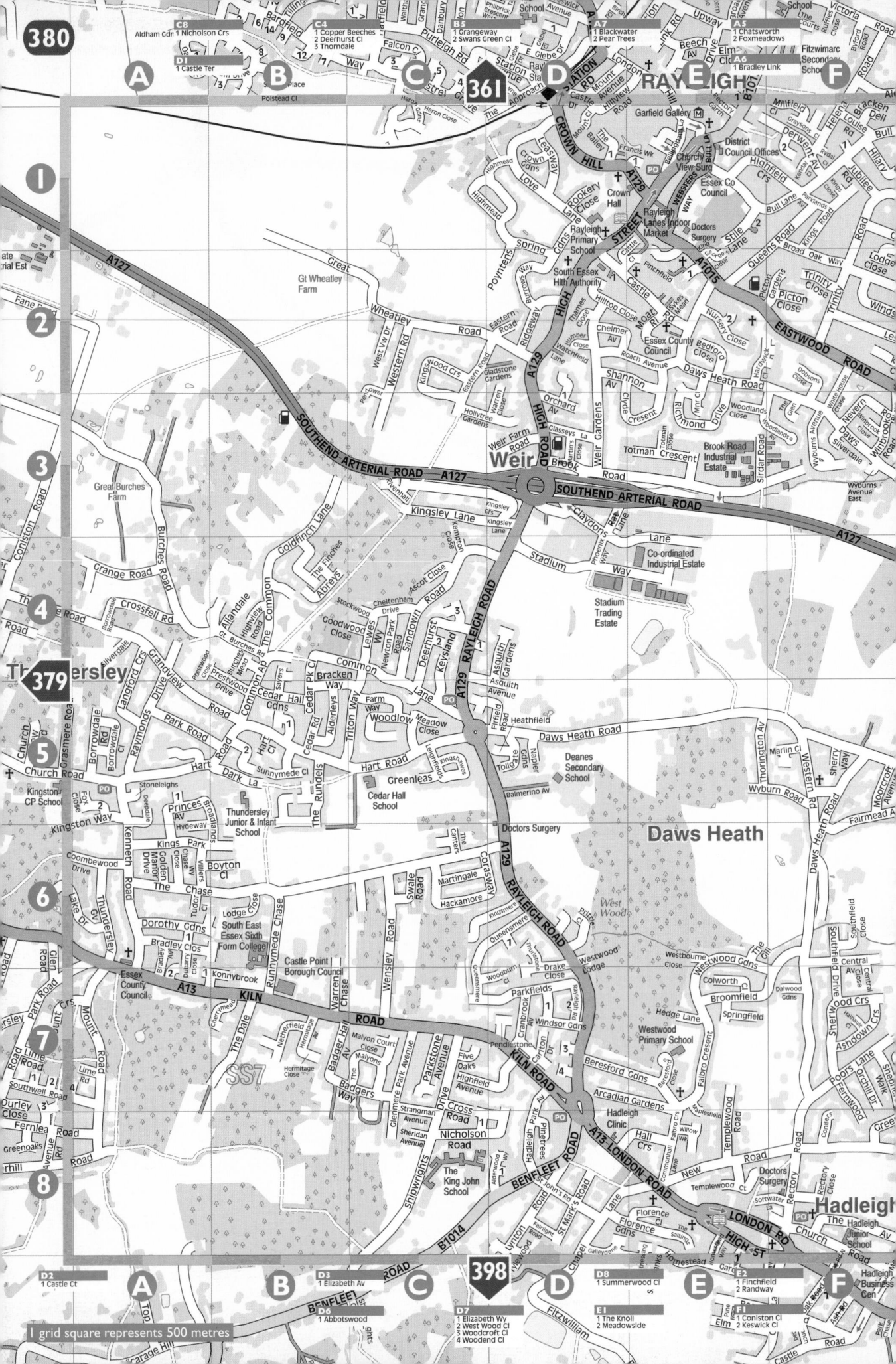

384

A   B   C   **365**   D   E   F

F7
1 Townfield Wk

1

Waldens

River Roach

2

Roper's Farm

Bolts
Farm

Mucking Hall Road

3

Mucking
Hall

Church Road

Barling

Barling Magna
Primary School

4

Magna Mead

Little Wakering Road

Barling Road

383

High
House

Carpenters

Kimberley Road

5

Blue
House
Farm

Stonebridge

PO

**Little
Wake**

Beauchamps

6

Essex County
Southend-on-Sea

Barrow Hall Road

The Crofts

Barrow
Hall Farm

Clay Street
Farm

7

Trotters

Oldbury
Farm

B10

Barling Road

Rebels Lane

STAR LANE

Essex County
Southend-on-Sea

Southend Road

8

ROYAL
ARTILLERY

B1017

Alleyn
Court & Eton
House School

402

Avenue

A   B   C   D   E   F

POYNTERS LANE B1017

1 grid square represents 500 metres

Thorpe
Hall School

Bournes

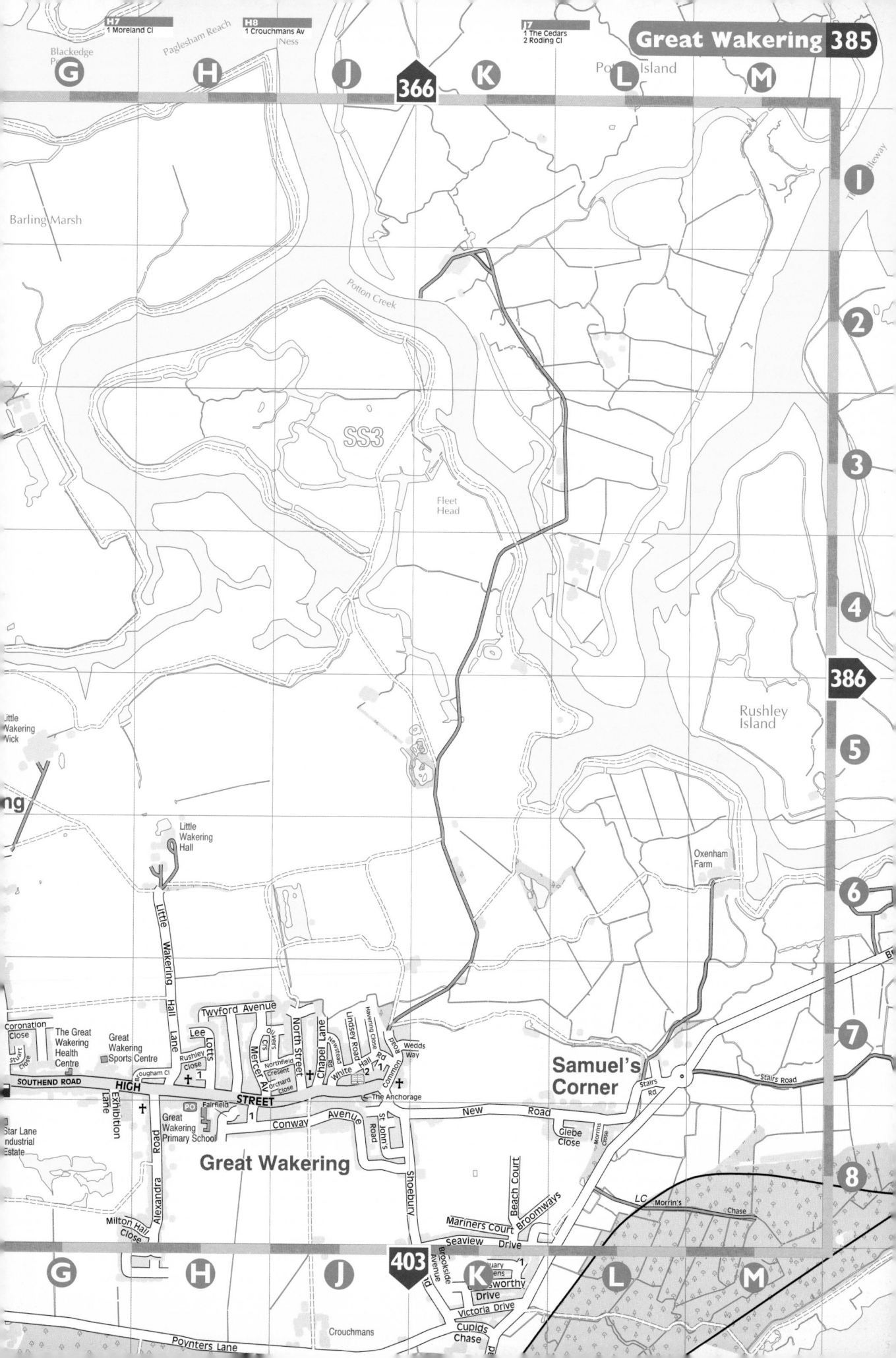

367

1

The Middleway

2

Shelford Creek

3

New England
Island

New England Creek

4

hley
nd

5

Havengore
Island

Sharpness
Head

6

Bridge Road

Havengore
Head

7

Haven
Point

Stairs Road

8

Wakering
Stairs

I grid square represents 500 metres

G H J **368** K L M

Great
Burwood Farm

Rugwood Head

Asplins
Head

Shelford
Head

1
2
3
4
5
6
7
8

G H J K L M

392

A   B   C   374   D   E   F

1

Old Englands
Farm

Thurrock
Havering

2

Dunnings Lane

Slose

3

Blankets
Farm

Home Farm

Fen Lane

China La

Hatch Farm

Mar Dyke

Dunnings Lane

4

Corner
Farm

Stone
Hall

Fen Lane

391

Havering
Thurrock

Fen Farm

5

6

7

Mar Dyke

8

Orsett
Fen

A   B   C   407   D   E   F
                                    Hobletts

1 grid square represents 500 metres

G H J **375** K L M

I

2

3

4

394

5

6

7

8

G H **408** J K L M

Peartree Lane

A128

BULPHAN

BY-PASS

Brentwood Road

Bulphan Primary School

Bulphan

PO

Church Road

Stanley Road

Albert Road

Victoria Road

Church Lane

The Elms Farm

Manor House

Noke Hall Farm

Doesgate Lane

Doesgate Lane

Lower Dunton Road

Lower Dunton Road

Doesgate Farm

Little Malgraves

Little Malgraves Industrial Estate

BRENTWOOD ROAD

A128

Ongar Hall Farm

Parker's Farm Road

Parker's Farm Road

CONWAY'S ROAD

B188

Lorkins Farm

Home Farm

Wyfields Farm

North Hill Business Park

Great Malgra

Hernd th Hi

Black Bush Lane

Robinson Road

Oxford Road

York Road

Hillcrest

Victoria Road

Orsett Road

G6
1 Ashdown Cl
2 Benton Gdns
3 Bracelet Cl
4 Hillview Gdns
5 Kenneth Gdns
6 Morley Link
7 Wood hurst Rd

G7
1 Bellmaine Av
2 Briceway
3 Nottage Cl
4 St Johns Ms
5 Tasman Cl

G8
1 Palmers
2 Pearsons

G H J K L M

377

I
2
3
396
4
5
6
7
8

SS16

Dry Street

STANFORD-LE-HOPE BY-PASS

Hovels Farm

One Tree Hill

A13

B1420 SOUTHEND ROAD

LAMPITS

Southend Road

Milton Road

Howell Road

Morley Hill

Gable Hall GM School

Brampton Close

York Avenue

Windsor Avenue

Lampits Hill Avenue

Balmoral Av

Arundel Drive

Carisbrooke Dr

Pembroke Dr

Montfort Av

Central Av

Bellmaine Av

Gardner Av

Giffards Co Junior & Infant Sch

Balstonia

Corringham

Swimming Pool

Springhouse Road

A1014

Springhouse Lane

Old Hall

410

Stanford

Kenwood Road

Woodbrooke Way

Kersbrooke Way

HILL

Wheatley Road

Ashway

Thames Crescent

Edith Way

Digby

Finches Close

Recreation Av

Larkswood

Woolfers Av

Corringham Cemetery

Ash Tree Surgery

The Surgery

Corringham Health Centre

CHURCH ROAD

Princes Avenue

Giffards Cross Rd

Rookery Hill

THE ROOKERY

East Thurrock Football Club

Corringham County Primary School

Fobbing Road

Hall Terrace

Lion Hill

The Avenue

Gildeborne Close

The Hawthorns

Wharf Rd

Fobbing

Wheelers Lane

High Road

Marsh Lane

Waterworks Lane

Mill Lane

Greathouse Chase

Patricia Drive

Whitehall Lane

Whitehall Farm

Inglefield Road

Mill Lane

Moores Avenue

Hertford Drive

Brook Drive

Woodlands Drive

A176 NETHER MAYNE

Hawkesbury Bush Lane

Bells Hill Road

Leonard Road

Fort William Road

Vange Corner Drive

Vange Park Road

Middle Drive

A13

Castle Rd

Park

London Road

Basildon Zoo

Hollands Wk

Victoria Rd

Marsh Farm

Southview Park Surgery

Merricks Lane

The Slades

LC

G H J K L M

J6
1 Fernside Cl
2 Glenfield Rd

J2
1 Highland Rd

H7
1 Langland Cl
2 Limeslade Cl

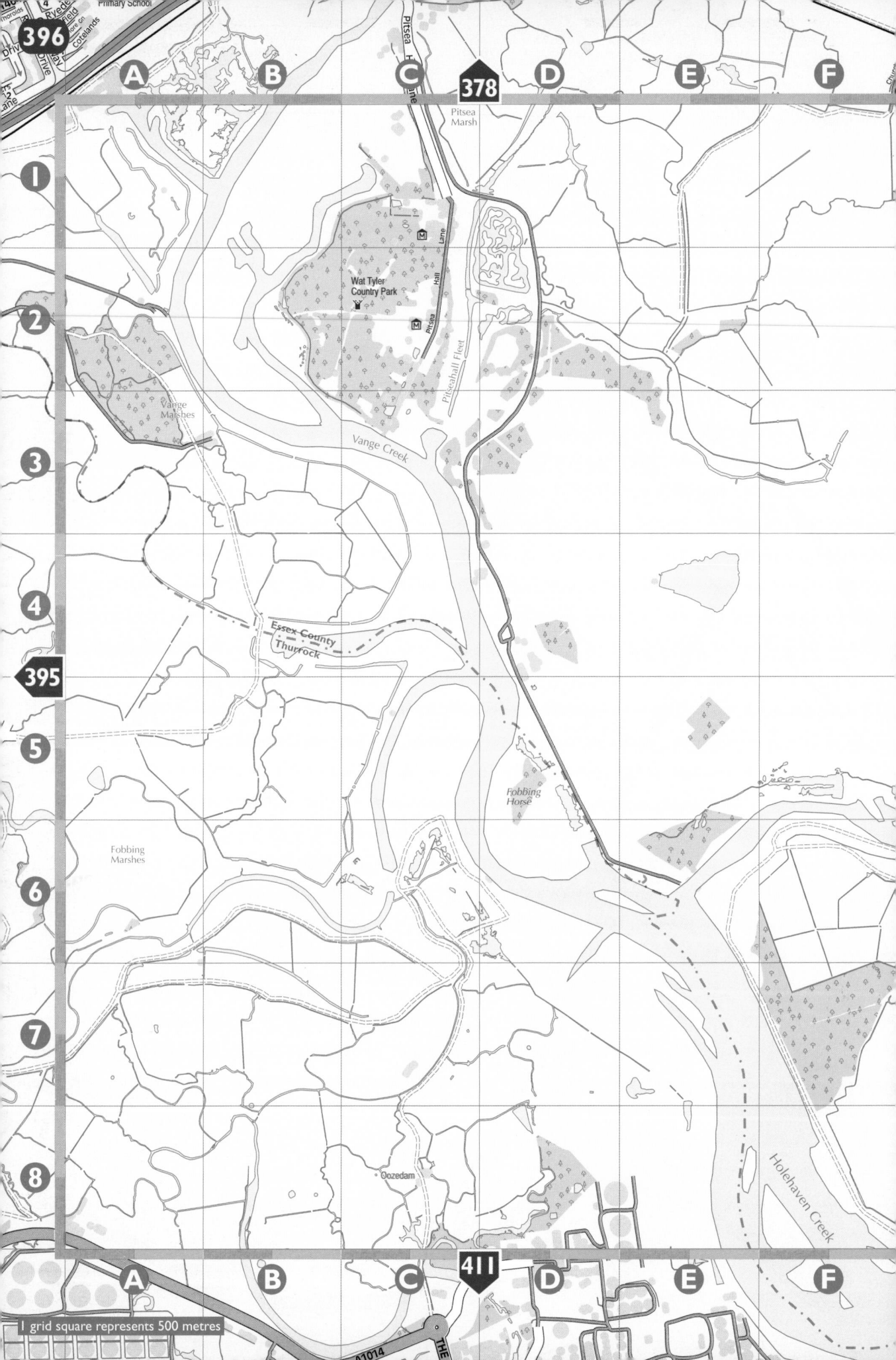

396

A   B   C   378   D   E   F

Pitsea Marsh

1

Pitsea Lane

M

Wat Tyler
Country Park

M

Pitsea Hall Lane

2

Vange
Marshes

Pitsehall Fleet

Vange Creek

3

4

Essex County
Thurrock

395

5

Fobbing
Horse

Fobbing
Marshes

6

7

8

Oozedam

Holehaven Creek

A   B   C   411   D   E   F

THE

B1014

1 grid square represents 500 metres

G H J 385 K L M

Great Wakering
1 New England Crs

H4
1 Southchurch Av

Industrial
Estate

Alexandra

Milton Hall
Close

Shoeb...

Seaview Drive

Marine Court

Beach Court

Broomways

Morrin's

Chas

Brookside Avenue

Estuary
Gardens

Goldsworthy
Drive

Victoria Drive

Cupids
Chase

LC

Cherrytree Chase

Black
Grounds

I

Poynters Lane

Crouchmans

North
Shoebury

Watkins
Way

Rowbank

Carmania Close

Fraser Close

Exeter Close

Cunningham
Close

PO

Centurion

Constable

Picasso Way

Raphael Drive

Wakering Road

Rembrandt Way

Goya Rise

Rubens

Whistler

Hogarth Drive

Ter Cl

Vermeer Crs

Tur

Friars County
Junior School

Brodie Road

LC

LC

Sandpit Road

Suttons Road

Boyce Road

I Butts Rd

Pig's Bay

LC

Essex County
Southend-on-Sea

2

3

Ashanti Close

Hermes Way

Elm Road

The Woodlands

Vanguard Way

Seedbed
Business
Centre

The Goslings

Newell Avenue

Castle Cl

Peel Avenue

Blackgate Road

LC

Suttons Road

Rossfser Road

Walker Way

4

The Vanguards

Friars St

Wallace

Shoebury Av

Terminal Close

Wakering Avenue

High Street

Gunners Road

Shoeburyness
Station

5

Primary
School

Rosewood

Lane

Hinguer St

Smith
Street

George St

John St

Rampart Street

Terrance

Chapel

Hospital Road

Shoeburyness

6

Field

Road

The Ter

Lane

Road

Dane's Av

Beach Sq Rd

Mess

Warrior

7

8

G H J K L M

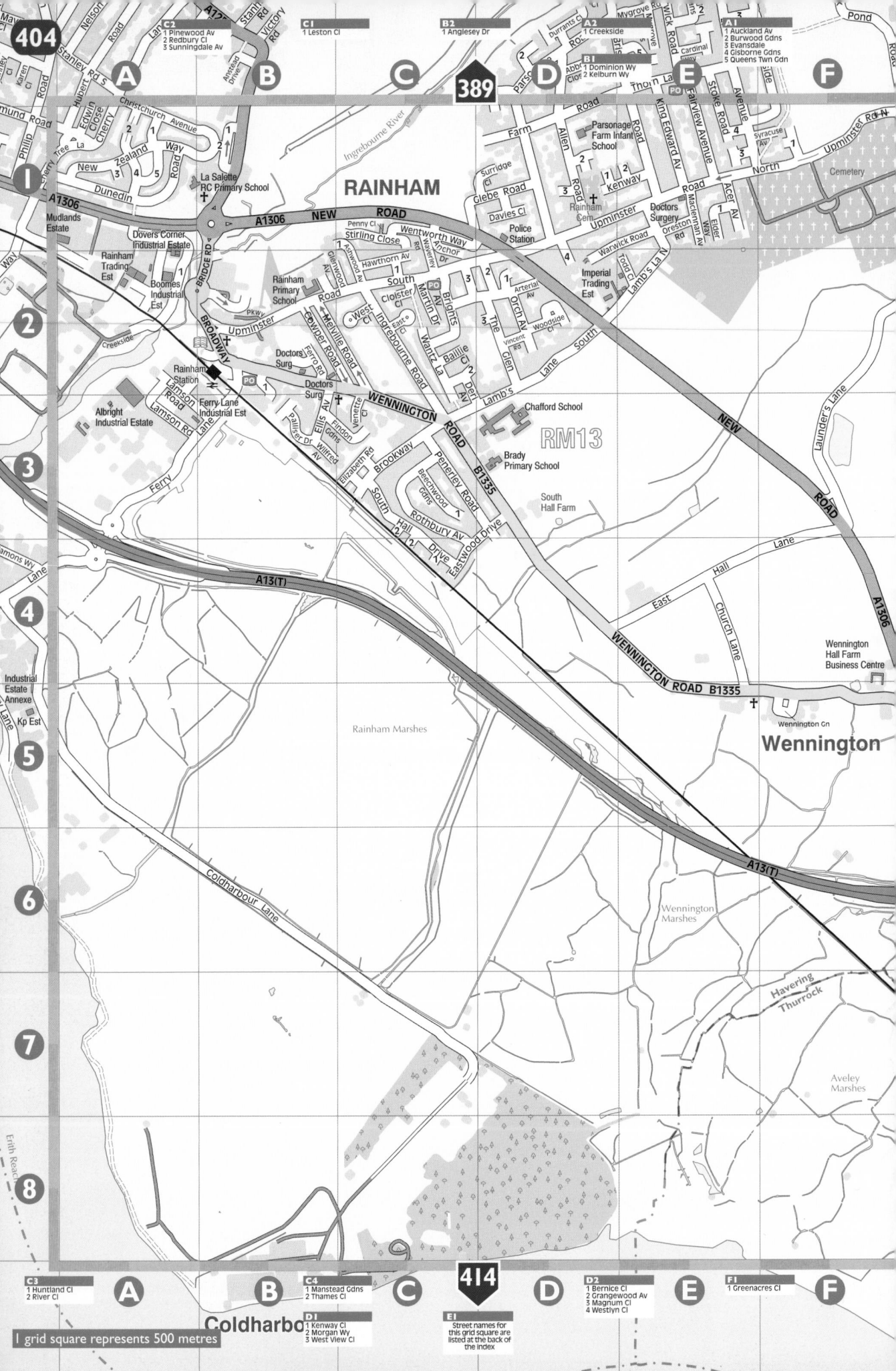

A **B** **C** **D** **E** **F**

1

RAINHAM

A1306 NEW ROAD

Rainham Primary School

2

Rainham Station

La Salette RC Primary School

WENNINGTON ROAD

RM13

Chafford School

Brady Primary School

South Hall Farm

3

Albright Industrial Estate

A13(T)

Rainham Marshes

4

Industrial Estate Annexe

Kp Est

Wennington Hall Farm Business Centre

WENNINGTON ROAD B1335

Wennington Gn

5

Wennington

Wennington Marshes

6

Coldharbour Lane

A13(T)

7

Havering Thurrock

Aveley Marshes

8

Erith Reach

A **B** **C** **D** **E** **F**

Coldharbo

1 grid square represents 500 metres

396

Oozedam

A1014

THE MANORWAY

Coryton

Oil Refinery

LC

Shell Haven

Cor
Wh

Thames Haven

Thurrock
Medway Towns

412

River   Thames

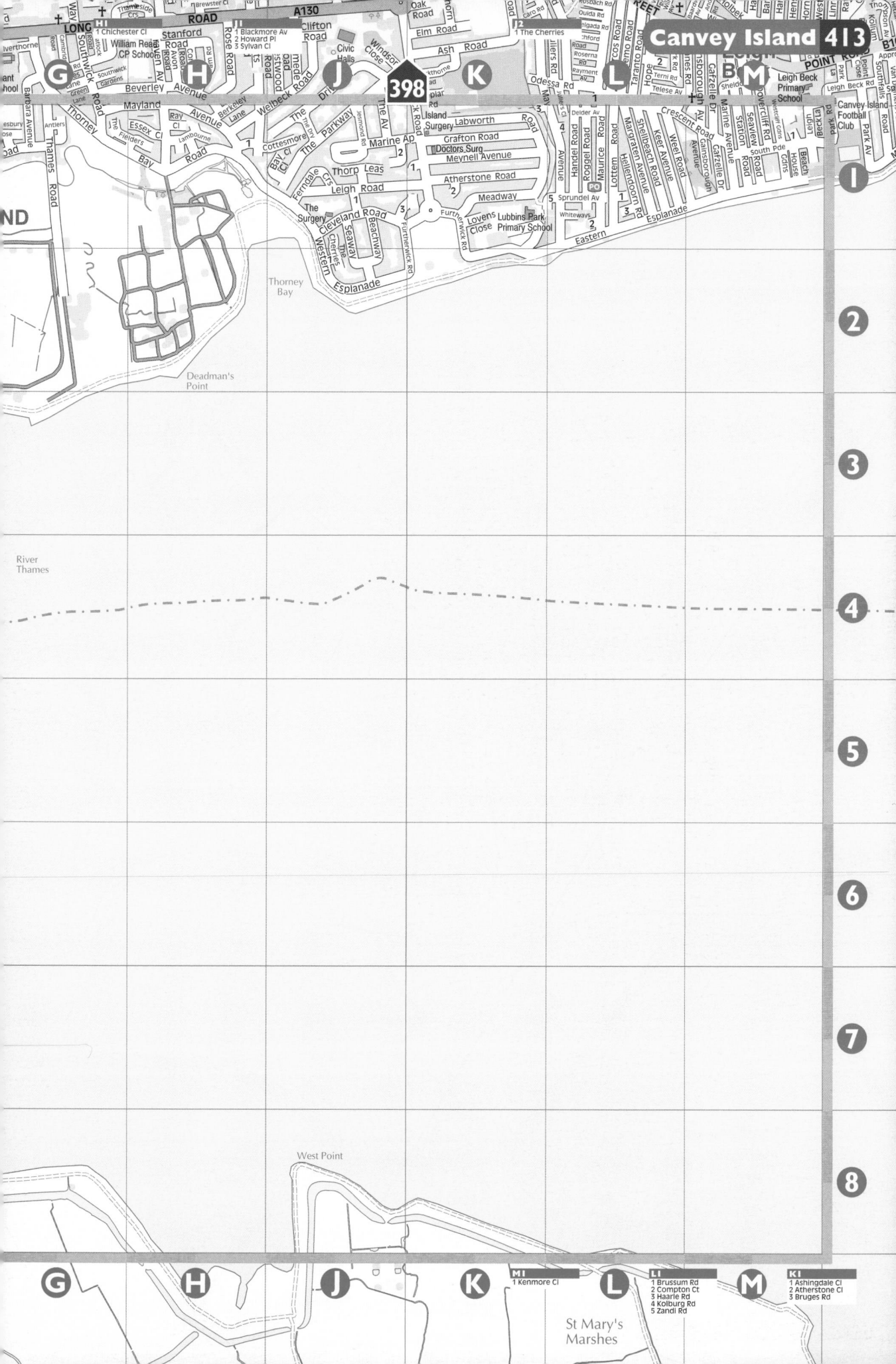

LONG

ROAD A130

J1 1 Blackmore Av
2 Howard Pl
3 Sylvan Cl

H1 1 Chichester Cl

William Read CP School

Clifton Road

Stanford Road

Rose Road

Civic Halls

Windsor Close

Elm Road

Ash Road

Oak Road

J2 1 The Cherries

Caro Rd
Ouida Rd

Canvey Island Football Club

Leigh Beck Primary School

Beverley

Mayland

Essex Cl

Thorney Bay

Avenue

Welbeck Road

The Parkway

Marine Ap

Grafton Road
Doctors Surg
Meynell Avenue

Atherstone Road

Odessa Road

Island Surgery Labworth

Handel Road

Roggel Road

Maurice Road

Crescent Dr

Marine Avenue

Seaview Station

Beach

South Pde

Thames Road

Ray Cl

Lambourne

Cottesmore

Thorp Leas

Leigh Road

Cleveland Road

The Surgery

The Cherries

Seaway

Beachway

Furtherwick Road

Lovens Close

Lubbins Park Primary School

Meadway

Whiteways

Sprundel Av

Eastern Esplanade

Shellbeach Road

Margraten Avenue

Keer Avenue

Weel Road

Esplanade

Gainsborough Avenue

Gafzelle Dr

Marine Avenue

I

Deadman's Point

2

3

River Thames

4

5

6

7

West Point

8

M1 1 Kenmore Cl

L1 1 Brussum Rd
2 Compton Ct
3 Haarle Rd
4 Kolburg Rd
5 Zandi Rd

K1 1 Ashingdale Cl
2 Atherstone Cl
3 Bruges Rd

St Mary's Marshes

G7
1 Mannock Rd
LC

H1
1 St Clements Ct

H2
1 Church Hollow

The Caravan
Site

G

H

J

405

RM19

K

Mar Dyke

L

M

Back La

South Way

UCI
Cinema

I

A282(T)

Junction 31

A13(T) ARTERIAL ROAD PURFLEET

Thurrock
Council

Marine
Court

Centurion
Way

Crusader
Close

Mulberry
Drive

Chieftan Drive

PO

A1090

Mardyke
Surg
Lane

Marlow Av

Quarry
Hill

Fanns Rise

Thamley

Comet

Tank   Lane

Purfleet
Primary School

Beacon Hill
Industrial Estate

Botany Way

Church Lane

The Lintons

Harrisons Wharf

Purfleet
Station

Beacon Hill
Industrial
Estate

Oakhill Rd

Beacon Hill

Linnet

Way

Wood

North   Road

Watts Crs

South Av

Cartel Cl

Brimfield

Stonehouse Lane

A1090

Fondu
Sports
Club

Armor Road

Hotel

Weston Avenue

East

2

Thames

Purfleet

LC

A1090   LONDON

Mill Road

ROAD

Joslin   Rd

Linden
Cl

PURFLEET

3

LC

LC

Long Reach

A282(T)

Canterbury Way

4

River C

Dartford
Marshes

416

5

Dartford
Tunnel

Queen Elizabeth II
Bridge

6

Street

Marsh

Joyce Green
Hospital

A&E

Marsh   Street

Littlebrook
Business Centre

A282(T)

Stone
Marshes

7

UNIVERSITY WAY

Grove

McCudden
Rd

Cornwall
Rd

Cemetery

A206

Bridge Close

Clipper Bvd West

Hotel

Clipper Bvd

8

Salmon

Green Lane

Strickland
Av

Barnwell Rd

Henderson

Chaucer Wy

Hardy Gv

Wodehouse
Road

Wordsworth Way

Drive

Cavell Crescent

Coleridge Rd

Shakespeare
Rd

Shaftesbury Lane

Hotel

A282(T)

Toll
Toll

Victory
Way

Masthead
Close

A206

Anchor Boulevard

Galleon

Newton's Ct

PO

Spelman Road

Browning
Road

Bronte Gv

Byron

Joyce Green Lane

Keyes Road

Trevelyan

Perry

Sheridan

Farnol Rd

Dickens

Dryden

Kingsley Av

Tennyson Rd

Bridges

Masefield
Rd

Junction 1a

St Mary's Road

A206

Stone Cross

Elizabeth Street

Charles

G

Trevithick Drive

Hilltop Cons

St Anselms
RC Primary
School

Doctors
Surgery

Thames
Primary
School

Littlebrook Manor Way

Lansbury Crs

H

J

K

Cotton   Lane

L

M

Stone Cross   LC

Bell Close

Cooper Cl

Sto

Temple Hill Sq

PO

A282(T)

Lansbury

Falcon

LC

Church Rd

Green Wk

Chalice

Swallow

Cross

Muckingford

409

East Tilbury

East Tilbury Station

Bata Medical Centre

East Tilbury Surgery

Bata Surgery

Doctors Surgery

Doctors Surgery

Low Street

Muckingford Road

Low Street Lane

Buckland

Bowaters Farm

Station Road

Love Lane

Princess Margaret Road

Linley Cl

Gordon Close

East Tilbury Marshes

Coalhouse Point

Farm Road

Gloucester Av

Queen Mary Av

Princess Rd

Coronation Av

Princess Margaret Road

Thomas Bata Av

King George VI Avenue

Queen Elizabeth Avenue

Alexandra Way

Stenning Av

Bundles Cl

Beechcroft Av

Halt Drive

Solway

Clyde

Tweed

Trent

Arun

Avenue

Coronation

H1
1 Hazelwood

K1
1 Qu Elizabeth Av
2 Strathmore

Lower

G H J K L M

I 2 3 4 5 6 7 8

G H J K L M

Abberton 191 H8
Abbess End 230 F8
Abbess Roding 230 E7
Abbey Field 162 F6
Abridge 328 D5
Acton 35 L5
Acton Place 35 H3
Aimes Green 278 A8
Aingers Green 194 F6
Albury 144 B5
Albury End 144 A7
Aldham 160 C3
Allen's Green 200 A5
Alphamstone 77 G8
Alresford 193 H3
Althorne 343 H1
Ardleigh 137 G4
Ardleigh Green 371 K3
Ardleigh Heath 136 F2
Ardley End 229 J2
Arkesden 87 M1
Armigers 121 K5
Ashdon 45 H3
Asheldham 321 J4
Ashen 50 E2
Ashingdon 363 L4
Audley End 65 J3
Audley End 74 F3
Aveley 405 L5
Aythorpe Roding 204 C8
Bacon End 204 F1
Baconend Green 177 M7
Baddow Park 312 F1
Baker Street 408 A4
Ballards Gore 365 G5
Ballingdon 4 A9
Balls Green 166 B6
Balstonia 395 G7
Bamber's Green 149 C8
Bannister Green 181 G6
Bardfield End Green 122 D1
Bardfield Saling 152 E2
Barleycroft End 116 C7
Barling 384 F4
Barnes Cray 414 C6
Barnston 179 G7
Bartholomew Green 181 M4
Bartlow 25 H4
Basildon 18 E6
Bath Side 7 J4
Battlesbridge 360 E1
Baythorne End 49 M1
Beacon End 161 L5
Beacon Hill 240 C5
Beauchamp Roding 260 B2
Beaumont 169 G4
Beazley End 126 D5
Bedlar's Green 175 H6
Beggar Hill 309 M4
Belchamp Otten 52 D3
Belchamp St Paul 52 A2
Belchamp Walter 53 H5
Bell Common 303 L4
Belstead 57 K4
Bentfield Bury 146 C3
Bentfield Green 146 D3
Bentley 78 F4
Bentley 331 M5
Berden 117 J3
Berechurch 190 F2
Berners Roding 260 F3
Bicknacre 315 G1
Biggin 418 D3
Billericay 357 J2
Birch 189 H7
Birchanger 174 F1
Birch Green 216 B1
Birchhall Corner 136 D1
Birdbrook 49 H4
Bird Green 86 F3
Birds Green 260 B5
Bishops Green 205 M3
Bishop's Stortford 173 K4
Blackheath 191 H8
Blackmore 309 G3
Blackmore End 126 C1
Black Notley 183 J6
Blacksmith's Corner 57 K5
Blake End 181 H1
Blasford Hill 235 J8
Bobbingworth 282 E3
Bocking 155 G7
Bocking Churchstreet 155 H3
Bocking's Elm 223 H6
Boreham 265 M3
Borley 34 A8
Borley Green 53 L1
Bournes Green 402 C1
Bovinger 282 A4
Bowers Gifford 378 F6
Boxted 105 G4
Boxted 105 H7
Boxted Cross 105 G3
Boyton Cross 262 C4
Boyton End 29 L6
Boyton End 92 C6
Bradfield 140 A1
Bradfield Heath 139 L3
Bradwell 184 E1
Bradwell on Sea 298 C1
Bradwell Waterside 274 A7
Braintree 155 H6
Braiswick 162 C1
Bramford 36 B1
Brandy Hole 340 B7
Bran End 151 K3
Brantham 108 E2
Brays Grove 256 B4
Breeds 234 E5
Brent Pelham 116 A1
Brewer's End 176 C4
Brick End 148 F2
Brick House End 117 J6
Brickkiln Green 96 B7
Bridge End 94 B8
Bridge Green 63 J5
Brightlingsea 220 E3
Brimsdown 324 F4

Broad Green 40 C8
Broad Green 158 F8
Broadley Common 254 E8
Broad's Green 234 F6
Broad Street Green 269 K3
Brock Hill 337 J6
Broke Hall 38 D8
Bromley Cross 137 K7
Brook Street 353 M5
Broomfield 264 C1
Broxbourne 253 H8
Broxted 149 G1
Brundon 54 D2
Buckhurst Hill 348 D4
Bucklesham 61 J3
Building End 62 B4
Bulls Cross 300 B8
Bulmer 54 A6
Bulmer Tye 54 A8
Bulphan 393 G2
Bumble's Green 278 B4
Bures 102 A3
Burnham-on-Crouch 344 E6
Burnt Heath 137 J6
Burnt Mills 378 D1
Burrsville Park 224 B4
Burton End 147 K7
Burton Green 157 J1
Bury Green 172 F4
Bury Green 300 C3
Bush End 176 B7
Bustard Green 123 J5
Buttsbury 334 F1
Butt's Green 290 A8
Calford Green 29 G4
California 38 C5
Cambridge Town 402 D5
Campions 228 A6
Camps End 46 B2
Canewdon 364 E1
Canfield End 177 J4
Cannon's Green 284 A2
Canvey Island 412 F1
Capel St Mary 78 A2
Cardinal's Green 26 C1
Carter's Green 257 M1
Castle Camps 26 F8
Castle Hedingham 73 M7
Catmere End 42 B7
Cattawade 108 E4
Causeway End 180 C7
Cavendish 32 E1
Chadwell St Mary 408 A8
Chalk End 261 M1
Chalkwell 400 B3
Chalvedon 378 B5
Chantry 36 F8
Chapel End 148 D5
Chapel Row 315 H6
Chappel 131 K5
Chase Cross 351 M7
Chatham Green 208 E8
Chatter End 145 J4
Chattisham 56 B2
Chelmer Village 265 J8
Chelmondiston 82 A4
Chelmsford 17 M6
Cherry Green 120 F3
Cheshunt 300 C2
Chickney 121 G7
Chignall Smealy 234 F3
Chignall St James 263 G3
Chigwell 349 J3
Chigwell Row 350 C3
Childerditch 374 A4
Chilton 5 K4
Chilton Street 30 F1
Chipping Hill 211 M8
Chipping Ongar 307 J1
Chitts Hills 161 L3
Chrishall 40 E7
Church End 45 G4
Church End 83 G6
Church End 121 H8
Church End 125 M6
Church End 172 E1
Churchend 150 F8
Churchend 368 D5
Churchgate 300 C1
Churchgate Street 228 A7
Church Langley 256 E3
Church Street 32 C8
Clacton-on-Sea 13 J7
Clapgate 144 B6
Clare 31 K3
Clatterford End 232 C4
Clatterford End 283 K1
Clatterford End 306 C2
Claverhambury 278 C7
Clavering 87 K6
Clifftown 20 E8
Coalhill 337 M4
Cobbs Fenn 97 L4
Cobler's Green 180 E8
Cock Clarks 316 A1
Cock Green 180 F7
Coggeshall 185 M1
Coggeshall Hamlet 186 B3
Colchester 10 A7
Coldharbour 414 A2
Cold Norton 316 F6
Cole End 66 E5
Coles Green 56 C3
Collier Row 370 D1
Colliers Hatch 305 G3
Colne Engaine 130 B2
Cook's Green 224 C1
Cooksmill Green 286 A2
Coopersale Common 304 C1
Coopersale Street 304 D3
Cooper's End 63 H6
Copdock 57 G4
Copford 160 D7
Copford Green 188 D1
Copthall Green 302 E5
Corbets Tey 390 C4
Cornard Tye 55 M4
Cornish Hall End 70 C6

Corringham 395 H7
Coryton 411 K2
Countess Cross 130 E1
Courtsend 369 G3
Coxtie Green 331 L7
Crabbs Green 116 E5
Cradle End 173 G3
Craig's End 71 K4
Cranham 372 F7
Crawley End 40 E6
Crays Hill 358 E6
Creeksea 343 M6
Cressing 184 A5
Cripple Corner 100 B1
Crockleford Heath 164 D1
Crockleford Hill 164 B2
Cross End 100 D3
Crow Green 332 B5
Crow's Green 152 F3
Cuckoo Tye 35 H5
Curling Tye Green 268 B8
Curtismill Green 330 A5
Cutlers Green 121 L1
Dagenham 388 E6
Danbury 290 E4
Danbury Common 290 F6
Daws Heath 380 E6
Debden 90 C4
Debden Green 91 G6
Debden Green 327 K2
Dedham 106 F4
Dedham Heath 107 H7
Deer's Green 87 H7
Delvin End 73 G8
Dengie 321 M3
Dewes Green 117 G2
Doddinghurst 332 C1
Dovercourt 7 H8
Downham 336 F7
Dry Street 395 G1
Duck End 94 D4
Duck End 151 L2
Duck End 174 F2
Duckend Green 153 M8
Duddenhoe End 63 H5
Dutch Village 397 L7
Duton Hill 149 M1
Earls Colne 130 D4
East End 108 E1
East End 116 F7
East End 274 C8
Eastend 14 A3
East Gores 159 H7
East Hanningfield 314 D4
East Horndon 375 G4
Easthorpe 246 E2
East Mersea 165 G8
East Tilbury 419 K4
Eastwick 226 C7
Eastwood 381 M6
Edney Common 286 D6
Eight Ash Green 161 J3
Elder Street 90 F2
Elkins Green 309 G3
Elmdon 41 H7
Elm Park 389 J4
Elmstead 165 H3
Elmstead Heath 165 G8
Elmstead Market 165 J5
Elsenham 147 J1
Emerson Park 371 M6
Enfield Highway 324 D4
Enfield Lock 325 G1
Enfield Wash 324 F2
Epping 279 H4
Epping Green 279 H4
Epping Upland 279 K6
Erith 414 A2
Erwarton 112 C1
Eversley 378 C4
Fairstead 210 C5
Fanner's Green 234 C4
Farmbridge End 232 D8
Farnham 145 K5
Farnham Green 145 J4
Farther Howegreen 316 F4
Faulkbourne 211 J4
Feering 186 D8
Felixstowe 9 L4
Felmore 378 B3
Felsted 180 C6
Fiddlers Hamlet 304 D4
Finchingfield 94 C5
Fingringhoe 192 B6
Flack's Green 237 J1
Flatstead End 276 C8
Fobbing 395 L7
Ford End 86 F7
Ford End 207 J4
Fordham 132 D5
Fordham Heath 132 D8
Fordstreet 132 D8
Forry's Green 97 H5
Forty Hill 324 A3
Foster Street 257 G4
Four Wantz 232 A8
Foxash Estate 137 K2
Foxearth 33 K5
Fox Hatch 332 A2
Fox Street 136 B7
Frating 193 M2
Frating Green 166 B8
Freezy Water 300 F3
Freston 58 F8
Frinkle Green 49 L1
Frinton-on-Sea 198 E7
Frogs' Green 67 G3
Fryerning 310 B6
Fryers 19 L2
Fryern's 147 K3
Fuller's End 147 K3
Fuller Street 209 L7
Furneux Pelham 116 B6
Further Ford End 86 E5
Fyfield 259 L8
Gainsborough 59 J3
Gainsford End 71 M7
Galleyend 288 C7
Galleywood 312 C5

Gallows Corner 371 L1
Gallows Green 122 E8
Gallows Green 160 D2
Gamble's Green 237 G1
Garnetts 206 A3
Gaston Green 201 J4
Gaunt's End 148 B3
Gay Bowers 291 H6
Gestingthorpe 74 F2
Gidea Park 371 G2
Gilston 226 E6
Gilston Park 226 D5
Gilwell Park 325 K5
Goldhanger 271 G4
Good Easter 232 E6
Gooseberry Green 334 F8
Goose Green 139 L8
Goose Green 167 M4
Goose Green 252 E4
Gore Pit 186 F7
Gosfield 127 M3
Grange Hill 349 L7
Gransmore Green 181 G2
Grass Green 72 C2
Gravesend 144 B3
Grays 417 H4
Great Baddow 288 E6
Great Bardfield 124 D2
Great Bentley 194 E3
Great Berry 376 B7
Great Braxted 240 D2
Great Bromley 165 M2
Great Burstead 357 K6
Great Canfield 204 D3
Great Chesterford 42 F1
Great Clacton 12 D2
Great Claydons 314 B2
Great Cornard 55 L6
Great Dunmow 178 D4
Great Easton 150 A4
Great Hallingbury 174 E7
Great Henny 76 D3
Great Holland 198 A8
Great Horkesley 134 B2
Great Leighs 209 G3
Great Maplestead 98 D1
Great Malgraves 394 A6
Great Notley 182 C4
Great Oakley 141 L7
Great Oxney Green 287 G2
Great Parndon 15 H8
Great Saling 153 H3
Great Sampford 69 H7
Great Stambridge 364 F3
Great Tey 159 K3
Great Tey 240 B7
Great Totham 240 F4
Great Wakering 385 H8
Great Waltham 234 F4
Great Warley 373 H1
Great Wigborough 216 F8
Great Yeldham 73 H1
Greenstead 11 M9
Greenstead Green 129 H6
Greensted 282 D8
Greensted Green 282 C8
Green Street 172 F2
Green Street 309 L7
The Green 183 K7
Greenwich 58 E2
Gubbion's Green 209 K3
Hacton 389 M4
Hadham Ford 172 C3
Hadleigh 380 F8
Hadstock 24 D5
Hailey 253 G1
Hainault 350 A8
Hallingbury Street 175 J7
Hallsford Bridge 307 J2
Halls Green 254 D5
Halstead 128 E1
Hamperden End 120 F1
Hanchet End 27 J2
Handley Green 310 E3
Hardy's Green 188 E5
Hare Green 166 B5
Hare Street 15 G7
Harkstead 111 J1
Harlow 15 M4
Harold Hill 352 F6
Harold Park 353 J7
Harold Wood 372 B1
Hartford End 207 L3
Harwich 7 H6
Hastingwood 257 G7
Hatfield Broad Oak 203 G6
Hatfield Heath 202 C8
Hatfield Peverel 238 C6
Haverhill 27 L3
Havering-atte-Bower 352 A4
Hawbush Green 184 A6
Hawkin's Hill 93 M3
Hawkspur Green 93 L6
Hawkwell 363 H6
Hay Green 309 G6
Hazeleigh 292 A7
Hazel End 146 B5
Hazel Stub 27 K4
Heath Park 371 J6
The Heath 79 J5
Heckfordbridge 189 H4
Helions Bumpstead 47 J3
Hellman's Cross 204 A1
Hemp's Green 132 C5
Hempstead 69 G2
Henham 119 M6
Henny Street 77 G2
Herongate 374 F1
Heybridge 269 J5
Heybridge 334 C1
Heybridge Basin 269 L8
Heydon 40 B6
High Beach 326 C3
High Easter 232 D1
Highfields 213 L4
High Garrett 155 K1
High Houses 234 E4
High Laver 258 C5

High Ongar 283 L7
High Roding 204 F4
Highstreet Green 97 H1
The High 15 L4
High Wych 227 J2
Hill Green 87 M5
Hinxton 22 B3
Hobbs Cross 257 H2
Hobbs Cross 304 E8
Hockerill 174 C5
Hockley 362 D4
Hoddesdon 252 F6
Holbrook 80 F5
Holder's Green 122 F5
Holland-on-Sea 224 F6
Holyfield 277 K8
Hook End 308 D7
Hope End Green 176 F6
Hope's Green 397 K1
Hornchurch 389 L1
Horndon on the Hill 394 A7
Horne Row 290 D5
Hornestreet 105 L6
Horseman Side 330 F6
Horsley Cross 139 H8
Horsleycross Street 139 H5
Housham Tye 257 L1
Howe Green 201 M1
Howe Green 289 K8
Howegreen 316 D3
Howe Street 95 G2
Howe Street 234 F1
Howlett End 91 H1
Hullbridge 339 M8
Hurst Green 221 H5
Hutton 333 K8
Hutton Mount 355 J2
Hyde Chase 291 L7
The Hythe 163 L7
Ickleton 22 B8
Ingatestone 310 D8
Ingrave 355 L6
Inworth 214 A3
Ipswich 3 H7
Ivy Chimneys 303 H4
Jack's Hatch 279 J1
Janke's Green 131 M3
Jasper's Green 153 L1
Jaywick 250 A3
Katherines 254 F6
Kedington 29 J1
Keelars Tye 164 F8
Keeres Green 231 L2
Kelvedon 213 L2
Kelvedon Hatch 331 L1
Kesgrave 39 K3
Keysers Estate 277 J1
Kingsmoor 255 K8
King Street 284 C8
Kingswood 19 H8
Kirby Cross 198 C4
Kirby-le-Soken 198 D2
Knowl Green 52 A4
Laindon 376 E4
Lakeside 416 A1
Lamarsh 77 K7
Lamb Corner 106 C7
Lambourne 328 E6
Lambourne End 350 F1
Langdon Hills 376 B7
Langenhoe 218 B1
Langford 268 E4
Langham 106 A7
Langley 86 D1
Langley Green 187 G3
Latchingdon 318 B6
Latchmore Bank 201 H1
Latton Bush 256 B7
Lawford 108 B8
Layer Breton 216 C1
Layer de la Haye 190 A6
Layer Marney 215 M3
Leaden Roding 231 L3
Lee Chapel 18 C8
Lee-over-Sands 248 D5
Leigh Beck 398 F8
Leigh-on-Sea 399 M1 *
Level's Green 145 M6
Levington 60 F8
Lexden 162 B3
Lindsell 123 H8
Linford 409 G7
Lippitts Hill 326 A4
Liston 34 B5
Liston Garden 33 M3
Little Baddow 266 E7
Little Bardfield 123 L1
Little Bentley 167 H3
Little Braxted 239 K1
Little Bromley 138 C5
Little Burstead 357 F4
Littlebury 42 F7
Littlebury Green 64 B2
Little Cambridge 122 C8
Little Chesterford 42 F3
Little Clacton 196 E8
Little Cornard 55 M8
Little Dunmow 179 M4
Little Easton 149 M6
Little End 306 F4
Little Hadham 172 D1
Little Hallingbury 201 K3
Little Henham 119 K2
Little Horkesley 103 H3
Little Laver 259 G3
Little Leighs 208 F5
Little London 70 C8
Little London 117 L3
Little Maplestead 99 H2
Little Mascalls 313 H2
Little Oakley 142 D4
Little Oxney Green 286 E3
Little Parndon 15 G2
Little Sampford 93 K3
Little Tey 159 K2
Little Thurrock 417 K1
Little Totham 241 H7
Little Wakering 384 F5

Little Walden 44 A3
Little Waltham 235 K5
Little Warley 374 A2
Little Wigborough 217 J8
Little Yeldham 51 M7
Littley Green 208 A4
Long Gardens 76 A6
Long Melford 34 E4
Loughton 327 G6
Loves Green 286 B6
Lower Bobbingworth Green 282 C4
Lower Falkenham 84 F1
Lower Green 86 C2
Lower Green 96 C8
Lower Green 289 K6
Lower Green 312 D2
Lower Holbrook 81 H8
Lower Nazeing 277 L3
Lower Sheering 228 B2
Lower Street 110 C2
Low Street 419 G3
Loyter's Green 258 A2
Lucking Street 98 F1
Mace Green 56 E4
Magdalen Laver 257 L6
Maggots End 117 M7
Maidenhall 58 C1
Maldon 269 J8
Mallows Green 145 K1
Manningtree 108 C7
Manuden 146 A1
Manwood Green 229 M6
Maple End 67 L4
Marden Ash 307 G2
Margaret Roding 231 L6
Margaretting 311 H3
Margaretting Tye 311 J4
Mark Hall North 227 H8
Mark Hall South 256 B1
Marks Tey 160 B8
Mashbury 233 K7
Matching 229 H7
Matching Green 229 L8
Matching Tye 229 G8
Mayland 319 K3
Maylandsea 318 F2
Maypole Green 190 E2
Meadowend 50 D6
Meesden 86 A6
Messing 214 D1
Middleton 54 F7
Mile End 134 F7
Millend Green 150 D3
Miller's Green 260 B7
Mill Green 26 D4
Mill Green 310 A4
Mill Hill 362 C4
Minnow End 235 H4
Mistley 109 H7
Mistley Heath 139 H1
Molehill Green 148 E5
Molehill Green 181 L6
Monk Street 122 C4
Montsale 346 C3
Moreton 282 D1
Mott's Green 201 L5
Moulsham 17 G7
Mount Bovers 362 E8
Mount Bures 101 M5
Mount End 305 G4
Mountnessing 333 L3
Mowden 266 E2
Mucking 409 L4
Mundon 317 M1
Nacton 60 D6
Navestock Heath 330 D4
Navestock Side 331 K4
Nayland 104 C2
Nazeing 278 C2
Nazeing Gate 278 D5
Nazeing Long Green 278 B5
Nazeing Mead 253 L7
Needham Green 203 H7
Nether Street 231 H7
Netteswell 255 M2
Nevendon 359 K8
New England 49 K1
Newman's End 229 G6
Newman's Green 35 H7
New Mistley 109 H8
Newney Green 286 C1
Newport 89 H3
New Thundersley 379 L4
Nine Ashes 308 E2
Noak Bridge 377 G2
Noak Hill 352 F3
Noak Hill 357 K7
North Benfleet 379 G3
North End 52 A8
North End 206 F1
North End 414 A5
Northend 43 H7
Northend 320 E6
North Fambridge 341 H4
North Ockendon 391 J4
North Shoebury 403 G2
North Stifford 406 F5
North Weald Bassett 281 G6
Norton Heath 284 F5
Norton Mandeville 284 A5
Norwood End 259 K6
Nosterfield End 27 G6
Nounsley 267 H1
Nuper's Hatch 351 M1
Old Felixstowe 85 L8
Old Harlow 227 K7
Old Heath 163 K8
Old Mead 119 L7
Olmstead Green 46 F4
Onslow Green 206 D1
Orsett 408 C3
Orsett Heath 408 A7
Ostend 343 M4
Ovington 51 J2
Oxen End 123 M5
Oxley Green 242 B2
Padham's Green 334 C4
Paglesham Churchend 365 L4
Paglesham Eastend 366 B6
Pale Green 47 L2
Panfield 154 B4
Pannel's Ash 50 F2
Parkeston 6 A4
Parkgate 206 F3
Park Green 117 J5
Parney Heath 106 C7
Parsonage Green 264 B3
Paslow Wood Common 308 C2
Passingford Bridge 329 L3
Passmores 15 L9
Paternoster Heath 215 H8
Patient End 116 A8
Patmore Heath 144 E3
Pattiswick 156 F6
Peartree Green 332 E1
Pebmarsh 100 A4
Pedlars End 282 C1
Peldon 217 L5
Pentlow 32 F5
Pentlow Street 33 H3
Pepper's Green 261 J2
Perry Green 184 E2
Pharisee Green 178 B6
Philpot End 205 H1
Piercing Hill 303 L7
Pigstye Green 285 G2
Pilgrims Hatch 332 C6
Pinnacles 14 F6
Pipps Hill 18 D1
Pitsea 378 C6
Pledgdon Green 148 D1
Pleshey 233 M1
Point Clear 248 C1
Ponders End 324 D7
Pond Street 63 G4
The Port of Felixstowe 8 A8
Potash 78 F4
Potter Street 256 E5
Powers Hall End 211 K8
Priory Heath 59 L2
Prittlewell 382 F8
Purfleet 415 H3
Purleigh 316 F2
Puttock End 52 E5
Puttock's End 176 E7
Queen's Park 335 H5
Quendon 119 G1
Racecourse 59 G1
Radley Green 285 K4
Radwinter 67 M4
Radwinter End 46 B7
Rainham 404 C1
Ramsden Bellhouse 358 F2
Ramsden Heath 336 E7
Ramsey 142 A1
Ramsey Island 296 C3
Rank's Green 209 L3
Raven's Green 166 D6
Rawreth 360 F4
Rawreth Shot 360 D4
Rayleigh 361 L8
Rayne 181 M1
Reader's Corner 288 F6
Rettendon 338 C2
Richmond's Green 122 E4
Rickling 88 C7
Rickling Green 118 E3
Ridgewell 50 B5
Ringtail Green 207 J6
Rise Park 370 F1
Rivenhall 212 C4
Rivenhall End 212 F5
Roast Green 87 G5
Robinhood End 71 J6
Rochford 383 H1
Rodbridge Corner 34 D7
Romford 370 E5
Rook End 90 B6
Roost End 29 H7
Rosedale 276 A8
Rose Green 131 M6
Rose Hill 3 M8
Rotten End 126 B4
Roundbush 317 H3
Roundbush Green 231 K1
Row Green 182 E5
Row Heath 196 B8
Rowhedge 191 M3
Roxwell 262 C5
Roydon 254 C2
Roydon Hamlet 254 D7
Rudley Green 292 D8
Runsell Green 291 H4
Runwell 359 M2
Rush Green 223 J8
Rush Green 370 F7
Rushley Green 74 A5
Rushmere St Andrew 38 E3
Rushmere Street 39 G2
Rye Meads 253 L2
Rye Park 253 J4
Sabine's Green 330 E4
Saffron Walden 66 B2
St Lawrence 297 G6
St Osyth 222 B7
St Osyth Heath 222 F2
St Vincent's Hamlet 353 H2
Salcott-cum-Virley 243 H3
Samuel's Corner 385 L7
Sandon 289 K5
Sawbridgeworth 227 J1
School Green 96 C8
Seawick 249 K4
Seven Star Green 161 G3
Sewards End 66 F2
Sewardstone 325 L4
Sewardstonebury 325 M7
Shalford 125 L4
Shalford Green 125 K8
Sheering 228 E3
Shelley 283 H4
Shellow Bowells 261 G7
Shenfield 354 F1
Shoeburyness 403 H5
Shop Corner 112 B2
Shotgate 360 C5
Shotley 82 F8
Shotley Gate 113 J2
Shrub End 162 C7
Shudy Camps 26 C5
Sible Hedingham 97 M1
Sibley's Green 122 C6
Silver End 184 F7
Skye Green 186 F2
Slade Green 414 B6
Smith's Green 48 A6
Smith's Green 176 E4
Smythe's Green 215 K1
South Benfleet 379 M8
Southchurch 401 M3
Southend-on-Sea 20 E4
Southey Green 97 K6
South Fambridge 341 J7
Southfields 408 E5
South Green 192 B8
South Green 357 L4
South Hanningfield 337 L3
South Heath 195 G8
South Hornchurch 388 E7
Southminster 320 C7
South Ockendon 406 D2
South Stifford 416 E2
South Weald 353 M3
South Woodham Ferrers 340 A2
Spellbrook 200 F3
Spitalbrook 253 H7
Springfield 264 E5
Springwell 43 H4
Sproughton 36 C5
Stafford's Corner 216 F6
Stagden Cross 233 G1
Stambourne 71 K1
Stambourne Green 71 H2
Stanbrook 121 M3
Stanford-le-Hope 410 A1
Stanford Rivers 306 D5
Stansted Mountfitchet 146 D4
Stanway 161 K6
Stanway Green 161 L8
Stapleford Abbotts 329 L8
Stapleford Tawney 305 K8
Starling's Green 87 G8
Start Hill 175 H4
Stebbing 151 M6
Stebbing Green 152 E8
Steeple 295 M8
Steeple Bumpstead 48 C3
Steventon End 45 K1
Stewards 255 M8
Steward's Green 304 C4
Stickling Green 87 L5
Stisted 156 D5
Stocking Green 67 J2
Stocking Pelham 116 E4
Stoke 2 E8
Stoke by Clare 30 D8
Stoke Park 58 A2
Stondon Massey 308 B6
Stonebridge 384 A5
Stones Green 168 E1
Stoneyhills 344 D4
Stow Maries 316 D7
Stratford St Mary 106 D2
Strethall 41 M7
Stroud Green 382 C1
Sturmer 28 F7
Stutton 110 A1
Suckstead Green 121 J5
Sudbury 4 F3
Sumners 255 H7
Sunken Marsh 398 D6
Sunnymede 357 L1
Surrex 186 F1
Swallows Cross 333 G1
Swan Street 131 K8
Takeley 176 C3
Takeley Street 176 A4
Tarpots 379 K6
Tattingstone 79 K4
Tattingstone White Horse 79 L2
Taverners Green 203 K3
Temple End 33 J8
Temple Fields 227 H7
Temple Hill 414 E8
Tendring 168 A6
Tendring Green 167 M3
Tendring Heath 167 K2
Terling 210 D8
Thaxted 92 C8
Theydon Bois 327 L1
Theydon Garnon 304 D8
Theydon Mount 305 H8
Thistley Green 181 J7
Thorley 200 D1
Thorley Houses 173 H6
Thorley Street 173 M8
Thornwood Common 280 C5
Thorpe Bay 402 C4
Thorpe Common 83 M3
Thorpe Green 169 G7
Thorpe-le-Soken 197 H2
Thorrington 194 C6
Threshers Bush 257 H4
Thundersley 379 M4
Tilbury 418 B5
Tilbury Green 50 E5
Tilbury Juxta Claire 51 J6
Tilegate Green 257 L5
Tilekiln Green 175 G5
Tilkey 158 A7
Tillingham 298 A7
Tilty 149 L2
Tindon End 92 C2
Tip's Cross 308 D6
Tiptree 214 C5
Tiptree Heath 214 C8
Tollesbury 272 D2
Tolleshunt D'Arcy 242 D7
Tolleshunt Knights 242 B1
Tolleshunt Major 241 M7
Toot Hill 306 A2
Toppesfield 72 C4
Totham Hill 240 F6
Totham Plains 241 J6
Trimley Lower Street 83 M5
Trimley St Martin 84 B2
Trimley St Mary 84 C6
Trims Green 200 D4
Turnford 276 E5
Twinstead 76 D5
Twinstead Green 76 B6
Tye Common 357 G4
Tye Green 67 K8
Tye Green 147 M5
Tye Green 183 M5
Tye Green 232 F5
Tyler's Green 281 L4
Ugley 119 G5
Ugley Green 119 H8
Ulting Wick 267 K4
Upminster 390 D1
Uppend 145 J2
Upper Dovercourt 112 F8
Upper Green 86 E1
Upper Street 109 M2
Upshire 302 D4
Upwick Green 144 F6
Vange 377 M7
Wakes Colne 131 J5
Wakes Colne Green 131 K2
Waltham Abbey 301 L4
Waltham Cross 300 D5
Waltham's Cross 124 F2
Walton 85 G8
Walton-on-the-Naze 198 F3
Warley 354 C6
Warren Heath 60 A2
Washall Green 116 C2
Washbrook 56 F2
Washbrook Street 56 F1
Watch House Green 180 F4
Water End 45 J5
Waterhales 330 E8
Watton's Green 330 C8
Weeley 196 A2
Weeley Heath 196 A5
Weir 380 D3
Wellstye Green 206 B1
Welshwood Park 164 A2
Wendens Ambo 64 F6
Wennington 404 F5
West Bergholt 133 M8
Westbourne 36 F2
Westcliff-on-Sea 400 D4
West Hanningfield 313 J7
West Horndon 374 D6
Westley Heights 394 D1
West Mersea 245 H5
West Thurrock 416 B2
West Tilbury 418 F3
Westwood Park 133 M2
Wethersfield 95 J8
Wherstead 58 C5
Whiteash Green 98 A8
White Colne 130 F5
White House 36 F1
White Notley 210 F2
White Roding or
White Roothing 230 D4
Wicken Bonhunt 88 C3
Wickford 360 A6
Wickham Bishops 239 L6
Wickham St Paul 75 K6
Widdington 89 K7
Widford 287 M5
Wiggens Green 47 M2
Willingale 260 D8
Willows Green 181 M7
Wimbish 67 K5
Wimbish Green 67 M8
Winter Gardens 397 M6
Witham 211 M7
Wivenhoe 192 C2
Wix 140 D6
Wixoe 29 L8
Woodend 259 M2
Woodend Green 120 C6
Woodford 348 C7
Woodford Bridge 349 G8
Woodford Green 348 B8
Woodford Wells 348 C4
Woodgates End 148 E4
Wood Green 302 D6
Woodham Ferrers 315 H7
Woodham Mortimer 291 L6
Woodham Walter 291 K1
Woodhill 290 C5
The Woodlands 80 C4
Woodside 280 E6
Woodside Green 202 A2
Woollensbrook 252 E2
Woolverstone 81 H2
Workhouse Green 77 M4
Workhouse Hill 104 F7
Wormingford 102 E6
Wormley 276 F4
Wormleybury 276 C3
Wormley West End 276 B2
Wrabness 111 G8
Wright's Green 201 L4
Writtle 287 H3
Young's End 182 B7

USING THE STREET INDEX

Street names are listed alphabetically. Each street name is followed by its postal town or area locality, the Postcode District, the page number, and the reference to the square in which the name is found.

Example: **Abbey Cl** *ROM* RM1 **371** H6 1

Some entries are followed by a number in a blue box. This number indicates the location of the street within the referenced grid square. The full street name is listed at the side of the map page.

GENERAL ABBREVIATIONS

ACC	ACCESS	CATH	CATHEDRAL	COMM	COMMISSION	CYN	CANYON	F/O	FLYOVER
ALY	ALLEY	CEM	CEMETERY	CON	CONVENT	DEPT	DEPARTMENT	FC	FOOTBALL CLUB
AP	APPROACH	CEN	CENTRE	COT	COTTAGE	DL	DALE	FK	FORK
AR	ARCADE	CFT	CROFT	COTS	COTTAGES	DM	DAM	FLD	FIELD
ASS	ASSOCIATION	CH	CHURCH	CP	CAPE	DR	DRIVE	FLDS	FIELDS
AV	AVENUE	CHA	CHASE	CPS	COPSE	DRO	DROVE	FLS	FALLS
BCH	BEACH	CHYD	CHURCHYARD	CR	CREEK	DRY	DRIVEWAY	FLS	FLATS
BLDS	BUILDINGS	CIR	CIRCLE	CREM	CREMATORIUM	DWGS	DWELLINGS	FM	FARM
BND	BEND	CIRC	CIRCUS	CRS	CRESCENT	E	EAST	FT	FORT
BNK	BANK	CL	CLOSE	CSWY	CAUSEWAY	EMB	EMBANKMENT	FWY	FREEWAY
BR	BRIDGE	CLFS	CLIFFS	CT	COURT	EMBY	EMBASSY	FY	FERRY
BRK	BROOK	CMP	CAMP	CTRL	CENTRAL	ESP	ESPLANADE	GA	GATE
BTM	BOTTOM	CNR	CORNER	CTS	COURTS	EST	ESTATE	GAL	GALLERY
BUS	BUSINESS	CO	COUNTY	CTYD	COURTYARD	EX	EXCHANGE	GDN	GARDEN
BVD	BOULEVARD	COLL	COLLEGE	CUTT	CUTTINGS	EXPY	EXPRESSWAY	GDNS	GARDENS
BY	BYPASS	COM	COMMON	CV	COVE	EXT	EXTENSION	GLD	GLADE

GLN GLEN
GN GREEN
GND GROUND
GRA GRANGE
GRG GARAGE
GT GREAT
GTWY GATEWAY
GV GROVE
HGR HIGHER
HL HILL
HLS HILLS
HO HOUSE
HOL HOLLOW
HOSP HOSPITAL
HRB HARBOUR
HTH HEATH
HTS HEIGHTS
HVN HAVEN
HWY HIGHWAY
IMP IMPERIAL
IN INLET
IND EST INDUSTRIAL ESTATE
INF INFIRMARY
INFO INFORMATION
INT INTERCHANGE
IS ISLAND
JCT JUNCTION
JTY JETTY
KG KING
KNL KNOLL
L LAKE
LA LANE
LDG LODGE
LGT LIGHT
LK LOCK
LKS LAKES
LNDG LANDING
LTL LITTLE
LWR LOWER
MAG MAGISTRATE
MAN MANSIONS
MD MEAD
MDW MEADOWS
MEM MEMORIAL
MKT MARKET
MKTS MARKETS
ML MALL
ML MILL
MNR MANOR
MS MEWS
MSN MISSION
MT MOUNT
MTN MOUNTAIN
MTS MOUNTAINS
MUS MUSEUM
MWY MOTORWAY
N NORTH
NE NORTH EAST
NW NORTH WEST
O/P OVERPASS
OFF OFFICE
ORCH ORCHARD
OV OVAL
PAL PALACE
PAS PASSAGE
PAV PAVILION
PDE PARADE
PH PUBLIC HOUSE
PK PARK
PKWY PARKWAY
PL PLACE
PLN PLAIN
PLNS PLAINS
PLZ PLAZA
POL POLICE STATION
PR PRINCE
PREC PRECINCT
PREP PREPARATORY
PRIM PRIMARY
PROM PROMENADE
PRS PRINCESS
PRT PORT
PT POINT
PTH PATH
PZ PIAZZA
QD QUADRANT
QU QUEEN
QY QUAY
R RIVER
RBT ROUNDABOUT
RD ROAD
RDG RIDGE
REP REPUBLIC
RES RESERVOIR
RFC RUGBY FOOTBALL CLUB
RI RISE
RP RAMP
RW ROW
S SOUTH
SCH SCHOOL
SE SOUTH EAST
SER SERVICE AREA
SH SHORE
SHOP SHOPPING
SKWY SKYWAY
SMT SUMMIT
SOC SOCIETY
SP SPUR
SPR SPRING
SQ SQUARE
ST STREET
STN STATION
STR STREAM
STRD STRAND
SW SOUTH WEST
TDG TRADING
TER TERRACE
THWY THROUGHWAY
TNL TUNNEL
TOLL TOLLWAY
TPK TURNPIKE
TR TRACK
TRL TRAIL
TWR TOWER
U/P UNDERPASS
UNI UNIVERSITY
UPR UPPER
V VALE
VA VALLEY
VIAD VIADUCT
VIL VILLA
VIS VISTA
VLG VILLAGE
VLS VILLAS
VW VIEW
W WEST
WD WOOD
WHF WHARF
WK WALK
WKS WALKS
WLS WELLS
WY WAY
YD YARD
YHA YOUTH HOSTEL

POSTCODE TOWNS AND AREA ABBREVIATIONS

ABR/ST Abridge/Stapleford Abbotts
BARK/HLT Barkingside/Hainault
BCAYE Billericay east
BCAYW Billericay west
BCTR Becontree
BKHH Buckhurst Hill
BOC Burnham-on-Crouch
BROX Broxbourne
BRTR Braintree
BRW Brentwood
BRWN Brentwood north
BSDN Basildon
BSF Bishop's Stortford
BUNT Buntingford
BURES Bures
BXLYHN Bexleyheath north
CBE/LIN Cambridge east/Linton
CBS Cambridge south
CDW/CHF Chadwell St Mary/Chafford Hundred
CHDH Chadwell Heath
CHES/WCR Cheshunt/Waltham Cross
CHESW Cheshunt west
CHIG Chigwell
CHING Chingford
CHLM/GWD Chelmsford/Galleywood
CHLM/WR Chelmsford/Writtle
CHONG Chipping Ongar
CHTY Chantry
CLAY Clayhall
COL Colchester
COLN Colchester north
COLS Colchester south
COLW Colchester west
COS Clacton-on-Sea
CRW Collier Row
CVI Canvey Island
DAGE Dagenham east
DAGW Dagenham west
DART Dartford
ED Edmonton
EMPK Emerson Park
EN Enfield
ENC/FH Enfield Chase/Forty Hill
EPP Epping
ERITH Erith
FOS Frinton-on-Sea
FRAM/WMKT Framlingham/Wickham Market
FX Felixstowe
GPK Gidea Park
GRAYS Grays
GRH Greenhithe
GTDUN Great Dunmow
GVW Gravesend west
HAR Harwich
HARH Harold Hill
HCH Hornchurch
HERT/BAY Hertford/Bayford
HLW Harlow
HLWE Harlow east
HLWS Harlow south
HLWW/ROY Harlow west/Roydon
HOC/HUL Hockley/Hullbridge
HOD Hoddesdon
HOO/HM Hoo St Werburgh/Higham
HSTD Halstead
HVHL Haverhill
ING Ingatestone
IP Ipswich
IPNE Ipswich northeast
IPSE Ipswich southeast
K/T/MI Kelvedon/Tiptree/Mersea Island
KESG Kesgrave
KIR/NAC Kirton/Nacton
LAIN Laindon
LOS Leigh-on-Sea
MAL Maldon
MGTR Manningtree
MHAD Much Hadham
NHMKT Needham Market
PEND Ponders End
PIT Pitsea
PUR Purfleet
RAIN Rainham (Gt Lon)
RAYL Rayleigh
RBRW/HUT Rural Brentwood/Hutton
RBSF Rural Bishop's Stortford
RCFD Rochford
RCHLM Rural Chelmsford
RCOLE Rural Colchester east
RCOLW Rural Colchester west
RCOS Rural Clacton-on-Sea
RIPS/CAP Rural Ipswich south/Capel St Mary
RIPW Rural Ipswich west
ROM Romford
ROMW/RG Romford west/Rush Green
ROY Royston
SAFWN Saffron Walden north
SAFWS Saffron Walden south
SBF/HAD South Benfleet/Hadleigh
SBN/FI Shoeburyness/Foulness Island
SBW Sawbridgeworth
SLH/COR Stanford-le-Hope/Corringham
SOCK/AV South Ockendon/Aveley
SOS Southend-on-Sea
SOSN Southend-on-Sea north
STDN Standon
STSD Stansted
SUD Sudbury
SWCM Swanscombe
SWFD South Woodford
TIL Tilbury
UED Upper Edmonton
UPMR Upminster
VGE Vange
WAB Waltham Abbey
WARE Ware
WCHMH Winchmore Hill
WDBR Woodbridge
WFD Woodford
WICKE Wickford east
WICKW Wickford west
WIT Witham
WOS/PRIT Westcliff-on-Sea/Prittlewell
WOTN Walton-on-the-Naze
WTHK West Thurrock

A

Aalten Av CVI SS8 399 G8
Abberton Rd COLS CO2 190 C6
K/T/MI CO5 192 B6
Abbess Cl CHLM/WR CM1 16 A4
Abbey Cl HOC/HUL SS5 361 L1
ROM RM1 371 H6
Abbey Ct WAB EN9 301 J6
Abbey Crs RCOS CO16 197 H2
Abbey Dale Cl HLWE CM17 256 D4
Abbey Flds RCHLM CM3 314 C4
Abbey Gate St COLS CO2 10 C9
Abbey La RCOLW CO6 186 B2
SAFWN CB10 65 L2
Abbey Meadow HSTD CO9 97 L1
Abbey Rd BAR EN8 300 F6
BCAYW CM12 357 G2
HOC/HUL SS5 361 L2
SUD CO10 4 C2
Abbey St RCOS CO16 197 H2
SAFWN CB10 22 B7
Abbey Turning MAL CM9 268 E8
Abbey Vw GTDUN CM6 149 M1
Abbeyview WAB EN9 301 J5
Abbey Wood La RAIN RM13 389 L8
Abbotsbury Cl CHTY IP2 58 B2
Abbots Cl BRWN CM15 355 H2
COS CO15 223 M5
MGTR CO11 140 D6
RAIN RM13 389 K8
Abbots Ct LAIN SS15 376 F2
Abbotsford Gdns WFD IG8 348 B8
Abbots Gdns RCOS CO16 222 D7
Abbots La COLW CO3 161 H4
Abbotsleigh Rd RCHLM CM3 339 L4
Abbotsmead MAL CM9 269 G6
Abbots Ride BCAYE CM11 357 K1
Abbot's Rd COLS CO2 163 K8
Abbots Wk SBN/FI SS3 402 D3
Abbotsweld HLWS CM18 255 L6
Abbots Wick La K/T/MI CO5 216 B8
Abbotswood SBF/HAD SS7 380 D6
Abbott Rd HAR CO12 143 G1
Abbotts Cl CHLM/WR CM1 17 L2
LOS SS9 381 M6
ROMW/RG RM7 370 C3
Abbotts Ct HVHL CB9 28 F6
Abbotts Dr SLH/COR SS17 409 M1
WAB EN9 302 B6
Abbotts Hall Cha SLH/COR SS17 409 M1
Abbotts Rd HVHL CB9 28 B2
Abbotts Wy BSF CM23 173 M8
Abbs Cross Gdns HCH RM12 371 K8
Abbs Cross La HCH RM12 389 K2
Abdy Av HAR CO12 142 F1
Abell Wy CHLM/GWD CM2 265 J7
Abels Rd HSTD CO9 128 E3
Abenberg Wy
RBRW/HUT CM13 355 H3
Abensburg Rd CVI SS8 398 E6
Abercorn Wy WIT CM8 239 H1
Abercrombie Dr EN EN1 324 B3
Abercrombie Wy
HLWW/ROY CM19 15 J7
Aberdare Rd PEND EN3 324 D6
Aberdeen Gdns LOS SS9 399 H1
Aberdeen Wy IPNE IP4 38 C2
Aberfoyle Cl IPNE IP4 38 D2
Abingdon Ct PIT SS13 378 B2
Abinger Cl RCOS CO16 223 K5
Abraham Dr WIT CM8 184 F7
Abram's La ROY SG8 40 D6
Abreys SBF/HAD SS7 380 B4
Abridge Cl BAR EN8 300 E7
Abridge Gdns CRW RM5 351 H7
Abridge Rd CHIG IG7 327 M8
EPP CM16 328 B1
Acacia Av COLN CO4 163 M3
HCH RM12 389 G1
Acacia Cl IPSE IP3 59 M2
Acacia Dr MAL CM9 292 F1
SOS SS1 402 B3
UPMR RM14 390 B3
Acacia Gdns UPMR RM14 373 G7
WIT CM8 212 C7
Acacia Rd PIT SS13 378 F3
Accommodation Rd
RCOLW CO6 134 E4
Acer Av RAIN RM13 404 E1
Acer Gv RIPW IP8 57 K2
Achilles Wy BRTR CM7 155 J6
Achnacone Dr COLN CO4 134 D8
Acland Av COLW CO3 162 B4
Acorn Av BRTR CM7 182 E1
HSTD CO9 128 E2
Acorn Cl HAR CO12 143 H2
RCOLE CO7 135 L7
RIPW IP8 57 K1
Acorn Pl VGE SS16 376 B6
The Acorns HOC/HUL SS5 362 F4
Acremore St STDN SG11 172 E4
Acre Rd DAGE RM10 388 D6
Acres Av CHONG CM5 283 G6
Acres End CHLM/WR CM1 263 M7
The Acres SLH/COR SS17 395 G8
Acton Cl BAR EN8 300 F3
RIPW IP8 36 B1
SUD CO10 4 E4
Acton Gn SUD CO10 4 C6
Acton La SUD CO10 4 E4
SUD CO10 5 G1
SUD CO10 35 G7
Acton Rd RIPW IP8 36 B1
Adair Rd IP IP1 36 E3
Adalia Crs LOS SS9 399 J1
Adalia Wy LOS SS9 399 J1
Adams Cl CHTY IP2 37 K8
Adams Ct SAFWS CB11 65 K3
Adamsfield CHESW EN7 276 A6
Adams Gld RCFD SS4 363 L5
Adams House HLW CM20 15 L3
Adams Pl KESG IP5 39 K4
Adams Rd SLH/COR SS17 409 M2
Adam Wy WICKE SS11 359 M3
Adastral Cl FX IP11 8 E9
Addington Rd FX IP11 84 D6
Addis Cl PEND EN3 324 E3
Addison Gdns GRAYS RM17 417 K1
Addison Rd FOS CO13 198 B6
PEND EN3 324 D3
SUD CO10 5 H3
Adelaide Dr COLS CO2 191 H2
Adelaide Gdns SBF/HAD SS7 397 L2
Adelaide Rd IPNE IP4 38 E5
TIL RM18 418 A5
Adelaide St HAR CO12 6 A5
Adelphi Crs HCH RM12 389 H1
Adelsburg Rd CVI SS8 398 D7
Aden Rd PEND EN3 324 F6
Admirals Wk CHLM/WR CM1 16 C1
HOD EN11 253 H7
SBN/FI SS3 402 E6
Admiral Ms WOS/PRIT SS0 400 D4
Adnams Wk RAIN RM13 389 H5
Adstock Wy GRAYS RM17 417 G1
Advice Av CDH/CHF RM16 407 H7
Aetheric Rd BRTR CM7 154 F8
Affleck Rd COLN CO4 163 M4
Afton Dr SOCK/AV RM15 406 C4
Agar Road Ap WOTN CO14 199 K3
Agate Cl IP IP1 36 E2
Agate Rd COS CO15 12 F8
Agincourt Rd COS CO15 12 C4
Agister Rd CHIG IG7 350 B6
Agnes Av LOS SS9 399 J1
Agricola Pl EN EN1 324 A7
Ailsa Rd WOS/PRIT SS0 400 D3
Ainger Rd HAR CO12 142 F1
Aingers Green Rd RCOLE CO7 195 G6
Ainsley Av ROMW/RG RM7 370 D6
Ainslie Rd IP IP1 2 B3
Aintree Gv UPMR RM14 390 A2
Aire Dr SOCK/AV RM15 406 C2
Airfield Wy HCH RM12 389 J5
Aisne Rd COLS CO2 162 E7
Aisthorpe RIPS/CAP IP9 78 A2
Ajax Cl BRTR CM7 155 J6
Akenfield Cl RCHLM CM3 339 M4
Alamein Cl BROX EN10 252 E8
Alamein Rd BOC CM0 344 D7
CHLM/WR CM1 264 A5
COLS CO2 190 D1
Alanbrooke Rd COLS CO2 191 L1
Alan Cl DART DA1 414 D8
LOS SS9 381 M5
Alan Dr RCOS CO16 223 L2
Alan Gdns ROMW/RG RM7 370 B7
Alan Gv LOS SS9 381 M5
Alan Rd IPSE IP3 3 M7
WIT CM8 238 F2
Alan Wy COLW CO3 162 A7
Albany Av WOS/PRIT SS0 20 D4
Albany Cl CHLM/WR CM1 263 M6
RCOLW CO6 133 M7
Albany Ct EPP CM16 304 A2
Albany Gdns East COS CO15 13 L4
Albany Gdns West COS CO15 13 K4
Albany Park Av PEND EN3 324 D3
Albany Rd BRWN CM15 332 C8
CHDH RM6 370 A6
HCH RM12 371 H8
PEND EN3 324 E1
RAYL SS6 381 H2
RCOLW CO6 134 A7
TIL RM18 418 B5
WICKW SS12 359 L5
The Albany IPNE IP4 37 M3
Albany Vw BKHH IG9 348 B2
Albemarle Av BAR EN8 276 D8
Albemarle Cl GRAYS RM17 407 H7
Albemarle Gdns BRTR CM7 155 K6
Albemarle St HAR CO12 7 K4
Alberta Cl KESG IP5 39 H4
Alberta Rd EN EN1 324 A8
Albert Cl CDH/CHF RM16 407 K8
RAYL SS6 381 G1
RCFD SS4 363 K4
Albert Dr LAIN SS15 376 D5
Albert Gdns COS CO15 13 K5
HLWE CM17 256 E4
RCOLW CO6 186 B1
Albertine Cl COLW CO3 161 K5
Albert Pl RCOLW CO6 186 B1
Albert Rd BCTR RM8 370 A8
BKHH IG9 348 E3
BOC CM0 344 D7
BRTR CM7 155 H8
RAYL SS6 381 G1
RCFD SS4 363 K5
RCHLM CM3 339 K4
RCOLE CO7 221 H5
ROM RM1 371 G6
SBF/HAD SS7 379 J5
SOS SS1 21 K7
UPMR RM14 393 G3
WIT CM8 212 B8
Albert St BRW CM14 354 D6
COL CO1 10 B5
HAR CO12 7 K5
Albion Cl ROMW/RG RM7 370 E6
Albion Gv COLS CO2 163 H6
Albion Hl IPNE IP4 3 L2
LOU IG10 326 D7
Albion Pk LOU IG10 326 E7
Albion Rd DAGE RM10 388 B4
SBF/HAD SS7 379 K7
WOS/PRIT SS0 20 C4
Albion St K/T/MI CO5 192 B4
Albrighton Cft COLN CO4 135 K7
Albury Grove Rd BAR EN8 300 E2
Albury Ride BAR EN8 300 E3
Albury Rd STDN SG11 172 D1
Albury Wk BAR EN8 300 D2
Albyns VGE SS16 376 D7
Albyns La ABR/ST RM4 329 L4
Alconbury BSF CM23 174 C2
Alcotes BSDN SS14 378 A6
Aldborough Rd DAGE RM10 388 D5
UPMR RM14 390 A1
Aldeburgh Cl HVHL CB9 27 M5
RCOS CO16 223 J7
Aldeburgh Gdns COLN CO4 135 J7
Aldeburgh Pl WFD IG8 348 B5
Aldeburgh Wy CHLM/WR CM1 264 E6
Alder Av UPMR RM14 390 A3
Alderbury Lea RCHLM CM3 315 G2
Alderbury Rd STSD CM24 146 F3
Aldercar Rd RCOLW CO6 189 G2
Alder Cl BSF CM23 173 L7
HOD EN11 253 J3
LAIN SS15 376 E2
Aldercroft Rd IP IP1 37 J1
Alder Dr CHLM/GWD CM2 288 C5
SOCK/AV RM15 406 D2
Alderford St HSTD CO9 97 M3
Alderlee CHTY IP2 58 A3
Alderleys SBF/HAD SS7 380 B5
Alderman Rd IP IP1 2 C5
Alderman's Hl HOC/HUL SS5 362 C6
Alderman Wk SLH/COR SS17 394 F6
Alderney Gdns WICKE SS11 359 K1
Alderney Rd ERITH DA8 414 B4
Alde Rd HVHL CB9 28 B3
Alders Wk SBW CM21 227 M1
Alderton Cl BRWN CM15 332 C7
GTDUN CM6 180 D5
LOU IG10 327 H6
Alderton Hall La LOU IG10 327 H6
Alderton Hl LOU IG10 327 G7
Alderton Ri LOU IG10 327 H6
Alderton Rd CDH/CHF RM16 408 E4
COLN CO4 11 K5
Alderton Wy LOU IG10 327 G7
Alderwood Dr ABR/ST RM4 328 C5
Alderwood Wy SBF/HAD SS7 380 D8
Aldham Gdns RAYL SS6 361 G8
Aldingham Gdns HCH RM12 389 H4
Aldon Cl HAR CO12 142 D2
Aldria Rd SLH/COR SS17 394 F6
Aldridge Av PEND EN3 325 H2
Aldridge Cl CHLM/GWD CM2 265 H7
Aldrin Cl SLH/COR SS17 409 M1
Aldringham Ms FX IP11 84 E8
Aldrin Wy LOS SS9 382 B5
Aldwych Cl HCH RM12 389 H1
Alexander La BRWN CM15 333 H7
Alexander Ms CHLM/GWD CM2 313 L1
Alexander Rd BRTR CM7 154 F7
VGE SS16 376 C7
Alexandra Av K/T/MI CO5 245 L5
Alexandra Cl CDH/CHF RM16 408 C7
Alexandra Dr RCOLE CO7 164 D8
Alexandra Rd BOC CM0 344 C6
COLW CO3 10 A9
COS CO15 12 F6
ERITH DA8 414 A3
FX IP11 84 F7
HAR CO12 7 K5
HSTD CO9 97 L2
IPNE IP4 3 K3
LOS SS9 399 M3
PEND EN3 324 E6

RAIN RM13 ... 389 G7
RAYL SS6 ... 361 M8
RCFD SS4 ... 363 K5
RCOS CO16 ... 196 A3
ROM RM1 ... 371 G6
SBF/HAD SS7 ... 397 L1
SBN/FI SS3 ... 385 H8
SOS SS1 ... 20 E7
SUD CO10 ... 5 G6
TIL RM18 ... 418 A6
Alexandra St *HAR* CO12 ... 7 K5
SOS SS1 ... 21 H7
Alexandra Ter *COLW* CO3 ... 162 F5
Alexandra Wy *BAR* EN8 ... 301 C6
TIL RM18 ... 419 J1
Alexandria Dr *RAYL* SS6 ... 361 H7
Alfells Rd *RCOLE* CO7 ... 165 C5
Alf Eounder Cl *COLN* CO4 ... 163 H5
Alfreda Av *HOC/HUL* SS5 ... 339 L8
Alfred Gdns *WICKE* SS11 ... 359 L2
Alfred Rd *BKHH* IG9 ... 348 E3
BRW CM14 ... 354 E3
SOCK/AV RM15 ... 405 K6
Alfred St *GRAYS* RM17 ... 417 K3
Alfred Ter *WOTN* CO14 ... 199 K3
Alfreg Rd *WIT* CM8 ... 238 E3
Algars Wy *RCHLM* CM3 ... 339 L3
Algers Cl *LOU* IG10 ... 326 E7
Algers Rd *LOU* IG10 ... 326 F7
Alghers Md *LOU* IG10 ... 326 E7
Alibon Gdns *DAGE* RM10 ... 388 B4
Alicia Av *WICKE* SS11 ... 360 B4
Alicia Cl *WICKE* SS11 ... 360 B4
Alicia Wk *WICKE* SS11 ... 360 B4
Alicia Wy *WICKE* SS11 ... 360 B4
Alienor Av *BRTR* CM7 ... 124 C2
Allandale *SBF/HAD* SS7 ... 380 B4
Allandale Rd *EMPK* RM11 ... 371 C7
PEND EN3 ... 300 E8
Allard Cl *CHESW* EN7 ... 276 A7
Allard Wy *BROX* EN10 ... 276 F1
Allectus Wy *WIT* CM8 ... 238 E3
Allenby Crs *GRAYS* RM17 ... 417 J2
Allenby Dr *EMPK* RM11 ... 371 M4
Allenby Rd *CHTY* IP2 ... 37 G5
Allendale Dr *RCOLW* CO6 ... 160 E7
Allen Rd *RAIN* RM13 ... 404 D1
Allens Cl *RCHLM* CM3 ... 266 A2
Allens Rd *BCAYE* CM11 ... 336 D6
PEND EN3 ... 324 D7
Allensway *SLH/COR* SS17 ... 395 C8
Allen Wy *RCOS* CO16 ... 221 H8
Allerton Cl *RCFD* SS4 ... 363 K5
Alley Dock *LOS* SS9 ... 399 L1
Alleyn Wy *COS* CO15 ... 250 B3
Alleyn Pl *WOS/PRIT* SS0 ... 400 D2
Allfields *HAR* CO12 ... 143 G1
Allington Cl *IPNE* IP4 ... 3 M2
Allington Wk *HVHL* CB9 ... 27 M3
Allison Cl *WAB* EN9 ... 302 B5
Allistonway *SLH/COR* SS17 ... 395 C8
Allmains Cl *WAB* EN9 ... 278 C5
Allnutts Rd *EPP* CM16 ... 304 B5
All Saints Av *COLW* CO3 ... 162 B7
All Saints Cl *BRWN* CM15 ... 308 C8
BSF CM23 ... 174 B3
CHIG IG7 ... 350 C4
CHLM/WR CM1 ... 264 F7
All Saints' Rd *IP* IP1 ... 2 A1
Allwood Rd *CHESW* EN7 ... 276 A7
Alma Av *HCH* RM12 ... 389 M2
Alma Cl *IPNE* IP4 ... 38 B2
SBF/HAD SS7 ... 399 C1
WICKE SS12 ... 359 H5
Alma Dr *CHLM/WR* CM1 ... 16 E3
Alma Rd *PEND* EN3 ... 324 F7
SBF/HAD SS7 ... 399 H1
Alma St *RCOLE* CO7 ... 192 C5 D3
Almere *SBF/HAD* SS7 ... 379 L7
Almond Av *WICKW* SS12 ... 359 J4
Almond Cl *CDH/CHF* RM16 ... 408 B8
COS CO15 ... 12 A6
K/T/MI CO5 ... 214 D5
RCOLE CO7 ... 192 D1
Almondhayes *CHTY* IP2 ... 2 C9
Almonds Av *BKHH* IG9 ... 348 B3
Almond Wk *CVI* SS8 ... 398 A7
Almond Wy *COLN* CO4 ... 163 M3
Almshouse La *EN* EN1 ... 324 C1
Alnwick Cl *VGE* SS16 ... 376 A6
Alpe St *IP* IP1 ... 2 C2
Alpha Cl *BRTR* CM7 ... 183 H1
PIT SS13 ... 379 C5
Alphamstone Rd *BURES* CO8 ... 77 J7
Alpha Pl *BSF* CM23 ... 174 A3
Alpha Rd *BOC* CM0 ... 344 D6
PIT SS13 ... 379 H6
RCOS CO16 ... 221 J8
Alport Av *COLS* CO2 ... 162 D7
Alresford Gn *WICKW* SS12 ... 359 M5
Alresford Rd *RCOLE* CO7 ... 192 F5
Alsa Gdns *RBSF* CM22 ... 147 K1
Alsa Leys *RBSF* CM22 ... 147 K1
Alsa St *STSD* CM24 ... 147 G2
Alston Dr *IPSE* IP3 ... 3 M8
Altar Pl *LAIN* SS15 ... 376 C4
Altbarn Cl *COLN* CO4 ... 135 K6
Altbarn Rd *COLS* CO2 ... 163 L6
Altham Gv *HLW* CM20 ... 255 M1
Althorne Cl *PIT* SS13 ... 378 C2
Althorne Wy *DAGE* RM10 ... 388 D1
RCFD SS4 ... 364 F1
Althorpe Cl *HOC/HUL* SS5 ... 362 E5
Alton Dr *COLW* CO3 ... 162 C5
Alton Gdns *SOSN* SS2 ... 382 F6
Alton Hall La *RIPS/CAP* IP9 ... 80 A7
Alton Park La *COS* CO15 ... 250 B2
Alton Park Rd *COS* CO15 ... 12 D7
Alton Rd *COS* CO15 ... 12 F8
Aluric Cl *CDH/CHF* RM16 ... 418 C1
Alverstoke Rd *HARH* RM3 ... 352 C4
Alverton Cl *BRTR* CM7 ... 182 C4
Alverton Wy *COLN* CO4 ... 135 J8
Alvis Av *COS* CO15 ... 249 M5
Alwen Gv *SOCK/AV* RM15 ... 406 C3
Alwyne Av *BRWN* CM15 ... 333 C4
Alyssum Cl *CHLM/WR* CM1 ... 265 C5
Amanda Cl *CHIG* IG7 ... 349 L7

Amberley Cl *RCOLE* CO7 ... 192 D2
Amberley Rd *BKHH* IG9 ... 348 D2
EN EN1 ... 324 A8
Amberley Wy *ROMW/RG* RM7 ... 370 C4
Amberry Ct *HLW* CM20 ... 15 M2
Ambleside *EPP* CM16 ... 304 B3
WICKE SS11 ... 360 C4
Ambleside Av *HCH* RM12 ... 389 J4
Ambleside Ct *COS* CO15 ... 13 K6
Ambleside Crs *PEND* EN3 ... 324 E5
Ambleside Dr *SOS* SS1 ... 21 L6
Ambleside Gdns *HOC/HUL* SS5 ... 361 L1
Ambleside Wk *CVI* SS8 ... 398 A7
Ambridge Rd *RCOLW* CO6 ... 157 M8
Ambrose Av *COLW* CO3 ... 162 A7
Ambrose Cl *DART* DA1 ... 414 A8
Amcotes Pl *CHLM/GWD* CM2 ... 17 K8
Ameland Rd *COLN* CO4 ... 135 L8
Amerells Rd *RCOS* CO16 ... 196 D7
America Rd *RCOLW* CO6 ... 158 C2
America St *MAL* CM9 ... 293 H1
Amersham Av *SOS* SS16 ... 376 A6
Amersham Cl *HARH* RM3 ... 353 C7
Amersham Rd *HARH* RM3 ... 352 F7
Amersham Wk *HARH* RM3 ... 353 C7
Amery Gdns *GPK* RM2 ... 371 L3
Amesbury *WAB* EN9 ... 302 A4
Amesbury Dr *CHLM* E4 ... 325 J8
Amesbury Rd *EPP* CM16 ... 304 A3
Amid Rd Hl *SUD* CO10 ... 76 C3
Amos Hl *SUD* CO10 ... 76 C3
Amoss Rd *CHLM/GWD* CM2 ... 289 C3
Ampers End *BSDN* SS14 ... 19 L7
Amwell Ct *HOD* EN11 ... 253 H4
WAB EN9 ... 301 M5
Amwell St *HOD* EN11 ... 253 H5
Ancaster Rd *CHTY* IP2 ... 2 E8
The Anchorage *SBN/FI* SS3 ... 385 J7
Anchor Bvd *GRH* DA9 ... 415 K8
Anchor Cl *BAR* EN8 ... 276 E8
Anchor Dr *RAIN* RM13 ... 404 C1
Anchor End *MGTR* CO11 ... 109 H7
Anchor Hl *RCOLE* CO7 ... 192 C4
Anchor La *CHONG* CM5 ... 230 C7
MAL CM9 ... 269 H6
MGTR CO11 ... 109 H7
RCFD SS4 ... 364 F2
Anchor Reach *RCHLM* CM3 ... 339 M6
Anchor Rd *COS* CO15 ... 12 D5
K/T/MI CO5 ... 214 D7
Anchor St *BSF* CM23 ... 174 B5
CHLM/GWD CM2 ... 17 G6
Anders Fall *LOS* SS9 ... 382 B5
Anderson Av *CHLM/WR* CM1 ... 264 A6
Anderson Cl *BSF* CM23 ... 146 A1
Andersons Ln *CHESW* EN7 ... 276 B8
Andrea Av *CDH/CHF* RM16 ... 407 C7
Andrew Cl *BARK/HLT* IG6 ... 349 L7
BRTR CM7 ... 155 C6
SLH/COR SS17 ... 394 E7
Andrews Cl *BKHH* IG9 ... 348 D3
Andrews Farm La *GTDUN* CM6 ... 150 D3
Andrew's La *CHESW* EN7 ... 276 B8
Andrews Pl *CHLM/WR* CM1 ... 16 E3
Andros Cl *IPSE* IP3 ... 59 H3
Anemone Cl *COLN* CO4 ... 162 D1
Anerley Rd *WOS/PRIT* SS0 ... 20 B5
Angel Cl *VGE* SS16 ... 377 L8
Angelgate Esp *HAR* CO12 ... 7 L3
Angel La *GTDUN* CM6 ... 178 E3
IPNE IP4 ... 3 H6
Angel Rd *RIPW* IP8 ... 57 K2
Angel Wy *ROM* RM1 ... 370 F5
Angle Rd *WTHK* RM20 ... 416 E3
Anglesea Rd *IP* IP1 ... 2 C2
RCOLE CO7 ... 192 D3
Anglesey Cl *BSF* CM23 ... 173 K4
Anglesey Dr *RAIN* RM13 ... 404 D3
Anglesey Gdns *WICKW* SS12 ... 360 A6
Anglesey Rd *PEND* EN3 ... 324 C6
Angle Side *BRTR* CM7 ... 183 J1
Anglia Cl *COLS* CO2 ... 162 C8
Anglia Wy *BRTR* CM7 ... 183 J1
Angus Cl *IPNE* IP4 ... 38 C2
Anita Cl East *CHTY* IP2 ... 36 F6
Anita Cl West *CHTY* IP2 ... 36 F6
Anjou Gn *CHLM/WR* CM1 ... 265 H4
Annabell Av *CDH/CHF* RM16 ... 408 A8
Annalee Gdns *SOCK/AV* RM15 ... 406 C3
Annalee Rd *SOCK/AV* RM15 ... 406 C3
Annan Wy *ROM* RM1 ... 370 E1
Ann Boleyn Dr *RCFD* SS4 ... 383 C4
Annbrook Rd *CHTY* IP2 ... 57 M2
Ann Coles Cl *HVHL* CB9 ... 48 D5
Anne Cl *RCOLE* CO7 ... 221 C5
Anne St *FX* IP11 ... 9 G4
Anne Wy *BARK/HLT* IG6 ... 349 K7
Ann St *IP* IP1 ... 2 C2
Ann Suckling Rd *HVHL* CB9 ... 28 B1
Ansgar Rd *SAFWS* CB11 ... 65 M4
Anson Cha *SBN/FI* SS3 ... 402 F3
Anson Cl *HAR* CO12 ... 143 H1
RCHLM CM3 ... 339 M5
ROMW/RG RM7 ... 370 C2
Anson Wy *BRTR* CM7 ... 155 K7
Anstead Dr *RAIN* RM13 ... 389 H4
Anstey Cl *LOS* SS9 ... 381 L4
Antelope Av *CDH/CHF* RM16 ... 407 H8
Anthony Cl *BCAYE* CM11 ... 357 L5
COLN CO4 ... 135 L3
Anthony Dr *SLH/COR* SS17 ... 394 F7
Antlers *CVI* SS8 ... 413 C1
Antlers Hl *CHING* E4 ... 325 K7
Antonia Ct *HVHL* CB9 ... 28 F4
Antonius Wy *COLN* CO4 ... 135 J5
Anton Rd *SOCK/AV* RM15 ... 406 C3
Antony Cl *CVI* SS8 ... 398 C6
Antrim Rd *IP* IP1 ... 36 E2
SBN/FI SS3 ... 402 E4
Anvil Wy *BCAYW* CM12 ... 335 J6
CHLM/WR CM1 ... 264 F7
Anzani Av *FX* IP11 ... 8 C2
Anzio Crs *COLS* CO2 ... 190 D1
Apeldoorn *SBF/HAD* SS7 ... 379 J4
Aperfield Rd *ERITH* DA8 ... 414 A4
Apollo Cl *HCH* RM12 ... 389 J1
Appleby Cl *RIPW* IP8 ... 57 K2

Appleby Dr *HARH* RM3 ... 352 D6
VGE SS16 ... 376 A6
Appledene Cl *RAYL* SS6 ... 361 L7
Appledore *SBN/FI* SS3 ... 402 D2
Appleford's Cl *HOD* EN11 ... 253 G3
Apple Ga *BRW* CM14 ... 332 A7
Applerow *LOS* SS9 ... 382 A5
Appleton Flds *BSF* CM23 ... 173 M7
Appleton Rd *LOU* IG10 ... 327 J5
SBF/HAD SS7 ... 379 J8
Appleton Wy *HCH* RM12 ... 371 L8
Appletree Cl *BRTR* CM7 ... 184 A6
SOSN SS2 ... 383 M8
Apple Tree Crs *BRWN* CM15 ... 332 D2
Apple Tree Wy *WICKE* SS11 ... 360 A3
Appleyard Av *HOC/HUL* SS5 ... 362 F3
Appold St *ERITH* DA8 ... 414 A3
Approach Rd *BCAYE* CM11 ... 358 E6
CVI SS8 ... 399 C8
The Approach *COS* CO15 ... 250 B3
EN EN1 ... 324 C4
RAYL SS6 ... 380 D1
UPMR RM14 ... 390 C2
Apsley Cl *BSF* CM23 ... 173 M7
Apton Ct *BSF* CM23 ... 174 A4
Apton Flds *BSF* CM23 ... 174 A5
Apton Hall Rd *RCFD* SS4 ... 364 B5
Apton Rd *BSF* CM23 ... 174 A4
Araglen Av *SOCK/AV* RM15 ... 406 C3
Aragon Cl *COS* CO15 ... 250 A3
SOSN SS2 ... 382 F7
Aragon Dr *BARK/HLT* IG6 ... 349 K8
Aragon Rd *RCHLM* CM3 ... 209 C4
Arakan Cl *COLS* CO2 ... 190 C2
Arbour Cl *BRW* CM14 ... 354 E6
Arbour La *CHLM/WR* CM1 ... 264 E7
WIT CM8 ... 239 M6
Arbour Rd *PEND* EN3 ... 324 E6
Arbour Wy *COLN* CO4 ... 135 K7
HCH RM12 ... 389 J4
Arcade Pl *ROM* RM1 ... 370 F5
Arcade St *IP* IP1 ... 2 E4
Arcadian Gdns *SBF/HAD* SS7 ... 380 D7
Arcadia Rd *BOC* CM0 ... 344 D6
CVI SS8 ... 398 E8
Arcany Rd *SOCK/AV* RM15 ... 406 C2
Archangel Gdns *CHTY* IP2 ... 36 F7
Archates Av *CDH/CHF* RM16 ... 407 H8
Archer Av *SOSN* SS2 ... 383 L8
Archer Cl *SOSN* SS2 ... 383 M8
Archer Rd *LAIN* SS15 ... 376 C3
Archers *EPP* CM16 ... 255 J8
Archers Cl *BCAYW* CM12 ... 357 H3
Archers Dr *PEND* EN3 ... 324 D4
Archers Flds *PIT* SS13 ... 378 C2
Archers Fields Cl *PIT* SS13 ... 378 B2
Archery Flds *COS* CO15 ... 13 K2
Archibald Rd *HARH* RM3 ... 372 B1
Archway *HARH* RM3 ... 352 D7
Arden Cl *COLN* CO4 ... 135 K8
Arderne Rd *HAR* CO12 ... 143 C1
Ardleigh *VGE* SS16 ... 18 A8
Ardleigh Gn *EMPK* RM11 ... 371 L3
Ardleigh Gdns *RBRW/HUT* CM13 ... 333 M8
Ardleigh Green Rd *EMPK* RM11 ... 371 L5
Ardleigh Rd *MGTR* CO11 ... 137 M6
RCOLE CO7 ... 106 E8
RCOLE CO7 ... 137 J7
Ardley Crs *RBSF* CM22 ... 229 J1
Ardley Wy *RAYL* SS6 ... 361 L7
Ardmore La *CHESW* EN7 ... 276 B8
Ardmore Rd *SOCK/AV* RM15 ... 406 C2
Argents La *COLW* CO3 ... 161 J1
Argent St *GRAYS* RM17 ... 417 J4
WTHK RM20 ... 416 F3
Argus Cl *ROMW/RG* RM7 ... 370 C1
Argyle Gdns *UPMR* RM14 ... 390 E2
Argyle Rd *BOC* CM0 ... 344 E7
RCOS CO16 ... 197 H1
Argyle St *IPNE* IP4 ... 3 H4
Argyll Rd *GRAYS* RM17 ... 417 H2
WOS/PRIT SS0 ... 20 B5
Ariel Cl *COLN* CO4 ... 163 M4
Arisdale Av *SOCK/AV* RM15 ... 406 C2
Arjan Wy *CVI* SS8 ... 397 K8
Ark Av *CDH/CHF* RM16 ... 407 H8
Ark La *RCFD* SS4 ... 382 B2
Arkle Ct *KESC* IP5 ... 39 L4
Arkwright Rd *CHTY* IP2 ... 36 F5
TIL RM18 ... 418 B6
Arlington Crs *BAR* EN8 ... 300 F6
Arlington Gdns *HARH* RM3 ... 371 M1
Arlington Rd *SOSN* SS2 ... 401 M2
WFD IG8 ... 348 C8
Arlington Wy *BCAYW* CM12 ... 335 G6
Armada Cl *LAIN* SS15 ... 376 E6
Armadale *CVI* SS8 ... 398 A7
Armagh Rd *SBN/FI* SS3 ... 402 E4
Armath La *VGE* SS16 ... 376 A7
Armidale Wk *COLS* CO2 ... 191 H1
Armiger Wy *WIT* CM8 ... 239 J1
Armitage Rd *SOS* SS1 ... 402 B2
Armonde Cl *RCHLM* CM3 ... 265 M2
Armond Rd *WIT* CM8 ... 211 M8
Armor Rd *PUR* RM19 ... 415 L1
Armourers Cl *BSF* CM23 ... 173 J7
Armoury Rd *RCOLW* CO6 ... 134 A7
Arms La *HVHL* CB9 ... 29 J2
Armstead Wk *DAGE* RM10 ... 388 B6
Armstrong Cl *RCHLM* CM3 ... 291 C3
SLH/COR SS17 ... 409 M1
Armstrong Rd *SBF/HAD* SS7 ... 379 C4
Arne Cl *SLH/COR* SS17 ... 394 E8
Arne Cl *LAIN* SS15 ... 376 D3
Arne Ms *LAIN* SS15 ... 376 D3
Arnheim Av *SOCK/AV* RM15 ... 405 K6
Arnheim Rd *COLN* CO4 ... 135 K5
Arnhem Av *SOCK/AV* RM15 ... 405 K6
Arnhem Gv *BRTR* CM7 ... 154 F6
Arnhem Rd *CHLM/WR* CM1 ... 263 M5
Arnold Av *SOS* SS1 ... 21 M7
Arnold Av East *PEND* EN3 ... 325 G2

Arnold Pl *TIL* RM18 ... 418 D5
Arnold Rd *COS* CO15 ... 12 C9
DAGW RM9 ... 388 A6
Arnolds Av *RBRW/HUT* CM13 ... 333 K7
Arnolds Cl *RBRW/HUT* CM13 ... 333 K7
Arnolds Farm La *RBRW/HUT* CM13 ... 333 M5
Arnolds Wy *RCFD* SS4 ... 363 K4
Arnold Vls *K/T/MI* CO5 ... 214 D5
Arnold Wy *CHLM/GWD* CM2 ... 288 D8
Arnstones Cl *COLN* CO4 ... 11 K6
Arran Ct *WICKW* SS12 ... 360 A5
Arras Rd *COLS* CO2 ... 162 E7
Arrendene Rd *HVHL* CB9 ... 28 A2
Arrow Rd *COLN* CO4 ... 164 A4
Arrowsmith Rd *CHIG* IG7 ... 350 A6
Arterial Av *RAIN* RM13 ... 404 D2
Arterial Road North Stifford *CDH/CHF* RM16 ... 406 F7
Arterial Road Purfleet *PUR* RM19 ... 415 K1
Arterial Road West Thurrock *WTHK* RM20 ... 406 A8
Artesian Rd *ROM* RM1 ... 371 G7
Arthur Ct *CHLM/WR* CM1 ... 264 A6
Arthur St *COL* CO1 ... 10 D9
ERITH DA8 ... 414 A4
GRAYS RM17 ... 417 K3
Arthy Cl *RCHLM* CM3 ... 238 B7
Artillery St *COL* CO1 ... 163 J5
Arun Cl *RCHLM* CM3 ... 238 B7
Arun Ct *TIL* RM18 ... 419 K1
Arundel Cl *CHLM/WR* CM1 ... 264 D6
BAR EN8 ... 276 C8
Arundel Dr *SLH/COR* SS17 ... 395 H7
WFD IG8 ... 348 B8
Arundel Gdns *RAYL* SS6 ... 361 J6
WOS/PRIT SS0 ... 382 B8
Arundel Rd *DART* DA1 ... 414 D8
HARH RM3 ... 353 C8
SBF/HAD SS7 ... 379 J4
WICKE SS11 ... 359 K2
Arundel Wy *BCAYW* CM12 ... 335 K5
IPSE IP3 ... 38 F8
Arwela Rd *FX* IP11 ... 9 J5
Arwen Gv *RCHLM* CM3 ... 339 K5
Asbury Cl *COLN* CO4 ... 11 L6
Asbury Dr *RCOLW* CO6 ... 160 A8
Ascension Rd *CRW* RM5 ... 351 K7
Ascot Cl *BARK/HLT* IG6 ... 349 M7
BSF CM23 ... 174 D3
SBF/HAD SS7 ... 380 C4
Ascot Dr *FX* IP11 ... 84 F7
IPSE IP3 ... 38 E3
Ascot Gdns *HCH* RM12 ... 389 M3
PEND EN3 ... 324 D1
Ashanti Cl *SBN/FI* SS3 ... 403 G3
Ashbeam Cl *RBRW/HUT* CM13 ... 354 D7
Ashbourne Rd *BROX* EN10 ... 277 G1
HARH RM3 ... 352 D5
Ashbrook Rd *DAGE* RM10 ... 388 C2
Ash Bungalows *BRTR* CM7 ... 154 F8
Ashburnham Gdns *UPMR* RM14 ... 372 C8
Ashburnham Rd *SOS* SS1 ... 20 F5
Ashby Cl *CDH/CHF* RM16 ... 408 A7
EMPK RM11 ... 372 B8
Ashby Ri *BSF* CM23 ... 174 C2
Ashby Rd *WIT* CM8 ... 239 H4
Ash Cl *BRWN* CM15 ... 332 A7
COS CO15 ... 12 A6
RCHLM CM3 ... 238 B7
RCOLE CO7 ... 220 F4
ROMW/RG RM7 ... 351 J2

Ashdale *BSF* CM23 ... 173 L7
Ashdale Rd *KESC* IP5 ... 39 L3
Ashdene Cl *HOC/HUL* SS5 ... 361 M1
Ashdon Cl *RBRW/HUT* CM13 ... 333 K8
SOCK/AV RM15 ... 406 C4
WFD IG8 ... 348 C7
Ashdon Rd *SAFWN* CB10 ... 44 E8
SAFWN CB10 ... 45 L7
SAFWN CB10 ... 65 M1
Ashdown Cl *SLH/COR* SS17 ... 395 C6
SBF/HAD SS7 ... 380 F7
Ashdown Crs *BAR* EN8 ... 276 F8
Ashdown Rd *PEND* EN3 ... 324 D4
SAFWN CB10 ... 68 A1
Ashdown Wk *ROMW/RG* RM7 ... 370 C1
Ashdown Wy *COLN* CO4 ... 11 M8
IPSE IP3 ... 38 E8
Ashen Cl *SUD* CO10 ... 50 E2
Ashen Hl *SUD* CO10 ... 50 D1
Ashen La *SUD* CO10 ... 30 D8
Ashen Rd *HSTD* CO9 ... 50 C3
SUD CO10 ... 31 J5
SUD CO10 ... 51 H2
Ashes Cl *FOS* CO13 ... 199 C3
Ashes Rd *BRTR* CM7 ... 184 A4
Ash Fall *WIT* CM8 ... 212 B6
Ashfield *RAYL* SS6 ... 361 C8
Ashfield Farm Rd *MAL* CM9 ... 267 C3
Ashfields *LOU* IG10 ... 327 L4
PIT SS13 ... 378 D4
Ashford Av *BRW* CM14 ... 354 C4
Ashford Crs *PEND* EN3 ... 324 D4
Ashford Rd *CHLM/WR* CM1 ... 16 B4
Ash Gn *RCFD* SS4 ... 364 F2
SAFWN CB10 ... 42 E2
Ash Ground Cl *FX* IP11 ... 84 C3
MGTR CO11 ... 108 C3
Ash Gv *BOC* CM0 ... 344 C5
CHLM/GWD CM2 ... 288 C4
COLS CO2 ... 191 G4
GTDUN CM6 ... 178 A4
HVHL CB9 ... 27 M2
MAL CM9 ... 269 J5
RCOLE CO7 ... 164 D8
RIPS/CAP IP9 ... 78 B2
SUD CO10 ... 55 J4
Ash Groves *SBW* CM21 ... 228 B1
Ashingdale Cl *CVI* SS8 ... 413 K1
Ashingdon Rd *HOC/HUL* SS5 ... 363 J2

Ashlea Cl *HVHL* CB9 ... 28 C5
Ashlea Rd *HVHL* CB9 ... 28 C5
Ashleigh Ct *SLH/COR* SS17 ... 398 B5
Ashleigh Dr *LOS* SS9 ... 400 A3
Ashleigh Gdns *UPMR* RM14 ... 390 E2
COLW CO3 ... 162 D5
Ashley Gn *RCHLM* CM3 ... 314 C4
Ashley Rd *HAR* CO12 ... 6 D8
PEND EN3 ... 324 D4
Ashley St *CHTY* IP2 ... 2 F8
Ashlong Gv *HSTD* CO9 ... 98 F8
Ashlyn Gv *EMPK* RM11 ... 371 L3
Ashlyns La *CHONG* CM5 ... 282 A1
Ashlyns Rd *EPP* CM16 ... 304 A2
FOS CO13 ... 199 H5
Ashmans Rw *RCHLM* CM3 ... 339 L5
Ashmere Gv *IPNE* IP4 ... 3 L3
Ashmere Ri *SUD* CO10 ... 5 G5
Ashmole Dr *FOS* CO13 ... 199 C5
Ashmour Gdns *ROM* RM1 ... 370 E2
Ashpole Rd *BRTR* CM7 ... 155 J2
Ash Ri *HSTD* CO9 ... 128 F3
RCOLW CO6 ... 104 A2
Ash Rd *CVI* SS8 ... 398 D8
RCOLE CO7 ... 193 J3
SBF/HAD SS7 ... 398 F1
Ashstead Cl *RCOS* CO16 ... 223 J5
Ashton Cl *CHTY* IP2 ... 57 K1
Ashton Pl *CHLM/GWD* CM2 ... 265 H8
Ashton Rd *HARH* RM3 ... 352 E8
PEND EN3 ... 300 F8
Ash Tree Cl *CHLM/WR* CM1 ... 16 B4
Ash Tree Ct *RCFD* SS4 ... 364 F1
Ash Tree Crs *CHLM/WR* CM1 ... 16 C4
Ash Tree Fld *HLW* CM20 ... 14 F1
Ashurst Av *SOSN* SS2 ... 402 A1
Ashurst Cl *DART* DA1 ... 414 A7
K/T/MI CO5 ... 192 K3
Ashurst Dr *CHLM/WR* CM1 ... 264 E4
BARK/HLT IG6 ... 349 K8
Ashvale Dr *UPMR* RM14 ... 390 F1
Ashvale Gdns *CRW* RM5 ... 351 L6
UPMR RM14 ... 390 F1
Ash Wk *SOCK/AV* RM15 ... 406 E1
SOS SS1 ... 21 K7
Ashway *COLW* CO3 ... 162 A8
HOC/HUL SS5 ... 362 F1
SLH/COR SS17 ... 395 J6
Ashwells Rd *BRWN* CM15 ... 332 A5
Ashwin Av *RCOLW* CO6 ... 160 E7
Ashwood Av *RAIN* RM13 ... 404 C1
Ashworth Pl *HLWE* CM17 ... 256 E3
Ashworths *CVI* SS8 ... 398 B5
RCFD SS4 ... 363 K5
Askews Farm Rd *GRAYS* RM17 ... 416 F2
Askwith Rd *RAIN* RM13 ... 388 E8
Aspen Cl *CVI* SS8 ... 397 M7
HVHL CB9 ... 27 M2
Aspen Ct *LAIN* SS15 ... 376 D2
Aspen Gv *UPMR* RM14 ... 390 B3
The Aspens *BSF* CM23 ... 174 C1
Aspen Wy *COLN* CO4 ... 11 M5
HAR CO12 ... 142 C4
PEND EN3 ... 300 E7
Aspin Ms *SAFWN* CB10 ... 43 M8
Asquith Av *SBF/HAD* SS7 ... 380 D5
Asquith Dr *COLN* CO4 ... 135 K6
Asquith Gdns *SBF/HAD* SS7 ... 380 C4
Assandune Cl *RCFD* SS4 ... 363 L4
Aster Cl *BSF* CM23 ... 173 L5
CHLM/WR CM1 ... 265 C5
COS CO15 ... 12 A4
Aster Rd *CHTY* IP2 ... 36 F7
Astley *GRAYS* RM17 ... 417 G3
Astley Rd *COS* CO15 ... 12 C5
Aston Rd *LAIN* SS15 ... 376 C5
Astor Av *ROMW/RG* RM7 ... 370 C6
Astra Cl *RAIN* RM13 ... 389 J5
Ataka Rd *FX* IP11 ... 85 C7
Athelstan Cl *HARH* RM3 ... 372 A1
Athelstan Gdns *WICKE* SS11 ... 359 C4
WICKE SS11 ... 360 A2
Athelstan Rd *COLW* CO3 ... 162 D6
HARH RM3 ... 372 A1
Atherstone Cl *CVI* SS8 ... 413 K1
Atherstone Rd *CVI* SS8 ... 413 K1
Atherton End *SBW* CM21 ... 200 F8
Atherton Gdns *CDH/CHF* RM16 ... 418 D1
Atherton Rd *IPSE* IP3 ... 57 L1
Athos Rd *CVI* SS8 ... 398 D6
Atlanta Bvd *ROM* RM1 ... 370 F6
Atlas Ct *RCOLW* CO6 ... 130 B4
Atlas Rd *DART* DA1 ... 415 C7
RCOLW CO6 ... 130 A4
Atridge Cha *BCAYW* CM12 ... 335 H7
Atterton Rd *HVHL* CB9 ... 27 L3
Attlee Ct *GRAYS* RM17 ... 407 H8
Attwood Cl *COLN* CO4 ... 135 C4
Attwoods Cl *CHLM/GWD* CM2 ... 288 C8
Aubrey Cl *CHLM/WR* CM1 ... 264 C4
Aubrietia Cl *HARH* RM3 ... 371 M1
Auckland Av *RAIN* RM13 ... 404 A1
Auckland Cl *CHLM/WR* CM1 ... 263 M6
EN EN1 ... 324 C1
TIL RM18 ... 418 B6
Audleigh Pl *CHIG* IG7 ... 349 H7
Audley End Rd *SAFWS* CB11 ... 65 H2
Audley Gdns *LOU* IG10 ... 327 L4
WAB EN9 ... 301 M3
Audley Rd *COLW* CO3 ... 162 D6
RCHLM CM3 ... 209 C4
SAFWS CB11 ... 65 L2
Audleys Cl *SOSN* SS2 ... 382 F6
Audley Wy *BSDN* SS14 ... 18 F5
FOS CO13 ... 199 H5
Audrey Gdns *BSF* CM23 ... 174 A8
Audwick Cl *BAR* EN8 ... 276 E8
Augustine Wy *RCHLM* CM3 ... 315 C3
Augustus Cl *COLN* CO4 ... 135 J5
HVHL CB9 ... 28 E5
Augustus Wy *WIT* CM8 ... 238 F3
Aukingford Gdns *CHONG* CM5 ... 283 G7
Aukingford Gn *CHONG* CM5 ... 283 G7
Auriel Av *DAGE* RM10 ... 388 C5
Austen Cl *BRTR* CM7 ... 183 H3

LOU IG10	327 L5
TIL RM18	418 D6
Austen Dr ING CM4	335 L1
Austin Av COS CO15	249 M5
Austin St CHTY IP2	2 F7
Austral Dr EMPK RM11	371 J4
Austral Wy RCHLM CM3	319 H8
Auton Cft SAFWS CB11	65 L4
Autoway COLN CO4	135 K7
Autumn Cl EN EN1	324 C4
RCOS EN EN1	12 A1
Avebury Rd WOS/PRIT SS0	20 D3
Aveley By-pass SOCK/AV RM15	405 K5
Aveley Cl ERITH DA8	414 A3
Aveley Rd ROM RM1	370 E4
UPMR RM14	390 C6
Aveline Rd RCOLE CO7	136 E4
Avelon Rd CRW RM5	351 L7
RAIN RM13	389 H7
Avenue Cl HARH RM3	353 G8
Avenue Rd BRW CM14	354 D5
BSF CM23	174 B5
CHLM/GWD CM2	288 E4
EPP CM16	303 L8
HARH RM3	353 G8
HOD EN11	253 L7
ING CM4	310 C8
LOS SS9	399 M3
SBF/HAD SS7	379 M8
WFD IG8	348 D7
WIT CM8	212 B8
WOS/PRIT SS0	20 D6
Avenue Ter WOS/PRIT SS0	20 D6
The Avenue BCAYW CM12	357 H1
BRTR CM7	155 C8
COLW CO3	162 D5
COS CO15	224 C4
CVI SS8	398 C8
FX IP11	84 C6
GTDUN CM6	178 F3
HAR CO12	141 J8
HCH RM12	389 L1
HOC/HUL SS5	339 L6
HOD EN11	253 G7
IP IP1	37 K2
LOU IG10	326 F8
RBRW/HUT CM13	354 F7
RCHLM CM3	291 G5
RCHLM CM3	341 H4
RCOLW CO6	133 L8
RIPW IP8	57 G4
ROM RM1	370 E4
SBF/HAD SS7	380 F8
SLH/COR SS17	395 L6
WAB EN9	278 D5
WIT CM8	212 B8
WIT CM8	213 H8
Avey La LOU IG10	326 A1
Aviation Wy SOSN SS2	382 D4
Avignon Cl COLS CO2	163 J7
Avila Cha CHLM/GWD CM2	312 C2
Avocet Cl FOS CO13	198 F5
K/T/MI CO5	213 L1
K/T/MI CO5	245 L4
Avocet Wy MAL CM9	269 K6
Avon Cl RCFD SS4	363 K6
RAYL SS6	381 G1
Avondale Crs PEND EN3	324 F5
Avondale Dr LOS SS9	382 A7
LOU IG10	327 G8
Avondale Gdns SLH/COR SS17	394 F6
LOU IG10	327 G8
Avondale Rd COS CO15	13 G5
IPSE IP3	59 J1
RAYL SS6	381 G1
SBF/HAD SS7	379 L8
VGE SS16	378 B7
Avon Gn SOCK/AV RM15	406 C4
Avon Rd CHLM/WR CM1	263 L7
UPMR RM14	372 D6
Avon Wy COLN CO4	164 A4
SBN/FI SS3	402 E5
Avro Rd SOSN SS2	382 E5
Aylands Rd PEND EN3	300 E8
Aylesbeare SBN/FI SS3	402 E3
Aylesbury Dr COS CO15	225 G5
VGE SS16	376 A6
Aylets Fld HLWS CM18	255 M6
Aylett Rd UPMR RM14	390 D1
Ayletts CHLM/WR CM1	235 J8
Ayley Cft EN EN1	324 B7
Ayloffe Rd COLN CO4	11 K4
DAGW RM9	388 A5
Ayloffs Cl EMPK RM11	371 M5
Ayloff's Wk EMPK RM11	371 M5
Aylsham La HARH RM3	352 D5
Aylsham Rd HOD EN11	253 K3
Aynsley Gdns HLWE CM17	256 C5
Aynsworth Av BSF CM23	174 B1
Ayr Gn ROM RM1	370 F1
Ayron Rd SOCK/AV RM15	406 C2
Ayr Rd IPNE IP4	38 C2
Ayr Wy ROM RM1	370 F1
Azalea Av WICKW SS12	359 K4

B

Baardwyk Av CVI SS8	398 F8
Baas Hl BROX EN10	276 F1
Baas Hill Cl BROX EN10	276 F1
Baas La BROX EN10	276 F1
Babergh Cl SUD CO10	35 L5
Babington Rd HCH RM12	371 J8
Back Hamlet IPSE IP3	3 J6
Back HI CBE/LIN CB1	24 C5
Back La BRTR CM7	156 D3
CDH/CHF RM16	406 D6
COLW CO3	161 M4
FX IP11	85 G8
GTDUN CM6	92 A8
HAR CO12	141 K8
ING CM4	310 B6
ING CM4	335 K1
KIR/NAC IP10	85 H2
PUR RM19	415 M1
RBSF CM22	201 J4
RBSF CM22	228 D3
RCFD SS4	382 F2
RCHLM CM3	207 H5
RCHLM CM3	233 M1
RCHLM CM3	235 K6
RCHLM CM3	314 B4
RIPS/CAP IP9	79 K5
RIPW IP8	56 F3
SAFWN CB10	22 B8
WAB EN9	278 D3
WIT CM8	240 A7
Back La East RCOLE CO7	166 B5
Back La West RCOLE CO7	166 A4
Back Rd CHLM/WR CM1	287 G2
MAL CM9	243 J7
RCOLE CO7	137 J6
Back Waterside La RCOLE CO7	221 G6
Bacon Link CRW RM5	351 J7
Bacons Cha BOC CM0	298 D2
Bacon's La RCOLW CO6	131 K8
Bacton Rd FX IP11	9 J3
Badburgham Ct WAB EN9	302 A5
Baddow Cl DAGE RM10	388 B7
WFD IG8	348 E7
Baddow Hall Av	
CHLM/GWD CM2	289 H4
Baddow Hall Crs	
CHLM/GWD CM2	289 H4
Baddow Place Av	
CHLM/GWD CM2	289 H5
Baddow Rd CHLM/GWD CM2	17 J5
CHLM/GWD CM2	289 H5
RCOS CO16	223 K1
SBN/FI SS3	402 F2
Baden Powell Dr COLW CO3	162 B8
Bader Cl IPSE IP3	59 L1
Bader Wy RAIN RM13	389 H5
Badger Gv BRTR CM7	155 J8
Badger Hall Av SBF/HAD SS7	380 B7
Badgers BSF CM23	173 M6
Badgers Cl CHLM/GWD CM2	312 C2
WOS/PRIT SS0	382 C7
Badgers Cft BROX EN10	276 F1
Badgers Gn RCOLW CO6	159 M8
Badgers Gv RCOLW CO6	134 C2
Badgers Keep BOC CM0	344 C3
Badgers Mt CDH/CHF RM16	408 A7
HOC/HUL SS5	362 D6
The Badgers VGE SS16	376 B7
Badgers Wy SBF/HAD SS7	380 B7
Badley Hall Rd RCOLE CO7	166 A1
Badminton PI BROX EN10	252 F8
Badminton Rd COS CO15	250 B4
Badshah Av IPSE IP3	38 C8
Bag La ING CM4	309 M7
Bagshaw Rd HAR CO12	7 J7
Bagshot Rd EN EN1	324 A8
Bailey Bridge Rd BRTR CM7	154 F6
Bailey Cl CHTY IP2	36 F5
HVHL CB9	28 E4
PUR RM19	415 L1
Bailey Dl COLW CO3	161 K7
Bailey La SUD CO10	31 K4
Bailey Rd LOS SS9	399 J1
The Bailey RBSF CM22	380 D1
Baillie Cl RAIN RM13	404 C2
Bainbridge Dr K/T/MI CO5	214 E7
Bainbridge Rd DAGW RM9	388 A3
Baines Cl COLW CO3	162 A6
Baird Cl CHTY IP2	37 G4
Baird Rd EN EN1	324 C5
Baker Av RCHLM CM3	238 B6
Baker Rd RIPS/CAP IP9	113 H3
Bakers Cl RCHLM CM3	339 L2
Baker's Ct BSDN SS14	378 B1
Bakers Farm Cl WICKE SS11	360 B4
Bakers Fld ING CM4	335 L1
Baker's La BRTR CM7	182 D6
CBE/LIN CB1	24 E1
CHLM/GWD CM2	312 C4
COLN CO4	162 C1
COLW CO3	162 B2
EPP CM16	304 A2
GTDUN CM6	180 D7
ING CM4	310 C7
MAL CM9	241 K7
RCHLM CM3	290 F4
Bakers Md RCHLM CM3	235 C4
Bakers Meadow BRWN CM15	332 D1
Bakers Ms ING CM4	310 C7
Bakers Rd CHESW EN7	300 C2
SUD CO10	52 A2
Baker St CDH/CHF RM16	407 M4
CHLM/GWD CM2	16 F5
Bakery Cl BOC CM0	297 M8
HLWW/ROY CM19	254 D3
Baldocks Rd EPP CM16	303 M7
Baldry Cl RIPW IP8	57 K2
Baldwin's Hl LOU IG10	327 G3
Baldwin's La RCOLW CO6	158 F3
Bale Cl COLW CO3	161 M7
Balfe Ct COLN CO4	163 M5
Balfour Cl WICKW SS12	359 M6
Balfour Rd GRAYS RM17	417 K1
Balgores Crs GPK RM2	371 J3
Balgores La GPK RM2	371 J4
Balgores Sq GPK RM2	371 J4
Balkerne Gdns COLW CO3	10 B8
Balkerne Hl COLW CO3	10 A8
Ballards Cl DAGE RM10	388 C7
Ballards Rd DAGE RM10	388 C7
Ballards Wk LAIN SS15	18 A4
Ballast Quay Rd K/T/MI CO5	192 C5
RCOLE CO7	192 D3
Ballingdon Hl SUD CO10	54 D1
Ballingdon St SUD CO10	4 A8
Ball La COLS CO2	191 H6
Ball's Cha HSTD CO9	129 G2
Ball's Chace RCOLW CO6	132 A1
Balmerino Av SBF/HAD SS7	380 D5
Balmoral Av COS CO15	12 C6
Balmoral Cl BAR EN8	300 E6
BCAYE CM11	357 M2
CHTY IP2	58 A2
Balmoral Gdns HOC/HUL SS5	362 D5
Balmoral Rd BRWN CM15	332 C8
GPK RM2	371 J4
HCH RM12	389 L2
PEND EN3	300 E8
WOS/PRIT SS0	20 D5
Balstonia Dr SLH/COR SS17	394 F6
Baltic Av COS CO15	21 H6
Bamford Wy HAR CO12	143 G1
Bampton Rd HARH RM3	352 F8
Bancrofts Rd RCHLM CM3	339 M3
Banes Down WAB EN9	277 M2
Banham Dr SUD CO10	4 F4
Banister Cl RCOS CO16	12 B1
Bankart La CHLM/GWD CM2	265 G7
Bankfoot GRAYS RM17	417 C1
Bankside Cl RCHLM CM3	339 M2
Bank La EPP CM16	304 F4
Bank St BRTR CM7	155 C8
Bann Cl SOCK/AV RM15	406 C5
Banner Wy PUR RM19	415 L1
Bannister Dr RBRW/HUT CM13	333 K8
Bannister Gn WICKW SS12	359 M5
Banson's La CHONG CM5	283 H8
Bansons Wy CHONG CM5	283 H8
Banters La RCHLM CM3	209 H2
Banton Cl EN EN1	324 C4
Bantoft Ter IPSE IP3	59 L1
Banton Cl EN EN1	324 C4
Banyard Cl KESG IP5	39 L4
Banyards EMPK RM11	371 M4
Banyardway RCFD SS4	363 K7
Banyards Av CVI SS8	398 A8
Barbara Cl RCFD SS4	363 L8
Barbel Cl BAR EN8	301 H6
Barbel Rd COLN CO4	164 A2
Barberry Rd HARH RM3	352 E8
Barbrook La K/T/MI CO5	214 E5
Barbrook Wy RCHLM CM3	314 F2
Barclay Cl CHLM/GWD CM2	289 C5
Barclay Ct HOD EN11	253 H6
Barclay Ov WFD IG8	348 B5
Barclay Pl PIT SS13	378 F2
Barclay Rd COLS CO2	163 H6
Barclay Wy WTHK RM20	416 A2
Bardenville Rd CVI SS8	398 F8
Bardeswell Cl BRW CM14	354 D3
Bardfield VGE SS16	377 M6
COLS CO2	191 H2
GTDUN CM6	123 G2
Bardfield Rd BRTR CM7	153 G2
RAYL SS6	361 H8
Bardfield Wy FOS CO13	199 G5
RAYL SS6	361 H8
Barfield Rd K/T/MI CO5	245 K5
Barfields LOU IG10	327 H6
Bargate La RCOLE CO7	107 J8
Barge Pier Rd SBN/FI SS3	402 F6
Barham Rd CDH/CHF RM16	406 A8
Barington Ct RBRW/HUT CM13	333 K8
Barker Cl CHTY IP2	36 E6
HVHL CB9	48 C5
MGTR CO11	108 C7
Barker Rd SUD CO10	4 D1
Barkis Cl CHLM/WR CM1	263 L4
Barkstead Rd COLN CO4	11 K3
Barkwood Cl ROMW/RG RM7	370 D5
Barlee Cl SAFWS CB11	87 K8
Barle Gdns SOCK/AV RM15	406 C5
Barley Cl RBSF CM22	229 M1
VGE SS16	376 B8
Barleycorn Wy EMPK RM11	372 A6
Barley Ct SAFWS CB11	65 L2
Barley Cft HLWS CM18	255 L7
Barley Fld BRWN CM15	332 A1
Barley Flds WIT CM8	239 H2
Barley Hills BSF CM23	173 M7
Barley Md CHLM/WR CM1	291 J5
Barley Wy CBE/LIN CB1	24 E1
COLW CO3	161 L6
Barling Rd SBN/FI SS3	384 D5
Barlon Rd RCFD SS4	138 A7
Barlow's Reach	
CHLM/GWD CM2	265 H7
Barnaby Rudge CHLM/WR CM1	264 A4
Barnaby Wy CHIG IG7	349 H4
Barnard Acres WAB EN9	277 M3
Barnard Cl SAFWS CB11	89 G3
VGE SS16	377 M8
Barnardiston Rd COLN CO4	11 K4
Barnardiston Wy WIT CM8	212 A8
Barnard Rd CHLM/GWD CM2	312 D1
EN EN1	324 C4
LOS SS9	399 J1
SBW CM21	200 F8
Barnards Av CVI SS8	398 E7
Barnards Fld GTDUN CM6	122 C1
Barncombe Cl SBF/HAD SS7	379 L5
Barncroft STDN SG11	144 D4
Barncroft Cl COLN CO4	135 J8
LOU IG10	327 H7
Barncroft Gn LOU IG10	327 H7
Barncroft Rd LOU IG10	327 H7
Barnes Cray Rd DART DA1	414 B8
Barnet Park Rd WICKE SS11	360 A1
Barnett Cl ERITH DA8	414 A6
Barnfield EPP CM16	280 B8
FX IP11	84 E7
K/T/MI CO5	186 E8
MGTR CO11	108 E7
RBSF CM22	203 H6
RIPS/CAP IP9	78 C2
Barnfield Cl HOD EN11	253 H3
WAB EN9	278 A2
Barnfield Ms CHLM/WR CM1	264 D5
Barnfield Rd RCOLW CO6	134 D5
Barn Flds COLW CO3	161 K5
Barn Gn COLN CO4	11 G8
Barn Hall Av COLS CO2	163 J7
Barnhall Rd MAL CM9	242 C1
Barnham Pl KESG IP5	39 G5
Barn HI HLWW/ROY CM19	254 C7
Barn La MGTR CO11	138 A4
Barn Md BRTR CM7	183 L1
BRWN CM15	308 D8
HLWS CM18	15 M9
Barnmead Gdns DAGW RM9	388 A4
Barnmead Rd DAGW RM9	388 A4
Barnmead Wy BOC CM0	344 C4
Barns Ct EPP CM16	255 J8
Barnsley Rd HARH RM3	353 G8
Barnstable Cl SOS SS1	402 E3
Barnstaple Rd HARH RM3	352 D6
SOS SS1	402 C3
Barnston Gn GTDUN CM6	179 H7
Barnston Wy	
RBRW/HUT CM13	333 K7
Barn View Rd RCOLW CO6	186 B2
Barnwell Dr HOC/HUL SS5	362 E5
Barnwell Rd DART DA1	415 G7
The Barnyard VGE SS16	376 B7
Baronia Cft COLN CO4	135 K8
Baron Rd RCHLM CM3	339 M4
Barons Cl FX IP11	85 L7
Baronsdale Cl IP IP1	37 J2
Baron's La RCHLM CM3	316 F2
The Barons BSF CM23	173 L6
Barons Wy VGE SS16	376 C7
Baronswood Wy COLS CO2	190 E1
Barrack La HAR CO12	7 L6
IP IP1	2 D3
RCHLM CM3	234 F3
Barrack Rd CHLM/WR CM1	233 H5
Barrack Sq CHLM/GWD CM2	17 H4
Barrack St COL CO1	163 J5
MGTR CO11	139 L3
Barra Gld WICKW SS12	360 A6
Barr Cl RCOLE CO7	192 D2
Barrel Cl RCOLE CO7	166 B8
Barrells Down Rd BSF CM23	173 M2
Barrett La BSF CM23	174 A5
Barrington Cl BSDN SS14	378 A3
CHLM/GWD CM2	289 H5
RCOS CO16	223 K1
SBN/FI SS3	402 F2
Barrington Gdns BSDN SS14	378 A3
COS CO15	224 D6
Barrington Gn LOU IG10	327 K6
Barrington Pl ING CM4	310 C8
Barrington Rd COLS CO2	163 H6
LOU IG10	327 K6
Barringtons Cl RAYL SS6	361 L8
Barron's Cl CHONG CM5	283 C7
Barrow Hall Rd SBN/FI SS3	384 D6
Barrow Hl SUD CO10	35 L4
Barrow La CHESW EN7	300 A3
Barrowsand SOS SS1	402 C5
Barrows Rd HLWW/ROY CM19	14 C5
Barry Cl CDH/CHF RM16	408 B8
Barryfields BRTR CM7	125 M4
Barsey Cl HVHL CB9	27 K2
Barstable Rd SLH/COR SS17	409 L1
Bartholomew Cl SAFWN CB10	42 F1
Bartholomew Dr HARH RM3	371 J2
Bartholomew Rd BSF CM23	174 A5
Bartholomew St IPNE IP4	3 L4
Bartlett Cl RCHLM CM3	319 G2
Bartletts RAYL SS6	381 H3
Bartley Cl SBF/HAD SS7	379 J5
Bartley Rd SBF/HAD SS7	379 J5
Bartlow End PIT SS13	378 C3
Bartlow Gdns CRW RM5	370 E1
Bartlow Rd CBE/LIN CB1	24 E1
CBE/LIN CB1	26 D7
Bartlow Side PIT SS13	378 C3
Barton Av RCHLM CM3	370 D8
Barton Cl CHIG IG7	349 K3
CHTY IP2	57 M1
RCHLM CM3	339 L2
Barton Cft HVHL CB9	29 J1
Barton Gv HVHL CB9	29 J1
Barton Cl FX IP11	115 J1
HCH RM12	371 H8
Bartram Av BRTR CM7	155 K8
Barwell Wy WIT CM8	239 H1
Baryta Cl SLH/COR SS17	409 K2
Basbow La BSF CM23	174 A3
Basildon Dr LAIN SS15	376 D4
Basildon Rd LAIN SS15	18 A2
Basin Rd MAL CM9	269 M7
Bassenthwaite Rd	
SBF/HAD SS7	379 M5
Bassett Gdns EPP CM16	281 J6
Bassett's La CHONG CM5	285 J3
MAL CM9	267 H7
Bassingbourne Cl	
BROX EN10	253 G8
Bassingbourn Rd STSD CM24	176 A1
Bassingbourn Rbt RBSF CM22	176 A2
Bata Av TIL RM18	419 J2
Batavia Rd CVI SS8	397 L7
Bate-dudley Dr BOC CM0	274 C8
Bateman Rd RCOLE CO7	220 F3
Bateman's Rd RCOS CO16	196 C7
Bates Rd HARH RM3	353 H8
MAL CM9	269 H7
Bath Rd FX IP11	115 J1
Bath St CHTY IP2	3 G9
RCOLE CO7	192 C3
Bathurst Cl COLS CO2	191 H2
Baton Cl PUR RM19	415 L1
Battery La RIPS/CAP IP9	113 J3
Battisford Dr RCOS CO16	223 H7
Battlesbrook Rd COLS CO2	191 L1
Battles La KESG IP5	39 L4
Battleswick BSDN SS14	377 M2
Batt's Rd BOC CM0	320 A2
Bawdsey Cl FX IP11	85 L6
Bawn Cl BRTR CM7	155 H7
Bawtree Wy COLW CO3	162 B6
Baxter Av SOSN SS2	20 E3
Baxters RCHLM CM3	291 H4
Bayard Av RCOLE CO7	221 G4
Bay Cl CVI SS8	413 J4
Bayleys Md RBRW/HUT CM13	355 K3
Bayley St HSTD CO9	74 A7
Bay Manor La WTHK RM20	416 A3
Baymans Wd BRWN CM15	354 F3
Baynards Crs FOS CO13	198 F5
Baynes Cl EN EN1	324 B3
Bay Rd HAR CO12	7 J7
Bay Tree Cl CHESW EN7	276 A7
Bay Vw BOC CM0	296 D3
Bay View Crs HAR CO12	142 D3
Baywood Sq CHIG IG7	350 C6
Beach Av LOS SS9	400 B3
Beach Cl SBN/FI SS3	385 K8
Beach Crs COS CO15	250 A5
Beachcroft Av RCOS CO13	198 E5
Beaches Cl HOC/HUL SS5	363 G5
Beach House Gdns CVI SS8	413 M1
Beach Rd COS CO15	13 H7
CVI SS8	398 E7
HAR CO12	7 G9
K/T/MI CO5	245 K5
RCOS CO16	248 D6
SBN/FI SS3	403 G6
SOS SS1	21 L8
Beach Rd East FX IP11	115 K1
Beach Rd West FX IP11	9 J5
Beach's Dr CHLM/WR CM1	263 L8
Beach Station Rd FX IP11	9 H7
Beach Wy COS CO15	250 A5
Beachway CVI SS8	413 J1
Beachy Dr BOC CM0	296 D3
Beacon Cl RCOLE CO7	220 F5
Beacon Fld FX IP11	84 F8
Beaconfield Av EPP CM16	304 A1
Beaconfield Rd EPP CM16	304 A1
Beaconfield Wy EPP CM16	304 B1
Beacon Hts RCOS CO16	248 C1
Beacon HI BRW CM14	331 K1
MAL CM9	292 F1
PUR RM19	415 J2
WIT CM8	240 B5
Beacon Hill Av HAR CO12	7 K6
Beacon Hill Rd BRW CM14	331 J1
Beacon Rd ERITH DA8	414 C4
Beaconsfield Av COLW CO3	162 F5
Beaconsfield Cl SUD CO10	4 C4
Beaconsfield Rd COS CO15	13 G6
IP IP1	37 G4
PEND EN3	324 C1
SUD CO10	4 C5
The Beacons LOU IG10	327 H2
Beacon Vw COLW CO3	161 K5
RCOS CO16	248 C1
The Beadles RBSF CM22	201 J3
Beadle Wy RCHLM CM3	209 G5
Beadon Dr BRTR CM7	183 H2
Beads Hall La BRWN CM15	332 D6
Beam Av DAGE RM10	388 C7
Beambridge PIT SS13	378 B3
Beamish Cl EPP CM16	281 K5
Beams Wy BCAYE CM11	357 K3
Beamway DAGE RM10	388 E6
Beanfield Rd SBW CM21	200 B7
Bear Cl ROMW/RG RM7	370 C6
Beard's La SAFWS CB11	63 H7
Beardsley Dr CHLM/WR CM1	264 F4
Bearing Cl CHIG IG7	350 B5
Bearing Wy CHIG IG7	350 B5
Bearsted Dr PIT SS13	378 D6
Bear St RCOLW CO6	104 A2
Beaton Cl GRH DA9	416 C8
Beatrice Av CVI SS8	398 C7
FX IP11	115 J1
Beatrice Cl HOC/HUL SS5	362 E5
IPSE IP3	38 B8
Beatrice Rd COS CO15	12 E8
WOTN CO14	199 L1
Beatty Gdns BRTR CM7	155 K7
Beatty La BSDN SS14	377 M5
Beatty Ri RCHLM CM3	340 A5
IPSE IP3	59 J1
SUD CO10	5 G2
Beauchamps BOC CM0	344 C4
Beauchamps Dr WICKE SS11	360 B4
Beaufort CDH/CHF RM16	407 C8
EPP CM16	281 H7
ROMW/RG RM7	370 D4
Beaufort Gdns BRTR CM7	155 H7
Beaufort Rd BCAYW CM12	357 G1
CHLM/GWD CM2	265 H7
Beaufort St IP IP1	2 B2
SOSN SS2	401 L2
Beaulieu Bvd CHLM/WR CM1	265 G4
Beaulieu Dr WAB EN9	301 J5
Beauly Wy ROM RM1	370 F1
Beaumont Av COS CO15	12 C5
RCOLE CO7	221 H4
Beaumont Cl COLN CO4	134 F7
FOS CO13	199 G4
GPK RM2	371 K2
Beaumont Ct HVHL CB9	28 C5
Beaumont Crs RAIN RM13	389 H5
Beaumont Gdns	
RBRW/HUT CM13	333 K8
Beaumont HI GTDUN CM6	178 E1
Beaumont Pk RCHLM CM3	290 D5
Beaumont Park Dr	
HLWW/ROY CM19	254 C3
Beaumont Pl BRTR CM7	155 J8
Beaumont Rd BROX EN10	276 A4
HAR CO12	169 K1
Beaumont V HVHL CB9	28 C5
Beaumont Wy MAL CM9	293 J3
Beaver Cl COLW CO3	161 M4
Beazley End WICKW SS12	359 M5
Bebington Cl BCAYW CM12	335 H8
Beccles Cl WICKE SS11	359 L3
Beche Rd COLS CO2	163 J6
Becker Rd COLW CO3	161 M7
Beckers Green Rd BRTR CM7	183 L1
Becket Cl RBRW/HUT CM13	354 D7
RCFD SS4	363 L6
Beckett Dr SLH/COR SS17	394 E7
Beckett Wy RCHLM CM3	339 M6
Beck Farm Cl CVI SS8	399 G8
Beckford Rd MGTR CO11	109 H7
Beckingham Rd MAL CM9	240 D6
MAL CM9	242 D7
Beckingham St MAL CM9	270 C1
Beck Rd CVI SS8	399 G8
SAFWN CB10	65 L2
Becontree Cl COS CO15	224 D4

Bedale Rd HARH RM3.....353 H6
Bedells Av BRTR CM7.....183 J6
Bedford Cl BRTR CM7.....155 J7
K/T/MI CO5.....214 C6 ⑤
RAYL SS6.....380 E2
Bedford Crs PEND EN3.....300 F7
Bedford Gdns HCH RM12.....389 K1
Bedford Rd COLN CO4.....135 G6
COS CO15.....224 E6
GRAYS RM17.....417 J2 ⑨
LAIN SS15.....376 C5
Bedford St IP IP1.....2 D3
Bedloes Av WICKE SS11.....360 F4 ⑤
Bedwell Rd RBSF CM22.....119 J8
Beecham Ct LAIN SS15.....376 D3
Beech Av BKHH IG9.....348 C3
BRTR CM7.....155 G6
HSTD CO9.....129 H1
RAYL SS6.....361 L8
RBRW/HUT CM13.....355 C4
RCOLE CO7.....192 C2
UPMR RM14.....390 C2
Beech Dr SBW CM21.....227 K3
Beeches Cl CHLM/WR CM1.....16 B3
SAFWS CB11.....65 K4
Beeches La CHLM/WR CM1.....16 A3
MAL CM9.....269 G6
WICKE SS11.....360 F1
The Beeches BRW CM14.....354 C4
IPS3.....3 L7
MGTR CO11.....108 D3
TIL RM18.....418 C6
Beechfield HOD EN11.....253 J5
SBW CM21.....228 A1
Beechfield Gdns
ROMW/RG RM7.....370 D7
Beech Gdns DAGE RM10.....388 C6
Beech Gn WIT CM8.....240 A6
Beech Gv BARK/HLT IG6.....349 M7
HAR CO12.....142 C4
HSTD CO9.....97 L2
HVHL CB9.....27 M2
IPS3.....3 M9
SOCK/AV RM15.....405 K7
Beech Hl COLW CO3.....162 B6
Beech Hill Gdns WAB EN9.....326 C1
Beechlands BSF CM23.....174 A6
Beechmont Gdns SOSN SS2.....382 F7
Beech Pl EPP CM16.....304 A3
Beech Ri RCHLM CM3.....238 B7
Beech Rd BSDN SS14.....377 M6
CHONG CM5.....260 E2
HOC/HUL SS5.....361 M1
KESG IP5.....39 G4
SBF/HAD SS7.....398 E1
SUD CO10.....5 K9
WIT CM8.....212 C4
Beech St ROMW/RG RM7.....370 D4
Beech Tree Gld CHING E4.....348 A2
Beech Wk DART DA1.....414 B8
Beech Wy CBE/LIN CB1.....24 D1
Beechwood Cl COLS CO2.....190 C1
Beechwood Dr WFD IG8.....348 A6
Beecroft Crs CVI SS8.....398 B5
Beedell Av WICKE SS11.....360 A5
WOS/PRIT SSO.....20 A3
Beehive Cha BRWN CM15.....308 E7
Beehive La RBSF CM22.....202 B8
Beehive La CHLM/GWD CM2.....288 C2
Beeleigh Av VGE SS16.....376 D8
Beeleigh Cha MAL CM9.....268 E7
Beeleigh Cl COLS CO2.....191 H2 ⑤
SOSN SS2.....382 F8
Beeleigh Cross BSDN SS14.....377 M4
Beeleigh East BSDN SS14.....377 M4
Beeleigh Link CHLM/GWD CM2.....289 C1
Beeleigh Rd MAL CM9.....269 C8
Beeleigh West BSDN SS14.....19 M2
Beeston Dr BAR EN8.....276 E2
Beggarhill ING CM4.....309 L4
Begonia Cl CHLM/WR CM1.....265 C5
Beke Hall Cha North RAYL SS6.....360 F7
Beke Hall Cha South RAYL SS6.....360 F8
Bekeswell La CHLM/GWD CM2.....288 A8
Belchamp St HSTD CO9.....51 J5
Belchamps Rd WICKE SS11.....360 A3
Belchamps Wy HOC/HUL SS5.....362 F6
Belcham's La SAFWS CB11.....118 T3
Belcher Rd HOD EN11.....253 H4 ⑤
Belchers La WAB EN9.....278 C4
Beldams Cl RCOS CO16.....197 H2 ⑤
Beldams La BSF CM23.....174 D5
Belfairs Cl LOS SS9.....399 L1
Belfairs Dr LOS SS9.....399 L1
Belfairs Park Cl LOS SS9.....381 K6
Belfairs Park Dr LOS SS9.....381 J6
Belgrave Av GPK RM2.....371 K3
Belgrave Cl IPNE IP4.....37 M2
LOS SS9.....381 J4
RAYL SS6.....361 J7 ⑨
Belgrave Rd BCAYW CM12.....335 J7
LOS SS9.....381 J5
Bellamy Cl FOS CO13.....198 C5
Bellamy Rd BAR EN8.....300 F1
Bell Av HARH RM3.....371 J1
Bell Cl CHTY IP2.....2 F7
COLS CO2.....191 L1
Bell Common EPP CM16.....303 M4
Bellcroft WIT CM8.....212 B8
Belle Vue CHLM/GWD CM2.....16 B6
Bellevue Av SOS SS1.....21 M5
Bellevue Pl SOS SS1.....21 M5
Belle Vue Rd COL CO1.....10 A4
CRW RM5.....351 K7
IPNE IP4.....3 K3
RCOLE CO7.....192 C3

SUD CO10.....4 E6
Bellevue Rd BCAYW CM12.....357 G1
EMPK RM11.....372 A8
SOSN SS2.....21 M4
Bellfield BSF CM23.....377 M8
Bellfield Av RCOLE CO7.....221 G5
Bellfield Cl RCOLE CO7.....221 H4
Bellfield Gdns HLWE CM17.....256 D4
Bellfield Rd RCOLE CO7.....221 H4
Bell Hl BURES CO8.....77 K7
RCHLM CM3.....290 D4
Bell Hill Cl BCAYW CM12.....357 J3
Bellhouse Crs LOS SS9.....381 L6
Bellhouse La BRW CM14.....331 M7
LOS SS9.....381 L7
Bellhouse Rd LOS SS9.....381 L5
Bell House Rd ROMW/RG RM7.....370 D8
Bellingham La RAYL SS6.....380 L1
Bell La BROX EN10.....276 F1
BRTR CM7.....124 D1
BRTR CM7.....154 B4 ⑩
CHTY IP2.....2 F7
GTDUN CM6.....92 B8 ⑩
HOD EN11.....253 H5
KESG IP5.....39 J3
PEND EN3.....324 E2
Bellmaine Av SLH/COR SS17.....395 C7 ⑦
Bellmead CHLM/GWD CM2.....17 C4
Bell Md ING CM4.....310 C8
SBW CM21.....227 M1
Bells Cha CHLM/GWD CM2.....288 F5
Bells Cl SAFWS CB11.....65 L3
Bells Hl BSF CM23.....173 M4
BURES CO8.....102 B7
Bells Hill Rd VGE SS16.....395 J1
Bell Rd SUD CO10.....53 G5
Bell St CHLM/GWD CM2.....289 G5
SBW CM21.....227 M1
Bell Wk WOS/PRIT SSO.....382 E7 ⑦
Belmer Rd STSD CM24.....147 L7
Belmonde Dr CHLM/WR CM1.....264 E4
WICKW SS12.....359 H5
Belmont Cl CHLM/WR CM1.....264 F4
WFD IG8.....348 C5
WICKW SS12.....359 J4
Belmont Crs COLN CO4.....135 K8
Belmont Hl SAFWS CB11.....89 H2
Belmont Pl COL CO1.....163 K7
Belmont Rd GRAYS RM17.....417 G2
HCH RM12.....389 L2
IPNE IP4.....57 K2
Belsize Av COS CO15.....249 L5
Belstead Av CHTY IP2.....2 D9
Belstead Rd CHTY IP2.....58 A2
Belsteads Farm La
CHLM/WR CM1.....264 C1
Belstedes LAIN SS15.....376 E5
Beltinge Rd HARH RM3.....372 A3
Beltona Gdns BAR EN8.....276 E7
Belton Br LOS SS9.....399 L3
Belton Gdns LOS SS9.....399 K3
Belton Wy East LOS SS9.....399 K3
Belton Wy West LOS SS9.....399 J3
Belvawney Cl CHLM/WR CM1.....263 M5
Belvedere Av HOC/HUL SS5.....362 D5 ⑤
Belvedere Cl RCHLM CM3.....291 C4
Belvedere Pl MAL CM9.....293 C3
Belvedere Rd BOC CM0.....344 D8
BRW CM14.....354 A4
IPNE IP4.....38 A3
RCHLM CM3.....291 H4 ⑤
RCHLM CM3.....291 G4 ⑦
The Belvoir ING CM4.....310 B8
Bembridge Cl COS CO15.....224 A3
Bemerton Gdns FOS CO13.....198 D5
Benacre Rd IPSE IP3.....59 H1
Benbow Dr RCHLM CM3.....339 M5
Bencroft CHESW EN7.....276 B6
Benderloch CVI SS8.....397 M7
Bendlowes Rd BRTR CM7.....124 C2
Benedict Dr CHLM/WR CM1.....16 A3
Benets Rd EMPK RM11.....372 B8
Benezet St IP IP1.....2 C2
Benfield Wy BRTR CM7.....183 J1
Benfleet Park Rd SBF/HAD SS7.....379 J8
Benfleet Rd SBF/HAD SS7.....398 B1
Benford Rd HOD EN11.....253 G7
Benhooks Av BSF CM23.....173 M6
Benhurst Av HCH RM12.....389 J3
Benjamin Cl EMPK RM11.....371 H6 ⑤
Bennet Ct COLN CO4.....163 M5
Bennett Cl BRTR CM7.....183 H3 ⑤
WOTN CO14.....199 H3
Bennett Rd IP IP1.....36 E3
Bennett's Av RCHLM CM3.....314 A8
Bennett's La GTDUN CM6.....206 E1
Bennett Wy RCHLM CM3.....238 B7
Bennions Cl HCH RM12.....389 L5 ⑤
Bennison Dr HARH RM3.....371 L2
Benrek Cl BARK/HLT IG6.....349 K4
Benskins Cl BSF CM23.....117 H3
Benskins La ABR/ST RM4.....352 E2
Benson Rd GRAYS RM17.....417 J3
Bentall Cl HSTD CO9.....129 C3 ⑤
Bentalls BSDN SS14.....18 F1
Bentalls Cl SOSN SS2.....383 H7
Bentfield End Cswy STSD CM24.....146 E4
Bentfield Gdns STSD CM24.....146 E4
Bentfield Rd STSD CM24.....146 E4
Bent Hl FX IP11.....9 M3
Bent La IPNE IP4.....38 F3
Bentley Av COS CO15.....249 M5
Bentley Cl BSF CM23.....174 A6
Bentley Dr HLWE CM17.....256 D4
Bentley La RIPS/CAP IP9.....79 L7
RIPW IP8.....57 K6
Bentley Wy MGTR CO11.....138 D7
RCOS CO16.....195 K6
WIT CM8.....211 M7 ⑤
The Bentleys LOS SS9.....382 A4
Bentley Wy WFD IG8.....348 B4
Benton Cl BRTR CM7.....183 M5 ⑤
WIT CM8.....239 H4
Benton Gdns SLH/COR SS17.....395 C6 ⑦
Benvenue Av LOS SS9.....382 A4
Benyon Pth SOCK/AV RM15.....406 D1 ⑤

Berberis Cl VGE SS16.....376 A7 ⑩
Berbice La GTDUN CM6.....178 D1
Berdens VGE SS16.....19 M8
Berechurch Hall Rd COLS CO2.....190 D2
Berechurch Rd COLS CO2.....190 E2
Berecroft HLWS CM18.....255 L8 ⑩
Beredens La RBRW/HUT CM13.....373 C2
Berens Cl WICKE SS11.....360 A2
Beresford Cl SBF/HAD SS7.....380 E7
Beresford Ct BCAYW CM12.....335 G6 ⑩
Beresford Dr WFD IG8.....348 D5
Beresford Rd SOS SS1.....21 L8
Berg Av CVI SS8.....398 E6 ⑩
Bergholt Rd COLN CO4.....162 E1
MGTR CO11.....108 C4
Beridge Rd HSTD CO9.....128 E1
Berkeley Av CRW RM5.....351 K8
Berkeley Cl IPNE IP4.....37 M2
UPMR RM14.....390 C1
Berkeley Dr BCAYW CM12.....335 H6 ⑩
EMPK RM11.....372 B8
Berkeley Gdns LOS SS9.....399 H2
Berkeley La CVI SS8.....413 H1
Berkeley Rd COS CO15.....13 G3
Berkley Dr CHLM/GWD CM2.....289 C1
Berkley Av BAR EN8.....300 E6
Berkley Cl COLN CO4.....135 K7
Berkley Hl SLH/COR SS17.....394 F7
Berkshire Cl LOS SS9.....381 K6
Berkshire Wy EMPK RM11.....372 B5
Bermuda Rd KIR/NAC IP10.....59 M4
TIL RM18.....418 B6
Bernard Cl BARK/HLT IG6.....349 L7
FOS CO13.....198 F5 ⑩
Bernard Crs IPSE IP3.....59 J1
Bernard Gv WAB EN9.....301 J5 ⑩
Bernard Rd ROMW/RG RM7.....370 D7
Berners End GTDUN CM6.....179 H7
Berners St IP IP1.....2 D3
Berners Wy BROX EN10.....277 G3
Bernice Cl RAIN RM13.....404 D2 ⑩
Bernside BRTR CM7.....183 C1 ⑩
Berrimans Cl COLN CO4.....11 M9 ⑩
Berry Cl HCH RM12.....389 L4 ⑩
IPSE IP3.....60 A2
VGE SS16.....376 C6
WICKW SS12.....359 J5
Berry La VGE SS16.....376 C7
Berry V RCHLM CM3.....339 M5
Bersham La GRAYS RM17.....417 C1
Berther Rd EMPK RM11.....371 M7
Bertram Av RCOS CO16.....223 L2
Bertram Rd EN EN1.....324 B6
Bert Wy EN EN1.....324 A6
Berwick Av CHLM/WR CM1.....264 B3
Berwick Cl BAR EN8.....301 H6 ⑩
Berwick La CHONG CM5.....305 M5
Berwick Pond Cl RAIN RM13.....389 L8 ⑩
Berwick Pond Rd RAIN RM13.....389 L8
UPMR RM14.....390 A5
Berwick Rd RAIN RM13.....389 L8
Berwood Rd SLH/COR SS17.....395 C8
Beryl Rd HAR CO12.....142 E2
Beslyns Rd BRTR CM7.....94 B8
Bethany St RCOLE CO7.....192 C4
Betjeman Cl BRTR CM7.....183 H3 ⑩
CHESW EN7.....276 B8 ⑩
RAYL SS6.....362 A8
Betjeman Wy CHONG CM5.....283 C6 ⑩
Betony Crs CHLM/GWD CM2.....335 C6
Betoyne Cl BCAYE CM11.....357 L1
Betsham Rd ERITH DA8.....414 A4
Betterton Rd RAIN RM13.....388 F8
Betts Green Rd RCOS CO16.....196 E6
Bett's La HOC/HUL SS5.....362 E5
WAB EN9.....278 D1
Beulah Rd EPP CM16.....304 B1
HCH RM12.....389 K2
Beult Rd DART DA1.....414 B7
Bevan Wy HCH RM12.....390 A2
Beveland Rd CVI SS8.....399 H8
Beverley Av CVI SS8.....398 A8
K/T/MI CO5.....245 L4
Beverley Cl CDH/CHF RM16.....408 E4 ⑩
EMPK RM11.....372 A7
Beverley Dr FOS CO13.....198 F4
Beverley Gdns CHESW EN7.....300 A3
EMPK RM11.....371 M7 ⑩
SOSN SS2.....382 F7
Beverley Ri BCAYE CM11.....357 K2
K/T/MI CO5.....245 L4
IPNE IP4.....38 A3
Beverly Cl BROX EN10.....276 F1
Bevington Ms WIT CM8.....239 J1 ⑩
Bewick Ct HSTD CO9.....97 M1 ⑩
Bewley Cl BAR EN8.....300 E3
Bexhill Cl COS CO15.....250 D3
Bexhill Dr GRAYS RM17.....416 F3
Bexley Av HAR CO12.....143 G2
Bexley Rd ERITH DA8.....414 A2 ⑩
Beyers Gdns HOD EN11.....253 H2
Beyers Prospect HOD EN11.....253 H2 ⑩
Beyers Ride HOD EN11.....253 H2
Bibb Wy IP IP1.....2 B5
Bibby Cl SLH/COR SS17.....395 H8
Bickenhall St HOC/HUL SS5.....362 E5
Bickenhall SBN/FI SS3.....402 E3
Bickerton Point RCHLM CM3.....340 A5
Bicknacre Rd RCHLM CM3.....290 E6
Bicknoller Rd EN EN1.....324 A4
Biddenden Ct PIT SS13.....378 D5 ⑩
Bideford Cl HARH RM3.....371 K1
WOS/PRIT SSO.....382 B6
Bideford Rd PEND EN3.....325 C2
Biggin La GRAYS RM17.....418 C3
The Bight RCHLM CM3.....340 A6
Bignalls Cft COLN CO4.....135 K7
Bigods La GTDUN CM6.....210 E5
Bijou Cl K/T/MI CO5.....214 B5 ⑩
Bilberry End CBE/LIN CB1.....24 D4
Bildeston Gdns IP IP3.....37 L2 ⑩
Billericay Rd RBRW/HUT CM3.....355 M8
Billet La EMPK RM11.....371 L8
SLH/COR SS17.....409 M2
Billy's La RCOLE CO7.....106 E1
Bilsdale Cl COLN CO4.....135 K7 ⑩
Bilton Rd CHLM/WR CM1.....16 C6
SBF/HAD SS7.....380 A7

Bilton Wy PEND EN3.....325 G3
Bingham Cl SOCK/AV RM15.....406 C4 ⑩
Bingley Rd HOD EN11.....253 K5
Binley Rd CHLM/GWD CM2.....288 F1
Birchalls STSD CM24.....146 F3 ⑩
Bircham Rd SOSN SS2.....21 C2
Birchanger La BSF CM23.....174 E1
Birch Av HAR CO12.....6 F8
RCOLE CO7.....194 F3
Birch Cl BKHH IG9.....348 C3 ⑩
BRTR CM7.....182 D1 ⑩
COS CO15.....12 A5
CVI SS8.....398 A8
RAYL SS6.....361 K8
RCFD SS4.....364 F2
ROMW/RG RM7.....370 C3
SBF/HAD SS7.....379 J4
SOCK/AV RM15.....406 E2
Birch Crs EMPK RM11.....371 M4
SOCK/AV RM15.....406 E1
Birchcroft Rd IP IP1.....37 J1
Birchdale HOC/HUL SS5.....339 L8
Birch Dr MGTR CO11.....108 E2
Birche Cl LOS SS9.....381 M7
The Birches EPP CM16.....281 J6
FOS CO13.....198 D5
RBRW/HUT CM13.....354 F4
SBF/HAD SS7.....379 K3
Birches Wk CHLM/GWD CM2.....312 B1
Birch Fall RCOLW CO6.....104 A2
Birchfield Rd BAR EN8.....300 C1
Birch Gdns DAGE RM10.....388 D2
Birch Gn WICKW SS12.....359 L4
Birch La ING CM4.....312 A4
Birch Ri WIT CM8.....239 M5
Birch Rd BOC CM0.....297 M7
COLS CO2.....189 L6
ROMW/RG RM7.....370 C3
RCOLW CO6.....104 B2
Birch St COLS CO2.....189 H8
Birchway COLS CO2.....216 B1
Birchwood BSF CM23.....174 E1
SBF/HAD SS7.....379 J4
Birchwood Cl K/T/MI CO5.....214 F7 ⑩
Birch Wood Cl K/T/MI CO5.....245 L5 ⑩
Birchwood Cl
RBRW/HUT CM13.....354 D7 ⑩
Birchwood Dr KESG IP5.....38 F2 ⑩
LOS SS9.....400 B1
Birchwood Rd COLN CO4.....106 B7
RCHLM CM3.....316 A1
RCOLE CO7.....106 C8
SLH/COR SS17.....395 J6
Birchwood Wy K/T/MI CO5.....215 C6
Birdbrook Rd DAGE RM10.....388 D6 ⑩
RBRW/HUT CM13.....333 J8
Birdbrook Rd HSTD CO9.....49 H8
Birdbush Av SAFWS CB11.....65 L4
Bird La K/T/MI CO5.....214 F7
RBRW/HUT CM13.....373 K2
UPMR RM14.....372 E5
Birds Cl SAFWN CB10.....22 A8
Birds Farm Av ROMW/RG RM7.....370 C1
Birds Gn CHONG CM5.....260 A4
Birkbeck Rd RBRW/HUT CM13.....333 L8
ROMW/RG RM7.....370 E6
Birkdale Av HARH RM3.....353 H8 ⑩
Birkdale Ri RCHLM CM3.....238 C7
Birkfield Av HARH RM3.....353 C6
Birkfield Cl CHTY IP2.....2 A8
Birkfield Dr CHTY IP2.....57 M2
Birkin Cl K/T/MI CO5.....214 C7
Biros Rd BCAYE CM11.....336 D6
Birs Cl WICKE SS11.....359 L2
Biscay SOSN SS2.....382 B4
Biscay Cl HVHL CB9.....28 C1
Bishop Rd CHLM/WR CM1.....17 C1
COLS CO2.....162 B8
Bishops Av BRTR CM7.....155 J8
BSF CM23.....174 A8
Bishops Cl EN EN1.....324 C4
FX IP11.....85 L7 ⑩
PIT SS13.....378 B1
Bishopscourt Gdns
CHLM/WR CM1.....264 F7 ⑩
Bishops Dr RCOS CO16.....249 J5
Bishopsfield HLWS CM18.....255 L8
Bishop's Hall Rd BRWN CM15.....332 C8
Bishop's Hl IPSE IP3.....3 K7
Bishop's La HSTD CO9.....76 C8
K/T/MI CO5.....214 A7 ⑩
Bishops Park Wy BSF CM23.....173 J4
Bishops Rd COLW CO3.....162 C5
SLH/COR SS17.....395 C8
WICKW SS12.....359 L8
Bishopsteignton SBN/FI SS3.....402 E3
Bishops Wk BRWN CM15.....355 C3
Bisley Cl BAR EN8.....300 E5
RCOS CO16.....223 J5 ⑩
Bittern Cl CHTY IP2.....36 F8 ⑩
K/T/MI CO5.....213 L1
Bixley Dr IPNE IP4.....38 F6
Bixley La IPNE IP4.....39 C6
Bixley Rd IPSE IP3.....38 E8
Blackacre Rd EPP CM16.....327 M1
Black Barns FX IP11.....84 D6
Blackberry Rd COLW CO3.....161 K7
Blackborne Rd DAGE RM10.....388 B5
Black Boy La MGTR CO11.....111 H7
Blackbrook Rd RCOLW CO6.....134 D4
Blackbushe BSF CM23.....174 D2
Black Bush La CDH/CHF RM16.....393 L7
Blackbush Spring HLWS CM18.....256 B2 ⑩
Black Chapel La GTDUN CM6.....206 F3
Blackdale CHESW EN7.....276 B6
Black Ditch Rd WAB EN9.....301 K8
Black Ditch Wy WAB EN9.....301 J8
Blackdown Av KESG IP5.....39 C5
Blackfriars SUD CO10.....4 B8
Blackgate Rd SBN/FI SS3.....403 H4
Blackheath COLS CO2.....191 H3
Black Horse La EPP CM16.....281 L5
Black Horse La IP IP1.....2 B4
Blackhouse La SUD CO10.....55 J8
Blacklands St SAFWS CB11.....65 K4
Black La BRTR CM7.....124 D1
Blackley La RCHLM CM3.....182 A8
Black Lion St HLWE CM17.....227 K7 ⑩
Blacklock CHLM/GWD CM2.....265 H8

Blackman Wy WIT CM8.....239 H2 ⑩
Blackmore Av CVI SS8.....413 J1 ⑩
Blackmore Cl HVHL CB9.....28 A2
Blackmore Ct WAB EN9.....302 B5
Blackmore Md ING CM4.....309 C3 ⑩
BRWN CM15.....308 C7
GRAYS RM17.....417 K2 ⑩
ING CM4.....308 D5
Blackmores LAIN SS15.....375 M5
Blackshots La CDH/CHF RM16.....407 K5
Blacksmith Cl BCAYW CM12.....335 J6 ⑩
CHLM/WR CM1.....264 F3 ⑩
Blacksmiths Aly ING CM4.....308 F3
Blacksmiths Cl BSF CM23.....173 J6
Blacksmiths Hl SUD CO10.....30 C7
Blacksmiths La CBE/LIN CB1.....26 D6
HAR CO12.....6 B9
RAIN RM13.....389 C7
SUD CO10.....76 A1
WIT CM8.....239 M6
Blacksmiths Wy SBW CM21.....227 J2 ⑩
Blackthorn Cl COLN CO4.....163 M3
Blackthorn Cl
CHLM/WR CM1.....287 H2 ⑩
IPSE IP3.....59 M1 ⑩
Blackthorn Ct VGE SS16.....376 B7
Blackthorne Rd CVI SS8.....398 D8
Blackthorn Rd CDH/CHF RM16.....407 J6
HAR CO12.....143 C1 ⑩
HOC/HUL SS5.....363 G3 ⑩
IPSE IP3.....59 M1
Blackthorn Wy BRW CM14.....354 E6 ⑩
MAL CM9.....242 B1
Blackwall Br CHLM/WR CM1.....262 E6
Blackwater SBF/HAD SS7.....380 A7 ⑩
Blackwater Cl BOC CM0.....344 D6 ⑩
CHLM/WR CM1.....264 C5
MAL CM9.....269 M8
SBN/FI SS3.....402 F2 ⑩
Blackwater Dr K/T/MI CO5.....245 H5
Blackwater La WIT CM8.....239 J3
Blackwater Wy BRTR CM7.....155 K7
Blackwood Chine RCHLM CM3.....339 M5
Bladen Dr IPNE IP4.....39 G6
Bladon Cl BRTR CM7.....154 F4
K/T/MI CO5.....214 F6
Blaine Dr FOS CO13.....198 F4
Blair Cl BSF CM23.....173 K4
IPNE IP4.....38 F6
Blake Av RIPS/CAP IP9.....113 H2
Blake Cl MGTR CO11.....108 C7
RAIN RM13.....389 C2
Blake Dr BRTR CM7.....155 K7
RCOS CO16.....223 L5
Blake Gdns DART DA1.....415 C8
Blake Hall Dr WICKE SS11.....360 B5
Blake Hall Rd CHONG CM5.....282 B6
Blake Rd WIT CM8.....212 A6
Blamsters Crs HSTD CO9.....128 E3
Blanchard Cl FOS CO13.....198 B4
Blanche St IPNE IP4.....3 H4
Blandford El ROMW/RG RM7.....370 C4
Blandford Rd IPSE IP3.....38 E8
Blatches Cha BSF CM23.....382 A5
Blenheim Cha LOS SS9.....381 L8
Blenheim Cl BRTR CM7.....154 F4 ⑩
HOC/HUL SS5.....362 F3
HVHL CB9.....28 C2
MGTR CO11.....108 E2
PIT SS13.....315 C1
ROMW/RG RM7.....370 D4
SBW CM21.....227 J3
UPMR RM14.....372 F8 ⑩
Blenheim Ct BSF CM23.....173 K4
WFD IG8.....348 C8
Blenheim Crs LOS SS9.....381 M8
Blenheim Dr COLS CO2.....191 H3 ⑩
SOCK/AV RM15.....405 J6
Blenheim Gdns RCHLM CM3.....319 H2
SOCK/AV RM15.....405 J6
Blenheim Ms LOS SS9.....381 M8
Blenheim Park Cl LOS SS9.....382 A7
Blenheim Rd BRWN CM15.....332 B8
COS CO15.....12 C8
IP IP1.....2 A1
Blenheim Wy EPP CM16.....281 H7
K/T/MI CO5.....214 F6
Blickling Cl CHTY IP2.....58 C1 ⑩
Blind La BCAYW CM12.....356 C5
CHLM/GWD CM2.....289 M7
CHLM/GWD CM2.....313 G6
K/T/MI CO5.....188 C8
MAL CM9.....242 C2
MAL CM9.....270 D4
MAL CM9.....317 J1
Blindman's La BAR EN8.....300 C5
Blockhouse Rd GRAYS RM17.....417 K3 ⑩
Blofield Rd FX IP11.....8 C1
Blois Rd HVHL CB9.....48 E3
Bloom Cl FOS CO13.....199 G5
Bloomfield Av FOS CO13.....198 F4 ⑩
Bloomfield St IPNE IP4.....38 C5
Blossom Cl DAGW RM9.....388 A4
Blountswood Rd HOC/HUL SS5.....362 B3
Blower Cl RAYL SS6.....362 A8
Blue Anchor La TIL RM18.....418 F1
Blue Barn Cl FX IP11.....84 B3
Bluebell Cl RCOS CO16.....12 A3
Bluebell Cl CHTY IP2.....36 F7 ⑩
ROMW/RG RM7.....388 F1
WIT CM8.....211 M8 ⑩
Bluebell Wd BCAYW CM12.....334 E7
Blueberry Cl WFD IG8.....348 B7 ⑩
Bluegate La RIPS/CAP IP9.....78 B4
Bluehouse Av RCOS CO16.....223 J7
Blue House Farm Cha
RCHLM CM3.....341 J4
Bluehouses VGE SS16.....18 E7
Bluemans EPP CM16.....281 L4
Bluemans End EPP CM16.....281 L4
Blue Mill La MAL CM9.....267 C4
Blue Mills Hl WIT CM8.....239 J4
Blue Rd K/T/MI CO5.....214 D6
Bluestem Rd IPSE IP3.....59 L3 ⑩
Blunts Hall Rd WIT CM8.....238 D2
Blunts Wall Rd BCAYW CM12.....356 F2

Blyford Rd *RCOS* CO16 — 223 H7
Blyford Wy *FX* IP11 — 8 D1
Blyth Av *SBN/FI* SS3 — 402 D4
Blyth Cl *CHTY* IP2 — 58 B2
Blythe La *RCOLE* CO7 — 192 C3
Blythe Rd *HOD* EN11 — 253 L7
  SLH/COR SS17 — 394 F7
Blyth's Wy *BRTR* CM7 — K4
Blyth's Meadow *BRTR* CM7 — 155 G8
Blyth's Wy *BRTR* CM7 — 182 A1
Blyth Wk *UPMR* RM14 — 372 F7
Blythwood Gdns *STSD* CM24 — 146 E5
Blyton Cl *WICKW* SS12 — 359 L6
Boadicea Wy *COLS* CO2 — 162 D7
Boardman Av *CHING* E4 — 325 J7
Boars Tye Rd *WIT* CM8 — 184 D5
Bobbing Rd *RCFD* SS4 — 383 G1
Bobbingworth MI *CHONG* CM5 — 282 B4
Bobbits La *RIPS/CAP* IP9 — 57 M3
Bobbits Wy *RCOLE* CO7 — 192 D3
Bober Ct *COLS* CO2 — 191 J4
Bocking End *BRTR* CM7 — 155 G8
Bockingham Gn *PIT* SS13 — 378 B3
Bocking's Gv *RCOS* CO16 — 223 J8
Bodell Cl *CDH/CHF* RM16 — 407 J7
Bodiam Cl *IPSE* IP3 — 38 E7
Bodiam Rd *IPSE* IP3 — 38 E7
Bodley Cl *EPP* CM16 — 304 A2
Bodmin Cl *KESG* IP5 — 39 H5
Bodmin Rd *CHLM/WR* CM1 — 264 E6
Bohemia Cha *LOS* SS9 — 399 G4
Bohun Rd *RCHLM* CM3 — 209 G4
Bois Hall Gdns *HSTD* CO9 — 129 G1
Boley Dr *COS* CO15 — 13 K3
Boleyn Av *EN* EN1 — 324 C3
Boleyn Cl *BCAYW* CM12 — 335 K6
  CDH/CHF RM16 — 407 G8
  LOS SS9 — 381 K4
Boleyn Ct *BKHH* IG9 — 348 B2
  BROX EN10 — 276 F1
Boleyn Gdns *DAGE* RM10 — 388 D6
  RBRW/HUT CM13 — 355 H4
Boleyns Av *BRTR* CM7 — 155 G5
Boleyn Wy *BARK/HLT* IG6 — 349 K7
  COS CO15 — 250 A3
  HVHL CB9 — 27 L4
  RCHLM CM3 — 266 A2
Boley Rd *RCOLW* CO6 — 131 C4
Bolford St *GTDUN* CM6 — 122 A1
Bolingbroke Cl *RCHLM* CM3 — 209 G4
Bolney Dr *LOS* SS9 — 381 K4
Bolton La *IPNE* IP4 — 3 G3
Bommel Wy *CVI* SS8 — 399 H8
Bonchurch Av *LOS* SS9 — 399 L1
Bond St *CHLM/GWD* CM2 — 17 J3
  GRAYS RM17 — 417 K3
  IPNE IP4 — 3 H5
Bonham Cl *COS* CO15 — 13 J1
Bonington Cha *CHLM/WR* CM1 — 264 F5
Bonington Rd *HCH* RM12 — 389 L4
Bonks Hi *SBW* CM21 — 227 L2
Bonner Wk *CDH/CHF* RM16 — 407 G8
Bonneting La *BSF* CM23 — 117 J3
Bonney Gv *CHESW* EN7 — 300 B2
Bonnington Av *IPSE* IP3 — 59 G2
Bonningtons *RBRW/HUT* CM13 — 355 J4
Bonnygate *BSDN* SS14 — 19 L4
Boone Pl *WIT* CM8 — 239 H1
Bootham Cl *BCAYW* CM12 — 357 G2
Bootham Rd *BCAYW* CM12 — 357 G2
Booth Av *COLN* CO4 — 11 K7
Booth La *KESG* IP5 — 39 M3
Borda Cl *CHLM/WR* CM1 — 264 B6
Border's La *LOU* IG10 — 327 H6
Boreham Av *WICKE* SS11 — 360 C6
Boreham Rd *RCHLM* CM3 — 209 J8
Borley Rd *SUD* CO10 — 34 C7
Borman Cl *LOS* SS9 — 382 B5
Borough La *SAFWS* CB11 — 65 L3
The Borough *CHONG* CM5 — 307 C1
Borradaile Ct *HVHL* CB9 — 48 C5
Borrell Cl *BROX* EN10 — 252 F4
Borrett Av *CVI* SS8 — 398 B7
Borrowdale Av *IPNE* IP4 — 37 L2
Borrowdale Cl *SBF/HAD* SS7 — 380 A5
Borrowdale Rd *SBF/HAD* SS7 — 380 A5
Borwick La *BCAYE* CM11 — 358 F7
  WICKW SS12 — 359 J7
Bosanquet Rd *HOD* EN11 — 253 K3
Boscawen Gdns *BRTR* CM7 — 155 J7
Boscombe Av *EMPK* RM11 — 371 L2
  GRAYS RM17 — 417 L1
  WICKW SS12 — 359 G3
Boscombe Rd *SOSN* SS2 — 21 K4
Boss Hall Rd *IP* IP1 — 36 F4
Bostock Rd *CHTY* IP2 — 58 D2
Boston Av *RAYL* SS6 — 361 J7
  SOS SS1 — 20 F5
  SOSN SS1 — 20 E3
Boston Rd *IPNE* IP4 — 3 M2
Boswell Av *RCFD* SS4 — 363 L6
Boswells Dr *CHLM/GWD* CM2 — 17 K3
Bosworth Cl *HOC/HUL* SS5 — 363 G7
Bosworth Crs *HARH* RM3 — 352 D7
Bosworth Rd *DAGE* RM10 — 388 B3
  LOS SS9 — 381 K4
Botanical Av *RCOS* CO16 — 222 B7
Botany La *RCOS* CO16 — 196 C6
Botany Wy *PUR* RM19 — 415 J2
Botelers *VGE* SS16 — 18 B9
Botney Hill Rd *BCAYE* CM11 — 356 D7
Bouchers Md *CHLM/WR* CM1 — 265 C5
Bouldrewood Rd *SBF/HAD* SS7 — 379 J6
The Boulevard *RCFD* SS4 — 364 A8
Boulter Gdns *RAIN* RM13 — 389 H5
Boult Rd *LAIN* SS15 — 376 D3
Boundary Dr *RBRW/HUT* CM13 — 355 M1
Boundary Rd *BSF* CM23 — 174 B6
  COLN CO4 — 164 A7
  ED N9 — 324 D2
  HVHL CB9 — 28 E4
  LOS SS9 — 381 J3
  ROM RM1 — 371 H6
  UPMR RM14 — 390 B2
Boundary St *ERITH* DA8 — 414 A4
Bounderby Gv
  CHLM/WR CM1 — 263 M5

Bounstead Hl *COLS* CO2 — 190 D6
Bounstead Rd *COLS* CO2 — 190 E4
Bourchier Avene *BRTR* CM7 — 155 L6
Bourchier Wy *HSTD* CO9 — 128 E3
Bourne Av *LAIN* SS15 — 376 B3
Bournebridge Cl *RBRW/HUT* CM13 — 355 M1
Bournebridge Hl *HSTD* CO9 — 128 D4
Bourne Cl *BROX* EN10 — 253 C8
  HSTD CO9 — 128 E3
  LAIN SS15 — 376 B3
Bourne End *EMPK* RM11 — 372 B7
Bourne Hl *CHTY* IP2 — 58 B7
Bournemouth Park Rd
  SOSN SS2 — 383 J8
Bournemouth Rd *COS* CO15 — 225 G5
Bourne Rd *COLS* CO2 — 163 H7
  HVHL CB9 — 28 C3
  RCOLW CO6 — 133 M8
Bournes Green Cha *SBN/FI* SS3 — 402 D1
  SOS SS1 — 402 C2
The Bourne *BSF* CM23 — 174 C3
Bouvel Dr *BOC* CM0 — 344 C3
Bouverie Rd *CHLM/GWD* CM2 — 17 H7
Bouvier Rd *PEND* EN3 — 324 D2
Bovey Wy *SOCK/AV* RM15 — 406 C3
Bovingdon Rd *BRTR* CM7 — 126 E7
Bovinger Wy *SOS* SS1 — 402 A2
Bowbank Cl *SBN/FI* SS3 — 403 H3
Bowden Dr *EMPK* RM11 — 371 M8
Bowdens La *RCOLW* CO6 — 103 C4
Bower Cl *CRW* RM5 — 351 L8
Bower Farm Rd *ABR/ST* RM4 — 351 K4
Bower Gdns *MAL* CM9 — 269 G8
Bower Hall Dr *HVHL* CB9 — 48 C5
Bower Hall La *K/T/MI* CO5 — 245 M2
Bower Hl *EPP* CM16 — 304 B4
Bower La *BSDN* SS14 — 377 M3
Bowerman Rd *CDH/CHF* RM16 — 418 B1
Bowers Cl *WIT* CM8 — 184 F8
Bowers Court Dr *PIT* SS13 — 379 C6
Bowers Rd *SBF/HAD* SS7 — 379 L6
Bower V *EPP* CM16 — 304 B4
Bowers Dr *CHONG* CM5 — 283 C7
Bowes Rd *RCOLE* CO7 — 192 D2
Bowfell Dr *VGE* SS16 — 376 B6
Bowhay *RBRW/HUT* CM13 — 355 J3
Bowland Dr *RIPW* IP8 — 57 K2
Bowland Rd *WFD* IG8 — 348 D3
Bowles Gn *EN* EN1 — 300 C8
Bowling Cl *BSF* CM23 — 174 A5
Bowman Av *LOS* SS9 — 381 J5
Bowmans Pk *HSTD* CO9 — 73 M7
Bowman Rd *RBRW/HUT* CM13 — 333 J8
Bowmont Rd *RBRW/HUT* CM13 — 333 J8
Bown Cl *TIL* RM18 — 418 C6
Bowness Rd *HCH* RM12 — 389 H4
Bowood Rd *PEND* EN3 — 324 E4
Bowsers La *SAFWN* SS10 — 44 C1
Bowthorpe Cl *IP* IP1 — 2 C2
Box Cl *LAIN* SS15 — 376 E2
Boxford Cl *RAYL* SS6 — 361 L8
Boxford St *FX* IP11 — 8 D2
Boxhouse La *RCOLE* CO7 — 106 C5
Box La *HOD* EN11 — 252 F4
Boxley La *RBSF* CM22 — 203 L3
Box Mill La *HSTD* CO9 — 98 F8
Boxmoor Rd *CRW* RM5 — 351 K6
Boxoll Rd *DAGW* RM9 — 388 A3
Boxted Av *RCOS* CO16 — 223 J7
Boxted Church Rd *RCOLW* CO6 — 104 D6
Boxted Cl *BKHH* IG9 — 348 F2
Boxted Rd *COLN* CO4 — 134 L6
  RCOLW CO6 — 104 D8
Boxted Straight Rd *COLN* CO4 — 105 H6
Boyce Gn *SBF/HAD* SS7 — 397 L1
Boyce Hill Cl *LOS* SS9 — 381 J6
Boyce Rd *SBN/FI* SS3 — 403 J3
  SLH/COR SS17 — 394 D8
Boyce View Dr *SBF/HAD* SS7 — 397 J1
Boyd Cl *BSF* CM23 — 174 C3
Boyd Ct *WICKW* SS12 — 360 A6
Boyden Cl *SOSN* SS2 — 402 A1
Boydlands *RIPS/CAP* IP9 — 78 B2
Boyles Ct *COLS* CO2 — 191 J4
Boyne Dr *CHLM/WR* CM1 — 264 E5
Boyne Rd *DAGE* RM10 — 388 B2
Boyton Cl *HVHL* CB9 — 28 B1
  SBF/HAD SS7 — 380 A6
Boyton Rd *IPSE* IP3 — 59 J3
Boytons *LAIN* SS15 — 18 B5
Boytons Acre - *SAFWS* CB11 — 65 L3
Boyton's La *SAFWN* SS10 — 69 G1
Brabant Rd *RCHLM* CM3 — 341 H4
Brabner Gdns *BCAYE* CM11 — 336 D7
Brace Wk *RCHLM* CM3 — 339 M6
Brackenbury Cl *IP* IP1 — 37 J3
Bracken La *LOU* IG10 — 327 J3
Brackendale *BCAYE* CM11 — 335 L8
Brackendale Av *PIT* SS13 — 378 D7
Brackendale Cl *HOC/HUL* SS5 — 362 E4
Brackendale Gdns *UPMR* RM14 — 390 D3
Bracken Dell *RAYL* SS6 — 380 F1
Brackenden Dr *CHLM/WR* CM1 — 264 E6
Bracken Dr *CHIG* IG7 — 349 J7
Brackenhayes Cl *CHTY* IP2 — 37 J8
Bracken Ms *ROMW/RG* RM7 — 370 B6
The Brackens *COLN* CO4 — 135 J4
Bracken Wy *K/T/MI* CO5 — 218 B1
  SBF/HAD SS7 — 380 B4
Brackley Cl *FX* IP11 — 84 E8
Brackley Crs *PIT* SS13 — 378 E2
Brackley Sq *WFD* IG8 — 348 E8
Bracks La *RCOLW* CO6 — 159 G8
Bradburne Av *GRAYS* RM17 — 417 J3
Bradbourne Wy *PIT* SS13 — 378 D6
Bradd Cl *SOCK/AV* RM15 — 406 D1
Bradfield Bury *LOS* SS9 — 381 K5
Bradfield St *BRTR* CM7 — 155 H7
  CHLM/GWD CM2 — 16 E6
Brading Av *COS* CO15 — 224 B4
Bradleigh Av *GRAYS* RM17 — 417 K1
Bradley Av *SBF/HAD* SS7 — 380 A7
Bradley Cl *CVI* SS8 — 398 B6

  GTDUN CM6 — 178 D1
  SBF/HAD SS7 — 380 A6
Bradley Common *BSF* CM23 — 146 D8
Bradley Link *SBF/HAD* SS7 — 380 A6
Bradley Ms *SAFWN* CB10 — 66 A1
Bradley Rd *PEND* EN3 — 324 F2
Bradley St *CHTY* IP2 — 2 E8
Bradley Wy *RCFD* SS4 — 382 F2
Bradshaw Rd *CDH/CHF* RM16 — 407 H6
Bradwell Av *DAGE* RM10 — 388 B1
Bradwell Ct *RCHLM* CM3 — 389 J5
Bradwell Gn
  RBRW/HUT CM13 — 333 K8
Bradwell Rd *BKHH* IG9 — 348 F2
  BOC CM0 — 296 F5
Brady Av *LOU* IG10 — 327 K4
Braemar Av *CHLM/GWD* CM2 — 16 F7
Braemar Crs *LOS* SS9 — 399 H1
Braemar Gdns *EMPK* RM11 — 372 B6
Braemore *CVI* SS8 — 398 A6
Braemore Cl *COLN* CO4 — 135 L8
Brain Rd *WIT* CM8 — 211 M8
Braintree Rd *BRTR* CM7 — 124 C3
  BRTR CM7 — 125 M5
  BRTR CM7 — 183 L4
  DAGE RM10 — 388 B2
  GTDUN CM6 — 178 F3
  HSTD CO9 — 127 M6
  RCHLM CM3 — 209 K6
  WIT CM8 — 212 B8
Brain Valley Av *BRTR* CM7 — 183 J5
Brairwood Cl *LOS* SS9 — 381 L6
Braiswick *COLN* CO4 — 162 C1
Braiswick La *COLN* CO4 — 134 E7
Braiswick Pl *LAIN* SS15 — 376 C3
Braithwaite Av *ROMW/RG* RM7 — 370 B7
Braithwaite Rd *PEND* EN3 — 325 C5
Bramble Cl *HVHL* CB9 — 27 L2
  LOS SS9 — 381 J4
Bramble Crs *SBF/HAD* SS7 — 381 H6
Bramble Dr *IPSE* IP3 — 59 M2
Bramble La *GTDUN* CM6 — 179 M2
  UPMR RM14 — 390 D7
Bramble Ri *HLW* CM20 — 15 K2
Bramble Rd *CVI* SS8 — 398 D7
  LOS SS9 — 381 L4
  SBF/HAD SS7 — 381 G5
  WIT CM8 — 211 M7
Brambles *WOTN* CO14 — 199 H4
The Brambles *BAR* EN8 — 300 E3
  BOC CM0 — 320 E8
  BSF CM23 — 173 K5
  CHIG IG7 — 349 K7
  COLW CO3 — 162 A8
Bramble Tye *LAIN* SS15 — 377 G2
Bramblewood *RIPW* IP8 — 57 K1
Bramerton Av *HOC/HUL* SS5 — 362 E5
Bramfield Rd East *RAYL* SS6 — 381 H1
Bramfield Rd West *RAYL* SS6 — 381 C1
Bramford La *IP* IP1 — 2 A2
Bramford Rd *IP* IP1 — 36 D3
Bramhall Cl *CHTY* IP2 — 57 L2
Bramley Cl *BRTR* CM7 — 183 H2
  COLW CO3 — 162 C4
  RCOLE CO7 — 193 J2
Bramley Gdns *LAIN* SS15 — 376 D3
Bramley Pl *DART* DA1 — 414 B8
Bramley Rd *HVHL* CB9 — 27 K3
Bramleys *SLH/COR* SS17 — 394 E8
Bramley Shaw *WAB* EN9 — 302 A5
The Bramleys *RCFD* SS4 — 363 L6
  RCOLW CO6 — 158 B8
Bramley Wy *RCHLM* CM3 — 319 H2
Brampstead *LAIN* SS15 — 376 B5
Brampton Cl *CHESW* EN7 — 276 B8
  SLH/COR SS17 — 395 H6
Bramston Cl *BARK/HLT* IG6 — 350 A7
  CHLM/GWD CM2 — 289 C3
Bramston Link *LAIN* SS15 — 375 M4
Bramston Wy *LAIN* SS15 — 375 M5
Bramwoods Rd *CHLM/GWD* CM2 — 288 F3
Branch Rd *BARK/HLT* IG6 — 289 C3
  SBF/HAD SS7 — 398 F1
Brancroft Wy *PEND* EN3 — 324 F3
Brand Ct *BRTR* CM7 — 155 G4
Brand Dr *K/T/MI* CO5 — 191 J8
Brandenburg Rd *CVI* SS8 — 398 E6
Brandeston Cl *SUD* CO10 — 35 M8
Brandon Cl *BCAYW* CM12 — 335 H6
Brandon Groves Av
  SOCK/AV RM15 — 406 D1
Brandon Rd *BRTR* CM7 — 182 E1
  FX IP11 — 8 D2
Brands Cl *SUD* CO10 — 55 K6
Bran End Flds *GTDUN* CM6 — 151 L4
Branfield Rd *UPMR* RM14 — 390 C1
Branksome Av *HOC/HUL* SS5 — 362 F3
  SLH/COR SS17 — 394 E7
  WICKW SS12 — 359 C4
Branksome Cl *SLH/COR* SS17 — 394 D8
Branksome Rd *SOSN* SS2 — 21 K4
Bransby Gdns *IPNE* IP4 — 3 J2
Branscombe Cl *FOS* CO13 — 198 E6
Branscombe Gdns *SOS* SS1 — 402 C3
Branscombe Sq *SOS* SS1 — 402 C2
Branscombe Wk *SOS* SS1 — 402 C2
Branston Rd *COS* CO15 — 12 B5
Brantham Hl *MGTR* CO11 — 108 D3
Brassingham Crs *K/T/MI* CO5 — 214 F6
Braxted Cl *RCFD* SS4 — 363 K7
Braxted La *WIT* CM8 — 240 D2
Braxted Rd *WIT* CM8 — 240 B5
Braxteds *LAIN* SS15 — 376 B5
Braybrooke *BSDN* SS14 — 19 G5
Bray Ct *RCOLW* CO6 — 134 A7
Brayers Ms *RCFD* SS4 — 383 G2
Brays La *RCFD* SS4 — 363 M6
Brays Md *HLWS* CM18 — 256 A5
Braziers Cl *CHLM/GWD* CM2 — 288 D8
Braziers Quay *BSF* CM23 — 174 B5
Brazier's Wood Rd *IPSE* IP3 — 59 J3
Breachfield Rd *COLS* CO2 — 190 C1
Breach La *GTDUN* CM6 — 150 C1
Breach Rd *WTHK* RM20 — 416 A3
Break Egg Hl *BCAYE* CM11 — 335 L8

Breams Fld *VGE* SS16 — 376 D7
Brecon Cl *CHTY* IP2 — 58 C1
  PIT SS13 — 378 D3
Brecon Rd *PEND* EN3 — 324 D6
Bredfield Cl *FX* IP11 — 84 E8
Bree Av *RCOLW* CO6 — 159 M8
Bree Hl *RCHLM* CM3 — 339 K5
Brempsons *BSDN* SS14 — 18 F4
Brendans CI *EMPK* RM11 — 371 M8
Brendon Dr *KESG* IP5 — 39 G5
Brendon Pl *CHLM/WR* CM1 — 16 A6
Brendon Wy *WOS/PRIT* SS0 — 382 B6
Brennan Rd *TIL* RM18 — 418 C6
Brent Av *RCHLM* CM3 — 339 L2
Brent Cl *FOS* CO13 — 199 C4
  WIT CM8 — 238 F1
Brent Hall Rd *BRTR* CM7 — 94 C5
Brentwood Pl *EMPK* RM11 — 354 E2
Brentwood Rd *CDH/CHF* RM16 — 408 D6
  CHONG CM5 — 307 H3
  COS CO15 — 224 D5
  GPK RM2 — 371 K5
  RBRW/HUT CM13 — 355 L8
  ROM RM1 — 371 G6
  UPMR RM14 — 393 H2
Bressey Av *EN* EN1 — 324 B3
Bressingham Gdns
  RCHLM CM3 — 339 K4
Bretten Cl *RCOS* CO16 — 223 H7
Brettenham Crs *IP* IP1 — 37 L2
Brettenham Dr *SOS* SS1 — 401 M3
The Bretts *KESG* IP5 — 39 M3
Brevet Cl *PUR* RM19 — 415 L1
Brewers Cl *BSF* CM23 — 173 K6
Brewery La *STSD* CM24 — 146 F4
Brewery Rd *HOD* EN11 — 253 H5
Brewster Cl *CVI* SS8 — 398 B8
Brian Bishop Cl *WOTN* CO14 — 199 J3
Brian Cl *CHLM/GWD* CM2 — 288 C5
  HCH RM12 — 389 J3
Briar Cl *BAR* EN8 — 300 D1
  BCAYE CM11 — 357 L4
  BKHH IG9 — 348 E3
  HOC/HUL SS5 — 363 G7
Briardale Av *HAR* CO12 — 6 A8
Briarfields *FOS* CO13 — 198 D3
Briarhayes Cl *CHTY* IP2 — 37 J8
Briarleas Gdns *UPMR* RM14 — 372 F7
Briarley La *BROX* EN10 — 277 C2
Briarley Cl *COLN* CO4 — 135 K6
Briar Md *LAIN* SS15 — 376 C4
Briar Rd *HARH* RM3 — 352 D8
  RCOLE CO7 — 137 J7
The Briars *BAR* EN8 — 300 F3
  HLWS CM18 — 255 M6
Briars Wk *HARH* RM3 — 352 D8
Briarswood *CHLM/WR* CM1 — 264 E4
  CVI SS8 — 398 B6
Briar Vw *BCAYE* CM11 — 357 L4
Briarwood *BRWN* CM15 — 332 A1
Briarwood Av *COS* CO15 — 224 F5
Briarwood Dr *LOS* SS9 — 381 L6
Briarwood End *COLN* CO4 — 135 J4
The Briary *WICKW* SS12 — 359 J4
Briceway *SLH/COR* SS17 — 395 C7
Brickburn Rd *GTDUN* CM6 — 180 D7
Brickcroft *BROX* EN10 — 276 F6
Brickfield Cl *CHTY* IP2 — 2 F9
  VGE SS16 — 395 L1
Brickfield Rd *EPP* CM16 — 304 C1
  VGE SS16 — 395 L1
Brickfields Rd *RCHLM* CM3 — 339 M4
Brickfields Wy *RCFD* SS4 — 383 H2
Brickhouse Cl *K/T/MI* CO5 — 245 J4
Brick House La *RCHLM* CM3 — 265 M2
Brickhouse Rd *RCOLW* CO6 — 100 B8
Brick Kiln Cl *FX* IP11 — 84 E8
  RCOLW CO6 — 158 B8
Brick Kiln La *GTDUN* CM6 — 151 K4
  RCOLE CO7 — 193 M6
  SAFWS CB11 — 118 E3
Brick Kiln Rd *CHLM/GWD* CM2 — 289 K4
  COL CO1 — 10 B3
  RCOLW CO6 — 134 C5
  RIPS/CAP IP9 — 81 J6
Brick Kiln Wy *BRTR* CM7 — 183 J5
Brick La *EN* EN1 — 324 C4
  PEND EN3 — 324 D4
Brickmakers La *COLN* CO4 — 10 C1
Brickman's Hl *MGTR* CO11 — 109 M8
Brickspring La *MAL* CM9 — 240 E4
Brick St *COLW* CO3 — 161 J2
Brickwall Ct *BOC* CM0 — 344 C7
Bridewell St *SUD* CO10 — 31 K3
Bridge Av *UPMR* RM14 — 390 B2
Bridgebrook Cl *COLN* CO4 — 11 M3
Bridge Cl *EN* EN1 — 324 C3
  GRH DA9 — 415 L7
  RBRW/HUT CM13 — 354 F4
  ROM RM1 — 370 F6
  SBN/FI SS3 — 402 F4
Bridgecote La *LAIN* SS15 — 377 C1
Bridge Cft *RCHLM* CM3 — 235 C1
Bridge End La *BRTR* CM7 — 182 D3
Bridgefield Cl *COL* CO1 — 11 B3
Bridge Hall Rd *BRTR* CM7 — 156 D8
Bridge Hl *EPP* CM16 — 304 A5
  RCOLW CO6 — 132 D4
Bridge House Cl *WICKW* SS12 — 359 K4
Bridgemans Gn *RCHLM* CM3 — 318 B5
Bridgemarsh La *RCHLM* CM3 — 341 M3
Bridgend Cl *RCHLM* CM3 — 339 M3
Bridgend Rd *EN* EN1 — 300 D7
Bridgenhall Rd *EN* EN1 — 324 A3
Bridge Rd *CHONG* CM5 — 282 D1
  ERITH DA8 — 414 B5
  FX IP11 — 85 H8
  GRAYS RM17 — 417 J3
  KIR/NAC IP10 — 61 G6
  RAIN RM13 — 404 A3
  SBN/FI SS3 — 386 A2
  WICKE SS11 — 360 B4
Bridge St *BRTR* CM7 — 94 D5
  BSF CM23 — 174 A4
  BURES CO8 — 102 A3
  CHLM/WR CM1 — 287 J2
  HSTD CO9 — 73 H2

  IP IP1 — 2 F7
  LAIN SS15 — 376 F1
  RCOLW CO6 — 186 A2
  SAFWN CB10 — 65 K1
  WIT CM8 — 239 G2
Bridgewick Rd *BOC* CM0 — 322 E8
Bridgwater Dr *LOS* SS9 — 382 A6
  WOS/PRIT SS0 — 382 B7
Bridgwater Dr *CHTY* IP2 — 57 L1
  HARH RM3 — 352 D6
Bridgwater Wk *HARH* RM3 — 352 E6
Bridle Cl *HOD* EN11 — 253 H1
  PEND EN3 — 325 C1
Bridleway *BCAYE* CM11 — 335 L6
Bridle Wy *HOD* EN11 — 253 H2
Bridle Way (North) *HOD* EN11 — 253 H1
Bridle Way (South) *HOD* EN11 — 253 H1
Bridon Cl *RCHLM* CM3 — 314 C5
Bridport Av *IPSE* IP3 — 38 E8
  ROMW/RG RM7 — 370 C6
Bridport Rd *CHLM/WR* CM1 — 264 E6
Bridport Wy *BRTR* CM7 — 155 L6
Brierley Av *K/T/MI* CO5 — 245 M4
Brierley Cl *EMPK* RM11 — 371 K6
Bright Cl *RCOS* CO16 — 223 L5
Brighten Rd *WOS/PRIT* SS0 — 20 D5
Brightlingsea Rd *RCOLE* CO7 — 164 D7
  RCOLE CO7 — 220 E1
Brighton Av *SOS* SS1 — 401 L2
Brighton Rd *RCOS* CO15 — 404 C2
Brights Av *RAIN* RM13 — 404 C2
Brightside *BCAYW* CM12 — 334 F7
  FOS CO13 — 198 F4
The Brightside *BCAYW* CM12 — 334 F7
Brightwell Av *WOS/PRIT* SS0 — 20 B3
Brightwell Rd *FX* IP11 — 8 D1
Brimfield Rd *PUR* RM19 — 415 L1
Brimsdown Av *PEND* EN3 — 324 F3
Brimstone Av *LAIN* SS15 — 376 C5
Brimstone Ct *BRTR* CM7 — 182 F5
Brindles *CVI* SS8 — 398 A7
  EMPK RM11 — 371 M4
Brindles Cl *RBRW/HUT* CM13 — 355 K3
  TIL RM18 — 419 H1
Brindley Rd *COS* CO15 — 224 C5
The Bringey *CHLM/GWD* CM2 — 289 H5
Brinkley Crs *COLN* CO4 — 11 M3
Brinkley Grove Rd *COLN* CO4 — 135 H6
Brinkley La *COLN* CO4 — 135 K6
Brinkley Wy *FX* IP11 — 8 D1
Brinkworth Ci *HOC/HUL* SS5 — 363 G5
Brinley Cl *BAR* EN8 — 300 E3
Brinsmead Rd *HARH* RM3 — 372 B2
Brisbane Rd *IPNE* IP4 — 38 E5
Brisbane Wk *COLS* CO2 — 191 H2
Briscoe Cl *HOD* EN11 — 253 G3
Briscoe Rd *HOD* EN11 — 253 G3
  PIT SS13 — 378 C4
  RAIN RM13 — 389 K8
Brise Cl *BRTR* CM7 — 183 H2
Bristol Cl *RAYL* SS6 — 361 K6
Bristol Ct *WIT* CM8 — 184 F8
Bristol Hl *RIPS/CAP* IP9 — 113 J3
Bristol Rd *COL* CO1 — 10 F6
  IPNE IP4 — 3 M8
  SOSN SS2 — 382 E5
Bristowe Av *CHLM/GWD* CM2 — 289 H6
Bristowe Dr *CDH/CHF* RM16 — 408 E4
Britannia Crs *RCOLE* CO7 — 192 C2
Britannia Gdns *WOS/PRIT* SS0 — 400 D3
Britannia Rd *BAR* EN8 — 301 G6
  BRW CM14 — 354 D6
  IPNE IP4 — 38 C5
  WOS/PRIT SS0 — 400 D3
British Legion Rd *CHING* E4 — 348 A3
Brittany Wy *COLS* CO2 — 163 J7
Britten Cl *COLN* CO4 — 163 M5
  VGE SS16 — 376 B6
Britten Crs *CHLM/GWD* CM2 — 289 G3
Brittons La *ING* CM4 — 336 A3
Brixham Cl *COS* CO15 — 250 D3
  RAYL SS6 — 361 L6
Brixton La *BSF* CM23 — 118 B6
  RBSF CM22 — 118 E4
Broad Cl *HOC/HUL* SS5 — 362 F5
Broadclyst Cl *LOS* SS9 — 381 L6
Broadclyst Gdns *SOS* SS1 — 402 B2
Broadcroft Crs *HVHL* CB9 — 27 M3
Broadfield *BSF* CM23 — 174 A1
  GTDUN CM6 — 204 F4
  HLW CM20 — 255 M2
Broadfield Rd *RBSF* CM22 — 176 F4
Broadfields *RCOLE* CO7 — 164 D7
  SBW CM21 — 227 J2
Broadfield Sq *EN* EN1 — 324 C5
Broadfield Wy *BKHH* IG9 — 348 D4
Broadgate *WAB* EN9 — 302 A5
Broadhope Rd *SLH/COR* SS17 — 409 K3
  GRAYS RM17 — 417 C2
  SBF/HAD SS7 — 380 A5
  RAYL SS6 — 361 L8
Broadlands Av *HOC/HUL* SS5 — 363 G4
  PEND EN3 — 324 D4
  RAYL SS6 — 361 L8
Broadlands Cl *PEND* EN3 — 324 D5
Broadlands Rd *HOC/HUL* SS5 — 363 G5
Broadlands Wy *COLN* CO4 — 135 J4
  IPNE IP4 — 39 G6
Broad La *RCOLW* CO6 — 134 D1
Broadlawn *LOS* SS9 — 381 K7
Broadleaf Av *BSF* CM23 — 173 K7
Bradley *HLW/ROY* CM19 — 255 F2
Broadmayne *BSDN* SS14 — 18 F6
Broad Meadow *BRWN* CM15 — 332 A1
  RIPW IP8 — 57 K1
Broadmead Rd *COLN* CO4 — 163 M2
  WFD IG8 — 348 D8
Broadmere Crs *COS* CO15 — 224 F4
Broadmere Rd *IP* IP1 — 36 F3
Broad Oak *WFD* IG8 — 348 D8
Broad Oaks *WICKW* SS12 — 359 M5
Broad Oaks Cl *SAFWN* CB10 — 90 E1
Broadoaks Crs *BRTR* CM7 — 155 L7
Broad Oaks Pk *COLN* CO4 — 135 M8

Broad Oak Wy RAYL SS6 — 380 F1
Broad Pde HOC/HUL SS5 — 363 G5
Broad Rd BRTR CM7 — 155 J5
  HSTD CO9 — 75 J4
Broadstone Rd HCH RM12 — 389 F1
Broad St DAGE RM10 — 388 B6
  HVHL CB9 — 28 A3
  RBSF CM22 — 203 C5
Broad Street Green Rd
  MAL CM9 — 269 K3
Broadstrood LOU IG10 — 327 L2
  RCOS CO16 — 222 B6
Broadview Av CDH/CHF RM16 — 407 L7
Broad Wk HOC/HUL SS5 — 363 G5
The Broad Walk (North)
  RBRW/HUT CM13 — 355 H4
The Broadwalk (South)
  RBRW/HUT CM13 — 355 H5
Broadwater Gdns
  RIPS/CAP IP9 — 113 H3
Broadwater Gn LAIN SS15 — 376 A5
Broadway COS CO15 — 250 B5
  GPK RM2 — 371 H3
  GRAYS RM17 — 417 K3
Broad Wy HOC/HUL SS5 — 363 G4
Broadway LOS SS9 — 399 M3
  RAIN RM13 — 404 B2
  TIL RM18 — 418 A6
  WIT CM8 — 184 E6
Broadway Av HLWE CM17 — 227 J7
Broadway Cl WFD IG8 — 348 C2
Broadway St WIT CM8 — 184 E6
The Broadway BCTR RM8 — 388 B1
  GTDUN CM6 — 151 C7
  HCH RM12 — 389 J3
  LOU IG10 — 327 K5
  SOS SS1 — 402 B5
  WFD IG8 — 348 C7
  WICKW SS12 — 359 L3
Broadway West LOS SS9 — 399 L3
Brock Cl WIT CM8 — 238 F3
Brockenhurst Dr
  SLH/COR SS17 — 409 K3
Brocket Cl CHIG IG7 — 350 A5
Brocket Rd HOD EN11 — 253 H5
Brockett Rd CDH/CHF RM16 — 408 C8
Brocket Wy CHIG IG7 — 349 M6
Brock Gn SOCK/AV RM15 — 406 C4
Brock Hl WICKE SS11 — 337 J6
Brock Hill Dr WICKE SS11 — 337 K8
Brockles Md WROY CM19 — 255 K7
Brockley Crs CRW RM5 — 351 K8
  IP IP1 — 36 E2
Brockley Gv RBRW/HUT CM13 — 355 H2
Brockley Rd CHLM/GWD CM2 — 17 L4
Brocksford Av RAYL SS6 — 381 G2
Brocks Md GTDUN CM6 — 149 M4
Brocksparkwood
  RBRW/HUT CM13 — 355 J4
Brockton Cl ROM RM1 — 371 G4
Brockwell La K/T/MI CO5 — 213 K7
Brodie Rd SBN/FI SS3 — 403 J2
Brodie Wk WICKW SS12 — 360 A6
Brograve Cl CHLM/GWD CM2 — 288 E8
Broke Av RIPW IP8 — 36 C1
Broke Hall Gdns IPSE IP3 — 38 E7
Broman's La K/T/MI CO5 — 247 H1
Bromefield Ct WAB EN9 — 302 B5
Bromeswell Rd IPNE IP4 — 37 M2
Bromfords Cl WICKW SS12 — 359 J6
Bromfords Dr WICKW SS12 — 359 J6
Bromleigh Cl BAR EN8 — 276 F8
Bromley GRAYS RM17 — 417 G3
Bromley Cl CHTY IP2 — 37 K8
Bromley La SAFWS CB11 — 89 J2
Bromley Ms RAYL SS6 — 361 H8
Bromley Rd COLN CO4 — 163 K4
  MGTR CO11 — 138 C4
  RCOLE CO7 — 165 J6
Brompton Cl CHLM/GWD CM12 — 335 H6
Brompton Dr ERITH DA8 — 414 C4
Brompton Gdns MAL CM9 — 292 F8
Bronte Cl BRTR CM7 — 183 H5
  TIL RM18 — 418 D6
Bronte Gv DART DA1 — 415 G8
Bronte Rd WIT CM8 — 212 A6
Brook Av DAGE RM10 — 388 C6
Brook Cl BRTR CM7 — 182 D1
  GPK RM2 — 371 G1
  K/T/MI CO5 — 215 G8
  MAL CM9 — 240 B8
  MAL CM9 — 291 L1
  RCFD SS4 — 383 H3
Brookdale Av UPMR RM14 — 390 B2
Brookdale Cl UPMR RM14 — 390 C2
Brook Dr SLH/COR SS17 — 395 K2
  WICKW SS12 — 359 K5
Brooke Av SAFWN CB10 — 43 M8
Brooke Gdns BSF CM23 — 174 D4
Brook End SBW CM21 — 227 L1
Brook End Rd
  CHLM/GWD CM2 — 265 H7
Brooke Rd GRAYS RM17 — 417 H3
Brooker Rd WAB EN9 — 301 K6
Brooke Sq MAL CM9 — 293 H2
Brook Farm La RIPS/CAP IP9 — 129 H2
Brook Farm La RIPS/CAP IP9 — 80 D5
Brookfield EPP CM16 — 280 D5
Brookfield Cl RBRW/HUT CM13 — 333 K8
Brookfield Gdns BAR EN8 — 276 E7
Brookfield La BAR EN8 — 276 E8
Brookfield La East BAR EN8 — 276 E7
Brookfield La West BAR EN8 — 276 D7
Brookfield IP IP1 — 37 G3
Brookfields CHONG CM5 — 283 G6
  GTDUN CM6 — 151 L5
  LOS SS9 — 384 L6
  PEND EN3 — 324 E4
  SBW CM21 — 227 L1
Brookfields Cl LOS SS9 — 381 L6
Brook Hall Rd K/T/MI CO5 — 192 C5
Brookhampton St SAFWN CB10 — 22 B6
Brook Hl GTDUN CM6 — 207 G2
  RCHLM CM3 — 235 J3
Brookhill Wy IPNE IP4 — 39 G7

Brookhouse Rd RCOLW CO6 — 159 H3
Brookhurst Cl CDH/CHF RM16 — 17 M1
Brookland K/T/MI CO5 — 214 D7
Brooklands COL CO1 — 10 F9
  COS CO15 — 249 M5
  WICKW SS12 — 359 J4
Brooklands Ap
  ROMW/RG RM7 — 370 E4
Brooklands Av LOS SS9 — 381 M5
Brooklands Cl
  ROMW/RG RM7 — 370 E4
Brooklands Gdns COS CO15 — 249 M5
  EMPK RM11 — 371 K5
Brooklands La
  ROMW/RG RM7 — 370 E4
Brooklands Pk LAIN SS15 — 376 A5
Brooklands Ri LAIN SS15 — 108 E3
Brooklands Rd MGTR CO11 — 108 D4
  ROMW/RG RM7 — 370 E4
Brooklands Sq CVI SS8 — 412 F1
Brooklands Wk CHLM/GWD CM2 — 16 E8
Brooklane Fld HLWS CM18 — 256 C6
Brooklyn Av LOU IG10 — 326 F6
Brooklyn Ri RAYL SS6 — 361 L6
Brooklyn Rd HAR CO12 — 7 H8
Brookman's Av CDH/CHF RM16 — 407 K6
Brookmans Ct UPMR RM14 — 372 F7
Brookmans Rd ING CM4 — 335 L1
Brook Md LAIN SS15 — 376 C4
  RCHLM CM3 — 234 F3
Brook Meadow HSTD CO9 — 97 L2
  HSTD CO9 — 97 M2
Brook Mdw K/T/MI CO5 — 214 D7
Brook Ri CHIG IG7 — 349 H4
Brook Rd BAR EN8 — 301 G6
  BKHH IG9 — 348 B3
  BOC CM0 — 297 L6
  BRW CM14 — 354 A4
  EPP CM16 — 304 B5
  GPK RM2 — 371 G2
  K/T/MI CO5 — 215 G8
  LOU IG10 — 326 F7
  RAYL SS6 — 380 D3
  RCOLW CO6 — 159 K4
  RCOLW CO6 — 160 C6
  SBF/HAD SS7 — 397 K2
  SBW CM21 — 227 L2
  STSD CM24 — 146 F5
Brook Service Rd HVHL CB9 — 28 B3
Brooks Hall Rd IP IP1 — 2 A1
Brookside BARK/HLT IG6 — 349 K7
  BCAYE CM11 — 335 K5
  CVI SS8 — 398 B6
  EMPK RM11 — 371 M5
  HLWW/ROY CM19 — 255 G6
  HOC/HUL SS5 — 363 G7
  HOD EN11 — 253 H5
  WAB EN9 — 301 M4
Brookside Av SBN/FI SS3 — 403 K1
Brookside Cl COLS CO2 — 163 J7
Brookside Gdns EN EN1 — 324 C1
Brooksies SAFWS CB11 — 63 G5
Brook St BRTR CM7 — 124 C1
  BRW CM14 — 353 M5
  CHLM/WR CM1 — 17 H1
  COL CO1 — 11 G8
  GTDUN CM6 — 179 L4
  MGTR CO11 — 108 E7
  RCOLE CO7 — 107 G4
  RCOLE CO7 — 165 M2
  RCOLE CO7 — 192 C5
  RCOLW CO6 — 129 M2
Brook Ter RCOS CO16 — 222 B7
Brook Va GTDUN CM6 — 289 K5
Brookview CHTY IP2 — 57 M3
Brook Vw GTDUN CM6 — 92 B8
Brook Wy CHIG IG7 — 349 H4
Brookway RAIN RM13 — 404 C3
Broom Cl CHESW EN7 — 276 B7
Broome Gv RCOLE CO7 — 192 C1
Broome Rd BCAYE CM11 — 335 L6
Broomer Pl BAR EN8 — 300 D1
Broom Farm Rd RBSF CM22 — 147 K1
Broom Fld FX IP11 — 84 F7
Broomfield HLW CM20 — 227 J8
  SBF/HAD SS7 — 380 C1
  WIT CM8 — 184 D6
Broomfield Av BROX EN10 — 276 F6
  LOS SS9 — 382 A6
  LOU IG10 — 327 G1
  RAYL SS6 — 361 H8
Broomfield Cl CRW RM5 — 351 L7
Broomfield Common RIPW IP8 — 36 C5
Broomfield Crs RCOLE CO7 — 192 C1
Broomfield Gn CVI SS8 — 398 A6
Broomfield Rd CHLM/WR CM1 — 16 F2
Broomfields PIT SS13 — 378 B5
  RBSF CM22 — 202 B8
Broomfords Dr WICKW SS12 — 359 J5
Broomhall Cl CHLM/WR CM1 — 264 C1
Broomhall Rd CHLM/WR CM1 — 264 B1
Broomhayes CHTY IP2 — 58 B1
Broom Hill Rd IP IP1 — 37 H3
Broomhill Rd WFD IG8 — 348 B7
Broomhills Cha BCAYW CM12 — 357 H6
Broomhills Rd K/T/MI CO5 — 245 L5
Broom Knoll MGTR CO11 — 108 D1
Broom Rd HOC/HUL SS5 — 361 M1
Broomstick Hall Rd WAB EN9 — 301 M4
Broom St SUD CO10 — 55 J6
Broom Wy K/T/MI CO5 — 218 C1
  RIPS/CAP IP9 — 78 B1
Broomways SBN/FI SS3 — 385 K8
Broomwood Gdns BRWN CM15 — 332 B8
Broomwood La ING CM4 — 336 B3
Broseley Gdns HARH RM3 — 352 F5
Broseley Rd HARH RM3 — 352 F5
Brotherton Av FX IP11 — 84 C5
Broton Dr HSTD CO9 — 128 F1

Brougham Cl SBN/FI SS3 — 385 H7
Brougham Glades COLW CO3 — 161 L6
Broughton Cl COLS CO3 — 162 D9
Broughton Rd IP IP1 — 2 D1
  RCHLM CM3 — 339 M1
  SBF/HAD SS7 — 399 G1
Browne Cl BRW CM14 — 354 C2
Browning Av SOSN SS2 — 21 L7
Browning Cl COLW CO3 — 162 A5
Browning Rd BRTR CM7 — 183 K5
  DART DA1 — 415 G8
  MAL CM9 — 293 H5
  RAYL SS6 — 380 E1
  SAFWS CB11 — 86 C1
  SUD CO10 — 34 F3
Brownings Av CHLM/WR CM1 — 264 B6
Brownlow Bend BSDN SS14 — 19 L6
Brownlow Cross BSDN SS14 — 19 M6
Brownlow Gn BSDN SS14 — 19 M6
Brownlows Cl GTDUN CM6 — 231 K4
Browns Av WICKE SS11 — 360 A1
Brownsea Wy COLW CO3 — 162 B7
Brown's End Rd GTDUN CM6 — 149 G4
Browns Gv KESG IP5 — 39 L4
Broxburn Dr SOCK/AV RM15 — 406 D5
Broxhill Rd ABR/ST RM4 — 352 B4
Broxted Dr WICKW SS12 — 359 M5
Bruce Av HCH RM12 — 389 K1
Bruce Gv CHLM/GWD CM2 — 288 B4
  WICKE SS11 — 360 B5
Bruce Rd CHLM/WR CM1 — 287 J2
Bruces Wharf Rd GRAYS RM17 — 417 H3
Bruce Wy BAR EN8 — 300 E5
Bruff Cl COLN CO4 — 10 B2
Bruff Dr FOS CO13 — 199 H4
Bruges Rd CVI SS8 — 413 K1
Brundells Rd RCOLE CO7 — 166 A6
Brundish PIT SS13 — 378 B6
Brundon La SUD CO10 — 4 A2
Brunel Dr BRTR CM7 — 183 K5
Brunel Av SBN/FI SS3 — 402 D5
Brunel Ct COLN CO4 — 135 K5
Brunel Rd BRTR CM7 — 183 H2
  CHTY IP2 — 36 F5
  COS CO15 — 224 C3
  LOS SS9 — 381 K4
  SBF/HAD SS7 — 379 L4
  WFD IG8 — 349 G6
Brunel Wy COLN CO4 — 135 K5
  RCHLM CM3 — 339 K4
Brunswick Av UPMR RM14 — 372 F7
Brunswick Gdns BARK/HLT IG6 — 349 K8
Brunswick House Cut
  MGTR CO11 — 109 H8
Brunswick Pl RAYL SS6 — 361 H6
Brunswick Rd IPNE IP4 — 3 L1
  SOS SS1 — 401 L3
  WAB EN9 — 325 H2
Brunwin Rd BRTR CM7 — 182 A1
Brunwins Cl WICKE SS11 — 360 A4
Brussels Cl HAR CO12 — 143 J2
Brussum Rd CVI SS8 — 413 L1
Bruton Av WOS/PRIT SS0 — 382 B6
Bryan Rd BSF CM23 — 174 A3
Bryanstone Rd BAR EN8 — 301 G6
Bryanston Rd TIL RM18 — 418 D6
Bryant Av HARH RM3 — 371 L2
  SOS SS1 — 401 M5
Bryant's La MAL CM9 — 291 L4
Brybank Rd HVHL CB9 — 27 K2
Bryn Farm Cl BSDN SS14 — 19 K1
Bryn-y-mawr Rd EN EN1 — 324 B6
Bryony Cl HVHL CB9 — 27 K8
Buchanan Cl SOCK/AV RM15 — 405 K6
Buchanan Gdns
  WICKW SS12 — 359 M6
Buchan Wy RCHLM CM3 — 318 B6
Buchan Cl BRTR CM7 — 183 H3
Buckenhoe Rd SAFWN CB10 — 43 M8
Buckeridge Wy BOC CM0 — 274 C8
Buckfast Av FOS CO13 — 198 E5
Buckfast Cl CHTY IP2 — 58 E1
Buckhatch La RCHLM CM3 — 314 E6
Buck Hl BRTR CM7 — 183 C5
Buckhurst Wy BKHH IG9 — 348 A6
Buckingham Cl EMPK RM11 — 371 L5
Buckingham Ct
  CHLM/GWD CM2 — 265 G7
Buckingham Dr COLN CO4 — 163 M4
Buckingham Hill Rd
  CDH/CHF RM16 — 409 G6
Buckingham Rd HOC/HUL SS5 — 362 E5
  HVHL CB9 — 27 M5
  LAIN SS15 — 18 A1
Buckland SBN/FI SS3 — 402 D2
Bucklebury Heath RCHLM CM3 — 339 L5
Bucklers Cl BROX EN10 — 277 G4
Bucklers Ct BRW CM14 — 354 D6
Bucklesham Rd IPSE IP3 — 60 A2
Buckles La SOCK/AV RM15 — 406 D3
Buckley Cl DART DA1 — 414 A6
  SLH/COR SS17 — 395 G6
Buckleys CHLM/GWD CM2 — 289 G4
Buckleys Cl WIT CM8 — 239 M6
Buckley's La RCOLW CO6 — 158 E5
Buck's Horns La RIPW IP8 — 57 J4
Buckwoods Rd BRTR CM7 — 183 G2
Buckwyns Cha BCAYW CM12 — 334 F5
Buckwyns Ct BCAYW CM12 — 335 G7
Buddleia Cl CHTY IP2 — 36 F7
Buddleia Ct RCOLE CO7 — 192 B1
Bude Cl KESG IP5 — 39 H5
Budna Rd CVI SS8 — 398 A6
Buffett Wy COLN CO4 — 163 M5
Buglers Ri CHLM/WR CM1 — 287 J3
Bugsby Wy KESG IP5 — 39 M4
Buick Av COS CO15 — 249 L5
Building End Rd ROY SG8 — 62 C4
Bulbecks Wk RCHLM CM3 — 339 L6
Bulford Mill La BRTR CM7 — 183 K6
Bullace Cl COLN CO4 — 135 L8
Bull Cl CDH/CHF RM16 — 407 G7
  VGE SS16 — 377 M6
Bullen Cl RIPW IP8 — 36 B1
Bullen La RIPW IP8 — 36 B1
Buller Rd LAIN SS15 — 376 C4

RCHLM CM3 — 341 H2
  SBW CM21 — 200 F8
Bullfinch Cl COLN CO4 — 164 A3
Bull Hill Rd COS CO15 — 13 H2
  HOC/HUL SS5 — 362 D5
  K/T/MI CO5 — 214 D7
  MAL CM9 — 269 G8
  RAYL SS6 — 380 E1
  SAFWS CB11 — 86 C1
  SUD CO10 — 34 F3
Bullocks La SAFWS CB11 — 89 H3
Bull's Cross ENC/FH EN2 — 300 B8
Bulls Cross Ride CHESW EN7 — 300 D7
Bullsmoor Cl BAR EN8 — 300 D7
Bullsmoor Gdns BAR EN8 — 300 C7
Bullsmoor La EN EN1 — 300 C7
  PEND EN3 — 300 E7
Bullsmoor Wy BAR EN8 — 300 C7
Bullwood Ap HOC/HUL SS5 — 362 C6
Bullwood Hall La HOC/HUL SS5 — 362 E6
Bullwood Rd HOC/HUL SS5 — 362 E6
Bulmer Rd SUD CO10 — 54 D5
Bulmer St SUD CO10 — 53 L7
Bulow Av CVI SS8 — 398 E8
Bulphan By-pass UPMR RM14 — 391 H4
Bulphan Cl WICKW SS12 — 359 M5
Bulstrode Rd CHTY IP2 — 3 C7
Bulwark Rd SBN/FI SS3 — 402 F7
Bulwer Rd IP IP1 — 2 B3
Bumbles Green La WAB EN9 — 278 C5
Bumfords La RCHLM CM3 — 267 H4
Bumpstead Rd HVHL CB9 — 28 C6
Bunces La WFD IG8 — 348 A8
Bundick's HI CHLM/WR CM1 — 16 B1
Bung Rw K/T/MI CO5 — 240 C2
Bunters Av SBN/FI SS3 — 402 D5
Bunting Cl CHLM/GWD CM2 — 288 C2
Bunting La BCAYE CM11 — 357 K1
Bunting Rd CHTY IP2 — 36 B8
Bunyan Rd BRTR CM7 — 154 F8
Burbage Cl BAR EN8 — 300 F1
Burches LAIN SS15 — 376 F2
Burches Md SBF/HAD SS7 — 380 B4
Burches Rd SBF/HAD SS7 — 379 L2
Burchett Wy CHDH RM6 — 370 A6
Burchwall Cl CRW RM5 — 351 K4
Burdett Av WOS/PRIT SS0 — 20 C5
Burdett Rd SOS SS1 — 21 L9
Burdetts Rd DAGW RM9 — 388 A7
Bure TIL RM18 — 409 K8
Bure Dr WIT CM8 — 211 L8
Buregate Rd FX IP11 — 9 J5
Buren Av CVI SS8 — 398 F8
Bures Rd RCOLW CO6 — 103 C3
  SUD CO10 — 55 H6
Burfield Cl LOS SS9 — 382 K5
Burfield Rd COLN CO4 — 382 A5
Burford Gdns HOD EN11 — 253 J4
Burford St HOD EN11 — 253 H5
Burgate Cl DART DA1 — 414 A7
  RCOS CO16 — 223 H7
Burges Cl EMPK RM11 — 372 A6
  SOS SS1 — 402 B5
Burges Rd SOS SS1 — 402 B5
Burgess Av SLH/COR SS17 — 409 M2
Burgess Fld CHLM/GWD CM2 — 265 G7
Burges Ter SOS SS1 — 402 A5
Burghley Av BSF CM23 — 173 K4
Burghley Cl BRTR CM7 — 182 C5
  CHTY IP2 — 58 B7
Burghley Rd CDH/CHF RM16 — 406 D8
Burghstead Cl BCAYW CM12 — 357 H2
Burgundy Gdns PIT SS13 — 378 C3
Burkitts La SUD CO10 — 4 C6
Burland Rd BRWN CM15 — 354 C2
  CRW RM5 — 351 K2
Burleigh Cl BCAYW CM12 — 335 J6
Burleigh Rd BAR EN8 — 300 F4
Burleigh Sq SOS SS1 — 402 C3
Burleigh Hl WICKW SS12 — 359 M6
Burley Hl CHLM/GWD CM2 — 265 H4
Burley Rd BSF CM23 — 174 B7
Burlington Av ROMW/RG RM7 — 370 D6
Burlington Ct PIT SS13 — 378 C3
Burlington Gdns SBF/HAD SS7 — 381 G8
Burlington Pl WFD IG8 — 348 B4
Burlington Rd COLW CO3 — 10 A9
  IP IP1 — 2 C2
Burmanny Cl COS CO15 — 12 B6
Burnaby Rd SOS SS1 — 21 M8
Burncroft Av PEND EN3 — 324 D4
  PEND EN3 — 324 E4
Burne Av WICKE SS11 — 359 J5
Burnell Ga CHLM/WR CM1 — 265 H4
Burnells Wy STSD CM24 — 146 E1
Burnell Wk RBRW/HUT CM13 — 354 D7
Burnett Pk HLWW/ROY CM19 — 255 J8
Burnett Rd ERITH DA8 — 414 A1
Burney Dr LOU IG10 — 327 K5
Burnham Av RCHLM CM3 — 317 H6
Burnham Cl FX IP11 — 84 D5
Burnham Crs DART DA1 — 414 D8
Burnham Rd BOC CM0 — 344 D1
  CHLM/WR CM1 — 264 E6
  HOC/HUL SS5 — 361 M1
  LOS SS9 — 399 K2
  MAL CM9 — 292 A6
  RCHLM CM3 — 318 E6
  RCHLM CM3 — 339 J3
  ROMW/RG RM7 — 370 D3
  WICKE SS11 — 338 F6
Burnham Road (Summerhill)
  RCHLM CM3 — 319 G7
Burnley Rd WTHK RM20 — 416 A5
Burnsall Cl SAFWS CB11 — 66 A3
Burns Av COLW CO3 — 162 A6
  PIT SS13 — 378 C6
Burns Cl ERITH DA8 — 414 A5

MAL CM9 — 293 H2
Burns Crs CHLM/GWD CM2 — 17 H7
Burnside CVI SS8 — 398 B6
  HOD EN11 — 253 G5
  SBW CM21 — 200 F8
Burnside Crs CHLM/WR CM1 — 264 C4
Burns Pl TIL RM18 — 418 C5
Burns Wy RBRW/HUT CM13 — 355 L1
Burnt Dick Hl COLN CO4 — 104 E4
Burnt Heath Cottages
  RCOLE CO7 — 137 H6
Burnthouse La ING CM4 — 334 A2
Burnthouse Rd RCOLW CO6 — 158 F2
Burntmill La HLW CM20 — 226 D8
Burntmill La HLW CM20 — 226 D8
Burnt Mills Rd PIT SS13 — 378 B3
Burntwood Av EMPK RM11 — 371 L6
Burntwood Cl BCAYW CM12 — 357 C1
  RBRW/HUT CM13 — 374 E6
Burnway EMPK RM11 — 371 M7
Burr Cl HAR CO12 — 142 D2
  VGE SS16 — 375 M6
Burrell Rd CHTY IP2 — 2 D7
Burr Hill Cha WOS/PRIT SS0 — 382 F8
Burroughs Piece Rd SUD CO10 — 4 E6
Burrow Gn CHIG IG7 — 350 A6
Burrow Rd CHIG IG7 — 350 B6
Burrows Cl MGTR CO11 — 108 C7
  RCOS CO16 — 223 L5
Burrows Rd RCOLW CO6 — 130 C5
Burrows Wy RAYL SS6 — 380 D2
Burrs Rd COS CO15 — 13 H1
Burr's Wy SLH/COR SS17 — 395 J7
Burrswood Pl MAL CM9 — 269 L8
Burses Wy RBRW/HUT CM13 — 355 J1
Bursland Rd PEND EN3 — 324 C5
Burslem Av RBRW/HUT CM13 — 350 B7
Burstall Cl RCOS CO16 — 223 J7
Burstead Dr BCAYE CM11 — 357 L4
Burton Cl HVHL CB9 — 27 M4
  SLH/COR SS17 — 395 G6
Burton End HVHL CB9 — 27 L4
Burton Pl CHLM/GWD CM2 — 265 G7
Burton Rd LOU IG10 — 327 K6
Burton's Green Rd HSTD CO9 — 129 H7
Burwell Av CVI SS8 — 398 A6
Burwood Gdns RAIN RM13 — 404 A1
Bury Cl COL CO1 — 10 F6
  RCOLW CO6 — 160 A8
Bury Farm La BCAYE CM11 — 358 E8
Bury Flds GTDUN CM6 — 180 B6
Bury Green Rd CHESW EN7 — 300 B3
Bury Holme BROX EN10 — 277 G3
Bury La EPP CM16 — 303 L2
  RCHLM CM3 — 234 E3
  RCHLM CM3 — 238 A6
  ROY SG8 — 62 E2
Bury Lodge La RBSF CM22 — 175 K3
  STSD CM24 — 147 H8
Bury Rd CHING E4 — 325 L6
  DAGE RM10 — 388 D4
  EPP CM16 — 303 M3
  HLWE CM17 — 227 K7
The Bury RCOS CO16 — 222 B7
Burywoods COLN CO4 — 162 C1
Bushbarns CHESW EN7 — 300 B1
Bushby Av BROX EN10 — 277 G2
Bushell Wy FOS CO13 — 198 F5
Bush Elms Rd EMPK RM11 — 371 H7
Bushey Cl RCHLM CM3 — 339 M4
  RIPS/CAP IP9 — 78 B2
Bushey Cft HLWS CM18 — 255 M5
Bushey Ley BRTR CM7 — 155 L8
Bushfields LOU IG10 — 327 H5
Bush Gv SUD CO10 — 54 D5
Bush Hall Rd BCAYW CM12 — 335 J6
Bush La SAFWN CB10 — 92 E1
Bushman Gdns RIPW IP8 — 36 B1
Bush Rd BKHH IG9 — 348 E5
  SAFWN CB10 — 92 F1
Bushy Md LAIN SS15 — 376 C3
Butcher Rw SAFWN CB10 — 65 L1
Butcher's HI SAFWN CB10 — 22 B7
Butchers La RIPS/CAP IP9 — 78 C2
  WOTN CO14 — 199 J4
Butchers Pasture GTDUN CM6 — 150 A6
Butler Cl SAFWS CB11 — 65 M2
Butler Rd HSTD CO9 — 128 E1
Butlers Cl CHLM/WR CM1 — 264 C1
Butlers Dr CHING E4 — 325 K2
Butlers Gv VGE SS16 — 376 C8
Butler's La MGTR CO11 — 140 F2
Butler Smith Gdns KESG IP5 — 39 K4
Butlers Wy HSTD CO9 — 73 H2
Butley Cl CHTY IP2 — 58 A3
Butley Rd FX IP11 — 9 H3
Butneys BSDN SS14 — 19 G3
Butterbur Rd RCHLM CM3 — 339 K5
Buttercross La EPP CM16 — 304 B2
Buttercup Cl BCAYW CM12 — 335 H7
  HARH RM3 — 371 L1
  RIPW IP8 — 57 K2
Buttercup Wk WIT CM8 — 211 M7
Buttercup Wy BOC CM0 — 320 D8
Butterfield Rd RCHLM CM3 — 265 M3
Butteridges Cl DAGW RM9 — 388 A7
Butter Market IP IP1 — 2 F4
Buttermere BRTR CM7 — 182 C5
Buttersweet Ri SBW CM21 — 227 M2
Butterworth Gdns WFD IG8 — 348 B6
Butterys SOS SS1 — 401 M3
Buttfield Cl DAGE RM10 — 388 C5
Butt La BSF CM23 — 145 L1
  MAL CM9 — 293 H1
Buttleys La GTDUN CM6 — 178 A3
Buttondene Crs BROX EN10 — 277 J2
Button Rd CDH/CHF RM16 — 417 C1
Butt Rd COLS CO2 — 162 E6
  SUD CO10 — 5 J8
Buttsbury ING CM4 — 334 F2
Butt's Green Rd
  CHLM/GWD CM2 — 290 A7
  EMPK RM11 — 371 L6
Butts La RCHLM CM3 — 290 F4
  SLH/COR SS17 — 409 K4
Butts Paddock RCFD SS4 — 364 E1

Butts Rd *SLH/COR* SS17 ... 409 K2
The Butts *BROX* EN10 ... 276 F4
Butts Wy *CHLM/GWD* CM2 ... 287 M8
Buxey Cl *K/T/MI* CO5 ... 245 J4
Buxton Cl *LOS* SS9 ... 381 H8
Buxton Cl *LOS* SS9 ... 381 H8
  WFD IG8 ... 348 E7
Buxton Link *LAIN* SS15 ... 375 M5
Buxton Rd *CDH/CHF* RM16 ... 407 M7
  COLS CO2 ... 163 H8
  EPP CM16 ... 303 M8
  RCOLW CO6 ... 158 A8
  WAB EN9 ... 302 B4
Buxton Sq *LOS* SS9 ... 381 H8
Buyl Av *CVI* SS8 ... 398 C6
Byfield *LOS* SS9 ... 382 A4
Byfletts *VGE* SS16 ... 378 A7
Byford Rd *RAYL* SS6 ... 361 M8
  SUD CO10 ... 5 H3
Byfam La *RIPS/CAP* IP9 ... 81 K4
Byland Cl *CHTY* IP2 ... 58 B1
Bylands Cl *BSF* CM23 ... 173 L5
Byng Crs *RCOS* CO16 ... 197 J2
Byng Gdns *BRTR* CM7 ... 155 K7
Bynghams *HLWW/ROY* CM19 ... 14 D9
Bypass Rd *RCOS* CO16 ... 222 C6
Byrd Ct *LAIN* SS15 ... 376 D3
Byrd's Farm La *SAFWN* CB10 ... 43 M8
Byrne Dr *SOSN* SS2 ... 382 F6
Byron Av *COLW* CO3 ... 162 A4
  SOSN SS2 ... 21 J2
Byron Cl *BRTR* CM7 ... 183 J1
  CVI SS8 ... 398 D7
Byron Ct *LAIN* SS15 ... 376 C5
Byron Dr *WIT* CM8 ... 239 M6
Byron Gdns *TIL* RM18 ... 418 E5
Byron Wk *CHLM/GWD* CM2 ... 17 M4
  DART DA1 ... 415 J8
  RBRW/HUT CM13 ... 355 L1
Byron Wy *HARH* RM3 ... 371 G7
Byrony Cl *WIT* CM8 ... 211 L7
Bywater Rd *RCHLM* CM3 ... 339 K5

C

Cabborns Crs *SLH/COR* SS17 ... 409 L3
Cabinet Wy *LOS* SS9 ... 381 K5
Cadenhouse Ms *COLW* CO3 ... 161 M3
Cadmore La *BAR* EN8 ... 276 F8
Cadogan Av *RBRW/HUT* CM13 ... 374 E6
  HOC/HUL SS5 ... 362 E5
Cage End *RBSF* CM22 ... 203 G6
Cage End *RBSF* CM22 ... 203 G6
Cagefield Rd *RCFD* SS4 ... 364 F7
Cage La *COLN* CO4 ... 105 J6
  FX IP11 ... 84 F8
Cairns Rd *WFD* IG8 ... 349 G7
Cairns Rd *COLS* CO2 ... 191 H1
Caister Dr *PIT* SS13 ... 378 C5
Caithness Cl *IPNE* IP4 ... 38 C3
Caladonia La *WICKW* SS12 ... 359 M6
Calamint Rd *WIT* CM8 ... 211 L8
Calbourne Av *HCH* RM12 ... 389 J4
Calcott Cl *BRW* CM14 ... 354 C2
Calcutta Rd *TIL* RM18 ... 418 A6
Callis St *SUD* CO10 ... 31 J3
Callowood Cft *RCHLM* CM3 ... 316 E2
Calmore Cl *HCH* RM12 ... 389 K4
Calshot Av *CDH/CHF* RM16 ... 407 G7
Calverley Cl *BSF* CM23 ... 173 M8
Calverley Crs *DAGE* RM10 ... 388 B1
Calvert Dr *PIT* SS13 ... 378 D2
Calvina Cl *LAIN* SS15 ... 377 L2
Camberley La *IPNE* IP4 ... 38 E4
Camberton Rd *BRTR* CM7 ... 154 F5
Cambeys Rd *DAGE* RM10 ... 388 D4
Camborne Av *HARH* RM3 ... 352 F8
Camborne Av *KESG* IP5 ... 39 J4
Camborne Wy *HARH* RM3 ... 353 C8
Cambrai Rd *COLS* CO2 ... 162 G6
Cambria Cl *CVI* SS8 ... 397 K8
  MGTR CO11 ... 109 J8
Cambridge Av *GPK* RM2 ... 371 K3
  HSTD CO9 ... 97 M3
Cambridge Cl *BAR* EN8 ... 300 D1
  HVHL CB9 ... 27 M2
  ING CM4 ... 335 L1
  VGE SS16 ... 376 A6
Cambridge Dr *CHTY* IP2 ... 57 M2
Cambridge Gdns
  CDH/CHF RM16 ... 418 B1
  EN EN1 ... 324 B4
  RCFD SS4 ... 363 K6
Cambridge Rd *CBE/LIN* CB1 ... 24 C1
  COLW CO3 ... 162 D6
  COS CO15 ... 12 F4
  CVI SS8 ... 398 A8
  FOS CO13 ... 199 H6
  FX IP11 ... 115 J1
  HLW CM20 ... 227 K5
  KESG IP5 ... 39 H5
  SAFWS CB11 ... 43 G7
  SBW CM21 ... 200 F6
  STSD CM24 ... 146 F3
  WOS/PRIT SS0 ... 20 E7
Cambridge Wy *BURES* CO8 ... 102 A3
  HVHL CB9 ... 27 M2
Camden Cl *CDH/CHF* RM16 ... 418 C1
Camden Rd *CDH/CHF* RM16 ... 406 F8
  IPSE IP3 ... 38 C2
Camellia Av *RCOS* CO16 ... 12 A3
Camellia Cl *CHLM/WR* CM1 ... 265 G5
  HARH RM3 ... 371 M1
Camellia Crs *RCOS* CO16 ... 12 A3

Camelot Cl *CHLM/WR* CM1 ... 264 A6
Camelot Gdns *PIT* SS13 ... 378 D5
Cameron Cl *BRW* CM14 ... 354 D5
  ING CM4 ... 310 C8
  LOS SS9 ... 399 K1
  SLH/COR SS17 ... 394 F5
Cameron Dr *BAR* EN8 ... 300 E6
Cameron Pl *WICKW* SS12 ... 359 M6
Cam Gn *SOCK/AV* RM15 ... 406 C4
Camoise Cl *HSTD* CO9 ... 72 C4
Camomile Dr *WICKE* SS11 ... 359 M3
Camomile Wy *COLN* CO4 ... 162 D1
Camomile Rd *ROM/RG* RM7 ... 388 E1
Campbell Cl *CHLM/GWD* CM2 ... 288 D4
  HLWE CM17 ... 256 C4
  ROM RM1 ... 351 M7
  WICKW SS12 ... 359 L6
Campbell Dr *COLN* CO4 ... 163 M1
Campbell Rd *IPSE* IP3 ... 59 K2
  WIT CM8 ... 212 A6
Camperdown Rd *CVI* SS8 ... 398 D6
Campernell Cl *RCOLE* CO7 ... 221 C3
Camper Rd *SOS* SS1 ... 401 L5
Campfield Rd *SBN/FI* SS3 ... 402 F8
Campine Cl *BRW* CM14 ... 276 E8
Campion Cl *ROM/RG* RM7 ... 388 E1
Campion Gdns *WFD* IG8 ... 348 B6
Campion Rd *CHTY* IP2 ... 37 G7
  COLS CO2 ... 163 H6
Campions *LOU* IG10 ... 327 H2
Campions Hl *RCOLW* CO6 ... 103 L2
The Campions *STSD* CM24 ... 146 F3
Campion Wy *WIT* CM8 ... 211 M8
Cample La *SOCK/AV* RM15 ... 406 C5
Camp Rd *RCOLE* CO7 ... 166 A4
Camps Rd *CBE/LIN* CB1 ... 25 J4
  HVHL CB9 ... 28 A4
  HVHL CB9 ... 47 J2
Camulodunum Wy *COLS* CO2 ... 190 D2
Camulus Cl *COLS* CO2 ... 190 B1
Cam Wy *WIT* CM8 ... 238 E1
Camwood Gdns *IPSE* IP3 ... 38 C7
Canada La *BROX* EN10 ... 276 F5
Canada Rd *ERITH* DA8 ... 414 C4
The Canadas *BROX* EN10 ... 276 F5
Canberra Cl *CHLM/WR* CM1 ... 263 M6
  COLS CO2 ... 191 H2
  DAGE RM10 ... 388 E6
  HCH RM12 ... 389 K3
  IPNE IP4 ... 38 E5
Canberra Crs *DAGE* RM10 ... 388 E6
Canberra Sq *TIL* RM18 ... 418 B6
Can Bridge Wy *CHLM/GWD* CM2 ... 17 J5
Cancer Wy *SOCK/AV* RM15 ... 406 C5
Candlet Gv *FX* IP11 ... 85 G8
Candlet Rd *FX* IP11 ... 84 F6
Candover Rd *HCH* RM12 ... 371 J8
Candytuft Rd *CHLM/WR* CM1 ... 265 G5
Cane Hl *HARH* RM3 ... 371 L2
Canes La *HLWE* CM17 ... 280 F2
Canewdon Cl *WICKE* SS11 ... 359 L1
Canewdon Gdns *WICKE* SS11 ... 359 L1
Canewdon Hall Cl *RCFD* SS4 ... 364 E1
Canewdon Rd *RCFD* SS4 ... 363 K3
  WOS/PRIT SS0 ... 20 B6
Canewdon View Rd *RCFD* SS4 ... 363 L5
Canfield *BSF* CM23 ... 173 M3
Canfield Rd *GTDUN* CM6 ... 204 E3
  RAIN RM13 ... 389 G7
  WFD IG8 ... 348 F8
Canford Av *WICKW* SS12 ... 359 C3
Canford Cl *CHLM/GWD* CM2 ... 288 F4
Canhams Rd *SUD* CO10 ... 55 J8
Canham St *IP* IP1 ... 2 D4
Canning St *HAR* CO12 ... 7 K5
Canning St *BOC* CM0 ... 295 K6
Cannon Cir *BRTR* CM7 ... 95 L5
Cannon Leys *CHLM/GWD* CM2 ... 288 D8
Cannon Ms *WAB* EN9 ... 301 K7
Cannon Rd *COL* CO1 ... 163 J5
Cannons Cl *BSF* CM23 ... 174 B3
  COLS CO2 ... 162 E7
Cannons La *CHONG* CM5 ... 283 M1
  RBSF CM22 ... 203 G6
Cannons Md *BRWN* CM15 ... 308 B5
  STSD CM24 ... 146 E4
Cannons Mill La *BSF* CM23 ... 174 B2
Canon Cl *HVHL* CB9 ... 28 A2
  SLH/COR SS17 ... 410 A1
Canon Pugh Dr *SUD* CO10 ... 35 K5
Canons Brook *HLWW/ROY* CM19 ... 14 F1
Canons Cl *RCHLM* CM3 ... 314 F2
Canons Ga *BAR* EN8 ... 277 G6
  HLW CM20 ... 14 F1
Cansleigh Crs *LOS* SS9 ... 399 M2
Cansey La *MGTR* CO11 ... 139 L3
Canterbury Av *SOSN* SS2 ... 383 M8
  UPMR RM14 ... 373 G8
Canterbury Cl *BSDN* SS14 ... 378 A3
  CHIG IG7 ... 350 A4
  CHTY IP2 ... 58 A3
  RAYL SS6 ... 361 K6
Canterbury Gra *BRTR* CM7 ... 155 G3
Canterbury Rd *COLS* CO2 ... 163 H6
  COS CO15 ... 224 D5
Canterbury Wy *CHLM/WR* CM1 ... 16 B1
  DART DA1 ... 415 K8
  RBRW/HUT CM13 ... 354 D7
  WTHK RM20 ... 415 M4
The Canters *SBF/HAD* SS7 ... 380 C6
Canuden Rd *CHLM/WR* CM1 ... 16 B5
Canute Cl *RCFD* SS4 ... 364 F1
Canvey Rd *CVI* SS8 ... 397 L4
  LOS SS9 ... 399 J2
  PIT SS13 ... 379 G5
Canvey Wk *CHLM/WR* CM1 ... 264 F5
Canvey Wy *CVI* SS8 ... 397 K4
  SBF/HAD SS7 ... 379 H8
Capadocia St *SOS* SS1 ... 401 M5
Cape Cl *COLN* CO4 ... 162 A6
Capel Cl *BRTR* CM7 ... 182 A1
  CHLM/WR CM1 ... 264 C4
  FX IP11 ... 84 C3
  SLH/COR SS17 ... 409 M1
Capel Dr *FX* IP11 ... 8 D1

Capel Hall La *FX* IP11 ... 84 D3
Capel Pk *FOS* CO13 ... 198 F4
Capel Rd *BRTR* CM7 ... 182 A1
  COLW CO3 ... 162 D6
  EN EN1 ... 300 C8
Capel Ter *SOS* SS1 ... 21 G7
Capon Cl *COLS* CO2 ... 189 G7
Capon Cl *BRW* CM14 ... 354 C2
Capons La *RCHLM* CM3 ... 291 H5
Cap Pillar Cl *RCOLE* CO7 ... 192 C1
Capstan Ct *GRH* GRA ... 415 K8
Captains Rd *K/T/MI* CO5 ... 245 J5
Captains Wood Rd *MAL* CM9 ... 269 H1
The Caravan Site
  SOCK/AV RM15 ... 405 L8
Caravel Cl *CDH/CHF* RM16 ... 407 L8
Carbonels *SUD* CO10 ... 35 M8
Carbury Cl *HCH* RM12 ... 389 K5
Cardew Drift *KESG* IP5 ... 39 L3
Cardiff Av *CHTY* IP2 ... 58 C2
Cardiff Rd *PEND* EN3 ... 324 C6
Cardigan Av *WOS/PRIT* SS0 ... 382 D8
Cardigan St *IP* IP1 ... 2 C2
Cardinal Cl *COLN* CO4 ... 164 B4
  CHESW EN7 ... 276 A6
Cardinal Dr *BARK/HLT* IG6 ... 349 K7
Cardinal St *IP* IP1 ... 2 E6
Cardinal Wy *HVHL* CB9 ... 28 A2
  RAIN RM13 ... 389 G5
Card's Rd *CHLM/GWD* CM2 ... 289 K5
Carfax Rd *HCH* RM12 ... 389 G3
Carisbrook Cl *EN* EN1 ... 324 A3
Carisbrooke Av *COS* CO15 ... 224 B3
Carisbrooke Cl *EMPK* RM11 ... 372 B8
  PIT SS13 ... 378 C5
Carisbrooke Dr *RCHLM* CM3 ... 339 K4
  SLH/COR SS17 ... 395 H7
Carisbrooke Rd *BRWN* CM15 ... 332 C8
  WOS/PRIT SS0 ... 20 C3
Carleton Rd *BAR* EN8 ... 276 E7
Carlina Gdns *WFD* IG8 ... 348 C6
Carlingford Dr *WOS/PRIT* SS0 ... 382 D8
Carlisle Cl *COL* CO1 ... 10 F5
Carlisle Rd *ROM* RM1 ... 371 G5
Carlisle Wy *PIT* SS13 ... 378 C5
Carlton Av *WOS/PRIT* SS0 ... 382 D7
Carlton Cl *HSTD* CO9 ... 73 H1
  HVHL CB9 ... 28 A2
  UPMR RM14 ... 390 C1
Carlton Dr *LOS* SS9 ... 400 A2
  SBF/HAD SS7 ... 380 D2
Carlton Rd *CDH/CHF* RM16 ... 408 A7
  COS CO15 ... 13 L3
  GPK RM2 ... 371 H5
  KESG IP5 ... 39 H4
  PIT SS13 ... 378 F3
  WICKE SS11 ... 359 K1
Carlton Wy *IPNE* IP4 ... 37 M3
Carlyle Gdns *BCAYW* CM12 ... 335 G6
  WICKW SS12 ... 359 M6
Carmania Cl *SBN/FI* SS3 ... 403 G2
Carmarthen Rd *CHTY* IP2 ... 58 B2
Carmel St *SAFWN* CB10 ... 42 E1
Carmen St *SAFWN* CB10 ... 22 E8
Carnaby Rd *BROX* EN10 ... 252 F8
Carnach Gn *SOCK/AV* RM15 ... 406 C5
Carnarvon Av *EN* EN1 ... 324 A4
Carnarvon Rd *COS* CO15 ... 13 C6
  SOSN SS2 ... 20 F3
Carnation Cl *CHLM/WR* CM1 ... 265 G6
  ROMW/RG RM7 ... 388 F1
Carnation Dr *SAFWN* CB10 ... 66 A1
Carnforth Gdns *HCH* RM12 ... 389 H4
Carnival Cl *BSDN* SS14 ... 377 J2
Carolbrook Rd *CHTY* IP2 ... 57 M2
Carol Cl *FX* IP11 ... 85 K8
  LAIN SS15 ... 376 E4
Carolina Wy *K/T/MI* CO5 ... 214 E6
Caroline Cl *RCOLE* CO7 ... 164 D8
Caroline's Cl *SOSN* SS2 ... 382 F6
Caro Rd *CVI* SS8 ... 398 D8
Carpenter Cl *BCAYW* CM12 ... 335 C7
Carpenter Pth
  RBRW/HUT CM13 ... 333 L7
Carpenters *SBN/FI* SS3 ... 384 E5
Carpenters Arms La *EPP* CM16 ... 280 C5
Carpenters Rd *EN* EN1 ... 300 D8
The Carpenters *BSF* CM23 ... 173 K7
Carraways *WIT* CM8 ... 239 J3
Carriage Cl *FX* IP11 ... 84 D5
Carriage Dr *CHLM/WR* CM1 ... 264 F3
Carriers Cl *K/T/MI* CO5 ... 245 H4
Carrigans *BSF* CM23 ... 173 M3
Carrington Ct *K/T/MI* CO5 ... 245 L4
Carringtons Rd *RCOLE* CO7 ... 137 J7
Carrington Wy *BRTR* CM7 ... 155 G3
Carroll Hl *LOU* IG10 ... 327 G5
Carron Md *RCHLM* CM3 ... 340 A5
Carr Rd *FX* IP11 ... 8 E9
Carrs Rd *COS* CO15 ... 12 C5
Carr St *IPNE* IP4 ... 3 G4
Carruthers Dr *WICKE* SS11 ... 359 L2
Carsey Cl *BCAYE* CM11 ... 336 D7
Carsey Hl *CBE/LIN* CB1 ... 26 C5
Carshalton End *COLW* CO3 ... 162 A7
Carsons Dr *BCAYE* CM11 ... 335 L6
Carsons Dr *SUD* CO10 ... 55 K6
Carswell Rd *RBRW/HUT* CM13 ... 333 L8
Cartbridge Cl *WOTN* CO14 ... 199 J3
Cartel *IP* IP1 RM19 ... 415 L1
Carte Pl *VGE* SS16 ... 376 B6
Carter Cl *CRW* RM5 ... 351 J8
Carter Dr *CRW* RM5 ... 351 J5
Carterhatch La *EN* EN1 ... 324 A3
  PEND EN3 ... 324 D4
Carterhatch Rd *PEND* EN3 ... 324 F4
Carters Cl *RCOS* CO16 ... 223 J8
Carters Cft *SAFWN* CB10 ... 45 J2
Cartersfield Rd *WAB* EN9 ... 301 K6
Carters Hl *BSF* CM23 ... 146 B2
Carters La *EPP* CM16 ... 279 J4
  RBSF CM22 ... 120 A6
  WIT CM8 ... 240 A5
Carters Leys *BSF* CM23 ... 173 L3
Carters Md *HLWE* CM17 ... 256 C4
Cartlodge Av *WICKE* SS11 ... 359 M3
Cartwright Rd *SBF/HAD* SS7 ... 379 L4

Cartwright Wk
  CHLM/CWD CM2 ... 289 G1
Carvers Wd *BCAYE* CM11 ... 357 K4
Cascade Rd *BKHH* IG9 ... 348 E5
Case La *RIPS/CAP* IP9 ... 78 E5
Casey La *BOC* CM0 ... 297 M7
Cashiobury Ter *SOS* SS1 ... 20 F7
Cashmere Wy *VGE* SS16 ... 377 K8
Cassandra Ga *BAR* EN8 ... 277 G7
Cassel Av *CVI* SS8 ... 398 D6
Cassino Rd *CHLM/WR* CM1 ... 263 M5
  COLS CO2 ... 162 D8
Castellan Av *GPK* RM2 ... 371 J3
Castell Rd *LOU* IG10 ... 327 K3
Castle Av *HVHL* CB9 ... 27 M3
  RAIN RM13 ... 388 F6
  SBF/HAD SS7 ... 398 E2
Castle Cl *FX* IP11 ... 85 L7
  HARH RM3 ... 352 D4
  HOD EN11 ... 253 K2
  RAYL SS6 ... 380 D2
  RCHLM CM3 ... 209 G5
  SBN/FI SS3 ... 403 H3
Castle Ct *RAYL* SS6 ... 380 D2
Castle Cross *SAFWN* CB10 ... 43 M8
Castledon Rd *BCAYE* CM11 ... 337 C8
Castle Dr *LOS* SS9 ... 399 J3
  RAYL SS6 ... 361 K8
Castlegate St *HAR* CO12 ... 7 L2
Castle Hl *RCOLE* CO7 ... 107 G7
Castle La *HSTD* CO9 ... 74 A7
  HVHL CB9 ... 27 M3
Castle Meadow *HSTD* CO9 ... 97 L1
Castle Rd *COL* CO1 ... 10 E6
  COS CO15 ... 12 E6
  GRAYS RM17 ... 416 F3
  HOD EN11 ... 253 J2
  IP IP1 ... 36 F2
  PEND EN3 ... 324 F5
  RAYL SS6 ... 380 D2
  SBF/HAD SS7 ... 398 F1
Castle St *BSF* CM23 ... 174 B4
  CHONG CM5 ... 307 H1
  SAFWN CB10 ... 65 L1
Castle Ter *RAYL* SS6 ... 380 D2
Castleton Rd *SOSN* SS2 ... 401 M2
Castle Vw *BSF* CM23 ... 174 B4
Castle View Rd *CVI* SS8 ... 398 B5
Castle Wk *HVHL* CB9 ... 27 M3
Castleward Cl *RCOLE* CO7 ... 192 C3
Castle Wy *RCOS* CO16 ... 222 B7
Caswell Cl *SLH/COR* SS17 ... 395 H7
Caswell Ms *CHLM/GWD* CM2 ... 289 C1
Catalina Av *CDH/CHF* RM16 ... 407 G7
Catchpole La *MAL* CM9 ... 240 B7
Catchpool Rd *COL* CO1 ... 10 C4
Caterham Cl *RCOS* CO16 ... 223 K5
Caterham Ct *WAB* EN9 ... 302 A6
Cater Wd *BCAYW* CM12 ... 335 J8
Catesbray *RIPS/CAP* IP9 ... 78 A2
Catharine Cl *CDH/CHF* RM16 ... 407 G7
Cathedral Dr *LAIN* SS15 ... 376 D4
Catherine Cl *BRWN* CM15 ... 332 B7
  COS CO15 ... 13 J1
Catherine Hunt Wy *COLS* CO2 ... 190 C1
Catherine Rd *GPK* RM2 ... 371 J5
  PEND EN3 ... 300 F8
  SBF/HAD SS7 ... 379 L7
Catherines Cl *RCHLM* CM3 ... 209 G5
Catisfield Rd *PEND* EN3 ... 324 F1
Catkin Cl *HVHL* CB9 ... 27 L2
Catons La *SAFWN* CB10 ... 43 L8
Cat's La *SUD* CO10 ... 5 H7
Cattawade End *BSDN* SS14 ... 19 L3
Cattawade Link *BSDN* SS14 ... 19 M3
Cattawade St *WOTN* CO14 ... 108 D4
Cattermole Cl *RCOS* CO16 ... 223 J8
Catts Cl *RIPS/CAP* IP9 ... 110 A1
Cattsfield *RIPS/CAP* IP9 ... 110 A1
Cauldwell Av *IPNE* IP4 ... 3 M3
Cauldwell Hall Rd *IPNE* IP4 ... 38 B4
Caulfield Rd *SBN/FI* SS3 ... 402 D4
Causeway *RCHLM* CM3 ... 208 A2
Causeway Br *SOCK/AV* RM15 ... 405 M8
Causeway End *MGTR* CO11 ... 108 C4
Causeway End Rd *GTDUN* CM6 ... 180 D8
Causeway Reach *RCOS* CO16 ... 223 M4
The Causeway *BRTR* CM7 ... 94 D5
  BRTR CM7 ... 155 G8
  BSF CM23 ... 174 A4
  BUNT SG9 ... 116 B2
  CHLM/GWD CM2 ... 289 C5
  CHLM/WR CM1 ... 286 E5
  COLN CO4 ... 11 K3
  GTDUN CM6 ... 178 E1
  HSTD CO9 ... 50 A3
  HSTD CO9 ... 72 C5
  HSTD CO9 ... 128 F2
  HVHL CB9 ... 27 M4
  MAL CM9 ... 267 L5
  MAL CM9 ... 269 H7
  RCOLW CO6 ... 134 C2
  SAFWS CB11 ... 90 C4
Causton Rd *COL* CO1 ... 10 B5
Caustons Cl *SUD* CO10 ... 55 K6
Caustonway *RAYL* SS6 ... 361 J2
Cavan Rd *IP* IP1 ... 36 E1
Cavell Crs *DART* DA1 ... 415 H8
Cavell Rd *CHESW* EN7 ... 276 A4
Cavendish Av *COLS* CO2 ... 163 K7
  RAIN RM13 ... 389 G1
  WFD IG8 ... 348 C8
Cavendish Crs *RAIN* RM13 ... 389 G1
Cavendish Dr *MGTR* CO11 ... 108 C8
  RCOS CO16 ... 223 H7
Cavendish Gdns *BRTR* CM7 ... 155 K6
  CHLM/GWD CM2 ... 264 D8
  WOS/PRIT SS0 ... 400 B1
Cavendish Rd *FX* IP11 ... 9 J4
  HOC/HUL SS5 ... 363 H2
  SUD CO10 ... 31 L4
Cavendish St *IPSE* IP3 ... 3 L7
Cavendish Wy *LAIN* SS15 ... 376 E2

Cavenham Gdns *EMPK* RM11 ... 371 K5
Caversham Av *SBN/FI* SS3 ... 402 F2
Caversham Park Av
  RAYL SS6 ... 361 K6
Cawdor Av *SOCK/AV* RM15 ... 406 B5
Cawkell Cl *STSD* CM24 ... 146 E4
Cawkwell Cl *CHLM/GWD* CM2 ... 265 G7
Caxton Ct *COLN* CO4 ... 135 K5
Caxton Rd *HOD* EN11 ... 253 J1
Cecil Av *CDH/CHF* RM16 ... 407 G7
  EMPK RM11 ... 371 M5
  EN EN1 ... 324 A6
Cecil Cl *BSF* CM23 ... 174 E4
Cecil Ct *HLWS* CM18 ... 255 K6
Cecilia St *IP* IP1 ... 2 E6
Cecil Rd *BAR* EN8 ... 300 E4
  HOD EN11 ... 253 K3
  IP IP1 ... 2 D3
Cecil Wy *RAYL* SS6 ... 381 G1
Cedar Av *BAR* EN8 ... 300 E5
  CHLM/WR CM1 ... 16 E2
  K/T/MI CO5 ... 214 D4
  KESG IP5 ... 39 H5
  PEND EN3 ... 324 D4
  RCOLE CO7 ... 220 E4
  UPMR RM14 ... 390 B3
  WICKW SS12 ... 359 K6
Cedar Av West *CHLM/WR* CM1 ... 16 E1
Cedar Cha *MAL* CM9 ... 269 K6
Cedar Cl *BKHH* IG9 ... 348 E3
  FOS CO13 ... 199 H4
  MGTR CO11 ... 108 E2
  RAYL SS6 ... 381 G3
  RBRW/HUT CM13 ... 355 L1
  ROMW/RG RM7 ... 370 D4
  SBW CM21 ... 227 M2
  SOSN SS2 ... 21 H1
Cedar Ct *BSF* CM23 ... 174 A2
  RCOLW CO6 ... 133 L6
Cedar Crs *MGTR* CO11 ... 108 E2
Cedarcroft Rd *IP* IP1 ... 37 G1
Cedar Dr *HOC/HUL* SS5 ... 361 M1
  LOU IG10 ... 327 J4
  WIT CM8 ... 212 B6
Cedar Gdns *UPMR* RM14 ... 390 D2
Cedar Gn *HOD* EN11 ... 253 H6
Cedar Gv *BOC* CM0 ... 344 C5
Cedar Hall Gdns *SBF/HAD* SS7 ... 380 B5
Cedar Ms *HOC/HUL* SS5 ... 362 D5
Cedar Pk *SBF/HAD* SS7 ... 380 B5
Cedar Ri *SOCK/AV* RM15 ... 406 E2
Cedar Rd *CDH/CHF* RM16 ... 408 B8
  CVI SS8 ... 398 A7
  ERITH DA8 ... 414 B5
  HCH RM12 ... 389 K2
  RBRW/HUT CM13 ... 333 L8
  ROMW/RG RM7 ... 370 D4
  SBF/HAD SS7 ... 380 B5
Cedars *SLH/COR* SS17 ... 409 M1
Cedars La *RIPS/CAP* IP9 ... 78 A3
Cedars Rd *COLS* CO2 ... 10 B9
The Cedars *BKHH* IG9 ... 348 B2
  RCHLM CM3 ... 339 L3
  SBF/HAD SS7 ... 385 J7
Cedar Wk *RCFD* SS4 ... 364 C2
Cedar Wy *RCOLE* CO7 ... 194 F3
Cedric Av *ROM* RM1 ... 370 F3
Celadon Cl *PEND* EN3 ... 324 F5
Celandine Cl *BCAYW* CM12 ... 335 G7
  SOCK/AV RM15 ... 406 D2
Celandine Ct *COLN* CO4 ... 162 D1
Celeborn St *RCHLM* CM3 ... 339 K5
Celedon Cl *CDH/CHF* RM16 ... 406 F7
Cement Block Cottages
  GRAYS RM17 ... 417 K2
Cemetery La *RCOLE* CO7 ... 107 H1
Cemetery Rd *BSF* CM23 ... 174 A6
  IPNE IP4 ... 3 H3
Centaur Wy *MAL* CM9 ... 293 H3
Centaury Cl *COLW* CO3 ... 161 K4
Centenary Cir *CHLM/GWD* CM2 ... 312 C2
  RCFD SS4 ... 265 H2
Centenary Wk *EPP* CM16 ... 303 K6
  LOU IG10 ... 326 C8
Centenary Wy *RCOS* CO16 ... 223 M2
Central Av *BAR* EN8 ... 300 F5
  BCAYW CM12 ... 335 J8
  CVI SS8 ... 397 M7
  EN EN1 ... 324 C4
  FOS CO13 ... 199 H5
  HOC/HUL SS5 ... 362 A2
  IPSE IP3 ... 59 L3
  RCFD SS4 ... 363 L6
  SBF/HAD SS7 ... 380 F6
  SLH/COR SS17 ... 394 F6
  SOCK/AV RM15 ... 405 K7
  SOSN SS2 ... 21 J3
  TIL RM18 ... 418 B5
  WTHK RM20 ... 416 A2
Central Cl *SBF/HAD* SS7 ... 380 F7
Central Dr *HCH* RM12 ... 389 M2
Central Park Av *DAGE* RM10 ... 388 D3
Central Rd *HLW* CM20 ... 227 H7
  SLH/COR SS17 ... 409 L2
Central Wall *CVI* SS8 ... 398 C6
Central Wall Rd *CVI* SS8 ... 398 C6
Centre Av *EPP* CM16 ... 304 A4
Centre Dr *EPP* CM16 ... 304 A4
Centre Gn *EPP* CM16 ... 304 A4
Centre Rd *DAGE* RM10 ... 388 C8
The Centre *HSTD* CO9 ... 128 F1
Centre Wy *WAB* EN9 ... 301 K7
Centurion Cl *SBN/FI* SS3 ... 403 G3
Centurion Wy *COLS* CO2 ... 190 B1
  PUR RM19 ... 415 G1
Century Rd *HOD* EN11 ... 253 H4
Ceylon Rd *WOS/PRIT* SS0 ... 20 B5
Chadacre Rd *SOS* SS1 ... 402 C2
Chadburn Rd *SUD* CO10 ... 34 E3
Chadfields *TIL* RM18 ... 418 B4
Chadville Gdns *ROM* RM6 ... 369 M1
Chadwell Av *BAR* EN8 ... 276 D8
Chadwell By-pass Cnr *GRAYS* RM17 ... 418 G2
Chadwell Hl *CDH/CHF* RM16 ... 418 C2
Chadwell Rd *GRAYS* RM17 ... 417 M1
Chadwick Dr *HARH* RM3 ... 371 L2
Chadwick Rd *RCHLM* CM3 ... 339 M2
  WOS/PRIT SS0 ... 4 A1

Chaffinch Cl SBN/FI SS3 ....402 F3
Chafford Gdns
  RBRW/HUT CM13 ....374 E6
Chafford Wy CDH/CHF RM16 .407 H6
Chailey Av EN EN1 ....324 A4
Chaingate Av SOSN SS2 ......401 M1
Chalfont Cl LOS SS9 ....381 L7
Chalfont Rd COLN CO4 ....135 K8
Chalforde Gdns GPK RM2 ....371 J4
Chalice Cl BSDN SS14 ....377 M5
Chalk End PIT SS13 ....378 B4
Chalklands CHLM/GWD 313 L1
  SAFWN CB10 ....43 M8
Chalk La HLWE CM17 ....257 H1
Chalkners Cl RIPS/CAP IP9 ...78 B2
Chalk Rd CVI SS8 ....398 B5
Chalks Av SBW CM21 ....200 E8
Chalks Rd WIT CM8 ....212 A8
Chalkstone Wy HVHL CB9 .....28 D5
Chalk St RCHLM CM3 ....338 A3
Chalkwell Av WOS/PRIT SS0 ..400 C4
Chalkwell Esp WOS/PRIT SS0 .400 C4
Chalkwell Park Dr LOS SS9 ..400 A1
Chalky La ROY SG8 ....62 E1
Challacombe SBN/FI SS3 .....402 D2
Challacombe Cl
  RBRW/HUT CM13 ....355 K2
Challenge Wy COL CO1 ......163 J5
Challinor HLWE CM17 ....256 F3
Challis La BRTR CM7 ....183 H3
Challock Lees PIT SS13 ......378 D6
Chalon St IP IP1 ....2 D5
Chalvedon Av PIT SS13 ......378 C4
Chamberlain Av CVI SS8 .....398 D7
  SLH/COR SS17 ....395 H6
  WOTN CO14 ....199 J4
Chamberlain Cl HLWE CM17 ..256 D3
Chamberlains Ride
  RCHLM CM3 ....339 L5
Chamberlain Wy RIPW IP8 ...57 K1
Champion Cl SLH/COR SS17 ..394 F8
  WICKW SS12 ....359 L5
Champion Rd UPMR RM14 ....390 C1
Champions Wy HOD EN11 ....253 H2
  RCHLM CM3 ....339 K3
Champlain Av CVI SS8 ....398 A6
Chance Cl CDH/CHF RM16 ...407 G8
Chancel Cl BOC CM0 ....297 M7
  LAIN SS15 ....376 D3
  SBF/HAD SS7 ....379 K5
Chancellor Av CHLM/GWD 265 J7
Chancellor Rd SOS SS1 ......21 H7
Chancery Gv COLS CO2 ......191 H3
Chancery Pl CHLM/WR CM1 ..287 J2
Chandler Rd LOU IG10 ......327 J3
Chandlers BOC CM0 ....344 B5
Chandlers Cl BSF CM23 ......173 K7
  RCOS CO16 ....223 J8
Chandlers Rw COL CO1 ......163 K6
Chandlers Wk BRWN CM15 ...331 M1
Chandlers Wy ROM RM1 .....370 F5
  SOSN SS2 ....383 G6
Chandos Cl BKHH IG9 ......348 C3
Chandos Pde SBF/HAD SS7 ..381 C3
Chaney Rd ROL CO7 ....192 B1
Chanlock Pth SOCK/AV RM15 406 C5
Channing Cl EMPK RM11 ....372 A7
Chanterelle COLN CO4 ......135 J8
Chanton Cl LOS SS9 ....381 L4
Chantress Rd DAGE RM10 ...388 D7
Chantreywood
  RBRW/HUT CM13 ....355 H4
Chantry Cl BSF CM23 ....173 M3
  COS CO15 ....223 M4
Chantry Dr ING CM4 ....310 C8
  LAIN SS15 ....376 D4
Chantry Gn CHTY IP2 ....36 E8
Chantry La RCHLM CM3 .....237 H8
Chantry Rd BSF CM23 ......173 M3
The Chantry COLW CO3 .....162 D4
  HLW CM20 ....227 H8
Chantry Wy BCAYW CM11 ...357 J1
  RAIN RM13 ....388 E3
Chanute Av BRTR CM7 ......95 K4
Chapel Cl RIPS/CAP IP9 .....78 B2
  SUD CO10 ....35 M8
  WTHK RM20 ....416 C3
Chapel Ct BCAYE CM11 .....357 J1
Chapel Cft ING CM4 ....310 C7
  RCOLE CO7 ....136 F7
Chapel Cut MGTR CO11 .....109 H7
Chapel Dr RCHLM CM3 ......235 J5
Chapel End HOD EN11 ......253 H6
Chapel End Wy HSTD CO9 ...71 J1
Chapel Fld RIPW IP8 ....36 B1
Chapelfields FOS CO13 ......198 F5
Chapel Flds HLWE CM17 .....256 D5
Chapel Hl BRTR CM7 ....183 J1
  HSTD CO9 ....128 E1
  SUD CO10 ....52 E7
Chapel La BOC CM0 ....297 M7
  CHIG IG7 ....350 A4
  CHLM/WR CM1 ....286 A2
  COLN CO4 ....105 H8
  FOS CO13 ....198 B5
  HLWE CM17 ....256 D5
  MAL CM9 ....293 M1
  RCHLM CM3 ....266 C8
  RCHLM CM3 ....316 E3
  RCOLE CO7 ....164 C2
  RCOLE CO7 ....165 H5
  RCOLE CO7 ....166 B6
  RCOLE CO7 ....194 B6
  RCOLW CO6 ....133 M8
  RCOS CO16 ....167 M3
  RCOS CO16 ....222 B7
  RIPW IP8 ....57 K4
  RIPW IP8 ....57 J1
  SAFWN CB11 ....89 H3
  SBN/FI SS3 ....385 J7
  STDN SG11 ....172 B3
  SUD CO10 ....77 K2
Chapel Rd BOC CM0 ....344 D7
  COLN CO4 ....105 H8
  COLW CO3 ....161 K5
  EPP CM16 ....304 A2

HSTD CO9 ....50 C4
K/T/MI CO5 ....214 F7
KIR/NAC IP10 ....61 M4
MAL CM9 ....240 E5
MAL CM9 ....242 F7
RCOLE CO7 ....192 C3
RCOLE CO7 ....221 H4
RCOLW CO6 ....133 L8
RCOS CO16 ....168 E4
SBN/FI SS3 ....403 C3
Chapel St BCAYW CM12 .....357 H1
  HSTD CO9 ....30 A8
  HSTD CO9 ....128 F1
  HVHL CB9 ....48 D4
  K/T/MI CO5 ....192 A3
Chapel St North COLS CO2 ..10 B9
Chapel St South COLS CO2 ..10 B9
  COLS CO2 ....162 F5
Chaplaincy Gdns
  EMPK RM11 ....371 M8
Chaplains Cl HVHL CB9 .....28 A2
Chaplemount Rd WFD IG8 ...349 G2
Chaplin Cl CHLM/GWD 312 C1
  LAIN SS15 ....376 F2
Chaplin Dr COLN CO4 ......11 M3
Chaplins FOS CO13 ....199 G4
Chapman Rd COS CO15 .....13 G6
  CVI SS8 ....399 H8
Chapmans Cl LOS SS9 ......399 J2
Chapmans La K/T/MI CO5 ...246 A2
Chapmans Wk LOS SS9 ......399 J2
Chappel Hl RCOLW CO6 ....131 K6
Chappel Rd RCOLW CO6 ....101 M8
  RCOLW CO6 ....132 C4
  RCOLW CO6 ....159 K1
Chapple Dr HVHL CB9 ......28 A2
Charcroft Gdns PEND EN3 ..324 C1
Charfinch Crs BCAYE CM11 .357 K2
Charfleets Cl CVI SS8 ......397 L8
Charfleets Rd CVI SS8 ......397 K8
Charfleets Service Rd CVI SS8 397 K8
Charity Farm Cha BCAYW CM12 535 G8
Charlbury Cl HARH RM3 ....352 D7
Charlbury Crs HARH RM3 ...352 D7
Charlecote Rd BRTR CM7 ...182 D4
Charles Cl WOS/PRIT SS0 ...382 A6
Charles Pell Rd COLN CO4 ..163 M5
Charles Rd DAGE RM10 .....388 E5
  FX IP11 ....9 H4
  RCOLE CO7 ....221 G5
Charles St COL CO1 ....163 H5
  EN EN1 ....324 A7
  EPP CM16 ....304 B4
  GRAYS RM17 ....417 J3
  IP IP1 ....2 E3
Charleston Av PIT SS13 ....378 D2
Charleston Ct PIT SS13 ....378 D2
Charlotte Av WICKW SS12 ..359 K4
Charlotte Cl RCHLM CM3 ...339 L5
Charlotte Dr FOS CO13 ....198 F5
Charlotte Gdns CRW RM5 ..351 J2
Charlotte Pl WTHK RM20 ..416 C3
Charlotte's RIPW IP8 ......57 G2
Charlotte Wy WIT CM8 ....239 J1
Charlton Av IP IP1 ....37 G1
Charlton Cl HOD EN11 ....253 H5
  PIT SS13 ....378 D4
Charlton Mead La HOD EN11 253 K6
Charlton St WTHK RM20 ...416 E3
Charlton Wy HOD EN11 ....253 H6
Charnock Cl FOS CO13 ....199 G5
Charnwood Av CHLM/WR CM1 16 B6
Charnwood Rd EN EN1 ....300 C3
Charteris Rd WFD IG8 .....348 G2
Charters Cross HLWS CM18 255 L6
The Charters GTDUN CM6 ..178 E1
Charter Wy BSF CM23 .....183 K2
Chartfield Dr FOS CO13 ....198 E3
Chartwell Cl BRTR CM7 ....154 F4
  IPNE IP4 ....38 C6
  WAB EN9 ....301 M5
Chase Cl HVHL CB9 ....28 B2
  SBF/HAD SS7 ....380 A6
Chase Ct COLN CO4 ....11 M9
  COLN CO4 ....163 M4
Chase Cross Rd CRW RM5 ..351 K8
Chase Dr RCHLM CM3 .....339 K3
Chase End RAYL SS6 ....381 G1
Chase Gdns WOS/PRIT SS0 .382 E8
Chase House Gdns EMPK RM11 372 A5
Chase La CHIG IG7 ....350 B4
  HAR CO12 ....142 F1
Chase Rd BRW CM14 ......354 D4
  SLH/COR SS17 ....395 H8
  SOS SS1 ....21 M5
Chase Rd East RCOLE CO7 ..166 D4
Chaseside RAYL SS6 ....380 F3
Chaseside Cl ROM RM1 ....351 M7
The Chase BCAYE CM11 ....357 K1
  BOC CM0 ....320 E7
  BRTR CM7 ....155 H4
  BRTR CM7 ....182 D6
  BRW CM14 ....354 C5
  BRW CM14 ....354 E4
  BSF CM23 ....173 K3
  CHIG IG7 ....349 J5
  CHLM/GWD CM2 ....289 G5
  COL CO1 ....11 L8
  COS CO15 ....224 F6
  DAGE RM10 ....388 E2
  DAGE RM10 ....389 G2
  GTDUN CM6 ....179 J7
  HVHL CB9 ....48 C4
  K/T/MI CO5 ....213 K1
  K/T/MI CO5 ....245 K5
  LAIN SS15 ....376 C1
  LOU IG10 ....348 D1
  MAL CM9 ....242 C7
  MAL CM9 ....272 E2
  MAL CM9 ....295 G1
  MGTR CO11 ....108 E8
  MGTR CO11 ....109 G2
  RAYL SS6 ....381 G2
  RBRW/HUT CM13 ......355 K6
  RBSF CM22 ....120 A5
  RCFD SS4 ....363 K4
  RCHLM CM3 ....265 M4

RCHLM CM3 ....339 K3
RCOLE CO7 ....107 H7
RCOLE CO7 ....165 J5
RCOLW CO6 ....159 K3
ROM RM1 ....370 F3
SBF/HAD SS7 ....380 A6
SBN/FI SS3 ....369 L8
SUD CO10 ....33 K5
UPMR RM14 ....390 F2
VGE SS16 ....376 F3
WICKE SS11 ....338 B8
WICKW SS12 ....359 M7
WICKW SS12 ....359 H4
WTHK RM20 ....416 E3
Chaseway VGE SS16 ....378 A7
Chaseways SBW CM21 .....227 J3
The Chase Wy COLW CO3 ..162 D2
The Chaseway ING CM4 ...336 B3
Chaters HI SAFWN CB10 ...65 M1
Chatham Hall La RCHLM CM3 235 H1
Chatley Rd RCHLM CM3 ...209 H3
Chatsworth SBF/HAD SS7 ..380 A5
Chatsworth Av BRTR CM7 ..182 C4
Chatsworth Cl BSF CM23 ..173 K4
Chatsworth Crs CHTY IP2 ..58 B1
  FX IP11 ....84 D6
Chatsworth Dr IPNE IP4 ...38 F6
Chatsworth Gdns COS CO15 12 C8
  HOC/HUL SS5 ....362 E5
Chatsworth Rd DART DA1 ..414 D8
  K/T/MI CO5 ....245 K4
Chatteris Av HARH RM3 ...352 C2
Chattisham Rd RIPW IP8 ...56 C3
Chatton Cl WICKW SS12 ...359 M6
Chaucer Cl COS CO15 ......250 B2
  MAL CM9 ....293 H3
  TIL RM18 ....418 D6
Chaucer Crs BRTR CM7 ....183 H5
Chaucer Rd CHLM/GWD CM2 17 M5
  FX IP11 ....9 J5
  HARH RM3 ....352 C8
  SUD CO10 ....4 A1
Chaucer Wk WICKW SS12 ..359 K6
Chaucer Wy COLW CO3 ....162 A4
  DART DA1 ....415 H8
  HOD EN11 ....253 H1
Chauntry Rd HVHL CB9 ....28 A4
Cheapside East RAYL SS6 ..361 K7
Cheapside West RAYL SS6 ..361 K7
Cheddar Av WOS/PRIT SS0 .382 B7
Chedington SBN/FI SS3 ....402 D3
Cheelson Rd SOCK/AV RM15 391 K8
Cheffins Rd HOD EN11 ....253 H2
Cheldon Barton SBN/FI SS3 402 D3
Chelmer Av RAYL SS6 ......380 C2
  RCHLM CM3 ....235 J6
Chelmer Cl FOS CO13 ......198 F4
  MAL CM9 ....241 J7
Chelmer Dr GTDUN CM6 ...178 F3
  RBRW/HUT CM13 ......333 M8
  SOCK/AV RM15 ....406 D5
Chelmer Lea CHLM/GWD CM2 288 F4
Chelmer Pl CHLM/WR CM1 .17 K2
Chelmer Rd BRTR CM7 ....183 L2
  CDH/CHF RM16 ....418 B2
  CHLM/GWD CM2 ....17 M6
  HVHL CB9 ....28 C3
  UPMR RM14 ....372 E6
  WIT CM8 ....238 F1
Chelmer Ter MAL CM9 ....293 J1
Chelmerton Av
  CHLM/GWD CM2 ....288 F4
Chelmer Valley Rd
  CHLM/WR CM1 ....264 C7
Chelmer Village Wy
  CHLM/GWD CM2 ....288 F1
Chelmer Wy BOC CM0 .....344 B5
  SBN/FI SS3 ....402 E4
Chelmsford Av CRW RM5 ..351 L8
  SOSN SS2 ....20 E3
Chelmsford Dr UPMR RM14 390 A2
Chelmsford Rd BRWN CM15 333 K5
  CHLM/WR CM1 ....287 K2
  CHONG CM5 ....283 J7
  COS CO15 ....224 D5
  GTDUN CM6 ....179 G5
  GTDUN CM6 ....232 A4
  ING CM4 ....309 H2
  MAL CM9 ....291 K4
  RBSF CM22 ....229 J1
  RCHLM CM3 ....235 H4
  RCHLM CM3 ....292 C8
  WICKE SS11 ....360 F3
Chelsea Av SOS SS1 ......401 L5
Chelsea Cl IP IP1 ....37 G2
Chelsea Ct SUD CO10 ....4 F6
Chelsea Flds HOD EN11 ..253 J1
Chelsea Gdns HLWE CM17 256 F4
Chelsea Rd SUD CO10 ....4 F6
Chelsworth Av IPNE IP4 ..37 L2
  SUD CO10 ....5 K8
Chelsworth Cl SOS SS1 ..402 A3
Chelsworth Dr HARH RM3 .371 H1
Chelsworth Rd FX IP11 ...8 E3
Cheltenham Av IP IP1 ....37 J2
Cheltenham Dr LOS SS9 ..400 A4
  SBF/HAD SS7 ....380 C4
Cheltenham Gdns LOU IG10 326 F8
Cheltenham Rd
  HOC/HUL SS5 ....363 G4
  SOS SS6 ....21 L6

Cheriton Rd BRTR CM7 ....183 K2
The Cherries CVI SS8 .....413 J2
Cherry Av RBRW/HUT CM13 355 C4
Cherry Blossom Cl RIPW IP8 57 J1
Cherry Blossom La RCHLM CM3 317 G6
Cherrybrook SOS SS1 .....402 D2
Cherry Cha K/T/MI CO5 ...214 E7
  HOC/HUL SS5 ....362 F4
Cherry Cl CVI SS8 ....397 M7
Cherrydene Cl HOC/HUL SS5 361 M1
Cherrydown CDH/CHF RM16 407 G7
  RAYL SS6 ....361 L7
Cherrydown East VGE SS16 18 F8
Cherrydown Wk
  ROMW/RG RM7 ....370 C2
Cherrydown West VGE SS16 18 E8
Cherrygarden La
  CHLM/GWD CM2 ....16 D7
Cherry Garden La RCHLM CM3 291 H4
  SAFWN CB11 ....89 G3
Cherry Garden Rd MAL CM9 292 F1
  RCHLM CM3 ....234 F4
Cherry Gdns BCAYW CM12 334 F7
  BSF CM23 ....173 J6
  DACW RM9 ....388 A4
  SBW CM21 ....200 F7
Cherry Gardens La IPNE IP4 38 C4
Cherry La HSTD CO9 .....73 H3
  WICKE SS11 ....360 A4
Cherry Orchard La RCFD SS4 382 B5
Cherry Orchard Wy RCFD SS4 382 C3
  SOSN SS2 ....382 C4
Cherry Rd PEND EN3 .....324 D2
Cherry Rw COLW CO3 .....162 A6
Cherry St ROMW/RG RM7 ..370 E5
Cherry Tree Av COS CO15 .12 B9
Cherrytree Cha SBN/FI SS3 403 K2
Cherry Tree Cl HAR CO12 .142 C4
  RAIN RM13 ....389 H8
Cherry Tree Dr
  SOCK/AV RM15 ....406 E1
Cherry Tree La COLS CO2 ..191 H5
  RAIN RM13 ....404 A1
Cherry Tree Ri BKHH IG9 ..348 E5
Cherry Tree Rd HOD EN11 253 H4
Cherrytree BCAYW CM12 ..357 C3
Cherrytrees BCAYW CM12 ..357 C3
Cherry Wk CDH/CHF RM16 408 B8
  RAIN RM13 ....389 C8
Cherrywood Dr COLW CO3 162 A6
Cherrywoods RCOLE CO7 ..194 E3
Chertsey Cl SBN/FI SS3 ..402 E2
Chervil Cl K/T/MI CO5 ....214 D7
Cherwell Dr CHLM/WR CM1 263 K6
Cherwell Gv SOCK/AV RM15 406 C5
Chesapeake Cl RIPS/CAP IP9 82 A4
Chesapeake Rd IPSE IP3 ..59 H3
Chesfield Cl BSF CM23 ....174 A6
Chesham Cl ROMW/RG RM7 370 E4
Chesham Dr LAIN SS15 ...376 C2
Chesham Rd CHTY IP2 ....2 D8
Cheshire Cl EMPK RM11 ..372 B5
Cheshunt Dr RAYL SS6 ....361 J5
Cheshunts PIT SS13 ......378 B5
Cheshunt Wash BAR EN8 ..276 F7
Chessington Av IP IP1 ....37 G3
Chess La WIT CM8 ....239 H1
Chester Av SOS SS1 ......401 L5
  UPMR RM14 ....390 F1
Chesterfield Av SBF/HAD SS7 379 L5
Chesterfield Crs LOS SS9 ..381 L5
Chesterfield Dr IP IP1 ....37 G1
Chesterfield Rd PEND EN3 324 F1
Chesterford Gdns
  BSDN SS14 ....378 A3
Chester Gdns ED N9 ......324 C8
Chester Hall La BSDN SS14 18 E1
Chester Pl CHLM/WR CM1 264 B6
Chester Rd CHIG IG7 .....349 H4
  FX IP11 ....85 G8
  LOU IG10 ....327 K3
Chesterton Cl CHTY IP2 ..58 A2
Chestnut Av BCAYW CM12 357 G1
  BKHH IG9 ....348 E4
  CDH/CHF RM16 ....407 J7
  COLS CO2 ....191 H3
  COS CO15 ....12 A7
  FOS CO13 ....198 D5
  HCH RM12 ....389 G1
  HSTD CO9 ....127 M3
  MAL CM9 ....269 K5
  RCHLM CM3 ....238 B8
  SAFWS CB11 ....64 D2
Chestnut Ct SAFWS CB11 ..89 H3
  VGE SS16 ....378 B7
Chestnut Farm Dr RCHLM CM3 342 F1
Chestnut Gln HCH RM12 ..389 G1
Chestnut Gv BARK/HLT IG6 349 M7
  BRTR CM7 ....182 F1
  BRW CM14 ....354 D3
  SBF/HAD SS7 ....379 J7
  SOSN SS2 ....21 H1
Chestnut Rd PEND EN3 ...300 F8
  RCOLE CO7 ....193 J5
  VGE SS16 ....378 B7
Chestnuts RBRW/HUT CM13 355 J2
The Chestnuts CHTY IP2 ..57 K1
  RAYL SS6 ....361 M7
Chestnut Wk CHLM/WR CM1 264 B6
  EPP CM16 ....279 J4
  GTDUN CM6 ....180 D5
  LOU IG10 ....327 H7
  MGTR CO11 ....138 C5
Chestnut Wy K/T/MI CO5 214 D5
  RBSF CM22 ....176 D4
  RCOLE CO7 ....220 F4
Chestwood Cl BCAYW CM12 335 J7

Chevalier Rd FX IP11 .....115 J1
Chevallier St IP IP1 ......2 A1
Cheveling Rd COLS CO2 ..191 L1
Chevely Cl EPP CM16 .....304 E1
Chevening Gdns
  HOC/HUL SS5 ....362 D5
Chevers Pawen PIT SS13 ..378 B6
Chevington Wy HCH RM12 389 J1
Cheviot Dr CHLM/WR CM1 263 L6
Cheviot Rd EMPK RM11 ...371 H7
Chevy Ct HAR CO12 ......142 D1
Cheyne Ct SUD CO10 ....4 C7
  WICKW SS12 ....359 M7
Chichester Cl BSDN SS14 ..378 A3
  CVI SS8 ....413 H1
  SOCK/AV RM15 ....405 K6
Chichester Dr CHLM/WR CM1 264 C7
Chichester Rd SAFWS CB11 65 M3
  SOSN SS2 ....21 H5
Chichester Wy MAL CM9 ..293 J3
Chickney Rd RBSF CM22 ..120 D5
Chieftan Dr PUR RM19 ...415 H1
Chigborough Rd MAL CM9 270 A4
Chignall Rd CHLM/WR CM1 263 L7
The Chignalls LAIN SS15 ..376 B5
Chigwell La CHIG IG7 ....327 K8
  LOU IG10 ....327 K6
Chigwell Park Dr CHIG IG7 349 H5
Chigwell Ri CHIG IG7 ....349 H3
Chigwell Rd WFD IG8 ....348 F7
Chilburn Rd COS CO15 ...224 A4
Childerditch Hall Dr
  RBRW/HUT CM13 ......374 A3
Childerditch La
  RBRW/HUT CM13 ......374 B3
Childerditch St
  RBRW/HUT CM13 ......374 B1
Childers Cl RIPS/CAP IP9 113 H2
Childers Fld FX IP11 ......84 E8
The Childers WFD IG8 ....349 G6
Childs Cl EMPK RM11 ....371 K6
Childwell Aly COL CO1 ...10 E9
Chilham Cl PIT SS13 ......378 C6
Chiltern Cl COL CO1 .....10 A4
  RAYL SS6 ....361 L8
Chiltern Gdns HCH RM12 389 K2
The Chilterns CVI SS8 ...398 A7
Chiltern Wy WFD IG8 ....348 B4
Chilton Cl CHLM/GWD CM2 17 L9
  RCOLW CO6 ....134 C4
Chilton Ct SUD CO10 ....5 G7
Chilton Lodge Rd SUD CO10 5 G7
Chilton Rd CDH/CHF RM16 408 B8
  IPSE IP3 ....38 D7
Chilworth Ga BROX EN10 277 G2
The Chimes SBF/HAD SS7 379 M7
Chimney Pot La RCHLM CM3 291 M8
Chimswell Wy HVHL CB9 ..27 L3
China La UPMR RM14 ....392 E3
Chinchilla Rd SOS SS1 ...401 L2
Chindit Cl BROX EN10 ...252 E8
Chindits La RBRW/HUT CM13 354 D6
Chingford Av COS CO15 ..224 A3
Chinnel La SAFWS CB11 ..64 E5
Chinnery Cl EN EN1 ......324 A3
Chinnery Hl BSF CM23 ...174 A4
Chinook COLN CO4 ....135 J7
Chippenham Gdns
  HARH RM3 ....352 E6
Chippenham Rd HARH RM3 352 F8
Chipperfield Cl UPMR RM14 372 F8
Chippetts La COLW CO3 ..160 D4
Chippingdell WIT CM8 ...212 A7
Chippingfield HLWE CM17 227 K8
Chipping HI HSTD CO9 ...129 G1
  WIT CM8 ....212 A8
Chipstead Wk RCOS CO16 223 K5
Chishill Rd ROY SG8 ....40 A8
Chisholm Ct WICKW SS12 359 M6
Chislett Rw CHLM/GWD CM2 17 K8
Chittenden Cl HOD EN11 253 J2
Chittock Cl RCOS CO16 ..223 J8
Chittock Ga BSDN SS14 ..377 M5
Chittock Md BSDN SS14 ..377 M5
Chitts HI COLW CO3 .....161 L4
Chivers Rd BRWN CM15 ..308 A6
  HVHL CB9 ....27 L4
Choats Wd RCOLW CO6 ..161 G2
Chorley Cl VGE SS16 ....376 A6
Chrismund Wy RCOLW CO6 159 K2
Christchurch Av RAIN RM13 389 G8
  WICKW SS12 ....359 H3
Christchurch Rd SOSN SS2 21 L4
  TIL RM18 ....418 B5
Christchurch St IPNE IP4 ..3 H2
Christie Cl BROX EN10 ...277 G1
Christina Rd WIT CM8 ...238 E3
Christine Cha COLW CO3 162 A6
Christmas Fld HSTD CO9 ..97 L1
Christopher Cl HCH RM12 389 H1
Christopher Dr RCOS CO16 223 L2
Christopher La SUD CO10 4 C7
Christopher Martin Rd
  BSDN SS14 ....377 M1
Christy Av CHLM/WR CM1 264 A7
Christy Wy LAIN SS15 ...375 M4
Chudleigh Rd HARH RM3 352 F5
Church Av CHLM/WR CM1 263 B1
Churchbury La EN EN1 ...324 A4
Church Cha RCHLM CM3 ..338 D6
  WIT CM8 ....213 G8
Church Cl BRW CM14 ....331 L1
  BRWN CM15 ....333 M3
  CVI SS8 ....398 A8
  KESG IP5 ....39 J3
  KIR/NAC IP10 ....61 H2
  RCOLW CO6 ....133 M7
  SBN/FI SS3 ....402 A5
  SLH/COR SS17 ....394 A8
  SUD CO10 ....32 E1
  WIT CM8 ....213 G8
Church Cnr SBF/HAD SS7 397 M1
Church Crs BRWN CM15 ..333 M3
  COS CO15 ....13 H7
  RIPW IP8 ....36 B5
  SOCK/AV RM15 ......406 D1
Church Dr BSF CM23 ....117 J3
Church Elm La DAGE RM10 388 B5

Church End *BRTR* CM7 ...... 154 C4
 GTDUN CM6 ...... 178 E1
 HLWW/ROY CM19 ...... 14 E9
Church End Av *WICKE* SS11 ...... 359 M1
Church End La *WICKE* SS11 ...... 359 L1
Church Farm Wy *COLN* CO4 ...... 134 F7
Church Fld *EPP* CM16 ...... 304 B1
Churchfield *HLW* CM20 ...... 256 B1
Church Fld *SAFWS* CB11 ...... 65 M4
Church Field Pth *BAR* EN8 ...... 300 D1
Churchfield Rd *SUD* CO10 ...... 5 J2
Churchfield Rd *RCOLW* CO6 ...... 158 B8
 WOTN CO14 ...... 199 K3
Church Flds *HSTD* CO9 ...... 73 G1
Churchfields *BROX* EN10 ...... 253 H8
 K/T/MI CO5 ...... 245 J5
 LOU IG10 ...... 326 F6
 SBN/FI SS3 ...... 402 F1
 STSD CM24 ...... 147 G5
Churchfields Av *COLW* CO3 ...... 161 K7
Churchfields Dr *HVHL* CB9 ...... 48 C5
Churchfields La *BROX* EN10 ...... 253 H8
Church Gdns *GTDUN* CM6 ...... 178 E1
Churchgate *BAR* EN8 ...... 300 C2
Churchgate Rd *BAR* EN8 ...... 300 C1
Churchgate St *HLWE* CM17 ...... 227 M7
Church Gn *CHLM/WR* CM1 ...... 262 C6
 HSTD CO9 ...... 51 L1
 RCFD SS4 ...... 364 E2
 RCOLW CO6 ...... 186 B1
 RIPW IP8 ...... 36 C2
 SAFWN CB10 ...... 22 C4
Church Gv *RCOLW* CO6 ...... 160 C3
Church HI *BRTR* CM7 ...... 94 E5
 EPP CM16 ...... 304 B1
 HAR CO12 ...... 142 B2
 HVHL CB9 ...... 47 K3
 K/T/MI CO5 ...... 192 A3
 LAIN SS15 ...... 376 E4
 LOU IG10 ...... 327 G5
 MAL CM9 ...... 291 L1
 MGTR CO11 ...... 108 A8
 RCHLM CM3 ...... 235 K5
 RCHLM CM3 ...... 316 C2
 RCOLW CO6 ...... 130 D5
 SAFWN CB10 ...... 45 H3
 SLH/COR SS17 ...... 409 K2
 WIT CM8 ...... 211 G3
Church Hollow *PUR* RM19 ...... 415 H2
Churchill Av *HSTD* CO9 ...... 99 H8
 HVHL CB9 ...... 28 C2
 IPNE IP4 ...... 38 C6
Churchill CI *CHONG* CM5 ...... 283 H7
 RCOLE CO7 ...... 221 C3
Churchill Dr *SUD* CO10 ...... 4 C1
Churchill Crs *SLH/COR* SS17 ...... 394 F7
Churchill Ri *CHLM/WR* CM1 ...... 264 F4
Churchill Rd *BRTR* CM7 ...... 154 F5
 GRAYS RM17 ...... 417 L3
 K/T/MI CO5 ...... 215 G6
Churchill Wy *COLS* CO2 ...... 163 J7
Church La *ABR/ST* RM4 ...... 328 E6
 ABR/ST RM4 ...... 329 K6
 BAR EN8 ...... 300 D1
 BCAYE CM11 ...... 358 C5
 BROX EN10 ...... 276 E3
 BRTR CM7 ...... 155 G4
 BRWN CM15 ...... 332 C1
 BSF CM23 ...... 200 E1
 CBE/LIN CB1 ...... 24 D1
 CBE/LIN CB1 ...... 26 E8
 CHLM/WR CM1 ...... 264 E7
 CHLM/WR CM1 ...... 287 J2
 CHONG CM5 ...... 283 H4
 COLW CO3 ...... 161 H7
 COLW CO3 ...... 162 A5
 DAGE RM10 ...... 388 C2
 EPP CM16 ...... 281 H5
 FOS CO13 ...... 198 C4
 FX IP11 ...... 84 C4
 FX IP11 ...... 84 F7
 GTDUN CM6 ...... 177 J4
 GTDUN CM6 ...... 230 D4
 HAR CO12 ...... 7 L3
 HSTD CO9 ...... 50 C5
 HSTD CO9 ...... 72 C4
 HSTD CO9 ...... 73 M7
 ING CM4 ...... 310 F5
 K/T/MI CO5 ...... 217 G8
 K/T/MI CO5 ...... 246 E2
 KIR/NAC IP10 ...... 60 F8
 KIR/NAC IP10 ...... 61 H2
 LOU IG10 ...... 327 G5
 MAL CM9 ...... 270 A3
 MAL CM9 ...... 270 C1
 MGTR CO11 ...... 108 F2
 MGTR CO11 ...... 108 F7
 MHAD SG10 ...... 172 A8
 PIT SS13 ...... 378 B1
 PUR RM19 ...... 415 H2
 RAIN RM13 ...... 404 E4
 RBRW/HUT CM13 ...... 356 A2
 RBRW/HUT CM13 ...... 373 K6
 RBSF CM22 ...... 147 M3
 RBSF CM22 ...... 176 C4
 RBSF CM22 ...... 228 E3
 RCHLM CM3 ...... 207 J5
 RCHLM CM3 ...... 208 D3
 RCHLM CM3 ...... 313 H7
 RCHLM CM3 ...... 316 D8
 RCHLM CM3 ...... 337 L3
 RCOLW CO6 ...... 104 C2
 RCOLW CO6 ...... 159 K8
 RCOLW CO6 ...... 160 B7
 RCOS CO16 ...... 169 H5
 RCOS CO16 ...... 196 B4
 RIPS/CAP IP9 ...... 81 J8
 RIPS/CAP IP9 ...... 112 D1
 RIPW IP8 ...... 56 C6
 RIPW IP8 ...... 56 E3
 ROM RM1 ...... 370 F4
 SAFWS CB11 ...... 90 B4
 SUD CO10 ...... 76 E3
 UPMR RM14 ...... 391 J4
 UPMR RM14 ...... 393 G4
Church Langley Wy
 HLWE CM17 ...... 256 D3
Church Leys *HLWS* CM18 ...... 256 A4

Church Md *HLWW/ROY* CM19 ...... 254 C2
 WIT CM8 ...... 211 G2
Church Mdw *BRTR* CM7 ...... 155 G5
Church Ms *LAIN* SS15 ...... 376 C4
Church Pde *CVI* SS8 ...... 397 M6
Church Pk *SUD* CO10 ...... 30 D8
Church Park Rd *PIT* SS13 ...... 378 C6
Church Pth *CBE/LIN* CB1 ...... 24 C5
Churchponds *HSTD* CO9 ...... 73 M7
Church Rd *ABR/ST* RM4 ...... 330 E3
 ABR/ST RM4 ...... 352 C2
 BCAYE CM11 ...... 336 D7
 BOC CM0 ...... 344 C5
 BRTR CM7 ...... 157 G6
 BRTR CM7 ...... 183 G5
 BRTR CM7 ...... 184 B5
 BRTR CM7 ...... 184 B1
 BRW CM14 ...... 331 K1
 BSDN SS14 ...... 19 L7
 CBE/LIN CB1 ...... 26 D6
 CHLM/GWD CM2 ...... 313 G7
 CHONG CM5 ...... 282 D1
 CHONG CM5 ...... 306 E5
 COLN CO4 ...... 105 H4
 COLS CO2 ...... 190 A7
 COLS CO2 ...... 13 J7
 FX IP11 ...... 85 K7
 HARH RM3 ...... 353 H8
 HLWE CM17 ...... 256 D6
 HOC/HUL SS5 ...... 362 C4
 HSTD CO9 ...... 71 L1
 HSTD CO9 ...... 73 G1
 HSTD CO9 ...... 75 J4
 HSTD CO9 ...... 127 L4
 HSTD CO9 ...... 129 H6
 K/T/MI CO5 ...... 213 K1
 K/T/MI CO5 ...... 214 D6
 K/T/MI CO5 ...... 217 L6
 K/T/MI CO5 ...... 245 J5
 KIR/NAC IP10 ...... 60 C7
 LAIN SS15 ...... 18 A1
 LAIN SS15 ...... 376 F2
 LOU IG10 ...... 326 B5
 MAL CM9 ...... 267 K5
 MAL CM9 ...... 269 L1
 MAL CM9 ...... 271 G1
 MGTR CO11 ...... 110 F7
 PEND EN3 ...... 324 D8
 PIT SS13 ...... 378 F6
 RAYL SS6 ...... 380 F1
 RBRW/HUT CM13 ...... 333 M3
 RBRW/HUT CM13 ...... 375 K6
 RBSF CM22 ...... 175 H6
 RBSF CM22 ...... 201 K1
 RCFD SS4 ...... 363 K4
 RCHLM CM3 ...... 237 J1
 RCHLM CM3 ...... 238 B8
 RCHLM CM3 ...... 265 M3
 RCHLM CM3 ...... 341 G4
 RCOLE CO7 ...... 165 H5
 RCOLE CO7 ...... 167 G4
 RCOLE CO7 ...... 193 J4
 RCOLE CO7 ...... 193 L1
 RCOLE CO7 ...... 194 B6
 RCOLE CO7 ...... 220 F2
 RCOLW CO6 ...... 104 F5
 RCOLW CO6 ...... 132 G6
 RCOLW CO6 ...... 188 F1
 RIPS/CAP IP9 ...... 78 F4
 RIPS/CAP IP9 ...... 79 J5
 RIPS/CAP IP9 ...... 80 F7
 RIPS/CAP IP9 ...... 110 B1
 ROY SG8 ...... 40 E8
 SAFWN CB10 ...... 69 G3
 SBF/HAD SS7 ...... 379 K5
 SBF/HAD SS7 ...... 380 F4
 SBN/FI SS3 ...... 384 F4
 SBN/FI SS3 ...... 402 D5
 SLH/COR SS17 ...... 395 J8
 SOS SS1 ...... 21 H7
 STSD CM24 ...... 147 G6
 SUD CO10 ...... 53 M6
 SUD CO10 ...... 54 A8
 SUD CO10 ...... 50 B5
 TIL RM18 ...... 417 M5
 TIL RM18 ...... 418 F3
 UPMR RM14 ...... 393 H3
 VGE SS16 ...... 378 F8
 WICKE SS11 ...... 360 E4
 WIT CM8 ...... 212 C2
 WIT CM8 ...... 239 L6
 WOTN CO14 ...... 199 K3
Church Sq *BURES* CO8 ...... 102 A2
 RCOS CO16 ...... 222 B7
Church St *BCAYE* CM11 ...... 357 K6
 BCAYW CM12 ...... 357 J6
 BRTR CM7 ...... 155 H2
 BSF CM23 ...... 174 A4
 CHLM/GWD CM2 ...... 289 H5
 CHLM/WR CM1 ...... 17 H3
 COLN CO4 ...... 105 H4
 COLW CO3 ...... 10 B8
 DAGE RM10 ...... 388 C6
 GRAYS RM17 ...... 417 K3
 GTDUN CM6 ...... 178 E1
 HAR CO12 ...... 7 K3
 HSTD CO9 ...... 74 F3
 HSTD CO9 ...... 97 L2
 HSTD CO9 ...... 98 E2
 HVHL CB9 ...... 48 C4
 ING CM4 ...... 308 F3
 K/T/MI CO5 ...... 192 A3
 K/T/MI CO5 ...... 213 J1
 MAL CM9 ...... 242 E7
 MAL CM9 ...... 270 F5
 MAL CM9 ...... 272 C2
 MAL CM9 ...... 293 J1
 RBSF CM22 ...... 119 M5
 RCOLW CO6 ...... 130 B2
 RCOLW CO6 ...... 186 B1
 RIPS/CAP IP9 ...... 81 M4
 SAFWN CB10 ...... 22 B7
 SAFWN CB10 ...... 42 E1
 SAFWN CB10 ...... 65 L1
 SAFWS CB11 ...... 64 F6
 SAFWS CB11 ...... 89 L7
 SAFWS CB11 ...... 89 H2

 SBW CM21 ...... 227 M1
 SUD CO10 ...... 4 B8
 SUD CO10 ...... 31 J3
 SUD CO10 ...... 52 C1
 WAB EN9 ...... 301 K5
 WIT CM8 ...... 212 A7
Church Vw *BROX* EN10 ...... 253 C8
 RCOLE CO7 ...... 136 F4
 SOCK/AV RM15 ...... 405 K7
 UPMR RM14 ...... 390 C1
Church View Rd *SBF/HAD* SS7 ...... 379 M5
Church Wk *COLW* CO3 ...... 10 B8
 HVHL CB9 ...... 28 F7
 SAFWS CB11 ...... 43 G7
 SBW CM21 ...... 228 A1
 SUD CO10 ...... 4 C5
 SUD CO10 ...... 34 E1
Churchway *SBF/HAD* SS7 ...... 399 C1
Churchwell Av *K/T/MI* CO5 ...... 188 B4
Churnwood Rd *COLN* CO4 ...... 11 M4
Chuzzlewit Dr
 RCHLM CM3 ...... 263 M4
Cillocks CI *HOD* EN11 ...... 253 H4
Cimarron CI *RCHLM* CM3 ...... 339 L4
Cinque Port Rd *RCOLE* CO7 ...... 221 C4
Circular Rd East *COLS* CO2 ...... 163 G6
Circular Rd North *COLS* CO2 ...... 162 F6
Circular Rd South *COLS* CO2 ...... 162 F7
Circular Rd West *COLS* CO2 ...... 162 F6
City Rd *K/T/MI* CO5 ...... 245 H4
Civic Dr *IP* IP1 ...... 2 D4
Civic Sq *TIL* RM18 ...... 418 B6
Clachar CI *CHLM/GWD* CM2 ...... 265 H8
Clacton Rd *FOS* CO13 ...... 225 H2
 HAR CO12 ...... 142 B6
 MGTR CO11 ...... 139 C2
 RCOLE CO7 ...... 164 D6
 RCOLE CO7 ...... 165 J4
 RCOLE CO7 ...... 194 B6
 RCOS CO16 ...... 196 B5
 RCOS CO16 ...... 222 C7
Claire CI *RBRW/HUT* CM13 ...... 355 H5
Claire Rd *FOS* CO13 ...... 198 C5
Clairmont CI *BRTR* CM7 ...... 183 G1
Clairmont Rd *COLW* CO3 ...... 161 M6
Clairvale *EMPK* RM11 ...... 371 M7
Clapgate Dr *RCOS* CO16 ...... 223 K1
Clapgate La *IPSE* IP3 ...... 38 B8
Clapton Hall La *GTDUN* CM6 ...... 178 E6
Clara Reeve CI *COLW* CO3 ...... 162 A7
Clare Av *WICKE* SS11 ...... 359 L1
Clare CI *HSTD* CO9 ...... 128 F4
Clare Ct *GTDUN* CM6 ...... 92 A8
Clare Ms *CHONG* CM5 ...... 283 H6
Claremont CI *UPMR* RM14 ...... 372 E8
Claremont La *WHVL* CB9 ...... 27 L4
Claremont CI *CDH/CHF* RM16 ...... 407 K8
 WOS/PRIT SS0 ...... 20 C4
Claremont Dr *VGE* SS16 ...... 378 A7
Claremont Gdns *UPMR* RM14 ...... 372 E8
Claremont Gv *WFD* IG8 ...... 348 D7
Claremont Hts *COL* CO1 ...... 10 A3
Claremont Rd *EMPK* RM11 ...... 371 H6
 LAIN SS15 ...... 376 C4
 RCOLE CO7 ...... 192 D3
 WOS/PRIT SS0 ...... 20 B4
Clarence Av *UPMR* RM14 ...... 390 B1
Clarence CI *CHLM/GWD* CM2 ...... 265 H7
 SBF/HAD SS7 ...... 379 L7
Clarence Rd *BRWN* CM15 ...... 332 C8
 GRAYS RM17 ...... 417 H3
 IPSE IP3 ...... 59 J2
 PEND EN3 ...... 324 D7
 PIT SS13 ...... 379 G4
 RAYL SS6 ...... 381 H2
 SBF/HAD SS7 ...... 379 L7
 SLH/COR SS17 ...... 395 K7
 SOS SS1 ...... 21 G7
 STSD CM24 ...... 146 F4
 SUD CO10 ...... 4 C4
 SUD CO10 ...... 31 J2
Clarence Rd North
 SBF/HAD SS7 ...... 379 L7
Clarence St *SOS* SS1 ...... 21 G7
Clarendon Pk *COS* CO15 ...... 13 L2
Clarendon Rd *BAR* EN8 ...... 300 C1
 CVI SS8 ...... 398 D7
 HVHL CB9 ...... 28 A4
 PIT SS13 ...... 378 D4
 RBSF CM22 ...... 176 F4
Clarendon Wy *COL* CO1 ...... 10 B4
Clare Rd *BRTR* CM7 ...... 182 E1
 IPNE IP4 ...... 38 A3
 SBF/HAD SS7 ...... 379 H5
 SUD CO10 ...... 31 J1
Clare Wy *RCOS* CO16 ...... 223 J6
Clarkbourne Dr *GRAYS* RM17 ...... 417 L3
Clark CI *ERITH* DA8 ...... 414 B5
Clarke Ri *RCHLM* CM3 ...... 317 G6
Clarkesmead *K/T/MI* CO5 ...... 214 D7
Clarke's Rd *HAR* CO12 ...... 6 B8
Clarkhill *HLWS* CM18 ...... 255 M7
Clarks Farm Rd *RCHLM* CM3 ...... 291 G3
Clarks La *EPP* CM16 ...... 304 A3
Clarkson St *IP* IP1 ...... 2 C3
Clarks Wood Dr *BRTR* CM7 ...... 155 L8
Clark Wy *CHLM/WR* CM1 ...... 264 B2
Claters CI *SOSN* SS2 ...... 402 A1
Clatterbury La *SAFWS* CB11 ...... 87 M4

Claybrick Av *HOC/HUL* SS5 ...... 362 E6
Clayburn Cir *BSDN* SS14 ...... 19 L6
Clayburn Gdns
 SOCK/AV RM15 ...... 406 C5
Claybury Rd *WFD* IG8 ...... 348 F8
Claydon CI *CBE/LIN* CB1 ...... 26 F7
Claydon Crs *BSDN* SS14 ...... 19 K4
Claydons La *SBF/HAD* SS7 ...... 380 D3
Claygate CI *HCH* RM12 ...... 389 H3
Clayhall La *SUD* CO10 ...... 35 M5
Clayhall PI *SUD* CO10 ...... 35 L5
Clayhall Rd *COS* CO15 ...... 13 J2
Clay HI *SUD* CO10 ...... 76 D3
Clay Hill Rd *VGE* SS16 ...... 19 G8
 VGE SS16 ...... 377 M7
Clayhive Dr *HVHL* CB9 ...... 28 A4
Clay La *GTDUN* CM6 ...... 151 L4
 RCOS CO16 ...... 222 D3
Claypit HI *RBSF* CM22 ...... 147 M6
 WAB EN9 ...... 302 D8
Clay Pit Piece *SAFWS* CB11 ...... 65 M5
Clayshotts Dr *WIT* CM8 ...... 239 J3
Clayside *CHIC* IG7 ...... 349 L7
Clay's La *LOU* IG10 ...... 327 H3
Clayponds *BSF* CM23 ...... 174 B4
Clays Rd *WOTN* CO14 ...... 199 H3
Clayspring CI *HOC/HUL* SS5 ...... 362 C4
Clay Tye Rd *UPMR* RM14 ...... 391 K2
Claywall Br *HVHL* CB9 ...... 48 C4
Cleall Av *WAB* EN9 ...... 301 K6
Clearwater *COLS* CO2 ...... 163 J7
Cleland Pth *LOU* IG10 ...... 327 J3
Clematis CI *HARH* RM3 ...... 352 D8
Clematis Gdns *WFD* IG8 ...... 348 B6
Clematis Wy *COLN* CO4 ...... 163 M4
Clemence Rd *DAGE* RM10 ...... 388 D7
Clement Rd *BAR* EN8 ...... 276 F7
Clements CI *CHLM/GWD* CM2 ...... 265 J8
 HVHL CB9 ...... 28 A4
Clements Dr *HVHL* CB9 ...... 28 A4
Clements Gdns *HOC/HUL* SS5 ...... 363 H6
Clements Green La
 RCHLM CM3 ...... 339 L3
Clements Hall La *HOC/HUL* SS5 ...... 363 H6
Clements Hall Wy
 HOC/HUL SS5 ...... 363 H7
Clement's La *HVHL* CB9 ...... 27 K3
Clement Wy *HCH* RM12 ...... 390 A2
Clench CI *IPNE* IP4 ...... 3 H4
Clench Rd *RIPS/CAP* IP9 ...... 80 E4
Clerks Piece *LOU* IG10 ...... 327 G5
Clermont Av *SUD* CO10 ...... 4 C1
Clevedon CI *BRTR* CM7 ...... 182 D4
Cleveland CI *COLN* CO4 ...... 135 K7
Cleveland Dr *WOS/PRIT* SS0 ...... 382 E8
Cleveland Rd *BSDN* SS14 ...... 19 K6
 CVI SS8 ...... 413 J1
Cleves Av *BRW* CM14 ...... 354 C2
Cleves Ct *RCHLM* CM3 ...... 265 M2
Cleves Rd *HVHL* CB9 ...... 27 L4
Cleves Wk *BARK/HLT* IG6 ...... 349 K8
Clevis Dr *RCHLM* CM3 ...... 340 A6
Clicket HI *BURES* CO8 ...... 102 C3
Clickett End *BSDN* SS14 ...... 19 K6
Clickett HI *BSDN* SS14 ...... 19 J6
Clickett Side *BSDN* SS14 ...... 19 J6
Clieveden Rd *SOS* SS1 ...... 402 A5
Cliff Av *WOS/PRIT* SS0 ...... 20 D4
 WOS/PRIT SS0 ...... 400 B3
Cliff CI *WOS/PRIT* SS0 ...... 400 B3
Cliff Gdns *LOS* SS9 ...... 400 B3
Cliffield *BRTR* CM7 ...... 125 M4
Cliff La *IPSE* IP3 ...... 38 A4
Clifford CI *LAIN* SS15 ...... 376 E6
Clifford Rd *CDH/CHF* RM16 ...... 407 C7
 ED N9 ...... 324 D8
 IPNE IP4 ...... 3 L5
Cliff Pde *LOS* SS9 ...... 399 M3
 WOTN CO14 ...... 199 M1
Cliff PI *SOCK/AV* RM15 ...... 406 D1
Cliff Rd *COS* CO15 ...... 224 F6
 FX IP11 ...... 85 L8
 HAR CO12 ...... 7 H3
 IPSE IP3 ...... 3 J9
 WOS/PRIT SS0 ...... 400 B3
Cliffsea Gv *LOS* SS9 ...... 400 A3
Clifftown Pde *SOS* SS1 ...... 20 E8
Clifftown Rd *SOS* SS1 ...... 21 G7
Cliff Wy *FOS* CO13 ...... 199 H6
Clifton Av *SBF/HAD* SS7 ...... 379 K7
Clifton CI *BAR* EN8 ...... 300 F1
 SBF/HAD SS7 ...... 379 L7
Clifton Dr *WOS/PRIT* SS0 ...... 20 A7
Clifton Hatch *HLWS* CM18 ...... 256 B6
Clifton Ms *SOS* SS1 ...... 21 G8
Clifton Rd *CVI* SS8 ...... 398 C8
 EMPK RM11 ...... 371 H6
 LOU IG10 ...... 326 F6
 PIT SS13 ...... 379 G4
 RCFD SS4 ...... 363 K4
Clifton Ter *SOS* SS1 ...... 21 G8
Clifton Wy *CHTY* IP2 ...... 57 L1
 RBRW/HUT CM13 ...... 355 L2
 SBF/HAD SS7 ...... 379 K7
Clifton Wd *RIPS/CAP* IP9 ...... 80 E5
Climmen Rd *CVI* SS8 ...... 398 C6
Clinton CI *RCHLM* CM3 ...... 314 D4
Clinton Crs *BARK/HLT* IG6 ...... 349 M7
Clinton Rd *CVI* SS8 ...... 397 H3
Clipped Hedge *RBSF* CM22 ...... 202 B8
Clipper Bvd *GRH* DA9 ...... 415 M8
Clipper Bvd West *GRH* DA9 ...... 415 L7
Clitheroe Rd *CRW* RM5 ...... 351 K6
Clive Av *IP* IP1 ...... 37 J1
Cliveden CI *BRWN* CM15 ...... 355 C1
 CHLM/WR CM1 ...... 16 A1
Clive Rd *COLS* CO2 ...... 163 G6
 EN EN1 ...... 324 B6

 GPK RM2 ...... 371 J5
 RBRW/HUT CM13 ...... 354 D8
Clive Wy *EN* EN1 ...... 324 B6
Clockhouse La *CDH/CHF* RM16 ...... 406 F6
 CRW RM5 ...... 351 K8
Clock House Rd *BCAYW* CM12 ...... 356 F6
Clockhouse Wy *BRTR* CM7 ...... 183 J1
Cloes La *RCOS* CO16 ...... 223 H4
Cloister CI *RAIN* RM13 ...... 404 C2
Cloisters *SLH/COR* SS17 ...... 409 M1
The Cloisters *BRTR* CM7 ...... 155 H6
 K/T/MI CO5 ...... 213 J2
 LAIN SS15 ...... 376 D5
Cloncurry Gdns *FX* IP11 ...... 8 E4
Clopton Dr *SUD* CO10 ...... 34 D5
The Close *BRTR* CM7 ...... 183 M5
 BRW CM14 ...... 354 E4
 CDH/CHF RM16 ...... 407 J7
 COS CO15 ...... 250 B4
 FOS CO13 ...... 198 B8
 FOS CO13 ...... 198 F6
 HAR CO12 ...... 6 C7
 RBSF CM22 ...... 202 B8
 RIPS/CAP IP9 ...... 79 L4
 SAFWS CB11 ...... 90 C4
 SUD CO10 ...... 4 F4
Cloudberry Rd *HARH* RM5 ...... 352 E7
Clouded Yellow CI *BRTR* CM7 ...... 182 F3
Cloudesley CI *ERITH* DA8 ...... 414 A5
Clough Rd *COLN* CO4 ...... 135 K5
Clova Rd *LOS* SS9 ...... 400 A1
Clovelly CI *IPNE* IP4 ...... 39 G7
Clovelly Gdns *ROMW/RG* RM7 ...... 370 C3
 WICKE SS11 ...... 359 K3
Clover Av *BSF* CM23 ...... 173 J5
Clover CI *CHTY* IP2 ...... 37 G7
 VGE SS16 ...... 377 M8
Clover Ct *CBE/LIN* CB1 ...... 24 E1
 SUD CO10 ...... 5 L3
Clover Dr *RCOLE* CO7 ...... 194 B6
Clover Fld *HLWS* CM18 ...... 256 B6
 HVHL CB9 ...... 27 K3
Cloverlands *COLN* CO4 ...... 11 K3
Clover Leas *EPP* CM16 ...... 304 A1
Cloverley Rd *CHONG* CM5 ...... 307 H2
Clovers *HSTD* CO9 ...... 128 E2
Clover Wy *RCOLE* CO7 ...... 136 C6
 VGE SS16 ...... 377 M8
Cluanie Orch *SUD* CO10 ...... 32 F2
Club Pde *RCOS* CO16 ...... 249 J5
Clunas Gdns *GPK* RM2 ...... 371 L3
Cluny Sq *SOSN* SS2 ...... 21 L1
Clydale Rd *EN* EN1 ...... 324 A5
Clyde *TIL* RM18 ...... 419 K1
Clyde Crs *CHLM/WR* CM1 ...... 263 L7
 RAYL SS6 ...... 380 D2
 UPMR RM14 ...... 372 F6
Clyde Rd *HOD* EN11 ...... 253 L7
Clydesdale *PEND* EN3 ...... 324 E6
Clydesdale Rd *BRTR* CM7 ...... 154 F8
 EMPK RM11 ...... 371 G7
Clyde Wy *ROM* RM1 ...... 370 F1
Clyfton CI *BROX* EN10 ...... 277 G3
Coach House Wy *WIT* CM8 ...... 239 G1
Coach La *MAL* CM9 ...... 269 G8
Coachman's Paddock
 RIPS/CAP IP9 ...... 80 E5
Coach Ms *BCAYE* CM11 ...... 335 L6
Coach Rd *RCOLE* CO7 ...... 193 J4
 RCOLW CO6 ...... 133 M3
 SAFWN CB10 ...... 68 F1
Coalport CI *HLWE* CM17 ...... 256 D4
Coan Av *COS* CO15 ...... 250 E2
Coast Rd *K/T/MI* CO5 ...... 245 H5
Coates CI *MAL* CM9 ...... 269 J7
Coats Hutton Rd *COLS* CO2 ...... 162 C8
Cobbett CI *PEND* EN3 ...... 300 D8
Cobbin's Br *EPP* CM16 ...... 279 J7
Cobbins Cha *BOC* CM0 ...... 344 C4
Cobbins CI *BOC* CM0 ...... 344 C3
Cobbinsend Rd *WAB* EN9 ...... 302 E1
The Cobbins *BOC* CM0 ...... 344 C3
 WAB EN9 ...... 301 M4
Cobbins Wy *HLWE* CM17 ...... 227 M7
The Cobbles *BRWN* CM15 ...... 354 C5
 UPMR RM14 ...... 373 G7
Cobbold Ms *IPNE* IP4 ...... 3 H3
Cobbold Rd *FX* IP11 ...... 9 K1
Cobbold St *IPNE* IP4 ...... 3 G3
Cobbs La *RBSF* CM22 ...... 149 G8
Cobbs PI *CHLM/WR* CM1 ...... 17 L1
Cobden PI *IPNE* IP4 ...... 3 H4
Cobham Rd *CDH/CHF* RM16 ...... 407 J7
Cobham Rd *IPSE* IP3 ...... 38 D8
 WOS/PRIT SS0 ...... 400 D4
Cobill CI *EMPK* RM11 ...... 371 K4
Coblers Wy *SUD* CO10 ...... 35 K5
Coburg La *VGE* SS16 ...... 376 A7
Coburg PI *RCHLM* CM3 ...... 339 L5
Cock And Bell La *SUD* CO10 ...... 34 D3
Cockaynes La *RCOLE* CO7 ...... 193 L2
Cockerell CI *PIT* SS13 ...... 378 C2
Cocker Rd *EN* EN1 ...... 300 C8
Cockethurst CI *WOS/PRIT* SS0 ...... 382 B7
Cockett Wick La *RCOS* CO16 ...... 249 K2
Cock La *BROX* EN10 ...... 252 D7
 CHLM/WR CM1 ...... 310 A1
 SAFWS CB11 ...... 87 G8
Cockrell's Rd *RCOLW* CO6 ...... 103 J7
Cock Rd *HSTD* CO9 ...... 99 J2
Cockrobin La *HLW* CM20 ...... 226 B4
Codenham Gn *VGE* SS16 ...... 19 G9
Codenham Straight *VGE* SS16 ...... 19 G9
Codham Hall La
 RBRW/HUT CM13 ...... 373 J5
Codham Little Park Dr
 BRTR CM7 ...... 126 C5
Cody Rd *IPSE* IP3 ...... 59 K2
Coeur De Lion *COLN* CO4 ...... 10 D1
Coggeshall Rd *BRTR* CM7 ...... 155 G8
 K/T/MI CO5 ...... 186 C5
 RCOLE CO7 ...... 137 G1
 RCOLW CO6 ...... 130 D7
 RCOLW CO6 ...... 185 H1
Coggeshall Road (Feering)
 ...... 186 C2
Coggeshall Wy *HSTD* CO9 ...... 129 H1
Cogmore *SAFWS* CB11 ...... 63 J9

Cohen Cl *BAR* EN8 .... 300 F4
Cohort Dr *COLS* CO2 .... 190 B1
Cokefield Av *SOSN* SS2 .... 383 K8
Coker Rd *CVI* SS8 .... 412 E1
Coke St *HAR* CO12 .... 7 K4
Colam La *RCHLM* CM3 .... 266 D7
Colbert Av *SOSN* SS1 .... 401 M4
Colbourne Cl *SLH/COR* SS17 .... 395 G8
Colchester Cl *WOS/PRIT* SS0 .... 20 E1
Colchester Rd *BURES* CO8 .... 102 A4
　CHLM/GWD CM2 .... 265 H5
　COLN CO4 .... 164 B6
　COS CO15 .... 224 D6
　HAR CO12 .... 140 B8
　HARH RM3 .... 352 F8
　HSTD CO9 .... 129 G2
　IPNE IP2 .... 37 M2
　K/T/MI CO5 .... 245 K4
　MAL CM9 .... 240 E6
　MGTR CO11 .... 108 C8
　RCOLE CO7 .... 106 F6
　RCOLE CO7 .... 136 D5
　RCOLE CO7 .... 164 C7
　RCOLW CO6 .... 130 F4
　RCOS CO16 .... 195 L2
　SOSN SS2 .... 20 E2
　WIT CM8 .... 212 C8
Cold Hall Cha *RCOLE* CO7 .... 165 M5
Coldham Gv *PEND* EN3 .... 324 F1 🖪
Coldharbour La *RAIN* RM13 .... 404 B6
Coldharbour Rd
　HLWW/ROY CM19 .... 14 D6
Coldnailhurst Av *BRTR* CM7 .... 155 G6 🖪
Cold Norton Rd *RCHLM* CM3 .... 317 L6
Cold Store Rd *FX* IP11 .... 8 B5
Cole Av *CDH/CHF* RM6 .... 418 D1
Colebrook Gdns *LOU* IG10 .... 327 J4 🖪
Colebrook La *LOU* IG10 .... 327 J4
Cole Hl *RCHLM* CM3 .... 209 J7
Colehills Cl *SAFWS* CB11 .... 87 K7
Colemans Av *WOS/PRIT* SS0 .... 382 E7
Colemans La *RCHLM* CM3 .... 290 E4
　WAB EN9 .... 277 L6
Coleman St *SOSN* SS2 .... 21 H4
Cole Ness Rd *IPSE* IP3 .... 59 H3
Coleridge Cl *CHESW* EN7 .... 276 A7
Coleridge Rd *DART* DA1 .... 415 H8
　HARH RM3 .... 352 C8
　MAL CM9 .... 293 H2
　TIL RM18 .... 418 C5
Coleridge Wk *RBRW/HUT* CM13 .... 355 K1 🖪
Coles Gn *LOU* IG10 .... 327 J3
Coles La *CBE/LIN* CB1 .... 24 D1
　WOTN CO14 .... 171 H8
Coles Oak La *RCOLE* CO7 .... 106 D5
Colet Rd *RBRW/HUT* CM13 .... 333 L7
Collard Av *LOU* IG10 .... 327 K4
College Av *GRAYS* RM17 .... 417 J1
College Cl *BSF* CM23 .... 173 L4
College Ct *BAR* EN8 .... 300 D2 🖪
College Rd *BAR* EN8 .... 300 E2
　BRTR CM7 .... 154 F8
　COS CO15 .... 13 J5
　CHESW EN7 .... 300 C2
　GRAYS RM17 .... 417 K1
　HERT/BAY SG13 .... 252 D1
　HOD EN11 .... 253 G3
College Sq *HLW* CM20 .... 15 K4
College Wy *SOS* SS1 .... 21 G5
Coller Rd *HAR* CO12 .... 6 A4
Colles Brook Rd *RCOLE* CO7 .... 195 G6
Collet Cl *BAR* EN8 .... 276 E8 🖪
Colletts Cha *RCOLW* CO6 .... 103 G7
Colley Rd *CHLM/GWD* CM2 .... 289 H5
Collier Row La *CRW* RM5 .... 370 C1
Collier Row Rd *CRW* RM5 .... 370 B1
　ROMW/RG RM7 .... 370 A1
The Colliers *RM* 269 M8
Collimer Cl *RIPS/CAP* IP9 .... 81 M3
Collindale Cl *CVI* SS8 .... 398 E7
Collingdale Gdns *COS* CO15 .... 224 D6
Collingwood *SBF/HAD* SS7 .... 379 M7 🖪
Collingwood Cl *BRTR* CM7 .... 155 K6
Collingwood Cl *COLW* CO3 .... 161 M1
　COS CO15 .... 250 E2
　RCHLM CM3 .... 340 A5
　VGE SS16 .... 19 L9
　WIT CM8 .... 239 H1
Collingwood Wk *VGE* SS16 .... 19 M8
Collingwood Wy *SBN/FI* SS3 .... 402 J2 🖪
Collins Cl *BRTR* CM7 .... 183 G1 🖪
　SLH/COR SS17 .... 409 M1
Collins Cross *BSF* CM23 .... 174 C2
Collins Meadow
　HLWW/ROY CM19 .... 15 G6
Collinson's *CHTY* IP2 .... 36 D6
Collins Rd *HSTD* CO9 .... 99 M1
Collins Wy *LOS* SS9 .... 382 B5
　RBRW/HUT CM13 .... 333 M7
Collinwood Av *PEND* EN3 .... 324 D5
Colman Cl *SLH/COR* SS17 .... 394 C4
Colmore Rd *PEND* EN3 .... 324 D5
Colne *TIL* RM18 .... 409 K8
Colne Bank Av *COLW* CO3 .... 10 A5
Colne Cha *WIT* CM8 .... 238 F1
Colne Cl *RCHLM* CM3 .... 339 L4
　SOCK/AV RM15 .... 406 D5 🖪
Colne Dr *HARH* RM3 .... 353 G7
　SBN/FI SS3 .... 402 F2
Colneford Hl *RCOLW* CO6 .... 130 E5
Colneis Rd *FX* IP11 .... 85 H7
Colne Park Rd *RCOLW* CO6 .... 130 E5
Colne Rd *BURES* CO8 .... 101 M3
　COS CO15 .... 13 G7
　HSTD CO9 .... 97 M3 🖪
　HSTD CO9 .... 129 G1
　RCOLE CO7 .... 220 F5
　RCOS CO16 .... 158 B8
Colne Springs *HSTD* CO9 .... 50 C4
Colne Va *UPMR* RM14 .... 372 F6
Colne Valley Rd *HSTD* CO9 .... 128 E1

Colne Valley Rd *HVHL* CB9 .... 28 B4
Colne Vw *RCOS* CO16 .... 248 B1
Colne Wy *RCOS* CO16 .... 221 G2
Colneys Cl *SUD* CO10 .... 4 B2
The Colonnade *BAR* EN8 .... 276 E8 🖪
Colson Pth *LOU* IG10 .... 327 H6
Colson Rd *LOU* IG10 .... 327 J6
Colthorpe Rd *COS* CO15 .... 224 A3
Coltishall Cl *WICKE* SS11 .... 360 C5 🖪
Coltishall Rd *RCHLM* CM12 .... 389 K5
Coltsfield *STSD* CM24 .... 146 F4
Coltsfoot Cl *COLN* CO4 .... 162 D1
　GRAYS RM17 .... 417 L3
Coltsfoot Pth *HARH* RM3 .... 352 E8
Coltsfoot Rd *CHTY* IP2 .... 36 F7
The Colts *BSF* CM23 .... 173 M8
Columbia Cl *KESG* IP5 .... 39 H4
Columbia Wharf Rd
　GRAYS RM17 .... 417 H3
Columbine Gdns *CHTY* IP2 .... 36 F6
　FOS CO13 .... 199 J4
Columbine Ms *SUD* CO10 .... 32 F1
The Columbines *SUD* CO10 .... 32 F1
Columbine Wy *HARH* RM3 .... 371 M1
Colvers *HLWE* CM17 .... 258 D1
Colville Cl *BRTR* CM7 .... 182 D4 🖪
　SLH/COR SS17 .... 395 G8
Colville Ms *BCAYW* CM12 .... 335 C6 🖪
Colvin Cha *CHLM/GWD* CM2 .... 312 C2
Colvin Cl *COLW* CO3 .... 162 A5
Colvin Gdns *BAR* EN8 .... 300 D1
　BARK/HLT IG6 .... 349 K8
Colwall Gdns *WFD* IG8 .... 348 B6 🖪
Colworth Cl *SBF/HAD* SS7 .... 380 E7
Colyers Reach *CHLM/GWD* CM2 .... 289 H1
Combes Rd *DAGW* RM9 .... 388 B6
Comet Cl *PUR* RM19 .... 415 H1
Comfrey Ct *GRAYS* RM17 .... 417 L3
Comma Cl *BRTR* CM7 .... 182 F2
Commerce Pk *COLS* CO2 .... 163 J7
Commerce Wy *COLS* CO2 .... 163 L7
　MGTR CO11 .... 108 D6
Commercial Rd *IP* IP1 .... 2 D7
　WOS/PRIT SS0 .... 382 E8
Common Ap *SBF/HAD* SS7 .... 380 B5
Commonfields *HLW* CM20 .... 255 M2
Commonhall La *SBF/HAD* SS7 .... 380 E8
Common Hl *SAFWN* CB10 .... 65 L1 🖪
Common La *ING* CM4 .... 335 M1
　MAL CM9 .... 291 J1
　RCHLM CM3 .... 290 F1
　ROY SG8 .... 62 C4
　SBF/HAD SS7 .... 380 B4
Common Rd *ING* CM4 .... 311 M8
　RBRW/HUT CM13 .... 355 K6
　SBN/FI SS3 .... 385 J7
　WAB EN9 .... 278 F1
Commonside Rd *HLWS* CM18 .... 256 A7
The Commons *COLW* CO3 .... 162 B6
Common St *SUD* CO10 .... 31 J3
The Common *RCHLM* CM3 .... 314 C3
　RCHLM CM3 .... 290 F5
　SBF/HAD SS7 .... 380 B4
Como St *ROMW/RG* RM7 .... 370 E5
Compasses Rd *BRTR* CM7 .... 157 G6
Compton Av *GPK* RM2 .... 371 J3
　RBRW/HUT CM13 .... 355 K6
Compton Ct *CVI* SS8 .... 413 L1 🖪
Compton Pl *ERITH* DA8 .... 414 A3
Compton Rd *COLN* CO4 .... 11 J6
Comyns Pl *CHLM/WR* CM1 .... 287 J2 🖪
Comyns Rd *DAGW* RM9 .... 388 B6
Conan Doyle Cl *BRTR* CM7 .... 183 H3 🖪
Concord Rd *CVI* SS8 .... 398 A6
　PEND EN3 .... 324 D7
Conder Wy *COLS* CO2 .... 163 K7
Conduit La *HOD* EN11 .... 253 H5
　MAL CM9 .... 291 M5
Conduit La East *HOD* EN11 .... 253 J5
Coney Gn *SBW* CM21 .... 200 E8
Congreve Rd *IP* IP1 .... 37 J1
　WAB EN9 .... 301 M5
Conies Rd *HSTD* CO9 .... 128 E4
Conifer Av *CRW* RM5 .... 351 J6 🖪
Conifer Cl *COLN* CO4 .... 11 M6
　CHESW EN7 .... 300 A1
　RCOLE CO7 .... 193 L6
Conifer Dr *BRW* CM14 .... 354 E6
Conifers *SBF/HAD* SS7 .... 380 F8
Coniston Cl *COS* CO15 .... 250 E2
　RCHLM CM3 .... 340 A5
　VGE SS16 .... 19 L9
Coniston Av *UPMR* RM14 .... 390 D5
Coniston Cl *BRTR* CM7 .... 182 D5
　FX IP11 .... 85 M6 🖪
　IPSE IP3 .... 59 J1
　SBF/HAD SS7 .... 379 M4
Coniston Wy *HCH* RM12 .... 389 H4
Connaught Av *CDH/CHF* RM16 .... 407 J7
　FOS CO13 .... 199 G7
　LOU IG10 .... 326 E6
Connaught Cl *COS* CO15 .... 13 M5
Connaught Dr *RCHLM* CM3 .... 339 K4 🖪
Connaught Gdns *BRTR* CM7 .... 155 J7
　SBN/FI SS3 .... 402 D5
Connaught Gdns East *COS* CO15 .. 13 L4
Connaught Gdns
　West *COS* CO15 .... 13 L4
Connaught Hl *LOU* IG10 .... 326 E6
Connaught Rd *HCH* RM12 .... 389 L2
　HVHL CB9 .... 27 M4
　IP IP1 .... 36 E1
　RAYL SS6 .... 381 J3
　RCOS CO16 .... 196 C6
Connaught Wy *BCAYW* CM12 .... 335 J5
Connop Rd *PEND* EN3 .... 324 E2
Connor Rd *DAGW* RM9 .... 388 A3
Conquerors Cl *SAFWN* CB10 .... 238 C8 🖪
Conrad Cl *BRW* CM14 .... 354 D6
Conrad Gdns *CDH/CHF* RM16 .... 407 H7
Conrad Rd *SLH/COR* SS17 .... 409 M1
　WIT CM8 .... 212 A6
Consort Cl *BRW* CM14 .... 354 D6
Constable Av *RCOS* CO16 .... 223 K5
Constable Cl *COLN* CO4 .... 134 F7
　K/T/MI CO5 .... 245 L4
　MGTR CO11 .... 108 C7 🖪
Constable Rd *IP* IP11 .... 115 J1

HVHL CB9 .... 27 L2
IPNE IP4 .... 3 H1
SUD CO10 .... 4 D4
Constantine Rd *COLW* CO3 .... 162 E6
IP IP1 .... 2 C6
WIT CM8 .... 238 F3 🖪
Constitution Hl *IP* IP1 .... 37 J3
　SBF/HAD SS7 .... 379 L8
　SUD CO10 .... 4 E5
Convalescent Hl *FX* IP11 .... 9 L4
Convent Cl *LAIN* SS15 .... 376 D7 🖪
Convent Hl *BRTR* CM7 .... 155 H6
Convent La *BRTR* CM7 .... 155 H6
Convent Rd *CVI* SS8 .... 398 C8
Con Wy *SBF/HAD* SS7 .... 379 L8
Conway Av *SBN/FI* SS3 .... 385 J8
Conway Cl *CHTY* IP2 .... 58 C1
　FX IP11 .... 85 K6
　RAIN RM13 .... 389 H6 🖪
　RCOLE CO7 .... 192 D5
Conway Gdns *GRAYS* RM17 .... 417 J4
Conway's Rd *CDH/CHF* RM16 .... 393 H7
Conybury Cl *WAB* EN9 .... 302 B4
Conyer Cl *MAL* CM9 .... 293 C3
Conyers Hl *HLW* CM20 .... 255 K1
Conyers Wy *LOU* IG10 .... 327 J5
Cook Cl *HAR* CO12 .... 143 M2
Cookham St *SBN/FI* SS3 .... 402 F1 🖪
Cook Pl *CHLM/GWD* CM2 .... 265 G8
Cook's Cl *CRW* RM5 .... 370 D1
　HSTD CO9 .... 129 G3
　KESG IP5 .... 39 M3
Cooks Gn *CHTY* IP2 .... 378 D2 🖪
Cook's Hall Rd *RCOLW* CO6 .... 133 M8
Cooks Hl *COLN* CO4 .... 105 J4
Cook's La *BRTR* CM7 .... 93 M7
Cooks Spinney *HLW* CM20 .... 256 B1
Coolgardie Av *CHIG* IG7 .... 349 H4
Coolyne Wy *COS* CO15 .... 224 C4
Coombe Dr *VGE* SS16 .... 394 D2
Coombe Ri *BRWN* CM15 .... 355 G2
　CHLM/WR CM1 .... 264 C4
　SLH/COR SS17 .... 409 M1
Coombe Rd *BOC* CM0 .... 320 E7
　HARH RM3 .... 372 A3
Coombers *RIPS/CAP* IP9 .... 78 A2
Coombes Cl *BCAYW* CM12 .... 335 G7
Coombes Gv *RCFD* SS4 .... 383 H1
Coombes Rd *DAGW* RM9 .... 388 A7
Coombe-wood Dr *CHDH* RM6 .... 370 A6
Coombewood Dr *SBF/HAD* SS7 .. 379 M6
Coopersale Common
　EPP CM16 .... 280 E8
Coopersale La *EPP* CM16 .... 328 E1
Coopersales *LAIN* SS15 .... 376 A5
Coopers Av *MAL* CM9 .... 269 K6
Coopers Cl *BSF* CM23 .... 173 J7
　CHIG IG7 .... 350 C3
　DAGE RM10 .... 388 C5
Coopers Crs *RCOLW* CO6 .... 134 A7
Coopers Dr *BCAYE* CM11 .... 357 K5
Coopers End Rd *RBSF* CM22 .... 148 B8
Coopers End Rbt *RBSF* CM22 .... 148 C8
Cooper Shaw Rd *TIL* RM18 .... 418 E4
Coopers La *COS* CO15 .... 12 A5
　RCHLM CM3 .... 209 G4
　RCOLE CO7 .... 107 G6
Coopers Rd *SBN/FI* SS3 .... 385 G7
　SBF/HAD SS7 .... 380 C4
Coopers Vls *RBSF* CM22 .... 176 C1
Coopers Wy *SOSN* SS2 .... 383 H6
Coote Rd *BCTR* RM8 .... 388 A2
Copdoek *BSDN* SS14 .... 19 J4
Copelands *RCFD* SS4 .... 363 L5 🖪
Copellis Cl *HVHL* CB9 .... 28 B1
Copeman Rd
　RBRW/HUT CM13 .... 355 L1 🖪
Copford Av *RAYL* SS6 .... 381 G2
Copford Rd *BCAYE* CM11 .... 357 K1 🖪
Copland Cl *CHLM/GWD* CM2 .... 289 G3
　CHLM/WR CM1 .... 264 B2
Copland Rd *SLH/COR* SS17 .... 409 L2
Copleston Rd *IPNE* IP4 .... 38 C5
Coploe Rd *SAFWN* CB10 .... 22 B8
Coppen Rd *BCTR* RM8 .... 370 A7
Coppens Gn *WICKW* SS12 .... 359 L5
Copper Beeches *COLW* CO3 .... 161 L6
Copper Beech Rd
　SOCK/AV RM15 .... 406 D1 🖪
　CHIG IG7 .... 349 L7
Copperfield *BCAYE* CM11 .... 357 L5 🖪
Copperfield Gdns *BRW* CM14 .... 354 C2
Copperfield Rd *CHLM/WR* CM1 .. 263 L5
　CHTY IP2 .... 36 F6
Copperfields *LAIN* SS15 .... 376 D4 🖪
　SAFWS CB11 .... 65 K3
Copperfields Wy *HARH* RM3 .... 371 L1 🖪
Coppice Cl *GTDUN* CM6 .... 178 E2
Coppice End *COLN* CO4 .... 135 J8
Coppice La *GTDUN* CM6 .... 206 F3
　LAIN SS15 .... 377 G2
Coppice Pth *CHIG* IG7 .... 350 C5
Coppice Rd *RCOLE* CO7 .... 193 J3
Coppice Rw *EPP* CM16 .... 303 L8
The Coppice *COS* CO15 .... 250 E2
Coppingford End *RCOLW* CO6 .... 160 E6
The Coppings *HOD* EN11 .... 253 H3 🖪
Coppins Cl *CHLM/WR* CM1 .... 264 F7
Coppins Rd *COS* CO15 .... 12 A4
Coprolite St *IPSE* IP3 .... 3 J6
Copse Hl *HLWW/ROY* CM19 .... 255 J6
The Copse *BCAYW* CM12 .... 335 H7 🖪
　BSF CM23 .... 174 D3 🖪
　CHING E4 .... 348 A2
　GTDUN CM6 .... 181 G5
Copshall Cl *HLWS* CM18 .... 255 M7
Coptfold Cl *SOS* SS11 .... 402 A2 🖪
Coptfold Rd *BRW* CM14 .... 354 D3
Copthall La *GTDUN* CM6 .... 92 B8
Copt Hall La *K/T/MI* CO5 .... 217 J8
Copt Hl *RCHLM* CM3 .... 290 F5
Copthorne Av *BARK/HLT* IG6 .... 349 J7

BROX EN10 .... 253 G8
Copthorne Gdns *EMPK* RM11 .... 372 B5
Copy Hl *HVHL* CB9 .... 27 M8
Coral Cl *RCHLM* CM3 .... 339 K3 🖪
Coral Dr *IP* IP1 .... 36 E2
Coralin Wk *COLW* CO3 .... 161 K5
Coram Gn *RBRW/HUT* CM13 .... 333 L8
Corans *BRWN* CM15 .... 332 C8
Carasway *SBF/HAD* SS7 .... 380 C6
Corbets Av *UPMR* RM14 .... 390 C2
Corbets Tey Rd *UPMR* RM14 .... 390 C2
Cordelia Crs *RAYL* SS6 .... 361 K8
Cordell Cl *BAR* EN8 .... 276 F8 🖪
Cordell Pl *SUD* CO10 .... 34 E3
Cordell Rd *SUD* CO10 .... 34 D3
Corder Rd *IPNE* IP4 .... 37 L3
The Cordwainers *SOSN* SS2 .... 383 H6
Cordwinders *RCOLE* CO7 .... 107 M2
Cordy's La *FX* IP11 .... 84 C7
Corfe Cl *PIT* SS13 .... 378 C5
Coriander Rd *K/T/MI* CO5 .... 214 D7
Cornard Rd *SUD* CO10 .... 4 E7
Cornec Av *LOS* SS9 .... 381 K5
Cornec Cha *LOS* SS9 .... 381 K5
Cornel Cl *WIT* CM8 .... 211 L7
Cornelius V *CHLM/GWD* CM2 .... 333 J1
Cornells La *SAFWS* CB11 .... 89 M8
Cornell Wy *CRW* RM5 .... 351 J6
Corner Meadow *HLWS* CM18 .... 256 B7
Corner Pk *BCAYE* CM11 .... 43 M8
Corner Rd *BCAYE* CM11 .... 358 E5
Cornerth Crs *SUD* CO10 .... 5 J9
Cornfields *RCHLM* CM3 .... 339 J3
　COLW CO3 .... 161 K4
Cornflower Cl *CHTY* IP2 .... 36 F7
Cornflower Dr *CHLM/WR* CM1 .... 265 G6
Cornflower Gdns *BCAYW* CM12 .... 335 G6
Cornflower Rd *COS* CO15 .... 250 B4
Cornflower Wy *HARH* RM3 .... 371 M1
Cornford Wy *MGTR* CO11 .... 108 C7
Cornhill Av *HOC/HUL* SS5 .... 362 F4
Cornhill Dr *PEND* EN3 .... 324 F1 🖪
Cornish Gv *RCHLM* CM3 .... 339 M5
Cornish Hall End Rd *BRTR* CM7 .... 70 E4
Cornsland *BRW* CM14 .... 354 E4
Cornwall Cl *BAR* EN8 .... 300 F5
　EMPK RM11 .... 372 B4 🖪
　MGTR CO11 .... 108 C8
Cornwall Crs *CHLM/WR* CM1 .... 264 B4
Cornwall Gdns *BRTR* CM7 .... 155 J7
　RCFD SS4 .... 363 K6
Cornwallis Cl *ERITH* DA8 .... 414 A3
Cornwallis Dr *RCHLM* CM3 .... 340 A4
Cornwallis Pl *SAFWN* CB10 .... 43 M8 🖪
　SAFWN CB10 .... 65 M1 🖪
Cornwallis Rd *HVHL* CB9 .... 28 A4
Cornwall Rd *BRWN* CM15 .... 332 C7
　DART DA1 .... 415 G7
　FX IP11 .... 84 F8
　PIT SS13 .... 379 C4
Cornwalls Dr *RCOLW* CO6 .... 160 A8 🖪
Cornwall Crs *SLH/COR* SS17 .... 394 C4
Cornworthy *SBN/FI* SS3 .... 402 D3
Corona Rd *CVI* SS8 .... 398 D6
　VGE SS16 .... 376 C8
Coronation Av *BRTR* CM7 .... 183 G1
　COLS CO2 .... 191 H2
　TIL RM18 .... 419 J1
Coronation Cl *SBN/FI* SS3 .... 385 G7
Coronation Dr *FX* IP11 .... 8 F3
　HCH RM12 .... 389 J4
Coronation Hl *EPP* CM16 .... 304 A2
Coronation Rd *BOC* CM0 .... 344 C7
　BSF CM23 .... 173 M6
　COS CO15 .... 12 B5
　IPNE IP4 .... 38 C6
Corporation Av *CHTY* IP2 .... 58 B3
Corporation Rd *CHLM/WR* CM1 .... 264 B7
Corran Wy *SOCK/AV* RM15 .... 406 C5
Corringham Rd *SLH/COR* SS17 .... 409 L2
Corsel Rd *CVI* SS8 .... 398 C4
Cortoncroft Cl *FOS* CO13 .... 199 C4
Corton Rd *IPSE* IP3 .... 59 J2
Corve La *SOCK/AV* RM15 .... 406 C5
Cory Dr *RBRW/HUT* CM13 .... 355 J1
Cosgrove Av *LOS* SS9 .... 381 J8
Cossington Rd *WOS/PRIT* SS0 .... 20 C7
Costead Manor Rd *BRW* CM14 .... 354 C2
Cotelands *VGE* SS16 .... 378 A8
Coteright Rd *ROMW/RG* RM7 .... 370 E6
Cotman Av *CHLM/GWD* CM2 .... 264 B7
Cotman Rd *COLW* CO3 .... 162 B6
　IPSE IP3 .... 59 H2
　RCOS CO16 .... 223 L5
Cotswold Av *IP* IP1 .... 37 J2
　RAYL SS6 .... 361 L8
Cotswold Ct *COLN* CO4 .... 135 K7 🖪
Cotswold Dr *SUD* CO10 .... 34 C5
Cotswold Gdns
　RBRW/HUT CM13 .... 355 M1
Cotswold Rd *COS* CO15 .... 13 G2
　HARH RM3 .... 372 A2
　WOS/PRIT SS0 .... 20 A5
Cottage Cl *COLS* CO10 .... 163 K8
Cottage Gdns *BAR* EN8 .... 300 D1
Cottage Gn *RCOS* CO16 .... 223 K5 🖪
Cottage Pl *CHLM/WR* CM1 .... 17 H2
Cottage Wk *RCOS* CO16 .... 223 J5
Cottesmore Cl *CVI* SS8 .... 413 H1
Cottesmore Rd *LOS* SS9 .... 399 H2
Cottingham Rd *RIPW* IP8 .... 57 J2
Cottis Cl *VGE* SS16 .... 376 B8
Cottons Ap *ROMW/RG* RM7 .... 370 F5
Cottonwood Cl *COLS* CO2 .... 190 E1
Coulde Dennis *RCHLM* CM3 .... 314 C4 🖪
Coulsdon Cl *RCOS* CO16 .... 223 M5
Council Rd *BSF* CM23 .... 174 C4
Counting House La
　GTDUN CM6 .... 178 E2
County Pl *CHLM/GWD* CM2 .... 17 C8
Coupals Cl *HVHL* CB9 .... 28 D5
Coupals Rd *HVHL* CB9 .... 28 D5
Courage Cl *EMPK* RM11 .... 371 K6 🖪

Courtauld Cl *HSTD* CO9 .... 129 G2
Courtauld Rd *BRTR* CM7 .... 155 H7
　PIT SS13 .... 378 C1
Court Av *HARH* RM3 .... 353 H8
Courtenay Cl *SUD* CO10 .... 4 C7
Courtenay Dr
　CDH/CHF RM16 .... 407 G8 🖪
Courtenay Gdns *UPMR* RM14 .... 390 F1
Courtfield Cl *BROX* EN10 .... 253 H8 🖪
Courtland Dr *CHING* E4 .... 348 A3
Courtland Dr *CHIG* IG7 .... 349 K4
Courtland Ms *MAL* CM9 .... 293 G3
Courtland Pl *MAL* CM9 .... 293 G3
Courtlands *BCAYW* CM12 .... 356 F1
　CHLM/WR CM1 .... 264 B5
Courtney Park Rd *VGE* SS16 .... 376 C8
Courtney Rd *CDH/CHF* RM16 .... 408 D7
Court Rd *CHLM/WR* CM1 .... 235 H7
The Courts *RAYL* SS6 .... 361 M8
Court St *RCOLW* CO6 .... 104 B2
Court Vw *ING* CM4 .... 334 A2 🖪
Court Wy *HARH* RM3 .... 371 M2
Coval Av *CHLM/WR* CM1 .... 16 E3
Coval La *CHLM/WR* CM1 .... 16 E3
Covenbrook *RBRW/HUT* CM13 .... 355 H4
Coventry Cl *COL* CO1 .... 10 E6
　HOC/HUL SS5 .... 362 A4
Coventry Hill Lower Rd
　HOC/HUL SS5 .... 361 M8
Coverley Cl *RBRW/HUT* CM13 .... 354 D7
Covert Cl *HVHL* CB9 .... 28 B2
Covert Rd *BARK/HLT* IG6 .... 350 A7
The Coverts *CHLM/WR* CM1 .... 287 J2
　K/T/MI CO5 .... 245 L5
　RBRW/HUT CM13 .... 355 H2
Cowdray Av *COL* CO1 .... 10 C4
Cowdray Crs *COL* CO1 .... 10 D7
Cowdray Wy *HCH* RM12 .... 389 H3
Cowell Av *CHLM/WR* CM1 .... 263 M6
Cowell St *CHTY* IP2 .... 37 K8
Cowels Farm La *GTDUN* CM6 .... 122 F6
Cowland Av *PEND* EN3 .... 324 D6
Cow La *RCOS* CO16 .... 221 K8
　SAFWN CB10 .... 23 G8
Cowles *CHESW* EN7 .... 276 A7
Cowley Rd *FX* IP11 .... 9 L1
　HARH RM3 .... 352 C8
Cowlins *HLWE* CM17 .... 227 L7 🖪
Cowper Av *TIL* RM18 .... 418 C5
Cowper Rd *RAIN* RM13 .... 404 B2
Cowper St *IPNE* IP4 .... 38 C5
Cowslip Cl *CHTY* IP2 .... 36 F7
Cowslip Cl *COLW* CO3 .... 161 K4
Cow Watering La
　CHLM/WR CM1 .... 263 G8
Coxbridge Ct *BCAYW* CM12 .... 357 H1
Coxes Cl *SLH/COR* SS17 .... 394 E8
Coxes Farm Rd *BCAYE* CM11 .... 357 M4
Coxhall Rd *RIPS/CAP* IP9 .... 79 L2
Cox La *IPNE* IP4 .... 3 C5
Cox Ley *RBSF* CM22 .... 202 B8
Coxs Cl *RCHLM* CM3 .... 339 M3
Coxs HI *MGTR* CO11 .... 108 B8
Coxtie Green Rd *BRW* CM14 .... 331 H8
Coytes Gdns *IP* IP1 .... 2 E5
Cozens La East *BROX* EN10 .... 277 G2
Cozens La West *BROX* EN10 .... 276 F2
Crabbe St *IPNE* IP4 .... 38 B5
Crabb's HI *RCHLM* CM3 .... 267 G2
Crabb's La *BUNT* SG9 .... 116 F4
Crabs Cft *BRTR* CM7 .... 155 K8
Crabtree *FOS* CO13 .... 198 D3 🖪
Crabtree La *RCOLW* CO6 .... 133 K1
Cracknell Cl *RD EN* EN1 .... 324 A5
Craddock Rd *EN* EN1 .... 324 A5
Craftsmans Sq *SOSN* SS2 .... 383 H6
Craig Cl *FX* IP11 .... 84 C3
Craigdale Rd *ROM* RM1 .... 371 G6
Craigfield Av *COS* CO15 .... 224 A5
Craig's La *BURES* CO8 .... 101 M5
Craiston Wy *CHLM/GWD* CM2 .... 289 G6
Crammavill St *CDH/CHF* RM16 .... 407 H6
Cramphorn Wk *CHLM/WR* CM1 .. 16 D2
Cranborne Cha *IPNE* IP4 .... 38 B2
Cranborne Gdns *UPMR* RM14 .... 390 C1
Cranborne Rd *BAR* EN8 .... 300 E4 🖪
　HOD EN11 .... 253 J4
Cranbourne Dr *HOD* EN11 .... 253 J1
Cranbrook La *SBF/HAD* SS7 .... 380 D7
Cranbrook Dr *GPK* RM2 .... 371 J4
Cranbrook La *SUD* CO10 .... 34 A2
Crane Cl *DAGE* RM10 .... 388 B5
Cranes Cl *BSDN* SS14 .... 378 A2
Cranes Farm Rd *BSDN* SS14 .... 18 C2
Cranes La *BSDN* SS14 .... 19 J1
　K/T/MI CO5 .... 213 G2
Cranfield Park Av *WICKW* SS12 .... 378 F1
Cranfield Park Rd *WICKW* SS12 .. 359 M7
Cranford Cl *FOS* CO13 .... 198 D4
Cranham Gdns *UPMR* RM14 .... 373 G7
Cranham Rd *EMPK* RM11 .... 371 J6
　GTDUN CM6 .... 149 G1
Cranleigh Cl *CHESW* EN7 .... 276 B8
　RCOS CO16 .... 223 J5
Cranleigh Dr *LOS* SS9 .... 399 H1
Cranleigh Gdns *HOC/HUL* SS5 .... 361 L2 🖪
　LOU IG10 .... 327 G8
Cranley Av *WOS/PRIT* SS0 .... 20 A4
Cranley Gdns *SBN/FI* SS3 .... 402 C5
Cranley Rd *WOS/PRIT* SS0 .... 20 A5
Cranmer Cl *BCAYW* CM12 .... 335 J5
Cranmer Gdns *DAGE* RM10 .... 388 D3
Cranmer's La *RCOLW* CO6 .... 158 F5
Cranmore Cl *RBSF* CM22 .... 147 K1 🖪
Cranston Av *WOS/PRIT* SS0 .... 382 E6
Cranston Park Av *UPMR* RM14 .... 390 D4
Cranwell Crs *CRS* IP9 .... 59 K2
Cranwell Gdns *BSF* CM23 .... 174 D2
Cranwell Gv *KESG* IP5 .... 39 K4
Craven Av *CVI* SS8 .... 398 B8
Craven Cl *RCFD* SS4 .... 363 L6
Craven Dr *COLN* CO4 .... 135 K8
Craven Gdns *CRW* RM5 .... 351 H6
　HARH RM3 .... 353 K7
Crawford Av *CDH/CHF* RM16 .... 407 J6

Crawford Cha WICKW SS12 — 359 M6
Crawford Cl BCAYW CM12 — 335 K6
Crawford La KESG IP5 — 39 K4
Crawley Cl SLH/COR SS17 — 395 H6
Crawley End ROY SG8 — 40 F1
Craword Compton Cl HCH RM12 — 389 K5
Craydene Rd ERITH DA8 — 414 A5
Crayfields BSDN SS14 — 378 A4
Crayford Cl MAL CM9 — 292 F3
Crayford Wy DART DA1 — 414 B8
Craylands BSDN SS14 — 378 A4
Crays HI BCAYE CM11 — 358 C7
Crays Hill Rd BCAYE CM11 — 358 D6
Crays Vw BCAYW CM12 — 357 J3
Crealock Gv WFD IG8 — 348 A6
Creasen Butt Cl MAL CM9 — 269 H7
Creasey Cl HCH RM12 — 389 J1
Credon Cl COS CO15 — 224 A4
Credon Dr COS CO15 — 224 A4
Credo Wy WTHK RM20 — 416 C3
Creekhurst Rd RCOLE CO7 — 221 H5
Creek Rd CVI SS8 — 398 E7
Creeksea Ferry Rd RCFD SS4 — 365 G3
Creeksea La BOC CM0 — 344 A5
Creekside RAIN RM13 — 404 A2
Creek Vw VGE SS16 — 377 M8
Creek View Rd HOC/HUL SS5 — 339 K8
Creekview Rd RCHLM CM3 — 340 A4
Creephedge La RCHLM CM3 — 314 E6
Cree Wy ROM RM1 — 351 M8
Creffield Rd COLW CO3 — 135 J5
Crepping Hall Dr RIPS/CAP IP9 — 110 C1
  HCH RM12 — 389 J1
Crescent Av GRAYS RM17 — 417 L2
Crescent Cl BCAYW CM12 — 335 G7
Crescent Dr BRWN CM15 — 354 F2
Crescent Gdns BCAYW CM12 — 335 G7
Crescent Rd BCAYW CM12 — 335 G7
  BRW CM14 — 354 C5
  BSF CM23 — 174 B7
  CHLM/GWD CM2 — 289 H4
  CVI SS8 — 413 L1
  DAGE RM10 — 388 C2
  ERITH DA8 — 414 A3
  FX IP11 — 9 L2
  IP IP1 — 2 C3
  LOS SS9 — 399 J2
  MAL CM9 — 269 G6
  MAL CM9 — 272 F2
  SBF/HAD SS7 — 397 L1
  SOCK/AV RM15 — 405 K7
  WOTN CO14 — 199 K3
The Crescent COLN CO4 — 135 K4
  COS CO15 — 224 C4
  EPP CM16 — 304 A4
  FOS CO13 — 199 G5
  HLWE CM17 — 227 K5
  LOU IG10 — 326 E8
  RCHLM CM3 — 208 F6
  RCOLW CO6 — 133 L6
  RCOLW CO6 — 134 C2
  RCOLW CO6 — 160 B8
  RCOS CO16 — 197 G1
  SBF/HAD SS7 — 399 C1
  UPMR RM14 — 372 F7
Crescent Vw LOU IG10 — 326 E8
Crescent Wk SOCK/AV RM15 — 405 K7
Crescent Wy SOCK/AV RM15 — 405 L6
Cressages Cl GTDUN CM6 — 180 F5
Cress Cft BRTR CM7 — 183 L2
Cressells LAIN SS15 — 18 D7
Cressing Rd BRTR CM7 — 183 J1
  WIT CM8 — 211 L3
Crest Av GRAYS RM17 — 417 J4
  PIT SS13 — 378 D5
Crest Dr PEND EN3 — 324 D2
Cresthill Av GRAYS RM17 — 417 K2
Crestlands RCOLE CO7 — 193 J4
The Crest LOS SS9 — 381 L5
  SBW CM21 — 227 L1
Crest Vw GRH DA9 — 416 B8
Creswick Av RAYL SS6 — 361 K8
Cricketers Cl CHLM/WR CM1 — 264 C1
Cricketers La RBRW/HUT CM13 — 355 L8
Cricketers Rw RBRW/HUT CM13 — 355 L8
Cricketers Wy PIT SS13 — 378 C1
Cricketfield La BSF CM23 — 173 L3
Cricket Hill Rd FX IP11 — 84 B8
Crickhollow RCHLM CM3 — 339 K6
Cricklade Av HARH RM3 — 352 F2
Cringle Lock RCHLM CM3 — 339 M6
Cripplegate BOC CM0 — 320 F6
Cripsey Av CHONG CM5 — 283 G6
Crispin Cl HVHL CB9 — 28 C1
Crittall Cl WIT CM8 — 184 F7
Crittall Rd WIT CM8 — 212 C8
Croasdaile Rd STSD CM24 — 146 F3
Croasdale Cl STSD CM24 — 146 F3
Crocus Cl CHTY IP2 — 36 F7
Crocus Flds SAFWN CB10 — 43 M8
Crocus Wy CHLM/WR CM1 — 264 C1
Croft Cl BRTR CM7 — 155 H8
  LOS SS9 — 381 H7
  SBF/HAD SS7 — 379 K6
Croft Ct CHLM/WR CM1 — 264 C1
Crofters SBW CM21 — 200 F8
Crofters End SBW CM21 — 200 F7
Croft La HVHL CB9 — 28 C5
  RCHLM CM3 — 207 G8
Croft Lodge Cl WFD IG8 — 348 C7
Crofton Av SLH/COR SS17 — 395 G7
Crofton Rd CDH/CHF RM16 — 407 M7
  IPNE IP4 — 38 C4
Croft Rd COS CO15 — 12 D4
  K/T/MI CO5 — 213 J1
  PEND EN3 — 324 F3
  SBF/HAD SS7 — 380 B7
  SUD CO10 — 4 C5
The Crofts SBN/FI SS3 — 384 F7
Croft St CHTY IP2 — 2 E9
The Croft BROX EN10 — 276 F5
  BURES CO8 — 102 A2
  HSTD CO9 — 73 H1
  LOU IG10 — 327 H4
  RAYL SS6 — 381 G3

RBSF CM22 — 147 K2
RCOLW CO6 — 130 B5
Croft Wy WIT CM8 — 212 B8
Cromarty Rd IPNE IP4 — 38 C3
Crome Cl COLW CO3 — 162 B6
Cromer Av LAIN SS15 — 376 C3
Crome Rd LAIN SS15 — 376 C3
Crome Rd RCOS CO16 — 223 L5
Cromer Rd EMPK RM11 — 371 L7
  IP IP1 — 37 G3
  ROMW/RG RM7 — 370 D6
  SOS SS1 — 21 K6
Crompton Rd CHTY IP2 — 36 F4
Crompton St CHLM/WR CM1 — 16 C1
Cromwell Av BCAYW CM12 — 335 H8
Cromwell Cl BSF CM23 — 173 J4
Cromwell HI MAL CM9 — 269 G8
Cromwell La MAL CM9 — 269 G8
Cromwell Pk GTDUN CM6 — 180 C5
Cromwell Rd BRW CM14 — 354 C5
  COLS CO2 — 163 G5
  GRAYS RM17 — 417 H1
  HOC/HUL SS5 — 362 F5
  SAFWS CB11 — 65 M4
  SOSN SS2 — 383 H8
Cromwell Sq IP IP1 — 2 E5
Crondon Park La ING CM4 — 311 M7
Crooked Mile WAB EN9 — 301 K2
Crooked Wk CVI SS8 — 398 C6
Cropenburg Wk CVI SS8 — 398 C6
Croppath Rd DAGE RM10 — 388 B3
Croquet Gdns RCOLE CO7 — 192 D2
Crosby Rd DAGE RM10 — 388 C2
  WOS/PRIT SS0 — 400 C3
Cross Av WICKW SS12 — 359 K5
Crossbow Rd CHIG IG7 — 350 A6
Crossbrook St BAR EN8 — 300 E2
Crosby Cl BRWN CM15 — 333 M3
Crossfell Rd SBF/HAD SS7 — 380 A4
Crossfield Rd COS CO15 — 12 F5
  HOD EN11 — 253 J3
  SOSN SS2 — 401 L1
Cross Field Wy COLN CO4 — 105 J6
Crossfield Wy FOS CO13 — 198 C5
Crossgate Fld FX IP11 — 84 F8
Cross HI HAR CO12 — 169 K2
Crossing Rd EPP CM16 — 304 B4
Cross La K/T/MI CO5 — 246 A4
Crossley Av COS CO15 — 249 M4
Crossley Gdns IP IP1 — 36 D1
Cross Rd BAR EN8 — 300 F5
  EN EN1 — 324 A6
  MAL CM9 — 293 H2
  PIT SS13 — 379 G4
  ROMW/RG RM7 — 370 B3
  SBF/HAD SS7 — 380 C7
  WFD IG8 — 349 G7
  WIT CM8 — 212 A7
Cross Roads LOU IG10 — 326 C4
Cross St FX IP11 — 84 F7
  SAFWN CB10 — 65 L2
  SUD CO10 — 4 B8
Crosstree Wk COLS CO2 — 163 H8
Cross Wy K/T/MI CO5 — 245 M4
Crossways BRWN CM15 — 333 H8
  CBE/LIN CB1 — 24 E1
  CHLM/GWD CM2 — 288 D4
  COS CO15 — 250 A3
  GPK RM2 — 371 J3
  RCOLW CO6 — 130 B8
The Crossways WOS/PRIT SS0 — 400 B3
Crotchets Cl RIPS/CAP IP9 — 78 B2
Crouch Av HOC/HUL SS5 — 361 M2
Crouch Beck RCHLM CM3 — 339 M4
Crouch Dr WICKE SS11 — 359 L3
Croutel Rd FX IP11 — 85 J8
Crowborough Rd SOSN SS2 — 383 M4
Crowe Hall La RIPS/CAP IP9 — 110 B1
Crow Green La BRWN CM15 — 332 B7
Crow Green Rd BRWN CM15 — 332 A7
Crowhall La MGTR CO11 — 139 L3
Crowhurst Rd COLW CO3 — 10 A8
Crowland Cl CHTY IP2 — 58 B1
Crowland Rd HVHL CB9 — 28 A3
Crowlands Av ROMW/RG RM7 — 370 C6
Crow La RCOS CO16 — 196 A1
  ROMW/RG RM7 — 370 A7
  ROMW/RG RM7 — 370 D7
Crown Av PIT SS13 — 378 D4
Crown Bays Rd COLN CO4 — 11 K5
Crown Cl PIT SS13 — 378 D5
  RBSF CM22 — 228 D3
Crownfield BROX EN10 — 277 H1
Crown Gdns RAYL SS6 — 380 D1
Crown Ga COLN CO4 — 135 L5
  HLW CM20 — 15 L4
Crown HI RAYL SS6 — 380 D1
  WAB EN9 — 303 G5
Crownhill Rd WFD IG8 — 348 F8
Crown La RCOS CO16 — 167 L8
Crown La North RCOLE CO7 — 135 M4
Crown La South RCOLE CO7 — 136 B7
Crown Meadow BRTR CM7 — 155 L7
Crown Rd BCAYE CM11 — 357 J1
  BRW CM14 — 331 L3
  COS CO15 — 12 B9
  EN EN1 — 324 B5
  GRAYS RM17 — 417 H3
  HOC/HUL SS5 — 362 C6
  RCHLM CM3 — 317 G5
Crown St BRTR CM7 — 124 C1

BRW CM14 — 354 D3
DAGE RM10 — 388 D5
FX IP11 — 84 F3
HSTD CO9 — 73 H7
IP IP1 — 2 E3
RCOLE CO7 — 107 C5
Crown Ter BSF CM23 — 174 B4
Crown Wy BOC CM0 — 320 D7
Crow Pond Rd RCHLM CM3 — 237 K1
Crowsheath La BCAYE CM11 — 336 F5
Crows La RCHLM CM3 — 315 J5
Crows Rd EPP CM16 — 304 A2
Crowstone Av WOS/PRIT SS0 — 400 D4
Crowstone Cl WOS/PRIT SS0 — 400 D2
Crowstone Rd CDH/CHF RM16 — 407 K7
  WOS/PRIT SS0 — 400 D3
Crow St RBSF CM22 — 120 A6
Crowswell Ct FX IP11 — 84 C3
Croxford Wy ROMW/RG RM7 — 370 E8
Croxon Wy BOC CM0 — 344 C4
Crozier Av BSF CM23 — 173 K3
Cruce Wy RCOS CO16 — 221 G8
Cruick Av SOCK/AV RM15 — 406 D4
Crummock Cl BRTR CM7 — 182 D5
Crunch Cft HVHL CB9 — 28 F6
Crusader Cl PUR RM19 — 415 H1
Crusader Wy BRTR CM7 — 183 L1
Crushes Cl RBRW/HUT CM13 — 333 M8
Crystal Av HCH RM12 — 389 M3
Cuba Dr PEND EN3 — 324 D4
Cuckfield Av IPSE IP3 — 38 F8
Cuckoo HI BURES CO8 — 102 A2
  HSTD CO9 — 97 J3
Cuckoo La CDH/CHF RM16 — 407 C6
Cuckoos La GTDUN CM6 — 204 A1
Cuckoo Wy BRTR CM7 — 182 C5
Culford Rd CDH/CHF RM16 — 407 K7
Cullen Sq SOCK/AV RM15 — 406 D5
Cullingham Rd IP IP1 — 2 A4
Cullings Ct WAB EN9 — 302 A5
Culpepper Cl CHIG IG7 — 349 J7
Culverdown BSDN SS14 — 18 F5
Culver Ri RCHLM CM3 — 339 M4
Culver St East COL CO1 — 10 D8
Culver St West COL CO1 — 10 D8
Cumberland Av HCH RM12 — 389 M2
  MAL CM9 — 292 F2
  SBF/HAD SS7 — 379 K8
  SOSN SS2 — 21 M1
Cumberland Cl BRTR CM7 — 155 J7
  FX IP11 — 85 L7
Cumberland Crs CHLM/WR CM1 — 264 B4
Cumberland Dr LAIN SS15 — 376 B5
Cumberland St IP IP1 — 2 C2
Cumley Rd CHONG CM5 — 305 M2
Cumming Rd BCAYE CM11 — 359 H1
Cummings Hall La ABR/ST RM4 — 352 D4
Cunningham Av PEND EN3 — 300 F8
Cunningham Cl SBN/FI SS3 — 403 G2
Cunningham Dr WICKW SS12 — 359 M6
Cunningham Ri EPP CM16 — 281 L5
Cunningham Rd BAR EN8 — 276 F7
Cunnington Rd BRTR CM7 — 155 K8
Cunobelin Wy COLS CO2 — 190 A1
Cupids Cha SBN/FI SS3 — 403 K1
Cuppers Cl WIT CM8 — 238 F2
Curds Rd RCOLW CO6 — 130 B8
Curlew Av RCHLM CM3 — 319 H3
Curlew Cl COS CO15 — 224 A5
  K/T/MI CO5 — 213 L1
  MAL CM9 — 269 K6
Curlew Crs VGE SS16 — 377 J8
Curlew Cft COLN CO4 — 164 A3
Curlew Dr SBF/HAD SS7 — 397 K1
Curlew Rd CHTY IP2 — 36 E8
Curling La GRAYS RM17 — 417 G2
Curling Tye La MAL CM9 — 268 A8
Curling Wk BSDN SS14 — 19 M4
Currants Farm Rd BRTR CM7 — 154 F6
Curriers' La IP IP1 — 2 D5
Curteys HLWE CM17 — 227 L6
Curtis Cl RCOS CO16 — 223 J8
  RIPW IP8 — 57 K2
Curtis Mill La ABR/ST RM4 — 329 M6
Curtis Rd EMPK RM11 — 372 A8
Curtisway RAYL SS6 — 361 M7
Curzon Av PEND EN3 — 324 E7
Curzon Dr GRAYS RM17 — 417 K4
Curzon Rd SUD CO10 — 5 J5
Curzon Wy CHLM/GWD CM2 — 289 H1
Cusak Rd CHLM/GWD CM2 — 289 G1
Cussons Cl CHESW EN7 — 300 B1
Cut-a-thwart La MAL CM9 — 268 C8
Cutforth Rd SBW CM21 — 200 F8
Cuthbert Cl CHESW EN7 — 300 A1
Cut Hedge BRTR CM7 — 182 D5
Cuthedge La RCOLW CO6 — 185 J4
Cutlers Rd RCHLM CM3 — 339 M3
Cutler St IP IP1 — 2 E6
Cutmore Pl CHLM/GWD CM2 — 16 D8
Cuton Hall La CHLM/GWD CM2 — 265 H6
The Cut K/T/MI CO5 — 214 D6
Cut Throat La WIT CM8 — 212 B8
Cutting Dr HSTD CO9 — 128 F2
Cygnet Cl BSF CM23 — 174 A5
  HSTD CO9 — 97 M2
Cygnet Vw WTHK RM20 — 406 A8
Cymbeline Way (Colchester By- Pass) COLW CO3 — 162 A4
Cymbeline Way (Colchester by Pass) COLW CO3 — 162 C3
Cypress Cl COS CO15 — 223 M4
  WAB EN9 — 301 L6
Cypress Dr CHLM/GWD CM2 — 288 D5
Cypress Gv BARK/HLT IG6 — 349 M7
  COLN CO4 — 163 M3
Cypress Ms K/T/MI CO5 — 245 J4
Cyril Child Cl COLN CO4 — 163 M4

D

Daarle Av CVI SS8 — 398 B8
Dabbling Cl ERITH DA8 — 414 C4
Dacre Av SOCK/AV RM15 — 405 L6
Dacre Cl CHIG IG7 — 349 K5
Dacre Crs SOCK/AV RM15 — 405 L6
Dacre Gdns CHIG IG7 — 349 K5
Daen Ingas RCHLM CM3 — 290 D4
Daffodil Av BRWN CM15 — 332 C2
Daffodil Cl CHTY IP2 — 36 F8
Daffodil Wy CHLM/WR CM1 — 264 C4
Dagenham Rd DAGE RM10 — 388 D3
  RAIN RM13 — 388 C4
  ROMW/RG RM7 — 370 E7
Dagmar Rd DAGE RM10 — 388 D6
Dagnam Park Cl HARH RM3 — 353 H6
Dagnam Park Dr HARH RM3 — 352 F6
Dagnam Park Gdns HARH RM3 — 353 H7
Dagnam Park Sq HARH RM3 — 353 J7
Dagnets La BRTR CM7 — 182 D7
Dagwood La BRWN CM15 — 332 C2
Dahlia Cl CHLM/WR CM1 — 265 G6
  COS CO15 — 12 A3
Daiglen Dr SOCK/AV RM15 — 406 B5
Daimler Av COS CO15 — 249 L4
Daimler Rd IP IP1 — 36 D1
Daines Cl SOCK/AV RM15 — 406 B2
  SOS SS1 — 402 C3
Daines Rd BCAYE CM11 — 357 J1
Daines Wy SOS SS1 — 402 C2
Dains Pl FX IP11 — 84 D6
Dairy Farm Rd RCHLM CM3 — 319 L8
Dairyglen Av BAR EN8 — 300 E3
Dairyhouse La MGTR CO11 — 139 M3
Daisleys La RCHLM CM3 — 236 B1
Daisy Green Rd COLW CO3 — 160 E3
Daisyley Rd GTDUN CM6 — 123 H8
Dakyn Dr ING CM4 — 311 L8
Dale Cl HVHL CB9 — 161 J4
  SOCK/AV RM15 — 406 B4
Dale Ct SBW CM21 — 227 L2
Dale Gdns WFD IG8 — 348 C5
Dale Hall La IP IP1 — 37 J1
Dalen Av CVI SS8 — 398 B8
Dale Rd LOS SS9 — 399 J2
Daleside Gdns CHIG IG7 — 349 K4
Dales Rd IP IP1 — 37 H2
The Dales HAR CO12 — 143 C2
  RCFD SS4 — 363 L8
Dales Vw RIPW IP8 — 56 F3
Dales View Rd IP IP1 — 37 H3
Dale Vw ERITH DA8 — 414 B6
Daleview Av MGTR CO11 — 139 L6
Dalewood Cl EMPK RM11 — 371 M7
Dallwood Wy BRTR CM7 — 155 J8
Dalmatia Rd SOS SS1 — 401 L2
Dalmeney VGE SS16 — 376 C7
Dalroy Cl SOCK/AV RM15 — 406 B4
Dalrymple Cl CHLM/GWD CM2 — 17 M1
Daltes La RCOS CO16 — 222 C8
Dalton Gdns BSF CM23 — 173 M8
Dalton Rd IP IP1 — 2 C4
Daltons Fen PIT SS13 — 378 D3
Dalwood SBN/FI SS3 — 402 E3
Dalwood Gdns SBF/HAD SS7 — 380 F7
Dalys Rd RCFD SS4 — 382 F1
Damant's Farm La FOS CO13 — 197 L3
Damases La RCHLM CM3 — 266 C1
Damask Rd COLW CO3 — 161 K4
Dampier Rd RCOLW CO6 — 158 A8
Danacre LAIN SS15 — 376 C5
Danbury Cl BRW CM14 — 332 A7
  LOS SS9 — 382 A7
Danbury Crs SOCK/AV RM15 — 406 C4
Danbury Down BSDN SS14 — 19 M2
Danbury Rd LOU IG10 — 326 F8
  RAIN RM13 — 389 C7
  RAYL SS6 — 361 J8
Danbury V RCHLM CM3 — 291 H5
Danbury Wy WFD IG8 — 348 D7
Dancing Dicks La WIT CM8 — 238 B1
Dandalan Cl IP IP1 — 36 E4
Dandies Cha LOS SS9 — 381 L4
Dandies Cl LOS SS9 — 381 L4
Dandies Dr LOS SS9 — 381 L4
Dane Acres BSF CM23 — 173 L3
Dane Br MHAD SC10 — 172 C8
Dane Cl HVHL CB9 — 29 H1
Dane Common HVHL CB9 — 29 H1
Danemead HOD EN11 — 253 H2
Dane O'coys Rd BSF CM23 — 173 L3
Dane Pk BSF CM23 — 173 L3
Dane Rd CHLM/WR CM1 — 16 B4
Dane's Av SBN/FI SS3 — 403 G5
Danes Cl SUD CO10 — 55 J7
Danescroft Cl LOS SS9 — 381 L7
Danescroft Dr LOS SS9 — 381 L7
Danesfield SBF/HAD SS7 — 397 J1
Danesleigh Gdns LOS SS9 — 381 L7
Danes Rd ROMW/RG RM7 — 370 D7
Dane St BSF CM23 — 174 B5
  SBN/FI SS3 — 403 H5
Danes Wy BRWN CM15 — 332 A7
Danette Gdns DAGE RM10 — 388 A1
Daniel Cl CDH/CHF RM16 — 406 F7
  CDH/CHF RM16 — 408 C5
Daniel Cole Rd COLS CO2 — 190 C1
Daniell Cl RCOS CO16 — 223 K5
Daniells Cl COLS CO2 — 190 C1
Daniels Cl SUD CO10 — 35 K5
Daniel Wy WIT CM8 — 184 F7
Danyon Cl RAIN RM13 — 389 C7
Daphne Cl BRTR CM7 — 182 D4
Dapifer Dr BRTR CM7 — 155 J4
Darby Dr WAB EN9 — 301 K5
D'arcy Av MAL CM9 — 293 J3
D'arcy Cl BAR EN8 — 300 F3
  BOC CM0 — 344 D5
  FOS CO13 — 199 G5
  RBRW/HUT CM13 — 355 J1
D'arcy Gdns DAGW RM9 — 388 A7

D'arcy Hts COLS CO2 — 163 K8
Darcy Ri RCHLM CM3 — 290 F2
D'arcy Rd COLS CO2 — 163 K8
  K/T/MI CO5 — 215 G8
  RCOS CO16 — 222 C6
D'arcy Wy MAL CM9 — 242 F7
  RCOLE CO7 — 220 F4
Darell Wy BCAYE CM11 — 357 L2
Darenth La SOCK/AV RM15 — 406 B4
Darenth Rd LOS SS9 — 399 J2
Darent Valley Pth DART DA1 — 414 E2
Darkhouse La K/T/MI CO5 — 192 B5
Dark La BRW CM14 — 354 B8
  CHESW EN7 — 300 B3
  SBF/HAD SS7 — 380 B5
Darlinghurst Gv LOS SS9 — 400 B1
Darlington Ct BRWN CM15 — 332 B8
Darlington Gdns HARH RM3 — 352 E6
Darlton Cl DART DA1 — 414 A6
Darnel Wy COLW CO3 — 161 J4
Darnet Rd MAL CM9 — 272 F2
Darnley Cl CHLM/WR CM1 — 264 C5
Darrell Cl CHLM/WR CM1 — 264 C5
Darrell Rd FX IP11 — 8 E8
Darsham Cl FX IP11 — 8 E1
Dart Cl UPMR RM14 — 372 E6
  WIT CM8 — 238 E1
Dartfields HARH RM3 — 352 E7
Dartford Av ED N9 — 324 D8
Dart Gn SOCK/AV RM15 — 406 C4
Dartmouth Rd RAYL SS6 — 361 L6
Dartmouth Rd CHLM/WR CM1 — 266 F1
Dartview GRAYS RM17 — 417 M1
Darwin Cl BRTR CM7 — 183 G2
  COLS CO2 — 191 J2
Darwin Rd IPNE IP4 — 3 M5
  TIL RM18 — 418 A5
Dash End HVHL CB9 — 29 J1
Dash End La HVHL CB9 — 29 J1
The Dashes HLW CM20 — 255 M2
Dashwood Cl RIPW IP8 — 57 L2
Datchet Dr SBN/FI SS3 — 402 F1
Daundy Cl CHTY IP2 — 36 E6
Davall Cl HAR CO12 — 142 D2
Davenants PIT SS13 — 378 C3
Davenport HLWE CM17 — 256 F4
Daventry Gdns HARH RM3 — 352 D6
Daventry Rd HARH RM3 — 352 D6
Davey Cl COL CO1 — 11 K9
  IPSE IP3 — 59 G2
David Av WICKE SS11 — 359 L1
David Dr HARH RM3 — 353 H7
Davidson Cl SUD CO10 — 55 K7
Davidson Rd WICKW SS12 — 359 M6
Davidson Wy ROMW/RG RM7 — 370 F6
David's Wk BCAYE CM11 — 357 K1
Davids Wy BARK/HLT IG6 — 349 M8
Davies Cl RAIN RM13 — 404 D1
Davinia Cl WFD IG8 — 349 G7
Davison Cl BAR EN8 — 276 E8
Davison Dr BAR EN8 — 276 E8
Davis Rd CDH/CHF RM16 — 407 G8
  SOCK/AV RM15 — 405 L6
Davy Rd COS CO15 — 224 D3
Dawes Av HCH RM12 — 389 L2
Dawes Cl RIPS/CAP IP9 — 78 A2
Dawes La K/T/MI CO5 — 245 M2
Dawley Gn SOCK/AV RM15 — 406 B4
Dawlish Crs RAYL SS6 — 361 L6
Dawlish Dr LOS SS9 — 399 M2
Dawlish Rd COS CO15 — 250 D3
Dawn Cl MAL CM9 — 293 J3
Dawnford Cl COLW CO3 — 161 K4
Daws Cl CHLM/WR CM1 — 287 C2
Daws Heath Rd RAYL SS6 — 380 E2
  SBF/HAD SS7 — 380 D5
Daws HI CHING E4 — 325 K5
Dawson Cl SAFWN CB10 — 66 A1
Dawson Drift KESG IP5 — 39 K4
Dawson Pth FX IP11 — 84 D5
  RAIN RM13 — 389 C6
Daw St BRTR CM7 — 94 F7
  HSTD CO9 — 49 J6
Daylop Dr CHIG IG7 — 350 C4
Days Cl CHLM/GWD CM2 — 264 C3
Days Gn RIPS/CAP IP9 — 78 A2
Days Rd RIPS/CAP IP9 — 78 A1
Dayton Dr ERITH DA8 — 414 E2
Dazeley's La RCOLE CO7 — 108 A3
Deacon Cl FX IP11 — 85 L7
Deacon Dr LAIN SS15 — 376 D4
Deacon Wy WFD IG8 — 349 G8
Dead La BURES CO8 — 102 F1
  MGTR CO11 — 138 C1
  RCOLE CO7 — 136 D3
  RCOS CO16 — 222 A1
  RCOS CO16 — 223 J2
Deadman's La CHLM/GWD CM2 — 288 F7
Deal Cl BRTR CM7 — 154 F5
  COS CO15 — 250 D3
Dealtree Cl BRWN CM15 — 308 C2
Deal Wy RCOLE CO7 — 220 F2
Deanery Gdns BRTR CM7 — 155 G4
Deanery HI BRTR CM7 — 154 F4
Deane's Cl HAR CO12 — 143 H1
Deanhill Av COS CO15 — 13 M2
Dean Rd CBE/LIN CB1 — 25 J4
Dean Rogers Pl BRTR CM7 — 155 G4
Deans Cl HVHL CB9 — 28 A2
Deans Rd BRW CM14 — 354 C4
Dean St RCOLE CO7 — 220 F4
Dearsley Rd EN EN1 — 324 B5
Debden Cl WFD IG8 — 348 E8
Debden Cl SAFWN CB10 — 90 F1
Debden Gn VGE SS16 — 376 D7
Debden La LOU IG10 — 327 J2
  SAFWS CB11 — 65 L3
  SAFWS CB11 — 89 H3
Debden La LOU IG10 — 327 J2
Debden Rd COLN CO4 — 163 M2
  HVHL CB9 — 28 C3
  IP IP1 — 37 G2

Deben Valley Dr *KESG* IP5 .... 39 K4
Deben Wk *RCOS* CO16 .... 223 K5 ⊡
Deben Wy *FX* IP11 .... 9 H3
De Bohun Ct *SAFWN* CB10 .... 65 M1
De Burgh Pl *SUD* CO10 .... 31 J2
De Burgh Rd *COLW* CO3 .... 161 M5
Dedham Av *RCOS* CO16 .... 223 J7
Dedham Cl *BCAYE* CM11 .... 357 J7
Dedham Meade *RCOLE* CO7 .... 107 G8
Dedham Rd *BCAYE* CM11 .... 357 K1
  COLN CO4 .... 105 J5
  MGTR CO11 .... 107 M7
  RCOLE CO7 .... 107 G2
Dee La *UPMR* RM14 .... 372 E6
Deepdale *SBF/HAD* SS7 .... 380 A5
Deepdale Rd *HAR* CO12 .... 6 D7
Deepdene *ING* CM4 .... 310 C3
Deepdene Av *RAYL* SS6 .... 361 K6
Deepdene Pth *LOU* IG10 .... 327 J6
Deepdene Rd *LOU* IG10 .... 327 H6
Deeping Wk *RCOS* CO16 .... 222 K5
Deepwater Rd *FX* IP11 .... 412 F1
Deerbank Rd *BCAYE* CM11 .... 335 K8
Deere Av *RM13* 389 H5
Deerhurst Cha *RCHLM* CM3 .... 315 G2
Deerhurst *SBF/HAD* SS7 .... 380 C4
Deerhurst Cha *RCHLM* CM3 .... 315 G2
Deerhurst *SBF/HAD* SS7 .... 380 C4 ⊡
Deerleap Gv *CHING* E4 .... 325 J7
Deerleap Wy *BRTR* CM7 .... 155 L7
Deer Pk *HLWW/ROY* CM19 .... 255 H6
Dee Wy *ROM* RM1 .... 370 F1
Defoe Crs *COLN* CO4 .... 134 D1
Defoe Pde *CDH/CHF* RM16 .... 408 C8
Defoe Wy *CRW* RM5 .... 351 H7
Deford Rd *WIT* CM8 .... 238 E3
De Greys Rd *SUD* CO10 .... 55 K6
Deirdre Av *WICKW* SS12 .... 359 J4
Deirdre Cl *WICKW* SS12 .... 359 J4
Delafield Rd *GRAYS* RM17 .... 417 L2
Delamare Rd *BAR* EN8 .... 301 G1
Delamere Rd *CHLM/WR* CM1 .... 16 B6
  COLN CO4 .... 135 L8
Delargy Cl *CDH/CHF* RM16 .... 408 C8
Delaware Crs *SBN/FI* SS3 .... 402 E4
Delaware Rd *SBN/FI* SS3 .... 402 D4
Delder Av *CVI* SS8 .... 413 L1
Delft Rd *CVI* SS8 .... 398 B7
Delfzul Rd *CVI* SS8 .... 398 B7
Delgada Rd *CVI* SS8 .... 398 E8
Delhi Rd *PIT* SS13 .... 378 D5
Delimands *LAIN* SS15 .... 18 C6
Dell Cl *WFD* IG8 .... 348 C4
Dell La *BSF* CM23 .... 174 B4
  RBSF CM22 .... 201 H3
Dellows La *RBSF* CM22 .... 147 H1
Dell Rd *GRAYS* RM17 .... 417 L1
  PEND EN3 .... 324 D2
Dells Wood Cl *HOD* EN11 .... 253 G2
The Dell *BRW* CM14 .... 354 C7
  CHLM/GWD CM2 .... 289 G4
  COL CO1 .... 10 E9
  GTDUN CM6 .... 178 D7
  VGE SS16 .... 377 J8
  WFD IG8 .... 348 C4
  WICKW SS11 .... 359 M4
Dellwood Av *FX* IP11 .... 85 H8
Delmar Gdns *WICKE* SS11 .... 359 K1
Delmores *VGE* SS16 .... 376 D8
Delta Rd *RBRW/HUT* CM13 .... 333 L8
Delvers Md *DAGE* RM10 .... 388 D3 ⊡
Delview *CVI* SS8 .... 398 A6
Delvins *PIT* SS13 .... 378 B3
Delvyn's La *HSTD* CO9 .... 74 D5
De Mandeville Rd *PIT* SS13 .... 378 B3
De Mandeville Rd *RBSF* CM22 .... 147 K1
De-marci Ct *BRTR* CM7 .... 155 L8
Denbigh Cl *EMPK* RM11 .... 372 A1
Denbigh Rd *LAIN* SS15 .... 376 C6
Denby Gra *HLWE* CM17 .... 256 F3
Dencourt Crs *BSDN* SS14 .... 378 A6
Dendridge Cl *EN* EN1 .... 324 C1
Dene Cl *RAYL* SS6 .... 361 L7
Dene Ct *CHLM/WR* CM1 .... 263 L6
Denecroft Gdns *GRAYS* RM17 .... 407 L8
Dene Gdns *RAYL* SS6 .... 361 L7
Denehurst Gdns *VGE* SS16 .... 375 M7
  WFD IG8 .... 348 C5
Deneway *VGE* SS16 .... 395 L1
Dengayne *BSDN* SS14 .... 19 M6
Dengie Cl *WIT* CM8 .... 239 G3
Denham Cl *RCOLE* CO7 .... 192 D3
Denham Rd *PIT* SS13 .... 378 B4
Denham V *RAYL* SS6 .... 361 H8
Denholm Ct *WIT* CM8 .... 239 G3
Denholme Wk *RAIN* RM13 .... 389 G5
Denmark Gdns *RIPS/CAP* IP9 .... 80 E5
Dennises La *UPMR* RM14 .... 391 J7
Dennis Rd *UPMR* RM14 .... 391 H7
Denny Av *WAB* EN9 .... 301 L6
Denny Ct *BSF* CM23 .... 174 C1
Denny Ga *BAR* EN8 .... 277 G7
Dent Cl *SOCK/AV* RM15 .... 406 B4 ⊡
Denton Ap *WOS/PRIT* SS0 .... 382 B6 ⊡
Denton Av *WOS/PRIT* SS0 .... 382 C5
Denton Cl *CHTY* IP2 .... 57 L1
  WOS/PRIT SS0 .... 382 B6
Denver Dr *PIT* SS13 .... 378 D2
Denys Dr *BSDN* SS14 .... 378 A2
Derby Av *ROMW/RG* RM7 .... 370 C4
  UPMR RM14 .... 390 A2
Derby Cl *BCAYE* CM11 .... 335 L6
  IPNE IP4 .... 38 B6
  RCHLM CM3 .... 319 G2
  VGE SS16 .... 376 A7 ⊡
Derbydale *RCFD* SS4 .... 363 K5
Derby Rd *HOD* EN11 .... 253 L7
  IPSE IP3 .... 38 B7
  PEND EN3 .... 324 C7
Derby Road Br *GRAYS* RM17 .... 417 J2
Dereham Av *DART* DA1 .... 415 H6
Dereham Cl *COLS* CO2 .... 162 D8
Derek Gdns *SOSN* SS2 .... 382 F6
Derham Gdns *UPMR* RM14 .... 390 D2
Deri Av *RAIN* RM13 .... 404 C2
Dering Crs *LOS* SS9 .... 381 L4

Derry Av *SOCK/AV* RM15 .... 406 B3 ⊡
Derventer Av *CVI* SS8 .... 398 B5
Derwent Av *RAYL* SS6 .... 380 F1
Derwent Gdns *COS* CO15 .... 224 D5
Derwent Pde *SOCK/AV* RM15 .... 406 B4
Derwent Rd *COLN* CO4 .... 135 K6
  IPSE IP3 .... 38 A8
Derwent Wy *BRTR* CM7 .... 182 D5
  HCH RM12 .... 389 J4
De Staunton Cl *RCOLE* CO7 .... 193 J4 ⊡
Detling Cl *HCH* RM12 .... 389 K4 ⊡
Devereaux Cl *FOS* CO13 .... 199 G3
Devereaux Pl *COLN* CO4 .... 134 D8
De Vere Av *MAL* CM9 .... 293 J2
De Vere Cl *RCHLM* CM3 .... 238 C8
  RCOLE CO7 .... 192 C3
De Vere La *RCOLE* CO7 .... 192 C3
De Vere Rd *COLW* CO3 .... 162 A6
  RCOLW CO6 .... 130 A4
Devereux Rd *CDH/CHF* RM16 .... 407 G8
  SOS SS1 .... 21 G8
Devereux Wy *BCAYW* CM12 .... 335 G6
De Vere Wy *HAR* CO12 .... 143 G1 ⊡
Deveron Gdns
  SOCK/AV RM15 .... 406 B3 ⊡
Deveron Wy *ROM* RM1 .... 370 F1
De Vigier Av *SAFWN* CB10 .... 66 B1
Devlin Rd *RIPW* IP8 .... 57 J2
Devoils La *BSF* CM23 .... 174 A4 ⊡
Devon Cl *BKHH* IG9 .... 348 C5
Devon Gdns *RCFD* SS4 .... 363 K6
Devon Rd *COLS* CO2 .... 162 C8
  FX IP11 .... 85 G8
Devonshire Cl *LAIN* SS15 .... 376 B3
Devonshire Gdns *BRTR* CM7 .... 155 J7
  SLH/COR SS17 .... 409 H8
Devonshire Rd *BOC* CM0 .... 344 C6
  CDH/CHF RM16 .... 416 F1
  HCH RM12 .... 389 L7
  IPSE IP3 .... 3 L6
  LAIN SS15 .... 376 B3
Devon Wy *COS* CO15 .... 224 F4 ⊡
  CVI SS8 .... 398 B6
  HAR CO12 .... 142 E1 ⊡
Dewar La *IP* IP1 .... 2 F4
Dewes Green Rd *BSF* CM23 .... 117 G2
Dewey Rd *DAGE* RM10 .... 388 C5
Dewgrass Gv *BAR* EN8 .... 300 E7 ⊡
Dewhurst Rd *BAR* EN8 .... 300 D1
Dewlands *BRTR* CM7 .... 183 J6
Dewsbury Gdns *HARH* RM3 .... 352 E7 ⊡
Dewsbury Rd *HARH* RM3 .... 352 F7 ⊡
Dewsgreen *VGE* SS16 .... 377 M7
Dewyk Rd *CVI* SS8 .... 398 D6
Dexter Cl *GRAYS* RM17 .... 407 H8
Deyncourt Gdns *UPMR* RM14 .... 390 D1
Deynes Rd *SAFWS* CB11 .... 90 C4
Dial La *IP* IP1 .... 2 F4
Dial Rd *RCOLE* CO7 .... 194 F3
Diamond Cl *CDH/CHF* RM16 .... 407 G8
  IP IP1 .... 36 D2
Diana Cl *CDH/CHF* RM16 .... 407 G8
Diana Wy *COS* CO15 .... 12 B8
Diban Av *HCH* RM12 .... 389 J3
Dickens Av *DART* DA1 .... 415 H6
  TIL RM18 .... 418 C5
Dickens Cl *BRTR* CM7 .... 183 H3 ⊡
  SOSN SS2 .... 21 J1
Dickens Dr *LAIN* SS15 .... 376 D4
Dickens Pl *CHLM/WR* CM1 .... 263 L4
Dickens Ri *CHIG* IG7 .... 349 H4
Dickens Rd *CHTY* IP2 .... 36 F5
Dickens Wy *ROM* RM1 .... 370 F1
Dickins Cl *CHESW* EN7 .... 276 B7
Dickinson Ter *KESG* IP5 .... 39 L4 ⊡
Dickson *CHESW* EN7 .... 276 A7
Dicky Moors *RCHLM* CM3 .... 235 G4
Didsbury Cl *CHTY* IP2 .... 57 L1
Digby Gdns *DAGE* RM10 .... 388 B7
Digby Rd *IPNE* IP4 .... 38 D4
  SOS SS17 .... 395 J6
Dig Dag Hl *CHESW* EN7 .... 276 A7
Dilbridge Rd East *COLN* CO4 .... 11 J5
Dilbridge Rd West *COLN* CO4 .... 11 H5
Dillwyn St *IP* IP1 .... 2 B4
Dillwyn St West *IP* IP1 .... 2 B4
Dilston *RCHLM* CM3 .... 291 H5
Dimsdale Crs *BSF* CM23 .... 174 C6
Dinant Av *CVI* SS8 .... 397 M6
Dinant Link Rd *HOD* EN11 .... 253 K4
Dinants Crs *RCOLW* CO6 .... 159 M8
Dinsdale Cl *COLN* CO4 .... 11 K6
The Dismals *RCHLM* CM3 .... 237 J1
Disney Cl *ING* CM4 .... 310 C7
Dison Cl *PEND* EN3 .... 324 E3 ⊡
Disraeli Rd *RAYL* SS6 .... 381 J3
Distillery La *COLS* CO2 .... 163 L7
Ditchfield Rd *HOD* EN11 .... 253 H3
Ditchingham Gv *IPNE* IP4 .... 38 F5
Ditton Court Rd *WOS/PRIT* SS0 .... 20 A6
Dixon Av *CHLM/WR* CM1 .... 264 A7
  RCOS CO16 .... 223 K5
Dixon Cl *MGTR* CO11 .... 108 C7
Dixon Rd *RCOLE* CO7 .... 164 B8
Dobbies La *RCOLW* CO6 .... 160 A8
Dobbs La *KESG* IP5 .... 39 M3
Dobb's Weir Rd *HOD* EN11 .... 253 L6
Dobsons Cl *LOS* SS9 .... 400 A1
  RAYL SS6 .... 380 F2
Dock Approach Rd
  CDH/CHF RM16 .... 408 A6
  GRAYS RM17 .... 417 M2
Dockfield Av *HAR* CO12 .... 6 A8
Docklands Av *ING* CM4 .... 310 D7
Dock La *HAR* CO12 .... 142 B7
Dock Rd *GRAYS* RM17 .... 417 L3
  TIL RM18 .... 417 M5
Dock St *CHTY* IP2 .... 2 F4
Dockwra La *RCHLM* CM3 .... 291 G4
Doctor's La *SUD* CO10 .... 59 E1
Doddenhill Cl *SAFWN* CB10 .... 43 M8 ⊡
Doddinghurst Rd *BRWN* CM15 .... 332 D1
Dodmans *RIPS/CAP* IP9 .... 78 B2 ⊡

Dodson V *KESG* IP5 .... 39 K4
Doesgate La *UPMR* RM14 .... 393 J2
Doeshill Dr *WICKW* SS12 .... 359 M8
Dog Cha *BRTR* CM7 .... 95 K8 ⊡
Dogden La *BSF* CM23 .... 145 M1
Doggetts Cha *RCFD* SS4 .... 364 B3
Doggetts Cl *RCFD* SS4 .... 364 A3
Doggetts La *RCOLW* CO6 .... 188 A3
Doghouse Rd *BRTR* CM7 .... 156 F6
Dog Kennel La *ING* CM4 .... 310 C4
Dogs Head St *IPNE* IP4 .... 2 F5
Dolby Ri *CHLM/GWD* CM2 .... 289 C1
Dollant Av *CVI* SS8 .... 398 B8
Dolphin Ap *ROM* RM1 .... 371 G4
Dolphin Cl *CBE/LIN* CB1 .... 24 E1 ⊡
Dolphin Gdns *CHLM/GWD* CM2 .... 335 G6 ⊡
Dolphins *WOS/PRIT* SS0 .... 382 E6
Dolphin Wy *BSF* CM23 .... 174 B3
Dombey Cl *CHLM/WR* CM1 .... 264 A4
Dombey Rd *CHTY* IP2 .... 36 F6
Dominion Dr *CRW* RM5 .... 351 J7
Dominion Wy *RAIN* RM13 .... 404 B1 ⊡
Domitian Cl *COLN* CO4 .... 135 J6
Domsey Bank *RCOLW* CO6 .... 159 M8
Domsey Cha *K/T/MI* CO5 .... 187 J3
Domsey La *RCHLM* CM3 .... 235 M8
Doms La *RCHLM* CM3 .... 237 H1
Donald Thorn Cl *WICKX* SS12 .... 359 L5 ⊡
Donald Wy *CHLM/GWD* CM2 .... 288 D4
Donard Dr *RCOLW* CO6 .... 133 L7
Doncaster Wy *UPMR* RM14 .... 390 A2
Don Ct *WIT* CM8 .... 238 E1
Donegal Rd *IP* IP1 .... 36 E1
Donkey La *EN* EN1 .... 324 B4
Donne Dr *COS* CO15 .... 250 B3
Donovan's Gdn
  RBRW/HUT CM13 .... 355 M8 ⊡
Don Wy *ROM* RM1 .... 351 M8
Donyland Wy *K/T/MI* CO5 .... 192 A4
Dooley Rd *HSTD* CO9 .... 128 E2
Dorchester Av *HOD* EN11 .... 253 H3
Dorchester End *COLS* CO2 .... 162 A6
Dorchester Rd *BCAYW* CM12 .... 335 H6 ⊡
  IPSE IP3 .... 38 E8
Dorewards Av *BRTR* CM7 .... 155 G4
Dorian Rd *HCH* RM12 .... 371 H8
Doric Av *RCFD* SS4 .... 363 L6
Dorking Crs *RCOS* CO16 .... 223 K5
Dorking Ri *HARH* RM3 .... 352 E5
Dorking Rd *HARH* RM3 .... 352 E5
Dorking Wk *HARH* RM3 .... 352 E5
Dorkins Wy *UPMR* RM14 .... 391 J7
Dorothy Farm Rd *RAYL* SS6 .... 381 H2 ⊡
Dorothy Gdns *SBF/HAD* SS7 .... 380 A6
Dorothy Sayers Dr *WIT* CM8 .... 212 A6
Dorrington Gdns *HCH* RM12 .... 371 L8
Dorset Av *CHLM/GWD* CM2 .... 288 E5
  ROM RM1 .... 370 E3
Dorset Cl *CHLM/GWD* CM2 .... 288 D5
  COS CO15 .... 224 F5 ⊡
  IPNE IP4 .... 38 A2
Dorset Gdns *RCFD* SS4 .... 363 K6
Dorset Rd *BOC* CM0 .... 344 D7
  MAL CM9 .... 293 G2
Dorset Wy *BCAYW* CM12 .... 335 H6
Dorvis La *SAFWN* CB10 .... 45 J2
Doubleday Dr *MAL* CM9 .... 269 G6
Doubleday Gdns *BRTR* CM7 .... 155 J6
Doubleday Rd *LOU* IG10 .... 327 K5
Doublegate La *WICKE* SS11 .... 360 D6
  WICKW SS12 .... 360 C7
Doublet St *BCAYE* CM11 .... 335 L6
Douglas Av *HARH* RM3 .... 371 M2
Douglas Cl *CDH/CHF* RM16 .... 406 F8
  CHLM/GWD CM2 .... 288 E3 ⊡
Douglas Dr *WICKW* SS12 .... 359 L8
Douglas Gv *WIT* CM8 .... 238 E1 ⊡
Douglas Rd *COS* CO15 .... 12 B4
  HAR CO12 .... 6 E7
  ROM RM1 .... 371 G6
  SBF/HAD SS7 .... 381 G8
Douglas Wk *CHLM/GWD* CM2 .... 16 D8
Doug Siddons Ct
  GRAYS RM17 .... 417 K3 ⊡
Doulton Cl *HLWE* CM17 .... 256 F4
Doulton Wy *RCFD* SS4 .... 363 K5
Dove Cl *BSF* CM23 .... 173 M8
  STSD SM24 .... 146 F4
Dovecote *SBN/FI* SS3 .... 402 F2 ⊡
Dove Crs *HAR* CO12 .... 142 E1
Dovedale *CVI* SS8 .... 398 E6 ⊡
  FX IP11 .... 8 F4
Dovedale Cl *BCAYE* CM11 .... 336 D7 ⊡
  VGE SS16 .... 376 B7 ⊡
Dovedale Gdns *COS* CO15 .... 224 D5
Dove Dr *SBF/HAD* SS7 .... 397 J1
Dovehouse Cft *HLW* CM20 .... 256 B1 ⊡
Dove House Rd *HVHL* CB9 .... 28 B3 ⊡
Dove La *CHLM/GWD* CM2 .... 288 B5
Dovercliff Rd *CVI* SS8 .... 398 E5
Dover Cl *BRTR* CM7 .... 154 F5
  COS CO15 .... 224 F4 ⊡
  ROMW/RG RM7 .... 370 D2
Dover Rd *IPSE* IP3 .... 38 C7
Dovervelt Rd *CVI* SS8 .... 398 C6
Dover Wy *PIT* SS13 .... 378 C5
Dovesgate *SBF/HAD* SS7 .... 379 J7 ⊡
Doves La *GTDUN* CM6 .... 205 H1
Doves Ms *LAIN* SS15 .... 376 E2 ⊡
Dove St *IPNE* IP4 .... 3 J4
Dowches Dr *K/T/MI* CO5 .... 186 D8
Dowches Gdns *K/T/MI* CO5 .... 186 D8 ⊡
Dow Ct *BOC* CM0 .... 320 D7
Dowding Rd *RAIN* RM13 .... 389 J6
Dowland Cl *SLH/COR* SS17 .... 394 D8 ⊡
Dowling Rd *BURES* CO8 .... 102 A8
Downer Rd *SBF/HAD* SS7 .... 379 L7
Downer Rd North *SBF/HAD* SS7 .... 379 M6
Downesway *SBF/HAD* SS7 .... 379 L8
Downey Cl *BSDN* SS14 .... 19 K4
Downfield Rd *BAR* EN8 .... 300 F3
Downhall Cl *RAYL* SS6 .... 361 L7
Downhall Park Wy *RAYL* SS6 .... 361 K8
Down Hall Rd *RAYL* SS6 .... 361 K8
Downhall Rd *RBSF* CM22 .... 229 J3
Downham Cl *CRW* RM5 .... 351 H8
Downham Rd *BCAYE* CM11 .... 336 E6

  CVI SS8 .... 398 B8
  ING CM4 .... 312 B7
  WICKE SS11 .... 359 K1
Downing Cl *CHTY* IP2 .... 58 A1
Downing Rd *DAGW* RM9 .... 388 A6
Downlands *WAB* EN9 .... 301 M6 ⊡
Downleaze *CHLM/GWD* CM2 .... 339 M8
Downs Crs *GTDUN* CM6 .... 178 D2
  HVHL CB9 .... 28 A3
Downs Gv *VGE* SS16 .... 377 M8
Downside Cl *CHTY* IP2 .... 58 A3
Downsland Dr *BRW* CM14 .... 354 D4
Downs Rd *MAL* CM9 .... 269 H8
The Downs *FX* IP11 .... 84 E8
  GTDUN CM6 .... 178 D2
  HLW CM20 .... 255 H3
Downsway *CHLM/WR* CM1 .... 264 E4
Downton Dr *HVHL* CB9 .... 27 M3
Dowsetts La *BCAYE* CM11 .... 336 C3
Dragon Cl *BOC* CM0 .... 344 B6
Dragon's Gn *SAFWN* CB10 .... 66 E2 ⊡
Drake Av *IPSE* IP3 .... 59 J1
  RCHLM CM3 .... 319 H3
Drake Cl *BRW* CM14 .... 354 C6
  SBF/HAD SS7 .... 380 D7
Drake Gdns *BRTR* CM7 .... 155 K7 ⊡
Drake Ms *RAIN* RM13 .... 389 H5
Drakes Ap *COS* CO15 .... 250 B3
Drakes Cl *BAR* EN8 .... 276 E3 ⊡
Drakes La *RCHLM* CM3 .... 236 A4
Drake Sq North *IPSE* IP3 .... 59 J1
Drake Sq South *IPSE* IP3 .... 59 J1
The Drakes *SBN/FI* SS3 .... 402 F3 ⊡
Drakes Wy *RAYL* SS6 .... 361 M7
Drapers Cha *BRTR* CM7 .... 181 L2
  MAL CM9 .... 269 L7
Drapers La *HVHL* CB9 .... 47 J1
Drapers Rd *RAIN* RM13 .... 339 M3
Drayman's Cl *BSF* CM23 .... 173 J6
Drayson Cl *WAB* EN9 .... 301 L4
Drayton Av *MAL* CM9 .... 293 H2 ⊡
Drayton Cl *LOU* IG10 .... 327 G8
Drewsteignton *SBN/FI* SS3 .... 402 E3
The Dreys *SUD* CO10 .... 34 C6
Drayton Av *MAL* CM9 .... 293 H2 ⊡
The Dreys *SAFWN* CB10 .... 66 E3
Driberg Wy *BRTR* CM7 .... 183 H2
Driffield Cl *K/T/MI* CO5 .... 186 E7
The Drift *IPNE* IP4 .... 38 B5
  IPSE IP3 .... 59 K2
  RIPS/CAP IP9 .... 82 D6
  SUD CO10 .... 55 K6
Driftway *VGE* SS16 .... 378 A8
The Driftway *IPNE* IP4 .... 38 C5
The Drive *BKHH* IG9 .... 348 D1
  CHLM/WR CM1 .... 264 B5
  COS CO15 .... 224 C4
  CRW RM5 .... 370 E1
  CHESW EN7 .... 276 C8
  GTDUN CM6 .... 92 A8
  HAR CO12 .... 143 J1
  HARH RM3 .... 371 M1
  HLW CM20 .... 255 M2
  HOC/HUL SS5 .... 339 L8
  HOD EN11 .... 253 H3
  LOU IG10 .... 326 F5
  RAYL SS6 .... 381 J3
  RBRW/HUT CM13 .... 354 D7
  RCFD SS4 .... 383 G1
  RCHLM CM3 .... 319 G3
  SBW CM21 .... 227 M1
  WIT CM8 .... 212 F5
  WOS/PRIT SS0 .... 400 C3
The Driveway *CVI* SS8 .... 413 J1
Droitwich Av *SOSN* SS2 .... 401 L2 ⊡
Drood Cl *CHLM/WR* CM1 .... 264 A4
Drover's Ct *FX* IP11 .... 84 C5
Drovers Wy *BSF* CM23 .... 173 K7 ⊡
The Druce *SAFWS* CB11 .... 87 L7
Drum Fld *RCOLE* CO7 .... 106 F7
Drummond Av
  ROMW/RG RM7 .... 370 E4 ⊡
Drummond Pl *WICKW* SS12 .... 359 M6 ⊡
Drummond Rd *ROMW/RG* RM7 .... 370 D4
The Drummonds *EPP* CM16 .... 304 B2 ⊡
Drury La *BRTR* CM7 .... 155 G8 ⊡
  GTDUN CM6 .... 231 J1
  HSTD CO9 .... 50 B5
Drury Rd *COLS* CO2 .... 162 D6
Dryden Av *SOSN* SS2 .... 21 J2
Dryden Cl *BARK/HLT* IG6 .... 350 A7
  MAL CM9 .... 293 H3 ⊡
Dryden Pl *TIL* RM18 .... 418 C5
Drysdale Av *CHING* E4 .... 325 J8
Dry St *VGE* SS16 .... 394 D1
  VGE SS16 .... 395 H1
Drywoods *RCHLM* CM3 .... 339 L6 ⊡
Duarte Pl *CDH/CHF* RM16 .... 407 G8
Dubarry Cl *SBF/HAD* SS7 .... 380 A7
Du Cane Pl *WIT* CM8 .... 239 H7
Duchess Cl *BSF* CM23 .... 173 J4 ⊡
Duckamere *RIPW* IP8 .... 36 B2
Ducker's La *CHLM/WR* CM1 .... 233 K4
Ducketts Md *HLWW/ROY* CM19 .... 254 C2
  RCFD SS4 .... 364 C1
Ducking Stool Ct *ROM* RM1 .... 370 F4 ⊡
Duck La *EPP* CM16 .... 280 D6
Duck Lees La *PEND* EN3 .... 324 F6
Duckling La *SBW* CM21 .... 227 M1 ⊡
Duck St *GTDUN* CM6 .... 150 A6
  SAFWS CB11 .... 64 F6
Dudbrook Rd *BRW* CM14 .... 331 H2
Duddery Hl *HVHL* CB9 .... 28 A4
Duddery Rd *HVHL* CB9 .... 28 B4
Dudley Av *BAR* EN8 .... 300 E4
Dudley Cl *CDH/CHF* RM16 .... 406 F7
  COLS CO2 .... 163 H7
  RCHLM CM3 .... 265 M2
Dudley Rd *COS* CO15 .... 12 D5
  HARH RM3 .... 352 E7
  K/T/MI CO5 .... 191 M8
  RCOLW CO6 .... 130 A4
Duffield Cl *CDH/CHF* RM16 .... 407 G8
Duffield Rd *CHLM/GWD* CM2 .... 288 E5

Duffries Cl *RCHLM* CM3 .... 234 F4
Dugard Av *COLW* CO3 .... 161 M7
Duggers La *BRTR* CM7 .... 183 H2
Dugmore Av *FOS* CO13 .... 198 D3
Duke Pl *LAIN* SS15 .... 18 A1
Dukes Av *BOC* CM0 .... 320 E8
  CDH/CHF RM16 .... 407 H8
  EPP CM16 .... 303 M7
Dukes Cl *EPP* CM16 .... 281 J7
  FX IP11 .... 85 L7
Dukes Farm Cl *BCAYE* CM12 .... 335 K6
Dukes Farm Rd *BCAYW* CM12 .... 335 J7
Dukes La *CHLM/GWD* CM2 .... 265 G7
  CHONG CM5 .... 260 D5
Dukes Orch *RBSF* CM22 .... 203 G5
Dukes Ride *RCFD* SS4 .... 173 K4
Dukes Rd *BCAYE* CM11 .... 335 K7
  BRTR CM7 .... 155 G6 ⊡
Duke St *CHLM/WR* CM1 .... 16 F7
  HOD EN11 .... 253 H4
  IPSE IP3 .... 3 J7
  RCOLE CO7 .... 220 F5
Dulverton Av *WOS/PRIT* SS0 .... 382 B5
Dulverton Cl *WOS/PRIT* SS0 .... 382 B6
Dulverton Rd *HARH* RM3 .... 352 F7
Dulwich Rd *COS* CO15 .... 224 D7
Dumbarton Av *BAR* EN8 .... 300 E6 ⊡
Dumbarton Cl *IPNE* IP4 .... 38 C3
Dumney La *RCHLM* CM3 .... 181 J8
Dumont Av *RCOS* CO16 .... 248 C3
Dunbar Av *DAGE* RM10 .... 388 B2
Dunbar Gdns *DAGE* RM10 .... 388 B4
Dunbar Pl *WICKW* SS12 .... 359 M6 ⊡
Duncan Av *WICKW* SS12 .... 360 A6 ⊡
Duncan Ri *HSTD* CO9 .... 73 G1 ⊡
Duncan Rd *COLS* CO2 .... 162 C7
Dundee Av *LOS* SS9 .... 399 J1
Dundee Cl *LOS* SS9 .... 399 K1
Dundee Ct *BSDN* SS14 .... 378 A3
Dundee Wy *PEND* EN3 .... 324 F5
Dundonald Dr *LOS* SS9 .... 400 A2
Dunedin Rd *RAIN* RM13 .... 404 A1
Dunfane *BCAYW* CM12 .... 335 K6
Dungannon Cha *SOS* SS1 .... 402 C5
Dungannon Dr *SOS* SS1 .... 402 C5
Dunkellin Gv *SOCK/AV* RM15 .... 406 B4 ⊡
Dunkellin Wy *SOCK/AV* RM15 .... 406 B4
Dunkin Rd *DART* DA1 .... 415 H8
Dunkirk Rd *BOC* CM0 .... 344 D7
Dunlin Cl *MAL* CM9 .... 269 K6 ⊡
  RCHLM CM3 .... 339 L3
Dunlin Ct *K/T/MI* CO5 .... 213 K1
Dunlin Rd *CHTY* IP2 .... 57 M1
Dunlop Cl *CHTY* IP2 .... 37 G5
  TIL RM18 .... 418 A5
Dunmore Rd
  CHLM/GWD CM2 .... 265 H8 ⊡
Dunmow Dr *RAIN* RM13 .... 389 G7
Dunmow Gdns
  RBRW/HUT CM13 .... 374 E6
Dunmow Rd *BRTR* CM7 .... 123 M4
  BRTR CM7 .... 181 K2
  BSF CM23 .... 174 C4
  CHONG CM5 .... 260 A2
  GTDUN CM6 .... 122 B2
  GTDUN CM6 .... 205 G3
  RBSF CM22 .... 175 H4
Dunning Cl *MGTR* CO11 .... 119 H5
  SOCK/AV RM15 .... 406 B4 ⊡
Dunningford Cl *HCH* RM12 .... 389 G4 ⊡
Dunnings La *RBRW/HUT* CM13 .... 392 C1
Dunnock Wy *COLN* CO4 .... 164 B4
Dunoon Cl *BRTR* CM7 .... 155 L7 ⊡
Dunsey Wood Cl *HVHL* CB9 .... 27 L2
Dunstable Rd *HARH* RM3 .... 352 E7
  SLH/COR SS17 .... 394 D8
Dunstalls *HLWW/ROY* CM19 .... 255 H7
Dunster Av *WOS/PRIT* SS0 .... 382 B6
Dunster Cl *ROMW/RG* RM7 .... 370 D2
Dunster Crs *UPMR* RM14 .... 390 B1
Dunster Dr *HVHL* CB9 .... 27 M3
Dunthorne Rd *COLN* CO4 .... 163 M1
Dunthorpe Rd *RCOS* CO16 .... 223 J5
Dunton Rd *RBRW/HUT* CM13 .... 375 L2
  ROM RM1 .... 370 F4
Dupont Cl *RCOS* CO16 .... 223 L5 ⊡
Durants Park Av *PEND* EN3 .... 324 E6
Durants Rd *PEND* EN3 .... 324 E6
Durban Gdns *DAGE* RM10 .... 388 D6 ⊡
Durban La *LAIN* SS15 .... 377 G1 ⊡
The Durdans *VGE* SS16 .... 376 C7
Durham Av *GPK* RM2 .... 371 K4
  WFD IG8 .... 348 C4
Durham Cl *BRTR* CM7 .... 124 B2
  SBW CM21 .... 227 K2 ⊡
Durham Rd *DAGE* RM10 .... 388 D4
  LAIN SS15 .... 375 M5
  RCFD SS4 .... 363 J6
  SOSN SS2 .... 401 L1
Durham Sq *COL* CO1 .... 10 F7
Durham Wy *RAYL* SS6 .... 361 L6
Durley Av *WICKW* SS12 .... 359 G3
Durley Cl *SBF/HAD* SS7 .... 379 M7
Durnell Wy *LOU* IG10 .... 327 H5
Durrants Cl *RAIN* RM13 .... 389 K8
Durrington Cl *VGE* SS16 .... 19 J7
Dury Falls Cl *EMPK* RM11 .... 372 A8 ⊡
Duxford *WICKE* SS11 .... 360 B5
Duxford Cl *HCH* RM12 .... 389 J3
Duxford Rd *SAFWN* CB10 .... 22 A6
Dyer's Rd *COLW* CO3 .... 161 K8
  HSTD CO9 .... 71 M2
  MAL CM9 .... 293 H1
Dyers Wy *HARH* RM3 .... 352 B8
Dyke Crs *CVI* SS8 .... 397 L7
Dykes Cha *MAL* CM9 .... 268 F8
Dyke St *IP* IP1 .... 2 E2
Dymoke Rd *ROM* RM1 .... 371 G7
Dymokes Wy *HOD* EN11 .... 253 H2
Dyneor Gdns *LOS* SS9 .... 399 J2
Dysons Cl *BAR* EN8 .... 300 E5
Dytchleys Rd *BRW* CM14 .... 331 G6

E

Eagle Av *WOTN* CO14 .... 199 L2
Eagle Cl *PEND* EN3 .... 324 D6
  RAIN RM13 .... 389 J5
  WAB EN9 .... 302 B6
Eagle La *BRTR* CM7 .... 155 G6
  BRWN CM15 .... 331 M1
Eagles Cl *FX* IP11 .... 9 K1
Eagles Rd *GRH* DA9 .... 416 C8
Eagle St *IPNE* IP4 .... 3 G5
Eagle Ter *WFD* IG8 .... 348 C8
Eagle Wy *RBRW/HUT* CM13 .. 354 D7
  SBN/FI SS3 .... 402 F3
Eardemont Cl *DART* DA1 .... 414 A8
Earlhams Cl *HAR* CO12 .... 143 G1
Earl Mountbatten Dr
  BCAYW CM12 .... 335 G8 ▣
Earls Cl *BSF* CM23 .... 173 L5
  FX IP11 .... 85 L7
Earls Colne Rd *RCOLW* CO6 .. 159 G1
Earlsfield Dr *CHLM/GWD* CM2 ... 265 G8
Earls Hall Av *SOSN* SS2 .... 382 F8
Earls Hall Rd *RCOS* CO16 ...... 222 F7
Earls Hall Pde *SOSN* SS2 .... 382 F7
Earlsmead *WIT* CM8 .... 212 A8 ▣
Earl's Pth *LOU* IG10 .... 326 D5
Earlswood *SBF/HAD* SS7 .... 379 L7
Earlswood Wy *COLS* CO2 .... 190 E1
Easedale Dr *HCH* RM12 .... 389 J4
Easington Wy *SOCK/AV* RM15 ... 406 B3
East Bay *COL* CO1 .... 11 G8
Eastbourne Gv *WOS/PRIT* SS0 ... 382 D8
East Bridge Rd *RCHLM* CM3 ... 339 L3
Eastbrook Rd *DAGE* RM10 ...... 388 D3
Eastbrook Dr *DAGE* RM10 .... 388 F2
Eastbrook Rd *WAB* EN9 .... 301 M5
Eastbrooks *PIT* SS13 .... 378 C4
Eastbury Av *RCFD* SS4 .... 363 L7
Eastbury Rd *ROMW/RG* RM7 ... 370 E6
Eastby Cl *SAFWS* CB11 .... 66 A3
Eastcheap *RAYL* SS6 .... 361 K7
Eastcliff Av *RAYL* SS6 .... 361 J8
Eastcliff Av *COS* CO15 .... 13 M3
East Cl *RAIN* RM13 .... 404 C2
Eastcote Gv *SOSN* SS2 .... 383 L8
East Crs *CVI* SS8 .... 398 A7
East Dene Dr *HARH* RM3 .... 352 E6
East Dock Rd *HAR* CO12 .... 6 B3
East Dr *SBW* CM21 .... 227 M2
Eastend La *RBSF* CM22 .... 148 C2
East End La *RCOLE* CO7 .... 78 D8
Eastend Rd *BOC* CM0 .... 298 C1
East End Rd *RCOLE* CO7 .... 108 D1
East Entrance *DAGE* RM10 ...... 388 C8
Easterford Rd *K/T/MI* CO5 .... 213 K1
Easterling Cl *HAR* CO12 .... 6 D7
Eastern Av *BAR* EN8 .... 301 G6
  HVHL CB9 .... 28 A3
  SBF/HAD SS7 .... 379 K6
  SOCK/AV RM15 .... 405 K7
  SOSN SS2 .... 383 K8
  WTHK RM20 .... 416 A2
Eastern Av East *GPK* RM2 ...... 371 G4
  ROM RM1 .... 370 E3
Eastern Av West
  ROMW/RG RM7 .... 370 D4
  SOSN SS2 .... 383 H8
Eastern Cl *IPNE* IP4 .... 39 G7 ▣
  SOSN SS2 .... 383 H8
Eastern Crs *CHLM/WR* CM1 ... 264 A6
Eastern Esp *CVI* SS8 .... 413 L1
  SOS SS1 .... 21 L8
Eastern Rd *BOC* CM0 .... 344 D5
  GRAYS RM17 .... 417 L1 ▣
  RAYL SS6 .... 380 C3
  RCOLE CO7 .... 220 F5
  ROM RM1 .... 370 F5
Eastern Wy *GRAYS* RM17 .... 417 H3
Eastfield Gdns *DAGE* RM10 .... 388 B3 ▣
Eastfield Rd *BAR* EN8 .... 301 G4
  BRW CM14 .... 354 E3
  CVI SS8 .... 398 E6
  DAGE RM10 .... 388 B3
  LAIN SS15 .... 377 G1
  PEND EN3 .... 324 E2
East Ga *HLW* CM20 .... 15 L3 ▣
Eastgate *SAFWN* CB10 .... 42 E1
Eastgate St *HAR* CO12 .... 7 K2
East Glebe Dr *RAYL* SS6 .... 361 K8
East Gores Rd *RCOLW* CO6 .... 159 G7
East Hall La *RAIN* RM13 .... 404 C4
East Ham Crs *RBRW/HUT* CM13 .. 355 H5
East Hanningfield Rd
  CHLM/GWD CM2 .... 289 M8
  RCHLM CM3 .... 338 C2
Easthorpe Rd *K/T/MI* CO5 ...... 187 M7
Eastland Ct *FX* IP11 .... 84 E6
East Lawn *IPNE* IP4 .... 38 D3
Eastleigh Rd *SBF/HAD* SS7 .... 397 M3
Eastley *VGE* SS16 .... 18 D9
East Mayne *BSDN* SS14 .... 378 B1
  PIT SS13 .... 378 A4
East Mersea Rd *K/T/MI* CO5 ... 245 L1
East Mill Gn *RIPS/CAP* IP9 .... 78 F5
Easton End *LAIN* SS15 .... 376 B5 ▣
Easton Rd *WIT* CM8 .... 212 B8
Easton Wy *COS* CO15 .... 199 J5
East Pk *HLWE* CM17 .... 227 K8
  SBW CM21 .... 227 M2
East Philbrick Crs *RAYL* SS6 ... 361 K8 ▣
East Rd *BSF* CM23 .... 174 C4
  HLW CM20 .... 227 J7
  K/T/MI CO5 .... 245 L4
  PEND EN3 .... 324 D2
  ROMW/RG RM7 .... 370 C4
East Side *COLN* CO4 .... 105 H7
East Stockwell St *COL* CO1 ...... 10 C7
East St *BRTR* CM7 .... 155 H8
  COL CO1 .... 11 G7
  HAR CO12 .... 7 J6
  LOS SS9 .... 399 M3
  MAL CM9 .... 272 C4
  RCFD SS4 .... 383 G1
  RCOLE CO7 .... 192 C6

RCOLW CO6 .... 186 B1
SAFWN CB10 .... 65 M2
SOSN SS2 .... 20 F1
SUD CO10 .... 4 E5
WTHK RM20 .... 416 F3
East Ter *WOTN* CO14 .... 199 L2
East Thorpe *BSDN* SS14 .... 19 J7
East Thurrock Rd *GRAYS* RM17 ... 417 J3
East Tilbury Rd *SLH/COR* SS17 ... 409 H7
East Vw *CHLM/WR* CM1 .... 287 G2
East View Cl *SAFWN* CB10 ...... 68 A4
East Wy *WAB* EN9 .... 301 L7
Eastways *CVI* SS8 .... 398 A6
  WIT CM8 .... 212 B7
Eastwick Hall La *HLW* CM20 ... 226 B5
Eastwick Rd *HLW* CM20 .... 226 C7
Eastwoodbrook *SOSN* SS2 ...... 382 E5
Eastwoodbury Cl *SOSN* SS2 ... 382 F5
Eastwoodbury La *SOSN* SS2 ... 382 E5
Eastwood Dr *COLN* CO4 .... 135 J8
  RAIN RM13 .... 404 C4
Eastwood La South
  WOS/PRIT SS0 .... 400 C1
Eastwood Old Rd *LOS* SS9 ...... 381 K6
  SBF/HAD SS7 .... 381 H4
Eastwood Park Dr *LOS* SS9 ..... 381 M5
Eastwood Ri *LOS* SS9 .... 381 K4
Eastwood Rd *LOS* SS9 .... 381 L8
  RAYL SS6 .... 380 F2
Eastwood Rd North *LOS* SS9 ... 381 L7
Eaton Cl *BCAYW* CM12 .... 335 H6
  FX IP11 .... 84 D6
Eaton Dr *CRW* RM5 .... 351 J8
Eaton Gdns *FX* IP11 .... 9 H6
Eaton Ms *COLS* CO2 .... 163 J8
Eaton Rd *LOS* SS9 .... 399 K1
  UPMR RM14 .... 390 F1
Eaton Wy *MAL* CM9 .... 240 E4
Ebenezer Cl *WIT* CM8 .... 211 M6
Ebony Cl *COLS* CO2 .... 190 E1
Eccles Rd *CHTY* IP2 .... 57 L1
Eccleston Gdns
  BCAYW CM12 .... 335 H6 ▣
Eckersley Rd *CHLM/WR* CM1 ... 17 J2
Eddy Cl *ROMW/RG* RM7 .... 370 C6
Eden Gn *SOCK/AV* RM15 .... 406 C3
Edenhall Rd *HARH* RM3 .... 352 D6
Eden Rd *HVHL* CB9 .... 28 B4
  IPNE IP4 .... 38 C6 ▣
Edens Cl *BSF* CM23 .... 174 C4
Edenside *FOS* CO13 .... 199 G4
Edgecotts *VGE* SS16 .... 18 A9
Edgefield Av *MGTR* CO11 .... 108 C8
Edgehill Gdns *DAGE* RM10 ...... 388 B3 ▣
Edgeworth Rd *CHTY* IP2 .... 57 M1 ▣
Edgware Rd *COS* CO15 .... 12 C2
Edgworth Rd *SUD* CO10 .... 4 D8
Edinburgh Av *LOS* SS9 .... 399 J1
  SLH/COR SS17 .... 395 G7
Edinburgh Cl *RAYL* SS6 .... 361 J6 ▣
  WIT CM8 .... 239 H3 ▣
Edinburgh Crs *BAR* EN8 .... 300 F5
Edinburgh Gdns *BRTR* CM7 .... 155 J7
Edinburgh Ms *TIL* RM18 .... 418 C6 ▣
Edinburgh Pl *HLW* CM20 .... 227 H7
Edinburgh's Dr *ROMW/RG* RM7 .. 370 D4
Edinburgh Wy *HLW* CM20 .... 227 J7
  HLWE CM17 .... 227 K6 ▣
  PIT SS13 .... 378 C5
Edington Rd *PEND* EN3 .... 324 D4 ▣
Edison Av *HCH* RM12 .... 371 G4
  HCH RM12 .... 371 G8
Edison Cl *BRTR* CM7 .... 183 G2 ▣
  HCH RM12 .... 371 G8
Edison Gdns *COLN* CO4 .... 11 J4
Edison Rd *COS* CO15 .... 224 F5
  PEND EN3 .... 325 G4
Edith Cavell Wy *HVHL* CB9 ...... 48 C5
Edith Cl *CVI* SS8 .... 397 M8
Edith Rd *COS* CO15 .... 12 F8
  CVI SS8 .... 397 L8
  FOS CO13 .... 198 E3
  SOSN SS2 .... 20 E1
Edith Wy *SLH/COR* SS17 .... 395 H6
Edmonton Cl *KESG* IP5 .... 39 H4
Edmonton Rd *KESG* IP5 .... 39 H3
Edmund Cl *HVHL* CB9 .... 28 A3 ▣
Edmund Gn *HSTD* CO9 .... 127 M3 ▣
Edmund Rd *CDH/CHF* RM16 .... 406 E1
  WIT CM8 .... 238 F3 ▣
Edridge Cl *HCH* RM12 .... 389 L4 ▣
Edward Av *RCOLE* CO7 .... 221 G4
Edward Cl *WAB* EN9 .... 302 A5
Edward Dr *CHLM/GWD* CM2 ... 288 D4
Edward Gdns *WICKE* SS11 .... 359 L3
Edward Marke Dr *K/T/MI* CO5 ... 191 J8
Edward Rd *RCOS* CO16 .... 197 G8
  RBRW/HUT CM13 .... 333 M8
Edward St *HAR* CO12 .... 112 F6
Edward Wy *RBRW/HUT* CM13 ... 333 M8
Edwin Cl *RAIN* RM13 .... 404 A1
Edwin Hall Vw *RCHLM* CM3 ... 339 K2
Edwin's Hall Rd *RCHLM* CM3 ... 315 K8
Egbert Gdns *WICKE* SS11 .... 359 L2
Egerton Dr *VGE* SS16 .... 376 M6
Egerton Green Rd *COLS* CO2 ... 162 B8
Egg Hall *EPP* CM16 .... 179 M7
Eggleston Cl *CHTY* IP2 .... 58 A2
Eggshell La *HSTD* CO9 .... 48 F8
Egremont Wy *COLW* CO3 .... 161 M4
Egret Crs *COLN* CO4 .... 164 B3
Ehringshausen Wy *HVHL* CB9 .... 28 B4
Eight Acre La *COLS* CO2 .... 190 D1
Eisel Rd *SOCK/AV* RM15 .... 406 B3 ▣
Eldeland *LAIN* SS15 .... 18 B3
Elder Av *WICKW* SS12 .... 359 J5
Elderbeck Cl *CHESW* EN7 .... 276 B8
Elderberry Cl *VGE* SS16 .... 376 C3 ▣

Elderberry Gdns *WIT* CM8 .... 212 C7 ▣
Elder Fld *BRTR* CM7 .... 182 C6 ▣
Elderfield *HLWE* CM17 .... 227 L7
Elderstep Av *CVI* SS8 .... 398 F8 ▣
Elderton Rd *WOS/PRIT* SS0 ...... 20 A5
Elder Wy *RAIN* RM13 .... 404 E1
  WICKW SS12 .... 359 K5
Eldon Cl *COLN* CO4 .... 163 M2
Eldon Rd *HOD* EN11 .... 253 L7
Eldon St *HOC/HUL* SS5 .... 362 E5
Eldred Av *COLS* CO2 .... 162 C8
Eldred Dr *SUD* CO10 .... 55 K7
Eldred Gdns *UPMR* RM14 .... 372 F7
Eleanor Cha *WICKW* SS12 ...... 359 K4
Eleanor Cl *K/T/MI* CO5 .... 214 E5 ▣
Eleanor Cross Rd *BAR* EN8 ..... 300 F6
Eleanor Rd *BAR* EN8 .... 300 F5
Eleanor Wy *BAR* EN8 .... 301 G6
  BRW CM14 .... 354 E6
Electric Av *WOS/PRIT* SS0 .... 400 D1
Eleven Acre Ri *LOU* IG10 .... 327 C5
Elgar Cl *BKHH* IG9 .... 348 E3
  LAIN SS15 .... 376 E3
  SBF/HAD SS7 .... 379 J5
Elgar Gdns *TIL* RM18 .... 418 B5
Elgin Av *CHLM/WR* CM1 .... 16 E3
  HARH RM3 .... 353 J8
Elgin Rd *BAR* EN8 .... 300 D2
  BROX EN10 .... 277 C4
Elham Dr *PIT* SS13 .... 378 D6
Elianore Rd *COLW* CO3 .... 162 C4
Eliot Wy *MAL* CM9 .... 293 H2
Elizabeth Av *RAYL* SS6 .... 380 D3 ▣
  WIT CM8 .... 239 H4
Elizabeth Cl *COLN* CO4 .... 135 K7
  HOC/HUL SS5 .... 362 F7
  ROMW/RG RM7 .... 370 C1
  SAFWN CB10 .... 66 A1
  TIL RM18 .... 418 C6 ▣
  WAB EN9 .... 277 L3
Elizabeth Dr *EPP* CM16 .... 303 M8
  WICKW SS12 .... 359 J3
Elizabeth Rd *BRWN* CM15 .... 332 C8
  BSF CM23 .... 173 M6
  CDH/CHF RM16 .... 407 C8
  HAR CO12 .... 6 D9
  RAIN RM13 .... 404 C3
Elizabeth Wy *FX* IP11 .... 8 F4
  HLWW/ROY CM19 .... 14 D5
  HSTD CO9 .... 128 F1 ▣
  LAIN SS15 .... 376 E4
  MAL CM9 .... 269 H6
  RCHLM CM3 .... 238 B7 ▣
  RCOLE CO7 .... 164 D8
  RCOLE CO7 .... 221 G5
  SAFWN CB10 .... 66 A1
  SBF/HAD SS7 .... 380 D7 ▣
  SUD CO10 .... 54 D6
The Elkins *ROM* RM1 .... 370 F2
Ellenborough Cl *BSF* CM23 ..... 173 L6
Ellenbrook Cl *LOS* SS9 .... 381 M8
Ellenbrook Rd *CHTY* IP2 .... 57 L2
  RIPW IP8 .... 57 M3
Ellen Wy *BRTR* CM7 .... 182 D4
Ellerman Rd *TIL* RM18 .... 418 A6 ▣
Ellesmere Rd *CVI* SS8 .... 397 M8
Elliot Cl *RCHLM* CM3 .... 340 A5 ▣
Elliots Dr *WOTN* CO14 .... 199 J3
Elliott Gdns *HARH* RM3 .... 371 J1
Elliott St *IP* IP1 .... 2 B3
Ellis Av *RAIN* RM13 .... 404 B3
Ellis Cl *CDH/CHF* RM16 .... 408 E4
Ellis Rd *COLN* CO4 .... 105 G7
  COS CO15 .... 12 F8
  MGTR CO11 .... 139 L3
Ellmore Cl *HARH* RM3 .... 371 J1
Elm Av *MAL* CM9 .... 269 J6
  UPMR RM14 .... 390 C2
Elmbridge *HLWE* CM17 .... 228 A8
Elmbridge Rd *BARK/HLT* IG6 ... 350 B7
Elmbrook Dr *BSF* CM23 .... 173 M7 ▣
Elm Bungalows *BRTR* CM7 ...... 154 E7
Elm Cl *BKHH* IG9 .... 348 E3
  CHLM/GWD CM2 .... 288 F5
  EPP CM16 .... 279 J4
  HSTD CO9 .... 97 L1 ▣
  HVHL CB9 .... 28 A3
  K/T/MI CO5 .... 214 D4
  MGTR CO11 .... 108 E2
  RAYL SS6 .... 361 L8
  RBSF CM22 .... 147 K1
  RBSF CM22 .... 176 D4
  RCOLE CO7 .... 192 D7
  ROMW/RG RM7 .... 370 C1
  SBN/FI SS3 .... 402 F4
  WAB EN9 .... 301 L6
Elm Close Extension
  RBSF CM22 .... 176 D4 ▣
Elm Ct *HVHL* CB9 .... 28 F6
  SAFWS CB11 .... 41 J7
Elm Crs *COLN* CO4 .... 11 M7
Elmcroft Av *RCOLE* CO7 .... 165 G5
Elmcroft La *FX* IP11 .... 85 K6
Elmcroft Rd *IP* IP1 .... 37 L1
Elmdale Dr *MGTR* CO11 .... 108 E7
Elmden Ct *COS* CO15 .... 12 F1
Elmdene Av *HARH* RM3 .... 372 A5
Elmdon Rd *SOCK/AV* RM15 .... 406 B3
Elm Dr *BAR* EN8 .... 276 F8
  HAR CO12 .... 6 F8
  HSTD CO9 .... 129 G2
  RAYL SS6 .... 361 L8
  RCOLE CO7 .... 220 E4
Elmer Ap *SOS* SS1 .... 21 G6
Elmer Av *ABR/ST* RM4 .... 351 M4
  SOS SS1 .... 21 G6
Elmer Cl *RAIN* RM13 .... 389 H6 ▣
Elmer Gdns *RAIN* RM13 .... 389 H6
Elmers La *KESG* IP5 .... 39 L4
Elmfield Cl *COS* CO15 .... 224 F4
Elm Gdns *EPP* CM16 .... 281 J6
England's La *LOU* IG10 .... 327 H4
Englefield Cl *HOC/HUL* SS5 .... 363 H7
Englefields *BOC* CM0 .... 297 M8
Engleric *ROY* SG8 .... 40 E7
Enid Wy *COLN* CO4 .... 162 E1
Ennerdale Av *BRTR* CM7 .... 182 D5

HCH RM12 .... 389 H4
Ennerdale Cl *FX* IP11 .... 85 L6
Ennismore Gdns *SOSN* SS2 ..... 383 H8
Ensign Cl *LOS* SS9 .... 400 B2 ▣
Enterprise Ct *BRTR* CM7 .... 183 J1
Enterprise Wy *WICKW* SS12 ... 360 A5
Enville Wy *COLN* CO4 .... 135 J7
Epping Cl *CHLM/WR* CM1 .... 16 B6
  COS CO15 .... 223 K5
  LOS SS9 .... 381 M4 ▣
  ROMW/RG RM7 .... 370 C3
Epping Gld *CHING* E4 .... 325 K8
Epping La *ABR/ST* RM4 .... 328 C4
Epping New Rd *BKHH* IG9 .... 348 C1
  LOU IG10 .... 326 E2
Epping Rd *CHONG* CM5 .... 282 A4
  EPP CM16 .... 279 J4
  LOU IG10 .... 303 G7
  WAB EN9 .... 255 G8
Epping Wy *CHING* E4 .... 325 K8
  WIT CM8 .... 238 F3
Epsom Cl *RCOS* CO16 .... 223 K5
Epsom Wy *HCH* RM12 .... 390 A3
Erbury Pl *SUD* CO10 .... 31 J3
Erick Av *CHLM/WR* CM1 .... 264 C4
Eric Rd *PIT* SS13 .... 379 G5
Eridge Cl *CHLM/WR* CM1 .... 264 E4 ▣
Eriswell Rd *HVHL* CB9 .... 28 C3
Erith Cl *PUR* RM19 .... 415 H1
Erith Crs *CRW* RM5 .... 351 H8
Erith High St *ERITH* DA8 .... 414 A3
Erle Havard Rd *RCOLW* CO6 ... 133 M7
Ermine Cl *CHESW* EN7 .... 300 C3 ▣
Ermine Side *EN* EN1 .... 324 B7
Ernan Cl *SOCK/AV* RM15 .... 406 B3
Ernan Rd *SOCK/AV* RM15 .... 406 B3
Ernest Rd *EMPK* RM11 .... 371 M6
  RCOLE CO7 .... 192 D2
Ernleigh Rd *IPNE* IP4 .... 38 C5
Erriff Dr *SOCK/AV* RM15 .... 406 B3
Errington Ct *CDH/CHF* RM16 ... 408 C8 ▣
Errington Rd *COLW* CO3 .... 162 B6
Erroll Rd *ROM* RM1 .... 371 G4
Erskine Pl *WICKW* SS12 .... 359 M5 ▣
Erskine Rd *MGTR* CO11 .... 108 E7
Erwarton Wk *RIPS/CAP* IP9 .... 82 E8
Esdaile Gdns *UPMR* RM14 ...... 372 E7
Esdaile La *HOD* EN11 .... 253 H6
Esher Av *ROMW/RG* RM7 .... 370 D6 ▣
Eskley Gdns *SOCK/AV* RM15 ... 406 B3
Esk Wy *ROM* RM1 .... 351 M8
Esmond Cl *RAIN* RM13 .... 389 J6 ▣
Esplanade *FOS* CO13 .... 199 G8
Esplanade Gdns *WOS/PRIT* SS0 ... 400 C2
The Esplanade *COS* CO15 .... 225 H5
  HOC/HUL SS5 .... 339 K8
  RCHLM CM3 .... 318 F2
Essex Av *CHLM/WR* CM1 .... 264 B4
  COS CO15 .... 249 M5
  SUD CO10 .... 4 F1
Essex Cl *CVI* SS8 .... 413 H1
  LAIN SS15 .... 376 C5
  RAYL SS6 .... 381 G2
  ROMW/RG RM7 .... 370 C4
Essex Gdns *EMPK* RM11 .... 372 B5
  LOS SS9 .... 381 M7
  SLH/COR SS17 .... 409 H7
Essex Hall Rd *COL* CO1 .... 10 A3
Essex HI *SAFWS* CB11 .... 41 H8
Essex Regiment Wy
  RCHLM CM3 .... 235 H1
Essex Rd *BOC* CM0 .... 344 D6
  BRTR CM7 .... 155 J7 ▣
  CVI SS8 .... 398 C7
  DAGE RM10 .... 388 D4
  HOD EN11 .... 253 J5
  MAL CM9 .... 293 G2
  ROMW/RG RM7 .... 370 C4
  WTHK RM20 .... 416 B3
Essex St *SOSN* SS2 .... 21 H5
Essex Wy *BRTR* CM7 .... 184 A7
  CHONG CM5 .... 260 F8
  CHONG CM5 .... 261 J2
  COLN CO4 .... 106 B3
  EPP CM16 .... 304 B4
  HAR CO12 .... 143 K1
  IPSE IP3 .... 59 M2
  MGTR CO11 .... 109 G8
  RBRW/HUT CM13 .... 354 D7
  RCOLW CO6 .... 104 E6
  RCOLW CO6 .... 131 M8
  SBF/HAD SS7 .... 397 M2
  WIT CM8 .... 184 D5
Essex Yeomanry Wy *COLW* CO3 ... 161 J4
Estate Rd *SBF/HAD* SS7 .... 381 G8
Estella Md *CHLM/WR* CM1 ...... 263 M4
Estfeld Cl *HOD* EN11 .... 253 J2 ▣
Estuary Cl *COLN* CO4 .... 134 F7
Estuary Crs *COS* CO15 .... 12 D6
  RIPS/CAP IP9 .... 113 J3
Estuary Dr *FX* IP11 .... 85 L6
Estuary Gdns *SBN/FI* SS3 .... 403 K1
Estuary Ms *MAL* CM9 .... 272 E1 ▣
Estuary Park Rd *K/T/MI* CO5 ... 245 M5
Estuary Rd *RIPS/CAP* IP9 .... 113 H3
Ethelburga Rd *HARH* RM3 .... 372 A1
Ethelred Gdns *WICKE* SS11 ..... 359 M2
Ethel Rd *RAYL* SS6 .... 381 J3
Etheridge Rd *LOU* IG10 .... 327 K5
Eton Cl *CVI* SS8 .... 398 C6
Eton Rd *COS* CO15 .... 13 G4
  FOS CO13 .... 199 H6
Eton Wk *SBN/FI* SS3 .... 402 F2
Etton Wy *DART* DA1 .... 414 A8
Etton Cl *HCH* RM12 .... 389 M1
Euclid Wy *WTHK* RM20 .... 416 A1
Eudo Rd *COLS* CO2 .... 162 D7
Eugene Cl *GPK* RM2 .... 371 G4
Europa Pl *HAR* CO12 .... 6 B6
Europa Wy *HAR* CO12 .... 6 B6
Eustace Rd *IP* IP1 .... 36 F3
Euston Av *IPNE* IP4 .... 39 G5
Euston Wy *IP* IP1 .... 8 D2
Evabrook Cl *CHTY* IP2 .... 57 M2 ▣
Evansdale *RAIN* RM13 .... 404 A1 ▣
Evelyn Rd *HOC/HUL* SS5 .... 362 F6
  RCHLM CM3 .... 181 L7
Evelyn Sharp Cl *GPK* RM2 .... 371 L3 ▣

Evelyn Wood Rd BRTR CM7 ...... 183 M5
Everard Rd BSDN SS14 ...... 378 A3
Everest RAYL SS6 ...... 361 L6
Everest Ri BCAYW CM12 ...... 357 G5
Everest Wy MAL CM9 ...... 269 J6
Evergreen Dr RCOLE CO7 ...... 135 L7
Everitt Rd SAFWN CB10 ...... 66 A1
Everitt Wy HSTD CO9 ...... 97 M1
Eversleigh Gdns UPMR RM14 ..... 372 E6
Eversley Rd PIT SS13 ...... 378 E6
  SBF/HAD SS7 ...... 379 J4
Everton Crs IP IP1 ...... 37 G2
Eves Cnr RCHLM CM3 ...... 290 F4
Eves Ct HAR CO12 ...... 142 E2
Eves Crs CHLM/WR CM1 ...... 264 B6
Evesham Cl CHTY IP2 ...... 58 B1
Ewan Cl COLW CO3 ...... 161 K5
  LOS SS9 ...... 381 H8
Ewanrigg Ter WFD IG8 ...... 348 D6
Ewan Rd HARH RM3 ...... 371 L2
Ewan Wy COLW CO3 ...... 161 K5
  SBF/HAD SS7 ...... 381 H8
Ewell Hall Cha K/T/MI CO5 ...... 213 K3
Exchange St ROM RM1 ...... 370 F5
Exeter Cl BRTR CM7 ...... 155 J6
  BSDN SS14 ...... 378 A4
  RCOLW CO6 ...... 134 C4
  SBN/FI SS3 ...... 403 G2
Exeter Dr COL CO1 ...... 10 F7
Exeter Rd CHLM/WR CM1 ...... 264 F6
  DAGE RM10 ...... 388 C5
  FX IP11 ...... 85 G8
  IPSE IP3 ...... 38 C7
  PEND EN3 ...... 324 E5
Exford Av WOS/PRIT SS0 ...... 382 B6
Exhibition La SBN/FI SS3 ...... 385 G7
Exley Cl ING CM4 ...... 310 C7
Exmoor Cl CHLM/WR CM1 ...... 287 J2
Exmoor Rd FX IP11 ...... 85 G7
Exmouth Dr RAYL SS6 ...... 361 L6
Exmouth Rd GRAYS RM17 ...... 417 J3
Eyhurst Av HCH RM12 ...... 389 H2
Eynesham Wy PIT SS13 ...... 378 B2
Eyre Cl GPK RM2 ...... 371 J4

F

Fabians Cl RCOLW CO6 ...... 158 B8
Factory Hl K/T/MI CO5 ...... 214 F8
Factory La MGTR CO11 ...... 108 D4
Factory La East HSTD CO9 ...... 128 F2
Factory La West HSTD CO9 ...... 128 F2
Fagbury Rd FX IP11 ...... 114 B1
Faggotters La HLWE CM17 ...... 257 M2
Fagus Av RAIN RM13 ...... 404 E1
Fairbairn Rd KESG IP5 ...... 39 L4
Fairburn Cl SOS SS1 ...... 21 K5
Fair Cl RCOLE CO7 ...... 221 H5
Fairclough Av RCOS CO16 ...... 223 J8
Faircross Av CRW RM5 ...... 351 L8
Fairfax Av PIT SS13 ...... 378 D3
Fairfax Dr WOS/PRIT SS0 ...... 400 D1
Fairfax Md CHLM/GWD CM2 ...... 289 G1
Fairfax Rd COLS CO2 ...... 163 C5
  GRAYS RM17 ...... 417 J2
  TIL RM18 ...... 418 A5
Fairfield ING CM4 ...... 310 D7
  SBN/FI SS3 ...... 385 H8
Fairfield Av CDH/CHF RM16 ...... 407 K6
  FX IP11 ...... 85 H8
  UPMR RM14 ...... 390 D2
Fairfield Cl HCH RM12 ...... 371 H8
  PEND EN3 ...... 324 F6
Fairfield Crs LOS SS9 ...... 382 A4
Fairfield Dr BROX EN10 ...... 277 G4
Fairfield Gdns COLN CO4 ...... 11 J6
  LOS SS9 ...... 381 M4
Fairfield Ri BCAYW CM12 ...... 357 G3
Fairfield Rd BRTR CM7 ...... 183 G1
  BRW CM14 ...... 354 D4
  CHLM/WR CM1 ...... 16 F2
  CHONG CM5 ...... 307 G1
  COS CO15 ...... 12 F5
  EPP CM16 ...... 304 C1
  HOD EN11 ...... 253 H3
  IPSE IP3 ...... 59 H1
  LOS SS9 ...... 381 M4
  WFD IG8 ...... 348 B7
Fairford Cl HARH RM3 ...... 353 J7
Fairford Wy HARH RM3 ...... 353 J7
Fairham Av SOCK/AV RM15 ...... 406 B5
Fairhaven Av K/T/MI CO5 ...... 245 J5
Fairhead Rd North COLN CO4 ...... 11 J5
Fairhead Rd South COLN CO4 ...... 11 J5
Fairholme Av GPK RM2 ...... 371 H5
Fairholme Gdns UPMR RM14 ...... 373 G7
Fairkytes Av EMPK RM11 ...... 371 L8
Fairland Cl RAYL SS6 ...... 361 M6
Fairlands Av BKHH IG9 ...... 348 B3
Fairlawn Dr WFD IG8 ...... 348 B8
Fairlawn Gdns SOSN SS2 ...... 382 F6
Fairlawns Cl EMPK RM11 ...... 372 A7
Fairleads RCHLM CM3 ...... 291 G3
Fair Leas SAFWN CB10 ...... 43 M8
Fairleigh Av PIT SS13 ...... 378 E6
Fairleigh Dr LOS SS9 ...... 399 L2
Fairleigh Rd PIT SS13 ...... 378 E6
Fairley Wy CHESW EN7 ...... 276 C8
Fairlight Av WFD IG8 ...... 348 B7
Fairlight Rd SBF/HAD SS7 ...... 380 D8
Fairlop Av CVI SS8 ...... 398 B7
Fairlop Cl COS CO15 ...... 224 A3
  HCH RM12 ...... 389 J3
Fairlop Gdns BARK/HLT IG6 ...... 349 K8
  BSDN SS14 ...... 19 J1
Fair Md BSDN SS14 ...... 19 J1
Fairmead RAYL SS6 ...... 361 J7
Fairmead Av SBF/HAD SS7 ...... 380 F6
  WOS/PRIT SS0 ...... 400 D1
Fairmead Rd LOU IG10 ...... 326 C6
Fairmeads LOU IG10 ...... 327 J4
Fairoak Gdns ROM RM1 ...... 370 F2
Fairoaks Gv PEND EN3 ...... 324 E1
Fairstead Hall Rd RCHLM CM3 ...... 210 B5
Fairstead Rd RCHLM CM3 ...... 210 D5

Fairview BCAYW CM12 ...... 357 H2
  CVI SS8 ...... 398 A6
  ERITH DA8 ...... 414 A4
Fairview Av RAIN RM13 ...... 389 L8
  RBRW/HUT RM13 ...... 355 M1
  SLH/COR SS17 ...... 409 K2
Fairview Cha SLH/COR SS17 ...... 409 K3
  SBF/HAD SS7 ...... 379 K4
Fairview Crs SBF/HAD SS7 ...... 379 K4
Fairview Dr CHIG IG7 ...... 349 M6
  WOS/PRIT SS0 ...... 382 D7
Fairview Gdns LOS SS9 ...... 399 K1
Fairview Rd BSDN SS14 ...... 19 L6
  BSDN SS14 ...... 377 M5
  CHIG IG7 ...... 349 M5
Fairway BSF CM23 ...... 174 D5
  CDH/CHF RM16 ...... 407 J6
  CHLM/GWD CM2 ...... 288 E4
  SBW CM21 ...... 228 A1
  WFD IG8 ...... 348 D6
  WICKW SS12 ...... 359 M8
Fairway Dr BOC CM0 ...... 344 C6
Fairway Gdns LOS SS9 ...... 381 K6
Fairway Gardens Cl LOS SS9 ...... 381 K6
  COLN CO4 ...... 134 C8
The Fairways IPNE IP4 ...... 38 F6
  RCHLM CM3 ...... 317 C6
The Fairway HLWS CM18 ...... 256 A6
  LOS SS9 ...... 381 K6
  SBF/HAD SS7 ...... 379 K4
  UPMR RM14 ...... 372 D7
Fairycroft Rd SAFWN CB10 ...... 65 L1
Fairy Hall La BRTR CM7 ...... 182 B2
Falbro Crs SBF/HAD SS7 ...... 380 E8
Falbro Cresent SBF/HAD SS7 ...... 380 E7
Falcon Av HVHL CB9 ...... 28 D3
  LOS SS9 ...... 381 M6
  RAYL SS6 ...... 361 J8
  SBW CM21 ...... 227 K2
Falcon Crs COL CO1 ...... 163 J6
  PEND EN3 ...... 324 E7
Falcon St FX IP11 ...... 84 F7
  IP IP1 ...... 2 E5
Falcon Flds MAL CM9 ...... 293 G3
Falcon Ms MAL CM9 ...... 293 G3
Falcon Pk BSDN SS14 ...... 18 D1
Falcon Rd BOC CM0 ...... 320 D7
  PEND EN3 ...... 324 E7
Falconer Rd BARK/HLT IG6 ...... 350 C6
  HVHL CB9 ...... 28 B1
Falconers Pk SBW CM21 ...... 227 L2
Falconer St BSF CM23 ...... 173 K6
Falcon Yd RCOLE CO7 ...... 192 C3
Fal Dr WIT CM8 ...... 238 F1
Falkenham End BSDN SS14 ...... 19 J3
Falkenham Ri BSDN SS14 ...... 19 J3
Falkenham Rw BSDN SS14 ...... 19 J3
Falkirk Cl EMPK RM11 ...... 372 B8
Falkland Cl RCHLM CM3 ...... 338 F7
Falkland Dr MGTR CO11 ...... 108 E7
Falklands Rd BOC CM0 ...... 344 C6
  HVHL CB9 ...... 28 B1
Falkner Cl ING CM4 ...... 312 A8
Fallow Cl CHIG IG7 ...... 350 A6
Fallowden La SAFWN CB10 ...... 44 F3
Fallowfield SBN/FI SS3 ...... 402 E3
Fallowfield Cl HVHL CB9 ...... 28 C3
Fallowfield Cl COLS CO2 ...... 190 D1
Fallow Flds LOU IG10 ...... 348 E1
The Fallows CVI SS8 ...... 398 A5
Falmouth Cl KESG IP5 ...... 39 J5
Falmouth Rd CHLM/WR CM1 ...... 264 F6
Falstones LAIN SS15 ...... 376 E5
Fambridge Cha WIT CM8 ...... 211 G1
Fambridge Dr MAL CM9 ...... 293 H2
Fambridge Dr WICKW SS12 ...... 359 M5
Fambridge Rd BCTR RM8 ...... 370 B8
  MAL CM9 ...... 293 G1
  RCFD SS4 ...... 341 J8
  RCHLM CM3 ...... 317 K7
  RCHLM CM3 ...... 343 G1
Fane Rd SBF/HAD SS7 ...... 379 L3
Fanns Ri PUR RM19 ...... 415 H1
Fanny's La RCOS CO16 ...... 222 E1
Fanshawe Crs EMPK RM11 ...... 371 L6
Fanshawe Rd CDH/CHF RM16 ...... 408 B8
Fanton Av WICKW SS12 ...... 360 A8
Fanton Cha WICKE SS11 ...... 360 B5
Fanton Gdns WICKE SS11 ...... 360 B5
Fanton Wk WICKE SS11 ...... 360 C4
Faraday Cl BRTR CM7 ...... 183 G2
  COS CO15 ...... 224 B3
Faraday Rd IPSE IP3 ...... 3 M6
  LOS SS9 ...... 381 K5
Faringdon Av HARH RM3 ...... 371 K1
Farmadine Crs SAFWN CB11 ...... 65 M2
Farmadine Gv SAFWS CB11 ...... 65 M2
Farmbridge End Rd CHLM/WR CM1 ...... 232 E8
Farm Cl BAR EN8 ...... 300 D2
  BKHH IG9 ...... 348 D4
  DAGE RM10 ...... 388 D6
  RBRW/HUT RM13 ...... 355 K1
Farm Crs RCHLM CM3 ...... 338 F7
Farm End E4 ...... 325 M7
Farmer Ct WAB EN9 ...... 302 B5
Farmers Wy RCOS CO16 ...... 223 J8
Farmfield Rd RCOLW CO6 ...... 159 J2
Farm Hill Rd WAB EN9 ...... 301 L6
Farmhouse Cl BROX EN10 ...... 277 G5
Farm La WTHK RM20 ...... 416 F3
Farmleigh Av COS CO15 ...... 224 A3
Farm Pl DART DA1 ...... 414 B8
Farm Rd CDH/CHF RM16 ...... 408 A7
  CVI SS8 ...... 398 C6
  HAR CO12 ...... 141 K7
  RAIN RM13 ...... 404 D2
  TIL RM18 ...... 419 K1
Farm Vw RAYL SS6 ...... 361 L6
Farm Wk RCOLE CO7 ...... 220 F3
Farm Wy BKHH IG9 ...... 348 D5

  HCH RM12 ...... 389 J3
  SBF/HAD SS7 ...... 380 C5
Farnes Av WICKW SS12 ...... 359 K4
Farnes Dr GPK RM2 ...... 371 K2
Farnham Cl SBW CM21 ...... 227 K2
Farnham Rd HARH RM3 ...... 352 E6
Farnol Rd DART DA1 ...... 415 H8
Farriers Dr BCAYW CM12 ...... 335 H6
Farriers End BROX EN10 ...... 277 G6
  COLW CO3 ...... 161 L6
Farriers Wy SOSN SS2 ...... 383 G6
Farrington Service Rd SOS SS1 ... 21 G6
  COL CO1 ...... 163 K5
Farrow Gdns CDH/CHF RM16 ...... 407 J6
Farthingale La WAB EN9 ...... 302 B6
Farthing Cl BRTR CM7 ...... 155 L7
Farthing Rd IP IP1 ...... 36 D4
Farthings Went RIPS/CAP IP9 ... 78 C1
Fastnet SOSN SS2 ...... 382 B4
Fastnet Cl HVHL CB9 ...... 28 C3
Faulkbourne Rd WIT CM8 ...... 211 K7
Faulkeners Wy FX IP11 ...... 84 D5
Fauners VGE SS16 ...... 18 E8
Faverolle Gn BAR EN8 ...... 276 E8
Faversham Cl CHIG IG7 ...... 350 C3
Fawkner Cl CHLM/GWD CM2 ...... 289 G1
Fawley Cl IPNE IP4 ...... 38 D4
Fawn Rd CHIG IG7 ...... 350 A6
Fawters Cl RBRW/HUT RM13 ...... 333 L8
Faymore Gdns SOCK/AV RM15 ...... 406 B4
Featherby Wy RCFD SS4 ...... 383 H2
Feathers Fld FX IP11 ...... 84 E8
Feathers Hl RBSF CM22 ...... 202 F5
Feedhams Cl RCOLE CO7 ...... 164 D8
Feenan Hwy TIL RM18 ...... 418 C4
Feering Dr BSDN SS14 ...... 378 A4
Feering Gn BSDN SS14 ...... 378 A6
Feering Hl K/T/MI CO5 ...... 186 E8
Feering Rd BCAYE CM11 ...... 357 K1
Feering Rw BSDN SS14 ...... 378 A6
Felaw St CHTY IP2 ...... 3 G8
Felhurst Crs DAGE RM10 ...... 388 D3
Felicia Wy CDH/CHF RM16 ...... 418 C1
Felipe Rd CDH/CHF RM16 ...... 406 D8
Felix Cl KESG IP5 ...... 39 J4
Felix Rd FX IP11 ...... 115 J1
  IPSE IP3 ...... 59 K1
Felixstowe Cl RCOS CO16 ...... 223 H7
Felixstowe Rd IPSE IP3 ...... 38 D7
  KIR/NAC IP10 ...... 60 B3
Fellbrigg Av KESG IP5 ...... 39 G5
Fell Christy CHLM/WR CM1 ...... 264 C6
Fell Rd HSTD CO9 ...... 49 J3
Felmongers HLW CM20 ...... 256 C1
Felmores PIT SS13 ...... 378 B3
Fels Cl DAGE RM10 ...... 388 C2
Fels Farm Av DAGE RM10 ...... 388 D2
Felstead Cl COLS CO2 ...... 191 H3
  RBRW/HUT RM13 ...... 333 K8
  SBF/HAD SS7 ...... 379 L7
Felstead Rd BAR EN8 ...... 300 F4
  CRW RM5 ...... 351 L4
  LOU IG10 ...... 348 F1
  SBF/HAD SS7 ...... 379 L7
Felsted Rd BCAYE CM11 ...... 357 K1
Felton Cl BROX EN10 ...... 277 G5
Fen Br RCOLE CO7 ...... 107 J3
Fenbridge La RCOLE CO7 ...... 107 J3
Fencepiece Rd BARK/HLT IG6 ...... 349 K7
  CHIG IG7 ...... 349 K7
Fen Cl BRWN CM15 ...... 333 K6
  UPMR RM14 ...... 393 G4
Fengates Rd RCHLM CM3 ...... 339 K3
Fen La CDH/CHF RM16 ...... 408 A2
  RCOLE CO7 ...... 136 E2
Fenn Cl SLH/COR SS17 ...... 395 K6
Fen Meadow FX IP11 ...... 84 D5
Fenn Cl RCHLM CM3 ...... 339 K3
  RCOLE CO7 ...... 166 B8
Fennell Cl K/T/MI CO5 ...... 214 D6
Fennells HLWW/ROY CM19 ...... 255 J8
Fennels Cl HVHL CB9 ...... 28 B4
Fenner Rd CDH/CHF RM16 ...... 406 D8
Fenners Wy PIT SS13 ...... 378 B1
Fennes Rd BRTR CM7 ...... 127 G7
  BRTR CM7 ...... 155 G2
Fennfields Rd RCHLM CM3 ...... 339 J3
Fenton Av HVHL CB9 ...... 28 C3
Fentiman Wy EMPK RM11 ...... 371 M8
Fenton Gra EMPK RM11 ...... 256 D4
Fenton Rd HVHL CB9 ...... 28 C3
Fenton Wy KESG IP5 ...... 39 K4
Fen Vw RIPW IP8 ...... 56 F3
Fenwick Wy CVI SS8 ...... 398 B5
Ferguson Av GPK RM2 ...... 371 K2
Ferguson Cl SAFWS CB11 ...... 66 B1
Ferguson Ct GPK RM2 ...... 371 L2
Fermoy Rd SOS SS1 ...... 402 B4
Fernbank BCAYW CM12 ...... 357 G2
  BKHH IG9 ...... 348 C2
Fernbank Av HCH RM12 ...... 389 K3
Fernbrook Av SOS SS1 ...... 401 L3
Fern Cl BCAYW CM12 ...... 335 J5
  BROX EN10 ...... 277 G3
  ERITH DA8 ...... 414 C5
Ferndale Cl COS CO15 ...... 224 A5
  LAIN SS15 ...... 376 C5
Ferndale Crs CVI SS8 ...... 398 C6
Ferndale Rd CRW RM5 ...... 370 D2
  HAR CO12 ...... 7 K5
  PEND EN3 ...... 324 A7
  RAYL SS6 ...... 361 L5
  SOSN SS2 ...... 21 L2
Fernden Wy ROMW/RG RM7 ...... 370 C6
Ferndown EMPK RM11 ...... 372 B6
Ferndown Rd FOS CO13 ...... 198 F6
  FX IP11 ...... 85 K7
Ferndown Wy RCHLM CM3 ...... 238 C7
Fern Gv HVHL CB9 ...... 37 M3
Fernhall La WAB EN9 ...... 302 E3

Fernhayes Cl CHTY IP2 ...... 37 H8
Fernhill HLWS CM18 ...... 255 M7
Fern Hl VGE SS16 ...... 376 D7
Fern Hill La HLWS CM18 ...... 256 D7
Fernlea COLN CO4 ...... 162 D1
Fernlea Rd BOC CM0 ...... 344 C6
  HAR CO12 ...... 7 H9
  SBF/HAD SS7 ...... 379 M8
Ferns Cl LOS SS9 ...... 400 B2
Fernside BKHH IG9 ...... 348 C2
Fernside Cl SLH/COR SS17 ...... 395 J6
Fern Wk VGE SS16 ...... 375 M7
Fern Wy COS CO15 ...... 250 A4
Fernwood SBF/HAD SS7 ...... 380 F7
Fernwood Av COS CO15 ...... 225 G6
Ferrers Rd RCHLM CM3 ...... 339 K3
Ferris Av RCHLM CM3 ...... 317 G6
Ferro Rd RAIN RM13 ...... 404 B2
Ferry La FX IP11 ...... 8 E3
  RAIN RM13 ...... 404 A3
Ferrymead CVI SS8 ...... 398 A6
Ferry Rd BOC CM0 ...... 343 M6
  FX IP11 ...... 85 K6
  HOC/HUL SS5 ...... 361 L1
  K/T/MI CO5 ...... 192 C5
  RCHLM CM3 ...... 341 H4
  SBF/HAD SS7 ...... 397 L3
  TIL RM18 ...... 418 B6
Feryby Rd CDH/CHF RM16 ...... 408 C8
Fesants Cft HLW CM20 ...... 227 J8
Festival Cl ERITH DA8 ...... 414 A4
Festival Gdns MAL CM9 ...... 242 E7
Festival Link BSDN SS14 ...... 19 G1
Festival Wy BSDN SS14 ...... 19 H1
Fetherston Rd SLH/COR SS17 ... 409 L1
Feverills Rd RCOS CO16 ...... 196 D7
Fiat Av COS CO15 ...... 249 L5
Fiddlers Cl GRH DA9 ...... 416 C8
Fiddlers Folly RCOLW CO6 ...... 160 F2
Fiddlers Hl COLW CO3 ...... 160 F1
Field Cl ABR/ST RM4 ...... 328 C5
  BKHH IG9 ...... 348 D4
  CBE/LIN CB1 ...... 24 C1
The Fielders CVI SS8 ...... 413 C1
Fieldfare BCAYW CM12 ...... 357 K3
Field Gdns CHONG CM5 ...... 306 F6
Field Gate La RBSF CM22 ...... 119 H7
Fielding Av TIL RM18 ...... 418 C5
Fieldings Rd BAR EN8 ...... 301 C1
Fielding Wy RBRW/HUT RM13 ...... 333 K8
Field Kiln BRWN CM15 ...... 308 E7
Field Rd SOCK/AV RM15 ...... 405 K6
Fields Cl RCOS CO16 ...... 196 A4
Fields Farm Rd COLS CO2 ...... 190 C7
Field Vw KIR/NAC IP10 ...... 61 H3
Field View Dr MAL CM9 ...... 241 K6
Fieldway CDH/CHF RM16 ...... 407 H6
  PIT SS13 ...... 378 C7
  WICKW SS12 ...... 359 L8
Field Wy HOD EN11 ...... 253 J1
  RCOLE CO7 ...... 192 D1
Fife Rd IPNE IP4 ...... 38 C2
Fifth Av CHLM/WR CM1 ...... 264 C5
  CVI SS8 ...... 397 M7
  FOS CO13 ...... 198 F6
  HSTD CO9 ...... 129 J2
  WICKE SS11 ...... 360 B5
  WTHK RM20 ...... 416 B3
Fifth Avenue Allende Av HLW CM20 ...... 15 L2
Filey Rd BOC CM0 ...... 344 B1
Fillebrook Wy LOS SS9 ...... 400 B1
Finbars Wk IPNE IP4 ...... 3 L5
Finborough Cl KESG IP5 ...... 39 G5
Fincham's Cl CBE/LIN CB1 ...... 24 E1
Finchdale COS CO15 ...... 224 A5
Finch Dr RCOLE CO7 ...... 194 E2
Finches Cl SLH/COR SS17 ...... 395 K6
The Finches SBF/HAD SS7 ...... 380 B5
Finchfield RAYL SS6 ...... 380 E2
Finch Hl SUD CO10 ...... 54 B4
Finchingfield Wy COLS CO2 ...... 191 H3
  WICKW SS12 ...... 359 K6
Finchland Vw RCHLM CM3 ...... 339 J3
Finchley Av CHLM/GWD CM2 ...... 16 F8
Finchley Rd GRAYS RM17 ...... 417 J3
  IPNE IP4 ...... 3 J3
  WOS/PRIT SS0 ...... 20 A5
Finchmoor HLWS CM18 ...... 255 L6
Finch's WIT CM8 ...... 240 A5
Findley Cl RIPS/CAP IP9 ...... 110 A1
Fine Cl RCOS CO16 ...... 12 B2
Fingringhoe Rd COLS CO2 ...... 191 L1
  K/T/MI CO5 ...... 191 J8
Fingrith Hall La ING CM4 ...... 284 F7
Finham Cl COLN CO4 ...... 164 A4
Finney's Drift KIR/NAC IP10 ...... 60 D6
Finucane Gdns RAIN RM13 ...... 389 H5
Firbank Rd CRW RM5 ...... 351 J4
Fircroft Rd IP IP1 ...... 37 H1
Firebronds Rd RIPS/CAP IP9 ...... 80 E6
Firecrest Rd CHLM/GWD CM2 ... 288 D6
Firfield Rd SBF/HAD SS7 ...... 380 D5
Firham Park Av HARH RM3 ...... 353 H8
Firlands BSF CM23 ...... 173 H5
The Firle VGE SS16 ...... 376 D8
Firle Wk COLS CO2 ...... 191 H1
Firmans Cl CVI SS8 ...... 398 C6
Firmins Ct RCOLW CO6 ...... 133 L7
First Av BCAYW CM12 ...... 356 F4
  BRWN CM15 ...... 308 D6
  CHLM/WR CM1 ...... 264 C6

  COS CO15 ...... 13 M4
  CVI SS8 ...... 397 L8
  DAGE RM10 ...... 388 C8
  EN EN1 ...... 324 A7
  FOS CO13 ...... 198 F7
  HAR CO12 ...... 7 H9
  HOC/HUL SS5 ...... 362 A2
  HSTD CO9 ...... 129 J2
  RCOS CO16 ...... 196 A2
  RCOS CO16 ...... 249 K5
  SLH/COR SS17 ...... 394 E8
  SUD CO10 ...... 5 G3
  WICKE SS11 ...... 360 B5
  WOS/PRIT SS0 ...... 400 C3
  WOTN CO14 ...... 171 L8
  WTHK RM20 ...... 416 B3
First Avenue Mandela Av HLW CM20 ...... 15 L2
  HLWE CM17 ...... 227 J8
The Firs BRWN CM15 ...... 332 B8
  CDH/CHF RM16 ...... 407 K6
  CVI SS8 ...... 398 A6
Firstore Dr COLW CO3 ...... 161 M4
Firs Wk WFD IG8 ...... 348 B6
Fir Tree Cl COLN CO4 ...... 135 J7
  ROM RM1 ...... 370 E3
Fir Tree Hl RIPS/CAP IP9 ...... 80 F6
Fir Tree La RCHLM CM3 ...... 290 F2
Fir Tree Ri CHLM/GWD CM2 ...... 288 B5
  RIPW IP8 ...... 57 K1
Fir Trees ABR/ST RM4 ...... 328 C5
Fir Tree Wk MAL CM9 ...... 269 K6
Fir Wy COS CO15 ...... 250 B5
Firwood's Rd HSTD CO9 ...... 128 F3
Fishbane Cl IPSE IP3 ...... 59 H3
Fisher Cl HVHL CB9 ...... 28 E4
Fishers Cl BAR EN8 ...... 301 H6
Fisher's La RCOLE CO7 ...... 78 C3
Fisher Wy BRTR CM7 ...... 155 K7
Fishmarket St GTDUN CM6 ...... 122 A1
Fish Pond Hl RIPS/CAP IP9 ...... 81 K8
Fishponds Hl RCOLW CO6 ...... 103 M6
Fishponds La RIPS/CAP IP9 ...... 80 F6
Fish St MAL CM9 ...... 270 F5
Fisin Wk COLW CO3 ...... 161 M8
Fitches Crs MAL CM9 ...... 293 J2
Fitzgerald Cl MGTR CO11 ...... 108 C7
Fitzgerald Rd RIPW IP8 ...... 36 B2
Fitzgilbert Cl COLS CO2 ...... 162 D7
Fitzilian Av HARH RM3 ...... 372 A1
Fitzmaurice Rd IPSE IP3 ...... 38 C8
Fitzpiers SAFWN CB10 ...... 65 M1
Fitzroy Cl BCAYW CM12 ...... 335 H4
Fitzroy St IP IP1 ...... 2 F3
Fitzwalter La RCHLM CM3 ...... 290 E5
Fitzwalter Pl CHLM/WR CM1 ...... 16 A1
Fitzwalter Rd COLW CO3 ...... 162 C5
  RCHLM CM3 ...... 266 A3
Fitzwarren SBN/FI SS3 ...... 402 E2
Fitzwilliam Cl CHTY IP2 ...... 58 A1
Fitzwilliam Ct COLW CO3 ...... 162 C4
  SBF/HAD SS7 ...... 398 D1
Fitzwilliams Ct HLWE CM17 ...... 227 M7
Five Acres HLWS CM18 ...... 255 M6
  RCHLM CM3 ...... 291 G8
  RCHLM CM3 ...... 315 G1
  STSD CM24 ...... 146 F3
  WOTN CO14 ...... 199 J3
Fiveash La BRTR CM7 ...... 184 F2
Five Elms Rd DAGW RM9 ...... 388 C4
Five Oaks SBF/HAD SS7 ...... 380 C7
Five Oaks La CHIG IG7 ...... 350 F7
Flag Hl RCOS CO16 ...... 222 A2
Flagstaff Cl WAB EN9 ...... 301 J5
Flagstaff Rd COLS CO2 ...... 163 G5
  WAB EN9 ...... 301 J4
Flail Cl RCOLE CO7 ...... 165 G5
Flambird's Cha RCHLM CM3 ...... 316 A4
Flamboro Cl LOS SS9 ...... 381 L5
Flamingo Wk RAIN RM13 ...... 389 H6
Flamstead End Rd BAR EN8 ...... 276 C8
Flanders Cl BRTR CM7 ...... 154 F6
Flanders Fld COLS CO2 ...... 163 J8
Flatford Dr RCOS CO16 ...... 223 J7
Flatford Rd RCOLE CO7 ...... 107 K2
Flavian Cl HVHL CB9 ...... 28 E4
Fleet Av UPMR RM14 ...... 372 E6
Fleet Cl UPMR RM14 ...... 372 E6
Fleethall Gv CDH/CHF RM16 ...... 407 H6
Fleethall Rd RCFD SS4 ...... 383 H3
Fleet Rd SBF/HAD SS7 ...... 397 L3
Fleetwood Av COS CO15 ...... 224 F4
  FX IP11 ...... 85 J8
  WOS/PRIT SS0 ...... 400 D1
Fleetwood Cl COS CO15 ...... 224 F4
Fleetwood Rd FX IP11 ...... 85 J8
Fleming Cl BRTR CM7 ...... 183 G2
  CHESW EN7 ...... 276 B6
Fleming Gdns HARH RM3 ...... 371 J2
  TIL RM18 ...... 418 C6
Fleming Rd CDH/CHF RM16 ...... 408 A7
Flemings RBRW/HUT RM13 ...... 354 D7
Flemings Farm Rd LOS SS9 ...... 381 L3
Flemming Av LOS SS9 ...... 381 L8
Flemming Crs LOS SS9 ...... 381 L8
Fletcher Dr WICKW SS12 ...... 359 L5
Fletcher Rd CHIG IG7 ...... 350 A6
  IPSE IP3 ...... 59 H3
Fletchers VGE SS16 ...... 376 E7
Fletchers La KESG IP5 ...... 39 L3
Fletchers Sq SOSN SS2 ...... 383 H5
Flex Meadow HLWW/ROY CM19 .. 14 D7
Flindell Dr RIPW IP8 ...... 36 B1
Flint Cl CHTY IP2 ...... 58 C1
  VGE SS16 ...... 376 A6
Flint St WTHK RM20 ...... 416 C3
Flintwich Mnr CHLM/WR CM1 ... 263 M4
Flitch La GTDUN CM6 ...... 178 F4
Flitch Wy BRTR CM7 ...... 181 H5
  GTDUN CM6 ...... 149 M1
  RBSF CM22 ...... 175 L4
  RBSF CM22 ...... 177 G5
Flixton Cl RCOS CO16 ...... 223 H7
Flora Rd WIT CM8 ...... 211 G6
Florence Cl HCH RM12 ...... 389 H1
  HLWE CM17 ...... 256 D5
  SBF/HAD SS7 ...... 380 E8
  WTHK RM20 ...... 416 F3

Florence Gdns SBF/HAD SS7....380 D8
Florence Rd CVI SS8....398 C7
  WOTN CO14....199 L1
Florence Wy VGE SS16....376 C6
Florie's Rd RCOLW CO6....159 C3
Flower Cl SOS SS1....21 L5
Flowers Wy COS CO15....250 B4
Flowmere Rd ROY SG8....40 B6
Flux's La EPP CM16....304 B5
Fobbing Farm Cl VGE SS16....377 H8
Fobbing Rd SLH/COR SS17....395 K7
Fodderwick BSDN SS14....18 F6
Foden Av IP IP1....36 D1
Foksville Rd CVI SS8....398 C6
Fold Cft HLW CM20....14 F3
Folkards La RCOLE CO7....221 G3
Folkes La UPMR RM14....373 C5
Folly Cha HOC/HUL SS5....362 C5
Folly La HOC/HUL SS5....362 C5
  RIPW IP8....56 E7
Folly Mill La GTDUN CM6....122 A5
The Folly COLS CO2....190 B5
  K/T/MI CO5....242 A1
  RCOLE CO7....192 C4
Fonnereau Rd IP IP1....2 E2
Fontayne Av CHIG IG7....349 K5
  RAIN RM13....388 F6
  ROM RM1....370 F2
Fonteyn Cl LAIN SS15....376 D3
Fontwell Park Gdns
  HCH RM12....389 M3 [1]
Forbes Cl HCH RM12....371 J8
Ford Cl LAIN SS15....376 B5
  RAIN RM13....389 G6
Ford End WFD IG8....348 C7
Ford Fld STDN SG11....172 B3
Fordham Cl EMPK RM11....372 B7 [1]
Fordham Pl IPNE IP4....39 G6 [1]
Fordham Rd RCOLW CO6....132 A1
Fordhams Rw CDH/CHF RM16....408 D7
Ford Hl STDN SG11....172 C3
Ford La COLN CO4....134 D6
  RAIN RM13....389 G6
  RCOLE CO7....193 J6
Ford Rd COS CO15....12 D6
  DAGE RM10....388 D6
  DAGW RM9....388 A6
Fords La COLN CO4....134 E6
Fordson Rd CHLM/GWD CM2....265 J5
Ford St RCOLW CO6....132 B7
Fordwater Cl STSD CM24....29 J8
Fordwich Rd RCOLE CO7....220 F2
Fordyce Cl EMPK RM11....372 B7
Forebury Av SBW CM21....228 A1
The Forebury SBW CM21....228 A1
Fore Fld BRTR CM7....155 L8 [1]
Forefield Gn CHLM/WR CM1....265 G4
Fore Hamlet IPSE IP3....3 J6
Foremark Rd BARK/HLT IG6....350 A6 [1]
Foresight Rd COLS CO2....191 L1
Forest Ap WFD IG8....348 A8
Forest Av CHIG IG7....349 H6
Forest Cl WAB EN9....326 C1
  WFD IG8....348 C5 [1]
Forest Ct CHING E4....348 A2
Forest Dr CHLM/WR CM1....16 A5
  EPP CM16....303 M8
Forest Edge BKHH IG9....348 D4
Foresthall Rd STSD CM24....146 E7
Forest La CHIG IG7....349 H6
Forest Park Av COS CO15....223 M4
Fore Fld HLWE CM17....227 K7
  IPNE IP4....3 H6
  LAIN SS15....376 F1
Forest Rd BAR EN8....300 E1
  BARK/HLT IG6....350 C7
  COLN CO4....11 L7
  ERITH DA8....414 B5
  LOU IG10....326 E6
  PEND EN3....300 F8
  ROMW/RG RM7....370 D3
  WFD IG8....348 B4
  WIT CM8....212 B7
Forest Side BKHH IG9....348 C2
  CHING E4....348 A1
  EPP CM16....303 L5
Forest Vw CHING E4....325 L8
Forest View Dr LOS SS9....381 H8
Forest Wy HLWE CM17....256 C7
  LOU IG10....326 D2
  WAB EN9....302 F3
  WFD IG8....348 C5
Forfar Cl IPNE IP4....38 C2
  LOS SS9....399 J1
Forge Cl KIR/NAC IP10....61 H2 [1]
Forge Crs BRTR CM7....156 D8
Forge St RCOLE CO7....107 C5
Forres Rd HOD EN11....253 H5
Forrest Cl RCHLM CM3....339 K4
Forsyth Dr BRWN CM15....183 H7
Forsythia Cl CHLM/WR CM1....264 F4 [1]
Fortescue Cha SOS SS1....402 A2
Forth Rd UPMR RM14....372 E6
Forties Cl HVHL CB9....28 E3
Fortinbras Wy CHLM/GWD CM2....17 K3
Fortin Cl SOCK/AV RM15....406 B5
Fortin Wy SOCK/AV RM15....406 B5
Fort Rd TIL RM18....418 C7
Fortune Cl RCHLM CM3....209 H4 [1]
The Fortunes HLWS CM18....256 F5
Fort William Rd SLH/COR SS17....395 J1
Forty Hl EN EN1....324 A1
Fossetts La RCOLE CO7....132 E6
Fossetts Wy SOSN SS2....383 K8
Fostal Cl LOS SS9....381 M8
Foster Cl BAR EN8....300 F2 [1]
Foster Rd CVI SS8....398 D7
  HAR CO12....112 F6
  MAL CM9....240 B7
Fosters Cl CHLM/WR CM1....287 C2
Foster St HLWE CM17....257 K7
Fotheringham Rd EN EN1....324 A6
Foulgar Cl RCHLM CM3....339 M3 [1]

Foundation St IPNE IP4....3 G6
Foundry La BOC CM0....344 B6
  IPSE IP3....2 F6
  RCOLW CO6....130 C5
  RCOLW CO6....160 E6
Fountain Farm HLWS CM18....256 A5 [1]
Fountain La HOC/HUL SS5....362 C6
  K/T/MI CO5....188 E3
Fountain Pl WAB EN9....301 K6 [1]
Fountain Rd CHLM/WR CM1....232 C8
Fountains Rd CHTY IP2....58 A2
Fouracres PEND EN3....324 F3
Four Acres SAFWN CB10....22 E8
  SAFWS CB11....65 M2
The Four Acres SBW CM21....228 B1
Four Ash Hl HSTD CO9....49 M2
Four Sisters Cl LOS SS9....382 A6 [1]
Four Sisters Wy LOS SS9....382 A5
Fourth Av CHLM/WR CM1....264 B6
  COS CO15....224 D7
  COS CO13....199 C7
  HLW CM20....15 L3
  HLWW/ROY CM19....14 D5
  HSTD CO9....129 J2
  RCOS CO16....249 J5
  ROMW/RG RM7....370 D3
  SLH/COR SS17....394 F6
  WICKE SS11....360 B5
  WTHK RM20....416 B3
Fourways RBSF CM22....147 K2
Fowe's La SUD CO10....52 C4
Fowler Cl SOS SS1....21 L5
Fowler Rd BARK/HLT IG6....350 D6
Fowley Cl BAR EN8....301 G6 [1]
Foxborough Cha INC CM4....312 B6
Foxburrow Cl HVHL CB9....28 A2
Fox Burrow Rd CHIG IG7....350 A5
Fox Burrows La CHLM/WR CM1....287 J1
Fox Cl CRW RM5....351 J6
  SBF/HAD SS7....380 A5
Fox Crs CHLM/WR CM1....264 A7
Foxdells La BSF CM23....174 A1
Foxden WIT CM8....212 E5
Foxes Dr CHESW EN7....300 A1
Foxes Gn CDH/CHF RM16....408 B7
Foxes Gv RBRW/HUT CM13....356 C1
Foxes La RCOLW CO6....160 E3
  SUD CO10....50 E2
Foxes Rd SUD CO10....50 E2
Foxfield Cl HOC/HUL SS5....363 H5 [1]
Foxfield Dr SLH/COR SS17....394 F6 [1]
Foxglove Cl BSF CM23....173 K5
  COS CO15....224 A4
  WIT CM8....211 L8
Foxglove Rd SOCK/AV RM15....406 D4 [1]
Foxglove Wy CHLM/WR CM1....265 G5
Foxgrove Gdns FX IP11....85 K8
Foxgrove La FX IP11....85 K8
Foxhall Rd BOC CM0....320 C4
  IPNE IP4....3 L6
  IPNE IP4....38 F7
  IPSE IP3....38 B6
  UPMR RM14....390 D4
Fox Hatch BRWN CM15....331 M2
Foxhills Rd CDH/CHF RM16....407 L6 [1]
Foxholes Rd
  CHLM/GWD CM2....289 G5 [1]
Foxlands Crs DAGE RM10....388 D4
Foxlands Rd DAGE RM10....388 D4
Fox Lea KESC IP5....39 M3
Foxleigh BCAYW CM12....357 H5 [1]
Foxleigh Cl BCAYW CM12....357 H3
Foxley Dr BSF CM23....174 B3
Fox Manor Wy WTHK RM20....416 C3
Foxmead WIT CM8....212 E5
Foxmeadows SBF/HAD SS7....380 A5 [1]
Foxtail Rd IPSE IP3....59 L3
Foxton Rd HOD EN11....253 G5
  WTHK RM20....416 B3
Foxwood Cl RCOLE CO7....137 J1
Foxwood Crs IPNE IP4....39 G6
Foxwood Pl LOS SS9....399 L1
Foyle Dr SOCK/AV RM15....406 B3
Foys Wk BCAYE CM11....357 K4 [1]
Frambury La SAFWS CB11....89 G3
Framlingham Wy BRTR CM7....182 D4 [1]
Frampton Rd BSDN SS14....378 B2 [1]
  EPP CM16....280 B8
  IPSE IP3....59 H3
Frances Cl RCOLE CO7....192 C1
Frances Gdns SOCK/AV RM15....406 A4 [1]
Frances Ga CHLM/WR CM1....265 H4
Franciscan Wy IP IP1....2 E5
Francis Cl HVHL CB9....28 A3
  K/T/MI CO5....214 D7
  KESC IP5....39 M3
  SLH/COR SS17....394 A8
Francisco Rd CDH/CHF RM16....406 D8
Francis Ct WIT CM8....184 D6
Francis Ms MAL CM9....293 J3 [1]
Francis Rd BRTR CM7....182 E1
  SUD CO10....4 D7
Francis St RCOLE CO7....221 G6 [1]
Francis Wk RAYL SS6....380 D1
Francis Wy COLN CO4....11 M3
  WIT CM8....184 D7
Francombe Gdns ROM RM1....371 H6
Frank Clater Cl COLN CO4....11 J6
Frankland Cl WFD IG8....348 D6 [1]
Franklin Av CHESW EN7....300 B2
Franklin Rd HCH RM12....389 K5 [1]
  IPSE IP3....59 J1
  RCHLM CM3....341 J3
Franklins Wy WICKE SS11....359 H4 [1]
Franklyn Gdns BARK/HLT IG6....349 L7
Frank Martin Ct CHESW EN7....300 B2
Franmil Rd EMPK RM11....371 M4
Fraser Cl CHLM/GWD CM2....17 K3 [1]
  LAIN SS15....375 M4 [1]
  SBN/FI SS3....403 G2
Fraser Rd BAR EN8....276 F8 [1]
  IP IP1....37 G4
Frating Abbey Farm Rd
  RCOLE CO7....194 D5

Frating Crs WFD IG8....348 C7 [1]
Frating Hl RCOLE CO7....165 L8
Frating Rd RCOLE CO7....137 G6
Frayes Cha CHLM/WR CM1....231 H8
Frazer Rd ROMW/RG RM7....371 G7
Frederick Crs PEND EN3....324 D4
Frederick Rd RAIN RM13....388 E8
Freebore Gdns RAIN RM13....389 H5 [1]
Freebournes Rd WIT CM8....239 J2
Freehold Rd IPNE IP4....38 B5
Freeland Rd COS CO15....12 E9
Freelands RCOLE CO7....221 K5
Freeland Wy ERITH DA8....414 B5
Freemantle Av PEND EN3....324 E7
Freeman Wy EMPK RM11....371 M6
Freewood La SAFWS CB11....41 H8
Fremantle SBN/FI SS3....402 E6
Fremantle Cl RCHLM CM3....339 L2 [1]
Fremantle Rd COLS CO2....191 J2 [1]
The Fremnells BSDN SS14....19 M3
French Rd RCHLM CM3....341 C2
Frensham Cl COLW CO3....161 L4 [1]
Frensham Dr CHONG CM5....259 G8
Frere Wy K/T/MI CO5....192 C5
Frerichs Cl WICKW SS12....359 L6
Freshfields HAR CO12....143 C2
Freshfields CHLM/GWD CM2....289 K5
  SAFWN CB10....65 K1 [1]
Freshwell St SAFWN CB10....65 L1 [1]
Fresian Cl BRTR CM7....182 D1 [1]
Freston Hl RIPS/CAP IP9....58 F7
Freston St RIPS/CAP IP9....58 E8
Frettons BSDN SS14....377 M6
Friar Cl CHLM/GWD CM2....28 A2
Friars RIPS/CAP IP9....78 C3
Friar's Av BRWN CM15....355 H1
Friars Bridge Rd IP IP1....2 D5
Friar's Cl BRWN CM15....355 H1
  COLN CO4....11 J1
  FX IP11....85 L7
  HSTD CO9....97 K1
  LAIN SS15....376 D5 [1]
  RCOLE CO7....192 D3
  RCOS CO16....223 M5
Friarscroft BROX EN10....253 H8
Friars Gate WFD IG8....348 B5
Friars La BRTR CM7....155 G7
  MAL CM9....293 G1 [1]
  RBSF CM22....229 J2
Friars St IP IP1....2 E5
  SBN/FI SS3....403 G4
  SUD CO10....4 C7
The Friars CHIC IG7....349 M5
Friars Wk CHLM/GWD CM2....17 H5
Friars Wd BSF CM23....174 D3
Friary La WFD IG8....348 B5
Friday Wood Gn COLS CO2....191 H3 [1]
Friedberg Av BSF CM23....173 L6
Friends Av BAR EN8....300 E4
Friends Fld BURES CO8....102 A2
Friends Wk KESC IP5....39 L3
  SAFWS CB11....88 A2
Friern Gdns WICKW SS12....359 J4
Friern Pl WICKW SS12....359 J5
Friern Wk WICKW SS12....359 J4
Frietuna Rd FOS CO13....198 F5
Frimley Av EMPK RM11....372 B8
Frinton Rd COS CO15....225 G5
  CRW RM5....351 H8
  FOS CO13....198 D5
  RCOS CO16....197 J2
Frithwood Cl BCAYW CM12....357 G4
Frithwood La BCAYW CM12....357 G3
Fritton Cl CHTY IP2....58 B2
Frizlands La DAGE RM10....388 C2
Frobisher Dr COS CO15....250 A2
Frobisher Rd ERITH DA8....414 B4
  HAR CO12....143 G2
  IPSE IP3....59 J3
Frobisher Wy BRTR CM7....155 K7
  GRH DA9....416 C8
  SBN/FI SS3....402 F2
Froden Brook BCAYE CM11....357 K4
Froden Cl BCAYE CM11....357 K5 [1]
Frogge St SAFWN CB10....42 C1
Frog Hall Cl K/T/MI CO5....192 C5
Frog St BRWN CM15....331 M3
Frogs Aly RIPS/CAP IP9....83 G6
Frome Cl TIL RM18....419 K1
Fronk's Av HAR CO12....143 K1
Fronk's Rd HAR CO12....143 J1
Front La UPMR RM14....390 F1
Front Rd IPSE IP3....59 L3
Frowick La RCOS CO16....222 C1
Fryatt Av HAR CO12....6 C7
Fry Cl CRW RM5....351 H6
Fryerning La ING CM4....310 C2
Fryth Cl HVHL CB9....28 B2
The Fryth BSDN SS14....377 M3
Fuchsia La IPNE IP4....38 B6
Fulbrook La SOCK/AV RM15....406 A5
Fulcher Av CHLM/GWD CM2....265 C8
Fulfen Wy SAFWS CB11....65 L4
Fulford Dr LOS SS9....382 B5
Fullarton Crs SOCK/AV RM15....406 A4 [1]
Fullbridge MAL CM9....269 H8
Fuller Ct BSF CM23....174 B4 [1]
Fuller's Av WFD IG8....348 A8
Fullers Cl CRW RM5....351 K8
  K/T/MI CO5....213 J1
  WAB EN9....302 A5
Fullers Md HLWE CM17....256 C6
Fullers Rd COLS CO2....191 L1
Fulmar Cl COLN CO4....164 B3 [1]
Fulmar Rd RAIN RM13....389 J5
Fulmar Wy WICKE SS11....360 B6
Fulton Crs BSF CM23....174 D2
Fulton Rd SBF/HAD SS7....379 L4
Furlongs COS CO15....19 L9
The Furlongs ING CM4....310 C8
Furneaux La K/T/MI CO5....192 A6

Furner Cl DART DA1....414 A7
Furness Rd CDH/CHF RM16....418 C2
  CHTY IP2....58 A3
Furness Wy HCH RM12....389 H4
The Furrells CBE/LIN CB1....24 D1
Furriers Cl BSF CM23....173 K6
Furrow Cl COLW CO3....161 M6 [1]
Furrowfelde VGE SS16....377 H7
Further Meadow
  CHLM/WR CM1....287 H1
Furtherwick Rd CVI SS8....413 J1
Furze Crs RCOLE CO7....193 H4
Furze Gld VGE SS16....376 C6 [1]
Furze La ING CM4....336 D3
  RCOLE CO7....166 B6
Fusedale Wy SOCK/AV RM15....406 A5 [1]
Fyefields PIT SS13....378 D3
Fyfield Av WICKW SS12....359 K6
Fyfield Cl RBRW/HUT CM13....374 E6
Fyfield Dr SOCK/AV RM15....406 A5
Fyfield Rd CHONG CM5....259 G8
  RAIN RM13....389 G7
  WFD IG8....348 D8

G

Gabion Av PUR RM19....415 L1
Gablefields CHLM/GWD CM2....289 K5
The Gables PIT SS13....378 C3
  SBF/HAD SS7....381 H4
Gabriel Cl CRW RM5....351 K8
Gaces Acre SAFWS CB11....89 H2
Gadsden Cl UPMR RM14....372 F6 [1]
Gadwall Reach K/T/MI CO5....213 L1 [1]
Gafzelle Dr CVI SS8....398 F8
Gager Dr K/T/MI CO5....214 F6
Gage's Rd SUD CO10....51 M4
Gaiger Cl CHLM/WR CM1....264 E4
Gainsborough Av CVI SS8....398 F8
  K/T/MI CO5....245 L5
  RCOS CO16....223 K5
Gainsborough Crs
  CHLM/GWD CM2....264 F8
Gainsborough Dr MGTR CO11....108 C7
  WOS/PRIT SS0....20 C1
Gainsborough La IPSE IP3....59 G3
Gainsborough Pl
  RBRW/HUT CM13....355 L2
Gainsborough St COLW CO3....162 C6
  FX IP11....9 M1
  HVHL CB9....27 L2
  IPNE IP4....37 L3
  RAIN RM13....389 H7
  SUD CO10....4 C5
  WFD IG8....348 F7 [1]
Gainsborough St SUD CO10....4 C7
Gains Cl CVI SS8....398 F7
Gainsford Av COS CO15....13 M3
Gainsford End HSTD CO9....72 C5
Gainsthorpe Rd CHONG CM5....282 E3
Galadriel RCHLM CM3....339 J5
Galahad Cl BOC CM0....344 C6
Gales Wy WFD IG8....348 F8 [1]
Galey Gn SOCK/AV RM15....406 C4 [1]
Gall End La STSD CM24....147 C4
Galleon Bvd GRH DA9....415 L8
Galleons Hill Vicarage Rd
  CHLM/WR CM1....262 C6
Galleydene SBF/HAD SS7....380 D8
Galley Gn HERT/BAY SG13....253 H [1]
Galleyhill Rd WAB EN9....301 M4 [2]
Galleywood Crs CRW RM5....351 L7 [1]
Galliford Rd MAL CM9....269 H7
Gallows Cl BSF CM23....174 B3
The Gallops VGE SS16....376 C6
Galloway Cl BROX EN10....277 G6
  BSF CM23....174 A3
Galloway Dr RCOS CO16....196 D8
Galloway Rd BSF CM23....174 A3
Gallows Green Rd GTDUN CM6....122 E8
Gallows Hl SAFWS CB11....65 K4
Galsworthy Cl BRTR CM7....183 H4 [1]
Galsworthy Rd TIL RM18....418 D5
Galton Rd WOS/PRIT SS0....400 D3
Galway Av IP IP1....36 F2
Gambleside VGE SS16....377 M8
Gandalf's Ride RCHLM CM3....339 K5
Gandish Rd RCOLE CO7....107 M1
Ganels Cl BCAYE CM11....357 K4 [1]
Ganels Rd BCAYE CM11....357 K4
Ganges Rd RIPS/CAP IP9....113 H3
Gangies Hl SBW CM21....200 B8
Gannet Cl HVHL CB9....28 D3
Gannet Rd CHTY IP2....36 F8
Gant Ct WAB EN9....302 A6
Ganwick Cl HVHL CB9....28 A1
Gaol La SUD CO10....4 D6
The Gap COS CO15....225 H5
  SAFWS CB11....88 A2
Garbutt Rd UPMR RM14....390 D1 [1]
Garden Cl RCHLM CM3....319 C7
  RIPS/CAP IP9....82 F8
Garden End ING CM4....336 A1
Gardeners CHLM/GWD CM2....288 E6
Gardeners La RCFD SS4....364 F2
Gardeners Rd HSTD CO9....129 G2
Garden Flds K/T/MI CO5....245 L3
Garden Fld FX IP11....84 E8
  RCHLM CM3....238 A7
Garden Flds BOC CM0....296 A8
  GTDUN CM6....151 L5
  RCOLW CO6....159 K3
Gardenia Wy WFD IG8....348 B6 [1]
Garden Rd COS CO15....250 B4
  FOS CO13....199 G4
The Gardens BRWN CM15....308 C8
Garden Terrace Rd HLWE CM17....227 K7
Garden Wy LOU IG10....327 H2 [1]
Gardiner Cl PEND EN3....324 E8
Gardiners Cl BSDN SS14....377 L2 [1]
Gardiners La North
  BCAYE CM11....358 C6
Gardiners La South BSDN SS14....377 M1
Gardiners Link BSDN SS14....377 L1 [1]
The Gardiners HLWE CM17....256 C6

Gardiners Wy BSDN SS14....377 L1 [1]
Gardner Av BSF/COR SS17....395 C6
Garfield Cl FX IP11....9 K3
Garfield Rd FX IP11....9 K3
  PEND EN3....324 D6
Garland Cl BAR EN8....300 F3 [1]
Garland Rd HAR CO12....6 B5
Garland Wy EMPK RM11....371 M4
Garnault Rd EN EN1....324 A2
Garner Dr BROX EN10....276 F6
Garnetts RBSF CM22....176 C3
Garnetts La GTDUN CM6....180 D5
Garnon Md EPP CM16....280 E8
Garnons Cha RCOLW CO6....103 H6
Garrettlands CHLM/GWD CM2....290 A5
Garrison La FX IP11....9 J3
  SUD CO10....35 M8
Garrod Ct COLS CO2....191 J4 [1]
Garrods RIPS/CAP IP9....78 C2 [1]
Garron La SOCK/AV RM15....406 A4
Garry Cl ROM RM1....351 M8
Garry Wy ROM RM1....351 M8
Garth Rd SOCK/AV RM15....406 D2
Garthwood Cl RCOLW CO6....133 M7
Gartons Cl PEND EN3....324 D7
Gascoigne Rd COLN CO4....11 J5
Gascoyne Cl HARH RM3....371 L1
Gascoyne Dr DART DA1....414 A7
Gaston St RCOLE CO7....107 K1
Gatacre Rd IP IP1....2 A1
Gate Farm Rd RIPS/CAP IP9....113 J2
Gatefield Cl FOS CO13....199 G4
Gatehouse Dr SOCK/AV RM15....406 A4
Gatehouse Ms INC CM4....310 C8
Gatekeeper Cl BRTR CM7....183 G2 [1]
Gate Lodge Cl LAIN SS15....377 G1 [1]
Gate Lodge Sq LAIN SS15....377 G1 [1]
Gate Lodge Wy LAIN SS15....377 G1 [1]
Gate St MAL CM9....269 G8
Gate Street Ms MAL CM9....269 G8
Gateway BSDN SS14....19 H6
Gatscombe Cl HOC/HUL SS5....362 E5 [1]
The Gattens RAYL SS6....362 A7
Gatwick Cl BSF CM23....174 C2 [1]
Gatwick Vw BCAYW CM12....357 J3
Gauden Rd BRTR CM7....155 G4 [1]
Gavenny Pth SOCK/AV RM15....406 A4
Gavin Wy COLN CO4....135 J6
Gay Bowers BSDN SS14....19 M2
  HOC/HUL SS5....362 C5 [1]
Gay Bowers La RCHLM CM3....291 G5
Gay Bowers Rd RCHLM CM3....290 F7
Gay Bowers Wy WIT CM8....239 H4 [1]
Gaye St IP IP1....2 C3
Gay Gdns DAGE RM10....388 D3
Gayleighs RAYL SS6....361 L7
Gaylor Rd TIL RM18....417 M5
Gaymers La FX IP11....84 C5
Gaynes Ct UPMR RM14....390 C3
Gaynesford VGE SS16....376 F7
Gaynes Hill Rd WFD IG8....348 F8
Gaynes Park Rd UPMR RM14....390 C3
Gaynes Rd UPMR RM14....390 C3
Gays La RCFD SS4....364 F1
Gayton Rd SOSN SS2....21 H2
Gaywood LAIN SS15....376 B4
Gaywood Av BAR EN8....300 E2
Gazelle Ct COLN CO4....135 K7 [1]
Geary Dr BRWN CM15....332 A7
Geddings Rd HOD EN11....253 J5
The Geerings SLH/COR SS17....395 C7
Geesh Rd CVI SS8....398 D6 [1]
Geisthorp Ct WAB EN9....302 B5
Gelsthorpe Rd CRW RM5....351 J8
Generals Ms FX IP11....84 E8 [1]
The Generals Wk PEND EN3....324 F1 [1]
Genesta Cl MAL CM9....272 L1
Genesta Rd WOS/PRIT SS0....400 D3
Geneva Rd IP IP1....2 D3
Genk Cl CVI SS8....398 C6
Gennep Rd CVI SS8....398 C6
Gentian Ct COLN CO4....162 D1 [1]
Gentry Cl SLH/COR SS17....409 K1 [1]
Geoffrey Av HARH RM3....353 H7
Geoff Seaden Cl COL CO1....11 K9
George Av RCOLE CO7....221 C4
George Avey Cft EPP CM16....281 J6
George Cardnell Wy
  RCHLM CM3....318 F2
George Cl COS CO15....12 B7
  CVI SS8....398 A5
George Cut RCOLE CO7....221 G5 [1]
George Frost Cl IPNE IP4....3 G1
George Gent Cl HVHL CB9....48 C5 [1]
George La BRTR CM7....182 E1
Georges Dr BRWN CM15....332 A7
George St CHLM/GWD CM2....17 G6
  COL CO1....10 C7
  GRAYS RM17....417 H3
  HAR CO12....7 L4
  ROM RM1....371 G6
  SBN/FI SS3....403 H5
Gepps Cl CHLM/WR CM1....232 E1
Gerald Rd BCTR RM8....388 A1
Geralds Av IPNE IP4....38 B6
Gerard Av BSF CM23....173 M7
Gerard Gdns RAIN RM13....388 F3 [1]
Gerard Rd RCOS CO16....223 K5
  RAIN RM13....389 L8 [1]
Gernon Cl CHLM/WR CM1....235 J8 [1]
  RAIN RM13....389 L8 [1]
Gernon Rd RCOLE CO7....136 F4
Gernons VGE SS16....18 D9
  VGE SS16....377 G7 [1]
Gerpins La UPMR RM14....390 A4
Gerrard Crs BRW CM14....354 D4
Gestingthorpe Rd SUD CO10....53 L8
Gew's Cnr BAR EN8....300 E1
Geylen Rd CVI SS8....398 E7
Ghyllgrove BSDN SS14....19 G4
Ghyllgrove Cl BSDN SS14....19 G4
Gibb Cft HLWS CM18....255 M7
Gibbons Ct GTDUN CM6....178 E2 [1]
Gibbons St IP IP1....2 B4
Gibbs Cl BAR EN8....300 E1
Gibbs Fld BSF CM23....173 L6
Gibbs Fld BSDN SS14....377 M5
Gibcracks BSDN SS14....377 M5
Gibraltar Cl RBRW/HUT CM13....354 C7 [1]
Gibson Cl EPP CM16....281 K5 [1]

SAFWN CB10 ... 65 L2
Gibson Gdns SAFWN CB10 ... 65 L2
Gibson Rd HSTD CO9 ... 97 L3
Gibson Wy SAFWN CB10 ... 65 L2
Gidea Av GPK RM2 ... 371 H3
Gidea Cl GPK RM2 ... 371 H3
Gideons Wy SLH/COR SS17 ... 394 E8
Giffins Cl BRTR CM7 ... 182 F2
Gifford Cl RIPS/CAP IP9 ... 80 E5
Gifford Gn PIT SS13 ... 378 C6
Gifford Rd SBF/HAD SS7 ... 379 L6
Giffords Cross Av
   SLH/COR SS17 ... 395 H7
Giffords Cross Rd
   SLH/COR SS17 ... 395 H8
Giffordside CDH/CHF RM16 ... 418 C2
Giffords Pl IPNE IP4 ... 39 G5
Gifhorn Rd CVI SS8 ... 398 F8
Gilbert Ct COLN CO4 ... 135 K5
Gilberd Rd COLS CO2 ... 163 J3
Gilbert Cl RAYL SS6 ... 381 G1
Gilbert Dr VGE SS16 ... 376 B6
Gilbert Rd CDH/CHF RM16 ... 406 D8
   ROM RM1 ... 371 G4
   SUD CO10 ... 31 J2
Gilbert St PEND EN3 ... 324 D1
Gilden Cl HLWE CM17 ... 227 M7
Gilden Wy HLWE CM17 ... 227 L8
Gilderdale Cl COLN CO4 ... 135 L8
Gilders SBW CM21 ... 227 L1
Gilders Wy RCOS CO16 ... 12 B1
Giles Cl RAIN RM13 ... 389 L8
Gillam Wy RAIN RM13 ... 389 H5
Gill Cl MAL CM9 ... 269 C5
Gillian Crs GPK RM2 ... 371 K2
Gills Av CVI SS8 ... 398 D7
The Gill SBF/HAD SS7 ... 380 E6
Gilman Dr SBN/FI SS3 ... 402 D4
Gilmore Wy CHLM/GWD CM2 ... 289 J3
Gilmour Cl ENC/FH EN2 ... 300 B7
Gilmour Ri BCAYE CM12 ... 357 C2
Gilpin Wy BRTR CM7 ... 182 D4
Gilroy Cl RAIN RM13 ... 389 G5
Gilsland WAB EN9 ... 301 M7
Gilwell Cl CHING E4 ... 325 L6
Gilwell La CHING E4 ... 325 L6
Gilwell Park Cl COLW CO3 ... 162 B7
Gimson Cl WIT CM8 ... 238 F1
Ginns Rd BUNT SG9 ... 116 E5
Gippeswyck BSDN SS14 ... 19 J4
Gippeswyk Av CHTY IP2 ... 2 B8
Gippeswyck Rd CHTY IP2 ... 2 C8
Gipping Cl HVHL CB9 ... 27 M5
Gippingstone Rd RIPW IP8 ... 36 B2
Gipping Wy RIPW IP8 ... 36 B1
   RIPW IP8 ... 36 C5
Gipson Park Cl LOS SS9 ... 381 L5
Gipsy La BSF CM23 ... 146 D7
   GRAYS RM17 ... 417 K3
Girling St SUD CO10 ... 4 D5
Girton Ct BAR EN8 ... 300 F2
Girton Rd HVHL CB9 ... 28 C4
Girton Wy CHTY IP2 ... 58 A2
Gisborne Gdns RAIN RM13 ... 404 A1
Gladden Rd HLWS CM18 ... 255 M7
Gladden Flds RCHLM CM3 ... 339 K5
The Glade COLN CO4 ... 163 M1
   RBRW/HUT CM13 ... 334 C5
   UPMR RM14 ... 390 D4
   VGE SS16 ... 377 K7
   WFD IG8 ... 348 C4
Gladeview COS CO15 ... 224 A4
The Gladeway WAB EN9 ... 301 L5
Gladiator Wy COLS CO2 ... 190 B1
Gladstone Cl CHLM/GWD CM2 ... 17 H6
Gladstone Gdns RAYL SS6 ... 380 C2
Gladstone Rd BKHH IG9 ... 348 D2
   COL CO1 ... 163 H6
   HOC/HUL SS5 ... 362 F6
   HOD EN11 ... 253 J4
   IPSE IP3 ... 3 L6
   K/T/MI CO5 ... 214 E7
Gladwin Rd COLS CO2 ... 162 D7
Glamis Cl CHESW EN7 ... 300 B1
Glamis Dr EMPK RM11 ... 371 M8
Glamorgan Rd CHTY IP2 ... 58 C2
Glanmead BRWN CM15 ... 354 F2
Glanmire BCAYE CM11 ... 335 L5
Glanthams Rd BRWN CM15 ... 355 G3
Glanville Dr EMPK RM11 ... 372 A4
Glanville Pl KESG IP5 ... 39 J5
Glasseys La RAYL SS6 ... 380 D3
Glastonbury Av WFD IG8 ... 348 E8
Glastonbury Cha
   WOS/PRIT SS0 ... 382 C6
Glastonbury Cl CHTY IP2 ... 58 A2
Glebe Av BRTR CM7 ... 154 F4
   WFD IG8 ... 348 B7
Glebe Cl MGTR CO11 ... 140 D6
   RAYL SS6 ... 361 K8
   RCOLE CO7 ... 165 H5
   RIPS/CAP IP9 ... 79 K4
   RIPW IP8 ... 36 C5
   SBN/FI SS3 ... 385 L8
   SOS SS1 ... 401 M3
Glebe Ct BSF CM23 ... 174 C3
   WIT CM8 ... 211 M7
Glebe Crs CHLM/WR CM1 ... 264 C2
Glebe Dr RAYL SS6 ... 361 K8
Glebe End RBSF CM22 ... 147 L2
   RIPS/CAP IP9 ... 78 C1
Glebefield Rd RCHLM CM3 ... 238 C7
Glebe Gdns K/T/MI CO5 ... 186 F6
   RBRW/HUT CM13 ... 355 M8
Glebelands CHIG IG7 ... 350 C4
   DART DA1 ... 414 A8
   HLW CM20 ... 227 C8
   RCOLW CO6 ... 134 C2
   SBF/HAD SS7 ... 379 J4
Glebe La BOC CM0 ... 321 L2

GTDUN CM6 ... 150 A6
RIPS/CAP IP9 ... 81 H3
Glebe Meadow RCHLM CM3 ... 234 F4
Glebe Rd BCAYE CM11 ... 358 F5
   CHLM/WR CM1 ... 17 C1
   CHONG CM5 ... 307 G1
   COLS CO2 ... 190 D1
   DAGE RM10 ... 388 C7
   K/T/MI CO5 ... 213 J1
   K/T/MI CO5 ... 214 D6
   MAL CM9 ... 269 K6
   RAIN RM13 ... 404 C1
   WICKE SS11 ... 359 M4
The Glebe HVHL CB9 ... 28 B2
   RCHLM CM3 ... 316 D2
   SAFWS CB11 ... 65 M4
Glebe Wy BOC CM0 ... 344 C5
   COS CO15 ... 250 B4
   EMPK RM11 ... 371 M7
   FOS CO13 ... 199 C6
   SBF/HAD SS7 ... 381 G8
Glebeway WFD IG8 ... 348 D6
Glemham Dr IPNE IP4 ... 39 G7
Glemsford Cl FX IP11 ... 8 E4
Glen Av COLW CO3 ... 162 C4
Glenavon Rd IPNE IP4 ... 38 E4
Glenbervie Dr LOS SS9 ... 400 A1
Glencoe Dr DAGE RM10 ... 388 C3
   WICKE SS11 ... 360 B3
Glencoe Rd IPNE IP4 ... 38 D2
Glencree BCAYE CM11 ... 335 L5
Glen Crs WFD IG8 ... 348 C7
Glen Cft HOC/HUL SS5 ... 363 D6
Glendale RCHLM CM3 ... 339 M2
Glendale Cl BRWN CM15 ... 354 F2
Glendale Gdns LOS SS9 ... 399 L2
Glendale Gv COLN CO4 ... 135 K8
Glendale Rd BOC CM0 ... 344 D5
Gleneagles SBF/HAD SS7 ... 379 J6
   HARH RM3 ... 353 C8
Gleneagles Dr IPNE IP4 ... 38 E6
Gleneagles Rd LOS SS9 ... 381 K6
Gleneagles Wy RCHLM CM3 ... 238 C7
Glenester Cl HOD EN11 ... 253 F2
Glen Faba Rd HLWW/ROY CM19 ... 254 A5
Glenfield Av FX IP11 ... 7 L8
Glenfield Rd SLH/COR SS17 ... 395 J6
Glengall Rd WFD IG8 ... 348 C7
Glen Hazel BRWN CM15 ... 308 E7
Glenhurst Av IPNE IP4 ... 38 C3
Glenhurst Rd SOSN SS2 ... 21 G1
Glenloch Rd PEND EN3 ... 324 D4
Glenmere VGE SS16 ... 395 L1
Glenmere Park Av
   SBF/HAD SS7 ... 380 C8
Glenmore St SOSN SS2 ... 401 L2
Glenridding SBF/HAD SS7 ... 379 L6
Glen Ri WFD IG8 ... 348 C7
Glen Rd LOS SS9 ... 400 B3
   SBF/HAD SS7 ... 379 M6
Glenside BCAYE CM11 ... 357 L1
   CHIG IG7 ... 349 J7
   SUD CO10 ... 5 H9
The Glen RAIN RM13 ... 404 D2
   RAYL SS6 ... 380 F3
   SLH/COR SS17 ... 395 G8
   VGE SS16 ... 378 B7
Glenton Cl ROM RM1 ... 351 M4
Glenton Wy ROM RM1 ... 351 M4
Glentress Cl COLN CO4 ... 135 L8
Glenwood BROX EN10 ... 253 C7
Glenwood Av HOC/HUL SS5 ... 363 C6
   LOS SS9 ... 381 J4
   RAIN RM13 ... 404 B2
   WOS/PRIT SS0 ... 20 B2
Glenwood Dr GPK RM2 ... 371 H5
Glenwood Gdns VGE SS16 ... 375 M7
Gleten Rd CVI SS8 ... 398 E7
Glisson Sq COLS CO2 ... 162 C7
Globe Cl K/T/MI CO5 ... 214 E5
Globe Crs BSF CM23 ... 145 L5
Globe Rd EMPK RM11 ... 371 H6
   WFD IG8 ... 348 D7
Gloucester Av BAR EN8 ... 300 F5
   CDH/CHF RM16 ... 407 K7
   CHLM/GWD CM2 ... 288 C5
   COLS CO2 ... 162 C8
   EMPK RM11 ... 372 B5
   MAL CM9 ... 293 G3
   RAYL SS6 ... 381 H3
   TIL RM18 ... 419 K2
Gloucester Crs CHLM/WR CM1 ... 264 B6
Gloucester Gdns BRTR CM7 ... 155 J8
Gloucester Pl BCAYW CM12 ... 335 H5
Gloucester Rd BRWN CM15 ... 332 C7
   HVHL CB9 ... 27 M4
   IPSE IP3 ... 59 H1
   ROM RM1 ... 370 F6
Gloucester Ter SOS SS1 ... 402 A3
Gloucester Wy SUD CO10 ... 4 F7
Glover Cl CHESW EN7 ... 276 A7
Glovers Fld BRWN CM15 ... 332 A1
Glovers La HLWE CM17 ... 256 F8
Glynde Wy SOSN SS2 ... 402 A2
Glynn Rd BOC CM0 ... 344 C5
Glyn Rd PEND EN3 ... 324 D6
Goat Hall La CHLM/GWD CM2 ... 288 A8
Goat House La RCHLM CM3 ... 291 M8
Goat La EN EN1 ... 324 A2
Goat Lodge Rd MAL CM9 ... 240 B6
Goatsmoor La BCAYE CM11 ... 335 M6
Goatswood La ABR/ST RM4 ... 352 C1
Gobions VGE SS16 ... 18 E9
Gobions Av CRW RM5 ... 351 L8
Godbold Cl KESG IP5 ... 39 L4
Goddard Cl CDH/CHF RM16 ... 407 M6
Goddard Wy CHLM/GWD CM2 ... 289 J1
   SAFWN CB10 ... 43 M8
Godfrey Wy GTDUN CM6 ... 178 E1
Godlings Wy BRTR CM7 ... 182 F1
Godman Rd CDH/CHF RM16 ... 408 C8
Godmans La RCOLW CO6 ... 159 M8
Godric Rd WIT CM8 ... 238 F3
Godwin Cl CHING E4 ... 325 K2
   HSTD CO9 ... 128 C2
Goff's La CHESW EN7 ... 300 A1
   RCOS CO16 ... 169 G3

Goings La K/T/MI CO5 ... 245 L5
Goirle Av CVI SS8 ... 398 D7
Goldace GRAYS RM17 ... 417 G3
Goldberry Md RCHLM CM3 ... 339 K5
Golden Cl BROX EN10 ... 252 F8
   RBSF CM22 ... 119 J8
Goldcrest Cl COLN CO4 ... 164 A3
Goldcrest Dr BCAYE CM11 ... 357 K2
Goldcrest Rd CHTY IP2 ... 36 B1
Goldenacres CHLM/WR CM1 ... 265 G3
Golden Cross Rd RCFD SS4 ... 363 L5
Golden Dawn Wy COLN CO4 ... 10 A1
Golden La RCOS CO16 ... 169 C8
   SAFWN CB10 ... 68 A1
Golden Lion La HAR CO12 ... 7 L3
Golden Manor Dr SBF/HAD SS7 ... 380 A6
Golden Noble HI COLS CO2 ... 163 H5
Goldfinch Cl COLN CO4 ... 164 A4
Goldfinch La SBF/HAD SS7 ... 380 B4
Goldhanger Rd RAYL SS6 ... 361 H8
Goldhanger Cross BSDN SS14 ... 377 M4
Goldhaze Cl WFD IG8 ... 348 E8
Golding Crs SLH/COR SS17 ... 394 F8
Goldingham Av LOU IG10 ... 327 K4
Goldingham Dr BRTR CM7 ... 183 H5
Goldings BSF CM23 ... 174 C3
Goldings Cl HVHL CB9 ... 28 B1
Goldings Crs VGE SS16 ... 377 M8
Golding's Hl LOU IG10 ... 327 G2
Goldings Ri LOU IG10 ... 327 H3
Goldings Rd LOU IG10 ... 327 H3
Goldsmith GRAYS RM17 ... 417 G3
Goldsmith Av ROMW/RG RM7 ... 370 B7
Goldsmith Dr RAYL SS6 ... 361 J4
Goldsmiths Av SLH/COR SS17 ... 395 H8
Gold St WANT CM0 ... 65 L2
Goldsworthy Dr SBN/FI SS3 ... 403 K1
Golf Green Rd COS CO15 ... 250 B3
Golf Ride SBF/HAD SS7 ... 379 L8
Golf Rd FX IP11 ... 85 L8
Goodchild Wy HSTD CO9 ... 73 H1
Goodey Cl COL CO1 ... 163 H6
Goodlake Cl HAR CO12 ... 142 F1
Goodliffe Pk BSF CM23 ... 174 C1
Goodmans La RCHLM CM3 ... 208 F6
Goodview Rd LAIN SS15 ... 377 H1
Goodwin Cl BAR EN8 ... 276 F8
Goodwins Cl SAFWS CB11 ... 42 F8
Goodwin Stile BSF CM23 ... 173 L6
Goodwood Av HCH RM12 ... 389 M2
   PEND EN3 ... 324 D1
   RBRW/HUT CM13 ... 334 A4
Goodwood Cl HOD EN11 ... 253 G4
Goojerat Rd COLS CO2 ... 162 E6
Goose La BSF CM22 ... 201 L4
Gooshays Dr HARH RM3 ... 352 F7
Gooshays Gdns HARH RM3 ... 352 F7
Gordon Av HCH RM12 ... 389 G1
Gordon Cl BCAYW CM12 ... 335 G8
Gordon Dr COLN CO4 ... 135 J6
Gordon Pl SOS SS1 ... 20 F6
Gordon Rd BAR EN8 ... 301 H6
   BRWN CM15 ... 355 H2
   BSDN SS14 ... 19 M7
   CDH/CHF RM16 ... 407 M7
   CHDH RM6 ... 370 A6
   CHLM/GWD CM2 ... 288 B5
   HAR CO12 ... 143 J1
   IPNE IP4 ... 38 B4
   LOS SS9 ... 399 J1
   SLH/COR SS17 ... 395 G8
   SOS SS1 ... 20 F5
Gordons PIT SS13 ... 378 B6
Gordon Wy HAR CO12 ... 143 J1
Gorefield Rd RBSF CM22 ... 148 C7
Gore La BRTR CM7 ... 182 A1
Gore Rd BRTR CM7 ... 182 B1
   RCFD SS4 ... 364 F5
The Gore BSF CM23 ... 18 F5
Goring Cl CRW RM5 ... 370 D1
Goring Rd COLN CO4 ... 11 J4
   DAGE RM10 ... 388 E5
   IPNE IP4 ... 38 C5
Gorsehayes CHTY IP2 ... 2 C9
Gorse La COS CO15 ... 224 A4
Gorse Rd IPSE IP3 ... 59 J1
Gorse Wy COLW CO3 ... 161 L7
   COS CO15 ... 250 A4
Gorseway ROMW/RG RM7 ... 388 F1
Gosbecks Rd COLS CO2 ... 162 B8
Gosbecks Vw COLS CO2 ... 190 B1
Gosfield Cl RAYL SS6 ... 361 H8
Gosfield Rd BCTR RM8 ... 370 B8
   BRTR CM7 ... 127 L8
   COLS CO2 ... 191 H3
Gosford Cl SUD CO10 ... 31 J3
Gosford Wy FX IP11 ... 85 K7
Goshawk Dr
   CHLM/GWD CM2 ... 288 C6
The Goslings SBN/FI SS3 ... 403 H4
   WIT CM8 ... 184 D6
Gosling Pl KESG IP5 ... 39 M3
Gotsfield Cl SUD CO10 ... 35 K4
Gough Rd EN EN1 ... 324 C4
Gould Cl CHONG CM5 ... 282 D1
Gouldings Av WOTN CO14 ... 199 J3
Goulds Rd BURES CO8 ... 100 F7
Goulton Rd CHLM/WR CM1 ... 264 B2
Gourney Gv CDH/CHF RM16 ... 407 J5
Government Rw PEND EN3 ... 325 H1

Gowan Brae SBF/HAD SS7 ... 379 J6
Gowan Cl SBF/HAD SS7 ... 379 J6
Gowers Av CHLM/GWD CM2 ... 288 F5
Gowers Cl KESG IP5 ... 39 M4
Gowers La CDH/CHF RM16 ... 408 A7
The Gowers HLW CM20 ... 256 B1
Gower St CHTY IP2 ... 2 F7
Goya Ri SBN/FI SS3 ... 403 H3
Goyfield Av FX IP11 ... 9 J2
Grace Cl BARK/HLT IG6 ... 350 A7
Grace Gdns BSF CM23 ... 174 A7
Graces Cl WIT CM8 ... 239 H4
Graces La RCHLM CM3 ... 290 C2
Graces Wk FOS CO13 ... 199 H5
   RCHLM CM3 ... 290 A1
Grafton Pl CHLM/GWD CM2 ... 265 H7
Grafton Rd CVI SS8 ... 413 K1
   HAR CO12 ... 7 K6
Grafton Wy IP IP1 ... 2 E6
Graham Av BROX EN10 ... 252 F8
   IP IP1 ... 37 J3
Graham Cl CHLM/GWD CM2 ... 335 J6
   HOC/HUL SS5 ... 362 F4
   RBRW/HUT CM13 ... 333 K7
   SLH/COR SS17 ... 394 E7
Graham Rd IP IP11 ... 85 C8
   IP IP1 ... 2 C1
Grailands BSF CM23 ... 173 L3
Grainger Cl SOSN SS2 ... 21 G2
Grainger Rd SOSN SS2 ... 21 G2
Grammar School Pl SUD CO10 ... 4 C7
Grampian Gv CHLM/WR CM1 ... 263 L5
The Granaries WAB EN9 ... 301 M5
Granary Cl RCHLM CM3 ... 318 C6
The Granary HLWW/ROY CM19 ... 254 C2
   SUD CO10 ... 31 J5
Granby Park Rd CHESW EN7 ... 276 A8
Grand Dr LOS SS9 ... 400 A3
Grand Pde LOS SS9 ... 400 A3
Grandview Rd SBF/HAD SS7 ... 380 C4
Grange Av LOS SS9 ... 381 H6
   RCHLM CM3 ... 319 J4
   WICKW SS12 ... 359 J5
Grange Cl FOS CO13 ... 199 H4
   FX IP11 ... 8 E1
   HSTD CO9 ... 128 F4
   KESG IP5 ... 39 M3
   LOS SS9 ... 381 M8
   RBRW/HUT CM13 ... 355 H6
   WFD IG8 ... 348 A6
Grange Ct WAB EN9 ... 301 K6
Grange Crs CHIG IG7 ... 349 L6
Grange Farm Av FX IP11 ... 8 E1
Grange Gdns RAYL SS6 ... 361 J8
   SOS SS1 ... 21 J5
Grange HI RCOLW CO6 ... 186 A2
Grange La GTDUN CM6 ... 179 J4
   HLWW/ROY CM19 ... 254 D3
   KESG IP5 ... 39 M3
Grange Pk BSF CM23 ... 174 A2
Grange Park Dr LOS SS9 ... 400 A1
Granger Av MAL CM9 ... 293 C2
Grange Rd BCAYE CM11 ... 357 K4
   BOC CM0 ... 298 A8
   BSF CM23 ... 174 B4
   FX IP11 ... 8 E3
   GRAYS RM17 ... 417 J3
   HAR CO12 ... 143 H1
   HARH RM3 ... 352 C7
   IPNE IP4 ... 3 K5
   K/T/MI CO5 ... 214 B6
   LOS SS9 ... 399 L2
   MGTR CO11 ... 137 M4
   PIT SS13 ... 378 F3
   RCHLM CM3 ... 233 M1
   RCOLW CO6 ... 134 C4
   SAFWN CB10 ... 41 H3
   SBF/HAD SS7 ... 379 M8
   SOCK/AV RM15 ... 405 K6
   WICKE SS11 ... 359 K1
   WIT CM8 ... 239 L7
Granger Wy EMPK RM11 ... 371 H6
Grangeside BSF CM23 ... 174 A1
Grange Wk BSF CM23 ... 174 B4
Grange Wy COLS CO2 ... 163 L7
   ERITH DA8 ... 414 C4
Grangeway SBF/HAD SS7 ... 380 B5
   WFD IG8 ... 348 D5
Grangewood Av
   CDH/CHF RM16 ... 407 M8
   RAIN RM13 ... 404 D2
Grangewood Cl
   RBRW/HUT CM13 ... 355 H4
Granites Cha BCAYE CM11 ... 358 A5
Granta Cl SAFWN CB10 ... 42 E2
Granta V CBE/LIN CB1 ... 24 E1
Grantchester Pl KESG IP5 ... 39 M3
Grant Cl WICKW SS12 ... 359 M6
Grantham Crs CHTY IP2 ... 2 B8
Grantham Gdns CHDH RM6 ... 370 A6
Grantham Rd CDH/CHF RM16 ... 407 H6
Grantley Cl RCOLW CO6 ... 160 E6
Granton Av HCH RM12 ... 390 A1
Granville Cl BCAYW CM12 ... 335 G6
   RCOLW CO6 ... 133 M8
   SBF/HAD SS7 ... 379 M7
Granville Gdns HOD EN11 ... 253 H1
Granville Rd COL CO1 ... 163 J6
   COS CO15 ... 304 C1
   EPP CM16 ... 304 C1
   FX IP11 ... 9 K4
Granville St IP IP1 ... 2 C3
Granville Wy RCOLE CO7 ... 221 H4
Grapnells VGE SS16 ... 378 A7
Grasby Cl RCOLE CO7 ... 192 C1
Grasmead Av LOS SS9 ... 400 A1
Grasmere Av FX IP11 ... 85 L7
   HOC/HUL SS5 ... 339 L7
   IPSE IP3 ... 59 J2
   LOU IG10 ... 327 G4
Grasmere Gdns FOS CO13 ... 199 G4
Grasmere Rd CVI SS8 ... 397 K5
   SBF/HAD SS7 ... 380 B5
Grasmere BRTR CM7 ... 182 D5

Gratmore Gn VGE SS16 ... 377 M8
Gravel Cl CHIG IG7 ... 350 B3
Gravel HI RCOLW CO6 ... 104 B1
Gravel La CHIG IG7 ... 328 B8
Gravelly La CHLM/WR CM1 ... 262 C6
Gravelpit La MGTR CO11 ... 78 F8
Gravel Pit La MGTR CO11 ... 108 F1
Gravel Rd LOS SS9 ... 381 J3
The Gravel RCOLW CO6 ... 186 A1
Gray Av BCTR RM8 ... 370 A8
Gray Gdns RAIN RM13 ... 389 H5
Grayling Cl BRTR CM7 ... 182 F2
Grayling Dr COLN CO4 ... 164 A2
Gray Rd COLW CO3 ... 162 E5
Grays Av VGE SS16 ... 394 D2
Grays Cl K/T/MI CO5 ... 245 K5
Grays Ct BSF CM23 ... 173 M3
Grays End Cl CDH/CHF RM16 ... 407 H8
Gray's La BRTR CM7 ... 95 M7
Grays Md HSTD CO9 ... 97 L1
Graysons Cl RAYL SS6 ... 380 F1
Grays Wk RBRW/HUT CM13 ... 355 L1
Great Bentley Rd RCOLE CO7 ... 194 B3
Great Berry Farm Cha
   VGE SS16 ... 376 B7
Great Berry La VGE SS16 ... 376 B7
Great Brays HLWS CM18 ... 256 B4
Great Burches Rd SBF/HAD SS7 ... 380 B4
Great Cambridge Rd BAR EN8 ... 300 D6
   BROX EN10 ... 276 F6
Great Canfield Rd RBSF CM22 ... 176 E4
Great Cob CHLM/WR CM1 ... 264 F6
Great Colman St IPNE IP4 ... 2 F4
Great Cullings ROMW/RG RM7 ... 388 F5
Great Eastern Cl BSF CM23 ... 174 B5
Great Eastern Rd BRW CM14 ... 354 D5
   HOC/HUL SS5 ... 362 F6
   SUD CO10 ... 4 E7
Great Fld FX IP11 ... 84 D5
Great Fox Meadow
   BRWN CM15 ... 332 A1
Great Gardens Rd EMPK RM11 ... 371 J6
Great Gipping St IP IP1 ... 2 D5
Great Godfreys CHLM/WR CM1 ... 287 C2
Great Gregorie VGE SS16 ... 18 B8
Great Gregories La EPP CM16 ... 303 M5
Great Hadham Rd BSF CM23 ... 173 K6
Great Harlings RIPS/CAP IP9 ... 113 H2
Great Harrods FOS CO13 ... 199 H4
Great Hays LOS SS9 ... 381 M8
Great Holland Common Rd
   COS CO15 ... 224 C1
Greathouse Cha SLH/COR SS17 ... 395 K5
Great House Farm Rd
   COLS CO2 ... 190 B6
Great Knightleys LAIN SS15 ... 18 A6
Great Lawn CHONG CM5 ... 283 H7
Great Leighs Wy PIT SS13 ... 378 D2
Great Leylands HLWS CM18 ... 256 B4
Great Meadow BROX EN10 ... 277 H2
Great Mistley VGE SS16 ... 19 K8
Great Nelmes Cha EMPK RM11 ... 372 A1
Great Notley Av BRTR CM7 ... 182 D6
   BRTR CM7 ... 182 E6
Great Oak Ct HSTD CO9 ... 73 H2
Great Oaks BSDN SS14 ... 18 F6
   CHIG IG7 ... 349 K5
   RBRW/HUT CM13 ... 333 J8
Great Owl Rd CHIG IG7 ... 349 H4
Great Plumtree HLW CM20 ... 256 A1
Great Ranton PIT SS13 ... 378 D3
Great Ropers La BRW CM14 ... 354 B7
Great Saling WICKE SS11 ... 360 B1
Great Smials RBRW/HUT CM13 ... 339 K5
Great Spenders BSDN SS14 ... 19 L2
Great Sq BRTR CM7 ... 155 C8
Great Tey Rd RCOLW CO6 ... 159 K6
Great Totham Rd WIT CM8 ... 240 C6
Great Tufts RIPS/CAP IP9 ... 78 C2
Great Warley St
   RBRW/HUT CM13 ... 373 H1
Great Wheatley Rd RAYL SS6 ... 380 D5
Great Whip St CHTY IP2 ... 2 F7
Great Yeldham Rd HSTD CO9 ... 72 C3
Grebe Cl CHTY IP2 ... 57 M1
   RCHLM CM3 ... 319 H3
Grebe Crest WTHK RM20 ... 416 B1
Greding Wk RBRW/HUT CM13 ... 355 J3
Green Acre SUD CO10 ... 35 M8
Greenacre La INC CM4 ... 335 M3
Greenacre Ms LOS SS9 ... 399 M7
Greenacres COLN CO4 ... 134 F8
   COS CO15 ... 13 K2
   EPP CM16 ... 280 A8
   RCOLW CO6 ... 186 A2
   SBF/HAD SS7 ... 379 M7
Greenacres Cl RAIN RM13 ... 404 F1
Green Acres Rd COLS CO2 ... 190 A6
Greenall Cl BAR EN8 ... 300 F5
Green Av CVI SS8 ... 397 M8
Greenbank CHESW EN7 ... 276 C8
Greenbank Cl HARH RM3 ... 352 E4
Greenbanks LOS SS9 ... 400 B1
   UPMR RM14 ... 390 F4
Green Cl BAR EN8 ... 300 F4
   CHLM/WR CM1 ... 264 C1
   EPP CM16 ... 279 J4
   RCHLM CM3 ... 238 C2
Green Crs KIR/NAC IP10 ... 71 H1
Greendyke CVI SS8 ... 398 A6
Green End La FOS CO13 ... 198 B6
Greene Vw BRTR CM7 ... 183 J3
Green Farm Rd RCOLW CO6 ... 130 C1
Greenfield WIT CM8 ... 239 H7
Greenfield Dr BCAYW CM12 ... 357 G3
Greenfield St WAB EN9 ... 301 K6
Greenfields Wy HVHL CB9 ... 27 M5
Greenfinch Av CHTY IP2 ... 36 E8
Greenfinch End COLN CO4 ... 164 A3
Greenford Rd COS CO15 ... 12 B6

Green Gld EPP CM16 327 M1
Green Glades EMPK RM11 372 A6
Greenhill BKHH IG9 348 D2
Greenhill Pk BSF CM23 173 L6
Greenhills HLW CM20 255 M3
Greenhurst Rd RCOLE CO7 221 H5
Greenlands RCFD SS4 363 L7
Green La BCAYW CM12 356 D7
BCAYW CM12 357 H8
BCTR RM8 388 A1
BOC CM0 344 A4
BROX EN10 277 J3
BRW CM14 331 L3
BRW CM14 354 B2
BRWN CM15 332 D8
CBE/LIN CB1 24 D1
CDH/CHF RM16 407 K3
CHIG IG7 349 M4
CHLM/WR CM1 262 C7
COLN CO4 135 M8
CVI SS8 398 A8
GTDUN CM6 178 D2
HLWE CM17 257 J4
K/T/MI CO5 214 E5
K/T/MI CO5 241 M2
LOS SS9 381 L4
MAL CM9 241 K7
RBRW/HUT CM13 354 B8
RCHLM CM3 319 H5
RCOLE CO7 136 E5
RCOLE CO7 164 D2
RCOLW CO6 104 E6
RCOLW CO6 134 D5
RCOLW CO6 160 C5
RCOS CO16 196 B6
RIPS/CAP IP9 79 K4
VGE SS16 376 E7
WAB EN9 302 E7
WIT CM8 210 B1
WOTN CO14 199 L1
Greenleas SBF/HAD SS7 380 C5
Green Man La WIT CM8 240 A5
Green Md RCHLM CM3 339 K4
Greenmoor Rd PEND EN3 324 D4
Greenoaks SBF/HAD SS7 379 M8
Greenock Wy ROM RM1 351 M8
Green Ride LOU IG10 326 B8
Green Rd SBF/HAD SS7 397 L2
The Greens Cl LOU IG10 327 H4
Greens Farm La BCAYE CM11 357 K2
Greenshaw BRW CM14 354 C2
Greensmill MGTR CO11 108 C6 2
Greenspire Gv RIPW IP8 57 J1 1
Greenstead SBW CM21 227 M2
Greenstead Av WFD IG8 348 D7
Greenstead Cl
RBRW/HUT CM13 355 M1 2
Greenstead Gdns WFD IG8 348 D7
Greenstead Rd COL CO1 11 J7
COLS CO2 11 L9
Greensted Cl BSDN SS14 378 A6
Greensted Rd CHONG CM5 282 B8
LOU IG10 348 F1
The Greensted BSDN SS14 378 A6
The Greens IPNE IP4 39 G7
Green St GTDUN CM6 176 F8
ING CM4 309 K5
PEND EN3 325 E5
Greensward La HOC/HUL SS5 363 G5
The Green BAR EN8 276 D8
BSF CM23 174 A8 1
CDH/CHF RM16 408 B3
CHLM/WR CM1 264 A7
CHLM/WR CM1 287 J2
COS CO15 250 C1
EPP CM16 327 M1
ING CM4 308 F3
LOS SS9 381 M4
MGTR CO11 109 G7
SLH/COR SS17 409 L2 1
Green Trees EPP CM16 304 B3
Green Trees Av RCHLM CM3 317 G6
Greenview Pk COS CO15 224 B4
Green Wk CHONG CM5 307 G2
DART DA1 414 A8
WFD IG8 348 F7 2
Greenway BCAYE CM11 357 L2
BSF CM23 174 D5
FOS CO13 199 G6
HARH RM3 353 J7
HLWW/ROY CM19 14 A4
RBRW/HUT CM13 355 H1
Green Wy RCOLW CO6 130 B1
Greenway Gdns BRTR CM7 182 E4
Greenways CHLM/WR CM1 264 C5
CVI SS8 398 A6 3
HSTD CO9 127 M4 1
K/T/MI CO5 186 E8
MAL CM9 293 G1 2
RCFD SS4 383 G1
SAFWS CB11 65 M4
SBF/HAD SS7 397 J1
SOS SS1 401 M4
Greenways Cl IP IP1 37 J3
The Greenways RCOLW CO6 158 B8
The Greenway COS CO15 224 C4
PEND EN3 300 E7 3
WICKE SS11 337 K8
Greenwich Cl IPSE IP3 58 F1
Greenwich Rd IPSE IP3 58 E1
Greenwood Av DAGE RM10 388 C3
CHESW EN7 300 C3
PEND EN3 324 F3
SBF/HAD SS7 397 L2
Greenwood Cl CHESW EN7 300 C3 2
HVHL CB9 27 M4 2
Greenwood Gdns
BARK/HLT IG6 349 K8
Greenwood Gv COLN CO4 135 K8
Greenwood Rd CHIG IG7 350 C5
Greenyard WAB EN9 301 K5 3
Gregory Cl HOC/HUL SS5 363 G7 2
Gregory St SUD CO10 4 C6
Grenadine Cl CHESW EN7 276 A7 3
Grendel Wy COS CO15 225 G5
Grenfell Av COS CO15 224 F4
HCH RM12 371 G8
Grenfell Cl COLN CO4 11 J4
Grennan Cl RBRW/HUT CM13 355 L7
Grenville Av BROX EN10 277 G1
Grenville Cl BAR EN8 300 E4
Grenville Gdns WFD IG8 348 D8
Grenville Rd BRTR CM7 154 F8
SUD CO10 4 F1
Gresham Ct BRW CM14 354 D4
Gresham Rd BRW CM14 354 D4
Gresley Cl COLN CO4 10 D2
Gresley Gdns CHTY IP2 2 F9
Greville Cl WOTN CO14 199 M1
Greyfriars RBRW/HUT CM13 355 J1
Grey Friars Rd IP IP1 2 E6
Greygoose Pk
HLWW/ROY CM19 255 J6 1
Greyhound Hl COLN CO4 105 M7
Greyhound La CDH/CHF RM16 408 B7
Greyhound Wy SOSN SS2 21 H3
Grey Ladys CHLM/GWD CM2 288 C8
Greys Cl SUD CO10 32 D2
Greys Hollow SAFWS CB11 118 E3
Greystones Cl COLW CO3 162 B8
Grey Towers Av EMPK RM11 371 L8
Grey Towers Gdns
EMPK RM11 371 K7 1
Gridiron Pl UPMR RM14 390 C1
Grieves Ct COLW CO3 161 K7
Griffin Av CVI SS8 398 D6
UPMR RM14 372 F6
The Griffins CDH/CHF RM16 407 J7
Grifon Cl CDH/CHF RM16 406 D8 1
Grifon Rd CDH/CHF RM16 406 D8
Griggs Gdns HCH RM12 389 K4 2
Grimshaw Wy ROM RM1 371 G5 2
Grimston La FX IP11 84 A4
Grimston Rd BSDN SS14 378 A2
COLS CO2 163 H7
Grimston Wy WOTN CO14 199 J4
Grimwade Cl MGTR CO11 108 E4
Grimwade St IPNE IP4 3 H6
The Grindle RIPW IP8 36 A4
Grinstead La RBSF CM22 201 K5
The Grip CBE/LIN CB1 24 C2
Groom Pk COS CO15 12 E3
Groom Rd BROX EN10 277 G6
Groomside BRTR CM7 183 H1 1
Grooms La WIT CM8 184 F7
Grosvenor Cl BSF CM23 173 L8
CHLM/GWD CM2 17 L9
IPNE IP4 37 M3 1
K/T/MI CO5 214 E6
LOU IG10 327 J3
Grosvenor Dr EMPK RM11 371 K8
LOU IG10 327 J4
Grosvenor Gdns BCAYW CM12 335 H7
UPMR RM14 390 E1
WFD IG8 348 B7
Grosvenor Ms WOS/PRIT SS0 400 D4
Grosvenor Rd BCTR RM8 370 A8
BROX EN10 253 G8
CDH/CHF RM16 408 E4
RAYL SS6 361 J7 2
ROMW/RG RM7 370 E7
SBF/HAD SS7 397 M2
SUD CO10 54 E1
WOS/PRIT SS0 400 D4
Grove Av K/T/MI CO5 245 K6
VGE SS16 376 C8
WOTN CO14 199 J3
Grove Cl RAYL SS6 381 G1
Grove Ct RAYL SS6 381 H2
WAB EN9 301 J5
Grovedale Cl CHESW EN7 300 A2
Grove Farm Rd WIT CM8 241 G2
Grove Fld BRTR CM7 155 K1
Grove Gdns DAGE RM10 388 D2 1
PEND EN3 324 E3
The Grove; Henley Roa IP IP1 37 K1
Groveherst Rd DART DA1 415 G7
Grove Hl COLN CO4 106 A7
LOS SS9 381 J4
RCOLE CO7 106 E7
RIPW IP8 57 K4
STSD CM24 146 F4
Grovelands Rd WICKW SS12 359 L5
Grovelands Wy GRAYS RM17 417 G2
Grove La CHIG IG7 350 A4
EPP CM16 304 B2 1
IPNE IP4 3 K5
RIPS/CAP IP9 81 L6
Grove Orch BRTR CM7 155 K2
Grove Park Rd RAIN RM13 389 H7
Grove Rd BCAYW CM12 357 G1
CHLM/GWD CM2 17 H6
CVI SS8 398 D7
FX IP11 85 H7
GRAYS RM17 417 K3
K/T/MI CO5 214 E6
MGTR CO11 108 E3
RAYL SS6 381 G1
RCOS CO16 196 E6
RIPS/CAP IP9 78 F5
SBF/HAD SS7 397 L1
SLH/COR SS17 409 L3
Grove Rd West PEND EN3 324 D1
Grover St SOS SS1 21 H7
Groves Cl SOCK/AV RM15 406 A5 2
The Grove BCAYE CM11 335 K6
BRW CM14 354 A5
CHLM/GWD CM2 289 J6
COS CO15 13 G7
RBSF CM22 175 G7
RCHLM CM3 315 G2
SOSN SS2 21 L2
STDN SG11 172 F4
UPMR RM14 390 B3
WIT CM8 239 H1
Grove Wk SBN/FI SS3 402 F4 1
Grovewood Av LOS SS9 381 J4
Grovewood Cl LOS SS9 381 J4
Grovewood Pl WFD IG8 349 G7
Gryme's Dyke Wy COLW CO3 161 L8
Guardian Cl HCH RM12 389 J1
Guardsman Cl BRW CM14 354 E6
Gubbins La HARH RM3 372 A1
Guelph's La GTDUN CM6 92 B8
Guernsey Gdns WICKE SS11 359 K2
Guernsey Wy BRTR CM7 182 E1
Guildford Rd COL CO1 10 F6
HARH RM3 352 F7
SOSN SS2 21 H4
Guildhall Wy SAFWN CB10 45 H4
Guild Rd ERITH DA8 414 A4
The Guilfords HLWE CM17 227 L6
Guinea Cl BRTR CM7 155 L7 4
Guinevere Gdns BAR EN8 300 F2 2
Guithavon Ri WIT CM8 239 G1 2
Guithavon Rd WIT CM8 239 G2
Guithavon St WIT CM8 239 G1
Guithavon Va WIT CM8 239 G1
Gulls Cft BRTR CM7 155 K8
Gull's La RCOLE CO7 107 H8
Gulpher Rd FX IP11 84 F7
Gumley Rd WTHK RM20 416 E3
Gunfleet Cl K/T/MI CO5 245 J4
Gun Hl COLN CO4 106 C4
TIL RM18 418 E3
Gun Hill Pl VGE SS16 19 J8
Gunners Rd SBN/FI SS3 403 H4
Gurdon Rd COLS CO2 163 G8
Gurlings Cl HVHL CB9 28 B1
Gurney Benham Cl COLS CO2 162 C7 1
Gurton Rd RCOLW CO6 158 B8
Gustedhall La HOC/HUL SS5 381 M1
Gutteridge Hall La RCOS CO16 195 M4
Gutteridge La ABR/ST RM4 329 K8
Gutters La CHLM/WR CM1 264 C4
Guy Cook Cl SUD CO10 55 K6
Guys Farm Rd RCHLM CM3 339 L4
Guysfield Cl RAIN RM13 389 H7 1
Guysfield Dr RAIN RM13 389 H7
Gwendalen Av CVI SS8 398 E7
Gwendoline Rd IPNE IP4 38 F7
Gwyn Cl RCHLM CM3 265 M2 3
Gwynne Park Av WFD IG8 349 G7
Gwynne Rd HAR CO12 7 K6
Gymnasium St IP IP1 2 C3
Gypsy La K/T/MI CO5 187 J4

H

Haarlem Rd CVI SS8 397 L7
Haarle Rd CVI SS8 413 L1 3
Haase Cl CVI SS8 398 B5
Habgood Rd LOU IG10 326 F5
Hackamore SBF/HAD SS7 380 C6
Hackmans La RCHLM CM3 291 M8
Hacton Dr HCH RM12 389 M3
Hacton La HCH RM12 390 A1
UPMR RM14 390 A4
Haddestoke Ga BROX EN10 277 G6
Haddon Cl EN EN1 324 B8 1
RAYL SS6 361 H8
Haddon Md RCHLM CM3 339 L6
Haddon Pk COL CO1 11 K9
Hadfield Rd SLH/COR SS17 409 L2
Hadham Ct BSF CM23 173 L3
Hadham Gv BSF CM23 173 K3
Hadham Rd BSF CM23 173 L3
Hadleigh Ct BROX EN10 277 G2
Hadleigh Park Av SBF/HAD SS7 380 D8
Hadleigh Rd FOS CO13 199 H6
LOS SS9 399 K2
RCOS CO16 223 J6
RIPW IP8 36 D7
WOS/PRIT SS0 20 C7
Hadley Cl BRTR CM7 155 J2
Hadley Gra HLWE CM17 256 D4
Hadrian Cl COLN CO4 135 J5
HVHL CB9 28 E4 2
Hadrians Cl WIT CM8 238 F3 2
Hadrian's Ride EN EN1 324 A7
Hadrians Wy MAL CM9 269 H6
Hadstock Rd CBE/LIN CB1 24 C2
Haggars La RCOLE CO7 166 A8
Hagg Hl RCHLM CM3 316 D6
Haglemere Dr IPNE IP4 3 K2
Haig Ct CHLM/GWD CM2 16 E6
Haig Rd CDH/CHF RM16 408 B8
Hailes Wd RBSF CM22 147 L1
Hailey Av HOD EN11 253 H1
Haileybury Av EN EN1 324 A8
Hailey La HOD EN11 252 E2
Hailsham Cl HARH RM3 352 D6
Hailsham Rd HARH RM3 352 D6
Hainault Av RCFD SS4 363 K7
WOS/PRIT SS0 20 B2
Hainault Cl SBF/HAD SS7 380 F7
Hainault Gv CHIG IG7 349 K5
CHLM/WR CM1 16 A5
Hainault Rd CHDH RM6 350 C8
CHIG IG7 349 K5
RCHLM CM3 341 H2
ROMW/RG RM7 370 E3
Halbutt St DAGW RM9 388 A3
Halcyon Wy EMPK RM11 372 A8
Hale Cl CHTY IP2 57 L1
Hale End HARH RM3 352 C7
Halesowen Cl CHTY IP2 58 A3 1
Halesworth Cl HARH RM3 352 F7 2
Halesworth Rd HARH RM3 352 F7
Half Acres BSF CM23 174 A3
Halfacres WIT CM8 239 H4
Halfhide La BAR EN8 276 E6
Halfhides WAB EN9 301 L5
Half Moon La EPP CM16 304 A3 2
Halford Ct RIPW IP8 57 K1
Halfway Ct PUR RM19 415 H1
Halidon Ri HARH RM3 353 J7
Halifax Rd CHTY IP2 58 C1
Hallam Cl BRWN CM15 332 C1
Hallam Ct BCAYW CM12 335 G7 2
Hall Av SOCK/AV RM15 405 K6
Hall Bridge Ri MAL CM9 269 K7
Hall Cha GTDUN CM6 206 E3
RCOLW CO6 160 C8
Hall Cl CHLM/GWD CM2 289 H5
COS CO15 225 G5 2
SLH/COR SS17 394 F7
Hall Crs SBF/HAD SS7 380 E8
SOCK/AV RM15 405 K7
Hallcroft Cha COLN CO4 135 K7 4
Hall Cut RCOLE CO7 221 G5 2
Hall Dr HSTD CO9 127 L3
Hallet Rd CVI SS8 398 F8
Hall Farm Cl K/T/MI CO5 186 F7
SBF/HAD SS7 397 L2
Hall Farm Rd SBF/HAD SS7 397 L1
Hall Fld FX IP11 84 E8
Hall Green La RBRW/HUT CM13 355 L1
Hallingbury Cl RBSF CM22 201 J2
Hallingbury Rd BSF CM23 174 C7
SBW CM21 201 H7
Halling Hl HLW CM20 256 A2
Halliwell Rd IPNE IP4 38 C5
Hall La BRWN CM15 333 G8
CHLM/GWD CM2 289 K5
CHLM/GWD CM2 312 E6
CHLM/WR CM1 264 C7 1
HAR CO12 143 H1
HARH RM3 372 D2
HSTD CO9 50 C5
ING CM4 334 D1
RCOS CO16 197 H3
ROY SG8 62 A1
UPMR RM14 372 D5
WOTN CO14 199 L2
Hallmores BROX EN10 253 H7 1
Hallowell Down RCHLM CM3 339 M5
Hall Park Av WOS/PRIT SS0 400 C3
Hall Park Rd UPMR RM14 390 D4 1
Hall Pond Wy FX IP11 84 E8
Hall Ri SUD CO10 54 D6
Hall Rd BOC CM0 321 J4
BRTR CM7 154 A4
BURES CO8 101 M6
DART DA1 415 G8
GPK RM2 371 J3
HOC/HUL SS5 382 B1
K/T/MI CO5 214 D8
KESG IP5 39 M1
KIR/NAC IP10 39 M7
MAL CM9 240 C8
MAL CM9 269 J7
MAL CM9 272 E2
RBSF CM22 147 L2
RCFD SS4 383 D2
RCOLE CO7 165 K1
RCOLW CO6 132 E6
RCOLW CO6 133 L6
RCOLW CO6 160 F7
SOCK/AV RM15 405 K7
SUD CO10 54 B1
Hallside Rd EN EN1 324 A2
Hall St CHLM/GWD CM2 17 H5
SUD CO10 34 D4
Hall Ter SOCK/AV RM15 405 L7
Hall View Rd RCOLE CO7 194 F4
Hall Wk RIPW IP8 36 A1
Hallwood Crs BRWN CM15 354 F1
Halstead Ct WICKW SS12 359 K6 2
Halstead Rd BRTR CM7 127 M8
COLW CO3 161 J4
FOS CO13 198 D3
HSTD CO9 98 B5
HSTD CO9 127 M3
RCOLW CO6 130 A4
RCOLW CO6 132 B7
Halstead Wy RBRW/HUT CM13 333 J8
Halston Pl MAL CM9 293 G3
Halstow Wy PIT SS13 378 D6
Halt Dr TIL RM18 419 H1
Halton Crs IPSE IP3 59 K2 1
Halton Rd CDH/CHF RM16 408 C8
Haltwhistle Rd RCHLM CM3 339 K3
Halyard Reach RCHLM CM3 339 L6
Hamberts Rd RCHLM CM3 339 L2
Hamble Cl WIT CM8 238 F1 3
Hamble La SOCK/AV RM15 406 A3
Hamble Wy BOC CM0 344 B5 3
Hamboro Gdns LOS SS9 399 J2
Hambro' Av RAYL SS6 361 L7
Hambro Cl RAYL SS6 361 M7
Hambro Hl RAYL SS6 361 M6
Hambro Rd BRW CM14 354 E3
Hamburgh Ct BAR EN8 276 E8 3
Hamden Crs DAGE RM10 388 C2
Hamel Wy SAFWS CB11 89 L7
Hamford Cl WOTN CO14 199 L1 1
Hamford Dr HAR CO12 141 K8
Hamilton Av HOD EN11 253 H3
ROM RM1 370 E2
Hamilton Cl LOS SS9 399 H1
Hamilton Crs BRW CM14 354 D6
Hamilton Dr EMPK RM11 371 M2
Hamilton Gdns FX IP11 9 M3
HOC/HUL SS5 362 F4
Hamilton Ms RAYL SS6 362 A8
SAFWS CB11 66 A1 3
Hamilton Rd COLW CO3 162 E6
FOS CO13 198 B6
FX IP11 9 M2
GPK RM2 371 J5
IPSE IP3 38 C8
RBSF CM22 177 G3
RCOLE CO7 192 C3
SUD CO10 4 D7
Hamilton St FX IP11 84 F8 4
HAR CO12 6 B4
Hamlet Cl CRW RM5 351 H8
Hamlet Ct BURES CO8 101 M3 1
Hamlet Court Ms WOS/PRIT SS0 20 C4
Hamlet Court Rd WOS/PRIT SS0 20 B6
Hamlet Dr COLN CO4 164 A4
Hamlet Hl HLWW/ROY CM19 254 D7
Hamlet Rd CHLM/GWD CM2 17 G6
CRW RM5 351 H8
HVHL CB9 28 B4
WOS/PRIT SS0 20 E7
Hamley Cl SBF/HAD SS7 379 J5
Hammarskjold Rd HLW CM20 15 K2
Hammond Cl CHESW EN7 276 A6
Hammond Rd EN EN1 324 C5
Hammonds La BCAYE CM11 357 K4 1
RBRW/HUT CM13 354 C7 1
Hammonds Rd
CHLM/GWD CM2 289 L2
RBSF CM22 203 H5
Hampden Cl EPP CM16 281 H7
Hampden Crs BRW CM14 354 D6 1
CHESW EN7 300 C3
Hampden Rd GRAYS RM17 417 J2
Hampit Rd SAFWS CB11 87 L1
Hampshire Rd EMPK RM11 372 B4 2
Hampstead Av COS CO15 12 C2
Hampstead Gdns HOC/HUL SS5 363 G4
Hampton Cl SOSN SS2 382 F7
Hampton Ct HOC/HUL SS5 362 E5 3
Hampton Gdns SBW CM21 227 J4
SOSN SS2 382 F7
Hampton Rd CHLM/GWD CM2 288 F5
IP IP1 37 G4
Hamstel Rd HLW CM20 15 H2
SOSN SS2 383 L8
Hamsters Cl HSTD CO9 100 A3 1
Hanbury Cl BAR EN8 300 E2
Hanbury Gdns COLN CO4 135 J6
Hanbury Rd CHLM/WR CM1 16 A8
Hance La BRTR CM7 182 A1
Hanchetts Orch GTDUN CM6 92 B8 2
Handel Crs TIL RM18 418 B4
Handel Rd CVI SS8 413 L1
Handford Cut IP IP1 2 B4
Handford Rd IP IP1 2 B4
Hand La SBW CM21 227 K2
Handleys Cha LAIN SS15 377 G1
Hanford Rd SOCK/AV RM15 405 K6 3
Hanging Hill La
RBRW/HUT CM13 355 J4
Haning Hill La
RBRW/HUT CM13 333 K8
Hankin Av HAR CO12 142 D2
Hanlee Brook CHLM/GWD CM2 289 G6
Hannah Cl CVI SS8 398 B5 4
Hannards Wy CHIG IG7 350 C6
Hannett Rd CVI SS8 398 F8
Hanningfield Cl RAYL SS6 361 H8 3
Hanningfield Wy COLN CO4 135 J6 1
Hanover Br K/T/MI CO5 187 G6
Hanover Cl BSDN SS14 377 M6 1
Hanover Dr BSDN SS14 377 M6
Hanover Gdns BARK/HLT IG6 349 K8
Hanover Ms HOC/HUL SS5 362 E5 3
Hansells Md HLWW/ROY CM19 254 B3
Hanson Dr LOU IG10 327 K4
Hanwell Cl RCOS CO16 12 C1
Ha'penny Fld RIPS/CAP IP9 80 E6
Harberts Rd HLWW/ROY CM19 15 H6
Harberts Wy RAYL SS6 361 K6
Harborough Hall Rd
K/T/MI CO5 214 E1
Harbour Crs HAR CO12 7 L4
Harbourer Rd BARK/HLT IG6 350 C6
Harcamlow Wy GTDUN CM6 91 M7
RBSF CM22 118 D3
RBSF CM22 175 K6
ROY SG8 40 C7
SAFWN CB10 44 E6
SAFWS CB11 65 K8
Harcourt Av HAR CO12 6 C7
SOSN SS2 20 E3
Harcourt Ms ROM RM1 371 G5 3
Hardie Rd DAGE RM10 388 D2
SLH/COR SS17 409 L1
Harding Rd CDH/CHF RM16 408 B8
Hardings Cl RCOLW CO6 160 C3
Harding's Elms Rd BCAYE CM11 358 C7
Harding's La ING CM4 310 A4
Hardley Crs EMPK RM11 371 L4
Hardwick Cl IPNE IP4 38 F6
RAYL SS6 380 E2
Hardwick Rd HVHL CB9 28 C3
Hardy Cl BRTR CM7 183 H3 3
MGTR CO11 108 D4
Hardy Gv DART DA1 415 H8
Hardys Wy CVI SS8 398 B5
Harebell Cl BCAYW CM12 335 G7
COLN CO4 135 J8 2
Harebell Dr WIT CM8 211 M8
Harebell Rd CHTY IP2 37 G7
Harebell Wy HARH RM3 352 E8
Harefield HLW CM20 256 B2
SUD CO10 34 E1
Harefield Rd CBE/LIN CB1 24 F1
Hare Hall La GPK RM2 371 J4 2
Hares Cha BCAYW CM12 335 G8
Haresfield Rd DAGE RM10 388 B5 1
Haresland Cl SBF/HAD SS7 381 G6
Hare St HLWW/ROY CM19 15 H5
Hare Street Springs
HLWW/ROY CM19 15 H5
Harewood Av RCFD SS4 363 K6
Harewood Hl EPP CM16 303 M7
Harewood Rd BRWN CM15 332 C8
CHLM/WR CM1 16 A6
Harfred Av MAL CM9 269 M8
Hargrave Cl STSD CM24 146 F3
Hargreaves Av CHESW EN7 300 C3
Hargreaves Cl CHESW EN7 300 C3 3
Harkilees Wy BRTR CM7 155 G6
Harkness Cl HARH RM3 353 G6
Harkstead La RIPS/CAP IP9 81 H2
Harkstead Rd RIPS/CAP IP9 81 G7
Harlech Rd PIT SS13 378 C6
Harlesden Cl HARH RM3 353 G8
Harlesden Rd HARH RM3 353 G7
Harley St LOS SS9 399 K2
Harlings Gv CHLM/WR CM1 17 H2
The Harlings HERT/BAY SG13 252 D1
Harlow Common HLWE CM17 256 E6
Harlow Gdns CRW RM5 351 K7
Harlow Rd CHONG CM5 258 D8
HLWE CM17 228 C4
HLWW/ROY CM19 254 D2
RAIN RM13 389 G7
SBW CM21 227 K3
Harman Av WFD IG8 348 A8
Harman Rd EN EN1 324 A7
Harness Cl CHLM/WR CM1 264 F4
Harnham Dr BRTR CM7 182 D4 4
Harold Cl HSTD CO9 129 G2
Harold Court Rd HARH RM3 353 J7
Harold Crs WAB EN9 301 K4
Harold Gdns WICKE SS11 359 L2
Harold Gv FOS CO13 199 G7
Harold Rd BRTR CM7 154 F8
COS CO15 13 H6
FOS CO13 199 G7
Harolds Rd HLWW/ROY CM19 14 C6
Harold Vw HARH RM3 372 A2

Harold Wy FOS CO13 ..... 199 G7
Haron Cl CVI SS8 ..... 398 C8
Harpclose Rd SUD CO10 ..... 4 E4
Harper's Hl RCOLW CO6 ..... 103 M1
Harper's Hill Est RCOLW CO6 ..... 104 A2
Harpers La BRWN CM15 ..... 332 E1
Harrap Cha RAYL SS6 ..... 361 K8 [2]
Harrap Cha GRAYS CM17 ..... 417 G2
Harridge Cl LOS SS9 ..... 381 M8
Harridge Rd LOS SS9 ..... 381 M8
Harrier Cl RAIN RM13 ..... 389 J5 [1]
Harrier Wy WAB EN9 ..... 302 B6
Harrierscourt WAB EN9 ..... 302 B4
Harrington Cl K/T/MI CO5 ..... 214 C6
Harris Cl SLH/COR SS17 ..... 395 J7
 WICKW SS12 ..... 360 A6
Harrison Ct RBRW/HUT CM13 ..... 333 L7
Harrison Dr BRTR CM7 ..... 183 H2 [2]
 EPP CM16 ..... 281 J6
Harrison Gdns HOC/HUL SS5 ..... 361 L1
Harrison Gv KESG IP5 ..... 39 G3
Harrison Rd COLS CO2 ..... 163 C8
 DAGE RM10 ..... 388 C5
Harrisons BSF CM23 ..... 174 E1
Harrisons Whf PUR RM19 ..... 415 H2
Harrison Wk BAR EN8 ..... 300 E1
Harris Rd DAGW RM9 ..... 388 A4
Harrods Ct BCAYE CM11 ..... 357 H1
Harrogate Dr HOC/HUL SS5 ..... 363 C3
Harrogate Rd HOC/HUL SS5 ..... 363 C4
Harrow Av EN EN1 ..... 324 A8 [2]
Harrow Cl HOC/HUL SS5 ..... 363 H6
 IPNE IP4 ..... 38 B6
Harrow Crs HARH RM3 ..... 352 C8
Harrow Dr EMPK RM11 ..... 371 K7
Harrow Gdns HOC/HUL SS5 ..... 363 H6
Harrow Hl HSTD CO9 ..... 72 A5
Harrow Rd COS CO15 ..... 13 C4
 CVI SS8 ..... 398 C6
 HVHL CB9 ..... 27 M4
 WICKW SS12 ..... 379 H1
Harrow Wy CHLM/GWD CM2 ..... 289 H5
Harsnett Rd COL CO1 ..... 163 J6
Harston Dr PEND EN3 ..... 325 H2
Hartest Wy SUD CO10 ..... 5 K9
Hartford Cl RAYL SS6 ..... 361 H1
Hartford End PIT SS13 ..... 378 B6
Hartington Pl SOS SS1 ..... 21 K8
Hartington Rd SOS SS1 ..... 21 J7
Hartland Cl LOS SS9 ..... 381 L4
Hartland Rd BAR EN8 ..... 300 E2
 EPP CM16 ..... 304 B3
 HCH RM12 ..... 389 H1
Hartley Cl CHLM/GWD CM2 ..... 265 H7
Hartley St CHTY IP2 ..... 2 F9
Hartmoor Ms PEND EN3 ..... 324 E1 [1]
Hart Rd HLWE CM17 ..... 227 K6
 SBF/HAD SS7 ..... 380 A5
Harts Gv WFD IG8 ..... 348 B6
Hart's La RCOLE CO7 ..... 136 A2
Hart St BRW CM14 ..... 354 D3
 CHLM/GWD CM2 ..... 16 E5
Hartsway PEND EN3 ..... 324 C1
Hartswood Cl BRW CM14 ..... 354 F5
Hartswood Rd BRW CM14 ..... 354 F5
Harty Cl CDH/CHF RM16 ..... 407 J6
Harvard Ct COLN CO4 ..... 135 J7
Harvest Cl RCHLM CM3 ..... 339 L4
Harvest Ct K/T/MI CO5 ..... 186 F7 [1]
Harvest End COLW CO3 ..... 161 L6
Harvesters' Wy RCOLW CO6 ..... 159 J3
Harvest La LOU IG10 ..... 348 E1
Harvest Rd CVI SS8 ..... 398 C6
Harvest Wy MAL CM9 ..... 269 G6
 RCOLE CO7 ..... 165 C5
Harvey CDH/CHF RM16 ..... 407 J6
Harvey Cl MGTR CO11 ..... 108 D7 [1]
Harvey Crs COLW CO3 ..... 161 K6
Harvey Gdns LOU IG10 ..... 327 J5
Harvey Rd COLS CO2 ..... 190 C1
 MAL CM9 ..... 240 B7
 PIT SS13 ..... 378 C1
 RCOLE CO7 ..... 192 C2
Harvey's La ROMW/RG RM7 ..... 388 C2
Harvey St HSTD CO9 ..... 129 C1
Harvey Wy SAFWN CB10 ..... 66 A1
 SAFWN CB10 ..... 69 C2
Harwater Dr LOU IG10 ..... 327 C4
Harwich Rd COLN CO4 ..... 11 K5
 HAR CO12 ..... 142 C4
 MGTR CO11 ..... 109 H7
 RCOLE CO7 ..... 136 F3 [2]
 RCOLE CO7 ..... 166 A5
 RCOS CO16 ..... 196 D7
Harwood Av EMPK RM11 ..... 371 M3
Harwood Cl COLS CO2 ..... 163 H7 [2]
Harwood Hall La UPMR RM14 ..... 390 C7
Haselfoot Rd RCHLM CM3 ..... 266 A3
Haselmere Gdns FOS CO13 ..... 199 C8
Haskell Ms BRTR CM7 ..... 183 H3 [2]
Haskins SLH/COR SS17 ..... 410 A1 [4]
Haskins Wk KESG IP5 ..... 39 M4
Haslemere BSF CM23 ..... 174 B7
Haslemere Rd WICKE SS11 ..... 359 K1
Hasler Rd MAL CM9 ..... 272 E1
Haslers La GTDUN CM6 ..... 178 E3
Haslewood Av HOD EN11 ..... 253 H4
Hassell Rd CVI SS8 ..... 398 C4
Hassenbrook Rd SLH/COR SS17 ..... 409 L1
Hastings Av COS CO15 ..... 250 C3
Hastings Cl WTHK RM20 ..... 416 F3
Hastings Pl COLW CO3 ..... 162 B7
Hastings Rd COLW CO3 ..... 162 B7
 GPK RM2 ..... 371 J5
 SOS SS1 ..... 21 K6
The Hastings WICKE SS11 ..... 359 L2
Hastingwood Rd HLWE CM17 ..... 256 F8
Hatches Farm Rd BCAYW CM12 ..... 356 E6
Hatchfields RCHLM CM3 ..... 235 C4
Hatch Gn RBSF CM22 ..... 201 J3
Hatch Rd BRWN CM15 ..... 332 B7
Hatch Side CHIG IG7 ..... 349 H6 [1]

The Hatch PEND EN3 ..... 324 E3
Hatchwoods WFD IG8 ..... 348 A5 [1]
Hatfield Cl HCH RM12 ..... 389 L4 [1]
 RBRW/HUT CM13 ..... 355 L1 [2]
Hatfield Dr BCAYE CM11 ..... 357 L1 [1]
Hatfield Gv CHLM/WR CM1 ..... 287 L2
Hatfield Rd IPSE IP3 ..... 38 B7
 MAL CM9 ..... 268 C4
 RAYL SS6 ..... 361 J8
 RCHLM CM3 ..... 210 D8
 WAB EN9 ..... 238 E5
Hatfields LOU IG10 ..... 327 J5
Hathaway Rd GRAYS CM17 ..... 407 J8
The Hatherley BSDN SS14 ..... 19 L3
Hatley Gdns SBF/HAD SS7 ..... 379 K6
Hatterill LAIN SS15 ..... 18 A8
 LAIN SS15 ..... 376 E6
Hatton Cl CDH/CHF RM16 ..... 406 E8
Hatton Rd BAR EN8 ..... 300 E1
Haubourdin Ct HSTD CO9 ..... 129 H1 [2]
Haughley Dr IPNE IP4 ..... 39 C5 [2]
Havana Cl ROM RM1 ..... 370 F6
Havana Dr RAYL SS6 ..... 361 J5
Havengore CHLM/WR CM1 ..... 264 F6
 PIT SS13 ..... 378 D3
Haven Pl CDH/CHF RM16 ..... 407 K7
Haven Ri BCAYE CM11 ..... 357 L5
Haven Rd COLS CO2 ..... 163 L7
 CVI SS8 ..... 412 E1
Havenside SBN/FI SS3 ..... 384 F6
The Havens KIR/NAC IG10 ..... 59 M4
The Haven GRAYS CM17 ..... 418 A2 [1]
Haverhill Rd HVHL CB9 ..... 28 C1
 HVHL CB9 ..... 47 K3
Havering Cl COLN CO4 ..... 11 G4
 COS CO15 ..... 223 M4
 SBN/FI SS3 ..... 385 J7
Havering Dr ROM RM1 ..... 370 F4
Havering Rd ROM RM1 ..... 370 E3 [2]
Havers La BSF CM23 ..... 174 A6
Havisham Wy CHLM/WR CM1 ..... 263 L4
Havis Rd SLH/COR SS17 ..... 394 F7
Haward Rd HOD EN11 ..... 253 K3
Hawbridge RIPS/CAP IP9 ..... 78 B1
Hawes La WAB EN9 ..... 325 K2
Hawes St CHTY IP2 ..... 3 C9
Hawfinch Rd COLS CO2 ..... 190 B6
Hawkbush Gn PIT SS13 ..... 378 C2 [1]
Hawk Cl WAB EN9 ..... 302 B6
Hawkdene CHING E4 ..... 325 J8
Hawkenbury Rd HLWW/ROY CM19 ..... 14 F9
Hawkendon Rd RCOS CO16 ..... 223 H7
Hawke Rd IPSE IP3 ..... 58 F7
Hawkesbury Bush La VGE SS16 ..... 395 H1
Hawkesbury Cl VGE SS16 ..... 412 F1 [1]
Hawkesbury Rd CVI SS8 ..... 397 M8
Hawkes Dr GRAYS CM17 ..... 417 J3 [5]
Hawkes La FX IP11 ..... 84 E7
Hawkes Rd RCOLW CO6 ..... 158 A4
Hawkeswary COS CO15 ..... 224 A5
Hawk Hl WICKE SS11 ..... 338 D8
Hawkins Cl RCHLM CM3 ..... 315 M1
 WICKE SS11 ..... 360 A4 [1]
Hawkins Dr COLS CO2 ..... 163 L5
 RCOLE CO7 ..... 193 J3
 SUD CO10 ..... 5 G1
Hawkins Wy BRTR CM7 ..... 155 K7
Hawk La WICKE SS11 ..... 360 E1
Hawkridge SBN/FI SS3 ..... 402 D3
Hawks Cl RCHLM CM3 ..... 291 H6
Hawks La HOC/HUL SS5 ..... 362 F6
Hawksmead Ct PEND EN3 ..... 300 E7 [1]
Hawksmoor Gn
 RBRW/HUT CM13 ..... 333 L7
Hawksway VGE SS16 ..... 377 J7
Hawkswood Rd BCAYE CM11 ..... 337 G4
Hawkwell Cha HOC/HUL SS5 ..... 362 F7
Hawkwell Park Dr
 HOC/HUL SS5 ..... 363 G6
Hawkwell Rd HOC/HUL SS5 ..... 362 F5
Hawkwood Cl RCHLM CM3 ..... 339 M2
Hawkwood Crs CHING E4 ..... 325 J8
Hawkwood Rd HSTD CO9 ..... 97 M3 [2]
Hawlmark End RCOLW CO6 ..... 159 M8
Hawsted BKHH IG9 ..... 348 C1 [1]
Hawthorn Av COLN CO4 ..... 163 M3
 RAIN RM13 ..... 404 C3 [2]
 RBRW/HUT CM13 ..... 355 G4
Hawthorn Cl
 CHLM/GWD CM2 ..... 288 D5 [1]
 HOC/HUL SS5 ..... 363 H6 [3]
 HSTD CO9 ..... 129 H1 [1]
 RBSF CM22 ..... 176 D4
Hawthorn Dr CHTY IP2 ..... 37 C9
Hawthorne Av CHESW EN7 ..... 300 C2
Hawthorne Cl CHESW EN7 ..... 300 C3
Hawthorne Gdns HOC/HUL SS5 ..... 362 C6
Hawthorne Rd SLH/COR SS17 ..... 395 C7
Hawthornes RCHLM CM3 ..... 316 E2
Hawthorn Ri BSF CM23 ..... 174 A8
Hawthorn Rd BKHH IG9 ..... 348 C5
 COS CO15 ..... 223 M4
 CVI SS8 ..... 398 D8
 HOD EN11 ..... 253 J5
 HVHL CB9 ..... 27 M2 [7]
 MAL CM9 ..... 242 B1
 RCHLM CM3 ..... 238 B6
 SUD CO10 ..... 5 J7
The Hawthorns RCHLM CM3 ..... 291 H4
 SLH/COR SS17 ..... 395 K7
Hawthorn Wk RCHLM CM3 ..... 339 M2
Hawthorn Wy RAYL SS6 ..... 381 G3 [7]
Hawtree Cl SOS SS1 ..... 21 L8

Hayburn Wy HCH RM12 ..... 371 G8
Haycocks La CHLM/WR CM1 ..... 246 A2
Haycocks Rd HVHL CB9 ..... 27 K2
Haycroft BSF CM23 ..... 174 D5
Haydens Rd HLWW/ROY CM19 ..... 15 K5
Hayden Wy CRW RM5 ..... 370 D2
Haydock Cl HCH RM12 ..... 390 A4
Haye La K/T/MI CO5 ..... 191 K7
Hayes Barton SOS SS1 ..... 402 D3
Hayes Cha RCHLM CM3 ..... 339 C6
 WICKE SS11 ..... 339 G7
Hayes Cl CHLM/GWD CM2 ..... 17 C5
 WTHK RM20 ..... 416 D3
Hayes Dr RAIN RM13 ..... 389 J6
Hayes La CVI SS8 ..... 398 A8
Hayes Rd COS CO15 ..... 12 F7
Hay Gn RCHLM CM3 ..... 291 G3
Hay Green La BRWN CM15 ..... 308 E7
 ING CM4 ..... 309 G6
Hayhill Rd IPNE IP4 ..... 3 J2
Hayhouse Rd RCOLW CO6 ..... 130 B6
Hay La BRTR CM7 ..... 155 K8
Hayle TIL RM18 ..... 409 H4
Hayley Bell Gdns BSF CM23 ..... 174 A8
Hayman Rd IPSE IP3 ..... 59 G2
Haymeads La BSF CM23 ..... 174 D5
Haynes Green Rd K/T/MI CO5 ..... 215 H3
Haynes Rd EMPK RM11 ..... 371 L5
Hayron's La CHLM/WR CM1 ..... 232 C3
Haysoms Cl ROM RM1 ..... 370 F4
Haytor Cl BRTR CM7 ..... 183 K1
The Haywain COLW CO3 ..... 161 L6 [8]
Haywards Cl RBRW/HUT CM13 ..... 333 M8
Haywards Flds KESG IP5 ..... 39 L3 [3]
Hayword Ct WAB EN9 ..... 302 A4
Hazelbrouck Gdns
 BARK/HLT IG6 ..... 349 L8
Hazel Cl HCH RM12 ..... 389 J2 [2]
 HVHL CB9 ..... 27 M4
 LAIN SS15 ..... 377 G1
 LOS SS9 ..... 399 K2
 RCOLE CO7 ..... 194 B6
 SBF/HAD SS7 ..... 399 G1
Hazelcroft Rd IP IP1 ..... 37 J1
Hazeldene BAR EN8 ..... 300 F4
Hazeldon Cl RCHLM CM3 ..... 235 K5 [8]
Hazel Dr ERITH DA8 ..... 414 B5
 IPSE IP3 ..... 59 M2
 SOCK/AV RM15 ..... 406 D1
Hazeleigh RBRW/HUT CM13 ..... 355 J4
Hazeleigh Gdns WFD IG8 ..... 348 F6
Hazeleigh Hall La MAL CM9 ..... 292 D6
Hazelend Rd BSF CM23 ..... 146 C8
Hazel Gdns CDH/CHF RM16 ..... 407 M8
Hazel Gv BRTR CM7 ..... 182 F2
 EN EN1 ..... 324 B8 [1]
Hazell Av COLS CO2 ..... 162 B8
Hazell Crs ROMW/RG RM7 ..... 370 C1
Hazelmere PIT SS13 ..... 378 B7
Hazelmere EMPK RM11 ..... 371 J5
Hazel Ri EMPK RM11 ..... 371 K6
Hazel Rd ERITH DA8 ..... 414 B5
Hazelton Rd COLN CO4 ..... 11 L3
Hazelville Cl HAR CO12 ..... 142 F2
Hazel Wy CHING E4 ..... 325 H8
Hazelwood Ct MAL CM9 ..... 269 J5 [6]
Hazelwood Crs RCOS CO16 ..... 223 K2
Hazelwood Gdns
 BRWN CM15 ..... 332 B8 [2]
Hazelwood Gv LOS SS9 ..... 381 M6
Hazelwood Park Cl
 BARK/HLT IG6 ..... 349 M6
Hazelwood Rd EN EN1 ..... 324 A8
Hazlemere Rd COS CO15 ..... 224 D7
 SBF/HAD SS7 ..... 379 L6
Headcorn Cl PIT SS13 ..... 378 D6
Headgate COL CO1 ..... 10 B9
Headingham Cl CHTY IP2 ..... 58 B1 [3]
Headingley Cl CHESW EN7 ..... 276 A6 [2]
Headland Av HVHL CB9 ..... 27 M4
Headley Cha BRW CM14 ..... 354 D5
Headley Rd BCAYE CM11 ..... 335 K7
Head St COL CO1 ..... 10 B8
 HSTD CO9 ..... 129 G1
 K/T/MI CO5 ..... 192 A3
 MAL CM9 ..... 270 F5
Heard's La BRTR CM7 ..... 70 E6
 BRTR CM7 ..... 70 D5
 BRWN CM15 ..... 333 G5
Hearn Rd ROM RM1 ..... 371 G6
Hearsall Av CHLM/WR CM1 ..... 264 C4
 SLH/COR SS17 ..... 409 M1
Heath Cl BCAYW CM12 ..... 357 G2
 GPK RM2 ..... 371 H3
Heathcote Gdns HLWE CM17 ..... 256 F3
Heath Ct FX IP11 ..... 84 C3 [2]
Heath Dr CHLM/GWD CM2 ..... 288 C5
 EPP CM16 ..... 303 M7
 GPK RM2 ..... 371 H1
Heather Av IPSE IP3 ..... 38 D8
Heather Bank BCAYE CM11 ..... 357 K1 [8]
Heather Cl BRWN CM15 ..... 332 C7 [1]
 BSF CM23 ..... 173 L5
 COLS CO2 ..... 190 A5
 COS CO15 ..... 224 C4
 ROM RM1 ..... 370 F2
Heather Ct CHLM/WR CM1 ..... 265 C5 [5]
Heathercroft Rd WICKE SS11 ..... 360 B5 [1]
Heather Dr COLW CO3 ..... 162 A6
 ROM RM1 ..... 370 E2
 SBF/HAD SS7 ..... 399 G1
Heather Gdns ROM RM1 ..... 370 E2
Heather Gln ROM RM1 ..... 370 E2
Heatherhayes CHTY IP2 ..... 37 H8
Heatherfield SBF/HAD SS7 ..... 380 D5
Heathfield Rd CHLM/WR CM1 ..... 264 C3
 RIPS/CAP IP9 ..... 80 E6
Heathfields COLW CO3 ..... 161 J3
 FX IP11 ..... 84 B7
Heathgate WIT CM8 ..... 239 L5
Heathgate Piece FX IP11 ..... 84 D5 [8]
Heathlands BCAYE CM11 ..... 357 G2
Heathlands Cl RCOLE CO7 ..... 194 B6
Heathlands Pk IPNE IP4 ..... 38 F7
Heath La HERT/BAY SG13 ..... 252 D1

IPNE IP4 ..... 38 D6
Heathleigh Dr VGE SS16 ..... 376 C7
Heath Park Rd GPK RM2 ..... 371 H5
 CDH/CHF RM16 ..... 408 A6
 COLW CO3 ..... 161 G2
 IPNE IP4 ..... 38 D4
 K/T/MI CO5 ..... 192 A3
 MGTR CO11 ..... 139 L3
 RCOLE CO7 ..... 192 C1
 RCOS CO16 ..... 193 J3 [2]
 RCOS CO16 ..... 167 L2
 RCOS CO16 ..... 222 F2
Heath Rw BSF CM23 ..... 174 C2
Heathside RCOLW CO6 ..... 133 M7 [1]
The Heath COLS CO2 ..... 190 B5
 RCOLE CO7 ..... 107 G7
 SUD CO10 ..... 35 M7
Heath Vw KESG IP5 ..... 39 H5
Heath View Gdns
 CDH/CHF RM16 ..... 407 K7
Heath View Rd CDH/CHF RM16 ..... 407 K7 [2]
Heathway DAGW RM9 ..... 388 A3
Heath Wy SUD CO10 ..... 35 M7
Heathway WFD IG8 ..... 348 D5
Heatley Wy COLN CO4 ..... 164 A3
Heaton Av HARH RM3 ..... 352 C8
Heaton Cl HARH RM3 ..... 352 D8
Heaton Grange Rd GPK RM2 ..... 371 C1
 K/T/MI CO5 ..... 214 E5
Heckford's Rd RCOLE CO7 ..... 194 F1
Heckworth Av COLN CO4 ..... 135 K5
Hedge Dr COLS CO2 ..... 190 C1
Hedgehope Av RAYL SS6 ..... 361 C1
Hedgelands COLW CO3 ..... 160 E6
Hedge La SBF/HAD SS7 ..... 380 E7
Hedgerows SBW CM21 ..... 228 A1
Hedingham Rd EMPK RM11 ..... 372 B8
 HSTD CO9 ..... 75 H4
 HSTD CO9 ..... 127 M3
 SUD CO10 ..... 75 K3
Hedley Av WTHK RM20 ..... 416 D4
Hedworth Av BAR EN8 ..... 300 E5
Heeswyk Rd CVI SS8 ..... 398 E6 [1]
Heideburg Rd CVI SS8 ..... 398 D6
Heighams HLWW/ROY CM19 ..... 255 C6
The Heights LOU IG10 ..... 327 C4
 RCHLM CM3 ..... 290 D4
 WAB EN9 ..... 278 C5
Heilsburg Rd CVI SS8 ..... 398 E6
Helden Av CVI SS8 ..... 398 C6
Helena Cl HOC/HUL SS5 ..... 363 C6
Helena Ct RCHLM CM3 ..... 339 L5
Helena Rd IPSE IP3 ..... 3 J8
 RAYL SS6 ..... 380 C1
 SBW CM21 ..... 227 L2
Helen How RCHLM CM3 ..... 209 G4 [1]
Helen Rd EMPK RM11 ..... 371 L5
Helens Ga BAR EN8 ..... 277 G6 [2]
Helford Ct WIT CM8 ..... 238 E1
Helford Wy UPMR RM14 ..... 372 E6
Helions Bumpstead Rd
 HVHL CB9 ..... 28 B6
Helions Park Av HVHL CB9 ..... 28 B4
Helions Park Gdns HVHL CB9 ..... 28 B4 [1]
Helions Park Gv HVHL CB9 ..... 28 B4 [1]
Helions Rd HLWW/ROY CM19 ..... 15 C5
 HVHL CB9 ..... 48 B5
Helions Service Rd HVHL CB9 ..... 28 B4
Helions Wk HVHL CB9 ..... 28 B4 [1]
Helleborine GRAYS CM17 ..... 417 C2
Hellendoorn Rd CVI SS8 ..... 413 L1
Helm Cl RCOLW CO6 ..... 134 D4
Helmons La CHLM/GWD CM2 ..... 313 H7
Helmores LAIN SS15 ..... 376 A5
Helmsdale CVI SS8 ..... 398 A6 [4]
Helmsdale Cl ROM RM1 ..... 351 M8
Helmsdale Rd ROM RM1 ..... 351 M8
Helpeston BSDN SS14 ..... 19 M6
Helston Cl KESG IP5 ..... 39 J5
Helston Rd CHLM/GWD CM2 ..... 264 F6
Hemingway Rd WIT CM8 ..... 211 M6
Hemley Rd CDH/CHF RM16 ..... 408 E4
Hemmells LAIN SS15 ..... 376 C3
Hemmings Ct MAL CM9 ..... 292 F3 [3]
Hemnall St EPP CM16 ..... 304 A3
Hempstead Cl BKHH IG9 ..... 348 B5
Hempstead Rd HVHL CB9 ..... 27 K2
Henderson Cl HVHL CB9 ..... 27 K2 [1]
 RIPW IP8 ..... 36 B2 [1]
Henderson Dr DART DA1 ..... 415 M4 [2]
Henderson Gdns WICKW SS12 ..... 359 M6
Hendersons La HCH RM12 ..... 389 H1 [2]
Hendon Cl RCOS CO16 ..... 12 C1
 WICKW SS12 ..... 359 L5
Hendon Gdns CRW RM5 ..... 351 K7
Hengist Gdns WICKE SS11 ..... 359 L2
Hengrave Cl CHTY IP2 ..... 58 B1 [4]
Henham Cl BCAYE CM11 ..... 357 L1 [3]
Henham Rd RBSF CM22 ..... 147 M2
 SAFWS CB11 ..... 120 E1
Henley Ct COLW CO3 ..... 161 M5
Henley Crs WOS/PRIT SS0 ..... 382 F7
Henley Rd IP IP1 ..... 37 K1
Henney Cl RCHLM CM3 ..... 317 C5 [1]
Henniker Ga CHLM/GWD CM2 ..... 265 G4
Henniker Rd IP IP1 ..... 36 E3
Henny Back Rd BURES CO8 ..... 76 F7
Henny Rd BURES CO8 ..... 77 J5
Henrietta Rd RCOLE CO7 ..... 164 D7
Henry Cl COS CO15 ..... 12 B8
Henry Dixon Rd WIT CM8 ..... 212 E5
Henry Dr LOS SS9 ..... 399 J1
Henry Rd CHLM/WR CM1 ..... 264 C7
 IPSE IP3 ..... 59 J1
Henry's Av IG8 ..... 348 A6
Henry St GRAYS CM17 ..... 417 K3 [2]
Henslow Rd IPNE IP4 ..... 3 H2
Henson Av CVI SS8 ..... 398 B6
Henstead Gdns IPSE IP3 ..... 59 H1
Henwood Side WFD IG8 ..... 349 G1 [1]
Herald Cl BSF CM23 ..... 173 L5
Herbage Park Rd MAL CM9 ..... 291 K2
Herbert Gv SOS SS1 ..... 21 J7
Herbert Rd COS CO15 ..... 12 E5
 CVI SS8 ..... 398 D7 [3]
 EMPK RM11 ..... 371 M7
 KESG IP5 ..... 39 M3

SBN/FI SS3 ..... 402 D5
Herd La SLH/COR SS17 ..... 395 K7
Hereford Ct CHLM/GWD CM2 ..... 289 C6
 COS CO15 ..... 224 F6 [1]
Hereford Rd COL CO1 ..... 10 F7
 COS CO15 ..... 224 F5
Hereward Cl RCOLE CO7 ..... 164 D8
 WAB EN9 ..... 301 K4 [1]
Hereward Gdns WICKE SS11 ..... 359 L2
Hereward Gn LOU IG10 ..... 327 K3 [1]
Hereward Wy BRTR CM7 ..... 95 K8
Herga Cl CDH/CHF RM16 ..... 408 B3
Herington Gv RBRW/HUT CM13 ..... 355 H1
Heriot Cl BOC CM0 ..... 344 C6 [2]
Heritage Wy RCFD SS4 ..... 382 F1
 RCHLM CM3 ..... 318 C6
Hermes Dr BOC CM0 ..... 344 C6 [2]
Hermes Wy SBN/FI SS3 ..... 403 G3
Hermitage Av SBF/HAD SS7 ..... 380 B7
Hermitage Cl SBF/HAD SS7 ..... 380 B7
Hermitage Dr LAIN SS15 ..... 376 D5
Hermitage Mdw SUD CO10 ..... 31 K2
Hermitage Rd WOS/PRIT SS0 ..... 20 C6
Hernen Rd CVI SS8 ..... 398 C6
Hernshaw RBRW/HUT CM13 ..... 355 L8
Heron Av WICKE SS11 ..... 360 A5
Heron Cha RBRW/HUT CM13 ..... 355 M8
Heron Cl BKHH IG9 ..... 348 B2
 RAYL SS6 ..... 380 C1
 SBW CM21 ..... 227 L2
Heron Ct BSF CM23 ..... 174 B4
Heron Di BSDN SS14 ..... 19 L3
Heron Flight Av RAIN RM13 ..... 389 J6 [2]
Heron Gdns RAYL SS6 ..... 361 J8
 SBN/FI SS3 ..... 402 F3
Herongate Rd BAR EN8 ..... 276 E7
Heron Rd COS CO15 ..... 224 A4
 K/T/MI CO5 ..... 186 E8
Heronsgate FOS CO13 ..... 199 C5
Herons La CHONG CM5 ..... 283 K2
Heron Wd FOS CO13 ..... 198 F4
Heron Wy FOS CO13 ..... 198 F4
 MAL CM9 ..... 269 K6
Heronway RBRW/HUT CM13 ..... 355 J2
Heron Wy RCHLM CM3 ..... 319 H3
 UPMR RM14 ..... 372 F6
 WTHK RM20 ..... 416 C2
Herrick Cl COLW CO3 ..... 162 B5
Herring's Wy RCOLW CO6 ..... 132 E5
Herschell Rd LOS SS9 ..... 399 K1
Hertford Dr SLH/COR SS17 ..... 395 K2
Hertford La ROY SG8 ..... 40 E6
 SAFWS CB11 ..... 41 G7
Hertford Rd CVI SS8 ..... 398 A8
 HOD EN11 ..... 252 F3
 PEND EN3 ..... 300 E7
 PEND EN3 ..... 324 D2 [1]
 PEND EN3 ..... 324 D4 [2]
 SUD CO10 ..... 31 J2
Hertford Road High St
 PEND EN3 ..... 324 D6 [1]
Hertfordshire Wy STDN SG11 ..... 144 F7
Hervey Cl RIPS/CAP IP9 ..... 113 H2
Hervey St IPNE IP4 ..... 3 H2
Hervilly Wy WOTN CO14 ..... 199 J4 [1]
Hesselyn Dr RAIN RM13 ..... 389 J6 [1]
Hester Pl BOC CM0 ..... 344 D6
Hetherington Cl COLS CO2 ..... 191 H3 [1]
Hetzand Rd CVI SS8 ..... 399 C8
Hever Cl HOC/HUL SS5 ..... 362 E5
Hewes Cl COLN CO4 ..... 164 A4
Hewitt Rd HAR CO12 ..... 142 D2
Hexham Cl CHTY IP2 ..... 58 B1 [7]
Heybridge Ap MAL CM9 ..... 269 J5 [4]
Heybridge Dr WICKW SS12 ..... 359 M4
Heybridge St MAL CM9 ..... 269 H6
Heybridge St ING CM4 ..... 334 A2
Heycroft Dr BRTR CM7 ..... 183 L5
Heycroft Rd HOC/HUL SS5 ..... 363 C6
 LOS SS9 ..... 382 A4
Heycroft Wy CHLM/GWD CM2 ..... 289 C6
 K/T/MI CO5 ..... 214 E5
 RCOLW CO6 ..... 104 A2
Heydon La ROY SG8 ..... 40 C6
 SAFWS CB11 ..... 41 G7
Heygate Av SOS SS1 ..... 21 J7
The Heythrop
 CHLM/WR CM1 ..... 264 F7 [2]
 ING CM4 ..... 310 B8
Heywood Cl CHTY IP2 ..... 57 M2 [5]
Heywood Ct MAL CM9 ..... 269 J5 [2]
Heywood La GTDUN CM6 ..... 178 E4
Heywood Wy MAL CM9 ..... 269 J5
Hibbard Rd RIPW IP8 ..... 36 D1
Hickford Hl SUD CO10 ..... 31 L5
Hickling Cl LOS SS9 ..... 381 J5
Hickman Cl BROX EN10 ..... 252 F8 [1]
Hickory Av COLN CO4 ..... 11 M7
Hickstars La BCAYE CM11 ..... 357 K4 [8]
Hicks Wy HVHL CB9 ..... 28 F5 [1]
Hidcote Wy BRTR CM7 ..... 182 C4
The Hides HLW CM20 ..... 15 M3
Higham Rd WFD IG8 ..... 348 B7
Highams Cha MAL CM9 ..... 271 G3
Highams Rd HOC/HUL SS5 ..... 362 F6
Higham Vw EPP CM16 ..... 281 J6
High Ash Cl TIL RM18 ..... 409 H8
High Bank VGE SS16 ..... 376 A7 [2]
Highbank Cl LOS SS9 ..... 382 A6
High Beach RAYL SS6 ..... 381 H1 [1]
High Beeches SBF/HAD SS7 ..... 379 J8
High Bridge Rd SBF/HAD SS7 ..... 380 D5
High Bridge Rd CHLM/GWD CM2 ..... 17 J5
Highbirch Rd RCOS CO16 ..... 195 L6
Highbridge St WAB EN9 ..... 301 J5
Highbury Wy SUD CO10 ..... 5 K9
Highclere Rd BRTR CM7 ..... 182 C5 [1]
 COLN CO4 ..... 135 J7
Highcliff Crs RCFD SS4 ..... 363 K4
High Cliff Dr LOS SS9 ..... 400 K3
Highcliff Dr WICKW SS12 ..... 359 C3
Highcliffe Cl WICKE SS11 ..... 360 A3 [3]
Highcliffe Rd WICKE SS11 ..... 360 A4 [4]
Highcliffe Rd SBF/HAD SS7 ..... 397 M2

High Cloister BCAYE CM11 ... 357 J1
High Cl ROY SG8 ... 40 B6
High Cross La GTDUN CM6 ... 177 J2
Highcross La GTDUN CM6 ... 177 K6
High Cross La East GTDUN CM6 ... 177 M6
High Easter Rd GTDUN CM6 ... 206 A1
GTDUN CM6 ... 231 M5
High Elms CHIG IG7 ... 349 M5
UPMR RM14 ... 372 F8
WFD IG8 ... 348 B6
High Elms Rd HOC/HUL SS5 ... 361 M2
Highfield HLWS CM18 ... 256 B4
SUD CO10 ... 31 K4
Highfield Ap BCAYE CM11 ... 357 L3
IP IP1 ... 37 G2
Highfield Av BSF CM23 ... 174 D5
HAR CO12 ... 6 E8
SBF/HAD SS7 ... 380 C7
Highfield Cl BRTR CM7 ... 155 H5
CRW RM5 ... 351 K7
RCHLM CM3 ... 290 E5
WOS/PRIT SS0 ... 20 B1
Highfield Crs HCH RM12 ... 390 A1
RAYL SS6 ... 380 C1
WOS/PRIT SS0 ... 20 B1
Highfield Dr BROX EN10 ... 276 F1
COLW CO3 ... 162 D5
WOS/PRIT SS0 ... 20 B1
Highfield Gdns CDH/CHF RM16 .. 407 L7
WOS/PRIT SS0 ... 382 B8
Highfield Gn EPP CM16 ... 303 M3
Highfield Gv WOS/PRIT SS0 ... 382 B8
Highfield Link CRW RM5 ... 351 K7
Highfield Pl EPP CM16 ... 303 M3
Highfield Ri RCHLM CM3 ... 319 H8
Highfield Rd BCAYE CM11 ... 357 L4
CHLM/WR CM1 ... 263 M7
CRW RM5 ... 351 K7
FX IP11 ... 9 M2
HCH RM12 ... 390 A1
IP IP1 ... 36 F1
SUD CO10 ... 5 G3
WFD IG8 ... 348 F8
High Flds GTDUN CM6 ... 178 E3
Highfields HSTD CO9 ... 73 H1
HSTD CO9 ... 128 F3
RBSF CM22 ... 120 A5
RIPS/CAP IP9 ... 78 F5
SAFWN CB10 ... 65 M1
SAFWS CB11 ... 90 C4
Highfields La K/T/MI CO5 ... 213 L4
Highfields Md RCHLM CM3 ... 314 C3
Highfields Rd WIT CM8 ... 211 M8
Highfield Stile Rd BRTR CM7 ... 155 H5
Highfield Wy WOS/PRIT SS0 ... 382 B8
High Garrett BRTR CM7 ... 155 K2
Highgate Gv SBW CM21 ... 227 L1
High Hall Cl FX IP11 ... 84 B5
High House La CDH/CHF RM16.. 408 E8
Highland Av BRW CM14 ... 354 D2
DAGE RM10 ... 388 D2
LOU IG10 ... 327 G8
Highland Gv BCAYE CM11 ... 335 J8
Highland Rd BSF CM23 ... 174 A8
SLH/COR SS17 ... 395 J2
WAB EN9 ... 277 M2
Highlands HSTD CO9 ... 127 M2
Highlands Av VGE SS16 ... 19 M9
Highlands Bvd LOS SS9 ... 381 H8
Highlands Crs PIT SS13 ... 379 C5
Highlands Dr MAL CM9 ... 292 F1
Highlands Hl RCHLM CM3 ... 319 L5
Highlands Rd PIT SS13 ... 379 C5
WICKE SS11 ... 361 J1
High La RBSF CM22 ... 228 F5
STSD CM24 ... 146 F3
HOC/HUL SS5 ... 362 F6
Highmead RAYL SS6 ... 380 D1
STSD CM24 ... 146 F3
High Meadow BCAYE CM11 ... 357 K1
GTDUN CM6 ... 178 D3
High Mdw CHIG IG7 ... 349 L6
High Oaks VGE SS16 ... 376 C4
High Pastures RBSF CM22 ... 228 D3
High Rd BKHH IG9 ... 348 C3
BROX EN10 ... 253 C8
CDH/CHF RM16 ... 406 F6
CDH/CHF RM16 ... 408 A3
CHDH RM6 ... 370 A6
CHIG IG7 ... 349 J4
COLS CO2 ... 190 A6
EPP CM16 ... 280 C4
EPP CM16 ... 303 K5
FX IP14 ... 84 C4
HOC/HUL SS5 ... 362 B6
LAIN SS15 ... 376 C6
RAYL SS6 ... 380 D3
SBF/HAD SS7 ... 379 J7
SLH/COR SS17 ... 394 A8
SLH/COR SS17 ... 395 K2
SLH/COR SS17 ... 410 B2
VGE SS16 ... 376 D8
VGE SS16 ... 378 A7
VGE SS16 ... 394 C2
High Road Broxbourne
BROX EN10 ... 277 G1
High Rd East FX IP11 ... 85 J3
High Rd North LAIN SS15 ... 376 D2
High Road Ongar
(Chelmsford Road)
CHONG CM5 ... 283 J7
High Road Turnford
BROX EN10 ... 276 F6
High Rd West FX IP11 ... 85 G7
High Road Woodford Gn
WFD IG8 ... 348 B6
High Road Wormley
BROX EN10 ... 277 G4
High Row Fld FX IP11 ... 85 K8
High Silver LOU IG10 ... 326 E6
High Stile GTDUN CM6 ... 178 D3
High St BAR EN8 ... 300 F6
BCAYW CM12 ... 357 H1
BOC CM0 ... 274 B8
BOC CM0 ... 320 E7
BOC CM0 ... 344 C0
BROX EN10 ... 276 F5

BRTR CM7 ... 95 K8
BRTR CM7 ... 124 C1
BRTR CM7 ... 155 G8
BRW CM14 ... 354 D3
BSF CM23 ... 174 A4
BURES CO8 ... 102 A2
CBE/LIN CB1 ... 24 C1
CBE/LIN CB1 ... 26 F8
CHLM/GWD CM2 ... 289 G4
CHLM/WR CM1 ... 17 H3
CHONG CM5 ... 307 H1
COL CO1 ... 10 B8
COLN CO4 ... 105 L7
COS CO15 ... 13 H7
CVI SS8 ... 398 D7
EMPK RM11 ... 371 L8
EPP CM16 ... 304 A3
FX IP11 ... 84 F7
GRAYS RM17 ... 417 H2
GRH DA9 ... 416 C8
GTDUN CM6 ... 151 L6
GTDUN CM6 ... 178 E3
HAR CO12 ... 7 J7
HAR CO12 ... 141 K7
HLWE CM17 ... 227 K7
HLWW/ROY CM19 ... 254 C2
HOD EN11 ... 253 H5
HOD EN11 ... 253 H7
HSTD CO9 ... 73 H2
HSTD CO9 ... 128 F1
HVHL CB9 ... 28 B4
ING CM4 ... 310 D6
ING CM4 ... 310 C8
ING CM4 ... 335 M1
IP IP1 ... 2 E3
K/T/MI CO5 ... 192 B3
K/T/MI CO5 ... 213 K1
K/T/MI CO5 ... 245 J5
LOS SS9 ... 399 K3
MAL CM9 ... 269 G8
MAL CM9 ... 272 D2
MGTR CM11 ... 108 E7
MHAD SG10 ... 172 A8
RAYL SS6 ... 380 C1
RBSF CM22 ... 120 A6
RBSF CM22 ... 203 G5
RCFD SS4 ... 364 E1
RCOLE CO7 ... 106 F5
RCOLE CO7 ... 192 C3
RCOLE CO7 ... 221 G5
RCOLW CO6 ... 104 C2
RCOS CO16 ... 197 G1
RIPW IP8 ... 36 B5
ROM RM1 ... 370 F5
ROY SG8 ... 40 E8
SAFWN CB10 ... 22 B4
SAFWN CB10 ... 42 F1
SAFWN CB10 ... 65 L2
SAFWN CB10 ... 68 F2
SAFWS CB11 ... 43 G7
SAFWS CB11 ... 87 K7
SAFWS CB11 ... 89 L7
SAFWS CB11 ... 89 H3
SAFWS CB11 ... 90 C4
SBF/HAD SS7 ... 380 E8
SBF/HAD SS7 ... 397 L2
SBN/FI SS3 ... 385 G7
SBN/FI SS3 ... 403 H4
SLH/COR SS17 ... 409 L2
SOCK/AV RM15 ... 405 K6
SOS SS1 ... 21 G6
SUD CO10 ... 31 J4
SUD CO10 ... 32 E2
WICKW SS12 ... 359 L4
WOTN CO14 ... 199 K3
High St North K/T/MI CO5 ... 245 J5
High Tree La WOTN CO14 ... 199 L1
Hightrees ING CM4 ... 335 L1
High Vw BOC CM0 ... 296 D3
BSF CM23 ... 146 D8
High View Av COS CO15.. ... 223 M5
GRAYS RM17 ... 417 K2
Highview Av COS CO15 ... 375 M7
High View Cl COS CO15 ... 223 M5
LOU IG10 ... 326 D7
Highview Cl SUD CO10.. ... 4 C1
Highview Crs RBRW/HUT CM13.. 333 K8
High View Gdns GRAYS RM17 ... 417 K2
Highview Gdns UPMR RM14... 390 C1
High View Ri BCAYE CM11 ... 358 D6
High View Rd IP IP1 ... 36 E3
Highview Rd SBF/HAD SS7 ... 380 B4
Highwood Cl BRW CM14 ... 354 C1
LOS SS9 ... 382 A7
Highwood La LOU IG10 ... 327 H8
Highwood Rd CHLM/WR CM1 .. 286 A7
High Wood Rd HOD EN11 ... 253 G2
Highwoods Ap COLN CO4 ... 135 J7
Highwoods Sq COLN CO4 ... 135 J8
High Wych La SBW CM21 ... 227 H1
High Wych Rd HLW CM20 ... 226 F5
SBW CM21 ... 227 L2
Hilary Cl HCH RM12 ... 389 L4
RCFD SS4 ... 363 M6
Hilary Crs RAYL SS6 ... 380 F1
Hilbery Rd CVI SS8 ... 398 D8
Hildabrook Cl CHTY IP2 ... 57 M2
Hildaville Dr WOS/PRIT SS0 ... 400 D1
Hilden Dr ERITH DA8 ... 414 C4
Hillary Cl CHLM/WR CM1 ... 264 E7
IPNE IP4 ... 38 B6
MAL CM9 ... 269 J6
Hillary Mt BCAYW CM12 ... 357 G2
Hill Av WICKE SS11 ... 360 A4
Hillborough Rd WOS/PRIT SS0 382 E8
Hill Cl SBF/HAD SS7 ... 379 M7
SUD CO10 ... 34 E3
Hill Crs CHLM/GWD CM2 ... 17 L4
EMPK RM11 ... 371 K6
HVHL CB9 ... 28 B2
Hillcrest COS CO15 ... 224 A5
FOS CO13 ... 198 E3
RCHLM CM3 ... 319 H2
Hillcrest Ap RIPW IP8 ... 36 C1
Hillcrest Av HOC/HUL SS5 ... 361 M1
WTHK RM20 ... 416 B3
Hillcrest Cl SLH/COR SS17 ... 394 A7

Hillcrest Ct HAR CO12 ... 7 H8
Hill Crest Rd CHONG CM5 ... 305 M2
Hillcrest Rd EMPK RM11 ... 371 H7
HOC/HUL SS5 ... 362 F6
LOU IG10 ... 326 E8
RCHLM CM3 ... 339 K4
SLH/COR SS17 ... 393 M8
SOS SS1 ... 21 J6
SUD CO10 ... 4 D1
Hillcrest Vw VGE SS16 ... 377 L8
Hillcrest Wy EPP CM16 ... 304 B3
Hilldene Av HARH RM3 ... 352 D7
Hilldene Cl HARH RM3 ... 352 E6
Hill Farm La RIPS/CAP IP9 ... 82 A4
Hillfoot Av CRW RM5 ... 370 D1
Hillfoot Rd CRW RM5 ... 370 D1
Hill Gv ROM RM1 ... 370 F3
Hillhouse WAB EN9 ... 302 A5
Hillhouse Cl BCAYW CM12 ... 335 J7
Hillhouse Dr BCAYW CM12 ... 335 J7
Hillhouse La RCOS CO16 ... 168 C8
Hilliards Rd RCOLE CO7 ... 166 D7
Hillie Bunnies RCOLW CO6 ... 130 C4
Hill La HOC/HUL SS5 ... 363 G6
HVHL CB9 ... 29 G7
Hillman Av COS CO15 ... 249 M5
Hillman Cl EMPK RM11 ... 371 L3
Hillridge COLN CO4 ... 135 J8
Hill Ri ED N9 ... 324 C8
UPMR RM14 ... 390 B1
Hill Rd CRW RM5 ... 351 K7
UPMR RM14 ... 390 B1
Hill Rd BRW CM14 ... 354 B4
CHLM/GWD CM2 ... 17 L4
COS CO15 ... 223 M5
EPP CM16 ... 327 M1
HAR CO12 ... 7 H7
HAR CO12 ... 141 M3
RCOLW CO6 ... 186 C1
SAFWN CB10 ... 68 E3
SBF/HAD SS7 ... 379 M8
SOSN SS2 ... 20 E1
Hill's Chace BRW CM14 ... 354 D5
Hills Cl BRTR CM7 ... 155 G7
Hills Crs COLW CO3 ... 162 B6
Hillside FOS CO13 ... 198 F7
GRAYS RM17 ... 417 L1
HLWE CM17 ... 256 D5
HOD EN11 ... 253 G4
Hillside Av BAR EN8 ... 300 E3
BSF CM23 ... 174 B4
HOC/HUL SS5 ... 362 F6
WFD IG8 ... 348 D6
Hillside Cl BCAYE CM11 ... 357 J2
WFD IG8 ... 348 D6
Hillside Crs BAR EN8 ... 300 E3
COS CO15 ... 224 D6
IPSE IP3 ... 38 C8
LOS SS9 ... 400 B3
Hillside Gdns BRTR CM7 ... 183 G2
Hillside Gv CHLM/GWD CM2 ... 288 B5
Hillside Ms CHLM/GWD CM2 ... 16 F9
Hillside Rd BCAYW CM12 ... 357 J2
BOC CM0 ... 320 D7
BOC CM0 ... 344 C6
GTDUN CM6 ... 180 A5
HOC/HUL SS5 ... 362 C6
LOS SS9 ... 381 K3
SBF/HAD SS7 ... 397 L2
SUD CO10 ... 5 G6
Hillside Wk BRW CM14 ... 354 B4
Hill's Rd BKHH IG9 ... 348 C2
HSTD CO9 ... 97 L3
Hill St SLH/COR SS17 ... 395 K6
Hill Ter SLH/COR SS17 ... 395 K6
The Hill HLWE CM17 ... 227 K7
Hill Top LOU IG10 ... 327 H5
Hilltop Cl COLS CO2 ... 163 L7
CHESW EN7 ... 276 A6
Hill Top Cl LOU IG10 ... 327 H5
Hilltop Cl RAYL SS6 ... 380 D2
Hilltop Crs RCOS CO16 ... 196 A2
Hill Top La SAFWS CB11 ... 65 L4
Hilltop Ri RCOS CO16 ... 195 M2
Hill Top Ri VGE SS16 ... 376 A7
Hill Top Vw WFD IG8 ... 349 G7
Hill Tree Cl SBW CM21 ... 227 L2
Hill Vw RCHLM CM3 ... 315 C2
Hillview Av EMPK RM11 ... 371 K6
Hill View Cl K/T/MI CO5 ... 192 A3
Hillview Gdns BAR EN8 ... 276 F1
SLH/COR SS17 ... 395 G6
Hill View Rd CHLM/WR CM1 ... 264 D7
Hillview Rd RAYL SS6 ... 380 D1
Hillway BCAYE CM11 ... 357 L1
CBE/LIN CB1 ... 24 D1
WOS/PRIT SS0 ... 400 B3
The Hill Wy BRWN CM15 ... 333 M3
Hillwood Cl RBRW/HUT CM13... 355 J2
Hillwood Gv RBRW/HUT CM13... 355 J2
WICKW SS12 ... 359 M4
Hilly Fld HLWS CM18 ... 256 A7
Hillyfields LOU IG10 ... 327 H4
Hilton Cl MGTR CM11 ... 108 E7
Hilton Rd CVI SS8 ... 398 B6
IPSE IP3 ... 59 K2
Hilton Wk CVI SS8 ... 398 B6
Hilton Wy HSTD CO9 ... 97 M3
Hilversum Wy CVI SS8 ... 398 C6
Hind Cl CHIG IG7 ... 350 A6
Hindles Rd CVI SS8 ... 398 E7
Hines St SBN/FI SS3 ... 403 G5
Hintesham Cl IPNE IP4 ... 39 G6
Hintlesham Dr FX IP11 ... 84 E8
Hipkins BSF CM23 ... 173 M7
Histon Cl KESG IP5 ... 39 G4
Hitcham Rd RCOLW CO6 ... 158 A8
Hitch Common Rd
SAFWS CB11 ... 89 G3
Hitchin Cl HARH RM3 ... 352 D5
Hitchin Ms BRTR CM7 ... 183 J3

Hither Blakers RCHLM CM3 ... 339 L3
Hitherwood Cl HCH RM12 ... 389 L3
Hitherwood Rd COLS CO2 ... 190 D1
Hobart Cl CHLM/WR CM1 ... 263 M6
Hobart Rd TIL RM18 ... 418 B5
Hobbs Cl BAR EN8 ... 300 E1
Hobbs Cross Rd HLWE CM17 ... 228 A8
Hobhouse Rd SLH/COR SS17 ... 394 F7
Hobbs Dr COLN CO4 ... 105 K6
Hobleythick La WOS/PRIT SS0 ... 382 E8
Hobsons Cl HOD EN11 ... 253 G2
Hobtoe Rd HLW CM20 ... 14 F2
Hockerill St BSF CM23 ... 174 B4
Hockley Cl BOC CM0 ... 298 D1
BSDN SS14 ... 19 L5
Hockley Dr GPK RM2 ... 371 J2
Hockley Rd BSDN SS14 ... 377 M5
Hockley La BOC CM0 ... 274 D8
Hockley Ri HOC/HUL SS5 ... 362 F6
Hockley Rd BSDN SS14 ... 19 M5
RAYL SS6 ... 361 M8
Hockney Gdns IPSE IP3 ... 59 H3
Hodges Holt WIT CM8 ... 239 H4
Hodgson Ct WICKW SS12 ... 360 B6
Hodgson Wy WICKW SS12 ... 360 A5
Hodings Rd HLW CM20 ... 14 F2
Hoecroft WAB EN9 ... 278 A2
Hoe Dr COLW CO3 ... 162 B6
Hoe La ABR/ST RM4 ... 328 C5
EN EN1 ... 324 C2
PEND EN3 ... 324 D2
RCHLM CM3 ... 234 F5
RCHLM CM3 ... 338 A5
SUD CO10 ... 33 G3
WAB EN9 ... 278 A2
Hoe Mill Rd MAL CM9 ... 267 L7
Hoestock Rd SBW CM21 ... 227 L1
Hoe St CHLM/WR CM1 ... 262 D7
The Hoe BCAYW CM12 ... 357 J7
Hogarth Av BRW CM14 ... 354 F4
Hogarth Dr SBN/FI SS3 ... 403 H3
Hogarth End FOS CO13 ... 198 F4
Hogarth Reach LOU IG10 ... 327 C7
Hogarth Rd CDH/CHF RM16 ... 407 H6
IPSE IP3 ... 59 G2
Hogarth Sq IPSE IP3 ... 59 G2
Hogarth Wy RCFD SS4 ... 363 K5
GRAYS RM17 ... 417 H1
Hogg La CDH/CHF RM16 ... 407 H8
Hog Hill Rd CRW RM5 ... 351 G8
Hog's La ROY SG8 ... 40 E8
Hogwell Cha RCHLM CM3 ... 340 C2
Holbech Rd BSDN SS14 ... 378 A3
Holbeck La CHESW EN7 ... 276 A6
Holbek Rd CVI SS8 ... 398 F8
Holborough Cl COLN CO4 ... 164 A4
Holbrook Cl BCAYE CM11 ... 357 L1
EN EN1 ... 324 A3
RCHLM CM3 ... 339 L4
RCOS CO16 ... 223 J7
SUD CO10 ... 35 M8
Holbrook Crs FX IP11 ... 8 F1
Holbrook Rd HVHL CB9 ... 27 M5
IPSE IP3 ... 58 F2
RIPS/CAP IP9 ... 110 D1
RIPS/CAP IP9 ... 111 H1
Holcombe Crs CHTY IP2 ... 57 L1
Holdbrook Wy HARH RM3 ... 372 A2
Holden Cl CHTY IP2 ... 3 G1
Holden Gdns BRW CM14 ... 354 E6
BSDN SS14 ... 378 A2
COLN CO4 ... 10 C1
Holden Wy UPMR RM14 ... 372 E8
Holecroft WAB EN9 ... 301 M6
Holford Rd CDH/CHF RM16.. 408 F8
TIL RM18 ... 418 E1
Holgate PIT SS13 ... 378 D3
Holgate Rd DAGE RM10 ... 388 B4
Holkham Av RCHLM CM3 ... 339 L6
Holkham Cl IPNE IP4 ... 39 G6
Holland Av CVI SS8 ... 397 L6
Holland Cl ROMW/RG RM7 ... 370 D5
FOS CO13 ... 198 F8
FOS CO13 ... 198 C6
FX IP11 ... 9 J5
IPNE IP4 ... 3 M3
RCOS CO16 ... 224 B1
WOS/PRIT SS0 ... 20 B7
Hollands Rd HVHL CB9 ... 28 B5
Hollands Wk VGE SS16 ... 395 L1
Holledge Crs FOS CO13 ... 198 F5
Holliday Hl CHLM/GWD CM2 ... 312 F7
Hollidge Wy DAGE RM10 ... 388 C5
Hollies Rd BRTR CM7 ... 156 D8
The Hollies SLH/COR SS17 ... 409 K2
Holliland Cft RCOLW CO6 ... 159 K3
Hollingtons Gv COLS CO2 ... 216 B1
Hollis Lock CHLM/GWD CM2 ... 265 H8
Hollis Pl GRAYS RM17 ... 407 H8
Holliwel Cl COLW CO3 ... 161 L5
Holloway Crs GTDUN CM6 ... 231 K4
Holloway Rd MAL CM9 ... 269 G5
Hollowfield Av GRAYS RM17 ... 417 L1
Hollow La CHLM/WR CM1 ... 263 L4
RIPS/CAP IP9 ... 82 A4
Hollow Rd GTDUN CM6 ... 181 J6
K/T/MI CO5 ... 213 G1
RIPW IP8 ... 56 E3
ROY SG8 ... 62 E2
SAFWS CB11 ... 41 J7
SAFWS CB11 ... 89 K8
The Hollow WFD IG8 ... 348 A5
Hollybank WIT CM8 ... 239 G2
Hollybush Dr FX IP11 ... 85 L6
Hollybush Hi HOC/HUL SS5 ... 194 F8
Hollybush Wy CHESW EN7 ... 276 B6
Holly Cl BKHH IG9 ... 348 E4
BOC CM0 ... 344 C5
COLS CO2 ... 190 D1
Holly Dr SOCK/AV RM15 ... 406 E2
Holly Fld HLWW/ROY CM19... 15 H9

HLWW/ROY CM19 ... 255 K6
Hollyfields BROX EN10 ... 276 F6
Hollyfield BCAYE CM11 ... 335 K6
Holly Gv VGE SS16 ... 376 A6
Hollyhock Rd SAFWN CB10 ... 65 M1
RCOLW CO6 ... 104 D7
RIPS/CAP IP9 ... 79 M8
RIPW IP8 ... 57 K3
Hollymead SLH/COR SS17 ... 394 F7
Hollymead Cl COLN CO4 ... 135 G8
Holly Oaks RCOLW CO6 ... 102 F7
Holly Rd COLW CO3 ... 161 K7
IP IP1 ... 2 D1
KESG IP5 ... 39 G4
PEND EN3 ... 300 E8
Hollytree Ct COLS CO2 ... 162 D8
Hollytree Gdns RAYL SS6 ... 380 C3
Hollyview Cl RCOS CO16 ... 168 A6
Holly Wy CHLM/GWD CM2 ... 288 C4
K/T/MI CO5 ... 214 D6
RCOLE CO7 ... 165 C5
Hollywood Cl CHLM/GWD CM2 .. 288 F5
Hollywood Wy ERITH DA8... 414 C5
Holman Crs COLW CO3 ... 162 B7
Holman Rd HSTD CO9 ... 128 F2
Holmans RCHLM CM3 ... 265 M3
Holmbridge Gdns PEND EN3 ... 324 E6
Holmbrook Wy FOS CO13 ... 198 F6
Holme Cl BAR EN8 ... 300 F3
Holme Rd EMPK RM11 ... 372 B6
Holmes Cl SLH/COR SS17 ... 394 A8
Holmesdale BAR EN8 ... 300 D7
Holmes Meadow EPP CM16 ... 279 J1
Holmes Rd HSTD CO9 ... 128 F3
Holme Wk WICKW SS12 ... 360 A6
Holmleigh Av DART DA1 ... 414 D8
Holmsdale Cl WOS/PRIT SS0 ... 382 C8
Holmwood CVI SS8 ... 398 F6
Holmwood Dr BRWN CM15 ... 333 H7
Holmwood Cl RCOS CO16 ... 223 J5
Holmwood Rd PEND EN3 ... 300 E8
Holst Av LAIN SS15 ... 376 D3
Holst Cl SLH/COR SS17 ... 394 A8
Holt Cl CHIG IG7 ... 350 A6
WIT CM8 ... 239 M6
Holt Dr COLS CO2 ... 191 H4
WIT CM8 ... 239 M6
Holt Farm Wy RCFD SS4 ... 363 L7
Holton Rd CVI SS8 ... 399 G8
RAYL SS6 ... 381 H2
Holt's Rd RCOLW CO6 ... 103 J8
The Holt BARK/HLT IG6 ... 349 K7
Holt Wy CHIG IG7 ... 350 K6
Holtynge SBF/HAD SS7 ... 379 K7
Holybread La RCHLM CM3 ... 266 D7
Holy Cross HI BROX EN10 ... 276 B3
Holyfield Rd WAB EN9 ... 301 K1
Holyoak La HOC/HUL SS5 ... 362 F7
Holyrood HAR CO12 ... 143 G1
Holyrood Cl CHTY IP2 ... 58 A2
Holyrood Dr WOS/PRIT SS0 ... 400 C1
Holyrood Gdns CDH/CHF RM16 .. 418 D1
Holywells Cl IPSE IP3 ... 3 K8
Holy Wells Rd IPSE IP3 ... 3 J9
Homebridge SAFWN CB10 ... 69 H8
Home Cl BROX EN10 ... 277 G4
HLW CM20 ... 256 A3
HVHL CB9 ... 48 D4
Homecroft Gdns LOU IG10 ... 327 J6
Home Farm La RCOLE CO7 ... 137 H3
Home Farm Rd
RBRW/HUT CM13 ... 373 M1
Homefield BOC CM0 ... 320 F6
RIPS/CAP IP9 ... 78 C2
WAB EN9 ... 302 B4
Homefield Cl BCAYE CM11 ... 357 L5
CHLM/WR CM1 ... 263 L6
EPP CM16 ... 304 B1
Homefield Rd COLS CO2 ... 190 D2
HVHL CB9 ... 27 M6
WIT CM8 ... 212 B7
Homefields Av SBF/HAD SS7 ... 379 J6
Homefield Wy BRTR CM7 ... 183 L4
RCOLW CO6 ... 130 C4
Home Gdns DAGE RM10 ... 388 D2
Homelands Gv BCAYE CM11 ... 336 D7
Homeleigh Ct BAR EN8 ... 300 C2
Homelye Cha GTDUN CM6 ... 179 J2
Home Md CHLM/GWD CM2 ... 312 D1
LAIN SS15 ... 287 H2
Home Mdw BCAYW CM12 ... 357 H1
Home Pastures RBSF CM22 ... 202 A8
Homerton Cl COS CO15 ... 224 A3
Homestead CHLM/WR CM1 ... 264 C6
Homestead Dr VGE SS16 ... 394 D1
Homestead Gdns SBF/HAD SS7 .. 398 E1
Homestead Rd BCAYE CM11.. 358 E3
BCTR RM8 ... 388 A1
PIT SS13 ... 378 F4
SBF/HAD SS7 ... 398 E1
Homestead Wy SBF/HAD SS7 ... 398 E1
Homeway HARH RM3 ... 353 J7
Homing Rd RCOS CO16 ... 196 D7
Honeybourne BSF CM23 ... 173 M7
Honey Brook WAB EN9 ... 301 M5
Honey Cl BRWN CM15 ... 308 E7
CHLM/GWD CM2 ... 288 E5
DAGE RM10 ... 388 D5
Honeycroft LOU IG10 ... 327 H6
Honey La BAR EN8 ... 301 C6
SAFWS CB11 ... 87 G8
WAB EN9 ... 301 M6
Honeymeade HLW CM20 ... 227 K4
Honeypot La BRW CM14 ... 354 D3
BSDN SS14 ... 19 H5
ING CM4 ... 335 K2
MAL CM9 ... 242 C2
MGTR CM11 ... 140 A7
Honey Pot La RCHLM CM3 ... 316 F8
Honeypot La RCOS CO16 ... 196 B7
Honeypots CHLM/GWD CM2 ... 288 D5
Honeysuckle Cl BRWN CM15 ... 332 C7
BSF CM23 ... 173 K5
HARH RM3 ... 352 E7
HVHL CB9 ... 27 M2
Honeysuckle Gdns CHTY IP2 ... 36 F7
Honeysuckle Wy COLN CO4 ... 163 M5

RCOLE CO7 .... 194 B6 🗓
WIT CM8 .... 211 L7
Honeywood Av RCOLW CO5 .... 158 B8
Honiley Av WICKW SS12 .... 378 F1
Honington Cl WICKE SS11 .... 360 C5 🗓
Honiton Rd ROMW/RG RM7 .... 370 E6
SOS SS1 .... 21 L6
Honorius Dr COLN CO4 .... 135 J6
Honywood Rd RCOLW CO6 .... 159 M8 🗓
Honywood Rd BSDN SS14 .... 359 G8
COLW CO3 .... 162 E5
Honywood Wy FOS CO13 .... 199 C4
Hood Cl WICKW SS12 .... 359M5
Hood Gdns BRTR CM7 .... 155 K7 🗓
Hood Rd IPSE IP3 .... 58 F2
RAIN RM13 .... 388 F7
Hood Wk ROMW/RG RM7 .... 370 C1
Hook End La BRWN CM15 .... 308 D6
Hook End Rd BRWN CM15 .... 308 D7
Hook Fld HLWS CM18 .... 255M5
Hook Ga EN E1 .... 324 C1
Hook La ABR/ST RM4 .... 329 C8
Hooks Hall Dr DAGE RM10 .... 388 D2 🗓
Hookstone Wy WFD IG8 .... 348 E8
Hooley Dr RAYL SS6 .... 361 K5
The Hoo HLWE CM17 .... 227 K6
Hoover Dr LAIN SS15 .... 376 A1
Hope Av SLH/COR SS17 .... 394 F6
Hope Cl BRWN CM15 .... 333 M3 🗓
Hope Rd BCAYE CM11 .... 358 D6
CVI SS8 .... 398 E8
SBF/HAD SS7 .... 397 K2
Hop Gardens La MAL CM9 .... 268 A7
The Hopgrounds BRTR CM7 .... 94 E5
Hopkins Cl CHLM/GWD CM2 .... 265 H8 🗓
FOS CO13 .... 199 C5 🗓
GPK RM2 .... 371 K3
Hopkins Md CHLM/GWD CM2 .... 289 C1
Hopkirk Cl RCHLM CM3 .... 291 C3
Hop Meadow RCOLE CO7 .... 107 J1
Hopping Jacks La RCHLM CM3 .... 291 C4
Hoppit Rd BRTR CM7 .... 183 C2
The Hoppitt CHONG CM5 .... 258 D8
Hopton Ri HVHL CB9 .... 27 K3
Horace Av ROMW/RG RM7 .... 370 E6
Horace Rd BCAYE CM11 .... 335 J7
SOS SS1 .... 21 J7
Hordle Pl HAR CO12 .... 7 J7 🗓
Hordle St HAR CO12 .... 7 J7 🗓
Horkesley Hl RCOLW CO6 .... 104 B3
Horkesley Rd RCOLW CO6 .... 104 B3
RCOLW CO6 .... 134 E3
Horkesley Wy WICKW SS12 .... 359 M5 🗓
Horksley Gdns
RBRW/HUT CM13 .... 333 K8 🗓
Horley Cl RCOS CO16 .... 223 K5
Hornbeam Av UPMR RM14 .... 390 B3
Hornbeam Cha SOCK/AV RM15 .... 406 C1
Hornbeam Cl CHLM/GWD CM2 .... 288 B5
COLS CO2 .... 190 E1
EPP CM16 .... 327M1
RBRW/HUT CM13 .... 355 J4
Hornbeam La CHING E4 .... 325M7
Hornbeam Rd BKHH IG9 .... 348 E4
EPP CM16 .... 327 L1 🗓
Hornbeams SBF/HAD SS7 .... 379 J3
Hornbeams Av EN EN1 .... 300 D7
The Hornbeams HAR CO12 .... 142 C4
HLW CM20 .... 15 J1
Hornbeam Wy CHESW EN7 .... 300 A1
LAIN SS15 .... 376 C2
Hornby Av WOS/PRIT SS0 .... 382 D6
Hornby Dr WOS/PRIT SS0 .... 382 E6
Hornchurch Cl WICKE SS11 .... 360 B5 🗓
Hornchurch Rd EMPK RM11 .... 371 J8
HCH CM12 .... 371 H8
Horndon Cl CRW RM5 .... 370 D1
Horndon Gn CRW RM5 .... 370 D1
Horndon Rd RCHLM CM3 .... 370 D1
SLH/COR SS17 .... 409 H2
Horne Rw WOS/PRIT SS0 .... 382 E6
Horner Pl WIT CM8 .... 239 H1 🗓
Hornet Wy BOC CM0 .... 344 C6
Hornford Wy ROMW/RG RM7 .... 370 C7
Horn Hl HSTD CO9 .... 97 K6
Horn La CBE/LIN CB1 .... 24 C1
WFD IG8 .... 348 B7
Hornminster Gln
EMPK RM11 .... 390 B1 🗓
Hornsby La CDH/CHF RM16 .... 408 B5
Hornsby Sq LAIN SS15 .... 375M4
Hornsby Wy LAIN SS15 .... 376 A4
Hornsland Rd CVI SS8 .... 398 F8
Horrocks Cl COLS CO2 .... 163 H7
Horscroft Pl HLWW/ROY CM19 .... 14 B6
Horscroft Rd HLWW/ROY CM19 .... 14 B6
Horseheath Gn CBE/LIN CB1 .... 26 D2
Horseheath Rd CBE/LIN CB1 .... 24 E1
Horseman Side BRW CM14 .... 330 A3
Horseshoe Cl BCAYW CM12 .... 335 H6
SAFWS CB11 .... 41 J7
Horseshoe Hl WAB EN9 .... 302 D5
Horseshoe La HVHL CB9 .... 27 M4 🗓
Horsey Rd FOS CO13 .... 198 D3
Horsham Av IPSE IP3 .... 38 E8
Horsham Cl HVHL CB9 .... 27 K2 🗓
Horsley Cross BSDN SS14 .... 19 H4
Hospital Ap CHLM/WR CM1 .... 235 J8
Hospital La COLW CO3 .... 162 E5 🗓
Hospital Rd COLW CO3 .... 162 E5 🗓
SBF/FI SS3 .... 403 C5
Hossack Rd IPSE IP3 .... 59 H3
Houblons Hl EPP CM16 .... 304 E3
Houchin Dr CHONG CM5 .... 283 L1
Houchin's La RCOLW CO6 .... 158 F8
Houghton Pl IPNE IP4 .... 39 C6 🗓
Hove Cl GRAYS RM17 .... 417 H3 🗓
RBRW/HUT CM13 .... 355 K3
WICKW SS12 .... 359 L8
Hovefields Av PIT SS13 .... 378 E1
Hovefields Dr WICKW SS12 .... 359 L8
Howard Av HAR CO12 .... 143 C1
Howard Cha BSDN SS14 .... 18 D1
Howard Cl BRTR CM7 .... 155 J8
WAB EN9 .... 301 L6
Howard Crs PIT SS13 .... 378 D6
Howard Dr CHLM/GWD CM2 .... 289 G1 🗓

Howard Pl CVI SS8 .... 413 J1 🗓
Howard Rd CDH/CHF RM16 .... 406 D8
COS CO15 .... 224 D7
SAFWN CB10 .... 65M1
UPMR RM14 .... 390 D1
Howards Cha WOS/PRIT SS0 .... 20 D2
Howards Cl RCHLM CM3 .... 265 M3 🗓
Howards Cft COLN CO4 .... 134 E6
Howard's La CBE/LIN CB1 .... 26 B1
Howard St IPNE IP4 .... 38 C4
Howards Wy KESC IP5 .... 39 M3
Howard Vyse Ct COS CO15 .... 12 F1
Howard Wy HLW CM20 .... 256 A1
Howbridge Hall Rd WIT CM8 .... 239 G3
Howbridge Rd WIT CM8 .... 239 G3
Howbury La ERITH DA8 .... 414 B6
Howbury Rd DART DA1 .... 414 B6
Howe Av IPSE IP3 .... 38 D8
Howe Cha HSTD CO9 .... 98 F7
Howe Cl COLN CO4 .... 11 L8
ROMW/RG RM7 .... 370 B1 🗓
Howe Green Rd RCHLM CM3 .... 316 F5
Howe La SAFWN CB10 .... 69 H7
Howell Rd SLH/COR SS17 .... 395 C5
Howe Rd HVHL CB9 .... 27 M2
Howfield Gn HOD EN11 .... 253 C2
Hows Md EPP CM16 .... 281 L4
Hoxter Wy SUD CO10 .... 4 D1
Hoxton Cl COS CO15 .... 12 C3
Hoylake Gdns HARH RM3 .... 353 H8 🗓
Hoynors RCHLM CM3 .... 291 H4
Hubbards Cha EMPK RM11 .... 372 B5
WOTN CO16 .... 199 J2
Hubbards Cl EMPK RM11 .... 372 B5
COLW CO3 .... 162 C3
RAIN RM13 .... 404 A1
Hucklesbury Av COS CO15 .... 224 F4 🗓
Hucknall Cl HARH RM3 .... 353 C7
Hudson Cl HAR CO12 .... 143 H2
HVHL CB9 .... 28 D5 🗓
RCOS CO16 .... 12 A2
Hudson Crs LOS SS9 .... 381M5
Hudson Rd LOS SS9 .... 381 L5
Hudsons Cl SLH/COR SS17 .... 394 E8 🗓
Hudson Wy CVI SS8 .... 398 B5
Hugh Dickson Rd COLN CO4 .... 10 A1
Hughes Rd CDH/CHF RM16 .... 408 B8
Hugo Gdns RAIN RM13 .... 389 C5
Hullbridge Rd RAYL SS6 .... 361 L3
RCHLM CM3 .... 339 L5
Hullett's La BRWN CM15 .... 332 A6
Hull Gn HLWE CM17 .... 258 E1
Hull Gv HLWW/ROY CM19 .... 255 H8
Hull La RCHLM CM3 .... 237 H1
Hull's La CHLM/GWD CM2 .... 289M5
Hulse Av ROMW/RG RM7 .... 370 C1
Hulton Cl RCHLM CM3 .... 265M3
Humber Av COS CO15 .... 249M5
SOCK/AV RM15 .... 406 A4
Humber Cl RAYL SS6 .... 380 C2
Humber Doucy La IPNE IP4 .... 38 B1
Humber Dr UPMR RM14 .... 372 E6
Humber Rd CHLM/WR CM1 .... 264 D6
WIT CM8 .... 238 E1
Hume Av TIL RM18 .... 418 C2
Hume Cl TIL RM18 .... 418 B7
Humphrey's Farm La
RCHLM CM3 .... 234 D4
Humphries Cl DAGW RM9 .... 388 A3 🗓
Humphry Rd SUD CO10 .... 4 D4
Hundon Rd HVHL CB9 .... 29 K1
Hundred La COLN CO4 .... 105 J7
Hungerdown La MGTR CO11 .... 137M1
RCOLE CO7 .... 137 K4
Hunnable Rd BRTR CM7 .... 154 F8
Hunt Av MAL CM9 .... 269 J6
Hunt Cl K/T/MI CO5 .... 186 E7
Hunt Dr RCOS CO16 .... 12 C1
Hunter Av BRWN CM15 .... 333 H8
Hunter Dr HCH RM12 .... 389 K3
MGTR CO11 .... 108 C8
WICKW SS12 .... 359M6
Hunter Rd BRTR CM7 .... 183 K1
Hunters Av BCAYW CM12 .... 357 J4
Hunters Cha RBRW/HUT CM13 .... 356 D2
RCOLE CO7 .... 136 F1
Hunters End FX IP11 .... 84 D6
Hunter's Gv CRW RM5 .... 351 J6
Hunters Hall Rd DAGE RM10 .... 388 B3
Hunters Reach CHESW EN7 .... 300 A1
Hunters Ridg COLN CO4 .... 135 J7
Hunters Sq DAGE RM10 .... 388 B3
Hunters Wy CHLM/WR CM1 .... 265 G4 🗓
SAFWN CB11 .... 65 J4
Huntingdon Cl BROX EN10 .... 276 F4
Huntingdon Rd SOS SS1 .... 401 L3
Huntingdon Wy COS CO15 .... 223M5
Hunting Ga COL CO1 .... 11 L8
Huntings Rd DAGE RM10 .... 388 B5 🗓
Huntland Cl RAIN RM13 .... 404 C3
Hunt Rd RCOLW CO6 .... 130 A5
Hunt's Cl CHLM/WR CM1 .... 287 J3
Hunt's Dr CHLM/WR CM1 .... 287 J3
Hunts Farm Cl MAL CM9 .... 272 E1
Hunts La SAFWN CB10 .... 22 C4
Huntsman Rd BARK/HLT IG6 .... 350 C7
Huntsmans Dr UPMR RM14 .... 390 E4
Hunts Md BCAYW CM12 .... 357 G2
PEND EN3 .... 324 F5
Hunt Wy FOS CO13 .... 198 F5
Hunwicke Rd COLN CO4 .... 163M5
Hurlock Rd BCAYE CM11 .... 357 J1 🗓
Hurnard Dr COLW CO3 .... 162 B4
Hurrell Down COLN CO4 .... 135 H7
RCHLM CM3 .... 266 A2 🗓
Hurrells La RCHLM CM3 .... 266 B8
Hurricane Cl WICKE SS11 .... 360 C5
Hurricane Wy EPP CM16 .... 281 C7
WICKE SS11 .... 360 C6
Hursley Rd CHIG IG7 .... 350 A6
Hurst Cl RCOLE CO7 .... 221 H5
Hurst Dr BAR EN8 .... 300 E6
Hurstlands Cl HARH RM11 .... 371 K6 🗓
Hurst Park Av HCH RM12 .... 389 M3 🗓
Hurst Rd BKHH IG9 .... 348 L2
Hurst Wy CHLM/GWD CM2 .... 289 G1 🗓

LOS SS9 .... 382 A7
Hurstwood Av BRWN CM15 .... 354 C1
Hutchins Cl HCH RM12 .... 389 M2 🗓
Hutland Rd IPNE IP4 .... 3 M2
Hutton Cl WFD IG8 .... 348 C7
Hutton Dr RBRW/HUT CM13 .... 355 L1
Hutton Ga RBRW/HUT CM13 .... 355 J1
Hutton Rd BRWN CM15 .... 355 C1
Hutton Village
RBRW/HUT CM13 .... 355M1
Huxtables Cl COLW CO3 .... 161 H2
Hyacinth Cl MAL CM9 .... 272 F2
RCOS CO16 .... 12 A3
Hyams La RIPS/CAP IP9 .... 80 D6
RIPS/CAP IP9 .... 110 A2
Hycliffe Gdns CHIG IG7 .... 349 K5
Hyde Cha MAL CM9 .... 291 K7
Hyde Gn RCHLM CM3 .... 291 J4
Hyde La BRTR CM7 .... 126 C2
Hyde Md WAB EN9 .... 277M3
Hyde Rd SUD CO10 .... 4 C7
Hyder Rd CDH/CHF RM16 .... 408 D8
The Hyde VGE SS16 .... 376 D7
Hydeway SBF/HAD SS7 .... 380 A6
Hyde Wy WICKW SS12 .... 359 L5
Hyde Wood La RCFD SS4 .... 364 A4
Hydewood Rd HSTD CO9 .... 51 J8
Hyem's La FX IP11 .... 85 J6
Hyland Cl EMPK RM11 .... 371 J7
Hylands Cl GTDUN CM6 .... 179 H7 🗓
The Hylands HOC/HUL SS5 .... 362 E6
Hyland Wy EMPK RM11 .... 371 J7
Hyll Cl SAFWN CB10 .... 22 E8
Hyntle Cl CHTY IP2 .... 36 F6
Hythe Cl BRTR CM7 .... 154 F5
COS CO15 .... 250 E3
Hythe Gv RCOLE CO7 .... 220 F2 🗓
Hythe Hl COL CO1 .... 163 K5
Hythe Station Rd COLS CO2 .... 11 L9
The Hythe MAL CM9 .... 293 J1

I

Ian Rd BCAYW CM12 .... 335 G7
Ibbetson Pth LOU IG10 .... 327 J5
Ibscott Cl DAGE RM10 .... 388 D5
I Butts Rd SBN/FI SS3 .... 403 A3
Iceni Wy COLS CO2 .... 162 C8
Ickleton Rd SAFWN CB10 .... 22 B6
SAFWN CB11 .... 41 H7
Icknield Cl SAFWN CB10 .... 22 B8 🗓
Icknield Wy ROY SG8 .... 40 E8
SAFWN CB11 .... 41 H7
Icknield Way Pth SAFWN CB10 .... 42 C3
Ickworth Cl COLN CO4 .... 164 A2 🗓
Ickworth Crs IPNE IP4 .... 39 C6
Ilex Cl COLS CO2 .... 190 E1
Ilfracombe Av PIT SS13 .... 378 E6
SOS SS1 .... 401 L3
Ilfracombe Crs HCH RM12 .... 389 K3
Ilfracombe Rd SOSN SS2 .... 21 M4
Ilgars Rd WICKE SS11 .... 359M2
Ilmington Dr PIT SS13 .... 378 B2
Imogen Cl COLN CO4 .... 164 A2 🗓
Imperial Av RCHLM CM3 .... 318 F2
WOS/PRIT SS0 .... 400 C2
Imphal Cl COLS CO2 .... 190 D2
Inchbonnie Rd RCHLM CM3 .... 339M5
Ingarfield Rd COS CO15 .... 224 F5
Ingatestone By-pass ING CM4 .... 310 C6
Ingatestone Rd CHLM/WR CM1 .... 309M1
ING CM4 .... 335 G2
ING CM4 .... 335 G2
WFD IG8 .... 348 C8
Ingaway VGE SS16 .... 18 C8
Ingelrica Av RCHLM CM3 .... 238 C8 🗓
Ingels Md EPP CM16 .... 304 A1
Ingersoll Rd PEND EN3 .... 324 D2
Ingestre St HAR CO12 .... 7 K6
Ingham Rd HVHL CB9 .... 28 C3
Ingleby Gdns CHIG IG7 .... 350 C4
Ingleby Rd CDH/CHF RM16 .... 408 C8
DAGE RM10 .... 388 C5
Inglefield Rd SLH/COR SS17 .... 395 J3
Ingleglen EMPK RM11 .... 372 B7 🗓
Inglenook Ct SAFWS CB11 .... 65 L2 🗓
Inglenook Cl BARK/HLT IG6 .... 350 A7
HCH RM12 .... 389 L3 🗓
Inglis Rd COLW CO3 .... 162 C5
Ingram Ms BRTR CM7 .... 183 J3 🗓
Ingram Rd GRAYS RM17 .... 417 K1
Ingram's Piece RCOLE CO7 .... 136 F4 🗓
Ingrave Cl WICKW SS12 .... 359 M5 🗓
Ingrave Rd BRW CM14 .... 354 F4
ROM RM1 .... 370 F4 🗓
Ingrebourne Gdns UPMR RM14 .... 372 D8
Ingrebourne Rd RAIN RM13 .... 404 C2
Ingreway HARH RM3 .... 353 J7
Inkerpole Hl CHLM/GWD CM2 .... 265 G7
Inmans Rw WFD IG8 .... 348 B5
Innes Cl WICKW SS12 .... 359 L6
Innham Hl HSTD CO9 .... 97 K5
Inskip Dr EMPK RM11 .... 371 M8 🗓
Institute Rd EPP CM16 .... 304 E1
Inverness Av WOS/PRIT SS0 .... 20 B2
Inverness Cl COL CO1 .... 10 E6
Inverness Dr BARK/HLT IG6 .... 349M7
Inverness Rd IPNE IP4 .... 38 B1
Invicta Ct BCAYW CM12 .... 334 F7
Inworth La RCOLW CO6 .... 131 L1
Inworth Rd K/T/MI CO5 .... 186 F7
Inworth Wk COLS CO2 .... 191 H2 🗓
Iona Wy WICKW SS12 .... 360 A6
Ipswich Ms VGE SS16 .... 376 A6 🗓
Ipswich Rd COL CO1 .... 11 H7
COLN CO4 .... 11 J2
COLN CO4 .... 106 C5
COS CO15 .... 224 E5
KIR/NAC IP10 .... 60 A5
MGTR CO11 .... 108 E2
RCOLE CO7 .... 106 F1
RIPS/CAP IP9 .... 80 E1
Ireland Rd IPSE IP3 .... 59 G2
Ireton Pl GRAYS RM17 .... 417 H1

Ireton Rd COLW CO3 .... 162 E6
Iris Cl BRWN CM15 .... 332 C7
CHLM/WR CM1 .... 265 G6
CHTY IP2 .... 37 G6
Irkdale Av EN EN1 .... 324 A3
Irlam Rd CHTY IP2 .... 57 L1
Iron Latch La CDH/CHF RM16 .... 161 K3
Iron Mill Cl DART DA1 .... 414 A8
Iron Mill Pl DART DA1 .... 414 A8
Irons Av CRW RM5 .... 351 K8
Ironwell La HOC/HUL SS5 .... 363 H8
RCFD SS4 .... 382 E1
Irvine Gdns SOCK/AV RM15 .... 406 A4
Irvine Pl WICKW SS12 .... 360 A6 🗓
Irvine Rd COLW CO3 .... 162 D6
Irvine Wy BCAYW CM12 .... 357 H2 🗓
Irving Cl BSF CM23 .... 173 L7 🗓
Irvington Cl LOS SS9 .... 381 L7
Irvon Hill Rd WICKW SS12 .... 359 K4
Irye Md VGE SS16 .... 376 D7
Isabel Ga BAR EN8 .... 277 C6
Isbourne Rd COLN CO4 .... 135 J6
Ishams Cha WIT CM8 .... 239 K4
Isis Dr UPMR RM14 .... 372 F6
Island La FOS CO13 .... 198 F2
Island Rd WOTN CO14 .... 170 F8
Ives Gdns ROM RM1 .... 371 C4
Ivy Barns La ING CM4 .... 310 B2
Ivybridge BROX EN10 .... 253 H7
Ivy Chimneys Rd EPP CM16 .... 303M4
Ivy La K/T/MI CO5 .... 220 C8
Ivy Lodge La HARH RM3 .... 372 D2
Ivy Lodge Rd RCOLW CO6 .... 134 D3
Ivy Rd SBF/HAD SS7 .... 379 H5
Ivy Ter HOD EN11 .... 253 K5
Ivy Todd Hl SAFWS CB11 .... 90 B3
Ixworth Rd HVHL CB9 .... 27M5

J

Jacaranda Cl CHLM/WR CM1 .... 265 C5
Jack Andrews Dr COLN CO4 .... 135 J6 🗓
Jackdaw Cl BCAYE CM11 .... 357 K3
SBN/FI SS3 .... 402 F3
Jack Evans Ct
SOCK/AV RM15 .... 406 B4 🗓
Jack Hatch Wy RCOLE CO7 .... 164 B8
Jack's La WICKE SS11 .... 360 A4
Jack's La RBSF CM22 .... 176 E4
Jackson Cl EMPK RM11 .... 372 A2 🗓
Jackson Pl CHLM/GWD CM2 .... 288 E5
Jackson Rd COS CO15 .... 12 F8
WDBR IP12 .... 61 M2
Jacksons Cl CHONG CM5 .... 307 H1 🗓
Jacksons Dr CHESW EN7 .... 276 B8
Jacksons La BCAYE CM11 .... 335 J8
SAFWN CB10 .... 22 E8
Jacksons Ms BCAYE CM11 .... 357 K1 🗓
Jack Stevens Cl HLWE CM17 .... 256 D5 🗓
Jacobs Av HARH RM3 .... 371M2
Jacobs Cl DAGE RM10 .... 388 C3
Jacquard Wy BRTR CM7 .... 183 H3 🗓
Jacqueline Gdns BCAYW CM12 .... 335 J7
Jaggards Rd RCOLW CO6 .... 158 B8
James Av BCTR RM8 .... 370 A8
James Boden Cl FX IP11 .... 84 F8 🗓
James Carter Rd COLW CO3 .... 161M8
James Cl GPK RM2 .... 371 H5
RCOLE CO7 .... 164 D8
James Cft CHLM/GWD CM2 .... 312 C1
James Gdns RCOS CO16 .... 222 C6
Jameson Rd COS CO15 .... 12 B8
James Rd COS CO15 .... 12 B8
James St COL CO1 .... 163 H5 🗓
EN EN1 .... 324 A7
EPP CM16 .... 280 A8
James Watt Wy ERITH DA8 .... 414 A3
Janebrook Rd CHTY IP2 .... 57 M1 🗓
Janette Av CVI SS8 .... 397M8
Janmead RBRW/HUT CM13 .... 355 J1
WIT CM8 .... 212 B8
Janus Cl HVHL CB9 .... 28 E5 🗓
Jardine Rd PIT SS13 .... 378 D3
Jarmin Rd COL CO1 .... 10 C5
Jarndyce CHLM/WR CM1 .... 264 A5
Jarvis Cleys CHESW EN7 .... 276 A6 🗓
Jarvis Fld RCHLM CM3 .... 266 E6
Jarvis Rd CVI SS8 .... 398 B5
SBF/HAD SS7 .... 379M7
Jarvis Wy HARH RM3 .... 371M2
Jasmin Cl BSF CM23 .... 173 K5
Jasmine Cl CHTY IP2 .... 37 G8 🗓
COLN CO4 .... 11 M6
FX IP11 .... 84 C3
VGE SS16 .... 376 A7
Jasmine Rd ROMW/RG RM7 .... 388 F1
Jasmine Wy COS CO15 .... 250 B4
Jason Cl CDH/CHF RM16 .... 408 F4
CVI SS8 .... 398 B7
Jasons Cl BRW CM14 .... 354 A5
Jasper Cl PEND EN3 .... 324 D1
Jays Cl RCOLW CO6 .... 160 A8
Jays La RCOLW CO6 .... 160 A8
Jaywick Cl RCOS CO16 .... 250 B1
Jaywick Rd HVHL CB9 .... 265M3
Jeans Cl BSF CM23 .... 173M4
Jefferies Rd IPNE IP4 .... 3 J4
Jefferson Av LAIN SS15 .... 376 B5
Jefferson Cl COLN CO4 .... 161 M6
Jeffery Rd CHLM/GWD CM2 .... 289 H4
Jeffrey Cl CHLM/WR CM1 .... 162 A6
Jeffrey's Rd BRTR CM7 .... 183 L5
PEND EN3 .... 325 C4
Jekylls La DAGW RM9 .... 70 E7
Jena Cl SBN/FI SS3 .... 402 F4
Jenkins Dr RBSF CM22 .... 119 K8
Jenkins La BSF CM23 .... 174 D6
Jenner Cl BRTR CM7 .... 183 G2 🗓
Jenner Md CHLM/WR CM1 .... 264 A5
Jenningham Dr CDH/CHF RM16 .... 407 H6
Jenningtree Rd ERITH DA8 .... 414 C4
Jericho Pl ING CM4 .... 308 F3

Jermayns LAIN SS15 .... 18 A5
Jermyns Cl RIPS/CAP IP9 .... 78 C1 🗓
Jerounds HLWW/ROY CM19 .... 15 G9
Jersey Cl HOD EN11 .... 253 H4
Jersey Gdns WICKE SS11 .... 359 L3
Jersey Rd MAL CM9 .... 293 J2
RAIN RM13 .... 389 H6
Jersey Wy BRTR CM7 .... 182 C1
Jervis Av RCOLE CO7 .... 300 F7
Jervis Rd BSF CM23 .... 174 A5
Jesmond Rd CDH/CHF RM16 .... 407 L6
CVI SS8 .... 413 J1
Jessel Dr LOU IG10 .... 327 K4
Jessica Cl COLN CO4 .... 164 A4 🗓
Jetty Wk GRAYS RM17 .... 417 H3 🗓
Jewell Vw KESC IP5 .... 39 L4
Jimmy's La MGTR CO11 .... 79 G8
Jocelyns HLWE CM17 .... 227 K7
Jodrell Wy WTHK RM20 .... 416 A2
Joes Rd SUD CO10 .... 55M4
Johnby Cl PEND EN3 .... 324 F1 🗓
John Eliot Cl WAB EN9 .... 277M2
John English Av BRTR CM7 .... 154 E7
John Harper St COL CO1 .... 10 B5 🗓
John Kent Av COLS CO2 .... 190 C1
John Raven Ct K/T/MI CO5 .... 186 E8
John Ray St BRTR CM7 .... 155 H8 🗓
Johnson Cl BRTR CM7 .... 183 H4 🗓
CHTY IP2 .... 37 K8
RCFD SS4 .... 363 L6
WICKW SS12 .... 359 L6 🗓
Johnson Rd CHLM/GWD CM2 .... 289 G6
RCOS CO16 .... 222 C7
Johnson's Dr RCOLE CO7 .... 165 H5
Johns Rd BSF CM23 .... 174 B2
The Johns CHONG CM5 .... 283 H7
Johnston Cl COS CO15 .... 224 F4 🗓
HSTD CO9 .... 129 C3
Johnston Rd SOS SS1 .... 402 B4
Johnston Rd WFD IG8 .... 348 B6 🗓
Johnston Wy MAL CM9 .... 293 H3 🗓
John St EN EN1 .... 324 A7
GRAYS RM17 .... 417 K3
RCOLE CO7 .... 221 C5
SBN/FI SS3 .... 403 H5
John Tibauld Ct HVHL CB9 .... 48 C5 🗓
Joiner's Cl CBE/LIN CB1 .... 24 C1
Joiner's Rd CBE/LIN CB1 .... 24 C1
Jollyboys La North GTDUN CM6 .... 180 D5
Jollyboys La South GTDUN CM6 .... 180 D7
Jones Cl SOSN SS2 .... 382 F8
Jonquil Wy COLN CO4 .... 162 C1
Jordans Cl DAGE RM10 .... 388 C3 🗓
Jordans Wy RAIN RM13 .... 389 L8
Joseph Gdns WIT CM8 .... 184 F7 🗓
Joslin Rd PUR RM19 .... 415 K2
Joslyn Cl PEND EN3 .... 325 H2
Josselin Cl PIT SS13 .... 378 D1 🗓
Josselin Cl RCOLW CO6 .... 130 C4
Josselin Ct PIT SS13 .... 378 D1 🗓
Josselin Rd PIT SS13 .... 378 D1
The Josselyns FX IP11 .... 84 D5
Jotmans La SBF/HAD SS7 .... 379 H8
Journeymans Wy SOSN SS2 .... 383 H1
Joyce Ct WAB EN9 .... 301 L6 🗓
Joyce Green La DART DA1 .... 414 E5
Joyce's Cha MAL CM9 .... 271 H3
Joyners Fld HLWS CM18 .... 255 K7
Joyners Rd DAGW RM9 .... 388 A3
Jubilee Av CHLM/WR CM1 .... 264 C5
COS CO15 .... 223M4
ROMW/RG RM7 .... 370 C5
Jubilee Cl FX IP11 .... 84 C3
HAR CO12 .... 142 F2
HOC/HUL SS5 .... 362 F6
ROMW/RG RM7 .... 370 C5
Jubilee Ct GTDUN CM6 .... 178 D2
HSTD CO9 .... 97 H3 🗓
Jubilee Dr WICKW SS12 .... 359 K3
Jubilee End MGTR CO11 .... 108 D6
Jubilee La RCOLE CO7 .... 136 D8
Jubilee Ri RCHLM CM3 .... 291 C5
Jubilee Rd BCAYE CM11 .... 358 C7
RAYL SS6 .... 380 F1
SUD CO10 .... 4 E4
WTHK RM20 .... 416 C3
Jubilee Wy FOS CO13 .... 199 C5
Judith Av CRW RM5 .... 351 J7
Julian Av COLN CO4 .... 135 J3
Julian Cl CHLM/WR CM1 .... 264 C2
HVHL CB9 .... 28 E4
Julian Court Rd BRTR CM7 .... 155 H7
Juliers Cl CVI SS8 .... 398 E8
Juliers Rd CVI SS8 .... 398 E8
Juliette Wy PUR RM19 .... 405 C7
Junction Rd BRW CM14 .... 354 D5
RCHLM CM3 .... 317 H5
ROM RM1 .... 371 C4
VGE SS16 .... 378 C7
June Av IP IP1 .... 37 J1
Juniper Cl BCAYE CM11 .... 335 K7
BROX EN10 .... 277 C5 🗓
HSTD CO9 .... 128 E3
Juniper Ct GTDUN CM6 .... 178 C2 🗓
Juniper Crs WIT CM8 .... 212 B7
Juniper Dr CHLM/GWD CM2 .... 288 C5
SOCK/AV RM15 .... 406 F1
Juniper Rd COLW CO3 .... 161 K6
LOS SS9 .... 382 A7
RCHLM CM3 .... 265M3
Juniper Wy COLN CO4 .... 11 M6
HARH RM3 .... 371M1
Jupes Hl RCOLE CO7 .... 107 K6
RCOLW CO6 .... 131 L1
Jupiter Cl HVHL CB9 .... 28 D5 🗓
Jupiter Rd IPNE IP4 .... 38 C4
Justinian Cl HVHL CB9 .... 28 E4
Jute La PEND EN3 .... 324 F4
Jutsums Av ROMW/RG RM7 .... 370 C6
Jutsums La ROMW/RG RM7 .... 370 C6
Juvina Cl WIT CM8 .... 239 G4 🗓

K

Kale Cft COLW CO3 .... 161 L6
Kale Rd SBF/HAD SS7 .... 379M7

Kamerwyk Av CVI SS8 398 D7
Kandlewood RBRW/HUT CM13 355 J1
Karen Cl BRWN CM15 354 D1
IP IP1 37 J2
RAIN RM13 388 F8
SBF/HAD SS7 397 L3
SLH/COR SS17 409 K2 3
WICKW SS12 359 K5
Karina Cl CHIG IG7 349 M6
Kate's La SAFWN CB10 45 K3
Katherine Cl RAYL SS6 381 H2
Katherine Gdns BARK/HLT IG6 349 K8
Katherine Rd PIT SS13 378 F4
Katherine's Wy
HLWW/ROY CM19 14 F8
Kathleen Cl SLH/COR SS17 394 E7
Kathleen Dr LOS SS9 400 A1
Kathleen Ferrier Crs LAIN SS15 376 D3
Katonia Av RCHLM CM3 319 G2
Kavanaghs Rd BRW CM14 354 B4
Kavanaghs Ter BRW CM14 354 C4
Kay Cl RCHLM CM3 209 H4
Keable Rd RCOLW CO6 159 M8
Keating Cl MGTR CO11 108 C7 3
Keats Av BRTR CM7 183 G3
HARH RM3 352 C8
Keats Cl CHIG IG7 349 K7
MAL CM9 293 H3
PEND EN3 324 E7
Keats Gdns TIL RM18 418 C6
Keats Rd COLW CO3 162 A5
Keats Wk RBRW/HUT CM13 355 L1
Keats Wy WICKW SS12 359 K4
Keble Cl COLW CO3 162 E5 3
Kecksy's SBW CM21 201 G7
Kedington Hl SUD CO10 77 J1
Keeble Cl K/T/MI CO5 214 F6
Keeble Ct RCOLE CO7 194 F4
Keeble Pk MAL CM9 293 G3
Keeble Wy BRTR CM7 155 H8
Keegan Pl CVI SS8 398 D7 3
Keelars La RCOLE CO7 192 F1
Keelers Wy RCOLW CO6 134 C4
Keelings La BOC CM0 321 M3
Keelings Rd BOC CM0 321 L3
Keene Wy CHLM/GWD CM2 288 C8
Keepers Gn COLN CO4 134 C8
Keeper's La FX IP11 84 B6
Keer Av CVI SS8 413 L1
Keighley Ms SBN/FI SS3 402 E1
Keith Av WICKE SS11 359 L2
Keith Cl COS CO15 224 C3
Keith Wy EMPK RM11 371 M7
SOSN SS2 382 F6
Kelburn Wy RAIN RM13 404 B1 2
Kellington Rd CVI SS8 398 D6 3
Kelly Rd CHTY IP2 36 F6
PIT SS13 378 F5
Kelman Cl BAR EN8 300 E3 1
Kelsie Wy BARK/HLT IG6 349 M7
Kelso Cl RCOLW CO6 134 D5
Kelvedon Cl CHLM/WR CM1 264 B5
RAYL SS6 361 H8 7
RBRW/HUT CM13 333 M8
Kelvedon Dr IPNE IP4 39 G6
Kelvedon Gn BRWN CM15 332 A1
Kelvedon Hall La BRW CM14 307 K6
K/T/MI CO5 213 L6
Kelvedon Rd BCAYE CM11 357 K1 2
K/T/MI CO5 214 C4
MAL CM9 242 D5
RCOLW CO6 186 B3
WIT CM8 240 A6
Kelvedon Wy WFD IG8 349 G7 4
Kelvin Rd IP IP1 37 G2
SBF/HAD SS7 379 L4
TIL RM18 418 B6
Kelvinside SLH/COR SS17 394 F6
Kemball St IPNE IP4 38 B6
Kembles RAYL SS6 361 M6
Kempe Rd BRTR CM7 94 E5
EN EN1 300 C8
Kempson Dr SUD CO10 55 K6
The Kempsters FX IP11 84 E6 1
Kempton Av HCH RM12 390 A3
Kempton Cl SBF/HAD SS7 380 C3
Kempton Pk RCOS CO16 196 C6
Kemsley Rd FX IP11 85 G8
RCOLW CO6 130 B5
Kendal Av EPP CM16 304 B2
Kendal Cl HOC/HUL SS5 361 M2
RAYL SS6 380 F1
WFD IG8 348 A3
Kendal Ct WICKE SS11 360 B6
Kendal Cft HCH RM12 389 H4
Kendale CDH/CHF RM16 408 C8
Kendall Rd COL CO1 163 H5
Kendal Wy LOS SS9 381 M4
Kenholme LOS SS9 381 M7
Kenilworth Av HARH RM3 353 J6
Kenilworth Cl BCAYW CM12 356 F1 1
Kenilworth Gdns HCH RM12 389 K2
LOU IG10 327 G8
RAYL SS6 361 K8
WOS/PRIT SS0 382 B8
Kenilworth Gv RCOS CO16 197 H1
Kenilworth Pl LAIN SS15 376 F2 2
Kenilworth Rd COS CO15 224 F5
Kenley Cl WICKE SS11 360 B5
Kenley Gdns HCH RM12 390 A1
Kenmore Cl CVI SS8 413 M1 1
Kennedy Av HOD EN11 253 G5
LAIN SS15 376 A5
PEND EN3 324 D8
Kennedy Cl BAR EN8 276 F8
IPNE IP4 38 B5
RAYL SS6 381 H3
SBF/HAD SS7 379 J4
Kennedy Wy COS CO15 13 K1
Kennel La BCAYW CM12 357 J4
Kennels Rd KIR/NAC IP10 60 F1
Kennet Cl UPMR RM14 372 F6
Kenneth Gdns SLH/COR SS17 395 G6 3
Kenneth Rd PIT SS13 378 D4
SBF/HAD SS7 380 A6
Kenning Rd HOD EN11 253 H3
Kennington Av SBF/HAD SS7 379 K6
Kennylands Rd BARK/HLT IG6 350 B8
Kensington Gdns
BCAYW CM12 335 H7 2
Kensington Rd BRWN CM15 332 B8
IP IP1 37 H3
ROMW/RG RM7 370 D6
SOS SS1 401 L3
Kent Av CVI SS8 398 C6 4
LOS SS9 400 A1
Kent Cl LAIN SS15 376 C5
RCOLE CO7 221 G4
Kent Crs BSF CM23 173 M7
Kent Dr HCH RM12 389 L3
Kent Elms Cl SOSN SS2 382 A6
Kentford Rd FX IP11 8 E2
Kent Gdns BRTR CM7 155 J7
Kent Green Cl HOC/HUL SS5 363 G6
The Kentings BRTR CM7 182 F1 2
Kentmere COLN CO4 135 M8
Kenton Wy VGE SS16 376 A6
Kent Rd DAGE RM10 388 C4
GRAYS RM17 417 K3
Kent's Av COS CO15 224 F5
Kents Farm La
CHLM/GWD CM2 312 E7
Kents Grass MAL CM9 272 E1
Kents Hill Rd SBF/HAD SS7 379 L8
Kents Hill Rd North
SBF/HAD SS7 379 L6
Kents La EPP CM16 281 L1
Kents Yd SAFWS CB11 43 G7 1
Kent Vw SOCK/AV RM15 405 K7
Kent View Av LOS SS9 400 B3
Kent View Rd VGE SS16 378 A6
Kent Wy RAYL SS6 381 H3
Kentwell Cl IPNE IP4 39 G7
Kenway RAIN RM13 404 D1
ROMW/RG RM7 370 D2
SOSN SS2 21 G1
Kenway Cl RAIN RM13 404 D1 1
Kenway Wk RAIN RM13 404 E1 2
Kenwood Gdns CBE/LIN CB1 24 F1
Kenwood Rd SLH/COR SS17 395 J7
Kenworth Cl BAR EN8 300 E5
Kenworthy Rd BRTR CM7 182 F1
Kenyon Cl RCOLE CO7 106 E2
Kenyon St CHTY IP2 2 F8
Kerby Ri CHLM/GWD CM2 289 G1
Kerridge's Cut MGTR CO11 109 H7 2
Kerril Cft HLW CM20 14 F2
Kerry Av IP IP1 36 E1
PUR RM19 405 G7
Kerry Cl UPMR RM14 373 G7
Kerry Ct COL CO1 11 J7
Kerry Dr UPMR RM14 373 G7
Kerry Rd CDH/CHF RM16 407 L6
Kersbrooke Wy SLH/COR SS17 395 J6
Kersey Av SUD CO10 5 K8
Kersey Dr RCOS CO16 223 J6
Kersey Gdns HARH RM3 352 F8
Kersey Rd FX IP11 8 E3
Kershaw Cl CDH/CHF RM16 406 D8
EMPK RM11 371 L7
Kershaw Rd DAGE RM10 388 B2
Kershaws Cl WICKW SS12 359 K6
Kessler Av BRTR CM7 95 L4 1
Kesteven Cl BARK/HLT IG6 350 A7
Kesteven Rd CHTY IP2 2 B8
Kestrel Cl BARK/HLT IG6 350 D5 1
RAIN RM13 389 J6 5
Kestrel Gdns BSF CM23 173 K5
Kestrel Gv RAYL SS6 361 J8
Kestrel Ri HSTD CO9 129 G2
Kestrel Rd CHTY IP2 36 E8
WAB EN9 302 B6
Kestrel Wy COS CO15 224 A5
Keswick Av COS CO15 224 D5
EMPK RM11 371 L8
HOC/HUL SS5 361 M1
Keswick Cl FX IP11 85 K7
RAYL SS6 380 F1 1
Keswick Dr PEND EN3 300 D8
Keswick Rd SBF/HAD SS7 379 M5
Ketleys CHLM/GWD CM2 288 D8
Ketleys Vw BRTR CM7 154 B4
Kettering Rd HARH RM3 352 F8
PEND EN3 324 E1
Kettlebaston Wy IP IP1 37 L2 2
Kettlebury Wy CHONG CM5 307 G2
Kevin Cl BCAYE CM11 357 L4
Kew La FOS CO13 198 B7
Keyes Cl SBN/FI SS3 402 F2
Keyes Rd DART DA1 415 H8
Keyes Wy BRTR CM7 155 K7
Keymer Wy COLW CO3 162 A7 1
Keynes Wy HAR CO12 143 G2
Key Rd COS CO15 12 E5
Keysers Rd BROX EN10 277 H2
Keysland SBF/HAD SS7 380 C4
Key St IPSE IP3 3 G6
Khartoum Rd IPNE IP4 3 M2
Kibcaps VGE SS16 18 C9
Kidder Rd BRTR CM7 182 A2
Kielder Cl BARK/HLT IG6 350 A7
Kilburn Gdns RCOS CO16 12 C1
Kildare Av IP IP1 36 E1
Kildermorie Cl COLN CO4 135 L8
Kilmaine Rd HAR CO12 143 G2
Kilmartin Wy HCH RM12 389 J4
Kilmington Cl RBRW/HUT CM13 355 J3
Kiln Barn Av COS CO15 224 A4
Kiln Dr SUD CO10 5 H8
Kilnfield CHONG CM5 307 G1 1
Kiln Fld FX IP11 84 E8 5
Kiln La HLWE CM17 256 E4
Kiln Rd EPP CM16 281 H7
SBF/HAD SS7 380 B7
Kiln Wy GRAYS RM17 417 G2
Kilnwood Av HOC/HUL SS5 362 E6
Kilowan Cl VGE SS16 376 A7
Kilsmore La BAR EN8 276 E8
Kiltie Rd K/T/MI CO5 214 F6
Kilworth Av BRWN CM15 333 H8
SOS SS1 21 K6
Kimberley Av ROMW/RG RM7 370 C6
Kimberley Cl BSF CM23 174 B6 1
Kimberley Gdns EN EN1 324 A5
Kimberley Rd COL CO1 163 J5
SBF/HAD SS7 379 K8
SBN/FI SS3 384 F5
Kimberly Dr LAIN SS15 377 G1
Kimpton Av BRWN CM15 354 C1
Kimpton's Cl CHONG CM5 283 G6 2
Kincaid Rd RCOS CO16 222 B7
Kinfauns Av EMPK RM11 371 K6
Kingaby Gdns RAIN RM13 389 H6
King Alfred Rd HARH RM3 372 A2
King Arthur Ct BAR EN8 300 F3
King Charles Rd K/T/MI CO5 245 L5
King Coel Rd COLW CO3 161 L4
King Edward Av BOC CM0 344 C5
RAIN RM13 389 L8
King Edward Dr
CDH/CHF RM16 407 M8
GRAYS RM17 417 M1
King Edward Quay COLS CO2 163 L6
King Edward Rd BAR EN8 300 F5
BRW CM14 354 D4 1
GRH DA9 416 B8
IPSE IP3 38 C8
LAIN SS15 376 C3
ROM RM1 371 G6 2
King Edward's Rd PEND EN3 324 E6
RCHLM CM3 339 M3 3
SLH/COR SS17 409 L3
King Edward Vii Dr
RIPS/CAP IP9 113 J3
King Edward Wy WIT CM8 238 F3
Kingfisher Av CHTY IP2 36 E8
Kingfisher Cl COLN CO4 164 A3
HVHL CB9 28 D3 1
MAL CM9 269 K6
RBRW/HUT CM13 355 H1
SBN/FI SS3 402 F2
Kingfisher Crs RAYL SS6 361 J8 3
Kingfisher Dr SBF/HAD SS7 397 K1
Kingfisher Ga BRTR CM7 155 H6 1
Kingfisher Mdw HSTD CO9 129 G2 1
Kingfisher Rd UPMR RM14 373 G8
Kingfishers COS CO15 224 A5
VGE SS16 19 J9
Kingfisher Wy BSF CM23 174 B4
K/T/MI CO5 213 K1 1
King George Cl ROMW/RG RM7 370 D3
King George Rd COLS CO2 163 H7
WAB EN9 301 K6 2
King George's Av HAR CO12 6 F7
King George's Cl RAYL SS6 380 E2
King George's Rd BRWN CM15 332 C8
King George Vi Av TIL RM18 419 J1
King Harold Rd COLW CO3 162 B7
King Henry's Dr RCFD SS4 383 G4
King Henry's Ms PEND EN3 325 H1 1
Kingley Cl WICKW SS12 359 J4
Kingley Dr WICKW SS12 359 J4
Kings Acre RCOLW CO6 186 A1
Kings Av CHDH RM6 370 A6
COS CO15 224 D6
IPNE IP4 3 J5
WFD IG8 348 D6
Kingsbridge Cl BRTR CM7 155 G3 1
Kingsbridge Rd BSF CM23 174 B3
HARH RM3 352 F7 3
Kingsbury Cl RCOLW CO6 160 A8 2
Kingsbury Rd FX IP11 84 D6
King's Cha BRW CM14 354 D4
WIT CM8 239 H2
Kings Cl CVI SS8 397 K8
MGTR CO11 108 D7
RAYL SS6 380 F1
RCOS CO16 222 B8
SUD CO10 35 K5
Kings Ct BSF CM23 174 B3
Kings Crs LAIN SS15 376 C2
Kings Cft BOC CM0 320 D7
Kingsdon La HLWE CM17 256 D4
Kingsdown Cl PIT SS13 378 D5
Kings Farm RAYL SS6 361 M6
Kingsfield HOD EN11 253 H3
Kingsfield Av IP IP1 37 L2
Kingsfield Dr PEND EN3 300 E7
Kingsfield Wy PEND EN3 300 E7 3
Kings Fleet Rd FX IP11 9 G3
Kingsford Dr CHLM/GWD CM2 265 J8
Kings Gdns UPMR RM14 372 F7
Kingsgate Dr IPNE IP4 38 A3
King's Gn LOU IG10 326 F5 1
Kings Gv ROM RM1 371 H5
Kingshawes SBF/HAD SS7 380 C5
Kings Head Ct COL CO1 10 B5
King's Head St HAR CO12 7 K3
King's Hl HVHL CB9 29 H2
Kingshill Av CRW RM5 351 K7
Kingsland HLWS CM18 15 K8
RIPS/CAP IP9 112 F1
Kingsland Beach K/T/MI CO5 245 K6
Kingsland Cl K/T/MI CO5 245 K6 1
Kingsland Rd K/T/MI CO5 245 K6
Kings La BRTR CM7 155 M7
SUD CO10 35 G4
Kingsley Av BAR EN8 300 C1
Kingsley Cl DAGE RM10 388 C3
Kingsley Ct EMPK RM11 371 J6 1
Kingsley Crs SBF/HAD SS7 380 C3
Kingsley Gdns EMPK RM11 371 L4
Kingsley La SBF/HAD SS7 380 C3
Kingsley Rd LOU IG10 327 L5
RBRW/HUT CM13 355 L1
Kingsley Wk CDH/CHF RM16 418 B1
Kings Lynn Dr HARH RM3 352 E7
Kingsman Dr CDH/CHF RM16 407 J5 1
RCOS CO16 12 A2
Kingsman Rd SLH/COR SS17 409 J2
Kingsmans Farm Rd
HOC/HUL SS5 340 A7
Kingsmead BAR EN8 276 E8
Kings Md HSTD CO9 100 B4
Kingsmead SBW CM21 227 M2
Kingsmead Av ROM RM1 371 G6 3
Kingsmead Cl
HLWW/ROY CM19 254 C4
Kings Meadow HVHL CB9 29 H1
SUD CO10 5 G8
Kings Meadow Rd COL CO1 10 C5
Kingsmere SBF/HAD SS7 380 D6
Kingsmere Cl
K/T/MI CO5 245 L5
Kings Ms RCOLE CO7 164 D7
Kingsmill Gdns DAGW RM9 388 A4
Kingsmill Rd DAGW RM9 388 A4
Kingsmoor Rd
HLWW/ROY CM19 255 J6
Kings Pde COS CO15 224 E7
Kings Pk SBF/HAD SS7 380 A6
Kings Pl BKHH IG9 348 D3 1
King's Quay St HAR CO12 7 L2
King's Rd BAR EN8 300 F6
BOC CM0 320 E8
BOC CM0 344 C7
BRTR CM7 154 F5 2
BRW CM14 354 D4
CHLM/WR CM1 264 A7
COS CO15 250 E2
CVI SS8 397 K8
HAR CO12 6 E9
HSTD CO9 128 F2
LAIN SS15 376 C2
MAL CM9 240 E4
RAYL SS6 380 F1
ROM RM1 371 H5
SBF/HAD SS7 397 M1
WOS/PRIT SS0 400 C2
Kingsteignton SBN/FI SS3 402 D2
King Stephen Rd COL CO1 163 J5
Kingston Av CHLM/GWD CM2 264 F8
SBN/FI SS3 402 F1
Kingston Cha MAL CM9 269 G5
Kingston Crs CHLM/GWD CM2 264 F8
Kingston Hl VGE SS16 394 E1
Kingston Rd IP IP1 37 G3
ROM RM1 371 G4
Kingston Wy SBF/HAD SS7 379 M6
King St BSF CM23 174 A4
CHONG CM5 284 C8
FX IP11 84 F8
HSTD CO9 74 A7 2
IP IP1 2 E4
MAL CM9 293 H2
MGTR CO11 139 K3
SLH/COR SS17 409 K2
SUD CO10 4 D6
Kings Wk MAL CM9 272 F2
Kingsway HAR CO12 7 J7
HOC/HUL SS5 361 L2
K/T/MI CO5 214 D5
PEND EN3 324 C7
WOS/PRIT SS0 400 B1
Kings Wy BCAYE CM11 357 L5
IPSE IP3 59 J1
RCHLM CM3 339 K2
Kingsway Ms WOS/PRIT SS0 400 C1 1
Kingswood Cha LOS SS9 381 L8
Kingswood Cl BCAYE CM11 335 K8
EN EN1 324 A7 2
Kingswood Ct BOC CM0 274 B8
Kingswood Crs RAYL SS6 380 C2
Kingswood Rd COLN CO4 135 G7
VGE SS16 19 J8
Kingwell Av COS CO15 12 F2
Kinlett Cl COLN CO4 135 J7
Kinloch Cha WIT CM8 239 G4 2
Kinnaird Wy WFD IG8 349 G7
Kino Rd WOTN CO14 199 L3 1
Kinross Rd IPNE IP4 38 C2
Kipling Av TIL RM18 418 C5
Kipling Cl CHLM/WR CM1 264 B6
Kipling Wy BRTR CM7 183 H3
Kirby Cl BARK/HLT IG6 349 M7
HARH RM3 353 H6
IPNE IP4 38 B4
LOU IG10 348 F1 2
Kirby Hall Rd HSTD CO9 73 L6
Kirby Rd BSDN SS14 377 M5
FOS CO13 198 B7
FOS CO13 199 H3
Kirby St IPNE IP4 38 B4
Kirkbaye FOS CO13 198 F5
Kirkham Av SLH/COR SS17 394 A4
Kirkham Cl CHTY IP2 58 B1
Kirkham Rd SLH/COR SS17 394 A4
Kirkham Shaw SLH/COR SS17 394 A3
Kirkhurst Cl RCOLE CO7 221 H5 1
Kirkmans Rd CHLM/GWD CM2 288 E8
Kirk Pl CHLM/GWD CM2 265 G8 2
Kirkton Cl RIPS/CAP IP9 113 H2
Kirton Cl HCH RM12 389 K5
Kirton Rd KIR/NAC IP10 61 M4
KIR/NAC IP10 84 C1
Kitchener Rd IP IP1 37 G3
RCHLM CM3 341 H2
Kitchener Wy RIPS/CAP IP9 113 H3
Kitchen Fld BRTR CM7 155 L8
Kitchen Hl SUD CO10 54 C5
Kitkatts Rd CVI SS8 398 B8
Kitson Wy HLW CM20 15 K3
Kittiwake Cl CHTY IP2 36 F8
Kittiwake Dr MAL CM9 269 K6 5
Knapton Cl CHLM/WR CM1 264 E4
The Knares VGE SS16 18 A9
Knightbridge Wk BCAYW CM12 335 H8
Knighton Cl ROMW/RG RM7 370 E6 1
WFD IG8 348 C5
Knighton Dr WFD IG8 348 C5
Knighton La BKHH IG9 348 C3
Knighton Rd ROMW/RG RM7 370 D6
Knights LAIN SS15 376 E4
Knightsbridge Cl COLS CO2 162 D8 1
Knightsbridge Gdns
ROMW/RG RM7 370 E5
Knights Cl BSF CM23 173 J3
FX IP11 85 L7
K/T/MI CO5 215 G8
MGTR CO11 108 D7
Knightsdale Rd IP IP1 37 H2
Knights La KESG IP5 39 L4
Knights Rd BRTR CM7 183 K2
RCOLW CO6 186 A1
Knight St RCHLM CM3 339 M4
SBW CM21 227 M1
Knights Wk ABR/ST RM4 328 C5
Knights Wy BARK/HLT IG6 349 K7
GTDUN CM6 178 E2
RBRW/HUT CM13 355 H5
Knightswick Rd CVI SS8 398 C7
Knivet Cl RAYL SS6 380 F2
Knole La SAFWS CB11 63 H4
Knollcroft SBN/FI SS3 402 E6
The Knoll BCAYW CM12 335 J7
RAYL SS6 380 E1 1
Knowles Cl HSTD CO9 128 F2
The Knowle HOD EN11 253 H6 2
VGE SS16 19 K9
Knox Cl MAL CM9 293 H3
Knox Ct WICKW SS12 360 A6 5
Knox Gdns COS CO15 12 F2
Knox Rd COS CO15 12 E1
Knutsford Cl RIPW IP8 57 K2
Kohima Rd COLS CO2 190 C2
Kolburg Rd CVI SS8 413 L1 4
Kollum Rd CVI SS8 399 G8
Koln Cl CVI SS8 397 K8
Komberg Crs CVI SS8 398 D6
Konnybrook SBF/HAD SS7 380 B7
Korndyk Av CVI SS8 398 D7
Kreswell Gv HAR CO12 143 J1
Kursaal Wy SOS SS1 21 L7
Kyme Rd ROM RM1 371 G6
Kynance Cl HARH RM3 352 D4
Kynaston Pl WIT CM8 239 J1 2
Kynaston Rd BRTR CM7 154 A3
Kynoch Ct SLH/COR SS17 409 M2

L

Laars Av CVI SS8 398 D7
Laburnham Cl UPMR RM14 373 H7
Laburnham Gdns UPMR RM14 373 G7
Laburnum RCHLM CM3 238 B8
Laburnum Av HCH RM12 389 H1
WICKW SS12 359 K5
Laburnum Cl BAR EN8 300 E3
COS CO15 12 A6
HOC/HUL SS5 362 D5 2
IPSE IP3 59 M1 1
RCOLE CO7 194 F3 1
RIPW IP8 57 K1 3
WICKW SS12 359 K4 4
Laburnum Crs FOS CO13 198 E5
Laburnum Dr CHLM/GWD CM2 288 C5
SLH/COR SS17 395 H8
Laburnum Gdns KESG IP5 38 F2 2
Laburnum Gv COLN CO4 163 M3
CVI SS8 397 L8
HOC/HUL SS5 362 C6
SOCK/AV RM15 406 E2 2
Laburnum Rd EPP CM16 304 D1
HOD EN11 253 J3 1
Laburnum Wk HCH RM12 389 K4
Laburnum Wy RAYL SS6 361 J5 1
RCOLW CO6 104 A2
WIT CM8 212 B7 2
Labworth Rd CVI SS8 413 K1
Lacey St IPNE IP4 3 J3
Lackmore Rd EN EN1 300 D7 2
Lacon Rd RIPW IP8 36 B1
Ladbroke Rd EN EN1 324 A8
Ladbrook Dr COLS CO2 163 H8
Ladbrooke Rd RCOS CO16 223 L5
Ladell Cl COLW CO3 161 M8
Ladram Cl SOS SS1 402 D3
Ladram Rd SOS SS1 402 C3
Ladram Wy SOS SS1 402 C3
Ladyfields LOU IG10 327 J6
Lady La CHLM/GWD CM2 17 J7
IP IP1 2 D4
Ladyshot HLW CM20 256 B2
Ladysmith Av RCOLE CO7 220 F4
Ladysmith Rd EN EN1 324 A4
Ladysmith Wy LAIN SS15 377 G2 1
Ladywell La CHLM/GWD CM2 289 J6
Ladywell Prospect SBW CM21 228 A2
Ladywood Rd IPNE IP4 38 D4
Lagonda Av BARK/HLT IG6 350 A7 2
Lagonda Wy DART DA1 414 D8
Laindon Common Rd
BCAYW CM12 357 G6
Laindon Link LAIN SS15 18 B8
Laindon Rd BCAYW CM12 357 H3
Laindon West LAIN SS15 375 M5 1
Laing Cl CHIG IG7 349 L7
Laing Rd COLN CO4 163 M5
Laird Av CDH/CHF RM16 407 L7
Lake Av BCAYW CM12 335 H8
COS CO15 12 A5
RAIN RM13 389 L8
Lake Dr SBF/HAD SS7 379 M6
Lakefields Cl RAIN RM13 389 L8 3
Lake Gdns DAGE RM10 388 B4
Lakeland Cl CHIG IG7 350 C5
Lake Ri ROM RM1 371 G3
WTHK RM20 416 B1
Lake Rd WAB EN9 277 M1
Lakeside RAIN RM13 389 M8
RAYL SS6 361 L7 2
Lakeside Cl CHIG IG7 350 A5
Lakeside Crs BRW CM14 354 E4
CVI SS8 398 E6 3
Lakeside Rd BAR EN8 276 D8
CHTY IP2 57 M1
Lakes Meadow RCOLW CO6 186 B2
Lakes Rd BRTR CM7 183 J1
Lakeview CVI SS8 398 B6
Lake Vw VGE SS16 376 A7
Lake Wk COS CO15 12 A5
Lake Wy COS CO15 250 A4
Lakforth SUD CO10 34 E3
Lakin Cl CHLM/GWD CM2 265 H8
Lamarsh Hl BURES CO8 77 J4
Lamarsh Rd BURES CO8 77 H8
Lamb Cl TIL RM18 418 D6
Lambert Cross SAFWN CB10 43 M8
Lambert Dr SUD CO10 35 L5
Lamberts La KESG IP5 38 D1
Lambert's Rd RCOLW CO6 159 G1
Lambeth Ms HOC/HUL SS5 362 D5 3
Lambeth Rd LOS SS9 381 M5
SBF/HAD SS7 379 K5
Lamb La HSTD CO9 97 L4
Lambourne CVI SS8 413 H1

Lambourne Cl *CHIG* IG7 .... 350 C4
  COLW CO3 .... 161 L7
  COS CO15 .... 224 A3
Lambourne Crs *BSDN* SS14 .... 378 A6
  CHIG IG7 .... 350 C3
Lambourne Dr
  RBRW/HUT CM13 .... 388 M3
  HCH RM12 .... 389 L1
Lambourne Gdns *EN* EN1 .... 324 A4
Lambourne Gv *MAL* CM9 .... 293 G3
Lambourne Hall Rd *RCFD* SS4 .... 365 C2
Lambourne Rd *CHIG* IG7 .... 350 A5
Lambourini Cl *SBN/FI* SS3 .... 402 F1 ▣
Lamb's La North *RAIN* RM13 .... 404 A3
Lamb's La South *RAIN* RM13 .... 404 D1
Lambton Av *BAR* EN8 .... 300 E5 ▣
Lammasmead *BROX* EN10 .... 277 G3
Lammas Wy *RCOLE* CO7 .... 164 D8
Lamont Cl *WICKW* SS12 .... 359 M6 ▣
Lampern Crs *BCAYW* CM12 .... 335 K5
Lampits *HOD* EN11 .... 253 J5
Lampits La *SLH/COR* SS17 .... 395 H5
Lampits Hill Av *SLH/COR* SS17 .... 395 H6
Lampits La *SLH/COR* SS17 .... 395 J5
Lamplighters Cl *WAB* EN9 .... 302 B6 ▣
Lamson Rd *RAIN* RM13 .... 404 A3
Lanark Rd *IPNE* IP4 .... 38 C2
Lancaster Cl *BRWN* CM15 .... 332 B7
Lancaster Dr *HCH* RM12 .... 389 J4
  LOU IG10 .... 326 F8
  VGE SS16 .... 376 A6 ▣
Lancaster Gdns *RAYL* SS6 .... 381 H3 ▣
  SOS SS1 .... 21 J3
Lancaster Gdns East *COS* CO15 .... 13 K4
Lancaster Gdns West *COS* CO15 .... 13 K4
Lancaster Rd *EPP* CM16 .... 281 H6
  IPNE IP4 .... 3 J4
  RAYL SS6 .... 381 J4
  SUD CO10 .... 54 E1
Lancaster Wy *BRTR* CM7 .... 154 F7
  BSF CM23 .... 173 J3
  RCOLW CO6 .... 158 A1
Lancelot Rd *BARK/HLT* IG6 .... 349 M7 ▣
Lancer Wy *BCAYW* CM12 .... 335 K5
Lanchester Av *COS* CO15 .... 249 L5
Lancing Av *IPNE* IP4 .... 38 B3
Lancing Rd *HARH* RM3 .... 352 F8
Landau Wy *BROX* EN10 .... 277 C6
  ERITH DA8 .... 414 C2
Land Cl *RCOS* CO16 .... 12 A1
Landermere *BSDN* SS14 .... 19 G3
Landermere Rd *RCOS* CO16 .... 197 H2
Lander Rd *GRAYS* RM17 .... 417 L2
Landguard Rd *FX* IP11 .... 9 G9
Landisdale *RCHLM* CM3 .... 291 H4
Land La *COL* CO1 .... 10 E7
Landmead Rd *BAR* EN8 .... 300 F1 ▣
Landsburg Rd *CVI* SS8 .... 398 E6
Landscape Rd *WFD* IG8 .... 348 C8
Landscape Vw *SAFWS* CB11 .... 65 L5
Landsdown Rd *SUD* CO10 .... 5 G3
Landseer Cl *HCH* RM12 .... 371 J8 ▣
  IPSE IP3 .... 59 H2
Landseer Rd *COLW* CO3 .... 162 C6
  EN EN1 .... 324 B7
  IPSE IP3 .... 58 F1
Landview Gdns *CHONG* CM5 .... 307 C2
Landwick La *BOC* CM0 .... 322 A4
Lane End *HLWE* CM17 .... 256 F4
Lanercost Wy *CHTY* IP2 .... 58 B2
Lane Rd *RCOLW* CO6 .... 131 J5
Laneside Av *BCTR* RM8 .... 370 A7
The Lane *K/T/MI* CO5 .... 213 L1 ▣
  MGTR CO11 .... 109 G7
Langdale *BRTR* CM7 .... 182 D4 ▣
Langdale Cl *FX* IP11 .... 85 L7
Langdale Dr *COLN* CO4 .... 135 J7
Langdale Gdns *CHLM/GWD* CM2 .... 17 K7
  HCH RM12 .... 389 H4
  PEND EN3 .... 300 E7
Langdon Rd *RAYL* SS6 .... 361 J8
Langdon Wy *SLH/COR* SS17 .... 395 J6
Langemore Wy *BCAYE* CM11 .... 357 J1
Langenhoe *WICKW* SS12 .... 359 M5
Langenhoe Hall La *K/T/MI* CO5 .... 218 C4
Langenhoe Pk *K/T/MI* CO5 .... 218 C1
Langer Rd *FX* IP11 .... 9 H6
Langfield Cl *WAB* EN9 .... 277 M2 ▣
Langford Br *CHONG* CM5 .... 307 J4
Langford Crs *SBF/HAD* SS7 .... 380 A5
Langford Gn *RBRW/HUT* CM13 .... 333 K8
Langford Gv *PIT* SS13 .... 378 D3
Langford Rd *MAL* CM9 .... 268 F5
  WFD IG8 .... 348 D7 ▣
  WIT CM8 .... 239 K8
Langfords *BKHH* IG9 .... 348 G3
Langham Ct *EMPK* RM11 .... 371 L7
Langham Crs *BCAYW* CM12 .... 357 J3
Langham Dr *RAYL* SS6 .... 361 H8 ▣
  RCOS CO16 .... 223 J7
Langham La *COLN* CO4 .... 135 J3
Langham Wy *HVHL* CB9 .... 27 J2
Langhorne Rd *DAGE* RM10 .... 388 B6
Langland *SLH/COR* SS17 .... 395 H7 ▣
Langley Av *BRTR* CM7 .... 95 L4
  FX IP11 .... 9 G1
Langley Cl *HAR* CO12 .... 7 G9
  HARH RM3 .... 352 E8 ▣
  LOS SS9 .... 381 J4
  SOS SS1 .... 21 L5
Langley Dr *BRW* CM14 .... 354 B4
Langley Hl *BURES* CO8 .... 77 K8
Langleys *VGE* SS16 .... 19 G9
Langport Dr *WOS/PRIT* SS0 .... 382 B7
Langside Cl *LAIN* SS15 .... 376 C3 ▣
Langstons *FX* IP11 .... 84 E5
Langthorne Crs *GRAYS* RM17 .... 417 K1
Langton Av *CHLM/WR* CM1 .... 263 M6
Langton Rd *HOD* EN11 .... 253 G5
Langton Wy *CDH/CHF* RM16 .... 418 C7 ▣
Langwood *K/T/MI* CO5 .... 245 K4 ▣
Lanhams *PIT* SS13 .... 378 D3
Lansbury Rd *PEND* EN3 .... 324 E3
Lansdown Av *SBF/HAD* SS7 .... 381 G5
Lansdowne Av *LOS* SS9 .... 400 B2
Lansdowne Cl *K/T/MI* CO5 .... 214 D5 ▣

Lansdowne Dr *RAYL* SS6 .... 361 K8
Lansdowne Rd *FX* IP11 .... 85 J7
  IPNE IP4 .... 38 B6 ▣
Lansdun Rd *TIL* RM18 .... 418 A6
Lanvalley Rd *COLW* CO3 .... 161 M5
La Plata Gv *BRW* CM14 .... 354 C4
Lappmark Rd *CVI* SS8 .... 398 E8
Lapwing Cl *ERITH* DA8 .... 414 C4 ▣
Lapwing Dr *K/T/MI* CO5 .... 213 L1 ▣
  MAL CM9 .... 269 K6
Lapwing Rd *CHTY* IP2 .... 36 E8 ▣
  WICKE SS11 .... 359 K1 ▣
Larch Cl *COLN* CO4 .... 11 M5
  LAIN SS15 .... 376 D2
Larchcroft Cl *IP* IP1 .... 37 J1
Larchcroft Rd *IP* IP1 .... 37 H1
Larches Av *EN* EN1 .... 300 D7
The Larches *RCHLM* CM3 .... 265 M3 ▣
  SBF/HAD SS7 .... 379 J3
Larch Gv *CHLM/GWD* CM2 .... 288 D5
  RCOLW CO6 .... 104 A2
  WIT CM8 .... 212 B6 ▣
Larch Wk *MAL* CM9 .... 269 K5
Larch Wy *GTDUN* CM6 .... 178 B2
Larchwood *BSF* CM23 .... 173 L6
Larchwood Av *CRW* RM5 .... 351 J2
Larchwood Cl *CHTY* IP2 .... 36 D6
  CRW RM5 .... 351 K7
  LOS SS9 .... 381 J5
Larchwood Gdns *BRWN* CM15 .... 332 B8
Largent Gv *KESG* IP5 .... 39 M3
Larke Ri *RBRW/HUT* SS0 .... 382 E7
Larkfield *SLH/COR* SS17 .... 395 K7
Larkfield Cl *RCFD* SS4 .... 363 L7
Larkfield Rd *RCOLE* CO7 .... 194 E2
Larkhill Av *RCFD* SS4 .... 364 B1
Larkhill Rd *RCFD* SS4 .... 364 A2
Larkhill Wy *FX* IP11 .... 84 E8 ▣
Larkin Cl *RBRW/HUT* CM13 .... 355 K1
Lark Ri *SUD* CO10 .... 54 E6 ▣
Larks Cl *HVHL* CB9 .... 28 D4
Larksfield Crs *HAR* CO12 .... 6 F7
Larksfield *RIPS/CAP* IP9 .... 80 B8
Lark's La *RCHLM* CM3 .... 235 G6
Larkspur *BSF* CM23 .... 173 L5
  SOCK/AV RM15 .... 406 D1 ▣
  WIT CM8 .... 211 M7 ▣
Larkspur Cl *CHTY* IP2 .... 37 G8
Larkway *BSF* CM23 .... 173 K5
  FX IP11 .... 8 F4
Larkswood *HLWE* CM17 .... 256 D5 ▣
Larkswood Cl *ERITH* DA8 .... 414 A5
Larkswood Rd *SLH/COR* SS17 .... 395 J7
Larkway *FOS* CO13 .... 198 K4 ▣
Larmans Rd *PEND* EN3 .... 300 D8 ▣
The Larneys *FOS* CO13 .... 198 K4 ▣
Larsen Dr *WAB* EN9 .... 301 L6 ▣
Larup Av *CVI* SS8 .... 398 C7 ▣
Lascelles Cl *BRWN* CM15 .... 332 C7
Lascelles Gdns *RCFD* SS4 .... 363 K6
Latchetts Shaw *VGE* SS16 .... 19 G9
Latchford Pl *CHIG* IG7 .... 350 C5
Latchingdon Cl *RAYL* SS6 .... 361 H8 ▣
Latchingdon Gdns *WFD* IG8 .... 348 F7 ▣
Latchingdon Rd *RCHLM* CM3 .... 317 C6
Latchmore Bank *RBSF* CM22 .... 201 J1
Lathcoates Crs
  CHLM/GWD CM2 .... 288 F3
Latimer Dr *HCH* RM12 .... 389 L2
  LAIN SS15 .... 376 C2
Lattice Av *IPNE* IP4 .... 38 D5
Latton Gn *HLWS* CM18 .... 256 A7
Latton Hall Cl *HLW* CM20 .... 256 C6
Latton House *HLWS* CM18 .... 256 C6
Latton St *HLW* CM20 .... 256 C3
  HLWE CM17 .... 256 D6
Laud's Cl *FX* IP11 .... 84 C5
Launceston Cl *COLS* CO2 .... 191 J2
  HARH RM3 .... 371 K1
Launder's La *RAIN* RM13 .... 404 F3
Laundry La *BRWN* CM15 .... 333 L3
  WAB EN9 .... 278 A5
Laurel Av *HAR* CO12 .... 6 B9
  KESG IP5 .... 39 H4
  WICKW SS12 .... 359 K4
Laurel Cl *BARK/HLT* IG6 .... 349 K7
  COS CO15 .... 224 C4
  HVHL CB9 .... 27 L2
  LOS SS9 .... 399 L3
  RBRW/HUT CM13 .... 333 J7
Laurel Crs *ROMW/RG* RM7 .... 370 F8
Laurel Dr *GTDUN* CM6 .... 178 C2 ▣
  SOCK/AV RM15 .... 406 D2 ▣
  SUD CO10 .... 34 D4
Laurel Gv *CHLM/GWD* CM2 .... 16 D8
Laurelhayes *CHTY* IP2 .... 37 H8
The Laurels *RAYL* SS6 .... 381 G3
  RCHLM CM3 .... 339 L3
Laurence Av *WIT* CM8 .... 239 H5
Laurence Cl *RCOLE* CO7 .... 165 G5
Laurence Cft *CHLM/WR* CM1 .... 287 J2
Lavender Av *BRWN* CM15 .... 332 C7
Lavender Cl *BSF* CM23 .... 173 L5
  CHESW EN7 .... 276 A7 ▣
  HARH RM3 .... 352 E8
  HLW CM20 .... 255 M2
  K/T/MI CO5 .... 214 D7 ▣
  SOCK/AV RM15 .... 406 F2 ▣
  WIT CM8 .... 211 M7 ▣
Lavender Ct *CHLM/WR* CM1 .... 265 G6 ▣
Lavender Dr *BOC* CM0 .... 320 D8
Lavender Gv *WOS/PRIT* SS0 .... 382 B7
Lavender Hl *CHTY* IP2 .... 37 G7
Lavender Ms *WOS/PRIT* SS0 .... 382 B7
Lavender Wk *COLN* CO4 .... 162 D1 ▣
  WICKW SS12 .... 359 K4 ▣
Lavenham Cl *RCOS* CO16 .... 223 J7
Lavenham Rd *CHTY* IP2 .... 36 F6
  SUD CO10 .... 35 H2
Lawford Cl *HCH* RM12 .... 389 K3 ▣
Lawling Av *MAL* CM9 .... 269 K6
Lawlinge Rd *RCHLM* CM3 .... 318 C6
Lawn Av *SOSN* SS2 .... 21 K1
Lawn Cha *WIT* CM8 .... 239 G7
Lawn La *CHLM/WR* CM1 .... 264 E5 ▣
Lawns Cl *K/T/MI* CO5 .... 245 K4

Lawnscourt *SBF/HAD* SS7 .... 379 J4 ▣
Lawns Crs *GRAYS* RM17 .... 417 L3
The Lawns Dr *BROX* EN10 .... 277 C2
The Lawns *CHLM/WR* CM1 .... 264 E6
  IPNE IP4 .... 38 D3
  SBF/HAD SS7 .... 379 K4
Lawn Wy *FX* IP11 .... 84 F8
Lawrance Av *SBW* CM21 .... 200 F7
Lawrence Av *CRW* RM5 .... 351 K8
Lawrence Crs *DAGE* RM10 .... 388 C2
Lawrence Rd *TIL* RM18 .... 418 C4
Lawrence Moorings *SBW* CM21 .... 228 A2
Lawrence Rd *GPK* RM2 .... 371 J5
  LAIN SS15 .... 376 D4
Laws Cl *SAFWS* CB11 .... 65 L4
Law's Drift *KIR/NAC* IP10 .... 61 M7
Lawshall's Hl *RCOLW* CO6 .... 130 E3
Lawson Rd *DART* DA1 .... 414 E8
  PEND EN3 .... 324 D3
Lawton Rd *LOU* IG10 .... 327 J5
Laxton Gv *LOS* SS13 .... 198 B6
Laxton Rd *RCOLE* CO7 .... 193 J5
Laxtons *SLH/COR* SS17 .... 394 E8 ▣
Layard Rd *EN* EN1 .... 324 A3
Layer Breton Hl *COLS* CO2 .... 216 B2
Layer Rd *COLS* CO2 .... 190 C1
  HVHL CB9 .... 27 M4
  K/T/MI CO5 .... 190 F7
  K/T/MI CO5 .... 216 E7
Layzell Cft *SUD* CO10 .... 55 K7
Leach Cl *CHLM/GWD* CM2 .... 289 J4
Leaden Cl *GTDUN* CM6 .... 231 K3
Leaforis Rd *CHESW* EN7 .... 276 B8
Leafy Wy *RBRW/HUT* CM13 .... 355 L2
Lea Gv *BSF* CM23 .... 174 C2
  MAL CM9 .... 268 A2
Lea La *WIT* CM8 .... 240 A2
Leam Cl *COLN* CO4 .... 164 A4 ▣
Leamington Rd *HARH* RM3 .... 353 H6
  HOC/HUL SS5 .... 363 G4
  SOS SS1 .... 21 L6
Leapingwell Cl
  CHLM/GWD CM2 .... 265 H8 ▣
Lea Rd *CDH/CHF* RM16 .... 418 B2
  HOD EN11 .... 253 K3
  SBF/HAD SS7 .... 379 K6
  WAB EN9 .... 301 H6
Leas Cl *WOS/PRIT* SS0 .... 400 C3
Leas Gdns *WOS/PRIT* SS0 .... 400 C3
Lea Side *K/T/MI* CO5 .... 245 L5
Leaside *SLH/COR* SS17 .... 410 B7
Leas La *COLS* CO2 .... 189 K5
Leas Rd *COLS* CO2 .... 190 D2
  COS CO15 .... 12 C8
The Leas *BOC* CM0 .... 344 D5
  FOS CO13 .... 199 J5
  ING CM4 .... 334 B1
  UPMR RM14 .... 372 E7
  WOS/PRIT SS0 .... 400 D4
  WICKW SS12 .... 359 J5
The Leasway *WOS/PRIT* SS0 .... 400 C3
Leat Cl *SBW* CM21 .... 201 G8
Leathart Cl *HLW* CM20 .... 389 J6 ▣
Leatherbottle Hl *ING* CM4 .... 312 B8
Leather La *EMPK* RM11 .... 371 L8
  HSTD CO9 .... 73 H2
  HVHL CB9 .... 27 M4
Lea Valley Rd *CHING* E4 .... 325 G8
Lea Valley Wk *WAB* EN9 .... 277 H6
Leaview *WAB* EN9 .... 301 J5
Lea Wy *BCAYW* CM12 .... 357 J3
Le Cateau Rd *COLS* CO2 .... 162 F5
Lechmere Av *CHIG* IG7 .... 349 K6
Leda Av *PEND* EN3 .... 324 E3
Lede Rd *CVI* SS8 .... 398 C7 ▣
Lee Chapel La *VGE* SS16 .... 376 D8
Leech's La *COLN* CO4 .... 134 E7
Leecon Wy *RCFD* SS4 .... 363 L8
Lee Gardens Av *EMPK* RM11 .... 372 B8 ▣
Lee Gv *CHIG* IG7 .... 349 J3
Lee Lotts *SBN/FI* SS3 .... 385 H7
Lee Rd *EN* EN1 .... 324 B8
  HAR CO12 .... 7 G9
  IPSE IP3 .... 38 A8
  PIT SS13 .... 379 G5
Leeward Rd *RCHLM* CM3 .... 339 M6
The Leeway *RCHLM* CM3 .... 291 G4
Lee Woottens La *VGE* SS16 .... 18 E4
Leez La *K/T/MI* CO5 .... 207 L2
Leggatt Dr *RIPW* IP8 .... 36 B1
Legg St *CHLM/WR* CM1 .... 17 H2
Legions Wy *BSF* CM23 .... 174 A3
Legon Av *ROMW/RG* RM7 .... 370 D8
Legra Av *HOD* EN11 .... 253 H5 ▣
Leicester Av *SBW* CM21 .... 383 G3
Leicester Cl *CHTY* IP2 .... 58 A7 ▣
  COL CO1 .... 10 E6
Leicester Ct *WIT* CM8 .... 184 E8 ▣
Leicester Rd *TIL* RM18 .... 418 A5
Leige Av *CVI* SS8 .... 398 B5 ▣
Leigham Court Dr *LOS* SS9 .... 400 A1
Leighams Rd *RCHLM* CM3 .... 314 F6
Leigh Beck La *CVI* SS8 .... 413 M1
Leigh Beck Rd *CVI* SS8 .... 399 C8 ▣
Leigh Cliff Rd *LOS* SS9 .... 400 A3
Leighcroft Gdns *LOS* SS9 .... 381 M7
Leigh Dr *HARH* RM3 .... 352 E5
Leigh Fells *PIT* SS13 .... 378 D5
Leighfields *SBF/HAD* SS7 .... 380 C5
Leighfields Av *LOS* SS9 .... 381 L5
Leighfields Rd *LOS* SS9 .... 381 K5
Leigh Hall Rd *LOS* SS9 .... 399 M2
Leigh Hts *SBF/HAD* SS7 .... 381 G8 ▣
Leigh Hl *LOS* SS9 .... 399 M3
Leigh Hill Cl *LOS* SS9 .... 399 M3
Leighlands Rd *RCHLM* CM3 .... 339 L4

Lilliput Rd *ROMW/RG* RM7 .... 370 E7
Lillyville Wk *RAYL* SS6 .... 381 H2 ▣
Lily Cl *BKHH* IG9 .... 265 G5
Limbourne Av *ROMW/RG* RM7 .... 370 E4
Limbourne Dr *MAL* CM9 .... 269 K6
Limburg Rd *CVI* SS8 .... 397 L7
Lime Av *COLN* CO4 .... 11 M5
  HAR CO12 .... 6 F7
  LOS SS9 .... 399 K1
  RBRW/HUT CM13 .... 355 G4 ▣
  UPMR RM14 .... 390 B3
Limebrook Wy *MAL* CM9 .... 293 H4
Lime Cl *BKHH* IG9 .... 348 C3
  COS CO15 .... 12 A6
  ROMW/RG RM7 .... 370 D5
  SOCK/AV RM15 .... 406 D1 ▣
  WIT CM8 .... 212 B6
Limefields *SAFWN* CB10 .... 43 L7 ▣
Lime Gv *BARK/HLT* IG6 .... 350 A7
  BRWN CM15 .... 332 D2
  SUD CO10 .... 54 D6
Limekiln La *STSD* CM24 .... 146 D5
Limerick Cl *IP* IP1 .... 36 F1
Limerick Ct *IP* IP1 .... 36 F1 ▣
Lime Rd *SBF/HAD* SS7 .... 379 M7
Limes Av *CHIG* IG7 .... 349 K6
  RIPW IP8 .... 36 D1
Limes Ct *HOD* EN11 .... 253 H5 ▣
Limes Crs *BSF* CM23 .... 174 B4
Limeslade Cl *SLH/COR* SS17 .... 395 H7 ▣
Limes Rd *BAR* EN8 .... 300 E4
The Limes *CHLM/GWD* CM2 .... 312 C1
  HSTD CO9 .... 127 M4
  ING CM4 .... 310 D7
  KESG IP5 .... 38 E2
  PUR RM19 .... 415 H2
  RAYL SS6 .... 381 G3
  RBRW/HUT CM13 .... 355 G4 ▣
  RCOLE CO7 .... 137 G4 ▣
  SUD CO10 .... 34 D4
Lime St *RCOLE* CO7 .... 221 G6
Limetree Av *SBF/HAD* SS7 .... 379 J7
Limetree Rd *CVI* SS8 .... 398 E7
Lime Wk *CHLM/GWD* CM2 .... 288 D5
Lime Wy *BOC* CM0 .... 344 B5
Lincefield *VGE* SS16 .... 376 C8 ▣
Linclon Cl *ERITH* DA8 .... 414 A6
Lincoln Av *COS* CO15 .... 249 L5
  ROMW/RG RM7 .... 370 F8
Lincoln Cha *SOSN* SS2 .... 383 M8
Lincoln Cl *BSF* CM23 .... 173 L6
  EMPK RM11 .... 372 B5
Lincoln La *RCOLW* CO6 .... 134 D2
Lincoln Rd *BSDN* SS14 .... 378 A4
  ERITH DA8 .... 414 A6
  RCFD SS4 .... 363 J5
Lincolns Fld *EPP* CM16 .... 304 A1
Lincolns La *BRW* CM14 .... 331 K8
Lincoln Ter *FX* IP11 .... 9 J4
Lincoln Wy *COL* CO1 .... 10 F7
  CVI SS8 .... 397 M7
  EN EN1 .... 324 C7
  RAYL SS6 .... 361 K6
Linda Gdns *BCAYW* CM12 .... 334 F7
Lindbergh Rd *IPSE* IP3 .... 59 K2
Linden Av *EN* EN1 .... 324 B3 ▣
Linden Cl *CHLM/GWD* CM2 .... 288 D4
  COLN CO4 .... 163 M2
  CHESW EN7 .... 300 C3 ▣
  MGTR CO11 .... 108 C8
  PUR RM19 .... 415 K3
  RAYL SS6 .... 381 G2
  SBF/HAD SS7 .... 379 K6
Linden Crs *WFD* IG8 .... 348 C7
Linden Dr *COS* CO15 .... 223 M5
Linden Gdns *EN* EN1 .... 324 B3
Linden Leas *SBF/HAD* SS7 .... 379 K5 ▣
Linden Ri *BRW* CM14 .... 354 C6
Linden Rd *SBF/HAD* SS7 .... 379 K5
The Lindens *BRTR* CM7 .... 183 H2 ▣
  BSF CM23 .... 174 A5
  ING CM4 .... 335 M4
  LOU IG10 .... 327 K4 ▣
  VGE SS16 .... 376 B6 ▣
Linden St *ROMW/RG* RM7 .... 370 E4
Linden Wy *CVI* SS8 .... 398 A7
Linde Rd *CVI* SS8 .... 398 C7
Lindfield Rd *HARH* RM3 .... 352 F6
Lindhill Cl *PEND* EN3 .... 324 E4 ▣
Lindhurst Dr *BCAYE* CM11 .... 336 D7
Lindisfarne Av *LOS* SS9 .... 400 B1
Lindisfarne Cl *CHTY* IP2 .... 58 B2 ▣
Lindon Rd *WICKE* SS11 .... 337 K8
Lindsay Pl *CHESW* EN7 .... 300 C2 ▣
Lindsell Gn *BSDN* SS14 .... 377 M6 ▣
Lindsell La *BSDN* SS14 .... 377 M6 ▣
  GTDUN CM6 .... 123 J8
Lindsey Av *SUD* CO10 .... 5 J8
Lindsey Cl *BRW* CM14 .... 354 B5
  BSF CM23 .... 174 A2
Lindsey Rd *BSF* CM23 .... 174 A2
  IPNE IP4 .... 38 D4
  SBN/FI SS3 .... 385 J7
Lindsey St *EPP* CM16 .... 304 B1
Lindsey Wy *EMPK* RM11 .... 371 K5 ▣
Linfold Cl *BRTR* CM7 .... 155 L7
Linford Cl *HLWW/ROY* CM19 .... 15 J9
Linford Dr *BSDN* SS14 .... 377 M6
Linford End *HLWW/ROY* CM19 .... 15 J9
Linford Ms *MAL* CM9 .... 292 F3 ▣
Linford Rd *CDH/CHF* RM16 .... 418 C2
Lingcroft *VGE* SS16 .... 377 H8
Lingfield Av *UPMR* RM14 .... 390 A2
Lingfield Dr *RCFD* SS4 .... 364 B8
Lingmere Cl *CHIG* IG7 .... 349 K3
Ling's La *RIPS/CAP* IP9 .... 81 M5
Lingwood Rd *RCHLM* CM3 .... 290 F4
Link Cl *COLN* CO4 .... 134 F7
Linkdale *BCAYW* CM12 .... 357 J3
Link La *RIPS/CAP* IP9 .... 78 E5
Link Rd *BSF* CM23 .... 174 A3
  COS CO15 .... 12 D8
  CVI SS8 .... 397 M7
  DAGW RM9 .... 388 C8 ▣
  HSTD CO9 .... 128 E3
  RAYL SS6 .... 361 L8
  RCOLE CO7 .... 221 H5

RIPS/CAP IP9 78 B2
RIPS/CAP SS17 113 H2
SLH/COR SS17 394 E3
Links Av FX IP11 85 H7
  GPK RM2 371 J2
Links Dr CHLM/GWD CM2 288 A4
Linksfield KESG IP5 38 F4
Linksfield Gdns KESG IP5 38 F4
Linkside CHIG IG7 349 K6
Links Rd BRTR CM7 184 D4
  RCOS CO16 249 J5
  WFD IG8 348 B6
The Links BAR EN8 276 E6
  BCAYW CM12 334 F7
Linksway LOS SS9 381 K7
Links Wy SBF/HAD SS7 381 C8
The Link PEND EN3 324 F3
  RIPS/CAP IP9 78 E5
Linkway BSDN SS14 19 G5
Link Wy BSF CM23 173 M5
  EMPK RM11 371 M8
Linkway Rd BRW CM14 354 A4
Linley Cl TIL RM18 419 L4
Linley Crs ROMW/RG RM7 370 C3
Linley Gdns COS SS15 12 C8
Linnet Cl SBN/FI SS3 402 F2
Linnet Dr CHLM/GWD CM2 288 C5
  SBF/HAD SS7 397 K1
Linnet Rd CHTY IP2 36 E7
Linnets COS CO15 224 A5
  VGE SS16 377 H8
Linnetts La HVHL CB9 29 H7
Linnet Wy PUR RM19 415 J2
  RCOLE CO7 194 E3
Linroping Av RCOS CO16 223 H7
Linstead Cl RCOS CO16 223 H7
Linton Cl SAFWS CB11 66 A3
Linton Ct ROM RM1 370 F2
Linton Rd CBE/LIN CB1 24 C3
  SBN/FI SS3 402 F5
The Lintons CHLM/GWD CM2 289 L5
Linwood SBW CM21 227 M1
Linwood Crs EN EN1 324 B3
Lionel Hurst Cl SUD CO10 55 K6
Lionel Rd CVI SS8 398 B8
Lionfield Ter CHLM/WR CM1 17 L1
Lion Hl SLH/COR SS17 395 L7
Lion La BCAYW CM12 357 H1
Lion Meadow HVHL CB9 48 C4
Lion St IP IP1 2 D3
Liphook Cl HCH RM12 389 G3
Lippitts Hl LOU IG10 325 M4
Lisa Cl BCAYW CM12 335 J5
Lisle Pl GRAYS RM17 407 H8
Lisle Rd COS CO15 163 H6
Lister Av HARH RM3 371 L2
Lister Rd BRTR CM7 183 G3
  IP IP1 37 G2
  TIL RM18 418 B6
Lister Tye CHLM/GWD CM2 17 K9
Listonhall Cha HSTD CO9 97 J6
Liston La SUD CO10 34 C4
Listowel Rd DAGE RM10 388 B2
Litchborough Pk RCHLM CM3 291 C3
Litchfield HAR CO12 142 F1
Litchfield Cl COS CO15 12 E1
Littell Tweed CHLM/GWD CM2 265 H8
Little And Great Sir Hughes La
  CHLM/GWD CM2 313 H1
Little Aston Rd HARH RM3 353 C8
Little Baddow Rd MAL CM9 267 K8
  RCHLM CM3
Little Bakers FOS CO13 199 H4
Little Belhus Cl SOCK/AV RM15 406 B2
Little Bentley BSDN SS14 19 H4
Little Bentley Rd RCOLE CO7 167 J2
Little Berry La VGE SS16 376 B7
Little Braxted La WIT CM8 212 D8
Little Brays HLWS CM18 256 B5
Little Bromley Rd RCOLE CO7 137 M8
  RCOLE CO7 137 H4
Littlebrook Gdns BAR EN8 300 E2
Little Brook Rd
  HLWW/ROY CM19 254 D3
  PIT SS13 378 B3
Littlebury Gdns COS CO2 163 K7
Littlebury Gn PIT SS13 378 B3
Littlebury Green Rd
  SAFWS CB11 42 D8
Little Cattins HLWW/ROY CM19 255 G7
Little Charlton PIT SS13 378 D5
Little Chittock BSDN SS14 377 M5
Little Clacton Rd FOS CO13 224 F1
  RCOS CO16 223 J4
Littlecotes COLN CO4 134 E7
Littlecroft RCHLM CM3 339 L5
Little Croft St CHTY IP2 2 E9
Little Dorrit CHLM/WR CM1 263 M4
Little Dragons LOU IG10 326 E6
Littlefield Rd COLS CO2 190 D2
Little Flds RCHLM CM3 291 H4
Little Garth PIT SS13 378 B6
Little Gaynes Gdns
  UPMR RM14 390 C3
Little Gaynes La UPMR RM14 390 A3
Little Gerpins Rd UPMR RM14 390 F7
Little Gipping St IP IP1 2 D1
Little Gregories La EPP CM16 303 L7
Little Gv RIPS/CAP IP9 78 B3
Little Grove Fld
  HLWW/ROY CM19 15 J5
Little Gulls RIPS/CAP IP9 78 A2
Little Gypps Cl CVI SS8 398 A8
Little Gypps Rd CVI SS8 398 A8
Little Harrods FOS CO13 199 H4
Little Hays LOS SS9 381 J5
Little Hayes Cha RCHLM CM3 340 D2
Little Heath RBSF CM22 202 A8
Little Horkesley Rd RCOLW CO6 103 G7
Littlehurst LAIN SS15 377 G1
Little Hyde Cl HSTD CO9 73 H1
Little Hyde La ING CM4 310 C5
Little Hyde Rd HSTD CO9 73 H1
Little Larchmount
  SAFWS CB11 65 L3
Little Laver Rd CHONG CM5 259 G8

HLWE CM17 258 F1
Little London Hl BRTR CM7 94 E3
Little London La MAL CM9 267 K6
Little Lullaway LAIN SS15 18 B4
Little Meadow CHLM/WR CM1 287 K2
Little Mdw MAL CM9 291 M5
Little Nell CHLM/WR CM1 263 M4
Little Norsey Rd BCAYW CM12 335 K7
Little Oaks BSDN SS14 18 F5
Little Oxcroft LAIN SS15 376 D6
Little Pluckett's Wy BKHH IG9 348 E2
Little Pynchons HLWS CM18 256 A6
Little Russets
  RBRW/HUT CM13 355 M1
Little St Mary's SUD CO10 34 D5
Little's Crs CHTY IP2 2 F8
Little Searles PIT SS13 378 C4
Little Spenders BSDN SS14 19 L2
Little Stambridge Hall Rd
  RCFD SS4 383 J1
Little Stile CHLM/WR CM1 287 H3
Little Stone Ct COS CO15 250 D3
Little Tey Rd K/T/MI CO5 187 G4
Little Thorpe SOS SS1 402 B2
Littlethorpe VGE SS16 378 A7
Littleton Av CHING E4 348 A2
Little Totham Rd MAL CM9 270 D2
Little Tufts RIPS/CAP IP9 78 C2
Little Wakering Hall La
  SBN/FI SS3 385 H6
Little Wakering Rd SBN/FI SS3 384 F4
Little Walden Rd SAFWN CB10 43 L7
  SAFWN CB10 65 L1
Little Waltham Rd
  CHLM/WR CM1 264 E2
Little Warley Hall La
  RBRW/HUT CM13 373 M5
Little Wheatley Cha RAYL SS6 361 H8
Little Whip St CHTY IP2 2 D7
Little Wd FOS CO13 198 F5
Little Yeldham Rd HSTD CO9 73 J1
Llewellyn Cl CHLM/GWD CM2 264 C7
Lloyd Rd DAGW RM9 388 A5
  RIPS/CAP IP9 113 H3
Lloyds Av IP IP1 2 F4
The Lloyds KESG IP5 39 K4
Lloyd-taylor Cl STDN SC11 172 C1
Lloyd Wise Cl SOSN SS2 383 L8
Loamy Hill Rd WIT CM8 241 G2
Lobelia Cl CHLM/WR CM1 265 G5
Locarno Cl WICKE SS11 359 M2
Locarno Rd IPSE IP3 38 C8
Locke Cl RAIN RM13 389 G5
  SLH/COR SS17 394 D8
Lockfield Av PEND EN3 324 F4
Lockhart Av COLW CO3 162 D4
Lockram La WIT CM8 239 H1
Lock Rd HSTD CO9 128 F3
Locksley Cl SOSN SS2 402 A1
Lockyer Rd PUR RM19 415 K4
Lodge Av BRTR CM7 183 G3
  CHLM/WR CM1 287 G3
  EPP CM16 303 H6
  HAR CO12 142 D3
  K/T/MI CO5 187 L8
  MAL CM9 292 C4
  RCHLM CM3 292 B7
  RCHLM CM3 314 F5
  RCOLE CO7 220 F3
  RCOS CO16 197 G5
Lodge Cl RCOLW CO6 134 A7
Lodge Crs BAR EN8 300 F6
  RCHLM CM3 265 M3
Lodge Farm Cl LOS SS9 381 L6
Lodge Farm Dr FX IP11 85 K8
Lodge Farm La RCOS CO16 222 E7
Lodge Hall HLWS CM18 255 M7
Lodgelands Cl RAYL SS6 361 G2
Lodge La CDH/CHF RM16 407 H7
  COLN CO4 135 L3
  CRW RM5 351 H7
  GRAYS RM17 407 K8
  K/T/MI CO5 217 L3
  K/T/MI CO5 218 D2
  RCHLM CM3 316 C1
  RCOLE CO7 136 D5
  RCOLE CO7 220 E4
  RCOS CO16 168 A5
  WAB EN9 301 L7
Lodge Rd BRTR CM7 183 G2
  CHLM/WR CM1 287 G3
  EPP CM16 303 H6
  HAR CO12 142 D3
  K/T/MI CO5 187 L8
  MAL CM9 292 C4
  RCHLM CM3 292 B7
  RCHLM CM3 314 F5
  RCOLE CO7 220 F3
  RCOS CO16 197 G5
Lodge Vls WFD IG8 348 A8
Lodwick SBN/FI SS3 402 D6
Loewen Rd CDH/CHF RM16 408 B8
Loftin Wy CHLM/GWD CM2 17 L9
Logan Cl PEND EN3 324 E3
Logan Link WICKW SS12 360 A6
Loman Pth SOCK/AV RM15 406 A4
Lombard Av PEND EN3 324 D3
Lombard St IPNE IP4 3 M2
Lombards Cha
  RBRW/HUT CM13 374 E6
Lombardy Rd SUD CO10 54 L1
Lonbarn Hl MGTR CO11 140 B1
London Cl CHLM/GWD CM2 312 B1
  RAYL SS6 361 K8
London Rd ABR/ST RM4 328 B5
  BCAYE CM11 358 F5
  BCAYW CM12 356 F1
  BRTR CM7 182 E3
  BRW CM14 354 B4
  BSF CM23 174 B6
  CHDH RM6 370 B6
  CHLM/GWD CM2 16 C9
  CHONG CM5 306 E6
  CHTY IP2 36 F6
  COLW CO3 161 J5
  COS CO15 12 E2
  EPP CM16 280 C2
  GRAYS RM17 416 F3
  HLWE CM17 227 K8

  IP IP1 2 A4
  K/T/MI CO5 187 K3
  MAL CM9 292 C1
  PIT SS13 378 E6
  RAYL SS6 361 J7
  RCHLM CM3 209 J1
  RCOLW CO6 133 M3
  RCOLW CO6 160 B8
  RCOS CO16 223 L3
  RIPS/CAP IP9 56 D8
  RIPW IP8 57 H2
  ROMW/RG RM7 370 D6
  SAFWN CB10 42 D1
  SAFWS CB11 65 L3
  SBF/HAD SS7 379 H6
  SBW CM21 227 M1
  SLH/COR SS17 409 J2
  SOCK/AV RM15 405 H7
  SOS SS1 21 G5
  TIL RM18 418 C6
  VGE SS16 395 L1
  WICKE SS11 360 E6
  WTHK RM20 416 E3
London Road Purfleet
  PUR RM19 415 J3
London Road West Thurrock
  WTHK RM20 416 A3
Londons Cl UPMR RM14 390 D4
Lone Barn Ct IP IP1 36 E3
Longacre BSDN SS14 19 H4
Longacre Rd BRTR CM7 183 M5
Longacres BRTR CM7 183 H2
Long Acres K/T/MI CO5 187 C5
Longaford Wy
  RBRW/HUT CM13 355 K2
Long Banks HLWS CM18 255 L6
Long Border Rd RBSF CM22 175 M2
Longborough Cl PIT SS13 378 B2
Long Brandocks
  CHLM/WR CM1 287 G2
Long Common MAL CM9 269 G6
Long Ct PUR RM19 415 H1
Longcroft FX IP11 84 F7
  RBSF CM22 176 D4
  SAFWN CB10 68 F3
Long Cft STSD CM24 146 E3
Long Croft Dr BAR EN8 301 G6
Longcroft Ri LOU IG10 327 J7
Longcroft Rd COLN CO4 11 K6
Longfellow Dr
  RBRW/HUT CM13 355 K1
Longfellow Rd MAL CM9 293 H2
Long Fld FX IP11 84 E7
Long Field HLWS CM18 256 B5
  LOU IG10 326 D7
  WIT CM8 211 M6
Longfield Av EMPK RM11 371 C7
  PEND EN3 324 D1
Longfield Cl WICKE SS11 360 B4
Longfield La CHESW EN7 276 C8
Longfield Rd CHLM/GWD CM2 288 F4
  RCHLM CM3 339 L3
  RIPS/CAP IP9 78 B1
  WICKE SS11 360 B4
Long Flds CHONG CM5 307 H2
Longfields RCOS CO16 222 C7
Long Gn BRTR CM7 183 M3
  CHIG IG7 349 M5
Long Green La BRTR CM7 152 D1
Long Gv HARH RM3 371 M2
Longhams Dr RCHLM CM3 339 L3
Longhedges SAFWS CB11 65 M2
Longhouse Rd CDH/CHF RM16 408 C8
Longlands Cl BAR EN8 300 E4
Long La BRTR CM7 182 A3
  CBE/LIN CB1 24 C2
  CDH/CHF RM16 407 M6
  FOS CO13 198 D8
  HOC/HUL SS5 340 A7
  SAFWS CB11 64 A6
Longleaf Dr BRTR CM7 183 C3
Longleat Cl CHLM/WR CM1 264 A4
Long Ley CHLM/WR CM1 256 A3
Longmead Av CHLM/GWD CM2 289 C3
Longmead Cl BRWN CM15 354 F2
Long Meadow WIT CM8 239 M6
Long Mdw BAR EN8 300 F1
Long Moor BAR EN8 300 F1
Longmore Av CHLM/GWD CM2 288 F3
Long Perry RIPS/CAP IP9 78 C2
Longport Cl BARK/HLT IG6 350 B7
Longreach Rd ERITH DA8 414 C4
Longridge COLN CO4 164 A3
Long Riding BSDN SS14 19 J5
Long Ridings Av
  RBRW/HUT CM13 333 J7
Longrise BCAYW CM12 357 J3
Long Rd CVI SS8 397 M8
  MGTR CO11 108 D8
Long Rd East RCOLE CO7 107 H8
Long Rd West RCOLE CO7 106 F8
Longsands SBN/FI SS3 402 A4
Longship Wy MAL CM9 292 F3
Longshots Cl CHLM/WR CM1 264 B2
Longs La RCHLM CM3 236 A2
Longstomps Av
  CHLM/GWD CM2 288 B5
Longstraw Cl COLW CO3 161 L5
Long St IPNE IP4 3 J6
  WAB EN9 302 F2
Longtail BCAYE CM11 335 K6
Longtown Rd HARH RM3 352 D6
Longview Wy CRW RM5 370 E1
Longwick VGE SS16 376 D7
Long Wd HLWS CM18 255 L8
Longwood Rd UPMR RM14 390 D4
Long Wyre St COL CO1 10 D3
The Loning PEND EN3 324 D2
Lonsdale CBE/LIN CB1 24 F1
Lonsdale Av RBRW/HUT CM13 333 L8

ROMW/RG RM7 370 D6
Lonsdale Cl IPNE IP4 3 M1
Lonsdale Rd RCOS CO16 197 H1
  SOSN SS2 401 L1
Looe Rd FX IP11 85 K8
Loompits Wy SAFWS CB11 65 K4
Loop Rd WAB EN9 301 J4
Lophams Cl RAIN RM13 388 D8
Loraine Cl PEND EN3 324 D7
Loraine Wy RIPW IP8 36 B2
Lord Holland Rd COLS CO2 163 G8
Lord Roberts Av LOS SS9 400 A2
Lords Av BSF CM23 173 J4
Lordship Cl RBRW/HUT CM13 355 L2
Lordship Rd CHLM/WR CM1 287 J1
  CHESW EN7 300 C2
Lordsland La BRTR CM7 156 D2
Lord St HOD EN11 252 F5
Lordswood Rd COLS CO2 190 D1
Lordswood Vw GTDUN CM6 231 L4
Lorien Gdns RCHLM CM3 339 K5
Lorkin's La HSTD CO9 76 C8
Lorkin Wy RCOLW CO6 134 A7
Lorne Rd BRW CM14 354 D5
Lornes Cl SOSN SS2 383 L8
Lorraine Cl RBRW/HUT CM13 357 J5
Lorrimore Cl BCAYW CM12 335 C6
Loten Rd SBF/HAD SS7 397 J1
Lottem Rd CVI SS8 413 L1
Lott's Rd RCOS CO16 196 C7
Loughton La EPP CM16 327 L1
Loughton Wy BKHH IG9 348 E2
Louisa Av SBF/HAD SS7 379 J5
Louis Dr RAYL SS6 361 J8
Louis Dr East RAYL SS6 361 J8
Louis Dr West RAYL SS6 361 H7
Louise Cl WOTN CO14 171 M8
Louise Rd RAYL SS6 380 F1
Louse La RCOLE CO7 106 F8
Louvaine Av WICKW SS12 359 J4
Louvain Rd HAR CO12 143 H2
Lovelace Av SOS SS1 401 L3
Lovelace Gdns SOSN SS2 401 L2
Love La CHONG CM5 283 H8
  RAYL SS6 380 D1
  RCOLE CO7 220 F3
  SOCK/AV RM15 405 K7
  TIL RM18 419 K3
  WFD IG8 349 G7
Lovens Cl CVI SS8 413 K1
Lover's La GRH DA9 416 E8
  RCOLE CO7 195 H4
  RIPS/CAP IP9 81 K7
Loves Wk CHLM/WR CM1 287 J3
Lovetofts Dr IP IP1 36 E1
Lovet Rd HLWW/ROY CM19 14 E6
Love Wy RCOS CO16 223 K5
Lowe Cha WOTN CO14 199 J2
Lowe Cl CHIG IG7 350 B6
Lowefields RCOLW CO6 130 E6
Lowen Rd RAIN RM13 388 E8
Lower Anchor St
  CHLM/GWD CM2 16 E5
Lower Av PIT SS13 378 F3
Lower Barn Rd RIPW IP8 56 B2
Lower Bedfords Rd ROM RM1 352 E7
Lower Broad St IPNE IP4 2 F5
Lower Burnham Rd
  RCHLM CM3 341 L1
Lower Bury La EPP CM16 303 M3
Lower Cha RCHLM CM3 319 C7
Lower Church Rd SBF/HAD SS7 379 J5
Lower Cloister BCAYE CM11 357 J1
Lower Crs SLH/COR SS17 409 H8
Lower Dales View Rd IP IP1 37 H3
Lower Downs Slade HVHL CB9 28 B3
Lower Dunton Rd
  RBRW/HUT CM13 375 L5
Lower Farm Rd COLN CO4 105 J3
Lower Gn CHLM/GWD CM2 312 C2
  RCOLW CO6 131 K2
Lower Harlings RIPS/CAP IP9 113 H3
Lower Holt St RCOLW CO6 130 D5
Lower House La WDBR IP12 61 M1
Lower Houses Rd RIPS/CAP IP9 81 L8
Lower Island Wy WAB EN9 301 J7
Lower King BRTR CM7 183 L2
Lower Lambricks RAYL SS6 361 L7
Lower Langley RCOLW CO6 131 K2
Lower Mardyke Av RAIN RM13 388 D2
Lower Marine Pde HAR CO12 143 K1
Lower Meadow BAR EN8 276 E7
  HLWS CM18 255 M7
Lower Ml GTDUN CM6 178 F4
Lower Noke Cl BRW CM14 352 F3
Lower Orwell St IPNE IP4 3 C1
Lower Park Crs BSF CM23 174 A6
Lower Park Rd LOU IG10 326 E7
  RCOLE CO7 220 F5
  WICKW SS12 359 K7
Lower Queen's Rd BKHH IG9 348 F3
Lower Rd BRWN CM15 333 L5
  BURES CO8 102 C6
  COLS CO2 189 H6
  GVW DA11 417 H8
  HOC/HUL SS5 361 L2
  K/T/MI CO5 216 A2
  K/T/MI CO5 217 L6
  KIR/NAC IP10 85 G2
  LOU IG10 327 H3
  RBSF CM22 201 K4
  SUD CO10 33 J1
  SUD CO10 34 C8
  TIL RM18 418 B8
Lower Southend Rd
  WICKE SS11 359 L3
Lower Stock Rd ING CM4 312 C8
Lower St LAIN SS15 376 F2
  RCOLE CO7 106 D2
  RIPS/CAP IP9 110 D1
  RIPW IP8 56 B2
  STSD CM24 147 G4
  SUD CO10 32 E1
Lower Swaines EPP CM16 303 M2

The Lowe CHIG IG7 350 B6
Lowfield SBW CM21 227 M2
Lowfield La HOD EN11 253 H5
Low Hill Rd HLWW/ROY CM19 254 A5
Lowland Gdns ROMW/RG RM7 370 C5
Lowlands Rd SOCK/AV RM15 405 K6
Low Rd HAR CO12 143 G2
Lowry Cl HVHL CB9 27 J7
Lowry Gdns IPSE IP3 59 H3
Lowshoe La ROMW/RG RM7 370 C1
Low Street La TIL RM18 419 G2
Loxford PIT SS13 378 B3
Luard Wy COLS CO2 189 G2
  WIT CM8 239 G2
Lubbards Cl RAYL SS6 361 L6
Lubberhedges La GTDUN CM6 123 L8
Lucas Av CHLM/GWD CM2 288 D5
  RCOLW CO6 132 E6
Lucas Rd COLS CO2 163 G5
  GRAYS RM17 407 H8
  SUD CO10 4 F7
Lucas's La RCOS CO16 168 C5
Lucerne Dr WICKE SS11 360 B4
Lucerne Rd RCOLE CO7 165 H5
Lucerne Wk WICKE SS11 360 B4
Lucerne Wy CHLM/WR CM1 287 J3
  HARH RM3 352 E7
Luces La HSTD CO9 74 A7
Luck's La RCHLM CM3 235 C7
Luckyn La BSDN SS14 18 C1
Luctons Av BKHH IG9 348 D2
Lucy Cl COLW CO3 161 K5
Lucy La North COLW CO3 161 J4
Lucy La South COLW CO3 161 K4
Lucy Rd SOS SS1 21 J8
Ludgores La RCHLM CM3 290 E6
Ludgrove RCHLM CM3 318 B5
Ludham Hall La BRTR CM7 182 C4
Ludlow Pl GRAYS RM17 407 J8
Luff Wy FOS CO13 199 G4
Lufkin Rd COLN CO4 135 G8
Lugar Cl COLN CO4 163 M5
Luker Rd SOS SS1 21 G6
Lukin's Dr GTDUN CM6 178 E4
Lulworth Av IPSE IP3 38 E8
Lulworth Cl COS CO15 250 D3
  SLH/COR SS17 409 J3
Lulworth Dr CRW RM5 351 J6
  HVHL CB9 27 M3
Lumber Leys FOS CO13 199 H4
Lummis V KESG IP5 39 K4
Luncies Rd BSDN SS14 377 M6
Lundy Cl HVHL CB9 28 E4
  SOSN SS2 382 C4
Lunnish Hl HAR CO12 112 A8
Lupin Cl ROMW/RG RM7 388 E1
Lupin Dr CHLM/WR CM1 265 G5
Lupin Rd CHTY IP2 36 F7
Lupin Wy RCOS CO16 12 B3
Luppits Cl RBRW/HUT CM13 355 H2
Lushes Ct LOU IG10 327 J7
Lushes Rd LOU IG10 327 J7
Lushington Av LOS SS9 198 C5
Lushington Rd MGTR CO11 108 D7
Lutea Cl LAIN SS15 376 E2
Luther King Rd HLW CM20 15 L5
Luther Rd CHTY IP2 2 D8
Luthers Cl BRWN CM15 331 M1
Lutus Cl SUD CO10 31 H5
Luxborough La CHIG IG7 349 C5
Luxford Pl SBW CM21 228 A2
Lych Ga LAIN SS15 376 D5
Lydford Rd WOS/PRIT SS0 20 C7
Lydgate St MGTR CO11 108 C7
Lydia Dr RCOS CO16 248 B1
Lydia Rd ERITH DA8 414 A3
Lylt Rd CVI SS8 398 B8
Lyme Rd SOSN SS2 21 L3
Lymington Av COS CO15 224 A3
  LOS SS9 399 M1
Lympstone Cl WOS/PRIT SS0 382 B6
Lynbrook Cl RAIN RM13 388 E8
Lynceley Gra EPP CM16 304 B1
The Lynch HOD EN11 253 J5
Lyndale Av SBF/HAD SS7 379 J6
Lyndale Av SOSN SS2 383 J8
Lyndene SBF/HAD SS7 379 J6
Lyndhurst Av IPNE IP4 38 D5
Lyndhurst Dr EMPK RM11 371 K8
  RCHLM CM3 315 G2
Lyndhurst Ri CHIG IG7 349 H5
Lyndhurst Rd COS CO15 224 D7
  SLH/COR SS17 395 C7
Lyndhurst Wy
  RBRW/HUT CM13 355 K2
Lynfords Av WICKE SS11 338 A8
Lynfords Dr WICKE SS11 338 A8
Lynmouth Av CHLM/GWD CM2 17 J7
  EN EN1 324 A8
Lynmouth Gdns
  CHLM/GWD CM2 17 J6
Lynne Cl FOS CO13 198 C5
Lynn View Cl SBF/HAD SS7 379 K6
Lynross Cl HARH RM3 371 M2
Lynstede BSDN SS14 378 B6
Lynton Av ROMW/RG RM7 370 C1
Lynton Cl HAR CO12 6 E7
Lynton Dr CHLM/WR CM1 264 F6
Lynton Rd SBF/HAD SS7 380 D8
  SOS SS1 402 A5
Lynwood Av FX IP11 85 J8
Lynwood Dr CRW RM5 351 J8
Lynwood Gn RAYL SS6 381 H3
Lyon Cl CHLM/GWD CM2 288 C8
  COS CO15 13 K3
Lyon Rd ROM RM1 371 G7
Lyons Hall Rd BRTR CM7 155 L3
Lyster Av CHLM/GWD CM2 289 H4
Lytchet Wy PEND EN3 324 D3
Lytton Av PEND EN3 324 E2
Lytton Rd CDH/CHF RM16 418 B1
  GPK RM2 371 J5
Lyttons Wy HOD EN11 253 H2

M

Mabbitt Wy COLN CO4 135 J6 3
Maberly Ct SAFWN CB10 65 L1 4
Mabey's Wk SBW CM21 227 J2
Macaulay Rd VGE SS16 376 B6 2
Macbeth Cl COLN CO4 164 A4
Macdonald Av DAGE RM10 388 C2
EMPK RM11 371 M4
WOS/PRIT SS0 20 C1
Macdonald Wy EMPK RM11 371 M4 2
Macer's La BROX EN10 277 G4
Mace Wk CHLM/WR CM1 16 D1
Macgregor Dr WICKW SS12 359 M6
Macintyres Wk RCFD SS4 363 K5
Mackay Ct COLS CO2 191 J1 1
Mackenzie Cl WICKW SS12 359 M5 5
Mackenzie Dr KESG IP5 39 J3
Mackley Dr SLH/COR SS17 395 G6
Maclarens WIT CM8 240 B5
Maclaren Wy WICKW SS12 359 M6 5
Maclennan Av RAIN RM13 404 E1
Macleod Cl GRAYS RM17 417 L1 2
Macmurdo Cl LOS SS9 381 L4
Macmurdo Rd LOS SS9 381 L4
Macon Wy UPMR RM14 373 G6
Maddox Rd HLW CM20 255 M3
Madeira Av LOS SS9 399 M1
Madeira Gv WFD IG8 348 D7 5
Madeira Rd COS CO15 224 E6
Madeline Pl CHLM/WR CM1 263 M5
Madells EPP CM16 304 A3
Madgements Rd BRTR CM7 156 D3
Madles La ING CM4 336 A2
Madrid Av RAYL SS6 361 H4
Mafeking Rd EN EN1 324 A5
Magazine Farm Wy
COLW CO3 162 B6 1
Magazine Rd SBN/FI SS3 402 F5
Magdalen Cl COS CO15 12 E4
Magdalene Cl CHTY IP2 58 A1
Magdalene Crs WIT CM8 184 E8
Magdalen Gdns
RBRW/HUT CM13 333 M8 2
Magdalen Gn GTDUN CM6 122 B1
Magdalen Rd COS CO15 12 E4
Magdalen St COL CO1 10 E9
Magenta Cl BCAYW CM12 334 F8
Magingley Crs KESG IP5 39 G5 3
Magna Md SBN/FI SS3 384 E4
Magnaville Rd BSF CM23 173 M7
Magnet Rd WTHK RM20 416 D3
Magnolia Cl CHLM/GWD CM2 288 C5
SOCK/AV RM15 406 F2
WIT CM8 212 B6 4
Magnolia Dr COLN CO4 164 A3
Magnolia Rd HOC/HUL SS5 363 J6
Magnolias BCAYE CM11 357 K5 2
Magnolia Wy BRWN CM15 332 C7
RCFD SS4 383 J3
Magnum Cl RAIN RM13 404 D2 3
Magpie Cl EN EN1 324 B3
RIPW IP8 57 K1 1
Magpie La RBRW/HUT CM13 373 L2
Magpies EPP CM16 279 H4
Magwitch Cl CHLM/WR CM1 264 A4
Mahon Cl EN EN1 324 A3
Mahonia Dr VGE SS16 376 A6
Maidenburgh St COL CO1 10 D8 1
Maidenhall Ap CHTY IP2 58 C1
Maiden La DART DA1 414 B7
Maidment Crs WIT CM8 239 G3
Maidstone Av CRW RM5 370 D2
Maidstone Rd FX IP11 84 F8 5
GRAYS RM17 417 H3
Mailers La BSF CM23 146 A1
Main Av EN EN1 324 A7
Maine Crs RAYL SS6 361 J7
Main Rd BOC CM0 296 D3
CHLM/WR CM1 264 C2
FOS CO13 198 B8
GPK RM2 371 K2
HAR CO12 6 E8
HOC/HUL SS5 362 E5
KESG IP5 39 H3
KIR/NAC IP10 61 G2
RCHLM CM3 290 B4
RCHLM CM3 314 D7
RCHLM CM3 338 C5
RCOLW CO6 103 G7
RIPS/CAP IP9 81 H1
RIPS/CAP IP9 81 M4
ROM RM1 371 G4
Main St CBE/LIN CB1 26 A5
Maitland Pl SBN/FI SS3 402 F2
Maitland Rd STSD CM24 146 F5
WICKW SS12 359 M6
Maizey Ct BRWN CM15 332 B7
Makemores BRTR CM7 182 A1 2
Makins Rd HAR CO12 6 A4
Malan Sq RAIN RM13 389 J5
Maldon Ct SUD CO10 5 J6
Maldon Rd BOC CM0 297 K4
BOC CM0 343 M3
COLS CO2 188 F8
COLW CO3 162 D6
ING CM4 311 J3
K/T/MI CO5 213 K2
MAL CM9 240 C7 1
MAL CM9 268 A3
RCHLM CM3 238 C7
RCHLM CM3 290 F4
RCHLM CM3 319 K3
ROMW/RG RM7 370 D7
SOSN SS2 21 H4
WIT CM8 239 G6
Maldon Wk WFD IG8 348 D7
Maldon Wy RCOS CO16 223 J7
Malgraves PIT SS13 378 C4
Malgraves Pl PIT SS13 378 C4
Malin Cl HVHL CB9 28 E4
Mallard Cl BRTR CM7 182 D6
COLS CO2 190 B6
K/T/MI CO5 186 D8 2
MAL CM9 272 E1
UPMR RM14 373 G7 1
Mallard Rd CHLM/GWD CM2 288 B6
Mallards RCHLM CM3 319 H3
SBN/FI SS3 402 F2
Mallards Ri HLWE CM17 256 D3
Mallards Rd WFD IG8 348 C8
Mallard Wy CHTY IP2 57 M1
RBRW/HUT CM13 355 H1
SUD CO10 55 K6
Mallinson Cl HCH RM12 389 K4 3
Mallion Ct WAB EN9 302 A5
Mallory Wy BCAYW CM12 357 H2 4
Mallow Ct GRAYS RM17 417 L3
Mallow Gdns BCAYW CM12 335 G6
Mallowhayes Cl CHTY IP2 2 C9
Mallows Fld HSTD CO9 129 G2
Mallows Gn HLWW/ROY CM19 255 H8
Mallows Green Rd BSF CM23 145 K1
Mallows La HSTD CO9 72 A8
The Mall HCH RM12 371 J8
Malmesbury Cl CHTY IP2 58 B1
Malmsmead SBN/FI SS3 402 D3
Malpas Rd CDH/CHF RM16 408 D8
Malta Rd TIL RM18 418 A6
Maltby Dr EN EN1 324 C2
Maltese Rd CHLM/WR CM1 264 B7
Malthouse Rd MGTR CO11 108 E7
Malting Farm La RCOLE CO7 136 D1
Malting Green Rd COLS CO2 190 A6
Malting La CDH/CHF RM16 408 B2
FOS CO13 198 D2
SUD CO10 31 J4
Malting Rd COLS CO2 190 D2
K/T/MI CO5 217 M4
Maltings Cha ING CM4 310 C8
Maltings Cl BURES CO8 101 M2
Maltings Ct WIT CM8 239 G3 2
Maltings Hl CHONG CM5 258 E8
Maltings La EPP CM16 304 B1 3
WIT CM8 239 G3
Maltings Rd
CHLM/GWD CM2 289 H6 1
RCOLE CO7 220 F3
WICKE SS11 360 F1
The Maltings BOC CM0 320 F7
BRTR CM7 182 B1
GTDUN CM6 122 B1
GTDUN CM6 178 E2
HAR CO12 141 M3
ROMW/RG RM7 371 G7 2
Maltings Vw BRTR CM7 155 H8 2
Malting Villas Rd RCFD SS4 383 G1
Malting Yd RCOLE CO7 192 C3 3
Maltings Park Rd RCOLW CO6 134 A7
Malvern Av CVI SS8 397 L8
Malvern Cl IPSE IP3 38 C7
KESG IP5 39 G4 3
RAYL SS6 361 L7
Malvern Dr WFD IG8 348 D6
Malvern Gdns LOU IG10 327 G8
Malvern Rd EMPK RM11 371 H6
GRAYS RM17 417 M1
HOC/HUL SS5 363 G3
PEND EN3 324 F1
Malvern Wy RCOLW CO6 134 C4
Malwood Dr SBF/HAD SS7 379 J6
Malwood Rd SBF/HAD SS7 379 J6
Malyon Court Cl SBF/HAD SS7 380 C7
Malyon Rd WIT CM8 239 G3
Malyons PIT SS13 378 C4
Malyons Cl PIT SS13 378 C3
Malyons Gn PIT SS13 378 C3
Malyons La HOC/HUL SS5 361 L1
Malyons Ms PIT SS13 378 C4
Malyons Pl PIT SS13 378 C3
The Malyons SBF/HAD SS7 380 C7
Manchester Dr LOS SS9 399 L1
Manchester Rd CHTY IP2 57 L1
COS CO15 224 F5
Mandeville Cl BROX EN10 253 G8
Mandeville Rd PEND EN3 324 F1
RCOLW CO6 159 M8
SAFWS CB11 65 L3
Mandeville Wy CHLM/WR CM1 235 J8
FOS CO13 199 G4
SBF/HAD SS7 379 K4 1
VGE SS16 18 A8
Mandy Cl IPNE IP4 38 B5
Manfield Gdns RCOS CO16 222 C6
Manford Cl CHIG IG7 350 C5
Manford Cross CHIG IG7 350 B6
Manford Wy CHIG IG7 350 B6
Mangapp Cha BOC CM0 344 B3
Mangrove La HERT/BAY SG13 252 A4
Manilla Rd SOS SS1 21 M8
Manly Dixon Dr PEND EN3 324 F1
Mannall Wk KESG IP5 39 M3
Mannering Gdns WOS/PRIT SS0 382 C8
Manners Wy SOSN SS2 382 F6
Manning Gv VGE SS16 376 D7
Manning Rd DAGE RM10 388 B6
FX IP11 9 J5
Mannings Cl SAFWS CB11 65 M4 3
Mannings La RIPS/CAP IP9 81 H1
Manning St SOCK/AV RM15 405 K6
Mannington Cl IPNE IP4 39 G6 3
Manningtree Rd RCOLE CO7 107 H5
RCOLE CO7 167 G3
RIPS/CAP IP9 109 M1
Mannock Dr LOU IG10 327 K4
Mannock Rd DART DA1 415 G7 1
Manns Wy RAYL SS6 361 K6
Manor Av EMPK RM11 371 K5
PIT SS13 378 D5
Manor Cl BCAYE CM11 336 D8
DAGE RM10 388 E5 1
RAYL SS6 380 E3
RCOLW CO6 134 D4
ROM RM1 371 H5
SOCK/AV RM15 405 K6
SUD CO10 32 D1 1
Manor Ct EN EN1 300 C8
Manor Crs EMPK RM11 371 K5
RCHLM CM3 235 J6
Manor Dr CHLM/GWD CM2 289 G4
Manor Farm Rd EN EN1 300 C7
Manor Hatch HLWS CM18 256 B4
Manor Hatch Cl HLWS CM18 256 C4
Manor House Wy RCOLE CO7 220 F4
Manor La HAR CO12 143 H1
RIPS/CAP IP9 109 M1
SAFWN CB10 42 E1
Manor Links BSF CM23 174 D4
Manor Rd ABR/ST RM4 350 E2
BOC CM0 321 L2
BSF CM23 174 B4
CHIG IG7 349 H7
CHLM/GWD CM2 17 H6
COLW CO3 162 E4 1
DAGE RM10 388 D5
ERITH DA8 414 A3
FOS CO13 198 B8
FX IP11 9 G8
FX IP11 84 C5
GRAYS RM17 417 K3
GTDUN CM6 150 A6
HAR CO12 6 D9
HLWE CM17 227 K6
HOC/HUL SS5 362 D5
HOD EN11 253 H3
HVHL CB9 28 C4
IPNE IP4 37 L3
LAIN SS15 376 C4
LOU IG10 326 C3
MAL CM9 267 M6
RCHLM CM3 267 K2
RCHLM CM3 339 K3
RCOLE CO7 192 D2
RCOLW CO6 133 M6
ROM RM1 371 H5
SBF/HAD SS7 379 K5
SLH/COR SS17 409 L1
STSD CM24 146 F6
SUD CO10 4 D2
TIL RM18 418 B6
WAB EN9 301 L5
WIT CM8 212 B7 3
WOS/PRIT SS0 20 A7
WTHK RM20 416 D3
Manor St BRTR CM7 155 G8
Manors Wy WIT CM8 184 D7
Manor Ter FX IP11 9 H5
Manor Wy BRW CM14 354 B4
COS CO15 225 H5
GRAYS RM17 417 K4
GVW DA11 417 H7
SWCM DA10 416 F8
Manorway WFD IG8 348 D6 4
The Manorway SLH/COR SS17 411 J1
Mansard Cl HCH RM12 389 H1
Manse Cha MAL CM9 293 H2
Mansel Cl LOS SS9 381 M5
Mansfield SBW CM21 227 H2
Mansfield Av IP IP1 37 G1 1
Mansfield Cl ED N9 324 B8
Mansfield Gdns HCH RM12 389 L1
Mansfields CHLM/WR CM1 287 G2 1
Manstead Gdns RAIN RM13 404 C4 1
Manstead Gdns RCFD SS4 363 L6
Manston Cl BAR EN8 300 D2 2
Manston Dr BSF CM23 174 C2
Manston Rd HLW CM20 255 M3
Manston Wy HCH RM12 389 J5
Manwick Rd FX IP11 9 H6
Maple Av BRTR CM7 182 E1
BSF CM23 173 L3
LOS SS9 400 A3
MAL CM9 269 K5
UPMR RM14 390 C2
Maple Cl BARK/HLT IG6 349 M6 1
BKHH IG9 348 E4
BSF CM23 173 L3
CHTY IP2 2 A9
COS CO15 12 A5
HAR CO12 6 F8
HCH RM12 389 J2 3
HSTD CO9 129 H1
RBRW/HUT CM13 355 G4 2
Maplecroft La WAB EN9 277 M1
Mapledene Av HOC/HUL SS5 361 M1
Maple Dr CHLM/GWD CM2 288 C5
FOS CO13 198 E5
RAYL SS6 361 K4
SOCK/AV RM15 406 E2 2
WIT CM8 212 B6 5
Mapleford Sweep VGE SS16 19 L9
Maple Ga LOU IG10 327 H4 1
Maple Gv BSF CM23 173 L3
Maple Hl SUD CO10 30 E1
Maple Leaf K/T/MI CO5 214 D4
Mapleleaf Cl HOC/HUL SS5 363 G4 2
Mapleleaf Gdns WICKW SS12 359 J5
Maple Md BCAYW CM12 357 K3 1
Maple Rd GRAYS RM17 417 K3
SUD CO10 55 J6
Maplesfield SBF/HAD SS7 380 E7
Maple Spring BSF CM23 173 K3
Maple Springs WAB EN9 302 B5
Maple Sq SOSN SS2 21 J2
Maplestead BSDN SS14 19 M1
The Maples HLWW/ROY CM19 255 J8
KESG IP5 38 F3
Maple St ROMW/RG RM7 370 D4
Mapleton Crs PEND EN3 324 D2
Mapleton Rd EN EN1 324 C4
Mapletree La ING CM4 310 A4
Maple Tree La VGE SS16 376 A6 7
Maple Wy BOC CM0 344 B5
COLS CO2 163 H7 2
CVI SS8 397 M8
Maplin Cl SBF/HAD SS7 379 K4
Maplin Gdns BSDN SS14 377 M6
Maplin Wy SOS SS1 402 D4
Maplin Wy North SBN/FI SS3 402 D3
Marasca End COLS CO2 191 J4 2
Maraschino Crs COLS CO2 191 H4 1
Marauder Wy RCOLW CO6 158 A1
Marchmant Cl HCH RM12 389 K2 1
March Pl SUD CO10 31 J2
Marconi Rd CHLM/WR CM1 17 G1
Marcos Rd CVI SS8 398 E8
Marcus Av SOS SS1 402 C5
Marcus Cha SOS SS1 402 C4
Marcus Cl COLN CO4 135 J5
HVHL CB9 28 E4 3
Marcus Gdns SOS SS1 402 C4
Marcus Rd FX IP11 85 L8
Marden Ash LAIN SS15 376 B5 3
Marden Rd ROM RM1 370 F6 2
Mardyke Rd HLW CM20 256 B1
Marenes Crs RCOLE CO7 220 F4
Mareth Rd COLS CO2 190 D1
Margaret Av BRWN CM15 355 G1 1
CHING E4 325 J8
Margaret Cl GPK RM2 371 J5 1
RCOLE CO7 221 G5
WAB EN9 301 L5 1
Margaret Dr EMPK RM11 372 A8
Margaret Rd COL CO1 10 B5
EPP CM16 304 B1 4
GPK RM2 371 J5
Margaret St FX IP11 84 F8
GTDUN CM6 92 A8
Margaretting Rd
CHLM/GWD CM2 312 B1
CHLM/WR CM1 287 H3
ING CM4 312 A2
Margaret Wy SAFWN CB10 65 L2 5
Margarite Wy WICKW SS12 359 J3
Margate Rd IPSE IP3 38 C8
Margeth Rd BCAYW CM12 357 K8
Margherita Pl WAB EN9 302 A6
Margraten Av CVI SS8 413 L1
Marguerite Dr LOS SS9 400 A2
Marguerite Wy BSF CM23 173 K5
Mariam Gdns HCH RM12 390 A1
Marian Cl BARK/HLT IG6 349 L8
CDH/CHF RM16 406 F6
Maria St HAR CO12 7 K4
Marigold Av CHTY IP2 36 F8
COS CO15 12 B2
Marigold Cl CHLM/WR CM1 265 G5
COLN CO4 163 M3
Marigold La ING CM4 335 M3
Marigold Pl HLWE CM17 227 J7 1
Marina Av RAYL SS6 361 K8
Marina Cl SOSN SS2 382 F7
Marina Gdns BAR EN8 300 D2
COS CO15 224 D6
FX IP11 9 H5
ROMW/RG RM7 370 C5
Marina Ms WOTN CO14 199 K3
Marina Rd RCHLM CM3 238 B7
Marine Ap CVI SS8 413 J1
Marine Av CVI SS8 398 F8
LOS SS9 399 L2
WOS/PRIT SS0 20 D8
Marine Cl LOS SS9 399 H2
Marine Ct PUR RM19 415 G1
Marine Pde HAR CO12 7 J8
LOS SS9 399 H2
RCHLM CM3 318 F2
SOS SS1 21 J8
Marine Pde East COS CO15 13 G8
Mariners Ct SBN/FI SS3 385 K8
Mariners Wy MAL CM9 293 H3
Marion Av RCOS CO16 223 M5
Marisco Cl CDH/CHF RM16 418 C1
Mariskals PIT SS13 378 B6
Maritime Av MAL CM9 269 M8 1
Marjorams Av LOU IG10 327 H4
Mark Av CHING E4 325 J8
Market Av WICKW SS12 359 K3
Market Cl COLW CO3 10 B6
Market End RCOLW CO6 186 A1
Market Gv HSTD CO9 73 G2
Market Hl HVHL CB9 28 B3
MAL CM9 269 H8
RCOLW CO6 186 B1 1
SUD CO10 4 D6
Market La CBE/LIN CB1 24 C1
Market Link ROM RM1 370 F4
Market Pl BRTR CM7 155 G8 4
GTDUN CM6 178 E2 2
ING CM4 310 C7 1
ROM RM1 370 F5
SOS SS1 21 H7
Market Rd CHLM/WR CM1 17 G3
IP IP1 2 D5
WICKW SS12 359 K4
Market Rw SAFWN CB10 65 L2
Market Sq BSDN SS14 18 F7
BSF CM23 174 A4
Market St BSF CM23 174 A4 3
HAR CO12 7 L3
HLWE CM17 227 K7
SAFWN CB10 65 L1
Mark Hall Moors HLW CM20 227 J8
Markhams SLH/COR SS17 395 G8
Markhams Cha LAIN SS15 376 E4 1
Markhams Cl HVHL CB9 28 A2 5
Marking's Fld SAFWN CB10 65 M1 2
Markland Dr MAL CM9 292 F2 2
Marklay Dr RCHLM CM3 339 K4
Mark Rd BOC CM0 298 A5
Mark's Av CHONG CM5 283 G7
Marks Cl BCAYW CM12 334 F7
ING CM4 334 A2 2
Marks Gdns BRTR CM7 155 K8
Marks Hall La GTDUN CM6 231 M8
Marks Hall Rd RCOLW CO6 158 A6
Marks La RCHLM CM3 338 A3
Marks Rd ROMW/RG RM7 370 D5
Markwells RBSF CM22 147 L1
Markwell Wd EPP CM16 279 J1
Marlborough Av BOC CM0 297 M8
Marlborough Cl BSF CM23 174 A6
CDH/CHF RM16 407 K7
COS CO15 12 B6
SBF/HAD SS7 379 L4
UPMR RM14 372 F8 2
Marlborough Dr SUD CO10 4 F5
Marlborough Gdns
UPMR RM14 372 F8
Marlborough Rd BRTR CM7 155 H7
BRWN CM15 332 B8
CHLM/GWD CM2 16 F7
IPNE IP4 3 M5
ROMW/RG RM7 370 B4
SOS SS1 401 L3
Marlborough Wk
HOC/HUL SS5 362 D5 6
Marlborough Wy BCAYW CM12 335 H6
Marle Gdns WAB EN9 301 K4
Marlescroft Wy LOU IG10 327 J7
Marlin Cl SBF/HAD SS7 380 F5
Marlow Av PUR RM19 415 H1
Marlowe Cl BCAYW CM12 335 J6
BRTR CM7 183 H4 3
MAL CM9 293 H3
Marlowe Rd COS CO15 250 B2
Marlowe Wy COLW CO3 162 A4
Marlow Gdns SOSN SS2 382 F7
Marlow Rd IP IP1 36 E2
Marlpits Rd MAL CM9 291 M7
Marlyon Rd BARK/HLT IG6 350 C6
Marne Rd COLS CO2 162 F7
Marney Cl CHLM/GWD CM2 288 F3 1
Marney Dr BSDN SS14 378 A6
Marney Wy FOS CO13 199 J5
Marquis Cl BSF CM23 173 J4
Marram Cl COLW CO3 161 J5
Marrilyne Av PEND EN3 325 G2
Mar Rd SOCK/AV RM15 406 D2
Marryat Rd EN EN1 300 C7
Marshall Cl K/T/MI CO5 186 E7 1
KESG IP5 39 K3 1
LOS SS9 381 H8
Marshalls RCFD SS4 363 L7
Marshalls Cl RAYL SS6 381 G1
Marshalls Dr ROM RM1 370 F3
Marshalls Piece GTDUN CM6 151 L5
Marshalls Rd BRTR CM7 182 F2
ROMW/RG RM7 370 E4
Marshbarns BSF CM23 173 K3
Marsh Cl BAR EN8 301 G5
Marsh Crs K/T/MI CO5 192 A3
Marshcroft Dr BAR EN8 300 F2
Marsh Farm La RCOLE CO7 221 L1
Marsh Farm Rd RCHLM CM3 339 L6
Marshfoot Rd GRAYS RM17 418 A2
Marsh Green Rd DAGE RM10 388 B7
Marsh Hl WAB EN9 277 M7
Marsh La FX IP11 85 L4
HLWE CM17 227 M6
RBRW/HUT CM13 334 B4
SLH/COR SS17 395 L5
Marsh Rd BOC CM0 298 B6
BOC CM0 344 D5
Marsh St DART DA1 415 H7
Marsh View Ct VGE SS16 377 M8 3
Marsh Wy RCOLE CO7 220 F5
Marshy La SUD CO10 51 K4
Marston Av DAGE RM10 388 B2
Marston Beck CHLM/GWD CM2 289 H1
Marston Cl DAGE RM10 388 B2 1
Marston Rd HOD EN11 253 J4 1
Martello La FX IP11 85 L8
Martello Rd WOTN CO14 199 K3
Martens Meadow BRTR CM7 155 L8
Martin Cl BCAYE CM11 357 J2
Martindale Av LAIN SS15 376 E1
Martin Dr RAIN RM13 404 C2
Martin End COLS CO2 190 B6
Martingale SBF/HAD SS7 380 C6
Martingale Cl BCAYE CM11 335 L6 1
Martingale Dr CHLM/WR CM1 265 G4
Martingale Rd BCAYE CM11 335 L6
Martin Rd CHTY IP2 2 E8
SOCK/AV RM15 405 L6
Martins Cl SLH/COR SS17 394 E8
Martinsdale COS CO15 224 A5
Martins Dr BAR EN8 276 F8
Martins La CBE/LIN CB1 24 F1
Martins Ms SBF/HAD SS7 379 K7
Martin's Rd HSTD CO9 128 F2 3
SUD CO10 5 K3
Martin Wk HOC/HUL SS5 363 G7
Martlesham Cl HCH RM12 389 K4 4
Martock Av WOS/PRIT SS0 382 B6
Martyns Gv WOS/PRIT SS0 400 C1
Martyns Ri SUD CO10 34 D6
Marvens CHLM/GWD CM2 288 E8
Marwell Cl ROM RM1 371 H6
Maryborough Gv COLS CO2 191 J1
Marylands Av HOC/HUL SS5 362 E4
Mary La North RCOLE CO7 166 A3
Mary La South RCOLE CO7 166 C4
Mary Mcarthur Pl
STSD CM24 146 F3 4
Maryon Rd IPSE IP3 59 J3
Mary Park Gdns BSF CM23 174 A7
Mary Warner Rd RCOLE CO7 136 F4
Mascalls Gdns BRW CM14 354 A5
Mascalls La BRW CM14 354 A5
Mascalls Wy CHLM/GWD CM2 288 F3
Masefield Cl ERITH DA8 414 A5
HARH RM3 371 J1
Masefield Crs GPK RM2 371 K1
Masefield Dr COLW CO3 162 A5
UPMR RM14 372 D7
Masefield Rd BRTR CM7 183 G3
CDH/CHF RM16 407 M7
MAL CM9 293 H2
Mashay Rd HSTD CO9 51 L7
SUD CO10 51 K5
Mashbury Rd RCHLM CM3 234 A4
Mashiters Hl CRW RM5 370 E1
Mashiters Wk ROM RM1 370 F3
Mason Cl COLS CO2 162 C8
Mason Dr HARH RM3 371 M2
Mason Rd COL CO1 10 C4
RCOS CO16 223 J8
Masons Ct BSF CM23 173 M4
Masons Rd EN EN1 300 C8
Mason Wy WAB EN9 301 M5
Masthead Cl GRH DA9 415 K8
Matching Fld BRWN CM15 332 A1 5
Matching Gn BSDN SS14 19 M1
Matching La BSF CM23 173 L3
Matching Rd HLWE CM17 228 C7
RBSF CM22 229 J2
Matfield Cl CHLM/WR CM1 264 E4 5
Mathams Dr BSF CM23 173 L6
Mather Wy CHTY IP2 3 G8
Mathews Cl HSTD CO9 99 H8 1
RCOLE CO7 106 D2
Matlock Cl RIPW IP8 57 K1 5
Matlock Gdns HCH RM12 389 M2 2
Matlock Rd CVI SS8 398 A8
Matson Rd IP IP1 37 G3 2
Maudlyn Rd COL CO1 163 K5
Maudsley Rd IP IP1 36 D1

Maugham Cl WICKW SS12 359 L6
Maunds Hatch HLWS CM18 255 L7
Maurice Rd CVI SS8 398 E8 1
Mavis Gv HCH RM12 389 M1
Mawney Cl ROMW/RG RM7 370 C2
Mawney Rd ROMW/RG RM7 370 C3
Maya Cl SBN/FI SS3 402 F4
May Av CVI SS8 398 D7
Maybank Av HCH RM12 389 J4
Mayberry Wk COLS CO2 163 H8
Maybrick Rd EMPK RM11 371 K5
Maybury Av BAR EN8 276 C8
CHESW EN7 276 C8 1
Maybury Cl RCOLW CO6 160 A8 3
Maybury Rd IPSE IP3 59 J2
Maybush La FX IP11 85 K8
Maybush Rd EMPK RM11 371 M7
Maycroft Av GRAYS RM17 417 L2
Maycroft Gdns GRAYS RM17 417 L2
Mayda Cl HSTD CO9 128 E2
Maydells PIT SS13 378 C6
Mayes Cl BSF CM23 174 E3
Mayes La CHLM/GWD CM2 289 M5
HAR CO12 142 C2
RCHLM CM3 290 F5
Mayes Pl GTDUN CM6 122 B5
Mayfair Av PIT SS13 378 D3
Mayfair Gdns WFD IG8 348 B8
Mayfield Av HOC/HUL SS5 361 M1
SOSN SS2 382 F7
WFD IG8 348 B7
Mayfield Cl COLN CO4 11 J3
HLWE CM17 228 A7
Mayfield Crs ED N9 324 C8
Mayfield Gdns BRW CM14 354 C2 1
BRW CM14 354 D2 1
Mayfield Pk BSF CM23 173 L8 1
Mayfield Rd CHLM/WR CM1 287 H1
IPNE IP4 38 D4
PEND EN3 324 E4
Mayfields CDH/CHF RM16 407 K7
Mayflower Av HAR CO12 7 L5
Mayflower Cl SOCK/AV RM15 406 D2
SOSN SS2 382 C5
WAB EN9 277 M3
Mayflower Dr MAL CM9 293 H4
Mayflower Gdns BSF CM23 173 J5
Mayflower Rd BCAYE CM11 357 J1 4
Mayflowers SBF/HAD SS7 379 J4 3
Mayflower Wy CHONG CM5 283 H7
SUD CO10 4 E1
Mayford Wy RCOS CO16 223 J5
Maygreen Crs EMPK RM11 371 H7
Mayland Av CVI SS8 413 G1
Mayland Cl MAL CM9 269 L7
RCHLM CM3 319 H4
Mayland Gn RCHLM CM3 319 J3
Mayland Hl RCHLM CM3 319 K5
Mayland Rd WIT CM8 239 H1 3
Maylands Av HCH RM12 389 J3
Maylands Dr BRTR CM7 182 E3
Maylands Wy HARH RM3 353 K7
Maylins Dr SBW CM21 227 L1
Maynard Cl ERITH DA8 414 A4
GTDUN CM6 178 E2 3
Maynards EMPK RM11 371 M7
Mayne Crest CHLM/WR CM1 264 F4
Mayo Cl BAR EN8 276 D8
Mayplace Av DART DA1 414 B8
Maypole Cl SAFWS CB11 65 K4 1
Maypole Crs BARK/HLT IG6 349 L8
ERITH DA8 414 E3
Maypole Dr CHIG IG7 350 B4
RCOS CO16 222 B7
Maypole Green Rd COLS CO2 190 D2
Maypole Rd K/T/MI CO5 214 D5
MAL CM9 269 G2
WIT CM8 240 A6
The Maypole GTDUN CM6 92 A8
May Rd IPSE IP3 59 K1
Maysent Av BRTR CM7 155 G6
May's La RCOLE CO7 106 F7
Mayswood Gdns DAGE RM10 388 D5 1
Maytree Cl RAIN RM13 388 F8
May Wk CHLM/GWD CM2 288 D4 1
STSD CM24 147 H2
Maywin Dr EMPK RM11 372 A8
Maze Green Hts BSF CM23 173 K4
Maze Green Rd BSF CM23 173 L4
The Maze LOS SS9 381 L4
Mazoe Cl BSF CM23 174 A6
Mazoe Rd BSF CM23 174 A6
Mcadam Cl HOD EN11 253 H3 1
Mccalmont Dr RAYL SS6 361 K4
Mccudden Rd DART DA1 415 G7
Mcdivitt Wk LOS SS9 382 B5 3
Mcintosh Cl ROM RM1 370 F3 1
Mcintosh Rd ROM RM1 370 F3
Mc Kenzie Rd BROX EN10 253 H8
Mead Barn EPP CM16 303 M8
Mead Cl CDH/CHF RM16 407 J7
GPK RM2 371 H2
LOU IG10 327 J4
Mead Ct WAB EN9 301 J6
Meade Rd BCAYE CM11 335 L6
Meadgate PIT SS13 378 D3 2
Meadgate Av CHLM/GWD CM2 17 L7
WFD IG8 348 F6
Meadgate Rd HOD EN11 253 L8
Mead Monks RCHLM CM3 315 G1
Meadow Clays SAFWS CB11 43 G7 2
Meadow Cl BRTR CM7 154 B4
COS CO15 224 C4
FX IP11 84 C3
HSTD CO9 129 G3
PEND EN3 324 F3
RCOLE CO7 166 B5
SBF/HAD SS7 380 C5
SLH/COR SS17 409 H8
Meadow Ct WICKE SS11 359 M3
Meadowcroft STSD CM24 146 F4 2
Meadowcroft Wy FOS CO13 199 G4
Meadowcross WAB EN9 301 M6
Meadow Dr SOS SS1 401 M3
VGE SS16 394 C3
Meadowford SAFWS CB11 89 G2
Meadowgate ING CM4 311 H4
Meadow Grass Cl COLW CO3 161 J5 1
Meadowland Rd WICKE SS11 360 B5
Meadowlands BSF CM23 174 B2
EMPK RM11 371 M7 3
Meadow La CBE/LIN CB1 24 C1
K/T/MI CO5 245 K6
SUD CO10 4 D7
WICKE SS11 337 M8
Meadow Ms RCHLM CM3 339 J3 1
Meadow Ri BCAYE CM11 357 K1
ING CM4 308 F3
Meadow Rd CDH/CHF RM16 407 K6
COLS CO2 190 E2
DAGW RM9 388 A5
EPP CM16 304 A1
HOC/HUL SS5 361 M1
LOU IG10 326 F7
RCHLM CM3 338 D6
ROMW/RG RM7 370 D8
SAFWN CB10 22 E8
SBF/HAD SS7 398 F1
Meadows Cl
RBRW/HUT CM13 355 K7 1
RCOLE CO7 165 G5
Meadows Gn RCHLM CM3 291 H5
Meadowside BRTR CM7 154 F6
CHLM/GWD CM2 17 K2
Meadow Side CHLM/WR CM1 17 G1
Meadowside RAYL SS6 380 E1 2
Meadowside Gdns IPNE IP4 38 F3
Meadowside Rd UPMR RM14 390 D4
The Meadows BSF CM23 173 M6
RBRW/HUT CM13 355 K7
SBW CM21 228 B1
Meadowsweet Cl BSF CM23 173 K5 1
HVHL CB9 27 M2 3
The Meadow HERT/BAY SG13 252 F1
Meadowvale Cl IPNE IP4 3 M1
Meadow Vw EPP CM16 304 B1 3
K/T/MI CO5 214 C6 1
VGE SS16 375 M7
Meadow View Cl COLW CO3 161 M6
Meadow View Rd SUD CO10 4 A9
Meadow Wk DAGW RM9 388 A5
Meadow Wy BOC CM0 344 B5
BRTR CM7 183 K6
CHIG IG7 349 K3
COS CO15 250 A4
HOC/HUL SS5 362 F6
K/T/MI CO5 218 C1
RCHLM CM3 318 B5
SBW CM21 228 B2
UPMR RM14 390 D2
WICKW SS12 359 L8
The Meadow Wy BCAYE CM11 357 K1
Mead Pastures MAL CM9 267 L8
Mead Pth CHLM/GWD CM2 16 D8
Meads Cl ING CM4 310 C7
Meads Rd PEND EN3 324 F3
The Meads ING CM4 310 C7
UPMR RM14 390 F1 3
VGE SS16 378 B8
Meadsway RBRW/HUT CM13 354 D7 3
The Mead ABR/ST RM4 328 C5
BAR EN8 300 D1
GTDUN CM6 92 B8
GTDUN CM6 178 D1
LAIN SS15 376 C3
SUD CO10 55 J7
Mead Vw BUNT SG9 116 F5
Mead Wk CHONG CM5 307 G2
Meadway CVI SS8 413 K1
GPK RM2 371 H2
GRAYS RM17 417 L1
HOD EN11 253 H7
HSTD CO9 127 M3
MAL CM9 293 J2
MGTR CO11 108 B8
PEND EN3 300 E8
RAYL SS6 381 G2
SBF/HAD SS7 379 K4
WFD IG8 348 D6 3
The Meadway BKHH IG9 348 E2
WOS/PRIT SS0 400 C3
Meakins Cl LOS SS9 382 A5
Mearns Pl CHLM/GWD CM2 265 G7
Medcalf Rd PEND EN3 325 G1
Medebridge Rd CDH/CHF RM16 407 G4
Mede Wy RCOLE CO7 164 D8
Medick Ct GRAYS RM17 417 M3
Medina Rd GRAYS RM17 417 L2
Medlar Dr SOCK/AV RM15 406 F2 2
Medlar Rd GRAYS RM17 417 L3
Medlars Md RBSF CM22 203 G6
Medley Rd BRTR CM7 182 A1
Medoc Cl PIT SS13 378 D3
Medora Rd ROMW/RG RM7 370 E4
Medway Av WIT CM8 238 E1
Medway Cl CHLM/WR CM1 263 L7
Medway Crs LOS SS9 399 J2
Medway Rd DART DA1 414 B7
IPSE IP3 59 G1
Meekings Rd SUD CO10 5 J5
The Meers FOS CO13 198 F5
Meeson Mdw MAL CM9 292 F3
Meesons La GRAYS RM17 417 G1
Meesons Md RCFD SS4 363 L8
Meeting Fld SUD CO10 34 D4
Meeting La HSTD CO9 50 C4
K/T/MI CO5 246 D1
Meggison Wy SBF/HAD SS7 379 K8
Megs Wy BRTR CM7 183 J2
Melba Ct CHLM/WR CM1 287 K2
Melba Gdns TIL RM18 418 B4
Melbourne Av CHLM/WR CM1 263 L6
Melbourne Cha COLS CO2 191 J2
Melbourne Rd COS CO15 12 D4
IPNE IP4 38 E4
TIL RM18 417 M5
Melbourne Wy EN EN1 324 A8
Melcombe Rd SBF/HAD SS7 379 K8
Melford Cl IPNE IP4 39 G6
Melford Rd SUD CO10 32 F1
SUD CO10 35 J3
SUD CO10 54 D1
Melford Wy FX IP11 8 D4
Melksham Cl HARH RM3 353 G8 4
Melksham Gdns HARH RM3 352 F8
Melksham Gn HARH RM3 352 F8 1
Melling Dr EN EN1 324 B3
Mellis Cl HVHL CB9 27 J2
Mellis Ct FX IP11 84 E8
Mellish Gdns WFD IG8 348 B6
Mellor Cha COLW CO3 161 M4
Mellor Cl ING CM4 310 C7 3
Mellow Purgess Cl LAIN SS15 376 D5
Mellow Purgess End LAIN SS15 376 D5
Mell Rd MAL CM9 272 F3
Melplash Cl IPSE IP3 38 F7 2
Melplash Rd IPSE IP3 38 F7
Melrose Gdns COS CO15 224 D6
IPNE IP4 38 C3
Melrose Rd K/T/MI CO5 245 J5
Melstock Av UPMR RM14 390 D3
Melton Cl RCOS CO16 223 H7
Melton Gdns ROM RM1 371 G7
Melville Dr WICKW SS12 359 L6
Melville Heath RCHLM CM3 339 M5
Melville Rd IPNE IP4 3 L5
RAIN RM13 404 B2
ROMW/RG RM7 370 C1 1
Memory Cl MAL CM9 293 H4 1
Mendip Cl RAYL SS6 361 L8
WICKE SS11 359 M4 1
Mendip Crs WOS/PRIT SS0 382 B6
Mendip Dr KESG IP5 39 G5
Mendip Rd CHLM/WR CM1 263 L5
EMPK RM11 371 H7
LOS SS9 382 B7
Mendlesham Cl RCOS CO16 223 J7
Mendoza Cl EMPK RM11 371 M5
Menin Rd COLS CO2 162 E7
Mentmore VGE SS16 376 C7
Menzies Av LAIN SS15 376 A5
Meon Cl CHLM/WR CM1 264 E5
Meppel Av CVI SS8 398 B5
Mercer Av SBN/FI SS3 385 H7
Mercer Rd BCAYE CM11 335 L6
Mercers HLWW/ROY CM19 255 H6
Mercers Av BSF CM23 173 J7
Mercers Wy COL CO1 10 B5
Merchant St RCHLM CM3 339 M4 3
Mercia Cl CHLM/GWD CM2 289 H6
Mercury Cl WICKE SS11 360 A3
Mercury Gdns ROM RM1 371 G5
Meredene BSDN SS14 378 A6
Meredith Rd CDH/CHF RM16 418 B1
COS CO15 12 E6
IP IP1 36 F1
Merefield SBW CM21 227 M2 2
Meres Cl WIT CM8 238 F2
Meriadoc Dr RCHLM CM3 339 L5
Merilies Cl WOS/PRIT SS0 382 C8
Merilies Gdns WOS/PRIT SS0 382 C8
Merivale Cl MGTR CO11 108 C8
Merivale Rd MGTR CO11 108 C8
Merlin Cl CRW RM5 351 L7
WAB EN9 302 B6
Merlin Ct CVI SS8 398 C8 2
Merlin End COLN CO4 164 A2
Merlin Gdns CRW RM5 351 L7 2
Merlin Gv BARK/HLT IG6 349 J8
Merlin Pl CHLM/WR CM1 264 A6 3
Merlin Rd CHTY IP2 36 D8
CRW RM5 351 L7
Merlin Wy EPP CM16 281 H5
WICKE SS11 359 L2
Mermagen Dr RAIN RM13 389 J6
Mermaid Wy MAL CM9 293 J3 3
Merriam Cl MGTR CO11 108 E3
Merricks La VGE SS16 395 M1
Merrielands Crs DAGW RM9 388 A8
Merrilees Crs COS CO15 224 E5
Merrion Cl RIPW IP8 57 K1 3
Merrivale SBF/HAD SS7 397 K1
Merryfield Ap LOS SS9 381 M7
Merryfields Av HOC/HUL SS5 362 E4
Merrylands LAIN SS15 376 B4
Merrymount Gdns COS CO15 13 M1
Mersea Av K/T/MI CO5 245 J5
Mersea Crs WICKW SS12 360 A5
Mersea Fleet Wy BRTR CM7 183 K2
Mersea Rd COLS CO2 191 H2
K/T/MI CO5 217 M6
Mersea Vw RCOS CO16 221 H8
Mersey Av UPMR RM14 372 E6
Mersey Rd IPSE IP3 38 A8
WIT CM8 211 M8
Merstham Dr RCOS CO16 223 K5
Merton Ct COLS CO2 191 H4 2
Merton Pl CDH/CHF RM16 418 B1
RCHLM CM3 340 A5
Merton Rd HOC/HUL SS5 362 B3
SBF/HAD SS7 379 K7
Messant Cl GPK RM2 371 L2 3
Messines Rd COLS CO2 162 E7
Mess Rd SBN/FI SS3 403 G6
Meteor Rd WOS/PRIT SS0 20 A6
Meteor Wy CHLM/WR CM1 16 D4
Methersgate BSDN SS14 19 J4
Metsons La CHLM/WR CM1 309 L1
Metz Av CVI SS8 398 B7
Meux Cl CHESW EN7 300 B3
Mews Ct CHLM/GWD CM2 17 G6
Mews Pl WFD IG8 348 B5
The Mews HOC/HUL SS5 362 D5
ROM RM1 370 F5 3
SBW CM21 200 F8 1
Meyel Av CVI SS8 398 D6
Meyer Gn EN EN1 324 B2
Meynell Av CVI SS8 413 K1
Meynell Rd HARH RM3 352 C7
Meyrick Crs COLS CO2 163 G6
Mey Wk HOC/HUL SS5 362 D5
Micawber Wy CHLM/WR CM1 263 L4
Michael Gdns EMPK RM11 371 L4
Michaelstowe Cl HAR CO12 142 D1
Michaelstowe Dr HAR CO12 142 D1
Michigan Cl KESG IP5 39 J4
Mickfield Ms FX IP11 84 E8 3
Micklegate Rd FX IP11 9 H6
Middleborough COLW CO3 10 A6
Middle Boy ABR/ST RM4 328 C5
Middle Dr SLH/COR SS17 395 J2
Middlefield HSTD CO9 129 G2
Middlefield Av HOD EN11 253 H3
Middlefield Cl HOD EN11 253 H3 2
Middlefield Rd HOD EN11 253 H3
MGTR CO11 109 H8
Middle Gn BRWN CM15 332 D1
RCOLW CO6 131 K2
Middle King BRTR CM7 183 L2
Middlemead
CHLM/GWD CM2 313 G7 1
Middle Md RCFD SS4 383 G1 1
Middlemead RCHLM CM3 337 K3
Middle Mead Cl
CHLM/GWD CM2 313 G7 2
Middle Mill Rd COL CO1 10 C6
Middle Rd RBRW/HUT CM13 355 K5
WAB EN9 301 J4
Middle Rw BSF CM23 174 A5
Middlesburg CVI SS8 397 M6
Middlesex Av LOS SS9 400 A1
Middle St SAFWS CB11 87 K7
WAB EN9 278 A3
Middleton Cl CHTY IP2 57 L1
RCOS CO16 223 L5
Middleton Hall La BRWN CM15 354 F3
Middleton Rd BRWN CM15 354 F2
SUD CO10 4 A9
Middleton Rw RCHLM CM3 339 M5
Middle Wy SUD CO10 34 E3
Middlewick Cl COLS CO2 191 H2 3
Midguard Wy MAL CM9 292 F3
Midhurst Av WOS/PRIT SS0 382 E7
Midhurst Cl HCH RM12 389 H3 2
Midland Cl COLS CO2 163 G7
Midsummer Meadow
SBN/FI SS3 402 F2 4
Midway COS CO15 249 M5
Midway Rd COLS CO2 190 D1
Milbanke Cl SBN/FI SS3 402 F2 5
Milburn Crs CHLM/WR CM1 287 L2
Milch La RCHLM CM3 181 M6
Milden Rd CHTY IP2 36 F6
Mildmayes VGE SS16 376 D7
Mildmay Rd BOC CM0 344 D6
CHLM/GWD CM2 17 H7
IPSE IP3 59 H2
ROMW/RG RM7 370 D5
Mildmays RCHLM CM3 290 D3
Mile Cl WAB EN9 301 K5 4
Mile End Rd COLN CO4 134 F8
Miles Cl COLW CO3 161 K5
HLWW/ROY CM19 15 H7
Miles Gray Rd BSDN SS14 376 F2
Milford Cl RCOLE CO7 192 D2
Milford Rd CDH/CHF RM16 407 L6
Milkwell Gdns WFD IG8 348 C8
Millais Pl TIL RM18 418 B4
Millais Rd EN EN1 324 A7
Millars Cl RCHLM CM3 339 M3 4
The Millars CHLM/WR CM1 235 H8 1
Millbank Av CHONG CM5 307 G1
Millbridge Rd WIT CM8 239 G1
Millbrook Gdns GPK RM2 370 F2
Mill Cswy ROY SG8 40 D6
Mill Cha HSTD CO9 128 F1
HVHL CB9 48 D6
Mill Cl BOC CM0 297 M7
BRTR CM7 124 C1
CHLM/WR CM1 262 B6
FX IP11 8 F2
FX IP11 84 B3
K/T/MI CO5 214 D5
RBSF CM22 147 K2
Mill Ct GTDUN CM6 177 J4
Millcroft BSF CM23 174 B2
Mill End GTDUN CM6 122 B1
Millennium Wy BRTR CM7 183 K2
Miller's Barn Rd COS CO15 250 B2
Millers Cl BRTR CM7 155 H3
BSF CM23 173 K6
CHIG IG7 350 C3
COLW CO3 161 K5
GTDUN CM6 179 H7 2
RCOLW CO6 134 C4
Millers Cft CHLM/GWD CM2 289 G5
GTDUN CM6 178 F2
Millersdale HLWW/ROY CM19 255 J7
Millers Green Rd CHONG CM5 260 C7
Miller's La CHIG IG7 350 C2
COLW CO3 161 L5
Millers Md K/T/MI CO5 186 F7
Millers Rw BRTR CM7 70 D5
Millfield CHONG CM5 283 K8
Mill Fld GTDUN CM6 179 H7
HLWE CM17 227 K7
RIPW IP8 36 C1
Millfield Cl RAYL SS6 361 M8
Millfield Gdns IPNE IP4 38 B5
Millfield La STDN SG11 172 E3
Millfields CHLM/WR CM1 287 H2
Mill Flds RCHLM CM3 291 H5
Millfields SBW CM21 201 G8
STSD CM24 146 F5 1
Millfields Wy HVHL CB9 28 C3
Mill Gra BOC CM0 344 C4
Mill Gn PIT SS13 378 B5
Mill Green Pl PIT SS13 378 B4
Mill Green Rd ING CM4 310 A3
Millhead Wy RCFD SS4 383 J2
Mill Hl BRTR CM7 183 J1
BRWN CM15 354 F1
BSF CM23 145 M6
CHLM/GWD CM2 312 A1
HVHL CB9 28 A4
MGTR CO11 107 L7
MGTR CO11 108 D7
RCHLM CM3 316 D3
RCOLW CO6 102 F5
SBF/HAD SS7 397 M2
STSD CM24 146 E5
SUD CO10 4 B7
Mill Hill Dr BCAYW CM12 335 J6
Millhurst Ms HLWE CM17 227 M7
Milligans Cha CHLM/GWD CM2 312 C2
Milliners Wy BSF CM23 173 K7
Mill La ABR/ST RM4 330 D4
BAR EN8 276 F8
BCAYE CM11 336 C6
BROX EN10 277 G1
BRTR CM7 71 G8
BRTR CM7 181 M3
BRTR CM7 183 L5
BRWN CM15 308 E7
BRWN CM15 331 M1
BUNT SG9 86 B6
CBE/LIN CB1 24 D1
CDH/CHF RM16 408 B4
CHING E4 325 J5
CHLM/WR CM1 264 C2
CHONG CM5 258 D6
CHONG CM5 305 M1
CHONG CM5 307 K1
COLS CO2 189 G8
COLS CO2 190 C6
FOS CO13 197 M8
FX IP11 9 H2
FX IP11 84 B3
GTDUN CM6 151 L6
GTDUN CM6 178 E3
HAR CO12 7 J7
HLWE CM17 227 M7
HSTD CO9 51 H8
HSTD CO9 98 F3
HSTD CO9 100 B4
ING CM4 310 B5
ING CM4 336 A1
K/T/MI CO5 187 G1
MAL CM9 241 M8
MAL CM9 243 J3
MAL CM9 269 G8
MGTR CO11 108 E7
MGTR CO11 139 L2
RBSF CM22 202 A7
RCFD SS4 383 J2
RCHLM CM3 207 L4
RCHLM CM3 209 J4
RCHLM CM3 210 B8
RCHLM CM3 316 D2
RCOLE CO7 107 G4
RCOLE CO7 137 J7
RCOLW CO6 130 B2
RCOS CO16 196 A5
RCOS CO16 197 G2
RIPW IP8 36 C2
RIPW IP8 57 G2
SAFWN CB10 22 B4
SAFWN CB10 22 C7
SAFWN CB10 65 M1
SAFWS CB11 43 G8
SBW CM21 201 G8
SLH/COR SS17 394 A8
SLH/COR SS17 395 K5
STDN SG11 144 E5
SUD CO10 4 B7
SUD CO10 32 C3
WFD IG8 348 A6
WIT CM8 239 G1
WOTN CO14 199 K2
WTHK RM20 416 E2
Mill Lane Cl BROX EN10 277 G1
RCOS CO16 196 B5
Millmarsh La PEND EN3 324 F4
Mill Park Av HCH RM12 389 M1
Mill Park Dr BRTR CM7 183 J2
Mill Piece KIR/NAC IP10 60 C5
Mill Pl DART DA1 414 B8
Mill Ri RIPS/CAP IP9 80 E6
Mill Rd BCAYE CM11 357 L5
BOC CM0 297 M7
BOC CM0 344 C4
BRTR CM7 94 E6
BRTR CM7 124 C1
CHLM/WR CM1 232 E6
COLN CO4 105 G7
COLN CO4 134 F7
COLN CO4 135 H5
GTDUN CM6 180 B8
HSTD CO9 49 K8
HSTD CO9 49 M1
HVHL CB9 28 B4
HVHL CB9 29 H1
HVHL CB9 47 K3
ING CM4 335 M1
IPSE IP3 60 A2
K/T/MI CO5 245 K3
MAL CM9 240 E4
MAL CM9 293 J2
PUR RM19 415 J3
RBSF CM22 119 M7
RCHLM CM3 319 J3
RCOLW CO6 132 E7
SAFWN CB10 91 H1
SAFWS CB11 90 B3
SOCK/AV RM15 405 K5
SUD CO10 31 K4
SUD CO10 33 K6
Mills Ct PIT SS13 378 D2
Mill Side STSD CM24 146 E5
Mills La SUD CO10 34 D7
Millsmead Wy LOU IG10 327 G4
Millson Bank
CHLM/GWD CM2 265 H7 3
Mills Rd SUD CO10 5 H5
The Mills IPNE IP4 38 F3
Mill St BSF CM23 174 B6
COLS CO2 163 H5
HLWE CM17 256 F6
RCOLE CO7 221 H5
RCOLW CO6 104 B2
RCOS CO16 222 A7
Mills Wy RBRW/HUT CM13 355 K2
Mill Tye SUD CO10 55 H7
Millview Mdw RCFD SS4 383 G2
Mill Vue Rd CHLM/GWD CM2 288 F1
Mill Wk K/T/MI CO5 214 D5 3
Millways MAL CM9 240 C7
Millwell Crs CHIG IG7 349 L6
Millwrights K/T/MI CO5 214 D5
Milner Pl BCAYW CM12 335 G6
Milner Rd SUD CO10 5 K4
Milner St IPNE IP4 3 J5
Milnrow RIPW IP8 57 K1
Milton Av BRTR CM7 183 H3
HCH RM12 389 G1
VGE SS16 375 M7
WOS/PRIT SS0 20 C7
Milton Cl COLW CO3 162 A5
RAYL SS6 381 G1
Milton Ct WAB EN9 301 K6 3

Milton Crs CHONG CM5 ... 283 G6
Milton Gdns TIL RM18 ... 418 C5
Milton Hall Cl SBN/FI SS3 ... 385 G8
Milton Pl CHLM/WR CM1 ... 264 A6
  SOS SS1 ... 20 F7
Milton Rd BRW CM14 ... 354 C4
  GRAYS RM17 ... 417 J1
  HAR CO12 ... 7 J7
  MAL CM9 ... 293 H3
  MGTR CO11 ... 138 C1
  ROM RM1 ... 371 H6
  SLH/COR SS17 ... 395 C5
  WIT CM8 ... 212 A6
  WOS/PRIT SS0 ... 20 D6
Milton St IPNE IP4 ... 38 B4
  SOSN SS2 ... 21 G4
Miltsin Av CVI SS8 ... 398 D6
Milwards HLWW/ROY CM19 ... 255 J7
Mimosa Cl BRWN CM15 ... 332 C7
  CHLM/WR CM1 ... 265 G5
  HARH RM3 ... 352 D8
Minchen Rd HLW CM20 ... 256 B2
Minden Rd SUD CO10 ... 4 E6
Minerva Cl HAR CO12 ... 143 C1
  HVHL CB9 ... 28 E5
Minsmere Rd RCOS CO16 ... 223 K5
Minsmere Wy SUD CO10 ... 5 L9
Minster Rd HVHL CB9 ... 28 A2
  LAIN SS15 ... 376 D5
Minster Wy EMPK RM11 ... 372 A8
  MAL CM9 ... 292 F5
Minton Hts RCFD SS4 ... 363 K5
Minton La HLWE CM17 ... 256 D5
Miramar Av CVI SS8 ... 397 M8
Miramar Wy HCH RM12 ... 389 L4
Mirosa Dr MAL CM9 ... 293 J3
Mirosa Reach MAL CM9 ... 293 K3
Mission La RCOLE CO7 ... 78 C8
Mistley End VGE SS16 ... 19 K8
Mistley Pth VGE SS16 ... 19 K8
Mistley Rd HLW CM20 ... 256 B1
Mistley Side VGE SS16 ... 19 K7
Mitchell Av CVI SS8 ... 128 F2
Mitchell Cir BRTR CM7 ... 95 K5
Mitchell Cl RAIN RM13 ... 389 K8
Mitchells Av CVI SS8 ... 398 E4
Mitchell Wy RCHLM CM3 ... 339 L3
Mitre Gdns BSF CM23 ... 174 B7
Mitton V CHLM/GWD CM2 ... 289 G1
Moat Cl BCAYE CM11 ... 336 C8
Moat Edge Gdns BCAYW CM12 ... 335 H7
Moat End SOS SS1 ... 402 C2
Moat Farm Cha WIT CM8 ... 212 A8
Moat Farm Cl IPNE IP4 ... 38 A3
Moat Fld BSDN SS14 ... 19 J1
Moat Flds RCOLW CO6 ... 132 E5
Moat La BURES CO8 ... 77 H7
  ERITH DA8 ... 414 B5
Moat Ri RAYL SS6 ... 380 E2
Moat Rd HSTD CO9 ... 49 K4
  RCOLW CO6 ... 132 E5
Moat Side PEND EN3 ... 324 D6
Modlen Rd WOTN CO14 ... 199 H4
Moffat Av IPNE IP4 ... 38 C2
Mole Hall La SAFWS CB11 ... 90 A8
Molehill Green Rbt RBSF CM22 ... 148 D6
Molesworth HOD EN11 ... 253 H1
Mollands VGE SS16 ... 378 A7
Mollands Cl SOCK/AV RM15 ... 406 F2
Mollands La SOCK/AV RM15 ... 406 F2
Mollison Av PEND EN3 ... 300 F7
Molrams La CHLM/GWD CM2 ... 289 J1
Momples Rd HLW CM20 ... 256 B2
Monarch Cl TIL RM18 ... 418 C6
Monarch Pl BKHH IG9 ... 348 D3
Monarch's Wy BAR EN8 ... 300 E5
Monastery Rd LAIN SS15 ... 376 D5
Moneypiece Cl HVHL CB9 ... 28 A2
Monkchester Cl LOU IG10 ... 327 H3
Monkdowns Rd RCOLW CO6 ... 158 C3
Monkham's Av WFD IG8 ... 348 C6
Monkham's Dr WFD IG8 ... 348 C6
Monkham's La WFD IG8 ... 348 C5
Monklands Ct HSTD CO9 ... 128 E2
Monks Cha HLWS CM18 ... 256 B6
Monks Cha RBRW/HUT CM13 ... 355 K6
Monks Cl BROX EN10 ... 253 H8
  FX IP11 ... 85 L7
Monks Ct WIT CM8 ... 211 M8
Monksford Dr HOC/HUL SS5 ... 361 L2
Monks Ga RIPW SS6 ... 36 B5
Monksgrove LOU IG10 ... 327 H7
Monks Hl SAFWS CB11 ... 66 A3
Monk's La RCOLE CO7 ... 106 E7
Monks Lodge Rd HSTD CO9 ... 74 E8
Monks Rd RCOLW CO6 ... 130 C4
Monks Wk MAL CM9 ... 272 F3
Monkswick Rd HLW CM20 ... 256 A1
Monkswood Av WAB EN9 ... 301 L6
Monkswood Dr BSF CM23 ... 173 L5
Monkwick Av COLS CO2 ... 191 H2
Monkwood Cl ROM RM1 ... 371 H5
Monmouth Ms VGE SS16 ... 376 A6
Monmouth Rd DAGW RM9 ... 388 A4
Monnow Rd SOCK/AV RM15 ... 405 K5
Monoux Cl BCAYE CM11 ... 357 L2
Monroe Crs EN EN1 ... 324 C3
Mons Av BCAYE CM11 ... 357 L1
Monson Rd BROX EN10 ... 253 G8
Mons Rd COLS CO2 ... 162 E7
Montague Av LOS SS9 ... 399 J1
Montague Pl CVI SS8 ... 397 M8
Montague Rd FX IP11 ... 9 M2
Montague Wy BCAYW CM12 ... 335 H6
Montalt Rd WFD IG8 ... 348 A6
Montana Rd KESG CM9 ... 39 H4
Montayne Rd BAR EN8 ... 300 E4
Montbretia Cl SLH/COR SS17 ... 395 H7
Montefiore Av RAYL SS6 ... 361 K3
Montfort Gdns BARK/HLT IG6 ... 349 K7
Montgomery Cl
  CHLM/WR CM1 ... 264 F4
  COLS CO2 ... 163 J7
Montgomery Ct SBN/FI SS3 ... 402 F2
Montgomery Crs HARH RM3 ... 352 E6

Montgomery Dr BAR EN8 ... 276 F8
Montgomery Rd CHTY IP2 ... 58 C2
Monton Ri CHTY IP2 ... 57 L1
Montpelier Rd TIL RM18 ... 418 B7
Montreal Rd TIL RM18 ... 418 B7
Montrose Av GPK RM2 ... 371 K2
Montrose Cl WFD IG8 ... 348 B5
Montrose Rd CHLM/GWD CM2 ... 265 G7
Montsale PIT SS13 ... 378 D3
Monument Farm Rd
  KIR/NAC IP10 ... 39 K7
Moon Hall La HVHL CB9 ... 28 A6
Moons Cl RCFD SS4 ... 363 L4
Moorcroft RCFD SS4 ... 363 K5
Moorcroft Rd SBF/HAD SS7 ... 380 F5
Moore Av TIL RM18 ... 418 C6
  WTHK RM20 ... 416 F2
Moore Cl BCAYE CM11 ... 335 L6
Moores Av SLH/COR SS17 ... 395 K2
Moorescroft BRWN CM15 ... 331 M1
Moorfield Cl KESG IP5 ... 39 K4
Moorfield Rd PEND EN3 ... 324 D3
Moorfields HLWS CM18 ... 255 K8
Moor Hall La RCHLM CM3 ... 290 F8
Moor Hall Rd HLWE CM17 ... 228 A7
Moorhen Av BOC CM0 ... 296 D3
Moorhen Cl ERITH DA8 ... 414 C4
Moorhouse Gn RCOLE CO7 ... 136 F3
The Moorings BSF CM23 ... 174 B5
Moorland Cl ROMW/RG RM7 ... 370 C1
Moor La UPMR RM14 ... 373 J6
Moor Park Cl LOS SS9 ... 381 K6
Moor Park Gdns LOS SS9 ... 381 K6
Moor Rd COLN CO4 ... 105 L8
  RCOLW CO6 ... 159 K3
Moors Cl RCOLE CO7 ... 194 F2
Moor's Farm Cha MAL CM9 ... 241 H8
Moorsfield SUD CO10 ... 55 J7
Moorside COL CO1 ... 11 H8
Moors La BRTR CM7 ... 153 L8
  GTDUN CM6 ... 179 L4
Mope La WIT CM8 ... 239 L3
Mopsies Rd BSDN SS14 ... 377 M5
Moran Av CHLM/WR CM1 ... 264 C4
Morant Gdns CRW RM5 ... 351 J6
Morant Rd CDH/CHF RM16 ... 408 C8
  COL CO1 ... 163 J6
Moray Cl CHLM/WR CM1 ... 264 E4
Moray Wy ROM RM1 ... 351 L8
Morebarn Rd RCOLE CO7 ... 165 M1
Morecambe Cl HCH RM12 ... 389 J4
Moreland Av SBF/HAD SS7 ... 379 K4
Moreland Cl SBF/HAD SS7 ... 379 K5
Moreland Rd WICKE SS11 ... 359 K1
Morelands Av
  CDH/CHF RM16 ... 407 K7
Morella Cl RCOLE CO7 ... 194 F4
Morello Ct COLS CO2 ... 191 H4
Moremead WAB EN9 ... 301 L5
Mores La BRW CM14 ... 331 L5
Moreton Br CHONG CM5 ... 282 D1
Moreton Cl CHESW EN7 ... 276 C7
Moreton Gdns WFD IG8 ... 348 F6
Moreton Rd CHONG CM5 ... 282 B3
Moretons CHLM/GWD CM2 ... 312 C1
  PIT SS13 ... 378 B5
Morgan Cl DAGE RM10 ... 388 B6
Morgan Crs EPP CM16 ... 303 M8
Morgan Rd RAIN RM13 ... 404 D1
  WFD IG8 ... 348 F7
Morice Rd HOD EN11 ... 253 H1
Morland Rd DAGE RM10 ... 388 B6
  IPSE IP3 ... 59 G3
Morland Wy BAR EN8 ... 276 F8
Morley Gv HLW CM20 ... 15 K2
Morley Hl SLH/COR SS17 ... 395 C5
Morley Link SLH/COR SS17 ... 395 G6
Morley Rd HSTD CO9 ... 129 C1
  K/T/MI CO5 ... 214 E7
Morley Sq CDH/CHF RM16 ... 418 B1
Morleys Rd RCOLW CO6 ... 130 B5
Mornington Av IP IP1 ... 37 G2
Mornington Crs CVI SS8 ... 398 E7
  SBF/HAD SS7 ... 381 C8
Mornington Rd CVI SS8 ... 398 C6
  HLWW/ROY CM19 ... 255 J7
Morrells VGE SS16 ... 377 C7
Morrin's Cha SBN/FI SS3 ... 385 L8
Morrins Cl SBN/FI SS3 ... 385 L8
Morris Av BCAYE CM11 ... 357 L2
  COS CO15 ... 249 M5
Morris Cl LAIN SS15 ... 376 C4
  WAB EN9 ... 302 A6
Morris Harp SAFWN CB10 ... 43 M8
Morrison Rd BCTR RM8 ... 388 A1
Morrow La RCOLE CO7 ... 137 H5
Mors End RCOLE CO7 ... 106 E1
Morses La RCOLE CO7 ... 221 C3
Morson Rd PEND EN3 ... 324 F8
Morston Hall Rd FX IP11 ... 83 M2
Morten Rd COL CO1 ... 10 A4
Mortimer Ga BAR EN8 ... 277 G7
Mortimer Pl SUD CO10 ... 31 J2
Mortimer Rd RAYL SS6 ... 361 L6
  RCHLM CM3 ... 238 B7
Morton Rd MAL CM9 ... 240 B7
Morton Wy HSTD CO9 ... 99 H8
Mosbach Gdns
  RBRW/HUT CM13 ... 355 J3
Moseley St SOSN SS2 ... 401 L2
Moss Bank GRAYS RM17 ... 417 C1
Moss Cl VGE SS16 ... 377 M8
Moss Dr VGE SS16 ... 377 M8
Mossfield Cl COLW CO3 ... 162 D5
Moss La ROM RM1 ... 371 C6
Moss Rd COLW CO3 ... 161 M7
  DAGE RM10 ... 388 D6
  SOCK/AV RM15 ... 406 D3
  WIT CM8 ... 212 C8
Moss Wy RCOLW CO6 ... 133 M8
Motehill VGE SS16 ... 376 D7
Motherwell Wy WTHK RM20 ... 416 B2
Mottingham Rd ED N9 ... 324 E8
Mottram Cl RIPW SS6 ... 57 K1

Motts Cl BRTR CM7 ... 154 F7
Mott's La RCOLW CO6 ... 159 L7
  WIT CM8 ... 212 B7
Mott St CHING E4 ... 325 M3
Motts Yd GTDUN CM6 ... 151 M6
Moules La CBE/LIN CB1 ... 24 D5
Moulsham Cha CHLM/GWD CM2 ... 17 K8
Moulsham Dr CHLM/GWD CM2 ... 17 K8
Moulsham Hall La RCHLM CM3 ... 181 M8
Moulsham St CHLM/GWD CM2 ... 16 F8
Moulsham Thrift
  CHLM/GWD CM2 ... 288 D5
Moultrie Wy UPMR RM14 ... 372 F7
Mountain Ash Cl COLN CO4 ... 11 K2
  SBF/HAD SS7 ... 381 J5
Mountain's Farm Rd
  GTDUN CM6 ... 178 D7
Mountains Cl MAL CM9 ... 240 C5
Mount Av HARH RM3 ... 353 K7
  HOC/HUL SS5 ... 362 E5
  RAYL SS6 ... 361 K8
  RBRW/HUT CM13 ... 355 J1
  WOS/PRIT SS0 ... 400 B3
Mountbatten Cl SUD CO10 ... 4 F1
Mountbatten Ct BKHH IG9 ... 348 E3
Mountbatten Dr COLS CO2 ... 163 J8
  SBN/FI SS3 ... 402 F2
Mountbatten Rd BRTR CM7 ... 155 J7
  SUD CO10 ... 4 F1
Mountbatten Wy
  CHLM/WR CM1 ... 264 E4
Mount Bovers La HOC/HUL SS5 ... 362 F8
Mount Cl RAYL SS6 ... 380 D1
  WICKE SS11 ... 359 M3
Mount Crs BRW CM14 ... 354 E5
  HOC/HUL SS5 ... 362 F5
  SBF/HAD SS7 ... 379 M7
Mountdale Gdns LOS SS9 ... 382 A7
Mount Dr IPSE IP3 ... 60 A2
  STSD CM24 ... 146 F7
Mountfield Cl SLH/COR SS17 ... 394 F8
Mountfields PIT SS13 ... 378 C7
Mountfitchet Rd STSD CM24 ... 146 F6
Mount Hl HSTD CO9 ... 128 E2
Mounthill Av CHLM/GWD CM2 ... 17 M1
Mount Lodge Cha MAL CM9 ... 240 E5
Mountnessing SBF/HAD SS7 ... 398 E1
Mountnessing La BRWN CM15 ... 332 F2
Mountnessing Rd BCAYW CM12 ... 334 E4
  BCAYW CM12 ... 357 C1
  BRWN CM15 ... 309 H8
Mountney Cl ING CM4 ... 334 A2
Mount Pleasant HSTD CO9 ... 128 F2
  MAL CM9 ... 293 C1
Mount Pleasant Av
  RBRW/HUT CM13 ... 333 M8
Mount Pleasant Est MAL CM9 ... 240 F5
Mount Pleasant Rd CHIC IG7 ... 349 K5
  CRW RM5 ... 351 L7
  RCHLM CM3 ... 339 L4
  SAFWS CB11 ... 65 L3
Mount Ri HSTD CO9 ... 128 E2
Mount Rd BCTR RM8 ... 370 A1
  BRTR CM7 ... 155 H8
  EPP CM16 ... 304 F4
  HVHL CB9 ... 28 C4
  RCOLW CO6 ... 186 C1
  SBF/HAD SS7 ... 380 A7
  WICKE SS11 ... 359 M3
The Mount BCAYE CM11 ... 335 M8
  BRW CM14 ... 354 D4
  COLW CO3 ... 162 A5
  HARH RM3 ... 352 D4
  MAL CM9 ... 272 F2
  SLH/COR SS17 ... 395 G8
Mount Vw BCAYE CM11 ... 357 M1
Mountview Cl VGE SS16 ... 377 M8
Mount View Crs BOC CM0 ... 296 D2
Mountview Rd COS CO15 ... 13 K1
Mount Wy WICKE SS11 ... 359 M3
Moverons La RCOLE CO7 ... 220 C1
Mowbray Rd HLW CM20 ... 256 A1
Mowbrays Cl CRW RM5 ... 351 J6
Mowbrays Rd CRW RM5 ... 370 D2
Mowbrey Gdns LOU IG10 ... 327 K3
Mowlands LAIN SS15 ... 18 A6
Moxom Av BAR EN8 ... 300 F2
Moy Rd COLS CO2 ... 191 H2
Muckingford Rd TIL RM18 ... 419 C1
Mucking Hall Rd SBN/FI SS3 ... 384 D3
Mucking Wharf Rd
  SLH/COR SS17 ... 409 K4
Muggeridge Rd DAGE RM10 ... 388 C3
Muirway SBF/HAD SS7 ... 379 J4
Mulberry Av COLS CO2 ... 163 H7
Mulberry Cl BROX EN10 ... 277 G4
  GPK RM2 ... 371 J4
Mulberry Ct BSF CM23 ... 174 B6
Mulberry Dr PUR RM19 ... 415 G1
Mulberry Gdns WIT CM8 ... 212 C7
Mulberry Gn HLWE CM17 ... 227 L7
Mulberry Hl BRWN CM15 ... 355 G1
Mulberry Rd CVI SS8 ... 397 K8
Mulberry Wy CHLM/WR CM1 ... 264 E6
Mulberry Gdns VGE SS16 ... 376 C6
Mullein Cl GRAYS RM17 ... 417 L3
Mullins Rd BRTR CM7 ... 155 C5
The Mullions BCAYW CM12 ... 335 G8
Multon Lea CHLM/WR CM1 ... 265 H4
Mumford Cl RCOLW CO6 ... 133 L7
Mumford Rd IP IP1 ... 36 F3
  COLW CO3 ... 133 L8
Mumfords La FOS CO13 ... 198 B4
Mundells CHESW EN7 ... 276 B7
Mundon Rd BRTR CM7 ... 183 L3
  MAL CM9 ... 293 H2
Mungo Park Rd RAIN RM13 ... 389 J6
Munnings Cl HVHL CB9 ... 27 L2
  IPSE IP3 ... 59 J3
Munnings Dr COLW CO3 ... 162 B6
Munnings Rd COLW CO3 ... 161 M4
Munro Ct WICKW SS12 ... 359 M6
Munro Rd WIT CM8 ... 212 A6
Munsons Aly BOC CM0 ... 320 E7
Munsterburg Rd CVI SS8 ... 398 E6
Murchison Cl CHLM/WR CM1 ... 263 M6
Murchison Rd HOD EN11 ... 253 J3

Murfitt Wy UPMR RM14 ... 390 B3
Murray Cl BRTR CM7 ... 154 F5
Murray Rd IPSE IP3 ... 38 B8
Murrell Lock CHLM/GWD CM2 ... 265 H7
Murrels La HOC/HUL SS5 ... 362 B4
Murrills Rd IPSE IP3 ... 60 A2
Murthering La ABR/ST RM4 ... 330 B6
Murton Slade HVHL CB9 ... 28 B3
Murtwell Dr CHIC IG7 ... 349 K7
Muscade Cl K/T/MI CO5 ... 214 E5
Museum St COL CO1 ... 10 D7
  IP IP1 ... 2 E4
  SAFWN CB10 ... 65 L1
Musgrave Cl CHESW EN7 ... 276 A7
  HAR CO12 ... 143 C2
Muskalls Cl CHESW EN7 ... 276 B7
Musk Cl COLW CO3 ... 161 L4
Musket Gv LOS SS9 ... 381 J4
Muskham Rd HLW CM20 ... 227 H8
Mutlow Hill London Rd
  SAFWS CB11 ... 65 G6
Mutton Rw CHONG CM5 ... 306 D2
Mychett Cl RCOS CO16 ... 223 J5
Mygrove Cl RAIN RM13 ... 389 L8
Mygrove Gdns RAIN RM13 ... 389 L8
Mygrove Rd RAIN RM13 ... 389 L8
Myland Hall Cha COLN CO4 ... 135 K8
Mylne Cl BAR EN8 ... 276 D7
Myln Meadow ING CM4 ... 336 A1
Mynchens LAIN SS15 ... 18 A6
Myneer Pk RCOLW CO6 ... 186 C1
Myrtle Cl COLS CO2 ... 163 J6
  SOCK/AV RM15 ... 405 K7
Myrtle Rd BRW CM14 ... 354 D5
  HARH RM3 ... 352 D7
  IPSE IP3 ... 3 K8

N

Nabbott Rd CHLM/WR CM1 ... 16 A3
Nacton Crs IPSE IP3 ... 59 J1
Nacton Rd FX IP11 ... 9 G7
  IPSE IP3 ... 3 M8
  KIR/NAC IP10 ... 59 M4
Naffenton Ri LOU IG10 ... 326 E7
Nag's Head La UPMR RM14 ... 372 D1
Nags Head Rd PEND EN3 ... 324 D6
Nails La BSF CM23 ... 174 A4
Nalla Gdns CHLM/WR CM1 ... 264 D5
Namur Rd CVI SS8 ... 398 D6
Nancy Smith Cl COLS CO2 ... 163 G6
Nansen Av RCFD SS4 ... 363 L5
Nansen Rd COS CO15 ... 224 E5
  IPSE IP3 ... 59 J1
Napier Av COS CO15 ... 249 L5
  SOS SS1 ... 20 D6
Napier Cl HCH RM12 ... 371 J8
Napier Crs WICKW SS12 ... 359 M6
Napier Gdns SBF/HAD SS7 ... 380 D5
Napier Rd COLS CO2 ... 163 C5
  PEND EN3 ... 324 F7
  RAYL SS6 ... 362 A8
Narboro Ct ROM RM1 ... 371 H6
Nare Rd SOCK/AV RM15 ... 405 K5
Narvik Cl MAL CM9 ... 292 F3
Naseby Rd DAGE RM10 ... 388 C1
Nash Cl COLW CO3 ... 162 C6
  MGTR CO11 ... 108 C2
Nash Dr CHLM/WR CM1 ... 235 H8
Nassau Rd RCOS CO16 ... 222 C7
Nathan Cl UPMR RM14 ... 372 F8
Nathan Ct COLS CO2 ... 191 J3
Nathan's La CHLM/WR CM1 ... 286 E6
Nats La SAFWS CB11 ... 64 F1
Naunton Wy HCH RM12 ... 389 L2
Navarre Gdns CRW RM5 ... 351 J7
Navarre St IP IP1 ... 2 F3
Navestock Cl RAYL SS6 ... 361 M8
Navestock Gdns SOS SS1 ... 402 A2
Navestock Side BRW CM14 ... 331 K4
Navestock Ter WFD IG8 ... 348 D8
Navigation Rd CHLM/GWD CM2 ... 17 K3
Nayland Cl WICKW SS12 ... 359 M4
Nayland Dr RCOS CO16 ... 223 J7
Nayland Rd BURES CO8 ... 102 A3
  COLN CO4 ... 134 E6
  FX IP11 ... 8 D3
  HVHL CB9 ... 27 M5
  RCOLW CO6 ... 104 A4
  RCOLW CO6 ... 133 L5
Nayling Rd BRTR CM7 ... 182 D1
Naylor Gv PEND EN3 ... 324 E7
Nazeingbury Cl WAB EN9 ... 277 L2
Nazeing Common WAB EN9 ... 278 D3
The Nazeing BSDN SS14 ... 377 M5
Naze Park Rd WOTN CO14 ... 199 L1
Neale Rd HSTD CO9 ... 128 F2
Neale St IP IP1 ... 2 F1
Neasden Av COS CO15 ... 12 C1
Neath Dr CHTY IP2 ... 58 B2
Neave Crs HARH RM3 ... 371 K1
Neil Armstrong Wy LOS SS9 ... 382 B4
Nelmes Cl EMPK RM11 ... 372 A5
Nelmes Crs EMPK RM11 ... 372 A5
Nelmes Rd EMPK RM11 ... 371 M7
Nelmes Wy EMPK RM11 ... 371 M4
Nelson Cl BRW CM14 ... 354 E6
  RAYL SS6 ... 362 A7
  ROMW/RG RM7 ... 370 C2
Nelson Dr LOS SS9 ... 400 A1
Nelson Gdns BRTR CM7 ... 155 K7
  RAYL SS6 ... 362 A7
Nelson Gv CHLM/WR CM1 ... 16 D2
Nelson Ms SOS SS1 ... 21 G7
Nelson Pl RCHLM CM3 ... 339 M5
Nelson Rd BSDN SS14 ... 19 M6
  BSF CM23 ... 174 B6
  CDH/CHF RM16 ... 408 E4
  COLW CO3 ... 161 M4
  COS CO15 ... 12 E1
  HAR CO12 ... 7 H7
  IPNE IP4 ... 38 B4
  PEND EN3 ... 324 D8
  RAIN RM13 ... 389 G8
  RAYL SS6 ... 362 A8

  RCFD SS4 ... 363 L5
  SOCK/AV RM15 ... 391 K8
  SUD CO10 ... 5 H2
  WOS/PRIT SS0 ... 400 B1
Nelson St RCOLE CO7 ... 220 F6
  SOS SS1 ... 21 G7
Nelwyn Av EMPK RM11 ... 372 A5
Ness Rd RIPS/CAP IP9 ... 112 B2
  SBN/FI SS3 ... 402 F6
Ness Wk WIT CM8 ... 238 E1
Nesta Rd WFD IG8 ... 348 A7
Nestuda Wy WOS/PRIT SS0 ... 382 C5
Nethan Dr SOCK/AV RM15 ... 405 K5
Nether Ct HSTD CO9 ... 129 H2
Netherfield SBF/HAD SS7 ... 380 B7
Nethergate St SUD CO10 ... 31 J5
Netherhall Rd
  HLWW/ROY CM19 ... 254 A5
Nether Hl HSTD CO9 ... 52 E8
Nether Mayne LAIN SS15 ... 18 E7
  VGE SS16 ... 377 J8
Netherpark Dr GPK RM2 ... 371 G2
Nether Priors BSDN SS14 ... 19 H6
Nether Rd SUD CO10 ... 32 D1
Netley Cl CHTY IP2 ... 58 A3
Nettesbury Farm
  HLWS CM18 ... 256 A4
Netteswell Orch HLW CM20 ... 15 L2
Netteswell Rd HLW CM20 ... 255 M1
Nevada Rd CVI SS8 ... 398 D6
Nevell Rd CDH/CHF RM16 ... 408 C8
Nevendon Ms PIT SS13 ... 378 B1
Nevendon Rd PIT SS13 ... 378 B1
  WICKW SS12 ... 359 K5
Nevern Cl RAYL SS6 ... 381 G3
Nevern Rd RAYL SS6 ... 380 F3
Neville Rd SAFWN CB10 ... 65 H1
Neville Shaw BSDN SS14 ... 19 G4
Nevill Wy LOU IG10 ... 326 F8
Nevis Cl ROM RM1 ... 351 M7
Newark Cl CHTY IP2 ... 58 A2
New Av VGE SS16 ... 376 B7
New Barn La RBSF CM22 ... 201 K2
Newbarn Rd RCOLW CO6 ... 159 J2
New Barns Wy CHIC IG7 ... 349 J4
Newbery Rd ERITH DA8 ... 414 A4
Newbiggen St GTDUN CM6 ... 92 A8
New Bowers Wy
  CHLM/WR CM1 ... 265 G5
Newbridge Hl RCOLW CO6 ... 161 L1
Newbridge Rd K/T/MI CO5 ... 215 G6
Newbury Av PEND EN3 ... 325 G1
Newbury Cl BSF CM23 ... 173 M3
  HARH RM3 ... 352 D7
Newbury Gdns HARH RM3 ... 352 E7
  UPMR RM14 ... 390 A2
Newbury Rd HARH RM3 ... 352 D6
  IPNE IP4 ... 38 C6
Newbury Wk HARH RM3 ... 352 E6
Newby Dr IPNE IP4 ... 39 G6
New Captains Rd K/T/MI CO5 ... 245 J5
New Cardinal St IP IP1 ... 2 D6
Newcastle Av BARK/HLT IG6 ... 350 B7
  COLW CO3 ... 161 M7
New Century Rd LAIN SS15 ... 376 C5
New Church Rd RCOLW CO6 ... 133 L7
Newcomen Rd COLN CO4 ... 135 J5
Newcourt Rd CHLM/GWD CM2 ... 17 M1
Newcroft SAFWN CB10 ... 65 M2
New Cut BURES CO8 ... 101 M3
  COLS CO2 ... 190 A6
  RCOLE CO7 ... 194 F3
New Cut West CHTY IP2 ... 3 G7
New Dukes Wy
  CHLM/GWD CM2 ... 265 G7
Newell Av SBN/FI SS3 ... 403 H3
New England Cl RCHLM CM3 ... 315 G2
New England Crs SBN/FI SS3 ... 403 K1
New Farm Dr ABR/ST RM4 ... 328 D5
New Farm Rd COLW CO3 ... 161 L5
New Ford Rd BAR EN8 ... 301 G6
New Forest La CHIC IG7 ... 349 H7
Newgate St WOTN CO14 ... 199 K3
Newhall RCFD SS4 ... 363 K5
New Hall Dr HARH RM3 ... 371 M1
New Hall La MAL CM9 ... 293 M8
Newhouse Av WICKW SS12 ... 359 G4
New House La SAFWN CB10 ... 45 H8
Newhouse Rd RCOLW CO6 ... 130 A7
Newington Av SOSN SS2 ... 401 M1
Newington Cl SOSN SS2 ... 402 A1
Newington Gdns COS CO15 ... 224 A3
New Kiln Rd COLW CO3 ... 162 D4
Newland Av BRTR CM7 ... 124 C2
Newland Dr EN EN1 ... 324 C3
Newland Pl WIT CM8 ... 239 H2
Newlands Cl BCAYW CM12 ... 335 J7
  RBRW/HUT CM13 ... 355 L3
Newlands Dr WIT CM8 ... 239 G1
Newlands End LAIN SS15 ... 376 C3
Newlands La RCOLW CO6 ... 104 C2
Newlands Rd BCAYW CM12 ... 335 J7
  CVI SS8 ... 398 E6
  WFD IG8 ... 348 A3
  WICKW SS12 ... 359 L7
Newland St WIT CM8 ... 239 H1
New La K/T/MI CO5 ... 187 G6
New Lodge Cha RCHLM CM3 ... 360 D5
New London Rd
  CHLM/GWD CM2 ... 16 E8
Newman Cl EMPK RM11 ... 371 M5
Newmans Dr RBRW/HUT CM13 ... 355 K1
Newmans La LOU IG10 ... 327 H5
Newman's Rd SUD CO10 ... 4 D5
Newmarket Rd SAFWN CB10 ... 22 D8
Newmarket Wy HCH RM12 ... 389 M3
New Meadgate Ter
  CHLM/GWD CM2 ... 17 L2
Newmill La MGTR CO11 ... 109 M4
New Moor Cl BOC CM0 ... 320 F7
New Moor Crs BOC CM0 ... 320 F7
New Nabbotts Wy
  CHLM/WR CM1 ... 264 F4
Newnham Cl BRTR CM7 ... 182 F1
  LOU IG10 ... 326 E8
Newnham Ct CHTY IP2 ... 57 M2

Newnham Gn MAL CM9 .... 268 F8
Newnham Pl CDH/CHF RM16 ... 418 B1
New Nth Rd BARK/HLT IG6 ... 349 L8
New Park Rd HOC/HUL SS5 ... 363 H3
  SBF/HAD SS7 .... 379 K6
New Park St COL CO1 .... 163 J5
Newpasture La GTDUN CM6 ... 152 D7
Newpiece LOU IG10 .... 327 J5
New Pier St WOTN CO14 ..... 199 K3
New Place Av UPMR RM14 .... 390 E1
New Pond La SAFWN CB10 .... 65 K1
Newport Av RCHLM CM3 ...... 317 J6
Newport Cl CHLM/GWD CM2 ... 289 C5
  HAR CO12 .... 143 H2
  PEND EN3 .... 324 F1
Newport Dr COS CO15 .... 224 B4
Newports SBW CM21 .... 227 K2
Newport Wy FOS CO13 .... 199 H5
Newpots Cl K/T/MI CO5 ..... 217 L6
Newpots La K/T/MI CO5 ..... 217 M6
Newquay Cl KESG IP5 .... 39 C5
New Queens Rd SUD CO10 .... 4 C3
New River Cl HOD EN11 ..... 253 J4
New Rd ABR/ST RM4 .... 328 E8
  BCAYW CM12 .... 357 H8
  BOC CM0 .... 344 D6
  BROX EN10 .... 253 C7
  BRTR CM7 .... 182 A2
  BRW CM14 .... 354 E3
  CBE/LIN CB1 .... 26 C5
  CHLM/GWD CM2 .... 289 H5
  CHLM/WR CM1 .... 264 C2
  CVI SS8 .... 397 M8
  DAGW RM9 .... 388 B7
  FX IP11 .... 84 D6
  GRAYS RM17 .... 417 H3
  HLWE CM17 .... 227 L1
  HSTD CO9 .... 127 M6
  ING CM4 .... 310 D7
  K/T/MI CO5 .... 213 J1
  K/T/MI CO5 .... 214 E6
  LOS SS9 .... 399 L3
  MAL CM9 .... 272 E7
  MGTR CO11 .... 108 E8
  RAIN RM13 .... 404 B1
  RAIN RM13 .... 405 C5
  RBSF CM22 .... 147 J1
  RCHLM CM3 .... 210 D8
  RCHLM CM3 .... 238 B8
  RCOLW CO6 .... 160 C1
  RIPS/CAP IP9 .... 81 H6
  SAFWN CB10 .... 22 C5
  SAFWN CB10 .... 65 M2
  SBF/HAD SS7 .... 380 E8
  SBN/FI SS3 .... 385 K8
  STDN SC11 .... 172 B4
  SUD CO10 .... 34 C4
Newry Av FX IP11 .... 9 J1
Newson St IP IP1 .... 2 D2
Newstead Rd SBN/FI SS3 .... 385 J7
New St BRTR CM7 .... 183 G1
  CHLM/WR CM1 .... 17 H3
  GTDUN CM6 .... 178 E3
  HSTD CO9 .... 128 E2
  MAL CM9 .... 293 G1
  RCOLE CO7 .... 221 G6
  SBW CM21 .... 200 F8
  SUD CO10 .... 4 C5
New Street Flds GTDUN CM6 . 178 E3
Newsum Gdns RAYL SS6 ...... 361 H8
Newteswell Dr WAB EN9 ..... 301 L4
New Thorpe Av RCOS CO16 ... 197 H1
Newton Cl BRTR CM7 .... 183 G3
  HOD EN11 .... 253 J1
Newton Cft SUD CO10 .... 5 G6
Newton Dr SBW CM21 .... 227 L2
Newton Gn RCHLM CM3 .... 178 C2
Newton Hall Gdns RCFD SS4 . 363 L5
Newton Park Rd SBF/HAD SS7 380 C4
Newton Rd HAR CO12 .... 6 C9
  IPSE IP3 .... 38 B7
  SUD CO10 .... 4 F6
  TIL RM18 .... 418 B6
Newtons Cl RAIN RM13 ...... 388 F6
Newton's Ct GRH DA9 .... 415 L8
Newton St IPNE IP4 .... 3 H4
Newton Wy RCOS CO16 .... 222 B6
Newtown Rd BSF CM23 .... 174 A5
  RCOS CO16 .... 197 C1
New Waverley Rd LAIN SS15 . 376 F2
New Wy CHTY IP2 .... 37 G5
  RCOS CO16 .... 221 C8
New Way La HLWE CM17 ...... 257 L2
New Writtle St CHLM/GWD CM2 16 E5
New Zealand Wy RAIN RM13 .. 404 A1
Niagara Cl BAR EN8 .... 300 E1
Nicholas Cl CHLM/WR CM1 ... 287 J3
  SOCK/AV RM15 .... 406 D1
Nicholas Ct WIT CM8 .... 239 C1
Nicholas Ms RAYL SS6 ......
  FX IP11 .... 8 C1
Nicholl Rd EPP CM16 .... 304 A3
  LAIN SS15 .... 376 C4
Nicholls Fld HLWS CM18 .... 256 C4
Nichols Cl MGTR CO11 ...... 108 C8
Nicholson Crs SBF/HAD SS7 . 380 C8
Nicholson Gv WICKW SS12 ... 359 M6
Nicholson Pl RCHLM CM3 .... 314 C4
Nicholson Rd SBF/HAD SS7 .. 380 C8
Nickleby Rd CHLM/WR CM1 ... 263 L4
Nickolsons Gv COL CO1 ..... 10 F9
Nicola Ms RAYL SS6 ....
Nicola Cl BARK/HLT IG6 .... 349 J7
Nightingale Av UPMR RM14 .. 373 C8
Nightingale Cl COLN CO4 ... 164 B3
  COS CO15 .... 13 H1
  HAR CO12 .... 143 C5
  RAYL SS6 .... 361 J8
  SOSN SS2 .... 382 F5
  WIT CM8 .... 238 F3
Nightingale Hl COLN CO4 ... 106 A5
Nightingale Ms SAFWN CB10 . 66 K1
Nightingale Pl COLW CO3 ... 161 K7
  IPSE IP3 .... 59 H3
Nightingale Rd CVI SS8 .... 398 D6
  IPSE IP3 .... 59 H3
Nightingales VGE SS16 ..... 376 A6
Nightingales Sq IPSE IP3 .. 59 H3

Nightingale Wy COS CO15 ... 13 H1
Nineacres BRTR CM7 .... 183 H2
Nine Acres CHTY IP2 .... 36 E5
Nine Ashes Rd BRWN CM15 ... 308 C5
  ING CM4 .... 308 D1
Ninefields WAB EN9 .... 302 A5
Nipsells Cha RCHLM CM3 .... 319 C1
Nita Rd BRW CM14 .... 354 D6
Niven Cl WICKW SS12 .... 359 M6
Noakes Av CHLM/GWD CM2 .... 288 C6
Noak Hill Cl BCAYW CM12 ... 357 K8
Noak Hill Rd BCAYW CM12 ... 357 J6
  HARH RM3 .... 352 E4
Nobel Sq PIT SS13 .... 378 D1
Nobles Green Cl LOS SS9 ... 381 M4
Nobles Green Rd LOS SS9 ... 381 M4
The Nobles BSF CM23 .... 173 L5
Nonsuch Cl CHIG IG7 .... 349 J7
Nonsuch Meadow SUD CO10 ... 4 C8
The Nook RCOLE CO7 .... 192 D2
Norbury Rd RCOLW CO6 ...... 160 A7
Norbury Rd IPNE IP4 .... 38 C4
Nordland Rd CVI SS8 .... 398 E7
Nordmann Pl SOCK/AV RM15 .. 406 E2
Noredale SBN/FI SS3 .... 402 E5
Nore Rd LOS SS9 .... 381 K3
Norfolk Av COS CO15 .... 224 F5
  K/T/MI CO5 .... 245 L4
  LOS SS9 .... 382 A8
Norfolk Cl CVI SS8 .... 398 B6
  LAIN SS15 .... 376 B5
  MAL CM9 .... 292 F2
Norfolk Crs COLN CO4 ...... 11 H3
Norfolk Dr CHLM/WR CM1 .... 264 B4
Norfolk Gdns BRTR CM7 ..... 155 J7
  IPNE IP4 .... 3 H3
  MAL CM9 .... 292 F2
  PEND EN3 .... 324 C8
  ROMW/RG RM7 .... 370 D6
  UPMR RM14 .... 390 B2
Norfolk Wy BSF CM23 .... 174 A6
  CVI SS8 .... 398 A6
Norman Av BSF CM23 .... 173 L5
Norman Cl FX IP11 .... 85 L7
  RCOLW CO6 .... 159 M8
  RCOS CO16 .... 222 B7
  ROMW/RG RM7 .... 370 C2
  WAB EN9 .... 301 L5
Norman Crs IPSE IP3 .... 59 H1
  RAYL SS6 .... 361 M6
  RBRW/HUT CM13 .... 355 H4
Normandie Wy BURES CO8 .... 101 M3
Normandy Av BOC CM0 .... 344 D6
  COLS CO2 .... 163 H8
Norman Hi RCHLM CM3 .... 237 J1
Normanhurst
  RBRW/HUT CM13 .... 333 K8
Norman Rd COS CO15 .... 224 E5
  EMPK RM11 .... 371 H7
  MGTR CO11 .... 108 E7
Normansfield GTDUN CM6 .... 178 F4
Normans Rd CVI SS8 .... 398 E7
Norman's Wy STSD SC24 ..... 146 F4
Norman Wy COLW CO3 .... 162 C6
  RCOS CO16 .... 221 G8
Norris Cl BRTR CM7 .... 155 K6
  BSF CM23 .... 174 D4
Norris Gv BROX EN10 .... 252 F8
Norris La HOD EN11 .... 253 H4
Norris Ri HOD EN11 .... 253 C4
Norris Rd HOD EN11 .... 253 H5
Norris Wy DART DA1 .... 414 A7
Norsey Cl BCAYE CM11 ...... 335 J8
Norsey Dr BCAYE CM11 ...... 335 K8
Norsey Rd BCAYE CM11 ...... 335 J8
Norsey View Dr BCAYW CM12 . 335 J5
Northallerton Wy HARH RM3 . 352 E6
Northampton Gv VGE SS16 ... 376 A7
Northampton Meadow
  BRTR CM7 .... 124 B1
Northampton Rd PEND EN3 ... 324 F6
North Av CHLM/WR CM1 ...... 264 A6
  CVI SS8 .... 398 A7
  HVHL CB9 .... 27 M3
  SOSN SS2 .... 21 J3
North Barn BROX EN10 ...... 277 J2
North Benfleet Hall Rd
  WICKW SS12 .... 379 G2
Northbourne Rd COS CO15 ... 13 H5
Northbrooks HLWW/ROY CM19 . 15 J7
North Cl CHIG IG7 .... 350 B6
  DAGE RM10 .... 388 B7
  IPNE IP4 .... 37 M3
North Colne VGE SS16 ...... 19 L9
North Crs HVHL CB9 .... 48 C3
  SOSN SS2 .... 382 D6
  WICKW SS12 .... 359 L4
North Crockerford VGE SS16 377 M6
Northcroft SUD CO10 .... 4 C6
North Dell CHLM/WR CM1 .... 264 E4
Northdene CHIG IG7 .... 349 L6
North Dr CHLM/GWD CM2 ..... 289 C4
  GPK RM2 .... 371 K3
  RBRW/HUT CM13 .... 334 C8
  RCHLM CM3 .... 319 G1
North End BKHH IG9 .... 348 D1
  BOC CM0 .... 320 E6
Northend RBRW/HUT CM13 .... 354 D6
Northend Rd ERITH DA8 ..... 414 A5
North End Rd HSTD CO9 ..... 51 M8
  SAFWN CB10 .... 22 C3
Northern Av RUD SS7 .... 379 K6
Northern Rd SUD CO10 ...... 5 K6
Northfalls Rd CVI SS8 ..... 399 C8
North Farm LOU IG10 .... 326 D8
Northfield BRTR CM7 .... 94 C8
Northfield Cl BCAYE CM11 .. 357 K1
Northfield Crs SBN/FI SS3 . 385 H7
Northfield Gdns COLN CO4 .. 135 H7
Northfield Rd BAR EN8 ..... 300 F4
  DAGW RM9 .... 388 A7
  PEND EN3 .... 324 C7
  SAFWS CB11 .... 65 M3
  SBW CM21 .... 200 F7
Northfields GRAYS RM17 .... 417 K1
North Ga HLW CM20 .... 15 K3

Northgate End BSF CM23 .... 174 A3
Northgate St COL CO1 ...... 10 B7
  IPNE IP4 .... 2 F4
North Gv HLWS CM18 .... 256 B4
North Gunnels BSDN SS14 ... 19 C6
North Hall Rd RBSF CM22 ... 119 J4
North Hl COL CO1 .... 10 B7
  RCHLM CM3 .... 266 E5
  SLH/COR SS17 .... 394 A7
North Hill Dr HARH RM3 .... 352 E5
North Hill Gdns IPNE IP4 .. 3 K3
North Hill Rd IPNE IP4 .... 3 K3
Northlands Ap VGE SS16 .... 394 D2
Northlands Cl SLH/COR SS17 394 F6
Northlands Farm Cha
  SLH/COR SS17 .... 394 F4
North La RCOLW CO6 .... 160 C7
North Lawn IPNE IP4 .... 38 C3
Northolme Cl
  CDH/CHF RM16 .... 407 K8
Northolt Av DAGE RM10 ..... 174 C2
Northolt Wy HCH RM12 ...... 389 K4
North Pl HLW CM20 .... 227 H6
  WAB EN9 .... 301 J5
North Ri SUD CO10 .... 5 H9
North Rd ABR/ST RM4 .... 351 M3
  BAR EN8 .... 300 F5
  BCAYE CM11 .... 358 E6
  BRW CM14 .... 354 D2
  COS CO15 .... 223 M5
  HOD EN11 .... 253 H4
  HSTD CO9 .... 73 G1
  MAL CM9 .... 272 D1
  PUR RM19 .... 415 K1
  RBSF CM22 .... 176 D3
  RCOLE CO7 .... 221 G4
  SOCK/AV RM15 .... 391 L6
  SUD CO10 .... 55 J6
  WOS/PRIT SS0 .... 20 D4
North Road Av BRW CM14 .... 354 D2
North Service Rd BRW CM14 . 354 D3
North Shoebury Rd SBN/FI SS3 402 E2
North Station Rd COL CO1 .. 10 B5
North St BOC CM0 .... 297 M6
  BOC CM0 .... 320 E7
  BSF CM23 .... 174 A3
  EMPK RM11 .... 371 L7
  GTDUN CM6 .... 178 E2
  HVHL CB9 .... 48 C4
  LOS SS9 .... 399 M3
  MAL CM9 .... 242 E6
  MAL CM9 .... 293 J1
  MGTR CO11 .... 108 E7
  RCFD SS4 .... 383 C1
  ROMW/RG RM7 .... 370 E4
  SBN/FI SS3 .... 385 J7
  SUD CO10 .... 4 D5
  WAB EN9 .... 277 M2
  WOTN CO14 .... 199 K3
  WOTN CO14 .... 199 K2
North Street Pde SUD CO10 . 4 D6
North Ter BSF CM23 .... 174 A3
Northumberland Av
  EMPK RM11 .... 371 K5
  EN EN1 .... 324 C2
  LAIN SS15 .... 376 D6
  SOS SS1 .... 21 M8
Northumberland Cl
  CHLM/GWD CM2 .... 265 G7
Northumberland Crs SOS SS1 401 L4
Northumberland Rd
  SLH/COR SS17 .... 409 G7
North View Av TIL RM18 .... 418 B5
Northview Dr WOS/PRIT SS0 . 20 A7
Northville Dr WOS/PRIT SS0 382 D7
North Wall RCOS CO16 ...... 221 G8
North Weald Cl WICKE SS11 . 360 C5
Northwick Rd CVI SS8 ...... 397 H7
Northwood CDH/CHF RM16 .... 408 C7
Northwood Av HCH RM12 ..... 389 H3
Northwood Cl CHESW EN7 .... 276 A7
Norton Av CVI SS8 .... 398 F8
Norton Cl SLH/COR SS17 .... 395 G7
Norton Heath Rd CHONG CM5 . 284 E3
Norton La CHONG CM5 .... 284 B5
Norton Rd CHLM/WR CM1 ..... 16 E2
  DAGE RM10 .... 388 E5
  HVHL CB9 .... 27 M5
  ING CM4 .... 310 C7
Norway Crs HAR CO12 .... 6 B8
Norwich Av SOSN SS2 .... 383 K8
Norwich Cl COL CO1 .... 10 F6
  RCOS CO16 .... 223 L5
  SOSN SS2 .... 21 L1
Norwich Crs RAYL SS6 ...... 361 K6
Norwich Rd IP IP1 .... 2 B2
Norwood Av COS CO15 .... 13 M2
  ROMW/RG RM7 .... 370 E7
Norwood Dr SBF/HAD SS7 .... 397 M2
Norwood End BSDN SS14 ..... 19 M3
  CHONG CM5 .... 259 K4
Norwood Rd BAR EN8 .... 300 F2
Norwood Wy WOTN CO14 ...... 199 H4
Notcutts RCOLE CO7 .... 107 M2
Notley Rd HVHL CB9 .... 27 J2
Notley Gn BRTR CM7 .... 182 C6
Notley Rd BRTR CM7 .... 183 G1
Nottage Cl SLH/COR SS17 ... 395 G7
Nottidge Rd IPNE IP4 ...... 3 K4
Nottingham Rd COS CO15 .... 224 F5
Nottingham Wy VGE SS16 .... 376 A6
Nounsley Rd RCHLM CM3 ..... 267 J2
Nunnery St HSTD CO9 .... 73 L7
Nunns Cl RCOLW CO6 .... 186 B1
Nunn's Rd COL CO1 .... 10 B7
Nuns Meadow HSTD CO9 ...... 127 M3
Nuns Wk HSTD CO9 .... 73 G1
Nunsbury Dr BROX EN10 ..... 276 F5
Nun's Meadow HSTD CO9 ..... 127 M3
Nunty's La BRTR CM7 .... 157 G3
Nursery Cl COLW CO3 .... 161 K6
  PEND EN3 .... 324 E3
  RAYL SS6 .... 380 E2
  SOCK/AV RM15 .... 406 D2
  WFD IG8 .... 348 C6

Nursery Dr BRTR CM7 .... 155 H6
Nursery Flds SBW CM21 ..... 227 L1
Nursery Gdns LAIN SS15 .... 376 D3
  PEND EN3 .... 324 E3
Nursery La K/T/MI CO5 ..... 291 C5
Nursery Ri GTDUN CM6 ...... 178 E4
Nursery Rd BROX EN10 ...... 276 F5
  BRWN CM15 .... 308 D6
  BSF CM23 .... 174 A5
  CHLM/GWD CM2 .... 17 G7
  HOD EN11 .... 253 J2
  LOU IG10 .... 326 E6
  SLH/COR SS17 .... 394 E8
  SUD CO10 .... 55 J6
  WAB EN9 .... 277 L2
The Nursery ERITH DA8 ..... 414 A4
Nursery Wk FX IP11 .... 9 K1
Nutberry Av CDH/CHF RM16 .. 407 H7
Nutberry Cl CDH/CHF RM16 .. 407 H7
Nutbrowne Rd DAGW RM9 ..... 388 A7
Nutcombe Crs RCFD SS4 ..... 363 L7
Nuthatch Cl BCAYE CM11 .... 357 K3
Nyssa Cl WFD IG8 .... 349 G7
Nyth Cl UPMR RM14 .... 372 E6

O

Oakapple Cl COLS CO2 ...... 190 E2
Oak Av BCAYE CM11 .... 358 D7
  COS CO15 .... 250 B1
  UPMR RM14 .... 390 C2
  WICKE SS11 .... 360 D4
Oakbank RBRW/HUT CM13 ..... 333 M7
Oak Bungalows BRTR CM7 .... 154 F8
Oak Cl FX IP11 .... 9 G1
  MAL CM9 .... 293 J3
  RCOLW CO6 .... 133 M8
  RCOS CO16 .... 197 H2
  WAB EN9 .... 301 L6
Oakdene BAR EN8 .... 300 F2
Oak Dene Cl ROM RM1 .... 371 J6
Oakdene Rd PIT SS13 .... 378 C3
Oak Dr SBW CM21 .... 227 K3
Oak End HLWS CM18 .... 256 A5
Oaken Grange Dr SOSN SS2 .. 382 F4
Oak Fall WIT CM8 .... 212 B6
Oak Farm Rd MAL CM9 .... 291 L1
Oakfield Cl SBF/HAD SS7 ... 379 K8
Oakfield La RCHLM CM3 ..... 237 H1
Oak Fld HOC/HUL SS5 .... 363 H3
  RIPW IP8 .... 57 G5
  SBF/HAD SS7 .... 379 K8
Oak Gld EPP CM16 .... 304 E1
Oak Gln EMPK RM11 .... 371 M3
Oakham Cl VGE SS16 .... 376 A6
Oak Hl BRTR CM7 .... 126 B3
Oak Hill La CHTY IP2 ...... 2 C9
Oak Hill Rd ABR/ST RM4 .... 351 L1
Oakhill Rd PUR RM19 .... 415 J2
Oak Holm COLS CO2 .... 163 H8
Oakhurst Cl WICKW SS12 .... 359 K6
Oakhurst Dr WICKW SS12 .... 359 J5
Oakhurst Gdns CHING E4 .... 348 A2
Oakhurst Rd PEND EN3 ...... 300 E8
  RAYL SS6 .... 381 G3
  SOSN SS2 .... 21 G1
Oakland Gdns
  RBRW/HUT CM13 .... 333 K7
Oakland Pl BKHH IG9 .... 348 B3
Oakland Rd HAR CO12 .... 7 H8
Oaklands Av COLW CO3 ...... 161 M6
  ED N9 .... 324 C8
  ROM RM1 .... 370 F3
Oaklands Cl BRTR CM7 ...... 182 E3
  BSF CM23 .... 174 C1
Oaklands Crs CHLM/GWD CM2 . 17 G8
Oaklands Dr BSF CM23 ...... 174 C2
  HLWE CM17 .... 256 D4
  SOCK/AV RM15 .... 406 D3
Oaklands Gv BROX EN10 ..... 276 F4
Oaklands Ms RCFD SS4 ...... 363 K7
Oaklands Pk BSF CM23 ...... 174 C1
Oaklands Wy RCHLM CM3 ..... 290 F1
Oak La BCAYE CM11 .... 358 D6
  WFD IG8 .... 348 A5
Oaklea Av CHLM/GWD CM2 .... 264 F7
Oakleigh Av HOC/HUL SS5 ... 361 M1
  SOS SS1 .... 401 L3
Oakleigh Park Dr LOS SS9 .. 399 M2
Oakleigh Rd COS CO15 ...... 224 A3
Oakleighs SBF/HAD SS7 ..... 379 K7
Oakley Av RAYL SS6 .... 361 G8
Oakley Cl WTHK RM20 .... 416 D3
Oakley Dr BCAYW CM12 ...... 335 G6
  HARH RM3 .... 353 H6
Oakley Rd BRTR CM7 .... 155 G4
  HAR CO12 .... 142 E2
  MGTR CO11 .... 141 G6
Oak Lodge Av CHIG IG7 ..... 349 L6
Oak Lodge Tye CHLM/WR CM1 . 265 H5
Oakmead Rd RCOS CO16 ...... 221 H8
Oakmoor Wy CHIG IG7 .... 349 M6
Oak Piece EPP CM16 .... 281 K5
Oak Rdg HAR CO12 .... 142 C4
Oak Ri BKHH IG9 .... 348 E4
Oak Rd BCAYE CM11 .... 336 E6
  BCAYE CM11 .... 358 D7
  CVI SS8 .... 398 D8
  EPP CM16 .... 304 A2
  ERITH DA8 .... 414 B5
  GRAYS RM17 .... 417 K3
  HARH RM3 .... 372 A1
  HSTD CO9 .... 99 H3
  HSTD CO9 .... 100 A2
  HSTD CO9 .... 128 E3
  K/T/MI CO5 .... 214 D4
  MAL CM9 .... 269 J5
  RCFD SS4 .... 382 E1
  RCOLW CO6 .... 159 J1
  SUD CO10 .... 5 K9
  WIT CM8 .... 212 D4
Oak Rd North SBF/HAD SS7 .. 398 F1
Oak Rd South SBF/HAD SS7 .. 398 F1
Oakroyd Av GTDUN CM6 ...... 178 F3
Oaks Av CRW RM5 .... 370 D2

Oaks Dr COLW CO3 .... 162 E4
Oaksmere Gdns CHTY IP2 .... 58 B1
Oaks Pl COLN CO4 .... 134 F8
Oakstead Cl IPNE IP4 ...... 3 M3
The Oaks BCAYE CM11 .... 357 K5
  FOS CO13 .... 199 G5
Oak St BSF CM23 .... 174 A5
  ROMW/RG RM7 .... 370 F5
Oaktree Cl BSF CM23 .... 174 A4
Oak Tree Cl LOU IG10 ...... 327 K3
Oaktree Cl RBRW/HUT CM13 .. 355 C4
Oak Tree Rd RCOLE CO7 ..... 193 J3
Oakview HAR CO12 .... 143 C2
Oakview Cl CHESW EN7 ...... 276 C8
Oak Wk HOC/HUL SS5 .... 362 F4
  HSTD CO9 .... 97 L1
  SBF/HAD SS7 .... 379 J5
Oakway CDH/CHF RM16 .... 407 J6
Oakwood Av COS CO15 .... 224 F5
  K/T/MI CO5 .... 245 L4
  LOS SS9 .... 381 M7
  RBRW/HUT CM13 .... 333 M8
Oakwood Cha EMPK RM11 ..... 372 A7
Oakwood Cl FOS CO13 .... 198 F5
  SBF/HAD SS7 .... 379 J6
  WFD IG8 .... 348 F7
Oakwood Ct RCHLM CM3 ...... 319 H8
Oakwood Dr BCAYW CM12 ..... 335 K6
  K/T/MI CO5 .... 245 L4
Oakwood Gdns K/T/MI CO5 ... 245 L4
Oakwood Gv PIT SS13 .... 378 C5
Oakwood Hl LOU IG10 .... 327 H8
Oakwood Hill Industrial Est
  LOU IG10 .... 327 J7
Oakwood Rd RAYL SS6 .... 361 K7
  SLH/COR SS17 .... 395 J7
Oasthouse Ct SAFWN CB10 ... 65 L2
Oast Wy RCFD SS4 .... 383 G1
Oates Rd CRW RM5 .... 351 J6
Oatfield Cl COLW CO3 ...... 161 L5
Oatlands RCOLE CO7 .... 165 G5
Oatlands Rd PEND EN3 ...... 324 D3
Oban Cl WICKE SS11 .... 360 C6
Oban Rd SOSN SS2 .... 21 L4
Oban St IP IP1 .... 2 C2
Oberon Cl COLN CO4 .... 164 A4
Obrey Wy BSF CM23 .... 173 M8
Observer Wy K/T/MI CO5 .... 186 C7
Ockelford Av CHLM/WR CM1 .. 264 A6
Ockendon Rd UPMR RM14 ..... 390 E5
Ockendon Wy WOTN CO14 ..... 199 H3
Octavia Dr WIT CM8 .... 238 F3
Oddcroft RCOLW CO6 .... 130 A2
Odessa Rd CVI SS8 .... 398 D8
Office La MAL CM9 .... 241 H6
Ogard Rd HOD EN11 .... 253 K3
Ogilvie Ct WICKW SS12 ..... 359 M6
Oglethorpe Rd DAGE RM10 ... 388 B2
Okehampton Sq HARH RM3 .... 352 D7
Old Barn La RCHLM CM3 ..... 338 A2
Old Barn Rd BURES CO8 ..... 102 A5
Old Barns La ING CM4 ...... 285 J5
Old Bell Cl STSD CM24 ..... 146 E5
Old Bell La RCHLM CM3 ..... 338 C2
Oldbury Av CHLM/GWD CM2 ... 289 G4
Old Burylodge La STSD CM24 147 L1
Oldbury Rd EN EN1 .... 324 B4
Old Cattle Market IPNE IP4 2 F5
Old Church Rd VGE SS16 .... 394 A2
Old Church La
  SUD CO10 .... 54 A8
Oldchurch Ri ROMW/RG RM7 .. 370 F2
Old Church Rd PIT SS13 .... 379 G6
  RBRW/HUT CM13 .... 334 A4
  RCHLM CM3 .... 314 C6
Oldchurch Rd ROMW/RG RM7 .. 370 F6
Old Coach Rd COL CO1 ...... 11 H7
Old Ct CHLM/WR CM1 .... 17 L1
Old Court Rd CHLM/WR CM1 .. 17 L1
Old Crown La BRW CM14 ..... 331 L4
Oldfield Rd RIPW IP8 ...... 57 J2
Old Forge Rd COLS CO2 ..... 190 A6
  EN EN1 .... 324 A2
  RCHLM CM3 .... 265 M3
Old Foundry Rd IPNE IP4 ... 3 G4
Old Hall La MAL CM9 .... 243 K7
  RIPS/CAP IP9 .... 57 C8
  WOTN CO14 .... 171 M7
Old Hall Ri HLWE CM17 ..... 256 F5
Oldhall Rd RIPS/CAP IP9 ... 83 G7
Old Heath Rd BOC CM0 ...... 344 B1
  COLS CO2 .... 163 K7
Old Hwy HOD EN11 .... 253 J3
Old Hill Av VGE SS16 ...... 394 C3
Oldhouse Cft HLW CM20 ..... 255 M1
Old House La COLN CO4 ..... 135 G1
  HLWW/ROY CM19 .... 254 E6
Old House Rd RCOLW CO6 .... 134 A3
Old Ipswich Rd RCOLE CO7 .. 135 M4
Old Jenkins Cl SLH/COR SS17 409 J2
Old Kirton Rd FX IP11 ..... 84 B3
Old Leigh Rd LOS SS9 ...... 400 B2
Old London Rd MAL CM9 ..... 291 L3
  RIPS/CAP IP9 .... 78 A4
  WICKE SS11 .... 360 E5
The Old Maltings BSF CM23 . 174 B4
Old Md LOS SS9 .... 382 B4
Old Mead Rd RBSF CM22 ..... 119 K7
Old Mill La K/T/MI CO5 .... 186 E4
  RBSF CM22 .... 201 J5
Old Mill Rd COLN CO4 ...... 105 K6
  SAFWS CB11 .... 65 K1
Old Nazeing Rd BROX EN10 .. 277 H1
  WAB EN9 .... 277 K2
Old Oaks WAB EN9 .... 301 M4
Old Orch HLWS CM18 .... 15 L9
Old Parsonage Wy FOS CO13 . 199 G6
Old Pier St WOTN CO14 ..... 199 K3
Old Rectory Rd CHONG CM5 .. 306 C5
Old River La BSF CM23 ..... 174 A4
Old Rd ABR/ST RM4 .... 330 E4
  BRTR CM7 .... 156 F6
  COS CO15 .... 12 E6
  FOS CO13 .... 199 G7
  HLWE CM17 .... 227 K5
  HSTD CO9 .... 75 L6

PEND EN3 324 D3
RCOLW CO6 186 E1
Old Rope Wk HVHL CB9 27 M4
Old Rose Gdns COLN CO4 134 E7 1
Old School Cl RCOS CO16 222 B7
Old School Ct RCHLM CM3 238 C8 3
Old School Fld CHLM/WR CM1 264 F7
Old School La RCOLE CO7 165 H5
Old School Meadow
SBN/FI SS3 384 F7
Old Ship La RCFD SS4 383 G1 2
Old Shire La WAB EN9 302 B6
Old Southend Rd
CHLM/GWD CM2 313 L2
SOS SS1 21 K7
Old Station Rd LOU IG10 326 F7
Old Street Hl RBSF CM22 202 D6
The Old St RIPS/CAP IP9 78 C2
Old Vicarage Cl CHLM/WR CM1 232 D1
Old Vicarage Rd HAR CO12 6 F9
Old Wy FOS CO13 199 G7
Old Wickford Rd RCHLM CM3 339 J3
Oldwyk VGE SS16 377 M7
Olive Av LOS SS9 399 H1
Olive Gv COLS CO2 190 E1
Oliver Cl WTHK RM20 416 A4
Oliver Pl WIT CM8 239 J1 5
Oliver Rd BRWN CM15 333 H7
RAIN RM13 389 G7
WTHK RM20 416 A5
Olivers Cl COS CO15 12 F4
SUD CO10 34 E4
Olivers Crs SBN/FI SS3 385 H7
Olivers Dr WIT CM8 239 H4
Olivers La COLS CO2 190 A4
Olivers Rd COS CO15 12 F4
Oliver Wy CHLM/WR CM1 264 A4
Olive St ROMW/RG RM7 370 E5
Olivewood Rd GTDUN CM6 178 E4 1
Olivia Dr LOS SS9 400 A1
Ollard's Gv LOU IG10 326 E6
Olympus Cl IP IP1 36 D1
Onehouse La IP IP1 37 J2
One Tree Hl SLH/COR SS17 395 G2
Ongar Cl RCOS CO16 223 J7
Ongark Rd CHLM/WR CM1 287 J2 2
Ongar Pl BRW CM14 354 E3
Ongar Rd ABR/ST RM4 328 D4
BRWN CM15 307 J5
CHLM/WR CM1 286 A4
CHONG CM5 283 J4
GTDUN CM6 178 E5
GTDUN CM6 260 E1
Ongar Wy RAIN RM13 388 F7
Onslow Crs COLS CO2 191 H2
Onslow Gdns CHONG CM5 283 H7
Opal Av IP IP1 36 E2
Ophir Rd RCOLE CO7 221 G6
Orange Gv CHIG IG7 349 K7
Orange Rd CVI SS8 398 E7
Orange St GTDUN CM6 122 B1 1
Orange Tree Cl
CHLM/GWD CM2 288 D5
Orange Tree Hl ROM RM1 351 L6
Orchard Av BCAYE CM11 358 E1
BCAYW CM12 335 K6
HOC/HUL SS5 362 F4
HSTD CO9 128 E2
RAIN RM13 404 D2
RAYL SS6 380 D3
RBRW/HUT CM13 355 G4
Orchard Cl CHLM/GWD CM2 288 D5
CHLM/WR CM1 287 J1
GTDUN CM6 92 B8
HAR CO12 141 K8
HAR CO12 142 B1
HOC/HUL SS5 363 G4 3
HSTD CO9 50 C5
HVHL CB9 28 A4
MAL CM9 272 F2
MAL CM9 293 G1
RBSF CM22 228 D3
RCHLM CM3 238 B7
RCOLE CO7 165 H5
RCOLW CO6 188 E1
RCOS CO16 12 A1
SAFWS CB11 65 L4
SAFWS CB11 89 G3
SBN/FI SS3 385 H7
SOCK/AV RM15 406 D2
Orchard Crs EN EN1 324 A3
Orchard Cft HLW CM20 256 B1
Orchard Dr BRTR CM7 183 H2
EPP CM16 303 M8
FOS CO13 198 B7
GRAYS RM17 407 H7
RCHLM CM3 319 H2
Orchard Gdns WAB EN9 301 J6
Orchard Ga CHTY IP2 36 D6
Orchard Gv KESG IP5 39 H4
LOS SS9 382 A5
Orchard La BRWN CM15 332 A7
WFD IG8 348 D5
Orchardleigh Av PEND EN3 324 D4
Orchard Md LOS SS9 381 M6
Orchard Piece ING CM4 309 G3
Orchard Pightle CBE/LIN CB1 24 C4
Orchard Rd BOC CM0 320 E7
BOC CM0 344 D7
BSF CM23 174 C2
COL CO1 10 A5
DAGE RM10 388 B7
K/T/MI CO5 186 D8
MAL CM9 293 C1
PEND EN3 324 D7
RCOLE CO7 193 J3
RIPW IP8 36 B1
ROMW/RG RM7 370 C2
SBF/HAD SS7 379 J5
SOCK/AV RM15 406 D3
Orchards WIT CM8 239 G2 1
Orchard Side LOS SS9 382 A5
Orchard Sq BROX EN10 277 G4 1
The Orchards EPP CM16 304 B4
SBW CM21 227 M1 1
Orchard St CHLM/GWD CM2 17 H5
IPNE IP4 3 H4
The Orchard GTDUN CM6 180 D6
WICKW SS12 359 J4
Orchard Wy CHIG IG7 350 B4
Orchid Av WIT CM8 211 M7
Orchid Cl CHTY IP2 36 F7
Orchid Pl RCHLM CM3 339 L3
Orchill Dr SBF/HAD SS7 380 F7
Orchis Gv GRAYS RM17 417 G1
Orchis Wy HARH RM3 353 G7
Ordnance Rd PEND EN3 324 E1
Oregon Rd KESG IP5 39 H5
Oreston Rd RAIN RM13 404 E1
Orford Crs CHLM/WR CM1 264 D6
Orford Rd FX IP11 9 G7
HVHL CB9 28 A5
Orford St IP IP1 2 C2
Oriel Cl SUD CO10 5 J9
Oriole Wy BSF CM23 173 K5
Orion Wy BRTR CM7 155 J7 5
Orkney Cl HVHL CB9 28 E4
Orkney Rd IPNE IP4 38 B2
Orlando Ct WOTN CO14 199 K3 3
Orlando Dr PIT SS13 378 D2 5
Ormesby Chine RCHLM CM3 339 L6
Ormonde Av RCFD SS4 363 M8 1
SBF/HAD SS7 399 H1
Ormonde Cl RCOLW CO6 133 M7
Ormonde Gdns LOS SS9 399 H1
Ormonde Ri BKHH IG9 348 D2
Ormonds Crs RCHLM CM3 315 J7
Ormsby Rd CVI SS8 412 E1
Orpen Cl RCOLW CO6 133 L7
Orpen's Hl COLS CO2 189 H5
Ormo Rd CVI SS8 399 G8
Orsett Av LOS SS9 381 K6
Orsett End BSDN SS14 19 K3
Orsett Heath Crs
CDH/CHF RM16 408 B8
Orsett Rd CDH/CHF RM16 408 E2
GRAYS RM17 417 J2
Orsett Ter WFD IG8 348 D8 1
Orton Cl ING CM4 311 H3
Orvis La RCOLE CO7 107 M2
Orwell Cl COLN CO4 163 M2
Orwell Ct WICKE SS11 360 C6
Orwell Pl IPNE IP4 3 G5
Orwell Ri RIPS/CAP IP9 82 A3
Orwell Rd COS CO15 13 G8
FX IP11 9 M2
HAR CO12 7 K7
IPSE IP3 38 B7
Orwell View Rd RIPS/CAP IP9 83 G8
Orwell Wy RCOS CO16 12 A1
Osbert Rd WIT CM8 238 F3
Osborne Cl COS CO15 224 B4
EMPK RM11 371 J6 3
Osborne Rd BAR EN8 276 F7 2
BKHH IG9 348 C2
BROX EN10 253 H7
BRWN CM15 332 C8
EMPK RM11 371 J6
IPSE IP3 38 B7 1
K/T/MI CO5 245 M5
PEND EN3 324 F4
PIT SS13 378 F3
VGE SS16 19 K7
WOS/PRIT SS0 20 C4
Osborne Sq DAGW RM9 388 A3
Osborne St COL CO1 10 D9
Osbourne Av HOC/HUL SS5 362 D5
Osea Rd MAL CM9 270 C8
Osea Wy CHLM/WR CM1 265 G6
Osprey Cl SBN/FI SS3 402 F2 7
Osprey Ms PEND EN3 324 C7
Osprey Rd HVHL CB9 28 D4
WAB EN9 302 B6
Ospreys COS CO15 224 A5
Osprey Wy CHLM/GWD CM2 288 B6 1
Osterberg Rd DART DA1 415 G8
Osterley Dr VGE SS16 376 A6 10
Osterley Pl RCHLM CM3 339 L6
Ostler Cl BSF CM23 173 K7 4
Ostler's Gn SAFWS CB11 63 J6
Othello Cl COLN CO4 164 A3
Otley Ct FX IP11 84 E8 2
Ottawa Gdns DAGE RM10 388 E6 1
Ottawa Rd TIL RM18 418 B6
Otten Rd SUD CO10 52 C2
Ottershaw Wy RCOS CO16 223 J5
Oudle La MHAD SG10 172 A8
Ouida Rd CVI SS8 398 E8
Oulton Cl HAR CO12 6 B9
Oulton Rd IPSE IP3 58 F1
Ousden Cl BAR EN8 300 F2
Ousden Dr BAR EN8 300 F2
Ouse Cha WIT CM8 238 E1 3
Outing Cl SOS SS1 21 L7
Outing's La BRWN CM15 308 C8
Outpart Eastward HAR CO12 7 L3 4
Outwood Common Rd
BCAYE CM11 357 K4
Outwood Farm Cl BCAYE CM11 357 M1
Outwood Farm Rd
BCAYE CM11 357 M3
Oval Gdns GRAYS RM17 407 K8
Oval Rd North DAGE RM10 388 C7
Oval Rd South DAGE RM10 388 C8
The Oval BROX EN10 276 F5
Overcliff Rd GRAYS RM17 417 L2
Overhall Hl RCOLW CO6 130 D1
Over Hall La SAFWN CB10 45 L1
Overlord Cl BROX EN10 252 F8 3
Overmead Dr RCHLM CM3 339 M3
Overshot Br RCHLM CM3 290 F7
Overton Cl SBF/HAD SS7 379 K5
Overton Dr SBF/HAD SS7 379 K5
Overton Rd SBF/HAD SS7 379 J4 5
Overton Wy SBF/HAD SS7 379 J5
Ovington Gdns BCAYW CM12 335 H6
Owen Cl CRW RM5 351 J7 1
Owen Gdns WFD IG8 348 F7
Owen Ward Cl COLS CO2 162 B8
Owlets Hall Cl HARH RM3 372 A3 1
Owl's Hl RCHLM CM3 210 C8
Owls Retreat COLN CO4 164 A3
Oxborrow Cl FOS CO13 198 B5 1
Oxcroft BSF CM23 174 A8
Oxendon Dr HOD EN11 253 H6
Oxenford Cl HAR CO12 143 G2 5
Oxford Av CDH/CHF RM16 418 B1
EMPK RM11 372 B4
Oxford Cl BAR EN8 300 D1
SUD CO10 5 H9
VGE SS16 376 A6 11
Oxford Ct BRW CM14 354 E5
CHLM/GWD CM2 264 F7 5
RCOLW CO6 130 C5
Oxford Crs COS CO15 12 F3
Oxford La HSTD CO9 97 K1
Oxford Meadow HSTD CO9 97 L1
Oxford Rd COLW CO3 162 E5
COS CO15 13 G4
CVI SS8 398 D7
FOS CO13 199 H6
HARH RM3 353 G7
HSTD CO9 128 E2 5
IPNE IP4 3 J5
KESG IP5 39 H4
MGTR CO11 108 E7
PEND EN3 324 C7
RCFD SS4 363 M7
SLH/COR SS17 393 M7
SLH/COR SS17 409 J3
WFD IG8 348 E6
Oxley Cl GPK RM2 371 K2 1
Oxley Gdns SLH/COR SS17 394 E7
Oxley Hl K/T/MI CO5 191 G7
MAL CM9 242 B2
Oxleys Rd WAB EN9 302 B5
The Oxleys HLWE CM17 227 L7
Oxlip Rd WIT CM8 211 M7
Oxlow La DAGE RM10 388 B3
DAGW RM9 388 A3
Oxney Md CHLM/WR CM1 287 G3
Oxney Vls GTDUN CM6 180 E4
Oxwich Cl SLH/COR SS17 395 H7
Oysterbed Rd FX IP11 114 A1
Oyster Pl CHLM/GWD CM2 265 G7
Oyster Tank Rd RCOLE CO7 220 F6
Ozier Ct SAFWS CB11 65 M4 4
Oziers RBSF CM22 147 K1
Ozonia Av WICKW SS12 359 K6
Ozonia Cl WICKW SS12 359 J6
Ozonia Wy WICKW SS12 359 K6

P

Paarl Rd CVI SS8 398 B7
Paceheath Cl CRW RM5 351 L7 3
Packard Av IPSE IP3 59 J1
Packard Pl RIPW IP8 36 C1
Packards La RCOLW CO6 132 F1
Packe Cl K/T/MI CO5 186 E7 2
Paddick Cl HOD EN11 253 G4
Paddock Cl BCAYE CM11 357 K4 6
CDH/CHF RM16 408 C3 1
HAR CO12 7 H7
LOS SS9 381 M4
Paddock Dr CHLM/WR CM1 264 F4
Paddock Md HLWS CM18 255 K8
The Paddocks ABR/ST RM4 330 A8
BURES CO8 101 M3
CDH/CHF RM16 408 C3 2
GTDUN CM6 204 F4
ING CM4 310 C8
MAL CM9 240 B7 1
RAYL SS6 381 G1
RCOLE CO7 195 G6 1
WIT CM8 239 H1
The Paddock BROX EN10 253 H8
BSF CM23 173 L8 2
ING CM4 335 M1
Paddock Wy RCOLE CO7 164 D8
Padgetts Wy HOC/HUL SS5 339 L8
Padham's Green Rd ING CM4 334 D3
Padstow Rd KESG IP5 39 H5
Pageant Cl TIL RM18 418 D5
Page Crs ERITH DA8 414 A4
Page Gdns KESG IP5 39 M3
Page Rd COS CO15 12 E5
PIT SS13 379 G4
Pages Cl BSF CM23 174 A6 1
Pages La MAL CM9 272 A3
Paget Ct RBSF CM22 147 K2
Paget Dr BCAYW CM12 335 H6
Paget Rd IP IP1 2 C1
K/T/MI CO5 192 A4
RCOLE CO7 192 D3 3
Pagette Wy GRAYS RM17 417 H2
Paglesfield RBRW/HUT CM13 333 K8 7
Paglesham Rd RCFD SS4 365 G5
Paignton Av CHLM/WR CM1 264 E6
Paignton Cl RAYL SS6 361 L6 2
Paines Brook Wy HARH RM3 353 G7
Painswick Av SLH/COR SS17 395 G6
Painters La PEND EN3 300 F7
Pakes Wy EPP CM16 327 M1
Palace Gdns BKHH IG9 348 E2
BSF CM23 173 M6 1
Palace Gv LAIN SS15 18 A1
Palatine Pk LAIN SS15 376 A5 2
Paley Gdns LOU IG10 327 J5
Palins Wy CDH/CHF RM16 407 H6
Palliser Dr RAIN RM13 404 B3
Pallister Rd COS CO15 13 G8
Pall Ml LOS SS9 399 M2
Palm Cl CHLM/GWD CM2 288 D5
WIT CM8 212 B6 7
Palmeira Av WOS/PRIT SS0 20 B8
Palmer Cl LAIN SS15 376 E5 1
Palmers SLH/COR SS17 395 G8 1
Palmer's Av GRAYS RM17 417 K2
Palmers Cl CBE/LIN CB1 24 C1
Palmers Cft CHLM/GWD CM2 289 H1 1
Palmers Dr GRAYS RM17 417 K1
Palmers Gv WAB EN9 278 A2
Palmers Hl EPP CM16 304 B1
Palmers La PEND EN3 324 D3
ROY SG8 40 D7
Palmerstone Rd CVI SS8 397 L8 1
RAIN RM13 389 K8 2
Palmerston Gdns WTHK RM20 416 E2
Palmerston Ldg
CHLM/GWD CM2 289 G4
Palmerston Rd BKHH IG9 348 D3
IPNE IP4 3 J4
RCOS CO16 197 H1
WOS/PRIT SS0 20 A7
WTHK RM20 416 E2
Palmers Wy BAR EN8 300 F1
Palmerswent Cl SUD CO10 34 E3
Palm Ms LAIN SS15 376 E2
Palm Rd ROMW/RG RM7 370 D5
Pamela Gdns BSF CM23 174 A8
Pampas Cl COLN CO4 135 H7
Panadown LAIN SS15 18 D6
Pancroft ABR/ST RM4 328 C5
Panfield La BRTR CM7 154 F7
Panfields LAIN SS15 376 B5
Pan La RCHLM CM3 314 B6
Pantile Av SOSN SS2 383 K8
Pantile Cl WIT CM8 239 H4
Pantile Hl BOC CM0 320 D7
Pantlings La K/T/MI CO5 186 B6
Panton Crs COLN CO4 163 M4
Panton Ms BRTR CM7 183 H3 11
Papenburg Rd CVI SS8 398 B5
Paper Mill Br RCHLM CM3 266 E5
Papillon Rd COLW CO3 162 E4 2
Paprills VGE SS16 18 B9
Parade Rd IPNE IP4 3 L2
The Parade WOTN CO14 199 L3 2
Paradise Cl CHESW EN7 276 C8
Paradise Rd CHLM/WR CM1 287 J3
WAB EN9 301 K6 5
Pardoe Pl IPNE IP4 38 F6
Pargat Dr LOS SS9 381 K4
Pargetters Hyam
HOC/HUL SS5 363 G5 3
Paringdon Rd
HLWW/ROY CM19 255 J7
Parish Cl HCH RM12 389 J1 3
Parish Wy LAIN SS15 376 D4
Parkanaur Av SOS SS1 402 C5
Park Av BSF CM23 174 A8
CHLM/WR CM1 16 C1
FX IP11 85 J8
HLWE CM17 256 D6
LOS SS9 381 M6
RBRW/HUT CM13 355 K2
UPMR RM14 372 F7
WFD IG8 348 C6
WTHK RM20 416 B3
Park Bvd COS CO15 224 F5
GPK RM2 371 G1
Park Cha RCOS CO16 222 D6
SBF/HAD SS7 398 F1
Park Cl EPP CM16 281 H7
SUD CO10 5 G4
WICKW SS12 359 K5 1
Park Ct HLW CM20 15 M2
Park Crs EMPK RM11 371 H7
WOS/PRIT SS0 20 E6
Parkdale RCHLM CM3 290 D4
Park Dr BRTR CM7 183 H3
DAGE RM10 388 D2
HSTD CO9 128 F2
ING CM4 310 D7
MAL CM9 293 J2
RBSF CM22 229 J1
RCOLE CO7 220 F4
ROM RM1 370 E4
UPMR RM14 390 D3
WICKW SS12 359 L5
Park End Rd ROM RM1 370 F4
Parker Av FX IP11 8 A3
TIL RM18 418 D5
Parker Rd CHLM/GWD CM2 17 J6
GRAYS RM17 417 G2
Parker's Farm Rd UPMR RM14 393 G6
Parker's Wy RCOLW CO6 104 B2
Parker Wy HSTD CO9 128 F3
Parkes Rd CHIG IG7 350 A6
Parkeston Rd FX IP11 8 F1
HAR CO12 6 B4
Park Farm Rd UPMR RM14 390 A4
Park Flds HLWW/ROY CM19 254 B3
Parkfields HSTD CO9 97 L2 2
SBF/HAD SS7 380 D7
Parkfield St K/T/MI CO5 192 A4
Park Gdns HOC/HUL SS5 363 G6
Park Gate Rd SLH/COR SS17 395 H3
WIT CM8 185 H8
Parkhall Rd BRTR CM7 126 E4
Park Hl CBE/LIN CB1 26 E1
HLWE CM17 227 J8
LOU IG10 326 E7
Parkhill Cl HCH RM12 389 K1
Parkhurst Dr RAYL SS6 361 K5
Parkhurst Rd PIT SS13 378 C6
Parkland Av ROM RM1 370 F2
UPMR RM14 390 C4
Parkland Cl HOD EN11 253 J2 3
Parkland Rd WFD IG8 348 C8
Parklands BCAYE CM11 335 J8 1
BRTR CM7 183 H3
CHIG IG7 349 K4
CVI SS8 398 B6 3
RCFD SS4 363 L7
RCOLW CO6 186 B1
WAB EN9 301 M4
Parklands Av RAYL SS6 380 F1
Parklands Dr CHLM/WR CM1 17 L1 2
Parkland Wy CHONG CM5 307 G2 3
Park La BAR EN8 300 E5
BCAYE CM11 336 D7
BROX EN10 252 F7
BSF CM23 174 A7
CBE/LIN CB1 26 F8
COLN CO4 105 M8
CVI SS8 399 G8
CHESW EN7 276 B7
EMPK RM11 371 H7
HLW CM20 15 M1
HSTD CO9 72 C4
HSTD CO9 128 A4
MAL CM9 215 J8
RAIN RM13 389 J5
RBRW/HUT CM13 355 L8
RCHLM CM3 207 G7
RCOLW CO6 130 C5
SAFWN CB10 65 L2
SAFWS CB11 86 B1
SOCK/AV RM15 405 L6
SOS SS1 21 M6
SUD CO10 76 A1
WOS/PRIT SS0 20 E7
Park Lane Cl RCOLW CO6 130 C5
Park Lane Paradise BROX EN10 276 B4
Park Md HLW CM20 15 H2
Parkmead LOU IG10 327 H7
Park Meadow BRWN CM15 332 E2
Parkmill Cl SLH/COR SS17 395 H7
Park North IP IP1 37 L3
Park Rd BAR EN8 300 E5 4
BOC CM0 344 C7
BRW CM14 354 C2
CHLM/WR CM1 17 G3
COLN CO4 164 B7
COLW CO3 162 D5
COS CO15 12 D7
GTDUN CM6 149 M7
HAR CO12 7 K6
HOD EN11 253 H5
HVHL CB9 27 L2
IP IP1 37 K3
LOS SS9 399 J2
MAL CM9 293 G2
PEND EN3 300 F8
RBSF CM22 147 L1
RCOLE CO7 108 C1
RCOLE CO7 137 G7
RCOLE CO7 166 D3
RCOLE CO7 192 C3
RCOLW CO6 104 C4
SAFWN CB10 22 F6
SBF/HAD SS7 380 A5
SLH/COR SS17 395 H8
SLH/COR SS17 409 J2
STSD CM24 146 F5
SUD CO10 5 G4
UPMR RM14 390 B3 2
WIT CM8 185 H8
WOS/PRIT SS0 20 E5
Park Side BCAYE CM11 357 K1 11
BKHH IG9 348 C3
GTDUN CM6 151 L5
PIT SS13 378 B4
WOS/PRIT SS0 400 B2
Parkside BAR EN8 300 F6
CDH/CHF RM16 407 L8
Parkside Av IPNE IP4 3 G1
ROM RM1 370 E2
TIL RM18 418 C6
Park Sq East COS CO15 250 A3
Park Sq West COS CO15 250 A2
Parkstone Av EMPK RM11 371 M6
SBF/HAD SS7 380 C7
WICKW SS12 359 G3
Parkstone Dr SOSN SS2 382 F8
Park St GTDUN CM6 122 B2
WOS/PRIT SS0 20 E6
Park Ter WOS/PRIT SS0 20 E6
Park Vale Cl HSTD CO9 73 M7
Park Vw HOD EN11 253 H6
SOCK/AV RM15 405 L6
Park View Crs CHLM/GWD CM2 289 G6
Park View Dr LOS SS9 381 J6
Park View Gdns GRAYS RM17 417 J2 3
Park View Rd IP IP1 37 H2
Park Wy BRWN CM15 355 G2
COS CO15 250 E2
Parkway CBE/LIN CB1 26 D5
CDH/CHF RM16 408 B3
CHLM/GWD CM2 17 H4
CHLM/WR CM1 16 F1
GPK RM2 371 G2
HLWW/ROY CM19 14 B4
RAIN RM13 404 B2
RAYL SS6 380 F3
SBW CM21 227 M2
SLH/COR SS17 395 K6
WFD IG8 348 D6 6
Parkway Cl LOS SS9 382 A4
The Parkway CVI SS8 413 J1
Parkwood Av RCOLE CO7 192 C2
Parkwood Cl HOD EN11 252 F7
Parkwood Dr SUD CO10 4 C1
Park Wood La MAL CM9 241 H8
Parliament Rd IPNE IP4 38 C6
Parmenter Dr SUD CO10 55 K6
Parnall Rd HLWS CM18 255 L7
Parndon Mill La HLW CM20 226 C8
Parndon Wood Rd
HLWW/ROY CM19 255 K8
Parnell Cl COLS CO2 191 H2
Parnham Pl IPNE IP4 39 G6
Parr Cl BRTR CM7 155 L7
Parr Dr COLW CO3 161 M7
Parrington Wy MGTR CO11 108 B8
Parrotts Fld HOD EN11 253 J4
Parry Cl SLH/COR SS17 394 E8
Parry Dr RCOS CO16 12 A2
Parsloe Rd EPP CM16 279 H1
Parsonage Cha MAL CM9 317 L3
Parsonage Cl CHLM/WR CM1 264 B2 2
FX IP11 8 F2
Parsonage Farm La
SAFWN CB10 69 J7
Parsonage Fld BRWN CM15 332 E1
Parsonage Gv BURES CO8 101 M3 2
Parsonage La BSF CM23 174 C3
GTDUN CM6 179 L8
ING CM4 311 H4
LAIN SS15 376 D5
RCHLM CM3 235 H1 1
RCHLM CM3 290 E1
RCOS CO16 167 L3
SAFWS CB11 87 J8
STDN SG11 144 A5
STSD CM24 147 G7
Parsonage Leys HLW CM20 256 A3
Parsonage Rd RAIN RM13 389 K8
RBSF CM22 176 C3
WTHK RM20 416 D3
Parsonage St HSTD CO9 129 G2
Parsonage Wy CBE/LIN CB1 24 E1
Parson's Fld RCOLE CO7 107 H5
Parson's Heath COLN CO4 163 M1
Parson's Hl COLW CO3 162 B5
Parsons La COL CO1 163 K5

Parsons Lawn SBN/FI SS3 ... 402 E2
Parsons Rd SBF/HAD SS7 ... 379 L4
Parsons Yd MGTR CO11 ... 108 E7
Partridge Av CHLM/WR CM1 ... 264 A5
Partridge Cl HAR CO12 ... 141 L7
Partridge Dr HLWS CM18 ... 255 M5
Partridge Dr DAGW RM9 ... 132 E6
  HLWS CM18 ... 15 M9
Parvills WAB EN9 ... 301 L4
Paschal Wy CHLM/GWD CM2 ... 288 F3
Pasfield WAB EN9 ... 301 L5
Paske Av HVHL CB9 ... 28 A4
Paslowes VGE SS16 ... 378 A7
Passingham Av CHLM CM11 ... 357 K5
Passingham Cl BCAYE CM11 ... 357 K4
Pasteur Dr HARH RM3 ... 371 L2
Paston Cl RCHLM CM3 ... 339 M2
Pasture High RCHLM CM3 ... 266 E8
Pasture Loates STSD CM24 ... 146 E3
Pasture Rd DAGW RM9 ... 388 A4
The Pastures IPNE IP4 ... 39 C6
Paternoster Cl WAB EN9 ... 302 A4
Paternoster Hl WAB EN9 ... 302 A4
Paternoster Rw ABR/ST RM4 ... 352 D2
  WOTN CO14 ... 199 K3
Pathfields Rd COS CO15 ... 12 D4
The Path RCOLE CO7 ... 194 E3
Pathways BSDN SS14 ... 377 M6
Patmore Cl BSF CM23 ... 173 K3
Patmore Flds RBSF CM22 ... 118 F5
Patmore Rd COLN CO4 ... 11 M5
  WAB EN9 ... 301 M3
Patmore Wy CRW RM5 ... 351 J6
Patricia Dr EMPK RM11 ... 371 M8
Patricia Gdns BCAYE CM11 ... 357 L4
  BSF CM23 ... 173 M6
Patten Cl RCOLW CO6 ... 159 M8
Patterdale SBF/HAD SS7 ... 379 J4
Pattern Bush Cl MGTR CO11 ... 108 E3
Patteson Rd IPSE IP3 ... 3 J8
Pattison Cl WIT CM8 ... 239 H3
Pattiswick Cnr BSDN SS14 ... 377 M4
Pattiswick Sq BSDN SS14 ... 377 M4
Pattocks BSDN SS14 ... 19 M6
Pattocks La RCOLW CO6 ... 159 K1
Pattrick's La HAR CO12 ... 7 H7
Pauline Cl COS CO15 ... 224 C5
Pauline Gdns BCAYW CM12 ... 335 C7
Pauline St CHTY IP2 ... 2 F9
Pauls Crs RCOLW CO7 ... 165 G5
Pauls La HOD EN11 ... 253 H5
Paul Spendlove Ct
  COLN CO4 ... 163 M2
Paul's Rd CHTY IP2 ... 37 G6
  LAIN SS15 ... 376 D3
Pavet Cl DAGE RM10 ... 388 C5
Pavilion Cl SOSN SS2 ... 401 M2
Pavilion Dr LOS SS9 ... 400 A1
The Pavilions EPP CM16 ... 281 K5
Pavillion Pl BCAYW CM12 ... 335 G7
Pavitt Meadow
  CHLM/GWD CM2 ... 312 D1
Pawle Cl CHLM/GWD CM2 ... 288 F3
Paxfords LAIN SS15 ... 376 A5
Paxman Av COLS CO2 ... 162 B8
Paxton Rd COS CO15 ... 224 C3
Paycocke Cl BSDN SS14 ... 378 A1
Paycocke Wy RCOLW CO6 ... 158 B8
Paycock Rd HLWW/ROY CM19 ... 14 F9
Payne Pl RCHLM CM3 ... 314 C5
Payne's La RCOLE CO7 ... 138 D8
  WAB EN9 ... 277 K4
Paynters Md VGE SS16 ... 377 M8
Peace Cl COLW CO3 ... 161 L4
Peach Av HOC/HUL SS5 ... 362 F4
Peacock Cl BRTR CM7 ... 183 G2
  EMPK RM11 ... 371 M4
Peacocks HLWW/ROY CM19 ... 14 D9
Peacocks Cl SUD CO10 ... 32 D1
Peacocks Rd SUD CO10 ... 32 C1
Peake Av FOS CO13 ... 198 B5
Peakes Cl K/T/MI CO5 ... 214 C7
Peakes La CHESW EN7 ... 276 A7
Peakes Wy CHESW EN7 ... 276 A7
Pea La UPMR RM14 ... 391 H5
Peal Rd SAFWS CB11 ... 66 A4
Pearce Mnr CHLM/GWD CM2 ... 16 D8
Pearce Rd IPSE IP3 ... 38 B6
Pearceswood Rd ERITH DA8 ... 414 A5
Pearl Rd IP IP1 ... 36 D3
Pearmain Cl WICKE SS11 ... 359 L4
Pearmain Wy COLW CO3 ... 161 K7
Pearse Wy IPSE IP3 ... 59 M2
Pearson Rd IPNE IP4 ... 28 F6
Pearsons SLH/COR SS17 ... 395 G8
Pearsons Av RAYL SS6 ... 361 J7
Pearsons Wy RIPW IP8 ... 57 G2
Peartree Cl BRTR CM7 ... 183 H2
  BRWN CM15 ... 332 E2
  MAL CM9 ... 270 F5
  SOCK/AV RM15 ... 391 K8
  SOSN SS2 ... 383 K8
Peartree Gdns ROMW/RG RM7 ... 370 C2
Peartree Hl BURES CO8 ... 102 B7
Peartree La BRWN CM15 ... 332 D1
  RCHLM CM3 ... 291 C8
  UPMR RM14 ... 393 G2
Pear Tree Md HLWS CM18 ... 256 B5
Peartree Rd COLW CO6 ... 161 L7
Peartrees RBRW/HUT CM13 ... 355 K7
Pear Trees SBF/HAD SS7 ... 380 A7
Peartree Wy RCOS CO16 ... 223 K1
Pease Cl HCH RM12 ... 389 C8
Pease Pl RCHLM CM3 ... 314 C5
Peaslands SAFWS CB11 ... 65 M3
Pebmarsh Cl COLS CO2 ... 191 H3
Pebmarsh Dr WICKW SS12 ... 359 M5
Pebmarsh Rd BURES CO8 ... 100 F2
  RCOLW CO6 ... 130 A1
Peck's Hl WMBF SS14 ... 55 K6
Pedder's Cl COLW CO3 ... 162 A8
Pedlars Cl RCHLM CM3 ... 291 H5
Pedlars End CHONG CM5 ... 282 C1
Pedlars Pth RCHLM CM3 ... 291 H5

Peel Av SBN/FI SS3 ... 403 H4
Peel Crs BRTR CM7 ... 154 F8
Peel Rd CHLM/GWD CM2 ... 264 F7
Peel St IP IP1 ... 2 E3
Peerage Wy EMPK RM11 ... 371 M7
Peerswood Rd COLS CO2 ... 190 E1
Peewit Hl FX IP11 ... 8 F5
Peewit Rd CHTY IP2 ... 36 D8
Pegasus Wy BRTR CM7 ... 154 F6
  COLN CO4 ... 11 K3
Pegelm Gdns EMPK RM11 ... 372 A4
Peggotty Cl CHLM/WR CM1 ... 264 A5
Peggy's Wk SAFWS CB11 ... 42 F8
Peg Millar's La RCHLM CM3 ... 210 D5
Pegrams Rd HLWS CM18 ... 255 K6
Pelham Cl HAR CO12 ... 143 G1
Pelham Pl SLH/COR SS17 ... 394 F7
Pelham Rd SAFWS CB11 ... 87 J7
Pelican Cl CHTY IP2 ... 36 F8
Pelly Av WIT CM8 ... 239 H3
Pelly Ct EPP CM16 ... 304 A3
Pemberton Av GPK RM2 ... 371 J3
  ING CM4 ... 310 C7
Pemberton Fld RCFD SS4 ... 341 J7
Pembrey Wy HCH RM12 ... 389 K5
Pembridge La BROX EN10 ... 276 A1
Pembroke Av EN EN1 ... 324 C3
  MAL CM9 ... 293 C2
  SLH/COR SS17 ... 395 H7
Pembroke Cl BCAYW CM12 ... 335 H6
  BROX EN10 ... 276 F4
  CHTY IP2 ... 37 J8
  COLS CO2 ... 163 K8
  EMPK RM11 ... 372 B4
Pembroke Gdns COS CO15 ... 224 F5
  DAGE RM10 ... 388 C2
Pembroke La CBE/LIN CB1 ... 24 F1
Pembroke Ms PIT SS13 ... 378 D3
Pembroke Pl CHLM/WR CM1 ... 264 B4
  SUD CO10 ... 54 E1
Pembury Rd WOS/PRIT SS0 ... 400 D4
Pendar Av BSDN SS14 ... 378 B2
Pendle Dr BSDN SS14 ... 378 A2
Pendlestone SBF/HAD SS7 ... 380 D7
Pendleton Rd CHTY IP2 ... 57 L2
Pendower RAYL SS6 ... 380 C5
Penerley Rd RAIN RM13 ... 404 C3
Penfold Rd COS CO15 ... 12 F8
  FX IP11 ... 9 M1
Pengelly Cl CHESW EN7 ... 300 C2
Penhurst Av SOSN SS2 ... 20 F1
Penhurst Dr RCHLM CM3 ... 339 L6
Penhurst Rd BARK/HLT IG6 ... 349 J8
Penlan Hall La RCOLW CO6 ... 132 C5
Penlow Rd HLWS CM18 ... 255 K6
Penn Cl CDH/CHF RM16 ... 408 C2
  RIPS/CAP IP9 ... 78 C1
Penn Gdns CRW RM5 ... 351 H8
Pennial Rd CVI SS8 ... 398 B7
Pennine Rd CHLM/WR CM1 ... 263 L5
Pennington Cl CRW RM5 ... 351 H7
Pennington La STSD CM24 ... 146 E3
Penningtons BSF CM23 ... 173 K6
Penn Ms BRTR CM7 ... 183 H1
Pennsylvania La K/T/MI CO5 ... 214 C6
Penny Cl RAIN RM13 ... 404 C3
Penny Flds BRW CM14 ... 354 D5
Penny La IPSE IP3 ... 60 A2
Pennymead HLW CM20 ... 256 B5
Penny Meadow RIPS/CAP IP9 ... 78 B2
Pennyroyal Crs WIT CM8 ... 211 M7
Pennyroyal Gdns CHTY IP2 ... 36 F7
Penny Royal Rd RCHLM CM3 ... 290 E5
Pennystone Rd SAFWS CB11 ... 65 M3
Penrice Cl COLN CO4 ... 163 M5
Penrith Crs RAIN RM13 ... 389 H4
Penrith Rd BARK/HLT IG6 ... 350 A7
  HARH RM3 ... 353 H7
Penrose Md CHLM/WR CM1 ... 287 J3
Penryn Rd KESG IP5 ... 39 G4
Penshurst Av HLWE CM17 ... 227 J8
Penshurst Pl BRTR CM7 ... 182 C5
Penshurst Rd IPSE IP3 ... 38 E7
Penson's La CHONG CM5 ... 282 B5
Penticton Rd BRTR CM7 ... 182 E1
Pentire Cl UPMR RM14 ... 372 F6
Pentland Av CHLM/WR CM1 ... 264 B5
  SBN/FI SS3 ... 402 D5
Pentlow Dr SUD CO10 ... 32 F2
Pentlow Hawke Cl HVHL CB9 ... 28 C4
Pentlow Hl SUD CO10 ... 33 H3
Pentlow Wy BKHH IG9 ... 348 F1
Penton Dr BAR EN8 ... 300 E1
Pentrich Av EN EN1 ... 324 B2
Penzance Cl CHLM/WR CM1 ... 264 F6
  COS CO15 ... 250 D3
Penzance Gdns HARH RM3 ... 353 H7
  KESG IP5 ... 39 H5
Peppercorn Cl COLN CO4 ... 10 C2
Peppercorn Wy CHTY IP2 ... 2 F9
Pepper's Rd RCOLW CO6 ... 134 F2
Pepples La SAFWN CB10 ... 91 H2
Pepys Cl TIL RM18 ... 418 D7
Pepys St HAR CO12 ... 7 K4
Percival Rd EMPK RM11 ... 371 K6
  EN EN1 ... 324 A6
  FOS CO13 ... 198 E2
  WOTN CO14 ... 199 L1
Percy Cottis Rd RCFD SS4 ... 363 M8
Percy Gdns PEND EN3 ... 324 E7
Percy Rd LOS SS9 ... 399 L1
  ROMW/RG RM7 ... 370 D3
Percy St GRAYS RM17 ... 417 K3
Peregrine Cl BSF CM23 ... 173 L5
  COS CO15 ... 224 A5
  SBN/FI SS3 ... 402 F2
  VGE SS16 ... 19 H9
Peregrine Ct COLN CO4 ... 164 A3
Peregrine Dr CHLM/GWD CM2 ... 288 B6
  SBF/HAD SS7 ... 397 K1

Peregrine Gdns RAYL SS6 ... 361 J8
Peregrine Rd BARK/HLT IG6 ... 350 C5
Peregrin Rd WAB EN9 ... 302 B6
Perkins Wy IPSE IP3 ... 59 C2
Perram Ct BROX EN10 ... 276 F6
Perriclose CHLM/GWD CM2 ... 264 E4
Perrin Pl CHLM/GWD CM2 ... 276 B7
Perriors Cl CHESW EN7 ... 276 B7
Perry Cl RAIN RM13 ... 388 E3
Perryfield Rd HLWE CM17 ... 258 D1
Perry Gn BSDN SS14 ... 19 C3
Perry Hl CHLM/WR CM1 ... 17 L1
  WAB EN9 ... 278 A3
Perry La COLN CO4 ... 106 A7
Perry Rd HLWS CM18 ... 255 K6
  K/T/MI CO5 ... 214 C6
  SBF/HAD SS7 ... 379 J8
  WIT CM8 ... 239 J2
Perry Spring HLWE CM17 ... 256 D5
Perry St BCAYW CM12 ... 335 C8
Perry Wy SOCK/AV RM15 ... 405 K5
  WIT CM8 ... 239 J2
Persardi Ct COLS CO2 ... 191 H4
Pershore End COLW CO3 ... 161 M6
Perth Cl COLS CO2 ... 191 H7
Pertwee Cl RCOLE CO7 ... 220 F3
Pertwee Dr CHLM/GWD CM2 ... 289 C5
  RCHLM CM3 ... 339 K4
Pertwee Wy K/T/MI CO5 ... 218 C1
Pesthouse La HAR CO12 ... 141 K8
Peterborough Av UPMR RM14 ... 372 F8
Peterborough Wy BSDN SS14 ... 378 A3
Peter Bruff Av RCOS CO16 ... 127 M6
Peterfield's La HSTD CO9 ... 57 M1
Peterhouse Cl EPP CM16 ... 304 A3
Petersfield CHLM/WR CM1 ... 264 C5
Petersfield Av HARH RM3 ... 352 F7
Petersfield Rd HARH RM3 ... 353 H7
Peter's Gv RIPS/CAP IP9 ... 78 B2
Peter St ING CM4 ... 336 A2
Peto Av COLN CO4 ... 10 C2
Petre Cl ING CM4 ... 334 B1
  RBRW/HUT CM13 ... 374 D6
Petrel Wy CHLM/GWD CM2 ... 288 D5
Petresfield Wy
  RBRW/HUT CM13 ... 374 D6
Petrolea Cl COL CO1 ... 10 B3
Pettit Cl HCH RM12 ... 389 J1
Pettit La BRTR CM7 ... 184 B7
Pettits Bvd GPK RM2 ... 370 F2
Pettits La ROM RM1 ... 370 F2
  ROM RM1 ... 370 F3
Pettits La North ROM RM1 ... 370 E1
Pettit's Pl DAGE RM10 ... 388 A4
Pettit's Rd DAGE RM10 ... 388 A4
Pettley Gdns ROMW/RG RM7 ... 370 E5
Petts La SAFWN CB10 ... 43 M2
Pettys Cl BAR EN8 ... 300 E1
Petunia Crs CHLM/WR CM1 ... 265 C5
Petworth Cl BRTR CM7 ... 182 C4
  RCOLE CO7 ... 192 D3
Petworth Gdns SOSN SS2 ... 402 A1
Petworth Wy HCH RM12 ... 389 C3
Pevensey Dr COS CO15 ... 250 D3
Pevensey Gdns HOC/HUL SS5 ... 362 A3
Pevensey Wy PIT SS13 ... 378 C5
Peverel Av RCHLM CM3 ... 267 K2
Pewterers Av BSF CM23 ... 173 K7
Pharos La K/T/MI CO5 ... 245 K5
Pheasant Ri RIPW IP8 ... 57 C3
Pheasant Rd CHTY IP2 ... 36 F8
Phelips Rd EPP CM16 ... 255 H8
Philan Wy CRW RM5 ... 351 L7
Philbrick Crs West RAYL SS6 ... 361 J8
Philip Av FX IP11 ... 8 F4
  ROMW/RG RM7 ... 370 D4
Philip Cl BRWN CM15 ... 332 C8
  WOTN CO14 ... 199 H3
Philip Rd CHTY IP2 ... 238 F3
  WIT CM8 ... 238 F3
Philips Cl BRTR CM7 ... 182 A1
Philips Rd BRTR CM7 ... 182 A1
Phillida Rd HARH RM3 ... 372 B2
Phillip Rd RCOLE CO7 ... 192 C3
Phillips Cha BRTR CM7 ... 155 H6
Phillips Field Rd SUD CO10 ... 55 H6
Philmead Rd SBF/HAD SS7 ... 397 J1
Philpot End La GTDUN CM6 ... 178 C8
Philpott Av SOSN SS2 ... 401 L1
Phoenix Gv CHLM/GWD CM2 ... 16 D7
Phoenix Rd IPNE IP4 ... 38 B4
Phoenix Wy SBF/HAD SS7 ... 380 D4
Picasso Wy SBN/FI SS3 ... 403 H2
Piccotts La BRTR CM7 ... 153 H3
Pickers Wy COS CO15 ... 224 F4
Picketts CVI SS8 ... 397 L7
Picketts Av LOS SS9 ... 381 M7
Picketts Cl LOS SS9 ... 381 M7
Picketts Rd FX IP11 ... 85 K8
Pick Hl WAB EN9 ... 302 C4
Pickpocket La BRTR CM7 ... 182 E5
Pickwick Av CHLM/WR CM1 ... 263 L5
Pickwick Cl LAIN SS15 ... 376 L4
Pickwick Rd CHTY IP2 ... 36 F5
Picton Av IP IP1 ... 37 L2
Picton Gdns RAYL SS6 ... 380 F2
Pier Ap WOTN CO14 ... 199 K4
Pier Av COS CO15 ... 12 E6
Pierce Gld K/T/MI CO5 ... 214 D6
Piercing Hl EPP CM16 ... 303 L7
Piercys PIT SS13 ... 378 B6
Pier Gap COS CO15 ... 13 G8
Pierrefitte Wy BRTR CM7 ... 154 F8
Pier Rd GRH DA9 ... 416 C8
Pigeon's La RIPW IP8 ... 56 E1
Piggotts Wy BSF CM23 ... 173 M6
The Pightle BRTR CM7 ... 94 E5
  HVHL CB9 ... 28 B3
  RIPS/CAP IP9 ... 78 C1
Pightle Wy FOS CO13 ... 199 H4
Pig La BSF CM23 ... 174 B8

Pigstye Green Rd CHONG CM5 ... 285 G3
Pike La UPMR RM14 ... 391 G4
Pike Wy EPP CM16 ... 281 H7
Pilborough Wy COLW CO3 ... 161 M8
Pilcox Hall La RCOS CO16 ... 167 K4
Pilgrim Cl BCAYE CM11 ... 357 J3
  BRWN CM15 ... 332 A7
  SAFWN CB10 ... 42 E1
  SOS SS1 ... 401 M2
Pilgrim's La BRW CM14 ... 331 M6
  CDH/CHF RM16 ... 406 D6
Pilgrims Ms SBF/HAD SS7 ... 381 G8
Pilgrim Wy LAIN SS15 ... 376 D5
Pilkingtons HLWE CM17 ... 256 F5
Pimblett Rw RBSF CM22 ... 120 A6
Pimpernel Cl CHTY IP2 ... 37 G8
Pinceybrook Rd HLWS CM18 ... 255 K7
Pincey Rd STSD CM24 ... 148 A8
Pinchpools Rd BSF CM23 ... 118 B3
Pindar Rd HOD EN11 ... 253 K4
Pine Av GTDUN CM6 ... 178 C2
  IP IP1 ... 37 J2
Pine Cl BAR EN8 ... 276 D8
  CVI SS8 ... 397 M8
  LOS SS9 ... 381 J6
  MGTR CO11 ... 108 E3
  RCOLE CO7 ... 195 G3
Pine Crs RBRW/HUT CM13 ... 333 L7
Pinecroft GPK RM2 ... 371 K4
  RBRW/HUT CM13 ... 355 J1
Pinecroft Gdns COLN CO4 ... 135 J8
Pinecroft Ri SUD CO10 ... 54 D6
Pinecroft Rd IP IP1 ... 37 H1
Pine Dr ING CM4 ... 310 D7
Pine Gv BSF CM23 ... 174 C5
  K/T/MI CO5 ... 245 J7
  WIT CM8 ... 212 B6
Pinelands BSF CM23 ... 174 A2
Pine Rd SBF/HAD SS7 ... 398 E1
Pines Av EN EN1 ... 300 D8
Pines Hl STSD CM24 ... 146 E6
The Pines CDH/CHF RM16 ... 407 J6
  FX IP11 ... 85 M7
  LAIN SS15 ... 376 D2
  RCHLM CM3 ... 238 B6
  WFD IG8 ... 348 A4
Pinetree Cl KESG IP5 ... 39 G4
Pinetrees SBF/HAD SS7 ... 380 D8
Pine View Rd IP IP1 ... 37 H5
Pinewood Av LOS SS9 ... 381 L6
  RAIN RM13 ... 404 C2
Pinewood Cl COS CO15 ... 223 M4
  FOS CO13 ... 198 E5
  HLWE CM17 ... 256 D5
  HOC/HUL SS5 ... 361 M1
  TIL RM18 ... 409 J8
Pinewood Rd ABR/ST RM4 ... 351 K5
Pinewood Wy
  RBRW/HUT CM13 ... 333 L7
Pinkeneys ROY SG8 ... 40 E6
Pinkham Dr WIT CM8 ... 239 G3
Pink La WIT CM8 ... 210 E4
Pinkney Cl SAFWN CB10 ... 90 F1
Pinkuah La SUD CO10 ... 33 G5
Pin Mill Cl RIPW IP8 ... 57 K2
Pinmill Rd RIPS/CAP IP9 ... 82 A3
Pinnacles WAB EN9 ... 301 M6
Pinners Cl BOC CM0 ... 344 A4
Pintail Cl CHTY IP2 ... 57 M1
Pintail Crs BRTR CM7 ... 182 C5
Pintail Rd WFD IG8 ... 348 C8
Pintols RCHLM CM3 ... 339 L5
Pipchin Rd CHLM/WR CM1 ... 263 M5
Piper Rd COLW CO3 ... 162 C4
Pipers Cl HVHL CB9 ... 28 D5
Piper's Tye CHLM/GWD CM2 ... 288 E8
Pippins Dr BOC CM0 ... 344 D5
The Pippins HSTD CO9 ... 128 E1
Pipps Hill La BSDN SS14 ... 377 J2
Pipps Hill Rd North
  BCAYE CM11 ... 358 C5
Pipps Hill Rd South BSDN SS14 ... 19 C1
Pirie Rd RCOLW CO6 ... 133 M7
Pishiobury Dr SBW CM21 ... 227 L3
Pitcairn Ct ROMW/RG RM7 ... 370 B4
Pitcairn Rd IP IP1 ... 36 F3
Pitfield Wy PEND EN3 ... 324 D3
Pit La K/T/MI CO5 ... 214 D5
Pitmans Cl SOS SS1 ... 21 H6
Pitmire La BURES CO8 ... 77 J5
Pitsea Hall La VGE SS16 ... 378 C8
Pitsea La PIT SS13 ... 378 B5
Pitsea Vw Rd BCAYE CM11 ... 358 E7
Pitseaville Gv VGE SS16 ... 377 M6
Pitt Av WIT CM8 ... 239 H3
Pitt Cha CHLM/GWD CM2 ... 288 C5
Pittfields VGE SS16 ... 376 B6
Pittman Ct RBRW/HUT CM13 ... 355 K5
Pittman's Fld HLW CM20 ... 256 A2
Place Farm La BRWN CM15 ... 332 B1
Plains Farm Cl RCOLE CO7 ... 135 L5
Plains Fld BRTR CM7 ... 183 L2
Plains Rd MAL CM9 ... 241 G5
The Plain EPP CM16 ... 304 C1
Plaistow Cl SLH/COR SS17 ... 409 L1
Plaistow Green Rd HSTD CO9 ... 128 D6
Plane Tree Cl BOC CM0 ... 344 C5
  CHLM/GWD CM2 ... 288 C5
Plane View Cl COS CO15 ... 250 C1
Plantaganet Pl MAL CM9 ... 301 J5
Plantation Cl SAFWS CB11 ... 65 M5
Plantation Rd ERITH DA8 ... 414 B5
  RCHLM CM3 ... 266 A2
Planton Wy COS CO15 ... 250 C1
Plashet Gdns RBRW/HUT CM13 ... 355 H5
Plashets RBSF CM22 ... 228 D2
Plas Newydd SOS SS1 ... 401 M5
Platford Gn EMPK RM11 ... 371 M4
Platters Cl IP IP1 ... 59 H4
Platters Rd FX IP11 ... 9 M1
Platts Rd PEND EN3 ... 324 D3
Plaw Hatch Cl BSF CM23 ... 174 C3
Players Ct GTDUN CM6 ... 180 D5
Playfield Av CRW RM5 ... 370 D1

Playfield Rd RIPS/CAP IP9 ... 78 C1
Playford La KESG IP5 ... 38 F2
Playford Rd IPNE IP4 ... 38 E4
Playhouse Sq HLW CM20 ... 15 K4
Playle Cha MAL CM9 ... 240 B7
Pleasant Dr BCAYW CM12 ... 334 F7
Pleasant Ms SOS SS1 ... 21 K8
Pleasant Rd BSF CM23 ... 173 M3
Pleasant Rw IPNE IP4 ... 3 G6
Pleasant Va BCAYW CM11 ... 65 L4
Pleshey Cl SOS SS1 ... 402 A3
  WICKW SS12 ... 359 M5
Pleshey Rd RCHLM CM3 ... 207 H3
Plough Dr COLW CO3 ... 162 B6
Plough La SUD CO10 ... 4 B7
Ploughmans Cl BSF CM23 ... 173 K6
Ploughmans Headland
  COLW CO3 ... 161 M6
Plough Ri UPMR RM14 ... 372 F7
Plough Rd RCOLE CO7 ... 194 F3
  RIPS/CAP IP9 ... 78 A2
Plough St IPSE IP3 ... 3 K7
Plover Cl FOS CO13 ... 198 F5
Plover Gdns UPMR RM14 ... 373 G8
Plover Rd CHTY IP2 ... 36 F8
Plovers Md BRWN CM15 ... 308 E8
The Plovers BOC CM0 ... 296 E4
Plowmans RAYL SS6 ... 361 M7
Ployters Rd HLWW/ROY CM19 ... 255 K7
Plumberow Av HOC/HUL SS5 ... 362 F4
Plumberow Mount Av
  HOC/HUL SS5 ... 362 F3
Plume Av COLW CO3 ... 162 B7
  MAL CM9 ... 293 G2
Plumleys PIT SS13 ... 378 C4
Plummers Rd RCOLW CO6 ... 132 F5
Plumpton Av HCH RM12 ... 390 A2
Plumpton Rd HOD EN11 ... 253 K3
Plump Tree La RCHLM CM3 ... 290 E6
Plumptre La RCHLM CM3 ... 290 E6
Plums La BRTR CM7 ... 124 F7
Plumtree Av CHLM/GWD CM2 ... 288 D5
Plumtree Cl DAGE RM10 ... 388 D5
Plymouth Rd CHLM/WR CM1 ... 264 F6
  FX IP11 ... 85 G7
Plymtree SOS SS1 ... 402 D2
Pochard Wy BRTR CM7 ... 182 D6
Pocklington Cl
  CHLM/GWD CM2 ... 265 H7
Pod's Brook Rd BRTR CM7 ... 182 E2
Pods La BRTR CM7 ... 181 L1
Point Clear Rd RCOS CO16 ... 248 E1
Point Cl CVI SS8 ... 399 G8
Point Rd CVI SS8 ... 398 F8
Pointwell La RCOLW CO6 ... 186 B4
Pole Barn La FOS CO13 ... 199 G6
Polecat Rd BRTR CM7 ... 154 F8
Pole La WIT CM8 ... 183 K8
Poley Rd SLH/COR SS17 ... 409 K2
Pollard Cl CHIG IG7 ... 350 B6
Pollard Hatch
  HLWW/ROY CM19 ... 255 J6
Pollards Cl LOU IG10 ... 326 D7
  RCFD SS4 ... 382 F7
Pollards Gn CHLM/GWD CM2 ... 289 G1
Pollard Wk RCOS CO16 ... 12 B2
Polley Cl FOS CO13 ... 198 F4
Polstead Cl RAYL SS6 ... 361 H8
Polsteads VGE SS16 ... 377 M8
Polstead Wy RCOS CO16 ... 223 J7
Pomfret Md BSDN SS14 ... 18 F5
Pompadour Cl BRW CM14 ... 354 D8
Pond Cha COLW CO3 ... 162 B7
Pond Cl FX IP11 ... 85 K8
Pond Cross Farm SAFWS CB11 ... 89 H3
Pond Crss Wy SAFWS CB11 ... 89 H3
Ponders Rd RCOLW CO6 ... 132 D8
Pondfield La COLN CO4 ... 11 M3
Pondfield Rd DAGE RM10 ... 388 C4
Pondholton Dr WIT CM8 ... 239 G4
Pond La RBSF CM22 ... 202 B8
Ponds Rd CHLM/GWD CM2 ... 312 C1
Pond Wk UPMR RM14 ... 390 F1
Poney Cha WIT CM8 ... 240 A6
Poole Cl IPSE IP3 ... 38 E8
Poole Rd EMPK RM11 ... 372 A7
Pooles La HOC/HUL SS5 ... 339 M8
Poole St HSTD CO9 ... 73 H4
  SUD CO10 ... 32 D2
Pool's La CHLM/WR CM1 ... 286 A7
Poors Rd SAFWS CB11 ... 21 H6
Poors La SBF/HAD SS7 ... 380 F7
Poors La North SBF/HAD SS7 ... 381 H6
Poperinghe Rd COLS CO2 ... 163 G7
Popes Ct HVHL CB9 ... 28 F6
Popes Crs PIT SS13 ... 378 B6
Pope's La COLW CO3 ... 10 A8
Pope's Rd RCOLW CO6 ... 131 K7
Popes Wk RAYL SS6 ... 381 G1
Poplar Av COS CO15 ... 250 B1
Poplar Cl CHLM/GWD CM2 ... 288 D5
  COS CO15 ... 250 C1
  HSTD CO9 ... 129 G3
  HVHL CB9 ... 27 L2
  ING CM4 ... 308 F3
  ING CM4 ... 334 B1
  RCHLM CM3 ... 339 K3
  SOCK/AV RM15 ... 406 C2
  WIT CM8 ... 212 B6
Poplar Dr RBRW/HUT CM13 ... 333 G8
Poplar Gv BOC CM0 ... 344 B6
Poplar Grove Cha MAL CM9 ... 269 J4
Poplar La RIPW IP8 ... 36 B8
Poplar Rd CVI SS8 ... 398 D8
  RAYL SS6 ... 381 G3
  SUD CO10 ... 5 J7
Poplar Rw EPP CM16 ... 327 M1
Poplars Av HOC/HUL SS5 ... 362 F7
Poplars Cl RCOLE CO7 ... 193 J4
Poplar Shaw WAB EN9 ... 302 A5
The Poplars ABR/ST RM4 ... 328 C5
  GTDUN CM6 ... 178 D1
  MGTR CO11 ... 108 E1
Poplar St ROMW/RG RM7 ... 370 D4
Poplar Wy FOS CO13 ... 198 E5
Poppy Cl CHTY IP2 ... 36 F8

Poppyfield Cl *LOS* SS9 .... 381 L5
Poppy Gdns *COLS* CO2 .... 163 K8
Porchester Cl *EMPK* RM11 ... 371 M6 🔟
Porchester Rd *BCAYW* CM12 ... 335 H6
Pork La *FOS* CO13 .... 197 M5
Porlock Av *WOS/PRIT* SS0 ...... 382 D7
Porter Cl *WTHK* RM20 ...... 416 E3 🔟
Porters *PIT* SS13 .... 378 D3
Porters Brook Wk *COLN* CO4 ... 11 K2
Porters Cl *BRW* CM14............. 354 D2
COLW CO3................................ 161 G1
Porter's La *COLW* CO3 .... 161 G1
Porter's Pk *RCHLM* CM3 .... 266 B1
Porter Wy *RCOS* CO16 .... 223 J7
Portland Av *HAR* CO12 .... 7 H8
SOS SS1 .... 21 J7
Portland Cl *BRTR* CM7 .... 155 J8 🔟
Portland Crs *HAR* CO12 .... 7 G8
Portland Dr *CHESW* EN7 .... 300 B3
Portland Pl *BSF* CM23 .... 174 A4 🔟
Portland Rd *BSF* CM23 .... 174 A4
COLS CO2 .... 10 D9
COLS CO2 .... 163 G5
Port La *COL* CO1 .... 163 J5
RBSF CM22 .... 201 J1
Portlight Cl *MGTR* CO11 .... 109 H7
Portman Dr *BCAYW* CM12 ... 335 J6
Portman Pl *IP* IP1 .... 2 D4
Portman's Wk *IP* IP1 .... 2 C5
Portmore Gdns *CRW* RM5 .... 351 H6
Portnoi Cl *ROM* RM1 .... 370 E2
Portobello Rd *WOTN* CM14 ...... 199 K3
Port of Felixstowe Rd *FX* IP11.. 8 D3
Portreath Pl *CHLM/WR* CM1 ... 264 B4
Portsea Rd *TIL* RM18 .... 418 C5
Portsmouth Rd *COS* CO15 ...... 250 D3
Portway *CHLM/GWD* CM2 .... 265 J7
Portway Ct *HSTD* CO9 .... 99 G8
Posford Ct *COLN* CO4.............. 135 G6
Postman's La *RCHLM* CM3 ...... 266 F8
Post Mill Cl *IPNE* IP4 .... 3 L3
Post Meadow *BCAYE* CM11 ..... 357 L5
Post Office La *MAL* CM9 .... 241 J7
Post Office Rd *CHLM/WR* CM1 ... 264 C5
HLW CM20.............................. 15 L3
ING CM4 .... 310 C8
MAL CM9 .... 291 M6
Potash La *RIPS/CAP* IP9......... 78 E3
Potash Rd *BCAYE* CM11 .... 357 J5
HLWE CM17 .... 229 L8
Pot Kiln Cha *HSTD* CO9 .... 75 G1
Pot Kiln Rd *SUD* CO10 .... 5 J9
The Pot Kilns *SUD* CO10 .... 5 J9
Potters Cl *LOU* IG10 .... 326 F4
RCHLM CM3 .... 291 H5
Potters Fld *HLWE* CM17 .... 256 E5
Potters La *RCHLM* CM3 .... 338 E1
Potter St *BSF* CM23 .... 174 A4
HLWE CM17 .... 256 D4
HSTD CO9 .... 97 M4
Potters Wy *SOSN* SS2............ 383 G6
Pottery La *CHLM/WR* CM1 ..... 264 B6
HSTD CO9 .... 74 A8
Pouch Mt *FX* IP11 .... 84 C5
Poulk Hall La *RCHLM* CM3 ..... 209 H5
Poulteney Rd *STSD* CM24 ...... 146 E3 🔟
Poulton Cl *MAL* CM9 .... 293 H3
Pound Cl *WAB* EN9 .... 277 M3
Poundfield Rd *LOU* IG10 .... 327 H7
Pound Flds *CHLM/WR* CM1 ..... 287 J3
Pound Ga *GTDUN* CM6 .... 151 L5
Pound La *CDH/CHF* RM16 ...... 408 D2
LAIN SS15 .... 376 E3
PIT SS13 .... 379 G5
RIPS/CAP IP9 .... 78 A3
RIPW IP8 .... 57 H4
WICKW SS12 .... 379 G2
Pound Lane Central *LAIN* SS15... 376 E2
Pound La North *LAIN* SS15 .... 376 E1
Pound Wk *SAFWN* CB10 .... 65 J1
Powdermill La *WAB* EN9 .... 301 J5
Powdermill Ms *WAB* EN9 ... 301 J5 🔟
Powdermill Wy *WAB* EN9 .... 301 J5
Powell Gdns *DAGE* RM10 .... 388 B3
Powell Rd *BKHH* IG9............... 348 D1
LAIN SS15 .... 376 C4
Powers Hall End *WIT* CM8 ..... 211 L8
Powling Rd *IPSE* IP3 .... 59 H1
Pownall Crs *COLS* CO2 .... 163 G7
Poynder Rd *TIL* RM18 .... 418 C5
Poynings Wy *HARH* RM3 .... 371 M1 🔟
Poyntens *RAYL* SS6 .... 380 D2
Poynter Cl *FOS* CO13 .... 198 M4 🔟
Poynter Rd *EN* EN1 .... 324 A7
Poynters La *SBN/FI* SS3 .... 402 E1
Pratts Farm La *RCHLM* CM3 ... 235 K7
Pratt's La *RIPS/CAP* IP9 .... 81 H1
Premier Av *CDH/CHF* RM16 .... 407 K7
Prentice Cl *RCFD* SS4 .... 383 C1
Prentice Hall La *MAL* CM9 ..... 272 B3
Prescott *VGE* SS16 .... 376 D8
Prescott Cl *HCH* RM12 .... 371 J8 🔟
Prescott Rd *BAR* EN8 .... 276 F7
President Rd *COLW* CO3 .... 161 M6
Preston Dr *IP* IP1 .... 2 C7
Preston Gdns *PEND* EN3 .... 324 F1
RAYL SS6 .... 361 L2
Preston Rd *COS* CO15 .... 224 E6
HARH RM3 .... 352 E5
WOS/PRIT SS0 .... 20 B6
Prestwick *FX* IP11 .... 85 K7
Prestwick Dr *BSF* CM23 .... 174 C2
Prestwood Cl *SBF/HAD* SS7 .... 380 A5
Prestwood Dr *CRW* RM5 .... 351 K6
SBF/HAD SS7 .... 380 B4
Pretoria *LAIN* SS15 .... 377 G2 🔟
Pretoria Rd *HSTD* CO9 .... 129 G1
ROMW/RG RM7 .... 370 D4
Prettygate Rd *COLW* CO3 .... 162 B6
Pretyman Rd *FX* IP11 .... 9 H7
IPSE IP3 .... 38 D1
Priests Av *ROM* RM1 .... 370 E2
Priests Fld *RBRW/HUT* CM13 ... 355 K6
Priest's La *BRWN* CM15 .... 354 F3
Primley La *RBSF* CM22 .... 228 D2

Primrose Cl *BSF* CM23 .... 173 K5
CVI SS8 .... 398 B5
VGE SS16 .... 376 C7
Primrose Fld *HLWS* CM18 ...... 256 A6
Primrose Gln *EMPK* RM11 ...... 371 M4
Primrose Hl *BRW* CM14 .... 354 D4
CHLM/WR CM1....................... 16 D1
CHTY IP2 .... 37 G7
HVHL CB9 .... 28 A4
RIPS/CAP IP9 .... 80 E7
Primrose La *K/T/MI* CO5 ..... 214 D5 🔟
MGTR CO11........................... 141 H2
Primrose Pth *CHESW* EN7 .... 300 B3
Primrose Pl *WIT* CM8 .... 211 M7 🔟
Primrose Rd *COS* CO15 .... 224 F5
Primrose Wk *BOC* CM0 .... 320 D8
Primula Wy *CHLM/WR* CM1 ... 265 G5
Prince Albert Rd *K/T/MI* CO5 ... 245 L5
Prince Av *WOS/PRIT* SS0 .... 382 A6
Prince Charles Av
CDH/CHF RM16 .... 408 C2
Prince Charles Cl *COS* CO15 ... 12 B9
SUD CO10 .... 4 E4
Prince Charles Rd *COLS* CO2 ... 191 G2
Princedale Cl *IP* IP1 .... 37 H2
Prince Edward Rd *RCOLE* CO7 ... 107 G4
Princel La *RCOLE* CO7 .... 107 G4
Prince of Wales Dr *CHTY* IP2 ... 58 B1
Prince of Wales Rd *WIT* CM8 ... 240 F7
Prince Philip Av *BOC* CM0 ...... 320 E7
PEND EN3 .... 300 F8
RCHLM CM3 .... 319 H3
SBF/HAD SS7 .... 380 A5
SLH/COR SS17 .... 395 H8
WFD IG8 .... 348 C5
Prince Philip Rd *COLS* CO2 ..... 191 G2
Princes Av *BOC* CM0 .... 320 E7
PEND EN3 .... 300 F8
RCHLM CM3 .... 319 H3
SBF/HAD SS7 .... 380 A5
SLH/COR SS17 .... 395 H8
WFD IG8 .... 348 C5
Princes Cl *BCAYW* CM12 .... 335 K5
EPP CM16 .... 281 K5
LAIN SS15 .... 376 E6
Princes Ct *BCAYW* CM12 ... 335 K5 🔟
BSF CM23 .... 173 K4 🔟
Prince's Esp *WOTN* CM14 ...... 199 L3
Princesfield Rd *WAB* EN9 ...... 302 C5
Princes Gdns *FX* IP11 .... 9 K2
Princes Ga *BSF* CM23 .... 173 K4
Princes Ms *BCAYW* CM12 ... 335 K5 🔟
Princes Pk *BKHH* IG9 .... 348 D3
BOC CM0 .... 344 C5
BRW CM14 .... 331 H4
CHLM/GWD CM2...................... 16 E9
COS CO15 .... 224 E6
CVI SS8 .... 398 A5
FX IP11 .... 9 K3
HAR CO12 .... 6 E8
MAL CM9 .... 293 H1
ROM RM1 .... 371 H5
Princess Anne Cl *COS* CO15 ... 250 D2
Princess Av *TIL* RM18 .... 419 K1
Princess Gdns *RCFD* SS4 .... 363 K6
Princess Margaret Rd *RM18* RM18... 419 J1
Princess Rd *RAYL* SS6 .... 362 A8
Princess St *HAR* CO12 .... 6 B4
Princes St *CHTY* IP2 .... 2 C7
IP IP1 .... 2 F4
WOS/PRIT SS0 .... 20 F5
Princess Wy *HVHL* CB9 .... 27 M3
Prince St *SUD* CO10 .... 4 C5
Princes Wy *BKHH* IG9 .... 348 D3
RBRW/HUT CM13.................... 355 H3
Princethorpe Rd *IPSE* IP3 ...... 38 D7
Princeton Ms *COLN* CO4 ... 135 J7 🔟
Prince William Av *CVI* SS8 ..... 398 A5
Printers Wy *HLW* CM20 .... 227 H6
Prior Cha *GRAYS* RM17 .... 417 G1
Priori Cl *HSTD* CO9 .... 128 E3
The Priories *HOC/HUL* SS5 ..... 361 L2
Priors Cl *BSDN* SS14 .... 19 J5
Priors East *BSDN* SS14 .... 19 K6
Priors Pk *HCH* RM12 .... 389 K2
Prior's Wy *COLN* CO4 .... 162 E1
Prior's Wood Rd *RBSF* CM22 ... 176 D4 🔟
Prior Wy *COLN* CO4 .... 162 E1
Priory Av *HLWE* CM17 .... 227 K6
HVHL CB9 .... 28 A4 🔟
SOSN SS2 .... 383 G8 🔟
Priory Cl *BROX* EN10 .... 276 F4 🔟
BRWN CM15 .... 332 B7
CHLM/WR CM1 .... 16 B4
HOD EN11 .... 253 H6
RCHLM CM3 .... 267 J2
RCOS CO16 .... 249 H5
SAFWN CB10 .... 22 B8
Priory Ct *BSF* CM23 .... 173 M4 🔟
HLWS CM18 .... 256 C6
Priory Crs *SOSN* SS2 .... 382 F7
Priory Dr *STSD* CM24 .... 146 F6
Priory Farm Rd *RCHLM* CM3 ... 267 J1
Priory Ga *BAR* EN8 .... 277 G7 🔟
Priory Gv *HARH* RM3 .... 352 E6
Priory La *RCHLM* CM3 .... 315 G2
Priory Md *BRWN* CM15 .... 308 D8
Priory Ms *HCH* RM12 .... 371 J8 🔟
Priory Pth *HARH* RM3 .... 352 F4 🔟
Priory Rd *COS* CO15 .... 12 E6
DART DA1 .... 414 E8
FX IP11 .... 85 L3 🔟
HARH RM3 .... 352 F4
LOU IG10 .... 326 F6
RCHLM CM3 .... 314 F2
RCOLW CO6 .... 131 J8
SLH/COR SS17 .... 394 F8
SUD CO10 .... 4 B2
WIT CM8 .... 214 A8
Priory St *COL* CO1 .... 10 E8
RCOLW CO6 .... 130 C4
The Priory *BCAYW* CM12 ...... 335 K6 🔟
CHLM/WR CM1 .... 16 B4
Priory View Rd *LOS* SS9 .... 381 M6 🔟
Priory Wk *SUD* CO10 .... 4 C7
Priory Wd *HSTD* CO9 .... 73 M7
Priory Wood Crs *LOS* SS9 ...... 381 M6
Priory Wood Rbt *RBSF* CM22 ... 175 H3

Prittle Cl *SBF/HAD* SS7 .... 380 D6
Prittlewell Cha *WOS/PRIT* SS0 ... 382 D8
Prittlewell Cl *CHTY* IP2............ 58 A2
Prittlewell Sq *SOS* SS1 .... 20 F8
Prittlewell St *SOSN* SS2 .... 21 H4
Proctor Cl *K/T/MI* CO5 .... 218 C1
Proctors Wy *BSF* CM23 .... 174 B7
Proctor Wy *RCOLW* CO6 .... 159 M8
Progress Ct *BRTR* CM7 .... 154 F8
Progress Rd *LOS* SS9 .... 381 K5
Progress Wy *EN* EN1 .... 324 B7
RCOS CO16 .... 223 K2
Promenade *COS* CO15 .... 249 L5
HAR CO12 .... 143 K1
RCHLM CM3 .... 319 G1
Promenade Wy *RCOLE* CO7 ... 220 E6
Prospect Av *SLH/COR* SS17 ... 409 J2
Prospect Cl *RCHLM* CM3 ... 238 B8 🔟
SOS SS1 .... 21 M8
Prospect Hl *SUD* CO10 .... 55 L8
Prospect Pl *CRW* RM5 .... 370 D2 🔟
GRAYS RM17 .... 417 J3 🔟
SAFWS CB11 .... 66 A2
Prospect Rd *BAR* EN8 .... 300 D1
EMPK RM11 .... 372 A3
IP IP1 .... 2 A3
WFD IG8 .... 348 D6
Prospect St *IP* IP1 .... 2 A3
Prospect Wy *RBRW/HUT* CM13 ... 333 L6
Prospero Cl *CVI* SS8 .... 398 C7
Protea Wy *CVI* SS8 .... 398 C7
Provence Cl *COLW* CO3 .... 161 K4
Providence *BOC* CM0 .... 344 D7
Providence La *IP* IP1 .... 2 B1
Providence Rd *ROMW/RG* RM7 ... 370 A1
Providence St *IP* IP1 .... 2 E4
Provident Sq *CHLM/GWD* CM2 ... 17 J4
Prower Cl *BCAYE* CM11 .... 357 J2
Prunus Ct *COLS* CO2 .... 191 H4 🔟
Prykes Dr *CHLM/WR* CM1 ...... 16 D3
Pryor Cl *WIT* CM8 .... 239 H2
Pryors Cl *BSF* CM23 .... 174 A5
Pryors Rd *BSF* CM23 .... 174 B5
Puckleside *VGE* SS16 .... 376 D7 🔟
Pudding La *CHIG* IG7 .... 327 M8 🔟
COLS CO2 .... 189 J8
Pudsey Hall La *RCFD* SS4 ...... 364 B1
Puffin Pl *SBN/FI* SS3 .... 402 F2
Puffinsdale *COS* CO15 .... 13 H1
Pugh Pl *SLH/COR* SS17 .... 394 E7
Pulham Av *BROX* EN10 .... 252 F8
Pulpitfield Cl *FOS* CO13 .... 199 H3 🔟
Pulpits Cl *HOC/HUL* SS5 .... 363 G4
Pump Hl *BUNT* SG9 .... 116 B1
CHLM/GWD CM2.................. 289 G5 🔟
LOU IG10 .... 327 G4
RCOS CO16 .... 222 D7
Pump La *EPP* CM16 .... 279 J4
RCHLM CM3 .... 233 M2
RCHLM CM3 .... 316 E3
Pump Mead Cl *BOC* CM0 .... 320 E7
Pump St *SLH/COR* SS17 .... 409 H7
Punchard Wy *FX* IP11 .... 84 D5
Purbeck Rd *EMPK* RM11 .... 371 H7
Purcell Cl *CHLM/WR* CM1 ...... 287 J7
COLN CO4 .... 163 M5 🔟
LAIN SS15 .... 376 E5
SLH/COR SS17 .... 394 D8
Purdeys Wy *RCFD* SS4 .... 383 H3
Purdis Av *IPSE* IP3 .... 60 A2
Purdis Farm La *IPSE* IP3 .... 60 A1
Purfleet By-pass *PUR* RM19 ... 415 K2
Purfleet Rd *SOCK/AV* RM15 ... 405 J6
Purford Gn *HLWS* CM18 .... 256 B4
Purland Ct *BCTR* RM8 .... 370 A4
Purleigh Av *WFD* IG8 .... 348 F7
Purleigh Cl *PIT* SS13 .... 378 D2
Purleigh Gv *RCHLM* CM3 .... 317 J6
Purleigh Rd *RAYL* SS6 .... 361 J8
Purleigh St *RCHLM* CM3 .... 317 G2
Purley Wy *RCOS* CO16 .... 223 J5
WOS/PRIT SS0 .... 382 D6
Purlieu Wy *EPP* CM16 .... 303 M7
Purplett St *CHTY* IP2 .... 3 G8
Purvis Wy *COLN* CO4 .... 135 J6
Putney Rd *PEND* EN3 .... 300 E8
Pyefleet Cl *K/T/MI* CO5 .... 192 D5
RCOLE CO7 .... 220 F4
Pyefleet Vw *K/T/MI* CO5 .... 191 M8
Pyenest Rd *HLWW/ROY* CM19 ... 15 H9
Pyesand *FOS* CO13 .... 198 D3
Pygot Pl *BRTR* CM7 .... 154 F7
Pym Pl *GRAYS* RM17 .... 417 H1
Pyms Rd *CHLM/GWD* CM2 ...... 288 C8
Pynchbek *BSF* CM23 .... 173 M8
Pynchon Ms *CHLM/WR* CM1 ... 17 L2
Pynchon Paddocks *RBSF* CM22... 201 L4
Pyne Ga *CHLM/GWD* CM2 ...... 312 C2
Pynest Green La *WAB* EN9 ..... 326 B1
Pyrles La *LOU* IG10 .... 327 J3 🔟
Pyrles La *LOU* IG10 .... 327 J4
Pytt Fld *HLWE* CM17 .... 256 C4

Q

Quadling St *IP* IP1 .... 2 D6
The Quadrant *PUR* RM19 .... 415 K1
Quaker La *WAB* EN9 .... 301 K6
Quaker's La *HVHL* CB9 .... 28 B4
Quale Rd *CHLM/GWD* CM2 ..... 265 J7
Quantock Cl *KESG* IP5 .... 39 G4
Quarles Cl *CRW* RM5 .... 351 H8 🔟
Quarry Hl *GRAYS* RM17 .... 417 H2
Quarry Ms *PUR* RM19 .... 415 H1
Quarry Springs *HLW* CM20 ..... 256 B3
Quarry Wy *WTHK* RM20 .... 416 A3
Quarter Ga *RCHLM* CM3 ..... 339 M6 🔟
Quay La *FOS* CO13 .... 198 C2
GRH DA9 .... 416 C8
RCOS CO16 .... 169 J7
SUD CO10 .... 4 C8
Quay Rd *MGTR* CO11 .... 108 E7
RCOLE CO7 .... 192 C4 🔟
The Quay *BOC* CM0 .... 344 D7 🔟
HAR CO12 .... 7 K2

Quebec Av *SOS* SS1 .... 21 H6
Quebec Cl *SOS* SS1 .... 21 J6
Quebec Dr *KESG* IP5 .... 39 J3
Quebec Rd *TIL* RM18 .... 418 B6
The Queech *RIPS/CAP* IP9 ...... 78 C1 🔟
Queen Anne Dr *K/T/MI* CO5 ... 245 L5 🔟
Queen Anne Gdns
K/T/MI CO5 .... 245 L5 🔟
Queen Anne Rd *K/T/MI* CO5 ... 245 L5
Queen Anne's Dr
WOS/PRIT SS0 .... 382 D7
Queen Anns Gv *HOC/HUL* SS5 ... 361 L3
Queenborough La *BRTR* CM7 ... 182 B2
Queenborough Rd *BOC* CM0 ... 320 E7
Queenbury Cl *K/T/MI* CO5 ..... 245 M5 🔟
Queen Edith Dr *HVHL* CB9 ...... 48 C5
Queen Elizabeth Av *COS* CO15... 250 D2
TIL RM18 .... 419 K7 🔟
Queen Elizabeth Cha *RCFD* SS4 ... 383 G4
Queen Elizabeth Dr
SLH/COR SS17 .... 395 G6
Queen Elizabeth Ii Br
WTHK RM20 .... 415 M6 🔟
Queen Elizabeth Wy *COLS* CO2 ... 191 H2
Queen Mary Av *TIL* RM18 ...... 419 K1
Queen Mary Cl *ROM* RM1 ...... 371 G6
Queen's Av *LOS* SS9 .... 399 M2 🔟
MAL CM9 .... 293 H2
WFD IG8 .... 348 C6
Queensberry Rd *IPSE* IP3 .... 59 H2 🔟
Queensbury Av *RCOLW* CO6 ... 160 E6
Queenscliffe Rd *CHTY* IP2 .... 2 B9
Queens Crs *BSF* CM23 .... 173 M6 🔟
Queensdale Cl *IP* IP1 .... 37 J2
Queen's Dr *BAR* EN8 .... 301 H6
Queen's Gdns *BRTR* CM7 ...... 154 B4
RAIN RM13 .... 388 E8
UPMR RM14 .... 373 C6
Queensgate Dr *IPNE* IP4 .... 38 C1
Queen's Gate Ms
BCAYW CM12 .... 335 C6
Queen's Head Rd *RCOLW* CO6 ... 134 E1
Queensland Av *RCFD* SS4 ...... 383 C4
Queensland Crs *CHLM/WR* CM1... 263 L6
Queensland Dr *COLS* CO2 ...... 191 H2
Queensmere *SBF/HAD* SS7 .... 380 C6
Queens Park Av *BCAYW* CM12... 335 H6
Queens Park Rd *HARH* RM3 ... 372 A1
Queen's Rd *BAR* EN8 .... 300 F6
BCAYE CM11 .... 358 C7
BKHH IG9 .... 348 C5
BOC CM0 .... 344 C6
BRTR CM7 .... 155 C6
BRW CM14 .... 354 D4
CHLM/GWD CM2...................... 17 L4
COLW CO3 .... 162 D5
COS CO15 .... 12 B9
EPP CM16 .... 281 K5
FOS CO13 .... 199 G7
FX IP11 .... 9 L2
HAR CO12 .... 143 H1
LAIN SS15 .... 376 E5
LOS SS9 .... 399 M3 🔟
LOU IG10 .... 327 G5
RAYL SS6 .... 380 E2
RCOLE CO7 .... 192 C3
RCOLW CO6 .... 130 C4
RCOLW CO6 .... 133 L8
SBF/HAD SS7 .... 397 L1
SUD CO10 .... 4 C4
WOS/PRIT SS0 .... 20 F4
Queen's Sq *IPSE* IP3 .... 59 J1
Queens St *HVHL* CB9 .... 28 B3
Queens Town Gdns
RAIN RM13 .... 404 A1 🔟
Queen St *BOC* CM0 .... 320 C7 🔟
BRW CM14 .... 354 D6
CHLM/GWD CM2...................... 16 F6
CHONG CM5 .... 283 M1
COL CO1 .... 10 D8
FX IP11 .... 84 F7
HSTD CO9 .... 73 M8
HSTD CO9 .... 98 A4
IP IP1 .... 2 E5
MAL CM9 .... 293 H1
RCOLE CO7 .... 221 C5
RCOLW CO6 .... 186 B1
ROMW/RG RM7 .... 370 E6
Queens Wy *BAR* EN8 .... 301 G6 🔟
IPSE IP3 .... 59 J1
Queensway *CHONG* CM5 .... 283 G6
COS CO15 .... 224 E6
HVHL CB9 .... 27 M3
K/T/MI CO5 .... 214 D5
MGTR CO11........................... 108 D7
PEND EN3 .... 324 D6
SOS SS1 .... 21 J7
SOSN SS2 .... 20 F5
SUD CO10 .... 35 K5
SUD CO10 .... 55 J6
Queenswood Av
RBRW/HUT CM13.................... 333 L7
Queen Victoria Dr
RIPS/CAP IP9 .... 113 J3
Quendon Av *BROX* EN10 .... 301 L5
Quendon Rd *BSDN* SS14 ..... 377 M3
Quendon Rd *FOS* CO13 .... 199 H5
Quennell Wy *RBRW/HUT* CM13... 355 K1
Quentin Cl *IP* IP1 .... 36 F7
Quickset Rd *SAFWS* CB11 ...... 41 G8
Quilp Dr *CHLM/WR* CM1 .... 264 A4
Quilter Pl *RIPW* IP8 .... 57 K2
Quilter Rd *HLWE* CM17 .... 115 J1
Quilters Cl *BSDN* SS14 .... 19 M2
COS CO15 .... 225 G5 🔟
Quilters Dr *MGTR* CO11 ...... 108 E2 🔟
Quilters Straight *BSDN* SS14... 19 M2
Quince Cl *MGTR* CO11 .... 108 E2 🔟
Quince Tree Cl
SOCK/AV RM15 .... 406 D2 🔟
Quinion Cl *CHLM/WR* CM1...... 263 L4
Quinton's La *FX* IP11 .... 85 K8
Quinton Wy *WAB* EN9 .... 301 K7

Quorn Gdns *LOS* SS9 .... 399 H2
The Quorn *ING* CM4 .... 334 B1

R

Rachael Clarke Cl
SLH/COR SS17 .... 394 F7 🔟
Rachael Gdns *WIT* CM8 .... 184 F7 🔟
Rackenford *SBN/FI* SS3 .... 402 E3 🔟
Radburn Rd *HLWS* CM18 .... 256 B7
Radcliffe Dr *CHTY* IP2 .... 57 L1
Radford Ct *BCAYW* CM12 ... 335 J8 🔟
Radford Crs *BCAYW* CM12 ..... 335 H8
Radford Rd *BCAYW* CM12 ...... 335 H8
Radiator Rd *SUD* CO10 .... 55 H6
Radley Green Rd *ING* CM4...... 285 K5
Radleys Md *DAGE* RM10 .... 388 C3
Radstocks *BCAYW* CM12 .... 335 J8
Radwinter Av *WICKW* SS12 .... 359 L6
Radwinter Rd *SAFWN* CB10 ... 45 J3
SAFWS CB11 .... 66 A2
Raeburn Cl *FOS* CO13 .... 199 G4 🔟
Raeburn Rd *IPSE* IP3 .... 59 G2
Raeburn Rd South *IPSE* IP3 ... 58 F2
Raglan Av *BAR* EN8 .... 300 E6
Raglan Ms *COS* CO15 .... 12 A6
Raglan Rd *FOS* CO13 .... 199 G6
Rags La *CHESW* EN7 .... 276 A7
Rahn Rd *EPP* CM16 .... 304 B3
Raider Cl *ROMW/RG* RM7 ...... 370 C1 🔟
Raile Wk *SUD* CO10 .... 34 E3
Railey Rd *SAFWS* CB11 .... 65 M4
Railway Ap *FX* IP11 .... 85 H8 🔟
LAIN SS15 .... 376 B5
Railway Rd *BAR* EN8 .... 301 C5
Railway Sq *CHLM/WR* CM1 .... 16 F2
Railway St *BRTR* CM7 .... 155 H8
CHLM/WR CM1....................... 16 F2
MGTR CO11........................... 108 E7
Railway Ter *SOSN* SS2 .... 383 H8
Rainbow Av *CVI* SS8 .... 398 C7
Rainbow La *SLH/COR* SS17 .... 410 A2
Rainbow Md *RCHLM* CM3 ...... 238 A6
Rainbow Ms *MAL* CM9 .... 269 G6 🔟
CVI SS8 .... 398 D7
HLWE CM17 .... 228 F8
K/T/MI CO5 .... 245 L5
Rainbow Wy *RCOLW* CO6 ...... 130 K2
Raine Av *HVHL* CB9 .... 27 L3
Rainer Cl *BAR* EN8 .... 300 E1
Rainham Rd *RAIN* RM13 .... 389 G6
Rainham Rd North *DAGE* RM10... 388 E4
Rainham Rd South *DAGE* RM10... 388 D5
DAGE RM10 .... 388 E6 🔟
Rainham Wy *FOS* CO13 .... 199 J5
Rainsford Av *CHLM/WR* CM1 ... 16 C3
Rainsford La *CHLM/WR* CM1 ... 16 D2
Rainsford Rd *CHLM/WR* CM1 ... 16 E2
STSD CM24 .... 146 E3
Rainsford Wy *HCH* RM12 .... 371 J5
Raleigh Cl *ERITH* DA8 .... 414 A3
SUD CO10 .... 5 G1
Raleigh Rd *SUD* CO10 .... 5 G1
Ralegh Dr *LAIN* SS15 .... 376 E6
Rambler Cl *COLW* CO3 .... 161 L4
Ramblers Wy *BOC* CM0 .... 344 C6
Ram Gorse *HLW* CM20 .... 15 H1
Ramney Dr *PEND* EN3 .... 300 F8
Ramparts Cl *RCOLW* CO6 ...... 134 C4
The Ramparts *RAYL* SS6 .... 380 F1
Rampart St *SBN/FI* SS3 .... 403 G5
Rampart Ter *SBN/FI* SS3 .... 403 H5
Ramplings Av *COS* CO15 .... 12 F1
Ramsay Dr *BROX* EN10 .... 276 F1 🔟
Ramsay Dr *VGE* SS16 .... 377 M8 🔟
Ramsay Gdns *GPK* RM2 .... 371 J1
Ramsden Cl *COS* CO15 .... 13 K2
Ramsden Dr *CRW* RM5 .... 351 H8
Ramsden Park Rd *BCAYE* CM11... 358 C2
Ramsden View Rd *WICKW* SS12... 359 K1
Ramsey Cha *RCHLM* CM3 ...... 318 B5
WICKW SS12 .... 360 A6
Ramsey Cl *CHTY* IP2 .... 58 B2
MAL CM9 .... 269 L7
Ramsey Rd *HAR* CO12 .... 142 E1
HSTD CO9 .... 128 E3
Ramsgate Dr *IPSE* IP3 .... 38 C2
Ramshaw Dr *CHLM/GWD* CM2... 265 G8
Ramuz Dr *WOS/PRIT* SS0 ...... 20 A3
Rana Ct *BRTR* CM7 .... 155 H7
Rana Dr *BRTR* CM7 .... 155 G7
Randall Cl *GTDUN* CM6 .... 178 E2
KESG IP5 .... 39 M4 🔟
Randall Dr *HCH* RM12 .... 389 K1
Randalls Dr *RBRW/HUT* CM13... 333 M8 🔟
Randolph Cl *LOS* SS9 .... 381 M8 🔟
MAL CM9 .... 293 G3
Rands Rd *GTDUN* CM6 .... 205 G3
Rands Wy *IPSE* IP3 .... 59 J2
Randulph Ter *CHLM/WR* CM1... 17 L1
Randway *RAYL* SS6 .... 380 E2 🔟
Randwell Ct *IPNE* IP4 .... 38 C6
Ranelagh Rd *CHTY* IP2 .... 37 G6 🔟
FX IP11 .... 9 M2
Ranger Wk *COLS* CO2 .... 163 J8
Rangoon Cl *COLS* CO2 .... 190 C2
Ransome Cl *RIPW* IP8 .... 36 E5
Ransome Crs *IPSE* IP3 .... 59 J1
Ransome Rd *IPSE* IP3 .... 59 J1
Ransomes Wy *CHLM/WR* CM1... 264 C7
IPSE IP3 .... 59 L3
Ransom Rd *K/T/MI* CO5 .... 214 D6
Rantree Fold *VGE* SS16 ...... 377 C3 🔟
Ranulf Cl *HLWE* CM17 .... 227 K5
Ranworth Av *HOD* EN11 .... 253 J7
Raphael Av *ROM* RM1 .... 371 G3
TIL RM18 .... 418 D2 🔟
Raphael Dr *CHLM/WR* CM1 .... 265 G4
SBN/FI SS3 .... 403 H3
Raphaels *LAIN* SS15 .... 18 B7
Rapier Cl *PUR* RM19 .... 415 G1
Ratcliffe Ct *K/T/MI* CO5 ...... 213 J1 🔟
Ratcliffe Rd *COLW* CO3 .... 161 M6

Rat HI *RIPS/CAP* IP9 .... 112 A2
Rat La *SBF/HAD* SS7 .... 380 D3
Ratsborough Cha *BOC* CM0 .... 344 D1
Rat's La *LOU* IG10 .... 326 C2
Rattwick Dr *CVI* SS8 .... 399 G8
Ravel Av *SOCK/AV* RM15 ...... 405 K4
Ravel Rd *SOCK/AV* RM15 ...... 405 L4
Raven Cl *BCAYW* CM12 .... 335 G7
Raven Crs *BCAYW* CM12 .... 335 G7
Ravencroft *CDH/CHF* RM16 ... 408 C7 🆎
Ravendale *SBN/FI* SS3 .... 402 E1
Raven Dr *SBF/HAD* SS7 .... 397 J1
Ravenoak Wy *CHIG* IG7 .... 349 M6
Raven La *BCAYW* CM12 .... 335 G7
Ravens Av *HSTD* CO9 .... 129 C3
Ravensbourne Crs *HARH* RM3 .. 372 A3
Ravensbourne Dr
  CHLM/WR CM1 .... 16 A5
Ravensbourne Rd *DART* DA1 .. 414 B7
Ravenscourt Cl *HCH* RM12 ..... 389 M2 🆎
Ravenscourt Dr *HCH* RM12 .... 389 M2
  VGE SS16 .... 377 M6
Ravenscourt Gv *HCH* RM12 .... 389 M1
Ravens Crs *GTDUN* CM6 .... 180 F4
Ravensdale *COS* CO15 .... 224 A5
  VGE SS16 .... 377 J7
Ravensfield *BSDN* SS14 .... 378 A5
Ravensfield Rd *IP* IP1 .... 36 F1
Ravens La *RIPW* IP8 .... 36 B1
Ravensmere *EPP* CM16 .... 304 E7
Ravenswood Cha *RCFD* SS4 ... 583 G4
Ravenswood Cl *CRW* RM5 ...... 351 J6
Raven Wy *COLN* CO4 .... 134 F7
Rawden Cl *HAR* CO12 .... 6 E7
Rawdon Dr *HOD* EN11 .... 253 H6
Rawlings Crs *COLN* CO4 .... 135 J6
Rawreth La *RAYL* SS6 .... 361 K5
  WICKE SS11 .... 361 H4
Rawstorn Rd *COLW* CO3 .... 10 A8
Ray Av *HAR* CO12 .... 6 D7
Rayburn Rd *EMPK* RM11 .... 372 B7
Raycliff Av *RCOS* CO16 .... 223 M4
Ray Cl *CVI* SS8 .... 413 H1
  LOS SS9 .... 399 J2
Raydon Wy *SUD* CO10 .... 5 L8
Rayfield *EPP* CM16 .... 304 A2
Rayfield Cl *GTDUN* CM6 .... 179 H7
Rayhaven *HAR* CO12 .... 142 D1
Ray Lamb Wy *ERITH* DA8 ...... 414 C3
Ray La *HAR* CO12 .... 112 F6
Rayleigh Av *LOS* SS9 .... 381 J3
  WOS/PRIT SS0 .... 20 C3
Rayleigh Cl *BRTR* CM7 .... 155 K7
  COLN CO4 .... 11 G4
  RBRW/HUT CM13 .... 355 K1
Rayleigh Downs Rd *RAYL* SS6 .. 381 H4
Rayleigh Dr *LOS* SS9 .... 381 L8
Rayleigh Rd *IP* IP1 .... 36 F2
  LOS SS9 .... 381 K4
  RBRW/HUT CM13 .... 333 K8
  SBF/HAD SS7 .... 380 C4
  SLH/COR SS17 .... 409 K2
  WFD IG8 .... 348 D8
Rayley La *EPP* CM16 .... 281 H4
Ray Lodge Rd *WFD* IG8 .... 348 D7
Ray Md *RCHLM* CM3 .... 235 G4
Rayment Av *CVI* SS8 .... 398 E8
Rayment Drift *KESC* IP5 .... 39 K4
Raymond Gdns *CHIG* IG7 .... 350 C4
Raymonds Cl *RCHLM* CM3 ..... 339 K4
Raymonds Dr *SBF/HAD* SS7 ... 380 A5
Rayne Rd *BRTR* CM7 .... 154 E8
Rayner Rd *COLS* CO2 .... 162 C7
Rayner Wy *HSTD* CO9 .... 128 F2
Raynham Cl *BSF* CM23 .... 174 D4
Raynham Rd *BSF* CM23 .... 174 C3
Raynton Rd *PEND* EN3 .... 324 E1
Rayside *BSDN* SS14 .... 19 K6
The Ray *CHLM/WR* CM1 .... 264 F6
Ray Wk *LOS* SS9 .... 399 J2
Read Cl *HOC/HUL* SS5 .... 363 H4
Read Ct *WAB* EN9 .... 302 B5
Reade Rd *RIPS/CAP* IP9 .... 80 E5
Readers Ct *CHLM/GWD* CM2 .. 288 F5
Reading Cl *VGE* SS16 .... 376 A6 🆎
Reading Rd *IPNE* IP4 .... 38 C4
The Readings *HLWS* CM18 ..... 256 A6
Reaper Rd *COLS* CO2 .... 162 B7
Rebecca Gdns *WIT* CM8 .... 184 F7 🆎
Rebecca Meade *GTDUN* CM6 . 150 A3
Rebels La *SBN/FI* SS3 .... 384 A7
Rebow Rd *HAR* CO12 .... 143 H1
  RCOLE CO7 .... 192 C5
Rebow St *COL* CO1 .... 163 J5
Reckitts Cl *COS* CO15 .... 13 L4
Recreation Av *HARH* RM3 ...... 372 A2
  LOS SS9 .... 400 A1
  ROMW/RG RM7 .... 370 D5
  SLH/COR SS17 .... 374 C5
Recreation Cl *FX* IP11 .... 85 G7 🆎
Recreation Gnd *STSD* CM24 .. 146 E5
Recreation La *FX* IP11 .... 85 G7
Recreation Rd *COL* CO1 .... 163 J6
  COS CO15 .... 13 H5
  HSTD CO9 .... 97 L3
  HVHL CB9 .... 28 A4
Recreation Wk *BCAYE* CM11 .. 336 D6 🆎
  SUD CO10 .... 55 J6
Recreation Wy *IPSE* IP3 .... 59 J1
  RCOLE CO7 .... 221 G4 🆎
Rectory Av *RCFD* SS4 .... 363 K5
Rectory Cha *BRWN* CM15 ...... 332 D1
  RBRW/HUT CM13 .... 373 M4
  SOS SS1 .... 401 M2
Rectory Cl *COLN* CO4 .... 10 A1
  ING CM4 .... 310 C7
  ING CM4 .... 335 L1
  RCHLM CM3 .... 235 J5
  SAFWS CB11 .... 43 G7 🆎
  SBF/HAD SS7 .... 380 F8
Rectory Fld *HLWW/ROY* CM19 .. 15 G8
  RIPS/CAP IP9 .... 81 M4
Rectory Gdns *PIT* SS13 .... 378 D6 🆎
  UPMR RM14 .... 390 F1
Rectory Garth *RAYL* SS6 .... 361 L8
Rectory Gv *LOS* SS9 .... 399 L3

WICKE SS11 .... 360 A4
Rectory HI *RCOLE* CO7 .... 107 K2
  RCOLE CO7 .... 192 D2
Rectory La *BSF* CM23 .... 145 K5
  CHLM/WR CM1 .... 264 C5
  HAR CO12 .... 142 B2
  HLWW/ROY CM19 .... 15 G8
  HSTD CO9 .... 75 K5
  K/T/MI CO5 .... 191 G8
  LOU IG10 .... 327 H4
  MAL CM9 .... 292 A5
  MGTR CO11 .... 108 F2
  RBRW/HUT CM13 .... 355 M8 🆎
  RCHLM CM3 .... 208 E3
  RCHLM CM3 .... 318 C7
  SAFWN CB10 .... 45 H2
  WIT CM8 .... 212 B5
Rectory Meadow *BRTR* CM7 ... 184 D1
Rectory Park Dr *PIT* SS13 ...... 378 C6
Rectory Rd *BCAYW* CM12 ...... 357 G7
  BRTR CM7 .... 156 C4
  CDH/CHF RM16 .... 408 C3
  CDH/CHF RM16 .... 408 B2
  CHLM/WR CM1 .... 287 J3
  CHTY IP2 .... 2 E9
  COLN CO4 .... 106 A5
  DAGE RM10 .... 388 B5
  FOS CO13 .... 198 B8
  GRAYS RM17 .... 407 L8
  HAR CO12 .... 142 A4
  HOC/HUL SS5 .... 363 H6
  HSTD CO9 .... 97 L2
  HVHL CB9 .... 29 J1
  K/T/MI CO5 .... 191 M4
  K/T/MI CO5 .... 214 D6
  MAL CM9 .... 242 D2
  MAL CM9 .... 267 L8
  MGTR CO11 .... 111 H8
  PIT SS13 .... 378 D4
  RCHLM CM3 .... 341 H5
  RCOLE CO7 .... 166 F3
  RCOLE CO7 .... 192 D1
  RCOLE CO7 .... 193 M2
  RCOLW CO6 .... 160 A3
  RCOLE CO7 .... 188 D2
  RCOS CO16 .... 196 A8
  RCOS CO16 .... 196 B6
  RIPS/CAP IP9 .... 81 K8
  SBF/HAD SS7 .... 380 F8
  SLH/COR SS17 .... 409 K2
  SUD CO10 .... 54 F7
  TIL RM18 .... 418 E5
Rectory Wd *HLW* CM20 .... 15 J2
Redan St *IP* IP1 .... 2 C2
Red Barn La *HAR* CO12 .... 141 J8
Red Barn Rd *RCOLE* CO7 ...... 221 C3
Redbridge Rd *COS* CO15 ...... 224 A3
Redbury Cl *RAIN* RM13 .... 404 C2 🆎
Redcar Rd *HARH* RM3 .... 353 G6
Redcliff Dr *LOS* SS9 .... 400 A3
Redcliffe Rd *CHLM/GWD* CM2 . 16 F6
Redden Court Rd *HARH* RM3 . 371 M3
Reddings Cl *SAFWS* CB11 ..... 65 M4 🆎
Reddings La *BOC* CM0 .... 297 K8
Reddy Rd *ERITH* DA8 .... 414 A3
Rede Wy *SUD* CO10 .... 5 L9
Redfern Gdns *GPK* RM2 .... 371 L2
Redgate Cl *WICKE* SS11 .... 360 B3
Redgate La *RIPS/CAP* IP9 ..... 58 D6
Redgates La *SAFWN* CB10 ..... 44 E7
Redgates Pl *CHLM/WR* CM1 .. 264 F7 🆎
Redgrave Rd *VGE* SS16 .... 377 M7
Redhills Rd *RCHLM* CM3 .... 339 M3
Red House Cl *FX* IP11 .... 84 B3
Redhouse La *RCOLW* CO6 ..... 134 E1
  SUD CO10 .... 4 D7
Red House La *SUD* CO10 ...... 55 H7
Red House Wk *KIR/NAC* IP10 . 60 F7
The Redinge *BCAYE* CM11 ..... 357 L4
Redlands Rd *PEND* EN3 .... 324 F5
Red La *RIPS/CAP* IP9 .... 78 B3
Redlie Cl *SLH/COR* SS17 .... 394 E7
Red Lion Crs *HLWE* CM17 ..... 256 D5
Red Lion La *HLWE* CM17 ...... 256 D5
Redmayne Dr *CHLM/GWD* CM2 .. 16 D8
Redmill *COLW* CO3 .... 162 B8
Redricks La *HLW* CM20 .... 227 G5
Redriff Rd *ROMW/RG* RM7 .... 370 C2
Red Rd *BRW* CM14 .... 354 C5
Redrose La *ING* CM4 .... 308 F2
Redruth Cl *CHLM/WR* CM1 .... 264 F6
Redruth Rd *HARH* RM3 .... 353 C6
Redshank Cl *HVHL* CB9 .... 28 D4
Redshank Crs *RCHLM* CM3 .... 339 L2 🆎
Red Sleeve *RIPS/CAP* IP9 ..... 78 A2
Redstock Rd *SOSN* SS2 .... 21 H2
Redvers Cl *BSF* CM23 .... 174 B1
Red White And Blue Rd
  BSF CM23 .... 174 C1
Red Willow *HLWW/ROY* CM19 .. 255 G6
Redwing Cl *CHTY* IP2 .... 36 E8
Redwing Dr *BCAYE* CM11 ...... 357 K3
Redwood Cha
  SOCK/AV RM15 .... 406 E2 🆎
Redwood Cl *COLN* CO4 .... 163 M3
  WIT CM8 .... 212 B6 🆎
Redwood Dr *CHLM/WR* CM1 .. 287 G2
  LAIN SS15 .... 376 E2
Redwood Gdns *CHING* E4 ...... 325 J8 🆎
The Redwoods *CVI* SS8 .... 397 M8 🆎
Reed Cl *RCOS* CO16 .... 12 B2
Reede Rd *DAGE* RM10 .... 388 B5
Reed Wy *DAGE* RM10 .... 388 C5
Reed Hall Av *COLS* CO2 .... 162 E8
Reedings Wy *SBW* CM21 .... 201 G7
  VGE SS16 .... 376 C7 🆎
Reed Pond Wk *GPK* RM2 ...... 371 L1
Reeds La *HVHL* CB9 .... 28 B3
Reeds Wy *WICKW* SS12 .... 359 K4
Reeve Gdns *KESC* IP5 .... 39 K4
Reeves Cl *BRWN* CM15 .... 308 C6
  VGE SS16 .... 376 A7 🆎
Reeves La *HLWW/ROY* CM19 .. 254 D7
Reeves Pightle *ROY* SG8 .... 40 A4
Reeves Wy *RCHLM* CM3 .... 339 M4
Refinery Rd *HAR* CO12 .... 112 F6

Regal Cl *CHLM/GWD* CM2 ..... 17 L8
Regan Cl *SLH/COR* SS17 .... 394 F7
Regarder Rd *CHIG* IG7 .... 350 C6
Regarth Av *ROM* RM1 .... 370 F6
Regency Cl *BSF* CM23 .... 173 M4
  CHIG IG7 .... 349 K6 🆎
  CHLM/GWD CM2 .... 17 M1 🆎
  RCFD SS4 .... 382 F1
  WICKE SS11 .... 359 L1
Regency Ct *BRW* CM14 .... 354 D3 🆎
  HLWS CM18 .... 256 B6
  MAL CM9 .... 269 H6
Regency Gdns *EMPK* RM11 .... 371 K7
Regent Cl *CDH/CHF* RM16 .... 407 K7
Regent Gn *COLW* CO3 .... 162 A7
Regent Rd *EPP* CM16 .... 304 A2
  RCOLE CO7 .... 221 G4
Regents Cl *BOC* CM0 .... 320 E7 🆎
  COLN CO4 .... 135 K6
Regent Pl *LOU* IG10 .... 348 E1
Regent St *IPNE* IP4 .... 3 J4
  K/T/MI CO5 .... 192 A3
  MGTR CO11 .... 108 E7 🆎
Regina Cl *IPNE* IP4 .... 38 C6
Reginald Rd *HARH* RM3 .... 372 B1
Regina Rd *CHLM/WR* CM1 ..... 17 J1
Reigate Av *RCOS* CO16 .... 223 L5
Reigate Cl *BSF* CM23 .... 173 G3 🆎
Rembrandt Cl *CVI* SS8 .... 398 B8
  SBN/FI SS3 .... 403 H3
Rembrandt Gv *CHLM/WR* CM1 .. 264 F5
Rembrandt Wy *COLW* CO3 ..... 162 C6 🆎
Rembrow Rd *RIPS/CAP* IP9 .... 78 B2
Remembrance Av *BOC* CM0 ... 344 C7
  RCHLM CM3 .... 238 B8
Remercie Rd *MGTR* CO11 ..... 109 H8
Renacres *VGE* SS16 .... 18 C9
Rendlesham Rd *FX* IP11 .... 84 E8 🆎
  IP IP1 .... 2 B3
Renfrew Rd *IPNE* IP4 .... 38 D2 🆎
Rennie Pl *CHLM/GWD* CM2 ... 265 J8
Rennie Rd *CHLM/GWD* CM2 ... 17 L5
Rennison Cl *CHESW* EN7 ...... 276 A7 🆎
Renoir Pl *CHLM/WR* CM1 ...... 265 G4
Renown Cl *ROMW/RG* RM7 ... 370 C1 🆎
  RCHLM CM3 .... 238 B8 🆎
Repton Av *GPK* RM2 .... 371 H3
Repton Cl *PIT* SS13 .... 378 B2
Repton Dr *GPK* RM2 .... 371 H4
Repton Gdns *GPK* RM2 .... 371 H3
Repton Gv *LOS* SS9 .... 382 B4
Repulse Cl *ROMW/RG* RM7 ... 370 C1 🆎
Retford Cl *HARH* RM3 .... 353 H7
Retford Pth *HARH* RM3 .... 353 H7
Retford Rd *HARH* RM3 .... 353 H8
Retreat Wy *HOC/HUL* SS5 ..... 362 F5
The Retreat *BRW* CM14 .... 354 C2
  GRAYS RM17 .... 417 J3 🆎
  RBRW/HUT CM13 .... 333 J8
  RCOLW CO6 .... 133 M8
  WIT CM8 .... 239 H2
Retreat Wy *CHIG* IG7 .... 350 C4
Rettendon Gdns *WICKE* SS11 . 359 H2 🆎
Rettendon Vw *WICKE* SS11 ... 360 A3
Reubens Rd *RBRW/HUT* CM13 .. 333 J8
Review Rd *DAGE* RM10 .... 388 C8
Reymead Cl *K/T/MI* CO5 .... 245 K4
Reynard Copse *BSF* CM23 ..... 174 A2
Reynards Cl *FOS* CO13 .... 198 E5
Reynards Copse *COLN* CO4 ... 135 H8
Reynards Av *COLW* CO3 .... 162 C6
  IPSE IP3 .... 59 H3
Reynold's Cl *HVHL* CB9 .... 27 L2 🆎
Reynolds Ct *FX* IP11 .... 84 E8
Reynolds Ga *RCHLM* CM3 ..... 339 M5 🆎
Reynolds Rd *IPSE* IP3 .... 59 H3
Rhoda Rd *CHLM/WR* CM1 ..... 17 J1
Rhoda Rd North *SBF/HAD* SS7 .. 379 M6
Rhodes Av *BSF* CM23 .... 174 A6
Rhugarve Gdns *CBE/LIN* CB1 . 24 E1 🆎
Ribble Cl *WFD* IG8 .... 348 D7 🆎
Riby Rd *FX* IP11 .... 9 J3
Richard Av *RCOLE* CO7 .... 164 D8
Richard Burn Wy *SUD* CO10 ... 4 D1
Richards Av *ROMW/RG* RM7 .. 370 C2
Richardson La *RIPS/CAP* IP9 .. 81 L4
Richardson Pl *CHLM/WR* CM1 . 16 D1
Richardson Wk *COLW* CO3 .... 162 A6
Rich Cl *RCHLM* CM3 .... 209 G4 🆎
Riche Cl *GTDUN* CM6 .... 180 C6
Richmond Av *SBF/HAD* SS7 ... 397 K1
  SBN/FI SS3 .... 402 E5
  WOS/PRIT SS0 .... 20 C5
Richmond St *SOSN* SS2 .... 401 L2
Ricketts Dr *BCAYW* CM12 ..... 335 G8
Rickling *VGE* SS16 .... 18 F7
Rickling Green Rd *SAFWS* CB11 .. 118 F3
Rickling Rd *SAFWS* CB11 ...... 88 C5
Rickstones Rd *WIT* CM8 .... 212 B4
Riddiford Dr *CHLM/WR* CM1 .. 264 A7
Riddings La *HLWS* CM18 ...... 256 B7
Riddles Dr *COLN* CO4 .... 10 D2
The Ride *PEND* EN3 .... 324 D5
Ridgemount *SBF/HAD* SS7 .... 379 M7 🆎
The Ridge *RCHLM* CM3 .... 290 F1
  WOTN CO14 .... 199 J3 🆎
Ridgeway *BCAYW* CM12 .... 357 H3
  GRAYS RM17 .... 417 M1
  ING CM4 .... 334 B2
  MAL CM9 .... 293 H3 🆎
  RAYL SS6 .... 380 D2
  RBRW/HUT CM13 .... 355 J2

STDN SG11 .... 172 C1
  WFD IG8 .... 348 D5
Ridgeway Gdns
  WOS/PRIT SS0 .... 400 C3 🆎
Ridgeways *HLWE* CM17 .... 256 F5
The Ridgeway *BRTR* CM7 ...... 183 M5 🆎
  CBE/LIN CB1 .... 24 F1
  GPK RM2 .... 371 H4
  HAR CO12 .... 6 D8
  HARH RM3 .... 371 M1
  LOS SS9 .... 400 B3
  WOS/PRIT SS0 .... 400 C3
Ridgeway Valley Vw
  COLN CO4 .... 135 H7 🆎
Ridgewell Av *CHLM/WR* CM1 . 264 A7
Ridgewell Cl *DAGE* RM10 ..... 388 C7
Ridgewell Rd *HSTD* CO9 .... 49 M1
  SUD CO10 .... 50 D2
Ridgewell Wy *COLS* CO2 .... 191 G2
Ridgwell Av *CDH/CHF* RM16 .. 408 B2
The Ridings *BSF* CM23 .... 173 L2
  CHLM/GWD CM2 .... 288 E4
  CVI SS8 .... 398 B6 🆎
  RCFD SS4 .... 383 G2
Ridlands Cl *BRTR* CM7 .... 183 M5 🆎
Ridley Cl *HARH* RM3 .... 371 J1
Ridley Gdns *RBSF* CM22 .... 147 K1
Ridley Rd *CHLM/WR* CM1 ..... 264 C3
  PIT SS13 .... 378 D2
Riffams Ct *PIT* SS13 .... 378 D3 🆎
Riffams Dr *PIT* SS13 .... 378 D3
Riffhams *RBRW/HUT* CM13 ... 355 J4
Riffhams Cha *RCHLM* CM3 .... 290 E2
Riffhams Dr *CHLM/GWD* CM2 . 289 G4
Riffhams La *RCHLM* CM3 ...... 290 D3
Rifle HI *BRTR* CM7 .... 183 G2
Rigby Av *MGTR* CO11 .... 109 H8
Rigby Gdns *CDH/CHF* RM16 .. 418 C1
Rignals La *CHLM/GWD* CM2 .. 288 E3
Riley Av *RCOS* CO15 .... 249 M5
Riley Rd *PEND* EN3 .... 324 D2
Rimini Cl *COLS* CO2 .... 190 D1
Ringham Rd *IPNE* IP4 .... 38 B5
Ringwood Av *HCH* RM12 ...... 389 L1
Ringwood Dr *LOS* SS9 .... 381 J4
Ripley Cl *RCOS* CO16 .... 223 J5
Ripley Vw *LOU* IG10 .... 327 J2
Ripley Wy *CHESW* EN7 .... 300 C2
Rippleside *BSDN* SS14 .... 378 A6
Ripple Wy *COLN* CO4 .... 11 H4
Risby Cl *IPNE* IP4 .... 38 C5
  RCOS CO16 .... 223 H7
Risdens *HLWS* CM18 .... 255 K6 🆎
Risebridge Cha *ROM* RM1 ..... 352 A8
Risebridge Rd *GPK* RM2 .... 371 G2
Rise Pk LAIN* SS15 .... 18 C6
Rise Park Bvd *GPK* RM2 .... 371 G1
Rise Park Pde *ROM* RM1 ...... 370 F2
The Rise *BKHH* IG9 .... 348 E2 🆎
  COLW CO3 .... 161 H3
  DART DA1 .... 414 A8
Riseway *BRWN* CM15 .... 354 F4
The Rising *BCAYE* CM11 .... 357 K2
Ritabrook Rd *CHTY* IP2 .... 57 M2
Rivendell V *RCHLM* CM3 .... 339 K5
Rivenhall *SBF/HAD* SS7 .... 380 C1
  WICKE SS11 .... 360 B5
River Av *HOD* EN11 .... 253 J4
Riverbank Cl *SUD* CO10 .... 31 K4 🆎
River Cl *BAR* EN8 .... 301 H6
  HSTD CO9 .... 129 G2
  RAIN RM13 .... 404 C3 🆎
Riverdale *LOS* SS9 .... 381 L4
River Dr *UPMR* RM14 .... 372 D6
Riverfield La *SBW* CM21 .... 200 F8 🆎
River HI *RCHLM* CM3 .... 210 C8
River Md *BRTR* CM7 .... 155 H6
Rivermill *HLW* CM20 .... 15 J1
River Rd *BKHH* IG9 .... 348 F2
  BRW CM14 .... 353 M5
Riversdale Rd *CRW* RM5 .... 351 J8
Riverside *BRTR* CM7 .... 156 E8
  BSF CM23 .... 174 A4
  GTDUN CM6 .... 178 F2
Riverside Av *BROX* EN10 ...... 277 H2
Riverside Av East *MGTR* CO11 . 108 D6
Riverside Av West *MGTR* CO11 . 108 C6
Riverside Cl *CHING* E4 .... 325 J8 🆎
  HLW CM20 .... 227 K5
Riverside Rd *BOC* CM0 .... 344 D7 🆎
  IP IP1 .... 37 G4
Riverside Wk *WICKW* SS12 ... 359 J3
Riverside Wy *K/T/MI* CO5 ..... 213 K2
Riversmead *HOD* EN11 .... 253 H6 🆎
Rivers St *IPNE* IP4 .... 3 L2
Riverton Dr *BOC* CM0 .... 296 C2
Rivertons *LOS* SS9 .... 378 A7
River Vw *CDH/CHF* RM16 ..... 418 B2
Riverview *VGE* SS16 .... 378 B7
River Vw *WIT* CM8 .... 239 H3
Riverview Gdns *HOC/HUL* SS5 . 339 K8
River View Rd *RIPS/CAP* IP9 .. 111 J3
  SBF/HAD SS7 .... 397 L1
River View Ter *RCHLM* CM3 ... 342 F1
River Wy *HLW* CM20 .... 227 H6
  LOU IG10 .... 327 H8
Rivey Wy *CBE/LIN* CB1 .... 24 E1
Riviera Dr *SOS* SS1 .... 21 M5
Rivish La *SUD* CO10 .... 34 D4
Roach Av *RAYL* SS6 .... 380 D2
Roach V *COLN* CO4 .... 163 M2
  LOS SS9 .... 382 A4
Roach Valley Wy *HOC/HUL* SS5 . 362 D8
Robeck Rd *IPSE* IP3 .... 58 F2
Robert Rd *BCAYW* CM12 ...... 357 G1
  CHIG IG7 .... 350 A6
  CHLM/GWD CM2 .... 265 G7
Roberts Cl *BAR* EN8 .... 300 C7 🆎
  HARH RM3 .... 371 J1
Robert's HI *BURES* CO8 .... 102 A8
Robertson Cl *BROX* EN10 ..... 276 F6 🆎
Robertson Dr *WICKW* SS12 ... 359 M6 🆎
Roberts Rd *COLS* CO2 .... 163 G6 🆎
  LAIN SS15 .... 376 C4 🆎
  RCHLM CM3 .... 341 H4
Robert Wallace Cl *BSF* CM23 . 174 A2

Robin Cl *BCAYW* CM12 .... 335 K5
  CRW RM5 .... 351 L8
  RCOLE CO7 .... 194 E3
Robin Crs *COLW* CO3 .... 161 K7
Robin Dr *CHTY* IP2 .... 36 E8
Robin Hood Rd *BRWN* CM15 .. 354 C1
  RBSF CM22 .... 147 K2
Robinia Cl *BARK/HLT* IG6 ..... 349 M7
  LAIN SS15 .... 376 E2
Robinsbridge Rd *RCOLW* CO6 . 186 A1
Robinsdale *COS* CO15 .... 224 A5
Robinson Cl *BSF* CM23 .... 174 A6
  HCH RM12 .... 389 J6 🆎
Robinson Rd *CDH/CHF* RM16 . 393 L7
  DAGE RM10 .... 388 B3
  RCOLE CO7 .... 221 H4
The Robins *BRWN* CM15 ...... 308 E7
Robin Wy *CHLM/GWD* CM2 ... 288 C6
  SUD CO10 .... 54 D6
Robjohns Rd *CHLM/WR* CM1 . 16 A8
Robletts Wy *RCOLW* CO6 ...... 102 F7
Robsons Cl *BAR* EN8 .... 300 D1 🆎
Roche Av *RCFD* SS4 .... 382 F1
Rochefort Cl *RCFD* SS4 .... 383 G3
Rochehall Wy *RCFD* SS4 .... 383 J3
Rochelle Cl *GTDUN* CM6 .... 92 B8
Rochester Cl *BRTR* CM7 .... 155 L7
Rochester Dr *WOS/PRIT* SS0 . 382 D7
Rochester Ms *WOS/PRIT* SS0 . 382 D7
Rochester Wy *SUD* CO10 ...... 4 A1
Rocheway *RCFD* SS4 .... 383 H1
Rochford Av *BRWN* CM15 ..... 333 H7
  WAB EN9 .... 301 L6
  WOS/PRIT SS0 .... 20 C3
Rochford Cl *BROX* EN10 .... 276 F6
  HCH RM12 .... 389 J5 🆎
  WICKE SS11 .... 360 A5
Rochford Gn *LOU* IG10 .... 327 K5
Rochford Hall *RCFD* SS4 .... 383 C2
Rochford Rd *BSF* CM23 .... 174 C2
  CHLM/GWD CM2 .... 17 J5 🆎
  CVI SS8 .... 398 E8
  RCOS CO16 .... 222 C7
  SOSN SS2 .... 382 E7
Rochford Wy *FOS* CO13 .... 199 H4 🆎
Rockall *SOSN* SS2 .... 382 B4
Rockall Cl *HVHL* CB9 .... 28 E4
Rockchase Gdns
  EMPK RM11 .... 371 M6 🆎
Rockingham Av *EMPK* RM11 .. 371 J6
Rockingham Cl *COLN* CO4 .... 135 L8 🆎
Rockleigh Av *LOS* SS9 .... 400 B2
Rockleigh Ct *BRWN* CM15 ..... 355 H1
Rockwell Rd *DAGE* RM10 ...... 388 C4
Rockwood Gdns *LOU* IG10 .... 327 K5
Rodbridge Dr *SOS* SS1 .... 402 A3
Rodbridge HI *SUD* CO10 .... 34 C7
Roddam Cl *COLW* CO3 .... 162 D5
Roden Cl *HLWE* CM17 .... 228 A7
Rodeo Cl *ERITH* DA8 .... 414 C5
Roding Cl *CHONG* CM5 .... 283 L1 🆎
  SBN/FI SS3 .... 385 J7 🆎
Roding Dr *BRWN* CM15 .... 332 A1
Roding Gdns *LOU* IG10 .... 326 F8
Roding La *BKHH* IG9 .... 348 F2
  CHIG IG7 .... 349 H2
Roding Leigh *RCHLM* CM3 .... 339 M4 🆎
Roding Rd *LOU* IG10 .... 327 G7
Rodings Av *SLH/COR* SS17 .... 394 E7
The Rodings *LOS* SS9 .... 381 L4
  UPMR RM14 .... 372 E6
Roding Vw *BKHH* IG9 .... 348 E2
  CHONG CM5 .... 283 J7
Roding Wy *RAIN* RM13 .... 389 L8 🆎
  WICKW SS12 .... 359 M4
Rodney Crs *HOD* EN11 .... 253 H3
Rodney Gdns *BRTR* CM7 ...... 155 K7 🆎
Rodney Rd *CHONG* CM5 .... 307 C1
Rodney Wy *CHLM/WR* CM1 ... 16 B9
  ROMW/RG RM7 .... 370 C1
Roebuck La *BKHH* IG9 .... 348 D2
Roebuck Rd *BARK/HLT* IG6 ... 350 C7
Roedean Av *PEND* EN3 .... 324 D3
Roedean Cl *PEND* EN3 .... 324 D3
  SOSN SS2 .... 402 A1
Roedean Gdns *SOSN* SS2 ..... 402 A1
Rogation Cl *COLW* CO3 .... 161 L6
Rogers Cl *FX* IP11 .... 85 G7 🆎
Rogers Gdns *DAGE* RM10 ..... 388 B4
Rogers Rd *DAGE* RM10 .... 388 B4
  GRAYS RM17 .... 417 K1
Roggel Rd *CVI* SS8 .... 413 L1
Rokells *BSDN* SS14 .... 18 F4
Rokell Wy *FOS* CO13 .... 199 G5
Rokescroft *PIT* SS13 .... 378 B6
Roland Cl *CVI* SS8 .... 398 C7
Rollestons *CHLM/WR* CM1 .... 287 G2
Rolley La *K/T/MI* CO5 .... 213 K1
Rolph Cl *RCOS* CO16 .... 197 H1
Romagne Cl *SLH/COR* SS17 ... 394 A8
Romainville Wy *CVI* SS8 .... 397 K8
Roman Wy *BCAYW* CM12 ...... 357 H3
  BOC CM0 .... 344 C4
  *EN EN1 .... 324 A7
  FX IP11 .... 85 L7
  HVHL CB9 .... 28 E5
  RCOS CO16 .... 221 H8
  SUD CO10 .... 34 D5
Rom Crs *ROMW/RG* RM7 ...... 370 F7
Romeland *WAB* EN9 .... 301 K5
Romford Cl *COLN* CO4 .... 11 H5
Romford Rd *CHDH* RM6 .... 350 E7

CHIG IG7 .... 350 C5
CHONG CM5 .... 306 F5
CRW RM5 .... 350 F8
SOCK/AV RM15 .... 405 K1
Romney Cha EMPK RM11 .... 372 B6 ▣
FOS CO13 .... 198 F4 ▣
RCOLE CO7 .... 220 F2
RCOS CO16 .... 223 L5
Romney Rd BCAYW CM12 .... 357 G2
IPSE IP3 .... 59 H3
Romsey CI HOC/HUL SS5 .... 362 E5
SLH/COR SS17 .... 409 J2 ▣
Romsey Crs SBF/HAD SS7 .... 379 J4
Romsey Dr SBF/HAD SS7 .... 379 H6
Romsey Rd SBF/HAD SS7 .... 379 H6
Romsey Wy SBF/HAD SS7 .... 379 H5
Romulus CI RCOLN CO4 .... 135 C6
Rom Valley Wy ROMW/RG RM7 .. 370 F6
Ronald Dr RAYL SS6 .... 361 H7
Ronald Park Av WOS/PRIT SS0 ... 400 D1
Ronald Rd HARH RM3 .... 372 B1
HSTD CO9 .... 128 F3
Roneo Cnr ROMW/RG RM7 .... 371 G8
Roneo Link HCH RM12 .... 371 G8 ▣
Roodegate BSDN SS14 .... 18 E4
Rook End La SAFWS CB11 .... 90 C5
The Rookeries RCOLW CO6 .... 160 C7 ▣
Rookery Cha RCOLE CO7 .... 136 F1
Rookery CI SS6 .... 380 D1
RCHLM CM3 .... 238 B6 ▣
SAFWN CB10 .... 22 E8
SLH/COR SS17 .... 409 J2
Rookery HI SLH/COR SS17 .... 395 K8
Rookery La K/T/MI CO5 .... 214 D6
MAL CM9 .... 240 F4
RCHLM CM3 .... 340 F2
SAFWS CB11 .... 64 F7
Rookery Md RCHLM CM3 .... 339 L3 ▣
Rookery Rd INC CM4 .... 308 D1
The Rookery MGTR CO11 .... 108 D7 ▣
STSD CM24 .... 146 F3 ▣
WTHK RM20 .... 416 B3 ▣
Rookery Vw GRAYS RM17 .... 417 L2
Rookes SAFWN SB10 .... 43 L7
Rookwood Av LOU IG10 .... 327 K5
Rookwood CI GRAYS RM17 .... 417 J1
RCOS CO16 .... 223 L4
Rookwood Gdns CHING E4 .... 348 A3 ▣
Rookwood Wy HVHL CB9 .... 28 B5
Rookyards VGE SS16 .... 377 M6 ▣
Rookes SAFWN SS9 .... 43 L7
Roosevelt Av CVI SS8 .... 398 B7
Roosevelt Rd LAIN SS15 .... 376 B5
Roosevelt Wy COLS CO2 .... 163 J7
DAGE RM10 .... 388 E5 ▣
Roos Hill Debden Rd
SAFWS CB11 .... 65 M6
Roots Hall Av SOSN SS2 .... 20 E1
Roots Hall Dr WOS/PRIT SS0 ..... 20 D1
Roots La WIT CM8 .... 239 M7
Ropers La SUD CO10 .... 34 C7
Ropes Dr KESG IP5 .... 39 L3
Rope Wk IPNE IP4 .... 3 H5
MAL CM9 .... 293 H2
Rosabelle Av RCOLE CO7 .... 192 C2
Rosalind CI COLN CO4 .... 164 A4
Rosary Gdns WOS/PRIT SS0 ...... 382 C7
Rosbach Rd CVI SS8 .... 398 E8
Rosberg Rd CVI SS8 .... 398 F8 ▣
Roscommon Wy CVI SS8 .... 397 K7
Rose Acre BSDN SS14 .... 378 A5
Roseacre CI RBSF CM22 .... 176 D4
SBW CM21 .... 200 B8
Rose Av COLW CO3 .... 161 K7
Rose Bank BRW CM14 .... 354 E4
Rosebank HAR CO12 .... 9 M1
WAB EN9 .... 301 M6
Rosebank Av HCH RM12 .... 389 K4
Rosebank Rd K/T/MI CO5 .... 245 H5
Rosebay Av BCAYW CM12 .... 335 G6
Rosebay CI WIT CM8 .... 211 L8
VGE SS16 .... 376 C7
Roseberry Av SBF/HAD SS7 ..... 379 K5
VGE SS16 .... 376 C7
Roseberry CI UPMR RM14 .... 373 C6
Roseberry Gdns UPMR RM14 .... 373 C7
Rosebery BSF CM23 .... 174 D5
Rosebery Av COL CO1 .... 10 F8
Rosebery Rd CHLM/GWD CM2 ... 17 H7
FX IP11 .... 115 J1
GRAYS RM17 .... 416 F3
IPNE IP4 .... 3 L5
Rose CI WICKW SS12 .... 359 M6 ▣
Rose Ct CHESW EN7 .... 276 B7
RIPS/CAP IP9 .... 83 G8 ▣
Rose Crs COLN CO4 .... 162 E1
Rosecroft CI COS CO15 .... 223 M5
VGE SS16 .... 376 B7
Rosecroft Rd IP IP1 .... 37 H1
Rosedale Av CHESW EN7 .... 300 A1
Rosedale Rd CRW RM5 .... 370 D3
GRAYS RM17 .... 417 L3
Rosedale Wy CHESW EN7 .... 276 B8
Rose Dr BOC CM0 .... 320 E8
Rosefinch CI HVHL CB9 .... 28 D4
Rose Gdns BRTR CM7 .... 183 H1 ▣
RCOS CO16 .... 249 J5
Rose Gln ROMW/RG RM7 .... 370 F8
Rose HI BRTR CM7 .... 183 H1
Rosehill CI HOD EN11 .... 253 C5
Rosehill Crs IPSE IP3 .... 3 L7
Rosehill Rd IPSE IP3 .... 3 M7
Roselaine BSDN SS14 .... 19 C4
Roselands Rd HOD EN11 .... 253 L4
Rose La BCAYW CM12 .... 357 H1
IPNE IP4 .... 2 F6
MAL CM9 .... 243 J3
RCOLE CO7 .... 192 C4 ▣
SAFWN SB10 .... 42 F1
Rosemary Av BRTR CM7 .... 155 G7 ▣
FX IP11 .... 85 J7
ROM RM1 .... 371 J3
Rosemary Crs COS CO15 .... 13 H8
GTDUN CM6 .... 178 D2 ▣

K/T/MI CO5 .... 214 D6
Rosemary Cresecent
GTDUN CM6 .... 178 D2 ▣
Rosemary Gdns BCTR RM8 .... 370 A8
SUD CO10 .... 4 E1
Rosemary La GTDUN CM6 .... 151 K4
GTDUN CM6 .... 178 D2
HSTD CO9 .... 74 A6
HSTD CO9 .... 128 F1
RCOLE CO7 .... 194 C6
Rosemary Rd COS CO15 .... 12 F7
Rosemary Rd West COS CO15 ... 12 E7
Rosemary Wy COS CO15 .... 250 B4
Rosemead SBF/HAD SS7 .... 379 K4
Rosemead Gdns
RBRW/HUT CM13 .... 333 L6
Rosemount HLWW/ROY CM19 ... 255 J6
Rosemount CI WFD IG8 .... 349 G7 ▣
Roserna Av CVI SS8 .... 398 E8
Rosery Ms FOS CO13 .... 198 B7
Rose Va BRW CM14 .... 354 D4 ▣
Rose Valley Crs SLH/COR SS17 . 394 E7
Rose Wy RCFD SS4 .... 383 H3
Rosewood Av HCH RM12 .... 389 H4 ▣
Rosewood CI RCOLN CO4 .... 135 H7
SOCK/AV RM15 .... 406 F1 ▣
Rosewood La SBN/FI SS3 .... 403 G5
Rosilian Dr HOC/HUL SS5 .... 362 D2
Roslings CI CHLM/WR CM1 .... 263 L5
Roslyn CI BROX EN10 .... 276 F1
Roslyn Gdns GPK RM2 .... 371 G2
Rossall CI EMPK RM11 .... 371 H6
Ross Av BCTR RM8 .... 388 A1
Ross CI HVHL CB9 .... 28 D4
SAFWS CB11 .... 65 M5
Rossdale Dr ED N9 .... 324 D8
Rossdene Gdns GTDUN CM6 ..... 231 L4
Rossell Rd TIL RM18 .... 418 A6 ▣
Rossendale CHLM/WR CM1 .... 16 B6
Rossendale CI RCOLN CO4 .... 135 K8
Rossetta CI RCOLE CO7 .... 192 B1 ▣
Rossiter Rd SBN/FI SS3 .... 403 J3
Rosslyn Av BCTR RM8 .... 370 A7
CHING E4 .... 348 A3
HARH RM3 .... 371 M2
Rosslyn CI HOC/HUL SS5 .... 362 F4
Rosslyn Rd BCAYW CM12 .... 357 G1
HOC/HUL SS5 .... 362 F5
Ross Rd IPNE IP4 .... 38 C2
Ross Wy VGE SS16 .... 377 H4
Roswell CI BAR EN8 .... 300 F2 ▣
Rothbury Av RAIN RM13 .... 404 C3
Rothbury Rd CHLM/WR CM1 ...... 287 L2
Rotherfield Rd PEND EN3 .... 324 E1
Rothesay Av CHLM/GWD CM2 ... 16 F7
Rothmans Av CHLM/GWD CM2 .. 288 F5
Rothwell CI LOS SS9 .... 381 K5
Roughtallys EPP CM16 .... 281 G7
Roughtons CHLM/GWD CM2 ..... 288 D8
LAIN SS15 .... 18 E7
Roundbush Rd K/T/MI CO5 .... 215 L2
MAL CM9 .... 317 H3
Round CI COLW CO3 .... 162 C4
Round Coppice Rd RBSF CM22 . 175 H3
Roundcroft CHESW EN7 .... 276 A6
Round Hill Rd SBF/HAD SS7 ..... 398 B1
Roundhills WAB EN9 .... 301 M6
The Roundings HERT/BAY SG13 . 252 D1
Roundmead Av LOU IG10 .... 327 H5
Roundmoor Dr BAR EN8 .... 300 F1
Roundridge Rd RIPS/CAP IP9 .... 78 C1 ▣
Roundwood Av
RBRW/HUT CM13 .... 355 H2
Roundwood Gv
RBRW/HUT CM13 .... 355 J1
Roundwood Rd IPNE IP4 .... 38 B4
Rounton Rd WAB EN9 .... 301 M5
Rous Cha CHLM/GWD CM2 .... 312 C2
Rous Rd BKHH IG9 .... 348 F2
Routh Av IPSE IP3 .... 60 A2 ▣
Rover Av BARK/HLT IG6 .... 350 A7
COS CO15 .... 249 M4
Rowallan CI COLW CO3 .... 162 B8
Rowan CI COLW CO3 .... 161 L7
COS CO15 .... 12 A6
HAR CO12 .... 6 F8
RAYL SS6 .... 361 J3 ▣
RCOLE CO7 .... 195 C3 ▣
Rowan Dr BROX EN10 .... 277 L4
MAL CM9 .... 269 K6
Rowan Gn East
RBRW/HUT CM13 .... 355 G4 ▣
Rowan Gn West
RBRW/HUT CM13 .... 355 G4 ▣
Rowan Gv SOCK/AV RM15 .... 405 K5
Rowanhayes CI CHTY IP2 .... 37 J8
The Rowans BCAYE CM11 .... 357 L3
BROX EN10 .... 252 F7
SOCK/AV RM15 .... 405 K6 ▣
Rowans Wy LOU IG10 .... 327 G6
WICKE SS11 .... 359 M3
Rowan Wk EMPK RM11 .... 371 L4
LOS SS9 .... 381 L5
SBW CM21 .... 227 M1
Rowan Wy RCFD SS4 .... 364 F2
RCHLM CM3 .... 238 B8 ▣
SOCK/AV RM15 .... 406 E2
WIT CM8 .... 212 B6
Rowarth Av KESG IP5 .... 39 K4
Rowdowns Rd DAGW RM9 .... 388 A4
Rowell CI HVHL CB9 .... 28 B1
Rowenhall LAIN SS15 .... 376 A5
Rowhedge La RCOLE CO7 .... 167 G7
Rowhedge Rd COLS CO2 .... 191 L1
Rowhedge CI PIT SS13 .... 378 E1 ▣
Rowhedge Ferry Rd
RCOLE CO7 .... 192 B3
Rowhedge Rd COLS CO2 .... 191 L1
Rowherns La RCOLE CO7 .... 167 G7
Rowland Crs CHIG IG7 .... 349 M5
Rowlands CI BAR EN8 .... 300 E2
Rowlands Rd BCTR RM8 .... 388 A1
The Rowlands SBF/HAD SS7 ..... 379 M7 ▣
Rowland's Yd HAR CO12 .... 142 F1

Rowley CI MGTR CO11 .... 108 E3
Rowley Ct HVHL CB9 .... 28 F6
Rowley HI WFD IG8 .... 28 E6
Rowley Md EPP CM16 .... 280 D5
Rowley Rd CDH/CHF RM16 .... 408 B3
Rowney Av SAFWN CB10 .... 90 F1
Rowney Gdns SBW CM21 .... 227 K3
Rowney Wd SBW CM21 .... 227 K2
Rowntree Wy SAFWS CB11 .... 65 L4
The Row RCOLE CO7 .... 106 D1
Roxburgh Av UPMR RM14 .... 390 D2
Roxburgh Rd RCOS CO16 .... 196 A5
Roxburgh Rd IPNE IP4 .... 38 C2
Roxwell Gdns
RBRW/HUT CM13 .... 333 K7
Roxwell Rd CHLM/WR CM1 .... 262 A3
Roxwell Wy WFD IG8 .... 348 D8
Royal Artillery Wy SOSN SS2 ..... 383 M8
Royal Av BAR EN8 .... 300 F5
Royal CI RCFD SS4 .... 363 L6
Royal Ct COLN CO4 .... 163 M2 ▣
MAL CM9 .... 293 H2
Royal Ms SOS SS1 .... 21 G8
Royal Oak Dr WICKE SS11 .... 360 B3
Royal Oak Gdns BSF CM23 .... 173 M5
Royal Ter SOS SS1 .... 21 G8
Roy Av IPNE IP4 .... 38 C6
Royce CI BROX EN10 .... 277 C2 ▣
Roy CI KESG IP5 .... 39 J4
Roydon Br SBDN SS14 .... 19 M2
Roydon CI LOU IG10 .... 348 F1
Roydon Rd HLWW/ROY CM19 ... 14 C4
Royer CI HOC/HUL SS5 .... 363 H7 ▣
Royle CI GPK RM2 .... 371 J5
Royston Av LAIN SS15 .... 376 E2
SOSN SS2 .... 383 J8
Royston Dr CHTY IP2 .... 57 L7 ▣
Royston La SAFWN CB10 .... 41 H3
Royston Rd HARH RM3 .... 353 H8
SAFWS CB11 .... 64 D6
Ruaton Dr COS CO15 .... 12 A3
Rubens CI SBN/FI SS3 .... 403 H3
Rubens Ga CHLM/WR CM1 .... 265 C4
Rubens IPSE IP3 .... 59 H2
Rubicon Av WICKE SS11 .... 360 A3
Rudkin Rd COLN CO4 .... 135 G6
Rudlands RIPW IP8 .... 57 K2
Rudsdale Wy COLW CO3 .... 162 A6
Rue De St Lawrence
WAB EN9 .... 301 K6 ▣
Rue's La FX IP11 .... 85 K5
Ruffels Fld GTDUN CM6 .... 151 M7
Ruffles CI RAYL SS6 .... 361 M8
Rugby Rd SUD CO10 .... 55 J7
Rugosa CI COLW CO3 .... 161 K4
Rumbold Rd HOD EN11 .... 253 J1
Rumbullion Dr BCAYW CM12 .... 335 G8 ▣
Rumsey Flds RCHLM CM3 .... 291 G4
Rumsley CHESW EN7 .... 276 B7
Rundells HLWS CM18 .... 256 B7
Rundells Wk BSDN SS14 .... 377 M4 ▣
The Rundels SBF/HAD SS7 .... 380 B6
Runnacles St WIT CM8 .... 184 D6
Runnacles Wy FX IP11 .... 84 E8
Running Mare La
CHLM/GWD CM2 .... 288 B8
Running Waters
RBRW/HUT CM13 .... 355 H5
Runnymede Cha SBF/HAD SS7 .. 380 B7
Runnymede Rd CVI SS8 .... 398 C8
SLH/COR SS17 .... 409 K2
Runsell CI RCHLM CM3 .... 291 G4
Runsell La RCHLM CM3 .... 291 G3
Runsell Vw RCHLM CM3 .... 291 G3
Runwell Gdns WICKE SS11 .... 359 L1
Runwell Rd WICKE SS11 .... 359 L3
Runwell Ter SOS SS1 .... 20 F7
Rupert Rd BOC CM0 .... 320 D7
Rural CI HCH RM12 .... 371 J8
Rurik Ct MAL CM9 .... 292 F3
Rushbottom La SBF/HAD SS7 ... 379 J5
WICKW SS12 .... 379 J3
Rushbury CI IPNE IP4 .... 38 C3
Rush CI SBF/HAD SS7 .... 379 J5
Rushdene Rd BCAYW CM12 ...... 357 G3
BRWN CM15 .... 354 D1 ▣
Rushdon CI CDH/CHF RM16 ...... 407 H8
ROM RM1 .... 371 H5
Rushes La BOC CM0 .... 321 H2
Rushes Md HLWS CM18 .... 255 M5
Rushfield SBW CM21 .... 227 M1 ▣
Rush Green Gdns
ROMW/RG RM7 .... 370 D8
Rush Green Rd ROMW/RG RM7 . 370 D8
ROMW/RG RM7 .... 370 D8
Rush La RBSF CM22 .... 147 K3
Rushleigh Av BAR EN8 .... 300 E2
Rushleigh Gn BSF CM23 .... 173 L8
Rushley PIT SS13 .... 378 E3
Rushley CI CDH/CHF RM16 ...... 407 L6
SBN/FI SS3 .... 385 H7
Rushleydale CHLM/WR CM1 ..... 264 F6
Rushmeadow Wy FX IP11 .... 85 L6 ▣
Rushmere Av UPMR RM14 .... 390 D2
Rushmere CI K/T/MI CO5 .... 245 K5
Rushmere Rd IPNE IP4 .... 38 B4
Rushmere St KESG IP5 .... 38 E2
Rusholme Av DAGE RM10 .... 388 B2
Rushton Gv HLWE CM17 .... 256 E3
Ruskin Av SOSN SS2 .... 21 H1
UPMR RM14 .... 372 D7
WAB EN9 .... 301 M6
Ruskin CI FOS CO13 .... 198 F4 ▣
HVHL CB9 .... 27 L2 ▣
Ruskin Dene BCAYW CM12 ...... 335 H8
Ruskin Gdns HARH RM3 .... 371 J1 ▣
Ruskin Rd CDH/CHF RM16 .... 418 B1
CHLM/WR CM1 .... 264 F6
IPSE IP3 .... 3 M6
SLH/COR SS17 .... 409 K2
St Andrew's Av COLS CO2 .... 11 M9
HCH RM12 .... 389 C4
St Andrew's Avenue
(Colchester By-pass Road)
COLN CO4 .... 11 J7
St Andrews CI CVI SS8 .... 397 L7 ▣
EPP CM16 .... 281 K4
IPNE IP4 .... 38 E6 ▣
RCOLE CO7 .... 193 J4
St Andrew's Dr RIPS/CAP IP9 ... 81 M4
St Andrews Gdns COLN CO4 ..... 11 H6
St Andrews La LAIN SS15 .... 376 D4

Russell Gv RCFD SS4 .... 383 H1
Russell Rd BKHH IG9 .... 348 D2
COS CO15 .... 13 K5
EN EN1 .... 324 A2
IP IP11 .... 9 J5
IP IP1 .... 2 C5
Russell's Dr BAR EN8 .... 300 F3 ▣
Russell's Ride BAR EN8 .... 300 E3 ▣
Russell's Rd HSTD CO9 .... 128 C3
Russel Rd GRAYS RM17 .... 417 M1
Russet CI BRTR CM7 .... 183 H2 ▣
SLH/COR SS17 .... 394 E8
Russets EMPK RM11 .... 371 M4 ▣
The Russets RCFD SS4 .... 363 L6 ▣
Russetts VGE SS16 .... 376 B6
Russet Wy BOC CM0 .... 344 D5
HOC/HUL SS5 .... 362 F5
Rustic CI UPMR RM14 .... 372 F8
Rutherford CI BCAYW CM12 ...... 335 H6 ▣
LOS SS9 .... 381 K5
Rutherfords CHLM/WR CM1 ...... 264 C2
Ruthven Av BAR EN8 .... 300 F5
Ruthven CI WICKW SS12 .... 359 L5
Rutland Ap EMPK RM11 .... 372 B5
Rutland Av COLS CO2 .... 162 C8
SOS SS1 .... 401 M3
Rutland CI LAIN SS15 .... 376 B5
Rutland Dr EMPK RM11 .... 372 B5
RAYL SS6 .... 361 H8
Rutland Gdns BRTR CM7 .... 155 H7 ▣
RCFD SS4 .... 363 K6
Rutland Rd CHLM/WR CM1 .... 264 B5
RCHLM CM3 .... 341 H4 ▣
Rydal Av FX IP11 .... 85 L6
Rydal CI HOC/HUL SS5 .... 339 L8
RAYL SS6 .... 380 F1
Rydal Wk IPSE IP3 .... 59 H3 ▣
Rydal Wy BRTR CM7 .... 182 D5
PEND EN3 .... 324 E1
Ryde Av CVI SS8 .... 224 B4
Ryde CI LOS SS9 .... 381 G6
Ryde Dr SLH/COR SS17 .... 409 K3
Ryder Gdns RAIN RM13 .... 389 C5
Ryder Wy PIT SS13 .... 378 E1
The Ryde LOS SS9 .... 381 G6
Rye CI COLW CO3 .... 161 L6
HCH RM12 .... 389 K4 ▣
IPSE IP3 .... 38 E7
RCHLM CM3 .... 238 B8
RCOLE CO7 .... 220 F7
Ryecroft HLWW/ROY CM19 ...... 15 C5
Ryedene VGE SS16 .... 377 M8
Ryedene CI VGE SS16 .... 377 M8 ▣
Ryedene PI VGE SS16 .... 377 M8 ▣
Ryefeld CI HOD EN11 .... 253 J1
The Rye Fld RCHLM CM3 .... 266 E8
Rye Hill Rd HLWS CM18 .... 255 L8
Rye Hills HSTD CO9 .... 129 C3
Rye La COLS CO2 .... 190 B7
Rye Mill La K/T/MI CO5 .... 186 E7
Rye Rd HOD EN11 .... 253 J4
Ryes La RBSF CM22 .... 202 C4
SUD CO10 .... 76 B1
Rye St BSF CM23 .... 174 A2
Rye Wk INC CM4 .... 334 B1
Rygate Rd COL CO1 .... 10 D7
Rykhill CDH/CHF RM16 .... 408 C3
Rylands CI RIPS/CAP IP9 .... 78 B1
Rylands Rd SOSN SS2 .... 21 M1
The Ryle CHLM/WR CM1 .... 287 H3
Rylstone Wy SAFWS CB11 .... 66 A3
Rysley RCHLM CM3 .... 266 E7

S

Sabina Rd CDH/CHF RM16 .... 418 D1
Sabines Rd ABR/ST RM4 .... 331 C5
Sackville CI CHLM/WR CM1 .... 16 A1
Sackville Crs HARH RM3 .... 371 M1
Sackville Rd SOSN SS2 .... 401 M3
Sackville Wy RCOLW CO6 .... 133 L7
Saddle Ri CHLM/WR CM1 .... 264 F3 ▣
Saddleworth Sq HARH RM3 ...... 352 D7 ▣
Sadler CI COLS CO2 .... 163 J7
Sadlers SBF/HAD SS7 .... 379 J4
FOS CO13 .... 198 D5
Sadlers CI BCAYE CM11 .... 335 L6
Sadlers Md HLWS CM18 .... 256 B4
Saffory CI LOS SS9 .... 381 K4
Saffron CI BRTR CM7 .... 95 K8 ▣
HOD EN11 .... 253 C4
RBRW/HUT CM13 .... 374 E6
SLH/COR SS17 .... 394 E8
Saffron Ct SAFWS CB11 .... 65 L2
Saffron Gdns BRTR CM7 .... 95 J8
SLH/COR SS17 .... 409 C2
Saffron Rd CDH/CHF RM16 ...... 416 D1
CRW RM5 .... 370 E2
Saffron Wk BCAYE CM11 .... 357 J1 ▣
BRTR CM7 .... 95 J8
Saffron Wy K/T/MI CO5 .... 214 D7
Sage Rd COLS CO2 .... 191 H1
Sages End Rd HVHL CB9 .... 47 H3
St Agnes Dr CVI SS8 .... 397 L3
St Agnes Wy KESG IP5 .... 39 C5
St Albans Av UPMR RM14 .... 372 F8
St Alban's Rd COLW CO3 .... 162 E4
COS CO15 .... 13 J5
EPP CM16 .... 304 E1
WFD IG8 .... 348 D5
St Andrew's Av COLS CO2 .... 11 M9
HCH RM12 .... 389 C4
St Andrews La LAIN SS15 .... 376 D4

St Andrews PI BRWN CM15 .... 355 G3
RCOLE CO7 .... 220 F2
St Andrew's Ri SUD CO10 .... 53 M6
St Andrew's Rd COS CO15 .... 12 E5
FX IP11 .... 85 H8
HSTD CO9 .... 128 F1
RCFD SS4 .... 382 F1
RCHLM CM3 .... 238 B7
RCOS CO16 .... 196 A2
ROMW/RG RM7 .... 370 E6
SBN/FI SS3 .... 402 D5
SUD CO10 .... 5 H9
TIL RM18 .... 417 M6
St Annes CI CDH/CHF RM16 ..... 407 J6 ▣
CHESW EN7 .... 276 B7
RCOLW CO6 .... 186 C1
St Anne's Pk BROX EN10 .... 253 H8
St Anne's Rd BRWN CM15 .... 333 K3
COLN CO4 .... 11 H5
CVI SS8 .... 398 E8
St Anns Rd COS CO15 .... 12 E3
SOSN SS2 .... 21 H4
St Anthony's Av WFD IG8 .... 348 D7
St Anthony's Dr
CHLM/GWD CM2 .... 288 D4
St Aubyns Rd IPNE IP4 .... 38 B6
St Augustine Ms COL CO1 .... 10 E8
St Augustine Rd
CDH/CHF RM16 .... 418 C1
IPSE IP3 .... 38 E7
St Augustine's Av SOS SS1 .... 402 C5
St Augustines CI BROX EN10 ... 253 G8 ▣
St Augustines Dr BROX EN10 ... 253 H7
St Augustine's Gdn IPSE IP3 .... 38 D8
St Austell CI KESG IP5 .... 39 H5
St Austell Rd COLN CO4 .... 135 L2
St Austin's La HAR CO12 .... 7 L2 ▣
St Barbara's Rd COLS CO2 .... 162 E7
St Bartholomew CI
COLN CO4 .... 135 K8 ▣
St Bartholomews La SUD CO10 .. 4 B2
St Benet's Rd SOSN SS2 .... 383 C5
St Bernard Rd COLN CO4 .... 11 M1
St Botolph's Church Wk
COL CO1 .... 10 D7
St Botolph's St COL CO1 .... 10 D8
St Botolph's Ter
WOTN CO14 .... 199 K3 ▣
St Botolph's Wy HVHL CB9 .... 28 A3
St Bride CI COLN CO4 .... 11 L2
St Catharine's Rd BROX EN10 ... 253 H7
St Catherines CI COLS CO2 ...... 190 E2
WICKE SS11 .... 360 A3 ▣
St Catherine's Rd
CHLM/WR CM1 .... 16 A4
SUD CO10 .... 34 A2
St Cecilia Rd CDH/CHF RM16 ... 418 C1
St Chads CI LAIN SS15 .... 376 D4 ▣
St Chad's Rd TIL RM18 .... 418 B5
St Charles Dr WICKE SS11 .... 359 M4
St Charles Rd BRW CM14 .... 354 C3
St Christopher Rd COLN CO4 .... 11 L2
St Christophers CI CVI SS8 .... 397 L7
St Christophers Wy COS CO15 .. 250 A4
St Clair CI COS CO15 .... 224 A3
St Clair's Dr RCOS CO16 .... 222 C6
St Clair's Rd RCOS CO16 .... 222 C6
St Clare Dr COLW CO3 .... 162 B4
St Clare Meadow RCFD SS4 ..... 364 A8
St Clare Rd COLW CO3 .... 162 B5
St Clement CI COLN CO4 .... 11 L1
St Clements GTDUN CM6 .... 122 B1
St Clement's Av LOS SS9 .... 399 M1
WTHK RM20 .... 416 B3
St Clements CI HOC/HUL SS5 ... 363 H7
SBF/HAD SS7 .... 379 K6 ▣
St Clements Ct PUR RM19 .... 415 H1 ▣
St Clement's Crs SBF/HAD SS7 . 379 J3
St Clement's Dr LOS SS9 .... 381 M8
St Clement's SBF/HAD SS7 ...... 379 K6
WTHK RM20 .... 416 B4
St Cleres Crs WICKE SS11 .... 360 A4
St Cleres Hall La RCOS CO16 .... 249 J1
St Cleres Wy RCHLM CM3 .... 290 E5
St Columb CI COLN CO4 .... 11 K1
St Cross CI HOD EN11 .... 253 H7 ▣
St Cuthberts Rd HOD EN11 ...... 253 K2
St Davids CI COLN CO4 .... 11 K7
St David's Dr BROX EN10 .... 253 G7
SBF/HAD SS7 .... 381 H8
St David's Rd IPSE IP3 .... 38 C8
VGE SS16 .... 376 C7
St Davids Ter LOS SS9 .... 381 H4
St David's Wy WICKE SS11 .... 360 A4 ▣
St Denis CI HAR CO12 .... 143 H2
St Dominic Rd COLN CO4 .... 11 M1
St Edith's CI BCAYW CM12 .... 357 H2 ▣
St Ediths La BCAYW CM12 .... 357 H2 ▣
St Edmunds CI HAR CO12 .... 143 H2 ▣
SOSN SS2 .... 383 K8 ▣
St Edmund's Ct COLN CO4 .... 11 J6
St Edmunds Flds GTDUN CM6 .. 178 F1
St Edmund's HI SUD CO10 .... 77 L5
St Edmunds La BURES CO8 ...... 102 A2
GTDUN CM6 .... 178 F1
St Edmund's PI IP IP1 .... 37 K3
St Edmunds Rd DART DA1 .... 415 G8
FX IP11 .... 9 H6
IP IP1 .... 37 J3
St Edmund's Wy HLWE CM17 ... 227 K7 ▣
St Edwards Wy ROM RM1 .... 370 F4
St Fabian's Dr CHLM/WR CM1 ... 263 M7
St Faith Rd COLN CO4 .... 11 L2
St Fillan CI COLN CO4 .... 11 L1
Saint Francis Wy
CDH/CHF RM16 .... 418 D1
St Gabriels Ct PIT SS13 .... 378 C6 ▣
Saint George's Av EMPK RM11 .. 372 A8
St George's Av GRAYS RM17 .... 417 K1
HAR CO12 .... 7 G9
IP IP1 .... 143 K1 ▣
St Georges CI BRWN CM15 .... 308 C7
RCOLE CO7 .... 165 M2
St George's Dr WOS/PRIT SS0 .. 382 F8
St George's La SBN/FI SS3 .... 403 C5

St George's Park Av
  WOS/PRIT SS0..........400 C1
St Georges Rd *DAGW* RM9......388 A3
  EN EN1..........324 A2
  FX IP11..........85 K7
St George's St *IP* IP1..........2 E3
St Georges Wk *SBF/HAD* SS7 .. 379 J5
St Giles Av *DAGE* RM10..........388 C6
St Giles Cl *CDH/CHF* RM16......408 B3
  DAGE RM10..........388 C6
  HSTD CO9..........98 E1
  MAL CM9..........292 F1
St Giles Crs *MAL* CM9..........292 F1
St Gregory's Ct *SUD* CO10..........4 B5
St Helena Ms *COLW* CO3......162 E6
St Helena Rd *COLW* CO3......162 E6
St Helens Av *COS* CO15......224 B4
St Helen's Gn *HAR* CO12..........7 L3
St Helen's La *COL* CO1..........10 C7
St Helen's Rd *WOS/PRIT* SS0......20 B5
St Helen's St *IPNE* IP4..........3 J4
St Helens Wk *BCAYW* CM12......335 G7
Saint Isidores *KESG* IP5..........39 L4
St Ives Cl *HARH* RM3..........353 G8
  KESG IP5..........39 H5
  RCOS CO16..........223 J8
St Ives Rd *K/T/MI* CO5..........217 H3
St Ivians Dr *GPK* RM2..........371 H3
St James' Av *CHONG* CM5......307 C2
  SOS SS1..........402 C5
St James Av East
  SLH/COR SS17..........394 F8
St James Av West
  SLH/COR SS17..........394 F8
St James Cl *CVI* SS8..........397 L7
  WOS/PRIT SS0..........382 B8
St James Gdns *WOS/PRIT* SS0......382 B8
St James Ms *BCAYW* CM12......357 H1
St James Pk *CHLM/WR* CM1......263 L7
St James Rd *BRTR* CM7..........155 G6
  VGE SS16..........19 M7
St James's Rd *BRW* CM14......354 D4
St James's St *HSTD* CO9..........74 A7
St James's Wk *HOC/HUL* SS5......362 D1
St James Wy *BSF* CM23..........173 J6
St Johns Av *BRTR* CM7..........183 C5
  BRW CM14..........354 C5
  CHLM/GWD CM2..........17 G8
  COL CO1..........10 C9
  HLWE CM17..........227 K7
St John's Cl *COLN* CO4..........135 K7
  LAIN SS15..........376 D4
  RAIN RM13..........389 H6
  RCOLE CO7..........135 L7
  SAFWS CB11..........65 L4
St John's Ct *BKHH* IG9..........348 C2
  MAL CM9..........272 D2
St Johns Crs *CVI* SS8..........397 L7
  STSD CM24..........146 F4
St Johns Dr *RAYL* SS6..........361 J2
St John's Gn *CHLM/WR* CM1 ... 287 J2
St John's La *STSD* CM24......146 F4
St Johns Ms *SLH/COR* SS17......395 G7
St John's Rd *BCAYE* CM11......335 J8
  CDH/CHF RM16..........418 C2
  CHLM/GWD CM2..........17 G7
  CHLM/WR CM1..........287 J2
  COLN CO4..........135 L8
  COS CO15..........12 F1
  CRW RM5..........351 K6
  EPP CM16..........304 A2
  LOU IG10..........327 G4
  RCOLE CO7..........192 D4
  RCOS CO16..........223 J6
  SBF/HAD SS7..........380 D8
  SBN/FI SS3..........385 J8
  STSD CM24..........146 F4
  WOS/PRIT SS0..........20 D7
St John's St *COL* CO1..........10 B9
  MAL CM9..........272 D2
St Johns Wk *HLWE* CM17......227 K7
St John's Wy *SLH/COR* SS17......395 G7
St Joseph Rd *COLN* CO4......135 K8
St Jude Gdns *COLN* CO4......11 M1
St Judes Cl *COLN* CO4......11 M2
St Julian Gv *COL* CO1..........10 E9
St Laurence Dr *BROX* RM10......276 F3
St Lawrence Dr *BOC* CM0......296 C3
St Lawrence Gdns *ING* CM4......308 F3
  LOS SS9..........381 M5
St Lawrence Hl *BOC* CM0......296 F6
St Lawrence Rd *BOC* CM0......297 J4
  COLN CO4..........11 L1
  UPMR RM14..........390 D1
St Lawrence Wy *KESG* IP5......39 J3
St Leonard's Av *BROX* RM10......276 F3
St Leonards Cl *SAFWS* CB11......89 H1
St Leonard's Rd *COL* CO1......163 K5
  IPSE IP3..........38 C8
  SOS SS1..........21 J7
  WAB EN9..........277 L4
St Leonards Wy *HCH* RM12......371 J8
St Luke's Cha *K/T/MI* CO5......214 E7
St Luke's Cl *COLN* CO4..........11 L1
  CVI SS8..........397 L7
St Luke's Rd *SOSN* SS2......383 K8
St Margaret's Av *SLH/COR* SS17 .. 409 K3
St Margaret's Rd
  CHLM/GWD CM2..........264 F8
  WARE SG12..........253 H1
St Margaret's St *IPNE* IP4......3 G3
St Mark Dr *COLN* CO4..........11 L1
St Mark's Fld *RCFD* SS4......383 C1
St Marks Rd *COS* CO15......12 E3
  CVI SS8..........397 L7
  EN EN1..........324 A8
  SBF/HAD SS7..........380 C4
St Martins Cl *COLN* CO4......12 E4
  EN EN1..........324 C1
  GTDUN CM6..........230 D4
  RAYL SS6..........380 D3
  SBF/HAD SS7..........379 J4
St Martins Ct *KESG* IP5......39 M4
St Martins Gn *IPNE* IP4......84 B3
St Mary's Av *BCAYW* CM12......357 H1
  BRWN CM15..........333 H7
St Mary's Cl *BRTR* CM7......154 C4

CHLM/GWD CM2..........289 G5
FX IP11..........84 C5
GRAYS RM17..........417 L3
RIPW IP8..........36 B2
SBF/HAD SS7..........397 L2
SBN/FI SS3..........402 B2
St Mary's Crs *FX* IP11..........84 F7
  PIT SS13..........378 D4
St Mary's Dr *SBF/HAD* SS7......397 M2
  STSD CM24..........147 G5
St Mary's La *MAL* CM9..........293 J1
  UPMR RM14..........373 M8
  UPMR RM14..........390 B1
St Marys Md *CHLM/WR* CM1 ... 264 B2
St Marys Pk *KIR/NAC* IP10......61 H3
St Mary's Pl *GTDUN* CM6......179 L4
St Mary's Rd *BAR* EN8..........300 D1
  BOC CM0..........344 C5
  BRTR CM7..........155 J8
  CDH/CHF RM16..........418 C1
  COS CO15..........12 E4
  FOS CO13..........199 H6
  K/T/MI CO5..........213 K1
  RCOLE CO7..........195 G6
  SBF/HAD SS7..........397 L3
  SOSN SS2..........20 E1
  WICKW SS12..........359 J6
  WIT CM8..........212 C4
St Marys Vw *SAFWN* CB10......43 M7
St Mary's Wk *HVHL* CB9......48 C5
St Marys Wy *CHIG* IG7......349 H6
St Matthew's Ct *RAIN* RM13......389 H6
St Matthew's St *IPNE* IP4......2 D3
St Michael's Av *PIT* SS13......378 C7
St Michael's Cha *RCOLW* CO6 ... 188 E1
St Michael's Cl *HLW* CM20......255 M2
  KESG IP5..........39 H5
  RCHLM CM3..........318 B6
  SOCK/AV RM15..........405 K5
St Michaels Dr *CHLM/WR* CM1 .. 262 B6
St Michael's La *BRTR* CM7......183 G1
St Michael's Rd *BROX* RM10......253 C8
  BRTR CM7..........183 G1
  CDH/CHF RM16..........418 C2
  CHLM/GWD CM2..........17 G8
  COLS CO2..........190 D2
  CVI SS8..........397 L8
  HAR CO12..........143 J1
  RCOS CO16..........197 G1
  SBF/HAD SS7..........381 G5
St Mildreds Rd *CHLM/GWD* CM2 .. 17 G8
St Monance Wy *COLN* CO4......11 L2
St Nazaire Rd *CHLM/WR* CM1......263 M5
St Neots Cl *COLN* CO4..........11 M2
St Neot's Rd *HARH* RM3......353 C8
St Nicholas Av *HCH* RM12......389 H2
St Nicholas Cl *WIT* CM8......212 A7
St Nicholas La *BSF* CM23......117 J3
St Nicholas Gv
  RBRW/HUT RM13..........355 K6
St Nicholas La *LAIN* SS15......376 E4
St Nicholas Rd *BOC* CM0......297 M7
  WIT CM8..........212 A7
St Nicholas St *COL* CO1......10 D8
  IP IP1..........2 E5
St Nicholas Wy *RCOLW* CO6......158 B8
St Olaves Cha *KESG* IP5......39 K3
St Omar Cl *WICKW* SS12......359 L5
St Osyth Cl *CHTY* IP2..........58 A3
St Osyth Rd *COS* CO15......12 A5
  RCOS CO16..........223 J3
St Osyth Rd East *RCOS* CO16......223 K2
St Osyth Rd West *RCOS* CO16......223 J2
St Patrick's Pl *CDH/CHF* RM16 ... 418 C1
St Paul's Cl *SOCK/AV* RM15......405 K5
St Pauls Gdns *BCAYW* CM12......335 H7
St Paul's Pl *SOCK/AV* RM15......405 K5
St Paul's Rd *COL* CO1..........10 A5
  COS CO15..........13 J6
  CVI SS8..........397 L7
St Pauls Wy *WAB* EN9..........301 L5
St Peter's Av *CHONG* CM5......293 C1
St Peter's Cl *BRTR* CM7..........155 G7
St Peters Fld *BOC* CM0..........344 B4
St Peter's-in-the-fields
  BRTR CM7..........155 G7
St Peter's Pavement
  BSDN SS14..........378 A2
St Peter's Rd *BRTR* CM7......155 G7
  BRW CM14..........354 C5
  CDH/CHF RM16..........418 C1
  CHLM/WR CM1..........16 A4
  CVI SS8..........397 L7
  HOC/HUL SS5..........362 C4
  K/T/MI CO5..........245 J5
  RCOLW CO6..........158 C8
St Peter's St *COL* CO1......10 B6
  IPNE IP4..........2 F5
St Peters Ter *WICKW* SS12......359 K4
St Peters Vw *HSTD* CO9......97 L2
St Peters Wk *BCAYW* CM12......335 G7
  BRTR CM7..........155 G8
St Ronans Crs *WFD* IG8......348 B8
St Runwald St *COL* CO1......10 C7
St Saviour Cl *COLN* CO4......11 M2
St Stephens Crs
  RBRW/HUT RM13..........355 H5
St Stephen's Rd *PEND* EN3......324 E1
  RCHLM CM3..........317 C7
Saint's Wk *CDH/CHF* RM16......418 D1
St Teresa Wk *CDH/CHF* RM16......418 C1
St Thomas Cl *COLN* CO4......163 M1
St Thomas Rd *RCFD* SS4......341 H7
St Thomas's Cl *WAB* EN9......302 C5
St Thomas's Pl *GRAYS* RM17......417 K3
St Valery *RBSF* CM22..........176 D4
St Vincent Cha *BRTR* CM7......155 J6
St Vincent Rd *COS* CO15......250 E2
St Vincents Rd *CHLM/GWD* CM2 .. 17 G8
  WOS/PRIT SS0..........20 D7
St Winifred's Cl *CHIG* IG7......349 H6
Sainty Ct *RCOLE* CO7..........192 D3
Sairard Cl *LOS* SS9..........381 L4
Sairard Gdns *LOS* SS9......381 L4
Sakins Cft *HLWS* CM18......256 A6
Saladin Dr *PUR* RM19..........415 H1

Salary Cl *COLN* CO4..........163 M2
Salcombe Dr *CHDH* RM6......370 A6
Salcombe Rd *BRTR* CM7......183 K2
Salcott Crs *WICKW* SS12......359 M4
Salcott St *MAL* CM9..........243 J3
Salehurst Rd *IPSE* IP3..........38 F8
Salerno Crs *COLS* CO2......190 D1
Salerno Rd *CHLM/WR* CM1......263 M5
Salerno Wy *CHLM/WR* CM1......263 M5
Salforal Cl *RCHLM* CM3......338 C2
Saling Gn *LAIN* SS15..........377 G1
Salisbury Av *COLW* CO3......162 E5
  SLH/COR SS17..........409 L2
  WOS/PRIT SS0..........20 D4
Salisbury Cl *BSF* CM23......174 A6
Salisbury Crs *BAR* EN8......300 E4
Salisbury Rd *COS* CO15......224 F6
  DAGE RM10..........388 C5
  GPK RM2..........371 J5
  GRAYS RM17..........417 K3
  HOD EN11..........253 K4
  IPSE IP3..........38 B8
  LOS SS9..........399 K2
  PEND EN3..........325 C1
Salix Rd *GRAYS* RM17......417 L3
Sallows Cl *IP* IP1..........57 G4
Salmon Cl *COLW* CO3..........162 A7
Salmon's Gv *RBRW/HUT* CM13 .. 355 K6
Salmon Rd *DART* DA1......415 G7
Salmon's La *RCOLW* CO6......159 H7
Saltash Rd *BARK/HLT* IG6......349 L8
Saltcoats *RCHLM* CM3......339 L3
Saltcote Maltings *MAL* CM9 .. 269 M7
Salter Pl *CHLM/GWD* CM2......289 C1
Salters *BSF* CM23..........173 K7
Salter's Meadow *MAL* CM9......242 E7
Salthouse La *IPNE* IP4..........3 G6
The Saltings *SBF/HAD* SS7......380 E8
Salt's Gn *CHLM/WR* CM1......261 L1
Salvia Cl *COS* CO15..........12 B3
Salway Cl *WFD* IG8..........348 B8
Salwey Crs *BROX* EN10......253 G8
Samford Pl *RIPS/CAP* IP9......80 E4
Samford Pl *RIPW* IP8..........36 C5
Samphire Cl *WIT* CM8..........211 L8
Samphire Ct *GRAYS* RM17......417 M3
Sampson Dr *SUD* CO10......34 E3
Sampson's La *K/T/MI* CO5......217 M7
Samsons Ct *RCOLE* CO7......220 F3
Samson's Rd *RCOLE* CO7......220 F2
Samuel Ct *IPNE* IP4..........3 H4
Samuel Mnr
  CHLM/GWD CM2..........265 G8
Samuel Rd *VGE* SS16..........376 C7
Samuels Dr *SOS* SS1..........402 C3
Sanctuary Gdn
  SLH/COR SS17..........409 M1
Sanctuary Rd *LOS* SS9......381 H8
Sandbanks *SBF/HAD* SS7......398 E1
Sanderling Gdns *MAL* CM9 .. 269 K6
Sanderlings *SBF/HAD* SS7......397 K1
Sanders Dr *COLW* CO3......162 C4
Sanderson Cl
  RBRW/HUT RM13..........374 D6
Sanderson Ms *K/T/MI* CO5......192 A3
Sanders Rd *CVI* SS8..........398 B5
Sandford Av *IG10*..........327 K5
Sandford Cl *RCOLE* CO7......192 D3
Sandford Mill Rd
  CHLM/GWD CM2..........289 H1
Sandgate Cl *ROMW/RG* RM7......370 D7
Sandhill Rd *LOS* SS9..........381 J3
Sandhurst *CVI* SS8..........397 K8
Sandhurst Av *IPSE* IP3..........3 M8
Sandhurst Cl *LOS* SS9......382 A7
Sandhurst Crs *LOS* SS9......382 A7
Sandhurst Rd *ED* N9..........324 D8
  TIL RM18..........418 D6
Sandleigh Rd *LOS* SS9......400 B2
Sandling Crs *IPNE* IP4..........38 F6
Sandon Br *CHLM/GWD* CM2......290 A4
Sandon Cl *BSDN* SS14..........378 A6
  RCFD SS4..........363 J8
  RCOLW CO6..........134 D4
Sandon Ct *BSDN* SS14......378 A6
Sandon Hall Bridleway
  CHLM/GWD CM2..........289 L8
Sandon Hl *RCHLM* CM3......207 H4
Sandon Pl *CHONG* CM5......307 H2
Sandon Rd *BAR* EN8..........300 D2
  BSDN SS14..........378 A6
Sandown Av *DAGE* RM10......388 D5
  HCH RM12..........389 L1
  WOS/PRIT SS0..........400 C1
Sandown Cl *COS* CO15......224 B3
  WICKE SS11..........360 B4
Sandown Ct *DAGE* RM10......388 D5
Sandown Rd *CDH/CHF* RM16 ... 408 F3
  SBF/HAD SS7..........380 C4
  WICKE SS11..........360 B4
Sandpiper Cl *COLN* CO4......164 B4
  HVHL CB9..........28 C4
  SBN/FI SS3..........402 F3
Sandpiper Dr *ERITH* DA8......414 C4
Sandpiper Rd *CHTY* IP2......57 M1
Sandpit La *BOC* CM0..........344 D6
  BRW CM14..........332 A8
Sandpit Rd *SBN/FI* SS3......403 J3
Sandringham Av
  HLWW/ROY CM19..........14 B4
  HOC/HUL SS5..........362 D5
  SLH/COR SS17..........394 F8
Sandringham Dr *COLS* CO2......163 H7
Sandringham Pl
  CHLM/GWD CM2..........17 K3
Sandringham Rd *BRWN* CM15......332 C3
  LAIN SS15..........18 A1
  SOS SS1..........401 L3
Sandringham Wy *BAR* EN8......300 D6
Sands Wy *WFD* IG8..........349 G7
Sandwich Cl *BRTR* CM7......154 F5
Sandwich Rd *COS* CO15......250 E3
  RCOLE CO7..........221 G3
Sandy Cl *FX* IP11..........84 C3

Sandy Hl *RCOLW* CO6......102 E7
Sandyhill La *IPSE* IP3..........58 F2
Sandy La *CDH/CHF* RM16......418 C3
  SOCK/AV RM15..........405 H5
  SUD CO10..........54 A6
  WTHK RM20..........416 C3
San Remo Pde *WOS/PRIT* SS0......20 C8
San Remo Rd *CVI* SS8......398 E8
Sapling Pl *IPNE* IP4..........38 F6
Sappers Cl *SBW* CM21......228 A1
Sara Crs *GRH* DA9..........416 B8
Saran Ct *RCOLE* CO7..........192 B1
Sarcel *BRTR* CM7..........156 D5
Sargeant Cl *COLS* CO2......163 J8
Sarre Av *HCH* RM12..........389 K5
Sarre Wy *RCOLE* CO7......220 F3
Sassoon Wy *MAL* CM9......293 H2
Satanita Rd *WOS/PRIT* SS0......400 D3
Saul's Av *WIT* CM8..........239 H3
Saul's Bridge Cl *WIT* CM8......239 H3
Saunders Av *BRTR* CM7......154 E7
Saunders Cl *BAR* EN8..........276 D8
  RBSF CM22..........147 K2
Saunton Rd *HCH* RM12......389 H1
Savernake Rd *CHLM/WR* CM1......16 B6
  ED N9..........324 B8
Saville Cl *SAFWS* CB11......87 J7
Saville Rd *CHDH* RM6......370 A6
Saville St *WOTN* CO14......199 K2
Savill Rd *COLS* CO2..........191 K1
Savill Rw *WFD* IG8..........348 A7
Savoy Cl *VGE* SS16..........376 B6
Savoy Wd *EPP* CM16......279 J1
Sawbridgeworth Rd
  RBSF CM22..........201 K4
  SBW CM21..........201 K8
Sawells *BROX* EN10..........277 L1
Sawkins Av *CHLM/GWD* CM2......288 E5
Sawkins Cl *CHLM/GWD* CM2......288 E5
Sawkins Gdns *CHLM/GWD* CM2......288 E5
Sawmill La *KIR/NAC* IP10......60 C5
Sawney Brook *CHLM/GWD* CM1 .. 287 H2
Sawpit La *BSF* CM23..........117 L3
Sawston Cft *CHLM/GWD* CM2 ... 58 B1
Sawyers Cl *RIPS/CAP* IP9......78 B2
Sawyer's Hall La *BRWN* CM15 .. 354 C1
Sawyer's Rd *MAL* CM9......241 K7
Saxmundham Wy *RCOS* CO16 .. 223 K8
Saxon Bank *BRTR* CM7......183 J1
Saxon Cl *COLW* CO3..........162 A7
  FX IP11..........85 L7
  HARH RM3..........372 A2
  HSTD CO9..........129 G1
  RAYL SS6..........361 M6
  RBRW/HUT CM13..........355 H4
  WICKE SS11..........359 M2
Saxon Dr *WIT* CM8..........211 M8
Saxon Gdns *SBN/FI* SS3......402 D4
Saxon La *RIPW* IP8..........56 E3
Saxonville *SBF/HAD* SS7......379 J7
Saxon Wy *CHLM/WR* CM1......264 C4
  COS CO15..........225 G5
  MAL CM9..........293 J2
  SAFWN CB10..........65 K2
  SBF/HAD SS7..........397 K1
Sayers *SBF/HAD* SS7..........380 B5
Sayesbury Av *SBW* CM21......200 E8
Sayesbury Rd *SBW* CM21......227 M1
Sayes Gdns *SBW* CM21......228 A1
Saywell Brook
  CHLM/GWD CM2..........289 H1
Scalby Rd *BOC* CM0..........344 B1
Scaldhurst *PIT* SS13..........378 D3
Scarborough Rd *BOC* CM0......344 B1
  LOS SS9..........399 H4
Scarfe Wy *COLN* CO4..........163 M5
Scarletts *BSDN* SS14..........19 J2
Scarletts Cl *WIT* CM8..........239 H4
Scarletts Rd *COL* CO1......163 K6
Sceptre Cl *MAL* CM9..........272 E1
Schneider Cl *FX* IP11..........8 E9
School Cha *HSTD* CO9......128 F3
School Green La *EPP* CM16......281 K5
  RIPW IP8..........57 G3
Schoolfield Rd *WTHK* RM20......416 B3
School Green La
  CHIG IG7..........350 A5
  CHLM/WR CM1..........205 J8
  CHONG CM5..........230 F8
  CHONG CM5..........257 L5
  COLS CO2..........189 H8
  GTDUN CM6..........148 E5
  HLW CM20..........255 M1
  HVHL CB9..........27 L3
  ING CM4..........335 L1
  K/T/MI CO5..........216 F7
  MGTR CO11..........108 E2
  MGTR CO11..........109 G7
  MGTR CO11..........138 B1
  RBRW/HUT RM13..........355 K7
  RBSF CM22..........120 A6
  RCHLM CM3..........208 F3
  RCOLE CO7..........106 E1
  RCOLE CO7..........107 G4
  RCOLE CO7..........194 B3
  RCOLW CO6..........103 L6
  RCOLW CO6..........133 M7
  RCOLW CO6..........134 B1
  SAFWS CB11..........63 H4
  SAFWS CB11..........89 G2
  SBF/HAD SS7..........397 L3
  SUD CO10..........34 D2
  WICKW SS12..........379 H1
School Rd *BCAYE* CM11......337 G6
  BCAYW CM12..........357 J3
  BCAYW CM12..........357 J3
  BRTR CM7..........181 M4
  BRWN CM15..........331 M1
  CHLM/WR CM1..........232 D6
  CHONG CM5..........306 A2
  COLN CO4..........105 M7
  COLS CO2..........191 H1
  DAGE RM10..........388 B7
  FOS CO13..........198 F6
  HAR CO12..........141 K8

  HSTD CO9..........51 L8
  HSTD CO9..........75 J6
  HSTD CO9..........97 L3
  HSTD CO9..........99 J3
  HVHL CB9..........29 H1
  K/T/MI CO5..........214 D2
  MAL CM9..........240 C8
  MAL CM9..........270 C1
  RCOLE CO7..........165 H6
  RCOLW CO6..........103 L6
  RCOLW CO6..........188 E1
  RCOS CO16..........167 M6
  RIPS/CAP IP9..........79 L2
  RIPS/CAP IP9..........113 J3
  SUD CO10..........32 F5
  WIT CM8..........184 F8
  WIT CM8..........240 A6
School St *SAFWN* CB10......42 E1
  SUD CO10..........4 C7
  SUD CO10..........33 L5
School View Rd *CHLM/WR* CM1 .. 16 D1
School Wk *BRTR* CM7......155 G8
School Wy *LOS* SS9..........382 A8
Schooner Ct *GRH* DA9......415 K8
Schreiber Rd *IPNE* IP4......38 C4
Scimitar Pk *PIT* SS13..........378 E1
Scofield Ct *SUD* CO10..........5 H8
Scopes Rd *KESG* IP5..........39 K3
Scotland Green Rd *PEND* EN3 .. 324 E7
Scotland Green Rd North
  PEND EN3..........324 C6
Scotland Rd *BKHH* IG9......348 D2
Scott Av *BRTR* CM7..........95 K6
Scott Cl *BRTR* CM7..........183 L5
Scott Crs *ERITH* DA8......414 A5
Scott Dr *COLW* CO3..........162 A5
  WICKW SS12..........359 L6
Scott Rd *BSF* CM23..........173 M5
  CDH/CHF RM16..........418 B1
  IPSE IP3..........59 J7
Scotts Cl *HCH* RM12..........389 K4
Scotts Hall Rd *RCFD* SS4......364 E3
Scraley Rd *MAL* CM9..........269 K5
Scratton Rd *SLH/COR* SS17......409 L1
  SOS SS1..........20 F7
Scrip's Rd *RCOLE* CO7......186 B4
Scrivener Dr *RIPW* IP8......57 J1
Scrub La *SBF/HAD* SS7......380 F8
Scrub Ri *BCAYW* CM12......357 G3
Scurvy Hall La *RCHLM* CM3 ... 235 J2
Scylla Cl *MAL* CM9..........269 K5
Scythe Wy *COLW* CO3......162 A7
Seaborough Rd
  CDH/CHF RM16..........408 D8
Seabrook Gdns *RCHLM* CM3 .. 266 A2
  ROMW/RG RM7..........370 B7
Seabrook Rd *CHLM/GWD* CM2 .. 289 H5
Sea Crs *COS* CO15..........250 A5
Sea Cornflower Wy *COS* CO15 .. 250 B4
Seafield Av *MGTR* CO11......109 J7
Seafield Rd *HAR* CO12......143 J1
Seafields Gdns *COS* CO15......224 D6
Seafields Rd *COS* CO15......224 D6
Sea Flowers Wy *COS* CO15......250 B4
Seaforth Av *SOSN* SS2......21 M1
Seaforth Cl *ROM* RM1......351 M8
Seaforth Dr *BAR* EN8......300 E6
Seaforth Gdns *WFD* IG8......348 G5
Seaforth Gv *SOSN* SS2......401 L1
Seaforth Rd *WOS/PRIT* SS0......20 A7
Seagers *MAL* CM9..........240 C7
Sea Glebe Wy *COS* CO15......250 B4
Sea Holly Wy *COS* CO15......250 B5
Sea King Crs *RCOLN* CO4......135 J7
Sea Lavender Wy *COS* CO15......250 B4
Seamans La *ING* CM4..........336 C1
Seamer Rd *BOC* CM0..........344 B1
Seamore Av *SBF/HAD* SS7......379 K5
Seamore Cl *SBF/HAD* SS7......379 J5
Sea Pink Wy *COS* CO15......250 B5
Sea Reach *LOS* SS9..........399 M3
Searle Wy *COLW* CO3......161 J2
Sea Rd *FX* IP11..........9 H7
Sea Rosemary Wy *COS* CO15 .. 250 B4
Sea Shell Wy *COS* CO15......250 B5
Sea Thistle Wy *COS* CO15......250 B4
Seaton Cl *MGTR* CO11......108 C8
Seaton Rd *FX* IP11..........84 F8
Seaview Av *HAR* CO12......142 D4
  K/T/MI CO5..........245 M4
  VGE SS16..........377 L8
Seaview Dr *SBN/FI* SS3......403 K1
Seaview Hts *WOTN* CO14......199 K4
Sea View Pde *BOC* CM0......296 C8
  RCHLM CM3..........319 G1
Sea View Prom *BOC* CM0......296 C2
Seaview Rd *CVI* SS8..........413 M1
  LOS SS9..........399 M3
  RCOLE CO7..........221 G4
  SBN/FI SS3..........402 E5
Seaview Ter *RCOS* CO16......221 H8
  SBF/HAD SS7..........398 E2
Seaway *BOC* CM0..........296 D3
Sea Wy *COS* CO15..........250 A4
Seaway *CVI* SS8..........413 J1
  SOS SS1..........21 J8
Seawick Rd *RCOS* CO16......249 J5
Seax Ct *LAIN* SS15..........376 A4
Seax Wy *LAIN* SS15..........376 A4
Sebastian Av *BRWN* CM15......333 H8
Sebastian Cl *COLN* CO4......163 M4
Sebert Cl *BCAYE* CM11......357 L4
Seckford Cl *IPNE* IP4..........39 G3
Second Av *BCAYW* CM12......356 F4
  BRWN CM15..........308 D6
  CHLM/WR CM1..........264 B6
  COS CO15..........13 M4
  CVI SS8..........397 L7
  DAGE RM10..........388 C8
  EN EN1..........324 A7
  FOS CO13..........198 F7
  FX IP11..........84 C6
  HAR CO12..........7 H9
  HLWS CM18..........256 A3
  HOC/HUL SS5..........362 A3
  ING CM4..........129 J2
  RCOS CO16..........196 A3
  RCOS CO16..........221 G3

SLH/COR SS17 .... 394 E8
SUD CO10 .... 4 F2
WICKE SS11 .... 360 B5
WOS/PRIT SS0 .... 400 C4
WOTN CO14 .... 171 M8
WTHK RM20 .... 416 B3
Sedcote Rd PEND EN3 .... 324 D7
Seddons Wk HOC/HUL SS5 .... 362 F5
Sedgefield Crs HARH RM3 .... 353 C5
Sedgefield Crs HARH RM3 .... 353 G6
Sedgefield Wy BRTR CM7 .... 183 J2
WAB EN9 .... 253 M8
Sedge Gn HLWW/ROY CM19 .... 254 A7
Sedgemoor SBN/FI SS3 .... 402 E2
Sedgemoor Dr DAGE RM10 .... 388 B3
Sedley Ri LOU IG10 .... 327 G4
Sedop Cl SAFWS CB11 .... 65 L4
Seeleys HLWE CM17 .... 227 K7
SBF/HAD SS7 .... 379 L6
Selbourne Rd HOC/HUL SS5 .... 362 F5
Seldon Cl COLS CO2 .... 190 E2
Seldon Rd K/T/MI CO5 .... 214 L6
Selkirk Rd IPNE IP4 .... 38 D3
Selsdon Cl CRW RM5 .... 370 D1
Selsey Av COS CO15 .... 250 D3
Selvale Wy FX IP11 .... 9 G1
Selwood Rd BRW CM14 .... 354 A4
Selworthy Cl BCAYE CM11 .... 357 K4
Selwyn Cl CHTY IP2 .... 2 E8
Selwyn Rd SOSN SS2 .... 21 L2
TIL RM18 .... 418 A6
Semper Rd CDH/CHF RM16 .... 408 D7
Semples SLH/COR SS17 .... 410 A1
Serpentine Rd IPSE IP3 .... 59 J1
Serpentine Wk COL CO1 .... 10 B5
Settle Rd HARH RM3 .... 353 H5
Seven Acres WICKE SS11 .... 359 M3
Seven Arches Rd BRW CM14 .... 354 F4
Seven Ash Gn CHLM/WR CM1 .... 264 D6
Seven Cottages La KESG IP5 .... 38 D2
Seven Devils La SAFWS CB11 .... 65 L5
Sevenoaks Cl HARH RM3 .... 352 D5
Seventh Av CHLM/WR CM1 .... 264 C5
CVI SS8 .... 397 M7
Severalls La COLN CO4 .... 135 H4
Severn TIL RM18 .... 409 J8
Severn Av GPK RM2 .... 371 J3
Severn Dr EN EN1 .... 324 B2
UPMR RM14 .... 372 E6
Severn Rd COS CO15 .... 13 G2
IPSE IP3 .... 38 A8
SOCK/AV RM15 .... 405 K4
Severns Fld EPP CM16 .... 304 B1
Sewards End WICKW SS12 .... 359 M5
WAB EN9 .... 301 K6
Sewardstone Rd CHING E4 .... 325 J6
Sewardstone St WAB EN9 .... 301 K6
Sewardstone Wy WAB EN9 .... 301 K8
Sewell Harris Cl HLW CM20 .... 256 A2
Sewell's La SUD CO10 .... 52 B2
Sewell Wontner Cl KESG IP5 .... 39 K3
Sexton Cl COLS CO2 .... 191 J3
RAIN RM13 .... 389 G7
Sexton Rd TIL RM18 .... 418 A5
Sextons La WIT CM8 .... 240 C1
Seymer Rd ROM RM1 .... 370 E3
Seymour Rd CDH/CHF RM16 .... 406 D8
CHTY IP2 .... 2 E8
COS CO15 .... 250 A2
SBF/HAD SS7 .... 381 G8
TIL RM18 .... 418 A5
WOS/PRIT SS0 .... 400 D2
Seymours HLWW/ROY CM19 .... 255 H6
Seymour St CHLM/GWD CM2 .... 16 E4
Shackleton Cl HAR CO12 .... 143 G2
Shackleton Rd IPSE IP3 .... 38 C8
Shadowbush Cl HVHL CB9 .... 28 A2
Shafter Rd DAGE RM10 .... 388 D5
Shaftesbury LOU IG10 .... 326 E5
Shaftesbury Av HAR CO12 .... 6 E7
PEND EN3 .... 324 E4
Shaftesbury La DART DA1 .... 415 J8
Shaftesbury Rd EPP CM16 .... 304 A1
ROM RM1 .... 371 G6
Shafto Rd IP IP1 .... 36 E7
Shair La RCOLE CO7 .... 195 J1
Shakespeare Av
BCAYW CM11 .... 357 K1
RAYL SS6 .... 381 G1
TIL RM18 .... 418 C6
VGE SS16 .... 376 B6
WOS/PRIT SS0 .... 20 B1
Shakespeare Cl BRTR CM7 .... 183 H4
Shakespeare Dr MAL CM9 .... 293 H3
WOS/PRIT SS0 .... 20 D1
Shakespeare Rd COLW CO3 .... 162 A5
DART DA1 .... 415 H8
ROM RM1 .... 371 G6
Shakespeare Sq BARK/HLT IG6 .... 349 L7
Shakeston Cl CHLM/WR CM1 .... 287 J3
Shakletons CHONG CM5 .... 283 H8
Shalcross Dr BAR EN8 .... 301 G2
Shalford Rd BCAYE CM11 .... 357 L1
BRTR CM7 .... 153 L7
Shamrock Av CHTY IP2 .... 36 F7
Shamrock Cl MAL CM9 .... 272 E1
Shangani Rd DART DA1 .... 174 A6
Shanklin Av BCAYW CM12 .... 357 H1
Shanklin Cl COS CO15 .... 250 C3
CHESW EN7 .... 300 A1
Shanklin Dr WOS/PRIT SS0 .... 400 B1
Shannon Av RAYL SS6 .... 380 D2
Shannon Cl HVHL CB9 .... 28 E4
LOS SS9 .... 381 M7
Shannon Rd IPSE IP3 .... 59 H3
Shannon Wy CVI SS8 .... 397 L8
SOCK/AV RM15 .... 405 K4
Shardlow Cl HVHL CB9 .... 27 K2
Sharlands Cl WICKE SS11 .... 360 A3
Sharnbrook SBN/FI SS3 .... 402 E1
Sharon Rd PEND EN3 .... 324 F4
Sharpecroft HLWW/ROY CM19 .... 15 K5
Sharpington Cl
CHLM/GWD CM2 .... 288 D8
Sharp Wy DART DA1 .... 415 G7
Shatters Rd COLS CO2 .... 216 B2
Shawbridge HLWW/ROY CM19 .... 255 K6

Shaw Cl BAR EN8 .... 300 D1
FOS CO13 .... 199 G4
HCH RM12 .... 371 J8
WICKW SS12 .... 359 L6
Shaw Crs RBRW/HUT CM13 .... 333 L7
TIL RM18 .... 418 C5
Shaw Dr BRTR CM7 .... 95 K5
Shaw Rd PEND EN3 .... 34 E3
SUD CO10 .... 212 A6
WIT CM8 .... 212 A6
The Shaw RBSF CM22 .... 202 B8
The Shearers BSF CM23 .... 173 J7
Shearers Wy RCHLM CM3 .... 266 A2
Shears Crs K/T/MI CO5 .... 245 L6
Shearwood Cresent DART DA1 .... 414 A7
Sheds La SAFWN CB10 .... 65 M1
Sheepcoates La MAL CM9 .... 270 A1
Sheepcote La BOC CM0 .... 320 E6
RCHLM CM3 .... 235 K4
WIT CM8 .... 184 F6
Sheepcot Rd HSTD CO9 .... 73 M8
Sheepen Pl COLW CO3 .... 10 A6
Sheepen Rd COLW CO3 .... 162 E3
Sheepgate La KIR/NAC IP10 .... 85 G1
Sheering Ct RAYL SS6 .... 361 H8
Sheering Dr HLWE CM17 .... 227 M8
Sheering Lower Rd SBW CM21 .... 228 A3
Sheering Mill La SBW CM21 .... 228 A1
Sheering Rd HLWE CM17 .... 228 A6
Sheering Rd HLWE CM17 .... 228 A6
COLS CO2 .... 191 G1
Sheerwater Cl BOC CM0 .... 344 C3
Sheerwater Ms COLN CO4 .... 164 B3
Sheffield Dr HARH RM3 .... 353 H6
Sheila Rd CRW RM5 .... 351 J8
Shelbourn Br BRTR CM7 .... 156 D7
The Sheilings EMPK RM11 .... 372 A5
Sheldon Cl HLWE CM17 .... 256 F3
SLH/COR SS17 .... 395 J6
Sheldon Rd CVI SS8 .... 398 F8
Sheldrake Dr CHTY IP2 .... 57 M1
Shellbeach Rd CVI SS8 .... 413 L1
Shellcroft RCOLW CO6 .... 130 A2
Shellduck Crs BRTR CM7 .... 182 D6
Shelley Av HCH RM12 .... 389 C1
SUD CO10 .... 5 K8
Shelley Cl CHONG CM5 .... 283 J7
MAL CM9 .... 293 H3
Shelley Gv LOU IG10 .... 327 C6
Shelley La RCOS CO16 .... 224 A1
Shelley Pl RAYL SS6 .... 361 H8
TIL RM18 .... 418 C5
Shelley Rd CHLM/GWD CM2 .... 17 M4
COLW CO3 .... 162 A5
RBRW/HUT CM13 .... 355 L1
Shelley Sq SOSN SS2 .... 21 J2
Shelley St CHTY IP2 .... 2 F8
Shellow Rd CHONG CM5 .... 260 E7
Shelsley Dr VGE SS16 .... 376 D8
Shenfield Crs BRWN CM15 .... 354 F3
Shenfield Gdns
RBRW/HUT CM13 .... 333 J8
Shenfield Gn BRWN CM15 .... 355 H1
Shenfield Pl BRWN CM15 .... 354 F1
Shenfield Rd BRWN CM15 .... 354 F2
WFD IG8 .... 348 C8
Shenley Rd IPSE IP3 .... 59 J2
Shenstone Gdns HARH RM3 .... 371 K1
Shepard Cl LOS SS9 .... 382 B5
Shepeshall LAIN SS15 .... 18 A6
Shepherd Dr RPW IP8 .... 17 K3
Shepherds Cl BSF CM23 .... 173 K7
SBF/HAD SS7 .... 380 F7
Shepherds Cft COLW CO3 .... 161 L6
Shepherds Rd HARH RM3 .... 372 B2
Shepherds Wk SBF/HAD SS7 .... 380 F7
Shepherds Wy SAFWN CB10 .... 66 A1
Shepley Cl HCH RM12 .... 389 L4
Shepley Ms PEND EN3 .... 325 H2
Sheppard Cl EN EN1 .... 324 C2
RCOS CO16 .... 223 L5
Sheppard Dr CHLM/GWD CM2 .... 265 H7
Sheppards HLWW/ROY CM19 .... 255 G6
Sheppards Wy KESG IP5 .... 39 L4
Sheppey Cl ERITH DA8 .... 414 C4
Sherborne Av IPNE IP4 .... 38 B1
PEND EN3 .... 324 D4
Sherborne Rd CHLM/WR CM1 .... 264 E6
Sherbourne Cl FOS CO13 .... 199 G4
SOSN SS2 .... 382 F5
Sherbourne Dr PIT SS13 .... 378 B2
Sherbourne Gdns SOSN SS2 .... 383 G5
Sherbourne Rd COLN CO4 .... 164 A3
Sheredes Dr HOD EN11 .... 253 G6
Sherfield Rd GRAYS RM17 .... 417 J3
Sheridan Av SBF/HAD SS7 .... 380 C8
Sheridan Cl HARH RM3 .... 352 C8
RAYL SS6 .... 381 G1
Sheridan Ct DART DA1 .... 415 H8
Sheriden Wk BROX EN10 .... 252 F8
Sheriffs Wy RCOS CO16 .... 223 M4
Sheringham Av ROMW/RG RM7 .... 370 D6
Sheringham Cl SLH/COR SS17 .... 394 F8
Sheriton Sq RAYL SS6 .... 361 L7
Sherhbrook Rd WAB EN9 .... 302 A6
Sherrington Rd IP IP1 .... 37 H3
Sherry Wy SBF/HAD SS7 .... 380 F5
Sherwood Cl COLN CO4 .... 11 M8
VGE SS16 .... 376 B7
Sherwood Crs SBF/HAD SS7 .... 380 F7
Sherwood Dr CHLM/WR CM1 .... 287 L2
COS CO15 .... 223 M5
Sherwood Flds KESG IP5 .... 39 K4
Sherwood Wy K/T/MI CO5 .... 186 E7
SOSN SS2 .... 401 M1
Shetland Cl IPNE IP4 .... 38 B3
Shetland Rd HVHL CB9 .... 28 E3
Shevon Wy BRW CM14 .... 354 A5
Shillibeer Wk CHIG IG7 .... 350 A4
Shillingstone SBN/FI SS3 .... 402 E2
Shillito Cl COLW CO3 .... 162 A7
Shingle Ct MAL CM9 .... 302 B5
Ship La MGTR CO11 .... 109 M8
RIPW IP8 .... 36 C2
SOCK/AV RM15 .... 405 L7

Ship Launch Rd IPSE IP3 .... 3 H9
Ship Rd BOC CM0 .... 344 D7
CHLM/GWD CM2 .... 312 C6
Shipwrights Cl SBF/HAD SS7 .... 398 C1
Shipwrights Dr SBF/HAD SS7 .... 380 C8
Shirebourn V RCHLM CM3 .... 339 L5
Shire Cl BCAYE CM11 .... 335 L7
BROX EN10 .... 277 G6
DART DA1 .... 265 C4
Shire Hall Tard IPNE IP4 .... 3 C6
Shire HI SAFWS CB11 .... 66 A2
Shire Hill La SAFWN CB10 .... 66 B3
Shirley Cl BAR EN8 .... 300 D1
BROX EN10 .... 277 G4
DART DA1 .... 414 D8
Shirley Gdns HCH RM12 .... 389 K1
PIT SS13 .... 378 D3
Shirley Rd LOS SS9 .... 381 M6
Shoebridge's HI RCOLE CO7 .... 106 F5
Shoebury Av SBN/FI SS3 .... 403 G4
Shoebury Common Rd
SBN/FI SS3 .... 402 D6
Shoebury Rd SBN/FI SS3 .... 385 J8
SOS SS1 .... 402 B2
Shonks Mill Rd ABR/ST RM4 .... 330 C2
Shooters Dr WAB EN9 .... 277 M2
Shopland Hall Rd RCFD SS4 .... 385 L5
Shopland Rd RCFD SS4 .... 383 K4
Shop La K/T/MI CO5 .... 220 A8
Shop Rd MGTR CO11 .... 138 C5
Shorefield SBF/HAD SS7 .... 379 J8
Shorefield Gdns WOS/PRIT SS0 .... 20 B8
Shorefield Rd WOS/PRIT SS0 .... 20 B7
Shoreham Rd COS CO15 .... 250 D3
Shore La KIR/NAC IP10 .... 60 C8
MGTR CO11 .... 109 M8
RIPS/CAP IP9 .... 111 H1
Shore Rd BOC CM0 .... 344 D7
Shortacre BSDN SS14 .... 19 J5
Short Cft BRWN CM15 .... 332 A1
Shortcroft CHTY IP2 .... 57 L2
Short Cut Rd COL CO1 .... 10 B7
Shorter Av BRWN CM15 .... 333 C8
Shortlands Av CHONG CM5 .... 283 C6
Shortlands Pl BSF CM23 .... 174 A3
Short La BCAYE CM11 .... 336 D8
Shortmead Dr BAR EN8 .... 300 F3
Shortridge Ct WIT CM8 .... 238 F3
Short Rd CVI SS8 .... 398 C7
SBF/HAD SS7 .... 398 E1
Short St SOSN SS2 .... 21 G3
Shotley Cl FX IP11 .... 8 F1
RIPW IP8 .... 57 K1
Shotley Wk RIPS/CAP IP9 .... 82 F6
Shott Lower CHESW EN7 .... 276 A6
Shrewsbury Cl VGE SS16 .... 376 A6
Shrewsbury Dr SBF/HAD SS7 .... 379 L4
Shropshire Cl
CHLM/GWD CM2 .... 289 G6
CHLM/WR CM1 .... 289 H6
The Shrubberies CHIG IG7 .... 349 K6
CHLM/WR CM1 .... 287 G3
Shrubbery Cl LAIN SS15 .... 376 E3
The Shrubbery UPMR RM14 .... 390 D2
Shrub End Rd COLW CO3 .... 162 B8
Shrubland Av IP IP1 .... 36 F2
Shrubland Ct COS CO15 .... 13 M1
Shrubland Dr IPNE IP4 .... 39 G6
Shrubland Rd COLS CO2 .... 163 G5
MGTR CO11 .... 109 G8
Shrublands SAFWN CB10 .... 43 M8
Shrublands Cl CHIG IG7 .... 349 K7
Shrublands Farm Rd
CDH/CHF RM16 .... 408 C7
Shums HI FOS CO13 .... 198 D5
Shuttle Rd DART DA1 .... 414 B7
Siam Pl SUD CO10 .... 4 D6
Sibneys Gn HLWS CM18 .... 255 M8
Sicklefield Cl CHESW EN7 .... 276 A6
Sidegate Av IPNE IP4 .... 38 B3
Sidegate La IPNE IP4 .... 38 B3
Sidegate La West IPNE IP4 .... 38 A2
The Sidings BROX EN10 .... 277 G2
Sidmouth Av WOS/PRIT SS0 .... 382 B6
Sidmouth Rd CHLM/WR CM1 .... 264 F5
Sidney Rd EPP CM16 .... 303 L8
Sidney Ter BSF CM23 .... 174 A5
Sidwell Av SBF/HAD SS7 .... 397 M2
Sidwell Cha SBF/HAD SS7 .... 397 M2
Sidwell La SBF/HAD SS7 .... 397 M2
Sidwell Pk SBF/HAD SS7 .... 397 M2
Siena Ms COLS CO2 .... 163 J7
Sierra Dr BRW CM14 .... 388 C8
Siggin's La K/T/MI CO5 .... 220 C1
Silcock Cl COLN CO4 .... 11 K1
Silcott St RCOLE CO7 .... 220 F5
Silent St IPNE IP4 .... 2 F5
Silks Wy BRTR CM7 .... 183 G1
Sillett Cl RCOS CO16 .... 223 L5
Silva Island Wy WICKW SS12 .... 360 A6
Silvanus Cl COLW CO3 .... 162 E5
Silver Birch Av EPP CM16 .... 280 F7
Silver Birches RBRW/HUT CM13.. 355 H2
Silverlocke Rd GRAYS RM17 .... 417 L3
Silverdale RAYL SS6 .... 380 F3
SBF/HAD SS7 .... 380 A4
SLH/COR SS17 .... 394 E7
Silverdale Av WOS/PRIT SS0 .... 20 C2
Silverdale Cl IP IP1 .... 37 H2
Silverdale East SLH/COR SS17 .... 394 E7
Silverfield BROX EN10 .... 277 G2
Silver La CHONG CM5 .... 285 H1
Silver Leys RIPS/CAP IP9 .... 78 F5
Silvermere VGE SS16 .... 376 B6
Silverpoint Marine CVI SS8 .... 399 H8
Silver Rd WOS/PRIT SS0 .... 400 B1
Silversea Dr WOS/PRIT SS0 .... 400 B1
Silver St ABR/ST RM4 .... 328 C5
BRTR CM7 .... 95 J8
HVHL CB9 .... 29 J1
MAL CM9 .... 269 G8
STSD CM24 .... 146 E5
WAB EN9 .... 301 K6
WIT CM8 .... 184 E7
Silverthorn Cl RCFD SS4 .... 363 L7

Silverthorne CVI SS8 .... 398 A8
Silverthorne Cl COLS CO2 .... 163 H8
Silvertown Av SLH/COR SS17 .... 409 L1
Silvertree Cl HOC/HUL SS5 .... 362 C5
Silver Wy ROMW/RG RM7 .... 370 C3
WICKE SS11 .... 359 K3
Silverwood Cl
CDH/CHF RM16 .... 407 H5
Simmonds La MAL CM9 .... 317 K2
Simmonds Wy RCHLM CM3 .... 291 G3
Simmons Pl CDH/CHF RM16 .... 407 H6
Simons La COL CO1 .... 11 G9
Simpson Rd RAIN RM13 .... 389 G5
Simpsons La K/T/MI CO5 .... 214 B8
Sims Cl RCOLW CO6 .... 130 C4
ROM RM1 .... 371 G4
Sim's La HVHL CB9 .... 29 L2
Sinclair Cl COLN CO4 .... 10 D1
Sinclair Dr CHTY IP2 .... 37 K8
Sinclair Wk WICKW SS12 .... 359 L6
Sinclare Ct EN EN1 .... 324 A3
Singer Av COS CO15 .... 249 M4
Singleton Cl HCH RM12 .... 389 G3
Singleton Ct SUD CO10 .... 55 H6
Singleton Rd DAGW RM9 .... 388 A4
Sinnington End COLN CO4 .... 135 K7
Sioux Cl COLN CO4 .... 135 K7
Sirdar Rd IP IP1 .... 2 A3
RAYL SS6 .... 380 E3
Sir Francis Wy BRW CM14 .... 354 C3
Sir Isaac's Wk COL CO1 .... 10 B9
Sir Walter Raleigh Dr RAYL SS6 .... 361 K7
Siskin Cl COLN CO4 .... 164 A3
Sittang Cl COLS CO2 .... 190 D2
Sitwell Cl BRTR CM7 .... 108 C7
Siviter Wy DAGE RM10 .... 388 C5
Siward Rd WIT CM8 .... 238 E3
Six Bells Ct BRTR CM7 .... 155 G6
Sixth Av CHLM/WR CM1 .... 264 C5
CVI SS8 .... 397 M7
STSD CM24 .... 147 K8
Skarnings Ct WAB EN9 .... 302 B5
Skate's HI SUD CO10 .... 33 J1
Skeins Wy SAFWS CB11 .... 87 K7
Skelmersdale Rd COS CO15 .... 13 H5
Skelton Cl MGTR CO11 .... 108 D7
Skerry Ri CHLM/WR CM1 .... 264 C4
Sketty Rd EN EN1 .... 324 A5
Skiddaw Cl BRTR CM7 .... 182 E4
Skinner's La CHLM/GWD CM2 .... 288 C8
Skinners St BSF CM23 .... 173 K7
Skipper Ct BRTR CM7 .... 183 C3
Skitts HI BRTR CM7 .... 183 H1
Skreens Ct CHLM/WR CM1 .... 263 L7
Sky Hall HI COLN CO4 .... 105 K4
Skylark Cl BCAYE CM11 .... 357 K2
Skylark La RIPW IP8 .... 57 K1
Skyrmans Fee FOS CO13 .... 198 F5
Sladburys La COS CO15 .... 224 E4
Slade End EPP CM16 .... 303 M8
Slade Gdns ERITH DA8 .... 414 A5
Slade Green Rd ERITH DA8 .... 414 A6
Slade Rd COS CO15 .... 224 D5
Slade's La CHLM/GWD CM2 .... 288 B8
The Slades VGE SS16 .... 395 M1
Slade St IPNE IP4 .... 3 G1
The Slade SAFWN CB10 .... 44 A4
Slaney Rd ROM RM1 .... 370 F5
Slate HSTD CO9 .... 129 G2
Slaters Cl FOS CO13 .... 199 G5
Sleaford Cl CHTY IP2 .... 2 C9
Sleepers Farm Rd
CDH/CHF RM16 .... 408 C7
Slewins Cl EMPK RM11 .... 371 K5
Slewins La EMPK RM11 .... 371 K5
Slipe La BROX EN10 .... 277 G4
Sloe HI HSTD CO9 .... 128 D1
Slough Farm Rd HSTD CO9 .... 128 E1
Slough House Cl BRTR CM7 .... 136 F6
Slough La RCOLE CO7 .... 164 C5
SUD CO10 .... 35 L3
Slough Rd CHLM/WR CM1 .... 232 C1
MGTR CO11 .... 108 D1
RCHLM CM3 .... 315 K1
Slushy La RIPS/CAP IP9 .... 81 J8
Smaley La SUD CO10 .... 34 D3
Smallbridge Entry BURES CO8 .... 102 E3
Smallgains Av CVI SS8 .... 398 E7
Small Gains La INC CM4 .... 335 J3
Smallgains La INC CM4 .... 335 M3
Smallwood Rd COLS CO2 .... 162 C8
Smart Cl HARH RM3 .... 371 J1
Smarts Gn CHESW EN7 .... 276 A4
Smart's La LOU IG10 .... 326 F6
Smart St IPNE IP4 .... 3 G6
Smartt Av CVI SS8 .... 398 B7
Smeaton Cl COLN CO4 .... 135 K6
WAB EN9 .... 301 M4
Smeaton Rd WAB EN9 .... 325 H2
WFD IG8 .... 349 C6
Smeetham Hall La SUD CO10 .... 53 M5
Smither's Cha SOSN SS2 .... 383 J8
Smithers Cl RIPS/CAP IP9 .... 78 B2
Smithers Dr CHLM/GWD CM2 .... 289 H5
Smiths Av RCHLM CM3 .... 319 H3
Smiths Fld BRTR CM7 .... 182 A1
COL CO1 .... 163 K6
Smiths Pl KESG IP5 .... 39 L4
Smith St SBN/FI SS3 .... 403 G5
The Smithy STDN SC11 .... 172 C1
Smyatts Cl BOC CM0 .... 320 E8
Smythe Cl RCOS CO16 .... 223 K5
Smythe Rd BCAYE CM11 .... 335 L6
Smythies Av COL CO1 .... 10 E8
Snakes HI BRW CM14 .... 331 K5
Snakes La RBSF CM22 .... 147 H1
SOSN SS2 .... 382 B6
Snakes La East WFD IG8 .... 348 D7
Snakes La West WFD IG8 .... 348 B7
Snape Ct RCOS CO16 .... 223 H7
Snape Wy FOS CO13 .... 199 G4
Sneating Hall La FOS CO13 .... 197 M3
Snelling Gv CHLM/GWD CM2 .... 289 H3
Snipe Cl ERITH DA8 .... 414 C4
Sniveller's La K/T/MI CO5 .... 185 L8
Snoreham Gdns RCHLM CM3 .... 318 B6
Snowberry Ct BRTR CM7 .... 155 L7

Snowberry Gv COLS CO2 .... 163 H8
Snowcroft RIPS/CAP IP9 .... 78 B2
Snowdonia Cl PIT SS13 .... 378 D3
Snowdon Rd CHTY IP2 .... 58 C1
Snowdrop Cl BSF CM23 .... 264 F4
WIT CM8 .... 211 M7
Snow HI SUD CO10 .... 31 J2
Soames Md BRWN CM15 .... 308 B5
Soane St IPNE IP4 .... 3 G3
PIT SS13 .... 378 C3
Soft Rd SUD CO10 .... 53 G6
Softwater La SBF/HAD SS7 .... 380 E8
Soham Rd PEND EN3 .... 325 C1
The Soils HAR CO12 .... 141 M6
Solid La BRWN CM15 .... 332 A3
Solway TIL RM18 .... 409 K8
Somerby Cl BROX EN10 .... 277 H1
Somerset Av RCFD SS4 .... 363 M8
WOS/PRIT SS0 .... 382 C7
Somerset Cl COLS CO2 .... 162 C8
Somerset Crs WOS/PRIT SS0 .... 382 C7
Somerset Gdns EMPK RM11 .... 372 B8
PIT SS13 .... 378 C5
Somerset Pl CHLM/WR CM1 .... 264 B4
Somerset Rd IPNE IP4 .... 38 A3
LAIN SS15 .... 376 C5
PEND EN3 .... 325 H2
SLH/COR SS17 .... 409 H7
Somerset Wy COS CO15 .... 250 A2
Somers Rd COLW CO3 .... 162 B7
Somerton Av WOS/PRIT SS0 .... 382 B7
Somerville Gdns LOS SS9 .... 400 A3
Somme Rd COLS CO2 .... 162 C7
Somnes Av CVI SS8 .... 397 M5
Sonell Ct RCOLE CO7 .... 192 C1
Sonning Wy SBN/FI SS3 .... 402 E2
Sonters Down RCHLM CM3 .... 338 D6
Soper Ms PEND EN3 .... 325 H2
Sorrel Cl CHTY IP2 .... 37 G8
COLN CO4 .... 162 D1
Sorrell Cl MAL CM9 .... 270 F4
RCHLM CM3 .... 235 J5
The Sorrells SLH/COR SS17 .... 410 A1
The Sorrels SBF/HAD SS7 .... 379 L4
Sorrel Wk ROM RM1 .... 371 C3
Southall Wy BRW CM14 .... 354 A5
South Av HOC/HUL SS5 .... 361 M2
SOSN SS2 .... 21 J3
VGE SS16 .... 394 C4
South Beech Av
WICKE SS11 .... 359 L4
Southborough Dr
WOS/PRIT SS0 .... 400 C1
Southborough Rd
CHLM/GWD CM2 .... 16 E7
Southbourne Gdns
WOS/PRIT SS0 .... 382 C7
Southbourne Gv HOC/HUL SS5 ... 362 C5
WICKW SS12 .... 359 H3
WOS/PRIT SS0 .... 382 C8
Southbrook SBW CM21 .... 227 M2
Southbrook Dr BAR EN8 .... 276 E8
Southbury Av EN EN1 .... 324 B6
Southbury Cl HCH RM12 .... 389 L4
Southbury Rd EN EN1 .... 324 C6
South Charlton Mead La
HOD EN11 .... 253 L6
Southchurch Av SBN/FI SS3 .... 403 H4
SOS SS1 .... 21 K6
Southchurch Bvd SOS SS1 .... 401 M2
Southchurch Hall Cl SOS SS1 .... 21 M6
Southchurch Rd SOS SS1 .... 21 H5
Southcliff SBF/HAD SS7 .... 379 K7
WOTN CO14 .... 199 K4
Southcliff Pk COS CO15 .... 13 K3
Southcliff Prom WOTN CO14 .... 199 K4
South Cl DAGE RM10 .... 388 B7
HSTD CO9 .... 128 F3
IPNE IP4 .... 37 M3
RCOS CO16 .... 222 C7
South Colne VGE SS16 .... 19 M9
Southcote Crs BSDN SS14 .... 377 M3
Southcote Rd WIT CM8 .... 212 A7
Southcote Rw BSDN SS14 .... 378 A3
South Crs WOS/PRIT SS0 .... 382 E6
South Crockerford VGE SS16 .... 377 M7
Southcroft Cl FOS CO13 .... 198 D5
Southdale CHIG IG7 .... 349 L7
Southdown Rd EMPK RM11 .... 371 J7
South Dr BRW CM14 .... 354 C5
GPK RM2 .... 371 K3
Southend Arterial Rd
BSDN SS14 .... 377 J1
EMPK RM11 .... 371 M3
LAIN SS15 .... 376 A2
RAYL SS6 .... 380 B3
RBRW/HUT CM13.. .... 373 J5
SBF/HAD SS7 .... 380 D3
Southend La WAB EN9 .... 302 C6
South End Rd RAIN RM13 .... 389 H7
Southend Rd BCAYE CM11 .... 357 K4
BCAYW CM12 .... 357 J2
GRAYS RM17 .... 417 K1
MAL CM9 .... 291 K6
RCFD SS3 .... 383 C4
SBN/FI SS3 .... 384 D8
SLH/COR SS17 .... 394 E8
WICKE SS11 .... 360 C4
Southend Road Main Rd
HOC/HUL SS5 .... 362 E6
Souther Cross Rd
CHLM/WR CM1 .... 232 E6
Southern Dr LOU IG10 .... 327 C8
RCHLM CM3 .... 339 K4
Southernhay BSDN SS14 .... 18 F7
LOS SS9 .... 381 L6
LOU IG10 .... 326 E7
Southey Wk TIL RM18 .... 418 C6
Southfalls Rd CVI SS8 .... 399 G8
Southfield SAFWN CB10 .... 22 B8
Southfield Cha BCAYW CM12 .... 375 M2
Southfield Cl SBF/HAD SS7 .... 380 F6

Southfield Dr SBF/HAD SS7 ...... 380 F6
Southfield Rd BAR EN8 .... 300 F4
　HOD EN11 .... 253 H3
　PEND EN3 .... 324 C8
Southfields RCOLE CO7 .... 107 G5
Southfield Wy BOC CM0 .... 320 D7
South Ga HLW CM20 .... 15 L4
　PUR RM19 .... 415 K1
Southgate Crs K/T/MI CO5 ...... 214 F6
Southgate Gdns SUD CO10 ...... 34 D5
Southgate St SUD CO10 .... 34 D5
South Green Rd K/T/MI CO5 ..... 192 A8
South Hall Dr RAIN RM13 .... 404 C3
South Hanningfield Rd
　RCHLM CM3 .... 337 K3
South Hanningfield Wy
WICKE SS11 .... 337 L8
South Heath Rd RCOLE CO7 ..... 195 G8
South HI FX IP11 .... 9 K4
　SLH/COR SS17 .... 394 B8
South Hill Crs SLH/COR SS17 .... 394 B8
South House Cha MAL CM9 ..... 293 J4
Southland CI COLN CO4 .... 11 K3
Southlands Cha
　CHLM/GWD CM2 .... 313 M1
Southlands Rd BCAYE CM11 ..... 358 E5
South Mayne PIT SS13 .... 378 B5
Southmead Crs BAR EN8 .... 300 F2
Southmill Rd BSF CM23 .... 174 B5
Southminster Rd BOC CM0 ..... 297 C8
Southminster Road Button's HI
　RCHLM CM3 .... 319 H7
Southminster Road Scotts HI
　BOC CM0 .... 320 B7
South Ordnance Rd PEND EN3 .. 325 H1
South Pde CVI SS8 .... 413 M1
South PI HLW CM20 .... 227 H8
　PEND EN3 .... 324 D7
South Primrose HI
　CHLM/WR CM1 .... 16 D1
South Rdg BCAYE CM11 .... 357 K2
South Riding BSDN SS14 .... 377 M5
South Rd BCAYE CM11 .... 358 E6
　BSF CM23 .... 174 B6
　ERITH DA8 .... 414 A3
　HLW CM20 .... 227 H8
　RBSF CM22 .... 176 D3
　SAFWS CB11 .... 65 M2
　SOCK/AV RM15 .... 406 D1
Southsea Av LOS SS9 .... 399 L1
South Strd MGTR CO11 .... 108 D6
South St BOC CM0 .... 297 M8
　BOC CM0 .... 298 B1
　BRTR CM7 .... 183 H1
　BRW CM14 .... 354 D3
　BSF CM23 .... 174 A5
　COLS CO2 .... 162 F5
　IP IP1 .... 2 C2
　MAL CM9 .... 242 E7
　MGTR CO11 .... 108 E7
　PEND EN3 .... 324 E7
　RAIN RM13 .... 388 D8
　RCFD SS4 .... 383 G2
　RCHLM CM3 .... 234 F4
　ROM RM1 .... 370 F5
　ROMW/RG RM7 .... 370 F6
　SAFWN CB10 .... 42 E1
South Vw CDH/CHF RM16 ..... 408 C3
　GTDUN CM6 .... 178 D3
South View Av TIL RM18 .... 418 B5
South View CI RAYL SS6 .... 381 G3
Southview CI RCHLM CM3 .... 339 L3
South View Dr UPMR RM14 ..... 390 B2
Southview Dr COS CO15 .... 225 C5
　WOS/PRIT SS0 .... 400 D1
　WOTN CO14 .... 199 K4
South View Gn RIPS/CAP IP9 .... 78 F5
South View Rd LOU IG10 .... 327 G8
　RCHLM CM3 .... 338 D6
　SBF/HAD SS7 .... 379 K8
　WTHK RM20 .... 416 D3
Southview Rd HOC/HUL SS5 .... 363 G4
　RCHLM CM3 .... 290 E5
Southwalters CVI SS8 .... 398 A7
South Wash Rd LAIN SS15 ..... 376 F1
Southway COLS CO2 .... 10 C9
　COLW CO3 .... 10 A9
South Wy PUR RM19 .... 405 M8
Southway VGE SS16 .... 394 E1
South Wy WAB EN9 .... 325 J1
South Weald Dr WAB EN9 .... 301 L5
South Weald Rd BRW CM14 ..... 354 B4
Southwell Rd SBF/HAD SS7 ..... 379 M7
South Wharf Rd GRAYS RM17 .... 417 G3
Southwick Gdns CVI SS8 .... 398 A8
Southwick Rd CVI SS8 .... 398 A8
Southwold Crs SBF/HAD SS7 .... 379 K6
Southwold Wy RCOS CO16 ..... 223 H6
Southwood Cha RCHLM CM3 .... 291 H7
Southwood Gdns RAYL SS6 ..... 381 J3
Sovereign CI BRTR CM7 .... 155 L7
　RCFD SS4 .... 382 F1
Sowerberry CI CHLM/WR CM1 .. 264 A4
Sowrey Av RAIN RM13 .... 389 G5
Spa CI HOC/HUL SS5 .... 362 F5
Spa Dr BOC CM0 .... 296 C2
Spains Hall PI VGE SS16 .... 19 J8
Spains Hall Rd CHONG CM5 ..... 260 E8
Spalding Av CHLM/WR CM1 ..... 263 M6
Spalding CI BRTR CM7 .... 154 F7
Spalding Wy CHLM/GWD CM2 .. 289 G3
Spalt CI RBRW/HUT CM13 .... 355 H3
Spanbeek Rd CVI SS8 .... 398 C6
Spanbies Rd RCOLE CO7 .... 106 E2
Spareleaze HI LOU IG10 .... 327 G6
Sparepenny La North
　SAFWN CB10 .... 69 H7
Sparepenny La South
　SAFWN CB10 .... 69 J7
Sparkbridge LAIN SS15 .... 376 B5
Sparkey CI WIT CM8 .... 239 H4
Sparks La HSTD CO9 .... 50 B5
Spar La RCHLM CM3 .... 292 D8
Sparling CI COLS CO2 .... 190 C1
The Sparlings FOS CO13 .... 198 D3
Spa Rd HOC/HUL SS5 .... 362 F5
　K/T/MI CO5 .... 186 F7
　WIT CM8 .... 211 M8

Sparrow CI HSTD CO9 .... 97 L3
Sparrow Gn DACE RM10 .... 388 C2
Sparrow Rd SUD CO10 .... 5 K9
Sparrows CI ING CM4 .... 286 B6
Sparrowsend HI SAFWS CB11 .... 65 H6
Sparrows Herne COS CO15 ..... 224 A5
Sparrow's La HLWE CM17 .... 229 M6
　RBSF CM22 .... 229 M4
Speckled Wood Ct BRTR CM7 ... 182 F5
Speedwell CI WIT CM8 .... 211 L8
Speedwell Rd CHTY IP2 .... 37 G7
　COLS CO2 .... 191 L1
Spellbrook CI WICKW SS12 ..... 360 A5
Spellbrook La East BSF CM23 ... 201 C3
Spellbrook La West SBW CM21 .. 200 E4
Spells CI BOC CM0 .... 320 E7
Spencer CI MAL CM9 .... 293 H3
　RBSF CM22 .... 119 K8
　STSD CM24 .... 146 F5
　WFD IG8 .... 348 D6
Spencer Ct RCHLM CM3 .... 339 M4
Spencer Gdns RCFD SS4 .... 363 L6
Spencer Rd RCOS CO16 .... 197 H1
　SAFWN CB10 .... 22 E8
　SBF/HAD SS7 .... 379 L5
Spencers Cft HLWS CM18 ..... 256 B5
Spencer Wk TIL RM18 .... 418 B6
Spendells CI WOTN CO14 ..... 199 M1
Spenders CI BSDN SS14 .... 19 L1
Spenlow Dr CHLM/WR CM1 ..... 263 L4
Spenser Crs UPMR RM14 .... 372 D7
Spenser Wy COS CO15 .... 250 A2
Spey Wy ROM RM1 .... 351 M8
Spicersfield CHESW EN7 .... 276 B7
Spicers La SUD CO10 .... 34 D3
Spielman Rd DART DA1 .... 415 C8
Spillbutters BRWN CM15 .... 308 C8
Spilsby Rd HARH RM3 .... 352 F8
Spindle Beams RCFD SS4 .... 383 G2
Spindle Rd HVHL CB9 .... 27 L3
Spindles TIL RM18 .... 418 B4
Spindle Wd COLN CO4 .... 135 H7
Spingate CI HCH RM12 .... 389 L4
Spinks La WIT CM8 .... 238 F2
Spinnaker CI COS CO15 .... 250 E3
Spinnaker Dr MAL CM9 .... 269 M8
The Spinnakers SBF/HAD SS7 ... 379 J6
The Spinnaker RCHLM CM3 ..... 339 M6
Spinnel's HI MGTR CO11 .... 140 C2
Spinnel's La MGTR CO11 .... 140 D5
Spinner CI IP IP1 .... 36 E3
Spinney CI RAIN RM13 .... 388 F8
　WICKE SS11 .... 360 A4
Spinneyfields K/T/MI CO5 .... 214 E5
The Spinneys HOC/HUL SS5 ..... 362 E6
　LOS SS9 .... 382 A4
　RAYL SS6 .... 381 H2
The Spinney BCAYW CM12 ..... 335 J7
　BROX EN10 .... 253 C7
　BRTR CM7 .... 183 K2
　CDH/CHF RM16 .... 408 B2
　CHONG CM5 .... 307 G2
　IPNE IP4 .... 39 C7
　RBRW/HUT CM13 .... 333 K8
　SAFWS CB11 .... 89 H4
　STSD CM24 .... 146 F6
Spinning Wheel Md
　HLWS CM18 .... 256 B6
Spire Rd LAIN SS15 .... 376 D4
The Spires CHLM/GWD CM2 ..... 289 C5
Spital La BRW CM14 .... 354 A4
Spital Rd MAL CM9 .... 292 E4
Sporehams La CHLM/GWD CM2 .. 290 A7
Sporhams VGE SS16 .... 377 G7
Sportsmans La RCHLM CM3 ..... 267 H1
Sportsway COL CO1 .... 10 D5
Spout La SUD CO10 .... 77 L4
Spratts La MGTR CO11 .... 138 B7
Spriggs La ING CM4 .... 285 C8
Springbank Av HCH RM12 ..... 389 K4
　MGTR CO11 .... 108 C3
Spring Cha RCOLE CO7 .... 192 C1
　RCOLE CO7 .... 220 F4
Spring CI COLN CO4 .... 135 K8
　RCHLM CM3 .... 266 E6
　RCOS CO16 .... 12 A1
Spring Elms La RCHLM CM3 ..... 267 G8
Springett's HI BURES CO8 ..... 101 L1
Springfarm CI RAIN RM13 ..... 404 E1
Springfield EPP CM16 .... 304 A4
　SBF/HAD SS7 .... 380 E7
Springfield Av FX IP11 .... 85 H7
　RBRW/HUT CM13 .... 355 M1
Springfield CI CHONG CM5 ..... 283 G6
Springfield Dr WOS/PRIT SS0 .. 382 E8
Springfield Gdns UPMR RM14 .. 390 D2
　WFD IG8 .... 348 D8
Springfield Gn CHLM/WR CM1 .. 264 E7
Springfield La IP IP1 .... 37 G3
Springfield Lyons Ap
　CHLM/GWD CM2 .... 265 H6
Springfield Park Av
　CHLM/GWD CM2 .... 17 M3
Springfield Park HI
　CHLM/GWD CM2 .... 17 L3
Springfield Park La
　CHLM/GWD CM2 .... 264 F8
Springfield Park Pde
　CHLM/GWD CM2 .... 17 M3
Springfield Park Rd
　CHLM/GWD CM2 .... 17 M3
Springfield PI
　CHLM/WR CM1 .... 264 E6
Springfield Rd BAR EN8 .... 300 F4
　BCAYW CM12 .... 335 J6
　BOC CM0 .... 344 B5
　CDH/CHF RM16 .... 407 M7
　FOS CO13 .... 198 F5
　LOS SS9 .... 382 B5
　SLH/COR SS17 .... 409 H8
　CHLM/WR CM1 .... 17 L2
　CVI SS8 .... 399 G8
　SUD CO10 .... 4 C2
　WICKE SS11 .... 360 A3
Springfields BROX EN10 .... 253 C7
　BRTR CM7 .... 182 D1
　GTDUN CM6 .... 178 D3
　RCOLE CO7 .... 221 G5

VGE SS16 .... 378 A8
Spring Gdns HCH RM12 .... 389 J3
　RAYL SS6 .... 380 D1
　ROMW/RG RM7 .... 370 D5
　WFD IG8 .... 348 D8
Spring Gardens Rd RCOLW CO6 .. 131 L4
Spring Gv LOU IG10 .... 326 E8
Springhall La SBW CM21 .... 227 M2
Springhall Rd SBW CM21 .... 227 M1
Springhead Rd ERITH DA8 ..... 414 A3
Spring HI SAFWS CB11 .... 65 H2
Springhill CI RCOLE CO7 .... 165 M2
Springhill Rd SAFWS CB11 ..... 65 L3
Spring Hills HLW CM20 .... 14 F2
Springhouse La SLH/COR SS17 .. 395 H8
Springhouse Rd SLH/COR SS17 .. 394 F7
Springhurst CI IPNE IP4 .... 3 M4
Springland CI IPNE IP4 .... 38 B5
Springlands Wy SUD CO10 ..... 4 F1
Spring La COLW CO3 .... 161 H3
　COLW CO3 .... 162 B4
　MAL CM9 .... 240 E4
　MAL CM9 .... 269 J7
　RCHLM CM3 .... 268 A1
　RCOLE CO7 .... 192 C1
　RCOLW CO6 .... 133 M7
　WIT CM8 .... 239 H4
Springmead BRTR CM7 .... 182 E4
Spring Pond CI
　CHLM/GWD CM2 .... 288 F3
Spring Pond Meadow
　BRWN CM15 .... 308 D6
Spring Rd IPNE IP4 .... 3 K4
　K/T/MI CO5 .... 214 D7
　RCOLE CO7 .... 221 C4
　RCOS CO16 .... 222 B7
　RIPW IP8 .... 56 E1
Spring Sedge CI COLW CO3 ..... 161 K4
The Springs BROX EN10 .... 276 F5
Springvalley La RCOLE CO7 ..... 136 D8
Spring Wk BROX EN10 .... 276 D1
Springwater CI LOS SS9 .... 381 K4
Springwater Gv LOS SS9 .... 381 K4
Springwater Rd LOS SS9 .... 381 J3
Spring Wy HSTD CO9 .... 97 M2
Springwell Rd SAFWN CB10 .... 43 H6
Springwood CHESW EN7 .... 276 A6
Springwood Dr BRTR CM7 ..... 154 D7
Springwood Wy ROM RM1 ..... 371 H5
Sprites End FX IP11 .... 84 E6
Spriteshall La FX IP11 .... 84 E6
Sprites La CHTY IP2 .... 57 K1
　RIPW IP8 .... 57 K2
Sproughton Rd IP IP1 .... 36 D4
　RIPW IP8 .... 36 C4
Spruce Av COLN CO4 .... 11 M6
Spruce CI K/T/MI CO5 .... 245 J4
　LAIN SS15 .... 376 D2
　WIT CM8 .... 212 B7
Spruce HI HLWS CM18 .... 255 M8
Sprundel Av CVI SS8 .... 413 L1
Spur CI ABR/ST RM4 .... 328 C5
Spurgate RBRW/HUT CM13 ..... 355 H3
Spurgeon CI HSTD CO9 .... 97 M2
Spurgeon St COL CO1 .... 11 K9
Spurling Rd DAGW RM9 .... 388 A5
The Spur BAR EN8 .... 276 E8
Squadrons Ap HCH RM12 ..... 389 K5
The Square BOC CM0 .... 297 M7
　BROX EN10 .... 277 G3
　ING CM4 .... 335 M1
　SBW CM21 .... 227 M1
　WFD IG8 .... 348 B6
Squires CI BSF CM23 .... 173 K3
Squire St RCHLM CM3 .... 339 M4
Squirrells Ct CHLM/WR CM1 ..... 264 A6
Squirrels VGE SS16 .... 376 C8
Squirrel's Cha
　CDH/CHF RM16 .... 408 B7
Squirrels CI BSF CM23 .... 174 A3
Squirrels Fld COLN CO4 .... 135 C6
Squirrel's Heath Av GPK RM2 .. 371 J3
Squirrels Heath La EMPK RM11 .. 371 K4
Squirrels Heath Rd HARH RM3 .. 371 M2
The Squirrels RIPS/CAP IP9 ..... 78 B1
Stable CI COLW CO3 .... 161 L5
　K/T/MI CO5 .... 245 M4
Stablecroft CHLM/WR CM1 ..... 264 F3
Stablefield Rd FOS CO13 .... 199 H4
Stable Ms K/T/MI CO5 .... 245 M3
Stacey Dr VGE SS16 .... 394 D1
Stacey's Mt BCAYE CM11 .... 358 D6
Stackfield HLW CM20 .... 227 J8
The Stackyard SAFWN CB10 .... 22 B8
Staddles RBSF CM22 .... 201 J2
Stadium Rd SOSN SS2 .... 21 H2
Stadium Wy HLWW/ROY CM19 .. 14 C3
　SBF/HAD SS7 .... 380 C4
Staffa CI WICKW SS12 .... 360 A6
Stafford Av EMPK RM11 .... 371 L3
Stafford CI BAR EN8 .... 300 C1
　CDH/CHF RM16 .... 416 D1
　FOS CO13 .... 198 F5
　LOS SS9 .... 382 B5
　SLH/COR SS17 .... 409 H8
Stafford Crs BRTR CM7 .... 155 L7
Stafford Dr BROX EN10 .... 253 H8
Stafford Gn VGE SS16 .... 376 A7
Staffords HLWE CM17 .... 227 M7
Stagden Cross BSDN SS14 ..... 378 A6
Staggart Gn BARK/HLT IG6 ..... 350 B7
Stag La BKHH IG9 .... 348 C3
Stainers BSF CM23 .... 173 K6
Stains CI BAR EN8 .... 276 F8
Stainton Rd PEND EN3 .... 324 D3
Stairs Rd SBN/FI SS3 .... 385 L7
Stalin Rd COLS CO2 .... 163 J7
Stallards Crs FOS CO13 .... 198 F5
Stambourne Rd HSTD CO9 ..... 50 A6
　HSTD CO9 .... 72 C3
Stambridge Rd COS CO15 ..... 12 B3
　RCFD SS4 .... 364 F6
Stamford CI CHTY IP2 .... 58 A3
Stammers PI KESG IP5 .... 39 M3
Stammers Rd COLN CO4 .... 135 C7
Standard Av COS CO15 .... 249 L4
Standard Rd COL CO1 .... 163 K5
　PEND EN3 .... 324 F2

Standen Av HCH RM12 .... 389 L2
Standfield Rd DAGE RM10 ..... 388 B4
Standingford EPP CM16 .... 255 J8
Standley Rd WOTN CO14 .... 199 L2
Stane CI BSF CM23 .... 174 A3
Stane Fld RCOLW CO6 .... 159 M8
Stanes Rd BRTR CM7 .... 155 C5
Staneway VGE SS16 .... 18 A9
Stanfield CI COLW CO3 .... 161 M8
Stanfield Rd SOSN SS2 .... 21 H2
Stanford CI ROMW/RG RM7 .... 370 C6
　WFD IG8 .... 348 F6
Stanford Ct WAB EN9 .... 302 B5
Stanford Gdns SOCK/AV RM15 .. 405 M6
Stanford-le-hope By-pass
　CDH/CHF RM16 .... 408 D4
　SLH/COR SS17 .... 395 H3
Stanford Rivers Rd
　CHONG CM5 .... 307 H3
Stanford Rd CDH/CHF RM16 .... 408 F3
　CVI SS8 .... 398 B8
　SLH/COR SS17 .... 409 J2
Stanham PI DART DA1 .... 414 B8
Stanhope Rd BAR EN8 .... 300 F5
　BCTR RM8 .... 388 A1
　RAIN RM13 .... 389 H8
Stanier CI SOS SS1 .... 21 L5
Stanley Av BCTR RM8 .... 370 A8
　GPK RM2 .... 371 H4
　IPSE IP3 .... 38 B7
　RCOLE CO7 .... 221 H4
Stanley CI GPK RM2 .... 371 H4
　HCH RM12 .... 389 K1
Stanley PI CHONG CM5 .... 307 H1
Stanley Ri CHLM/GWD CM2 .... 265 G8
Stanley Rd COS CO15 .... 12 A7
　CVI SS8 .... 398 D7
　FX IP11 .... 9 M3
　GRAYS RM17 .... 417 J2
　HCH RM12 .... 389 K1
　HSTD CO9 .... 128 E1
　RCFD SS4 .... 363 K4
　RCOLE CO7 .... 192 D2
　SAFWN CB10 .... 22 F8
　SBF/HAD SS7 .... 379 L6
　SOS SS1 .... 21 K7
　SUD CO10 .... 4 D4
　UPMR RM14 .... 393 G3
Stanley Rd North RAIN RM13 .. 388 F7
Stanley Rd South RAIN RM13 .. 389 G8
Stanleys Farm Rd
　SAFWS CB11 .... 66 A3
Stanley Ter BCAYW CM12 ..... 357 H2
Stanley Wood Av SUD CO10 ... 4 F2
Stanley Wooster Wy COLN CO4 .. 163 M4
Stanmore CI COS CO15 .... 12 D1
Stanmore Rd WICKE SS11 ..... 360 C5
Stanmore Wy LOU IG10 .... 327 H3
　RCOS CO16 .... 222 C7
Stannard Wy SUD CO10 .... 5 H9
Stannetts LAIN SS15 .... 376 C3
Stansfield Rd SBF/HAD SS7 .... 379 J4
Stansgate Rd BOC CM0 .... 296 A6
　DAGE RM10 .... 388 B1
Stanstead Dr HOD EN11 .... 253 J3
Stanstead Rd HOD EN11 .... 253 J3
　HSTD CO9 .... 129 G3
Stansted CI BCAYE CM11 ..... 357 L1
　CHLM/WR CM1 .... 16 A6
　HCH RM12 .... 389 K5
Stansted Rd BSF CM23 .... 174 B3
　COLS CO2 .... 191 H2
　RBSF CM22 .... 147 K2
Stansted Wy FOS CO13 .... 199 H5
Stanstrete Fld BRTR CM7 .... 182 C6
Stanton Hughes Wy
　MGTR CO11 .... 108 C3
Stanway CI CHIG IG7 .... 349 M6
Stanway Rd SBF/HAD SS7 ..... 379 K6
　WAB EN9 .... 302 B5
Stanwell St COL CO1 .... 10 C9
Stanwyck Gdns HARH RM3 ..... 352 C6
Stanwyn Av COS CO15 .... 12 F5
Stapleford CI CHLM/GWD CM2 .. 16 F5
Stapleford End WICKE SS11 ... 360 C6
Stapleford Gdns CRW RM5 ..... 351 H7
Stapleford Rd ABR/ST RM4 ..... 329 J6
Staplegrove SBN/FI SS3 .... 402 D3
Staplers CI MAL CM9 .... 240 C7
Staplers Heath MAL CM9 .... 240 C6
Staplers Wk MAL CM9 .... 240 C6
Staples Rd LOU IG10 .... 326 F5
Stapleton Crs RAIN RM13 ..... 389 H5
Starboard Vw RCHLM CM3 ..... 339 M6
Starfield CI IPNE IP4 .... 38 C5
Star CI EPP CM16 .... 304 B2
　GTDUN CM6 .... 178 E2
　ING CM4 .... 310 D7
　IPNE IP4 .... 2 F6
　SBN/FI SS3 .... 384 F8
Starling CI BKHH IG9 .... 348 B2
Star Md GTDUN CM6 .... 122 B1
Starr Rd RBSF CM22 .... 120 A6
Station Ap BAR EN8 .... 300 F6
　BOC CM0 .... 344 C6
　BRTR CM7 .... 183 H1
　CVI SS8 .... 398 A5
　FOS CO13 .... 199 G6
　HOC/HUL SS5 .... 362 F5
　LAIN SS15 .... 376 D6
　RCHLM CM3 .... 339 K3
　RCHLM CM3 .... 341 J3
　SOS SS1 .... 21 G6
　SOSN SS2 .... 20 F1
　VGE SS16 .... 18 F8
　WICKE SS11 .... 359 L3
Station Approach Rd TIL RM18 .. 418 B8
Station Av RAYL SS6 .... 361 K8
　SOSN SS2 .... 383 H8
　WICKE SS11 .... 359 K2
Station Crs RAYL SS6 .... 361 L8
Station HI BURES CO8 .... 101 M3
Station La HAR CO12 .... 7 H7
　HCH RM12 .... 389 M1
　ING CM4 .... 310 C4
　PIT SS13 .... 378 D6
Station Pde HCH RM12 .... 389 J3

Station Rd BAR EN8 .... 301 H6
　BCAYW CM12 .... 357 G1
　BOC CM0 .... 320 E7
　BOC CM0 .... 344 C7
　BROX EN10 .... 253 G8
　BRTR CM7 .... 182 A2
　BSF CM23 .... 174 A4
　BSF CM23 .... 174 B5
　CBE/LIN CB1 .... 24 C1
　CHIG IG7 .... 349 J4
　COS CO15 .... 13 G6
　CVI SS8 .... 413 M1
　EPP CM16 .... 281 J7
　EPP CM16 .... 304 B3
　FOS CO13 .... 198 C5
　FX IP11 .... 84 D6
　GPK RM2 .... 371 J4
　GTDUN CM6 .... 178 F3
　GTDUN CM6 .... 180 A4
　HAR CO12 .... 6 A4
　HARH RM3 .... 372 A1
　HLWE CM17 .... 227 K7
　HOC/HUL SS5 .... 362 F5
　HSTD CO9 .... 49 L3
　HSTD CO9 .... 97 L1
　HVHL CB9 .... 28 B3
　K/T/MI CO5 .... 186 D8
　K/T/MI CO5 .... 214 D7
　LOS SS9 .... 381 M8
　LOS SS9 .... 399 M1
　LOU IG10 .... 326 F7
　MAL CM9 .... 242 F6
　MAL CM9 .... 269 H8
　MAL CM9 .... 272 E1
　MGTR CO11 .... 108 C6
　MGTR CO11 .... 109 M8
　MGTR CO11 .... 111 G8
　MGTR CO11 .... 139 M1
　RAYL SS6 .... 361 K8
　RBRW/HUT CM13 .... 374 F6
　RBSF CM22 .... 147 K1
　RBSF CM22 .... 176 D4
　RCHLM CM3 .... 238 A6
　RCHLM CM3 .... 317 H6
　RCHLM CM3 .... 343 G2
　RCOLE CO7 .... 192 C3
　RCOLE CO7 .... 193 H3
　RCOLE CO7 .... 194 B3
　RCOLE CO7 .... 194 A5
　RCOLE CO7 .... 194 F4
　RCOLW CO6 .... 220 F5
　RCOLW CO6 .... 130 B4
　RCOLW CO6 .... 130 F4
　RCOLW CO6 .... 130 A2
　RCOLW CO6 .... 131 L5
　RCOLW CO6 .... 160 B7
　RCOS CO16 .... 197 G3
　RIPS/CAP IP9 .... 78 E5
　SAFWS CB11 .... 64 F6
　SAFWS CB11 .... 65 L3
　SAFWS CB11 .... 89 H3
　SBF/HAD SS7 .... 397 L3
　SBW CM21 .... 201 G8
　SOS SS1 .... 402 C3
　STSD CM24 .... 146 F5
　SUD CO10 .... 4 E7
　SUD CO10 .... 31 K4
　SUD CO10 .... 34 D6
　TIL RM18 .... 419 J4
　UPMR RM14 .... 390 D1
　WAB EN9 .... 277 M7
　WICKE SS11 .... 359 K1
　WIT CM8 .... 211 G1
　WIT CM8 .... 212 B8
　WIT CM8 .... 239 K7
　WOS/PRIT SS0 .... 20 A7
Station St CHTY IP2 .... 2 F9
　SAFWS CB11 .... 65 L3
　WOTN CO14 .... 199 K4
Station Wy BKHH IG9 .... 348 C5
　VGE SS16 .... 18 F8
Staverton Rd EMPK RM11 ..... 371 L6
Stays La CHONG CM5 .... 261 H8
Steam Mill Rd MGTR CO11 ..... 139 K3
Stebbing Rd GTDUN CM6 ..... 180 C4
Stebbings VGE SS16 .... 376 D7
St Edmund Wy BURES CO8 ..... 102 B2
　RCOLE CO7 .... 107 L4
Steed CI HCH RM12 .... 389 J1
Steeds Meadow SUD CO10 ..... 34 D3
Steeds Wy LOU IG10 .... 326 F5
Steele CI RCOLW CO6 .... 160 A8
Steen CI ING CM4 .... 310 C7
Steeple Bumpstead Rd
　HVHL CB9 .... 47 L3
Steeple CI MAL CM9 .... 269 L7
　RCFD SS4 .... 363 L8
Steeplefield LOS SS9 .... 381 M5
Steeplehall PIT SS13 .... 378 B6
Steeple Hts SBF/HAD SS7 ..... 379 J5
Steeple Mdw BOC CM0 .... 320 C5
Steeple Rd BOC CM0 .... 320 C5
　RCHLM CM3 .... 318 C5
Steeple Vw BSF CM23 .... 174 A3
Steeple Wy BRWN CM15 .... 332 C1
Steerforth CI CHLM/WR CM1 ... 263 L4
Steli Av CVI SS8 .... 398 A6
Stella Maris CI CVI SS8 .... 399 G8
Stennetts CI FX IP11 .... 84 C5
Stenning Av TIL RM18 .... 419 J1
Stepfield WIT CM8 .... 239 J1
Stephen Av RAIN RM13 .... 389 H5
Stephen CI HVHL CB9 .... 28 A3
　SUD CO10 .... 34 C6
Stephen Cranfield CI
　K/T/MI CO5 .... 192 B4
Stephen Marshall Av BRTR CM7 .. 94 D5
Stephen Rd KESG IP5 .... 39 M3
Stephens CI HARH RM3 .... 352 D6
Stephen's Ct IPNE IP4 .... 38 C5
Stephens Crs SLH/COR SS17 ... 394 A8
Stephenson Av TIL RM18 .... 418 B5
Stephenson Rd BRTR CM7 ..... 183 H2
　COLN CO4 .... 135 L5
　COS CO15 .... 224 C3
　LOS SS9 .... 381 K5
　RCHLM CM3 .... 341 H3

Stephenson Rd West *COS* CO15.. 224 B2
Sterling Av *BAR* EN8 ... 300 E6
Sterling CI *COL* CO1 ... 161 M6
Sterry Crs *DAGE* RM10 ... 388 B4
Sterry Gdns *DAGE* RM10 ... 388 B5
Sterry Rd *DAGE* RM10 ... 388 B3
Stevens CI *CVI* SS8 ... 398 E7
Stevens La *GTDUN* CM6 ... 181 J5
Stevenson CI *ERITH* DA8 ... 414 C4
Stevenson Rd *IP* IP1 ... 2 C3
Stevenson Wy *WICKW* SS12 ... 359 K6
Stevens Wy *WIT* CM8 ... 238 F2
Steward CI *BAR* EN8 ... 300 F2
Stewards CI *EPP* CM16 ... 304 B5
  FOS CO13 ... 199 G4
Stewards Elm Farm La
  RCFD SS4 ... 364 E7
Stewards Green Rd *EPP* CM16.. 304 C4
Stewart Av *UPMR* RM14 ... 390 C2
Stewart PI *WICKW* SS12 ... 360 A5
Stewart Rd *CHLM/GWD* CM2 ... 288 B5
The Stewarts *BSF* CM23 ... 173 M4
Stewarts Wy *BSF* CM23 ... 146 A1
Stewart Young Gv *KESG* IP5 ... 39 L4
Steyning Av *SOSN* SS2 ... 401 M1
Stifford Clays Rd
  CDH/CHF RM16 ... 407 H5
  CDH/CHF RM16 ... 407 J5
Stifford HI *CDH/CHF* RM16 ... 406 E6
  SOCK/AV RM15 ... 406 D5
Stifford Rd *SOCK/AV* RM15 ... 406 D5
Stile Cft *HLWS* CM18 ... 256 B5
Stile La *RAYL* SS6 ... 380 E1
Stilemans *WICKE* SS11 ... 359 L3
Stilemans Wd *BRTR* CM7 ... 183 L3
The Stiles *MAL* CM9 ... 269 M8
Stirling Av *LOS* SS9 ... 399 J1
Stirling CI *RAIN* RM13 ... 404 C1
  RAYL SS6 ... 361 J6
Stirling Dr *HVHL* CB9 ... 27 M3
Stirling PI *PIT* SS13 ... 378 C3
Stirrup CI *CHLM/WR* CM1 ... 264 F4
Stivvy's Rd *MAL* CM9 ... 267 K8
Stock Cha *MAL* CM9 ... 269 J6
Stock CI *SOSN* SS2 ... 383 G7
Stockdale Rd *BCTR* RM8 ... 388 A1
Stockfield Av *HOD* EN11 ... 253 H6
Stockhouse CI *MAL* CM9 ... 242 B1
Stockhouse Rd *K/T/MI* CO5 ... 215 J4
Stockingswater La *PEND* EN3.. 324 F5
Stock La *ING* CM4 ... 310 D7
Stockley CI *HVHL* CB9 ... 28 D4
Stockmers End *RIPS/CAP* IP9.... 78 B2
Stock Rd *BCAYE* ... 335 J2
  BCAYW CM12 ... 357 J1
  CHLM/GWD CM2 ... 288 B8
  ING CM4 ... 312 A8
  SOSN SS2 ... 383 H7
Stocksfield *BRWN* CM15 ... 332 A1
Stocks La *BRWN* CM15 ... 332 A1
Stockwell *COL* CO1 ... 10 C7
Stockwell CI *BCAYE* CM11 ... 357 L5
  CHESW EN7 ... 276 A7
Stockwood *SBF/HAD* SS7 ... 380 B4
Stokeash CI *RCOS* CO16 ... 223 H8
Stoke Av *BARK/HLT* IG6 ... 350 B7
Stoke Br *IP* IP1 ... 2 F7
Stokefelde *PIT* SS13 ... 378 C4
Stoke Hall Rd *CHTY* IP2 ... 2 E7
Stoke Park Dr *CHTY* IP2 ... 57 M3
Stoke Rd *RAIN* RM13 ... 404 E1
  RCOLW CO6 ... 104 C2
  SUD CO10 ... 31 H5
The Stokes *WOTN* CO14 ... 199 J2
Stoke St *CHTY* IP2 ... 2 F7
Stollery CI *KESG* IP5 ... 39 K4
Stonards HI *EPP* CM16 ... 304 D3
  LOU IG10 ... 327 G8
Stondon Rd *CHONG* CM5 ... 307 J2
Stonebridge HI *RCOLW* CO6 ... 129 L4
Stonechat Rd *BCAYW* CM12 ... 357 K3
  CHTY IP2 ... 36 B8
Stonehall Dr *RCOS* CO16 ... 223 L2
Stonehall La *RCOS* CO16 ... 168 C2
Stoneham Av *RCOS* CO16 ... 223 H6
Stonehill CI *LOS* SS9 ... 382 K4
Stonehill Rd *CHLM/WR* CM1 ... 262 A7
  LOS SS9 ... 381 M7
Stonehill Wy *K/T/MI* CO5 ... 245 H4
Stonehorse Rd *PEND* EN3 ... 324 D7
Stonehouse La *PUR* RM19 ... 415 M2
Stone La *K/T/MI* CO5 ... 241 C1
  MGTR CO11 ... 111 G7
Stoneleigh *SBW* CM21 ... 200 E8
Stoneleigh Av *EN* EN1 ... 324 C2
Stoneleigh CI *BAR* EN8 ... 300 E5
Stoneleigh Dr *HOD* EN11 ... 253 J2
Stoneleigh Pk *COLW* CO3 ... 162 A8
Stoneleighs *SBF/HAD* SS7 ... 380 A5
Stone Lodge La *CHTY* IP2 ... 2 A9
Stone Lodge La West *CHTY* IP2.. 37 G8
Stone Lodge Wk *CHTY* IP2 ... 2 C9
Stoneness Rd *WTHK* RM20 ... 416 C3
Stone Path Dr *RCHLM* CM3 ... 238 A7
Stone Rd *RCOLE* CO7 ... 166 C2
Stones Green Rd *HAR* CO12 ... 168 L1
  HAR CO12 ... 169 H1
Stoney Common *STSD* CM24 ... 146 F6
Stoney Common Rd
  STSD CM24 ... 146 E6
Stoneycroft Rd *WFD* IG8 ... 348 F7
Stoneyfield Dr *STSD* CM24 ... 146 F6
Stoney Hills *BCAYE* CM11 ... 336 C6
  BOC CM0 ... 344 D3
Stoney La *RCOLE* CO7 ... 221 H3
Stonycroft CI *PEND* EN3 ... 324 F4
Stony La *CHONG* CM5 ... 282 C3
  GTDUN CM6 ... 122 B1
Stony Pth *LOU* IG10 ... 327 G3
Stonyshotts *WAB* EN9 ... 301 M6
Stopford Ct *IP* IP1 ... 2 B3
Stores Rd *K/T/MI* CO5 ... 214 D5
Stormonts Wy *VGE* SS16 ... 394 E1

Stornoway Rd *SOSN* SS2 ... 21 M3
Storr Gdns *RBRW/HUT* CM13 ... 333 L7
Stortford Hall Pk *BSF* CM23 ... 174 C3
Stortford Hall Rd *BSF* CM23 ... 174 C3
Stortford Rd *GTDUN* CM6 ... 177 J4
  GTDUN CM6 ... 231 H5
  HOD EN11 ... 253 J4
  RBSF CM22 ... 201 M7
  SAFWS CB11 ... 87 K7
  STDN CS11 ... 172 D1
Stort Ldg *BSF* CM23 ... 173 L3
Stort Ml *HLW* CM20 ... 227 J5
Stort Rd *BSF* CM23 ... 174 A5
Stort Valley Wy *HLW* CM20 ... 227 L4
  HLWE CM17 ... 257 M1
  HLWW/ROY CM19 ... 254 A3
  SBW CM21 ... 228 D1
Stour Av *FX* IP11 ... 9 H3
Stour CI *HAR* CO12 ... 142 C1
  SBN/FI SS3 ... 402 F5
  SUD CO10 ... 33 K1
Stourdale CI *MGTR* CO11 ... 108 B8
Stour Gdns *SUD* CO10 ... 55 H7
Stourmead CI *HVHL* CB9 ... 29 H1
Stour Rd *CDH/CHF* RM16 ... 418 B2
  DAGE RM10 ... 388 B1
  DART DA1 ... 414 B7
  K/T/MI CO5 ... 7 K5
Stourside *RIPS/CAP* IP9 ... 113 H3
Stour St *MGTR* CO11 ... 108 C7
  SUD CO10 ... 4 B7
  SUD CO10 ... 32 D3
Stourton Rd *WIT* CM8 ... 211 M8
Stour V *HSTD* CO9 ... 29 L8
Stour Valley Pth *BURES* CO8 ... 101 M1
  RCOLW CO6 ... 103 J1
  SUD CO10 ... 32 B1
Stour Valley Rd *HVHL* CB9 ... 28 C4
Stour Valley Wk *SUD* CO10 ... 4 A9
Stourview Av *MGTR* CO11 ... 109 H7
Stourview CI *MGTR* CO11 ... 109 J7
Stour Wy *UPMR* RM14 ... 372 F6
Stowe's La *BOC* CM0 ... 297 K7
Stow Rd *RCHLM* CM3 ... 316 E7
The Stow *HLW* CM20 ... 256 A1
St Peter's La *BOC* CM0 ... 298 B6
  CHLM/GWD CM2 ... 313 H6
  CHONG CM5 ... 307 M1
  ING CM4 ... 308 F3
  ING CM4 ... 311 K7
  ING CM4 ... 336 B1
  RCHLM CM3 ... 295 H7
  RCHLM CM3 ... 315 M2
Stradbroke Dr *CHIG* IG7 ... 349 J7
Stradbroke Gv *BKHH* IG9 ... 348 E2
Stradbroke Pk *BARK/HLT* IG6 .. 349 J7
  CHIG IG7 ... 349 J7
Stradbroke Rd *IPNE* IP4 ... 38 B4
Straight Rd *COLN* CO4 ... 105 H7
  COLW CO3 ... 161 M5
  HARH RM3 ... 352 C6
  KIR/NAC IP10 ... 60 D3
  MGTR CO11 ... 139 K2
  RCOLE CO7 ... 195 H8
Straight Wy *COLS* CO2 ... 216 B1
The Straits *WAB* EN9 ... 301 J4
The Strand *CHTY* IP2 ... 58 D3
Strangman Rd *SBF/HAD* SS7 ... 380 C7
Strasbourg Rd *CVI* SS8 ... 398 E6
Stratfield Dr *BROX* EN10 ... 252 F7
Stratford CI *DAGE* RM10 ... 388 D6
Stratford Gdns *SLH/COR* SS17.. 409 L1
Stratford PI *WOTN* CO14 ... 199 L3
Stratford Rd *COS* CO15 ... 224 E5
  IP IP1 ... 37 G1
  RCOLE CO7 ... 194 C6
Strathmore Rd *TIL* RM18 ... 419 K1
Strathmore Gdns *HCH* RM12 ... 371 C8
Strathmore Rd *RCHLM* CM3 ... 341 J3
Strattonhall Drift *KIR/NAC* IP10.. 83 C1
Stratton Dr *HARH* RM3 ... 353 H6
Stratton Wk *HARH* RM3 ... 353 H6
Strawberry St *BRTR* CM7 ... 183 H2
Strawberry Flds *HVHL* CB9 ... 27 L4
Strawberry La *K/T/MI* CO5 ... 214 F8
Strawbrook HI *RCHLM* CM3 ... 208 F7
Straw La *SUD* CO10 ... 4 B7
The Street *BOC* CM0 ... 319 M1
  BRTR CM7 ... 156 C5
  BRTR CM7 ... 181 M2
  BRTR CM7 ... 184 B5
  BRTR CM7 ... 184 E1
  BSF CM23 ... 117 J4
  BSF CM23 ... 146 A1
  BUNT SG9 ... 116 B7
  CHLM/GWD CM2 ... 312 C1
  CHLM/WR CM1 ... 262 B5
  CHONG CM5 ... 260 B8
  CHONG CM5 ... 283 L7
  FOS CO13 ... 198 D2
  GTDUN CM6 ... 179 L3
  GTDUN CM6 ... 204 F4
  HAR CO12 ... 142 B2
  HSTD CO9 ... 49 J5
  HSTD CO9 ... 72 C4
  HSTD CO9 ... 100 B4
  HSTD CO9 ... 127 M3
  K/T/MI CO5 ... 186 F6
  K/T/MI CO5 ... 214 C1
  KIR/NAC IP10 ... 60 D6
  MAL CM9 ... 241 J6
  MAL CM9 ... 243 H3
  MAL CM9 ... 291 L1
  MGTR CO11 ... 109 H2
  MGTR CO11 ... 139 M2
  RBSF CM22 ... 175 H6
  RBSF CM22 ... 228 E3
  RCHLM CM3 ... 210 D8
  RCHLM CM3 ... 233 H1
  RCHLM CM3 ... 235 J5
  RCHLM CM3 ... 238 A7
  RCHLM CM3 ... 315 J7
  RCHLM CM3 ... 316 D7
  RCHLM CM3 ... 318 A6
  RCOLE CO7 ... 106 D3
  RCOLE CO7 ... 107 J1
  RCOLE CO7 ... 136 F3
  RCOLW CO6 ... 131 K6

  RCOLW CO6 ... 159 J3
  RCOS CO16 ... 167 M6
  RCOS CO16 ... 196 D7
  RCOS CO16 ... 196 A3
  RIPS/CAP IP9 ... 58 B5
  RIPS/CAP IP9 ... 78 A2
  RIPS/CAP IP9 ... 80 E5
  RIPS/CAP IP9 ... 82 E8
  RIPS/CAP IP9 ... 111 J1
  RIPS/CAP IP9 ... 112 C1
  RIPW IP8 ... 36 B1
  RIPW IP8 ... 56 A3
  RIPW IP8 ... 57 K5
  RIPW IP8 ... 57 J5
  SUD CO10 ... 30 C8
  SUD CO10 ... 33 H3
  SUD CO10 ... 33 K5
  SUD CO10 ... 50 E2
  SUD CO10 ... 52 D3
  SUD CO10 ... 53 M6
  SUD CO10 ... 54 F8
  WIT CM8 ... 210 F2
  WIT CM8 ... 239 M6
Stretford Ct *WIT* CM8 ... 184 E8
Strethall Rd *SAFWS* CB11 ... 42 B6
Strickland Rd *DART* DA1 ... 415 C8
Strickmere *RCOLE* CO7 ... 106 D1
Stroma Gdns *SBN/FI* SS3 ... 402 E5
Stromburg Rd *CVI* SS8 ... 397 M6
Stromness PI *SOSN* SS2 ... 21 L5
Stromness Rd *SOSN* SS2 ... 21 M4
Strood Av *ROMW/RG* RM7 ... 370 E8
Strood CI *K/T/MI* CO5 ... 245 J4
The Strood *K/T/MI* CO5 ... 218 C7
Struan Av *SLH/COR* SS17 ... 394 F6
Strudwick CI *BRTR* CM7 ... 183 G1
Strutt CI *RCHLM* CM3 ... 238 B7
Stuart CI *BRWN* CM15 ... 332 C7
  CHLM/GWD CM2 ... 289 J5
  CVI SS8 ... 398 C7
  FX IP11 ... 85 L6
  IPNE IP4 ... 3 L2
  SBN/FI SS3 ... 385 G7
  SOSN SS2 ... 21 H1
Stuart Rd *GRAYS* RM17 ... 417 J2
  SOSN SS2 ... 21 H1
Stuart St *SOSN* SS2 ... 383 H8
Stuarts Wy *BRTR* CM7 ... 183 J1
Stuart Wy *BCAYE* CM11 ... 357 M2
  CHESW EN7 ... 300 C3
  WAB EN9 ... 301 K5
Stubbers La *UPMR* RM14 ... 390 F5
Stubbs CI *FOS* CO13 ... 198 F4
  HVHL CB9 ... 27 L2
  IPSE IP3 ... 59 H2
  MGTR CO11 ... 108 C7
Stubbs La *BRTR* CM7 ... 183 K1
Stublands *BSDN* SS14 ... 378 A5
Studd's La *COLN* CO4 ... 134 E7
Studland Av *WICKW* SS12 ... 359 G3
Stump La *CHLM/WR* CM1 ... 264 E7
Sturdee Av *IPSE* IP3 ... 38 C8
Sturlas Wy *BAR* EN8 ... 300 E5
Sturmer Rd *HVHL* CB9 ... 28 D5
Sturrick La *RCOLE* CO7 ... 194 E2
Sturrocks *VGE* SS16 ... 377 M8
Stutton CI *RIPS/CAP* IP9 ... 110 B1
Stutton Gn *RIPS/CAP* IP9 ... 110 D2
Stutton La *RIPS/CAP* IP9 ... 79 K6
Stutton Rd *MGTR* CO11 ... 109 H1
Styles *BRTR* CM7 ... 123 L1
Sudbourne Av *RCOS* CO16 ... 223 H7
Sudbourne Rd *FX* IP11 ... 84 E8
Sudbrook CI *WICKW* SS12 ... 359 L5
Sudbury CI *HOC/HUL* SS5 ... 363 C7
Sudbury Rd *BCAYE* CM11 ... 337 H6
  BURES CO8 ... 102 A2
  FX IP11 ... 8 D2
  HSTD CO9 ... 99 G8
  SUD CO10 ... 35 K5
Sudburys Farm Rd
  BCAYW CM12 ... 356 C5
Sudeley Gdns *HOC/HUL* SS5 ... 362 D5
Sudicamps Ct *WAB* EN9 ... 302 B5
Suez Rd *PEND* EN3 ... 324 F6
Suffolk Av *RCOS* CO16 ... 223 H7
  COS CO15 ... 224 F4
Suffolk CI *COLN* CO4 ... 11 H4
  COS CO15 ... 224 F4
Suffolk Coast & Heaths Pth
  FX IP11 ... 115 J2
  IPSE IP3 ... 59 H5
  KIR/NAC IP10 ... 59 L4
  RIPS/CAP IP9 ... 81 M2
  RIPS/CAP IP9 ... 110 D1
  RIPS/CAP IP9 ... 112 A4
Suffolk Crs *MAL* CM9 ... 292 F2
Suffolk Dr *LAIN* SS15 ... 376 C5
Suffolk Rd *DAGE* RM10 ... 388 C4
  IPNE IP4 ... 3 H2
  MAL CM9 ... 292 F2
  PEND EN3 ... 324 C7
  SUD CO10 ... 4 D5
Suffolk Wy *WOTN* CO14 ... 199 K3
Sugar La *HSTD* CO9 ... 96 E4
Sugden Av *WICKW* SS12 ... 359 H4
Sullivan CI *COLN* CO4 ... 163 M5
Sullivan Rd *TIL* RM18 ... 418 B5
Sullivan Wy *VGE* SS16 ... 376 B6
Summercourt Rd *WOS/PRIT* SS0.. 20 D5
Summerdale *BCAYW* CM12 ... 357 H1
  RCHLM CM3 ... 319 H8
Summerfield CI *IPNE* IP4 ... 38 E3
Summerfield Rd *LOU* IG10 ... 326 E8
Summerfields *HSTD* CO9 ... 97 M2
  ING CM4 ... 310 D8
Summer Hill Rd *SAFWS* CB11 ... 65 L3
Summerwood CI
  SBF/HAD SS7 ... 380 D8
The Summit *LOU* IG10 ... 327 G3
Sumners Farm CI *EPP* CM16 ... 255 H8
Sumpters Wy *SOSN* SS2 ... 383 G5
Sunbank *GTDUN* CM6 ... 178 F3
Sunbeam Av *COS* CO15 ... 249 M5
Sunbury CI *SBN/FI* SS3 ... 402 F1
Sunbury Wy *MAL* CM9 ... 293 G3
Sun Ct *ERITH* DA8 ... 414 A6

Sundale CI *COS* CO15 ... 225 G5
Sunderland Rd *FX* IP11 ... 8 E9
Sunfield CI *IPNE* IP4 ... 38 C5
Sunflower Wy *HARH* RM3 ... 371 L1
Sun Lido Square Gdns
  BRTR CM7 ... 182 D5
Sunnedon *VGE* SS16 ... 19 M7
  CVI SS8 ... 398 D7
Sunningdale *BSF* CM23 ... 173 M5
Sunningdale Av *IPNE* IP4 ... 38 E6
  LOS SS9 ... 400 B2
  RAIN RM13 ... 404 C2
Sunningdale Dr *FX* IP11 ... 85 J7
Sunningdale Fall
  RCHLM CM3 ... 238 C7
Sunningdale Rd
  CHLM/WR CM1 ... 263 M7
  RAIN RM13 ... 389 H6
  RCHLM CM3 ... 342 F1
Sunningdale Wy *FOS* CO13 ... 198 F4
Sunnings La *UPMR* RM14 ... 390 E5
Sunnybank CI *LOS* SS9 ... 382 A5
Sunny Cft *HLWS* CM18 ... 256 A6
Sunnycroft Gdns *UPMR* RM14 .. 373 C7
Sunnydene CI *HARH* RM3 ... 353 C5
Sunnyfield Gdns *HOC/HUL* SS5 .. 362 C5
Sunnyfields Rd *BRTR* CM7 ... 155 L1
Sunnymede *CHIG* IG7 ... 350 C4
Sunnymede CI *SBF/HAD* SS7 ... 380 B5
Sunny Point *WOTN* CO14 ... 171 M8
Sunny Rd *HOC/HUL* SS5 ... 362 F6
The Sunny Rd *PEND* EN3 ... 324 E9
Sunnyside *BRTR* CM7 ... 154 F8
  STSD CM24 ... 146 F5
  VGE SS16 ... 376 A7
  WAB EN9 ... 278 A2
Sunnyside Gdns *UPMR* RM14 ... 390 D2
Sunnyside Rd *EPP* CM16 ... 304 A4
  RCOLW CO6 ... 132 C6
Sunnyside Wy *RCOS* CO16 ... 223 K2
Sunny Wy *BOC* CM0 ... 296 D3
Sunray Av *CHLM/WR* CM1 ... 264 B6
  HCH RM12 ... 389 K2
Sunset Av *WFD* IG8 ... 348 B6
Sunset CI *ERITH* DA8 ... 414 C4
Sun St *BCAYW* CM12 ... 357 H2
  SBW CM21 ... 228 A2
  WAB EN9 ... 301 K5
Surbiton Av *SOS* SS1 ... 401 L3
Surbiton Rd *IP* IP1 ... 2 F7
  SOSN SS2 ... 401 L2
Surig Rd *CVI* SS8 ... 398 B7
Surman Crs *RBRW/HUT* CM13 .. 333 M8
Surrey Av *LOS* SS9 ... 382 A8
Surrey Dr *EMPK* RM11 ... 372 B5
Surrey La *K/T/MI* CO5 ... 214 D7
Surrey Rd *DAGE* RM10 ... 388 C4
  FX IP11 ... 9 J2
  IP IP1 ... 2 A4
Surrey Wy *LAIN* SS15 ... 376 B3
Surridge CI *RAIN* RM13 ... 404 D1
Susan CI *ROMW/RG* RM7 ... 370 D4
Sussex Av *HARH* RM3 ... 353 G8
Sussex CI *CVI* SS8 ... 398 C6
  HOD EN11 ... 253 H4
  LAIN SS15 ... 376 C5
  RCHLM CM3 ... 266 A3
Sussex Gdns *COS* CO15 ... 224 F5
Sussex Rd *BRW* CM14 ... 354 C5
  COLW CO3 ... 162 C4
  CVI SS8 ... 398 B6
Sussex Wy *BCAYW* CM12 ... 335 J5
Sutcliffe CI *WICKW* SS12 ... 359 L5
Sutherland Bvd *LOS* SS9 ... 399 J1
Sutherland PI *WICKW* SS12 ... 359 L6
Sutherland Rd *PEND* EN3 ... 324 E8
Sutton Acres *RBSF* CM22 ... 201 L4
Sutton CI *BROX* EN10 ... 252 F8
  LOU IG10 ... 348 F1
Sutton Court Dr *RCFD* SS4 ... 383 C4
Sutton Md *CHLM/GWD* CM2 ... 265 H7
Sutton Park Av *COLW* CO3 ... 162 B8
Sutton Rd *RCFD* SS4 ... 383 H3
  SOSN SS2 ... 21 J5
Suttons Av *HCH* RM12 ... 389 K2
Suttons Gdns *HCH* RM12 ... 389 L2
Suttons La *HCH* RM12 ... 389 L4
Suttons Rd *SBN/FI* SS3 ... 403 J3
Swale CI *SOCK/AV* RM15 ... 405 K4
Swale Rd *DART* DA1 ... 414 B7
  SBF/HAD SS7 ... 380 C6
Swallowcliffe *SBN/FI* SS3 ... 402 E2
Swallow CI *CDH/CHF* RM16 ... 190 B6
  COLS CO2 ... 190 B6
  FX IP11 ... 85 K6
  RAYL SS6 ... 361 J8
Swallowdale *COLS* CO2 ... 163 K8
  COS CO15 ... 224 A5
Swallow Dl *VGE* SS16 ... 377 J7
Swallow Dr *SBF/HAD* SS7 ... 397 L1
Swallow Fld *RCOLW* CO6 ... 130 C5
Swallow Rd *CHTY* IP2 ... 36 D8
  WICKE SS11 ... 359 K1
Swallows *HLWE* CM17 ... 227 K7
Swallow's Rw *RCOLE* CO7 ... 195 J2
The Swallows *BCAYE* CM11 ... 357 K3
Swallow Wk *HSTD* CO9 ... 129 G2
Swanage Rd *SOSN* SS2 ... 21 J4
Swan And Pike Rd *PEND* EN3 .. 325 J2
Swan Av *UPMR* RM14 ... 373 C8
Swanbourne Dr *HCH* RM12 ... 389 L3
Swan Cha *HSTD* CO9 ... 97 M3
Swan CI *COLN* CO4 ... 163 M5
  LAIN SS15 ... 18 A5
  RCHLM CM3 ... 238 A7
Swan Ct *BSF* CM23 ... 174 A5
  MAL CM9 ... 269 J7
  MGTR CO11 ... 109 H2
Swan DI *CO05* ... 224 A5
Swanfield *SUD* CO10 ... 34 D4
Swanfield Rd *BAR* EN8 ... 300 F5
Swan Gv *RCOLW* CO6 ... 131 K6
Swan HI *RIPW* IP8 ... 57 H1
Swan La *BRWN* CM15 ... 331 M1
  HVHL CB9 ... 28 B3
  RCHLM CM3 ... 238 A7

  LOU IG10 ... 348 D1
  SUD CO10 ... 34 D4
  WICKE SS11 ... 359 L2
Swan Md *VGE* SS16 ... 19 L9
Swan Pas *COL* CO1 ... 10 D7
Swan Rd *RCOS* CO16 ... 168 E6
Swanscomb Rd *RCOLW* CO6 .. 131 G6
Swansea Av *CHTY* IP2 ... 58 C2
Swansea Rd *PEND* EN3 ... 324 D6
Swans Green CI
  SBF/HAD SS7 ... 380 B5
Swanshope *LOU* IG10 ... 327 J4
Swan Side *BRTR* CM7 ... 155 G8
Swans Rd *BAR* EN8 ... 300 E6
Swanstead *VGE* SS16 ... 377 M7
Swanstead *VGE* SS16 ... 377 M7
Swan St *HSTD* CO9 ... 97 M2
  K/T/MI CO5 ... 186 E5
  RCOLW CO6 ... 131 K8
Swan Wy *PEND* EN3 ... 324 E4
Swan Yd *RCOLW* CO6 ... 186 B1
Swatchway CI *IPSE* IP3 ... 59 J3
Swaynes *RCOLE* CO7 ... 106 D1
Sweden CI *HAR* CO12 ... 6 B7
Sweet Briar *BSF* CM23 ... 173 J5
Sweet Briar Av *SBF/HAD* SS7 ... 397 L1
Sweet Briar Dr *LAIN* SS15 ... 376 E2
Sweet Briar Rd *COLW* CO3 ... 161 K4
Sweet Md *SAFWN* CB10 ... 43 M8
Sweyne Av *HOC/HUL* SS5 ... 363 H7
  WOS/PRIT SS0 ... 20 E4
Sweyne CI *RAYL* SS6 ... 361 J7
Swift Av *COS* CO15 ... 250 A5
Swift CI *BRTR* CM7 ... 183 H3
  UPMR RM14 ... 372 F8
Swiftsure Rd *CDH/CHF* RM16 .. 416 D1
Swinborne Ct *PIT* SS13 ... 378 C1
Swinborne Rd *PIT* SS13 ... 378 D2
Swinburne Gdns *TIL* RM18 ... 418 C6
Swindon Gdns *HARH* RM3 ... 353 C6
Swindon La *HARH* RM3 ... 353 C6
Swinton CI *CHTY* IP2 ... 57 L2
Swiss Av *CHLM/WR* CM1 ... 264 A7
Sworders Yd *BSF* CM23 ... 174 A4
Sycamore Av *UPMR* RM14 ... 390 B2
Sycamore CI *CVI* SS8 ... 398 A8
  CHESW EN7 ... 276 A7
  RAYL SS6 ... 361 J5
  RBSF CM22 ... 176 D4
  RIPW IP8 ... 57 K2
  TIL RM18 ... 418 A5
  WIT CM8 ... 212 B6
Sycamore Dr *BRW* CM14 ... 354 C2
Sycamore Fld
  HLWW/ROY CM19 ... 255 M7
Sycamore Gv *BRTR* CM7 ... 182 E1
  SOSN SS2 ... 21 J2
Sycamore PI *RCOLE* CO7 ... 194 F3
Sycamore Rd *COLN* CO4 ... 11 M5
  MAL CM9 ... 269 J5
  SUD CO10 ... 5 J7
The Sycamores *BSF* CM23 ... 174 C5
Sycamore Wy *CHLM/GWD* CM2 .. 12 A6
  COS CO15 ... 198 E5
  FOS CO13 ... 198 E5
  MGTR CO11 ... 108 E3
  RCFD SS4 ... 364 E2
  SOCK/AV RM15 ... 406 E2
Sydenham CI *ROM* RM1 ... 371 G4
Sydervelt Rd *CVI* SS8 ... 398 B7
Sydner CI *CHLM/GWD* CM2 ... 289 H6
Sydney Rd *LOS* SS9 ... 399 J1
  SBF/HAD SS7 ... 379 K7
  TIL RM18 ... 418 B6
Sydney St *COLS* CO2 ... 191 J2
  RCOLE CO7 ... 221 G6
Sykes Md *RAYL* SS6 ... 380 E2
Sylvan Av *CHDH* RM6 ... 370 A6
  EMPK RM11 ... 372 A6
Sylvan CI *CDH/CHF* RM16 ... 416 F1
  CHLM/GWD CM2 ... 288 C5
  CVI SS8 ... 413 J3
  LAIN SS15 ... 376 C5
Sylvan Tryst *BCAYW* CM12 ... 335 J7
Sylvan Wy *CHIG* IG7 ... 350 C4
  LAIN SS15 ... 376 A4
  LOS SS9 ... 381 H7
Sylvesters *HLWW/ROY* CM19 ... 14 C9
Sylvia Av *RBRW/HUT* CM13 ... 355 K3
Symmons CI *BRTR* CM7 ... 182 A7
Symonds Ct *BAR* EN8 ... 276 E8
Symons Av *LOS* SS9 ... 381 M4
Syracuse Av *RAIN* RM13 ... 404 E1

T

Tabora Av *CVI* SS8 ... 398 A6
Tabor Av *BRTR* CM7 ... 154 F8
Tabor CI *RCOLE* CO7 ... 220 F3
Tabor Rd *COLN* CO4 ... 11 K8
Tabors Av *CHLM/GWD* CM2 ... 289 C4
Tabrum's La *RCHLM* CM3 ... 339 J4
The Tabrums *RCHLM* CM3 ... 339 K2
Tabrums Wy *UPMR* RM14 ... 372 F7
Tacket St *IPNE* IP4 ... 2 F5
Tacon Rd *FX* IP11 ... 9 H7
Tadlows CI *UPMR* RM14 ... 390 C4
Tadworth Pde *HCH* RM12 ... 389 J3
Taffrail Gdns *RCHLM* CM3 ... 339 M6
Tailors Ct *SOSN* SS2 ... 383 G6
Tailors Wy *SOSN* SS2 ... 383 G6
Taits *SLH/COR* SS17 ... 410 A1
Takeley CI *CRW* RM5 ... 370 C1
  WAB EN9 ... 301 L5
Takely End *VGE* SS16 ... 18 F9
Takely Ride *VGE* SS16 ... 18 F8
Talbot Av *COS* CO15 ... 250 A5
  RAYL SS6 ... 361 J8
Talbot Rd *DAGW* RM9 ... 388 A6
  RCOS CO16 ... 196 D7
  SUD CO10 ... 5 J7
Talbot St *HAR* CO12 ... 7 J6
Talbrook *BRW* CM14 ... 354 A4
Talcott Rd *COLS* CO2 ... 191 H1
Talisman CI *K/T/MI* CO5 ... 214 E5
Tallboys CI *KESG* IP5 ... 39 K3

Tallis Cl *SLH/COR* SS17 .... **394** D8
Tallis Rd *LAIN* SS15 .... **376** E3
Tallon Rd *RBRW/HUT* CM13.......... **333** M7
Tallow Ga *RCHLM* CM3 .... **389** M4
Tall Trees *COLN* CO4 .... **134** F8
Tall Trees Rd *EMPK* RM11 .... **371** L6
Tally Ho *COLN* CO4 .... **135** J7 ⓑ
Tallyho Cnr *RCOLE* CO7 .... **106** E2 ⓑ
Tally-ho Dr *RBRW/HUT* CM13 .... **356** C2
Talus Cl *PUR* RM19 .... **415** L1
Talza Wy *SOSN* SS2 .... **383** C6
Tamage Rd *SUD* CO10 .... **35** K5
Tamar Cl *UPMR* RM14 .... **372** F6
Tamar Dr *SOCK/AV* RM15 .... **405** K4
Tamarisk *SBF/HAD* SS7 .... **379** K7
Tamarisk Rd *SOCK/AV* RM15 .... **406** D1 ⓑ
SOCK/AV RM15 .... **406** D2 ⓑ
SOCK/AV RM15 .... **406** D2 ⓑ
Tamarisk Wy *COLN* CO4 .... **163** M4 ⓑ
COS CO15 .... **250** A5
Tamar Ri *CHLM/WR* CM1 .... **264** D5
Tambour Cl *RCOLW* CO6 .... **159** K3 ⓑ
Tamfield Cl *CHESW* EN7 .... **276** B7 ⓑ
Tanfield Dr *BCAYW* CM12 .... **357** H1
Tangent Link *HARH* RM3 .... **371** L1
Tangent Rd *HARH* RM3 .... **371** L1 ⓑ
Tangham Wk *BSDN* SS14 .... **19** H3
Tangmere Cl *WICKE* SS11 .... **360** C5 ⓑ
Tangmere Crs *HCH* RM12 .... **389** J5
Tan House La *BRW* CM14 .... **331** H5
Tankerville Dr *LOS* SS9 .... **381** L8
Tanners Cl *RCOS* CO16 .... **223** J8 ⓑ
Tanners Meadow *BRTR* CM7 .... **183** L1 ⓑ
Tanners Wy *RCHLM* CM3 .... **339** K3 ⓑ
SAFWN CB10.......... **65** M2
Tannery Ct *DAGE* RM10 .... **388** C2 ⓑ
Tanswell Av *CVI* SS8 .... **398** E8 ⓑ
Tanswell Cl *PIT* SS13 .... **378** C5
Tansy Cl *HARH* RM3 .... **352** F7
The Tanyard *GTDUN* CM6 .... **122** B1 ⓑ
Tany's Dell *HLW* CM20 .... **227** H8
Tapley Rd *CHLM/WR* CM1 .... **264** A5
Tapsworth Cl *COS* CO15.......... **12** B2
Tapwoods *COLW* CO3.......... **162** B4
Tara Cl *COLN* CO4 .... **11** M4
Taranto Rd *CVI* SS8 .... **398** E8
Tarn Hows Cl *FX* IP11 .... **85** L7 ⓑ
Tarnwood Rd *HARH* RM3 .... **353** H6
Tarpan Wy *BROX* EN10 .... **277** C6
Tarragona Ms *COLS* CO2 .... **163** J7 ⓑ
Tarragon Cl *K/T/MI* CO5 .... **214** D6
Tasker Rd *CDH/CHF* RM16 .... **408** C8
Tasman Cl *SLH/COR* SS17 .... **395** G7 ⓑ
Tasmania Rd *IPNE* IP4 .... **38** E5
Tasman Rd *HVHL* CB9 .... **28** D4
Tatsfield Av *WAB* EN9 .... **277** L3
Tattenham Rd *LAIN* SS15 .... **376** C4
Tattersall Gdns *LOS* SS9 .... **399** H2
Tattersalls Cha *BOC* CM0 .... **320** F7
Taunton Cl *BARK/HLT* IG6 .... **350** A7 ⓑ
Taunton Dr *WOS/PRIT* SS0 .... **382** C7
Taunton Rd *CHLM/WR* CM1 .... **264** F6
FX IP11 .... **85** G8
HARH RM3 .... **352** D5
Taveners Green Cl
WICKW SS12 .... **359** M5 ⓑ
Taverners Wk *WIT* CM8 .... **212** A7 ⓑ
Taverners *HOD* EN11.......... **253** H5
Tavern St *IP* IP1.......... **2** F4
Tavistock Cl *HARH* RM3 .... **371** L1
Tavistock Dr *BCAYW* CM12 .... **356** E6 ⓑ
Tavistock Rd *CHLM/WR* CM1 .... **264** E6 ⓑ
LAIN SS15 .... **376** D3 ⓑ
LAIN SS15 .... **376** D4 ⓑ
Tawell Ms *K/T/MI* CO5 .... **214** E6 ⓑ
Tawney Cl *RIPS/CAP* IP9 .... **78** B2
Tawney Common *EPP* CM16 .... **305** H4
Tawney La *ABR/ST* RM4.......... **329** K3
EPP CM16 .... **305** K4
Tawneys Ride *BURES* CO8.......... **102** B2
Tawny Rd *HLWS* CM18 .... **256** A5
Tawny Av *UPMR* RM14 .... **390** C4
Taylifers *HLWW/ROY* CM19 .... **255** H8
Taylor Av *CHLM/WR* CM1 .... **263** M6
Taylor Cl *CRW* RM5 .... **351** K4
Taylor Ct *COL* CO1 .... **10** C7
Taylor Dr *MGTR* CO11 .... **108** D7
Taylors Av *HOD* EN11 .... **253** H6
Taylors End Rd *STSD* SS24 .... **175** M2
Taylor's Rd *K/T/MI* CO5 .... **192** A3
Tay Wy *ROM* RM1 .... **371** C1
Teagles *LAIN* SS15 .... **18** B5
Teal Av *RCHLM* CM3 .... **319** H3
Teal Cl *BRTR* CM7 .... **182** C6
CHTY IP2 .... **36** E8
RCOLE CO7 .... **164** B3
Teal Wy *K/T/MI* CO5 .... **213** L1
Tedder Cl *COLS* CO2 .... **163** H7 ⓑ
Tees Cl *UPMR* RM14 .... **372** E2
Tees Dr *HARH* RM3 .... **352** E4
Tees Rd *CHLM/WR* CM1 .... **264** D5
Teign Dr *WIT* CM8 .... **238** E1
Teigngrace *SBN/FI* SS3 .... **402** E3
Teignmouth Dr *RAYL* SS6 .... **361** L6
Telford Dr *BRTR* CM7 .... **184** C3 ⓑ
COS CO15 .... **224** C3
Telford Wy *COLN* CO4 .... **135** L5
Tempest Wy *RAIN* RM13 .... **389** H5 ⓑ
Templar Rd *BRTR* CM7 .... **183** L1
Templars Cl *WIT* CM8 .... **212** A7 ⓑ
Temple Av *BCTR* RM8 .... **370** B8
Temple Bank *HLW* CM20 .... **212** A8 ⓑ
Temple Cl *CHESW* EN7 .... **300** B3
FOS CO13 .... **199** H5
LAIN SS15 .... **376** D4 ⓑ
SBF/HAD SS7 .... **381** G8
Temple Ct *COLN* CO4 .... **11** M2
Temple Dr *BRTR* CM7 .... **184** D8
Temple Md *HLWW/ROY* CM19.......... **254** C3
Templemead *WIT* CM8 .... **212** A8 ⓑ
Temple Pattle *MGTR* CO11 .... **108** D4
Templer Av *CDH/CHF* RM16 .... **418** B1
Temple Rd *COLS* CO2 .... **190** B1 ⓑ

Temple Wy *MAL* CM9 .... **269** G6
Templewood Ct *SBF/HAD* SS7 .... **380** E8
Templewood Rd *COLN* CO4.......... **163** M2
PIT SS13 .... **378** C5
SBF/HAD SS7 .... **380** E8
Temptin Av *CVI* SS8 .... **398** F8
Ten Acre Ap *MAL* CM9 .... **269** G6
Tenby Rd *CHTY* IP2 .... **58** C2 ⓑ
PEND EN3 .... **324** D5
Tendring Av *RAYL* SS6 .... **361** H8
Tendring Rd *HLWS* CM18 .... **15** K3
RCOLE CO7 .... **167** H3
RCOS CO16 .... **168** A1
Tennand Cl *CHESW* EN7 .... **276** A6
Tenniswood Rd *EN* EN1 .... **324** A3
Tennyson Av *GRAYS* RM17 .... **407** J8
SOSN SS2 .... **21** J1
WAB EN9 .... **301** M6
Tennyson Cl *BRTR* CM7 .... **183** G3 ⓑ
LOS SS9 .... **399** H1
PEND EN3 .... **324** E7
Tennyson Dr *PIT* SS13 .... **378** C7
Tennyson Rd *CHLM/WR* CM1 .... **264** A6
HARH RM3 .... **352** D8
IPNE IP4 .... **3** M5
MAL CM9 .... **293** H2
RBRW/HUT CM13.......... **355** K1
Tennyson Wk *TIL* RM18 .... **418** C6
Tennyson Wy *HCH* RM12 .... **371** G8
Tenpenny Hl *RCOLE* CO7 .... **193** M5
Tensing Gdns *BCAYW* CM12 .... **357** C2
Tenterden Rd *BCTR* RM8 .... **388** A1
Tenterfield *GTDUN* CM6 .... **178** F2
Tenter Fld *RCOLE* CO7 .... **106** E2
Tenterfield Rd *MAL* CM9 .... **293** H1
Tenterfields *PIT* SS13 .... **378** D3
SAFWN CB11 .... **89** G2
Tenth Rd *KIR/NAC* IP10 .... **61** J5
Tentree Rd *SUD* CO10 .... **35** M6
Teramo Rd *CVI* SS8 .... **398** E8 ⓑ
Tercel Pth *CHIG* IG7 .... **350** C5
Terence Webster Rd
WICKW SS12 .... **359** L5
Teresa Gdns *BAR* EN8 .... **300** D6
Terling *VGE* SS16 .... **19** H8
Terling Cl *COLS* CO2 .... **191** H2
Terling Hall Rd *RCHLM* CM3 .... **237** G2
Terling Rd *BCTR* RM8 .... **388** B1
RCHLM CM3 .... **238** A5
WIT CM8 .... **238** B1
The Terlings *BRW* CM14.......... **354** B4
Terminal Cl *SBN/FI* SS3 .... **403** G4
Terminus Dr *VGE* SS16 .... **19** H7
Terminus St *HLW* CM20 .... **15** L3 ⓑ
Termitts Cha *RCHLM* CM3 .... **238** A4
WIT CM8 .... **238** D4
Terms Av *CVI* SS8 .... **398** B6 ⓑ
Tern Cl *HVHL* CB9 .... **28** D4
K/T/MI CO5 .... **186** E8
RCHLM CM3 .... **319** H3
Terndale *COS* CO15 .... **224** A5
Tern Gdns *UPMR* RM14 .... **372** F8 ⓑ
Terni Rd *CVI* SS8 .... **398** E8
Tern Rd *CHTY* IP2 .... **57** M1
Tern Wy *BRW* CM14 .... **353** M5
Terrace Hall Cha *RCOLW* CO6 .... **134** D5
The Terrace *SBN/FI* SS3 .... **403** G5
Teviot Av *SOCK/AV* RM15.......... **405** K4
Tew Cl *K/T/MI* CO5 .... **214** E5 ⓑ
Tewkesbury Rd *COS* CO15 .... **12** F3
Tewkes Rd *CVI* SS8 .... **398** E6
Tey Rd *RCOLW* CO6 .... **130** E5
RCOLW CO6.......... **158** C8
RCOLW CO6.......... **160** B3
Tey Road Cl *RCOLW* CO6 .... **130** D5
Thackeray Av *TIL* RM18 .... **418** C6
Thackeray Cl *BRTR* CM7 .... **183** H3
Thackeray Rw *WICKW* SS12 .... **359** L6 ⓑ
Thai Massing Cl
RBRW/HUT CM13.......... **355** J3
Thames Av *CHLM/WR* CM1 .... **263** K6
Thames Cl *BRTR* CM7 .... **183** L2
LOS SS9 .... **399** H2
RAIN RM13 .... **404** C4 ⓑ
RAYL SS6 .... **380** D2
SLH/COR SS17 .... **395** H4
Thames Crs *SLH/COR* SS17 .... **395** J6
Thames Dr *CDH/CHF* RM16 .... **418** B2
LOS SS9 .... **399** H2
Thames Haven Rd
SLH/COR SS17 .... **395** H8
Thameside Crs *CVI* SS8 .... **398** A8
Thames Rd *CVI* SS8 .... **413** G1
DART DA1 .... **414** B7
GRAYS RM17 .... **417** J4
Thames Vw *GRAYS* RM17 .... **418** B2
VGE SS16 .... **394** D2
Thames Wy *BOC* CM0 .... **344** B5
Thamley *PUR* RM19 .... **415** H1
Thanet Rd *IPNE* IP4 .... **38** C5
Thatchers Cl *LOU* IG10 .... **327** K4
Thatchers Cft *RCHLM* CM3 .... **317** M5
Thatchers Dr *RCOLE* CO7 .... **165** G5
The Thatchers *BSF* CM23 .... **173** K6
Thaxted Gn *RBRW/HUT* CM13 .... **333** K7
Thaxted Rd *BKHH* IG9 .... **348** F1
SAFWN CB11 .... **66** A4
Thaxted Wk *COLS* CO2 .... **191** M3
Thaxted Wy *WAB* EN9 .... **301** L5
Thear Cl *WOS/PRIT* SS0 .... **382** D7
Theberton Rd *IPSE* IP5 .... **59** J2
Theleway Cl *HOD* EN11 .... **253** J2 ⓑ
Thelma Av *CVI* SS8 .... **398** B7
Theobalds Av *GRAYS* RM17 .... **417** K2
Theobald's Gv *BAR* EN8 .... **300** E4 ⓑ
Theobald's La *BAR* EN8 .... **300** C4
Theobalds Rd *LOS* SS9 .... **399** K2
Thetford Pl *LAIN* SS15 .... **376** C2
Thetford Rd *IP* IP1 .... **37** G4 ⓑ
Theydon Ct *WAB* EN9 .... **302** C5
Theydon Crs *BSDN* SS14 .... **378** A2
Theydon Gdns *RAIN* RM13 .... **389** G6 ⓑ
Theydon Ga *EPP* CM16 .... **303** M8 ⓑ
Theydon Gv *EPP* CM16 .... **304** B2
WFD IG8 .... **348** D7
Theydon Park Rd *EPP* CM16 .... **327** M3
Theydon Pl *EPP* CM16 .... **304** A3

Theydon Rd *EPP* CM16 .... **303** L6
Thielen Rd *CVI* SS8 .... **398** B6
Thieves Cnr *CHLM/WR* CM1 .... **263** G7
Third Av *CHLM/WR* CM1 .... **264** C6
COS CO15 .... **13** M4
CVI SS8 .... **397** M7
DAGE RM10.......... **388** C7
EN EN1 .... **324** A7
FOS CO13 .... **198** F7
HAR CO12 .... **7** C9
HLWS CM18.......... **15** L5
HLWW/ROY CM19 .... **15** H7
HSTD CO9 .... **129** J2
RCOS CO16 .... **249** J4
SLH/COR SS17 .... **394** F7
WICKE SS11 .... **360** B5
WOTN CO14 .... **171** M8
WTHK RM20 .... **429** L3
Thirlmere Cl *BRTR* CM7 .... **182** E4 ⓑ
Thirlmere Rd *SBF/HAD* SS7 .... **379** M4
Thirslet Dr *MAL* CM9 .... **269** K7
Thirtieth St *STSD* SS24 .... **148** A8
Thirtle Cl *RCOS* CO16 .... **223** L5
Thisselt Rd *CVI* SS8 .... **398** B6
Thistle Cl *CHTY* IP2 .... **37** G7
Thistledene Av *CRW* RM5 .... **351** J4
Thistledown *BRTR* CM7 .... **154** B4
BSDN SS14 .... **19** K5
COLN CO4 .... **135** J8
Thistle Md *LOU* IG10 .... **327** H5 ⓑ
Thistley Cl *LOS* SS9 .... **382** A7
MAL CM9 .... **270** F5
Thistley Crs *SAFWS* CB11 .... **118** F2 ⓑ
Thistley Green Rd *BRTR* CM7 .... **155** J4
Thoby La *BRWN* CM15 .... **333** H1
Thomas Av *FX* IP11 .... **84** D5
Thomas Bata Av *TIL* RM18.......... **419** J1
Thomas Bell Rd *RCOLW* CO6 .... **130** B5
Thomas Cl *BRWN* CM15 .... **354** F3
CHLM/GWD CM2 .... **289** G1 ⓑ
Thomas Dr *CVI* SS8 .... **397** M6
Thomasin Rd *PIT* SS13 .... **378** D2
Thomas Rd *COS* CO15 .... **12** D4
PIT SS13 .... **378** F4
Thomas Rochford Wy *BAR* EN8.. **277** G7
Thomas St *RCOLE* CO7 .... **221** G5 ⓑ
Thomas Wakley Cl *COLN* CO4 ... **135** G6
Thomas Wk *SAFWS* CB11 .... **64** A2
Thompson Av *COLW* CO3 .... **162** A5
CVI SS8 .... **399** G8
Thompson Rd *DAGW* RM9 .... **388** A2
IP IP1 .... **37** G3
Thorington Av *SBF/HAD* SS7 .... **380** E5
Thorington Rd *RAYL* SS6 .... **381** M2 ⓑ
Thorington Wy *RCHLM* CM3 .... **339** K5
Thorley Hl *BSF* CM23 .... **174** A6
Thorley La *BSF* CM23 .... **173** J6
Thorley Park Rd *BSF* CM23 .... **174** A7
Thorley Rd *CDH/CHF* RM16 .... **407** H6
Thornbera Cl *BSF* CM23 .... **174** A7
Thornbera Gdns *BSF* CM23 .... **173** M7
Thornberry Av *RCOS* CO16 .... **196** A3
Thornborough Av *RCHLM* CM3 .. **339** M4
Thornbury Cl *HOD* EN11 .... **253** J7
Thornbury Rd *COS* CO15 .... **13** G3
Thornbush *LAIN* SS15 .... **18** A5
Thorncroft *EMPK* RM11 .... **371** H4
Thorndale *SBF/HAD* SS7 .... **380** C4 ⓑ
Thorndales *BRW* CM14 .... **354** E5
Thorndon Ap *RBRW/HUT* CM13 .. **355** L8
Thorndon Av *RBRW/HUT* CM13 .. **374** D5
Thorndon Ct *RCOS* CO16 .... **223** H7 ⓑ
Thorndon Park Cl *LOS* SS9 .... **381** K6
Thorndon Park Crs *LOS* SS9 .... **381** J6
Thorndon Park Dr *LOS* SS9 .... **381** J6
Thorne *K/T/MI* CO5 .... **213** J1
Thorney Bay Rd *CVI* SS8 .... **413** G1
Thorney Rd *RIPS/CAP* IP9 .... **78** B1
Thornfield Rd *BSF* CM23 .... **173** M3
Thornford Gdns *SOSN* SS2 .... **383** G6
Thorn Gv *BSF* CM23 .... **174** C5
Thornhayes Cl *CHTY* IP2 .... **37** H8 ⓑ
Thornhill *EPP* CM16 .... **281** K6
LOS SS9 .... **381** M7
RCHLM CM3 .... **316** C2
Thornhill Cl *FOS* CO13 .... **199** G4 ⓑ
Thorn La *RAIN* RM13.......... **389** L8
Thornley Dr *IPNE* IP4 .... **38** D3
Thornley Rd *FX* IP11 .... **115** K1
Thornridge *BRW* CM14 .... **354** C2 ⓑ
Thorns Wk *WOTN* CO14 .... **199** H4
Thornton Dr *COLN* CO4 .... **10** D2
Thornton Pl *ING* CM4 .... **335** M1
Thornton Rd *RBSF* CM22 .... **177** G3
Thorntons Farm Av
ROMW/RG RM7 .... **388** D1
Thornton Wy *LAIN* SS15 .... **376** B6
Thorn Wy *FX* IP11 .... **9** H2
Thornwood *COLN* CO4 .... **135** C7
Thornwood Rd *EPP* CM16 .... **280** C8
Thorogood Wy *RAIN* RM13 .... **388** F7
Thorolds *VGE* SS16 .... **377** M8
Thoroughgood Rd *COS* CO15.......... **13** J7
Thorpe Bay Gdns *SOS* SS1 .... **402** B5
Thorpe Esp *HOC/HUL* SS5 .... **363** C7
Thorpe Hall Av *SOS* SS1 .... **402** B3 ⓑ
Thorpe Hall Cl *SOS* SS1.......... **402** B3
Thorpe La *FX* IP11 .... **84** A7
Thorpe Park La *RCOS* CO16.......... **197** H4
Thorpe Rd *COS* CO15 .... **224** A4
FOS CO13 .... **198** A4
HOC/HUL SS5 .... **363** C7
RCOS CO16 .... **168** B6
RCOS CO16 .... **224** A1
Thorp Leas *CVI* SS8 .... **413** G4
Thorrington Rd *RCOLE* CO7 .... **194** D3
RCOS CO16 .... **196** D7
Thors Oak *SLH/COR* SS17 .... **409** M1
Thracian Cl *COLS* CO2 .... **190** B1 ⓑ

Threadneedle St *RCOLE* CO7 .... **107** G4
Three Acres *RCOS* CO16 .... **222** B7
Three Crowns Rd *COLN* CO4 .... **10** A2
Three Forests Wy *ABR/ST* RM4 .. **329** L1
CHONG CM5 .... **259** L7
Three forests Wy *CHONG* CM5 ... **259** L7
Three Forests Wy *GTDUN* CM6... **72** E3
HLWW/ROY CM19 .... **254** A3
LOU IG10 .... **326** E3
SBW CM21 .... **227** M2
WAB EN9 .... **278** E1
WAB EN9 .... **302** D8
Three Forest Wy *RBSF* CM22 .... **175** J6
Three Gates Cl *HSTD* CO9 .... **128** E3
Three Horseshoes Rd
HLWW/ROY CM19 .... **15** G9
Thremhall Av *RBSF* CM22 .... **176** A2
Threshelford *VGE* SS16 .... **18** D9
Thresher Cl *BSF* CM23 .... **173** K6
Threshers End *COLW* CO3 .... **161** L6 ⓑ
Thrifts Md *EPP* CM16 .... **327** M1
Thrift Wd *RCHLM* CM3 .... **314** F2
Through Jollys *KESC* IP5 .... **39** L3
Throwley Cl *PIT* SS13 .... **378** D6
Thrushdale *COS* CO15 .... **224** A5
Thundersley Church Rd
SBF/HAD SS7 .... **379** L6
Thundersley Gv *SBF/HAD* SS7 ... **380** A6
Thundersley Park Rd
SBF/HAD SS7 .... **379** L8
Thurgood Rd *HOD* EN11 .... **253** H3 ⓑ
Thurlby Cl *WFD* IG8 .... **349** G6 ⓑ
Thurloe Gdns *ROM* RM1 .... **370** F6
Thurloe Wk *GRAYS* RM17 .... **407** H8
Thurlow Dr *SOS* SS1 .... **402** A3
Thurlow Gdns *CHIG* IG7 .... **349** L7
Thurlston Cl *COLN* CO4 .... **11** M3
Thurlstone *SBF/HAD* SS7 .... **380** D6
Thurmans La *FX* IP11 .... **84** C5
Thurrock Park Wy *GRAYS* RM17.. **417** L4
Thurso Cl *HARH* RM3 .... **353** J7
Thurstable Cl *MAL* CM9 .... **272** F1
Thurstable Rd *MAL* CM9 .... **272** F1
Thurstable Wy *MAL* CM9 .... **272** F1
Thurstans *HLWW/ROY* CM19.......... **255** J8
Thurston Av *SOSN* SS2 .... **401** M2
Thurston Ct *FX* IP11 .... **8** D2
Thyme Rd *K/T/MI* CO5 .... **214** E6 ⓑ
Thynne Rd *BCAYE* CM11 .... **357** K1
Tiberius Cl *HVHL* CB9 .... **28** E4
Tiberius Gdns *WIT* CM8 .... **238** F3 ⓑ
Tickenhall Dr *HLWE* CM17 .... **256** C5
Tickfield Av *SOSN* SS2 .... **20** F2
Tideswell Cl *BRTR* CM7 .... **155** L7 ⓑ
Tideway *MAL* CM9 .... **293** J3 ⓑ
Tidings Hl *HSTD* CO9 .... **128** F3
Tidworth Av *WICKE* SS11 .... **359** M1
Tidy's La *EPP* CM16 .... **304** B1
Tiffin Dr *K/T/MI* CO5 .... **214** F6
Tighfield Wk *RCHLM* CM3 .... **339** K6
Tilburg Rd *CVI* SS8 .... **398** B7
Tilbury Gdns *TIL* RM18 .... **418** B8
Tilbury Md *HLWS* CM18 .... **256** B5
Tilbury Rd *HSTD* CO9 .... **50** D4
RBRW/HUT CM13.......... **374** F4
Tile Barn La *MGTR* CO11 .... **137** K1
Tilegate Rd *CHONG* CM5 .... **257** K7
HLWS CM18.......... **256** A5
Tile House Rd *RCOLW* CO6.......... **134** C3
Tilkey Rd *RCOLW* CO6 .... **158** A7
Tillingham Ct *WAB* EN9 .... **302** B5 ⓑ
Tillingham Gn *LAIN* SS15 .... **376** B5
Tillingham Rd *BOC* CM0 .... **321** G6
Tillingham Wy *RAYL* SS6 .... **361** H8
Tillwicks Rd *HLWS* CM18 .... **256** A4
Tilney Rd *DAGW* RM9 .... **388** A5
Tilney Turn *VGE* SS16 .... **377** M7
Timber Hl *COL* CO1 .... **163** K5 ⓑ
Timberlog Cl *BSDN* SS14 .... **377** M5
Timberlog La *BSDN* SS14 .... **377** M6
Timbermans Vw *VGE* SS16 .... **378** A8
Timbers Cl *BRTR* CM7 .... **182** C4 ⓑ
Timsons La *CHLM/GWD* CM2 .... **264** F7
Tinabrook Cl *CHTY* IP2 .... **57** M2
Tindall Cl *HARH* RM3 .... **372** A2
Tindal St *CHLM/WR* CM1 .... **17** H3
Tindon End Rd *SAFWN* CB10.......... **92** E1
Tine Rd *CHIG* IG7 .... **349** M6
Tinker Av *BRTR* CM7 .... **95** K5
Tinker's La *RCFD* SS4 .... **383** G2
Tinker St *HAR* CO12 .... **142** A2
Tinnocks La *BOC* CM0 .... **296** C2
Tintagel Wy *MAL* CM9 .... **292** F3
Tintern Av *WOS/PRIT* SS0 .... **400** D1
Tintern Cl *CHTY* IP2 .... **58** B1
Tiplers Br *BCAYE* CM11 .... **336** C6
Tippersfield *SBF/HAD* SS7 .... **379** M7 ⓑ
Tippett Cl *COLN* CO4 .... **163** M5
Tipps Cross La *BRWN* CM15 .... **308** C6
Tiptree Cl *EMPK* RM11 .... **372** B8
LOS SS9 .... **382** A7
Tiptree Ct *RBRW/HUT* CM13 .... **333** L7
Tiptree Gv *WICKW* SS12 .... **359** L4 ⓑ
Tiptree Hall La *K/T/MI* CO5 .... **214** C8
Tintern Cl *WIT* CM8 .... **240** C2
Tiree Cha *WICKW* SS12 .... **360** A6
Titania Cl *COLN* CO4 .... **164** A4
Titan Rd *GRAYS* RM17 .... **417** H2
Titchfield Rd *PEND* EN3 .... **324** F1
Tithe Cl *WIT* CM8 .... **211** M8
Tithelands *HLWW/ROY* CM19 .... **255** G6
The Tithe *WICKW* SS12 .... **359** J5
Titus Wy *COLN* CO4 .... **135** J5
Tiverton Gv *HARH* RM3 .... **353** H6
Tobruk Rd *CHLM/WR* CM1 .... **264** B8
COLS CO2 .... **162** E8
Toddbrook *HLWW/ROY* CM19 .... **15** H6
Toft Av *GRAYS* RM17 .... **417** L1
Tofts Cha *RCHLM* CM3 .... **266** F6
Tofts Wk *BRTR* CM7 .... **155** C8 ⓑ
Toga Cl *COLS* CO2 .... **190** B1
Tog La *RCOLW* CO6 .... **104** B8
Tokely Rd *RCOLE* CO7 .... **166** B8
Tokio Rd *IPNE* IP4 .... **3** M4
Toledo Cl *SOS* SS1 .... **21** J6
Toledo Rd *SOS* SS1 .... **21** J6

Toll *GRH* DA9 .... **415** K8
Toller Rd *IPSE* IP3 .... **3** J9
Tollesbury Cl *WICKW* SS12 .... **359** M5 ⓑ
Tollesbury Rd *MAL* CM9.......... **242** F7
Tolleshunt D'arcy Rd *MAL* CM9 .. **242** A8
Tollgate *SBF/HAD* SS7 .... **380** D5
Tollgate Dr *COLW* CO3 .... **161** J3
Tollgate East *COLW* CO3 .... **161** K5
Tollgate Rd *BAR* EN8 .... **300** E7
COLW CO3.......... **161** K5
Toll Gate Rd *RIPS/CAP* IP9 .... **78** B2
Tollgate West *COLW* CO3.......... **161** K6
Tolliday Cl *RCOLE* CO7 .... **192** B1 ⓑ
Tolworth Av *WICKE* SS11 .... **359** M1
Tomkins Cl *SLH/COR* SS17 .... **409** K1
Tomkyns La *UPMR* RM14 .... **372** E3
Tomline Rd *FX* IP11 .... **9** L3
IPSE IP3 .... **38** B6
Tomlyns Cl *RBRW/HUT* CM13 .... **333** M8
Tom's La *BRTR* CM7 .... **94** B5
Tomswood Hl *BARK/HLT* IG6 .... **349** J8
Tomswood Rd *CHIG* IG7 .... **349** H7
Tom Tit La *MAL* CM9 .... **291** M3
Tonbridge Rd *HARH* RM3 .... **352** E8
HOC/HUL SS5 .... **363** G4
Tongres Rd *CVI* SS8 .... **398** B7
Tony Webb Cl *COLN* CO4 .... **135** J7
Took Dr *RCHLM* CM3 .... **339** K5
Toot Hill Rd *CHONG* CM5 .... **306** A1
Toplands Av *SOCK/AV* RM15 .... **405** J6
Toppesfield Av *WICKW* SS12 .... **359** K6
Toppesfield Rd *HSTD* CO9 .... **73** G3
Top Rd *MAL* CM9 .... **242** B1
MAL CM9 .... **291** L1
SAFWN CB10 .... **68** B6
Tor Bryan *ING* CM4 .... **334** C1
Torney Cl *VGE* SS16 .... **376** A7
Toronto Rd *TIL* RM18 .... **418** B6
Torquay Cl *RAYL* SS6 .... **361** L6 ⓑ
Torquay Dr *LOS* SS9 .... **399** M2
Torquay Rd *CHLM/WR* CM1 .... **264** E6 ⓑ
Torrance Cl *HCH* RM12 .... **371** K8 ⓑ
Torrington *SBN/FI* SS3 .... **402** E3
Torrington Cl *CHLM/WR* CM1 .... **264** F6
Torrington Dr *LOU* IG10 .... **327** K6
Torrington Gdns *LOU* IG10 .... **327** K6
Torrington Rd *BCTR* RM8 .... **370** A8
Torsi Rd *CVI* SS8 .... **398** E8 ⓑ
Tortoiseshell Wy *BRTR* CM7 .... **182** F2
Tortosa Cl *COLS* CO2 .... **163** J7 ⓑ
Torver Cl *BRTR* CM7 .... **182** D5
Totham Hill Gn *MAL* CM9.......... **240** F5
Totlands Dr *COS* CO15 .... **224** A4
Tot La *BSF* CM23 .... **146** E8
Totman Cl *RAYL* SS6 .... **380** E3
Totman Crs *RAYL* SS6 .... **380** D3
Totnes Wk *CHLM/WR* CM1 .... **264** F5
Totteridge Cl *RCOS* CO16 .... **12** C1
Totteridge Rd *PEND* EN3.......... **324** E1
Toucan Cl *SBN/FI* SS3 .... **402** F2 ⓑ
Toucan Wy *COS* CO15 .... **224** A5
VGE SS16 .... **377** H8
Toulmin Rd *RCHLM* CM3 .... **238** B7
Tovell's Rd *IPNE* IP4 .... **3** M3
Tovey Av *HOD* EN11 .... **253** H3
Tovey Rd *WAB* EN9 .... **277** M3
Tower Av *CHLM/WR* CM1 .... **16** C1
LAIN SS15 .... **376** D4
Tower Cl *CHIG* IG7 .... **349** J7
EPP CM16 .... **281** L5
Tower Ct *BRW* CM14 .... **354** C3
Tower Court Ms *WOS/PRIT* SS0 ... **20** D7
Tower Cut *RCOLE* CO7 .... **221** G5
Towerfield Cl *SBN/FI* SS3 .... **402** F4
Towerfield Rd *SBN/FI* SS3 .... **402** F4
Tower Hl *BRW* CM14.......... **354** D3
Tower Mill Rd *IP* IP1 .... **37** G4
Tower Ramparts *IP* IP1 .... **2** F3
Tower Rd *CHLM/WR* CM1 .... **287** G2
COS CO15 .... **12** F9
EPP CM16 .... **303** M2 ⓑ
FX IP11 .... **9** K3
RCOLE CO7 .... **192** C1
Towers Rd *GRAYS* RM17 .... **417** K2
MAL CM9 .... **269** K6
Tower St *IP* IP1 .... **2** F4
RCOLE CO7 .... **221** G6
Town Cft *CHLM/WR* CM1 .... **264** B6 ⓑ
Town End Fld *WIT* CM8 .... **238** F3
Townfield Cl *CHLM/WR* CM1 .... **16** F2
Townfield St *CHLM/WR* CM1 .... **17** H2
Townfield Wk *SBN/FI* SS3 .... **384** F1
Towngate *BSDN* SS14 .... **18** E6
Town Mead Rd *WAB* EN9 .... **301** K6
Townsend Rd *K/T/MI* CO5 .... **214** D5
Town Sq *BSDN* SS14 .... **18** F6
Town St *GTDUN* CM6 .... **122** B1 ⓑ
Towse Rd *RCOS* CO16 .... **12** A2
Tracyes Rd *HLWS* CM18 .... **256** C5
Traddles Ct *CHLM/WR* CM1 .... **264** A5 ⓑ
Trafalgar Av *BROX* EN10 .... **277** C1
Trafalgar Cl *IPNE* IP4 .... **3** M3
Trafalgar Rd *COLW* CO3 .... **161** M5
COS CO15 .... **12** E9
RAIN RM13 .... **389** G3
SBN/FI SS3 .... **402** E4
SUD CO10 .... **5** H2
Trafalgar Wy *BCAYW* CM12 .... **335** J6
BRTR CM7 .... **155** J7
Trajan Cl *COLN* CO4 .... **135** J5
Tranmere Gv *IP* IP1 .... **37** G1
Trap's Hl *LOU* IG10 .... **327** G6
Travers Wy *PIT* SS13 .... **378** E5
Treebeard Copse
RCHLM CM3 .... **339** J5 ⓑ
Tree Cl *COS* CO15 .... **224** A4
Treecot Dr *LOS* SS9 .... **382** B7
Treelawn Dr *LOS* SS9 .... **382** A7
Treelawn Gdns *LOS* SS9 .... **382** A7
Tree Tops *BRWN* CM15.......... **354** D2
Treetops *FX* IP11 .... **84** F6
Trefgarne Rd *DACE* RM10 .... **388** B1
Trefoil Cl *CHTY* IP2 .... **37** G7
Tregelles Dr *HOD* EN11 .... **253** H3
Trehern Rd *BARK/HLT* IG6 .... **349** L8
Trelawney Rd *BARK/HLT* IG6 .... **349** L8
Trenchard Crs *CHLM/WR* CM1 .. **264** E4
Trenders Av *RAYL* SS6 .... **361** J5

Trenham Av *PIT* SS13 .... 378 E4
Trent *TIL* RM18 .... 419 K1
Trent Av *UPMR* RM14 .... 372 E6
Trentbridge Cl *BARK/HLT* IG6 .. 350 A7
Trent Cl *BOC* CM0 .... 344 B5
  WICKW SS12 .... 359 L5
Trent Rd *BKHH* IG9 .... 348 C2
  CHLM/WR CM1 .... 263 K6
  IPSE IP3 .... 59 G1
  WIT CM8 .... 238 F1 6
Trescoe Gdns *CRW* RM5 .... 351 K6
Tresco Wy *WICKW* SS12 .... 360 A6
Trevelyan Cl *DART* DA1 .... 415 G4
Trevithick Dr *DART* DA1 .... 415 G8
Trevor Cl *BCAYW* CM12 .... 357 G4
Trevor Rd *WFD* IG8 .... 348 B8
Trews Gdns *K/T/MI* CO5 .... 186 D8
Trimble Cl *ING* CM4 .... 310 C7
  RCOS CO16 .... 223 J7
Trindehay *LAIN* SS15 .... 18 A7
Trinder Wy *WICKW* SS12 .... 359 H5
Tring Cl *HARH* RM3 .... 353 C5
Tring Gdns *HARH* RM3 .... 352 F5
Trinidad Gdns *DAGE* RM10 .... 388 C6
Trinity Av *EN* EN3 .... 324 A8
  FX IP11 .... 8 B4
  WOS/PRIT SS0 .... 20 D7
Trinity Cl *BCAYE* CM11 .... 357 K5
  BSF CM23 .... 174 A5
  K/T/MI CO5 .... 245 K4
  KESG IP5 .... 39 G4
  LAIN SS15 .... 376 D5
  MGTR CO11 .... 108 E8
  RAYL SS6 .... 380 F2
  RCOLE CO7 .... 192 D3
Trinity La *BAR* EN8 .... 300 F4
Trinity Link *HVHL* CB9 .... 28 B2
Trinity Ms *K/T/MI* CO5 .... 245 K4 8
Trinity Rd *BCAYE* CM11 .... 357 K5
  CHLM/GWD CM2 .... 17 L3
  HSTD CO9 .... 128 E2
  MGTR CO11 .... 108 E8
  RAYL SS6 .... 380 F2
  SOSN SS2 .... 21 M3
Trinity St *BSF* CM23 .... 174 A15
  COL CO1 .... 10 C8
  HSTD CO9 .... 128 E2
Trinity Wy *BSF* CM23 .... 174 A5
Trinity Wood Rd *HOC/HUL* SS5 .. 363 H3
Tripat Cl *SLH/COR* SS17 .... 395 L6
Tripton Rd *CHLM* SS18 .... 255 M4
Triton Wy *SBF/HAD* SS7 .... 380 C5
Triumph Av *COS* CO15 .... 249 M4
Triumph Cl *CDH/CHF* RM16 .... 416 D1
Troon Gdns *IPNE* IP4 .... 38 C3
Troopers Dr *HARH* RM3 .... 352 E5
Trotters Fld *BRTR* CM7 .... 155 J8
Trotters Rd *HLWS* CM18 .... 256 B6
Trotwood *CHIG* IG7 .... 349 L6
Trotwood Cl *CHLM/WR* CM1 .... 263 M4
Troubridge Cl *RCHLM* CM3 .... 340 A4
Trowbridge Rd *HARH* RM3 .... 352 E7
Troys Cha *RCHLM* CM3 .... 210 D5
Trueloves La *ING* CM4 .... 333 M1
Truman Cl *LAIN* SS15 .... 376 B5 11
Trunette Rd *COS* CO15 .... 12 B6
The Trunnions *RCFD* SS4 .... 383 C2
Truro Crs *KESG* IP5 .... 39 H5 6
  RAYL SS6 .... 361 K6
Trusses Rd *BOC* CM0 .... 274 A8
Trustons Gdns *EMPK* RM11 ...... 371 H7
Trust Rd *BAR* EN8 .... 300 F6 8
Tucker Dr *WIT* CM8 .... 239 C3
Tucker's Rw *BSF* CM23 .... 174 A5
Tuck Rd *RAIN* RM13 .... 389 H5
Tuddenham Av *IPNE* IP4 .... 3 J2
Tuddenham La *IPNE* IP4 .... 38 C1
Tuddenham Rd *IPNE* IP4 .... 3 H2
Tudor Av *CHESW* EN7 .... 300 C3
  GPK RM2 .... 371 H3
  SLH/COR SS17 .... 394 F7
Tudor Cl *BRWN* CM15 .... 333 G8
  CHIG IG7 .... 349 H5
  COS CO15 .... 250 B2
  CHESW EN7 .... 300 C3
  ING CM4 .... 334 B1
  LOS SS9 .... 381 K4
  RAYL SS6 .... 381 G1
  RCOLE CO7 .... 220 F3 8
  RIPS/CAP IP9 .... 113 H2
  SBF/HAD SS7 .... 380 A6
  SUD CO10 .... 4 C2
  WFD IG8 .... 348 C6
  WIT CM8 .... 239 G3
  WOTN CO14 .... 199 L1 8
Tudor Cl *LAIN* SS15 .... 377 G2 7
Tudor Crs *BARK/HLT* IG6 .... 349 K7
Tudor Dr *GPK* RM2 .... 371 H4
Tudor Gdns *GPK* RM2 .... 371 H4
  LOS SS9 .... 381 L8
  SBN/FI SS3 .... 402 E3
  UPMR RM14 .... 390 D1
Tudor Gn *COS* CO15 .... 250 A2
  SUD CO10 .... 4 C1
Tudor Ri *BROX* EN10 .... 276 F1
Tudor Rd *CVI* SS8 .... 397 L8
  LOS SS9 .... 381 K4
  SUD CO10 .... 4 C2
  WOS/PRIT SS0 .... 20 D2
Tudor Rose Cl *COLW* CO3 .... 161 K4
Tudor Wy *HOC/HUL* SS5 .... 363 G7
  WAB EN9 .... 301 L6
  WICKW SS12 .... 359 H4
Tudwick Rd *K/T/MI* CO5 .... 214 F8
  MAL CM9 .... 241 M6
Tufnell Wy *COLN* CO4 .... 162 D1
Tufted Cl *BRTR* CM7 .... 182 D6
Tufter Rd *CHIG* IG7 .... 350 A6
Tugby Pl *CHLM/WR* CM1 .... 263 M5
Tukes Wy *SAFWS* CB11 .... 66 A3
Tulip Cl *BRWN* CM15 .... 332 C7
  CHLM/WR CM1 .... 264 F4 8
  HARH RM3 .... 352 D4
Tumbler Rd *HLWS* CM18 .... 256 B4
Tumulus Wy *COLS* CO2 .... 190 A1
Tunbridge Rd *SOSN* SS2 .... 20 F2
Tunfield Rd *HOD* EN11 .... 253 J2

Tunnmeade *HLW* CM20 .... 256 B2
Tunstall Av *BARK/HLT* IG6 ...... 350 B7
Tunstall Cl *PIT* SS13 .... 378 D6
  RCOS CO16 .... 222 C3
Turin St *CHTY* IP2 .... 2 F8
Turkentine Cl *SUD* CO10 .... 55 L6
Turkey Cock La *COLW* CO3 ...... 160 F5
  RCOLW CO6 .... 161 G3
Turkey Oaks *CHLM/WR* CM1 .. 17 K2
Turkey St *EN* EN1 .... 300 B8
Turner Av *MGTR* CO11 .... 108 C6
Turner Cl *HVHL* CB9 .... 27 L2
  RCOLE CO7 .... 192 D2
  SBN/FI SS3 .... 403 G3
Turner Gv *KESG* IP5 .... 39 L3
Turner Rd *COLN* CO4 .... 10 C2
  IPSE IP3 .... 59 H3
Turners Cl *CHONG* CM5 .... 307 G1
Turners Crs *BSF* CM23 .... 173 K7
Turner's Hi *BAR* EN8 .... 300 E2
Turnors *HLWW/ROY* CM19 .... 15 J4
Turnpike Cl *COLN* CO4 .... 135 M3
Turnpike La *CDH/CHF* RM16 .. 418 E2
Turnstone End *COLN* CO4 ...... 164 A3 8
Turold Rd *SLH/COR* SS17 .... 394 F7
Turp Av *CDH/CHF* RM16 .... 407 K7
Turpin Av *CRW* RM5 .... 351 H8
Turpin La *ERITH* DA8 .... 414 B3
Turpins Av *COS* CO15 .... 224 D6
Turpins Cl *COS* CO15 .... 224 D6
Turpins La *FOS* CO13 .... 198 F4
  WFD IG8 .... 349 G6
The Turpins *BSDN* SS14 .... 19 K3
Turret La *IPNE* IP4 .... 2 F5
Turstan Rd *WIT* CM8 .... 238 F3
Tusser Cl *WIT* CM8 .... 212 C4
Tusset Ms *COLN* CO3 .... 161 M4 8
Tutors Wy *RCHLM* CM3 .... 339 M4 8
Tweed *TIL* RM18 .... 419 K1
Tweed Cl *HSTD* CO9 .... 128 E4
Tweed Wy *ROM* RM1 .... 351 L8
Twelve Acre Ap *KESG* IP5 .... 39 J4
Twelve Acres *BRTR* CM7 .... 155 L8
Twentyfirst St *STSD* CM24 ...... 176 A1
Twentyman Cl *WFD* IG8 .... 348 B6 7
Twining Rd *COLW* CO3 .... 161 M7
Twin Oaks *CHLM/GWD* CM2 .. 265 H4
Twinstead *WICKW* SS12 .... 359 M5
Twitten La *CHLM/GWD* CM2 .. 312 C1 8
Twitty Fee *RCHLM* CM3 .... 291 H2
Twizzlefoot Br *BOC* CM0 .... 345 J4
Two Acres *RIPS/CAP* IP9 .... 78 C1
Twyford Av *SBN/FI* SS3 .... 385 H7
Twyford Bury La *BSF* CM23 ...... 174 B7
Twyford Cl *BSF* CM23 .... 174 B6
Twyford Gdns *BSF* CM23 .... 174 A7
Twyford Rd *BSF* CM23 .... 174 B6
Twyzel Rd *CVI* SS8 .... 398 D6 6
Tyberry Rd *EN* EN1 .... 324 C5
Tyburn Hl *RCOLW* CO6 .... 131 H5
The Tyburns *RBRW/HUT* CM13 .. 355 K3
Tycehurst Hl *LOU* IG10 .... 327 G6
Tydeman Cl *COLW* CO3 .... 161 K7
Tye Common Rd *BCAYW* CM12 .. 356 F6
Tyefields *PIT* SS13 .... 378 D4
Tye Green Rd *RBSF* CM22 .... 147 K4
Tye Green Village
  HLWS CM18 .... 256 A6 8
Tyehurst Crs *COLN* CO4 .... 11 K1
Tyelands *BCAYW* CM12 .... 357 G3
Tye La *RCOLE* CO7 .... 164 F8
Tye Rd *RCOLE* CO7 .... 164 F4
The Tye Rd *RCOLE* CO7 .... 195 J3
The Tye *RCHLM* CM3 .... 314 D4
Tyfield Cl *BAR* EN8 .... 300 D2 8
Tyle Gn *EMPK* RM11 .... 371 M5
Tyler Av *LAIN* SS15 .... 376 D5
  RCOS CO16 .... 223 J8
Tylers Av *BCAYW* CM12 .... 335 J3
  SOS SS1 .... 21 H6
Tylers Cl *CHLM/GWD* CM2 ...... 288 C5
Tylers Crs *HCH* RM12 .... 389 K4
Tylers Gn *FX* IP11 .... 84 D2
Tylers Ride *RCHLM* CM3 .... 339 M4
Tylers Rd *HLWW/ROY* CM19 ... 254 E8
Tyler St *CHTY* IP2 .... 3 G8
  HAR CO12 .... 6 A4
Tyler Wy *BRW* CM14 .... 354 C2
Tylewood *SBF/HAD* SS7 .... 398 D1
Tylney Av *RCFD* SS4 .... 363 M8
Tylney Cft *HLWW/ROY* CM19 .. 15 H9
Tylneys Rd *HSTD* CO9 .... 99 H8
Tyms Wy *RAYL* SS6 .... 361 M7 8
Tyndale Cl *HLWS* CM18 .... 256 B4
Tyndale Dr *COS* CO15 .... 250 B2
Tyndales La *RCHLM* CM3 .... 291 J6
Tyne Cl *UPMR* RM14 .... 372 E6
Tynedale Sq *COLN* CO4 .... 135 J7
Tyne Gdns *SOCK/AV* RM15 ...... 405 K5 8
Tynemouth Dr *EN* EN1 .... 324 B2
Tyrel Dr *SOS* SS1 .... 21 J3
Tyrells *HOC/HUL* SS5 .... 362 E7
Tyrells Cl *CHLM/WR* CM1 .... 264 F7
  UPMR RM14 .... 390 C1 8
Tyrells Wy *CHLM/GWD* CM2 .. 289 G4
Tyrone Cl *BCAYE* CM11 .... 357 K5
  IP IP1 .... 36 E1 8
Tyrone Rd *BCAYE* CM11 .... 357 K5
  SOS SS1 .... 402 B3
Tyrrell Rd *SBF/HAD* SS7 .... 397 J1
Tyrrells Hall Cl *GRAYS* RM17 ... 417 L3
Tyrrells Rd *BCAYE* CM11 .... 357 L5
Tysea Cl *HLWS* CM18 .... 256 H6
Tysea Hl *ABR/ST* RM4 .... 352 A2
Tysea Rd *HLWS* CM18 .... 256 A6
Tysoe Av *PEND* EN3 .... 301 G8
Tyssen Md *RCHLM* CM3 .... 265 M3
Tyssen Pl *SOCK/AV* RM15 ...... 406 D1 8
Tythe Barn Wy *RCHLM* CM3 .. 339 K3 8
Tythe Cl *CHLM/WR* CM1 .... 264 D1
The Tythings *HSTD* CO9 .... 128 E3 8

Uckfield Rd *PEND* EN3 .... 324 E1
Udall Gdns *CRW* RM5 .... 351 H7

Ullswater Av *FX* IP11 .... 85 L6
Ullswater Cl *BRTR* CM7 .... 182 D5
Ullswater Rd *SBF/HAD* SS7 ...... 379 M4
Ullswater Wy *HCH* RM12 .... 389 H4
Ulster Av *IP* IP11 .... 36 E2
  SBN/FI SS3 .... 402 D5
Ulting Hall Rd *MAL* CM9 .... 267 M4
Ulting La *MAL* CM9 .... 267 L5
Ulting Rd *RCHLM* CM3 .... 267 K2
Ulting Wy *WICKE* SS11 .... 360 B3
Una Rd *HAR* CO12 .... 112 F7
Undercliff Rd East *FX* IP11 ...... 115 K1
Undercliff Rd West *FX* IP11 ...... 9 M3
Underhill Rd *SBF/HAD* SS7 ...... 379 M8
Underwood Rd *WFD* IG8 .... 348 E8 8
Underwood Sq *LOS* SS9 .... 399 K1
Union La *RCOLE* CO7 .... 248 F1
Union Rd *COS* CO15 .... 250 B3
Union St *IPNE* IP4 .... 3 G4 8
Unity Cl *COLS* CO2 .... 163 J7
Unity Rd *PEND* EN3 .... 324 D1
Unity St *IPSE* IP3 .... 3 K8
University Wy *DART* DA1 .... 414 E7
Upland Cl *BCAYW* CM12 .... 335 G7 10
Upland Court Rd *HARH* RM3 .. 372 A2
Upland Crs *K/T/MI* CO5 .... 245 K4
Upland Dr *BCAYW* CM12 .... 335 G7
  COLN CO4 .... 11 K2
Upland Rd *BCAYW* CM12 .... 335 G7
  EPP CM16 .... 279 L5
  IPNE IP4 .... 38 B5
  K/T/MI CO5 .... 245 K4
  LOS SS9 .... 400 B3 8
Uplands Cl *HOC/HUL* SS5 .... 363 G6
  SBF/HAD SS7 .... 379 J7
Uplands Crs *SUD* CO10 .... 4 D2
Uplands Dr *CHLM/WR* CM1 ...... 264 E4
Uplands Park Rd *RAYL* SS6 .. 361 L7
Uplands Rd *COS* CO15 .... 12 C9
  HOC/HUL SS5 .... 363 G6
  SBF/HAD SS7 .... 379 J8
  SUD CO10 .... 4 D2
  WFD IG8 .... 348 F8
The Uplands *LOU* IG10 .... 327 G5
Upminster Rd *HCH* RM12 .... 390 A1
Upminster Rd North
  RAIN RM13 .... 404 D1
Upminster Rd South
  RAIN RM13 .... 404 D1
Upney Cl *HCH* RM12 .... 389 L4 10
Upper Acres *WIT* CM8 .... 212 A6
Upper Av *PIT* SS13 .... 378 F3
Upper Barclay St *IPNE* IP4 .... 3 G5
Upper Branston Rd *COS* CO15 .. 12 C4
Upper Brentwood Rd *GPK* RM2 .. 371 K4
Upper Bridge Rd
  CHLM/GWD CM2 .... 16 E7
Upper Brook St *IPNE* IP4 .... 2 F2
Upper Chapel St *HSTD* CO9 ...... 128 F1 8
Upper Cha *CHLM/GWD* CM2 .. 16 E7
  RCHLM CM3 .... 343 C1
Upper Cornsland *BRW* CM14 .... 354 E4
Upper East St *SUD* CO10 .... 4 E5
Upper Fenn Rd *HSTD* CO9 .... 129 H1
Upperfield Dr *FX* IP11 .... 85 J7
Upper Fourth Av *FOS* CO13 ...... 199 G6
Upper High St *IP* IP1 .... 2 E2
Upper Holt St *RCOLW* CO6 ...... 130 D5
Upper Hook *HLWS* CM18 .... 256 A5
Upper Lambricks *RAYL* SS6 ...... 361 M7
Upper Market Rd
  WICKW SS12 .... 359 L3 6
  WICKW SS12 .... 359 K3 6
Upper Marsh La *HOD* EN11 ...... 253 H6
Upper Mayne *LAIN* SS15 .... 18 B1
Upper Mealines *HLWS* CM18 .. 256 B6
Upper Mill Fld *GTDUN* CM6 ...... 178 F4
Upper Moors *RCHLM* CM3 ...... 235 G4
Upper Orwell St *IPNE* IP4 .... 3 G5
Upper Pk *HLW* CM20 .... 15 G3
Upper Park Rd *COS* CO15 .... 12 D6
  RCOLE CO7 .... 220 F4
  WICKW SS12 .... 359 L7
Upper Rainham Rd *HCH* RM12 .. 389 C3
Upper Rd *BCAYE* CM11 .... 358 E6
Upper Roman Rd
  CHLM/GWD CM2 .... 17 H6
Upper Ryle *BRW* CM14 .... 354 C1
Upper Second Av *FOS* CO13 .. 198 F6
Upper Shott *CHESW* EN7 .... 276 A6
Upper Stonyfield
  HLWW/ROY CM19 .... 15 H4
Upper St *RCOLE* CO7 .... 106 D2
Upper Swaines *EPP* CM16 ...... 304 A2
Upper Third Av *FOS* CO13 ...... 198 F6
Upshers *SAFWS* CB11 .... 66 A3
Upshire Rd *WAB* EN9 .... 302 A4
Upsons Wy *KESG* IP5 .... 39 M3 8
Upton Cl *IPNE* IP4 .... 3 K4
  RCOLW CO6 .... 133 L7
  SLH/COR SS17 .... 409 L1
Upway *RAYL* SS6 .... 361 L8
The Upway *BSDN* SS14 .... 19 H2
Urban Av *HCH* RM12 .... 389 K2
Urban Rd *BSF* CM23 .... 174 C4
Urmond Rd *CVI* SS8 .... 398 B7
Usk Rd *SOCK/AV* RM15 .... 405 K4
Usterdale Rd *SAFWN* CB10 .. 43 M8
Uttons Av *LOS* SS9 .... 399 L3
Uvedale Rd *DAGE* RM10 .... 388 D8
Uvedale Cl *WICKE* SS11 .... 360 A5
Uxbridge Crs *IPSE* IP3 .... 59 K2 8

Vaagen Rd *CVI* SS8 .... 398 C7
Vadsoe Rd *CVI* SS8 .... 398 C6 8
Valance Av *CHING* E4 .... 348 A2
Valance Rd *SAFWS* CB11 .... 87 H4
Vale Av *SOSN* SS2 .... 21 G2
Vale Cl *BRWN* CM15 .... 332 A4
  COLN CO4 .... 163 M1

Vale End *CHLM/GWD* CM2 ...... 288 D8
Vale La *RIPS/CAP* IP9 .... 79 J7
Valence Dr *CHESW* EN7 .... 276 B8
Valence Wy *VGE* SS16 .... 376 D7
Valentines *ING* CM4 .... 336 A1
Valentines Dr *COLN* CO4 .... 11 J4
Valentines Wy *DAGE* RM10 .. 388 F1
Valentine Wy *WIT* CM8 .... 184 E7
The Vale *BRW* CM14 .... 354 D2
  ING CM4 .... 335 M4
  VGE SS16 .... 377 L8
  WFD IG8 .... 348 B8
Valfreda Wy *RCOLE* CO7 .... 192 C2
Valiant Cl *ROMW/RG* RM7 ...... 370 C2 7
Valkyrie Cl *MAL* CM9 .... 272 E1
Valkyrie Rd *WOS/PRIT* SS0 ...... 20 A6
Vallance Cl *SOSN* SS2 .... 383 M8
Valletta Cl *CHLM/WR* CM1 ...... 16 E1
Valley Br *CHLM/WR* CM1 .... 264 C5
Valleybridge Rd *COS* CO15 ...... 13 J1
Valley Cl *COLW* CO3 .... 161 M8
  IP IP1 .... 37 K2
  LOU IG10 .... 327 G8
  MGTR CO11 .... 108 E2
  WAB EN9 .... 301 K4
Valley Crs *RCOLW* CO6 .... 133 M8
Valley HI *LOU* IG10 .... 348 F1 8
Valley La *RIPS/CAP* IP9 .... 58 A7
Valley Rd *BCAYE* CM11 .... 357 J1
  BRTR CM7 .... 155 H7
  COS CO15 .... 13 J1
  HAR CO12 .... 142 E1
  IPNE IP4 .... 37 L2
  RCOLE CO7 .... 192 D3
  SUD CO10 .... 55 M2
Valley Vw *BRTR* CM7 .... 94 C5
  RCOLW CO6 .... 133 M8
Valley View Cl *COLN* CO4 .... 135 H7
Valleyview Dr *IPNE* IP4 .... 39 C7
Valmar Av *SLH/COR* SS17 ...... 409 J2
Vandenbury Cir *BRTR* CM7 .. 95 L5 8
Vanderbilt Av *RAYL* SS6 .... 361 K3
Vanderwalt Av *CVI* SS8 .... 398 E8 8
Van Dieman's La
  CHLM/GWD CM2 .... 17 K7
Van Dieman's Rd
  CHLM/GWD CM2 .... 17 K7
Van Diemens Pass *CVI* SS8 ...... 399 C8
Van Dyck Rd *COLW* CO3 .... 162 B6
Vandyck Rd *IPSE* IP3 .... 59 H3 8
Vane La *RCOLW* CO6 .... 186 B1
Vanessa Dr *WIT* CM8 .... 212 C2
Vange Corner Dr *SLH/COR* SS17 .. 395 J2
Vange Hill Dr *VGE* SS16 .... 19 M9
Vange Park Rd *SLH/COR* SS17 .. 395 J2
Vanguard Cl *ROMW/RG* RM7 .. 370 C2
The Vanguards *SBN/FI* SS3 ...... 403 G3
Vanguard Wy *BRTR* CM7 .... 155 J7 8
  SBN/FI SS3 .... 403 G3
Vanners Rd *HVHL* CB9 .... 28 B4
Vansittart St *HAR* CO12 .... 7 K5
Vantorts Cl *SBW* CM21 .... 227 M1
Vantorts Rd *SBW* CM21 .... 227 M2
Varden Cl *CHLM/WR* CM1 ...... 264 A5
Vardon Dr *LOS* SS9 .... 381 J8
Varney Cl *CHESW* EN7 .... 276 B7
Vaughan Av *HCH* RM12 .... 389 L3
Vaughan Cl *BRTR* CM7 .... 182 A1
  RCFD SS4 .... 363 M6
Vaughan St *CHTY* IP2 .... 2 F8
Vaughan Williams Rd
  LAIN SS15 .... 376 D3 8
Vaulx Rd *CVI* SS8 .... 398 C7
Vauxhall Av *HAR* CO12 .... 143 G2
Vauxhall Av *COS* CO15 .... 249 M5
Vauxhall Dr *BRTR* CM7 .... 182 E1
Velizy Av *HLW* CM20 .... 15 L2
Vellacotts *CHLM/WR* CM1 ...... 264 C4
Venables Cl *CVI* SS8 .... 398 D8
  DAGE RM10 .... 388 C3 8
Venette Cl *RAIN* RM13 .... 404 C3
Venlo Rd *CVI* SS8 .... 398 C6 7
Venmore Dr *GTDUN* CM6 ...... 178 F3
Ventnor Dr *COS* CO15 .... 224 B3
Ventris Cl *CHTY* IP2 .... 36 E6
Veny Crs *HCH* RM12 .... 389 L4
Vera Rd *BCAYE* CM11 .... 359 H1
Verbena Cl *SOCK/AV* RM15 ...... 406 D4 8
Verderers Rd *CHIG* IG7 .... 350 B6
Vere Gdns *IP* IP1 .... 37 K1
Vere Rd *LOU* IG10 .... 327 K6
Vermeer Crs *SBN/FI* SS3 .... 403 H3
Vermeer Ride
  CHLM/WR CM1 .... 265 G4 8
Vermont Cl *COS* CO15 .... 13 K3
  PIT SS13 .... 378 D3
Vermont Crs *RCOLE* CO7 .... 192 C2
Vermont Rd *IPNE* IP4 .... 3 H1
Vernon Av *ING* CM4 .... 335 M4
Vernon Crs *RBRW/HUT* CM13 .. 355 H4
Vernon Rd *CRW* RM5 .... 351 K6
  LOS SS9 .... 399 K2
  RCHLM CM3 .... 341 H2
Vernon's Cl *RBSF* CM22 .... 120 A6
Vernons Rd *RCOLW* CO6 .... 131 M6
Vernon St *CHTY* IP2 .... 2 F8
Vernon Wy *BRTR* CM7 .... 155 K6
Veronica Cl *HARH* RM3 .... 352 D8
Veronica Wk *COLN* CO4 .... 11 M7
Vesta Cl *RCOLW* CO6 .... 186 A1
Vestry Cl *LAIN* SS15 .... 376 D4
Vexil Cl *PUR* RM19 .... 415 L1
Veyses End *RCOLE* CO7 .... 106 E1
Viaduct Rd *CHLM/WR* CM1 ...... 16 E5
Vian Av *PEND* EN3 .... 300 F7
Viborg Gdns *MAL* CM9 .... 292 F5 8
Vicarage Cl *BRTR* CM7 .... 153 H5
  BRW CM14 .... 353 M5
  CVI SS8 .... 397 L8
  LAIN SS15 .... 376 D5 8
  MAL CM9 .... 242 E1 7
  RIPW IP8 .... 36 C2
Vicarage Crs *RCHLM* CM3 ...... 238 C7
Vicarage Fld *SUD* CO10 .... 55 J6

Vicarage Gdns *COS* CO15 .... 12 D8
Vicarage Hl *SBF/HAD* SS7 .... 398 A1
Vicarage La *BOC* CM0 .... 297 M7
  BSF CM23 .... 117 J3
  CHIG IG7 .... 349 L4
  CHLM/GWD CM2 .... 289 C8
  EPP CM16 .... 281 J4
  GTDUN CM6 .... 92 B8
  MAL CM9 .... 293 M8
  RBSF CM22 .... 119 G6
  RCOS CO16 .... 197 G1
  RIPS/CAP IP9 .... 58 C6
  RIPW IP8 .... 36 C2
  SUD CO10 .... 35 K5
  SUD CO10 .... 35 J7
  WOTN CO14 .... 199 K3 11 8
Vicarage Meadow *BOC* CM0 .. 320 D8
  HSTD CO9 .... 128 F2
Vicarage Rd *BRTR* CM7 .... 94 C5
  CHLM/GWD CM2 .... 16 F8
  CHLM/WR CM2 .... 262 D6
  DAGE RM10 .... 388 C6
  EPP CM16 .... 304 D7
  FX IP11 .... 8 F2
  HCH RM12 .... 371 H8
  RCHLM CM3 .... 233 M1
  SUD CO10 .... 52 B2
  WFD IG8 .... 348 B8
Vicarage Sq *GRAYS* RM17 .. 417 H3 7
Vicars Orch *SUD* CO10 .... 53 M6
Vicars Cl *RCOLE* CO7 .... 173 L7
Vicerons Pl *BSF* CM23 .... 173 J3
Viceroy Cl *COLS* CO2 .... 163 J8
Vickers Rd *SOSN* SS2 .... 382 E5
Victor Ap *HCH* RM12 .... 371 L8
Victor Av *PIT* SS13 .... 378 E5
Victor Cl *HCH* RM12 .... 371 L8
Victor Dr *LOS* SS9 .... 400 A3
Victor Gdns *HCH* RM12 .... 371 L8
  HOC/HUL SS5 .... 363 G6
Victoria Av *CDH/CHF* RM16 .. 407 K7
  CRW RM5 .... 351 J7
  FOS CO13 .... 198 E3
  RAYL SS6 .... 361 J6
  SAFWS CB11 .... 65 M3
  SOSN SS2 .... 20 F3
  VGE SS16 .... 376 D8 8
  WICKW SS12 .... 359 J3
Victoria Cha *COLW* CO3 .... 10 A5
Victoria Cl *CDH/CHF* RM16 .. 407 K7
  LAIN SS15 .... 376 C4 8
  RCOLE CO7 .... 192 C1
Victoria Crs *CHLM/WR* CM1 .. 16 F1
  LAIN SS15 .... 376 D3 8
  MGTR CO11 .... 108 D7
  RBRW/HUT CM13 .... 355 J3
  WICKW SS12 .... 359 J4
Victoria Dr *LOS* SS9 .... 399 M2
  SBN/FI SS3 .... 403 K1
Victoria Esp *K/T/MI* CO5 .... 245 L6
Victoria Gdns *COLN* CO4 .... 135 J8
  SAFWS CB11 .... 65 M2 8
Victoria Ga *HLWE* CM17 .... 256 C3
Victoria Pl *COL* CO1 .... 163 G5
  RCOLE CO7 .... 221 G5
Victoria Rd *BKHH* IG9 .... 348 B8
  BRW CM14 .... 354 D5
  CHLM/WR CM1 .... 17 J2
  COLW CO3 .... 162 D6
  COS CO15 .... 13 K4
  DAGE RM10 .... 388 D4
  FX IP11 .... 9 K3
  HVHL CB9 .... 27 L4
  LAIN SS15 .... 376 C4 8
  LOS SS9 .... 399 M3
  MAL CM9 .... 293 H1
  RAYL SS6 .... 361 M8
  RCHLM CM3 .... 317 G5
  RCHLM CM3 .... 339 L5
  RCOS CO16 .... 196 C6
  ROM RM1 .... 371 G5
  SLH/COR SS17 .... 394 A8
  SLH/COR SS17 .... 409 K1
  SOS SS1 .... 21 M6
  UPMR RM14 .... 393 G2
  VGE SS16 .... 395 L1
  WAB EN9 .... 301 K6
  WOTN CO14 .... 199 K3
Victoria Rd South
  CHLM/WR CM1 .... 17 G3
Victoria St *BRTR* CM7 .... 183 C1
  FX IP11 .... 9 M2
  HAR CO12 .... 7 J6
  IP IP1 .... 2 B3
Victor Mew Cl *WICKW* SS12 .. 359 L6
Victor's Crs *RBRW/HUT* CM13 .. 355 J3
Victory Rd *COS* CO15 .... 12 D5
  IPNE IP4 .... 38 B4
  K/T/MI CO5 .... 245 H5
  RAIN RM13 .... 389 H8
Victory Wy *GRH* DA9 .... 415 K8
  ROMW/RG RM7 .... 370 C2
Vienna Cl *HAR* CO12 .... 143 H2
View Cl *CHIG* IG7 .... 349 L6
View Point Rd *FX* IP11 .... 114 E6
Vigerons Wy *CDH/CHF* RM16 .. 418 C1
Vignoles Rd *ROMW/RG* RM7 .. 370 B7
Viking Rd *MAL* CM9 .... 292 F5
Vikings Wy *CVI* SS8 .... 397 L8
Viking Wy *BRWN* CM15 .... 332 C8
  COS CO15 .... 225 G5
  WICKE SS11 .... 359 L6
Village Cl *FOS* CO13 .... 198 E4
Village Dr *CVI* SS8 .... 397 M8
Village Ga *CHLM/GWD* CM2 .. 265 H8
Village Green Rd *DART* DA1 .. 414 B8
Village Hall Cl *CVI* SS8 .... 397 L8 8
Villa Rd *COLW* CO3 .... 161 K6
Villas Rd *SBF/HAD* SS7 .... 379 K7
Villiers Pl *RCHLM* CM3 .... 265 M3
Villiers-sur-marne Av
  BSF CM23 .... 173 L6
Villiers Wy *SBF/HAD* SS7 .... 380 A6
Vince Cl *K/T/MI* CO5 .... 245 K5
Vincent Av *SLH/COR* SS17 ...... 394 A8
Vincent Cl *BAR* EN8 .... 276 F4

BARK/HLT IG6 .... 349 K7
IP IP1 .... 36 F3
SBN/FI SS3 .... 402 F4
SLH/COR SS17 .... 395 J8
Vincent Rd *RAIN* RM13...... 404 D2
Vincent Wy *BCAYW* CM12 .... 335 G6
Vine Ct *HLW* CM20 .... 226 E6
Vine Gv *HLW* CM20 .... 226 E6
Vine Rd *K/T/MI* CO5 .... 214 C5
Vinesse Rd *RCOLW* CO6 ..... 133 L2
Vine St *BRTR* CM7 .... 124 C1 ⑤
ROMW/RG RM7 .... 370 D5
Vineway *BRW* CM14 .... 354 D2
The Vineway *HAR* CO12...... 6 D7
Vineyard Ga *COL* CO1 ...... 10 C9 ⑥
Vineyard St *COL* CO1 .... 10 D9
Vint Crs *COL* CO3 .... 162 D5
The Vintners *SOSN* SS2 ..... 383 G6
Viola Cl *SOCK/AV* RM15 .... 406 D1
Violet Cl *CHLM/WR* CM1 .... 264 F4
CHTY IP2 .... 37 G7
Violets La *BUNT* SG9 .... 116 C7
Virgil Dr *BROX* EN10 .... 277 C3 ⑥
Virgil Rd *WIT* CM8 .... 212 A6
Virginia St *COS* CO15 ...... 250 B2
CRW RM5 .... 351 K8
SBF/HAD SS7 .... 379 J4
Virley Cl *MAL* CM9 .... 269 L7
Viscount Dr *COLN* CO4 ..... 135 K6
Vista Av *FOS* CO13 .... 198 E2
PEND EN3 .... 324 E4
Vista Rd *COS* CO15 .... 13 H4
WICKE SS11 .... 360 H4
Vitilus Cl *COLN* CO4 .... 135 J5 ⑥
Vivian Ct *WOTN* CM14 ...... 199 K3
Volwycke Av *MAL* CM9 ...... 293 C3
Voorburg Rd *CVI* SS8 ...... 398 E7 ⑥
Vowler Rd *VGE* SS16 .... 376 C7
Voysey Gdns *PIT* SS13 ..... 378 C2

W

Waalwyk Dr *CVI* SS8 .... 398 D7
Waarden Rd *CVI* SS8 .... 398 E7
Waarem Av *CVI* SS8 .... 398 B7
Wacketts *CHESW* EN7 .... 276 B7 ⑥
Waddesdon Rd *HAR* CO12..... 7 J6
Wade Reach *WOTN* CO14 .... 199 H3
Wade Rd *COS* CO15 .... 224 C3
Wade's La *RIPS/CAP* IP9 .... 82 E5
Wadgate Rd *FX* IP11 .... 9 G1
Wadham Cl *ING* CM4 .... 310 C7
Wadham Park Av *HOC/HUL* SS5.. 362 B5
Wadhurst Rd *IPSE* IP3 ...... 38 E8
Wadsworth Rd *PEND* EN3 .... 324 E7 ⑥
Wagon Md *RBSF* CM22 ...... 202 B8
Wagtail Dr *MAL* CM9 .... 269 K6
Wainfleet Av *CRW* RM5 ..... 370 D2
Wainwright Av
 RBRW/HUT CM13 .... 355 L1
Wainwright Wy *KESG* IP5 .... 39 L3
Wakefield Av *SAFWN* CB10 .. 22 E8 ⑥
Wakefield Av *BCAYW* CM12 .. 357 H1
Wakefield Cl *COL* CO1 ...... 10 E6
Wakelin Cha *ING* CM4 .... 310 B8
Wakelin Wy *WIT* CM8 .... 239 J1 ⑥
Wakerfield Cl *EMPK* RM11 .. 372 A4 ⑥
Wakering Av *SBN/FI* SS3 .... 403 G4
Wakering Rd *SBN/FI* SS3 .... 402 B1
Wakescoline *WICKE* SS11 ... 360 B5
Wakeshall La *SUD* CO10 .... 51 K4
Wakes St *RCOLW* CO6 .... 131 J5
Walcot Rd *PEND* EN3 .... 325 C4
Waldegrave *VGE* SS16 ...... 19 G9
Waldegrave Cl *MGTR* CO11 .. 108 C8
Waldegrave Gdns *UPMR* RM14.. 390 C1
Waldegrave Rd *MGTR* CO11 .. 108 D8
The Waldegraves *BURES* CO8.. 102 A3
Waldegrave Wy *MGTR* CO11 .. 108 C8
Walden Av *RAIN* RM13 ...... 388 E8
 SAFWN CB10 .... 90 F1
Walden House Rd *WIT* CM8 .. 240 B6
Walden Rd *MAL* CM9 .... 240 F7
Walden Rd *CBE/LIN* CB1 .... 24 C5
 EMPK RM11 .... 371 L6
 GTDUN CM6 .... 92 A6
 SAFWN CB10 .... 22 F8
 SAFWS CB11 .... 65 G5
Walden Wy *BARK/HLT* IG6 ... 349 M8
 EMPK RM11 .... 371 L6
 FOS CO13 .... 199 H5
Waldgrooms *GTDUN* CM6 .... 178 D2
Waldingfield Rd *SUD* CO10 .. 4 F4
 SUD CO10 .... 35 L5
Waldon *TIL* RM18 .... 419 J8
Waldringfield *BSDN* SS14 .. 19 H3
Walford Pl *CHLM/GWD* CM2 .. 289 C1
Walfords Cl *HLWE* CM17 .... 227 K4
Walford Wy *RCOLW* CO6 ..... 186 B1
Walker Av *CHONG* CM5 ...... 283 L1
 IPSE IP3 .... 38 D6
Walker Dr *LOS* SS9 .... 399 H1
Walkers Cl *CHLM/WR* CM1 ... 264 E4
Walkers Sq *SLH/COR* SS17 .. 409 L2
Walkey Wy *SBN/FI* SS3 ...... 403 J3
The Walk *COLW* CO3 .... 161 H3
 EMPK RM11 .... 390 A1
 HOC/HUL SS5 .... 339 L8
 KESG IP5 .... 39 J3
Wallace Binder Cl *MAL* CM9 .. 293 G2
Wallace Cl *HOC/HUL* SS5 .... 339 L8
Wallace Crs *CHLM/GWD* CM2 .. 17 K8
Wallace La *RCHLM* CM3 ..... 207 J4
Wallace Rd *GRAYS* RM17 .... 417 J1
 IP IP1 .... 36 F3
Wallace's La *RCHLM* CM3 ... 237 G7
Wallace St *SBN/FI* SS3 ..... 403 G4
Wallasea Gdns
 CHLM/WR CM1 .... 265 G6 ⑥
Wall Cha *RCHLM* CM3 .... 207 G4
Wallenger Av *GPK* RM2 ..... 371 J3
Waller's Cl *ROY* SG8 .... 62 A2

WFD IG8 .... 349 G7
Waller's Gv *CHTY* IP2 ...... 37 G7
Waller's Hoppet *LOU* IG10 .. 327 G4
Wallers Wy *HOD* EN11 ...... 253 J2
Wallflower Ct
 CHLM/WR CM1 .... 265 G5 ⑥
Wallhouse Rd *ERITH* DA8 .. 414 D4
Wallis Av *SOSN* SS2 .... 20 E2
Wallis Cl *RCH* RM12 .... 371 J8
Wallis Ct *COLW* CO3 .... 161 M8
Wall Rd *CVI* SS8 .... 399 G8
The Walls *MGTR* CO11 ...... 108 F7
Wall St *RCOS* CO16 .... 248 D5
Walmer Cl *ROMW/RG* RM7 ... 370 C2
Walnut Cl *FX* IP11 .... 85 L6
 SUD CO10 .... 35 K4
Walnut Ct *HOC/HUL* SS5 .... 362 F4 ⑥
 WIT CM8 .... 212 B7
Walnut Dr *BSF* CM23 .... 173 L8
 WIT CM8 .... 212 B7
Walnut Gv *BRTR* CM7 .... 182 F1
Walnut Tree Av *SBW* CM21 .. 200 F7
Walnut Tree Cl *BAR* EN8 ... 300 E3
Walnut Tree Crs *SBW* CM21 . 200 F8 ⑥
Walnut Tree La *RIPS/CAP* IP9 . 111 J1
 SUD CO10 .... 4 B6
Walnut Tree Wy *COLS* CO2 .. 162 C8
 K/T/MI CO5 .... 214 D4
Walnut Wy *BKHH* IG9 .... 348 L6
 COS CO15 .... 12 A6
 RCOLE CO7 .... 220 F4
Walpole La *GRAYS* RM17 .... 417 K1 ⑥
Walsingham Cl *LAIN* SS15 .. 376 D4 ⑥
 SUD CO10 .... 55 K6
 SOSN SS2 .... 383 J8
Walsingham Rd *COLS* CO2 .. 10 C9
 SOSN SS2 .... 383 J8
Walsingham Wy *BCAYW* CM12.. 335 J6
Walter Radcliffe Wy
 RCOLE CO7 .... 192 D4
 LOS SS9 .... 381 M5
Walters Cl *CHLM/WR* CM1 ... 288 D8
 LOS SS9 .... 381 M5
Walters Rd *PEND* EN3 ...... 324 D7
Walter Wy *WIT* CM8 .... 184 D6
Waltham Cl *CHTY* IP2 ...... 58 B1
 RBRW/HUT CM13 .... 333 K8 ⑥
Waltham Crs *SOSN* SS2 ..... 383 J8
Waltham Gdns *PEND* EN3 ... 324 D1 ⑥
Waltham Ga *BAR* EN8 .... 276 F6
Waltham Gln *CHLM/GWD* CM2.. 17 J9
Waltham Rd *RAYL* SS6 ...... 361 J8
 RCHLM CM3 .... 257 G2
 WAB EN9 .... 277 M6
 WFD IG8 .... 348 F7
Walthams *PIT* SS13 .... 378 C4
Walthams Pl *PIT* SS13 ..... 378 C4
Waltham Wy *FOS* CO13 ..... 199 H6
Walton Av *FX* IP11 .... 8 C4
Walton Cl *LAIN* SS15 ...... 376 D3 ⑥
Walton Gdns *RBRW/HUT* CM13.. 333 K7
 WAB EN9 .... 301 J5
Walton Rd *COS* CO15 .... 13 H5
 CRW RM5 .... 351 G8 ⑥
 FOS CO13 .... 197 M1
 HOD EN11 .... 253 J3
 RCOS CO16 .... 169 J8
 SOS SS1 .... 402 A5
Walton's Hall Rd *SLH/COR* SS17.. 409 J6
Wambrook *SBN/FI* SS3 ...... 402 E2
Wambrook Cl *RBRW/HUT* CM13.. 355 K3
Wamburg Rd *CVI* SS8 ...... 398 E7
Wannock Gdns *BARK/HLT* IG6.. 349 J8
Wansfell Gdns *SOS* SS1 .... 402 A2
Wansford Cl *BRW* CM14 ..... 354 A4
Wantz Cha *MAL* CM9 .... 293 H1
Wantz Hvn *MAL* CM9 .... 293 H1 ⑥
Wantz La *RAIN* RM13 .... 404 C2
Wantz Rd *DAGE* RM10 ...... 388 C3
 ING CM4 .... 311 G2
 MAL CM9 .... 293 H1
Wapping La *RCOLE* CO7 ..... 220 C1
Warburton Rd *HSTD* CO9 .... 97 L3 ⑥
Ward Av *GRAYS* RM17 ...... 417 J1
Ward Cl *CHESW* EN7 .... 276 B7 ⑥
Ward Crs *BSF* CM23 .... 173 M5
Warde Cha *WOTN* CO14 ..... 199 J3 ⑥
Warden Av *CRW* RM5 .... 351 K6
Ward Hatch *HLW* CM20 ..... 227 J8 ⑥
Wardle Wy *CHLM/WR* CM1 ... 263 M4 ⑥
Wardley Cl *CHTY* IP2 ...... 57 L2
Ward Pth *CHLM/GWD* CM2 .. 265 J7
Ward Rd *RIPW* IP8 .... 57 J1
Wards Cft *SAFWS* CB11 ..... 65 L4
Wareham Av *IPSE* IP3 ...... 38 E8
Ware Rd *HOD* EN11 .... 253 H3
Warehouse Rd *GTDUN* CM6 .. 152 A6
Ware St *HOD* EN11 .... 253 H3
Warescot Cl *BRWN* CM15 ... 354 C1
Warescot Rd *BRWN* CM15 ... 354 C1
Wares Rd *CHLM/WR* CM1 .... 233 G6
Warham Rd *HAR* CO12 ...... 142 F2
Wargrave Rd *COS* CO15 .... 12 C4
Warley Av *ROMW/RG* RM7 ... 370 D4
Warley Cl *BRTR* CM7 .... 155 K8
Warley Gap *RBRW/HUT* CM13.. 354 D6
Warley Hl *RBRW/HUT* CM13 .. 354 D6
Warley Mt *BRW* CM14 ...... 354 D5
Warley Rd *RBRW/HUT* CM13.. 372 C2
 WFD IG8 .... 348 C8
Warley St *UPMR* RM14 ...... 373 L7
Warley Wy *FOS* CO13 .... 199 J5
Warner Cl *BCAYW* CM11 .... 357 L2 ⑥
 BRTR CM7 .... 182 A2
Warners *GTDUN* CM6 .... 178 E3 ⑥
Warners Av *HOD* EN11 ..... 253 G7
Warners Bridge Cha *RCFD* SS4.. 383 G5
Warners Gdns *SOSN* SS2 ... 382 F5
Warner Wy *SUD* CO10 ...... 5 H5
Warnham Ct *RCOS* CO16 .... 223 J5
Warren Cl *CHLM/WR* CM1 ... 235 J8
 RAYL SS6 .... 380 D3
 RBSF CM22 .... 176 E4
Warren Ct *CHIG* IG7 .... 349 L5
Warren Dr *HCH* RM12 ...... 389 H2
 WICKE SS11 .... 360 B3
Warrene Cl *SLH/COR* SS17 .. 409 L2

Warren Fld *EPP* CM16 ...... 304 B4
Warrenfield Cl *CHESW* EN7 .. 300 B3 ⑥
Warren Heath Av *IPSE* IP3 .. 59 L1
Warren Heath Rd *IPSE* IP3 .. 59 L1
Warren Hl *LOU* IG10 .... 326 D7
Warren La *BRWN* CM15 ..... 331 M3
 COLW/CHF RM16 .... 416 E1
 COLW CO3 .... 189 J2
 RIPS/CAP IP9 .... 82 D7
Warren Pond *CHING* E4 ..... 348 A1
Warren Rd *BRTR* CM7 .... 183 K1
 HSTD CO9 .... 128 E2 ⑥
 LOS SS9 .... 381 H8
 RCHLM CM3 .... 337 J5
Warrenside *BRTR* CM7 ...... 183 J3
The Warrens *FOS* CO13 ..... 198 F5
 WIT CM8 .... 239 M6
The Warren *BCAYW* CM12 ... 334 F7
Warrington Av *HCH* RM12 ... 389 L1
Warrington Gdns *EMPK* RM11.. 371 K6
Warrington Rd *IP* IP1 ...... 2 D1
Warrior Sq *SOS* SS1 .... 21 H6
Warrior Sq East *SOS* SS1 .. 21 H5
Warrior Sq North *SOS* SS1 .. 21 H5
Warrior Square Rd *SBN/FI* SS3.. 403 G6
Warwick Bailey Cl *COLN* CO4.. 162 E1 ⑥
 CVI SS8 .... 398 D7
 MAL CM9 .... 293 H2 ⑥
 RAYL SS6 .... 381 C2
 SBF/HAD SS7 .... 379 L4
Warwick Crs *COS* CO15 .... 12 E4
 MAL CM9 .... 293 H2
Warwick Dr *BAR* EN8 .... 276 E8
 MAL CM9 .... 293 C2
Warwick Gdns *GPK* RM2 .... 371 K3
 RAYL SS6 .... 381 C2
Warwick Gn *RAYL* SS6 ...... 381 H2
Warwick La *RAIN* RM13 ..... 390 A8
Warwick Pl *BRW* CM14 ..... 331 K6
 VGE SS16 .... 376 A7
Warwick Rd *BSF* CM23 ..... 174 C5
 COS CO15 .... 12 D5
 IPNE IP4 .... 3 K3
 PEND EN3 .... 325 C1
 RAIN RM13 .... 404 D2
 RAYL SS6 .... 381 C2
 RBSF CM22 .... 176 F3
 SOS SS1 .... 402 A5
Warwick Sq *CHLM/WR* CM1 .. 264 A7
Washford Gdns *COS* CO15 .. 12 D8
Washington Av *LAIN* SS15 .. 376 B5
Washington Rd *MAL* CM9 ... 292 F2 ⑥
Washington Rd *HAR* CO12 .. 143 H1 ⑥
 MAL CM9 .... 293 C2
Wash La *MAL* CM9 .... 270 C2
Wash Rd *LAIN* SS15 .... 376 D2
 RBRW/HUT CM13 .... 333 M7
The Wash *BUNT* SG9 .... 116 E6
Watchfield La *RAYL* SS6 .... 380 D2
Watch House Rd *GTDUN* CM6.. 151 M8
Watchouse Rd
 CHLM/WR CM2 .... 312 C1
Waterdene *CVI* SS8 .... 397 M6
The Waterfalls *VGE* SS16 .. 376 C8 ⑥
Waterford Rd *IP* IP1 .... 36 E1
 SBN/FI SS3 .... 402 E5
Waterfront Wk *BSDN* SS14 . 377 J2
Waterhale *SOS* SS1 .... 402 B2
Water Hall La *BRTR* CM7 ... 126 A5
Waterhoose Moor *HLWS* CM18.. 255 M4
Waterhouse St *CHLM/WR* CM1.. 16 C7
Water La *BRTR* CM7 .... 126 A8
 BRTR CM7 .... 156 D7
 BSF CM23 .... 174 A3
 BURES CO8 .... 101 M2
 COLW CO3 .... 162 D3
 GTDUN CM6 .... 149 K4
 HLWW/ROY CM19 .... 254 F7
 HSTD CO9 .... 100 B4
 HVHL CB9 .... 29 C6
 HVHL CB9 .... 47 K4
 HVHL CB9 .... 48 B5
 PUR RM19 .... 415 H1
 RCOLW CO6 .... 104 A3
 SAFWN CB10 .... 67 M3
 SAFWS CB11 .... 89 H2
 SAFWS CB11 .... 90 C2
 STSD CM24 .... 146 F5
 WAB EN9 .... 302 B5 ⑥
Waterloo Gdns *ROMW/RG* RM7.. 370 E6
Waterloo La *CHLM/WR* CM1 .. 17 H3
 IP IP1 .... 2 A1
 ROMW/RG RM7 .... 370 E5
 SBN/FI SS3 .... 402 E4
Watermans Wy *EPP* CM16 ... 281 H7
Watermeadow Cl *ERITH* DA8.. 414 C5 ⑥
Watermill Rd *K/T/MI* CO5 ... 186 F7
Waterside *RCOLE* CO7 ...... 220 F6
 STSD CM24 .... 146 F5 ⑥
Waterside Rd *BOC* CM0 ..... 274 A8
 RCFD SS4 .... 366 B6
Watersmeet *HLWW/ROY* CM19.. 255 J7
Waterson Rd *CDH/CHF* RM16.. 418 C1
Waterson V *CHLM/GWD* CM2.. 17 J8
Waterville Dr *VGE* SS16 .... 378 B7
Waterville Ms *COLS* CO2 ... 163 J8 ⑥
Wat Tyler Wy *BRWN* CM15 .. 354 E2
Watkins Cl *PIT* SS13 ...... 378 E2
Watkins Wy *SBN/FI* SS3 .... 403 G2
Watling La *GTDUN* CM6 ..... 92 A7
Watling St *GTDUN* CM6 ..... 92 M8
Watlington Rd *HLWE* CM17 .. 227 L7

SBF/HAD SS7 .... 397 J1
Watson Cl *SBN/FI* SS3 ..... 402 E4
 WTHK RM20 .... 416 B5
Watson Rd *COS* CO15 ...... 12 E6
Watts Cl *GTDUN* CM6 ...... 179 J7
 STDN SG11 .... 172 C1
Watts Crs *PUR* RM19 ...... 415 K1
Watts Rd *COLS* CO2 .... 190 C1
Wavell Av *COLS* CO2 .... 162 D7
Wavell Cl *BAR* EN8 .... 276 F7
 CHLM/WR CM1 .... 264 E3 ⑥
Waveney Dr *CHLM/WR* CM1 .. 264 D5
Waveney Rd *FX* IP11 .... 9 H4
 IP IP1 .... 36 F3
Waveney Ter *HVHL* CB9 .... 28 B4 ⑥
Waverley Crs *HARH* RM3 ... 352 D7
 WICKE SS11 .... 337 K8
Waverley Rd *LAIN* SS15 .... 376 F2 ⑥
 RAIN RM13 .... 404 C1
 SBF/HAD SS7 .... 379 K6
Wavertree Rd *SBF/HAD* SS7.. 379 J7
Waxham Av *FOS* CO13 ...... 198 F4
Waxwell Rd *HOC/HUL* SS5 .. 361 M1
The Wayback *SAFWN* CB10 .. 65 M1
Way Bank La *HSTD* CO9 .... 29 M5
Waycross Rd *UPMR* RM14 .. 372 F6
Wayfarer Gdns *BOC* CM0 ... 344 B6 ⑥
Wayfaring Gn *GRAYS* RM17 . 417 G2 ⑥
Wayletts *LAIN* SS15 .... 376 B4
 LOS SS9 .... 381 J5
Wayside *CHLM/WR* CM1 ..... 264 C5
Wayside Av *HCH* RM12 ..... 389 L1
Wayside Cl *ROM* RM1 ...... 371 C3
Wayside Gdns *DAGE* RM10 . 388 B4
Waytemore Rd *BSF* CM23 ... 173 M6
Weald Br *EPP* CM16 .... 281 M2
Weald Bridge Rd *EPP* CM16.. 281 M2
Weald Cl *BRW* CM14 .... 354 B4
Weald Hall La *EPP* CM16 ... 280 D5
Weald Park Wy *EPP* CM16 .. 353 M4
Weald Rd *BRW* CM14 .... 353 H2
The Weald *CVI* SS8 .... 397 M7
Weald Wy *ROMW/RG* RM7 .. 370 C6
Wear Dr *CHLM/WR* CM1 ..... 264 C5
Weare Gifford *SBN/FI* SS3 .. 402 D3
Weaver Cl *IP* IP1 .... 36 E3
Weaverdale *SBN/FI* SS3 .... 402 F2 ⑥
Weaverhead Cl *GTDUN* CM6.. 92 B8
Weaverhead La *GTDUN* CM6.. 92 B8
Weavers *VGE* SS16 .... 378 A7
Weavers Cl *BCAYW* CM11 ... 357 J1 ⑥
 COLW CO3 .... 162 A6
Weaversfield *WIT* CM8 ..... 184 D6
Weavers Gn *RCOLW* CO6 ... 132 E5
Weavers La *SUD* CO10 ..... 4 C6
Weavers Rw *HSTD* CO9 ..... 129 G2
Weaver St *BSF* CM23 ...... 173 K7
Webber Cl *ERITH* DA8 ..... 414 C4 ⑥
Webbs Ct *KESG* IP5 .... 39 K4 ⑦
Webbscroft Rd *DAGE* RM10 . 388 C3
Webb St *CHTY* IP2 .... 2 F9
Webster Cl *HCH* RM12 ..... 389 L2 ⑦
 HSTD CO9 .... 97 L3 ⑥
 WAB EN9 .... 302 B5 ⑥
Webster Pl *ING* CM4 ...... 335 M1
Webster Rd *SLH/COR* SS17 . 409 M1
Websters Wy *RAYL* SS6 .... 380 E1
Weddell Rd *HVHL* CB9 ..... 28 D5
Wedds Wy *SBN/FI* SS3 ..... 385 J7
Wedgewood Cl *EPP* CM16 .. 304 B2
Wedgewood Dr *COLN* CO4 .. 10 A1
 HLWE CM17 .... 256 F4
Wedlake Cl *EMPK* RM11 .... 371 M8 ⑥
Wednesbury Gdns *HARH* RM3.. 353 C8
Wednesbury Gn *HARH* RM3 . 353 C8
Wednesbury Rd *HARH* RM3 . 353 C8
Wedow Rd *GTDUN* CM6 ..... 92 B8
Weeley By-pass Rd *RCOS* CO16.. 195 M2
Weeley Rd *RCOLE* CO7 ..... 195 G6
 RCOS CO16 .... 196 D7
Weelkes Cl *SLH/COR* SS17 .. 394 D8
Weel Rd *CVI* SS8 .... 413 L1
Weggs Willow *COLN* CO4 ... 11 K7
Weight Rd *CHLM/GWD* CM2.. 17 K3
Weir Farm Rd *RAYL* SS6 ... 380 D3
Weir Gdns *RAYL* SS6 ...... 380 D3
Weir La *COLS* CO2 .... 191 J4
 K/T/MI CO5 .... 191 M3
Weir Pond Rd *RCFD* SS4 ... 383 G1
Weir Wynd *BCAYW* CM12..... 357 H2
Welbeck Cl *FX* IP11 .... 84 E6 ⑥
 HOC/HUL SS5 .... 363 G7
Welbeck Dr *MAL* CM9 ...... 376 B7
Welbeck Ri *VGE* SS16 ...... 376 B7 ⑥
Welbeck Rd *CVI* SS8 .... 413 H1
Welch Cl *SOSN* SS2 .... 383 M8
Welcome Av *FOS* CO13 ..... 198 F4
Weller Gv *CHESW* EN7 ..... 276 B8 ⑥
Wellesley *EPP* CM16 ...... 255 H8
Wellesley Rd *BRW* CM14 ... 354 D2
 COLW CO3 .... 10 A9
 COS CO15 .... 12 F6
 IPNE IP4 .... 3 M5
Well Fld *CHLM/WR* CM1 .... 287 H2
 HSTD CO9 .... 129 G3
Wellfields *LOU* IG10 ...... 327 H5
Wellfield Wy *FOS* CO13 .... 198 E4
Well-green Cl *SAFWS* CB11 . 65 M4 ⑥
Wellingbury *SBF/HAD* SS7 .. 379 K6 ⑥
Wellington Av *HOC/HUL* SS5.. 361 L2
 WOS/PRIT SS0 .... 400 B2
Wellington Cl *BRTR* CM7 ... 155 K7
 CHLM/WR CM1 .... 263 L6
 DAGE RM10 .... 388 D6 ⑥
Wellington Dr *DAGE* RM10 . 388 D6
Wellington Hl *LOU* IG10 ... 326 C2
Wellingtonia Av *ABR/ST* RM4.. 351 M4
Wellington Ms *BCAYW* CM12.. 335 G6

Wellington Pl *BRW* CM14 .. 354 D6
Wellington Rd *EPP* CM16 .. 281 H7
 HAR CO12 .... 7 J3
 MAL CM9 .... 293 C3
 RAYL SS6 .... 362 A8
 TIL RM18 .... 418 B7
The Wellingtons *BOC* CM0 . 320 E8 ⑥
Wellington St *COLS* CO2 ... 10 B9
 IP IP1 .... 2 B2
 RCOLE CO7 .... 221 G5 ⑦
Well La *BRWN* CM15 .... 332 A5
 CDH/CHF RM16 .... 416 F6
 CHLM/GWD CM2 .... 312 C1
 HLW CM20 .... 14 E3
 HLWW/ROY CM19 .... 14 E5
 ING CM4 .... 335 M2
 K/T/MI CO5 .... 188 B5
 RCHLM CM3 .... 290 D5
 SUD CO10 .... 31 J4
Well Md *BCAYW* CM12 ...... 357 K4 ⑥
Wellmeads *CHLM/GWD* CM2 .. 17 G7
Wells Av *SOSN* SS2 .... 382 E5
Wells Cl *IPNE* IP4 .... 3 J4
Wells Ct *CHLM/WR* CM1 .... 264 E6
 GTDUN CM6 .... 178 D2 ⑥
Wellsfield *RAYL* SS6 ...... 361 M7
Wells Gdns *RAIN* RM13 .... 389 G5
Wells Hall Rd *SUD* CO10 ... 55 K7
Well Side *RCOLW* CO6 ...... 159 M8
Wells Rd *COL* CO1 .... 10 F6
Well's St *CHLM/WR* CM1 ... 16 F2
Wellstead Gdns *WOS/PRIT* SS0.. 382 C8
Well St *RCOLE* CO7 .... 220 F4
Wellstye Gn *BSDN* SS14 ... 377 M3
Welshwood Park Rd *COLN* CO4.. 163 M1
Welsummer Wy *BAR* EN8 ... 276 F7
Wembley Av *RCHLM* CM3 ... 319 G3
Wendene *VGE* SS16 .... 378 A7
Wenden Rd *SAFWS* CB11 ... 65 J3
Wendon Cl *SS4 .... 363 K7 ⑥
Wendover Gdns
 RBRW/HUT CM13 .... 355 J3
Wendover Wy *HCH* RM12 ... 389 K4 ⑦
Wendy Cl *EN* EN1 .... 324 A8
 RIPS/CAP IP9 .... 82 A4
Wenham Dr *WOS/PRIT* SS0 . 20 C2
Wenham Rd *RIPW* IP8 ...... 56 E4
Wenlock Rd *RCOS* CO16 .... 196 A5
Wenlocks La *ING* CM4 ..... 308 F5
Wennington Gn *RAIN* RM13 . 404 F5
Wennington Rd *RAIN* RM13 . 404 C3
Wensley Av *WFD* IG8 ...... 348 B8
Wensley Cl *CRW* RM5 ...... 351 H6
Wensley Rd *SBF/HAD* SS7 .. 380 C7
Wentford Vw *SUD* CO10 .... 31 J2
Wentworth Cl *RCHLM* CM3 . 238 C7
Wentworth Crs *BRTR* CM7 . 155 G6
Wentworth Dr *BSF* CM23 .. 173 L5
 FX IP11 .... 85 K7
 RIPW IP8 .... 57 K1
Wentworth Mdw *MAL* CM9 . 293 C1
Wentworth Pl
 CDH/CHF RM16 .... 407 L8 ⑥
Wentworth Rd *SOSN* SS2 .. 383 H8
Wentworth Wy *RAIN* RM13 . 404 C1
Wesel Av *FX* IP11 .... 8 B3
Wesley Av *COLN* CO4 ...... 11 K6
Wesley End Rd *HSTD* CO9 .. 49 L8
Wesley Gdns *BCAYW* CM12 . 335 G6 ⑥
Wesley Rd *SOS* SS1 .... 21 K7
Wessem Rd *CVI* SS8 .... 398 C5 ⑥
Westall Rd *LOU* IG10 ...... 327 J5
West Av *CHLM/WR* CM1 .... 264 A6
 COS CO15 .... 12 E4
 HOC/HUL SS5 .... 339 K8
 RCHLM CM3 .... 318 F2
 VGE SS16 .... 375 M7
West Beech Av *WICKE* SS11.. 359 L4
West Beech *WICKE* SS11 ... 359 M4
West Belvedere *RCHLM* CM3.. 291 G4
Westborough Rd
 WOS/PRIT SS0 .... 400 C1
Westbourne Rd *HOC/HUL* SS5.. 363 H4 ⑥
 SBF/HAD SS7 .... 380 E6
Westbourne Dr *BRW* CM14 . 354 A5
Westbourne Gdns
 BCAYW CM12 .... 335 J6 ⑥
Westbourne Gv
 CHLM/GWD CM2 .... 288 E4
 WOS/PRIT SS0 .... 382 E4
Westbourne Rd *IP* IP1 .... 37 G2
West Bowers Rd *MAL* CM9 . 267 K7
Westbury *BAR* EN8 .... 300 E2 ⑥
 RCFD SS4 .... 363 K7
Westbury Cl *RCOLW* CO6 .. 160 E6
Westbury Dr *BRW* CM14 ... 354 C4
Westbury La *BKHH* IG9 .... 348 D3
Westbury Ri *HLWE* CM17 .. 256 E4
Westbury Rd *BKHH* IG9 .... 348 D3
 BRW CM14 .... 354 D2
 FOS CO13 .... 198 B6
 IPNE IP4 .... 38 C3
 SOSN SS2 .... 21 M1
Westbury Ter *UPMR* RM14 . 390 F1
Westbush Cl *HOD* EN11 .... 253 G2
West Cha *MAL* CM9 .... 269 G4
 MAL CM9 .... 317 M2
Westcliff Av *WOS/PRIT* SS0.. 20 C7
Westcliff Gdns *CVI* SS8 ... 398 F8
Westcliff Pde *WOS/PRIT* SS0.. 20 C7
Westcliff Park Dr *WOS/PRIT* SS0.. 20 A3
West Cloister *BCAYE* CM11 . 357 J1 ⑦
West Cl *HOD* EN11 .... 253 H3
 RAIN RM13 .... 404 C2
Westcott Rd *RCOS* CO16 ... 223 L5
West Crs *CVI* SS8 .... 398 E8
West Cft *BCAYE* CM11 ..... 357 J2 ⑦
Westcroft Cl *PEND* EN3 ... 324 D2 ⑥
West Cft *BROX* EN10 ...... 253 H7 ⑥
West Dene Dr *HARH* RM3 .. 352 E6
West Dock Rd *HAR* CO12 .. 112 F6
West Dr *BRTR* CM7 .... 95 J8
West End La *HAR* CO12 .... 143 J7
Westend La *HVHL* CB9 ..... 29 J1
West End Rd *BROX* EN10 ... 276 A3
 IP IP1 .... 2 C6
 K/T/MI CO5 .... 214 M4

Westerdale CHLM/WR CM1.... 264 E4
Westerfield Rd IP IP1.... 37 L3
  IPNE IP4.... 3 G2
Westergreen Meadow
  BRTR CM7.... 182 F2
Westerings RCHLM CM3.... 315 G1
The Westerings
  CHLM/GWD CM2.... 289 G6
  HOC/HUL SS5.... 362 F6
  RCOLW CO6.... 104 A1
Westerland Av CVI SS8.... 398 E7
The Westerlings BRTR CM7.... 185 M5
Western Approaches LOS SS9.... 382 B4
Western Av BRW CM14.... 354 D2
  DAGE RM10.... 388 D5
  EPP CM16.... 304 A4
  FX IP11.... 85 L7
  GPK IP11.... 371 K2
  HVHL CB9.... 27 M2
Western CI IPNE IP4.... 39 G7
  WIT CM8.... 184 F8
Western Esp CVI SS8.... 413 J1
  WOS/PRIT SS0.... 20 C8
Western La WIT CM8.... 184 F8
Western Ms BCAYW CM12.... 357 H1
Western Prom RCOLE CO7.... 220 E6
Western Rd BCAYW CM12.... 357 H1
  BCAYW CM12.... 357 G2
  BOC CM0.... 344 C7
  BRW CM14.... 354 D3
  LOS SS9.... 399 H2
  RAYL SS6.... 380 C2
  RCOLE CO7.... 220 F5
  ROM RM1.... 370 F5
  SBF/HAD SS7.... 380 F5
  WAB EN9.... 277 M2
  WIT CM8.... 185 G8
Western's End MGTR CO11.... 108 E3
Westfield HLWS CM18.... 255 M4
  LAIN SS15.... 376 B3
  SUD CO10.... 31 H5
Westfield Av CHLM/WR CM1.... 264 B7
Westfield CI BAR EN8.... 301 G3
  BSF CM23.... 173 M3
  PEND EN3.... 324 F5
  RAYL SS6.... 361 J6
  WICKE SS11.... 360 A3
Westfield Rd DR RCOLW CO6.... 158 A8
Westfield Park Dr WFD IG8.... 348 F7
Westfield Rd BSF CM23.... 173 M3
  HOD EN11.... 253 G4
West Flds SAFWS CB11.... 65 M3
Westgate BSDN SS14.... 18 E6
West Ga MLW CM20.... 15 K4
Westgate St IP IP1.... 2 E4
  SUD CO10.... 34 D1
West Gn SBF/HAD SS7.... 379 J8
West Gv WFD IG8.... 348 D7
West Hanningfield Rd
  CHLM/GWD CM2.... 312 E5
West Hayes RBSF CM22.... 202 B8
West Hill Rd HOD EN11.... 253 G5
Westholme Rd IP IP1.... 37 H2
West Hook VGE SS16.... 376 A3
West House Est BOC CM0.... 320 D7
Westlake Av PIT SS13.... 378 F5
Westlake Crs RCOLE CO7.... 192 B1
Westland Av EMPK RM11.... 371 M8
Westland Vw
  CDH/CHF RM16.... 407 H6
West Lawn IPNE IP4.... 38 C3
Westlea CI BROX EN10.... 277 G4
Westlea Rd BROX EN10.... 277 C3
Westleigh Av LOS SS9.... 399 L1
Westleton Wy FX IP11.... 84 E9
West Ley BOC CM0.... 344 D6
Westley La SAFWB CB10.... 43 L6
Westley Rd VGE SS16.... 394 D1
West Lodge Rd COLW CO3.... 162 E5
Westlyn CI RAIN RM13.... 404 D2
West Malling Wy HCH SS8.... 389 J4
Westman Rd CVI SS8.... 398 F8
Westmarch RCHLM CM3.... 339 K5
West Mayne LAIN SS15.... 376 B5
Westmeade CI CHESW EN7.... 300 C1
Westmede BARK/HLT IG6.... 349 K7
  VGE SS16.... 376 D7
West Mill Gn RIPS/CAP IP9.... 78 E5
Westminster CI IPNE IP4.... 38 C6
Westminster Dr HOC/HUL SS5.... 362 D5
  WOS/PRIT SS0.... 400 C1
Westminster Gdns
  BRTR CM7.... 155 J7
Westmoor Gdns PEND EN3.... 324 E4
Westmoor Rd PEND EN3.... 324 E4
Westmoreland Av
  EMPK RM11.... 371 K5
Westmorland CI MGTR CO11.... 109 J8
Westmorland Rd FX IP11.... 85 L6
Weston Av WTHK RM20.... 416 A1
Weston CI RBRW/HUT CM13.... 355 K1
Weston Rd COLS CO2.... 163 J7
  SOS SS1.... 21 G7
West Park Av BCAYW CM12.... 335 H8
West Park Crs BCAYW CM12.... 335 H8
West Park Dr BCAYW CM12.... 357 H1
West Park HI BRW CM14.... 354 D4
West Point Pl CVI SS8.... 397 K8
West Rdg BCAYW CM12.... 357 H3
Westridge Rd COS SS15.... 224 B5
West Rd BSF CM23.... 173 M5
  COS SS15.... 250 C3
  HLW CM20.... 227 H7
  HSTD CO9.... 128 F2
  IPSE IP3.... 59 M3
  ROMW/RG RM7.... 370 E7
  SAFWS CB11.... 65 L3
  SBN/FI SS3.... 402 E4
  SBW CM21.... 200 C8
  SOCK/AV RM15.... 406 C1
  STSD CM24.... 146 F6
  WOS/PRIT SS0.... 20 B3
Westropps SUD CO10.... 34 D6
West Side BROX EN10.... 276 F5
West Sq MAL CM9.... 269 G8
West Station Yd MAL CM9.... 292 F2
West Stockwell St COL CO1.... 10 C7
West St GRAYS RM17.... 417 H3

HAR CO12.... 7 K3
K/T/MI CO5.... 192 A3
LOS SS9.... 399 M3
MAL CM9.... 272 C2
RCFD SS4.... 382 F1
RCOLE CO7.... 192 C3
RCOLW CO6.... 185 M2
WOS/PRIT SS0.... 20 D2
WOTN CO14.... 199 K3
West Thurrock Wy WTHK RM20.. 416 B1
West Vw LOU IG10.... 327 C5
West View CI COLN CO4.... 135 J8
  RAIN RM13.... 404 D1
West View Dr RAYL SS6.... 380 C2
Westward Deals HVHL CB9.... 29 J1
Westwater SBF/HAD SS7.... 379 J7
West Wy CHLM/WR CM1.... 16 B8
  COLW CO3.... 10 A4
  RCHLM CM3.... 339 K5
West Wy WAB EN9.... 325 J1
Westwood Av BRW CM14.... 354 B5
  IP IP1.... 37 H3
West Wood CI SBF/HAD SS7.... 380 D7
Westwood Dr K/T/MI CO5.... 245 M5
Westwood Gdns SBF/HAD SS7.... 380 E7
West Wood HI COLN CO4.... 162 C1
Westwood La CVI SS8.... 398 C8
West Yd HSTD CO9.... 128 F3
Wetherfield STSD CM24.... 146 E4
Wetherland VGE SS16.... 18 D8
Wetherly CI HLWE CM17.... 227 K8
Wethersfield Rd RAYL SS6.... 361 H8
Wethersfield Rd BRTR CM7.... 125 M4
  COLS CO2.... 191 H3
  HSTD CO9.... 97 K2
Wethersfield Wy WICKE SS11.... 360 C6
Wet La COLN CO4.... 104 F5
Wetzlar CI COLS CO2.... 163 J7
Wexford Rd IP IP1.... 36 E1
Weybourne St SOSN SS2.... 383 J8
Weybourne Gdns SOSN SS2.... 383 J8
Weybridge Wk SBN/FI SS3.... 402 E2
Weydale SLH/COR SS17.... 395 J6
Weylond Rd BTR RM8.... 388 A2
Weymarks LAIN SS15.... 376 E4
Weymouth CI COS SS15.... 250 E3
Weymouth Rd CHLM/WR CM1.... 264 F5
  IPNE IP4.... 3 M4
Whadden Cha ING CM4.... 310 B8
Whalebone Av CHDH RM6.... 370 A6
Whalebone Cnr COLN CO4.... 106 A4
Whalebone Gv CHDH RM6.... 370 A6
Whalebone La North
  CHDH RM6.... 350 F8
Whalebone La South
  BCTR RM8.... 370 A7
Whaley Rd COLN CO4.... 11 J7
Wharf CI SLH/COR SS17.... 409 L2
Wharfedale Rd IP IP1.... 37 H2
Wharf La BURES CO8.... 102 A3
Wharf Rd BROX EN10.... 277 G4
  BRW CM14.... 354 D4
  BSF CM23.... 174 A5
  CHLM/GWD CM2.... 17 K4
  GRAYS RM17.... 417 G3
  MAL CM9.... 270 A7
  PEND EN3.... 324 F8
  SLH/COR SS17.... 395 L7
  SLH/COR SS17.... 409 M4
Wharley Hook HLWS CM18.... 256 A6
Wheat Cft BSF CM23.... 173 M7
Wheatear PI BCAYE CM11.... 357 K2
Wheatfield Rd COLW CO3.... 161 L5
Wheatfields HLWE CM17.... 227 L5
  PEND EN3.... 324 F3
  RCFD SS4.... 364 E7
Wheatfield Wy CHLM/WR CM1.... 16 D2
  VGE SS16.... 376 B7
Wheatlands RCOLE CO7.... 165 G5
Wheatley Av BRTR CM7.... 155 K8
Wheatley Rd EMPK RM11.... 371 L5
  RCFD SS4.... 363 L7
  SBW CM21.... 227 K2
Wheatley Rd SLH/COR SS17.... 395 J6
Wheatley Terrace Rd
  ERITH DA8.... 414 A3
Wheaton Rd WIT CM8.... 239 J1
Wheatsheaf CI HLW CM20.... 6 A4
Wheatsheaf La MGTR CO11.... 110 E8
Wheatsheaf Rd ROM RM1.... 371 G6
Wheeler CI COLN CO4.... 163 M5
Wheelers EPP CM16.... 304 B1
Wheelers CI WAB EN9.... 277 M2
Wheelers Farm Gdns
  EPP CM16.... 281 J6
Wheeler's HI RCHLM CM3.... 235 K5
Wheelers La BRW CM14.... 331 J6
  SLH/COR SS17.... 395 L6
Wheel Farm Dr DAGE RM10.... 388 D2
Wheelwrights CI BSF CM23.... 173 K7
The Wheelwrights FX IP11.... 84 D5
  SOSN SS2.... 383 H6
Whernside Av CVI SS8.... 398 D6
Wherstead Rd CHTY IP2.... 2 F9
Whinchat CI CHTY IP2.... 36 E8
Whinfield Av HAR CO12.... 143 G2
Whinhams Wy BCAYW CM12.... 335 G8
The Whinneys KESC IP5.... 39 L3
Whinyard Wy FX IP11.... 85 L6
Whist Av WICKE SS11.... 360 A2
Whistler Ri SBN/FI SS3.... 403 H3
Whitakers Wy LOU IG10.... 327 G3
Whitbreads Farm La
  RCHLM CM3.... 208 E7
Whitby Rd BOC CM0.... 344 C1
  IPNE IP4.... 38 A3
Whitchurch Rd HARH RM3.... 352 F5
Whitcroft VGE SS16.... 376 D8
Whitebarn La DAGE RM10.... 388 B8
White Barns RCHLM CM3.... 207 J5
Whitebarns La BUNT SG9.... 116 B4
Whitebeam CI
  CHLM/GWD CM2.... 288 A4
Whitebeam Dr
  SOCK/AV RM15.... 406 D1

White Bear STSD CM24.... 146 F3
Whiteditch La SAFWS CB11.... 89 G1
White Elm Rd RCHLM CM3.... 315 H1
Whitefields Rd BAR EN8.... 276 D8
Whitefriars Crs WOS/PRIT SS0.... 400 D4
Whitefriars Wy COLW CO3.... 162 B6
Whitegate Rd RCOLE CO7.... 221 H5
  SOS SS1.... 21 H6
White Gates HCH RM12.... 389 K1
Whitehall CI CHIG IG7.... 350 B4
  COLS CO2.... 163 K7
White Hall CI SUD CO10.... 35 M8
Whitehall Rd WAB EN9.... 277 M2
Whitehall Ct WIT CM8.... 239 H1
Whitehall La BKHH IG9.... 348 B5
  BSF CM23.... 174 A2
  ERITH DA8.... 414 A6
  GRAYS RM17.... 417 K3
  RCOS CO16.... 168 D8
  SLH/COR SS17.... 395 K4
Whitehall Rd BSF CM23.... 173 M2
  COLS CO2.... 163 K8
  GRAYS RM17.... 417 K1
White Hall Rd SBN/FI SS3.... 385 J7
Whitehands CI HOD EN11.... 253 G5
White Hart La HOC/HUL SS5.... 362 F6
  RCOLW CO6.... 133 M6
  ROMW/RG RM7.... 370 B1
Whitehills Rd LOU IG10.... 327 H5
White Horse Av HSTD CO9.... 128 E3
White Horse CI FX IP11.... 85 K7
White Horse HI RIPS/CAP IP9.... 79 L2
White Horse La MAL CM9.... 293 G1
  SAFWS CB11.... 89 H2
  WIT CM8.... 212 A8
White Horse Rd HVHL CB9.... 29 H1
  RCOLE CO7.... 107 L2
  RIPS/CAP IP9.... 78 C2
White House Cha RAYL SS6.... 380 F3
Whitehouse Crs
  CHLM/GWD CM2.... 17 M7
Whitehouse HI MAL CM9.... 243 H4
Whitehouse La RCOLW CO6.... 133 L8
  SUD CO10.... 52 C2
Whitehouse Mdw LOS SS9.... 382 B5
Whitehouse Rd GTDUN CM6.... 152 A6
White House Rd LOS SS9.... 382 A5
Whitehouse Rd RCHLM CM3.... 339 L3
Whitelands SAFWN CB10.... 308 E7
Whitelands CI WICKE SS11.... 359 M2
Whitelands Wy HARH RM3.... 371 L1
White Lodge Crs RCOS CO16.... 197 K2
White Lyons Rd BRW CM14.... 354 D4
White Md CHLM/WR CM1.... 264 C1
White Post Fld SBW CM21.... 227 L1
Whitesbridge La ING CM4.... 311 L2
Whiteshott VGE SS16.... 377 H7
Whiteshot Wy SAFWN CB10.... 66 A1
Whites La RCHLM CM3.... 208 F5
Whitesmith Dr BCAYW CM12.... 334 F8
White St GTDUN CM6.... 178 E3
White Stubbs La BROX EN10.... 276 A1
Whitethorn Gdns
  CHLM/GWD CM2.... 288 D4
  EMPK RM11.... 371 K6
Whitethorn Rd IPSE IP3.... 60 A2
White Tree Ct RCHLM CM3.... 339 J5
Whitewaits HLW CM20.... 255 M2
Whiteways BCAYE CM11.... 357 L1
  CVI SS8.... 413 L1
  LOS SS9.... 382 A5
Whiteways Ct WIT CM8.... 211 M8
Whitewebbs La ENC/FH EN2.... 300 A7
Whitewell Rd COLS CO2.... 10 C9
Whitfields SLH/COR SS17.... 410 A1
Whit Hern Ct BAR EN8.... 300 D2
Whitland CI CHTY IP2.... 58 B3
Whitley Rd HOD EN11.... 253 J3
Whitlock Dr HSTD CO9.... 73 G2
Whitmore Av CDH/CHF RM16.... 407 J5
  HARH RM3.... 371 M2
Whitmore CI CDH/CHF RM16.... 408 F4
Whitmore Ct BSDN SS14.... 377 M2
Whitmore Crs CHLM/GWD CM2.... 265 J8
Whitmore Wy BSDN SS14.... 19 H4
Whittaker Wy K/T/MI CO5.... 245 J4
Whittingham Av SOSN SS2.... 401 M1
Whittingstall Rd HOD EN11.... 253 J8
Whittington Rd
  RBRW/HUT CM13.... 333 L8
Whittington Wy BSF CM23.... 173 M8
Whittle Rd CHTY IP2.... 37 G5
Whitton Leyer EPP CM16.... 36 D1
Whitworth CI CHTY IP2.... 57 L1
Whybrews SLH/COR SS17.... 410 A1
Whybridge CI RAIN RM13.... 388 F2
Whytewaters VGE SS16.... 378 A8
Whyverne CI CHLM/WR CM1.... 264 F5
Wick Beech Av WICKE SS11.... 359 M4
Wick Cha SOSN SS2.... 401 M2
Wick Crs WICKW SS12.... 359 M6
Wick Dr WICKW SS12.... 359 L4
Wicken Rd SAFWS CB11.... 88 A2
Wickets Wy BARK/HLT IG6.... 350 A7
Wick Farm Rd BOC CM0.... 296 D3
Wickfield Ash CHLM/WR CM1.... 263 L5
Wickford Av PIT SS13.... 378 B5
Wickford Dr HARH RM3.... 353 G6
Wickford Rd RCHLM CM3.... 339 H3
  WOS/PRIT SS0.... 20 C7
Wick Gln BCAYW CM12.... 335 G7
Wicklow Md SBW CM21.... 227 M2
Wickham Bishop Rd
  RCHLM CM3.... 238 E7
Wickhambrook Ct FX IP11.... 8 D2
Wickham CI EN EN1.... 324 C5
Wickham Crs CHLM/WR CM1.... 264 A5
Wickham Hall La WIT CM8.... 239 K8
Wickham PI VGE SS16.... 19 J8
Wickham Rd CDH/CHF RM16.... 408 D7
  COLW CO3.... 162 C6
  WIT CM8.... 239 C3
Wickham's Cha RCHLM CM3.... 315 K1
Wickhay LAIN SS15.... 18 C7
Wick La HAR CO12.... 143 J2
  K/T/MI CO5.... 192 E8
  RCOLE CO7.... 136 C3

RCOS CO16.... 195 K8
  WICKE SS11.... 359 M4
Wicklow Av CHLM/WR CM1.... 263 L5
Wicklow Rd IP IP1.... 36 E1
Wickmead CI SOSN SS2.... 401 M1
Wick Rd BOC CM0.... 344 E7
  COLN CO4.... 105 K1
  COLS CO2.... 191 L1
  RCOLE CO7.... 195 J6
Widbrook BRWN CM15.... 308 D8
Wid CI RBRW/HUT CM13.... 333 L7
Widecombe CI HARH RM3.... 371 L1
Widford Cha CHLM/GWD CM2.... 288 A4
Widford CI CHLM/GWD CM2.... 16 C9
Widford Gv CHLM/GWD CM2.... 288 A4
Widford Park Pl
  CHLM/GWD CM2.... 16 C9
Widford Rd CHLM/GWD CM2.... 288 A4
Widgeon CI CHTY IP2.... 37 G8
Widgeon Pl K/T/MI CO5.... 213 K1
Widgeon Rd ERITH DA8.... 414 C4
Widgeons PIT SS13.... 378 D1
Widleybrook La BRTR CM7.... 95 M8
Widworthy Hayes
  RBRW/HUT CM13.... 355 J2
Wigborough Rd COLS CO2.... 216 F1
  K/T/MI CO5.... 217 K7
Wigeon CI RBRW/HUT CM13.... 333 L7
Wigeon CI BRTR CM7.... 182 D6
Wiggin's La BCAYW CM12.... 356 F4
  BCAYW CM12.... 356 F5
Wigley Bush La BRW CM14.... 353 M3
Wigmore CI CHTY IP2.... 58 A2
Wignall St MGTR CO11.... 108 A8
Wigton Rd HARH RM3.... 352 F5
Wigton Wy HARH RM3.... 352 F5
Wilberforce St IP IP1.... 2 B3
Wilbye CI COLS CO2.... 162 C7
Wilde CI TIL RM18.... 418 C6
Wilding Dr KESG IP5.... 39 L4
Wilding Rd RIPW IP8.... 57 K2
Wilfred Av RAIN RM13.... 404 B3
Wilkes Rd RBRW/HUT CM13.... 333 L7
Wilkin Ct COLW CO3.... 162 B7
Wilkin Dr K/T/MI CO5.... 214 E6
Wilkinsons Md
  CHLM/GWD CM2.... 265 H7
Willett Rd COLS CO2.... 162 C8
Willetts Fld SAFWN CB10.... 69 H8
William Booth Wy FX IP11.... 84 E8
William Boys CI COLN CO4.... 11 M4
William CI CRW RM5.... 370 D1
  RCOLE CO7.... 164 D7
William Dr COS SS15.... 12 C7
William Groom Av HAR CO12.... 143 H1
William Rd PIT SS13.... 378 F7
Williamson CI SLH/COR SS17.... 395 C6
Williams Rd CHLM/WR CM1.... 264 C2
William St GRAYS RM17.... 417 K3
  IP IP1.... 2 A4
William's Wk COL CO1.... 10 C7
Willingale Av RAYL SS6.... 361 M8
Willingale CI
  RBRW/HUT CM13.... 333 M8
  CHONG CM5.... 260 B8
  LOU IG10.... 327 K3
The Willingales LAIN SS15.... 376 B5
Willingale Rd BRTR CM7.... 155 L7
Willinghall CI WAB EN9.... 301 L2
Willingham Wy COLN CO4.... 163 M4
Willmott Rd SOSN SS2.... 382 E5
Willoughby Av K/T/MI CO5.... 245 L5
Willoughby CI BROX EN10.... 276 F1
Willoughby Dr
  CHLM/GWD CM2.... 289 G1
  RAIN RM13.... 388 F6
Willoughby Rd CHTY IP2.... 2 D7
Willoughby's La BRTR CM7.... 155 K3
Willow Av FOS CO13.... 198 E5
  RCOS CO16.... 249 J5
Willowbank CHLM/GWD CM2.... 288 C8
Willow CI BKHH IG9.... 348 E4
  BOC CM0.... 344 C5
  BRWN CM15.... 332 E2
  BSF CM23.... 173 M3
  CHLM/WR CM1.... 264 C2
  CVI SS8.... 398 A8
  HCH RM12.... 389 J2
  HOC/HUL SS5.... 363 G5
  HVHL CB9.... 27 L2
  LOS SS9.... 381 M5
  RBRW/HUT CM13.... 333 M8
  RCOLE CO7.... 135 L5
  RCOLE CO7.... 220 E5
Willow Crs RCHLM CM3.... 238 B8
Willowcroft Rd IP IP1.... 37 H1
Willowdene BAR EN8.... 276 F7
  BRWN CM15.... 332 A7
  HSTD CO9.... 97 L1
Willowdene Ct BRW CM14.... 354 D5
Willow Dr RAYL SS6.... 361 K7
Willowfield HLWS CM18.... 15 L8
Willowfields LAIN SS15.... 376 D3
Willow Gn ING CM4.... 310 C7
Willow Gv RCHLM CM3.... 339 H2
  RCOLW CO6.... 104 A1
Willow Hall La MGTR CO11.... 140 E3
Willowhill SLH/COR SS17.... 394 F6
Willowmead BCAYE CM11.... 336 D6
  CHIG IG7.... 350 A2
Willow Md SBW CM21.... 227 M2
Willow Pk RCOLW CO6.... 160 F6
Willow Pl HLWE CM17.... 257 C7
Willow Rd EN EN1.... 324 A5
  ERITH DA8.... 414 B5
Willow Springs BSF CM23.... 173 L3
The Willows BCAYE CM11.... 357 L4
  COLS CO2.... 163 H8
  GRAYS RM17.... 417 J3
  RCHLM CM3.... 265 M3
  SAFWN CB10.... 22 E8
  SBF/HAD SS7.... 379 J7
  SOS SS1.... 402 B2

Willow Tree Wy RCOLW CO6.... 130 C5
Willow Wk HOC/HUL SS5.... 363 G5
  K/T/MI CO5.... 214 D4
  RCFD SS4.... 364 E3
  SBF/HAD SS7.... 380 E8
  UPMR RM14.... 372 F8
Willow Wy COS SS15.... 250 B4
  HAR CO12.... 143 G1
  HARH RM3.... 353 J7
  HSTD CO9.... 128 E2
Will's Ayley La SAFWN CB10.... 66 F1
Wills HI SLH/COR SS17.... 394 E8
Wilmington Rd COLN CO4.... 11 K1
Wilmot Gn RBRW/HUT CM13.... 354 D7
Wilmslow Dr RIPW IP8.... 57 K1
Wilmslowe CVI SS8.... 398 E6
Wilrich Av CVI SS8.... 398 E8
Wilshire Av CHLM/GWD CM2.... 265 G8
Wilsman Rd SOCK/AV RM15.... 391 K8
Wilsner PIT SS13.... 378 D4
Wilson CI BSF CM23.... 174 A6
  RCOLE CO7.... 192 B1
Wilson Marriage Rd COLN CO4.... 11 J3
Wilson Rd RIPW IP8.... 57 J2
  WOS/PRIT SS0.... 20 E8
Wilson's La RCOLW CO6.... 159 M8
Wilthorne Gdns DAGE RM10.... 388 C6
Wilton CI BSF CM23.... 174 C4
Wilton Dr CRW RM5.... 351 K4
Wiltshire Av EMPK RM11.... 372 A4
Wimarc Crs RAYL SS6.... 361 J7
Wimbish End PIT SS13.... 378 C5
Wimbish Wk SAFWN CB10.... 90 F1
Wimborne Av IPSE IP3.... 38 E7
Wimborne CI BKHH IG9.... 348 D3
  SBW CM21.... 227 L1
Wimborne Rd SOSN SS2.... 21 J4
Wimbourne LAIN SS15.... 376 B4
Wimbourne Gdns FOS CO13.... 199 C4
Wimhurst CI HOC/HUL SS5.... 362 F4
Wimpole CI KESG IP5.... 39 C5
Wimpole Rd COL CO1.... 163 J5
Winbrook CI RAYL SS6.... 380 F3
Winbrook Rd RAYL SS6.... 380 F3
Wincanton CI IPNE IP4.... 38 B2
Wincanton Rd HARH RM3.... 352 E4
Wincelow Hall Rd SAFWN CB10.... 68 E2
Winchcombe Cl LOS SS9.... 381 M8
Winchelsea Dr CHLM/GWD CM2.. 288 A4
Winchelsea PI RCOLE CO7.... 221 C3
Winchester Av UPMR RM14.... 373 G8
Winchester CI BSF CM23.... 173 L7
  LOS SS9.... 382 A4
Winchester Gdns LAIN SS15.... 376 D2
Winchester Rd COLS CO2.... 163 H6
  FOS CO13.... 199 H6
Winchester Wy CHTY IP2.... 58 A3
Winch Vw EPP CM16.... 304 C1
Winckford CI RCHLM CM3.... 235 J5
Wincoat CI SBF/HAD SS7.... 379 K8
Wincoat Dr SBF/HAD SS7.... 379 J8
Windermere Av HCH RM12.... 389 H4
  HOC/HUL SS5.... 361 L1
Windermere CI IPSE IP3.... 59 J3
Windermere Dr BRTR CM7.... 182 D5
Windermere Rd BRTR CM7.... 182 D4
  COS SS15.... 224 D5
  FX IP11.... 85 L6
  SBF/HAD SS7.... 379 M4
  SOS SS1.... 21 L5
  SUD CO10.... 5 G5
Windham Rd SUD CO10.... 5 J5
Windhill BSF CM23.... 173 M5
Wind HI CHONG CM5.... 258 B7
Windhill Old Rd BSF CM23.... 173 M4
Winding HI MHAD SG10.... 172 B7
Winding Piece RIPS/CAP IP9.... 78 B2
Windmill CI COLN CO4.... 105 G7
  GTDUN CM6.... 178 F2
  HAR CO12.... 142 A2
  UPMR RM14.... 390 B1
  WAB EN9.... 301 M6
Windmill Ct RCOLW CO6.... 160 E7
Windmill Flds HLWE CM17.... 228 A7
  RCOLW CO6.... 158 A8
Windmill Gdns BRTR CM7.... 155 H3
Windmill Hts BCAYW CM12.... 357 J3
Windmill HI SAFWN CB10.... 43 J8
  SUD CO10.... 34 C1
Windmill La BAR EN8.... 300 F2
Windmill Mdw GTDUN CM6.... 204 D8
Windmill Pk COS CO15.... 13 G2
Windmill Rd HSTD CO9.... 128 E2
  MGTR CO11.... 139 K2
Windmills RCOLW CO6.... 159 K3
The Windmills CHLM/WR CM1.... 235 H8
Windmill Vw K/T/MI CO5.... 214 D5
Windmill Wy BRWN CM15.... 331 M1
Windrush Gn CHLM/WR CM1.... 264 D5
Windrush Rd KESG IP5.... 39 K3
Windsor Av CDH/CHF RM16.... 407 J7
  COS CO15.... 12 C6
  SLH/COR SS17.... 395 H6
Windsor CI COLS CO2.... 191 H1
  CVI SS8.... 398 C8
  CHESW EN7.... 300 B2
Windsor Ct RCOLE CO7.... 221 C3
Windsor Gdns BRTR CM7.... 155 J7
  BSF CM23.... 173 K4
  HOC/HUL SS5.... 363 J7
  SBF/HAD SS7.... 380 D7
  WICKE SS11.... 359 L2
Windsor Rd BCAYE CM11.... 336 E6
  BRWN CM15.... 332 C8
  COS CO15.... 12 C7
  EMPK RM11.... 371 K7
  FX IP11.... 9 G4
  IP IP1.... 37 G4
  K/T/MI CO5.... 245 L4
  PEND EN3.... 300 D8
  PIT SS13.... 378 F3
  SOS SS1.... 20 C4
The Windsors BKHH IG9.... 348 F3
Windsor Wy RAYL SS6.... 380 F2
Windsor Wd WAB EN9.... 301 M5
Windward CI PEND EN3.... 300 E7
Windward Wy RCHLM CM3.... 340 M5

Windy HI *RBRW/HUT* CM13...... 355 K2
Winfields *PIT* SS13...... 378 D3
Winford Dr *BROX* EN10...... 277 G2
Winfrith Rd *IPSE* IP5...... 38 E7
Wingate CI *BRTR* CM7...... 154 F7 [1]
Wingfield *GRAYS* RM17...... 417 G2
Wingfield CI
  RBRW/HUT CM13...... 355 H4 [4]
Wingfield Gdns *UPMR* RM14...... 373 G6 [1]
Wingfield St *IPNE* IP4...... 3 G5
Wingletye La *EMPK* RM11...... 372 A8
Wingrave Crs *BRW* CM14...... 353 M5 [1]
Wingway *BRWN* CM15...... 354 D2 [1]
Winifred Av *HCH* RM12...... 389 L3
Winifred Rd *PIT* SS13...... 378 C5
Winmill Rd *BCTR* RM8...... 388 A2
Winnington Rd *PEND* EN3...... 324 D2
Winnock Rd *COL* CO1...... 163 H5
Winsey Cha *BRTR* CM7...... 94 D5
Winsford Gdns *WOS/PRIT* SS0...... 382 B7
Winsford Wy *CHLM/GWD* CM2...... 265 J5
Winsley Rd *COL* CO1...... 163 H5
Winstanley Rd *SAFWS* CB11...... 66 A4
Winstead Gdns *DAGE* RM10...... 388 D4
Winston Av *COLW* CO3...... 162 C7
  IPNE IP4...... 38 D3
  K/T/MI CO5...... 214 F6
Winston Churchill Wy *BAR* EN8...... 300 D5
Winston CI *BRTR* CM7...... 154 F5 [1]
  FX IP11...... 84 E8
  ROMW/RG RM7...... 370 C4
Winston Wy *HSTD* CO9...... 99 H8
Winstree *PIT* SS13...... 378 C3
Winstree Rd *BOC* CM0...... 344 C6
  COLW CO3...... 161 L5 [1]
Winstreet CI *COLS* CO2...... 190 A6
Winterbournes *WOTN* CO14...... 199 H4
Winter Folly *LAIN* SS15...... 18 A8
Winter Gardens Pth *CVI* SS8...... 397 M4
Winterscroft Rd *HOD* EN11...... 253 C4 [1]
Winter's Rd *K/T/MI* CO5...... 215 L2
Winters Wy *MAL* EN9...... 302 B5 [1]
Winterswyk Av *CVI* SS8...... 398 F8
Winton Av *WICKW* SS12...... 359 H3
  WOS/PRIT SS0...... 20 C7
Winton Dr *BAR* EN8...... 300 F1
Wiscombe HI *VGE* SS16...... 376 D8
Wisdoms Gn *RCOLW* CO6...... 158 B8
Wisdons CI *DAGE* RM10...... 370 C8
Wisemans Gdns *SBW* CM21...... 227 K2
Wistaria CI *BRWN* CM15...... 332 C7
Wistaria PI *COS* CO15...... 12 B2
Wiston Rd *RCOLW* CO6...... 103 M2
Witchards *VGE* SS16...... 19 C8
Witch Elm *HAR* CO12...... 143 C1
Witch La *RCOLW* CO6...... 158 C3
Witchtree La *SAFWN* CB10...... 47 C8
Witham CI *LOU* IG10...... 326 F8
Witham Gdns
  RBRW/HUT CM13...... 374 E6 [3]
Witham Ldg *WIT* CM8...... 238 E3
Witham Rd *BRTR* CM7...... 183 H5
  DAGE RM10...... 388 B4
  GPK RM2...... 371 J5
  MAL CM9...... 241 K6
  RCHLM CM3...... 237 M2
  WIT CM8...... 183 K7
The Witherings *EMPK* RM11...... 371 M5
Withersfield Rd *HVHL* CB9...... 27 M2
Withipoll St *IP* IP1...... 3 C3
Withrick Wk *RCOS* CO16...... 222 B6
Withypool *SBN/FI* SS3...... 402 E2 [1]
The Withywindle *RCHLM* CM3...... 339 K5
Witney Rd *BOC* CM0...... 344 D7
Wittem Rd *CVI* SS8...... 398 C6
The Witterings *CVI* SS8...... 398 B6
Witting CI *RCOS* CO16...... 12 C1
Witton Wood Rd *FOS* CO13...... 198 F6
Wivenhoe Rd *RCOLW* CO7...... 164 D2
Wix By-pass *MGTR* CO11...... 140 C6
Wix Rd *HAR* CO12...... 142 A2
  MGTR CO11...... 140 A4
  RCOS CO16...... 168 E3
Woburn Av *BSF* CM23...... 173 K4
  EPP CM16...... 327 M1
  FOS CO13...... 198 E4
  HCH RM12...... 389 H3
Woburn PI *BCAYW* CM12...... 335 G6 [11]
Wodehouse Rd *DART* DA1...... 415 H8
Wokindon Rd *CDH/CHF* RM16...... 408 C8
Wollaston Crs *PIT* SS13...... 378 E1
Wollaston Wy *PIT* SS13...... 378 D2 [2]
Wolmers Rd *RCHLM* CM3...... 235 G4
Wolseley Av *COS* CO15...... 250 A5
Wolseley Rd *CHLM/GWD* CM2...... 16 F4
  ROMW/RG RM7...... 370 D7
Wolsey Av *CHESW* EN7...... 300 A1 [1]
Wolsey Gdns *BARK/HLT* IG6...... 349 K7 [2]
  FX IP11...... 9 L3
Wolsey Rd *EN* EN1...... 324 C4
Wolsey St *IP* IP1...... 2 E6
Wolton Rd *COLS* CO2...... 162 C8
  KESC IP5...... 39 K4
Wolves Hall La *RCOS* CO16...... 167 M2
Wonston Rd *BOC* CM0...... 320 D7
Woodall Rd *PEND* EN3...... 324 E8
Wood Av *HOC/HUL* SS5...... 362 F3
  PUR RM19...... 415 K1
Wood Barn La *MGTR* CO11...... 137 L2
Woodberry CI *CVI* SS8...... 398 B5 [3]

LOS SS9...... 381 K6
Woodberry Down *EPP* CM16...... 304 B1
Woodberry Rd *WICKE* SS11...... 360 B5 [1]
Woodberry Wy *FOS* CO13...... 199 J4
Woodbine CI *HLWW/ROY* CM19...... 15 J8
Woodbridge CI *HARH* RM3...... 352 E5 [1]
Woodbridge Gv *RCOS* CO16...... 223 H7
Woodbridge La *HARH* RM3...... 352 E4
Woodbridge Rd *IPNE* IP4...... 3 M2
  KESC IP5...... 39 G3
Woodbridge Rd East *IPNE* IP4...... 38 D4
Woodbrooke Wy
  SLH/COR SS17...... 395 J6
Woodbrook Gdns *WAB* EN9...... 301 M5
Woodburn CI *SBF/HAD* SS7...... 380 C7
Woodbury HI *LOU* IG10...... 326 F4
Woodcock CI *COLN* CO4...... 163 M5
  HVHL CB9...... 28 D4
Woodcock Rd *CHTY* IP2...... 57 M1
Woodcot CI *ED* N9...... 324 D8
Woodcote Ap *SBF/HAD* SS7...... 379 J4 [1]
Woodcote Av *HCH* RM12...... 389 H5
Woodcote CI *BAR* EN8...... 300 D2
Woodcote Crs *PIT* SS13...... 378 E5
Woodcote Ms *LOU* IG10...... 348 E1
Woodcote Rd *LOS* SS9...... 400 B1
Woodcotes *SBN/FI* SS3...... 402 F2
Woodcote Wy *SBF/HAD* SS7...... 379 J4
Woodcroft *HLWS* CM18...... 15 L9
Woodcroft CI *SBF/HAD* SS7...... 380 D7 [1]
Woodcutters Av
  CDH/CHF RM16...... 407 K7 [1]
  LOS SS9...... 381 K6
Woodedge CI *CHING* E4...... 348 A2
Wood End Av *HOC/HUL* SS5...... 362 E6
Woodend CI *SBF/HAD* SS7...... 380 D7 [2]
Woodfall Dr *DART* DA1...... 414 A8
Wood Farm CI *LOS* SS9...... 381 L7
Woodfield CI *FOS* CO13...... 199 H4
  STSD CM24...... 146 F5 [1]
Woodfield Dr *GPK* RM2...... 371 H4
  K/T/MI CO5...... 245 J4
Wood Field End *COLS* CO2...... 190 B6
Woodfield Gdns *LOS* SS9...... 400 A3
Woodfield La *RIPS/CAP* IP9...... 109 M1
Woodfield Park Dr *LOS* SS9...... 400 B2
Woodfield Rd *BRTR* CM7...... 155 G8
  LOS SS9...... 400 B2
  SBF/HAD SS7...... 381 H8 [1]
Woodfields *STSD* CM24...... 146 F5
Woodfield Ter *STSD* CM24...... 146 F5 [3]
Woodfield Wy *HCH* RM12...... 371 L8 [1]
  RCHLM CM3...... 238 B7
The Woodfines *EMPK* RM11...... 371 L6
Woodford CI *COS* CO15...... 224 A3
Woodford CI *WAB* EN9...... 302 B5
Woodford New Rd *WFD* IG8...... 348 A8
Woodgrange Av *EN* EN1...... 324 B8
Woodgrange Dr *SOS* SS1...... 401 M3 [1]
Woodgrange Gdns *EN* EN1...... 324 B8
Wood Gn *PIT* SS13...... 378 C2
Woodgreen Rd *WAB* EN9...... 302 D5
Woodhall CI *SUD* CO10...... 4 D3
Woodhall Crs *EMPK* RM11...... 372 A7
Woodhall Gv *BSF* CM23...... 173 L5
Woodhall HI *CHLM/WR* CM1...... 234 C8
Woodhall Rd *CHLM/WR* CM1...... 264 B4
  SUD CO10...... 4 C3
Woodham Dr *RCHLM* CM3...... 238 C7 [3]
Woodham Halt *RCHLM* CM3...... 339 K3
Woodham Mortimer Rd
  MAL CM9...... 291 M3
Woodham Park Dr
  SBF/HAD SS7...... 397 J1
Woodham Rd *RCHLM* CM3...... 338 E8
  RCHLM CM3...... 340 B1
  SBF/HAD SS7...... 397 J1
Woodhill *HLWS* CM18...... 255 M6
Woodhill Common Rd
  RCHLM CM3...... 290 C6
Woodhill Rd *CHLM/GWD* CM2...... 289 K5
Wood House La *BROX* EN10...... 276 A1
Woodhouse La *CHLM/WR* CM1...... 235 H7
  KIR/NAC IP10...... 60 D1
Woodhurst Rd *CVI* SS8...... 398 C7
Wooding Gv *HLWW/ROY* CM19...... 15 G4
Woodland Av *RBRW/HUT* CM13...... 333 K7
Woodland Cha *COLW* CO3...... 161 G2
Woodland CI *RBRW/HUT* CM13...... 333 K7
  RCHLM CM3...... 238 B6
  SBF/HAD SS7...... 381 G8
  WFD IG8...... 348 C4
Woodland Dr *COLW* CO3...... 162 A6
Woodland Park Cha
  RCHLM CM3...... 319 H4
Woodland Rd *CHLM/WR* CM1...... 264 B7
  LOU IG10...... 326 F5 [1]
Woodlands *BRTR* CM7...... 155 J8
  BSF CM23...... 174 D3
  COLN CO4...... 164 A2
  COS CO15...... 250 B2
  HAR CO12...... 169 J1
  RCHLM CM3...... 319 H8
  RIPS/CAP IP9...... 81 M4
Woodlands Av *EMPK* RM11...... 371 L5
  RAYL SS6...... 380 A5
Woodlands CI *CDH/CHF* RM16...... 407 M8
  COS CO15...... 224 B3

HOC/HUL SS5...... 362 E6
HOD EN11...... 253 H6 [1]
ING CM4...... 310 D7
RAYL SS6...... 380 E5
VGE SS16...... 378 A7
Woodlands Dr *HOD* EN11...... 253 H7
  SLH/COR SS17...... 395 K2
Woodlands Pk *LOS* SS9...... 381 H8
Woodlands Park Dr
  GTDUN CM6...... 178 C2
Woodlands Ri *RCOS* CO16...... 196 A2 [3]
Woodlands Rd *HARH* RM3...... 372 B1
  HOC/HUL SS5...... 362 E6
  RIPS/CAP IP9...... 80 D4
  ROM RM1...... 371 G3
  WICKW SS12...... 359 L4
The Woodlands *RCOLE* CO7...... 220 F3 [3]
  SBN/FI SS3...... 403 G3
Woodland Wy *CHONG* CM5...... 307 G2
  EPP CM16...... 303 M7
  HSTD CO9...... 127 M3 [2]
  RCOLE CO7...... 192 C2
  WFD IG8...... 348 C4
Wood La *BSF* CM23...... 174 F1
  BUNT SG9...... 86 B5
  CHONG CM5...... 260 E8
  DAGE RM10...... 388 B1
  GTDUN CM6...... 231 L2
  HCH RM12...... 389 H4
  MAL CM9...... 269 H6
  MAL CM9...... 317 M2
  RCOLW CO6...... 161 G2
  WFD IG8...... 348 A6
Woodleigh Av *LOS* SS9...... 381 L8
Woodley Wk *SBN/FI* SS3...... 402 F1 [3]
Woodlow *SBF/HAD* SS7...... 380 C5
Woodmanhurst Rd
  SLH/COR SS17...... 395 G6 [3]
Woodman La *CHING* E4...... 325 L7
Woodman Pth *BARK/HLT* IG6...... 349 M6
Woodman Rd *BRW* CM14...... 354 D6
Wood Meads *EPP* CM16...... 304 B1
Woodpecker CI *BSF* CM23...... 173 K5 [3]
  COLN CO4...... 164 A3 [3]
  ED N9...... 324 C8
Woodpecker Rd *CHTY* IP2...... 36 E8
Woodpond Av *HOC/HUL* SS5...... 362 E6
Woodredon CI
  HLWW/ROY CM19...... 254 C4 [1]
Woodridden HI *WAB* EN9...... 302 E7
Wood Rd *MAL* CM9...... 269 J5
Woodroffe CI *CHLM/GWD* CM2...... 265 H8
Woodrolfe Farm La *MAL* CM9...... 272 F2
Woodrolfe Pk *MAL* CM9...... 273 G1
Woodrolfe Rd *MAL* CM9...... 272 F2
Woodrows La *RCOS* CO16...... 223 J6
Woodrow Wy *COLN* CO4...... 163 M4
Woodrush End *COLW* CO3...... 161 J5 [3]
Woodrush Rd *IPSE* IP5...... 59 L1
Woodshire Rd *DAGE* RM10...... 388 C2
Woodside *BKHH* IG9...... 348 D3
  BSF CM23...... 174 E3
  CHESW EN7...... 300 B3
  EPP CM16...... 280 E7
  FOS CO13...... 199 J5
  LOS SS9...... 381 J6
  MAL CM9...... 240 C8
  RCHLM CM3...... 290 F2
Woodside Av *SBF/HAD* SS7...... 379 J3
Woodside Cha *HOC/HUL* SS5...... 362 F7
Woodside CI *COLN* CO4...... 163 M2 [3]
  RAIN RM13...... 404 D2
  RBRW/HUT CM13...... 333 L7 [3]
  SBF/HAD SS7...... 381 H5
Woodside Rd *HOC/HUL* SS5...... 362 C6
  WFD IG8...... 348 B5
Woodside Vw *SBF/HAD* SS7...... 379 K3
Woodside Wy *GTDUN* CM6...... 178 F2
Woodspring CI *CHTY* IP2...... 58 B1 [3]
Woods Rd *RCHLM* CM3...... 207 J5
The Woods *SBF/HAD* SS7...... 381 G8
Woodstock *K/T/MI* CO5...... 245 K4
  LAIN SS15...... 376 A5 [3]
Woodstock Av *HARH* RM3...... 353 J6
Woodstock Crs *ED* N9...... 324 C8
  HOC/HUL SS5...... 362 E5 [3]
  LAIN SS15...... 376 A5
Woodstock Rd *BROX* EN10...... 252 F7
Woodstone Av *IP* IP1...... 37 K2
Wood St *CHLM/GWD* CM2...... 16 D9
  GRAYS RM17...... 417 K3
Wood Vw *GRAYS* RM17...... 417 M1
Woodview *VGE* SS16...... 375 M7 [1]
Woodview CI *RCOLE* CO7...... 135 L7
Woodview Dr *RCHLM* CM3...... 209 H4
Woodview Rd *GTDUN* CM6...... 178 D3
Woodville CI *RCFD* SS4...... 363 L7
Woodville Rd *CVI* SS8...... 398 E8
  IPNE IP4...... 3 L5
Woodward CI *GRAYS* RM17...... 417 J1
Woodward Hts *GRAYS* RM17...... 417 J1
Woodwards *HLWW/ROY* CM19...... 15 J8
Wood Wy *BRTR* CM7...... 182 C5
Woodway *RBRW/HUT* CM13...... 355 H2
Woodyards *BOC* CM0...... 274 A8
Woolards Wy *RCHLM* CM3...... 319 J3
Woolhampton Wy *CHIG* IG7...... 350 C4 [1]
Woolifers Av *SLH/COR* SS17...... 395 J7
Woollards CI *IP* IP1...... 2 A4
Woollards Gdns *SUD* CO10...... 4 D3

Woollard St *WAB* EN9...... 301 K6
Woollard Wy *ING* CM4...... 308 F2
Woollett CI *DART* DA1...... 414 B8
Woolmans CI *BROX* EN10...... 277 G4
Woolmergreen *LAIN* SS15...... 18 A4
Woolmers Md *RCHLM* CM3...... 233 M1
Woolmonger's La *ING* CM4...... 308 B3
Woolner Rd *RCOS* CO16...... 223 L5
Woolnough CI *HVHL* CB9...... 48 C5
The Woolnoughs *KESC* IP5...... 39 L4 [1]
Woolpack La *BRTR* CM7...... 155 H6 [3]
Woolpit's Rd *BRTR* CM7...... 152 F2
Woolshotts Rd *WICKW* SS12...... 359 G4
Woolverstone CI *CHTY* IP2...... 57 L2
Woolwich Rd *RCOS* CO16...... 12 A2
Wootton CI *EMPK* RM11...... 371 L5
Worcester Av *UPMR* RM14...... 373 G6
Worcester CI *BRTR* CM7...... 183 H2
  RCHLM CM3...... 319 J2
  SLH/COR SS17...... 394 E8 [3]
  VGE SS16...... 376 A6 [1]
Worcester Ct
  CHLM/GWD CM2...... 289 H6 [3]
Worcester Crs *RCOLE* CO7...... 193 J3
  WFD IG8...... 348 C4
Worcester Dr *RAYL* SS6...... 381 G2
Worcester Rd *BOC* CM0...... 344 D5
  COL CO1...... 10 E6
  IPSE IP5...... 59 H3
Worcesters Av *EN* EN1...... 324 B2
Wordsworth Av *MAL* CM9...... 293 H3
Wordsworth CI *HARH* RM3...... 371 K1 [1]
  SOSN SS2...... 21 J1
  TIL RM18...... 418 D6 [3]
Wordsworth Rd *BRTR* CM7...... 155 G4 [3]
  COLW CO3...... 162 A5
Wordsworth Wy *DART* DA1...... 415 H8
Workhouse HI *COLN* CO4...... 104 F7
Workhouse La *RCHLM* CM3...... 339 H1
Workhouse Rd *RCOLW* CO6...... 103 K8
Workshop La *KIR/NAC* IP10...... 60 C6
Worlds End La *K/T/MI* CO5...... 186 E8
Wormley Ct *WAB* EN9...... 302 B5 [3]
Wormley Lodge CI
  BROX EN10...... 277 G3 [3]
Wormyngford Ct *WAB* EN9...... 302 B5 [3]
Worrin CI *BRWN* CM15...... 355 G2
Worrin Rd *BRWN* CM15...... 355 G3
Worsdell Wy *COLN* CO4...... 10 C2
Worsley CI *CHTY* IP2...... 57 L1
Wortham PI *CHLM/WR* CM1...... 28 B3
Worthing Ms *COS* CO15...... 250 D3 [3]
Worthing Rd *LAIN* SS15...... 376 B5 [3]
Worthington Wy *COLW* CO3...... 162 A7
Wouldham Rd *WTHK* RM20...... 416 F3
Wrabness Rd *HAR* CO12...... 111 M8
The Wraglins *BSF* CM23...... 174 C6
Wrangley Ct *WAB* EN9...... 302 B5 [3]
Wratting Rd *HVHL* CB9...... 28 B3
Wray CI *EMPK* RM11...... 371 L7
Wraysbury Dr *LAIN* SS15...... 376 E2 [3]
Wren Av *CHTY* IP2...... 36 E8
  LOS SS9...... 381 K4
Wrenbrook Rd *BSF* CM23...... 174 A6
Wren CI *BCAYE* CM11...... 357 K2 [3]
  LOS SS9...... 381 L4
  RCOLE CO7...... 194 E2 [3]
  SBF/HAD SS7...... 379 J5
Wrendale *COS* CO15...... 224 A5
Wren Dr *WAB* EN9...... 302 B6
Wren Gdns *HCH* RM12...... 371 G8
Wren PI *BRW* CM14...... 354 E4
Wrens Pk *FX* IP11...... 85 L6 [3]
The Wrens *HLWW/ROY* CM19...... 15 H5
Wren Ter *LOU* IG10...... 327 J3
Wren Wk *TIL* RM18...... 418 C4
Wrexham Rd *HARH* RM3...... 352 E5
  LAIN SS15...... 376 C6
Wright La *KESC* IP5...... 39 L3
Wright Rd *IPSE* IP5...... 59 K1
Wright's Av *BRTR* CM7...... 183 M4
Wrightsbridge Rd *BRW* CM14...... 353 G2
Wrights CI *DAGE* RM10...... 388 C2
Wright's Green La *RBSF* CM22...... 201 K4
Wrights La *BRWN* CM15...... 308 E8
Wright's Piece *RBSF* CM22...... 120 B5
Writtle CI *RCOS* CO16...... 223 J7
Writtle Rd *CHLM/WR* CM1...... 16 A6
  ING CM4...... 287 G8
Wroths Pth *LOU* IG10...... 327 G3
Wroxham CI *COLW* CO3...... 162 C5
  SBF/HAD SS7...... 381 J5
Wroxham Rd *IPSE* IP3...... 38 A8
Wryneck CI *COLN* CO4...... 135 G8
Wyatt Rd *DART* DA1...... 414 A7
Wyatts Dr *SOS* SS1...... 402 A4
Wyatts Green La *BRWN* CM15...... 308 E8
Wyatt's Green Rd *BRWN* CM15...... 308 E8
Wyatts La *SUD* CO10...... 77 L3
Wyburn Rd *SBF/HAD* SS7...... 380 C5
Wyburns Av *RAYL* SS6...... 380 E5
Wyburns Av East *RAYL* SS6...... 380 F5
Wych Elm *HLW* CM20...... 15 J3
Wych Elm CI *EMPK* RM11...... 372 B6 [3]
Wych Elm Rd *EMPK* RM11...... 372 B6
Wychford Dr *SBW* CM21...... 227 K2
Wycke HI *MAL* CM9...... 292 E3
Wycke La *MAL* CM9...... 272 F3
Wycliffe Gv *COL* CO1...... 10 A4
Wycombe Av *SBF/HAD* SS7...... 379 H5 [1]

Wye Rd *IPSE* IP3...... 38 B8
Wykeham Av *EMPK* RM11...... 371 L6
Wykeham Rd *CHLM/WR* CM1...... 287 J2
Wykes Bishop St *IPSE* IP3...... 3 J8
Wykes Gn *BSDN* SS14...... 19 L4
Wyldwood CI *HLWE* CM17...... 227 K5
Wyncolls Rd *COLN* CO4...... 135 K6
Wyndham Crs *COS* CO15...... 13 J3
Wynters *VGE* SS16...... 377 J7
Wynterton CI *IPSE* IP5...... 59 J2
Wynyard Rd *SAFWN* CB10...... 43 M8
Wyse's Rd *ING* CM4...... 286 A5
Wythefield *PIT* SS13...... 378 B5
Wythenshawe Rd *DAGE* RM10...... 388 B2

Y

Yale Ms *COLN* CO4...... 135 J7
Yale Wy *HCH* RM12...... 389 H3
Yamburg Rd *CVI* SS8...... 398 E8 [3]
Yardley CI *CHING* E4...... 325 J7 [1]
Yardley Hall La *GTDUN* CM6...... 91 L5
Yardley La *CHING* E4...... 325 J7
Yare Av *WIT* CM8...... 211 L8
Yarmouth CI *COS* CO15...... 223 M5 [3]
Yarmouth Rd *IP* IP1...... 37 G5
Yarnacott *SBN/FI* SS3...... 402 D3
Yarwood Rd *CHLM/GWD* CM2...... 288 F1
Yeldham Lock
  CHLM/GWD CM2...... 289 H1 [3]
Yeldham PI *HVHL* CB9...... 28 B3
Yeldham Rd *HSTD* CO9...... 73 K7
Yellowpine Wy *CHIG* IG7...... 350 C5
Yelverton CI *HARH* RM3...... 371 K1
Yeoman Rd *FX* IP11...... 8 F3
Yeomans CI *BSF* CM23...... 173 L6
Yeomans La *EN* EN1...... 324 C4 [3]
Yeoman Wy *BARK/HLT* IG6...... 349 K7
Yeovil Cha *WOS/PRIT* SS0...... 382 C7
Yerril Gdn *HVHL* CB9...... 27 M4 [3]
Yevele Wy *EMPK* RM11...... 371 M7
Yew CI *BKHH* IG9...... 348 E3 [3]
  LAIN SS15...... 376 D2
  WIT CM8...... 212 C6
Yew Ct *CHTY* IP2...... 37 H8
Yewlands *HOD* EN11...... 253 H6
  SBW CM21...... 227 M2 [3]
Yewlands Dr *HOD* EN11...... 253 H6
Yews Av *EN* EN1...... 300 C8
Yew Tree CI *COLN* CO4...... 163 M4
  RBRW/HUT CM13...... 333 J8
  RCHLM CM3...... 238 B6
Yew Tree Gdns
  CHLM/GWD CM2...... 288 D5 [3]
  ROMW/RG RM7...... 370 C5
Yewtree Gv *KESC* IP5...... 39 G4
Yew Tree PI *BSF* CM23...... 174 A3
Yewtree Ri *RIPW* IP8...... 57 K2
Yew Wk *HOD* EN11...... 253 H6
Yew Wy *COS* CO15...... 250 A5
Yorick Av *K/T/MI* CO5...... 245 K5
Yorick Rd *K/T/MI* CO5...... 245 K5
York Av *SLH/COR* SS17...... 395 H6
York CI *BRWN* CM15...... 355 G1
  RAYL SS6...... 381 H3
  SUD CO10...... 4 D3
York Crs *LOU* IG10...... 326 F5
Yorkes *HLWS* CM18...... 256 K5
York Gdns *BRTR* CM7...... 155 J7
York HI *LOU* IG10...... 326 F5
York PI *COL* CO1...... 10 F6 [3]
  GRAYS RM17...... 417 H3 [3]
York Ri *RAYL* SS6...... 381 H3
York Rd *BAR* EN8...... 300 F6
  BCAYW CM12...... 335 H6
  BOC CM0...... 344 D7
  BRWN CM15...... 355 G1
  CHLM/GWD CM2...... 16 F7
  COS CO15...... 224 E6
  EPP CM16...... 281 H7
  FX IP11...... 9 M1
  HVHL CB9...... 27 M4
  IPSE IP3...... 38 B7
  RAIN RM13...... 388 E6 [3]
  RAYL SS6...... 381 H3
  RCFD SS4...... 363 K4
  RCOLE CO7...... 220 F5
  RCOLW CO6...... 130 C5
  SLH/COR SS17...... 394 A7
  SOS SS1...... 21 H7
  SUD CO10...... 4 D4
York St *MGTR* CO11...... 108 E7
Young CI *LOS* SS9...... 382 B5
  RCOS CO16...... 12 B2
Ypres Rd *COLS* CO2...... 162 D5

Z

Zambesi Rd *BSF* CM23...... 174 A6 [2]
Zandi Rd *CVI* SS8...... 413 L1 [2]
Zealand Dr *CVI* SS8...... 398 F8
Zelham Dr *CVI* SS8...... 399 G8
Zider Pass *CVI* SS8...... 399 G8

Index - featured places

Aaron House Clinic
  of Physiotherapy
  WOS/PRIT SS0...... 382 C8
Abbey Mead Industrial Park
  WAB EN9...... 301 J6
Abbey Road Surgery
  BAR EN8...... 300 F6

Abbotsweld Primary School
  HLWS CM18...... 15 M9
Abbotts Hall Infant School
  SLH/COR SS17...... 394 F8
Acorn Trading Centre
  WTHK RM20...... 416 E3
Acton Place Industrial Estate
  SUD CO10...... 35 J3

Acton Primary School
  SUD CO10...... 35 K5
Adams Business Centre
  BSDN SS14...... 378 A2
Adult Community College
  COL CO1...... 10 E7

Adult Community
  College Chelmsford
  CHLM/WR CM1...... 16 B3
Airborne Industrial Estate
  LOS SS9...... 381 M6
Albany School Grant
  Maintained
  PEND EN3...... 324 E2

The Albany School
  HCH RM12...... 389 J1
Albright Industrial Estate
  RAIN RM13...... 404 A3
Albury School
  STDN SG11...... 144 B5
Alderman Blaxill School
  COLS CO2...... 162 C8

Alderton County
  Junior & Infant School
  LOU IG10 .... 327 H7
The Alec Hunter High School
  BRTR CM7 .... 183 K2
Alleyn Court
  & Eton House School
  SBN/FI SS3 .... 384 B8
Alleyn Court Preparatory
  School
  WOS/PRIT SS0 .... 400 D2
All Saints Church
  of England Primary School
  HAR CO12 .... 141 J8
All Saints C of E Junior
  Middle & Infant School
  BSF CM23 .... 174 A7
All Saints C of E
  Primary School
  HAR CO12 .... 6 C9
All Saints School
  BCTR RM8 .... 370 B8
All Saints Vc Middle School
  SUD CO10 .... 55 H1
Alma Road Junior
  & Infant School
  PEND EN3 .... 324 C4
Alresford Business Centre
  RCOLE CO7 .... 193 J3
Alresford Primary School
  RCOLE CO7 .... 193 J4
Alsa Business Park
  STSD CM24 .... 147 G2
Alton Park CP School
  COS CO15 .... 12 C7
Alton Water Sports Centre
  RIPS/CAP IP9 .... 80 C8
Amberfield School
  KIR/NAC IP10 .... 60 D5
Ambresbury Banks Fort
  EPP CM16 .... 303 J6
Anchor Press Social
  & Sports Club
  K/T/MI CO5 .... 214 E6
Ancient House
  IP IP1 .... 2 F4
Andrews Lane Junior
  & Infant School
  CHESW EN7 .... 276 B8
Anglia Polytechnic University
  BRWN CM15 .... 354 E2
Anglia Polytechnic University
  CHLM/GWD CM2 .... 16 F3
Anglia Polytechnic University
  CHLM/WR CM1 .... 235 H8
Anglia University
  CHLM/WR CM1 .... 264 C7
Annandale Clinic
  WOS/PRIT SS0 .... 382 C8
Appleton School
  SBF/HAD SS7 .... 379 K7
Ardleigh Green Junior School
  EMPK RM11 .... 371 L3
Arena Sports & Leisure Club
  COLS CO2 .... 162 F6
Art Gallery
  GTDUN CM6 .... 123 H7
The Art Gallery
  LOS SS9 .... 399 M3
Arthur Bugler Junior
  & Infant School
  SLH/COR SS17 .... 394 F8
The Arthur Findlay College
  STSD CM24 .... 147 H6
The Artisan Gallery
  WFD IG8 .... 348 C7
Ashdon CP School
  SAFWN CB10 .... 45 J2
Ashfield Club House
  GTDUN CM6 .... 204 C1
Ash Industrial Estate
  HLWW/ROY CM19 .... 14 C7
Ashingdon School
  RCFD SS4 .... 363 J2
Ashingdon Surgery
  RCFD SS4 .... 363 K6
Ash Tree Surgery
  SLH/COR SS17 .... 395 J7
Asquith School
  PEND EN3 .... 324 C6
Audley End
  SAFWS CB11 .... 65 J2
August 12th Art Gallery
  SAFWN CB10 .... 65 L2
Aveley Football Club
  SOCK/AV RM15 .... 405 K5
Aveley Medical Centre
  SOCK/AV RM15 .... 406 D2
Aveley Primary School
  SOCK/AV RM15 .... 405 M6
The Aveley School
  SOCK/AV RM15 .... 405 L5
Avenue Industrial Estate
  CPK RM2 .... 371 L2
Avenue Road Surgery
  BRW CM14 .... 354 D5
Avon House School
  WFD IG8 .... 348 B5
Aylands School
  PEND EN3 .... 300 D8
Ayloff Primary School
  HCH RM12 .... 389 J3
Babergh District Council
  SUD CO10 .... 4 C6
Baddow Hall Junior
  & Infant School
  CHLM/GWD CM2 .... 289 H5
Balfour Medical Centre
  GRAYS RM17 .... 417 K1
Ballards Gore Golf Club
  RCFD SS4 .... 364 F5
Ballards Walk Surgery
  LAIN SS15 .... 18 B5
Ballingdon Hill Industrial Estate
  SUD CO10 .... 54 D7
Bancrofts School
  WFD IG8 .... 348 B4

The Banyards School
  K/T/MI CO5 .... 214 C4
Barbara Castle Health Centre
  HLWW/ROY CM19 .... 255 H7
Barking College
  ROMW/RG RM7 .... 388 E1
Barking & Dagenham Council
  DAGW RM9 .... 388 A5
The Barking Dog Theatre Co
  BSF CM23 .... 174 A6
Barling Magna
  Primary School
  SBN/FI SS3 .... 384 F4
Barnes Cray Primary School
  DART DA1 .... 414 B8
Barnes Farm County
  Junior School
  CHLM/GWD CM2 .... 265 H8
Barons Court Infant School
  WOS/PRIT SS0 .... 20 E6
Barrack Lane Medical Centre
  IP IP1 .... 2 D3
Barracks
  COLS CO2 .... 163 G5
Barstable School
  BSDN SS14 .... 378 A5
Bartlet Hospital
  FX IP11 .... 115 J1
Basildon College
  VGE SS16 .... 377 G8
Basildon District Council
  BCAYE CM11 .... 357 M7
Basildon District Council
  BCAYW CM12 .... 357 H2
Basildon District Council
  BSDN SS14 .... 18 F6
Basildon District Council
  LAIN SS15 .... 376 D5
Basildon District Council
  WICKW SS12 .... 359 K4
Basildon Hospital
  VGE SS16 .... 377 G8
Basildon Rugby Football Club
  BSDN SS14 .... 377 L2
Basildon & Thurrock
  Community Health Council
  BSDN SS14 .... 19 G6
Basildon United Football Club
  BSDN SS14 .... 377 K2
Basildon Zoo
  VGE SS16 .... 395 K1
Bata Medical Centre
  TIL RM18 .... 419 K1
Bates Industrial Estate
  HARH RM3 .... 353 H8
Battlesbridge
  Motorcycle Museum
  WICKE SS11 .... 360 E1
Beacon Hill Industrial Estate
  PUR RM19 .... 415 J1
Beacon Hill Special School
  CHTY IP2 .... 37 G8
Beam Primary School
  DAGE RM10 .... 388 D8
Bearwalden Business Park
  SAFWS CB11 .... 64 F6
Beauchamps High School
  WICKE SS11 .... 360 B3
Beckers Green County
  Primary School
  BRTR CM7 .... 183 L1
Beckingham Business Park
  MAL CM9 .... 270 E1
Beech Avenue Surgery
  UPMR RM14 .... 390 C3
Beecroft Art Gallery
  WOS/PRIT SS0 .... 20 C7
Beehive Lane County
  Primary School
  CHLM/GWD CM2 .... 288 D6
Belcon Industrial Estate
  HOD EN11 .... 253 K5
Belfairs Community College
  LOS SS9 .... 399 K1
Belfairs Swimming Pool
  LOS SS9 .... 399 K1
Belhus Golf Club
  & Leisure Centre
  SOCK/AV RM15 .... 405 M4
Belstead Special School
  RIPW IP8 .... 57 K1
Benbridge Industrial Estate
  MAL CM9 .... 269 H6
Benfleet Business Centre
  SBF/HAD SS7 .... 397 L1
Benhurst Jmi School
  HCH RM12 .... 389 J2
Bentalls Industrial Estate
  MAL CM9 .... 269 H6
Bentalls Shopping Centre
  MAL CM9 .... 269 J6
Bentfield County
  Primary School
  STSD CM24 .... 146 E3
Bentley Primary School
  RIPS/CAP IP9 .... 79 G4
Benyon CP School
  SOCK/AV RM15 .... 391 K8
The Billericay School
  BCAYW CM12 .... 357 J3
Billericay Swimming Pool
  BCAYW CM12 .... 335 H8
Billericay Town Council
  BCAYW CM12 .... 357 H1
Billericay Town Football Club
  BCAYW CM12 .... 356 F2
Birch C of E School
  COLS CO2 .... 189 H7
The Birches Medical Centre
  KESG IP5 .... 39 J4
Birch Grove Golf Club
  COLS CO2 .... 190 C3
Birchwood High School
  BSF CM23 .... 174 D3
The Bishops C of E
  & RC Primary School
  CHLM/WR CM1 .... 265 G5

Bishop's Park Health Centre
  BSF CM23 .... 174 A3
Bishops Stortford College
  BSF CM23 .... 173 M4
The Bishops Stortford
  High School
  BSF CM23 .... 174 A7
Bishops Stortford
  Town Council
  BSF CM23 .... 174 A7
Bishop Stopford School
  EN EN1 .... 324 C4
Bishop William Ward School
  RCOLW CO16 .... 134 C4
Blackall Industrial Estate
  RCHLM CM3 .... 340 A2
Blackmore CP School
  ING CM4 .... 308 F3
Black Notley Hospital
  BRTR CM7 .... 184 E1
Blackshots Leisure Centre
  CDH/CHF RM16 .... 407 L7
Blackwater Leisure Centre
  MAL CM9 .... 293 J2
Blackwater Sailing Club
  MAL CM9 .... 270 A8
Blackwater Trading Estate
  MAL CM9 .... 269 H7
Blake End Gallery
  BRTR CM7 .... 153 H8
Blenheim County
  Primary School
  LOS SS9 .... 382 A8
Blois Meadow
  Business Centre
  HVHL CB9 .... 48 D4
Bluebridge Industrial Estate
  HSTD CO9 .... 129 J2
Bluehouse County
  Infant School
  LAIN SS15 .... 376 D5
Blyth's Meadow Surgery
  BRTR CM7 .... 155 F8
Bocking Church Street County
  Primary School
  BRTR CM7 .... 155 G3
Bonneygrove Junior
  & Infant School
  CHESW EN7 .... 300 B2
Bonnygate CP School
  SOCK/AV RM15 .... 406 C3
The Book Gallery
  GTDUN CM6 .... 178 C3
Boomes Industrial Estate
  RAIN RM13 .... 404 A2
Boreham County
  Primary School
  RCHLM CM3 .... 266 A3
Borough of Broxbourne
  BAR EN8 .... 300 C2
The Boswells School
  CHLM/WR CM1 .... 264 C5
Bournemouth Park
  Junior & Infants School
  SOSN SS2 .... 21 K2
Bournes Green Junior School
  SOS SS1 .... 402 C3
Bower Park School
  ROM RM1 .... 351 M7
The Box Gallery
  RIPS/CAP IP9 .... 79 L4
Boxted C of E Primary School
  COLN CO4 .... 105 G4
Boyd School
  UPMR RM14 .... 390 F1
The Brackenbury
  Sports Centre
  FX IP11 .... 85 K8
Bradfield Primary School
  MGTR CO11 .... 139 M2
Bradwell Quay Yacht Club
  BOC CM0 .... 273 M7
Brady Primary School
  RAIN RM13 .... 404 D3
Braintree & Bocking
  Urban District Council
  BRTR CM7 .... 155 H6
Braintree College
  BRTR CM7 .... 155 H6
Braintree District Council
  BRTR CM7 .... 155 G8
Braintree District Council
  BRTR CM7 .... 155 G8
Braintree District Council
  BRTR CM7 .... 155 J8
Braintree District Council
  WIT CM8 .... 239 H1
Braintree & District
  Golf Club Ltd
  BRTR CM7 .... 156 B5
Braintree Rugby Club
  BRTR CM7 .... 183 L1
Braintree Town Football Club
  BRTR CM7 .... 183 K1
Bramford Primary School
  RIPW IP8 .... 36 B2
Bramston Sports Centre
  WIT CM8 .... 239 G2
Brandler Galleries
  BRW CM14 .... 354 E3
Brandy Hole Yacht Club
  HOC/HUL SS5 .... 340 B7
Branfil Junior & Infant School
  UPMR RM14 .... 390 B3
Brantham Athletic
  & Social Club
  MGTR CO11 .... 108 D4
Brays Grove
  Comprehensive School
  HLWS CM18 .... 256 C5
Brentwood Borough Council
  BRW CM14 .... 354 D3
Brentwood Borough Council
  RBRW/HUT CM13 .... 354 E7
Brentwood Chiropody
  Surgery
  BRW CM14 .... 354 D3
The Brentwood Clinic
  BRW CM14 .... 354 E2

Brentwood Community
  Hospital
  BRWN CM15 .... 354 F2
Brentwood County High
  School
  BRW CM14 .... 354 E4
Brentwood Preparatory
  School
  BRWN CM15 .... 354 F2
Brentwood Rugby
  Football Club
  BRW CM14 .... 354 F5
Brentwood School
  BRWN CM15 .... 354 E3
Brentwood Sports Ground
  BRWN CM15 .... 354 E2
Brentwood Ursuline
  High School
  BRW CM14 .... 354 E4
Briarswood Clinic
  CVI SS8 .... 398 A6
Brickfield Surgery
  RCHLM CM3 .... 339 M4
Bridge Hospital
  WIT CM8 .... 239 G3
Bridge View Industrial Estate
  WTHK RM20 .... 416 B3
Brightlingsea Infant School
  RCOLE CO7 .... 220 F5
Brightlingsea Junior School
  RCOLE CO7 .... 220 F5
Brightlingsea United
  Football Club
  RCOLE CO7 .... 221 G4
Brightside County Junior
  & Infant School
  BCAYW CM12 .... 334 F6
Brimsdown Junior
  & Infant School
  PEND EN3 .... 324 C4
Brinkley Grove Gm
  Primary School
  COLN CO4 .... 135 J6
Brisco County Junior
  & Infant School
  PIT SS13 .... 378 C3
Britannia Business Centre
  BAR EN8 .... 301 G4
Britannia Primary School
  IPNE IP4 .... 38 C6
Brittania Business Park
  BAR EN8 .... 301 G4
Brittons School
  RAIN RM13 .... 389 G6
Broadfield School
  HLW CM20 .... 255 M2
Broadford Primary School
  HARH RM3 .... 352 E7
Brocks Business Park
  WICKE SS11 .... 360 A5
Broke Hall CP School
  IPNE IP4 .... 38 F6
Bromfords School
  WICKW SS12 .... 359 J6
Bromfords Sports Centre
  WICKW SS12 .... 359 J6
Brook Craft Market
  IP IP1 .... 2 F4
Brooke Trading Estate
  ROM RM1 .... 371 G7
Brook Farm Industrial Estate
  ABR/ST RM4 .... 351 L1
Brook Gallery
  CHIG IG7 .... 349 J4
Brookhouse Business Park
  CHTY IP2 .... 37 G5
Brookland Junior
  & Infant School
  BAR EN8 .... 276 E6
Brooklands School
  MGTR CO11 .... 108 E3
Brook Natural Health Centre
  CVI SS8 .... 397 M8
Brook Road Industrial Estate
  RAYL SS6 .... 380 E3
Brookside Business Centre
  RBSF CM22 .... 201 G2
Brookside Junior
  & Infant School
  HARH RM3 .... 352 E8
Brook Street Business Centre
  COL CO1 .... 11 G9
Brookweald Cricket Club
  BRW CM14 .... 353 M2
Broomfield County
  Primary School
  CHLM/WR CM1 .... 264 C4
Broomfield Football Club
  CHLM/WR CM1 .... 264 C3
Broomfield Hospital
  CHLM/WR CM1 .... 235 H8
Broomgrove County
  Infant & Junior School
  RCOLE CO7 .... 164 C8
Broomhills Industrial Estate
  BRTR CM7 .... 182 E1
Broom Hill Swimming Pool
  IP IP1 .... 37 H3
Broxbourne Borough Council
  BAR EN8 .... 276 E6
Broxbourne Business Centre
  BAR EN8 .... 276 E6
Broxbourne C of E Jmi School
  BROX EN10 .... 277 G1
Broxbourne Sailing Club
  HOD EN11 .... 253 L8
The Broxbourne School
  BROX EN10 .... 276 F2
Broxbourne Sports Club
  BROX EN10 .... 277 G1
Brunel Court Industrial Estate
  COLN CO4 .... 135 K6
Buckhurst Hill CP School
  BKHH IG9 .... 348 D7
Buckhurst Hill Football Club
  BKHH IG9 .... 348 F7

Buckhurst Hill Reform
  Synagogue
  LOU IG10 .... 326 E7
Bucklesham Primary School
  KIR/NAC IP10 .... 61 K3
Bull Hill Industrial Estate
  COS CO15 .... 13 H2
Bull Lane Industrial Estate
  SUD CO10 .... 35 H3
Bulmer Road Industrial Estate
  SUD CO10 .... 54 D4
Bulmer Road Industrial Estate
  SUD CO10 .... 54 D5
Bulphan Primary School
  UPMR RM14 .... 393 G2
Bures C of E VC Primary School
  BURES CO8 .... 102 A3
Burleigh Primary School
  BAR EN8 .... 300 E2
Burlington Road Surgery
  IP IP1 .... 2 C3
Burnham Business Park
  BOC CM0 .... 344 A5
Burnham Clinic
  BOC CM0 .... 344 D6
Burnham Museum
  BOC CM0 .... 344 C7
Burnham-on-Crouch CP School
  BOC CM0 .... 344 E6
Burnham-on-Crouch Golf Club
  LOS SS9 .... 343 M5
Burnham Road Clinic
  LOS SS9 .... 399 K2
The Burnham Surgery
  BOC CM0 .... 344 C6
Burnham Trading Estate
  DART DA1 .... 414 E8
Burnside Industrial Estate
  BARK/HLT IG6 .... 350 C6
Burnt Mill Comprehensive
  School
  HLW CM20 .... 255 M1
Burntmill Industrial Estate
  HLW CM20 .... 226 D8
Burrsville County Junior
  & Infant School
  COS CO15 .... 224 B5
Burton End CP School
  HVHL CB9 .... 27 L4
Bus Depot
  IP IP1 .... 2 B5
Bush Hill Park Junior
  & Infant School
  EN EN1 .... 324 B7
Bush Hill Park Medical Centre
  EN EN1 .... 324 A8
Business Centre
  LOU IG10 .... 327 L6
The Business Centre
  HARH RM3 .... 352 E8
Butter Market
  Shopping Centre
  IP IP1 .... 2 F4
Buttsbury County
  Infant School
  BCAYW CM12 .... 335 J6
Buttsbury Junior Gm School
  BCAYW CM12 .... 335 J6
The Campion School
  EMPK RM11 .... 372 A4
Canewdon Endowed
  Primary School
  RCFD SS4 .... 364 F2
Canfield Cricket Club
  GTDUN CM6 .... 204 B2
Cann Hall Primary School
  RCOS CO16 .... 223 K5
Canons Brook Golf Club
  HLW CM20 .... 14 E2
Canvey County Junior
  & Infant School
  CVI SS8 .... 398 A8
Canvey Village Surgery
  CVI SS8 .... 397 M8
Capel Manor Primary School
  EN EN1 .... 300 B7
Capel St Mary School
  RIPS/CAP IP9 .... 78 B2
Capitol Industrial Centre
  WICKE SS11 .... 360 B6
Cardinal Park
  IP IP1 .... 2 E6
Car Ferry Terminal
  HAR CO12 .... 6 A3
Car Ferry Terminal
  HAR CO12 .... 112 F6
Carnarvon Medical Centre
  SOSN SS2 .... 20 F2
The Carpet Gallery
  CVI SS8 .... 398 D7
The Carpet Gallery
  HCH RM12 .... 371 J8
Carterhatch School
  EN EN1 .... 324 C3
Castle Camps Primary School
  CBE/LIN CB1 .... 26 F8
Castledon School
  WICKW SS12 .... 359 J6
Castle Garden Medical Centre
  COL CO1 .... 10 F7
Castle Manor Upper School
  HVHL CB9 .... 27 M3
Castle Middle School
  HVHL CB9 .... 27 L3
The Castle Museum
  COL CO1 .... 10 D7
Castle Point Borough Council
  SBF/HAD SS7 .... 380 B6
Castlepoint Museum
  CVI SS8 .... 399 G8
Castle Street Surgery
  SAFWN CB10 .... 65 L1
Castle View Clinic
  CVI SS8 .... 398 C5
Castle Walk Clinic
  STSD CM24 .... 147 G5
Cater Museum
  BCAYW CM12 .... 357 J1

Cathedral of St Mary
& St Helen
BRWN CM15 .... 354 E3
The Cathedral Primary School
CHLM/WR CM1 .... 17 J2
The Causeway Business Centre
BSF CM23 .... 174 A4
Causeway Industrial Estate
MGTR CO11 .... 108 C6
Causton County Junior School
FX IP11 .... 84 E7
Cavendish Primary School
SUD CO10 .... 32 D1
Cecil Avenue Surgery
EMPK RM11 .... 371 M3
Cecil Jones High School
SOSN SS2 .... 383 L8
Cedar Hall School
SBF/HAD SS7 .... 380 C5
Central Health Clinic
HARH RM3 .... 352 F6
Central Park Swimming Pool
FX IP11 .... 85 H8
Central Surgery
SBW CM21 .... 227 M1
Chadwell St Mary
Primary School
CDH/CHF RM16 .... 418 B1
The Chafford Hundred
Medical Centre
CDH/CHF RM16 .... 406 F8
Chafford School
RAIN RM13 .... 404 D3
Chalkstone Middle School
HVHL CB9 .... 28 B3
Chalkwell Hall Junior School
LOS SS9 .... 400 B2
Chalvedon School
PIT SS13 .... 378 C5
Channels Golf Club
RCHLM CM3 .... 235 M8
Chantry Clinic
CHTY IP2 .... 36 F8
Chantry Gallery
SUD CO10 .... 34 D3
Chantry High School
CHTY IP2 .... 37 G8
Chantry Junior & Infant School
CHTY IP2 .... 36 F7
Chapel Hill County
Primary School
BRTR CM7 .... 183 J1
Chappel C of E
(Controlled) Primary School
RCOLW CO6 .... 131 K6
Charfleet Industrial Estate
CVI SS8 .... 397 K8
Charterhouse Trading Estate
HVHL CB9 .... 28 D5
Chartwell Gallery
SOSN SS2 .... 21 G5
Chase Lane Primary School
HAR CO12 .... 142 F1
Chelmer Valley High School
CHLM/WR CM1 .... 264 B1
Chelmer Village Retail Park
CHLM/GWD CM2 .... 288 C4
Chelmondiston CP School
RIPS/CAP IP9 .... 81 M4
Chelmsford Athletics Club
CHLM/WR CM1 .... 263 M5
Chelmsford Cathedral
CHLM/WR CM1 .... 17 H2
Chelmsford College
CHLM/GWD CM2 .... 16 F7
Chelmsford County
High School
CHLM/WR CM1 .... 264 B7
Chelmsford District Council
CHLM/GWD CM2 .... 312 B1
Chelmsford & Essex Museum
CHLM/GWD CM2 .... 16 F8
Chelmsford Golf Club
CHLM/GWD CM2 .... 288 A5
Chelmsford Lawford
Mead County Junior School
CHLM/WR CM1 .... 263 L6
Chelmsford Road
Industrial Estate
GTDUN CM6 .... 179 G4
Chelmsford Rugby
Football Club
CHLM/WR CM1 .... 264 F7
Chelmsford Squash Club
CHLM/GWD CM2 .... 288 C4
Cherry Tree School
COLS CO2 .... 191 H3
Cherry Tree Surgery
FOS CO13 .... 199 G7
Cheshunt Community Hospital
BAR EN8 .... 300 D6
Cheshunt Football Club
BAR EN8 .... 300 D4
Cheshunt School
BAR EN8 .... 300 D3
Cheshunt & Waltham
Cross Council
BAR EN8 .... 300 F6
Chesterfield Junior
& Infant School
PEND EN3 .... 324 F1
Chetwood CP School
RCHLM CM3 .... 339 L5
Chief Clerk County Court
COLW CO3 .... 10 B9
Chigwell County
Primary School
CHIG IG7 .... 349 K3
Chigwell & Hainault Synagogue
CHIG IG7 .... 349 K6
Chigwell Row County
First School
CHIG IG7 .... 350 D3
Chigwell School
CHIG IG7 .... 349 K3

Childerditch Industrial Park
RBRW/HUT CM13 .... 374 A3
Chilton Industrial Estate
SUD CO10 .... 5 J3
Chinese Herbal Medical Centre
CHLM/GWD CM2 .... 17 H5
Chinese Herbal Medical Centre
WOS/PRIT SS0 .... 20 B5
Chinese Medical Centre
CHLM/WR CM1 .... 16 F2
Chinese Medical Centre
COL CO1 .... 10 B8
Chinese Medical Centre
HCH RM12 .... 389 M2
Chinese Medical Centre
IPNE IP4 .... 3 G4
Chinese Medical Centre
ROM RM1 .... 370 F6
Chinese Medical Centre
WOS/PRIT SS0 .... 20 E5
Chipping Hill County
Infant School
WIT CM8 .... 212 A8
Chipping Ongar
Primary School
CHONG CM5 .... 307 G2
Chirstchurch Mansion
IP IP1 .... 2 F3
Christchurch Park Hospital
IP IP1 .... 2 E2
Christmas Maltings Surgery
HVHL CB9 .... 28 A3
Churchgate C of E
Primary School
HLWE CM17 .... 228 A8
Church Lane School
UPMR RM14 .... 391 J4
Church Langley Primary School
HLWE CM17 .... 256 D3
Church of England
Primary School
SAFWN CB10 .... 42 E1
Church Trading Estate
ERITH DA8 .... 414 B4
Church View Surgery
RAYL SS6 .... 380 E1
Civic Centre
CHLM/WR CM1 .... 16 E2
Civic Centre
IP IP1 .... 2 D4
Civic Halls
CVI SS8 .... 398 C8
Civic Industrial Estate
HVHL CB9 .... 28 A6
Civic Theatre
CHLM/WR CM1 .... 16 E2
Civil Service Sports Club
KIR/NAC IP10 .... 60 D2
Clacton County High School
COS CO15 .... 13 J4
Clacton Covered Market
COS CO15 .... 13 G7
Clacton & District Hospital
COS CO15 .... 12 E9
Clacton Leisure Centre
COS CO15 .... 13 J3
Clacton on Sea Golf Club
COS CO15 .... 250 D3
Clacton Police Station
COS CO15 .... 12 E8
Clacton Rugby Club
COS CO15 .... 13 J2
Clair Gallery
BRWN CM15 .... 333 H8
Clare Middle School
SUD CO10 .... 31 L3
Clare Primary School
SUD CO10 .... 31 J3
Clarklands Industrial Estate
SBW CM21 .... 200 F6
Clavering Primary School
SAFWS CB11 .... 87 K7
Clements CP School
HVHL CB9 .... 27 M4
Clements Hall Leisure Centre
HOC/HUL SS5 .... 363 H7
Clements House Surgery
RCHLM CM3 .... 339 M4
Cliff Lane Primary School
IPSE IP3 .... 37 M8
Clifford Road Primary School
IPNE IP4 .... 3 M5
Clinic
HOC/HUL SS5 .... 361 M1
The Clinic
SBF/HAD SS7 .... 379 L8
Clockhouse Junior School
CRW RM5 .... 351 J7
Coastal Business Centre
COS CO15 .... 12 C6
Cockridden Farm
Industrial Estate
RBRW/HUT CM13 .... 375 G2
C of E Primary School
SUD CO10 .... 52 B2
Coggeshall Surgery
RCOLW CO6 .... 186 A1
Coggeshall Town Football Club
RCOLW CO6 .... 185 L2
Colbayns High School
COS CO15 .... 12 C3
Colchester Business Park
COLN CO4 .... 135 K5
Colchester County Court
COLS CO2 .... 162 F5
Colchester County Court
COLW CO3 .... 10 B9
Colchester County
High School for Girls
COLW CO3 .... 162 C5
Colchester District
General Hospital
COLN CO4 .... 134 F8
Colchester Golf Club
COLN CO4 .... 134 D8
Colchester Institute
COLW CO3 .... 162 E3

Colchester Jamiah Mosque
COL CO1 .... 10 E9
Colchester Mercury
Theatre Ltd
COLW CO3 .... 10 B8
Colchester Museums
COL CO1 .... 10 C7
Colchester Royal
Grammar School
COLW CO3 .... 162 E5
Colchester Rugby
Football Club
COLN CO4 .... 135 H5
Colchester Sixth Form School
COLW CO3 .... 10 B7
Colchester United
Football Club
COLS CO2 .... 162 D7
Colchester Zoo
COLW CO3 .... 189 K2
The Colin Dove Practice
ROM RM1 .... 371 G5
College Annexe
IPNE IP4 .... 3 G6
College of Teachers
EPP CM16 .... 303 L8
College St Pierre
LOS SS9 .... 400 B2
Collier Row Clinic
ROMW/RG RM7 .... 370 C1
Collier Row Football Club
ROMW/RG RM7 .... 370 A1
Collingwood Primary School
RCHLM CM3 .... 339 M5
The Colne Community School
RCOLE CO7 .... 220 F3
Colne Engaine C of E School
RCOLW CO6 .... 130 B1
Colneis County Junior School
FX IP11 .... 85 J7
Colne Medical Centre
RCOLE CO7 .... 220 F5
Colne View Retail Park
COL CO1 .... 10 F4
Colne Yacht Club
RCOLE CO7 .... 221 G6
Commonside School
HLWS CM18 .... 256 A7
Community Care
& Health Centre
COS CO15 .... 250 B3
Community Clinic
HLWS CM18 .... 256 A6
Community Health Centre
COL CO1 .... 10 D9
Coopersale Hall School
EPP CM16 .... 304 C5
Coopersale & Theydon Garnon
C of E Primary School
EPP CM16 .... 304 E1
Co-ordinated Industrial Estate
SBF/HAD SS7 .... 380 E4
Copdock CP School
RIPP IP8 .... 57 G2
Copdock Cricket Club
RIPP IP8 .... 57 G4
Copford C of E Primary School
RCOLW CO6 .... 188 D1
Copleston High School
IPNE IP4 .... 38 D6
Coppice Primary School
CHIG IG7 .... 350 B6
Coppins Green CP School
COS CO15 .... 12 E2
Corbets Tey School
UPMR RM14 .... 390 C4
Cornard Surgery
SUD CO10 .... 5 K8
Cornelius Vermuyden School
CVI SS8 .... 397 M6
Corneil Estate
CHLM/GWD CM2 .... 17 L4
Corn Exchange
and Film Theatre
IP IP1 .... 2 E4
Cornwallis Business Centre
BSDN SS14 .... 18 D1
Corringham County
Primary School
SLH/COR SS17 .... 395 K7
Corringham Health Centre
SLH/COR SS17 .... 395 J8
The Cottage Museum
BRTR CM7 .... 124 B2
Council Offices
COLW CO3 .... 162 D5
County Hall
CHLM/WR CM1 .... 17 G3
County Hall
IPNE IP4 .... 3 H5
County Junior & Infant School
BRWN CM15 .... 332 B8
County Junior School
CHLM/WR CM1 .... 287 H3
County Primary School
CHLM/WR CM1 .... 286 B7
County Primary School
FX IP11 .... 9 H6
County Primary School
FX IP11 .... 84 D6
County Primary School
RCHLM CM3 .... 317 G6
County Primary School
RCHLM CM3 .... 338 D6
County Primary School
RCOLE CO7 .... 106 D2
Coupals CP School
HVHL CB9 .... 28 E4
Coward Industrial Estate
CDH/CHF RM16 .... 418 C2
Cramphorn Theatre
CHLM/WR CM1 .... 16 F3
Cranbourne School
HOD EN11 .... 253 J2
Cranes Industrial Centre
BSDN SS14 .... 378 A1
Cranham Health Centre
UPMR RM14 .... 372 F7

Craylands Clinic
BSDN SS14 .... 377 M4
Crays Hill County
Primary School
BCAYE CM11 .... 358 C5
Crayside Industrial Estate
DART DA1 .... 414 B7
Crayside Industrial Estate
DART DA1 .... 414 C7
Creffield Road Surgery
COLW CO3 .... 162 E5
Cressing County
Primary School
BRTR CM7 .... 183 M5
Cricket Club
EPP CM16 .... 327 M1
Cricketers Retail Park
PIT SS13 .... 359 H8
Cricketers Retail Park
WICKW SS12 .... 359 L8
Cricket Squash Tennis
& Hockey Club
BSF CM23 .... 173 K3
Crishall C of E Primary School
ROY SG8 .... 40 D8
Criton Industrial Estate
CDH/CHF RM16 .... 408 F4
Crouch Yacht Club
BOC CM0 .... 344 C7
Crowlands Junior
& Infant School
ROMW/RG RM7 .... 370 D6
Crown College
WOS/PRIT SS0 .... 20 D4
Crown & County Court
BSDN SS14 .... 18 E5
Crown Court
SOSN SS2 .... 21 G3
Crownfield School
ROMW/RG RM7 .... 370 B2
Crown Hall
RAYL SS6 .... 380 D1
Crown Pools
IP IP1 .... 2 E3
Crowstone Preparatory School
RCFD SS4 .... 383 J3
Crowstone Preparatory School
WOS/PRIT SS0 .... 400 C3
Crusader Business Park
COS CO15 .... 224 B3
Curzon Avenue Surgery
PEND EN3 .... 324 E7
Dabchicks Sailing Club
K/T/MI CO5 .... 245 H4
Dacre Industrial Estate
BAR EN8 .... 300 F1
Dagenham Chest Clinic
BCTR RM8 .... 388 A2
Dagenham Civic Centre
DAGE RM10 .... 388 C1
Dagenham Priory School
DAGE RM10 .... 388 C6
Dagenham & Redbridge
Football Club
DAGE RM10 .... 388 C4
Dagenham Superbowl
DAGE RM10 .... 388 C8
Dagenham Swimming Pool
BCTR RM8 .... 388 A1
Dale Hall Primary School
IP IP1 .... 37 J1
Dame Johane Bradbury School
SAFWN CB10 .... 66 A1
Dame Tipping School
ABR/ST RM4 .... 351 L4
Danbury Clinic
RCHLM CM3 .... 291 G4
Danbury Park School
RCHLM CM3 .... 290 D4
D'arcy Gallery
IPNE IP4 .... 2 F5
Darlinghurst School
LOS SS9 .... 400 A1
Davenant Foundation School
LOU IG10 .... 327 K2
Deanes Secondary School
SBF/HAD SS7 .... 380 D5
Debden Sports Club
LOU IG10 .... 327 K7
Deben High School
FX IP11 .... 9 K1
Dedham C of E (Controlled)
School
RCOLE CO7 .... 107 H5
Dedham Sports Club
RCOLE CO7 .... 107 G5
De La Salle RC School
BSDN SS14 .... 19 H2
Deneholm CP School
CDH/CHF RM16 .... 407 K7
De Vere CP School
HSTD CO9 .... 73 M7
Dewhurst St Mary Junior
Middle & Infant School
CHESW EN7 .... 300 C1
Diane Matthews Clinic
ROMW/RG RM7 .... 370 E4
Dickens Place Surgery
CHLM/WR CM1 .... 263 L5
Dilkes CP School
SOCK/AV RM15 .... 406 A4
Dipple Medical Centre
PIT SS13 .... 378 C6
District Council Offices
RAYL SS6 .... 380 E1
Doctor Child's Surgery
HAR CO12 .... 141 M6
Doctors Chakrabarti Surgery
CRW RM5 .... 351 J8
Doddinghurst C of E
Junior School
BRWN CM15 .... 332 J5
Doddinghurst County
Infant School
BRWN CM15 .... 332 J5
Doggetts CP School
RCFD SS4 .... 364 A7

Dominoes Health Centre
GRAYS RM17 .... 417 H3
Doucecroft School
K/T/MI CO5 .... 186 D8
Dovercourt Swimming Pool
HAR CO12 .... 143 J2
Dovers Corner Industrial Estate
RAIN RM13 .... 404 A1
Downfield School
BAR EN8 .... 300 F3
Downhall Primary School
RAYL SS6 .... 361 L6
Downham C of E
Primary School
BCAYE CM11 .... 336 D7
Downing Primary School
CHTY IP2 .... 58 A1
The Downs CP School
HLW CM20 .... 15 M4
Drakes Lane Industrial Estate
RCHLM CM3 .... 236 C4
Drapers Sports Club
MAL CM9 .... 269 L6
Dr Guile Surgery
COS CO15 .... 224 B3
Dr Mirza Practice
COS CO15 .... 12 E5
Dry Ski Slope
RBRW/HUT CM13 .... 354 D4
Dukes Park Industrial Estate
CHLM/GWD CM2 .... 265 G7
The Dukes Priory Hospital
CHLM/WR CM1 .... 264 E7
Dunmow C of E Junior School
GTDUN CM6 .... 178 D3
Dunmow County
Infants School
GTDUN CM6 .... 178 E2
Dunmow Sports Centre
GTDUN CM6 .... 150 D8
Dunningford Primary School
HCH RM12 .... 389 G4
Durants School
EN EN1 .... 324 D3
Dycorts School
HARH RM3 .... 353 H5
Eagle House Surgery
PEND EN3 .... 324 D6
Earls Colne CP School
RCOLW CO6 .... 130 C5
Earls Hall Infant School
WOS/PRIT SS0 .... 382 E7
Earthworks Gallery
HCH RM12 .... 371 M8
East Anglian Railway Museum
RCOLW CO6 .... 131 L5
Eastbrook Secondary School
DAGE RM10 .... 388 D3
Eastern Angles Theatre Co
IP IP1 .... 2 A2
Eastern Angles Theatre Co
IP IP1 .... 37 G4
East Essex Adult
Community College
MAL CM9 .... 293 G1
East Essex Aviation
Society & Museum
RCOS CO16 .... 220 F7
Eastfield Primary
& Infant School
PEND EN3 .... 324 E2
Eastgate Business Centre
BSDN SS14 .... 19 G7
Eastgate Shopping Centre
IP IP1 .... 2 F4
East Hanningfield
C of E Primary School
RCHLM CM3 .... 314 C4
East Herts District Council
BSF CM23 .... 174 A3
East Herts District Council
SBW CM21 .... 227 M1
East Thurrock Football Club
SLH/COR SS17 .... 395 J8
East Tilbury Surgery
TIL RM18 .... 419 J1
Eastwood Gm Infant School
LOS SS9 .... 382 A6
Eastwood Gm Junior School
LOS SS9 .... 382 A5
Eastwood High School
LOS SS9 .... 382 A6
Eastwood Industrial Estate
LOS SS9 .... 381 K5
Edith Borthwick School
BRTR CM7 .... 155 G3
Edward Francis
Community Junior School
RAYL SS6 .... 361 M8
Edwards Hall Junior
& Infant School
LOS SS9 .... 381 K4
Edwin Lambert Schooll
EMPK RM11 .... 371 H6
Eight Ash Green C of E
Primary School
RCOLW CO6 .... 161 G2
Eldenwall Industrial Estate
BCTR RM8 .... 370 A8
Eldon Way Industrial Estate
HOC/HUL SS5 .... 362 F5
Eleanor Estate
BAR EN8 .... 301 G6
Elm Green School
RCHLM CM3 .... 266 E8
Elm Hall County
Primary School
WIT CM8 .... 212 A5
Elms Business Park
WICKW SS12 .... 359 M7
Elmstead Market Surgery
RCOLE CO7 .... 165 H6
The Elmwood CP School
RCHLM CM3 .... 339 L4
Elton Park Business Centre
CHTY IP2 .... 36 F5
Elton Park Industrial Estate
CHTY IP2 .... 36 F5

Elwyn House Felsted School
GTDUN CM6 .... 180 D5

Emerson Park School
EMPK RM11 .... 372 C7

Endeavour School
BRWN CM15 .... 355 G4

Enfield Business Centre
PEND EN3 .... 324 D4

Enfield College
PEND EN3 .... 324 D5

Enfield Football Club Ltd
EN EN1 .... 324 B5

Engaines Primary School
RCOS CO16 .... 223 L1

Engayne Junior School
UPMR RM14 .... 372 F6

Enterprise Trading Estate
BRTR CM7 .... 182 A2

Epping County Infant School
EPP CM16 .... 303 M1

Epping County Junior School
EPP CM16 .... 304 A2

Epping Forest District Council
CHIG IG7 .... 349 L6

Epping Forest District Council
EPP CM16 .... 304 A2

Epping Forest District Council
EPP CM16 .... 304 B2

Epping Forest District Council
LOU IG10 .... 327 K6

Epping & Ongar Rural
District Council
EPP CM16 .... 304 E5

Theydon Bois Golf Club
EPP CM16 .... 303 L6

Theydon Bois Golf Club
EPP CM16 .... 304 A3

Epping Town Council
EPP CM16 .... 304 A3

Epping Upland Cofe
Primary School
EPP CM16 .... 279 J5

Erith Small Business Centre
ERITH DA8 .... 414 A3

Erith Theatre Guild
ERITH DA8 .... 414 A2

Essex County Council
BKHH IG9 .... 348 E4

Essex County Council
BRW CM14 .... 353 L2

Essex County Council
BRW CM14 .... 354 E3

Essex County Council
BSDN SS14 .... 377 M4

Essex County Council
CHIG IG7 .... 349 K2

Essex County Council
CHONG CM5 .... 283 H6

Essex County Council
CVI SS8 .... 397 M7

Essex County Council
EPP CM16 .... 304 A2

Essex County Council
GRAYS RM17 .... 417 J2

Essex County Council
LOU IG10 .... 327 J5

Essex County Council
LOU IG10 .... 327 H4

Essex County Council
PIT SS13 .... 378 D1

Essex County Council
RAYL SS6 .... 380 E2

Essex County Council
RAYL SS6 .... 380 E1

Essex County Council
RBRW/HUT CM13 .... 354 C7

Essex County Council
RCFD SS4 .... 382 F1

Essex County Council
SBF/HAD SS7 .... 380 A7

Essex County Council
SOSN SS2 .... 383 H6

Essex County Council
TIL RM18 .... 418 B6

Essex County Council
WAB EN9 .... 301 K5

Essex County Cricket Club
CHLM/GWD CM2 .... 16 F4

Essex County Hospital
COLW CO3 .... 162 E5

The Essex Nuffield Hospital
BRWN CM15 .... 354 F2

Europa Trading Estate
WTHK RM20 .... 416 E2

Everest Sports Club
BAR EN8 .... 300 C1

Everik Business Centre
RBRW/HUT CM13 .... 333 M7

Eversley College
SBW CM21 .... 227 L1

Eversley CP School
PIT SS13 .... 378 D5

The Eye Clinic
LOS SS9 .... 399 H1

The Eye Clinic
SBN/FI SS3 .... 402 E5

Fairfield Clinic
BKHH IG9 .... 348 C2

Fairfield Infant School
FX IP11 .... 85 H8

Fairfields Junior Middle
& Infant School
CHESW EN7 .... 276 B7

Fairhouse Junior
& Infant School
BSDN SS14 .... 19 L6

Fairways Primary School
LOS SS9 .... 381 K7

The Fairways
BAR EN8 .... 276 E6

Farnham School
BSF CM23 .... 145 L5

Fawbert & Barnards
(UNDL) Primary School
HLWE CM17 .... 227 K8

Feering Primary School
K/T/MI CO5 .... 186 F7

Felixstowe Ferry Golf Club
FX IP11 .... 85 M6

Felixstowe International
College
FX IP11 .... 85 K8

Felixstowe Port & Town
Football Club
FX IP11 .... 8 E8

Felixstowe Rugby Club
FX IP11 .... 8 F3

Felmore County Infant School
PIT SS13 .... 378 C3

Felsted CP School
GTDUN CM6 .... 180 E4

Felsted Preparatory School
GTDUN CM6 .... 180 C6

Felsted School
GTDUN CM6 .... 180 C5

Felsted School
GTDUN CM6 .... 180 D5

Ferndale Surgery
WFD IG8 .... 348 D7

Fern House Surgery
WIT CM8 .... 239 G2

Ferry Lane Industrial Estate
RAIN RM13 .... 404 B3

Finchingfield C of E
Primary School
BRTR CM7 .... 94 E5

Fingringhoe C of E School
K/T/MI CO5 .... 192 A6

Fire Station
IP IP1 .... 2 C6

The Firs Junior School
BSF CM23 .... 173 M5

Fitzwimarc Secondary School
RAYL SS6 .... 361 M8

Five Elms School
DAGW RM9 .... 388 A4

Flamstead End Junior School
CHESW EN7 .... 276 B7

Fledgelings Pre-school
CHLM/GWD CM2 .... 288 B6

Flitch Industrial Estate
GTDUN CM6 .... 178 E4

Florance Nightingale
Health Centre
HLWE CM17 .... 256 D3

Follyfield Felsted School
GTDUN CM6 .... 180 D6

Fondu Sports Club
PUR RM19 .... 415 K1

Football Stadium
IPNE IP4 .... 39 H6

Ford End C of E Primary School
RCHLM CM3 .... 207 J1

Fordham C of E Primary School
RCOLW CO6 .... 132 E7

Forest Industrial Park
BARK/HLT IG6 .... 349 M8

Forest Medical Centre
LOU IG10 .... 326 F7

Forres CP School
HOD EN11 .... 253 J2

Forrester Park Golf
& Tennis Club
MAL CM9 .... 240 D6

Forty Hill C of E School
EN EN1 .... 324 B1

Four Hands Gallery
ING CM4 .... 310 D7

The Four Swanns Jmi School
BAR EN8 .... 300 F5

Foxearth Primary School
SUD CO10 .... 33 K5

The Foxhall Hospital
KIR/NAC IP10 .... 39 J7

Frances Bardsley
School for Girls
ROM RM1 .... 371 H6

Franklin Way Practice
RCHLM CM3 .... 338 A6

Franklin Way Practice
WICKE SS11 .... 359 M3

Freshwell Health Centre
BRTR CM7 .... 94 E5

Friars Clinic
SUD CO10 .... 4 C7

Friars County Junior School
SBN/FI SS3 .... 403 G3

Friars Grove Junior
& Infant School
COLN CO4 .... 11 K2

Friends School
SAFWS CB11 .... 65 M3

Frinton Golf Club
FOS CO13 .... 225 M1

Frinton on Sea CP School
FOS CO13 .... 198 F6

Frinton on Sea Lawn
Tennis Club
FOS CO13 .... 198 F8

Frinton Road Medical Centre
COS CO15 .... 224 E5

Frinton Summer Theatre
FOS CO13 .... 199 G6

The Frinton & Walton Heritage
Museum
WOTN CO14 .... 199 M2

Frinton & Walton
Swimming Pool
WOTN CO14 .... 199 L2

Frobisher Primary School
COS CO15 .... 250 A2

Frost Business Centre
BRTR CM7 .... 156 D3

The Fryerns Medical Centre
BSDN SS14 .... 377 M3

Furneux Pelham C of E School
BUNT SG9 .... 116 D3

Fyfield Dr Walkers
C of E Primary School
ING CM4 .... 283 L1

Gable Hall Gm School
SLH/COR SS17 .... 395 G6

Gainsborough Clinic
IPSE IP3 .... 59 H2

The Gallery at Lakeside
WTHK RM20 .... 416 C1

The Gallery
BOC CM0 .... 344 D7

The Gallery
CHLM/GWD CM2 .... 17 H5

The Gallery
COLW CO3 .... 161 M7

The Gallery
IPNE IP4 .... 3 G5

The Gallery
SBF/HAD SS7 .... 397 L2

The Gallery
SUD CO10 .... 31 J4

Galleywood County
Infant School
CHLM/GWD CM2 .... 312 C1

Galliard Primary School
ED N9 .... 324 B8

Ganges Museum
RIPS/CAP IP9 .... 113 K3

Garfield Gallery
RAYL SS6 .... 380 E1

Gaynes School
UPMR RM14 .... 390 D4

Geoffrey Whitworth Theatre
DART DA1 .... 414 A8

George Spicer Primary School
EN EN1 .... 324 A5

Gepps House Felsted School
GTDUN CM6 .... 180 C5

Ghyllgrove County
Junior School
BSDN SS14 .... 18 A4

Gidea Park College
GPK RM2 .... 371 H3

Gidea Park Primary School
GPK RM2 .... 371 G4

Gidea Park Sports Ground
GPK RM2 .... 371 K2

Giffards County Junior
& Infant School
SLH/COR SS17 .... 395 G7

Gilberd School
COLN CO4 .... 135 J6

The Glade Business Centre
WTHK RM20 .... 416 A2

Glebe Infant School & U H I
RAYL SS6 .... 361 K8

Glenwood School
WICKW SS12 .... 379 H4

Globe Industrial Estate
GRAYS RM17 .... 417 K3

Globe Works Industrial Estate
GRAYS RM17 .... 417 L2

Gobions Jmi School
CRW RM5 .... 351 L7

Goffs School
CHESW EN7 .... 300 B1

Goldings Hill Clinic
LOU IG10 .... 327 H4

Golds Nurseries Business Park
RBSF CM22 .... 119 J8

Gorse Lane Industrial Estate
COS CO15 .... 224 C3

Gosbecks Junior
& Infant School
COLS CO2 .... 162 B8

Gosfield Lake Golf Club
HSTD CO9 .... 127 K3

Gosfield Primary School
HSTD CO9 .... 127 M3

Gosfield School
HSTD CO9 .... 128 B1

The Gowan Gallery
SBW CM21 .... 227 M1

Grange Paddock
Swimming Pool
BSF CM23 .... 174 A2

Grange Park Industrial Estate
COLS CO2 .... 163 L8

Grange Primary School
WICKW SS12 .... 359 J5

Grange Road Primary School
FX IP11 .... 8 F1

Grange Way Business Park
COLS CO2 .... 163 L8

Grays Athletic Football Club
GRAYS RM17 .... 417 J3

Grays Business Centre
GRAYS RM17 .... 407 K8

Grays Convent High School
GRAYS RM17 .... 417 J1

Grays County Court
GRAYS RM17 .... 417 H3

The Grays GM School
GRAYS RM17 .... 407 J8

Grays Health Centre
GRAYS RM17 .... 417 H2

Great Baddow High School
CHLM/GWD CM2 .... 288 E5

Great Bardfield County School
BRTR CM7 .... 124 C1

Great Bentley CP School
RCOLE CO7 .... 194 E4

Great Berry CP School
VGE SS16 .... 376 A7

Great Bradfords County
Infant School
BRTR CM7 .... 155 J7

The Great Clacton Surgery
COS CO15 .... 224 A5

Great Cornard Middle School
SUD CO10 .... 55 K7

Great Cornard Upper School
SUD CO10 .... 55 J7

Great Dunmow Town Council
GTDUN CM6 .... 178 D3

Great Leighs CP School
RCHLM CM3 .... 209 H4

Great Oaks Clinic
BSDN SS14 .... 18 F6

Great Sampford County
Primary School
SAFWN CB10 .... 69 H8

Great Stony School
CHONG CM5 .... 283 H7

Great Tey Primary School
RCOLW CO6 .... 159 K2

Great Totham County
Primary School
MAL CM9 .... 240 B6

The Great Wakering
Health Centre
SBN/FI SS3 .... 385 G7

Great Wakering
Primary School
SBN/FI SS3 .... 385 H8

Great Wakering
Sports Centre
SBN/FI SS3 .... 385 G7

Great Waltham C of E School
RCHLM CM3 .... 234 F4

Greenstead Clinic
COLN CO4 .... 163 M3

Greensted County
Infant School
BSDN SS14 .... 377 M5

Greensward College
HOC/HUL SS5 .... 362 F4

Greensward Surgery
HOC/HUL SS5 .... 363 G4

Greenwich Business Park
IPSE IP3 .... 58 F1

Greenwood School
HSTD CO9 .... 99 G8

Greenwood Surgery
RCHLM CM3 .... 339 M4

The Group Surgery
COLW CO3 .... 162 E5

Grove Junior & Infant School
RAYL SS6 .... 381 H2

Grove Lodge Surgery
COS CO15 .... 224 E6

Grove Tennis Club
CHLM/GWD CM2 .... 17 G9

Grundy Park Leisure Centre
BAR EN8 .... 300 F2

Guardian Business Centre
HARH RM3 .... 352 E8

Guildhall & Museum
BRTR CM7 .... 94 E5

Guildhall Surgery
SUD CO10 .... 31 J4

Gulpher Business Park
FX IP11 .... 85 G5

Guru Gobind Singh
Khalsa College
CHIG IG7 .... 349 G2

Gusford Primary School
CHTY IP2 .... 57 L2

GX
CHLM/WR CM1 .... 287 M4

GX Superbowl
CHLM/WR CM1 .... 287 M4

Hacton Infant School
HCH RM12 .... 389 M3

Hadleigh Business Centre
SBF/HAD SS7 .... 398 F1

Hadleigh Castle
SBF/HAD SS7 .... 398 F2

Hadleigh Clinic
SBF/HAD SS7 .... 380 D8

Hadleigh Junior School
SBF/HAD SS7 .... 380 F8

Haileybury College
HERT/BAY SG13 .... 252 E1

Hailey Hall School
HOD EN11 .... 253 G1

Hainault Forest High School
CHIG IG7 .... 350 B6

Hainault Industrial Estate
BARK/HLT IG6 .... 350 D6

Halifax Primary School
CHTY IP2 .... 58 C1

Hallmark Industrial Estate
BOC CM0 .... 320 F7

Hall Mead School
UPMR RM14 .... 372 E7

Hall Road Industrial Estate
BOC CM0 .... 320 F8

Hallsford Bridge
Industrial Estate
CHONG CM5 .... 307 K3

Hallsford Business Centre
CHONG CM5 .... 307 K3

The Hall
SAFWS CB11 .... 89 M7

Halstead Business Centre
HSTD CO9 .... 128 F2

Halstead Hospital
HSTD CO9 .... 98 F8

Halstead Primary School
HSTD CO9 .... 129 G2

Halstead Town Football Club
HSTD CO9 .... 128 F1

Hamford CP School
FOS CO13 .... 199 G4

Hamilton School
COLW CO3 .... 162 E6

Hamstel Primary School
SOSN SS2 .... 401 L1

Handford Hall Primary School
IP IP1 .... 2 A3

Hare Street County Junior
& Infant School
HLWW/ROY CM19 .... 15 J5

Harlowbury School
HLWE CM17 .... 227 L7

Harlow Business Park
HLWW/ROY CM19 .... 14 A4

Harlow College
HLW CM20 .... 15 L5

Harlow College
HLW CM20 .... 255 M2

Harlow Museum
HLWS CM18 .... 15 K7

Harlow Rugby Football Club
HLW CM20 .... 255 J1

Harlow Sailing Club
RCHLM CM3 .... 319 G1

Harlow Sports Centre
HLW CM20 .... 15 K1

Harlow Sports Centre
HLW CM20 .... 15 L1

Harlow Sports Centre
HLW CM20 .... 255 L1

Harlow Urban District
Swimming Pool
HLW CM20 .... 255 M1

Harold Court School
HARH RM3 .... 353 H8

Harold Wood Clinic
HARH RM3 .... 372 A2

Harold Wood Jmi School
HARH RM3 .... 372 B3

The Hartswood Clinic
RBRW/HUT CM13 .... 354 C7

Harvey Centre
HLW CM20 .... 15 L4

Harwich County Primary School
HAR CO12 .... 7 K5

Harwich County Primary School
HAR CO12 .... 7 L5

Harwich & District Hospital
HAR CO12 .... 6 D9

Harwich Golf Club
HAR CO12 .... 6 A6

Harwich Industrial Estate
HAR CO12 .... 6 B5

Harwich & Parkeston
Football Club
HAR CO12 .... 7 G8

The Harwich School
HAR CO12 .... 143 H1

Harwich Sports Centre
HAR CO12 .... 143 H1

Harwich Town Sailing Club
HAR CO12 .... 7 L3

Haslemere Industrial Estate
BSF CM23 .... 174 B7

Haslemere Business Centre
EN EN1 .... 324 C1

Haslemere Industrial Estate
HLWW/ROY CM19 .... 14 E6

Haslewood Junior School
HOD EN11 .... 253 H4

Hassenbrook School
SLH/COR SS17 .... 409 M1

Hassengate Medical Centre
SLH/COR SS17 .... 394 D8

Hatfield Heath CP School
RBSF CM22 .... 202 B8

Hatfield Peverel County
Infant School
RCHLM CM3 .... 238 D7

Haven Health Surgery
FX IP11 .... 8 E1

Haverhill Golf Club Ltd
HVHL CB9 .... 28 F5

Haverhill Rovers Football Club
HVHL CB9 .... 28 B5

Haverhill Sports Centre
HVHL CB9 .... 28 C4

Havering College of
Further & Higher Education
EMPK RM11 .... 371 J7

Havering College of
Further & Higher Education
EMPK RM11 .... 371 M4

Havering College of
Further & Higher Education
HARH RM3 .... 353 G5

Havering Court Nursing Home
ROM RM1 .... 351 M2

Havering Cricket Club
ABR/ST RM4 .... 330 A5

Havering Hospitals N H S Trust
HARH RM3 .... 371 M1

Havering Magistrates Court
ROM RM1 .... 370 F4

Havering Sixth Form College
EMPK RM11 .... 372 A8

Havers Infant School
BSF CM23 .... 173 M6

Hawkesbury Road
Doctors Surgery
CVI SS8 .... 397 M8

Hawkswood School & Centre
CHING E4 .... 325 K7

The Hayward School
CHLM/WR CM1 .... 264 B7

Hazelmere Junior School
COLN CO4 .... 163 M3

The Health Centre
HARH RM3 .... 352 F6

Health Service Clinic
COLS CO2 .... 191 H2

Health & Welfare Clinic
RAIN RM13 .... 389 H7

The Heathcote School
RCHLM CM3 .... 290 F4

Heath CP School
KESC IP5 .... 39 J4

Heathlands Primary School
RCOLW CO6 .... 133 M6

Heath School
COLW CO3 .... 161 L6

Heathside Special School
IPNE IP4 .... 38 D5

Heathway Medical Centre
DAGW RM9 .... 388 A3

Heavitrees Surgery
CHLM/GWD CM2 .... 16 D3

Heddington Castle
HSTD CO9 .... 74 A7

Hedgerows Business Park
CHLM/WR CM1 .... 265 H5

Hedingham County
Secondary School
HSTD CO9 .... 73 L8

Hedley Walter High School
BRWN CM15 .... 354 D1

Helena Romanes School
GTDUN CM6 .... 178 D1

Helsinki Health Centre
IPSE IP3 .... 38 E9

Henham & Ugley CP School
RBSF CM22 .... 120 A6

The Hereward County School
LOU IG10 .... 327 L3

Herington House
  Preparatory School
    BRWN CM15 .... 333 H8
Herons Gate Trading Estate
    BSDN SS14 .... 378 B1
Herringham County
  Infant School
    CDH/CHF RM16 .... 418 C1
Hertfordshire & Essex General
  Hospital
    BSF CM23 .... 174 D5
Hertfordshire & Essex
  High School
    BSF CM23 .... 174 C4
Heybridge CP School
    MAL CM9 .... 269 K6
Heybridge House
  Industrial Estate
    MAL CM9 .... 269 J7
Heybridge Swifts Football Club
    MAL CM9 .... 269 L5
High Beech C of E
  Primary School
    LOU IG10 .... 326 B3
Highfields County
  Primary School
    MGTR CO11 .... 108 D7
Highlands Surgery
    LOS SS9 .... 399 J1
High Ongar CP School
    CHONG CM5 .... 283 K7
High Street Surgery
  & Medical Centre
    EPP CM16 .... 304 B2
Highwood Hospital
    BRWN CM15 .... 354 C2
Highwoods County
  Primary School
    COLN CO4 .... 135 J7
Highwoods Surgery
    COLN CO4 .... 135 J7
Hilldene Junior School
    HARH RM3 .... 352 D7
Hillgrove Business Park
    WAB EN9 .... 277 K2
Hillmead Jmi School
    BSF CM23 .... 174 C1
Hillside Primary School
    CHTY IP2 .... 2 E9
Hillside Special School
    SUD CO10 .... 4 E2
Hilltop Junior & Infant School
    WICKE SS11 .... 360 B3
Hilton House Surgery
    HSTD CO9 .... 97 M3
Hinguar Primary School
    SBN/FI SS3 .... 403 G4
Hm Customs and Excise
    IPNE IP4 .... 2 F5
Hoblongs Industrial Estate
    GTDUN CM6 .... 178 F5
Hockerill Anglo European
  GM School
    BSF CM23 .... 174 C4
Hockerill Sports Club
    BSF CM23 .... 174 C6
Hockley Primary School
    HOC/HUL SS5 .... 362 D5
Hoddesdon Health Centre
    HOD EN11 .... 253 H6
Hoddesdon Industrial Estate
    HOD EN11 .... 253 K4
Hoddesdon Lawn Tennis Club
    HOD EN11 .... 253 G5
Hoddesdon St Pauls
  Infant School
    HOD EN11 .... 253 H6
Hogarth Primary School
    BRWN CM15 .... 355 L4
Holbrook CP School
    RIPS/CAP IP9 .... 80 E5
Holbrook High School
    RIPS/CAP IP9 .... 80 E5
Holdbrook Junior Middle
  & Infant School
    BAR EN8 .... 301 G6
Holland Haven Primary School
    COS CO15 .... 224 F5
Holland Park Primary School
    COS CO15 .... 13 L2
Holly House Private Hospital
    BKHH IG9 .... 348 C3
The Holly Trees County
  Infant School
    BRW CM14 .... 354 C5
Hollytrees Junior School
    BRW CM14 .... 354 C5
Hollywood Bowl
    BSDN SS14 .... 377 J2
Holmwood House School
    COLW CO3 .... 161 L3
Holt Farm Infant School
    RCFD SS4 .... 363 L8
Holy Cross RC Primary School
    HLWS CM18 .... 256 B5
Holy Cross RC School
    SOCK/AV RM15 .... 406 C5
Holy Family RC
  Primary School
    WIT CM8 .... 239 G3
Holy Family School
    SBF/HAD SS7 .... 379 L4
Holy Trinity C of E
  Primary School
    BAR EN8 .... 300 E4
Holy Trinity C of E
  Primary School
    HSTD CO9 .... 128 E1
Holywells High School
    IPSE IP3 .... 59 K2
Home Farm CP School
    COLW CO3 .... 161 M5
Homestead School
    COLN CO4 .... 105 M7
The Honeywood School
    RCOLW CO6 .... 158 B8

Honilands Junior
  & Infant School
    EN EN1 .... 300 C8
Hornchurch Clinic
    EMPK RM11 .... 371 M8
Hornchurch Sports Centre
    HCH RM12 .... 389 K1
Horndon Industrial Park
    RBRW/HUT CM13 .... 374 D6
Horndon-on-the-Hill
  C of E Primary School
    SLH/COR SS17 .... 394 A7
Howard Business Park
    WAB EN9 .... 301 L6
Howbridge Infants School
    WIT CM8 .... 239 G3
Howbridge Juniors School
    WIT CM8 .... 239 G3
Howe Green House School
    RBSF CM22 .... 201 L1
Hullbridge Clinic
    HOC/HUL SS5 .... 361 L1
Hullbridge Parochial
  Church Council
    HOC/HUL SS5 .... 361 L1
Hullbridge Sports Club
    HOC/HUL SS5 .... 361 M2
Hunters Hall School
    DAGE RM10 .... 388 C4
Hurst Drive JMI School
    BAR EN8 .... 300 E6
Hutton All Saints
  C of E Primary School
    RBRW/HUT CM13 .... 333 L8
Hutton Clinic
    RBRW/HUT CM13 .... 333 L8
Hyland House & Park
    CHLM/WR CM1 .... 287 K6
Hylands School
    CHLM/WR CM1 .... 287 L2
Ilford Trading Estate
    BSDN SS14 .... 377 M1
Immanuel School
    ROM RM1 .... 351 M7
Imperial Trading Estate
    RAIN RM13 .... 404 D2
Industrial Centre
    CHTY IP2 .... 2 F7
Industrial Estate
    EPP CM16 .... 280 D5
Industrial Estate
    RCHLM CM3 .... 314 C5
Industrial Estate
    RCHLM CM3 .... 319 J3
Industrial Park
    BAR EN8 .... 301 H6
Ingatestone County
  Infant School
    ING CM4 .... 310 B7
Ingatestone & Fryerning C of E
  Primary School
    ING CM4 .... 310 B7
Ingrave Johnstone
  C of E School
    RBRW/HUT CM13 .... 355 K7
Ingrebourne CP School
    HARH RM3 .... 352 D5
International Business Centre
    CVI SS8 .... 397 L8
International Business Park
    CVI SS8 .... 397 K8
Ipswich BC Crown Court
    IP IP1 .... 2 D4
Ipswich Civic College
    IP IP1 .... 2 E3
Ipswich Golf Club
    IPSE IP3 .... 60 A1
Ipswich High School for Girls
    RIPS/CAP IP9 .... 81 K1
Ipswich Hospital N H S Trust
    IPNE IP4 .... 38 D5
Ipswich Museums & Art Gallery
    IP IP1 .... 2 E3
Ipswich Regent Theatre
    IPNE IP4 .... 3 G4
Ipswich Rugby Union
  Football Club
    IPNE IP4 .... 38 C1
Ipswich School
    IP IP1 .... 2 E1
Ipswich School
    IP IP1 .... 37 J3
Ipswich Sports Club
    IP IP1 .... 37 K2
Ipswich Town Football Club
    IP IP1 .... 2 C5
Ipswich Transport Museum
    IPSE IP3 .... 59 K1
Island Golf
    CVI SS8 .... 398 A5
Island Surgery
    CVI SS8 .... 413 K1
Ivry Street Medical Practice
    IP IP1 .... 2 D1
Ivy Chimneys Primary School
    EPP CM16 .... 304 A4
Jacques Hall School
    MGTR CO11 .... 110 B8
Janet Duke County
  Infant School
    LAIN SS15 .... 376 E5
Jerounds Junior
  & Infant School
    HLWW/ROY CM19 .... 255 J6
John Bramston Infant School
    BARK/HLT IG6 .... 350 B7
The John Bramston School
    WIT CM8 .... 239 G2
John Bunyan Junior
  & Infant School
    BRTR CM7 .... 154 D1
John Cotgrove Gallery
    LOS SS9 .... 399 M3
John Perry School
    DAGE RM10 .... 388 E5
John Ray CP School
    BRTR CM7 .... 183 G3

John Russell Gallery
    IPSE IP3 .... 3 H6
The John Warner School
    HOD EN11 .... 253 J2
The Jones Family Practice
    HOC/HUL SS5 .... 362 E6
Jotmans Hall Primary School
    SBF/HAD SS7 .... 379 J7
Joyce Green Hospital
    DART DA1 .... 415 G6
Katherine Semar Junior School
    SAFWS CB11 .... 65 M5
Katherines Primary School
    HLWW/ROY CM19 .... 14 E9
Kedington Primary School
    PEND CM3 .... 300 D7
Kelrose Swimming Pool Centre
    BRWN/HUT CM13 .... 373 M5
Kelvedon Hatch CP School
    BRWN CM15 .... 307 M8
Kelvedon St Marys C of E
  Primary School
    K/T/MI CO5 .... 213 K1
Kendall Primary School
    COL CO1 .... 163 K7
Kenneth Mark Practice
    SAFWN CB10 .... 65 L1
Kenningtons Primary School
    SOCK/AV RM15 .... 405 K4
Kent Kraft Industrial Estate
    GVW DA11 .... 417 G8
Kents Hill Junior School
    SBF/HAD SS7 .... 379 L7
Kents Hill Road Surgery
    SBF/HAD SS7 .... 379 L6
Kesgrave High School
    KESG IP5 .... 39 L2
Kestner Industrial Estate
    GRH DA9 .... 416 B8
King Edmunds School
    RCFD SS4 .... 363 M6
King Edward Grammer
  Sports Ground
    CHLM/WR CM1 .... 235 G7
King Harold Comprehensive
  School
    WAB EN9 .... 301 M5
The King John School
    SBF/HAD SS7 .... 380 C8
Kingsdale Industrial Estate
    CHLM/WR CM1 .... 17 J1
Kingsdown School
    CHLM/WR CM1 .... 17 J1
Kings Estate
    HCH RM12 .... 389 H3
Kingsfleet Primary School
    FX IP11 .... 85 K7
Kingsford County Junior
  & Infant School
    COLS CO2 .... 162 D8
Kingsmead School
    EN EN1 .... 324 B6
Kingsmoor Junior
  & Infant School
    HLWW/ROY CM19 .... 255 K7
Kingsmoor Recreation Centre
    HLWW/ROY CM19 .... 255 J7
Kings Road Junior School
    CHLM/WR CM1 .... 264 A7
Kingston CP School
    SBF/HAD SS7 .... 379 M5
Kingsway Hall Art and Theatre
    HAR CO12 .... 7 J7
Kingswode Hoe Special School
    COLW CO3 .... 162 D4
Kingswood County Junior
  & Infant School
    VGE SS16 .... 19 H8
Kingswood Medical Centre
    VGE SS16 .... 19 H9
Kings Wood School
    HARH RM3 .... 353 H5
Kingswood Surgery
    VGE SS16 .... 19 G8
Kirby Le Soken Primary School
    FOS CO13 .... 198 C4
Knightsmead School
    SOCK/AV RM15 .... 406 B5
K-P Skillion Business Centre
    BSDN SS14 .... 18 F1
Laburnum Health Centre
    DAGE RM10 .... 388 B1
Lady of Lourdes RC School
    LOS SS9 .... 400 B1
Laindon Health Centre
    LAIN SS15 .... 376 C5
Laindon Park CP School
    LAIN SS15 .... 18 A2
Laindon Road Clinic
    BCAYW CM12 .... 357 H3
The Laindon School
    LAIN SS15 .... 376 C3
Lakeside Shopping Centre
    WTHK RM20 .... 406 C8
Lambourne CP School
    ABR/ST RM4 .... 328 C6
Landseer Business Park
    IPSE IP3 .... 37 L8
Langenhoe CP School
    K/T/MI CO5 .... 218 B1
Langer Park Industrial Estate
    FX IP11 .... 9 H5
Langham Primary School
    COLN CO4 .... 106 A7
Langtons Junior
  & Infant School
    EMPK RM11 .... 371 M8
Lansdowne County
  Primary School
    TIL RM18 .... 418 A6
La Salette RC Primary School
    RAIN RM13 .... 404 B1
Laser Clinic
    CHESW EN7 .... 300 C2
Latchingdon C of E
  Primary School
    RCHLM CM3 .... 318 C5

Latton Bush Business Centre
    HLWS CM18 .... 256 A6
Latton Bush Recreation Centre
    HLWS CM18 .... 255 M6
The Laurels Surgery
    RCHLM CM3 .... 266 A3
Laurence Industrial Estate
    SOSN SS2 .... 382 C5
Lawford C of E GM
  Primary School
    MGTR CO11 .... 138 B1
Leas School
    COS CO15 .... 12 C1
Lea Valley High School
    PEND EN3 .... 300 D7
Lee Chapel CP School
    VGE SS16 .... 18 C2
Leigh Beck Primary School
    CVI SS8 .... 398 F8
Leigh Junior & Infant School
    LOS SS9 .... 399 M3
Leigh Parish Council
    LOS SS9 .... 399 M2
The Leventhorpe School
    SBW CM21 .... 200 F7
Lexden CP School
    COLW CO3 .... 161 M5
Lexden Springs School
    COLW CO3 .... 161 M4
Lexden Squash Club
    COLW CO3 .... 161 L2
Ley Park CP School
    BROX EN10 .... 277 G2
Leys Infant School
    DAGE RM10 .... 388 D6
Lime Grove Estate
    HVHL CB9 .... 28 D1
Limes Farm County Primary
  & Infant School
    CHIG IG7 .... 349 L7
The Limes Medical Centre
    EPP CM16 .... 281 J6
The Limes Medical Centre
    EPP CM16 .... 304 C1
Lincewood County Junior
  & Infant School
    VGE SS16 .... 376 D2
Lincoln Road Clinic
    EN EN1 .... 324 C7
Lingwood Clinic
    SLH/COR SS17 .... 409 K2
Links Business Centre
    BSF CM23 .... 174 D4
Linton C of E (Aided)
  Infant School
    CBE/LIN CB1 .... 24 D1
Linton Health Centre
    CBE/LIN CB1 .... 24 D1
Linton Heights Junior School
    CBE/LIN CB1 .... 24 E1
Linton Village College
    CBE/LIN CB1 .... 24 C1
Linton Zoological Gardens
    CBE/LIN CB1 .... 24 C2
Lionmede Bowling Club
  & Tennis Courts
    CHLM/GWD CM2 .... 17 M2
Lister Medical Centre
    HLWS CM18 .... 255 K6
Littlebrook Business Centre
    DART DA1 .... 415 K4
Littlegarth School
    RCOLW CO6 .... 104 C1
Little Hallingbury C of E
  Primary School
    RBSF CM22 .... 201 K3
Little Margraves
  Industrial Estate
    UPMR RM14 .... 394 A2
Little Oakley C of E School
    HAR CO12 .... 142 C4
Little Thurrock County
  Primary School
    GRAYS RM17 .... 407 L8
Little Waltham C of E
  Primary School
    RCHLM CM3 .... 235 J4
Llewelyn Surgery
    WAB EN9 .... 301 K5
London Road Surgery
    RAYL SS6 .... 361 J2
London Road Surgery
    WICKW SS12 .... 359 K4
London Stansted Airport
    RBSF CM22 .... 148 B8
Longfield Medical Centre
    MAL CM9 .... 269 J6
Longfield Medical Centre
    MAL CM9 .... 293 H1
Long Gallery
    BSDN SS14 .... 19 H7
Longlands Junior Middle
  & Infant School
    BROX EN10 .... 276 F5
The Long Melford Practice
    SUD CO10 .... 34 D3
Long Melford Primary School
    SUD CO10 .... 34 D4
Long Ridings Junior
  & Infant School
    RBRW/HUT CM13 .... 333 J7
Long Road Surgery
    CVI SS8 .... 397 M8
Lord Butler Leisure Centre
    SAFWS CB11 .... 66 C1
Loughton Cricket Club
    LOU IG10 .... 327 G5
Loughton Hall Clinic
    LOU IG10 .... 327 J3
Loughton Health Centre
    LOU IG10 .... 326 F7
Loughton Mental
  Health Centre
    LOU IG10 .... 326 F7
Lowewood Museum
    HOD EN11 .... 253 H6
Lowfield Sports Ground
    HOD EN11 .... 253 G5

Loyola Preparatory School
    BKHH IG9 .... 348 D2
Lubbins Park Primary School
    CVI SS8 .... 413 K1
Lychgate Industrial Estate
    SBF/HAD SS7 .... 379 M2
Lynn Tait Gallery
    LOS SS9 .... 399 L3
Lyons Hall County
  Primary School
    BRTR CM7 .... 155 L7
Madeira Grove Clinic
    WFD IG8 .... 348 C7
Magistrates' Court
    IP IP1 .... 2 D5
Magnet Estate
    WTHK RM20 .... 416 D2
Maidenhall Sports Centre
    CHTY IP2 .... 58 D1
Maidstone County
  Infant School
    FX IP11 .... 84 F8
Malden All Saints C of E
  Primary School
    MAL CM9 .... 292 F1
Maldon Agricultural Museum
    MAL CM9 .... 270 F4
Maldon Court School
    MAL CM9 .... 269 G8
Maldon District Council
    MAL CM9 .... 293 H1
Maldon Museum
    MAL CM9 .... 293 H1
Maldon Primary School
    MAL CM9 .... 293 H1
Maldon Town Council
    MAL CM9 .... 269 H8
The Maltings Industrial Estate
    BOC CM0 .... 320 F7
The Maltings Industrial Estate
    SBW CM21 .... 228 A1
Manford Industrial Estate
    ERITH DA8 .... 414 C3
Manford Way Health Centre
    BARK/HLT IG6 .... 350 A7
Mangapps Farm Railway
  Museum
    BOC CM0 .... 344 B3
Manifest Theatre
    MGTR CO11 .... 108 C1
The Manningtree Gallery
    MGTR CO11 .... 108 C1
Manningtree High School
    MGTR CO11 .... 108 D8
Manningtree Sports Centre
    MGTR CO11 .... 108 D7
Manor County Junior
  & Infant School
    BSDN SS14 .... 19 J2
Manor Fields JMI School
    BSF CM23 .... 173 L6
The Manor of Groves
    SBW CM21 .... 227 G1
The Manor Primary School
    ROM RM1 .... 371 G5
Manor Road Surgery
    DAGE RM10 .... 388 E5
Manor Trading Estate
    SBF/HAD SS7 .... 379 L4
Manor Way Industrial Estate
    GRAYS RM17 .... 417 K4
Manuden CP School
    BSF CM23 .... 146 B1
Maple River Industrial Estate
    HLW CM20 .... 227 J5
Mardyke Surgery
    PUR RM19 .... 415 H1
Margaretting C of E
  Primary School
    ING CM4 .... 310 F3
Marillac Hospital
    RBRW/HUT CM13 .... 354 C7
Market Field School
    RCOLE CO7 .... 165 H6
Market (Open Air)
    IP IP1 .... 2 D4
Mark Hall Comprehensive
  School
    HLWE CM17 .... 227 K8
Mark Hall Cycle Museum
    HLW CM20 .... 227 J8
Markhams Chase
  Leisure Centre
    LAIN SS15 .... 376 E5
Marks Hall Arboretum
    RCOLW CO6 .... 157 M4
Marshalls Park School
    ROM RM1 .... 370 F2
Marshalls Park Upper School
    ROM RM1 .... 370 F4
Marsh Green School
    DAGE RM10 .... 388 B8
Martells Industrial Estate
    RCOLE CO7 .... 136 F5
Martells Industrial Estate
    RCOLE CO7 .... 136 E6
Martinbridge Industrial Estate
    EN EN1 .... 324 B7
Matching Green C of E
  Primary School
    HLWE CM17 .... 258 E1
Matching Green Surgery
    BSDN SS14 .... 19 M1
Maunds Wood CP School
    HLWS CM18 .... 255 L7
Mawney Infant School
    ROMW/RG RM7 .... 370 E5
Mayfair Industrial Estate
    RCHLM CM3 .... 318 A5
Mayfield County Infant School
    BAR EN8 .... 276 F7
Mayflower Comprehensive
  School
    BCAYW CM12 .... 335 K6
Mayflower County Primary
  School
    HAR CO12 .... 6 F7

Mayflower Retail Park
　BSDN SS14 .... 377 L1
Mayland Branch Surgery
　RCHLM CM3 .... 319 G2
Maylandsea CP School
　RCHLM CM3 .... 319 G3
Maylandsea Medical Centre
　RCHLM CM3 .... 318 F2
Maylands Golf Club
　HARH RM3 .... 353 J6
Meadgate CP School
　CHLM/GWD CM2 .... 288 F3
Mead Industrial Park
　HLW CM20 .... 227 G7
Mead Infant School
　HARH RM3 .... 353 G7
The Mead School
　HLWS CM18 .... 255 M5
The Medical Centre
　K/T/MI CO5 .... 214 E6
Medical Surgery
　GTDUN CM6 .... 178 E3
Melbourne House Surgery
　CHLM/WR CM1 .... 263 M6
Merrylands Junior School
　LAIN SS15 .... 376 B5
Mersea Community
　& Sports Centre
　K/T/MI CO5 .... 245 K5
Mersea Island Gm School
　K/T/MI CO5 .... 245 K5
The Mersea Road Surgery
　COLS CO2 .... 191 H1
Messing CP School
　K/T/MI CO5 .... 214 D1
Midas Business Centre
　DAGE RM10 .... 388 B3
Midas Industrial Estate
　DAGE RM10 .... 388 B3
Mid Essex Adult
　Community College
　RBRW/HUT CM13 .... 333 J8
Mid Essex Magistrates Courts
　CHLM/WR CM1 .... 17 H3
Mildmay Industrial Estate
　BOC CM0 .... 344 C6
Milehams Industrial Estate
　PUR RM19 .... 405 H8
Millbrook Junior Middle
　& Infant School
　BAR EN8 .... 300 F1
Milldene School
　K/T/MI CO5 .... 214 E5
Millfields (GM) Primary School
　RCOLE CO7 .... 192 E2
Millhouse County Junior
　& Infant School
　LAIN SS15 .... 376 D3
Mill Road Surgery
　COLN CO4 .... 134 F7
Millside Industrial Estate
　DART DA1 .... 414 E8
Millwards CP School
　HLWW/ROY CM19 .... 255 J7
Milton Hall Junior School
　WOS/PRIT SS0 .... 20 D5
Mistley Norman C of E
　Primary School
　MGTR CO11 .... 109 H7
Mitchell Junior School
　HCH RM12 .... 389 J5
Monkwick Primary
　& Infant School
　COLS CO2 .... 191 L1
Monkwick Sports Centre
　COLS CO2 .... 191 L1
Monro Industrial Estate
　BAR EN8 .... 300 F6
Montessori School
　RBSF CM22 .... 148 C8
Montgomerie Infant School
　SBF/HAD SS7 .... 379 J4
Montgomery County
　Infant School
　COLS CO2 .... 190 D1
Moonhall Business Park
　HVHL CB9 .... 28 B6
Moreton Bay Industrial Estate
　GPK RM2 .... 371 L2
Moreton C of E Primary School
　CHONG CM5 .... 258 D8
Morland Primary School
　IPSE IP3 .... 59 H3
Mosque
　WOS/PRIT SS0 .... 20 D6
Moulsham High School
　CHLM/GWD CM2 .... 288 C4
Moulsham Infant School
　CHLM/GWD CM2 .... 17 H9
Moulsham Lodge Clinic
　CHLM/GWD CM2 .... 288 C5
The Mountfitchet School
　STSD CM24 .... 147 G7
Mountnessing C of E
　Primary School
　BRWN CM15 .... 333 L3
Mrs Lipmans School
　GTDUN CM6 .... 180 C6
M S F Whitehall College
　BSF CM23 .... 173 M2
Murrayfield Primary School
　IPSE IP3 .... 38 B8
Museum
　WAB EN9 .... 301 K6
The Museum
　SAFWN CB10 .... 65 L1
Myland CP School
　COLN CO4 .... 134 F7
Nabbotts County Junior
　School
　CHLM/WR CM1 .... 264 C1
Nacton Primary School
　KIR/NAC IP10 .... 60 D6
Natural History Museum
　COL CO1 .... 10 D8
Nayland CP School
　RCOLW CO6 .... 104 B2

Nazeing CP School
　WAB EN9 .... 277 M3
Nazeing Golf Club
　WAB EN9 .... 278 D4
Nazeing Parish Council
　WAB EN9 .... 278 C5
Nazeing Park (SCH)
　WAB EN9 .... 278 D2
Neil Graham Gallery
　BRWN CM15 .... 354 E3
Nelmes Primary & Junior
　School
　EMPK RM11 .... 372 A4
The Nest Branch Surgery
　FX IP11 .... 84 C5
Nevendon Trading Estate
　PIT SS13 .... 378 C2
New Cangle School
　HVHL CB9 .... 28 A2
New Court Business Park
　HLWW/ROY CM19 .... 255 K7
New England Industrial Estate
　HOD EN11 .... 253 K4
Newlands Spring Primary
　School
　CHLM/WR CM1 .... 263 L4
Newmans Estate
　COS CO15 .... 12 C6
Newport CP School
　SAFWS CB11 .... 89 G3
Newport Free Grammar
　School
　SAFWS CB11 .... 89 H2
Newport Gallery
　SAFWS CB11 .... 89 H2
The New Surgery
　BCAYW CM12 .... 335 J8
Newtons Primary School
　RAIN RM13 .... 388 E8
Nicholas Comprehensive
　School
　LAIN SS15 .... 376 E4
Nightingale House Surgery
　ED N9 .... 324 D8
Noak Bridge Medical Centre
　LAIN SS15 .... 377 G1
Noak Bridge Primary School
　LAIN SS15 .... 377 G2
Northwood Arts Gallery
　FX IP11 .... 9 M1
Northwood Arts Gallery
　FX IP11 .... 85 H8
North Crescent School
　WICKW SS12 .... 359 L4
Northend CP School
　ERITH DA8 .... 414 A5
North Fambridge Yacht Club
　RCHLM CM3 .... 341 G4
Northfleet Industrial Estate
　GVW DA11 .... 417 H8
Northgate Business Centre
　EN EN1 .... 324 C5
Northgate High School
　IPNE IP4 .... 38 A2
Northgate Industrial Park
　CHDH RM6 .... 370 A1
Northgate Jmi School
　BSF CM23 .... 173 M3
Northgate Sports Centre
　IPNE IP4 .... 38 A2
North Havering College
　of Adult Education
　ROM RM1 .... 370 F4
North Hill Business Park
　SLH/COR SS17 .... 394 A7
North House Gallery
　MGTR CO11 .... 108 E7
North School
　COLW CO3 .... 10 A5
North Shoebury Surgery
　SBN/FI SS3 .... 402 E2
North Weald Golf Club
　EPP CM16 .... 281 H3
North & West Essex
　Adult Community College
　HLW CM20 .... 15 J1
Northwick Park Junior
　& Infant School
　CVI SS8 .... 397 L7
Norwich Road Surgery
　IP IP1 .... 2 B1
Notley High School
　BRTR CM7 .... 183 G3
Oak Hair & Health Centre
　BRTR CM7 .... 183 J1
Oak Industrial Park
　GTDUN CM6 .... 179 G4
Oaklands County Infant School
　CHLM/GWD CM2 .... 17 G7
Oaklands Farm
　Industrial Estate
　BCAYE CM11 .... 335 M5
Oaklands School
　LOU IG10 .... 326 E7
Oaks Hospital
　COLN CO4 .... 134 F8
The Oaks Industrial Estate
　HLW CM20 .... 227 C8
Oakwood Business Park
　COS CO15 .... 224 B2
Oakwood County
　Infant School
　COS CO15 .... 12 C7
Oakwood Estate
　HLW CM20 .... 227 H8
Oakwood Hill
　Industrial Estate
　LOU IG10 .... 327 J7
Occupational Health Centre
　HAR CO12 .... 112 F6
Ockendon School
　SOCK/AV RM15 .... 406 B3
Odeon Cinema
　CHLM/GWD CM2 .... 17 J4
Odeon Cinema
　COLW CO3 .... 10 B9
Odeon Cinema
　HLW CM20 .... 15 K3

Odeon Cinema
　IPNE IP4 .... 3 G4
Odeon Cinema
　ROM RM1 .... 371 G5
Oglethorpe County
　Junior & Infant School
　UPMR RM14 .... 391 M4
Old Bancroftians FC
　BKHH IG9 .... 348 C5
Old Chigwellians Sports Club
　CHIG IG7 .... 349 J2
Oldchurch Hospital
　ROMW/RG RM7 .... 370 D7
Old Church School
　RIPS/CAP IP9 .... 81 K8
Old Club House
　BOC CM0 .... 344 D8
Old Customs House
　IPSE IP3 .... 3 G4
Old Grammar School
　RCOLE CO7 .... 107 G4
Old Harlow Health Centre
　HLWE CM17 .... 227 K7
Old Heath County
　Primary School
　COLS CO2 .... 163 K8
Old Westcliffians Rugby
　Football Club
　RCFD SS4 .... 382 D3
Olympic Business Centre
　BSDN SS14 .... 378 A1
Ongar & District Sports Club
　CHONG CM5 .... 283 H8
Ongar Health Centre
　CHONG CM5 .... 283 H8
Ongar Leisure Centre
　CHONG CM5 .... 283 H6
Ongar Parish Council
　CHONG CM5 .... 283 H8
Ongar Road Trading Estate
　GTDUN CM6 .... 178 C7
Ongar War Memorial Hospital
　CHONG CM5 .... 283 H6
Oriental Galleries
　BCAYE CM11 .... 336 A5
Orsett Church
　of England Primary School
　CDH/CHF RM16 .... 408 B3
Orsett Hospital
　CDH/CHF RM16 .... 408 B3
Orsett Industrial Estate
　CDH/CHF RM16 .... 409 G3
Orwell Business Centre
　IPSE IP3 .... 58 F1
Orwell High School
　FX IP11 .... 84 F8
Orwell Junior School
　IPSE IP3 .... 59 G2
Orwell Park School
　KIR/NAC IP10 .... 60 C8
Orwell Yacht Club
　CHTY IP2 .... 58 D2
Oxford House School
　COLW CO3 .... 162 E5
Palace Theatre
　WOS/PRIT SS0 .... 20 B4
Palmers College
　GRAYS RM17 .... 418 A1
Parklands School
　ROM RM1 .... 370 E3
Park Lane Gallery
　COL CO1 .... 10 D8
Park Lane Surgery
　BROX EN10 .... 253 G8
Park School
　RAYL SS6 .... 361 J5
Parkway Middle School
　HVHL CB9 .... 27 L3
Parndoni Mill Gallery
　HLW CM20 .... 226 C8
Parsloes School
　DAGW RM9 .... 388 A5
Parsonage Farm
　Industrial Estate
　STSD CM24 .... 147 G8
Parsonage Farm Infant School
　RAIN RM13 .... 404 D1
Parsons Heath
　Medical Practice
　COLN CO4 .... 163 M2
Parsons Heath Primary School
　COLN CO4 .... 163 M1
Passmores
　Comprehensive School
　HLWS CM18 .... 15 M8
Peartree Business Centre
　COLW CO3 .... 161 M7
Peartree Surgery
　SOCK/AV RM15 .... 391 L8
Pembroke Business Centre
　BSDN SS14 .... 377 M1
Perryfields County Junior
　& Infant School
　CHLM/WR CM1 .... 264 E5
Peterswood Junior
　& Infant School
　HLWS CM18 .... 255 L7
The Philip Morrant School
　COLW CO3 .... 162 C6
Phillips Gallery
　CHLM/WR CM1 .... 17 J4
The Picture Frame Gallery
　ROM RM1 .... 370 E5
The Picture House
　HLW CM20 .... 15 K3
Pinebrook Surgery
　RIPW IP8 .... 57 K1
Pinewood Primary School
　CRW RM5 .... 351 J6
Pipps Hill Retail Park
　LAIN SS15 .... 18 B2
Pitsea County Junior
　& Infant School
　PIT SS13 .... 378 B6
Pitsea Health Clinic
　PIT SS13 .... 378 B6
Pitsea Leisure Centre
　PIT SS13 .... 378 C6

Pitsea Swimming Pool
　PIT SS13 .... 378 C6
Place Farm School
　HVHL CB9 .... 28 A3
Plaza Business Centre
　PEND EN3 .... 325 G4
The Plume School
　MAL CM9 .... 293 G1
The Pompadour Gallery
　GPK RM2 .... 371 H4
Ponders End Industrial Estate
　PEND EN3 .... 325 G6
Porters Grange Junior
　& Infant School
　SOS SS1 .... 21 K5
Portmans Walk Industrial Centre
　IP IP1 .... 2 B5
Pot Kiln County Primary School
　SUD CO10 .... 5 H8
Potter Street Primary School
　HLWE CM17 .... 256 C5
Power Industrial Estate
　ERITH DA8 .... 414 B5
Powers Hall County
　Infant School
　WIT CM8 .... 211 L8
The Practice
　BKHH IG9 .... 348 D3
Prettygate Junior School
　COLW CO3 .... 162 B7
Primary School
　HSTD CO9 .... 73 G1
Prince Avenue Primary School
　WOS/PRIT SS0 .... 382 E6
Prince of Wales Junior
　& Infant School
　PEND EN3 .... 325 G2
Princess Alexandra Hospital
　HLW CM20 .... 15 J3
Priory Heath Infant School
　IPSE IP3 .... 59 K2
Priory Park Industrial Estate
　SOSN SS2 .... 383 H7
Priory School
　WOS/PRIT SS0 .... 382 F8
Prittlewell C of E School
　SOSN SS2 .... 20 F1
Prospect Business Park
　LOU IG10 .... 327 L6
Prout Industrial Estate
　CVI SS8 .... 399 G8
Public Baths
　IPSE IP3 .... 3 H6
Purdeys Industrial Estate
　RCFD SS4 .... 383 H3
Purdeys Industrial Estate
　RCFD SS4 .... 383 H2
Purfleet Primary School
　PUR RM19 .... 415 H1
Purford Green School
　HLWS CM18 .... 256 B5
Purleigh CP School
　RCHLM CM3 .... 316 E2
Quarry Hill County Junior
　School
　GRAYS RM17 .... 417 J2
The Quay Theatre
　SUD CO10 .... 4 C8
Queens Theatre
　EMPK RM11 .... 371 L7
Queen Street Dental Health
　Centre
　COL CO1 .... 10 D8
Queensway Business Centre
　PEND EN3 .... 324 D6
Quest End Industrial Centre
　RAYL SS6 .... 361 K5
Quilters Junior & Infant School
　BCAYW CM12 .... 357 H2
R A Butler Infant Grammar
　School
　SAFWS CB11 .... 65 M2
Radford Business Centre
　BCAYW CM12 .... 335 G8
Radwinter C of E Aided
　Primary School
　SAFWN CB10 .... 68 A4
Raeburn Infant School
　IPSE IP3 .... 59 G2
Rainham Primary School
　RAIN RM13 .... 404 B2
Rainham Trading Estate
　RAIN RM13 .... 404 A2
Rainsford High School
　CHLM/WR CM1 .... 263 M7
Ramsden Hall School
　BCAYE CM11 .... 336 A8
Ramsey County
　Primary School
　HAR CO12 .... 142 C3
Ramsey School
　HSTD CO9 .... 129 H1
Ranelagh Primary School
　CHTY IP2 .... 37 G6
Ransomes Industrial
　Estate Post Office
　IPSE IP3 .... 59 M3
Ranworth Surgery
　COS CO15 .... 12 E7
Raphael School
　EMPK RM11 .... 371 H6
Ravensbourne School
　HARH RM3 .... 371 L1
Ravenscroft School
　RCOS CO16 .... 223 J7
Rawreth Industrial Estate
　RAYL SS6 .... 361 J6
Rayleigh Lanes Indoor Market
　RAYL SS6 .... 380 E1
Rayleigh Primary School
　RAYL SS6 .... 380 D1
Ray Lodge Junior
　& Infant School
　WFD IG8 .... 348 E7
Rayne CP School
　BRTR CM7 .... 181 M1

Raynham Road
　Industrial Estate
　BSF CM23 .... 174 C3
Redburn Industrial Estate
　PEND EN3 .... 324 E8
Redden Court School
　HARH RM3 .... 372 A3
Regency Art Gallery
　COLS CO2 .... 163 H5
Regent Leisure Centre
　SLH/COR SS17 .... 409 L2
Regional Sports Centre
　TIL RM18 .... 418 C6
Register Office
　IPNE IP4 .... 3 H5
Rhodes Museum
　& Commonwealth Centre
　BSF CM23 .... 174 B6
Rice Bridge Industrial Estate
　RCOS CO16 .... 197 H4
Richard Alibon Infant School
　DAGE RM10 .... 388 B4
Richard Whittington
　Jmi School
　BSF CM23 .... 173 M7
Richmond Avenue
　Junior School
　SBN/FI SS3 .... 402 E4
Rickling C of E
　Primary School
　SAFWS CB11 .... 118 F3
Rickstones School
　WIT CM8 .... 212 A5
Ridgewell C of E
　(Aided) Primary School
　HSTD CO9 .... 50 C4
Rise Park Infant School
　ROM RM1 .... 370 E1
Rivenhall C of E
　Primary School
　WIT CM8 .... 212 C3
Rivenhall Oaks Golf Club
　WIT CM8 .... 212 C7
The Rivermead Gate
　Medical Centre
　CHLM/WR CM1 .... 264 C7
River Road Practice
　BKHH IG9 .... 348 F2
Riverside Business Park
　STSD CM24 .... 146 E5
Riverside Clinic
　IPSE IP3 .... 37 M8
Riverside Health Centre
　MGTR CO11 .... 108 D7
Riverside Ice & Leisure Centre
　CHLM/WR CM1 .... 17 J3
Riverside Industrial Estate
　ED N9 .... 324 F8
Riverside Industrial Estate
　MAL CM9 .... 269 G7
Riverside Industrial Estate
　RCFD SS4 .... 383 G2
Riverside Industrial Park
　CHTY IP2 .... 37 L8
Riverside Junior School
　HOC/HUL SS5 .... 339 M8
Riverside Retail Park
　CHLM/WR CM1 .... 17 K1
Roach Vale Primary School
　COLN CO4 .... 163 M2
Robert Clack School
　BCTR RM8 .... 370 A8
Robert Drake Primary School
　SBF/HAD SS7 .... 379 L4
The Robert Frew
　Medical Centre
　WICKW SS12 .... 360 A6
Rochford Adult
　Community College
　RCFD SS4 .... 383 H1
Rochford District Council
　RCFD SS4 .... 383 G1
Rochford Parish Council
　RCFD SS4 .... 382 F1
Rochford Primary School
　RCFD SS4 .... 382 F1
Rochford Swimming
　Pool Services
　RCFD SS4 .... 383 H1
Roding Primary School
　WFD IG8 .... 348 F8
Rodings Central
　Primary School
　GTDUN CM6 .... 231 K3
Roding Valley High School
　LOU IG10 .... 326 F7
Roding Valley High School
　LOU IG10 .... 327 J6
Roebuck Road Trading Estate
　BARK/HLT IG6 .... 350 C7
Rolph C of E Primary School
　RCOS CO16 .... 197 G2
Romford Clinic
　ROM RM1 .... 371 G4
Romford County Court
　ROM RM1 .... 371 G4
Romford Ice Rink
　ROMW/RG RM7 .... 370 F7
Rosedale Clinic
　CHESW EN7 .... 276 B7
Rose Hill Primary School
　IPSE IP3 .... 38 B7
Roseland Junior Middle
　& Infant School
　HOD EN11 .... 253 G2
Rose Villa Surgery
　PIT SS13 .... 378 C6
Rosewood Medical Centre
　HCH RM12 .... 389 J4
Rosshill Industrial Park
　SOSN SS2 .... 383 J7
Rowhedge Surgery
　K/T/MI CO5 .... 192 A3
Roxwell C of E Primary School
　CHLM/WR CM1 .... 262 B5
Royal Burnham Yacht Club
　BOC CM0 .... 344 D7

Royal Corinthian Yacht Club
BOC CM0 .... 344 D8
Royal Hospital School
RIPS/CAP IP9 .... 80 E8
Royal Liberty School
GPK RM2 .... 371 K3
Royal London Sports Centre
COLN C04 .... 135 J5
Royal Mail Sorting Office
IP IP1 .... 2 B7
Royal Navy
CHLM/WR CM1 .... 17 G2
The Royals Shopping Centre
SOS SS1 .... 21 H7
Royden Bury Industrial Estate
HLWW/ROY CM19 .... 14 C5
Roydon CP School
HLWW/ROY CM19 .... 254 C3
Roydon Leisure Park
HLWW/ROY CM19 .... 254 B2
Rugby Club
BSF CM23 .... 173 L2
Runwell CP School
WICKE SS11 .... 359 L1
Runwell Parish Council
WICKE SS11 .... 359 M1
Rush Green School
ROMW/RG RM7 .... 370 E8
Rush Green Sports Centre
RCOS C016 .... 223 J8
Rush Green Surgery
ROMW/RG RM7 .... 388 K1
Rushmere Golf Club
IPNE IP4 .... 38 E5
Rushmere Hall CP School
IPNE IP4 .... 38 C2
Rushmere Sports Club
KESG IP5 .... 38 F2
Russet House School
EN EN1 .... 324 C3
Ryedene County
Primary School
VGE SS16 .... 378 A4
Rye House Stadium
HOD EN11 .... 253 L3
Ryelands JMI School
HOD EN11 .... 253 J4
The Sacred Heart
of Mary RC School
UPMR RM14 .... 390 C1
Sacred Heart RC School
SOS SS1 .... 21 L5
Saffron Business Centre
SAFWN CB10 .... 66 B1
Saffron Walden
County High School
SAFWS CB11 .... 65 K3
Saffron Walden Golf Club
SAFWN CB10 .... 65 K1
Saffron Walden Hospital
SAFWS CB11 .... 66 B1
Saffron Walden
Town Football Club
SAFWN CB10 .... 65 L1
Sailing Club
RCOLE C07 .... 220 F6
St Albans RC Church & School
Presbytery
HCH RM12 .... 389 H4
St Albans RC High School
IPNE IP4 .... 38 E4
St Albans RC Primary School
HLW CM20 .... 256 A1
St Albans RC School
RAIN RM13 .... 389 J6
St Andrews Church
of England Primary School
RCOS C016 .... 195 M3
St Andrews C of E (GM) Primary
School
EPP CM16 .... 281 K4
St Andrews C of E
Primary School
RCOLW C06 .... 159 M8
St Andrews County
Junior School
COLN C04 .... 11 M8
St Andrews Junior School
RCHLM CM3 .... 238 C8
St Andrews School
SUD C010 .... 54 A8
St Anne Line Junior School
LAIN SS15 .... 18 C6
St Annes CP School
COLN C04 .... 11 K4
St Annes Preparatory School
CHLM/GWD CM2 .... 16 F6
St Antonys RC Primary School
WFD IG8 .... 348 B5
St Aubyns School
WFD IG8 .... 348 A8
St Benedicts College
COLW C03 .... 162 C5
St Bernards High School
WOS/PRIT SS0 .... 20 C4
St Cedds Primary School
BOC CM0 .... 298 C1
St Chads School
TIL RM18 .... 418 B5
St Christopher School
LOS SS9 .... 382 A7
St Clares Roman
Catholic School
RCOS C016 .... 223 J7
St Clements Hospital
IPSE IP3 .... 38 C7
St Clements Hospital Lodge
IPSE IP3 .... 38 D6
St Clements Mixed
Junior School
BAR EN8 .... 276 F7
St Cleres School
SLH/COR SS17 .... 409 K3
St Cross RC Primary School
HOD EN11 .... 253 H7
St Edwards C of E
Comprehensive School
CHDH RM6 .... 370 B6

St Edwards C of E
Primary School
ROM RM1 .... 370 E3
St Felix RC Primary School
HVHL CB9 .... 27 L4
St Francis RC Primary School
BRTR CM7 .... 155 G7
St Francis RC Primary School
MAL CM9 .... 269 G8
St George's C of E
Primary School
RCOLE C07 .... 165 M2
St Georges Hospital
HCH RM12 .... 389 M3
St Georges Infant School
COLS C02 .... 163 H6
St Georges Primary School
COLS C02 .... 163 H6
St Georges RC School
SBN/FI SS3 .... 402 F3
St Giles C of E Primary School
HSTD C09 .... 98 E1
St Gregory V CP School
SUD C010 .... 4 B7
St Helena School
COLW C03 .... 162 E3
St Helens Junior School
BRWN CM15 .... 354 E1
St Helens Primary School
IPNE IP4 .... 3 J4
St Helens RC Infant School
BRW CM14 .... 354 E3
St Hildas School
WOS/PRIT SS0 .... 400 D2
St Ignatius College
EN EN1 .... 324 B1
St James Church School
HLWS CM18 .... 255 L7
St James C of E Primary School
PEND EN3 .... 324 D4
St James School
COL C01 .... 11 G7
St James Surgery
COS C015 .... 12 E8
St John Fisher RC Junior School
LOU IG10 .... 327 K4
St John Payne RC
Comprehensive School
CHLM/WR CM1 .... 264 B5
St John Payne RC School
CHLM/WR CM1 .... 264 A5
St Johns C of E Controlled
Primary School
COLN C04 .... 135 L7
St Johns C of E Primary School
BKHH IG9 .... 348 C2
St Johns C of E Primary School
IPNE IP4 .... 38 B4
St Johns C of E Primary School
RCHLM CM3 .... 291 G4
St Johns C of E School
EPP CM16 .... 303 M2
St Johns Green County Primary
School
COLS C02 .... 10 C9
St John's Hospital
CHLM/GWD CM2 .... 288 A5
St Johns Industrial Estate
RBSF CM22 .... 176 F4
St Johns School
BCAYW CM12 .... 335 J8
St Johns Special School
WFD IG8 .... 349 H6
St John the Baptist
Primary School
HSTD C09 .... 100 C3
St Joseph School
DAGW RM9 .... 388 A3
St Josephs College
CHTY IP2 .... 37 H8
St Josephs RC Jmi School
BAR EN8 .... 300 F5
St Josephs RC Junior
Middle & Infant School
BSF CM23 .... 173 L5
St Josephs RC Primary School
HAR C012 .... 143 J1
St Josephs RC Primary School
SLH/COR SS17 .... 409 L1
St Josephs RC School
CVI SS8 .... 398 C7
St Josephs RC Va
Primary School
SUD C010 .... 4 B5
St Josephs School
UPMR RM14 .... 390 C1
St Joseph the Worker
RC Primary School
RBRW/HUT CM13 .... 333 K8
St Katherine School
CVI SS8 .... 398 B6
St Lawrence C of E
Primary School
K/T/MI C05 .... 192 A3
St Lawrence C of E School
WAB EN9 .... 302 A5
St Leonards C of E Va
Junior School
BOC CM0 .... 320 E7
St Leonards Hospital
SUD C010 .... 4 F6
St Lukes C of E Primary School
K/T/MI C05 .... 214 E6
St Lukes RC Primary School
HLWW/ROY CM19 .... 15 J9
St Lukes Special School
LOU IG10 .... 327 H6
St Margarets C of E V A
Primary School
IP IP1 .... 3 G3
St Margarets Hospital
EPP CM16 .... 304 C1
St Margarets Preparatory
School
HSTD C09 .... 127 L3
St Margarets Primary School
HSTD C09 .... 72 D4

St Margarets School
PIT SS13 .... 378 F6
St Marks College
SAFWS CB11 .... 65 H3
St Marks RC Comprehensive
School
HLWS CM18 .... 255 M4
St Marks RC Primary School
CHTY IP2 .... 37 C8
St Martins School
RBRW/HUT CM13 .... 355 K2
St Mary's Business Centre
COLW C03 .... 10 A9
St Mary's Business Centre
COLW C03 .... 162 E4
St Marys Catholic School
BSF CM23 .... 173 M4
St Marys C of E Aided Primary
School
RCHLM CM3 .... 315 J7
St Marys C of E Primary School
BRWN CM15 .... 333 G8
St Marys C of E Primary School
RBSF CM22 .... 203 G5
St Marys C of E Primary School
RCOLE C07 .... 136 E3
St Marys C of E Primary School
STSD CM24 .... 146 F4
St Marys Hare Park School
GPK RM2 .... 371 K3
St Marys High School
CHESW EN7 .... 300 C2
St Marys Primary School
IPNE IP4 .... 3 L2
St Marys Primary School
SAFWN CB10 .... 65 L1
St Marys RC Church & School
HCH RM12 .... 371 H8
St Marys RC County Primary
School
TIL RM18 .... 418 A6
St Marys RC Primary School
PEND EN3 .... 324 E6
St Marys School
COLW C03 .... 162 D4
St Marys School C of E Primary
School
COLW C03 .... 10 A9
St Marys School C of E Primary
School
COLW C03 .... 161 G6
St Matthews C of E Primary
School
PEND EN3 .... 324 D7
St Matthews C of E School
IP IP1 .... 2 C4
St Michaels C of E Junior School
CHLM/GWD CM2 .... 312 D1
St Michaels Hospital
BRTR CM7 .... 154 F8
St Michaels Preparatory School
LOS SS9 .... 399 K2
St Michaels Primary School
BSF CM23 .... 173 M4
St Michaels School
BRTR CM7 .... 182 E1
St Nicholas C of E Primary
School
WICKE SS11 .... 360 F4
St Nicholas School
HLWE CM17 .... 228 A8
St Nicholas School
SOSN SS2 .... 401 M1
St Osyth C of E Primary School
RCOS C016 .... 222 C7
St Pancras RC Primary School
IP IP1 .... 37 G1
St Patricks School
ROMW/RG RM7 .... 370 C1
St Pauls C of E Primary School
BRW CM14 .... 331 L5
St Pauls Roman Catholic
Jmi School
CHESW EN7 .... 276 C7
St Peters C of E Primary School
BRW CM14 .... 353 M3
St Peters C of E Primary School
HSTD C09 .... 97 L3
St Peters C of E Primary School
RCOLW C06 .... 186 B1
St Peters C of E School
CHLM/GWD CM2 .... 313 G7
St Peters High School
BOC CM0 .... 344 C5
St Peters Hospital
MAL CM9 .... 293 G1
St Peters RC Primary School
BCAYE CM11 .... 357 M5
St Peters RC Primary School
ROM RM1 .... 370 E3
St Peters RC School
DAGW RM9 .... 388 A7
St Philomenas Convent
Day School
FOS C013 .... 199 C6
St Pius RC Primary School
CHLM/WR CM1 .... 264 A5
St Teresa RC School
RCFD SS4 .... 363 L8
St Theresas RC Primary School
COLW C03 .... 161 M6
St Thomas Moore RC
Primary School
SAFWS CB11 .... 65 M3
St Thomas More High
School for Boys
WOS/PRIT SS0 .... 382 B8
St Thomas More RC School
COL C01 .... 10 F8
St Thomas of Canterbury Junior &
Infant School
BRWN CM15 .... 354 E1
St Thomas RC Primary School
GRAYS RM17 .... 417 J1
St Ursulas Junior School
HARH RM3 .... 352 C7
Salvation Army
IPNE IP4 .... 3 H6

Samuel Ward Upper School
HVHL CB9 .... 28 C2
Sanatorium Felixstowe College
FX IP11 .... 115 K1
The Sanders Draper
Secondary School
HCH RM12 .... 389 K3
Sandon School
CHLM/GWD CM2 .... 289 J5
Saracens House Business
Centre
IP IP1 .... 3 C3
Sarbir Industrial Park
HLW CM20 .... 227 K6
Sawbridge Health Clinic
SBW CM21 .... 227 M1
Schoolhouse
ABR/ST RM4 .... 352 E3
School House Aveley School
SOCK/AV RM15 .... 405 M6
Schooling Licensed
Conveyancers
GRAYS RM17 .... 417 L2
School Street Surgery
SAFWN CB10 .... 42 E1
Scimitar Park Industrial Estate
PIT SS13 .... 378 E1
Scott Park Surgery
LOS SS9 .... 382 A4
Scotts Primary School
HCH RM12 .... 389 K4
Seedbed Business Centre
SBN/FI SS3 .... 403 G4
Severall Hospital
COLN C04 .... 134 F6
Severalls Park Industrial
Estate
COLN C04 .... 135 L5
Sharon Crickitt
Complementary
Health Centre
RCOLE C07 .... 192 C3
Shaw County Junior
& Infant School
SOCK/AV RM15 .... 406 C4
Sheepen Road Retail Park
COLW C03 .... 10 A9
Sheering C of E
Primary School
RBSF CM22 .... 228 E3
Shelley County
Primary School
CHONG CM5 .... 282 F6
Shenfield Cricket Club
BRWN CM15 .... 333 G8
Shenfield High School
BRWN CM15 .... 333 H7
Shenfield Sports Centre
BRWN CM15 .... 333 H7
Shenval Industrial Estate
HLW CM20 .... 227 H7
Sheredes School
HOD EN11 .... 253 G6
Shoeburyness High School
SBN/FI SS3 .... 402 E4
Shotley Primary School
RIPS/CAP IP9 .... 83 G8
Shotley Sailing Club
RIPS/CAP IP9 .... 113 J3
Shrub End Clinic
COLS C02 .... 162 C8
Shrub End Surgery
COLW C03 .... 162 B7
Siam Surgery
SUD C010 .... 4 D5
Sidegate Primary School
IPNE IP4 .... 38 E3
Sikh Temple
IP IP1 .... 2 A4
Silver End County
Primary School
WIT CM8 .... 184 F8
The Silver Tree Craft Gallery
MGTR C011 .... 108 E7
Sir Charles Lucas School
COLN C04 .... 163 M3
Sir Charles Lucas School
COLN C04 .... 164 A3
Slade Green Football Club
ERITH DA8 .... 414 C5
Slade Green Infant School
ERITH DA8 .... 414 B4
Smilers Industrial Estate
PIT SS13 .... 379 G3
Snap Theatre
BSF CM23 .... 174 B4
Social History Museum
COL C01 .... 10 C8
Somers Heath School
SOCK/AV RM15 .... 406 B5
Sooriakumaran Surgery
SOSN SS2 .... 382 F7
Sopwith Crescent
WICKE SS11 .... 360 C5
South Benfleet GM
Primary School
SBF/HAD SS7 .... 397 K7
Southbourne Grove Surgery
WOS/PRIT SS0 .... 382 C7
Southbury Primary
& Infant School
PEND EN3 .... 324 D6
Southbury Primary School
PEND EN3 .... 324 C6
South East Essex College
SOSN SS2 .... 20 F3
South East Essex Sixth
Form College
SBF/HAD SS7 .... 380 B6
Southend Adult
Community College
SOS SS1 .... 21 M6
Southend Borough Council
SOSN SS2 .... 20 D1
Southend Borough
Football Club
WOS/PRIT SS0 .... 382 C5

Southend County Court
SOS SS1 .... 21 H6
Southend High School for Boys
SOSN SS2 .... 382 F8
Southend Hospital N H S Trust
WOS/PRIT SS0 .... 382 D8
Southend Rugby Football Club
SOSN SS2 .... 383 G5
Southend United Football Club
SOSN SS2 .... 20 D1
South Essex Clinical
Trials Centre
LOS SS9 .... 399 J1
South Essex Health Authority
RAYL SS6 .... 380 D2
South Essex Health Authority
RBRW/HUT CM13 .... 354 D6
Southfields Industrial Park
LAIN SS15 .... 376 A4
South Green County
Infant & Junior School
BCAYW CM12 .... 357 J4
South Green Surgery
BCAYE CM11 .... 357 K4
Southminster Infant School
BOC CM0 .... 320 E8
Southminster Medical Centre
BOC CM0 .... 320 E7
South Street Surgery
BSF CM23 .... 174 A5
South Suffolk Business Centre
SUD C010 .... 5 G6
Southview Park Surgery
VGE SS16 .... 377 L8
Southview School
WIT CM8 .... 212 A5
South West Essex
Magistrates Court
BSDN SS14 .... 18 E5
South Woodham
Ferrers Leisure Centre
RCHLM CM3 .... 339 M4
Sovereign Business Centre
PEND EN3 .... 325 G5
Spa Pavillion Theatre
FX IP11 .... 115 J2
Spellbrook JMI School
BSF CM23 .... 201 G4
The Spinney Junior School
HLW CM20 .... 256 B2
Springfield County
Primary School
IP IP1 .... 36 F3
Springfield Cricket Club
CHLM/GWD CM2 .... 264 F7
Springfield Industrial Estate
BOC CM0 .... 344 A6
Springfield Junior School
IP IP1 .... 37 G3
Springfield Medical Centre
CHLM/WR CM1 .... 264 E5
Springfield School
CHONG CM5 .... 307 K2
Spring Meadow
Primary School
HAR C012 .... 6 C8
Sprites Junior & Infant School
CHTY IP2 .... 57 K1
Sproughton Business Park
IP IP1 .... 36 D4
Sproughton VC Primary School
RIPW IP8 .... 36 C5
Squirrels Heath Junior School
GPK RM2 .... 371 J5
Squirrels Heath Junior School
ROM RM1 .... 371 H5
Stadium Trading Estate
SBF/HAD SS7 .... 380 D4
Stafford Industrial Estate
EMPK RM11 .... 371 L3
Stambridge Primary School
RCFD SS4 .... 383 L1
Stansted Clinic
STSD CM24 .... 146 F4
Stanway CP School
COLW C03 .... 161 K5
Stanway Fiveways CP School
COLW C03 .... 161 L6
The Stanway School
COLW C03 .... 161 L6
Stanway Surgery
COLW C03 .... 161 K5
Stanway Swimming Centre
COLW C03 .... 161 G6
Stapleford Abbotts
County Primary School
ABR/ST RM4 .... 329 J7
Staples Road Junior
& Infant School
LOU IG10 .... 326 F5
Staple Tye Shopping Centre
HLWS CM18 .... 255 L6
Star Lane Industrial Estate
SBN/FI SS3 .... 385 G8
Station Yard Industrial Park
GTDUN CM6 .... 178 F4
Steeple Bumpstead CP School
HVHL CB9 .... 48 C5
Sterling Industrial Estate
DAGE RM10 .... 388 C3
Stewards Comprehensive
School
HLWS CM18 .... 255 K7
Stifford Clays County
Junior School
CDH/CHF RM16 .... 407 J6
Stifford Clays Health Centre
CDH/CHF RM16 .... 407 J6
Stifford County
Primary School
GRAYS RM17 .... 416 F2
Stock C of E Primary
School
ING CM4 .... 311 L0
Stock Industrial Park
SOSN SS2 .... 383 F3
Stockwell Lodge
Medical Centre
CHESW EN7 .... 276 B8

Stoke College
SUD CO10 .... 30 D8
Stoke High School
CHTY IP2 .... 58 D1
Stonehall Surgery
SUD CO10 .... 31 J4
Stortford Hall Industrial Park
BSF CM23 .... 174 C4
Stort Valley Industrial Estate
BSF CM23 .... 174 C1
Stour Sailing Club
MGTR CO11 .... 108 E7
Strand Gallery
SOSN SS2 .... 401 L2
The Street Industrial Estate
MAL CM9 .... 269 J6
Strumer End Industrial Estate
HVHL CB9 .... 28 C5
Stuarts Industrial Estate
CHLM/GWD CM2 .... 17 L5
Stutton Primary School
RIPS/CAP IP9 .... 110 B1
Sudbury Bowl
SUD CO10 .... 5 H3
Sudbury Business Centre
SUD CO10 .... 4 C6
Sudbury Health Centre
SUD CO10 .... 4 E4
Sudbury Rugby Union
Football Club
SUD CO10 .... 55 J7
Sudbury Town Football Club
SUD CO10 .... 4 C8
Sudbury Tudor
Voluntary Controlled School
SUD CO10 .... 4 E3
Sudbury Uplands Middle School
SUD CO10 .... 4 E3
Sudbury Upper School
SUD CO10 .... 4 E2
Sue Ryder Foundation
SUD CO10 .... 32 E2
Suffolk County Council Offices
IPNE IP4 .... 3 J5
Suffolks Junior & Infant School
EN EN1 .... 324 C4
Summercroft Junior
& Infant School
BSF CM23 .... 174 D3
Sumners Community
Recreation Centre
HLWW/ROY CM19 .... 255 H7
Sunnymede County
Junior School
BCAYE CM11 .... 357 L2
Sutherland Lodge Surgery
CHLM/GWD CM2 .... 17 K7
Suttons JMI School
HCH RM12 .... 389 L3
Suttons Manor Clinic
ABR/ST RM4 .... 329 M2
Swaines Industrial Estate
RCFD SS4 .... 363 M8
Swan Business Park
DART DA1 .... 414 E8
Swan Mead Junior School
VGE SS16 .... 19 L7
The Sweyne Park School
RAYL SS6 .... 361 K7
Swimming Pool
SLH/COR SS17 .... 395 G7
Swimming Pool Centre
BCAYE CM11 .... 336 D7
Tabor High Upper School
BRTR CM7 .... 154 E7
Tabor Middle School
BRTR CM7 .... 154 F8
Takeley Business Centre
RBSF CM22 .... 176 D4
Takeley GM Primary School
RBSF CM22 .... 176 D1
Tanys Dell Junior School
HLW CM20 .... 227 H8
Tattingstone C of E V CP
School
RIPS/CAP IP9 .... 79 L4
Templars County Infant
School
WIT CM8 .... 212 A6
Templers County Junior
School
WIT CM8 .... 212 A6
Temple Sutton Primary
& Infant School
SOSN SS2 .... 383 K8
Tendring Adult Community
College
COS CO15 .... 12 F5
Tendring CP School
RCOS CO16 .... 167 M5
Tendring Sixth Form College
FOS CO13 .... 199 H4
Tendring Technology College
& Sixth Form College
RCOS CO16 .... 197 G1
Tennyson House Surgery
CHLM/WR CM1 .... 264 A5
Terling C of E Primary School
RCHLM CM3 .... 210 D8
Thameside Community
Health Care
VGE SS16 .... 19 M8
Thameside Community
Healthcare N H S Trust
BCAYW CM12 .... 335 J8
Thameside County
Infant School
GRAYS RM17 .... 417 K3

Thameside Theatre
GRAYS RM17 .... 417 H2
Thaxted Primary School
GTDUN CM6 .... 122 B1
Theydon Bois CP School
EPP CM16 .... 303 M8
Theydon Gallery
EPP CM16 .... 327 L1
Thomas Lord Audley School
COLS CO2 .... 191 G1
Thomas Rivers
Medical Centre
HLW CM20 .... 227 K4
The Thomas Rivers
Medical Centre
SBW CM21 .... 227 K2
Thomas Tallis School
WAB EN9 .... 302 A5
The Thomas Willingale
Gm School
LOU IG10 .... 327 K5
Thorley Hill Jmi School
BSF CM23 .... 174 A7
Thorn Grove Primary School
BSF CM23 .... 174 C5
Thorpe Bay School
SOS SS1 .... 402 A2
Thorpe Bay Surgery
SOS SS1 .... 402 B4
Thorpedene Gm Junior School
SBN/FI SS3 .... 402 D4
Thorpe Hall School
SBN/FI SS3 .... 402 B1
Three Rivers Golf Club
RCHLM CM3 .... 316 F6
Threshelfords Business Park
K/T/MI CO5 .... 186 F8
Thriftwood School
CHLM/GWD CM2 .... 288 B8
Thundersley Junior
& Infant School
SBF/HAD SS7 .... 380 B5
Thurrock Borough Council
GRAYS RM17 .... 417 J3
Thurrock Borough Council
SOCK/AV RM15 .... 406 B4
Thurrock Business Centre
WTHK RM20 .... 416 A3
Thurrock College
CDH/CHF RM16 .... 418 A1
Thurrock Council
PUR RM19 .... 415 G1
Thurrock Council for Voluntary
Services
GRAYS RM17 .... 417 J2
Thurrock Council Office
GRAYS RM17 .... 417 J2
Thurstable School
K/T/MI CO5 .... 214 E5
Tilbury Fort
TIL RM18 .... 418 D8
Tilbury Manor Infant School
TIL RM18 .... 418 C4
Tilbury Surgery
TIL RM18 .... 418 B6
The Tile Gallery
LOS SS9 .... 400 B2
Tile House Surgery
BRWN CM15 .... 354 E2
Tillingham Medical Centre
BOC CM0 .... 297 M8
Tillingham St Nicholas
C of E Primary School
BOC CM0 .... 297 L7
Tiptree Heath CP School
K/T/MI CO5 .... 214 C8
Tiptree Sports Centre
K/T/MI CO5 .... 214 E4
Titan Industrial Estate
GRAYS RM17 .... 417 H1
Tollesbury CP School
MAL CM9 .... 272 E2
Tollesbury Sailing Club
MAL CM9 .... 273 G1
Tolleshunt Darcy
C of E Primary School
MAL CM9 .... 242 E7
Tooley's & Smarts Almshouses
IPNE IP4 .... 3 G5
Toot Hill Golf Club
CHONG CM5 .... 306 A3
Torells County Secondary
School for Girls
CDH/CHF RM16 .... 408 A7
Tower Business Park
K/T/MI CO5 .... 214 C4
Tower Ramparts
Shopping Centre
IP IP1 .... 2 F4
Towers Infant School
EMPK RM11 .... 371 K7
Towers Junior School
EMPK RM11 .... 371 K7
Trading Estate
WTHK RM20 .... 416 B2
Trafalgar Trading Estate
PEND EN3 .... 325 G6
Treetops School
GRAYS RM17 .... 417 J1
Tricor Business Park
BAR EN8 .... 300 F6
Tricor Trading Estate
BAR EN8 .... 300 F6
Trident Industrial Estate
HOD EN11 .... 253 K5
Trimley St Martins County
Primary School
FX IP11 .... 84 C1

Trinity Catholic Lower
High School
WFD IG8 .... 348 B5
Trinity Catholic Upper
High School
WFD IG8 .... 348 B5
Trinity Road Primary School
CHLM/GWD CM2 .... 17 L2
Trinity School
DAGE RM10 .... 388 B2
Tudor Court CP School
CDH/CHF RM16 .... 407 G7
Tunnel Industrial Estate
WTHK RM20 .... 416 A1
Tunnel Industrial Estate
WTHK RM20 .... 416 A3
Turnford School
BAR EN8 .... 276 F8
Twyford Business Centre
BSF CM23 .... 174 B6
The Tyrrells CP School
CHLM/WR CM1 .... 264 F6
U C I Cinema
BSDN SS14 .... 377 J2
U C I Cinema
WTHK RM20 .... 416 A1
Unit 5 Airport Business Park
SOSN SS2 .... 382 F5
Uniterian Meeting House
IP IP1 .... 2 E5
Unit 1-2 Stanford
Industrial Estate
SLH/COR SS17 .... 409 K2
Unity Health Centre
SUD CO10 .... 4 D6
University College Suffolk
IPNE IP4 .... 3 J5
University College
Suffolk Annexe
IPNE IP4 .... 3 H4
University of Essex
COLN CO4 .... 164 A7
University of Essex
COLN CO4 .... 164 A5
University of London
ENC/FH EN2 .... 300 B8
University of Middlesex
PEND EN3 .... 324 C7
University Yacht Club
RCOLE CO7 .... 221 G6
Upminster Infant School
UPMR RM14 .... 390 C2
Upminster Primary School
UPMR RM14 .... 390 D2
Upper Clapton Rugby
Football Club
EPP CM16 .... 280 C4
Upshire CP School
WAB EN9 .... 302 C4
Uttlesford District Council
GTDUN CM6 .... 178 E3
Van & Car Surgery
PEND EN3 .... 324 E6
Viking Business Centre
ROMW/RG RM7 .... 370 D7
Vineyard Gallery
COL CO1 .... 10 D8
Virgin Cinema
IP IP1 .... 2 D6
Virgin Cinemas
HLW CM20 .... 227 G7
Walnut Tree Hospital
SUD CO10 .... 4 B6
Waltham Abbey
Swimming Pool
WAB EN9 .... 301 L7
Waltham Holy Cross Council
WAB EN9 .... 301 J5
Waltham Holy Cross
Junior School
WAB EN9 .... 301 L5
Walton & Frinton Yacht Club
WOTN CO14 .... 199 K2
Walton GM Primary School
WOTN CO14 .... 199 K2
Walton Surgery
FX IP11 .... 84 F7
Wansfell College
EPP CM16 .... 303 L7
Warden Lodge Surgery
BAR EN8 .... 300 E3
Wardmaster Infirmary
RIPS/CAP IP9 .... 80 E8
Warley County Junior School
BRW CM14 .... 354 D6
Warley Hill Business Park
RBRW/HUT CM13 .... 354 D7
Warley Hospital
BRW CM14 .... 354 C6
Warley Lodge Hospital
RBRW/HUT CM13 .... 373 L1
Warner Brothers Cinema
WTHK RM20 .... 406 B8
Warner Industrial Park
SUD CO10 .... 5 H5
Warren Golf Club
MAL CM9 .... 291 K2
Warren Junior School
CHDH RM6 .... 370 A5
Warren Primary School
CDH/CHF RM16 .... 406 D8
Warren School
CHDH RM6 .... 370 A5
Watermill Business Centre
PEND EN3 .... 325 G4
Waterside Business Park
WIT CM8 .... 212 C7

Waterside Farm Sports Centre
CVI SS8 .... 397 M5
Waterside Industrial Estate
HOD EN11 .... 253 L6
Waterside (School)
BSF CM23 .... 145 M4
Waverley School
PEND EN3 .... 324 D6
Wellesley Hospital
SOSN SS2 .... 383 K8
Well Lane Industrial Estate
RCHLM CM3 .... 290 D4
Wells Hall Primary School
SUD CO10 .... 55 J7
Wells Park School
CHIG IG7 .... 350 A5
Wells Primary School
WFD IG8 .... 348 C5
Wennington Hall Farm
Business Centre
RAIN RM13 .... 404 F4
Wentworth Primary School
MAL CM9 .... 293 G3
Westborough Primary School
WOS/PRIT SS0 .... 20 C2
Westbourne High School
IP IP1 .... 36 F2
Westbridge Infant School
IP IP1 .... 2 B3
Westcliff High School for Boys
WOS/PRIT SS0 .... 382 B8
Westcliff High School for Girls
LOS SS9 .... 382 B8
Westcliff Leisure Centre
WOS/PRIT SS0 .... 20 D8
West Cliff Theatre
COS CO15 .... 12 E9
Westerings Primary School
HOC/HUL SS5 .... 362 E7
Western Road Surgery
BCAYW CM12 .... 357 H1
Westfield Jmi School
HOD EN11 .... 253 G4
Westfield Primary School
HVHL CB9 .... 28 C4
Westfleet Trading Estate
WICKE SS11 .... 360 A5
West Ham United
Football Club
CHDH RM6 .... 370 A7
West Hatch High School
CHIG IG7 .... 349 G6
West Horndon CP School
RBRW/HUT CM13 .... 374 E5
Westlands County
Secondary School
CHLM/WR CM1 .... 287 L2
Westlands CP School
CHLM/WR CM1 .... 16 B3
West Leigh Junior
& Infant School
LOS SS9 .... 399 L1
Westmayne Industrial Park
LAIN SS15 .... 375 M5
West Mersea Museum
K/T/MI CO5 .... 245 J6
West Road Mosque
WOS/PRIT SS0 .... 20 D2
West Station Industrial Estate
MAL CM9 .... 292 F2
West Station Yard
MAL CM9 .... 292 F2
West Thurrock CP School
WTHK RM20 .... 416 B3
Westwood Primary School
SBF/HAD SS7 .... 380 E7
Wethersfield Primary School
BRTR CM7 .... 95 K8
The White Bridge County
Infant & Junior School
LOU IG10 .... 348 L1
White Court CP School
BRTR CM7 .... 182 D5
Whitehall Estate
HLWW/ROY CM19 .... 14 B7
Whitehall Industrial Estate
COLS CO2 .... 163 L8
White House Infant School
IP IP1 .... 36 E2
White House Junior School
IP IP1 .... 36 E2
White Notley C of E
Primary School
WIT CM8 .... 211 G2
Whitmore County Junior
& Infant School
BSDN SS14 .... 377 M3
Whitton Clinic
IP IP1 .... 36 F1
Whybridge Infant School
RAIN RM13 .... 389 H7
Whybridge Junior School
RAIN RM13 .... 389 G7
Wickford Health Centre
WICKW SS12 .... 359 K3
Wickford Junior School
WICKW SS12 .... 359 K4
Wickford Swimming Pool
WICKW SS12 .... 359 K3
Widford Industrial Estate
CHLM/WR CM1 .... 16 A9
Widford Lodge
Preparatory School
CHLM/GWD CM2 .... 16 D9
William Bellamy Junior
& Infant School
DAGE RM10 .... 388 B1

William De Ferrers School
RCHLM CM3 .... 339 M4
William Edwards Gm School
CDH/CHF RM16 .... 407 K5
William Ford School
DAGE RM10 .... 388 B6
William Julian
Courtald Hospital
BRTR CM7 .... 182 F1
William Read CP School
CVI SS8 .... 398 A8
Willis Coroon Building
IP IP1 .... 2 E5
Wimbish CP School
SAFWN CB10 .... 67 K7
Windsor School Clacton
COS CO15 .... 13 M3
Windsor Trading Estate
BCAYE CM11 .... 336 E7
Winter Gardens Junior School
CVI SS8 .... 398 A6
The Witham Health Centre
WIT CM8 .... 239 H1
Witham Rugby Union F C
WIT CM8 .... 238 F2
Witham Town Football
& Social Club
WIT CM8 .... 238 F1
Wivenhoe Business Centre
RCOLE CO7 .... 192 D3
Wivenhoe Family
Health Centre
RCOLE CO7 .... 192 C1
Wivenhoe Sailing Club
RCOLE CO7 .... 192 D4
Wivenhoe Town Cricket Club
RCOLE CO7 .... 192 D1
Wix CP School
MGTR CO11 .... 140 C6
Wolsey Theatre
IP IP1 .... 2 D4
Woodacre School
SOCK/AV RM15 .... 406 B3
Woodbridge High School
WFD IG8 .... 348 C8
Woodford County High
School for Girls
WFD IG8 .... 348 A7
Woodford Medical Clinic
RCHLM CM3 .... 290 D4
Woodgreen Animal Shelter
ROY SG8 .... 40 B8
Woodhall Business Park
SUD CO10 .... 55 G1
Woodhall Business Park
Drury Drive
SUD CO10 .... 55 G1
Woodhall County
Primary School
SUD CO10 .... 4 E1
Woodham Ley CP School
SBF/HAD SS7 .... 379 J5
Woodham Walter
C of E Primary School
MAL CM9 .... 267 L8
Woodlands Comprehensive
School
VGE SS16 .... 18 F9
Woodlands Preparatory
School
RBRW/HUT CM13 .... 373 L4
Woodlands School
CHLM/WR CM1 .... 264 A5
Wood Lane Sports Centre
BCTR RM8 .... 370 C8
Wood Lane Surgery
HCH RM12 .... 389 H4
Woodside County
Primary School
CDH/CHF RM16 .... 408 A8
Woodville Primary School
RCHLM CM3 .... 339 K2
Worcesters Infant
& Primary School
EN EN1 .... 324 A2
The Working Silk Museum
BRTR CM7 .... 183 G1
Wormingford C of E
Primary School
RCOLW CO6 .... 102 F6
Wormley Jmi School
BROX EN10 .... 276 F3
Writtle College
CHLM/WR CM1 .... 263 J8
Writtle Junior School
CHLM/WR CM1 .... 287 H3
The Writtle Surgery
CHLM/WR CM1 .... 287 J1
Wyburns City Junior School
RAYL SS6 .... 381 G3
Wycke Hill Business Park
MAL CM9 .... 292 F3
Wykeham Junior School
HCH RM12 .... 371 H8
Wyncroft Surgery
RCHLM CM3 .... 291 G4
Yale Business Park
IPSE IP3 .... 60 A3
Yardley Primary School
CHING E4 .... 325 J7
Yellow Dot Sports Club
SUD CO10 .... 5 G7

Notes

Notes